The College of Law
of England and Wales

LIBRARY & INFORMATION SERVICES

The College of Law, 133 Great Hampton Street, Birmingham B18 6AQ

This book MUST be returned on or before the last date stamped below.
Failure to do so will result in a fine.

D1514591

Birmingham • Chester • Guildford • London • York

UK MERGER CONTROL:
LAW AND PRACTICE

AUSTRALIA
Law Book Company—Sydney

CANADA and USA
Carswell—Toronto

NEW ZEALAND
Brookers—Auckland

SINGAPORE and MALAYSIA
Sweet and Maxwell Asia—Singapore and Kuala Lumpur

UK MERGER CONTROL:
LAW AND PRACTICE
Second Edition

BY

A. NIGEL PARR, LL.B., LL.M., PhD
SOLICITOR

ROGER J. FINBOW, M.A. (OXON)
SOLICITOR

MATTHEW J. HUGHES, B.A., MSc

LONDON
SWEET & MAXWELL
2005

First Edition 1995
Second Edition 2005
Published in 2005 by
Sweet & Maxwell Limited of
100 Avenue Road
London NW3 3PF
Typeset by J&L Composition,
Filey, North Yorkshire
Printed in Great Britain by
T.J. International, Padstow, Cornwall

No natural forests were destroyed to make this product;
only farmed timber was used and replanted.

A CIP catalogue record for this book is
available from the British Library

ISBN 0 421 86100 2

PREFACE

When we started the process of writing the second edition of *UK Merger Control: Law and Practice*, we knew that there would be a great deal to write about. Quite apart from the adoption of the Enterprise Act 2002, the body of case law and practice had expanded considerably in the nine years since the first edition was published, particularly from the late 1990s, when merger activity reached one of its cyclical high points. During this period the level of sophistication of scrutiny of mergers by the UK authorities continued to increase, with an even greater emphasis on economic assessment following the appointment of internationally renowned economists as Chairmen of the OFT and Competition Commission. There was also a marked trend towards greater transparency of process and analysis, with the publication of more detailed guidance, and publication of the Director General's advice to the Secretary of State under the Fair Trading Act 1973 from late 2000. Many of the reforms to the EC Merger Regulation were aimed at making the interplay between national and EC merger control more efficient and more effective and the relationship between the two regimes has developed considerably since 1995.

In addition to these general developments—which would have necessitated the preparation of a second edition in any event—the text of the first edition has had to be fully reworked to reflect the new Enterprise Act regime. Although the reforms which the new legislation introduced are, from the merger control practitioner's perspective, to some extent a natural evolution of the Fair Trading Act regime, there are nevertheless some fundamental changes, both substantive and procedural. The trend towards transparency has been emphasised by the issue of extensive detailed guidance on both procedure and substantive assessment by the OFT and the Competition Commission. The new jurisdiction of the Competition Appeal Tribunal to review merger control decisions is a particularly important issue to discuss, with the potential to rejuvenate judicial control of the merger regime, stifled under the FTA by the relatively poor prospect, historically, of successfully challenging a merger control decision.

With these points in mind, we were always expecting preparation of the second edition to require a substantial re-writing exercise. What we were not expecting was to have a major case—perhaps the most important case in the history of UK merger control—to discuss. The *IBA Health* case in the CAT and the Court of Appeal has provided a crucial early interpretation of the new Enterprise Act test for reference; the case includes an important discussion of the legal basis for judicial review; and considers the fundamental issue of adequacy of reasoning. It has also raised important questions about the case management practice of the CAT. We took the decision to delay publication to take *IBA Health* into account and this certainly proved to be the right decision given the depth and scope of the court of Appeal's judgment.

We have endeavoured to state the law and practice as at August 1, 2004, but have incorporated subsequent changes wherever possible. Some key proposed changes, such as the merger fees reform and the Competition Commission's consultation on remedies, were not sufficiently advanced for us to be able to make definitive statements about future plans, but we have endeavoured to identify these issues in the text to alert the reader to them.

We would like to acknowledge our debt and express our thanks to a number of people who have kindly reviewed and commented on various parts of the text: Simon Priddis, Director, and Bob Gaddes, Deputy Director, of the Mergers Branch for their invaluable comments on Chapters 2, 3 and 4 on the OFT's jurisdiction, its procedure and its duty to refer; Carole Begent, Legal Director at the Competition Commission for her comments and suggestions for Chapter 5 on the practice and procedure of the Commission; Rory Chisholm of Finsbury financial PR consultancy for his input into what became the revised Chapter 9 on Lobbying; and Ben Rayment, formerly a Referendaire at the Competition Appeal Tribunal and now of Monckton Chambers for his helpful comments on Chapter 10 on the judicial review jurisdiction of the CAT.

Our thanks also extend to our Ashurst colleagues without whom this book could not have been written, in particular to Catherine Chibnall, the senior professional development lawyer in the Competition Department at Ashurst and formerly a Referendaire at the Competition Appeal Tribunal, whose contribution across a wide range of areas has been invaluable. Our thanks also go to Euan Burrows, Neil Cuninghame, Emily Clark, Celia Foss, Ross Mackenzie, and Tom Mercer who all made important contributions to the drafting process. Thanks also to Tessa Dunne and Leila Box who undertook the process of checking references, to the secretaries of the Ashurst London Competition team, particularly Carol Howard, who cheerfully typed the manuscript, and finally to those members of our team not already named, who have more or less all contributed to the project to some degree, not least where they have worked harder as we worked on this book.

As always, we alone are responsible for any errors or omissions.

NIGEL PARR
ROGER FINBOW
MAT HUGHES
October 2004

TABLE OF CONTENTS

CONTENTS

CONTENTS

CONTENTS

CONTENTS

CONTENTS

CONTENTS

CONTENTS

CONTENTS

TABLE OF CASES

TABLE OF CASES

TABLE OF CASES

TABLE OF STATUTES

(References are to paragraph numbers with those in bold referring to Statutory Materials)

TABLE OF STATUTORY INSTRUMENTS

(References are to paragraph numbers with those in bold referring to Statutory Materials)

TABLE OF EUROPEAN LEGISLATION

(References are to paragraph numbers)

TABLE OF EUROPEAN DECISIONS AND CASES

(References are to paragraph numbers)

Commission Merger Decisions

European Court of Justice Cases

TABLE OF MONOPOLIES AND MERGERS COMMISSION REPORTS, PRESS RELEASES, REFERENCES LAID ASIDE, MERGERS IN RESPECT OF WHICH REFERENCE NOT MADE AND MERGERS ABANDONED

(References are to paragraph numbers with those in bold referring to Summary of MMC Merger Reports)

xlv

TABLE OF DECISIONS OF THE OFFICE OF FAIR TRADING, PRESS RELEASES AND DTI ADVICES

(References are to paragraph numbers)

CHAPTER 1

AN OVERVIEW OF THE
ENTERPRISE ACT REGIME

Background

The Enterprise Act 2002, which received Royal Assent on November 7, **1.001**
2002 and entered into effect as regards its merger control provisions on
June 20, 2003, has introduced a number of fundamental changes to the
control of mergers in the UK. Under the previous legislative regime
contained in the Fair Trading Act 1973,[1] the key decision maker was a
government minister, the Secretary of State for Trade and Industry, who
decided, on the advice of the Director General of Fair Trading, whether a
merger should be referred to the Competition Commission[2] for a detailed
second stage inquiry, and what action should be taken (if any) in the light
of the Commission's recommendations following an adverse report. The
statutory test against which mergers were assessed was the UK public
interest, although a succession of ministerial statements since the mid
1980s emphasised that mergers would be assessed primarily on competition
grounds.[3]

In 1999, the Government announced its intention to reform the merger
regime,[4] taking most decisions out of the political arena by conferring decision-making powers on independent competition authorities, whilst

---

[1] Although the United Kingdom has a relatively long tradition of regulating competition with
the first statute, the Monopolies and Restrictive Practices (Inquiry and Control) Act, being
given Royal Assent in 1948, it was not until 1965 that statutory provisions relating to the
control of mergers were introduced. In that year, legislation was introduced at a time of
growing public concern, following cases such as the hostile bid by ICI for Courtaulds, that the
Government was unable to regulate mergers and takeovers that might have a profound effect
on competition in the United Kingdom. The system that was introduced by the Monopolies
and Mergers Act 1965 remained in place under the provisions of the Fair Trading Act 1973.
[2] The Monopolies and Mergers Commission (or MMC), originally created in 1949, was
renamed the Competition Commission by the Competition Act 1998. This book generally
refers to the body as the Competition Commission or the Commission but where an inquiry
was conducted prior to the name change, reference may be made to the MMC.
[3] The so-called "Tebbitt Doctrine", issued by Norman Tebbitt in a statement of July 5, 1984,
stated that his policy "has been and will continue to be to make references primarily on
competition grounds". The policy was reaffirmed by a number of subsequent Secretaries of
State (see further the first edition of this book at pp.99 to 101). Despite statements to the
contrary by the Labour party whilst in opposition which indicated that merger control policy
would be redirected to protecting the stability of UK industry (see the first edition of this
book at p.102, n.13), reference policy did not materially alter when the Labour government
was elected in 1997 and indeed it is a Labour government which has now replaced the public
interest test with a solely competition-based test.
[4] *Mergers: a Consultation Document on Proposals for Reform*, August 1999.

ensuring that Ministers would continue to take final decisions in a small minority of cases raising defined public interest issues, such as national security. Alongside these changes it was decided that the public interest test would be replaced by a competition test: whether a merger would result in a substantial lessening of competition, having regard to whether the merger would nevertheless bring overall benefits to consumers. However, unlike the position under the FTA, where the Secretary of State had a discretion to make a reference, the Office of Fair Trading (OFT) would be under a duty to refer to the Competition Commission relevant mergers which had resulted or might be expected to result in a substantial lessening of competition in a UK market. The two-stage approach to investigations would be retained, with the OFT conducting the first stage investigation to decide whether a reference to the Commission for a detailed second stage inquiry was required. Remedies would be determined by the Commission, in discussion with the parties and third parties, following publication of the Commission's provisional findings on the competition aspects of the merger and a statement on proposed remedies. Following a further White Paper in 2001,[5] these reforms were enacted by the Enterprise Act, substantially as they were originally envisaged.

The Enterprise Act has maintained the generally permissive approach to mergers adopted by the FTA, with the consequence that the Act preserves the basic presumption that a merger should be permitted unless there is a real expectation that it is likely to have significant adverse effects. Accordingly, the parties to a merger which qualifies for investigation under the Act are not prevented from completing the merger prior to regulatory clearance[6]; indeed, in contrast to the majority of merger control regimes in the European Union and around the world, there is no obligation on the parties to seek clearance at all.[7] However, the Act has introduced a new power for the OFT to impose a "hold separate" order (or to accept undertakings in lieu of an order) on the parties whilst it is considering whether to refer a completed merger to the Commission, in order to prevent pre-emptive action that might prejudice the reference or impede any remedial action that may be required by the Commission.[8] These powers cannot, however, be used to prevent a merger from being completed during the OFT's investigation.

---

[5] *Productivity and Enterprise: World Class Competition Regime*, Cm. 5233 (July 2001).
[6] Water and sewerage industry mergers are subject to a special regime which prohibits completion prior to clearance (see further Ch.2). Newspaper mergers were subject to a compulsory clearance regime until the Communications Act 2003 brought them under the Enterprise Act regime. Since December 29, 2003, newspaper mergers (and other media sector mergers) are subject to the standard merger regime under Pt 3 of the Enterprise Act, although they also form one of the areas where the public interest and special public interest provisions can be used to allow the Secretary of State for Trade and Industry to intervene on public interest grounds. See further Ch.7 (in relation to newspaper mergers) and Ch.2 (in relation to other media mergers).
[7] However, it is sometimes advisable for commercial reasons for the parties to a merger to do so: see further Ch.3 below.
[8] See further Ch.3.

The regulatory bodies involved in the UK merger control process

Consistent with the objective of the Enterprise Act to remove most mergers   **1.002**
from the arena of political decision-making, there are now two main
administrative bodies involved in the regulation of mergers in the United
Kingdom.[8A] This reflects to some degree the piecemeal development of
legislative control, but more importantly, the continued desire to achieve a
separation of powers between the detection and preliminary investigation
of, and the power of final decision over, the regulation of mergers.

The Office of Fair Trading

Under the FTA, the OFT was a non-statutory body which supported the   **1.003**
Director General of Fair Trading in fulfilling the specific obligations and
duties imposed upon him by statute, including an overall responsibility for
keeping merger activity under review with the aim of identifying mergers
that might adversely affect the public interest. On April 1, 2003, the
Enterprise Act abolished the post of Director General and established the
OFT as a corporate body to carry out a number of functions on behalf of
the Crown.[9] The Board of the OFT, which is appointed by the Secretary of
State, consists of a Chairman and at least four other members. The
Secretary of State is also obliged to appoint a Chief Executive of the OFT
who, from 2005, must not be the same person as the Chairman. Currently,
John Vickers, the former Director General of Fair Trading under the FTA,
occupies both posts.

   The evaluation of mergers is carried out by the OFT's Mergers Branch,
CE2, whose Director reports to the Director of the OFT's Competition
Enforcement Division, who in turn reports to the Chairman. Despite the
considerable number of mergers that qualify for investigation under the
legislation each year (and others which after evaluation are found not to
qualify),[10] the Mergers Branch is relatively small, comprising as at June
2004, the head of the Branch, two Deputy Directors, five principal case officers and eleven other case officers, eight economists and five general office
staff. Legal support is drawn from the OFT's Legal Branch, as needed, and

---

[8A] App.1 provides a navigation guide to the websites of the OFT, the Competition
   Commission, the Department of Trade and Industry and the Competition Appeal Tribunal.
[9] In addition to its functions in relation to mergers under the Enterprise Act, the OFT
   carries out a range of other competition law related statutory roles including, *inter alia*,
   the investigation of anti-competitive agreements and the abuse of a dominant position
   under the Competition Act 1998 and the investigation of "hard-core" criminal cartels
   and market investigation inquiries under the Enterprise Act.
[10] As is set out in Table 2 of App.2, in 2003/2004, the OFT reviewed 270 cases of which 117
   were qualifying mergers, along with a further 153 which did not qualify for investigation
   (this category includes mergers which were found not to qualify, merger proposals which
   were abandoned and informal advice cases). These figures are lower than in previous years
   (in 1998 the OFT reviewed 425 cases). The reduction in cases is believed to be due, in part,
   to the economic cycle, and in part due to the change in jurisdictional thresholds under the
   Act which has reduced the proportion of mergers which qualify for investigation (in both
   respects, see Table 1 of App.2, which shows the scale of merger activity in the UK and the
   proportion of those mergers which qualified for investigation under the merger control
   regime). In practice, some qualifying mergers are never looked at by the OFT, as a result of
   clearance not being sought and the merger not otherwise coming to the OFT's attention.

the Mergers Branch staff can also draw on the expertise of the accountants and business analysts in the OFT's Markets and Policy Initiatives Division when required. The Branch comprises six sections: Section 1 which deals with ECMR case work and associated policy questions; four sections dealing with merger cases arising under the Act, with each focusing on particular industry sectors; and Section 6 which provides economic advice for the other five sections.

As explained further below, the key role of the OFT in relation to mergers is to obtain and review relevant information and to act in accordance with its duty to refer to the Competition Commission for further investigation relevant merger situations which have or may be expected to result in a substantial lessening of competition. The OFT is also under a duty to advise the Secretary of State on any mergers which might fall within the scope of the public interest or special public interest provisions of the Act.

The Secretary of State for Trade and Industry[10A]

1.004   Under the FTA, the Secretary of State was the Government Minister responsible for taking decisions in the merger control process, having the power to make merger references to the Competition Commission and the discretion as to whether and how to act upon an adverse Commission report. It was a key objective of the Enterprise Act for the Secretary of State to cease exercising these decision-making powers except in relation to certain exceptional cases raising public interest issues.

The Secretary of State's role in relation to public interest cases is considered in detail below.[11] Broadly, where a merger qualifies for investigation, the Secretary of State may take certain specified public interest factors into account and intervene in the merger control process to clear, refer or remedy a merger. The public interest considerations that the Secretary of State may take into account are limited by the Act. At the time of its enactment, s.58 of the Enterprise Act only specified national security issues as areas where the Secretary of State could intervene in the merger scrutiny process but the Act also provides that the Secretary of State may specify further public interest issues by statutory instrument. Chapter 2 of the Communications Act 2003, which came into force on December 29, 2003, added a number of additional media-related public interest considerations to s.58 of the Enterprise Act.[12]

The Secretary of State also has the power to intervene in so-called "special public interest" cases in circumstances where the jurisdictional thresholds of the Enterprise Act are not satisfied. These cases include:

(i)   mergers involving government contractors or sub-contractors who may hold or receive information of a confidential nature relating to defence; and

---

[10A] In this book "he" and "him", etc. are used when referring to the role of the Secretary of State in the abstract (as is the approach adopted in the legislation). Where reference is made to the decision of a particular minister, the appropriate gender form is used.

[11] See further Ch.2.

[12] At the time of coming into force of the Enterprise Act, the newspaper provisions of the FTA remained in force. These provisions were repealed and replaced by s.375 of the Communications Act 2003. At that time, newspapers became one of the media categories specified under the public interest provisions of the Enterprise Act.

(ii)   by virtue of c.2 of the Communications Act 2003, certain mergers in the broadcasting and newspaper sectors.

The OFT will not undertake a competition assessment in special public interest cases, as the jurisdictional thresholds of the Act are not met.

The Competition Commission

The Competition Commission is a statutory body, independent of the Government and funded by the Department of Trade and Industry, with a full-time chairman and a deputy chairman appointed by the Secretary of State and approximately 50 part-time members representing a range of relevant competition experience and including businessmen, academics and members of the professions.[13] Part-time members are appointed by the Secretary of State, for a period of up to eight years. They are normally required to devote one-and-a-half days per week to their duties. Three of the more senior and experienced members are presently designated as deputy chairmen. They share with the chairman the role of chairing inquiries and have a commitment of four days per week. Other members may also be asked to act as ad hoc chairman for a particular inquiry (or a particular meeting which the inquiry chairperson is unable to attend). The Commission is assisted by the Chief Executive and Secretary and, beneath him, a team of administrators, accountants, economists and lawyers, numbering about 145 in total.

    Under the FTA, the role of the Commission in relation to mergers was to establish whether a merger referred to it qualified for investigation and, if so, whether it operated against the public interest. It was required to report its conclusions to the Secretary of State making recommendations, in the case of an adverse report, as to how (if at all) the identified detriments could be remedied. Under the Enterprise Act, the function of the Commission in merger cases is very different as it is required to reach final determinations, having conducted a detailed investigation, on whether a merger should be permitted and to adopt remedies where required. A merger inquiry is normally carried out by a group comprising between three and six members of the Commission.

1.005

The Competition Appeal Tribunal (CAT)[14]

Under the FTA, those affected by merger control decisions of the UK authorities could seek leave to apply to the High Court for judicial review. Under the Enterprise Act, any person aggrieved by a decision of the OFT, the Secretary of State or the Competition Commission in connection with a reference or possible reference may apply to the CAT for review of that decision.

1.006

---

[13] The biographies of the various members of the Competition Commission are available on the Competition Commission's website (see App.1).
[14] The CAT was created by s.12 of and Sch.2 to the Enterprise Act 2002 which came into force on April 1, 2003. The predecessor to the CAT were the Competition Commission Appeal Tribunals which were created by the Competition Act 1998 to hear appeals in respect of decisions made under that Act.

Overview of the merger control process

General principles

1.007 Under the Enterprise Act, whenever the OFT believes that it is or may be the case that a merger satisfies the jurisdictional requirements of the Act and has resulted or may result in a substantial lessening of competition, it is under a duty to refer the transaction to the Competition Commission for a detailed investigation. The OFT's guidance on substantive assessment, which was amended following the Court of Appeal's decision in the *IBA Health* case[15] states that "the test for reference will be met if the OFT has a positive and reasonable belief, objectively justified by relevant facts that there is a realistic prospect that the merger will lessen competition substantially".[16] In practice, this means that a reference is likely to be made to the Commission where there is a prospect which is not fanciful but has less than a 50 per cent likelihood of occurring that a merger is expected to confer an enhanced degree of market power on the merged company or the leading firms in a market such that it/they are likely to be able to act to the detriment of its/their customers or suppliers (and ultimately the consumer) in terms of price and choice.[17] There are, broadly, three exceptions to the OFT's duty to make a reference to the Competition Commission: where the market or markets concerned is or are not of sufficient importance to justify a reference (an exception that is likely to apply very rarely even in relation to markets having a value of less than £1 million); where the merger results in the creation of clear and quantifiable customer benefits (defined by the Act as lower prices, higher quality, greater choice or greater innovation) which outweigh the substantial lessening of competition concerned; and where a proposed merger is insufficiently advanced or likely to proceed to justify the making of a reference.

Consistent with the practice under the FTA, it is likely that only a small proportion of mergers qualifying for investigation will be referred to the Commission.[18] In this connection, the Act has retained the statutory procedure, available since 1989, to avoid a reference of a merger which would otherwise have been made by offering to the OFT undertakings in lieu of a reference to the Competition Commission. This involves the acquirer entering into undertakings enforceable by the OFT (or the Secretary of State in relation to public interest cases), typically to dispose of the part of the businesses to be merged which gives rise to competition concerns. This

---

[15] *IBA Health Limited v Office of Fair Trading, supported by iSOFT PLC and Torex PLC* [2003] CAT 27; and [2004] EWCA Civ. 142 (Court of Appeal).
[16] *Mergers, Substantive Assessment Guidance*, OFT, May 2003, at para.3.2, as revised in May 2004 by OFT guidance note OFT 516. Note that, as at the time of writing, the wording was expected to change again, following consultation on the initial redrafting.
[17] The OFT stated at para.3.2 of its *Substantive Assessment Guidance* as originally drafted that the threshold against which a substantial lessening of competition will be assessed is "the same as that against which FTA reference advices were prepared".
[18] As at July 1, 2004, 14 (or 9 per cent) of the 156 mergers (not including confidential guidance and informal guidance cases but including mergers subsequently found not to qualify) considered by the OFT under the Act had been referred, with five of those references being cancelled subsequently. In four further cases, undertakings were sought in lieu of reference. See further Table 3 of App.2.

concept was extended in November 1994 to encompass behavioural undertakings given by the acquirer, and the Act preserves the scope for behavioural undertakings to be accepted by the OFT.

After a reference has been made, the Competition Commission has a statutory period of up to 24 weeks (subject to a possible extension of a further eight weeks at the Commission's discretion) to carry out its investigation and reach a decision. Within these limits, the Commission sets its own administrative timetable for an inquiry. The Act requires the Commission to consider a series of questions: first, whether a relevant merger situation has been or will be created; and secondly, if so, whether the creation of that merger situation has resulted, or may be expected to result, in a substantial lessening of competition within any market or markets in the United Kingdom for goods or services. If the Commission concludes that there will be an "anti-competitive outcome" (*i.e.* that a substantial lessening of competition will result), it is obliged to consider whether any action should be taken (and if so, what action) to remedy the substantial lessening of competition or any adverse effects resulting from it. In making this assessment the Commission may have regard to the effect of any remedial action on any relevant customer benefits. There is no obligation on the parties to demonstrate that positive benefits arise from the merger, and although in practice the parties may often seek to do so, the Commission will clear a merger if it finds that it will not result in a substantial lessening of competition, even if no positive benefits may be expected to arise. This is consistent with the policy that merger activity in general is positive for the economy and should not be discouraged.

The statutory framework

A "relevant merger situation" under the Enterprise Act arises where two or more "enterprises" (at least one of which is carried on in the United Kingdom) cease to be distinct (that is, they are brought under common control or ownership) or there is a proposal to this effect. Enterprises are defined as "the activities, or part of the activities, of a business" and the acquisition of assets alone will not normally, therefore, result in a merger taking place unless, for example, such a transfer enables a business activity to be continued. However, the sale of assets accompanied by the transfer of goodwill and/or the benefit of contracts will normally amount to a merger. It follows that as well as acquisitions (in whole or part) of businesses and companies, most joint ventures will constitute relevant merger situations under the Act, as will management and leveraged buy-outs and buy-ins (under which the target merges with, and ceases to be distinct from, the buy-out vehicle).   **1.008**

A merger will qualify for investigation where either one or both of the following criteria is satisfied:

(i)   as a result of the merger a share of at least 25 per cent of the supply of goods or services of any description in the United Kingdom or in a substantial part of it is created or enhanced (the "share of supply" test);

    or

(ii)   the value of the turnover in the United Kingdom of the enterprise being taken over exceeds £70 million (the "turnover test").

A target company will be brought under common control or ownership in three sets of circumstances: first, where one party acquires a controlling interest (more than 50 per cent) in the other party (legal or *de jure* control); secondly, where one party acquires the ability to control the policy of the other ("*de facto*" control), which may involve an interest of substantially less than 50 per cent, depending, *inter alia*, upon the fragmentation of shareholdings in the target company; and thirdly, where one party acquires the ability materially to influence the policy of the other. An acquisition of 15 per cent of the shares of the target company has been sufficient for a reference to the Commission to be made on the ground of material influence, as has the acquisition of significant non-voting convertible loan stock and other rights. The OFT's guidance states that "[a]ssessment of material influence requires a case by case analysis of the entire relationship between the acquiring entity and the target" and accordingly, the level of shareholding in a target company is not in itself determinative.[19]

Although the parties to a merger are under no obligation under the Act to seek "clearance" from the OFT (that is, confirmation that it will not be referred to the Competition Commission) either before or after a merger takes place, an acquisition that is not cleared in advance faces the possibility of a reference to the Commission being made at any time up to four months after the transaction has been announced or completed, whichever is the later. Moreover, a wide range of sanctions, including divestment, can be adopted by the Commission if it concludes that an anti-competitive outcome will result, aggravating the uncertainty brought about by completing a transaction in advance of obtaining clearance. Nevertheless, there may be good commercial reasons on the part of the purchaser for preferring not to seek clearance in advance, and a vendor may insist that the transaction should be unconditional on prior merger clearance, leaving the risk of subsequent regulatory interference with the purchaser alone. The issues that will need to be considered vary in the circumstances of each particular case but, except in the case of a merger to which the City Code on Takeovers and Mergers applies,[20] advisers may be unlikely to recommend seeking clearance in advance of completion if in their opinion the risk of a reference is low.

Obtaining clearance

1.009   There are two possible procedures for obtaining a merger clearance from the OFT: the pre-notification procedure introduced in 1989 and retained by the Act may be used for publicly announced but uncompleted mergers by filing a statutory Merger Notice setting out details of the proposal and the markets it will affect; alternatively the parties to a merger may simply present a written submission to the OFT containing much the same information and arguing in favour of clearance. If the pre-notification procedure

---

[19] See the OFT's *Substantive Assessment Guidance* at para.2.10.
[20] See further Ch.3.

is used, a merger will be deemed to have been cleared 20 working days after submission of the Merger Notice (subject to the possibility of extension of a further 10 working days), unless on or before that date it has been referred to the Commission.[21] A non-statutory filing is subject to a non-binding 40 day administrative timetable. The decision as to which method to use depends upon the circumstances of the merger; the "traditional" approach of a written submission not using the Merger Notice is generally the more appropriate method for difficult or controversial cases (for example, contested takeovers or mergers with significant market overlaps), as the advantage of a fixed timetable under the pre-notification procedure may be more than offset by the risk of provoking a premature reference to the Commission because the OFT has insufficient time to assess a complex case.

Confidential guidance and informal advice

It is possible to obtain formal "confidential guidance" in relation to a proposed but unannounced merger. Before a planned acquisition becomes public knowledge, the OFT is prepared to give guidance in confidence as to whether it is likely that the transaction, once announced, would be referred to the Commission. The procedure is sometimes useful in acquisitions raising sensitive competition issues where the parties do not wish to announce their intentions without obtaining comfort that their proposal is unlikely to be referred. The merger proposal is evaluated by the OFT following the same procedure as for publicly announced transactions and in difficult cases the final decision will usually be taken by the Chairman of the OFT. However, because of the confidential nature of the procedure, the OFT is precluded from seeking the views of interested third parties and is entirely dependent on published information or information supplied to it by the applicant. Consequently, the OFT may decide that guidance cannot be given, rather than take the risk of giving positive guidance but then, following announcement and third party consultation, reaching an adverse conclusion and referring the merger. Alternatively, the OFT's guidance may be that a reference to the Commission would be likely. Even if confidential guidance has been given, the OFT is free to take a different view of the matter once it becomes public knowledge and it is able to ascertain the views of all the interested parties; it would, however, be very unusual for a different view to be taken later in the absence of material changes[22] (which is a critical element of the commercial value of receiving positive confidential guidance).

Informal advice, which is generally given orally at a single meeting in relation to proposed but unannounced mergers, following submission of a short written paper outlining the proposals, is a less formal process whereby parties can request the view of the Mergers Branch as to the likelihood of a reference

1.010

---

[21] There is a third option where a merger is also being notified in either France or Germany to use the "common form of notification" agreed between the competition authorities of the three jurisdictions. This option, however, has rarely been used in practice, and the form is currently out of date and under review. See further Ch.3.

[22] *e.g.* material changes in the interim to the structure of the transaction or the competition conditions against which it is assessed.

being made. Such advice is usually given by the Director, Deputy Director or a senior case officer; it is not given by the Chairman or any other member of the OFT's Board. Like formal confidential guidance, informal advice is not binding on the OFT, and although the process is as rigorous as the time available and the information provided by the parties permits, it cannot be as reliable as formal confidential guidance.

The OFT's evaluation

1.011   The OFT's responsibility under the Act for monitoring merger activity means that in practice some OFT merger evaluations commence not through an application by the parties for clearance, but as a result of the OFT's monitoring of the press for merger announcements, or because a third party has drawn a merger to its attention. The manner of evaluation is the same however the procedure is commenced. OFT staff will consider the information and arguments provided by the parties as well as relevant published information on the parties and the markets in question; they will also seek the views of customers, suppliers, competitors and others with an interest in the effects of the merger. In cases that raise complex or material competition issues, the parties will be sent an issues letter setting out the potential concerns identified by the OFT following its consultation process, and invited to attend an issues meeting with the Mergers Branch two to three days later. For the first time, the Act confers on the OFT in relation to completed mergers the power to accept undertakings from the parties to a merger in order to prevent "pre-emptive action" being taken, that is action which might prejudice a reference to the Commission or any remedies being imposed. The OFT may also make an order to the same effect where it has reasonable grounds for suspecting, in relation to a completed merger, that pre-emptive action is in progress or in contemplation.

Implications of a reference to the Competition Commission

1.012   The announcement of a reference places an automatic prohibition on the purchaser acquiring any further shares in the target (if it is a company) without the consent of the Competition Commission. In relation to completed mergers, the Act provides that once a reference to the Commission has been made, no further steps may be taken to implement the merger or integrate the merging business without the consent of the Commission.

The Commission's investigation

1.013   In carrying out its investigation and as part of its general information gathering and analysis, the Commission will request the parties' views on the merger and its anticipated effects on competition in the form of written submissions and responses to questionnaires. Each of the main parties is asked to attend a hearing, which usually takes place about six weeks after the announcement of the reference. Before then, the Commission will have sought the views of third parties, by a general press release and either by advertisements in the relevant trade press, or by writing directly to interested parties identified by the Commission. Third parties are invited to express their views in writing and those thought to be most likely to be affected by the merger may be asked to attend individual hearings with the Commission.

The Enterprise Act introduced a new procedure whereby, having carried out its substantive assessment of the issues raised by the merger, the Commission publishes its "provisional findings" which, if they are adverse, indicate the commencement of the Commission's consideration of whether there are any countervailing benefits and/or possible remedies. The main parties will be invited to attend a further hearing with the Commission to discuss these issues.

Where the Commission concludes that a merger will result in an anti-competitive outcome, it is under a duty to take action by way of seeking undertakings or making orders to remedy, mitigate, or prevent the substantial lessening of competition and any resulting adverse effects. Such action may include prohibitions; the disposal of shares, interests in shares or the limitation of voting rights; the sale of assets; the control of the conduct of the merged entity; or the publication of information. Where the remedy falls short of outright prohibition, the merger will be cleared subject to the provisions of any undertakings or orders concluded as being necessary by the Commission. If the Commission concludes that the merger may not be expected to result in a substantial lessening of competition neither the Commission nor the OFT has power to interfere and the merger will be cleared.

Review by the Competition Appeal Tribunal

For the first time, the Act places on a statutory basis the right to seek judi- **1.014** cial review of decision-making by the OFT, the Competition Commission and, where relevant, the Secretary of State, by way of an application to the Competition Appeal Tribunal. When hearing applications against merger decisions, the CAT is required to apply the same principles as would be applied by a court on an application for judicial review, and therefore it has no jurisdiction to hear appeals on the merits. In relation to a successful application, the CAT may quash the whole or part of the decision in question and refer the matter back to the original decision maker (*i.e.* the OFT, Commission or Secretary of State as the case may be), with a direction to reconsider the original decision. The first application to the CAT under the new regime was made in November 2003[23] and resulted in an appeal to the Court of Appeal, whose decision set out important guiding principles in relation to the OFT's decision-making process and the scope of the CAT's power to review merger control decisions. It is clear that following the Court of Appeal's judgment, the CAT has retained consider-able scope to review merger control decisions, whether by the OFT, or the Commission, even though its rule is limited to applying established judicial review principles.

---

[23] The *IBA Health* case, cited above.

Summary

1.015   Under the provisions of the Fair Trading Act, the process of merger control in the United Kingdom was based on discretion and choice: on the part of the merging parties, in considering whether to seek clearance; and on the part of the Secretary of State, in deciding whether to make a reference and, following any adverse conclusions contained in the Commission's report, whether to accept the Commission's recommendations. The system had been criticised for being unpredictable, haphazard and lacking internal cohesion, for following procedures which were unnecessarily slow and cumbersome, and for requiring a multi-tiered evaluation process involving two separate bodies in addition to the Secretary of State, as well as for imposing an unnecessary burden on the parties to a merger over an extended period. The competition authorities themselves had been described as slow to focus on the real issues and as lacking commercial awareness, and there was little effective judicial control. On the other hand, the authorities were generally perceived to be fair and thorough; and in separating the investigation of mergers from the enforcement of remedial action, the system ensured that the Competition Commission was free from internal conflicts of interest and from any obligation to implement the policies or will of the government of the day.

The Enterprise Act has sought to maintain the benefits of voluntary filings and the resulting commercial flexibility that is highly valued by the business community, particularly compared with the system of compulsory prior notification under the EC Merger Regulation and the national merger laws of many of the other EU Member States. At the same time it has sought to remove ministerial involvement in the vast majority of cases, although since the announcement of the so-called Tebbit Doctrine in 1984,[24] such interference had been relatively rare. A welcome development has been the increased transparency of the merger control process through publication of the OFT's reasons underlying its clearance and reference decisions, as well as through publication of the OFT's and Commission's assessment guidelines. The Act has also sought to improve the process of negotiating and implementing remedies by the Commission announcing its provisional findings before the remedies stage, which will avoid the necessity of having to discuss remedies on a hypothetical basis at a time when the Commission previously had to assure the parties that it retained an open mind as to the substantive issues and had reached no conclusions. Similarly, the practical difficulties of having to negotiate and agree undertakings with the OFT on the basis of sometimes brief and unclear statements in the Commission's report will be avoided.

However, there arguably remains scope for improvement in the Commission's procedures. In particular, the merging parties are not permitted to have access to the Commission's file to review the evidence submitted by third parties. The extent to which such evidence is made available remains a matter for the Commission's discretion. Similarly, it is suggested that the Commission's "issues letter" which sets out the issues which the Commission considers to be relevant to its deliberations, should become a fully fledged "statement of objections", to which should be

---

[24] See n.3 to para.1.001 above.

appended all of the evidence upon which the Commission intends to rely.[25] The introduction of such procedural safeguards, would reduce the prospect that the main parties may seize upon the Commission's provisional findings as the first reasoned statement to which they can respond and submit a detailed rebuttal, rather than proceed to a discussion relating to remedies, which will take place shortly afterwards.

Finally, although the government's decision to deny a full right of appeal before the CAT in merger cases, particularly in the absence of the procedural safeguards identified above, might be regarded as a missed opportunity to ensure fully rigorous decision-making by the Commission given the difficulty in ascribing relative weight to often conflicting evidence and the difficulties inherent in an *ex ante* analysis, there would appear to be reasonable scope for the CAT to review the Commission's reasoning following the judgment of the Court of Appeal in the *IBA Health* case.

---

[25] These suggestions would bring the Commission's procedures into line with the procedure under UK law for investigating anti-competitive practices, and with the procedure under EC law for investigating both anti-competitive practices and mergers.

CHAPTER 2

JURISDICTION

Introduction

2.001 The purpose of this chapter is to consider the circumstances in which a "merger" or "acquisition" (whether in the form of the acquisition of assets or through the purchase of shares or by a public bid, joint venture, management/leveraged buy-out or buy-in or similar transaction) will qualify for investigation by the United Kingdom merger authorities. In this connection, one of the first issues that should be considered by the parties to a merger is which regulatory bodies will have jurisdiction to control the proposed transaction. A key question is whether the transaction will amount to a concentration having a Community dimension under the EC Merger Regulation ("EC Merger Regulation")[1] and therefore be subject to the exclusive jurisdiction of the European Commission, subject to the "referral back" provisions contained in Art.9 and Art.4(4) of the EC Merger Regulation and the ability of Member States to protect certain legitimate interests under Art.21(4).[2] If the UK merger control provisions apply, a further issue that needs to be considered is whether the residual public interest considerations (and associated ministerial involvement which can arise in the defence, newspaper[3] and media sectors) are relevant, or whether sector-specific rules apply such as those that govern mergers of water and sewage undertakings. In addition, approval mechanisms exist for those seeking to acquire control over banks and building societies; and mergers and related transactions involving regulated utilities such as electricity, gas, water, telecommunications, rail and air traffic services may require the modification of an operating licence or give rise to other issues falling within the jurisdiction of the relevant industry regulator.[4]

The provisions of the Act relating to jurisdiction mirror, to a large extent, the provisions of the FTA, with the key jurisdictional change being the replacement of the former assets test by a UK turnover test, which gave the OFT jurisdiction over mergers where the gross worldwide value

---

[1] Council Regulation 139/2004 on the control of concentrations between undertakings [2004] O.J. L24/1. Prior to May 1, 2004, the provisions of the EC Merger Regulation were set out in Council Regulation 4064/89 [1990] O.J. L257/13, with amendments introduced by Council Regulation 1310/97 of June 30, 1997, [1997] O.J. L180/1 ("the pre-reform EC Merger Regulation"). See para.2.034, below.

[2] Previously Art.21(3) of the pre-reform EC Merger Regulation. The interfaces between the EC Merger Regulation and UK merger control are considered below at para.2.038.

[3] An analysis of the law and practice relating to newspaper mergers is set out in Ch.7.

[4] A review of the key provisions that relate to mergers and related transactions in these "special sectors" is set out below at para.2.058.

of the assets acquired exceeded £70 million. The White Paper[5] justified the change on the basis that:

"with service industries and intangibles of increasing importance, a turnover test represents a sounder measure of the economic significance of a merger".

In order to ensure that the full range of commercial structures identified above is subject to regulatory scrutiny, the Act adopts the broad jurisdictional concept of a "relevant merger situation". Section 23 of the Act provides that a relevant merger situation will arise if two or more enterprises have ceased to be distinct enterprises or there are arrangements in progress or contemplation which will lead to enterprises ceasing to be distinct[6] *and* either:

(i)   the value of the turnover in the United Kingdom of the enterprise being acquired exceeds £70 million (the "turnover test")[7]; or

(ii)   as a result, at least 25 per cent of the supply of goods or services of any description in the United Kingdom or in a substantial part of the United Kingdom, are supplied by or to the same person or for one and the same person, or by or to the persons by whom the relevant enterprises are carried on (the "share of supply test").[8]

To qualify for investigation under the share of supply test, the merger must result in an increase in the share of supply or consumption above the 25 per cent level. Accordingly, an increase from 25 per cent to 25.5 per cent will satisfy the test, as will an increase from 24 per cent to 30 per cent, but an increase from 0 per cent to 30 per cent will not.[9]

The jurisdictional test comprises two main elements: the concept of a *merger situation*, defined in terms of separate enterprises ceasing to be distinct and the concept of *relevance*, defined in terms of the share of supply test or the turnover test. It is implicit in these criteria that at least one of the enterprises concerned must be active within the UK: this will be the case by definition where the enterprise being acquired satisfies the turnover test; and where the share of supply test is satisfied both of the enterprises that cease to be distinct must be active in supplying or acquiring goods or services within the UK or a substantial part of it. In addition, either the merger must not yet have taken place or, in relation to an announced completed merger, must have taken place not more than four months before a reference to the Competition Commission is made.[10] Finally, in determining whether enterprises cease to be distinct and therefore a merger situation arises, it is important to consider whether a transaction, particularly those such as co-operative

---

[5] DTI White Paper "*A World Class Competition Regime*", Cm. 5233 (July 2001), para.5.11.
[6] s.22 imposes a duty on the OFT to make references in relation to completed mergers, and s.33 imposes a similar duty in relation to anticipated mergers.
[7] s.23(1)(b).
[8] s.23(2), (3) and (4).
[9] This follows from s.23(2)(b) which refers to the 25 per cent share of supply criterion "prevail[ing] or prevail[ing] to a greater extent".
[10] s.24.

joint venture arrangements, falls to be assessed under the provisions relating to the control of anti-competitive agreements under the Competition Act 1998 rather than the merger provisions of the Enterprise Act. The remainder of this Chapter will examine each of these elements in turn.

Has a merger situation arisen?

2.002 As indicated above, s.23(1) of the Act provides that a merger situation will exist where "two or more enterprises have ceased to be distinct enterprises. . .". This subsection gives rise to two questions: what is an enterprise; and when will enterprises cease to be distinct?

"Enterprise"

2.003 The Act defines an enterprise as "the activities, or part of the activities, of a business".[11] A "business" is defined by s.129(1) as including "a professional practice and . . . any other undertaking which is carried on for gain or reward or which is an undertaking in the course of which goods or services are supplied otherwise than free of charge". This does not mean that the business must be profit-making and, indeed, it may be loss-making or not-for-profit.[11A] The Act defines the concept of "supply" in relation to goods as including sale, lease, hire or hire purchase.[12] The supply of services is expressly stated to exclude the rendering of any services under a contract of service or apprenticeship but includes the performing of any activity for gain or reward.[13] The construction of buildings and other structures for a third party is also identified as amounting to a supply.[14]

This definition has two main implications. First, enterprises may cease to be distinct if only part of a business' activities are acquired, and there is no requirement that a business should be a separate legal entity in order to constitute an enterprise. Secondly, the acquisition of assets alone would not constitute a qualifying merger, unless, as a matter of fact, part or all of a business' activities are transferred. The OFT's substantive assessment guidance indicates the factors that the OFT is likely to consider in assessing whether a particular group of assets amounts to an "enterprise":

"[a]n 'enterprise' may comprise any number of components, most commonly including the assets and records needed to carry on the busi-

---

[11] s.129(1).

[11A] In his advice dated March 26, 2002, in connection with the completed merger between the Imperial Cancer Research Fund and the Cancer Research Campaign under the FTA, the Director General stated that: ". . . certain fund-raising activities of charities (for example, collecting private donations and legacies) do not constitute a business for the purposes of the Act. Likewise, charitable activities that involve the provision of goods and services free of charge fall outside the scope of the Act. In this case, however, both charities carry on certain activities for gain or reward, for example, retailing activities and the licensing of intellectual property rights". The Director General went on to conclude in his advice that the share of supply test under the FTA was satisfied with respect to "the supply of retailing services in the cancer charity sector."

[12] s.129(1).

[13] s.128(2).

[14] s.129(1).

ness, together with the benefit of existing contracts and/or goodwill. The transfer of 'customer records' is likely to be important in assessing whether an enterprise has been transferred. In some cases, the transfer of physical assets alone may be sufficient to constitute an enterprise: for example, where the facilities or site transferred enables a particular business activity to be continued. Intangible assets such as intellectual property rights are unlikely, on their own, to constitute an 'enterprise' unless it is possible to identify turnover directly related to the transferred intangible assets that will also transfer to the buyer".[15]

The definition of "enterprise" adopted by the Act is the same as that contained in the FTA, and the OFT's guidance set out above reflects the OFT's and Competition Commission's practice under the FTA. In practice, it is clear that the acquisition by one business of another business as a going concern will result in enterprises ceasing to be distinct. Accordingly, the lease of over 700 public houses by Allied Breweries Limited to Brent Walker plc on long leases with Allied Breweries retaining the freehold reversion was regarded by the OFT as amounting to a merger situation within the meaning of the FTA, as each pub constituted an established trading unit with an ongoing business and customer goodwill. The position would almost certainly have been different if the pubs were leased simply as buildings without tenants or justices' licences. The sale of a factory with plant and equipment, employees, goodwill and the benefit of existing contracts with suppliers and customers will clearly amount to an enterprise, whether or not it constitutes a stand-alone legal entity or is part of a larger business retained by the vendor. "Assets deals" as well as share sales will, therefore, be caught by the Act, provided that the other jurisdictional requirements are satisfied. The sale of an asset or assets such as a building, item of plant or equipment or intellectual property right (such as a patent, but not necessarily a trademark) will not constitute the sale of an enterprise *per se*, so that, for example, the sale of a factory as an empty building, will not amount to the sale of an "enterprise". However, if, as indicated above, the sale were accompanied by the transfer of the benefit of contracts with employees, customers and suppliers, the sale of an enterprise would almost certainly take place. It should be noted that none of these elements, individually, is likely to be essential to the finding that an enterprise has been transferred, so that if employees were not transferred, for example, this would not necessarily mean that the transfer of an enterprise had not taken place; in this connection if the Transfer of Undertakings (Protection of Employment) Regulations apply, it is likely that the OFT would conclude that an enterprise has been transferred.[15A] If, for the purposes of s.49 of the Value Added Tax Act 1994, a collection of assets are expressed to be transferred "as a going concern", this may suggest to the OFT that the assets in question amount to an enterprise within the meaning of the Act.[16] Similarly,

---

[15] OFT guidance, *Mergers: Substantive Assessment Guidance*, para.2.8.
[15A] SI 1981/1794.
[16] The effect of s.49 of the Value Added Tax Act 1994 together with the regulations made under it (presently contained in para.5 of the VAT (Special Provisions) Order 1995, SI 1995/1268) is that where a business is transferred as a going concern, the supply of goodwill, premises, plant, stock, etc. by the vendor will not be treated as a supply of goods or

the acceptance of a restrictive covenant by the vendor of assets not to compete with the business sold would tend to indicate that goodwill and, therefore, an enterprise had been transferred, rather than a collection of assets, whether or not employees had been transferred, and whether or not trading contracts had been assigned. Nor is it necessary that the enterprise acquired should be trading at the date of acquisition.[17] The OFT's approach is further illustrated by the Duffield case,[18] in which the OFT found that the acquisition by Duffield of a customer list and records, together with customer contracts and orders and a three year licence for an animal feed formula was sufficient to constitute an "enterprise" for the purpose of the FTA. The OFT found that the combination of assets, contracts and goodwill "facilitated the seamless carrying on by Duffield of the ruminant feed business of Bury Nutrition".

The concept of an "enterprise" under the FTA was not interpreted by the courts, but has been considered by the Competition Commission and its predecessor the Monopolies and Mergers Commission in a number of reports.[19] As a general principle, the MMC stated that in addressing this issue the concept of an enterprise should be interpreted broadly:

---

services and will therefore be outside the scope of VAT. There have been a number of cases in which the question of whether an undertaking has been transferred as a "going concern" has been considered. The issue is a question of fact in each case. As the European Court of Justice stated in Case 24/85 *JMA Spijkers v Gebroders Benedik Abbatoir CV* [1986] E.C.R. 1119; [1986] II C.M.L.R. 296, at 303:

"[i]t is necessary to take account of all the factual circumstances of the transaction in question, including the type of undertaking or business in question, the transfer or otherwise of tangible assets . . . at the date of transfer, whether the majority of the staff are taken over by the new employer, the transfer or otherwise of the circle of customers and the degree of similarity between activities before and after the transfer and the duration of any interruption in those activities. It should be made clear however that each of these factors is only part of the overall assessment which is required and therefore they cannot be examined independently of each other."

[17] *AAH Holdings PLC/Medicopharma NV*, Cm. 1950 (May 1992) discussed below. Similarly in *Stora Kopparbergs Bergslags AB/Swedish Match NV/The Gillette Company*, Cm. 1473 (March 1991), the MMC concluded that the transfer of the Wilkinson Sword wet-shaving division to a shelf company (Eemland) immediately prior to a leveraged buy-out taking place did involve the acquisition of an enterprise. In reaching this view, the MMC stated that "we consider that the activities, or part of the activities, of a business include not only the actual supply of the goods and services concerned, but also the steps necessary to make such supply possible" (at para.7.47). The MMC found support for this view from s.77 of the FTA which provides, *inter alia*, that for the purpose of determining whether any two enterprises have been brought under common ownership or control, "associated persons" are to be treated as single persons. Under s.77(4)(d) of the FTA such persons included any two or more persons acting together to secure or exercise control of any enterprise or assets. (This provision is now contained in s.127(4)(d) of the Enterprise Act.) The MMC concluded that the participants in the "bidding group" (that is Gillette, a number of investors, banks and finance houses) could be regarded as acting together to secure or exercise control of an enterprise or assets, namely the wet-shaving division.

[18] Acquisition by W L Duffield & Sons Limited of the ruminant feed business of Bury Nutrition, part of ABNA Limited, DGFT's Advice dated December 20, 2002.

[19] *William Cook plc acquisitions*, Cm. 1196 (August 1990); *AAH Holdings PLC/Medicopharma NV*, Cm. 1950 (May 1992); and *Stagecoach Holdings PLC/Lancaster City Transport*, Cm. 2423 (December 1993).

". . . we believe that one of the intentions and purposes of the Act is to enable the MMC to consider commercial realities and results and not merely the results of legally enforceable agreements and arrangements (a point also made in the AAH report, paragraph 6.69). It is, we believe, our duty to look at substance, not form".[20]

In the report[21] on the acquisition by AAH Holdings plc, a pharmaceutical wholesaler, of certain assets of Medicopharma, another pharmaceutical wholesaler, the relevant facts were that on November 3, 1991, Medicopharma Ltd and Medicopharma (UK) BV (together referred to as "Medicopharma") resolved to cease trading in the light of financial difficulties encountered by their Dutch parent company. On the same day, the entire stock of Medicopharma, together with the leases on its three largest depots in the United Kingdom and certain assets, including two computer systems, were sold to AAH. AAH argued before the MMC that the transaction did not amount to a merger situation within the meaning of the FTA as it had acquired only assets, and in particular because Medicopharma had ceased to trade prior to the acquisition, Medico-pharma's wholesaler dealer licences had lapsed, no contracts with customers had been transferred, outstanding orders were not delivered, customers had to make new arrangements, and AAH installed its own branch managers at the depots. The MMC accepted[22] that all of these factors, on their face, favoured AAH's argument that it had acquired only assets and that no transfer of an enterprise had taken place, but neverthe-less reached the conclusion that the overall effect of the arrangements, agreements and understandings between Medicopharma and AAH was that the business carried on by AAH represented the continuation of a signifi-cant proportion of the business previously carried on by Medicopharma, and that accordingly an enterprise had been acquired by AAH.

2.004

In reaching this conclusion, the MMC paid particular attention to the fact that the acquisition of the assets in question carried with them an inevitable degree of goodwill, as local pharmacists tended to rely on their nearest wholesaling depot notwithstanding changes in ownership, and the need for twice daily deliveries of certain pharmaceuticals increased this local depend-ence. Moreover, although AAH did not specifically acquire customer lists, the computer system it had acquired contained customers' telephone and fax numbers. The fact that contracts were not formally transferred was largely irrelevant as orders were placed on a twice daily basis and retail pharmacists would need to find an immediate local source of supply. The arrangements also gave AAH exclusive prior knowledge of the fact and timing of the closure of Medicopharma, and AAH therefore had an advantage over its competitors in terms of soliciting customers. Medicopharma's redundancy arrangements and notices were structured in such a way that AAH could take on Medicopharma's ex-employees[23] at the depots it had acquired, thereby

---

[20] *Stagecoach Holdings PLC/Lancaster City Transport*, Cm. 2423 (December 1993), para.6.21.
[21] *AAH Holdings PLC/Medicopharma NV*, Cm. 1950 (May 1992).
[22] *AAH Holdings PLC/Medicopharma NV*, Cm. 1950 (May 1992), para.6.101.
[23] *AAH Holdings PLC/Medicopharma NV*, Cm. 1950 (May 1992), para.6.102. The MMC quoted a report submitted to AAH's Board which showed that AAH considered that there

gaining the benefit of these employees' knowledge of Medicopharma's customers as well as the benefit of the established, supplier/customer relationship. Moreover, under the purchase agreement, AAH undertook to become Medicopharma NV's agent in recovering trade debts. AAH also undertook to use its reasonable endeavours to assume the obligations of Medicopharma NV in respect of certain pharmacy loan guarantee schemes.

Similarly, in its report on the merger situation between Stagecoach Holdings PLC and Lancaster City Transport Ltd,[24] the MMC accepted that a number of the features of the transaction were consistent with Stagecoach's arguments that it had only acquired assets (primarily a bus depot and some buses). Moreover, there was no direct transfer of staff, and no assignment of goodwill or the benefit of contracts had taken place. Nevertheless, the MMC again emphasised that the FTA should be interpreted widely so as to enable commercial realities and results to be assessed by looking at the substance of transactions rather than their form. The MMC concluded that, effectively, all that was required to run the business was staff, buses and the depot, and that the acquisition of the depot had enabled Stagecoach to continue to operate all the commercial services previously operated by Lancaster, with no perceptible break in services. The MMC also considered that Stagecoach's willingness to pay a higher price for the depot than other bidders was a further indication that the business had inevitably been transferred with the depot.

More recently, the OFT concluded that enterprises had not ceased to be distinct as a consequence of arrangements entered into between Unum Limited and Swiss Life (UK) plc in connection with the reinsurance and claims administration of group income protection (GIP) claims.[25] The OFT reached this conclusion on the grounds that no employees, assets or liabilities would be transferred to Unum from Swiss Life; the agreements entered into between the parties did not involve the transfer of existing insurance policies or renewal rights; customers continued to pay premiums to Swiss Life; no Swiss Life assets or liabilities were transferred to Unum (save to the extent that the economic effect of the reinsurance agreement would be to transfer claims liabilities and related reserves to Unum); Swiss Life would retain all policy records; although Unum would have full control over the administration of claims, it would have no control over the terms of the GIP policies themselves; only limited information relating to GIP claims and closed GIP claims would be transferred to Unum; and no details relating to current and previous premium rates, risk profiles, profitability assessments or renewal dates would be passed to Unum.

In its decision in relation to the completed acquisition by Arcelor SA of Corus UK Limited's UK hot rolled steel sheet piling business,[25A] the OFT

---

was a risk that the use of the depots by AAH for trading purposes constituted a transfer of a business in the context of the Transfer of Undertakings legislation; at para.6.89.

[24] *Stagecoach Holdings PLC/Lancaster City Transport Ltd*, Cm. 2423 (December 1993), para.6.24. In their report on the *Acquisitions by William Cook plc of certain steel foundries*, Cm. 1196 (August 1990) the MMC concluded that the acquisition of the Armadale works constituted the transfer of an enterprise for a number of reasons including, *inter alia*, because Cook had acquired the goodwill of the business, orders would be forwarded to it, it had the right to represent itself as carrying on the business in succession to the vendor, and had acquired custody of the patterns belonging to customers (at paras 6.4–6.7).

[25] OFT decision of March 22, 2004, *Completed transaction between Unum and Swiss Life (UK) plc*.

[25A] OFT reference decision, September 9, 2004.

concluded that the acquisition of the following assets and related interests constituted an enterprise: goodwill and a small number of employees; supplier and customer lists, including mailing lists, customer credit limits, customer payment history and UK transport rates; product development and design information, including specifications, drawings, training manuals and handbooks; sales, marketing, promotional information and market forecasts; technical and other expertise; and the granting of a non-compete covenant by the vendor (the duration of which was excised from the OFT's decision).

In light of the reports and decisions considered above, it is possible to draw a number of general conclusions as to when the acquisition of assets will amount to the transfer of an enterprise under the Enterprise Act[25B]:

2.005

(i) the Competition Commission (and therefore the OFT) in deciding whether a qualifying merger has arisen will have regard to the effect of all agreements, arrangements, understandings and transactions between the parties, whether or not they are intended to be legally enforceable, and will not therefore focus solely on the legal agreement[26] providing for the acquisition of the assets in question;

(ii) the Commission's role is to investigate the facts of each case "on the basis of a balance of probabilities", and there is therefore no scope for it to carry the burden of proving that what has been acquired in a given case amounts to an enterprise[27]; and

(iii) the question of whether an enterprise has been acquired is one of fact and degree in each case; the absence of a formal transfer of customer contracts, for example, is not determinative if, as a matter of fact, customers would continue to contract with the purchaser of the assets in any event.[28] In this connection, the ability of the purchaser to continue the business activities of the vendor is particularly important. Similarly, the fact that the legal agreements state that goodwill is not included in the sale will not avoid a finding that an enterprise has been transferred if, for example, former employees are taken on by the purchaser with knowledge of customers' details and terms of trading.[29]

The Commission's previous analysis suggests that where an acquirer is able, as a consequence of a transaction, to carry on at least part of the business carried on previously by the vendor, it will not be possible to rely on the argument that no business activities were transferred and

---

[25B] In *IBA Health Limited v OFT* [2004] EWCA Civ. 142, para.80, the Court of Appeal cautioned, in the context of an analysis of the OFT's duty to refer, that the major changes introduced by the Enterprise Act made it unwise to seek assistance in the case law and practice under the FTA. However, it is suggested that the concept of an enterprise as defined under the FTA will continue to be relevant.

[26] *AAH Holdings PLC/Medicopharma NV*, Cm. 1950 (May 1992), para.6.70; and *Stagecoach Holdings PLC/Lancaster City Transport Ltd*, Cm. 2423 (December 1993), para.6.21.

[27] *AAH Holdings PLC/Medicopharma NV.*, Cm. 1950 (May 1992), at para.6.63.

[28] *AAH Holdings PLC/Medicopharma NV.*, Cm. 1950 (May 1992), at para.6.80.

[29] *AAH Holdings PLC/Medicopharma NV.*, Cm. 1950 (May 1992), at para.6.88.

therefore that no enterprises would cease to be distinct. This conclusion is supported by two clearances by the Secretary of State of trademark acquisitions under the FTA.[30] These decisions were taken under the FTA before the Director General began publishing his advice to the Secretary of State in mergers cases and no detailed reasoning is therefore available. However, it is suggested that they are compatible with the statement made at para.2.8 of the OFT's *Substantive Assessment Guidance*, on the basis that as trademarks are guarantees of quality/ origin and attract valuable consumer goodwill, it will be relatively straightforward in most cases to identify turnover directly related to the trademark that will be transferred to the purchaser.

"Ceased to be distinct enterprises"

2.006   It was indicated above[31] that a merger situation will arise where "two or more enterprises have ceased to be distinct".[32] Section 26(1) provides that two enterprises shall be regarded as ceasing to be distinct "if they are brought under common ownership or common control (whether or not the business to which either of them formerly belonged continues to be carried on under the same or different ownership or control)."

Common ownership or common control

2.007   A literal interpretation of s.26(1) would suggest that a distinction exists between "common ownership" on the one hand and "common control" on the other,[33] with ownership being a reasonably narrow concept as in, for example, "A" owning all the shares in "B", whereas control is a much broader concept which would encompass ownership (which equates effectively to total 100 per cent control).[34] In interpreting the equivalent provisions of the FTA,[35] the MMC noted that "control" may include a "controlling interest" which is not defined by the Act, and that in specifying instances of common control the FTA recognised that these were "without prejudice to the generality of" the expression. The equivalent provision of the Enterprise Act, s.26(2), adopts a similar approach by referring to the listed instances as being particular examples of common control. Similarly, the MMC observed that the word "brought" was not defined by the FTA (and is similarly not defined by the Act) and concluded that the FTA did not limit how the process of bringing two enterprises under common ownership or control could be achieved, which enabled the Commission to consider

---

[30] See DTI press notices P/94/553 (acquisition of "Haig" user rights) and P/94/461 (acquisition of "Haliborange" T.M.).

[31] See para.2.002, above.

[32] s.23(1)(a) and s.23(2)(a), or there are arrangements in progress or contemplation which will lead to enterprises ceasing to be distinct: s.33(1)(a).

[33] This distinction was first identified by J.P. Cunningham in *The Fair Trading Act 1973* (Sweet & Maxwell, 1974).

[34] The OFT's *Substantive Assessment Guidance* considers only the concept of control and does not distinguish between "common ownership and common control".

[35] s.65 of the FTA.

"commercial realities and results" and not merely legally enforceable agreements and arrangements.[36]

Section 26(2) identifies a number of circumstances in which enterprises shall be regarded as being under common control,[37] providing, in essence, that enterprises will cease to be distinct where the "control" of one enterprise is acquired by another. Control is identified by s.26(3) as including the ability:

(i)   directly or indirectly to control; or

(ii)   materially to influence the policy of an enterprise (but without having a controlling interest in that enterprise).

Section 26 therefore recognises three levels of control:

(i)   a controlling interest (*de jure* or legal control);

(ii)   the ability to control policy (*de facto* control); and

(iii)   the ability materially to influence policy.

As the MMC has observed,[38] for a finding that a merger situation has been created, it is not necessary for there to be evidence that control or material influence has been exercised, or even whether, at a particular time, it is intended that they should be exercised, provided that the ability to exercise such control exists.

The Act provides[39] that a person will be treated as bringing an enterprise under his control (and thereby creating a new merger situation) if he moves up through the levels of control, that is, from material influence to *de facto* control, or from *de facto* control to *de jure* control. However, further acquisitions of a company's shares by a person having a controlling interest will not give rise to a new merger situation.

---

[36] *AAH Holdings PLC/Medicopharma NV*, Cm. 1950 (May 1992), paras 6.67–6.69.

[37] s.26(2) identifies three sets of circumstances in which enterprises will be regarded as being under common control. This will arise if they are:

    (i)   enterprises of interconnected bodies corporate (defined by s.129(2) as being parent and subsidiary within the meaning of s.736 of the Companies Act 1985, *i.e.* broadly more than 50 per cent);

    (ii)   enterprises carried on by two or more bodies corporate of which one and the same person or group of persons has control; or

    (iii) an enterprise carried on by a body corporate and an enterprise carried on by a person or group of persons having control of that body corporate.

Accordingly, under (i), if a parent company acquires another company, the subsidiary enterprises of both companies will be regarded as being in common control, whether or not either or both parties have adopted a policy of not interfering in the running of their subsidiary companies. Situation (ii) will arise if a person holds sufficient shares or interest in two separate companies to control those companies. Situation (iii) is similar to (ii), but where different corporate structures are involved.

[38] *Government of Kuwait/The British Petroleum Company plc*, Cm. 477 (October 1988), para.8.5.

[39] s.26(4).

(i) A controlling interest — de jure control

2.008   A controlling interest is interpreted by the OFT generally to mean a share-holding carrying more than 50 per cent of the voting rights in the company concerned[40] and conferring, therefore, the ability on the holder of the shares to pass ordinary resolutions. The existence of a controlling interest vested in one person will not prevent another person exercising "control" in the wider sense identified above but self-evidently only one person can have a controlling interest. For example, if "A" owns 51 per cent of the shares in a company, but a shareholding of more than 25 per cent is vested in a third party, "B", who can therefore block special resolutions, B will almost certainly be regarded as having the ability materially to influence the policy of the company. Moreover, if B owned less than 25 per cent of the shares in the circumstances identified above, it could still exercise material influence over the company if other factors establishing such influence were present.

(ii) Control of policy — de facto control

2.009   There are no precise criteria contained in the Act for determining when a shareholding will give the holder the ability to control the policy of the company concerned (*de facto* control). The OFT's guidance states simply that "a view has to be taken case by case in the light of the particular circumstances".[41] Much will depend upon the fragmentation of sharehold-ings in the company in question; if all of the other shareholders have only small holdings and are not organised in any way, ownership or control of 25 per cent or 30 per cent of the voting rights could confer on such a share-holder *de facto* control of the company through the ability to exercise more than 50 per cent of the votes cast at a general meeting. The OFT's guidance refers to two other situations in which it suggests that *de facto* control might arise: (i) where a shareholder has the "ability to veto any shareholder resolution requiring a supra-majority for adoption"; and (ii) when an entity is clearly the controller of a company, for example, "when an investor's industry expertise leads to its advice being followed in nearly all cases".[42] The first example is essentially negative control through the exercise of a veto, and is akin to the concept of "decisive influence" developed under the EC Merger Regulation,[43] which it is suggested generally arises at a lower level of shareholding than that which typically may be thought of as confer-ring *de facto* control; the second example would appear to be a clear illus-tration of material influence (rather than *de facto* control) as arose, for example, in the *British Airways/Sabena* case.[44] It is suggested that *de facto* control will arise primarily in circumstances where a shareholder in a listed company holds less than a 50 per cent plus one share of the voting rights in the company but is nevertheless able to control more than 50 per cent of the votes typically cast in general meeting.

---

[40] OFT's: *Substantive Assessment Guidance*; para.2.12.
[41] OFT's: *Substantive Assessment Guidance*; para.2.11
[42] OFT's: *Substantive Assessment Guidance*; para.2.11.
[43] Discussed below at para.2.036.
[44] Discussed below at para.2.013.

(iii) Material influence

There are no criteria contained in the Act for identifying when a person has   **2.010**
achieved the ability materially to influence the policy of another enterprise.
The OFT has stated that the assessment of material influence requires a
"case by case analysis of the entire relationship between the acquiring entity
and the target" and that:

> "factors relevant to an assessment of a particular shareholding may
> include: the distribution and holders of the remaining shares; patterns of
> attendance and voting at recent shareholders' meetings; the existence of
> any special voting or veto rights attached to the shareholding under
> consideration; and any other special provisions in the constitution of the
> company conferring an ability materially to influence policy."[45]

As regards the level of shareholding at which material influence might
arise, the OFT has indicated that:

> ". . . a 25 per cent share of voting rights is likely to be seen as presump-
> tively conferring the ability materially to influence policy — even when
> all the remaining shares are held by only one person. The OFT may
> examine any case where there is a shareholding of 15 per cent or more in
> order to see whether the holder might be able materially to influence the
> company's policy. Occasionally, a holding of less than 15 per cent might
> attract scrutiny where other factors indicating the ability to exercise
> influence over policy are present."[46]

The OFT's statements set out in its substantive assessment guidance
reflect the practice of the MMC and the Competition Commission over
many years. In 1986, in its inquiry into the merger between P&O and
European Ferries,[47] the MMC concluded that the acquisition by P&O of a
controlling interest in a company which held 20.8 per cent of the shares and
16.1 per cent of the voting rights of European Ferries conferred on P&O
the ability materially to influence the policy of European Ferries in circumstances where the chairman of P&O obtained a non-executive seat on the
European Ferries board, and one of P&O's senior executives obtained a

---

[45] OFT's: *Substantive Assessment Guidance*, at para.2.10.
[46] OFT's: *Substantive Assessment Guidance*, at para.2.10. In practice, the question may arise
whether an investor, such as a venture capital fund investing in a management buy-out,
which acquires a significant shareholding in, say, a retail chain, and has already invested in
another retail chain, is likely to be regarded as being able to influence materially the policy
of both enterprises such that they are regarded as coming under common control. In
assessing the effect of the arrangements, the OFT will focus attention on the likelihood of
the investing fund being able to influence the commercial policy of both entities by examining the level of shareholding, minority protection provisions and degree of board representation, as well as the fragmentation of other shareholdings in each case. In principle, if
such an investor were found to have acquired a position of material influence (or control)
over each business, and significant competition concerns were identified by the OFT, there
is no reason why a reference to the Commission should not be made, provided that the
second transaction constituted a relevant merger situation.
[47] *The Peninsular and Oriental Steam Navigation Company/European Ferries Group PLC*,
Cm. 31 (December 1986).

seat on the board of the holding company.[48] Prior to this decision, all the cases in which the MMC had found material influence over policy to exist had involved voting rights in excess of 20 per cent.[49]

In its inquiry into the shareholding of the Government of Kuwait through the Kuwait Investment Office ("KIO") in The British Petroleum Company plc ("BP"),[50] the MMC concluded that the KIO's acquisition of some 21.6 per cent of the issued ordinary share capital of BP gave it the ability materially to influence the policy of BP. In reaching this conclusion, the MMC considered that the "size and nature"[51] of other shareholdings is an important factor to take into account and noted that the KIO's holding was over 12 times the size of the next largest shareholdings, Prudential Assurance, which held 1.8 per cent, and the United Kingdom Government which held 1.7 per cent. The MMC also found that had KIO submitted proxy forms at the 1988 AGM, it would have had around 65 per cent of the total proxy vote, and that under BP's articles of association, as the holder of more than 10 per cent of the total voting rights, KIO would have been able to require a poll in relation to any resolution put to a general meeting. The MMC summarised its views as follows:

". . . we consider that a shareholding of 21.6 per cent would, in the absence of any other large shareholdings, have been sufficient to allow the Government of Kuwait to ensure that the Board of BP and its senior management would have regard to the interest and wishes of Kuwait before finalising any major decisions . . . Its holding would have put it in a very strong position to tip the balance if differences arose between shareholders."[52]

2.011   In its decision in the Kingdom FM case,[53] the OFT was required to assess whether the 22.5 per cent stake in Kingdom FM acquired by Scottish Radio Holdings plc ("SRH") conferred material influence. SRH had no entitlement to appoint a director to the board or any special voting rights, and the parties told the OFT that SRH was not involved in the day to day running of the station and was not selling radio airtime on its behalf. The OFT found that SRH did have material influence, stating that:

---

[48] The MMC concluded that the fact that both companies agreed that P&O had material influence over the policy of European Ferries was "significant but not decisive" (at para.8.5). The fact that, *inter alia*, no other shareholder controlled five per cent or more of the voting rights, that P&O's auditors concluded that P&O had significant influence over European Ferries within the meaning of accounting standard SSAP 1, and because of the views of P&O's representatives, European Ferries did not proceed with certain plans and appointments that had been suggested by its management, as well as the fact that P&O had influenced the presentation of European Ferries' accounts in the MMC's view, gave "P&O the potential to influence the policy of European Ferries" (at para.8.12).

[49] These cases were: *Euro Canadian Shipholdings/Furness Withy/Manchester Liners* (1976 H.C. 639) 28.80 per cent; *GUS/Empire Stores*, Cm. 8777 (January 1983) 29.99 per cent; *Pleasurama/Trident/Grand Metropolitan*, Cm. 9108 (December 1983) 20.02 per cent; *Lonrho/House of Fraser*, Cm. 9458 (March 1985) 29.90 per cent.

[50] *Government of Kuwait/BP*, Cm. 477 (October 1988).

[51] *Government of Kuwait/BP*, Cm. 477 (October 1988) at para. 8.9.

[52] *Government of Kuwait/BP*, Cm. 477 (October 1988) at para. 8.16.

[53] *Completed acquisition by Scottish Radio Holdings plc of 22.5 per cent shareholding in Kingdom FM Radio Limited*, Director General's advice dated March 11, 2002.

"When seeking to assess whether material influence arises it is necessary to examine the individual circumstances, not only the size of the shareholding and whether a directorship is held, but also the position and diversity of other shareholders, how influential they might be, and where appropriate the voting patterns of the shareholders and company board. In this regard SRH, as a leading radio operator in Scotland, may be well placed through its knowledge and expertise to convince others to follow a certain strategy when voting their shares. It seems unlikely, therefore, that Kingdom FM would conduct business without regard to SRH's views. It is also possible that the parties could become more closely involved in the future through SRH seeking a directorship or Kingdom FM deciding to use SRH's sales house for the sale of airtime. It is appropriate to have due regard to such possibilities."

However, in its substantive assessment of the case, after observing that "were a single company to control both Kingdom FM and Forth [an FM station operated by SRH] it might well find it profitable to raise Kingdom's prices somewhat given that some of the lost revenue by Kingdom's customers switching away would be reclaimed by Forth", the OFT concluded that, "while it appears more likely than not that SRH will have material influence over Kingdom, it is not clear that that influence is so great as to enable SRH to determine the pricing policy of Kingdom's radio advertising."

Although the OFT is correct to observe that the incentives of a majority owner of a business are unlikely to be aligned with those of a minority owner in such matters as price determination, in concluding that material influence existed, the OFT noted the relevance of Kingdom conducting its business with regard to SRH's views and the possibility that SRH may obtain board representation in the future which, whilst arguably consistent with the conclusion that SRH could not *determine* Kingdom's pricing policy, appears to ignore the possibility that it could materially *influence* it, for example, though the possibility of information sharing, notwithstanding that such actions between competitors could amount to an infringement of the c.1 prohibition of the Competition Act 1998.

Similar issues were considered by the Competition Commission in its report on the Icopal Holdings merger although the discussion was framed in terms of the effects of the transaction on competition (the Commission having already found that there was a relevant merger situation).[54] In that case, the Commission considered the issue of whether the acquisition of Icopal a/s (a manufacturer of roofing materials) by an acquisition company, CAIK, established for the purpose of bidding for Icopal, had changed or was likely to change the relationship between IKO (a manufacturer of weatherproofing materials), one of four equal shareholders in CAIK, and Icopal (in which IKO had previously directly held a shareholding of 10.2 per cent). In this connection, the Commission concluded that:

". . . although the acquisition is not a full merger creating a single pricing unit in the UK, the shareholding arrangement and the information flows

---

[54] *Icopal Holdings A/S and Icopal a/s*, Cm. 5089 (April 2001)

that naturally spring from it create a relationship that could be used to encourage a degree of common interest that might lead to a different attitude by the parties to mutual competition. They also provide a mechanism by which decisions made among shareholders about Icopal's strategy could be transmitted to the operating subsidiaries in the UK; although we have found no evidence of this happening to date there are grounds for a reasonable expectation that this relationship would be likely to lead to such a development, if the parties were so minded.

Were this to happen, then IKO would be likely to receive the lion's share of any profits that might arise as a consequence, because it would obtain all of the benefit that came to Ruberoid [a subsidiary of IKO] as a result of any market cooperation and 25 per cent of that accruing to Icopal. The other shareholders would receive only 25 per cent each of the gains to Icopal. Given these circumstances we would expect IKO to have the greater interest in making use of the relationship to generate opportunities for cooperative behaviour. Nevertheless, all the parties have a positive incentive to engage in behaviour that would maximize the profits of Icopal."[55]

2.012 However, a majority of the Commission concluded that although the acquisition created "a relationship that could be used to sustain a mutual awareness and common interest that would adversely affect competition in the marketplace",[56] the structure of the market would be unlikely to permit such mutual awareness to lead to significant public interest detriments.

In its BUPA report in 2000,[57] the Commission was asked to examine whether Salomon Brothers, via its investment company SBUKE, had acquired material influence over Community Hospitals Group ("CHG") by acquiring 26.8 per cent of its issued share capital. Salomon recognised that a shareholding of 25 per cent or more was generally viewed by the Commission as conferring the ability to exercise material influence over policy as it could be used to block a special resolution. However, it suggested that it was "necessary to consider not simply the theoretical ability to block special resolutions, but the likelihood of CHG needing to propose special resolutions during the expected period of SBUKE's ownership. SSSB further suggested that it was unlikely that CHG would need to propose special resolutions during the expected lifetime of SBUKE's holding in CHG other than on matters of a purely routine nature". The Competition Commission rejected the argument that it should consider the *likelihood* that voting rights conferring the possibility of exercising material influence would be exercised. It concluded that, in determining whether the 26.8 per cent shareholding conferred the ability to exercise material influence, evidence that such voting rights would be used or were intended to be used to block a special resolution was not required; the *ability* to exercise material influence is all that must exist. The Commission also concluded that SBUKE's ability materially to influence CHG went beyond its power to block special resolutions, as the next largest shareholding was only 7 per cent.

---

[55] *Icopal Holdings A/S and Icopal a/s*, Cm. 5089 (April 2001) at paras 2.131 and 2.132.
[56] *Icopal Holdings A/S and Icopal a/s*, Cm. 5089 (April 2001) at para.2.157.
[57] *British United Provident Association Limited/Community Hospitals Group PLC and Salomon International LLC/Community Hospitals Group PLC*, Cm. 5003 (December 2000).

In considering whether low shareholding levels might give rise to material influence, the authorities have made it clear that this will depend on the factual situation before them. In 1999 and 2000, the OFT examined a number of acquisitions of shareholdings in Premiership football clubs by broadcasters. In relation to the acquisition by BSkyB of a 9.08 per cent stake in Leeds Sporting, the OFT concluded[58] that this shareholding did not confer material influence on BSkyB, although BSkyB and Leeds had revoked the ability of BSkyB to appoint a director to the Leeds board. The OFT noted that the decision to revoke the power to appoint a director indicated that no material influence had been acquired by BSkyB over Leeds, but also noted that "in any event, board directors are legally obliged to act in the interests of the company as a whole."[58A] The Secretary of State referred a similar transaction involving NTL and Newcastle United to the Competition Commission. In that case, NTL had acquired 6.3 per cent of the share capital of Newcastle United and, at the time of the reference, had entered into a further commitment to purchase an additional equity stake of 50.8 per cent. However, once the reference had been made, the commitment had lapsed. The Commission therefore had to report on whether a 6.3 per cent stake which gave no right to board representation amounted to material influence. It concluded that it did not, taking all of the circumstances into account, and particularly the fact that the commitment in relation to the further shareholding of 50.8 per cent had lapsed and that there were two larger shareholders.[59]

The determination as to whether a shareholding confers on a shareholder the ability materially to influence the policy of a company is sometimes complex where a joint venture vehicle is created. In the Elders/Grand Metropolitan transaction,[60] which the MMC considered involved three different merger situations,[61] the MMC concluded that the acquisition by Grand Met of a 50 per cent holding in IEL, with the other 50 per cent of the shares being held by Elders (through Courage) would result in neither party having a controlling interest in, or being able to control the policy of, IEL. Rather, both Elders and Grand Met would be able materially to influence the policy of IEL, with neither company having control.[62] In practice, many joint venture arrangements are structured around a shareholder's agreement which may contain various minority protection provisions relating, for example, to board representation, the approval of annual budgets and the business plan, the conclusion of material contracts, investment above a certain level, the development of new products and the recruitment of senior personnel. Clearly, the presence or absence of such provisions will be of central importance in determining whether a shareholding of less than 25 per cent will confer on the minority shareholder the

---

[58] OFT press release, PN 08/00, February 3 2000.
[58A] It is understood that relevant factors in the OFT's assessment included the fact that the proposed BSkyB director who would have joined the Leeds board was also a director at BSkyB and a media rights agreement had been concluded between the parties.
[59] *NTL Communications Corp/Newcastle United PLC*, Cm. 4411 (July 1999).
[60] *Elders IXL Ltd/Grand Metropolitan PLC*, Cm. 1227 (October 1990).
[61] The three merger situations identified by the MMC were: the acquisition by Elders, through Courage, of the brewing interests of Grand Met; the acquisition by Grand Met of a 50 per cent holding in Inntrepreneur Estates Ltd. (IEL); and the acquisition by Elders, though its 50 per cent holding in IEL, of 3,565 public houses owned by Grand Met (at para.8.2).
[62] *Elders IXL Ltd/Grand Metropolitan PLC*, Cm. 1227 (October 1990) at para.8.6.

ability materially to influence the policy of the company, where the other shareholder holds more than 75 per cent of the voting rights and therefore has the ability to pass special resolutions.

2.013   As well as assessing the size and importance of shareholdings, the OFT will consider the issue of board representation:

> "An important factor in the OFT's assessment of material influence is whether the acquiring entity has or will have board representation. In this connection, the OFT will review the proportion of board directors appointed by the acquiring entity and the corporate/industry expertise exercised by members of the board appointed by the acquirer. This in turn requires assessment of the identities, relative experience and incentives of other board members."[63]

In its inquiry into the merger between Sabena, British Airways (BA) and KLM,[64] which involved the creation of a new company, Sabena World Airlines (SWA) (owned as to 60 per cent by Sabena and 20 per cent each by BA and KLM) the MMC had to consider whether BA's 20 per cent shareholding enabled it materially to influence SWA's policy. In concluding that it did so, the MMC noted that although Sabena had six representatives on the board of SWA while BA and KLM each had two, "Lord King and Sir Colin Marshall, the two BA directors appointed to the Board, are influential figures in the air transport industry and forceful personalities".[65] After noting that BA's assistance could be required to raise additional capital to implement SWA's business plan, the MMC went on to conclude that:

> "We consider it unlikely that BA would have invested approximately £35 million in its shareholding, and with the possibility of further calls on BA's resources in the future, unless it had had a reasonable expectation of being able to influence the way in which SWA's business was developed, and in that way to protect its investment".[66]

Following the MMC's report on the proposed acquisition by BSkyB of Manchester United which recommended that the merger should be prohibited,[67] the Secretary of State accepted undertakings from BSkyB in which BSkyB undertook, *inter alia*, to "procure that no director or employee of BSkyB holds any directorship or managerial position in any undertaking having control of or carrying on the business of Manchester United."[68]

In addition to an analysis of voting rights and board representation, the OFT's guidance indicates that it is necessary to consider other relevant agreements and arrangements in determining whether material influence is likely to arise:

---

[63] OFT's: *Substantive Assessment Guidance* at para. 2.12.
[64] *British Airways/Sabena*, Cm. 1155 (July 1990).
[65] *British Airways/Sabena*, Cm. 1155 (July 1990) at para.7.9.
[66] *British Airways/Sabena*, Cm. 1155 (July 1990) at para.7.9.
[67] *British Sky Broadcasting Group plc/Manchester United PLC*, Cm. 4305 (April 1999).
[68] DTI press release, P/2001/416, August 2, 2001.

"The OFT may also consider whether any additional agreements with the company enable the holder to influence policy. These might include the provision of consultancy services to the target or might, in certain circumstances, include agreements between firms that one will cease production and source all its requirements from the other. Financial arrangements may confer material influence where the conditions are such that one party becomes so dependent on the other that it gains material influence over the company's commercial policy (for example, where a lender could threaten to withdraw loan facilities if a particular policy is not pursued, or where the loan conditions confer on the lender an ability to exercise rights over and above those necessary to protect its investment, say, by options to take control of the company or veto rights over certain strategic decisions)".[69]

In this connection the MMC has concluded that material influence may result from the existence of rights connected to non-voting convertible loan stock. In its inquiry into the leveraged buy-out of the Consumer Products Division of Stora[70] (which included the Wilkinson Sword wet-shaving business) by a number of Swedish investors, banks and finance houses, together with The Gillette Company (the world's leading supplier of wet-shaving products), the MMC had to consider whether the holding by Gillette of a number of important rights and interests in Swedish Match NV, the buy-out vehicle, including 22 per cent of the equity in the form of non-voting convertible loan stock, amounted to material influence. The MMC began its analysis by identifying the "main components of possible influence" as including the facts that: the non-voting loan stock could convert to ordinary shares in the event of a Stock Exchange listing, a sale of equity in certain circumstances or upon the winding up of the company; Gillette had certain pre-emption rights over the sale of equity, whether in the form of ordinary shares or convertible loan stock, to a third party, as well as certain pre-emption rights over the sale of the company's assets; Gillette was a major creditor of the company, with a subsidiary having contributed $69 million of mezzanine debt (about 12 per cent of the company's debt); and Gillette was, in the MMC's view "clearly the prime mover behind the whole transaction and worked closely with the other investors and management to set it up".[71] Although the MMC accepted Gillette's arguments that it had no voting rights or board representation and no right to attend shareholders' meetings or to receive internal information, it concluded that:

---

[69] OFT's: *Substantive Assessment Guidance*; para.2.10.
[70] *Stora/Swedish Match/Gillette*, Cm. 1473 (March 1991).
[71] *Stora/Swedish Match/Gillette*, Cm. 1473 (March 1991) at para.7.53. As indicated below at para.2.024, Gillette's submission that the various pre-emption and conversion rights and options constituted "conditional" rights within the meaning of s.66(5) of the FTA (now s.27(3) of the Enterprise Act) and should not be taken into account until the option was exercised or the condition was satisfied was rejected by the MMC. This was because, in the MMC's view, s.66(4) (now s.27(2) of the Act) and 66(5) had to be read together and are directed to the part of the arrangements that have not been completed, *i.e.* the possible future acquisition as a result of an option having been exercised and not to the effect of the arrangements that have already taken place. On this reasoning, the MMC concluded that where the mere existence of the right gives rise to an ability to influence or control policy, s.66(4) and (5) would not result in the right being disregarded.

"... a prudent Wilkinson Sword management would be bound constantly to take into account the fact that Gillette was a major shareholder in its parent company, Swedish Match NV, was its parent company's largest creditor and had important rights in relation to significant decisions affecting the future of the company, notwithstanding the limits to Gillette's rights."[72]

2.014   In the light of the consistent practice of the Competition Commission (and its predecessor, the MMC) and the OFT's guidance, it is clear that the question of whether material influence will be found to exist will depend upon the likely *potential* effect of the arrangements on the conduct of the entity in question, taking into account all the relevant circumstances, and that the presence or absence of an equity shareholding will be relevant, but not determinative.

Associated persons

2.015   Section 127(4)(d) of the Act provides that, for the purpose of deciding whether two enterprises have been brought under common ownership or common control within the meaning of s.26, "two or more persons acting together to secure or exercise control of a body of persons corporate or unincorporate or to secure control of any enterprise or assets shall be regarded as associated with one another" and should therefore be treated as one person. Section 127 also provides that spouses or relatives, trustees and settlors of a settlement or persons carrying on business as a partnership and their spouses, partners and relatives shall be considered to be associated persons and therefore treated as one person for the purpose of s.26 of the Act. The OFT notes in its *Substantive Assessment Guidance* that:

> "[f]or [the] purposes of considering whether an enterprise has ceased to be distinct, the Act allows the OFT to consider whether a number of persons acquiring an enterprise are in fact 'associated persons' and thus should be viewed as acting together."[72A]

It goes on to observe that the most common situation where this will arise is:

> "where the acquiring persons are related or have a signed agreement to act jointly to make an acquisition. It is also possible that separate entities may be considered to be 'associated persons' where they appear to have common incentives to act together for the purpose of gaining control over the acquired enterprise."[73]

The Competition Commission considered the application of the associated persons test under the FTA (the equivalent provision was contained in

---

[72] *Stora/Swedish Match/Gillette*, Cm. 1473 (March 1991) at para.1.6. This degree of perceived ongoing influence by Gillette in the business of its leading competitor was also one of the reasons why the MMC concluded that the merger could be expected to operate against the public interest.

[72A] See para.2.16.

[73] See the OFT's *Substantive Assessment Guidance*, paras 2.16 to 2.17.

s.77 of the FTA) in the Icopal Holdings A/S and Icopal a/s inquiry.[74] The issue that arose in that case was whether the four shareholders of CAIK, the company which acquired control of Icopal, were associated persons for the purpose of that acquisition by acting together to acquire control of the company. The shareholders argued that they were not *acting* together to secure control of Icopal, once they had actually obtained control of the acquisition vehicle. The Commission concluded that in the context of s.77, "to secure" does not only mean "to obtain", it also means "to safeguard". The Commission explained that s.77 is based on the proposition that persons, *e.g.* husband and wife or a trustee and a settlor:

"... are persons who commonly do not act independently of each other and hence can reasonably be expected to coordinate their behaviour. It accordingly requires such person[s] to be treated, for jurisdiction purposes, as a single entity without it having to be established that they are likely in fact to act as a single entity. The section proceeds on the footing that persons who act together to obtain control can also be expected not to act independently. Where parties have obtained control by acting together in accordance with a set of arrangements and they then safeguard control by continuing to act in accordance with that set of arrangements (which remains in place), it can for the same reasons similarly be expected that they might well coordinate their conduct. It is therefore consistent with the purpose of the section that those who have obtained control in concert, and then under the same arrangements continue to safeguard control in concert, should be treated as 'acting together to secure control' of the company."[75]

The main factors which led the Commission to conclude that that the four shareholders were associated persons by acting together to obtain control and thereafter to safeguard their control of Icopal were that:

(i)   both before and after the acquisition, the relationship of the four shareholders was governed by a shareholders' agreement and the articles of association of CAIK;

(ii)   the parties continued to operate under the shareholders' agreement and articles;

(iii)   the agreement prohibited share transfers for three years and by doing so prevented control passing to a third party; and

(iv)   even after expiry of the three year period, any shareholder wishing to dispose of its shares had to offer them to the other shareholders before they could be offered to a third party.

The Commission did not consider the ability of IKO (one of the shareholders of CAIK) materially to influence the policy of Icopal as a jurisdictional issue because it considered that the associated persons links which caused the transaction to be referred were different in kind from "a merger

---

[74] *Icopal Holdings A/S and Icopal a/s*, Cm. 5089 (April 2001).
[75] *Icopal Holdings A/S and Icopal a/s*, Cm. 5089 (April 2001) at para.2.36.

case where one party acquires control of another's enterprise."[76] The Commission did, however, consider the issue of influence in connection with its substantive assessment and conclusions on the public interest.

Does the merger situation qualify for investigation?

2.016 If a merger situation has arisen, it will be a relevant merger situation and qualify for investigation if two sets of criteria are satisfied. First, it must satisfy either the "share of supply test" by creating or adding to an existing share of supply (or purchase) of 25 per cent or more *or* the "turnover test" by involving the transfer of an enterprise with a turnover in the UK exceeding £70 million, and secondly, it must satisfy the timing requirements of the Act.

The share of supply test

2.017 The first jurisdictional threshold, the share of supply test, is contained in s.23(2) of the Act and is defined in relation to goods by s.23(3) and in relation to services by s.23(4), although the effect of the provisions is similar for both goods and services. In both cases the share of supply test will be satisfied where "at least one quarter" of the goods or services of any description "in the United Kingdom, or in a substantial part of the United Kingdom" are either:

(i) "supplied by one and the same person or are supplied to one and the same person"; or

(ii) "supplied by the persons by whom the relevant enterprises (so far as they continue to be carried on) are carried on, or are supplied to those persons."

The reference to supply "by" or "to" one and the same person catches aggregations in the share of supply above 25 per cent with regard to both the purchase and supply of goods or services and is therefore capable of controlling the creation or enhancement of buyer power as well as supplier market power (notwithstanding that it is commonly referred to as the "share of *supply*" test). Paragraph (i) deals with the position where the aggregated share of supply is held by one individual or company.[77] Paragraph (ii) effectively requires the shares of enterprises under common ownership or control to be aggregated in applying the share of supply test.

The OFT's Substantive Assessment Guidance states that "the share of supply test" is satisfied only if the merged enterprises:

"(i) both either supply or acquire goods or services of a particular description; and

---

[76] *Icopal Holdings A/S and Icopal a/s*, Cm. 5089 (April 2001), at para. 2.39.
[77] This is because the extended meaning given to "person" as including "associated persons" by s.127 does not apply for the purposes of s.23.

(ii) will, after the merger takes place, supply or acquire 25 per cent or more of those goods or services, in the UK as a whole or in a substantial part of it."

Where an enterprise already supplies or acquires 25 per cent of particular goods or services, the test is satisfied so long as its share is increased as a result of the merger. It does not matter how small an increase that may be, provided that there is some element of aggregation.[78] The Act gives the OFT and the Commission a wide discretion in applying the share of supply test. Section 23(5) provides that in determining whether the test is satisfied:

"... the decision-making authority shall apply such criterion (whether value, cost, price, quantity, capacity, number of workers employed or some other criterion, of whatever nature), or such combination of criteria, as the decision-making authority considers appropriate."[79]

The OFT's guidance acknowledges that "the Act allows wide discretion in describing the relevant goods or services"[80] and goes on to state that:

"Generally, the OFT will have regard to the narrowest reasonable description of a set of goods or services to determine whether the share of supply test is met."[81]

Although the Act contains references to both a product market criterion ("goods of any description") and a geographical market criterion (the United Kingdom or a "substantial part" of it), it is important to bear in mind that, in determining whether these criteria and therefore the share of supply test, are satisfied, and accordingly whether a given merger situation qualifies for investigation, the usual demand and supply substitutability analysis and tests for geographical market definition are not necessarily appropriate.[82] The "reference market" may not therefore coincide with the "relevant market" by reference to which the effect of the merger on competition will be assessed. The reference market is essentially a formalistic concept concerned simply with the issue of jurisdiction. The OFT's *Procedural Guidance* explains the position as follows:

---

[78] See the OFT's *Substantive Assessment Guidance* at paras 2.22 and 2.23.
[79] s.23(6) provides that where goods or services are the subject of different forms of supply, the share of supply test may be assessed by considering all forms of supply taken together, separately or in groups, whichever the decision-making authority considers appropriate. s.23(8) adds further to the degree of flexibility available to the decision-making authority in applying the share of supply test by providing that "the criteria for deciding when goods or services can be treated . . . [as being] of a separate description shall . . . [be those which] in any particular case the decision-making authority considers appropriate in the circumstances of that case."
[80] See the OFT's *Substantive Assessment Guidance* at para.2.24.
[81] See the OFT's *Substantive Assessment Guidance* at para.2.24.
[82] Such analyses are, however, clearly relevant in determining whether a merger situation that qualifies for investigation on the basis of the share of supply test raises substantive competition issues that merit detailed analysis. A consideration of how the OFT and Competition Commission assess the effects of a merger on competition is undertaken in Ch.6.

"Historically, the term 'market share test' has been commonly used among specialists to describe the share of supply test, but this is a somewhat ambiguous phrase. The goods or services described in determining whether the merger meets the share of supply test do not necessarily correspond to those that constitute the relevant economic market or markets."[83]

In its report on the merger between Eastman Kodak Company and ColourCare Limited,[84] the Competition Commission considered that the share of supply test was satisfied on the basis of the parties' share of processing amateur films that were the subject of wholesale supply in the UK. On this basis, for jurisdictional purposes, the parties were considered to have a combined share of supply of 78 per cent. However in its substantive conclusions, the Commission considered the relevant product market to be the market for the processing of overnight, next-day and longer services carried out through autonomous retail shops, of which the parties had a combined share of around 51 per cent.

In investigating the merger between Octagon Motorsports Limited and British Racing Driving Club,[85] for the purposes of jurisdiction, the Commission considered the supply in the UK of services for the provision of licensed circuits for motor racing and related activities, in relation to which the merged entity had a share of 72 per cent. However, in its substantive assessment, the Commission concluded that three relevant markets were affected:

(i) a downstream market for the supply to final consumers of motorsport activities based on licensed circuits;

(ii) an upstream market for the supply of track time at licensed circuits to organisations which offer motorsport activities to final consumers; and

(iii) an upstream market for the promotion of motorsport spectator events at licensed circuits.

2.018 In its inquiry into the acquisition by Sara Lee Corporation of Reckitt & Colman's shoe care business,[86] the reference market was defined by the Secretary of State and the MMC as "applied shoe care products" which comprised "polishes intended for use on any type of footwear in such form as paste, wax, cream, liquid, gel, or impregnated sponge or cloth". In its analysis, the MMC added to this definition "various other chemical products ... in particular whiteners for white shoes and aerosols for cleaning suede shoes and waterproofing."[87] No formal demand and supply substitutability analysis was undertaken in determining jurisdiction. In the inquiry into the acquisition by Avenir Havas Media of Brunton Curtis

---

[83] OFT's *Procedural Guidance*, at para.4.9.
[84] *Eastman Kodak Company/ColourCare Limited*, Cm. 5339 (December 2001).
[85] *Octagon Motorsports Limited/British Racing Drivers Club Limited*, Cm. 5252 (September 2001).
[86] *Sara Lee/Reckitt & Colman*, Cm. 2040 (August 1992).
[87] *Sara Lee/Reckitt & Colman*, Cm. 2040 (August 1992).

Outdoor Advertising,[88] the reference market was defined as the supply of roadside poster advertising display services which included large poster panels of 48–sheet and 96–sheet dimension as well as the smaller 32, 16, 12, 6 and 4–sheet panels. However, the demand substitutability analysis carried out by the MMC in assessing the effects of the merger led the MMC to conclude that 48–sheet and larger roadside panels were not substitutable by smaller panels.[89]

In practice, determining whether a merger qualifies for investigation under the share of supply test is largely a mechanistic exercise which does not generally focus upon demand and supply substitutability considerations.[90]

As indicated above, the share of supply test contains a geographical element given that, in order to be a relevant merger situation, a merger must result in the creation or enhancement of a share of supply of 25 per cent or more in the United Kingdom as a whole or in a "substantial part" of it. The Act gives no guidance as to the circumstances in which a part of the United Kingdom will be regarded as substantial, although in *R. v MMC Ex p. South Yorkshire Transport Limited,* the House of Lords held that a part of the United Kingdom would be substantial within the meaning of s.64(3) of the FTA 1973 (which employed the same wording as is now contained in the Enterprise Act), if it "was of such a size, character and importance as to make it worth consideration for the purposes of the Act".[91] The case arose out of the reference by the Secretary of State to the MMC of the acquisition by South Yorkshire Transport Company Limited of certain companies operating local bus services in South Yorkshire and parts of Derbyshire and Nottinghamshire. In its report, the MMC had concluded that the reference area, which accounts for 1.65 per cent of the total area of the United Kingdom and has a population of 3.2 per cent of the total United Kingdom population, was substantial having regard to the "social, political, economic, financial and geographic significance" of the area.[92] In the High Court it was held that the MMC had acted without jurisdiction as the relevant test was whether the area was substantial in the light of its area, its population and its economic activity as a proportion of the United Kingdom as a whole.[93] The Court of Appeal upheld this approach,[94] on the basis that the reference to a substantial part of the United Kingdom in the FTA was used in a comparative sense, with the comparator being the whole of the United Kingdom. On that basis, although the reference area might be important, special or significant, it could not amount to "a substantial part" of the United Kingdom within the meaning of the Act. In rejecting this approach, Mustill L.J., who gave the judgment in the House of Lords,

---

[88] *Avenir Havas Media/Brunton Curtis,* Cm. 1737 (November 1991).

[89] *Avenir Havas Media/Brunton Curtis,* Cm. 1737 (November 1991), at para.6.58.

[90] The question of market definition from an economic perspective is considered in detail in Ch.6, below.

[91] *R. v Monopolies & Mergers Commission Ex p. South Yorkshire Transport Ltd* [1993] 1 W.L.R. 23 at 32. The OFT guidance refers to this case as the correct interpretational tool for the geographic test under the Enterprise Act: see the OFT's *Substantive Assessment Guidance* at para.2.25.

[92] *South Yorkshire Transport acquisitions,* Cm. 1166 (August 1990), paras 2.5 to 2.6.

[93] *R. v MMC Ex p. South Yorkshire Transport Ltd* [1991] B.C.C. 347, judgment of Otton J., March 22, 1991.

[94] *R. v MMC Ex p. South Yorkshire Transport Ltd* [1992] 1 All E.R. 257.

warned against "the dangers of taking an inherently imprecise word, and by redefining it thrusting on it a spurious degree of precision",[95] and went on to state that he was "unable to accept that proportionality is the beginning and end of the matter."[96] In his view, the reference to a substantial part of the United Kingdom is "enabling not restrictive. Its purpose is simply to entitle the Secretary of State to refer to the Commission mergers whose effect is not nationwide."[97] In this connection, Mustill L.J. observed that like the assets test under the FTA, the "epithet 'substantial' is there to ensure that the expensive, laborious and time-consuming mechanism of a merger reference is not set in motion if the effort is not worthwhile."[98] He concluded as follows:

> "Accordingly, although I readily accept that the Commission can, and indeed should, take into account the relative proportions of the area by comparison with the United Kingdom as a whole, as regards surface area, population, economic activities and (it may be) in some cases other factors as well, when reaching a conclusion on jurisdiction, neither each of them on its own, nor all of them together, can lead directly to the answer."

He went on to state that he was reluctant to formulate a non-statutory definition of "substantial part" as to do so might unduly fetter the MMC's judgment in some unforeseen future situation. However, he was prepared to endorse as a "general guide" a modified version of the formulation of Nourse L.J. in his dissenting judgment in the Court of Appeal that to be substantial "the part must be of such size, character and importance as to make it worth consideration for the purposes of the Act". He added that "to this question an inquiry into proportionality will often be material but it will not lead directly to a conclusion."[99]

2.019   In applying this formulation to the MMC's reasoning, Mustill L.J. concluded that there was no ground for interference by the courts as the MMC's conclusion was "well within the permissible field of judgment"[1]; in any event, he stated that a court could only substitute its opinion for that of the MMC if their decision was "so aberrant that it cannot be classed as rational."[2]

Following the House of Lords decision, the Secretary of State referred another bus merger,[3] this time in relation to bus services in several districts in and around Glasgow, to the Competition Commission. The Commission considered the House of Lords' decision and concluded that the Strathclyde region:

---

[95] R. v MMC Ex p. South Yorkshire Transport Ltd, [1993] 1 All E.R. 289 at 295.
[96] South Yorkshire Transport, cited above, at 296.
[97] South Yorkshire Transport, cited above, at 296.
[98] South Yorkshire Transport, cited above, at 296.
[99] South Yorkshire Transport, cited above, at 297.
[1] South Yorkshire Transport, cited above, at 298.
[2] South Yorkshire Transport, cited above, at 298. A more detailed discussion of judicial review of the MMC's conclusions and the Secretary of State's decisions is set out in Ch.10, below.
[3] Stagecoach Holdings plc and S B Holdings Limited, Cm. 2845 (April 1995).

"represents 3.9 per cent of the UK population. The region includes Glasgow, one of the great cities of the UK, and the towns of Airdrie, Ayr, Clydebank, Coatbridge, Cumbernauld, Dumbarton, East Kilbride, Greenock, Hamilton, Kilmarnock, Motherwell, Paisley and Wishaw. We have no doubt that the reference area is 'worth consideration for the purposes of the Act' and hence 'a substantial part of the UK' for those purposes. SBH and Stagecoach did not contest this view."

Since the House of Lords judgment, references have regularly been made in relation to small, regional markets, particularly bus mergers.[4] The OFT's *Substantive Assessment Guidance* states that:

"Factors which have been taken into account in cases considered under the FTA include the size, population, social, political, economic, financial and geographic significance of the specified area or areas, and whether it is (or they are) special or significant in some way. The OFT expects to take similar factors into account under the Act."[5]

The OFT has indicated that as a rule of thumb, 1 per cent of the population is a bench mark, but that it has the discretion to consider smaller markets depending on the circumstances. In the Archant reference decision,[6] the OFT stated that:

"The OFT's approach ... takes into account a ruling of the House of Lords, past CC practice and OFT guidance. In terms of past CC practice, under the FTA ... the CC has considered population among other factors as relevant, finding an area representing 1.1 per cent of UK population as a "substantial part" of the UK [Report on Stagecoach Holdings plc/Chesterfield Transport (1989) Ltd, January 1996]. In this case, the parties' overlapping local newspaper activities exceed 25 per cent of supply in the contiguous London boroughs of Havering, Barking & Dagenham and Redbridge, which together represent just under 0.5 million residents over 15 years of age, or more than 1.1 per cent of the over 15 population of the UK, and as such represents an area of economic significance for local newspaper advertising."[6A]

In its decision to accept undertakings in lieu of reference in relation to the acquisition by Tesco plc of the Co-operative Group's "one-stop shop"   **2.020**

---

[4] For example the inquiry into *Arriva plc and Lutonian Buses Ltd*, Cm. 4074 (November 1998) concerned a reference area which represented 2.7 per cent of the UK population and 1.2 per cent of the UK land area. The inquiry into *National Express Group plc and Midland Main Line Ltd*, Cm. 3495 (December 1996) concerned a reference area representing around 2 per cent of the surface area of the UK.

[5] See the OFT's *Substantive Assessment Guidance* at para.2.25.

[6] OFT's decision of April 29, 2004, *Completed acquisition by Archant Limited of the London Regionals Division of Independent News & Media plc.*

[6A] In its report, the Competition Commission preferred to focus on the larger area in which the acquired titles circulated or were distributed, which had a population over 15 of approximately 2.5 million, equating to 5.2 per cent of the UK population (see a report on the acquisition by Archant Limited of the London Newspapers of Independent News and Media Limited (September 2004), App.C, para.26).

supermarket store in Slough, the OFT simply concluded that ". . . each Co-op store can be considered an 'enterprise' for the purposes of [section 23 of the Act] and . . . [the] acquisition is likely to qualify for investigation under the share of supply test".[7] No explanation is given in the OFT's decision as to the application of the "substantial part of the UK" test contained in s.23(3) of the Act. The OFT's substantive analysis focussed on the isochrone analysis developed by the Competition Commission in the Safeway report,[8] which identifies locally competing stores on the basis of drive time from a specific store or population centre. It is implicit in the OFT's analysis that the geographic area defined by isochrone analysis around the relevant stores in Slough was regarded as amounting to a substantial part of the United Kingdom in establishing jurisdiction for the purposes of s.23 of the Act; although it is also the case that as Tesco enjoyed 32 per cent of grocery sales from stores over 1,400 sq metres in the UK, the transaction amounted to a relevant merger situation on the basis of Tesco's national share of supply. In relation to the distinct issue of whether the market in question was of sufficient importance to warrant a reference, the OFT commented that: ". . . while the affected area would be Slough and the surrounding area, the affected sector appears to be sufficient [sic] important to justify reference, given the total expenditure on groceries at one-stop stores in this area".[9] Although the comment was directed at a different point of law, it does echo to some degree the formulation of Nouse L.J. in his judgment in the Court of Appeal in the *South Yorkshire Transport* case that an area must be "worthy of consideration for the purposes of the Act".[10]

The turnover test

2.021   The turnover test, which replaces the assets test under the FTA, is set out in s.23(1)(b) of the Act and provides that a relevant merger situation will be created where "the value of the turnover in the United Kingdom of the enterprise being taken over exceeds £70 million." The requirement that there must be turnover in the UK has the effect of providing a necessary territorial link to the UK and, as a consequence, the requirement under s.64(1) of the FTA that "one [enterprise] at least was carried on in the United Kingdom by or under the control of a body corporate incorporated in the United Kingdom" is no longer necessary.

Section 28 of the Act provides that the value of the turnover in the United Kingdom of the enterprise being taken over shall be calculated by taking the total value of the turnover in the UK of the enterprises which will cease, or have already ceased, to be distinct and deducting the UK turnover of any enterprise which continues to be carried out under the same ownership and control. Where the merger is the simple acquisition by one enterprise of

---

[7] See the OFT's decision of February 2, 2004, *Completed acquisitions by Tesco plc of the Co-Operative Group's stores in Uxbridge Road, Slough as well as Stapleford Lane, Toton, Nottingham and Towers Place, South Shields.*

[8] *Safeway plc and others*, Cm. 5950 (September 2003)

[9] OFT's decision of February 2, 2004, *Completed acquisitions by Tesco plc of the Co-Operative Group's stores in Uxbridge Road, Slough as well as Stapleford Lane, Toton, Nottingham and Towers Place, South Shields.*

[10] *South Yorkshire Transport*, cited above, at 265.

another enterprise, this formulation seems rather over-complex: essentially, the question is whether the enterprise being taken over has UK turnover in excess of £70 million.

Where none of the enterprises remain under the same ownership and control, for example following the formation of a joint venture or partnership, the Act provides[11] that the value of the turnover of the enterprise being taken over shall be calculated as the sum of the turnovers of all of the enterprises ceasing to be distinct, less the turnover of the enterprise with the highest turnover (*i.e.* the lowest turnover is determinative). For example, if "A" and "B" form a 50:50 joint venture company via a hive-down of their assets and businesses in a particular area of activity, each is likely to have material influence over the other's business that has been put into the joint venture, and neither enterprise will remain under the same ownership or control as previously. In deciding whether the merger situation qualifies for investigation under the turnover test, the highest value contribution is ignored so that, for example, if A's business had turnover of £100 million in the UK and B's business had turnover of £40 million, the merger would not qualify for investigation. In practice, therefore, the effect of s.28(1)(b) is to require that in the context of a joint venture or partnership as described above, the turnover of each of at least two of the enterprises being put into the joint venture, and thus ceasing to be distinct, should exceed £70 million.

Pursuant to powers conferred by s.28(2) of the Act, the Secretary of State has adopted the Enterprise Act 2002 (Merger Fees and Determination of Turnover) Order 2003[12] which sets out how turnover should be calculated for the purpose of the turnover test. The OFT has also issued guidance on the calculation of turnover.[13] The general rule, set out in para.3 of the Schedule to the Order, is that the applicable turnover is that which is derived from sales or the provision of services to businesses or consumers in the UK.[14] The relevant period for the turnover to be considered will ordinarily be the business year preceding either the date of the merger (if the acquisition is completed) or the date of the decision as to whether to refer the merger to the Competition Commission (if the acquisition is in contemplation). If the undertaking has carried out an acquisition or disposal since the end of the preceding business year, or another event has occurred which may have a significant impact on the turnover of the business, the value of that acquisition, disposal, or event should also be taken into account. Where company accounts do not provide a relevant figure, for example, because only part of a company's business is being acquired, the OFT's *Substantive Assessment Guidance* states that:

"[the] OFT will consider evidence presented by the parties and other interested parties to form its own view as to what it believes to be the value of UK turnover for jurisdictional purposes."[15]

---

[11] s.28(1)(b).

[12] SI 2003/1370.

[13] *Guidance note on the calculation of turnover for the purposes of Part 3 of the Enterprise Act 2002*, July 2003.

[14] After the deduction of sales rebates, value added tax and other taxes directly related to turnover.

[15] See the OFT's *Substantive Assessment Guidance*, at para.2.20.

2.022   The Order also sets out the specific rules which apply in relation to credit and financial institutions and insurance undertakings.[16]

It is important to note that whilst at first sight the provisions on the calculation of turnover appear very similar to the rules for calculating turnover under the EC Merger Regulation, potentially significant differences do exist. For example, para.4 of the Schedule states that where an enterprise consists of two or more enterprises which are under common ownership or control, the applicable turnover shall be calculated by adding together the turnover of each of the enterprises under common ownership or control. This is a similar concept to that found in the EC Merger Regulation.[17] However, the concept of "control" is defined differently under the Act from the definition for the purposes of the EC Merger Regulation. "Decisive influence", the key concept in the definition of control for EC Merger Regulation purposes,[18] is generally considered to be a higher threshold than "material influence" under the Act.[19] The turnover of an enterprise could therefore be *greater* when calculated in accordance with the Act by including enterprises over which the acquired enterprise has material influence than would be the case for the purposes of the EC Merger Regulation.

A further potentially significant difference of detail arises in relation to the allocation of joint venture turnover. The issue arises where the target business itself holds a stake in a joint venture: how should the turnover of that joint venture be allocated? Under the EC Merger Regulation the number of entities (including the target business) which have decisive influence over the joint venture is identified, and the joint venture's turnover is then divided equally between them, regardless of their respective shareholdings. Under the Enterprise Act, however, the OFT's approach to this issue is understood to be that where the target has at least material influence[19A] in the joint venture, 100 per cent of the joint venture's turnover is allocated to it, regardless of the target business' actual shareholding and regardless of how many other entities share control with it.[19B]

Time limits

2.023   A completed merger which constitutes a relevant merger situation cannot be referred to the Competition Commission more than four months after the date on which the enterprises ceased to be distinct.[20] However, the time

---

[16]   Art.5 applies to credit and financial institutions and Art.6 applies to insurance undertakings.
[17]   See Art.5(4) in particular.
[18]   See Art.3(2) of the EC Merger Regulation and para.12 of the European Commission's notice on the concept of concentration ([1998] O.J. C 66/5).
[19]   See further para.2.001, above.
[19A] The concept of material influence and the other concepts of "control" under the Enterprise Act are discussed at paras 2.007–2.014.
[19B] This approach is based on paras 4 and 6 of the Schedule to the Enterprise Act 2002 (Merger Fees and Determination of Turnover) Order 2003; and paras 1.15 and 1.16 of the OFT's *Guidance note on the calculation of turnover for the purposes of Part 3 of the Enterprise Act 2002*, in particular at example (ii) in para.1.16.
[20]   s.24(1)(a). It is important to bear in mind that under the Enterprise Act, time will stop running (including in relation to the four month period) in a number of circumstances, including where the parties fail to respond to an information request within the stipulated time frame; see further Ch.3 below.

period will not begin to run until "material facts" about the proposed arrangements have been notified to the OFT or have otherwise been "made public".[21] "Made public" is defined as meaning being "so publicised as to be generally known or readily ascertainable."[22] The courts have not been required to interpret these provisions or the equivalent provision of the FTA. The definition of "made public" as being "so publicised as to be generally known or readily ascertainable"[23] raises the question as to who should possess such knowledge. The structure of the Act clearly indicates that if sufficient publication has taken place, time will start running regardless of whether the OFT is actually aware of the merger. Neither of the OFT's guidance documents address this issue. However, in its Mergers Guide under the FTA, the OFT referred to disclosure being made to the OFT or the secretary of State "or otherwise made public".[24]

It is suggested that this statement was inaccurate in the context of the FTA insofar as it stated that the disclosure of material facts must be *to* the OFT; it is clear from the wording of s.24(2) of the Act that notice of material facts is given if "it is given to the OFT, *or* the facts are made public . . .".[25]

A robust stance has also been adopted by the Competition Commission.[26] In the Icopal case, the Commission considered the argument put forward by the parties that the enterprises in question had ceased to be distinct more than four months before the reference was made, as the public offer to Danish shareholders became unconditional on July 21, 2000 and the reference to the Commission was made on November 24, 2000. The Commission concluded, having taken Counsel's advice, that the fact that the offer had become unconditional was a "material fact" which was not disclosed to the OFT before July 25 when an announcement that the offer had become unconditional was made to the Copenhagen Stock Exchange.[27]

If, when a merger takes place, material facts are made available to firms and persons active in the industry and the relevant market(s) (particularly customers, but also competitors) it is arguable that sufficient disclosure is made. This is because, under the Act, there is no obligation on the parties to a merger to inform the OFT and seek clearance; the merger provisions of the Act are policed not only by the OFT, which is under a duty to keep itself

---

[21] s.24(2).
[22] s.24(3).
[23] s.24(3).
[24] OFT Mergers Guide (relating to the Fair Trading Act 1973), at para.5.16.
[25] s.24(2)(b), emphasis added.
[26] In their report on the acquisitions by South Yorkshire Transport, the MMC noted that the "normal period for reference of the acquisition" of SYT Ltd. had expired before the reference was made, but concluded that the acquisition still qualified for investigation as the time for the reference began on the later date on which material facts "were brought to the attention of the Secretary of State or the Director General of Fair Trading, or were made public"; *South Yorkshire Transport Ltd acquisitions*, Cm. 1166 (August 1990), para.3.3. In its Archant/INM report, the Competition Commission concluded that the exercise of a purchase option and the execution of a sale and purchase agreement were material facts which could not have been known to the OFT until the day on which the purchaser wrote to the OFT to advise that it had entered into the relevant agreements. On the same day Archant published a press release recording the acquisition of the titles which were the subject of the sale and purchase agreement. *Archant Limited/Independent News & Media Limited* (September 2004), App.C, para.21.
[27] *Icopal Holdings A/S/Icopal a/s*, Cm. 5089 (April 2001).

informed as to merger activity, but also by interested third parties (primarily the customers and competitors of the merged company) making complaints to the OFT. Effectively, therefore, the publication requirements of the Act are aimed not only at enabling the OFT to identify mergers that have taken place, but also at the customers and competitors of the merged firm being able to draw to the OFT's attention a merger which they consider warrants scrutiny.

When a merger has not been notified to the OFT, it is generally regarded that time will start running from the date on which the merger receives significant press coverage. Clearly such press coverage may not contain all the "material facts" which are required to be disclosed by s.24(1)(b) and a literal interpretation of the Act together with the approach of the Commission in the Icopal case suggest that the OFT would not be prevented from making a reference after that date if some material facts have not been disclosed. In practice, however, it would appear that the OFT is keen to ensure that where details of the merger have appeared in the national or trade press, any reference should be made before the expiry of four months from that event.

2.024   The Act contains a number of other provisions relating to timing considerations. Section 27(2) provides in relation to transactions that do not have immediate effect (that is completion of the transaction does not take place at the same time as contracts are exchanged) that enterprises shall be treated as having ceased to be distinct at completion rather than at the date that contracts are entered into. Section 27(3) provides that, for the purpose of determining the time at which a merger has taken place "no account shall be taken of any option or other conditional right until the option is exercised or the condition is satisfied."[28] The MMC was required to interpret a similar provision contained in s.66(5) of the FTA in its inquiry into the Wilkinson Sword/Gillette merger.[29] In that case, as explained above,[30] the MMC rejected Gillette's argument that the effect of s.66(5) was that options and conditional rights could not be taken into account (for example in determining whether material influence exists) until they were exercised, on the ground that s.66(5) was concerned only with the time at which an option or similar right should be regarded as giving rise to a merger.

Subsections 27(5) and (6) of the Act provide that the OFT (and the Commission following a reference) may treat successive events occurring within a period of two years between the same parties or interests as having occurred simultaneously on the date on which the latest of them occurred. The OFT considered the operation of these provisions in its decision relating to the acquisition by Tesco of three supermarket stores from the Co-op in Toton (in November 2002), in South Shields (in July 2003) and in Slough (in October 2003). In declining to exercise its discretion to consider all of the acquisitions as having occurred in October 2003, the OFT set out its reasons as follows:

---

[28] Note that The Enterprise Act 2002 (Anticipated Mergers) Order 2003 (SI 2003/1595) extends the provisions of s.27 (which concerns completed mergers) to anticipated mergers, with amended wording in ss.27(5) and (6) as set out in the statutory instrument.

[29] Stora/Swedish Match/Gillette, Cm. 1473 (March 1991).

[30] See para.2.013.

"Section 24 of the Act in principle excludes the Toton and South Shields acquisitions from the purview of the Act, as more than four months have elapsed since completion and since the respective relevant material facts were so publicised as to be generally known or readily ascertainable. The OFT therefore considered whether to treat these two earlier acquisitions as having occurred simultaneously on the date on which the latest of them occurred, *i.e.* the Slough acquisiton, under section 27(5) of the Act.

In considering whether to exercise its discretion under section 27(5) of the Act in this case, the OFT took account of the following:

— that each transaction was or is a relevant merger situation
— that each transaction involved or involves the acquisition of a single Co-op store in a different (non-proximate) local area within the UK; and
— that we have found no basis for concluding that these transactions were structured so as to avoid scrutiny under the merger control provisions of the Act or, previously, the Fair Trading Act 1973; in this respect, we observe that each transaction was contemplated at a time prior to the completed investigation and report by the Competition Commission (CC) on the proposed acquisition of Safeway (Cm. 5950; the CC Report).

In these circumstances the OFT has decided not to exercise its discretion under section 27(5) of the Act with respect to the Toton and South Shields acquisitions. These transactions will, therefore, not be considered further."

Conversely, in the Archant reference decision,[31] the OFT did exercise its discretion under s.27(5) of the Act to treat the acquisition by Archant of three of INM's London regional newspaper divisions on December 11, 2003 as having occurred simultaneously with Archant's acquisiton of two further divisions on December 30, 2003. As a consequence, the statutory deadline for considering the "consolidated" merger was April 29, 2004, the date on which both transactions were referred to the Competition Commission.

Section 29 safeguards against the gradual acquisition of a business, sometimes referred to as "creeping control", by providing that where a person acquires control of an enterprise, in any of the three senses identified above,[32] during a series of transactions which all occur within a period of two years, the Secretary of State or the Competition Commission may treat them as having occurred simultaneously on the date of the latest event.[33] Section 29(2), extends the range of transactions that can be made the subject of a reference, by including any direct or indirect "step towards" any of the levels of control. Accordingly, if company "A" acquires a 25 per cent interest in company "B" through five or six share purchases over a

---

[31] OFT's decision of April 29, 2004, *Completed acquisition by Archant Limited of the London Regionals Division of Independent News & Media plc.*

[32] *i.e.* material influence, *de facto* control or *de jure* control; see paras 2.007–2.010, above.

[33] Note that The Enterprise Act 2002 (Anticipated Mergers) Order 2003 (SI 2003/1595) extends the provisions of s.29 (which concerns completed mergers) to anticipated mergers, with amended wording in ss.29(1) to (4) as set out in the statutory instrument.

two-year period (for example in a situation where a stake is being built in a publicly listed company), the OFT and the Competition Commission are entitled to regard the 25 per cent shareholding as having been acquired at the expiry of the two-year period. In keeping with s.27(3), s.29(6) provides that in determining the time at which any transaction occurs "no account shall be taken of any option or other conditional right until the option is exercised or the condition is satisfied."

Public interest cases

2.025   As explained in Ch.1, a key objective of the Enterprise Act was to take the politics out of merger control. Whilst this has been largely achieved, there remain two sets of circumstances in which Ministers may become involved in merger cases, both of which relate to the protection of the public interest as defined in the Act[34]: public interest cases, and special public interest cases. Public interest cases arise when the Secretary of State issues an intervention notice in connection with a relevant merger situation raising defined public interest issues. Special public interest cases arise in connection with mergers that fall below the jurisdictional thresholds of the Act but raise issues of national security because one or more of the parties to the merger is a relevant government contractor or issues of media plurality arise because one of the parties to the merger has more than a quarter of broadcasting activities or newspapers of a particular description in the UK or a substantial part of it.

The rules applicable to public interest cases concern situations where enterprises cease to be distinct which both: (i) fall within the definition of relevant merger situation contained in s.23[35]; and (ii) raise public interest issues as set out in s.58 (or which, in the Secretary of State's opinion, ought to be included in s.58).[36]

The rules applicable to special public interest cases concern situations where enterprises cease to be distinct, and where such situations: (i) fall outside the definition of a relevant merger situation set out in s.23 because they do not meet either the turnover or share of supply thresholds[37]; and (ii) raise public interest issues as specified in s.58[38]; and (iii) either (a) one or more of the persons concerned is a "relevant government contractor", as defined in s.59(8)[39]; or (b) in relation to any description of newspapers, at least one quarter of all newspapers of that description was (prior to the merger) supplied by the person by whom one of the merging enterprises was carried on[39A]; or (c) in relation to any description of broadcasting, at least one quarter of all broadcasting of that description was (prior to the merger)

---

[34] Including media-related public interest considerations which are considered in Ch.7 below, as regards newspapers, and para.2.060, below, as regards other media including the broadcasting sector.

[35] s.42(1).

[36] s.42(3).

[37] s.59(3A)(a).

[38] s.59(2). The Enterprise Act does not provide for the possibility of additional public interest considerations to be specified in relation to special public interest cases as it does in relation to "ordinary" public interest cases.

[39] s.59(3B)(b).

[39A] s.29(3C), read with the provisions regarding construction of this section in s.59A.

supplied by the person by whom one of the merging enterprises was carried on.[39B] Section 59(8) defines relevant government contractors as current and former government contractors who have been notified by or on behalf of the Secretary of State that they may hold or receive confidential information, documents or other articles relating to defence (and have not had such notifications revoked).[40] Section 59(9) defines "defence" and "government contractor" by reference to the Official Secrets Act 1989,[41] and states that the definition of government contractor includes any sub-contractors. Section 59A provides greater detail on the construction of ss.59(3C) and 59(3D) in relation to newspaper and broadcasting mergers.

The key difference between the public interest and special public interest cases from a procedural point of view is that no new public interest considerations may be introduced by the Secretary of State by statutory instrument in relation to special public interest cases. New special public interest considerations can, of course, be introduced by primary legislation, as has already occurred under the Communications Act 2003 in relation to newspapers and broadcasting activities.[42]

Definition of public interest

Relevant public interest considerations are set out in s.58 of the Act. This section originally specified only "the interests of national security" as a public interest consideration. However, the Communications Act 2003 has since added a number of media public interest considerations. Newspaper mergers are considered in detail in Ch.7. Other media mergers (that is mergers involving broadcasting undertakings), are considered briefly at the end of this Chapter.   2.026

Section 58(2) defines national security as including public security which is identified as having "the same meaning as in article 21(4) of the EC Merger Regulation".[43] Art.21(4) does not define "public security" and there have been very few EC merger cases that have raised public security issues. In one

---

[39B] s.59(3D), read with the provisions regarding construction of this section in s.59A.
[40] s.59(8).
[41] s.2(4) of the Official Secrets Act 1989 defines "defence" as meaning:

"(a) the size, shape, organisation, logistics, order of battle, deployment, operations, state of readiness and training of the armed forces of the Crown;
(b) the weapons, stores or other equipment of those forces and the invention, development, production and operation of such equipment and research relating to it;
(c) defence policy and strategy and military planning and intelligence;
(d) plans and measures for the maintenance of essential supplies and services that are or would be needed in time of war."

The definition of "government contractor" in ss.12(2) and (3) of the Official Secrets Act 1989 covers persons who are not Crown servants but who provide, or are employed in the provision of, goods or services: (a) for the purposes of the government (including Ministers, the civil service, the military or the police); or (b) under an agreement certified by the Secretary of State as being one to which a government of a State other than the UK, or an international organisation (as defined in s.13 of the Official Secrets Act 1989) is a party.
[42] See s.378 of the Communications Act 2003.
[43] The phrase "EC Merger Regulation" is defined in s.129(1) of the Act as "Council Regulation (EC) No 139/2004 of 20th January 2004 on the control of concentrations between undertakings", i.e. the reformed EC Merger Regulation which came into force on May 1, 2004.

case, IBM France/CGI,[44] although there is no reference to public security issues in the European Commission's clearance decision, the European Commission's XXIIIrd Report on Competition Policy (1993) states that this case involved the first application of Art.21(4) (then Art.21(3) of the pre-reform EC Merger Regulation) and that "measures were taken in order to protect French legitimate interests linked to public security".[45] However, it is not clear precisely what measures were taken or what public security interests the measures were intended to protect.

Article 30 of the EC Treaty identifies public security as one of the grounds for an exception to the general prohibition on restrictions on imports and exports contained in Arts 28 and 29 of the EC Treaty.[46] A significant volume of case law has developed on the meaning of "public security" in this context, and it is not unreasonable to assume that the European Courts would interpret the reference to public security in Art.21(4) of the EC Merger Regulation in a manner that is consistent with their interpretation of the concept under Art.30.[47]

2.027   The European Court of Justice was required to interpret the Art.30 public security exception in *Campus Oil v Minister for Industry and Energy*.[48] The case concerned a requirement under Irish law that importers of petroleum products to Ireland purchase a certain percentage of their requirements for refined petroleum products from the Irish National Petroleum Corporation (which was owned by the Irish Government). The plaintiffs in the case argued that this amounted to a quantitative restriction on imports of such products to Ireland, contrary to Art.28. The Irish Government maintained that if the requirement did amount to such a restriction it was justified under Art.30 on the grounds of public policy and public security, since the policy was intended to safeguard the continued operation of Ireland's only oil refinery which was necessary to maintain Ireland's supply of petroleum products, and without which Ireland would have been dependent on foreign imports.[49]

---

[44] Case No.IV/M.336.

[45] The XXIIIrd Report on Competition Policy (1993), para.321, simply states that:

> "The French authorities informed the [European] Commission that they had taken certain appropriate measures relating to two CGI subsidiaries forming part of the merger that worked in particular with the French Ministry of Defence. The measures were taken in order to protect French legitimate interests linked to public security, pursuant to the second subpara. of Art.21(3)."

[46] Art.30 of the EC Treaty states:

> "The provisions of Articles 28 and 29 shall not preclude prohibitions or restrictions on imports, exports or goods in transit justified on grounds of public morality, public policy or public security; . . .".

[47] The range of grounds for exceptions to be made to the rules in relation to the free movement of goods contained in Art.30 is longer than that in Art.21(4) of the EC Merger Regulation. In addition to public morality, public policy and public security, Art.30 also contains specific references to:

> "the protection of health and life of humans, animals or plants; the protection of national treasures possessing artistic, historic or archaeological value; or the protection of industrial and commercial property."

[48] Case 72/83, *Campus Oil v Minister for Industry and Energy* [1984] E.C.R. 2727.

[49] Interestingly, the UK Government intervened in the case. Its view, as reported in the European Court of Justice's judgment, was that:

The European Court stated that due to petroleum products' "exceptional importance as an energy source in the modern economy", which was of "fundamental importance for a country's existence since not only its economy but above all its institutions, its essential public services and even the survival of its inhabitants depend upon them", an "interruption in supplies of petroleum products, with the resultant dangers for the country's existence, could therefore seriously affect the public security that Art.30 allows States to protect".[50] The court went on to emphasise that:

> "A Member State cannot be allowed to avoid the effects of measures provided for in the Treaty by pleading the economic difficulties caused by the elimination of barriers to intra-Community trade. However, in the light of the seriousness of the consequences that an interruption in supplies of petroleum products may have for a country's existence, the aim of ensuring a minimum supply of petroleum products at all times is to be regarded as transcending purely economic considerations and thus as capable of constituting an objective covered by the concept of public security."[51]

Advocate General Slynn stated in his Opinion that:

> "'Public security' is clearly not limited to external military security . . . Nor in my view is it limited to internal security, in the sense of the maintenance of law and order . . . though it may include this."[52]

He also stated, in deciding whether the restrictions in question were justifiable on the grounds of public security, that:

> ". . . there must be left out of account any economic advantages accruing, however desirable in themselves they may be. Thus the protection of employment, any improvement in the balance of payments, the financial return, the desirability of keeping in operation a domestic industry and, for commercial reasons, of avoiding purchasing from suppliers outside the State, do not go to establish that the measures are justified."[53]

This analysis gives some guidance as to how the UK courts are likely to interpret the concept of public security. In summary, it would appear that "public security" in the Act is limited to non-economic matters which threaten the well-being of the State, and although these may be related to particularly serious economic considerations which threaten a country's

---

"the term "public security" in Art.[30] of the Treaty covers the fundamental interests of the State such as the maintenance of essential public services or the safe and effective functioning of the life of the State. The exceptions provided for in that Article cannot be relied upon if the measures in question are designed predominantly to attain economic objectives. Those measures must not go beyond what is necessary to attain the objective protected by Art.[30]." (para.23)

[50] *Campus Oil*, cited above, at para.34.
[51] *Campus Oil*, cited above, at para.35.
[52] *Campus Oil*, cited above, at p.2764.
[53] *Campus Oil*, cited above, at pp.2764–2765.

existence, economic considerations in themselves are unlikely to be sufficient grounds for Government intervention.[54]

2.028   Those matters falling within Art.296(1)(b)[55] of the EC Treaty would also seem to fall within the meaning of "national security" in s.58(1). There have been a number of cases reviewed under the EC Merger Regulation involving undertakings engaged in the supply of defence products where the European Commission has accepted notifications in which the parties have, at the behest of the relevant Member State(s), not provided information in relation to certain military activities. Examples include Case No.IV/M.528, *British Aerospace/VSEL* and Case No.IV/M.1258, *GEC Marconi/Alenia*.[56] However, in the *Saab/Celsius* decision,[57] the Commission adopted a less accommodating approach:

"As a result of instructions, referring to Art.296(1)(b) of the EC Treaty, given by the Swedish Government to the notifying party, this notification provided only information relating to civil and dual use products. In this connection, the Swedish government informed the Commission that it regarded the proposed concentration as very important to Sweden's ability to protect its vital security interests and stated its view that the aspects of the concentration relating to defence products should not be investigated under the Merger Regulation. Following a request by the Commission, the notifying party provided additional information to enable the Commission to assess the impact of the proposed concentration on competition with respect to defence products. The Commission's assessments in relation to all aspects of the proposed concentration are set out below."

The Commission then went on to consider the effect of the merger on a wide range of military activities including ammunition; guided weapons

---

[54] One example of a UK case which considered the definition of public safety (which is hard to differentiate from public security) was *R. v Governor of Wormwood Scrubs Prison* [1920] K.B. 305 In that case, which involved an application for a writ of habeus corpus in relation to a suspect detained without trial on the grounds of public safety under the Defence of the Realm (Consolidation) Act 1914, Bray J. stated that public safety as defined in the Act was not "limited to securing the country against some foreign foe" (at p.313) but also applied to "any internal disturbance or rebellion" (at p.314).

[55] Art.296(1)(b) states:

"any Member State may take such measures as it considers necessary for the protection of the essential interests of its security which are connected with the production of or trade in arms, munitions and war material; such matters shall not adversely affect the conditions of competition in the common market regarding products which are not intended for specifically military purposes."

[56] In the former case the European Commission decision notes at para.1 that:

"the United Kingdom, relying on Art.[296(1)(b)] of the EC Treaty, has instructed British Aerospace not to notify the acquisition of the military activities of VSEL".

Similarly, the European Commission decision in *GEC Marconi/Alenia* notes at para.2:

"The United Kingdom and Italy, relying upon Art.[296(1)(b)] of the EC Treaty have instructed the parties not to notify the military aspects of this operation. The notification therefore relates only to the non-military applications of the products of the JV".

[57] Case No. IV/M1779, 4/2/2000 — *Saab/Celsius*, para.2.

systems, torpedo weapons systems, anti-armour systems, small arms, defence electronics, and naval vessels.

Notwithstanding the acquiescence of the Swedish government in the Saab/Celsius decision, the UK, French and Italian governments subsequently requested the parties to the creation of a joint venture manufacturing tactical guided weapons and guided weapons systems, BAE Systems, EADS and Finmeccanica, not to notify the military aspects of the merger to the European Commission under the EC Merger Regulation.[58]

The concept of national security was described by the relevant Minister, Melanie Johnson MP,[59] in terms of defence issues at the Committee Stage of the passage of the Enterprise Bill through Parliament:

"National security primarily concerns defence issues. It includes public security, but only matters of great importance to the state. As the Honourable Member for Eastbourne said earlier, national security is like an elephant: one knows it when one sees it."[60]

However, it is clear from decisions of the UK courts in other contexts   2.029
that the term "national security" potentially has a broad interpretation. A recent example is *Secretary of State for the Home Department v Rehman*[61] in which the House of Lords, considering an appeal against a deportation decision made on the grounds of national security, stated that the term was not limited to activities directed at the overthrow by internal or external force or other illegal means of the UK government or a foreign government which as a result threatens the UK government, but also included actions which were not direct or immediate. Lord Slynn of Hadley stated that the term "national security" related to "the interests of the state, . . . not merely military defence but [also] democracy, the legal and constitutional systems of the state".[62]

Finally, it is perhaps worth noting at this point that there is provision for the UK Government to prohibit the transfer into foreign ownership of an "important manufacturing undertaking".[62A] So far as the authors are aware,

---

[58] Advice of the Director General of Fair Trading dated March 26, 2002 to the Secretary of State for Trade and Industry. On the advice of the Director General, having consulted with the Ministry of Defence, the Secretary of State accepted undertakings in lieu of a reference to the Competition Commission which related to the maintenance of strategic capabilities and the protection of classified information. The recitals to these undertakings state, inter alia:

"(E) But for the requests referred to in recital (G), the merger would have come within . . . [the EC Merger Regulation]. . .

(G) BAE Systems, Finmeccanica and EADS were each requested by their respective national governments, under Art.296(1)(b) of the EC Treaty, not to notify the military aspects of the merger to the European Commission under the EC Merger Regulation."

[59] Parliamentary Under-Secretary of State for Competition, Consumers and Markets.
[60] *Hansard*, House of Commons Standing Committee B, April 30, 2002, col.356.
[61] *Secretary of State for the Home Department v Rehman* [2002] 1 All E.R. 122.
[62] *Rehman* at para.16.
[62A] See Pt II of the Industry Act 1975. Important manufacturing undertaking is defined in s.11(2) as "an undertaking which, in so far as it is carried on in the United Kingdom, is wholly or mainly engaged in manufacturing industry and appears to the Secretary of State to be of special importance to the United Kingdom or to any substantial part of the United Kingdom."

these powers have never been used, although they remain on the statute book. Of course it is highly unlikely that these provisions could be used to block the transfer of a UK business to a purchaser based in the EU without breaching the UK's obligations as a Member State of the European Union. Moreover, these powers have, for some years now, been out of line with UK industrial policy (whether under a Conservative or a Labour government). In practice if the Government had concerns about key UK manufacturing capacity coming under foreign ownership (whether EU or otherwise) it would seem far more likely that the national security provisions would be used to protect the UK public interest, or a new public interest consideration would be specified.[62B]

Specification of additional public interest criteria

2.030   Section 58 leaves the door open for additional public interest considerations to be specified by the Secretary of State at a later date.[63] The specification of such new considerations, whether or not in the context of an existing merger, must be laid before Parliament in the form of an Order which must be approved under the affirmative resolution procedure by both Houses of Parliament within 28 days of it being made.[64] Although this power exists, the Government made it clear during the Parliamentary debates relating to the Bill that it did not intend to use the powers to define additional public interest considerations. Indeed, at one point in the debate the Minister, Melanie Johnson, stated:

> "... we have no plans to specify new public interest specifications. Merger reform has been the subject of extensive consultation and we have considered thoroughly whether anything beyond national security should be in the Bill. We do not expect to specify further issues in relation to the current scope of the merger control regime. It would be unwise, however, to ensure that unforeseen circumstances could not be dealt with if there were a compelling case in the public interest. We must ensure that we can meet unforeseen circumstances and other legislation makes similar provision."[65]

Nevertheless, before the Act had entered into force, the Communications Act 2003 was enacted, which introduced both new public interest and new special public interest considerations in relation to newspaper and other media mergers. In broad terms, these additional public interest considerations are aimed at ensuring the accurate presentation of the news, free expression of opinion and plurality of the media, the maintenance of a wide range of broadcasting throughout the UK and that persons carrying on media enterprises have a genuine commitment to the maintenance of the television and radio standards objectives set out in s.319 of the Communications Act 2003.[66]

[62B] See further para.2.030.

[63] s.58(3) and (4).

[64] s.124(7).

[65] *Hansard*, House of Commons Standing Committee B, April 30, 2002, col.343.

[66] These provisions are contained in ss.58(2A) to (2C) of the Act which was inserted by s.375(1) of the Communications Act 2003; see further paras 2.060–2.065, below for a

The Communications Act also introduced additional special public interest considerations which enable the Secretary of State to issue a special intervention notice where immediately before the enterprises ceased to be distinct, in relation to the provision of broadcasting of any description or the supply of newspapers of any description, at least one quarter of all broadcasting or newspapers of that description in the UK or in a substantial part of the UK was provided by the person or persons by whom one of the enterprises was carried on.[67]

Identification of public interest considerations

The Act requires the OFT to bring to the attention of the Secretary of State any case which it is considering which may raise already specified public interest considerations unless it believes that the Secretary of State would consider any such consideration to be immaterial in the context of the particular case.[68] In addition, the OFT and the Competition Commission must bring to the attention of the Secretary of State any representations which they receive in relation to the exercise of the Secretary of State's power to specify additional public interest considerations.[69] It is also probable that public interest cases will come to the attention of the Secretary of State by the parties to the transaction, or interested third parties, making representations to this effect to him. Furthermore, as pointed out by the Minister during the course of the Commons Standing Committee debate, the Government assumes that the Ministry of Defence will be alert to the possibility of additional public interest issues arising and would be likely to raise them with the Secretary of State in cases where it is appropriate and the same can be assumed of other government departments and/or public bodies such as OFCOM.[70]

2.031

Intervention notices

In order for the Secretary of State to take any action in relation to public interest cases or special public interest cases he must issue an "intervention notice" to the OFT at any time prior to the case being referred to the Competition Commission. Section 42 requires four conditions to be fulfilled before the Secretary of State may issue an intervention notice to the OFT in relation to public interest cases. First, he must have reasonable grounds for suspecting that a relevant merger situation has been (or is about to be) created[71]; secondly, no reference to the Competition Commission may have been made by the OFT; thirdly, no decision may have been made by the OFT not to make such a reference or to have accepted undertakings in lieu of a reference; and finally, a reference is not prevented from being made on any other grounds (e.g. the merger satisfies the turnover thresholds contained in

2.032

---

discussion of the key provisions relating to media mergers, and Ch.7 below for a discussion of how the media provisions relate to newspaper mergers.
[67] ss.59(3C) and (3D) and s.59A of the Act, as inserted by s.378 of the Communications Act 2003; see further paras 2.064 et seq., below.
[68] s.57(1).
[69] s.57(2).
[70] Hansard, House of Commons Standing Committee B, April 30, 2002, col.351.
[71] The Secretary of State's powers to determine whether or not this is the case are considered below.

the EC Merger Regulation).[72] Only one intervention notice may be issued by the Secretary of State in relation to each relevant merger situation.[73]

In addition to specifying the relevant merger situation concerned,[74] intervention notices must also specify any public interest consideration(s) which the Secretary of State believes are relevant.[75] These include, not only public interest considerations already specified in s.58, but also public interest considerations which, in the opinion of the Secretary of State ought to be specified in s.58. Where public interest considerations are identified as relevant by the Secretary of State, but are not included in s.58, they are required to be 'finalised' — that is laid before and approved by both Houses of Parliament under the affirmative resolution procedure within a period of 28 days of being made by the Secretary of State.[76] In such cases the intervention notice must specify the timetable proposed by the Secretary of State for the finalisation of the relevant public interest consideration(s),[77] and the Secretary of State must, as soon as practicable, take such action as is within his power to ensure that it is finalised.[78] When the OFT receives an intervention notice it has a duty to publicise this fact and to invite representations on the public interest issues from interested parties with a view to preparing a report to the Secretary of State.[79] Under s.46(2) of the Act, the Secretary of State is obliged to accept the decisions of the OFT set out in its report pursuant to s.44(4) including as to the existence of a relevant merger situation.

Existence of relevant merger situation

2.033 The existence of a relevant merger situation, in respect of which an intervention notice may be issued, is determined under very similar powers to those applicable in normal cases under ss.23 to 32 of the Act.[80] However, there are a number of adjustments to the exercise by the Secretary of State and the OFT of the OFT's standard powers[81] reflecting the fact that deci-

---

[72] s.42(1).
[73] s.42(4).
[74] s.43(1)(a).
[75] s.42(2). However, under s.43(2), where the Secretary of State believes that two or more public interest considerations are relevant to the consideration of the merger, he may decide not to mention those of them as he considers appropriate. That being said, if a public interest consideration is not mentioned in the intervention notice, the Secretary of State has no power under s.45 to refer the merger to the Competition Commission on the basis that the merger may operate against the public interest due to that public interest consideration (and therefore no adverse public interest findings can be made by the Competition Commission in relation to it). Moreover, as noted, s.42(4) provides that only one intervention notice may be given under s.42 in relation to any relevant merger situation. Accordingly, if the Secretary of State decides not to mention one or more possible public interest considerations, he will forfeit the chance of referring the merger in relation to any of the public interest considerations that are not mentioned.
[76] s.42(8) and s.124(7).
[77] s.43(1)(c).
[78] s.42(7).
[79] s.44. The role of the OFT in public interest cases is considered in Ch.4, below.
[80] s.42(5).
[81] Contained in s.42(6). ss.23 to 32 set out the jurisdictional tests and time limits (including extensions to those time limits) applicable in relation to anticipated and completed mergers without public interest considerations.

sions on the existence of a relevant merger situation must be made by the Secretary of State when issuing an intervention notice, by the OFT when reporting to the Secretary of State under s.44 and, if a reference is made by the Secretary of State, by the Competition Commission when reporting to the Secretary of State.[82]

Does the European Commission have jurisdiction?

Under the EC Merger Regulation,[83] the European Commission has exclusive competence, subject to limited exceptions, to regulate certain large scale mergers, defined as "concentrations having a Community dimension".[83A] As a consequence, subject to limited exceptions mergers which exceed the relevant turnover thresholds set out in the EC Merger Regulation are not subject to the OFT's jurisdiction under the Act. The purpose of this section is to identify the main circumstances in which the jurisdiction of the United Kingdom authorities will be affected by provisions of the EC Merger Regulation.[84]   **2.034**

Article 21 of the EC Merger Regulation addresses the issue of jurisdiction between the Commission and the competition authorities of the Member States. Art. 21(3) maintains the concept of the "one-stop shop" by laying down the basic principle that "no Member State shall apply its national legislation on competition to any concentration that has a Community dimension". Since the Enterprise Act cannot apply where the EC Merger Regulation applies to a merger, the question of whether the European Commission has jurisdiction is considered in some detail in this section.   **2.035**

Concentrations having a Community dimension

Article 1(2) provides that a concentration has a Community dimension[85] where:

(a)   the combined aggregate worldwide turnover of all the undertakings concerned is more than €5,000 million; and

(b)   the aggregate Community-wide turnover of each of at least two of the undertakings concerned is more than €250 million,

unless each of the undertakings concerned achieves more than two-thirds of its aggregate Community-wide turnover within one and the same Member State.[86]

---

[82]   s.42(6)(a).

[83]   Council Regulation 139/2004 on the control of concentrations between undertakings ([2004] O.J. L24/1).

[83A]   Art.1(1) of the EC merger Regulation.

[84]   A detailed discussion of the EC Merger Regulation is outside the scope of this work.

[85]   On June 8, 2004 the EEA Joint Committee adopted Decisions No.78/2004 and No.79/2004 which set out the applicability of the EC Merger Regulation to the European Economic Area ("EEA"). The Annex to Decision 78/2004 sets out the consequences of the Decision which include, *inter alia*, that for the purposes of the EEA Agreement the EC Merger Regulation shall be read as referring to a concentration having an "EEA dimension" as well as a Community dimension as appropriate.

[86]   Art.1(2). As at July 1, 2004, €5,000 million amounted to approximately £3,321 million; €250 million amounted to approximately £166 million.

Pursuant to Art.1(3) concentration will also have a Community dimension where:

(a) the combined aggregate worldwide turnover of all the undertakings concerned is more than €2,500 million;

(b) in each of at least three Member States, the combined aggregate turnover of all the undertakings concerned is more than €100 million;

(c) in each of at least three Member States included for the purpose of point (b), the aggregate turnover of each of at least two of the undertakings concerned is more than €25 million; and

(d) the aggregate Community-wide turnover of each of at least two of the undertakings concerned is more than €100 million.

unless each of the undertakings concerned achieves more than two-thirds of its aggregate Community-wide turnover within one and the same Member State.[87]

Under the EC Merger Regulation, aggregate turnover comprises the revenue derived by the undertakings concerned in the preceding financial year (that is, the last year for which accounts were available) from the sale of products and/or the provision of services, after deduction, amongst other things, of turnover related taxes. In calculating turnover it is necessary, broadly, to assess total group turnover across all product/business sectors by aggregating the turnover of the whole group of which the undertakings concerned are a part, taking into account the specific definition of "control" for EC Merger Regulation purposes. The Commission has published a notice setting out the correct approach to the calculation of turnover, in particular as regards corporate groups as well as for credit and other financial institutions and insurance undertakings.[87A]

In December 2001, the Commission published a Green Paper on the review of the EC Merger Regulation,[88] in which it stated that the second test, which was introduced as part of the 1997 review of the EC Merger Regulation, "has fallen short of achieving its underlying objective" of conferring competence on the Commission in cases which affect three or more Member States.[89] The Commission indicated in the Green Paper that its preference for the reform of Art.1(3) of the EC Merger Regulation would be for a Community dimension to be presumed where a merger gave rise to three or more national notification requirements.[90] However, the Commission subsequently indicated that a more appropriate balance between national and Community jurisdiction might be achieved through greater use of the "referral back" and "referral up" mechanisms contained

---

[87] Art.1(3). As at July 1, 2004, €2,500 million amounted to approximately £1,661 million; €100 million amounted to approximately £66 million; and €25 million amounted to approximately £17 million.

[87A] European Commission's Notice on calculation of turnover [1998] O.J. C 66/25.

[88] *Green Paper on the Review of Council Regulation* (EEC) No. 4064/89, COM (2001) 745/6 final.

[89] See the *Green Paper on the Review of Council Regulation*, cited above, at para.24.

[90] See the *Green Paper on the Review of Council Regulation*, cited above, at para.62.

in Art.9 and Art.22 of the EC Merger Regulation.[91] This was the approach that was ultimately adopted, as the turnover thresholds were not amended as part of the 2004 reforms, but the procedures for referrals between the Commission and the competent authorities of the Member States were strengthened. The recitals to the revised EC Merger Regulation set out the intention that the referral procedures "should operate as an effective corrective mechanism in the light of the principle of subsidiarity".[92]

The first issue to be determined in considering whether a proposed trans- 2.036 action is subject to a compulsory notification to the European Commission under the EC Merger Regulation is whether the transaction amounts to a "concentration". Article 3(1) provides that a concentration will arise where a change of control on a lasting basis results from two or more previously independent undertakings (or parts of undertakings) merging or where one or more undertakings acquiring direct or indirect control of the whole or part of one or more other undertakings. The means by which control is obtained include the purchase of shares, assets, by contract or "any other means".[93] "Control" is defined by Art.3(2) as the possibility of exercising "decisive influence" on an undertaking, through the ownership of, or the right to use, all or part of the assets of an undertaking, through voting rights, or as a result of contracts (typically through shareholders agreements).

This definition of control is potentially wide reaching and given the possibility that potentially very large fines (of up to ten per cent of the turnover of the undertaking concerned) can be imposed for failing to notify a concentration having a Community dimension[94] as well as for implementing an unnotified concentration,[95] particular caution should be exercised in assessing transactions that involve minority shareholders. The Commission has issued a notice on the concept of a concentration[96] which sets out in detail the circumstances in which decisive influence may arise. As a general observation the Notice states that:

"Whether an operation gives rise to an acquisition of control depends on a number of legal and/or factual elements. The acquisition of property rights and shareholders' agreements are important, but are not the only elements involved: purely economic relationships may also play a decisive role. Therefore, in exceptional circumstances, a situation of economic dependence may lead to control on a *de facto* basis where, for example, very important long-term supply agreements or credits provided by suppliers or customers, coupled with structural links, confer decisive influence".[97]

Sole control will normally be acquired where an undertaking acquires a majority of the voting rights of a company (that is, more than 50 per cent), but can also arise on a *de facto* basis where, for example, an acquiring

---

[91] The Commission XXXII Report on Competition Policy (2002) points 283 to 317.
[92] Recital 11 of the EC Merger Regulation.
[93] Art.3(1).
[94] Art.14(2)(a).
[95] Art.14(2)(b).
[96] European Commission's Notice on the concept of concentration under Council Regulation 4064/89 on the control of concentrations between undertakings, [1998] O.J. C 66/02.
[97] See the Notice on the concept of concentration, cited above, at para.9.

shareholder is "highly likely to achieve a majority at the shareholders' meeting, given that the remaining shares are widely dispersed".[98] In making this assessment, the European Commission will look at evidence of votes cast at recent shareholders' meetings. The application of this principle has resulted in *de facto* sole control being identified at relatively low levels: 27.47 per cent in *Anglo American v Lonrho*[99]; and 19 per cent in *CCIE v GTE*.[1] The European Commission's notice states that an option to purchase or convert shares from one class to another, thereby attracting voting rights, cannot in itself confer sole control unless the option will be exercised "in the near future" according to legally binding agreements. However, the notice states that it will take into account the likely exercise of such an option as an additional element which, together with other factors, may lead to the conclusion that there is sole control.[2]

Joint control will exist where two or more undertakings have the possibility of exercising decisive influence over another undertaking, which the Commission's Notice describes as "normally . . . the power to block actions which determine the strategic commercial behaviour of an undertaking",[3] thereby requiring shareholders to reach a common understanding in determining the commercial policy of the business. In other words, the shareholders in question have the right (typically set out in the statutes of the joint venture company or in a shareholders' agreement or other understanding between the participants) to veto strategic decisions relating to the business policy of the joint venture, sometimes referred to as "negative control". The Commission's notice states that to confer decisive influence and therefore joint control, such rights must go beyond those that are normally accorded to minority shareholders in order to protect their financial interests as investors.[3A] Investor protection rights include those relating to changes in the company's statutes, an increase or decrease in the capital, as well as votes over the sale or winding up of the business. In contrast, veto rights which confer joint control typically relate to core strategic issues such as the budget, the business plan, major investments or the appointment of senior management, but do not need to confer the ability to exercise decisive influence over the day to day commercial decisions which are part of the normal process of running the business.[4]

A concentration will also occur where a transaction leads to a change in the *structure* of control of an undertaking, such as a change from joint control to sole control as well as an increase in the number of shareholders exercising joint control[5] or even a change in the respective control rights of the shareholders which alters the balance of control between them.[6]

2.037   The EC Merger Regulation applies to the creation of a joint venture which performs on a lasting basis all of the functions of an autonomous

---

[98] See the Notice on the concept of concentration, cited above, at paras 13–14.
[99] Case IV/M.754, *Anglo American/Lonrho*.
[1] Case IV/M.258, *CCIE/GTE*.
[2] See the Notice on the concept of concentration, cited above, at para.15.
[3] See the Notice on the concept of concentration, cited above, at para.19.
[3A] See the Notice on the concept of a concentration, cited above, at para.22.
[4] See the Notice on the concept of concentration, cited above, at paras 23 to 29.
[5] See the Notice on the concept of concentration, cited above, at para.40.
[6] See para.41 of the European Commission's Notice on the concept of undertakings concerned, [1998] O.J. C66/14.

economic entity (known as "full-function" joint ventures).[7] Joint ventures which fall short of being full function are not subject to the EC Merger Regulation and national competition authorities remain competent, as well as the European Commission itself under Art.81 of the EC Treaty. In the UK, the possibility exists that a non-full function joint venture may constitute a merger under the Enterprise Act if enterprises cease to be distinct and the jurisdictional thresholds are satisfied. As the Commission's notice on full-function joint ventures states,[8] a full-function joint venture must be an autonomous economic entity and operate on a market performing the functions normally carried out by undertakings operating on the same market and must have the staff and resources in terms of finance and tangible and intangible assets to conduct its business activities on a lasting basis. If the joint venture does not fulfil these basic criteria then it is unlikely to be regarded as full function. In practice, in cases where it is difficult to be certain whether an arrangement is full function, it is advisable to discuss the question of jurisdiction in advance with the European Commission (and the OFT if there is a prospect of a relevant merger situation being created).

Will the United Kingdom authorities have jurisdiction under the "referral-back" provisions?

Following the 2004 reforms to the EC Merger Regulation, there are now two alternative mechanisms by which a transaction which constitutes a concentration having a Community dimension may nevertheless be reviewed in whole or part by a national competition authority. As has always been the case, Art.9 of the EC Merger Regulation provides for referral back at the request of a Member State following notification on Form CO of the merger to the European Commission. The 2004 reforms, which strengthened this limb of the jurisdictional "corrective mechanisms" have added a further procedure under Art.4(4) whereby the parties themselves can notify the European Commission (before they have submitted Form CO) that a merger affects competition in a distinct market within a Member State and should therefore be referred back to that national authority.[9] These two procedures are considered below, followed by a

2.038

---

[7] Art.3(4), EC Merger Regulation.

[8] See Commission Notice on the concept of full-function joint ventures [1998] O.J. C 66/1.

[9] Para.5 of the Commission's Notice on Case Referral states that "the revisions made to the referral system in the Merger Regulation [*i.e.* those in relation to Art.9 and Art.22] were designed to facilitate the re-attribution of cases between the Commission and Member States, consistent with the principle of subsidiarity, so that the more appropriate authority or authorities for carrying out a particular merger investigation should in principle deal with the case". At para.8 the Notice states that "above all, in considering whether or not to exercise their discretion to make or accede to a referral, the Commission and Member States should bear in mind the need to ensure effective protection of competition in all markets affected by the transaction". However, the Notice also refers to the benefits inherent in the "one-stop-shop" system which lies at the heart of the Merger Regulation and warns against the risk of fragmentation of cases which "should be avoided where possible" (Notice at paras 11 and 12). This is consistent with the views expressed by the CFI in Case T-119/02, *Philips v Commission* [2003] E.C.R. II-1433, which referred to the risk of "inconsistent, or even irreconcilable" decisions by the Commission and the national competition authorities as being "inherent in the referral system established by Art.9" (see paras 350 and 380), cited by the Commission at n.17 of the Case Referral Notice.

consideration of the EC Merger Regulation provisions which relate to proceedings at the national level following a referral back.[10]

The wording of Arts 4(4) and 9 of the EC Merger Regulation do not rule out the possibility of splitting a case up and making more than one referral back to a Member State, and/or with the Commission retaining part of the case which it will review itself. Fragmentation of this type has occurred in the past: in *Leroy Merlin/Brico*, the European Commission referred parts of the case back to France, Spain and Portugal, and reviewed the remainder of the case itself.[11] However, when the European Court of First Instance considered the issue of partial referral back in *Philips v Commission*, it considered fragmentation of a case between various authorities to be undesirable, and to risk undermining the core EC Merger Regulation principle of the one-stop shop.[11A] The CFI's view in *Philips* is referred to in the Commission's notice on case referral, which comments that:

"Fragmentation of cases through referral should . . . be avoided where possible, unless it appears that multiple authorities would be in a better position to ensure that competition in all markets affected by the transaction is effectively protected. Accordingly, while partial referrals are possible under Articles 4(4) and 9, it would normally be appropriate for the whole of a case (or at least all connected parts thereof) to be dealt with by a single authority".[11B]

This is an important limitation on the use of Arts 4(4) and 9 as a "corrective mechanism" to transfer jurisdiction, particularly as regards distinct national markets which are nonetheless closely linked to other markets which are also affected by the merger in question.

Referral back prior to notification under Article 4(4) of the EC Merger Regulation

2.039   Under Art.4(4), those responsible for notifying a qualifying merger to the European Commission[12] are able to initiate the referral back process themselves, by informing the Commission "that [i] the concentration may significantly affect competition [ii] in a market within a Member State which presents all the characteristics of a distinct market".[13] The Commission's

---

[10]   The Commission's Notice on case referrals states that its purpose "is to describe in a general way the rationale underlying the case referral system in Arts 4(4), 4(5), 9 and 22 of the [EC Merger Regulation]. . ., to catalogue the legal criteria that must be fulfilled in order for referrals to be possible, and to set out the factors which may be taken into consideration when referrals are decided upon." (para.1).

[11]   Case COMP/M.2898. See European Commission's press release of December 13, 2002, IP/02/1881.

[11A]   Case T-119/02, *Royal Philips Electronics NV v Commission* [2003] E.C.R. II-1433 at para.350.

[11B]   See para.12 of the Notice.

[12]   Art.4(2).

[13]   This wording mirrors the provisions of Art.9(2)(a), described further below at 2.040. The question arises as to how requests under Art.4(4) of the EC Merger Regulation should be dealt with by the Commission when the concentration in question affects competition in a distinct market within a Member State which does not constitute a substantial part of the common market (*cf.* Art.9(2)(b)). In the context of Art.9, pursuant to Art.9(3) third para-

notice on case referrals observes that as regards these two legal requirements, the requesting parties are required to demonstrate that the transaction is liable to have a potential impact on competition on a distinct market in a Member State, which may prove to be significant, thus deserving close scrutiny. The notice recognises that such indications would of necessity be preliminary in nature and would be without prejudice to the outcome of the investigation. Although recital 16 of the EC Merger Regulation states that the undertakings concerned should not be required to demonstrate that the effects of the concentration would be detrimental to competition, the notice states that they should nevertheless "point to indicators which are generally suggestive of the existence of some competitive effects stemming from the transaction".[13A] As regards the second criterion, the notice states that the requesting parties should show that a geographic market in which competition is affected by the transaction is national or narrower than national in scope.[14] The notice goes on to provide as an example the Commission's referral of certain distinct oil storage markets for assessment by the French authorities.[15] The parties can make submissions to the Commission that the merger should be examined (in whole or part) by the authorities of the relevant Member State. Such a request must be made formally by way of a reasoned submission[16] on Form RS which is annexed to the implementing regulation to the EC Merger Regulation.[17] Since Art.4(4) requires Form RS to be submitted before any notification has been made, it constitutes a detailed and comprehensive document, reproducing many of the questions in Form CO.[17A] Reinforcing the formality of the process, and consistent with a Form CO notification, the European Commission has the power to impose fines for intentionally or negligently providing incorrect or misleading information in Form RS.[18] The introduction to Form RS encourages prior consultation with the Commission and the relevant Member State(s) in relation to the adequacy and type of information to be provided, further increasing the parallels between submitting a reasoned submission and a full Form CO.

---

graph, the Commission is obliged to refer the whole or part of the case relating to the distinct market concerned to the Member State. To be consistent with the obligation on the Commission to refer cases satisfying Art.9(2)(b) to the Member State in question, it would seem that the request under Art.4(4) in relation to such a concentration should be granted "as of right".

[13A] Case Referral Notice at para.17.

[14] At para.18. Note 23 states that in this connection that "the requesting parties should consider those factors which are typically suggestive of national, or narrower than national markets, such as, primarily, the product characteristics (*e.g.* low value of the product as opposed to significant costs of transport), specific characteristics of demand (*e.g.* end consumers sourcing in proximity of their centre of activity) and supply, significant variation of prices and market shares across countries, national consumers habits, different regulatory frameworks, taxation or other legislation".

[15] Case Referral Notice, at n.24.

[16] Art.4(4), first paragraph.

[17] Commission Regulation 802/2004 of April 7, 2004, [2004] O.J. L133/1.

[17A] Form CO is the prescribed pro-forma for notification of a concentration having a Community dimension under the EC Merger Regulation. It is annexed to the Implementing Regulation.

[18] Art.14(1)(a) of the EC Merger Regulation.

The Explanatory Memorandum to the European Commission's proposal for the reformed EC Merger Regulation[19] implies that the Commission expects the Art.4(4) (and Art.4(5)) procedure to reduce the costs and uncertainties in the referral system.[20] The notice on case referrals observes that the handling of the merger by a single competition agency increases administrative efficiency by avoiding duplication and fragmentation of enforcement effort by multiple authorities. The notice also notes that this "brings advantages to businesses, in particular to merging firms, by reducing the costs and burdens arising from multiple filing obligations and by eliminating the risk of conflicting decisions resulting from the concurrent assessment of the same transaction by a number of competition authorities under diverse legal regimes".[21] However, as noted above, the preparation and effort required in completing a Form RS submission may not be significantly less than would be required for a Form CO notification itself. Moreover, the parties may subsequently also have to prepare a national notification if a referral back is made (or, exceptionally, a series of notifications if the merger is referred back only in part or to more than one Member State). The primary advantage of the Art.4(4) procedure may therefore turn out to be not that it creates any significant reduction in cost or the information burden, but that it allows the parties to accelerate the timescale of a referral back that would have happened in any event.

The original signed Form RS must be submitted together with 35 hard copies and an electronic copy,[22] and the European Commission will forward a copy of the submission to all 25 Member States "without delay".[23] The Member State to which the parties have requested the case should be referred back must express any objection within 15 working days of receipt: silence is deemed to constitute agreement.[24]

Consistent with the position under Art.9(2)(a), if the European Commission agrees that the market in question is a distinct market, it has a discretion to refer the case back in whole or part.[25] Such a decision must be taken within 25 working days of receipt of the reasoned submission: silence is deemed to amount to a decision to refer in accordance with the parties' request.[26] A decision (or deemed decision) to refer the whole case removes the obligation to notify the concentration to the European

---

[19] The Explanatory Memorandum was published as part of the Commission Proposal for a Council Regulation on the control of concentrations between undertakings, [2003] O.J. C20/4 ("the Explanatory Memorandum").

[20] See paras 22, 23, 29 and 30 of the Explanatory Memorandum.

[21] Notice on case referrals, at para.11.

[22] Art.3(2) read with Art.6(12) of Commission Regulation 802/2004 of April 7, 2004, the implementing regulation.

[23] Para.56 of the Commission's Notice on case referrals states that the Commission would endeavour to transmit such documents within one working day from the day they are received or issued. Information within the network will be exchanged by various means, depending on the circumstances: email, surface mail, courier, fax, telephone. It should be noted that "sensitive information or confidential information exchanges will be carried out by secure email or by any other protected means of communication between these contact points".

[24] Art.4(4), second paragraph.

[25] Art.4(4), third paragraph. See para.2.038, above, regarding the limitations on the exercise of this discretion which the case law of the Court of First Instance has emphasised.

[26] Art.4(4), fourth paragraph.

Commission which would otherwise apply under Art.4(1).[27] Once the referral has been made, the provisions set out in Arts 9(6) to (9) regarding the actions and decisions of the relevant Member State's competition authority apply (discussed below).

Referral back following notification under Article 9 of the EC Merger Regulation

Article 9 of the EC Merger Regulation provides for the possibility of a referral 2.040 back to national competition authorities once a full notification of the concentration has been made to the European Commission. Where a concentration having a Community dimension either:

(i) threatens to affect significantly competition on a market within a Member State which presents all the characteristics of a distinct market[28]; or

(ii) affects competition in a market within a Member State, which presents all the characteristics of a distinct market and which does not constitute a substantial part of the common market[29];

the Commission may, at the request of the Member State concerned on its own initiative or upon the invitation of the Commission, having regard to the market for the products and services in question and the geographical reference market,[30] refer the whole or part of such concentration to the competent national authority of the relevant Member State. As is clear from the wording of Art.9, the Commission can only accede to a request by a Member State in circumstances where the "distinct market" constitutes a separate geographical market that is no larger than the Member State making the request and, additionally in relation to paragraph (b), where it does not form a substantial

---

[27] Art.4(4), fifth paragraph. A partial referral back does not remove the obligation to submit Form CO. In such circumstances, there is no express lifting of the obligation to complete Form CO for the concentration as a whole although it is reasonable to assume that where a partial referral back has been made, the European Commission will waive the obligation to include information in Form CO about the referred market(s), pursuant to Art.4(2) of the EC Merger Regulation implementing regulation.

[28] Art. 9(2)(a). The Commission's Notice on case referrals states at para.35 that in relation to the first criterion, the Member State is required to demonstrate that, based on a preliminary analysis, there is a real risk that the transaction may have a significant adverse impact on competition, and that it therefore deserves close scrutiny. The notice states that "such preliminary indications may be in the nature of prima facie evidence of such a possible significant adverse impact, but would be without prejudice to the outcome of a full investigation."

[29] Art.9(2)(b).

[30] Art.9(2). Art.9(7) defines the geographical reference market for the purpose of determining whether the referral requirements of Art.9(3) are satisfied:

"... the geographical reference market shall consist of the area in which the undertakings concerned are involved in the supply and demand of products or services, in which the conditions of competition are sufficiently homogeneous and which can be distinguished from neighbouring areas because, in particular, conditions of competition are appreciably different in those areas. This assessment should take account in particular of the nature and characteristics of the products or services concerned, of the existence of entry barriers or of consumer preferences, of appreciable differences of the undertakings' market shares between the area concerned and neighbouring areas or of substantial price differences".

part of the common market. In relation to this latter requirement, the Commission's notice refers to the past practice of the Commission and relevant case law and states that such situations are generally limited to markets with a narrow geographic scope within a Member State.[31]

The provisions of Art.9 were strengthened in two notable respects by the 2004 reforms in order to increase its effective use as a corrective mechanism. First, Art.9(2)(a) has been amended so that it is no longer necessary for the Member State seeking a referral back to show that the merger "threatens to create or strengthen a dominant position as a result of which effective competition would be significantly impeded". The relevant standard is now simply that the merger threatens to affect competition significantly. In its 2001 Green Paper,[32] the European Commission had proposed the deletion of Art.9(2)(a) in order to simplify the criteria for referral,[33] but ultimately did not pursue this option. The Commission's Explanatory Memorandum which accompanied its proposal for the revised EC Merger Regulation[34] commented that the revised wording of Art.9(2)(a), as now implemented in the EC Merger Regulation, would remove the obligation on Member States' authorities to present elaborate preliminary conclusions with regard to the competitive assessment of the case. The Commission's expectation was that this change would "facilitate a speedier use of Art. 9".[35]

The second notable change to Art.9(2) concerns the introduction of a power for the European Commission to propose a referral back on its own initiative by inviting the Member State concerned to request a referral.[36] Originally, a stronger power of initiative was envisaged. The 2001 Green Paper stated:

"In order ... to fully protect competition on markets within a Member State, the Commission should, in line with the principle of subsidiarity, be able to refer a case or part of a case to national authorities where the [Section 9(2)] criteria ... are fulfilled".[37]

---

[31] Notice on case referrals at para.40. By way of example, the Commission refers at n.35 to case COMP/M.2446, *Govia/Connex South Central*, where the operation affected competition on specific railway routes in the London/Gatwick — Brighton area in the UK; case COMP/M.2730, *Connex/DNVBVG*, where the transaction affected competition in local public transport services in part of Saxony in Germany; and case COMP/M.3130 *Arla Foods/Express Dairies*, where the transaction affected competition in the market for the supply of bottled milk to doorstep deliverers in the London, Yorkshire and Lancashire regions of the UK. The Notice also refers to the relevance of case law of the European Court, particularly in relation to Art.82 of the EC Treaty in defining the notion of a non-substantial part of the common market.

[32] Green Paper on the Review of Council Regulation 4064/89 COM(2001) 745/6 final ("the 2001 Green Paper").

[33] See para.81(a) of the 2001 Green Paper. The paper noted the difficulties with the Art.9(2) referral criteria under the pre-reform EC Merger Regulation and that "most respondents [to a review of recent referral requests] would favour the establishment of 'predictable', 'simple' or even 'automatic' criteria". The Commission noted also that "Art. 9(2)(b), which was introduced to facilitate referral requests by establishing a less demanding test, has only once been successfully used as a basis for a request" (see para.74 of the 2001 Green Paper).

[34] Cited above.

[35] Para.20 of the Explanatory Memorandum.

[36] Art.9(2).

[37] Para.81(6) of the 2001 Green Paper.

The 2001 Green Paper stated that the use of such a power to refer of its **2.041** own initiative could have "spare[d] the Member State the procedural steps needed in preparing a request",[38] thereby streamlining the process. However, notwithstanding this advantage, the proposed change was not implemented. Instead, Art.9(2) gives the European Commission a right of initiative to *invite* a Member State to request a referral back; the Member States retain control over whether any such request is made (assuming a request has not already been made by the parties themselves under Art.4).

Procedurally, any request by a Member State on its own initiative or following an invitation from the Commission must be submitted within 15 working days of the date on which it receives its copy of the Form CO notification.[39] This time limit is relatively tight, and accordingly, if it is possible that the relevant UK authority[40] may conclude that a distinct market exists, the parties to a merger (or interested third parties) should ensure that they are in a position to react to any such request speedily.[41] In considering the application, the European Commission is entitled to request information from the competent authorities of the Member States. In fulfilment of this requirement, the UK has adopted the EC Merger Control (Distinct Market Investigations) Regulations 1990,[42] which gives the OFT the power to require by notice any person to provide relevant documents, estimates, returns or other information.[43]

Where an application by the competent authority of a Member State has been made, Stage I of the European Commission's investigation is automatically extended from 25 working days to 35 working days.[44] If the Commission considers that a distinct national market does exist and competition is threatened on that market as set out in Art.9(2)(a), it has a discretion to deal with the case itself or to refer the matter to the competent authorities of the Member State concerned with a view to the application of that State's national competition law.[45] Where a Member State informs the European Commission pursuant to Art.9(2)(b) that a concentration affects competition in a distinct market within that Member State, which

---

[38] Para.80 of the 2001 Green Paper.

[39] Art.9(2); under Art.19(1) copies of the notification must be sent to the competent authorities of the Member States within three working days.

[40] In the UK, the OFT decides whether to apply to the European Commission under Art.9(2).

[41] Of course, now that the Art.4(4) procedure is available, the parties could initiate the referral back procedure themselves.

[42] SI 1990/1715, as amended by the Enterprise Act 2002 (Consequential and Supplemental Provisions) Order 2003, SI 2003/1398, and by the EC Merger Control (Consequential Amendments) Regulations 2004, SI 2004/1079.

[43] The OFT is also provided with sanctions to reinforce its information gathering powers. Reg.4 of the Regulations makes it a criminal offence punishable by two years imprisonment and/or a fine intentionally to alter, suppress or destroy a document which has been required by the OFT to be produced pursuant to the Regulations. Reg.5 extends the criminal offence relating to the provision of false or misleading information set out in s.117 of the Enterprise Act (see further para.3.054 of Ch.3) as well as the confidentiality provisions contained in Pt 9 of the Act (see further paras 3.078–3.080 of Ch.3).

[44] Art.10(1). Stage I is the initial investigation period within which the European Commission must decide whether the notified concentration falls within the scope of the EC Merger Regulation and, if so, whether serious doubts exist as to its compatibility with the common market such that a Stage II investigation is required (see Art.6(1)).

[45] Art.9(3). See para.2.038 above regarding the limitations on the exercise of this discretion which the case law of the Court of First Instance has emphasised.

does not form a substantial part of the common market, the Commission has no such discretion and is obliged to refer the case (or the relevant part of the case) back to the Member State, provided that the Commission agrees that such a distinct market is affected.[46] The Commission's decision to refer the matter to the relevant national authority must be taken, "as a general rule" within the 35 working day preliminary assessment period where the Commission itself decides not to initiate proceedings and commence a full Stage II investigation, or alternatively within a maximum of 65 working days of the date of notification where the Commission has initiated second stage proceedings, unless it has taken preparatory steps to remedy the adverse competitive consequences.[47] Where the Commission fails to take an appropriate decision or to take steps to remedy the position within 65 working days of notification, despite a reminder from the Member State concerned, Art.9(5) provides that the Commission shall be deemed to have taken a decision to refer the case to the Member State concerned.

Procedure at the national level following a reference back

2.042 Once a referral back to the national authorities has been made, they are required to take "only the measures strictly necessary to safeguard or restore effective competition on the market concerned".[48] This provision mirrors the wording of Art.9(8) of the pre-reform EC Merger Regulation, which was specifically considered by the English High Court in the *Interbrew* judicial review case[49] to impose an obligation to act proportionately in adopting remedial measures:

> "Since Art. 9(8) imposes a requirement only to take those measures which are strictly necessary to safeguard or restore effective competition, it is plain that the [Competition] Commission and The Secretary of State are under a duty to act in a proportionate manner. Such an obligation is reinforced by the provisions of Article 1 of the First Protocol to the European Convention on Human Rights".[50]

Moses J. went on to consider in more detail the meaning of "proportionality", which is discussed further in Ch.10.[51]

---

[46] Art.9(3), final paragraph.
[47] Art.9(4).
[48] Art.9(8).
[49] *Interbrew SA and Interbrew UK Holdings Ltd v the Competition Commission and the Secretary of State for Trade and Industry* [2001] EWHC Admin 367; [2001] U.K.C.L.R. 954.
[50] *Interbrew*, cited above, at p.10.
[51] See in particular pp.10–12. Moses J. cited with approval the comments of the European Court of Human Rights in *James v United Kingdom* [1986] 8 E.H.R.R. 123 at para.50, the statement of the European Court of Justice in *R. v MAFF and Secretary of State for Health Ex p. FEDESA* [1990] E.C.R. I-4023 at para.13, and the comments of the Privy Council in *De Freitas v Ministry of Agriculture* [1999] 1 A.C. 69 at 80. As regards the nature of the requirement of proportionality, Moses J. stated that: "the measure should not be disproportionate in the sense that the value of the remedy which the measure sought to achieve should not be exceeded by the burden imposed on the person against whom the remedy was directed" (at p.9).

Under the pre-reform EC Merger Regulation, the national authorities were required to conclude their examination of a case that had been referred to them not more than four months after the referral back. The European Commission recorded in its 2001 Green Paper comments by respondents to its review of recent referrals back that the pre-reform working of Art.9(6) left scope for national competition authorities to use more time for the national review than would have been the case had the matter remained in the hands of the European Commission.[52] The Commission's formal proposal for the revised EC Merger Regulation altered the four month period to 90 working days,[53] a relatively insignificant change given the concerns. However the revised EC Merger Regulation adopts a different approach altogether. The national authority must now inform the undertakings concerned of their "preliminary competition assessment and what further action if any, it proposes to take" within 45 working days of the referral back or the date on which any national notification was received.[54] It appears that this imposes an obligation on the national authority to complete a first phase investigation within 45 working days, that is, in the UK, the OFT's decision whether to refer the transaction to the Competition Commission must be taken within this period. This is confirmed by s.34A of the Enterprise Act[55] which requires the OFT to decide whether to make a reference under s.22 or s.33 of the Act, and inform the parties of its decision, within the 45 working day preliminary assessment period. The section also empowers the OFT to accept undertakings in lieu of reference in this context. Section 34B[55A] gives the OFT powers to obtain information from the parties to the merger and s.34A provides for the clock to stop on the 45 working day period where requested information is not provided. Overall, the national competition authority's scrutiny of the case must be completed "without undue delay".[56] These provisions would seem to be pragmatic in that they allow for sufficient time for a full second stage — in the UK, Competition Commission — inquiry to take place where it is warranted. There is also more time for the negotiation of undertakings in lieu of a reference to the Competition Commission.

Under the former regime, the OFT faced the risk that if it did not make a speedy reference to the Competition Commission there would be insufficient time for the Commission to carry out its inquiry. The pre-reform EC Merger Regulation timeframe created significant time pressure where a second stage inquiry was required. Following a referral back in the *Interbrew* case[57] on August 22, 2000, the Secretary of State referred the matter to the Competition Commission a little over two weeks later on September 6, 2000 — extremely quickly, considering that under the FTA, the Secretary of State typically took six working days to consider the OFT's advice on whether to

---

[52] See para.78 of the 2001 Green Paper, cited above.

[53] See Art.9(6) of the European Commission's proposal for the new EC Merger Regulation.

[54] Art.9(6), second and third paragraphs.

[55] Inserted by the EC Merger Control (Consequential Amendments) Regulations 2004, SI 2004/1079.

[55A] Also inserted by the EC Merger Control (Consequential Amendments) Regulations 2004.

[56] Art.9(6), first paragraph.

[57] See the European Commission's decision of August 22, 2000 in Case No.COMP/M.2044 *Interbrew/Bass* at para.2, and the subsequent report of the Competition Commission, *Interbrew SA and Bass plc*, Cm. 5014 (January 2001).

refer. The Competition Commission was given a period of three months within which to issue its report (which corresponded to its usual reference period), and the Secretary of State's decision was announced on January 3, 2001. In *Arla Foods/Express Dairies*,[58] the referral back was made on June 10, 2003. The Secretary of State referred the merger to the Competition Commission on July 7, 2003, requiring the Commission to report by September 24, 2003. In this case, the reference period was condensed to about two and a half months,[59] and again, the first stage decision whether to refer the merger was taken more quickly than under the normal domestic timetable. Under the FTA, any remedies required by the Secretary of State were negotiated outside this timeframe. If, as with many European jurisdictions, the detail of remedies or undertakings had been required to be announced with the substantive decision, the time pressure under a referral back would potentially have been considerable. The revised wording of Art.9(6) is therefore to be welcomed. However, the likely effect of the changes would appear to be that once a merger has been referred back to the UK authorities, the period from the referral back to the date on which the Competition Commission takes a final decision (in cases where a reference is made) may significantly exceed the original four month period.

It was anticipated by the Commission and the Council in their joint statement in relation to the original EC Merger Regulation in 1989 that in practice "Art. 9 should only be applied in exceptional cases", being "confined to cases in which the interests in respect of competition of the Member State could not be adequately protected in any other way".[60] However, in practice, as at the date of writing the Commission had made referrals to national authorities in some 62 cases,[61] with referrals reaching a peak of 10 and 11

---

[58] See the European Commission's decision of June 10, 2003 in Case No.COMP/M.3130 *Arla Foods/Express Dairies* at para.4, and the subsequent report of the Competition Commission, *Arla Foods amba and Express Dairies plc*, Cm. 5983 (October 2003).

[59] The Competition Commission noted that given the EC Merger Regulation time limit, there was little scope for an extension to their reporting deadline (see para.2.3 of the *Arla Foods/Express Dairies* report, cited above).

[60] Accompanying statements entered in the minutes of the European Council [1990] 4 C.M.L.R. 314.

[61] A number of references to national authorities under Art.9 have involved the retail sector; see, for example, *Promodes/Casino, Promodes/S21/Gruppo GS, Vendex/Bijenkorf, GEHE/ Lloyds Chemists, Alliance Unichem/ Unifarma*. Other cases have involved building materials such as clay tiles (*Steetley/Tarmac*); ready mixed concrete (*Holdercim/Cedest*) and aggregates (*Redland/Lafarge*). Examples of referrals back which have been made since the *Philips* judgment include *BAT/ETI* (decision of October 23, 2003, IP/03/1441) where the European Commission referred to the Italian competition authorities the acquisition of Italian tobacco company ETI by BAT on the basis that the transaction had no effect outside Italy; the transaction was also the final step in the privatisation of ETI by the Italian Government. The Commission has also referred to the Belgian authorities a number of transactions involving the supply of electricity or gas to customers in Belgium (see for example decision of December 19, 2003, IP/03/1803, *Electrabel/Brussels — capital local authority energy supplier*). An example of where *Philips* appears to have influenced the decision whether to refer back occurred on July 23, 2003 (IP/03/1078) when the Commission rejected a request by the French authorities that they should carry out an inquiry into the acquisition of Vivendi Universal Publishing by Lagardère on the basis that the markets involved in the "book chain" from the acquisition of author rights, to publishing and distribution were, on the whole, supranational in scope as they covered the whole of the French speaking area of Europe. The Commission considered that the sale of school books was national because of the existence of national educational programmes, was undecided as to

in 2003 and 2002 respectively. In 2003, however, the Court of First Instance's judgment in *Philips v Commission* highlighted that fragmentation of cases was undesirable and the number of referrals back has since dropped notably, with only two referrals back in 2004, as at the time of writing. It remains the case, however, that the referral back mechanisms should be seen as having a central role in the jurisdictional mechanisms of the EC Merger Regulation, operating alongside the turnover thresholds to ensure that so far as possible, a merger is scrutinised by the "best placed" competition authority.[62]

Referral to the European Commission under Article 4(5) and Article 22 of the EC Merger Regulation

The other limb of the jurisdictional corrective mechanisms of the EC Merger Regulation is found in Arts 4(5) and 22. Article 4(5) corresponds to Art.4(4) of the reformed EC Merger Regulation, and introduced the possibility for the parties themselves to initiate the referral mechanisms, prior to any of the legally required (or voluntary, in the UK) notifications having been made under national merger control rules. In fact, this mechanism, whereby a merger which does not have a Community dimension within the meaning of Art.1 of the EC Merger Regulation may nevertheless be referred to the Commission by the Member States, has seldom been used. It is therefore instructive to consider past use of Art.22 before examining the new regime which has applied since May 1, 2004 and how the recent reforms may improve the utility of this mechanism. 2.043

Past use of Article 22

The provisions of Art.22 have been little used and, at the time of writing, requests had been made in only seven cases.[63] This is arguably, at least in part, due to a lack of communication between Member States after they have received notifications, something which has been addressed by the formation of the European Competition Network (ECN) in an attempt 2.044

---

the status of the market for text books but concluded that given the substantial overlap between these markets and all of the other activities forming part of the book chain, the Commission was best placed as a single authority to review the impact of the transaction on the relevant markets as a whole. The Commission also took into account the view of Lagardère that it preferred not to have to deal simultaneously with two competition authorities for closely related markets, and the Belgian authorities had informed the Commission that they preferred the case to be dealt with at Community level.

[62] In a speech to the British Chamber of Commerce in Brussels on June 4, 2002 (*"Review of the EC Merger Regulation — Roadmap for the reform project"*), Commissioner Mario Monti commented:

"An optimisation of case allocation between the Commission and Member States is the starting point and remains at the core of this review exercise. The guiding criterion upon which any changes along these lines ought to be made should — in my view — be the principle that the authority best placed to carry out the investigation should deal with the case".

[63] Case No. IV M.278 *British Airways/Dan Air* (1993); Case No. IV M.553 *RTL/Veronica/ Endemol* (1995–6); Case No. IV M.784 *Kesko/Tuko* (1996–7); Case No. IV M.890 *Blokker/Toys "R" Us* (II) (1997); M.2698 *Promatech/Sulzer Textil* (2002); Case No. COMP M.2738 *Gees/Unison* (2002); and Case No. IV M.3136 (2003) *GE/AGFA NDT* (2003).

to ensure that requests are made within the requisite period set out in Art.22.[64]

Originally, Art.22 was intended for use in situations where a Member State had no domestic merger control but was concerned about a merger which did not fall under the jurisdiction of the European Commission. The first four requests for a referral to the Commission were made in line with this approach.[65] Indeed, until December 2001, the provision had never been used jointly by several Member States together to refer a merger notified to all of them to the Commission on the basis that it was the best placed authority to act. In a speech in October 2001,[66] John Vickers, then the UK Director General of Fair Trading, indicated that where markets are larger than individual Member States, a national authority may not be as well placed to remedy the adverse effects of a merger having international effects as the European Commission would be. He commented, by way of example, that he did not believe that an individual Member State could have imposed the European Commission's remedy of prohibition in the GE/Honeywell merger[67] even if it had reached the same conclusion.

Only two months later, in December 2001, the UK, together with Italy, Spain, Germany, France, Portugal and Austria, used the Art.22 procedure in co-ordinated requests for the first time in the Promatech/Sulzer case[68] to refer to the Commission the acquisition of the textile division of a Swiss company by the Italian leader in the same sector. None of the parties' activities in the production of weaving machines were located in the UK, but both were significant suppliers of products to the downstream UK textiles market. The Commission found that the merged business would have dominated the Western European market for weaving machines and required the divestment of plants in Italy and Switzerland.

Shortly afterwards, in February 2002, the proposed acquisition of Unison Industries by a subsidiary of General Electric, which was initially notified in the UK, Germany, France, Italy, Spain, Austria and Greece, was referred to the European Commission by the national competition authorities. The Commission considered the market in question to be the worldwide market for engine accessories and controls but concluded that the merger would not give rise to a dominant position on the market which would adversely affect competition and cleared the merger unconditionally.[69] In December 2003, the Commission conditionally cleared the proposed acquisition by General Electric of the non-destructive testing busi-

---

[64] Art.22(1) of the EC Merger Regulation provides that a request for a referral to the European Commission must be made within 15 working days of the date of notification.

[65] See Case No.IV/M.278 British Airways/Dan Air, referred by Belgium, Case No.IV/M.553 RTL/Veronica/Endemol, referred by the Netherlands, Case No.IV/M.784, Kesko/Tuko, referred by Finland and Case No.IV/M.890, Blokker/Toys "R" Us (II), referred by the Netherlands.

[66] Speech of John Vickers, "International Mergers: the view from a national authority", given to the 28th Annual Conference on International Antitrust Law and Policy, Fordham University School of Law, New York, on October 25, 2001.

[67] See the European Commission's decision of July 3, 2001 in Case No.COMP/M.2220 General Electric/Honeywell.

[68] Case No.COMP/M. 2698, Promatech/Sulzer.

[69] See the European Commission's decision of April 17, 2002 in Case No.COMP/M.2738, GEES/Unison.

ness of Agfa.[70] Seven Member States, not including the UK, referred the transaction to the Commission under Art.22.

The UK competition authorities, together with other national competi-   2.045
tion authorities in the European Union, have shown that they are willing to refer cases to the European Commission where the thresholds contained in the EC Merger Regulation are not met but the Commission is the best placed authority to act. The OFT's Chairman has indicated that he considers that this would be an appropriate step to take in situations where the UK is only part of a larger market — European or world-wide — and that, even if the UK competition authorities did reach an adverse conclusion, it would be unlikely that the UK authorities could impose an effective remedy, for example, because production facilities are located outside the UK. From the three cases in which joint referrals under Art.22 have been made, it seems that other European competition authorities share these views. Such an approach is clearly consistent with the policy of avoiding fragmentation of cases, as emphasised by the Court of First Instance in *Philips v Commission*[70A] and reflected in the European Commission's notice on case referrals.[70B]

One of the reasons why the Commission has not received many Art.22 requests may be because national competition authorities have not seen the Commission as being better placed to deal with the situation in question. In its Procedural Guidance, the OFT sets out the criteria that it will apply in assessing whether a case is suitable for an Art.22 request:

(i)   the merger is a concentration within the meaning of Art.3 of the EC Merger Regulation;

(ii)   the concentration is subject to filing in several Member States (the OFT has indicated at least three);

(iii)   a relevant geographic market affected is wider than national[71];

(iv)   the concentration threatens significantly to impede effective competition, in particular as a result of the creation or strengthening of a dominant position; and

(v)   the concentration affects trade between Member States.[72]

A question that arises is whether a Member State can refer a merger to the European Commission under Art.22 if the transaction does not meet its national jurisdictional thresholds. It is suggested that although the wording of Art.22 does not impose such a limitation, where the jurisdictional thresholds

---

[70]   See the European Commission decision of December 5, 2003 in Case No.COMP/M.3136, *GE/Agfa NDT.*
[70A]   Cited above.
[70B]   See further para.2.038 above.
[71]   In its discussion of the factors which are relevant to the consideration of referral requests under Art.4(5), the Commission's Case Referral Notice states at para.29 that "the Commission may be more appropriately placed to treat cases (including investigation, assessment and possible remedial action) that give rise to potential competition concerns in a series of national or narrower than national markets located in a number of different countries in the EU".
[72]   Para.9.13 of the OFT's *Procedural Guidance.*

under the Act are not met, as a matter of national law the OFT has no power (except exceptionally under the special public interest provisions (discussed above)) to intervene in connection with a particular merger and that accordingly a reference to the European Commission under Art.22 should not be made. In practice, of course, the OFT is likely to be able to claim jurisdiction by reference to the share of supply test in relation to transactions that give rise to horizontal (but not vertical) competition concerns. In its draft notice on case referrals (which concerns the position under EC law) the Commission observed that:

> "It should be noted that, in the absence of a requirement for national notification in Art. 22, a Member State can request the referral of a concentration even where the concentration does not fall within the scope of its national competition law (for example, where the Member State concerned has no merger control legislation or where the concentration falls outside the scope of its merger control legislation, for instance being below the relevant national thresholds). This ensures that any Member State without adequate powers to deal with a concentration which threatens to significantly affect competition within its territory, and which concentration affects trade between Member States, can request that the Commission examine it pursuant to Art. 22."[73]

However, this footnote was not included in the final version of the notice. The notice makes it clear that a pre-notification referral by the undertakings concerned under Art.4(5) can only be made in circumstances where the national authorities would be competent to review the merger under their national competition law in the absence of a referral.[74]

The revised Article 22

2.046 In wording which mirrors Art.9(2)(a) of the EC Merger Regulation, the revised Art.22 permits one or more Member States to request the European Commission to examine any concentration[75] which does not have a Community dimension[76] but nevertheless affects trade between Member States and threatens significantly to affect competition within the territory of the Member State or States making the request. Although recent Art.22 referral cases have involved joint requests by a number of Member States, the EC Merger Regulation retains the possibility of a referral by a single Member State, notwithstanding that its primary use is likely to be where a merger has a significant impact on competition beyond a single Member State.[77]

A request under Art.22 must be made within 15 working days of the date on which the concentration was notified to the Member State, or where, as in the UK, no notification is required, of the date on which the merger was made known to the Member State concerned.[78] The European

---

[73] Commission Notice on case referrals at n.45.
[74] Commission Notice on case referrals at n.42.
[75] As defined in Art.3.
[76] Within the meaning of Art.1.
[77] See the Explanatory Note at para.21.
[78] Art.22(1), second paragraph.

Commission must inform all other Member States and the parties concerned of any requests received without delay,[79] following which any other Member State can join the request within 15 working days of being so informed.[80] The EC Merger Regulation further provides that pending a Member State's response as to whether it wishes to join the referral request, the clock is stopped on any national proceedings in relation to the merger.[81] The Commission is able to invite a Member State to request a referral where the Commission considers that the criteria for referral from that State are met.[82] The European Commission then has 10 working days from the deadline for requests by additional Member States to decide whether to accept jurisdiction over the case: silence is deemed to constitute consent to a referral.[83]

If the European Commission decides to accept a case referred to it under Art.22, it may at its discretion request the parties to submit a completed Form CO.[84] Where national filings follow the format of Form CO (which is the case in many jurisdictions whose merger control legislation is modelled on the EC Merger Regulation), it may be that no further notification need be prepared. This is perhaps less likely to be the case in the UK, where submissions are typically tailored to the transaction and may not be as exhaustive as a Form CO filing, even where a Merger Notice[85] is used. It remains to be seen how practice develops in relation to this issue.

It was proposed as part of the 2004 reforms that where three or more Member States make a request that a particular merger should be referred to the European Commission, the Commission would gain exclusive jurisdiction throughout the European Economic Area.[86] This proposal was promoted as ensuring that the mechanism was efficient and to reduce legal uncertainty. However, the revised EC Merger Regulation provides only that those Member States which made the referral to the Commission lose jurisdiction to apply their domestic merger control provisions.[87] It is possible that this approach could create some difficulties in relation to remedies; for example, if the European Commission wished to impose a remedy which would affect the merged business in a jurisdiction where the national authority had elected to retain jurisdiction to apply its domestic rules and had concluded that a different approach to remedies was appropriate. Moreover, this outcome does undermine the principle of the "one-stop shop" which is generally of paramount importance and utility in EC Merger Regulation proceedings and whose importance has been emphasised by the Court of First Instance.[87A]

It remains to be seen whether the changes to Art.22 will encourage a greater use of the referral mechanism by the national authorities. The natural inclination of national authorities to review cases that fall within

2.047

---

[79] Art.22(2), first paragraph.
[80] Art.22(2), second paragraph.
[81] Art.22(2), third paragraph.
[82] Art.22(5).
[83] Art.22(3).
[84] Art.22(3), second paragraph.
[85] See Ch.3 below.
[86] See para.26 of the Explanatory Memorandum, cited above.
[87] Art.22(3) para.3.
[87A] See *Philips v Commission*, cited above, at para.350.

their jurisdiction may well continue, and it may be that, since replacing numerous national notifications with a single Form CO is typically in the parties' interests because of the reduced costs and the elimination of the risk of conflicting outcomes, the new Art.4(5) mechanism may prove to be the more significant reform.

Article 4(5): pre-notification referral to the Commission

2.048   Article 4(5) mirrors Art.4(4) in giving the merging parties a power of initiative to trigger the referral mechanisms. In order to make use of these provisions, the merger must constitute a concentration for EC Merger Regulation purposes[88]; self evidently, it must not have a Community dimension[89]; and it must be capable of being reviewed[90] under the domestic merger control legislation of at least three Member States.[91] It is therefore not enough that the merger qualifies for investigation in three Member States; it must also constitute a "concentration" for EC Merger Regulation purposes. This distinction could be significant in relation to Member States such as the UK and Germany, where a lower level of minority interest may qualify as a "merger" under domestic legislation than would be considered to constitute a "concentration" under the EC Merger Regulation.[92]

Where the three cumulative conditions are met, the parties may, even before any national notifications have been made, inform the Commission in a reasoned submission that the merger should be reviewed by the European Commission.[93] The Commission might apply an approach analogous to Art.4(1), second paragraph, and accept a reasoned submission from such time as the parties can demonstrate a good faith intention to conclude an agreement, or have announced the intention to make a public offer. However, a strict interpretation of Art.4(5), first paragraph, suggests that this point will be governed by national law: the transaction must have become "capable of being reviewed under the national competition laws of at least three Member States". In some Member States (but not the UK, where mergers in contemplation can be reviewed) jurisdiction under merger control legislation is not triggered until a legally binding agreement has been entered into. Since the referral mechanism in Art.4(5) is intended to be pragmatic and useful to the parties, it is suggested that the former interpretation based on Art.4(1) would be preferable to the uncertainties and possible delays involved in the "national law" approach, as it would provide a uniform rule across all Member States. The reasoned submission

---

[88] As defined in Art.3.

[89] Pursuant to Art. 1.

[90] "Capable of being reviewed" means a concentration which falls within the jurisdiction of a Member State under its national competition law; see the Case Referral Notice at para.71. This wording reflects the fact that notification and clearance are not compulsory in all Member States — including of course the UK.

[91] These three cumulative conditions are set out in Art.4(5), first paragraph.

[92] Under the Act, as explained above, "material influence" can potentially be found to exist at a lower level of control than "decisive influence" (see para.2.010, above). Under German merger control, it is understood that the acquisition of a direct or indirect significant competitive influence over another enterprise can qualify as a reviewable merger, which again is potentially a lower level of control than would qualify for scrutiny under the EC Merger Regulation.

[93] Art.4(5), first paragraph.

required for an Art.4(5) request by the parties[94] is the same Form RS which is used for an Art.4(4) request, discussed above.[95]

Following receipt of Form RS, the Commission must submit a copy to all Member States without delay.[96] Member States with jurisdiction to review the merger under their domestic legislation have 15 working days from receipt to object to the requested referral.[97] It is not expressly stated, but would appear to be implicit from the wording of Art.4(5)[98] that silence constitutes acceptance. This is the Commission's approach, as indicated in para.49 of the case referral notice. If *any* expression of disagreement is received from a Member State having jurisdiction (one is sufficient), the referral request must be rejected, and all Member States and the parties concerned must be informed.[99] Where no such disagreement is indicated, the concentration will be deemed to have a Community dimension and the Commission will gain exclusive jurisdiction to scrutinise it.[1] This is a significant difference from the position under Art.22, discussed above, where the usual "one stop shop" principle does not apply.

In contrast to the Art.22 procedure where it is a matter for the European Commission's discretion whether to require the completion of Form CO by the parties, Art.4(5), fifth paragraph, makes it clear that Form CO must be submitted. In practice, there will usually be pre-notification discussions with the relevant officials and it may be possible to obtain a waiver from re-submitting information already supplied in Form RS: practice in this respect remains to be developed. Once the Commission has accepted a referral to it following an Art.4(5) request, the proceedings continue as if the case had fallen under the Art.1 jurisdictional thresholds from the outset.

2.049

Will the United Kingdom authorities be able to protect their "legitimate interests"?

The Enterprise Act provides for the protection of the UK's legitimate interests in relation to mergers having a Community dimension within the meaning of the EC Merger Regulation. Section 67(2) of the Act provides for the Secretary of State to issue a "European intervention notice" to the OFT in cases which meet the thresholds of the EC Merger Regulation, which would otherwise have been capable of being referred to the Competition Commission under ss.22 or 33 of the Act and in relation to which the Secretary of State is considering taking appropriate measures to protect the legitimate interests of the UK under Art.21(4) of the revised EC Merger

2.050

---

[94] Art.6(1) of the implementing regulation, cited above.
[95] At para.2.039. The comments set out above in relation to the complexities of Form RS are perhaps less applicable in the context of an Art.4(5) request, where the parties are facing at least three national notifications: in such circumstances, the level of detail required to complete Form RS is comparatively less burdensome.
[96] Art.4(5), second paragraph. See also para.73 of the Case Referral Notice.
[97] Art.4(5), third paragraph.
[98] The third and fourth paras of Art.4(5) focus on expressions of disagreement: it would seem logical to infer that silence equates to the absence of any such expression.
[99] See Art.4(5), fourth paragraph.
[1] See Art.4(5), fifth paragraph. As at September 17, 2004, nine requests under Art.4(5) had been submitted to the Commission, of which two had been vetoed by Member States; see speech of Mario Monti at the 8th IBA Annual Competition Conference.

Regulation. Article 21(4) provides that Member States may take "appropriate measures to protect legitimate interests other than those taken into consideration by this Regulation and compatible with the general principles and other provisions of Community law." The Regulation lists "public security, plurality of the media and prudential rules" as being regarded as legitimate interests within the meaning of the first paragraph of Art.21(4).[2] The third paragraph of Art.21(4) provides that "any other public interest must be communicated to the Commission by the Member State concerned". The Commission must then, by a decision within one month, inform the Member State of its assessment of its "compatibility with the general principles and other provisions of Community law" before any national measures may be taken. The provisions of Art.21(4) are the same as those contained in Art.21(3) of the pre-reform EC Merger Regulation, Reg.4064/89, in relation to which the Commission issued the following interpretative statement:

> "The Commission considers that the three specific categories of legitimate interests which any Member State may freely cite under this provision are to be interpreted as follows:
>
> - the reference to 'public security' is made without prejudice to the provisions of Article 223 on National Defence, which allows a Member State to intervene in respect of a concentration which would be contrary to the essential interests of its security and is connected with the production of, or trade in, arms, ammunitions and war material. The restrictions set by that Article concerning products not intended for specifically military purposes should be complied with. There may be wider considerations of public security, both in the sense of Article 224 and in that of Article 36, in addition to defence interests in the strict sense. Thus the requirement for public security, as interpreted by the Court of Justice, could cover security of supplies to the country in question of a product or service considered of vital or essential interest for the protection of the population's health.
> - The Member States' right to plead the 'plurality of the media' recognises the legitimate concern to maintain diversified sources of information for the sake of plurality of opinion and multiplicity of views.
> - Legitimate invocation may also be made of the 'prudential rules' in Member States, which relate in particular to financial services; the application of these rules is normally confined to national bodies for the surveillance of banks, stock broking firms and insurance companies. They concern, for example, the good repute of individuals, the honesty of transactions, and the rules of solvency. These specific prudential criteria are also the subject of efforts aimed at a minimum degree of harmonisation being made in order to ensure uniform 'rules of play' in the community as a whole."

---

[2] The concept of public security is considered above at para.2.026 in the context of public interest cases under the Enterprise Act. Plurality of the media is discussed in para.2.064 and Ch.7, below.

In November 2000 the European Commission adopted a decision[3] finding that the refusal of the Portuguese Finance Minister to approve (pursuant to a Portuguese privatisation law) a takeover bid which had a Community dimension and which had been notified to the Commission, was in breach of Art.21 of the EC Merger Regulation. The Commission rejected the Finance Minister's argument that the action was justified because it was necessary to protect the development of the shareholding structures in companies undergoing privatisation on the grounds that it constituted a barrier to the freedom of establishment and free movement of capital enshrined in the EC Treaty and was "not warranted under any essential grounds of public interest recognised in the case-law of the Court of Justice."[4]

The ECJ dismissed the Portuguese government's appeal under Art.230 of the EC Treaty for annulment of the European Commission's decision. The Portuguese Government argued that as it had not informed the Commission of its intention to protect what it regarded as its legitimate interests, the Commission had no competence under Art.21(3) to determine whether the interests were legitimate in accordance with the general principles of EC law. The ECJ rejected this argument on the grounds that such an approach would render the third paragraph of Art.21(3) ineffective by giving Member States the possibility of circumventing the controls enacted by that provision with ease.[5] Accordingly, the Court concluded that the Commission must be recognised as having the power to decide whether the interests that a Member State is seeking to protect are legitimate and compatible with Community law, whether or not these interests have been communicated to it.[6]

Under s.68 of the Enterprise Act, where a European intervention notice has been given under s.67, the Secretary of State may by order provide for action to be taken to remedy, mitigate or prevent the adverse effects to the public interest which may be expected to result from the creation of a European relevant merger situation.[7] Any such order must include provisions requiring the OFT to report to the Secretary of State before a reference is made to the Competition Commission, as well as enabling the Secretary of State to make a reference and the Commission to investigate and report to the Secretary of State. Finally, the order must enable the taking of interim and final enforcement action.[8] The first notice under s.67 was issued to the OFT by the Competition Minister, Gerry Sutcliffe, on April 26, 2004 in relation to General Dynamics Corporation's proposed acquisition of Alvis plc. The notice was issued on the ground of national security as Alvis Vickers, the main UK subsidiary of Alvis plc, produces a

---

[3] Commission Decision Case No. COMP/M.2054 of November 22, 2000, Commission press release IP/00 1338.
[4] See the Commission's decision cited above, at para.58.
[5] Case C-42/01, *Portuguese Republic v Commission* (judgment of June 22, 2004) [2004] 5 C.M.L.R. 9.
[6] *Portuguese Republic v Commission*, at para.57.
[7] s.68(1).
[8] s.68(2). Pursuant to these provisions, the Enterprise Act 2002 (Protection of Legitimate Interests) Order 2003 (SI 2003/1592) was adopted. Under Art.5, the Secretary of State may make a reference to the Competition Commission and under para.3(2) of Sch.2 to the Order he may accept undertakings in lieu of reference.

range of armoured vehicles and, through a subsidiary, military bridges. The OFT was required to consider the national security aspects of the transaction and reported to the Secretary of State on May 20, 2004 (four days in advance of the deadline set by the Minister) that the Ministry of Defence (MOD) had expressed concerns in relation to the maintenance of strategic UK capabilities and the protection of classified information. In its request the OFT stated that it is "not expert in national security matters" and restricted its comments to summarising representations made by the MOD and other third parties. The OFT appended to its report draft undertakings in lieu of a reference to the Competition Commission prepared by the MOD which the MOD believed was the most effective means of remedying the national security concerns it had identified. On June 3, 2004 the Secretary of State announced the decision to seek undertakings in lieu of reference to the Competition Commission. This merger was ultimately abandoned and so the undertakings were not finalised. At the time of writing, only one other European intervention notice had been issued, which was also in relation to national security.[8A] Again, the proposed response to the UK public interest concerns was to require undertakings in lieu of reference (which, at the time of writing, were undergoing the consultation process).

Coal and steel mergers

2.051   Until July 24, 2002, under Art.66 of the Treaty of Paris which established the European Coal and Steel Community (the "ECSC Treaty"), all mergers (except certain *de minimis* transactions) involving undertakings engaged in the production or distribution of certain coal or steel products, as defined in the ECSC Treaty, required the prior authorisation of the European Commission. The ECSC Treaty expired on July 23, 2002. As a consequence, from July 24, 2002, the sectors previously governed by the ECSC Treaty (and the procedural rules and other secondary legislation derived from the ECSC Treaty) are now subject to the EC Treaty as well as the procedural rules and other secondary legislation derived from that Treaty. In practical terms this means that, whereas under the ECSC Treaty the European Commission had exclusive jurisdiction over all concentrations involving coal and steel undertakings, the EC Commission now has jurisdiction over such concentrations only where the turnover thresholds of the EC Merger Regulation are met. Coal and steel transactions which do not meet these thresholds will fall to be considered under national merger rules.

Does jurisdiction over mergers remain vested in the European Commission and the national courts under Articles 81 and 82 of the EC Treaty?

2.052   Prior to the adoption of the EC Merger Regulation in 1989, the European Court of Justice had held that Arts 81 and 82 could, in certain circumstances, apply to transactions that could amount to merger situations

---

[8A] See the DTI's press release of August 20, 2004, P/2004/311, in relation to the proposed acquisition by Finmeccanica of GKN's shareholding in AgustaWestland.

within the meaning of the Fair Trading Act.[9] With the entry into force of the original EC Merger Regulation in 1989, an attempt was made to introduce a single source of EC regulatory control for mergers. However, given that the European Court of Justice has ruled that Arts 81 and 82 have direct effect and can be invoked and relied on by individuals or undertakings before national courts, the aim of ensuring a single source of European control was not straightforward. Article 21(1) of the EC Merger Regulation provides that the various EC regulations that provide the necessary administrative structure for the European Commission to apply Arts 81 and 82 (including Reg.1/2003[9A]) shall not apply to concentrations as defined in Art.3 of the EC Merger Regulation except in relation to joint ventures that do not have a Community dimension and which have as their object or effect the co-ordination of the competitive behaviour of undertakings that remain independent. Prior to the adoption of Reg.1/2003, the exemption criteria contained in Art.81(3) could be applied only by the European Commission, and in the absence of implementing legislation it was likely that Art.81 could not be relied on in national courts in relation to mergers.[10] However, following the entry into force of the new "modernisation" regime introduced by Reg.1/2003, the European Commission's monopoly on granting exemptions under Art.81(3) has ended and it is now possible for the national courts and competition authorities of the Member States to apply the exemption criteria contained in Art.81(3) of the Treaty. It is arguable, therefore, that the principle established by the European Court of Justice in *BAT and Reynolds v Commission* that the acquisition of an equity interest in a competition could in certain circumstances infringe Art.81(1) could be applied by the national courts and authorities, although given that all the Member States except Luxemburg now have their own merger control regimes, such national intervention may be unlikely.

Whatever the position under Reg.1/2003 in relation to the application of Art.81, given that no exemption can be granted in relation to an infringement of Art.82,[11] Art.82 should, as a matter of EC law, be capable of application by the national courts [and authorities]. The English courts have in the past had to consider the extent to which Art.82 can be invoked in relation to a merger in *R. v Secretary of State for Trade and Industry Ex p. Airlines of Britain Holdings plc and Virgin Atlantic Airlines Ltd.*[12] The case arose in the context of an application for judicial review of the Secretary of State for Trade and Industry's decision not to take any action under Arts 82 and 84 of the EC Treaty (having already exercised his discretion under the FTA not to make a reference). After reviewing the relevant provisions of the EC Merger Regulation and of the EC Treaty, Neill L.J., who gave the judgment of the court, concluded that:

---

[9] See Case 6/72, *Europemballage and Continental Can v Commission* [1973] E.C.R. 215; and Cases 142 and 156/84, *BAT and RJ Reynolds v Commission* [1988] 4 C.M.L.R. 24.
[9A] Council Regulation (EC) 1/2003 on the implementation of the rules on competition laid down in Arts 81 and 82 of the Treaty, [2003] O.J. L1/1.
[10] In Case 31/61, *De Geus v Bosch* [1962] E.C.R. 45, the European Court ruled that in general in the absence of administrative implementing provisions, a national court is unable to strike down an agreement which infringes Art.81(1).
[11] Case 66/86, *Ahmed Saeed v Zentrale* [1989] E.C.R. 803.
[12] [1993] B.C.C. 89, CA.

"[T]he effect of the Regulation is to require the Commission to deal with all questions arising under Articles 8[1] and 8[2] and to leave it to the national courts to apply their own domestic competition legislation to concentrations within their purview."

The court then refused the application for leave to apply for review. Although the judgment of the court is a practical response to a difficult question of EC constitutional law, it is arguable that Art.82 may nevertheless apply and that the issue of the direct applicability of Art.81 in national courts in relation to mergers will remain uncertain until such time as the European Court of Justice is required to consider the point.

Relationship with the Competition Act 1998

2.053   The Competition Act 1998 came into force on March 1, 2000. A detailed analysis of its provisions is outside the scope of this work, but there are certain situations where it may be necessary to consider its application in the context of mergers. The Competition Act introduced the Chapter I[13] and Chapter II[14] prohibitions, which respectively mirror the terms of Arts 81 and 82 of the EC Treaty in relation to agreements or conduct which affect trade within the United Kingdom. In general the Chapter I and II prohibitions have no application to merger situations. Schedule I to the Competition Act provides that:

"To the extent to which an agreement . . . results, or if carried out would result, in any two enterprises ceasing to be distinct enterprises for the purposes of Part 3 of the Enterprise Act 2002 . . . the Chapter I prohibition does not apply to the agreement".[15]

This exclusion from the Chapter I prohibition also extends to "any provision directly related and necessary to the implementation of the merger provisions", generally referred to as "ancillary restrictions".[16]

The Competition Act provides, in relation to the Chapter II prohibition, that:

"To the extent to which conduct. . .

(a)   results in any two enterprises ceasing to be distinct enterprises for the purposes of Part 3 of the 2002 Act, or

(b)   is directly related and necessary to the attainment of the result mentioned in paragraph (a),

the Chapter II prohibition does not apply to that conduct."[17]

This exclusion is designed to avoid a "double jeopardy" situation where restrictions which are entered into in connection with a merger fall to be

---

[13] See s.2 of the Competition Act 1998.
[14] See s.18 of the Competition Act 1998.
[15] Competition Act 1998, Sch.1, para.1(1), as amended by the Enterprise Act, Sch.25.
[16] Sch.1, para.1(2). See further para.2.054 below.
[17] Sch.1, para.2(1) as amended by the Enterprise Act, Sch.25.

considered under both the Competition Act and the Enterprise Act. The exclusion is not expressed to be dependent on the merger qualifying for investigation under the Enterprise Act, and accordingly, restrictions which are ancillary to mergers that fall below the turnover or share of supply thresholds are also exempt from the Competition Act, subject to the possible withdrawal of the exclusion.[18]

Ancillary restrictions

The OFT's *Substantive Assessment Guidance* recognises that the concept of ancillary restrictions is one which is well developed under Community law and states that its approach to ancillary restrictions will follow the Commission's notice regarding restrictions directly related and necessary to concentrations[19] "as this constitutes a statement of the European Commission to which the authorities must have regard under section 60 of the Competition Act 1998".[20] **2.054**

In order to be considered as ancillary, a restriction must be both "directly related" to the merger and "necessary". The OFT states in its *Substantive Assessment Guidance* that, in order to be directly related "the restriction must be connected with the merger, but ancillary or subordinate to its main object."[21] Clearly, a restriction will not be directly related simply because it is agreed at the same time as the merger, or states that it is directly related; the element of connection with the merger is crucial. Furthermore, the OFT states that contractual arrangements which go to the heart of the merger are not subordinate, but form part of the merger agreement and will be considered as part of the assessment of the merger itself under the Act.

The element of necessity, the OFT states, will be considered in each case, but is:

". . . likely to be the case where, for example, in the absence of the restriction the merger would not go ahead or could only go ahead under more [un]certain [sic] conditions, at substantially higher costs, over an appreciably longer period, or with considerably higher difficulty. In determining the necessity of the restriction, account will also be taken of whether its duration, subject matter and geographical field of application are proportionate to the overall requirements of the merger".[22]

---

[18] This is consistent with the parallel position under the EC Merger Regulation: see Art.21(1) which does not require a concentration to have a Community dimension in order to fall outside Arts 81 and 82.

[19] European Commission's 2004 Notice on restrictions directly related and necessary to concentrations. At the time of writing the 2004 notice (which replaced the 2001 notice on this issue) had not yet been published in the Official Journal, but was available from the European Commission's website.

[20] Para.11.13 of the OFT's *Substantive Assessment Guidance*.

[21] Para.11.15 of the OFT's *Substantive Assessment Guidance*.

[22] Para.11.18 of the OFT's *Substantive Assessment Guidance*. It is interesting to observe the echoes in this paragraph of the analytical approach of the English common law doctrine of restraint of trade, which has found its way into the EC law-driven assessment of ancillary restraints—or restrictive covenants, to give them their English legal system nomenclature. In *Days Medical v Pihsiang Machinery Manufacturing Co* [2004] EWHC 44 (Comm); [2004] 1 All E.R. (Comm) 991, Langley J. concluded that—at least as regards competition law—

In its *Substantive Assessment Guidance* the OFT considers three types of commonly arising restrictions: non-competition clauses, licences of intellectual property rights and know-how, and purchase and supply agreements. The OFT recognises that any of these types of agreements may be viewed as ancillary, but that there are situations in which they will be so restrictive that they will cease to be ancillary; for example exclusive supply agreements will only exceptionally be ancillary, but non-exclusive supply agreements will generally be regarded as ancillary where they are necessary for the running of the acquired business for at least a transitional period.[23]

2.055 In practice, of the 87 qualifying mergers which the OFT had considered as at June 1, 2004, the issue of ancillary restrictions was referred to in only four cases, and then only briefly. It seems likely that the parties will typically take their own view as to what will be unobjectionable in competition law terms, and will tend to draft restrictive covenants for the protection of goodwill in terms which follow the guidance in the European Commission's Notice as to what will generally be considered to be directly related and necessary to the merger.

Even in the cases where ancillary restrictions have been discussed, the analysis has tended to be brief. Ancillary restrictions were considered in two cases concerning the reorganisation of P&O and Stena's Irish Sea businesses. In relation to the first case, a proposed sale of two routes operated by P&O to Stena, the OFT's decision[24] simply notes that P&O has announced the closure of another route and that Stena would charter the ships formerly used on this route and comments ". . . P&O has also accepted a restriction [that][25] is not ancillary to this merger situation as it is clearly not necessary to the transaction". No more comment is made on the nature or scope of the restriction in question. In its decision in relation to the second merger situation,[26] the OFT refers (presumably) to the same point again, noting: "The cessation of P&O's services from the Port of Mostyn is [XX][27] not ancillary to the merger situation as it is clearly not necessary to the JV, nor does it form a relevant merger situation in its own right".

In *Dräger Medical/Hillenbrand*, there is even less discussion and the OFT does not reach a decision about the restrictions, but simply notes "There are a number of restrictions to the purchase agreement which may or may not be ancillary to the merger".[28]

The only case as at June 1, 2004 in which any detail is provided regarding the analysis of ancillary restrictions is *Milk Link/Glanbia*, where

---

the doctrine of restraint of trade has been "emasculated" or even "trumped by Community competition law" (at para.254), although it might be perhaps more appropriate to conclude that the doctrine has to a large degree been subsumed within competition law as there is no inherent conflict between their respective purposes.

[23] Para.11.22 of the OFT's *Substantive Assessment Guidance*.

[24] OFT's decision of August 22, 2003, *Anticipated acquisition by Stena of certain assets operated by P&O on the Irish Sea*.

[25] The parentheses were added by the OFT to indicate that commercially confidential material had been deleted.

[26] OFT's decision of August 22, 2003, *Anticipated joint venture between Stena and P&O to acquire Cairnryan Port*.

[27] Again, this indicates the deletion of commercially confidential information by the OFT.

[28] OFT's decision of December 18, 2003, *Anticipated acquisition by Dräger Medical AG & Co KGaA of the airshields business of Hillenbrand Industries Inc.*

the OFT lists the restrictions agreed in the sale and purchase arrangements between the parties and comments:

> "The OFT generally follows the European Commission's Notice on ancillary restraints, which provides that restrictions that are 'directly related and necessary' are justified by the legitimate objective sought of implementing the concentration. The Commission Notice indicates that restrictions are acceptable for up to five years. The ancillary restraints agreed by the parties are within these time limits. The agreements largely reflect existing trade patterns and merely formalise the previous informal intra-group relationship. Therefore, the restrictions are directly related and necessary in order to implement the merger".[29]

The OFT's comment that the restrictions are necessary for the merger is interesting in this context, where in addition to a non-compete clause for three years, there were various supply and cross-supply arrangements, as well as a marketing agency arrangement, an ingredients agency arrangement and IT and shared services support agreements. The durations of these arrangements are not specified in the OFT's decision but presumably they are all short term (less than five years). Competition concerns might be raised if at the expiry of these agreements, they were renewed so that their significance became more than simply a mechanism for ensuring that there were no disruption to the supply lines and commercial support needed for the acquired business. **2.056**

The procedure followed by the OFT in considering ancillary restrictions is discussed in Ch.3 below.[30]

Withdrawal of the exclusion

As explained above, where an agreement results in two enterprises ceasing to be distinct (*e.g.* a sale and purchase agreement or similar constitutive contractual arrangement) or a restriction is considered to be directly related and necessary to a merger situation, it will benefit from the exclusion from the Chapter I prohibition. However, sch.1 to the Competition Act grants the OFT the power to withdraw the exclusion in certain circumstances.[31] The rationale for this power is the recognition that it might be possible for parties to anti-competitive agreements to structure their arrangements in such a way as to fall within the definition of a merger under the Act, but below the turnover and market share thresholds. There are two circumstances in which the OFT may make a direction withdrawing the exclusion. First, the OFT has the power, when considering whether to make a direction to disapply the exclusion, to request such information from any party to the agreement as it may require. A failure to comply with this requirement within the time set out in the Director's Rules[32] (10 working days **2.057**

---

[29] OFT's decision of May 17, 2004, *Completed joint venture between Milk Link Limited and Glanbia Foods Limited*.
[30] See para.3.077 of Ch.3.
[31] Sch.1, para.4.
[32] Set out in the schedule to the Competition Act 1998 (Director's rules) Order 2000, SI 2000/293 ("the Director's Rules"). At the time of writing, the Director's Rules were about

from the date of receipt of the notice[33]) without a reasonable excuse will allow the OFT to disapply the exclusion. Secondly, the OFT may make a direction where an agreement is not a "protected agreement" and the OFT considers that the agreement will, if not excluded, infringe the Chapter I prohibition.[34]

Paragraph 5 of Sch.1 lists four types of agreement which are protected agreements, in respect of which the OFT cannot withdraw the exclusion:

(a) a qualifying merger which the OFT or the Secretary of State has decided not to refer to the Competition Commission;

(b) an agreement which has been referred to the Competition Commission by the OFT or the Secretary of State and the Competition Commission has found that the agreement has given rise to, or if carried out would give rise to, a relevant merger situation or a special merger situation;

(c) an agreement which does not fall within paragraph (a) or (b) but has given rise to, or would if carried out give rise to, enterprises to which it relates being regarded under s.26 of the 2002 Act as ceasing to be distinct enterprises (*i.e.* a qualifying merger situation which has not been reviewed by the OFT or Competition Commission) but excluding mergers which involve the acquisition of *de facto* control or material influence, or an increase in the level of control from material influence to *de facto* control; or

(d) the OFT has made a reference to the Competition Commission under s.32 of the Water Industry Act 1991 and the Competition Commission has found that the agreement has given rise to, or would if carried out give rise to, a merger of any two or more water enterprises.

Accordingly, the OFT is not able to withdraw the Chapter I prohibition exclusion in relation to most mergers which have been reviewed by the OFT and/or the Competition Commission, as well as in relation to water and sewerage mergers. However, there remains a small class of merger situations which falls outside the protected agreements definition. These are, as noted, the acquisition of *de facto* control or material influence over policy (and the transition from material influence to *de facto* control) in the absence of a controlling interest and which either qualify for consideration under the Act but have not been reviewed by the OFT or which do not qualify for investigation. If the OFT considers that a particular agreement of this sort may infringe the Chapter I prohibition, and it would not satisfy the individual exemption criteria contained in the Competition Act, the agreement may be subject to the Chapter 1 prohibition, notwithstanding that the agreement would constitute a merger under the Enterprise Act. It would appear that the only way to avoid such a possibility (at least in relation to mergers that qualify for investigation) would be to notify any agreements which may come

---

to be replaced by the Competition Act 1998 (Office of Fair Trading's Rules) Order 2004 but the new statutory instrument was still in draft form.

[33] See r.22(3) of the Director's Rules.

[34] Sch.1, para.4(5).

within subss.3 or 4(b) of s.26 to the OFT for clearance. The OFT has stated in its *Procedural Guidance* that it is only likely to exercise its power to withdraw the exclusion in relation to such agreements rarely. The reason for this is that:

> "even where an agreement is not protected, the OFT must believe that it will infringe the Chapter I prohibition and is unlikely to qualify for an unconditional exemption before it can withdraw the benefit of the exclusion. To infringe the Chapter I prohibition, the agreement must have an appreciable effect on competition which is generally unlikely to be the case where the combined market share of the parties to the agreement is less than 25 per cent."[35]

Particular sectors

As explained in the introduction to this chapter, there are a number of sectors where mergers are governed by different approval mechanisms or sector specific rules either instead of, or in addition to, the general jurisdiction of the OFT under the Enterprise Act. Although a detailed examination of each of these sectors is outside the scope of this work, the principal issues which arise are outlined below.   2.058

Newspapers

The new regime governing newspaper mergers introduced by the Communications Act 2003 is dealt with in detail in Ch.7 below.   2.059

Television and Radio

The Communications Act 2003 introduced into the Enterprise Act a new regime for the ownership and control of radio and television. The relevant provisions of the Act came into force on December 29, 2003 and relaxed some of the previously strict rules relating to television and radio ownership. In addition, as explained above,[36] the Communications Act introduced further public interest and special public interest criteria which allow the Secretary of State to intervene in mergers between broadcasters, and mergers between broadcasters and newspaper publishers in certain circumstances. These changes are explained briefly below.   2.060

---

[35] Para.B.8 of OFT's *Procedural Guidance*. Note that the reference in this paragraph to "25 per cent" was taken from the OFT's guidance on "The Chapter I prohibition" (OFT 401). That document was being revised at the time of writing, and in the draft issued for consultation ("Article 81 and the Chapter I prohibition"), the reference to a 25 per cent threshold of appreciability was deleted and the draft guidelines cross-referred instead to the lower appreciability thresholds of 10 per cent combined market share in relation to horizontal agreements and 15 per cent market share in relation to vertical agreements, as set out in the European Commission's Notice on Agreements of Minor Importance [2001] O.J. C368/13.
[36] At para.2.025.

Media ownership restrictions removed or relaxed

2.061 The following principal liberalisation measures have been introduced by the Communications Act.[37]

(i) the rule restricting ownership of broadcasting (*i.e.* TV and radio) licences by persons not resident or established in the EEA is abolished;

(ii) religious bodies are no longer barred from owning any type of licence; the restriction now applies only to certain types, including Channel 3 and Channel 5 TV licences and national radio licences;

(iii) the prohibition on local authorities from owning broadcasting licences is relaxed, so that they are now able to hold a licence if the service they intend to provide relates solely to the provision by local authorities of information concerning their functions and services;

(iv) the bans on a single person owning both London Channel 3 licences, and Channel 3 and Channel 5 are removed;

(v) the limit of 15 per cent on any company's share of the total TV audience is removed;

(vi) the complicated points system for radio ownership, which limited licensees to 15 per cent of the total points in the system, is abolished (although, as noted below, new points systems have been introduced for local radio licences)[38];

(vii) common ownership of a national TV station (*i.e.* Channel 3 or Channel 5) and a national radio station is no longer prohibited;

(viii) similarly, the rule preventing common ownership of a local radio licence and an overlapping regional TV licence is also abolished; and

(ix) national newspaper owners with a national market share exceeding 20 per cent are no longer prohibited from owning Channel 5, or a national or local radio service.[39]

Retained/revised rules

2.062 The rules formerly contained in Pts III to V of Sch.2 to the Broadcasting Act 1990 are replaced by a new, more limited set of rules contained in Sch.14

---

[37] ss.348 to 350 of the Communications Act, amending Sch.2, Pts II-IV of the Broadcasting Act 1990 (the "1990 Act"), as amended.

[38] ss.350. The previous system under paras 8 and 9 of Pt III of Sch.2 to the 1990 Act allocated a certain number of points to different licences according to the number of adults resident in the coverage area, with national licences equating to 25 points, and regional licences accounting for 15, 8, 3 and 1 points respectively (adjustments were necessary in certain instances).

[39] ss.350. The previous restrictions were contained in para.4 of Pt IV of Sch.2 to the 1990 Act. Note that the previous regime also prevented ownership of a Channel 3 licence by such a national newspaper operator. This restriction has been retained, although it is now contained in Sch.14 to the Communications Act, rather than the 1990 Act.

to the Communications Act. These rules no longer regulate the ownership of Channel 5. However, a number of restrictions remain in respect of Channel 3 licences, and digital and local radio licences. The principal rules are set out below.

The main restrictions in relation to Channel 3 licences are as follows[40]:

(i) a person may not hold, directly or indirectly, any Channel 3 licence (or own a 20 per cent stake in a company holding such a licence) if it runs (or has at least a 20 per cent stake in) a national newspaper or newspapers with a national market share of 20 per cent or more, and vice versa; and

(ii) a person may not hold a regional Channel 3 licence if it runs local newspapers which together have a local market share of 20 per cent or more in the coverage area of the licence.

For these purposes, market share is defined as the percentage of total newspaper sales in the relevant area in the previous six months (with free newspapers being treated as if they had been sold).[41]

With respect to local radio licences, Pt III of Sch.14 to the Communications Act allows the Secretary of State to impose limits on the number of licences that any person may own. These limits were introduced by the Media Ownership (Local Radio and Appointed News Provider) Order 2003 (the "Local Radio Order") which also came into force on December 29, 2003.[42] The provisions are relatively complex, but broadly provide that a person may not acquire an additional local analogue radio licence in a particular area if he already owns two such licences and by doing so he would hold more than 55 per cent of the total points available. Points are attributed to a licence depending on the extent to which its coverage area overlaps with that of the licence which is being considered (which means that the same licence may have a different number of points allocated to it depending on which other, overlapping licence is being considered).[43] If the person seeking to acquire a new overlapping licence also owns a local newspaper with a market share above 30 per cent in the licence area, or a regional Channel 3 licence covering the licence area, the threshold is 45 per cent of the available points, rather than 55 per cent.[44]

Article 9 of the Local Radio Order prohibits joint ownership in the same area of a local radio broadcasting licence, a regional Channel 3 licence and a local newspaper (or newspapers) having a 50 per cent share of the market in that area. A similar points system to that described above also applies to local digital radio services, with the relevant threshold again being 55 per

2.063

---

[40] See paras 1 to 3 of Sch.14 to the Communications Act.
[41] Para.3 of Sch.14. Under the newspaper regime of the FTA, where the circulation or distribution levels of newspapers in the previous six months were also relevant for the purpose of deciding whether the consent of the Secretary of State was required, and also whether reference to the Commission was mandatory, in practice the DTI accepted figures for the latest six month period for which audited ABC figures were available. These are published for January-June and July-December of each year. It is assumed that reference to these figures will similarly be acceptable under the new cross-media regime.
[42] SI 2003/3299.
[43] Local Radio Order, Arts 5 and 8.
[44] Local Radio Order, Art.6.

cent, but a person is allowed to own up to four services before the rules apply; points are allocated primarily by reference to the number of hours per week the service is broadcast rather than the extent of overlap.[45]

Paragraphs 7 and 8 of Sch.14 to the Communications Act also impose restrictions with respect to national and local multiplex radio licences.

New media merger provisions

2.064   The Government's intention had simply been to introduce the new, more liberalised, media ownership rules described above. Accordingly, subject to satisfying the media ownership rules, TV, radio or cross-media mergers would have been subject only to the general merger provisions contained in the Enterprise Act. However, during the passage of the Communications Bill through Parliament, there was a strong consensus in the House of Lords that additional safeguards were needed in relation to broadcasting and cross-media mergers. As a consequence, the Government was forced to introduce an amendment to the Bill which allows the Secretary of State to intervene in mergers which raise issues of media plurality. These new rules operate alongside the intervention rights which the Secretary of State has in relation to other public interest mergers (including newspaper mergers, discussed in Ch.7 below). The provisions add new rights for the Secretary of State to give an intervention notice under s.42(2) of the Act or a special intervention notice under s.59(2) of the Act. The distinction between the types of intervention notice is explained above.

Accordingly, in addition to the newspaper public considerations considered in Ch.7 below, s.375(1) inserts a new subs.(2C) in s.58 as follows:

"The following are specified in this section:

(a)   the need, in relation to every different audience in the United Kingdom or in a particular area or locality of the United Kingdom, for there to be a sufficient plurality of persons with control of the media enterprises serving that audience;

(b)   the need for the availability throughout the United Kingdom of a wide range of broadcasting which (taken as a whole) is both of high quality and calculated to appeal to a wide variety of tastes and interests; and

(c)   the need for persons carrying on media enterprises, and for those with control of such enterprises, to have a genuine commitment to the attainment in relation to broadcasting of the standards objective set out in section 319 of the Communications Act 2003."[46]

---

[45] Local Radio Order, Arts 10–12.

[46] s.319 of the Communications Act introduces the following standards objectives:

(a)   that persons under the age of eighteen are protected;

(b)   that material likely to encourage or to incite the commission of crime or to lead to disorder is not included in television and radio services;

(c)   that news included in television and radio services is presented with due impartiality and that the impartiality requirements of s.320 are complied with;

(d)   that news included in television and radio services is reported with due accuracy;

(e)   that the proper degree of responsibility is exercised with respect to the content of programmes which are religious programmes;

It should be noted that s.58A(8) defines audience to include reader-ship, and that for the purposes of s.58(2C)(a) only, "media enterprise" is defined to include newspaper enterprises, provided that at least one of the enterprises ceasing to be distinct consists in or involves broad-casting.[47] The consequence of this is that s.58(2C)(a) applies to cross-media transactions involving newspapers (as well as pure broadcasting mergers). Subsections 58(2C)(b) and (c) only apply to broadcasting (*i.e.* TV and radio) mergers.

Section 378 of the Communications Act also added additional s.59(3D) of the Act, whereby a further special public interest intervention right is available to the Secretary of State in circumstances where, in relation to the provision of broadcasting of any description, at least one-quarter of all broadcasting of that description provided in the United Kingdom, or in a substantial part of the United Kingdom, was provided by the person or persons by whom one of the enterprises concerned was carried on. This is essentially equivalent to s.59(3C) in relation to newspapers (discussed in Ch.7, below), and allows the Secretary of State to intervene even where the standard merger thresholds are not met, provided at least one of the parties has a 25 per cent share of supply of broadcasting of any description, either in the whole of the UK or a substantial part of the UK (that is, a product or geographic overlap is not required). The meaning of substantial part of the UK is discussed above.[48] It should be recalled that in special intervention cases, no competition assessment will occur and the analysis will simply focus on the public interest issues.

When the additional media merger provisions were introduced by the Government, the relevant Minister, Lord Mackintosh of Haringey, stated that it would normally be the Government's intention to use its intervention powers only in situations where media regulation had been completely removed (for example, national newspaper owners owning Channel 5 or a national radio service, single ownership of London Channel 3 licences or Channel 3 and Channel 5, common ownership of national radio and

---

(f)   that generally accepted standards are applied to the contents of television and radio services so as to provide adequate protection for members of the public from the inclusion in such services of offensive and harmful material;

(g)   that advertising that contravenes the prohibition on political advertising set out in s.321(2) is not included in television or radio services;

(h)   that the inclusion of advertising which may be misleading, harmful or offensive in television and radio services is prevented;

(i)   that the international obligations of the United Kingdom with respect to advertising included in television and radio services are complied with;

(j)   that the unsuitable sponsorship of programmes included in television and radio services is prevented;

(k)   that there is no undue discrimination between advertisers who seek to have adver-tisements included in television and radio services; and

(l)   that there is no use of techniques which exploit the possibility of conveying a message to viewers or listeners, or of otherwise influencing their minds, without their being aware, or fully aware, of what has occurred.

[47] s.58A(2).
[48] At para.2.018. In relation to broadcasting, the Severn Estuary licence area, covering (*inter alia*) Bristol and Cardiff, was considered to be a substantial part of the UK in *Scottish Radio Holdings plc and GWR Group plc and Galaxy Radio Wales and the West Limited*, Cm. 5811 (May 2003), para.2.5.

national TV station etc.).[49] This position is reiterated in the DTI guidance on the new regime.[50] Accordingly, the scope for intervention in non-newspaper media mergers is narrower than in relation to newspaper mergers, although whether this will translate into fewer interventions in practice remains to be seen.

2.065   In deciding whether to intervene, the DTI's guidance indicates that the Secretary of State will have regard to any relevant information as to the track record both of the enterprise seeking to acquire a broadcaster (or newspaper in the case of the cross-media rules) and of those who control it.[51] Whilst the guidance recognises that the media public interest considerations are distinct from competition issues, it states that "there is a recognisable overlap between [the] competition assessment and at least the first of the broadcasting and cross-media public interest considerations, which posits the need for there to be a sufficient plurality of persons controlling media enterprises".[52] In view of this, the guidance indicates that in some cases, the Secretary of State may take the view that action to safeguard competition will be sufficient to protect plurality.[53]

In connection with the first broadcasting and cross-media public interest consideration (namely the need for a sufficient plurality of persons with control of media enterprises serving the same audience), the DTI's guidance states that this seeks to ensure that any one person does not control too much of the media such that they would have an ability to influence opinions and control the agenda.[54] The guidance indicates that in assessing this issue, the Secretary of State will consider the number of persons controlling media enterprises serving the relevant audience (the BBC will also be taken into account in this respect) but will also take into account audience shares.[55]

In connection with the second broadcasting public interest consideration relating to the need for the availability of a wide range of television and radio services, the DTI guidance indicates that this aims to safeguard the quality and diversity of programming. The guidance clarifies that the primary focus of the test will be on the assessment of future plans of the acquirer, but that past compliance with requirements imposed on other broadcasting enterprises of the acquirer to deliver a sufficient range and/or quality of broadcasting services will also be taken into account.[56]

The third media public interest consideration relates to the need for broadcasting enterprises and their controllers to have a genuine commitment to the broadcasting standards objectives set out in the Communications Act. The DTI guidance indicates that it will assess whether persons controlling or

---

[49] *Hansard*, House of Lords, July 2, 2003, col.914–915. Essentially the same language was used at *Hansard*, House of Lords, July 8, 2003, col.157.

[50] *Enterprise Act 2002: Public Interest Intervention in media mergers: Guidance on the operation of the public interest merger provisions relating to newspaper and other media mergers*, May 2004, Executive Summary and para.8.2. Para.8.4 clarifies that this also covers situations where there were no previous media ownership restrictions, *e.g.* mergers involving satellite and cable television and radio services.

[51] Para.7.2.

[52] Para.7.3.

[53] Para.7.4.

[54] Para.7.7.

[55] Paras 7.9 to 7.12.

[56] DTI guidance, paras 7.18 to 7.20.

carrying on media enterprises post-merger are likely to comply with the spirit as well as the letter of the standards. The guidance indicates that this may include a qualitative assessment of past compliance with UK broadcasting standards (for example, relating to due impartiality and accuracy of news), and may also take into account compliance with any broadcasting standards in other jurisdictions. Commitment to any applicable non-broadcasting standards may also be taken into account.[57]

Whilst it is the Secretary of State's policy to intervene only on the basis of the media public interest considerations where media ownership restrictions have been removed, the DTI guidance clarifies that if some of the remaining restrictions on media ownership were to be lifted in the future, the Secretary of State would consider intervening in those areas as well.[58] The guidance also indicates that in exceptional circumstances, the Secretary of State may consider it necessary to intervene in instances where there continue to be media ownership rules or where there have never been any such rules. The guidance states that this would be considered if such a merger might give rise to serious public interest concerns. The guidance indicates that this might include circumstances where a large number of news or educational channels would be coming under single control, or if someone were to take over all the music channels. Intervention may also be considered if a potential new entrant in local radio has not shown a genuine commitment to broadcasting standards in other media or other countries. The guidance also states that the "Secretary of State is not currently aware of any other types of cases in which exceptional circumstances might arise". The guidance indicates that a previous adverse public interest finding would not necessarily constitute an exceptional circumstance meriting intervention.[59]

The procedure with respect to broadcasting and cross-media mergers is essentially the same as for newspaper mergers considered in Ch.7 with the OFT and OFCOM fulfilling the same roles. As is the case for newspaper mergers, the information which OFCOM requests or may request is included in merger notifications with respect to broadcasting mergers (in addition to the information which is generally required) is set out at App.1 to its guidance on the new regime, a copy of which is set out in full at App.8 below.[60]

It should be noted that, in light of the Secretary of State's policy decision normally to consider intervention only in circumstances where media ownership restrictions have been removed, informal advice and confidential guidance from the DTI/Secretary of State (and OFCOM if relevant) will generally only be offered in cases which would previously have been regulated by media ownership restrictions. Nevertheless, the parties may be able to obtain guidance if they successfully persuade the Secretary of State/the DTI that the proposed merger is an exceptional case in which the Secretary of State might choose to intervene (such as the circumstances referred to in para.8.8 of the DTI's guidance discussed above).[61]

---

[57] DTI guidance, paras 7.22 to 7.25.
[58] Para.8.3.
[59] Para.8.8.
[60] OFCOM *guidance for the public interest test for media mergers*, May 2004.
[61] DTI guidance para.4.5. Whether it is sensible to make such an argument in a case other than those falling within para.8.8, or even in some cases which do fall within para.8.8, is debateable as it may conceivably encourage intervention which would not otherwise have occurred.

Water and sewerage

2.066   The Act preserves the existence of a modified merger regime for water and sewerage companies. Sections 32–35 of the Water Industry Act 1991 as amended by s.70 of the Enterprise Act provide that the OFT must refer all mergers between licensed water companies to the Competition Commission, unless the value of the turnover of one of the enterprises is below £10 million. However, s.70 of the Act has yet to be brought into force, with the consequence that the previous rules continue to apply. Under these rules, the *de minimis* threshold is that the value of the gross assets of one of the enterprises is below £30 million. In addition, references are made by the Secretary of State rather than the OFT. The authors understand from the DTI that s.70 is due to be brought into force on December 29, 2004. In assessing a merger, the substantive test for the Commission is broadly similar under both the current and future regimes, relating primarily to whether the Director General of Water Services' ability, in carrying out his functions under the Water Industry Act, to make comparisons between different water enterprises, would be (or has been) prejudiced by the relevant transaction.

Other utilities and regulated industries

2.067   The OFT notes in its *Procedural Guidance* that there are no special provisions under UK merger legislation for regulated utilities and that in principle mergers in these sectors are equally subject to the Act. However, the OFT notes that:

> "A merger in these industries may well require the modification of an operating licence or give rise to other issues falling within the ambit of the relevant regulator."[62]

Accordingly in such cases the OFT and the Competition Commission may be expected to work closely with the appropriate sectoral regulator in order to determine whether a substantial lessening of competition is likely, and in relation to the identification of appropriate Where, in connection with competition remedies, or for non-competition related reasons, a merger results in new licence conditions or the modification of existing licence conditions, the changes to the licence can themselves potentially be the subject of a reference to the Competition Commission.

Electricity

2.068   The Electricity Act 1989 regulates the electricity industry in the UK. However, notwithstanding this sector-specific legislation mergers in the electricity industry, of which there have been a number in recent years, are considered by the OFT and the Competition Commission under the Enterprise Act in the normal way. OFGEM (the sectoral regulator with responsibility for electricity) will typically hold its own third party consultation process in relation to a merger in this sector, and will then report to

---

[62] Para.8.14.

the OFT its views on the competitive impact of the merger (taking into account any third party representations received) in line with a Concordat agreed between the OFT and OFGEM which outlines their respective roles in this context. As noted, it is additionally possible that OFGEM will wish to consider licence modifications or the insertion of new licence conditions in the light of the merger.

Gas

The Gas Act 1986 regulates the gas industry in the UK. However, it leaves merger control in the gas industry with the OFT and Competition Commission under the normal Enterprise Act provisions. As in the electricity sector, however, OFGEM will typically hold its own third party consultation process in relation to a gas sector merger, and will then report its views on the impact of the merger to the OFT, in line with the Concordat between them. Again, it is also possible that OFGEM will consider licence modifications or the insertion of new licence conditions in the light of the merger.

2.069

Telecoms and Communications

There was no provision under the FTA 1973, nor is there any provision in the Act, which expressly creates a role for the telecommunications/communications regulatory body in merger cases. This lack of sector-specific control is consistent with the wider removal of regulation in the telecoms sector. However, in practice, the OFT and the Competition Commission have in the past paid particular regard to views expressed by OFTEL in reaching their conclusions on the competitive impact of mergers in this sector and it is likely that a similar approach will be followed under the Act through liaison with OFCOM (which has replaced OFTEL).

2.070

Rail

The Railways Act 1993, as amended by the Enterprise Act, provides that, for the purpose of the Enterprise Act merger provisions, where a person enters into a franchise agreement as franchisee for the operation of particular rail services, there is to be regarded as having been brought under his control an enterprise engaged in the supply of the railway services to which the agreement relates. Accordingly, on the grant of a franchise two enterprises cease to be distinct within the meaning of the Act, which may give rise to a merger qualifying for investigation if the share of supply or turnover tests are met. The OFT and the Competition Commission are responsible for the assessment of such mergers.

2.071

Aviation

Under the Act the OFT and Competition Commission remain competent to control mergers in the aviation industry (for example, the DGFT recommended clearance under the FTA of the proposed merger between easyJet and Go in July 2002). In relation to changes of control of airport facilities, the Enterprise Act introduced new provisions into the Airports Act 1986 which provide for orders made in light of merger decisions by the OFT and

2.072

Competition Commission to include provisions regarding the conditions under which the merging parties operate the airport(s) in question.

Financial Services

2.073   In addition to the application of the provisions of the Enterprise Act to mergers in the financial services sector, the provisions of the Financial Services and Markets Act 2000 may also be relevant. The 2000 Act sets out requirements in relation to the notification of mergers to, and their approval by, the Financial Services Authority. Similarly, the Building Societies Act 1986 requires building society mergers and amalgamations to be notified and approved by the Financial Services Authority.

CHAPTER 3

PROCEDURE OF THE OFFICE OF FAIR TRADING

Introduction

Unlike the position under the EC Merger Regulation, there is no standard   3.001
procedure which must be followed in all cases for obtaining the OFT's
confirmation that a merger will not be referred to the Competition
Commission.[1] In particular, there continues to be no legal requirement that
the parties to a merger should obtain clearance, either before its implementation or at all, except in the case of certain water and sewerage mergers.
Following changes introduced by the Communications Act 2003, it is no
longer a requirement to obtain the prior consent of the Secretary of State in
relation to newspaper mergers.[2] The parties may choose to seek clearance
for reasons of certainty, or may be required to do so for reasons outside the
Enterprise Act. The Act retains the ability of the OFT to refer qualifying
mergers where it believes that it may be the case that the merger has
resulted or may be expected to result in a substantial lessening of competition to the Competition Commission up to four months from the date on
which the merger was completed and/or was made public.[3] The result of
not seeking clearance in advance may, therefore, lead to a period of uncertainty before the parties can be sure that a reference will not be made. As
under the FTA, however, the Act also envisages the regulation of anticipated
mergers, which reflects the fact that for practical reasons most mergers
submitted to the OFT for clearance are in relation to mergers which have
not yet been completed or even where there are as yet no binding contracts
in place.

Clearance[4] may be sought from the OFT in any of the following
circumstances:

---

[1] The OFT has published guidance on the procedural aspects of the assessment of proposed or
completed mergers under the Act in its publication, *Mergers: Procedural Guidance*, May
2003.

[2] As described in Ch.2 and Ch.7. The Secretary of State's role in newspaper mergers changed
when s.375 of the Communications Act 2003 entered into force on December 29, 2003,
adding newspaper and media considerations into the public interest considerations set out in
s.58 of the Act.

[3] As described in Ch.2. There are various exceptional reasons why the four-month period may
be extended.

[4] The word "clearance" is used in this chapter to mean a decision by the OFT that it will not
refer to the Competition Commission a proposed or completed merger that has been publicly
announced. Confirmation on a confidential basis that on the facts presently known it would

(i)   upon or following announcement of a proposed merger (or before but in anticipation of announcement), with completion being conditional upon clearance; or

(ii)   upon or following announcement of a proposed merger as before, in the hope that clearance will be forthcoming before the transaction is completed; or

(iii)   upon or following announcement of a completed transaction.

The "traditional" method of seeking clearance is by means of a written submission which describes the transaction and the parties to it and their activities, and addresses in detail the competition issues that may be raised by it. In the case of a proposed merger that has been publicly announced, the so called "prenotification" procedure[5] may be used as an alternative to the traditional method, with the key difference being that the "prenotification" procedure follows a fixed statutory timetable and requires completion of a *pro-forma* notification (the "Merger Notice").

This chapter considers the points that need to be taken into account in considering if, when, and how to seek clearance, the procedures involved and the possible outcomes. How the OFT evaluates qualifying mergers and the information likely to be required by the OFT are discussed in Ch.6. The OFT's duty to refer mergers which it believes may be expected to result or have resulted in a substantial lessening of competition, and the circumstances where that duty does not apply, are discussed in Ch.4.

The relevance of the Takeover Code on the decision to seek clearance

Merger situations to which the Takeover Code applies

3.002   It is important to highlight at the outset that the flexibility of approach described in the introduction to this chapter on the question of whether to seek clearance is not in practice available to the prospective purchaser in the case of a public bid governed by the City Code on Takeovers and Mergers.[5A] Rule 12.1(a) of the Takeover Code provides that:

"Where an offer comes within the statutory provisions for possible reference to the Competition Commission, it must be a term of the offer that it will lapse if there is a reference before the first closing date or the date when the offer becomes or is declared unconditional as to acceptances, whichever is the later."

---

not propose to make a reference, *i.e.* positive confidential guidance or positive informal advice (discussed below at paras 3.004 *et seq.*) should not be regarded as clearance. Positive confidential guidance is at best an indication that clearance will be forthcoming after public announcement of the merger provided that no further information comes to light which might cause it to reach a different decision.

[5] See paras 3.028 *et seq.*, below.

[5A] It should be noted that as at the time of writing, the relevant Rules of the Takeover Code (Arts 5 and 9) were yet to be amended to reflect changes introduced to the UK merger control regime by the Act, or the reformed EC Merger Regulation (Council Regulation (EC) 139/2004 on the control of concentrations between undertakings).

Rule 12.1(c) then provides that:

"Except in the case of an offer under Rule 9, the offeror may, in addition, make the offer conditional on a decision being made that there will be no reference, initiation of proceedings or referral. It may state, if desired, that the decision must be on terms satisfactory to it."[6]

It should be noted that the Takeover Code requires an offer to be subject to the term set out in Rule 12.1(a) only where the Act applies. Accordingly, if the bid does not give rise to a qualifying merger because neither the turnover test nor the share of supply test[7] is satisfied, the term is not required. Frequently, however, it will be difficult for the bidder or its advisers to state with any certainty that the share of supply test is not satisfied, because the OFT applies great flexibility in how it calculates the share of supply, which is not necessarily calculated by reference to a properly defined relevant product/services and geographic market. In practice, therefore, it is not often that the term can be dispensed with. The condition permitted by Rule 12.1(c) is optional and may therefore be waived by the bidder if included in the offer document. Nevertheless it is customary to include such a condition, with the effect that the bidder will usually in practice seek clearance for the merger from the OFT. The bidder retains a choice as to how to seek clearance. In particular, it will be necessary to decide whether to use the prenotification procedure. The issues that need to be considered in exercising this choice are examined later in this chapter.[8]

Although the Act places no automatic restrictions on the purchaser's right to acquire shares (or otherwise complete the acquisition) while the OFT's evaluation is taking place, certain restrictions are imposed on a bidder in circumstances where Rule 5 of the Code applies[9] which will be lifted, *inter alia*, when the OFT announces that the offer is not to be referred to the Competition Commission (or that the offer does not come within the statutory provisions for possible reference).[10]

---

[6] Rule 9 addresses the Mandatory Offer and its terms.

[7] A detailed explanation of the share of supply test and the turnover test is set out in paras 2.017 *et seq.* and paras 2.021 *et seq.* of Ch.2.

[8] See para.3.021 below. Timing of the clearance is often of particular concern in the case of a public offer, both because of the offer timetable established by the Code and because the bidder may be incurring underwriting costs. As to the offer timetable, Note 3 of Rule 31.6 of the Code states that where there is a significant delay in the decision as to whether there is to be a reference to the Competition Commission (or an initiation of proceedings under the EC Merger Regulation) the Takeover Panel will normally extend Day 39 (*i.e.* stop the timetable for the offer at the 39th day) pending a decision being announced. (For the significance of Day 39, see Rule 31.9 of the Code).

[9] The effect of Rule 5 is to prevent a party, except under certain specified conditions, from (a) acquiring shares or rights over shares which would, together with shares already held by it, carry 30% or more of the voting rights exercisable at a general meeting of the company or, (b) a party already holds between 30% and 50% of the voting rights.

[10] Provided that, in the case of a hostile offer, the first closing date of the offer has passed: see Rule 5.2(c)(iii). One consequence of the operation of Rule 5.2(c)(iii) is that in relation to a hostile offer, the benefit of this exemption can only be obtained where the offer has been notified to the OFT-even where it is believed that the Act does not apply to the offer-because only then will the OFT make such an announcement. Other exceptions are available in the case of a recommended offer.

Merger situations outside the Takeover Code

3.003   In the case of merger situations which are not subject to the Takeover Code, the decision whether to notify the transaction for clearance will depend upon a wide range of issues and, frequently, a combination of them. In particular:

(i)   how essential is the need for certainty?

(ii)   how important is it that the transaction is completed without delay?

(iii) is the purchaser (who will often prefer an acquisition to be conditional upon clearance) in a stronger bargaining position than the vendor (who will generally prefer the sale to be unconditional), or vice versa?

(iv)   is there any doubt as to the OFT's jurisdiction?

At one extreme, a purchaser who is prepared to make a public statement of his intention to undertake a particular transaction only if he can be reasonably assured that no reference to the Competition Commission will result may be advised to seek confidential guidance or, at the very least informal advice, in relation to the transaction before any public announcement is made. At the other extreme, a purchaser who is not concerned by the prospect of a reference, or has been advised that a reference is unlikely, or is given no choice by circumstances or by the vendor but to proceed unconditionally, or has been advised that a reference is likely but believes that the risk is worth taking, may prefer to complete the transaction and deal with any regulatory questions if and when they arise.[11] These issues are considered in more detail at para.3.016 *et seq.*, below.

There are a number of ways in which the parties to a merger may ask the OFT to consider the merger. In relation to proposed mergers which have not been publicly announced, the parties may seek confidential guidance or, less reliably, informal advice. Where a decision is taken to seek clearance, it is possible to engage in prenotification discussions, typically to ensure that the notification is as comprehensive as the OFT would wish. Where a transaction has been publicly announced but not yet completed, the parties may notify it by means of a Merger Notice under the statutory prenotification procedure; alternatively they may notify the merger

---

[11] Once a transaction is completed the purchaser takes the risk of a reference and, ultimately, a divestment order as the statutory powers do not include requiring a seller to re-purchase (unless otherwise agreed between the parties). The acquisition in 1997 under the FTA by Ladbroke Group plc of the Coral betting business was such a case. The parties proceeded to complete without a merger notification and on the basis of an unconditional agreement, even though the purchaser and the target were competing businesses. It appears that Ladbroke had relied on the Commission's analysis in *Grand Metropolitan plc and William Hill Organisation Ltd*, Cm. 776 (August 1989). In *Ladbroke Group PLC and the Coral betting business*, Cm. 4030 (September 1998) the Commission found that there had been significant changes in the market since September, 1989 and recommended that Ladbroke divest the Coral business in full. This recommendation was accepted by the Secretary of State and Ladbroke was ordered to divest the whole of the Coral betting business within six months.

whether anticipated or completed, via the "traditional" route of an informal written submission.[12]

These various options are considered in turn below.

Confidential guidance

"Confidential guidance" is the name given to the procedure whereby one or 3.004 more of the parties to a proposed transaction may seek an indication, in confidence, from the OFT as to whether the transaction would be likely to be referred to the Competition Commission if it were to proceed. The procedure is not statutory; it is, rather, an administrative procedure that developed over a number of years under the FTA and which has been retained by the OFT under the reformed regime under the Act.[13]

It will often be the case that the parties to an agreed transaction, or the bidder for a potentially unwilling publicly quoted target, will not wish to proceed if there is a substantial likelihood that the merger will be held up for up to six months or so following the OFT making a reference to the Competition Commission. Similarly, a publicly quoted vendor selling part of its business, however willing to proceed, may not be prepared to risk the delay that a reference entails, for fear that uncertainty in the market may have an adverse effect on its share price. The directors of the target in an agreed bid may well not be prepared to risk the likelihood that a "For Sale" sign will effectively be erected above it, inviting potentially unwelcome advances from third parties; and a publicly quoted bidder may fear loss of credibility if its bid is referred, as well as uncertainty on the financial markets. Both vendors and purchasers may have a number of additional reasons for wishing to avoid the risk of a reference: customer and supplier uncertainty, the potentially prejudicial effect on employees, the inevitable and considerable cost and management time a reference requires, difficulties arising from the purchaser's need to raise finance, and so on. Accordingly, the possibility of being able to establish, if not with certainty then with a high degree of comfort, that the proposal in contemplation is not likely to be referred to the Competition Commission, without any facts about the possible merger entering the public domain, is often an attractive one.

Procedure

If the company or companies involved want to seek confidential guidance 3.005 they should prepare a submission "in much the same way as they would be were the merger already public",[14] including at least as much detail on the transaction and relevant markets.[15] The confidential guidance procedure

---

[12] Strictly speaking the parties may also notify the OFT on the basis of an informal written submission before public announcement. However, once an informal written submission is made to the OFT, the OFT will swiftly publish an invitation to comment. A party wishing to get the clearance process underway whilst maintaining the confidentiality of the merger would probably be best advised to use the pre-notification discussions procedure (see para.3.022, below).

[13] See paras 3.18 to 3.19 of the OFT's *Procedural Guidance*.

[14] See para.3.11 of the OFT's *Procedural Guidance*.

[15] By comparison to the informal advice process (discussed below), the information burden on parties wishing to seek confidential guidance is relatively heavy. This is perhaps the reason

involves the OFT evaluating the proposed transaction in the same way and following the same procedure as in notified public cases[15A] with the important limitation, which is sometimes critical, that the views of third parties (particularly customers, suppliers and competitors of the merged company) cannot normally be sought because of the confidential nature of the process. The OFT may, however, consult relevant government departments in relation to a confidential guidance request.[16] In some sectors where there has historically been a high level of government interest or involvement (for example the ex-utilities such as energy and telecommunications, or sectors such as milk), this may enable the OFT to gather a large amount of market information.

At the conclusion of the OFT's considerations, it will inform the applicant or applicants either that the proposal is unlikely to be referred to the Competition Commission, or that a reference is likely to be made. The confidential guidance process can also provide some indication on whether undertakings in lieu of a reference might be acceptable (see Ch.4 at paras 4.021 *et seq.*). Alternatively, the outcome may be that no guidance can be given on the information available and in the absence of knowledge of the views of interested third parties. Sometimes caveated guidance is given, for example, that positive guidance is subject to third party consultations subsequently confirming particular statements put forward by the parties such as the definition of the product or geographical market. Clearly by its nature, such guidance is less reliable than unconditional guidance. The OFT endeavours to respond to requests for confidential guidance within 30 working days,[17] and in some cases it may take up to eight weeks or more.

One of the strengths of confidential guidance (particularly over informal advice, discussed below) is that the response has been considered at the highest level within the OFT. Effectively, the OFT follows substantially the same internal procedure as would be followed in assessing a submission or Merger Notice requesting clearance, save that there is no third party consultation.[18] Accordingly, every request for confidential guidance will receive a very similar degree of attention as a notified merger. In complex cases that raise potential issues and which go to a case review meeting,[19] therefore, the confidential guidance request will receive the attention of the Chairman (or other decision-maker, where appropriate). That said, the outcome is not binding upon the OFT and its decision on a request for confidential guidance is always caveated that it is based only on such information as has been available to the OFT at that time (*i.e.* that supplied by the applicant, as supplemented by information already in the public domain, and that which is already known to the OFT).

---

for a decline in recent years in the number of confidential guidance requests, as parties and their advisers have declined the "Rolls Royce" option of confidential guidance and utilised instead the option of informal advice. (In 2003/4, only 13 confidential guidance requests were received, compared to 28 in 2002/3). The relative merits of informal advice and confidential guidance are discussed at para.3.012, below.

[15A] The procedure of the OFT in evaluating cases (both public and confidential guidance) is set out at para.3.044 and following below.

[16] As confirmed at para.3.12 of the OFT's *Procedural Guidance*.

[17] The authors understand that the original target of 20 working days, which is an internal administrative target only, has recently been increased.

[18] See para.3.12 of the OFT's *Procedural Guidance* and para.3.044 *et seq.*, below.

[19] See para.3.062, below.

The OFT's *Procedural Guidance* summarises the possible outcomes of a confidential guidance request as follows:

"1. the merger appears unlikely to raise any competition issues that would warrant reference to the [Competition Commission] at the public stage

2. it is not possible to say whether or not the merger would raise competition concerns that would warrant reference at the public stage

3. the merger appears to raise competition concerns that would warrant reference at the public stage but such concerns might be remedied by undertakings, or

4. the merger appears to raise competition concerns that would warrant reference at the public stage, and undertakings do not appear to be appropriate".[20]

The formal response to a request for guidance is not reasoned and will usually simply state the OFT's conclusions, although in some cases some detail may be added regarding the potential competition concerns that the OFT has identified. An example of the basic wording of a negative confidential guidance letter (*i.e.* that reference is likely) is set out in App.3. However, the OFT's *Procedural Guidance* indicates that a meeting would be available to the parties where the OFT will provide a more detailed explanation of the guidance.[21–22] In some cases, particularly where negative guidance is given, a brief written explanation may be offered. Whether in writing or, more usually, verbally, the additional explanation will briefly outline what the OFT sees as the "pressure points" in the case. These will essentially be the areas where the OFT would wish to consult with third parties, should the merger become public, to verify its understanding and analysis of areas of concern. This additional explanation is particularly helpful since the parties, who after all know the markets concerned well, may be able to reach their own conclusions about whether third parties are likely to be concerned about the particular issues on which the OFT has not been able to reach a conclusion or which have prompted a conclusion that the merger is likely to be referred.

3.006

The effect of confidential guidance

It will be apparent from the preceding discussion that positive confidential guidance is not the same as clearance, any more than negative guidance— that is, an indication that the merger proposal would be likely to be referred to the Competition Commission if it proceeded—amounts to a reference. Certainty will only be obtained once the proposal has been announced, and third parties have been given the opportunity to make their views known.

3.007

The views of third parties, the emergence of further material facts, or the implementation of a proposal different in some respects from that disclosed to the OFT in seeking confidential guidance, may all result in the OFT's ultimate decision being different from that expressed in the confidential

---

[20] See para.3.13 of the OFT's *Procedural Guidance*.
[21–22] See para.3.14 of the OFT's *Procedural Guidance*.

guidance on whether to refer the proposed transaction. Because of the limitations on the extent to which the OFT can verify the parties' submissions, the robustness of a confidential guidance "clearance" is strongly linked to the degree to which the parties have been full and frank in their submissions to the OFT. Where the parties express firm views during the confidential guidance process, for example, in relation to market definition knowing that others might define the market differently and consider it a success when their arguments on definition are accepted by the OFT, there is a clear risk that the alternative market definition might emerge in the subsequent third party consultations, which might cause the OFT to reach a different conclusion about the merger. As the OFT's *Procedural Guidance* warns, confidential guidance "is . . . premised on the parties' evidence being supported by third party enquiries once the merger becomes publicly known".[23] In practice, however, a reference following positive guidance would be very rare.[24]

Receipt of clearance following negative guidance is possibly less unusual because, faced with the likelihood of a reference, the parties may proceed on the basis of a restructured proposal which attempts to take account of the problems they believe the OFT has identified in the original proposal. As noted above, the OFT will give the parties, if they wish, a certain amount of detail on where the competition concerns have arisen.[25] That said, the OFT does not act as a consultancy and typically will not enter into detailed discussions about what hypothetically would or would not be acceptable in terms of restructuring a merger to avoid regulatory problems.

A difficulty that can arise for applicants seeking confidential guidance is where the OFT concludes, after evaluation, that no view can be expressed as to whether the proposal is likely to be cleared or referred in the absence of being able to seek the views of third parties. The cases in which no guidance can be given may well be those in which guidance is most necessary, in the sense that the parties' advisers themselves were least able to give a view on the likelihood of a reference. For that reason it is often unwise for parties to a proposed merger to organise their arrangements, their fund raising and their tactics uniquely around the assumption that confidential guidance will be forthcoming; it is better to assume that it may well not be.

3.008   The attraction of the guidance procedure—its confidentiality—is also its weakness. This may be particularly so when the subject matter of the proposal or the market within which the parties compete is one that the OFT has not had cause to investigate or consider before, and on which it therefore has no background knowledge. Similar difficulties can arise in the context of a proposed public takeover of which the target has no knowledge at that time, since the purchaser will inevitably not have full knowledge at that stage of the market position and strategies of the target and the OFT may feel unable to give guidance where information from the target itself is unavailable.

---

[23] See para.3.18 of the OFT's *Procedural Guidance*.
[24] There was press speculation that Ladbroke Group PLC's acquisition of the Coral betting business which was acquired unconditionally in 1997 but subsequently referred to the Commission, had received positive confidential or perhaps informal guidance.
[25] See para.3.006, above.

Where a proposed merger is agreed, applicants can sometimes assist the procedure and make guidance more likely than it might otherwise be by being prepared to accept a form of qualified confidentiality. The OFT may indicate during its evaluation that guidance might be easier to give if it could consult with third parties having knowledge of the transaction. There may, for example, sometimes be major customers whose reactions the parties have sought in confidence during the planning stages of the proposal and who could therefore be approached by the OFT. However, the parties and their advisers in each case need to consider whether there is anything to be gained by agreeing to such a course, bearing in mind that the nominated third party may not always say what might have been anticipated, and that the OFT will inevitably treat such third party views as having been given by a party who is, to some extent, favourably disposed towards the applicant.

It should also be borne in mind in deciding whether to seek confidential guidance that the views of third parties, given following announcement of a merger, might persuade the OFT to recommend clearance in circumstances where, in the absence of such consultation at the confidential guidance stage, it would be likely to conclude that negative guidance was appropriate. In such circumstances, it may well be better not to seek guidance, and instead to seek to persuade the OFT of the acceptability of the merger following announcement. In particular, the Act has formally introduced the possibility that the duty to refer might be overridden where the OFT identifies countervailing customer benefits.[26] In a confidential guidance application without the scope for third party consultation, it is likely to be difficult for the OFT to reach a firm conclusion on the existence and weight of any such claimed benefits.

The OFT's *Procedural Guidance* expressly notes that the confidential guidance process can "provide some indication of whether undertakings in lieu of a reference might be acceptable".[27] Whilst this might at first sight seem difficult, even in public cases the OFT does not necessarily "market test" proposed undertakings in lieu with third parties until it has reached and announced its own conclusion as to whether they are likely to remedy the competition concerns.[28]

The need for confidentiality

The confidentiality of the guidance procedure implies more than a simple requirement that the parties to a merger seek a view from the OFT without the public at large being aware of their plans; rather, the need for strict confidence is insisted upon by the OFT itself, both during evaluation of the proposal and after guidance has been given and the proposed merger has been made public. The OFT's *Procedural Guidance* states that:

3.009

---

[26] The OFT's discretion not to refer in such circumstances is described in detail at paras 4.015 *et seq.* of Ch.4.
[27] See para.3.11 of the OFT's *Procedural Guidance*.
[28] The key provisions of the Act regarding undertakings in lieu are discussed at paras 4.021 *et seq.* of Ch.4 and the procedure of the OFT in seeking them is discussed at paras 3.072 *et seq.*, below.

"the OFT requires any company seeking confidential guidance not to reveal the fact that guidance has been requested or given (or the contents of the guidance given) to any other party even after the merger proposal becomes public. The guidance given by the OFT is confidential and is only for the Board members (and not individual shareholders) of the company/companies making the request and their legal/financial advisers that were privy to the request.[29]

In this connection, neither the request for guidance nor its outcome may be disclosed to the other party to the transaction, unless the application for guidance was made jointly or the OFT has approved such disclosure. The underlying policy is that any disclosure that confidential guidance has been received might prejudice the OFT's full freedom of action to reach a different view in the light of new facts put forward once the proposed merger is in the public domain. A party which ignored this would almost certainly find itself prevented by the OFT from making use of the confidential guidance procedure in the future, as might its legal and/or financial advisers. Much of UK merger clearance procedure depends, rightly or wrongly, on the exercise of mutual goodwill between the OFT, the parties and their advisers.

The opportunity for confidential guidance to be granted in a particular case will be withdrawn if there is any breach of confidentiality by the applicant during the period of the OFT's evaluation. On one occasion under the FTA, a director of the applicant company, concerned at the length of time the evaluation was taking, raised the matter with his Member of Parliament who, ill-advisedly, made enquiries of the Secretary of State. The applicant was thereupon informed that no guidance could be given. More typically, an applicant will lose the possibility of obtaining confidential guidance if forced by exceptional share price movements, or by the Stock Exchange, or both, to make an announcement that "discussions are in progress between X and Y which may lead to an acquisition". Mere press speculation, however, will not usually preclude guidance from being given.

Once the merger is announced, and certainly once it is completed, the OFT should be informed. The parties may, in any case, have decided to make the sale conditional on clearance, in which case they will want the OFT to commence its formal, public investigation as quickly as possible. Even if the merger is unconditional, however, the OFT will wish to complete its inquiries and formally clear the transaction. Under the FTA it could not be ruled out that the OFT might exceptionally have to refer a merger on which guidance had been given if it did not discover that the merger had been completed until close to the expiry of the statutory deadline for reference, and was unable to conclude its analysis or third party consultation in time. Under the Enterprise Act, such an essentially unnecessary reference is unlikely, as the OFT now has power to extend the s.24 statutory deadline for a reference where necessary.[30]

3.010   Finally, it is perhaps worth highlighting that the OFT itself respects the confidentiality of this process and will not reveal whether confidential guid-

---

[29] See para.3.18 of the OFT's *Procedural Guidance*.
[30] See s.25 of the Act, and paras 3.052 *et seq.*, below.

ance has been given, far less make any public announcement about its outcome. The OFT has an excellent reputation for preserving confidentiality: indeed the offices and IT systems of the Mergers Branch are kept secure from other parts of the OFT because of the amount of market sensitive information which the division handles on a daily basis.

Conclusion

It is clearly the case that confidential guidance can be a useful tool in the hands of the parties to a proposed merger, if only to give added assurance and confidence to those for whom the implications of a reference to the Competition Commission would be seriously prejudicial, or when there are serious doubts as to how the OFT would assess the competitive effect of a merger within the relevant market. In some circumstances the parties may feel, following receipt of positive confidential guidance, that the risk of a reference is sufficiently low that any condition precedent in relation to clearance under the Act can be waived.   **3.011**

The disadvantage with the procedure, as discussed above, is that confidential guidance may not be available in just those situations where the parties and their advisers would find it most useful. To wait for several weeks for the outcome of an evaluation which reaches the conclusion that no guidance is possible will rarely be regarded as time (or money) well spent; and to receive negative guidance in circumstances where, had third parties been consulted, a more positive outcome might have been likely, may result in failure to complete a perfectly acceptable transaction.

When considering confidential guidance as an option in a particular transaction, therefore, the parties and their advisers must consider how likely it is that positive guidance will be given. It may be there are real doubts that such guidance will be forthcoming; that the circumstances are such that a conditional contract is not a feasible option; the commercial attractions of the deal are sufficient to outweigh the risks of a reference; and there is a reasonable chance that the Competition Commission will ultimately clear it or recommend remedies which would still permit the principal aims of the transaction to be fulfilled. In such a situation, it may be preferable not to seek guidance. Moreover, in cases where the degree of uncertainty, or the areas where comfort are needed, are more limited, it may be that informal advice from the OFT will be sufficient and a more cost-effective way of managing the regulatory risk.

Informal advice

The pros and cons of informal advice compared to confidential guidance

Informal advice, as the name suggests, is a simpler procedure than confidential guidance for canvassing the views of the OFT on a merger.[31]   **3.012**

---

[31] Informal advice would usually be an alternative to seeking confidential guidance: it would be rare for both types of guidance to be given in relation to a single transaction unless there had been material changes in the facts although there is no reason why a party receiving positive informal advice could not then request confidential guidance.

However, it produces a potentially less reliable result to the extent that the response is prepared to a much shorter timeframe and comes from the head of the Mergers Branch, or one of its senior staff members, and (unlike confidential guidance) does not carry the authority of the OFT Board or its Chairman, who will take the actual decision whether to refer.

As well as carrying the same limitations as confidential guidance of being conducted in confidence without the input of third parties, informal advice does not incorporate the procedural protections of having been through the OFT's internal checks and balances—the issues will not have been put to the OFT review group and no case review meeting (with a nominated "devil's advocate") will have been held.[32] Moreover, since the parties are not held to the discipline of effectively making a full submission on all relevant issues for the OFT's competition analysis,[33] there is perhaps a greater risk that key information will be omitted, so that the Mergers Branch staff provide their advice without full information. When making an informal advice submission it is crucial to bear this point in mind. Notwithstanding the informality of the process, the reliability of the response, as with confidential guidance, is dependent on the parties having brought to the OFT's case officers' attention all the factors which might be relevant to the conclusion. As the OFT's *Procedural Guidance* puts it:

". . . the quality and accuracy of the Branch's advice will, to a large extent, reflect the quality of the information provided".[34]

Against these disadvantages, the primary tactical advantage of informal advice is its speed. The OFT's *Procedural Guidance* indicates that the OFT aims to provide informal advice within the timeframe requested by the parties[35]; the more limited scrutiny within the OFT creates greater scope for a swift response. In many cases, there may be insufficient time in the underlying transactional timeframe to permit the preparation and consideration by the OFT of a full submission for confidential guidance.[36]

A further advantage of informal advice is its flexibility. Unlike the confidential guidance process, the focus of an informal advice request need not be the broad question of whether the merger is likely to be referred to the Competition Commission. It can also be used to obtain comfort on a specific area of the likely competition assessment.[37] For example, if the OFT's approach to market definition is critical to the risk of a reference to the Competition Commission, informal advice might be limited to that issue alone. The process can also be useful where the merger will take place in a market with which the OFT is familiar, for example, because it has

---

[32] The detailed procedure followed by the OFT is set out at paras 3.058 *et seq.*, below.

[33] Recently the annual number of confidential guidance requests has fallen materially (in 2003/4, only 13 confidential guidance requests were received, compared to 28 in 2002/3) and it is possible that the lower information burden in seeking informal advice may be a significant underlying factor.

[34] See para.3.6 of the OFT's *Procedural Guidance*.

[35] See para.3.7 of the OFT's *Procedural Guidance*.

[36] The OFT's internal target for dealing with a confidential guidance request is 30 working days. See further para.3.005 above.

[37] Clearly this approach is subject to the caveat that the OFT's assessment and advice might have been affected by other aspects of the proposal of which it was not informed.

recently considered another transaction in the same market. In such a situation, a full presentation of the relevant market definition and the prevailing market conditions, such as would usually be given in a request for confidential guidance, may not be needed. Similarly, the process can be used to verify jurisdictional analysis,[37A] for example where a small shareholding is acquired and it is necessary to evaluate whether it amounts to material influence. The process of informal advice can also be used in relation to the interplay between the EC Merger Regulation and UK merger control. It may be a useful way to discuss with the OFT the likelihood, in relation to a merger subject to notification to the European Commission under the EC Merger Regulation, that the OFT will lodge a request that the transaction be referred back pursuant to Art.9 of that regulation.[38] Alternatively, informal guidance can be used as a way of exploring the possibility that a merger notified for clearance in the UK might be transferred to the European Commission pursuant to Art.22 of the EC Merger Regulation.[39] Informal advice can also be an appropriate way to obtain the OFT's confirmation that, for example, a draft Merger Notice contains all required information, or to identify supplemental information which should be added before a Merger Notice is submitted,[40] although this type of dialogue is also what the prenotification discussion procedure is intended to be used for (see para.3.022, below).

The process is not, however, available as the framework for an on-going **3.013** process of discussion with the Mergers Branch: the OFT cannot be used as a consultant to the process of negotiating the transaction structure. Its *Procedural Guidance* states that the informal advice process is not available for hypothetical transactions, nor is it a discursive process.[41] To the extent that such a dialogue may be needed, there is a process of prenotification discussion, considered further below.[42]

Procedure for seeking informal advice

The informal advice procedure commences with the submission of a **3.014** briefing paper or letter outlining the issues on which the OFT's advice is sought. The length and detail required will clearly turn on the questions in issue, but the OFT's *Procedural Guidance* indicates that the information provided should be brief.[43] As noted above, the OFT seeks to adhere to the timeframe requested by the parties within which to give its response. Typically, it will need at least a couple of days and usually around one week

---

[37A] Note that the OFT may reject a request for informal advice where the parties present the issues in such a way that the point on which the OFT's advice is requested does not appear to be in doubt. For example, the OFT will typically decline to "rubber stamp" a conclusion by the parties that the jurisdictional thresholds are not met on any analysis. By contrast, informal advice would be likely to be forthcoming where the parties explain that on basis A, which they believe to be correct, the OFT would not have jurisdiction, although on basis B, which they would like the OFT to confirm is not the right approach, one of the thresholds would be met.

[38] See further paras 2.040 *et seq.* of Ch.2.

[39] See further paras 2.043 *et seq.* of Ch.2.

[40] The OFT itself acknowledges this use of the process at para.3.6 of its *Procedural Guidance*.

[41] See para.3.6 of the *Procedural Guidance*.

[42] See para.3.022, below.

[43] See para.3.6 of the OFT's *Procedural Guidance*.

to consider the issues raised and information provided and will then host a meeting with the parties. The OFT's advice will be given orally during the course of the meeting.

In all aspects of the informal advice process, the quality of the advice received is directly related to the quality of the material provided by the parties. As with confidential guidance, the OFT is not able to "market test" claims made by the parties with third parties and competitors. The quality of the response is inevitably also affected by the timetable—if the parties need a very quick response, clearly, there is a risk that it will be less considered than if more time had been available. Informal advice is given by the Mergers Branch only, and does not bind the OFT, which may subsequently reach a different view (although this would happen typically only where there has been a material change in the facts, or issues are revealed that were not previously known to the OFT).

The need for confidentiality

3.015   Finally, and as with confidential guidance, the confidentiality of the process is paramount. The OFT considers not only the outcome of a request for informal guidance but also the process of requesting it to be strictly confidential at all times, even where a merger has subsequently been formally cleared. The requirement of confidentiality weighs not only on the parties but also their advisers, and the OFT will withdraw the availability of the guidance processes in the future from any party or adviser—including legal and financial advisers—which it discovers to have broken the confidentiality requirement. Once the transaction has been completed, the OFT should be informed as it will wish to complete its analysis and deal with the merger on a formal basis (and collect the merger fee). The points made above in this respect regarding confidential guidance apply equally to informal advice.[44]

Deciding not to seek clearance

3.016   There is no obligation to notify proposed or completed qualifying mergers (and no stigma attached to a decision not to notify[45]) except in the special case of mergers involving water companies. Since December 29, 2003, when the media merger provisions of the Communications Act 2003 entered into force, newspaper mergers are no longer subject to compulsory notification and reference to the Competition Commission, and notification is now at the parties' discretion.[46]

As stated above, one option available to the parties to a proposed merger is to complete the transaction notwithstanding the potential regulatory consequences, to take the risk that the OFT may refer the matter to the

---

[44] See para.3.009, above.
[45] In the authors' experience, the OFT's analysis of a merger is wholly unaffected by the issue of whether it was notified by the parties. The position might be different where it is clear that the parties have been actively seeking to avoid scrutiny of the transaction under the Act, but this is rare and can in any event now be dealt with by the OFT's power to extend the deadline for reaching its decision whether to refer. See further paras 3.052 et seq.
[46] See further Ch.7 which discusses newspaper mergers.

Competition Commission which may subsequently decide that the merger may be expected to result in a substantial lessening of competition, requiring the purchaser to submit to behavioural undertakings or, more severely, to dispose of part of the merged enterprise.[47] There is certainly nothing unusual in completing a transaction without first receiving regulatory clearance. Of the 87 mergers which had been considered by the OFT under the Act as at June 1, 2004, just under half were completed mergers. Moreover, the question whether a merger has already been completed does not in itself affect the OFT's analysis of whether it can be expected to result in a substantial lessening of competition. The fact that a merger has been completed and that unscrambling the fully integrated businesses would be complex and difficult, will not prevent a reference. The fact that it would be difficult to restore the pre-merger position will also not prevent a reference: it may be that remedies could be devised which, whilst falling short of fully restoring competition, would at least reintroduce a greater degree of competition than has prevailed since the merger.

Under the FTA, the OFT moved with great speed to refer mergers to the Competition Commission, where necessary.[48] Under the Act, the OFT has a greater arsenal with which to counter-attack. First, it now has powers to require the merging businesses to be kept apart, even after they have come into the same ownership.[49] Secondly, the OFT has powers to extend the statutory deadline for a reference, either by agreement with the parties, or by notice to the parties where it is still waiting for information from them.[50]

When there is no choice

In some transactions there may be no choice but to proceed without seeking clearance. In some cases, a vendor will simply not be prepared to sell its interests on a conditional basis. For example, when Bass sought to sell its brewing interests to Interbrew in 2000, the sale was subject to the EC Merger Regulation and could not therefore be completed prior to clearance. However, it appears that Bass wished to carry as little of the regulatory risk as possible, because the Competition Commission's report records that one of the reasons why Bass selected Interbrew over two other bidders was that its offer was conditional upon the transaction being cleared by the European Commission or being referred back under Art.9 of the EC Merger Regulation to the competent UK authorities[51] but, crucially, Interbrew's offer was *not* conditional upon clearance by the UK authorities following a reference back from the European Commission. When the European Commission referred the matter to the UK authorities, the condition was fulfilled and the transaction was accordingly completed without waiting for the UK authorities' conclusions on the case. In the event, the UK aspects of the acquisition were referred to the Competition Commission and,

3.017

---

[47] The range and breadth of remedies which the Competition Commission may adopt are discussed in Ch.9, below.

[48] Under the FTA, the OFT took only thirteen working days in advising the Secretary of State that a completed merger should be referred in the case of *AAH Holdings/Medicopharma NV*, Cm. 1950 (May 1992).

[49] See para.3.055, below.

[50] See further para.3.052, below.

[51] See further paras.2.042 of Ch.2, above.

following an adverse finding,[52] were blocked by the Secretary of State,[53] whose decision was then challenged by Interbrew in the High Court. Bass, meanwhile, had been able to complete the sale and thus walked away from the regulatory complexities.

In some circumstances, the commercial imperative to complete the transaction may mean that there is simply insufficient time available to make the merger conditional on competition clearance. In *Octagon Motorsports/ British Racing Drivers Club*,[54] it appears that Octagon took a lease of the Silverstone Grand Prix racing circuit and acquired some of the associated businesses from the British Racing Drivers Club under time pressure to avoid being in breach of its contract with Formula One Ltd administration to hold the British Grand Prix. Although the merger was referred to the Competition Commission, it was ultimately cleared. The acquisition of Canadian Airlines Corporation by Canada Airlines occurred against a background of severe cash flow problems for Canadian Airlines Corporation, which would otherwise have been likely to have collapsed.[55] Similarly, Avenir Havas Media, a subsidiary of the French Havas Group, having kept the OFT informed over several months of its negotiations to acquire a minority stake in Brunton Curtis, a roadside poster company, acquired the whole of the company without clearance (though with the knowledge of the OFT) as the only means of avoiding the target's imminent insolvency. That acquisition was also referred to the MMC, which subsequently recommended that the assets acquired should be disposed of in their entirety.[56] When AAH Holdings, a pharmaceutical wholesaler, announced that it had acquired certain of the United Kingdom pharmaceutical wholesaling assets of Medicopharma B.V. upon an apparently sudden decision being made by the vendor to withdraw from the United Kingdom market, the argument was advanced that the transaction did not amount to a merger situation at all.[57] However, the OFT rejected that contention and the Secretary of State quickly referred the merger to the MMC which recommended a divestment remedy.[58]

Electing to run the risk of a reference

3.018   The purchaser may decide that the risk of a reference is worth taking if there is a reasonable chance of being able to persuade the OFT that no reference is needed or, in the event of a reference being made, of being able

---

[52] See *Interbrew SA and Bass PLC*, Cm. 5014 (January 2001).

[53] See DTI Press Release P/2001/11 of January 3, 2001.

[54] See *Octagon Motorsports Limited and British Racing Drivers Club Limited*, Cm. 5252 (September 2001).

[55] See *Air Canada and Canadian Airlines Corporation*, Cm. 4838 (August 2000).

[56] See *Avenir Havas Media SA/Brunton Curtis Outdoor Advertising Ltd*, Cm. 1737 (November 1991).

[57] See paras 2.004 *et seq.* of Ch. 2.

[58] See *AAH Holdings PLC/Medicopharma NV*, Cm. 1950 (May 1992). The MMC recommended that AAH dispose of that part of the business it had acquired which was based in Scotland. The Secretary of State accepted the MMC's recommendations but was later persuaded that the disposal was unnecessary due to the emergence of a new wholesaler in Scotland. See DTI press notice: October 23, 1992, P/92/679. The negotiation of undertakings following a full investigation by the Competition Commission is discussed in Ch.9, below.

to convince the Competition Commission that the proposed merger will not result in a substantial lessening of competition. This is effectively the choice made (often unconsciously) in relation to a great number of mergers where no substantive competition issues arise. This course of action may be particularly attractive to a prospective purchaser if the only alternative is not to proceed with the transaction at all.[59] It is also a strategy that might be taken for tactical reasons, for example in the case of auction sales where a prospective purchaser judges that its bid is unlikely to be selected if it is conditional on merger clearance, usually in circumstances where competing bidders would not have competition issues to deal with. This is a question often faced by trade buyers (or financial buyers who already have an investment in the sector concerned and are pursuing a "buy and build" strategy) competing in an auction process against financial buyers who do not face any competition issues; deciding to take the regulatory risk of an unconditional offer may be the only way of having a realistic chance of being selected as the successful bidder.

Ladbroke appears to have taken this approach when it purchased the Coral betting business from Bass unconditionally in 1997. The other bidders were Nomura, which already owned the William Hill business and two venture capital organisations, which were likely to have had no competition concerns in relation to their proposed bids for Coral. The MMC's report[60] records that one of the reasons why Ladbroke was selected as the successful bidder was because of the lack of any conditions to its proposals, suggesting that Nomura's bid may have been conditional on competition clearance. In this case, Ladbroke apparently took the view that it had a good prospect of receiving clearance in purchasing the Coral betting business unconditionally. It appears to have relied on the analysis in the MMC's 1989 report on the Mecca/William Hill merger[61] and used the MMC's 1989 analysis to identify 134 betting shops from the combined Ladbroke/Coral portfolio which it agreed to sell to the Tote, signing the sale and purchase agreement for this divestment on the same day that the purchase of the Coral business was agreed. It would appear that this approach was perceived to address any likely concerns which the competition authorities might have. However, this belief turned out to be misplaced, primarily because, following a reference, the MMC found that market conditions had materially changed since 1989 so that the methodology of the 1989 report was no longer an appropriate basis for analysing the impact of the merger on competition in 1997.[62]

A further example of completing prior to clearance in the hope that the regulatory risk is manageable is Scottish Radio Holdings plc and GWR

---

[59] See, e.g. *Group 4 Falck A/S and the Wackenhut Corporation*, Cm. 5624 (October 2002), which states thtat Group 4 Falck did not originally seek to acquire Wackenhut Corporation's 57% stake in Wackenhut Corrections Corporation, which was involved in the provision of custodial services in the UK (a market in which Group 4 Falck was also present), and had not originally sought to acquire it. However the vendor insisted on exiting from the interests held through the Wackenhut Corporation as a whole.

[60] *Ladbroke Group PLC and the Coral betting business*, Cm. 4030 (September 1998).

[61] This report concerned the acquisition of the William Hill betting business by Grand Metropolitan plc, which already owned Mecca Bookmakers Ltd. See *Grand Metropolitan plc and William Hill Organisation Limited*, Cm. 776 (August 1989).

[62] *Ladbroke Group PLC and the Coral betting business*, cited above.

Group plc's acquisition of the Galaxy 101 radio station. The transaction was completed prior to clearance but, following investigation by the Competition Commission, made subject to divestment undertakings. In this case, whilst no comment is made in the Competition Commission's report as to why the merger was not conditional on competition clearance, it is clear that the parties argued strongly that the relevant market for advertising was not limited to local radio. In taking this approach, they may well have been encouraged by the fact that in 2000, the Secretary of State had decided, in accordance with the Director General of Fair Trading's advice, not to refer GWR's acquisition of a regional radio station in East Anglia, where it already owned four local radio stations. The DTI's press release announcing the decision not to refer the merger specifically notes the Director General's view at that time that local radio advertisers could consider switching to local newspaper advertising.[63] By contrast, in relation to the acquisition of Galaxy 101, the Director General concluded that radio advertising was distinct from other types of advertising, and recommended a reference.[64]

These two examples show the difficulties in second-guessing the conclusions which the OFT and/or Competition Commission will reach. Whilst these difficulties may to some extent be addressed through the informal advice or confidential guidance process, there is no doubt that an assessment of likely customer and competitor reactions to the merger is an essential element in any evaluation of the risk of a reference to the Competition Commission and this is an area where the parties must reach their own conclusions. In particular, aggressive opposition to a merger by a third party may increase the level of scrutiny of a merger beyond that which was anticipated.[65] This is not to say, however, that it is never appropriate to complete a transaction on the basis that, whilst there may be a risk of a reference to the Competition Commission, the risk of the transaction ultimately being made the subject of divestment undertakings is sufficiently low to warrant purchasing unconditionally. For example, the merger of VNU Entertainment Media UK Ltd and Book Data Ltd was completed unconditionally and subsequently cleared by the Competition Commission, notwithstanding that it created a monopoly in the supply of commercial bibliographic data services.[66] Similarly, Linpac's completed acquisition of

---

[63] DTI press release P/2000/728 of November 2, 2000. See further the Director General's advice, which noted that the MMC had concluded in previous inquiries that radio advertising was a distinct economic market from other types of advertising but nevertheless stated a belief that on the facts of that case, there might be some substitutability for advertisers between local newspapers and local radio advertising, and that several advertisers had indicated that they would consider such a switch. See the Director General's advice of October 18, 2000, *Acquisition by GWR Group plc of the radio interests of the Daily Mail and General Trust plc.*

[64] See the Director General's advice of December 20, 2002, *Completed acquisition by Vibe Radio Services Ltd of Eastern Counties Radio Ltd and Galaxy Radio Wales and the West Ltd.* The approach of treating radio advertising as a distinct services market was consistent with a number of previous MMC/Competition Commission reports.

[65] A development under the Act, moreover, is that the parties must consider not only the risk that third parties might try to provoke a reference or argue to the Competition Commission that the transaction should be blocked, but also that, even where clearance is given by the OFT or the Competition Commission, third parties might seek to have it overturned by the Competition Appeal Tribunal. See further Ch.10 below.

[66] *VNU Entertainment Media UK Limited and Book Data Limited*, Cm. 5779 (March 2003).

the Paxton returnable transit packaging business was cleared despite creating shares in excess of 60 per cent in a number of the economic markets within the business sector.[67] In both cases, it was the high aggregate market share of the merged entity which prompted the reference, but an assessment of other aspects of the relevant market conditions resulted in positive outcomes.[68]

In other cases the purchaser may take the view that however likely the possibility of a reference to the Competition Commission, circumstances within the particular industry will have so changed by the time the Competition Commission comes to report its findings, as to make remedies requiring modification of the transaction or divestment substantially less likely. Whether that was the view of AAH in acquiring Medicopharma's pharmaceutical wholesaling assets[69] is not known; but it is notable that the recommendations for disposal made by the MMC were not in the end thought necessary by the Secretary of State (notwithstanding his earlier acceptance of them), due to the entry into the market of a new competitor.[70]

3.019

In some cases, the purchaser may be tempted to adopt the high risk strategy that in the time taken for third parties to complain and the OFT to evaluate the merger and refer it to the Competition Commission (particularly if no announcement has been made by the parties), it will have been possible to merge the business acquired with its existing business. In such circumstances the purchaser might hope that unravelling the merger if it were subsequently found to result in a substantial lessening of competition by the Competition Commission would be extremely difficult. However, the regulatory authorities now have extensive power to take steps to keep businesses separate pending their investigations, as is discussed at para.3.055 and Ch.5 below. Whilst under the FTA so-called "hold separate" orders or undertakings could only be made or accepted once a reference to the Competition Commission had been made, the OFT now has power to accept "initial undertakings" from the parties to a completed merger to prevent them from taking any "pre-emptive action", *i.e.* action which might prejudice a reference or any remedies ultimately required by the Competition Commission.[71] In situations where the parties refuse to give undertakings, the OFT also has powers to make orders to similar effect.[72] Accordingly, attempts to consolidate the businesses may now be thwarted at the earliest stages of the process of competition scrutiny. The new powers of the OFT to accept hold-separate undertakings or make orders increase the flexibility with which it can deal with completed merger cases where potential premature integration is a concern. Indeed in some cases where appropriate hold separate undertakings are offered, the OFT may be

---

[67] *Linpac Group Limited and McKechnie Paxton Holdings Limited* Cm. 5496 (May 2002).

[68] In the case of *VNU/Book Data*, the Commission found that, in the absence of the merger, VNU would have exited the market in any case, and that conditions of competition were thus better with the merger (see further paras 6.109 and 6.110 of Ch.6). In *Linpac/Paxton*, the Commission found that the merged entity would not be able to exercise market power because of strong countervailing purchaser power (see further paras 6.073, 6.074 and 6.088 of Ch.6).

[69] See para.3.071, above.

[70] See DTI press release P/92/679 of October 23, 1992.

[71] See s.71 of the Act, in particular ss.71(2) and 71(8) of the Act.

[72] These powers are discussed in detail at para.3.055, below.

prepared to consider a completed merger at greater length, which may enable a reference to be avoided. Moreover, the OFT now has powers to extend the statutory deadline for a reference, as is discussed at paras 2.023 and following of Ch.2. Again, this may enable discussions to reach the point where the OFT concludes that a reference is no longer necessary.

Finally, there remains the option of taking the regulatory risk, completing and seeking to keep a low profile, but then unravelling the transaction if it proves unacceptable to the OFT. This strategy might be possible in particular sectors where assets change hands relatively frequently and integrating—or extricating—assets from a parent group's portfolio is regularly achieved and does not involve wholesale restructuring of the business. Tesco purchased three stores as separate transactions at various times from the Co-op Group.[73] In relation to two of those acquisitions, the OFT concluded that the four month statutory deadline for reference under the Act had passed.[74] In relation to the third acquisition, the OFT concluded that its duty to refer was engaged. However Tesco offered an undertaking in lieu to divest the store altogether, and no reference was made; effectively, Tesco offered to unravel the acquisition.[75]

It should be borne in mind that the fact that a merger is referred does not mean that prohibition is inevitable—in fact, historically around half of all mergers referred to the Competition Commission (and its predecessor the MMC) are cleared unconditionally and only around a quarter are blocked outright.[76] Clearly, with only four merger references under the Act completed by the Commission at the time of writing, it is too early to predict whether this pattern is likely to change. However, given that the Director General based his advice to the Secretary of State under the FTA essentially on whether the merger could be expected to lead to a substantial lessening of competition,[77] and given that the Secretary of State has similarly based his decisions on competition considerations for a number of

---

[73] See the OFT's decision of February 2, 2004, "*Completed acquisitions by Tesco plc of the Co-Operative Group's stores in Uxbridge Road, Slough, as well as Stapleford Lane, Toten, Nottingham and Towers Place, South Shields*".

[74] See further para.2.020 of Ch.2.

[75] These unusual circumstances are perhaps explained by the OFT's note that Tesco's reason for purchasing the Slough store was to facilitate the renovation of Tesco's existing site in Slough over a number of months without the loss of a Tesco store in the area during the renovation period. Presumably the monthly revenues of a large store justified the transaction costs incurred in the purchase and then sale of the Co-op store.

[76] The proportion of mergers which are cleared unconditionally in any particular year varies considerably (in 2002, 65% of the 10 mergers reported on by the Competition Commission were cleared unconditionally (*i.e.* six outright clearances and one part clearance in relation to a newspaper merger where the sale of some of the titles was cleared unconditionally but the remainder were prohibited); whereas in 1998 only 16.7% (*i.e.* one) of the six mergers reported on were cleared unconditionally). However a clearer pattern emerges if the statistics are viewed over a longer period. Of the 95 merger references on which the MMC/Competition Commission reported from January 1, 1995 to July 1, 2004 (including four references under the Act), 47.4% were cleared unconditionally, 26.6% were cleared subject to conditions, 25.0% were prohibited and one was abandoned before the Secretary of State had reached her decision on the MMC's report (which had recommended prohibition). Of the five mergers reviewed by the Competition Commission as at the time of writing under the Act, two and part of the *Stena/P&O* case were cleared unconditionally, two were cleared subject to undertakings, and the other part of the *Stena/P&O* case was prohibited.

[77] See para.4.003 of Ch.4.

years in the overwhelming majority of cases,[78] there is no reason to expect a major shift in the likelihood of prohibition following reference. That said, one factor which might increase the likelihood of reference is the emphasis which the courts have placed on the adequacy of the evidence and reasoning in the OFT's decision[79]: this may mean that marginal cases which might have been cleared under the FTA are now referred because there is insufficient evidence to justify a clearance.[80] However, this factor should not affect the likelihood of a finding by the Competition Commission that a merger is expected to result in a substantial lessening of competition. It may therefore be that over time, the proportion of mergers which are cleared unconditionally following a reference slightly increases under the Act.

The OFT's approach in the absence of notification

The OFT investigates all mergers and proposed mergers which come to its attention, whether or not they are formally notified and even if they have already gone through the informal advice or confidential guidance processes. A merger may come to its attention through information provided by the parties themselves, through press reports,[81] through third party representations, via the European Commission or a national competition authority or sometimes, where another division within the OFT alerts the Mergers Branch of a merger occurring in a market which they are monitoring for other reasons. Increasingly, co-operation between the national competition authorities of the EU Member States through participation in the European Competition Network, as well as wider international co-operation through the International Competition Network, means that the OFT will become aware of a merger because it has been notified for clearance in another Member State or other jurisdiction.[82]

3.020

The initial step in the OFT's inquiry, when information has not been received from the parties themselves, is to send a preliminary letter to the parties, normally addressed to the Company Secretary at the registered office, requesting details of the transaction. Typically, such a letter will explain the basis on which the OFT may have jurisdiction to review the merger and will append an annex requesting information along the following lines:

(i)   names of the parties involved and a brief description of the transaction, including the reasons underlying it and the actual or intended date of completion;

---

[78] See para.1.001 of Ch.1.

[79] See paras 3.068 et seq., below.

[80] The OFT has indicated that it expects a slight increase in the number of references made each year, as is discussed in para.4.007 of Ch.4, below.

[81] The duty of the OFT to keep itself informed about mergers is inherent in its duty to refer all qualifying mergers, completed or anticipated, which have resulted or are expected to result in a substantial lessening of competition (see ss.22 and 33 of the Act). Section 5 of the Act also specifies that the OFT has the function of acquiring and reviewing information about matters related to carrying out its role, so as to ensure that it can take informed decisions and carry out its role effectively. In practice newspapers and trade journals are monitored regularly so as to identify reports on prospective and completed mergers which may qualify for investigation.

[82] This may be a relevant consideration in deciding whether to "keep quiet" about a merger in the UK.

(ii)   a brief description of the businesses of the parties and any areas of overlap between the purchaser and the target business;

(iii)   information needed to establish whether the OFT has jurisdiction to consider the merger, *i.e.* turnover of the target business and a brief description of the main products and services supplied by the parties, with estimates of share of supply in any areas where there is a overlap;

(iv)   details of any other countries where the merger has been notified;

(v)   contact details for the five main customers and competitors for each of the purchaser and the target business in each area of overlap of products or services supplied.

How the parties choose to respond to such an enquiry will depend upon the nature of the transaction and the extent of any perceived regulatory issues. For example, they may simply respond by way of a short letter providing the requested information; alternatively they may decide to prepare a detailed memorandum comparable to a notification informing the OFT of the transaction and seeking clearance (or indeed by means of a Merger Notice in relation to an uncompleted merger) Accordingly, the points which follow should be regarded as general guidelines only. The OFT's guidance on the content of submissions is set out in Ch.4 of its *Procedural Guidance*.

Seeking clearance

3.021   Whilst there are sometimes good commercial reasons why a merger is completed prior to clearance, it remains the case that in most cases where a merger may be thought to raise potential competition concerns, a prudent purchaser will seek to obtain clearance before committing itself unconditionally to complete an acquisition. It has been explained above[83] that in certain circumstances confidential guidance may be desirable, and in cases where timing constraints do not permit an application for guidance to be made, or it is thought that no positive guidance would be forthcoming, a purchaser is likely to wish to obtain the vendor's agreement to making the purchase conditional upon clearance by the OFT or the Competition Commission. An alternative strategy may be to arrange the timing of the transaction so as to allow sufficient opportunity to obtain clearance prior to entering into a binding contract, but this possibility would be unavailable if the sensitivity of the transaction, for one or both of the parties, were such that total confidentiality must be maintained prior to signing a binding sale and purchase agreement. The OFT is prepared to commence the evaluation of prospective mergers prior to contract, but cannot do so if it is unable to seek the views of third parties. In such circumstances, the purchaser must choose between relying on confidential guidance or informal advice, persuading the vendor to accept a conditional agreement, or proceeding unconditionally, with the risks that that involves.

---

[83] See paras 3.004 *et seq.*, above.

The Enterprise Act has preserved the option which was available under the FTA of notifying a merger using either the standardised pro-forma of the Merger Notice,[84] or submitting a written submission in an unprescribed form. Under the FTA, both styles of notification were regularly used to notify the OFT of a merger and to seek clearance and, except for certain limitations on the availability of the Merger Notice[85] prenotification procedure, the form of notification remains largely a matter of choice for the parties involved.

A third option has existed for mergers which require notification in at least two of the UK, France and Germany, of using a common notification form agreed between the competition authorities of these three jurisdictions. At the time of writing, the common notification form was still referred to in the OFT's *Procedural Guidance*,[86] but in fact it had fallen out of use and was no longer posted on the OFT's website. It had not been re-issued to reflect the merger regime reforms introduced by the Enterprise Act since it was originally issued. In practice, the form has rarely been used,[87] primarily because, at least as originally drafted, it covered the basic information required in all three jurisdictions, but not the *whole* of the information which is required by each of the three authorities. Moreover national notifications are always made in the local language and are usually drafted by lawyers in that jurisdiction. So since translations and supplemental submissions would be needed even where the form was used, it is not clear that it would have saved time and/or cost to any material degree. It remains to be seen whether the idea of a common notification form will be revived.

Prenotification discussions

The OFT's *Procedural Guidance* formally acknowledges the possibility for the parties to engage in prenotification discussions prior to submission of a notification.[88] This process is similar to the standard procedure in relation to EC Merger Regulation notifications, where it is considered to be "best practice" to supply the European Commission with at least one draft of Form CO for review and comment by the case officer who will handle the case, prior to the formal filing.   3.022

At the EC level (where there is no equivalent to the confidential guidance or informal advice procedures), it would be unusual *not* to have prenotification discussions; by contrast in the UK regime it is simply a facility available to the parties if they wish.[89] Prenotification discussions are not seen as

---

[84] s.96 of the Act provides for notification using a Merger Notice and empowers the OFT to prescribe the form of the Merger Notice (see in particular ss.96(2) and (5)). The OFT published the Merger Notice for the new regime in June 2003. The text of the Merger Notice and the accompanying guidance notes is set out in full in App.4.

[85] Primarily, the option of using the Merger Notice is not available in respect of completed mergers or those which remain confidential. See further para.3.028

[86] See para.3.26 of the OFT's *Procedural Guidance*.

[87] The authors understand that the common notification form has been used on only one occasion.

[88] See paras 3.19 and 3.20 of the OFT's *Procedural Guidance*.

[89] This difference of attitude towards pre-notification discussions perhaps reflects the different timetables within which the two authorities operate. In the context of the tight EC Merger Regulation deadlines, pre-notification discussions can be a very useful way to inform the European Commission about a merger and to facilitate commencement of its evaluation process before the clock has started to run.

"best practice" across the board by the OFT, and can be used or not, as the parties judge appropriate, although they may well be a beneficial approach in more complex cases involving detailed submissions. Prenotification discussions will usually involve submission of a reasonably finalised draft notification (whether a Merger Notice or a traditional written submission) followed by a meeting a few days later,[90] at which the OFT will discuss with the parties whether there are any parts of the notification where clarification or additional information is needed. This procedure is available whether or not the confidential guidance or informal advice procedures have been used, and is not subject to the same rigorous confidentiality requirements. That said, the process is limited to considering the completeness and usefulness of the draft submission, and whilst the process may shed light on the areas which the OFT is likely to focus on in assessing the merger (because, for example, additional information, evidence or explanation is requested on a particular point), it is not a route by which to receive a response, formal or informal, on the likelihood that a reference will be made.

The traditional written submission

3.023   As the OFT acknowledges in its Procedural Guidance, "over the years, companies and their advisers have generally preferred to advise the OFT of an anticipated or completed UK merger by means of an informal submission",[91] *i.e.* a traditional written submission. The question of when prenotification on a Merger Notice is appropriate is considered in more detail at para.3.037 below.

General principles

3.024   As a general principle, the OFT is prepared to discuss with the parties the nature of the information it will require in its evaluation and in any event often requests further information which it considers to be relevant during the course of its investigation.[92] The possibility of prenotification discussions has been highlighted above.[93] In all cases, whatever the level of complexity of the case, the OFT will wish to have details of the parties and the merger situation, including its nature, value and each party's reasons for entering into it. Administrative information, like contact details of the parties and their legal advisers should also be provided.[94] It would be normal for the OFT to request copies of the latest report and accounts of each of the parties and, where relevant, their respective parent companies, and so it is sensible for the party or parties submitting the written submission to supply these as annexes. The OFT is not normally interested in seeing the legal documentation recording the transaction. There may be reasons in a particular case why they might wish to do so, and the parties

---

[90] Para.3.19 of the OFT's *Procedural Guidance*.
[91] See para.3.26 of the OFT's *Procedural Guidance*.
[92] See also the OFT's *Procedural Guidance* at paras 4.4 to 4.6.
[93] See para.3.022, above.
[94] Increasingly, the OFT uses email to contact parties and their advisers and this information should be given alongside phone and fax numbers.

themselves may have reasons for wishing to append any relevant agreements,[94A] but in the majority of cases this is unnecessary. Where the transaction structure is complex, narrative explaining the structure is typically more helpful to the OFT than the contractual documents themselves.

Increasingly, the OFT requests copies of internal documents, including board papers, that were prepared for evaluating the merger, and in particular its competitive impact. The OFT now also routinely requests copies of customer research that either of the parties has undertaken in relation to the relevant products. These documents, which are required to be provided to the European Commission when completing Form CO in connection with mergers having a Community dimension, tended in the past to be requested only by the Competition Commission following a reference. The change in approach is sensible, given that these documents are available "off the shelf" (in the sense that they will either exist in any case, or will not, and do not have to be drafted specifically for the OFT's investigation) and will often be highly relevant to the OFT's competition analysis.

There is no statutory deadline for the assessment of a transaction which is notified on a traditional written submission, although the OFT sets itself a non-binding administrative deadline of 40 working days for its assessment such cases, as is confirmed in para.3.26 of the OFT's *Procedural Guidance*. The s.24 four-month deadline for a reference (see para.2.023 and following) will apply in the normal way and in some cases concerning completed mergers which are not notified or do not come to the OFT's attention until fairly late in the day this can effectively operate as a statutory deadline for the OFT's assessment (of course there are provisions enabling an extension of the deadline in such circumstances, as is discussed in para.3.052).

Jurisdiction

There may be a preliminary point to address in the written submission, as to whether the OFT has jurisdiction.[95] Sometimes, the issue may be whether a merger situation has arisen at all, although more often the question is whether the merger qualifies for investigation on the basis that at least one of the jurisdictional threshold tests set out in s.23 of the Act is satisfied.[96] Whilst it was usually relatively easy to evaluate whether the gross assets test

3.025

[94A] For example to seek confirmation that the restrictions in the agreements are considered to be ancillary: see further para.3.077 below.

[95] See further paras 4.7 to 4.9 of the OFT's *Procedural Guidance*.

[96] Of the various mergers under the Act which had been found not to qualify as at June 1, 2004, only one of the OFT's decisions contains a detailed discussion of whether there was a merger situation at all. See the OFT's decision of March 22, 2004 "*Completed transaction between Unum and Swiss Life (UK) plc*", where the OFT concluded that the enterprises had not ceased to be distinct and thus there was no merger situation. See para.2.004 of Ch.2, above. The detailed analysis provided by the OFT in this case may well reflect the fact that an earlier proposed merger between the same parties had been considered by the OFT the previous year and referred to the Competition Commission (see the OFT's decision of October 31, 2003, *Proposed acquisition by Unum Limited of the employee benefits business of Swiss Life (UK) plc*). The parties withdrew those merger plans (causing the reference to be cancelled) and then renegotiated the commercial transaction. The restructured arrangements were subsequently held by the OFT not to constitute a merger situation and thus fell outside its jurisdiction.

had been met under the FTA, the turnover test which has replaced it may involve a more complex assessment, because it may not be possible to identify the appropriate turnover figure from published accounts.[97] The share of supply test may raise some difficulties, although since the share of the merged entity is not calculated by reference to a properly defined relevant economic market, it is usually sufficient for the OFT to establish that the merged entity will have a 25 per cent share of some category of goods or services.[98] In the event that there is doubt as to whether the jurisdictional thresholds are met, it is possible to make submissions on this point alone, before adding submissions as to the substantive assessment of the case.[99] In general though, where there is doubt about jurisdiction, in the interests of efficiency it is usual for the written submission to argue both that the merger does not qualify for investigation but, in the alternative, that if it does qualify, it raises no issues which require further consideration by the Competition Commission. This ensures that there is no time delay while the parties prepare the second round of submissions.[1]

The other circumstance in which the OFT's jurisdiction may be in doubt is where it is thought possible or likely that the EC Merger Regulation applies or that there may be a transfer of jurisdiction between the OFT and the European Commission pursuant to the "corrective mechanisms" of the EC Merger Regulation. The issues that need to be considered in such a case, and the procedure that should be adopted, are explained in Ch.2. As a general rule, it is advisable to keep the OFT informed of notifications to and discussions with the European Commission in cases where there is doubt over jurisdiction, not least because the OFT will receive and comment on each Form CO that is lodged with the European Commission, and will express its views on questions of jurisdiction (including whether a full function joint venture has been created) and whether the market constitutes a distinct market within the UK for the purposes of Art.9 of the EC Merger Regulation.

The scope and contents of the submission where no substantial lessening of competition arises

3.026   Where the parties consider that it is clear that a completed or anticipated merger will not give rise to a substantial lessening of competition within any UK product or service market, the submission may be quite short (and is likely to be necessary at all only because the OFT has written to the parties requesting information, or because the terms and conditions of an offer to which the Takeover Code applies require that clearance be sought). In such circumstances it is normally sufficient, having described the parties and the transaction, to demonstrate that there is no horizontal overlap between the merged parties' businesses, or that such overlapping activities as there are between the merged enterprises are *de minimis*[1A] in nature and extent, that

---

[97] See further paras 2.021 *et seq.* of Ch.2, above.
[98] See further paras 2.017 *et seq.* of Ch.[2], above.
[99] The OFT cannot proceed to the substantive competition assessment if the jurisdictional tests are not met.
[1] Of course one option would be to seek informal advice on the jurisdictional issue in advance.
[1A] Under the Merger Notice, mergers which lead to a horizontal overlap of less than 10 per cent by value or volume are considered to be *de minimis*. See Question 16 of the Merger Notice, reproduced at App.4.

no material vertical relationship exists or is created and that no other issues are raised that might give rise to competition concerns. In relation to such cases the OFT will make its own enquiries and solicit the views of third parties, and may seek clarification from the parties on points of detail, but will generally not spend time on detailed market analysis where there is self-evidently no issue arising from the merger that could conceivably lead to a substantial lessening of competition.

There is no statutory timetable for assessment by the OFT of a traditional submission and so there is no risk, as there would be with a Merger Notice, that a submission which is too brief will be formally rejected by the OFT. That said, as the OFT highlights in its *Procedural Guidance*,[2] the OFT can (and does) suspend the administrative timetable for assessment of the merger where a submission has material gaps in it, or may not start the administrative clock running until it is satisfied that the submission is sufficiently detailed for it to start its analysis. Alternatively the OFT may elect to use its formal information gathering powers,[3] which again can cause the clock to be stopped until the parties have furnished what is required. Prenotification discussions may be a way to reduce the risk that a submission is considered inadequate, although in the simple cases discussed in this section, the risks may not be sufficiently great to warrant such an approach.

The scope and contents of the submission where a substantial lessening of competition may arise

Where the parties recognise that there are issues arising from the merger which may, at least on first analysis, appear to give rise to a possible substantial lessening of competition within any UK product or service market, there is a need for greater effort to be made in the preparation of the written submission, which may be followed by responses to supplementary questions and by meetings with OFT officials to discuss and expand upon points of difficulty. The manner in which the OFT evaluates a merger and the categories of information it requires for that purpose are described and discussed in detail in Ch.6, and it is relevant here to mention in outline only the areas that are likely to interest the OFT in all but the most straightforward cases.   **3.027**

As noted in Ch.1, and explained in more detail in Ch.6, the basic objective of merger policy in the United Kingdom is the maintenance and promotion of effective competition and the protection of consumers from any undue reduction in the competitiveness of markets brought about as a result of merger activity. It follows that the OFT will potentially require information from the parties a wide range of information relating to:

(i)   all the products and/or services which the merging enterprises both provide (overlapping products services);

(ii)   market definition for each of those overlapping products and/or services, in particular information to assess the issues of demand and supply substitutability and geographical market definition;

---

[2] See para.3.28 of the OFT's *Procedural Guidance*.
[3] See further para.3.052, below.

(iii) the position of the merging businesses in each of those relevant markets, including the value and volume of their sales, and the respective shares in each market enjoyed by each of the merging enterprises and their competitors (to the extent that the parties can estimate them) and details of any regional or local concentrations;

(iv) the nature and extent of any vertical or conglomerate links between the enterprises (*i.e.* supplier-customer relationships or where the merging businesses have common customers across a range of products) and information about the relevant upstream and downstream markets;

(v) trends in the market as to entry and exit, other mergers, the extent of imports and the potential for further imports;

(vi) the cost of market entry and expansion, and the nature and extent of any barriers to entry or growth;

(vii) the extent of any countervailing buyer power which may be exercised by the merged entity's customers; and

(viii) names, addresses and contact telephone numbers of principal customers, competitors and suppliers (to enable the OFT to seek their views).

Clearly the parties will wish to present this information in the light that most favours their case; but in doing so it should always be borne in mind that arguments put forward in support of the merger (and any put forward against it by third parties or an unwilling target) will be subject to close scrutiny and analysis by the OFT. It is likely to be counter-productive to present arguments that cannot be supported by facts or data, since the effect will be, at best, to overshadow or dilute the stronger arguments and, at worst, to undermine the credibility of the party and its advisers and cause those stronger points to be doubted. The OFT does not apply formal rules of evidence and arguments can be backed up with anecdotal evidence as well as more concrete data and evidence (although clearly the latter is preferable, where available). Where the evidence relates to third parties, the OFT may well check it with them if possible. Tactics such as making statements anticipating the likely reaction of customers or competitors can therefore be risky because the OFT may put the statement to that customer or competitor for its reaction. In general, untenable claims will usually come to light. Finally, whilst there are no strict requirements for the type of evidence which may be submitted, it is a criminal offence for either the notifying parties or third parties—including their advisers—knowingly or recklessly to supply false or misleading information to the competition authorities.[4]

Statutory prenotification

3.028   Sections 96 to 102 of the Act provide for the voluntary prenotification of mergers through the Merger Notice procedure, continuing the availability

---

[4] See further para.3.054, below.

of this procedure which was introduced under the FTA as from April 1, 1990.[5] This procedure may only be used to provide formal notification of an anticipated merger which has already been made public; it cannot be used either for completed mergers, or for anticipated mergers which have not yet been made public.[6] The Merger Notice procedure has the advantage over the non-statutory traditional submission procedure of offering a defined statutory period within which the merger situation has to be referred to the Competition Commission, which is of particular significance where completion must be achieved within a finite time frame. Under s.96(3), a merger is deemed to have been cleared if, by the end of the statutory period, it has not been referred to the Competition Commission— although in practice it is the OFT's policy to issue an announcement before the end of the period and mergers are not cleared by default through elapse of the statutory deadline.[7]

A party wishing to prenotify must do so on a prescribed standard form, known as a Merger Notice, which requires the provision of information about the parties, the transaction and the markets involved, being essentially the information required by the OFT in considering any merger of any complexity (the information burden is greater than that which would be required in relation to a merger where there is no material risk that a substantial lessening of competition might arise).[8] Normally the party which completes the form, the pre-notifier, will be the proposed purchaser, although there is no reason why the vendor should not do so.[9] The Merger Notice takes the form prescribed by the OFT under s.96(2)[10] and is reproduced at App.4.

---

[5] This procedure was introduced under the Companies Act 1989, amended by the FTA (Amendment) (Mergers Prenotification) Regulations 1994, and, under the new regime under the Act, is now governed by ss.96 to 102 of the Act and the Enterprise Act 2002 (Merger Pre-notification) Regulations 2003 (SI 2003/1369) (referred to in this chapter as the "Merger Prenotification Regulations").

[6] This is because the OFT will wish to seek the views of third parties with an interest in the merger.

[7] The authors are aware of one case under the FTA where a merger was cleared because of a mistake over the deadline for a reference. The OFT's *Prior Notice of Publicly Proposed Mergers* guidance indicates that the statutory deadline takes effect at 5pm on the last day of the consideration period. In fact, the time of day of a reference decision is not usually an issue as the Press Office of the OFT has continued the practice of the Secretary of State of releasing the vast majority of decisions on merger reference (and clearance) at 11.00am or (less frequently) 3.00pm. Moreover, the Act does not actually specify the time of day at which the deadlines set out in s.97 expire. By contrast, the Merger Prenotification Regulations specify in a number of places that the deadline for various other steps taken by the parties, the OFT or the Secretary of State is 5pm (see, for example, Regs 5, 8(3), 11, 12 and 13(3)). Since there is no statutory time deadline for the decision whether to refer, strictly speaking, the OFT has until midnight on the final day of the period to reach its decision. However, in practice, the OFT applies the same 5pm deadline to its final decision as is imposed by the Merger Prenotification Regulations on various other steps under the Merger Notice procedure.

[8] See para.3.026, above which discusses the reduced information required in such circumstances.

[9] Note, however that the merger fee is payable by the acquiring party. For that reason the acquirer and its advisers will often wish to lead on the drafting of the Merger Notice. The merger fee is discussed at paras 3.083 *et seq.*, below.

[10] The Merger Notice and accompanying guidance notes are published by the OFT on its website. The OFT has also published guidance on these procedures generally: *Prior notice of publicly proposed mergers* (June 2003) available on the OFT's website.

Timing

3.029 The statutory timeframe for consideration by the OFT of a Merger Notice takes the following form:

(i) initial deadline: 20 working days from receipt of the Merger Notice or of the merger fee, if later[11];

(ii) possible extension of 10 working days, as required, at the OFT's discretion[12];

(iii) possible extension of 20 working days in public interest cases[13];

(iv) power for the OFT to "stop the clock" if a person has failed to provide information by a specified deadline[14];

(v) power for the OFT to "stop the clock" in order to negotiate undertakings in lieu of reference. If the parties refuse to give undertakings, the OFT will then have 10 working days to decide whether to make a reference[15];

(vi) power for the OFT to "stop the clock" where the European Commission is considering whether to assume jurisdiction over the merger[16] following a request under Art.22 of the EC Merger Regulation[17];

(vii) possible extensions and suspensions of the timeframe where the public interest provisions of the Act are activated.

The prescribed time period for consideration of a Merger Notice by the OFT begins at 9.00am on the first working day after receipt and acceptance by the OFT of the completed Merger Notice[18] and fee, provided that by that date the proposed merger has been publicly announced.[19] If it has not, the Notice will be rejected, and a further Notice will not be accepted until after a public announcement. It should be noted that any Notice received after 5.00pm or on a day which is not a working day[19A] will be deemed received

---

[11] s.97(1) of the Act. The merger fee is described below at paras 3.083 *et seq.*
[12] s.97(2) of the Act. This possibility does not apply in public interest cases.
[13] See ss.97(3) and (4) of the Act. See further para.3.083, below.
[14] See ss.97(5) and (6) of the Act and paras 3.052 *et seq.*, below.
[15] See ss.97(7) and 97(8) of the Act.
[16] See ss.97(11) to (13) of the Act.
[17] The procedures for passing jurisdiction to the EC Commission under Art.22 are discussed at paras 2.043 *et seq.* of Ch.2, above.
[18] Note that the Merger Notice will not be considered complete if the Declaration in Pt 3 is not signed.
[19] S.97(1). If, for strategic reasons, it is felt that the OFT should be put on notice of a merger prior to its announcement, the Merger Notice could be submitted as an unsigned confidential final draft by way of pre-notification discussions with the OFT. Under these circumstances the merger fee would not be paid and the clock would not start to run. The completed and signed Merger Notice would then be submitted with the merger fee on announcement of the proposed transaction.
[19A] Reg.2(1) of the Merger Prenotification Regulations specifies that for the purposes of the Regulations, "working day" means a day that is not Saturday, Sunday, Good Friday or Christmas Day, or a bank holiday in England and Wales. The same definition is set out in s.98(3) in relation to the various time limits set out in s.97.

the following working day, with time beginning to run from 9.00am on the first working day after that.[20] As noted above, time will also not start to run if the merger fee has not yet been received.[21]

The OFT's policy is that a Merger Notice is deemed to be validly received once delivered to them by post, by hand, by fax, or by email.[22] Where delivery is made by hand, delivery to the ground floor reception desk at Fleetbank House is sufficient to constitute valid receipt. In any case, it is advisable, particularly if delivery is likely to be made late in the day, to give advance warning by telephone to the Mergers Branch of its impending arrival, and to ensure that the reception desk issues a receipt recording the time of arrival. There is no prescribed form for a receipt; typically a photocopy of the covering letter to the Merger Notice might be used, on which the reception staff will stamp and mark the time of receipt.

The OFT will subsequently confirm by letter that the Merger Notice has been accepted and will indicate at the same time the date on which the initial 20 working days consideration period will expire.[23] If the consideration period is extended, the OFT will inform the pre-notifier in writing, though usually such written notification will have been preceded by a telephone call from the case officer responsible for the matter. The OFT also announces acceptance of a Merger Notice, together with any extensions of the statutory consideration period, via the Regulatory News Service.

It should be noted that the prescribed period for evaluation does not coincide with the bid timetable set down by the Takeover Code. The OFT once aimed, under the FTA, to advise the Secretary of State whether reference was warranted by the first closing date (21 days after posting of the offer document). This did not prove a feasible aim, because the length of the period between initial announcement and the posting of the offer document, which may be as much as 28 days, causes considerable variation to the period between the initial public announcement of the bid and the first closing date. If the bidder wishes to be able to declare its offer unconditional immediately following the first closing date, it will need to have announced its offer some time before posting the offer document and have filed its Merger Notice at that time in order to allow the OFT's decision to coincide with the first closing date, assuming no extension in the OFT's evaluation period is made.[24] However, the OFT is not bound by the offer

3.030

---

[20] See Reg.5 of the Merger Prenotification Regulations 2003.

[21] Art.9(1) of the Enterprise Act 2002 (Merger Fees and Determination of Turnover) Order 2003 (SI 2003/1370) ("the Merger Fees and Turnover Order") specifies that the fee becomes payable when the Merger Notice is submitted. Payment can be made by cheque, in which case the fee is deemed paid when the cheque is received (not when it later clears). If the cheque is subsequently dishonoured the statutory timetable does not stop, provided that the full fee is validly paid within the 20 working day initial period (see Reg.13 of the Merger Prenotification Regulations). Alternatively, payment may be sent to the OFT via the BACS system. In this case, information relating to this transfer must be forwarded to the Mergers Branch at the same time as the completed merger notice so that the payment can be matched with the appropriate submission. Any delay in matching the transferred fee with the merger notice may result in a delay in registering the notice and hence a delay in starting the clock.

[22] See the OFT's *Prior notice of publicly proposed mergers* at p.2.

[23] As noted above (at para.3.028), the OFT has indicated that the period for consideration expires at 5pm.

[24] See p.3 of the OFT's guidance *Prior notice of publicly proposed mergers*. The Takeover Code provides (at n.3 of Rule 31.6) that the Takeover Panel will normally extend Day 39 in

timetable and, if necessary, it has the discretion to extend the consideration period.

Completion of a Merger Notice

3.031   A detailed explanation of the relevance of the information required to be supplied in a Merger Notice is set out in Ch.6 in the context of an analysis of the evaluation and analysis of mergers by the OFT. This chapter explains in broad outline how the Notice should be completed, and by whom.

A Merger Notice may be given only by an authorised person; that is, a party carrying on an enterprise to which the notified arrangements relate.[25] However, the authorised person may then appoint a representative (typically its legal advisors) to act on its behalf in completing and delivering the Merger Notice and communicating with the OFT thereafter. Such an appointment must be notified to the OFT in writing[26]; in practice confirmation of authorisation is incorporated into the declaration and signature page at the end of the Merger Notice. Part One of the Merger Notice requires disclosure of the identity of the authorised person and the representative (if any), a brief description of the merger proposal, and a description of how the proposal has been publicised. The latter requirement is included because the prenotification procedure only applies to merger proposals that have been made public, and accordingly time will not begin to run until an announcement has been made.[27] A copy of the press release or other announcement of the proposed merger is required to be submitted with the Notice. As indicated above, the OFT invariably announces the receipt of a Merger Notice via the Regulatory News Service, indicating that the proposal has been notified to the OFT on the relevant date and indicating the date on which the period for considering the merger will end (unless subsequently extended).

Part Two of the Notice requires the authorised person to describe the merger proposal in detail by responding to a series of 18 questions covering:

(i)   the merger situation (the proposed arrangements, ownership and control of the merging enterprises before and following the merger, other enterprises which may cease to be distinct);

(ii)   jurisdiction (UK turnover of the target, description and share of supply for the main products or services supplied by each of the merging enterprises);

(iii)   financial information (most recent annual report and accounts, UK turnover of the acquirer and the value and form of the consideration for the acquisition[28]);

---

the event of a significant delay in the decision as to whether there is to be a reference to the Commission, pending the decision being announced; see para.3.002 above.

[25] See Reg.3 of the Merger Prenotification Regulations.

[26] See Reg.14 of the Merger Prenotification Regulations.

[27] The day following public announcement, assuming announcement before 5.00pm.

[28] In contrast to the FTA Merger Notice, information about gearing following the acquisition is not required. Although rarely an issue which would warrant reference on its own, where a purchaser with a high level of gearing acquires a business whose financial stability is a matter of public interest, this could give rise to concerns: see for example *PacifiCorp and The Energy Group plc*, Cm. 3816 (December 1997), where the MMC was concerned that

(iv)   the timing of exchange of contracts and completion;

(v)   the applicability of the Takeover Code[29] (effective closing date, and whether the merger has been recommended by the target's board[30]);

(vi)   the plans and motives behind the merger (reasons for the merger and plans for the merged businesses[31]);

(vii)   markets (this is the most detailed part of the Merger Notice and asks for detailed information necessary for market definition, information about market shares, the extent of rivalry in the market, import levels, barriers to entry, countervailing customer power, local competition issues, efficiencies and customer benefits, as well as any purchasing power which will be enjoyed by the merged entity and any vertical links between the parties).

The section on markets is likely to require the greatest effort in practice, since what is required is an economic analysis of each of the markets in which the merging enterprises are active, either horizontally or through downstream or upstream activities. How this analysis should be undertaken is explained in detail in Ch6.
    3.032

Part Three of the Notice comprises a declaration to be signed by the authorised person confirming that the Notice contains no information that is false or misleading in any material respect[32] and confirming the appointment (if any) of the authorised representative. If the declaration is signed by the representative of the acquirer itself, then the appointment of the authorised representative will be confirmed by a second signature on the same page. If the Merger Notice is signed by the acquirer's legal advisers, then it will be necessary to annex a letter from the acquirer confirming the

---

the high level of gearing of the Pacificorp holding company intended to take control of The Energy Group (a generator, supplier and distributor of electricity), would create significant financial pressures on the acquired energy business, potentially forcing higher dividends to be paid to the holding company than would otherwise be the case, and to under-investment, poorer service standards and/or higher prices in the longer term. In this case, the MMC found that the regulatory financial ring-fencing provisions in place would protect the electricity business from any such pressures and the acquisition was accordingly permitted. The issue of gearing was raised as a possible concern in relation to the entrepreneur Philip Green's proposed bid for Safeway plc, although the OFT concluded that it was unfounded. See OFT's advice *"Proposed acquisition by Trackdean Investments Limited of Safeway plc"* of March 13, 2003.

[29] To enable the OFT to confirm that the merger is not expected to take place prior to the end of the consideration period, which might result in the merger remaining liable for reference to the Competition Commission; see s.100(1)(b) of the Act and para.3.036, below.

[30] Two copies of the offer document and, where relevant, listing particulars are required to be enclosed, or the latest drafts of those documents, with final versions to be supplied when available.

[31] The OFT also requires copies of analyses, reports, studies and surveys submitted to or prepared for any member(s) of the Board, the conditions of competition or for shareholders' meetings, for the purposes of assessing or analysing the proposed transaction as regards competitors and market conditions. These documents may be of particular significance in assessing the likely impact of the merger on the conditions of competition.

[32] Under the Act, it is a criminal offence for a person to supply information which he knows to be false or misleading in any material respect. See further s.117 of the Act and para. 3.054, below.

appointment of the legal adviser and giving authorisation to sign the Merger Notice on its behalf. In practice, it is important to ensure that arrangements are made in good time to obtain all required signatures and authorisations. A Notice will be regarded as incomplete if it is not accompanied by the required documentation. It will also be deemed defective if not accompanied by the correct fee,[33] and the period for considering the Notice will not begin until the first working day after the fee has been received.

Whilst the intention of the Merger Notice is that it should be completed in the prescribed form, the ordering and division of subject matter between the various questions do not always coincide with the most appropriate way in which the case for the merger might be put to the OFT. Moreover, the decision to use the prenotification procedure may be taken at a fairly late stage in the proceedings, since it is essentially a strategic decision.[34] It is possible to draft a submission in the traditional, non-Merger Notice style, and then append it to a Merger Notice. The Merger Notice itself will then be completed with a series of cross-references to the main submission, supplemented with additional information where required to answer the Merger Notice questions fully, so that the answers to the various Merger Notice questions can be precisely identified by the OFT. If this format is adopted, it is essential that the cross-referencing between the Merger Notice questions and the traditional-style submission is appropriately pin-pointed and precise, because the OFT is entitled to reject the Merger Notice and the fixed statutory timeframe will not begin to run where the OFT considers that all the information required by the Merger Notice questions has duly been supplied.

Rejection of a Merger Notice

3.033   The Act identifies four sets of circumstances in which a Merger Notice may be rejected by the OFT at any time during the consideration period[35]:

(i)   where the OFT suspects that any information given in the Merger Notice, or any information given subsequently in respect to requests for further information, is in any material respect false or misleading[36];

(ii)   where the OFT suspects that the parties do not propose to carry the proposed merger into effect;

(iii) where the parties fail adequately to provide the information specified in the Notice, or any subsequently requested information, or delay doing so;

(iv)   where the notified arrangements appear to fall within the EC Merger Regulation, being a concentration with a Community

---

[33] A discussion of the fees payable for merger clearances is set out below at paras 3.083 *et seq.*
[34] See further para.3.037, below.
[35] See s.99(5) of the Act. See also p.4 of the OFT's guidelines *Prior notice of publicly proposed mergers.*
[36] This may also give rise to a criminal offence: see s.117 of the Act and para.3.054, below.

dimension, which would remove jurisdiction from the UK (and any other EU Member State's) competition authorities to consider the merger.

Note also that if the merger fee is not paid,[37] the Merger Notice will not be rejected, but the statutory clock will not start to run.[37A]

The OFT may reject a Merger Notice at any time, whether during the original consideration period or any extension. The rejection is required to be in writing (by fax, email or in a letter sent by first class post), although advance notice would normally be given by telephone by the case officer. In practice, the power to reject was used sparingly under the FTA, with OFT officials preferring, where possible, to deal with omissions from and defects in a Merger Notice informally in discussion with the notifying parties and there is no reason to believe that this pragmatic approach will not continue.

Further information

The OFT may require clarification of certain points or generally request further information under s.99(2) of the Act and will specify the time by which the information must be provided. If the information is not supplied by 5pm on the specified day, the OFT may reject the Merger Notice[38] or stop the clock on the consideration period.[39] Such requests are normally made in the first instance by telephone, though this is followed up by written notice specifying the date by which such information is to be provided. In reality, it will normally be in the interests of the parties to supply the requested information as quickly as possible, and the notifier is therefore unlikely to exceed the time limit specified. Clearly, if there were a danger of that happening, because of the time needed to prepare the information requested, for example, it would be prudent to inform the OFT by telephone as soon as possible, with a view to negotiating an extension of time. Inevitably, if further information is requested which cannot be supplied immediately, the chances increase that the OFT will "stop the clock" and thereby extend the prescribed consideration period. If essential information requested by the OFT is not supplied, the risk of a reference to the Competition Commission will increase, unless the Merger Notice is withdrawn so that the statutory time limits no longer bind the OFT. The issues surrounding withdrawal of a Merger Notice are discussed in the next paragraph.

3.034

Withdrawal of a Merger Notice

A party filing a Merger Notice may withdraw it at any time, by writing to the OFT to that effect.[40] This might be necessary if the terms of the proposal have changed, if the information given in the Notice is found to have been materially misleading, if the merger is no longer to be proceeded with or if

3.035

---

[37] See para.3.083 and following.
[37A] See s.97(1) of the Act.
[38] See s.99(5)(c) of the Act.
[39] See s.97(5) and (6) of the Act.
[40] See Reg.7 of the Merger Prenotification Regulations.

it appears that the timing of the OFT investigation may become too tight. In the latter case, the parties may decide, tactically, that it is better to lose the certainty of the Merger Notice timeframe than run the risk that the OFT is forced to make a reference because there is insufficient remaining time to persuade them that the merger will not lead to a substantial lessening of competition. However, the merger fee cannot be refunded unless the merger is caught by the EC Merger Regulation, is found not to qualify, or is referred to the European Commission under Art.22 of the EC Merger Regulation.[41]

In practice, the OFT may be prepared to accept amendments to a Merger Notice provided that the timetable is not threatened. Alternatively, if requested, the OFT will continue to evaluate the merger outside the prenotification procedure, where the Merger Notice is withdrawn. In the full year 2003, 32 mergers were notified using a Merger Notice. Seven of these were subsequently withdrawn, of which one appears to have been withdrawn because the transaction was abandoned; one was ultimately cleared; one was cleared subject to undertakings in lieu; and four were referred (and in each case subsequently abandoned).[42] The fact that in over half of the examples where a Merger Notice was withdrawn, the parties were unable to persuade the authorities that a reference was not appropriate demonstrates the risks of filing a Merger Notice with a view to withdrawing it if the case becomes difficult. The constraints of the Merger Notice timeframe can mean that there is not a great deal of flexibility in the later stages for the OFT to re-open the investigation and take a more leisurely look at the issues or to process large amounts of new information. Beyond a certain point in the investigation, a withdrawal may not make any difference to the outcome of the OFT's decision because the OFT's internal procedures will be too far advanced. Withdrawal cannot therefore be relied upon as a means, towards the end of the consideration period or at the point at which a reference to the Competition Commission begins to appear likely, to give the OFT further time to consider its decision.

Circumstances in which a reference remains possible notwithstanding clearance under a Merger Notice

3.036   Although the principle of prenotification is that avoidance of a reference can be presumed if a reference has not been made by the end of the prescribed period (or any extension), under s.100 of the Act there are certain situations in which this presumption ceases to apply, making the merger liable to reference to and investigation by the Competition Commission. Apart from the Merger Notice being withdrawn by the pre-notifier[43] or rejected by the OFT under s.99(5),[44] this might occur where:

---

[41] See Art.10 of the Merger Fees and Turnover Order, and para.3.085, below. In practice, if a Merger Notice is withdrawn in circumstances where no refund is possible, the OFT will credit the fee which has already been paid against the invoice which will be issued as a matter of course (in non-Merger Notice cases) when the OFT's decision on whether to refer the merger is announced.

[42] The authors are grateful to the OFT for providing these statistics.

[43] See s.100(1)(f) of the Act.

[44] See s.100(1)(a) of the Act.

(i) before the expiry of the evaluation period, or any extension of it, two or more of the enterprises to which the Merger Notice relates cease to be distinct from one another (*i.e.* the merger between them is completed)[45];

(ii) one of the enterprises to which the Merger Notice relates enters into a merger with a third party before the arrangements which are the subject of the Notice are carried into effect (clearly this further merger might cause the OFT to view the pre-notified transaction differently)[46];

(iii) the merger is not carried into effect within six months of the expiry of the evaluation period (since competitive conditions in the market might have changed by then)[47];

(iv) information supplied by the pre-notifier or any associated company (whether in the Notice or otherwise) is subsequently found to be materially false or misleading (which might have caused the Notice to have been rejected if such information had been known during the evaluation period)[48]; or

(v) any material information which is or ought to have been disclosed by the notifying party, its associate or subsidiary, and which is material to the notified arrangements, has not been disclosed at least five working days before the end of the original period or the extension. Such information must be given in writing.[49]

In addition, the Act provides that where a number of different transactions are treated under the Act as having all occurred on the same date and s.96(3) does not operate to prevent a reference in relation to the last of those transactions,[49A] then a reference may be made in relation to any of those transactions that occurred within six months prior to that date, or within the six months prior to the actual occurrence of any of the transactions so grouped together.[50]

As far as the authors are aware, as at the time of writing no merger cleared under the prenotification procedure had subsequently been referred to the Competition Commission under the FTA or the Act, and indeed such an event would be exceptional.

When is prenotification appropriate?

When the provisions introducing prenotification under the FTA were originally laid before Parliament, it was suggested by the Minister that the

3.037

---

[45] See s.100(1)(b) of the Act.
[46] See s.100(1)(d) of the Act.
[47] See s.100(1)(e) of the Act.
[48] See s.100(1)(g) of the Act.
[49] See s.100(1)(c) of the Act and Reg.4 of the Merger Prenotification Regulations.
[49A] Which presumably could be the case either because the pre-notification procedure was not used in relation to the last merger in the series, or because it was used, but the statutory consideration period has not yet expired.
[50] See ss.100(2) to (5) of the Act. A full discussion of the circumstances in which different transactions may be treated as a single transaction is set out in Ch.2 at paras 2.023 *et seq.*

changes being introduced were far-reaching and demonstrated the Government's commitment to accelerating the merger control process.[51] That claim seemed somewhat extravagant at the time, and in practice, the prenotification procedure has not been heavily used. In 1991, the first full year of the prenotification procedure, 38 Merger Notices were submitted (out of 285 merger situations considered by the OFT): thus, somewhat under 15 per cent of all cases examined that year were notified to the OFT under the new procedure. This level of usage is significantly lower than the Government originally anticipated,[52] although not materially different from the OFT's expectations. The OFT and many practitioners quickly realised that the prenotification procedure is often inappropriate: in particular, it is not ideally suited to mergers requiring a material degree of detailed analysis and investigation by the OFT, and is largely irrelevant and burdensome in cases that do not. This view has remained unchanged amongst most practitioners. The proportion of mergers which are pre-notified under the Act remains low[53] and the change in legislation has not significantly altered the factors which go into the decision of which notification route to use. Of the 87 qualifying mergers reviewed by the OFT under the Act to June 1, 2004, only nine are clearly indicated in the OFT's decisions as having been notified on a Merger Notice,[54-55] of which two were subsequently withdrawn to be treated as traditional written submissions. In the full year 2003 (during which cases were dealt with under both the FTA and, from June 20, 2003, the Act), 264 cases were considered, of which 32 (or 12 per cent) were notified under the prenotification Merger Notice procedure. Of these, seven were subsequently withdrawn. In both 2002 and 2001, 15 per cent of cases considered were filed using a Merger Notice.[56]

The prenotification procedure is probably most useful in three sets of circumstances: first, where there is some overlap between the businesses of

---

[51] The DTI's Blue Paper, *Merger Policy* (1988). The Blue Paper described the case for a non-mandatory prenotification arrangement in terms of efficiency:

> "The vast majority of merger cases considered by the OFT—well over 95 per cent—are cleared without reference to the MMC, and the aim of the proposed procedure is to facilitate the more rapid and efficient handling of those cases where it can be established at an early stage that there is no serious ground for contemplating a reference".

The Blue Paper, para.3.9.

[52] The Government had originally anticipated creating a strong incentive for using the Merger Notice pre-notification procedure by rendering "Mergers which are not pre-notified . . . liable to reference to the MMC for a period of up to five years", see the DTI's Blue Paper, "Merger Policy" (1988) at para.3.10. This has never, however, been introduced.

[53] In percentage terms, the proportion of mergers which are notified using a Merger Notice may increase under the Act, because the changes to the jurisdictional thresholds have reduced the total number of mergers over which the OFT has jurisdiction. See further [55].

[54-55] Table 1 in App.2 which shows that the proportion of all UK mergers which qualified for merger control scrutiny in 2003/2004 (18 per cent) was approximately half the historical level (typically around 35 per cent). The financial year 2003/2004 spanned the period of change from the FTA to the Act and the corresponding figures for 2004/2005, which will only include cases considered under the Act, may therefore show a further decline in the proportion of mergers which meet the jurisdictional thresholds. There are a further six cases where a Merger Notice may have been used, although it is unclear from the OFT's decision whether this was in fact the case.

[56] The authors are grateful to the OFT for providing the statistics for this analysis.

the merging enterprise so that full market information will be needed in any submission for clearance in any event, but either the overlap is not large, and the risk of a reference is judged to be low; secondly, where certainty as to the timeframe is essential; and thirdly, where the likelihood of a reference is considered to be high, in which case it is sometimes felt by the parties to be preferable to proceed to a reference as swiftly as possible and by a known deadline.

There are a number of limitations on the procedure's suitability in practice. First, as stated above, it can only be used for mergers in contemplation; completed mergers must still be notified to the OFT (if notified at all) in the traditional way. Secondly, prenotification would often not be appropriate in difficult or controversial cases, for example, in the case of a contested bid, or a merger involving significantly overlapping interests. In such cases the traditional procedure is likely to be preferable, giving the party or parties fewer constraints in putting forward their arguments, and placing the OFT under no time constraints to decide whether it is under a duty to make a reference to the Competition Commission, whereas under the prenotification system the OFT may be prompted to make a premature reference having insufficient time to assess a complex case.

It is important to note that the prenotification Merger Notice procedure does not provide an easy means of obtaining clearance in borderline cases. The OFT will not be hurried by impending time constraints into clearing a merger that might otherwise have been referred: indeed, it is probably more likely that the OFT would be persuaded by timing limitations to refer a merger that might have been cleared had the OFT had more time. If a proposal raises difficult issues regarding a substantial lessening of competition, therefore, it is likely to be preferable to use the traditional notification method. Where no significant issues arise, prenotification may be appropriate in some, but by no means all, cases. In the case of a straightforward private transaction, for example, it will often be regarded as appropriate not to seek clearance at all; and where clearance is sought in a simple case it is frequently sufficient (and acceptable) to provide the OFT with significantly less information than is required by the Merger Notice.[57]

Triggering the public interest regime and its impact on notification

As described in paras 2.025 and following of Ch.2 above, the Secretary of State retains power under the Act to decide to takeover from the OFT in the role of decision-maker in certain prescribed circumstances. At the time of writing, this power existed in relation to national security issues (including defence) and newspaper and media mergers, although the Secretary of State has power under s.58(3) of the Act to prescribe additional public interest considerations. The procedure followed by the OFT, the DTI/ Secretary of State and OFCOM in newspaper mergers is considered in detail in Ch.7 below, and a brief outline only will be given in this section in relation to those sectors. In relation to national security, no guidance has been published on the approach of the DTI/Secretary of State (or the Ministry of Defence) but such comment as can be made will follow below. At the time

3.038

---

[57] See further para.3.026, above.

of writing, the public interest regime provisions of the Act had not yet been used.[58]

Where the Secretary of State wishes to intervene in a merger under consideration by the OFT, he will issue an intervention notice under s.42 of the Act. It is not necessary that the merger should already be under scrutiny by the OFT, and it is certainly not the case that the merger needs to have been completed, before the Secretary of State can issue an intervention notice. The wording of s.42 does not preclude the Secretary of State taking the initiative to issue an intervention notice as soon as he becomes aware that "arrangements are in contemplation which, if carried into effect, will result in a relevant merger situation".[58A] This point is reflected in the DTI's guidance on media mergers, where it confirms that "the Secretary of State retains the ability to look at cases on [his] own initiative",[59] in addition to the duty of the OFT to inform the Secretary of State of any cases where he might wish to consider exercising the intervention powers.[60]

At the other end of the scale, an intervention notice can be issued at any time up to the point at which the OFT makes its decision whether to refer the merger. The DTI's guidance in relation to media mergers indicates that the Secretary of State will, as a matter of policy and precisely to avoid the undue uncertainty which would otherwise prevail, aim to take an initial decision on whether to intervene within 10 working days of the transaction being notified to the OFT or of the merger being brought to the Secretary of State's attention.[61] There is no such guidance in relation to mergers raising national security issues, although it is strongly to be hoped that the Secretary of State would apply the same approach.

Consultation on whether an intervention notice should be issued

3.039   The DTI's guidance on media mergers states at para.4.13 that the parties will be informed that the Secretary of State is considering issuing an intervention notice and will be invited to submit any views they may have on this point in writing. In reaching his decision whether to intervene in relation to a newspaper or media merger, the Secretary of State will not be advised by OFCOM (although he may request relevant information from it) but will take into account the following factors:

(i)   the parties' written submissions;

---

[58]   However, the European public interest regime under ss.67 and 68 of the Act, which mirrors the UK public interest regime where the UK wishes to intervene on public interest grounds under Art.21 of the EC Merger Regulation, had been used on two occasions at the time of writing, and certain analogies can be drawn from those cases.

[58A]   The authors understand, for example, that during 2004 the DTI kept a close watch on progress in relation to the negotiations for the sale of *The Daily Telegraph* national daily newspaper (and associated titles), well in advance of the transaction being reviewed by the OFT. In the end, the sale of *The Daily Telegraph* was cleared by the OFT without an intervention notice being issued by the Secretary of State. See the OFT's decision of October 11, 2004, *Completed acquisition by Press Acquisitions Limited of Telegraph Group Limited.*

[59]   See para.4.2 of the DTI's guidance *Public interest intervention in media mergers* (May 2004).

[60]   See s.57(1) of the Act.

[61]   See para.4.14 of the DTI's guidance *Public interest intervention in media mergers* (May 2004).

(ii)   complaints to and action taken by the Press Complaints Commission;

(iii)   relevant information or conclusions in any previous regulatory decisions;

(iv)   relevant published articles; and

(v)   any third-party representations received.[62]

As noted above, there is no guidance in relation to the approach of the Secretary of State in relation to national security issues, and no s.42 intervention notices had been issued as at the time of writing. However, it is to be hoped that the procedure would mirror the procedure for media mergers, particularly as regards informing the parties of the fact that issue of an intervention notice is being considered, and giving them an opportunity to submit observations. As regards the two examples of European intervention notices which had, at the time of writing, been issued and which both related to national defence considerations[63], it is not known whether the parties were given advance warning that the intervention notices were being considered, or what particular factors were taken into account in reaching the decision to intervene in each case.

Confidential guidance and informal advice on public interest considerations

The DTI's guidance in relation to newspaper and media mergers states that   3.040
informal advice and/or confidential guidance can be sought from the DTI as to the likelihood that an intervention notice will be served and from the DTI and OFCOM on whether a reference to the Competition Commission is likely.[64] These processes broadly mirror the informal advice and confidential guidance procedures of the OFT and are discussed in more detail in Ch.7.

In relation to national security mergers, there is no similar written guidance and at the time of writing it is not known whether the DTI/Secretary of State will offer informal advice or confidential guidance in relation to the possibility of intervention and/or the risk of a reference on public interest grounds.

To the extent that a merger in these sectors may raise competition issues, it is of course still the role of the OFT to advise the Secretary of State and so in relation to both national security mergers and newspaper and media mergers, informal advice or confidential guidance on any competition issues (as opposed to wider public interest issues) could be sought from the OFT in the normal way.

---

[62] See para.4.13 of the DTI's guidance *Public interest intervention in media mergers* (May 2004).

[63] See the DTI's press release P/2004/161 of April 26, 2004, *European intervention notice in relation to General Dynamics/Alvis* and the European intervention notice of the same date and the DTI's press release P/2004/311 of August 20, 2004 *Jacqui Smith issues European Intervention Notice in relation to proposed acquisition* and the intervention notice of the same date in relation to the proposed acquisition by Finmeccanica of GKN's shareholding in AgustaWestland.

[64] See paras 4.5 to 4.8 of the DTI's guidance *Public interest intervention in media mergers* (May 2004).

Submissions on public interest considerations

3.041　Even where the Secretary of State does decide to intervene, it is still the role of the OFT to investigate the extent to which competition issues may be raised by the merger. Accordingly, the basic considerations discussed above regarding the type of submission which might be appropriate and the content of any such submission—as regards competition issues, at least—are unchanged.

The parties may wish to make additional submissions to address public interest issues. In cases where a public interest intervention notice has been served before any notification has yet been submitted, or where an intervention notice seems very likely, the parties may prefer to include a discussion of public interest issues in their main submission to the OFT on competition issues[65], or at least to prepare separate submissions on competition and public interest issues in parallel.[65A] Conversely in cases where intervention is technically possible but where it is not clear whether the Secretary of State will wish to intervene, the parties may decide to keep their powder dry until they know whether public interest issues need to be dealt with. This would obviously reduce the risk of wasted time, effort and costs on preparing submissions which subsequently prove to be unnecessary. In *Archant/London Regionals Division of Independent News & Media plc*, a newspaper merger, the OFT's decision makes no reference to public interest considerations, suggesting that no submissions on such issues were received.[66]

In relation to newspaper and media mergers where the Secretary of State has issued an intervention notice, the Act provides that OFCOM shall prepare a report for the Secretary of State on the public interest considerations arising out of the merger.[67] OFCOM's guidance on media mergers indicates the type of information which it would wish to receive from the parties.[68] In these situations, the process by which the parties can make their views heard in relation to public interest considerations has been mapped out by the authorities in their guidance and is discussed in detail in Ch.7.

In relation to defence mergers, there is no nominated body charged with advising the Secretary of State on the public interest issues. It would seem

---

[65] The OFT may, if it wishes, advise on public interest issues as well as any competition concerns (see s.44(6) of the Act), although this is a discretion only and it tends to view its expertise as being primarily the competition analysis rather than any wider public interest considerations. See further para.3.066, below.

[65A] The latter approach would allow the public interest parts of the parties submissions to be copied to other relevant bodies, such as the DTI.

[66] See the OFT's decision of April 29, 2004, *Completed acquisition by Archant Ltd of the London Regionals Division of Independent News & Media plc*. It is not possible to infer from the silence in the OFT's advice that no public interest representations were made as s.57(1) provides that the OFT does not need to report to the Secretary of State on public interest issues raised which it believes the Secretary of State would consider immaterial in the context of the case in question. Compare the OFT's decision of March 24, 2004, *Anticipated merger of the Technical Services Divisions of Scottish Courage Limited and Carlsberg-Tetley Brewing Limited*, where the decision reports that, as required under s.57(2), the OFT had brought to the attention of the Secretary of State submissions made by third parties on possible public interest issues.

[67] See s.44A of the Act.

[68] See further in this respect Ch.7, below.

that the DTI will investigate these itself in consultation with other relevant government departments including, no doubt, the Ministry of Defence (MOD) (certainly in *General Dynamics/Alvis* and in *Finmeccanica/ Agustawestland*, the main advice on public interest issues was provided by the MOD).[69] There is also no guidance on what information the DTI would wish to consider under such circumstances, which bodies any submissions should be made to, and what the procedure will be. Under the FTA, the DTI did not enter into any discussion with the parties in relation to the Secretary of State's decision whether to refer. It remains to be seen whether the DTI will accept submissions directly from the parties on public interest considerations, or a different approach is appropriate. The issue of lobbying is discussed in more detail in Ch.8 below. There is a duty on the OFT, where a public interest intervention notice has been issued, to report to the Secretary of State in its advice on competition issues, representations which have been made to it in relation to the public interest issues.[70] The parties could therefore, as a minimum, make their submissions to the OFT in national security mergers, although the OFT is only obliged to submit a summary to the Secretary of State of the representations that it has received.

The nature of the national security/defence sector is such that businesses **3.042** in this sector usually have close relations with the MOD, which is likely to be one of their key customers. The MOD may have been consulted at the planning stages of the merger and may therefore be fully aware of the proposals before they come to the attention of the OFT or the DTI/ Secretary of State. The parties may therefore wish to make submissions on the public interest directly to the MOD, which can in turn be expected to liaise with the DTI and the Secretary of State and/or the OFT[71] in reaching the decision on whether public interest issues are raised by the merger which would warrant further investigation by the Competition Commission. If the MOD is supportive of a merger, this may well assist the parties in obtaining regulatory clearance.

The impact of the public interest regime on prenotification using a Merger Notice

In cases which raise possible competition concerns as well as possible public **3.043** interest issues, a Merger Notice can be used to notify the merger, subject to the usual limitations that the merger must be in the public domain and must

---

[69] See the report of the OFT pursuant to Arts 4(2) to (5) of the Enterprise Act 2002 (Protection of Legitimate Interests) Order 2003 (SI 2003/1592) of May 20, 2004, *Anticipated acquisition by General Dynamics Corporation of Alvis plc*, published on the DTI's website, which sets out the views of the MOD on the public interest issues. See also the report of the OFT of September 29, 2004, *Anticipated acquisition by Finmeccanica Societa Per Azioni of Agustawestland NV*, which similarly is primarily a summary of the MOD's views on the public interest issues arising out of the merger.

[70] See s.44(3)(b) of the Act. As noted, however, s.57(1) provides that the OFT does not have to report on issues raised which it does not believe the Secretary of State would consider to be material in the context of the transaction in question.

[71] Certainly in *General Dynamics/Alvis*, the OFT's report to the Secretary of State is focussed heavily on the views of MOD, but it is not possible to tell whether the MOD restricted itself to channelling its views through the OFT or also liaised directly with the DTI.

not have been completed.[72] The Merger Notice will need to be supplemented with any submissions which the parties wish to make on the public interest considerations.

As regards the statutory timetable for consideration of a Merger Notice case, the OFT has power to extend the deadline for the reference decision by a further 20 working days beyond the basic 20 day review period.[73] The Secretary of State has a further limited power to extend the period for considering a Merger Notice in circumstances where he decides to delay his decision whether to refer the merger.[74]

The OFT's evaluation procedure

3.044   As explained above, the OFT's investigation of a qualifying merger is usually initiated by the parties informing the OFT about the merger, and providing a written submission which describes the transaction and discusses any competition issues that the merger may raise. Alternatively, the OFT may become aware of a merger from the press, or third parties (such as competitors or customers) or from other Competition Policy divisions within the OFT, or from the European Commission or through communications with other members of the European Competition Network or International Competition Network. Once the OFT has become aware of a qualifying merger, the head of the Mergers Branch will appoint a case officer who will make an initial assessment of the merger from the parties' submission(s) and any further information available to the Office.[75]

An economist from the OFT will be assigned to the case and will consider, in conjunction with the case officer, whether the merger will potentially give rise to a substantial lessening of competition in any UK product or service market. If such issues arise, the economist will draw up a list of questions on such matters as market definition, market shares, barriers to entry and other aspects of the transaction for discussion with the parties, customers, competitors and other interested third parties such as trade associations, consumer associations and interested government departments.

In addition to information obtained in this way, the OFT also has access to a substantial amount of information on markets from a number of other sources:

(i)   industry files held in the OFT;

(ii)   files relating to other mergers;

(iii)   Competition Commission reports under the FTA and the Act (including both merger and monopoly/market investigations);

(iv)   past OFT decisions and judgments of the Competition Appeal Tribunal under the Competition Act 1998;

---

[72] See further paras 3.028 *et seq.*, above.
[73] See ss.97(3) and (4) of the Act.
[74] See ss.97(9) and (10) of the Act.
[75] For a description of the composition of the Mergers Branch, see Ch.1, above.

(v)   past decisions of the European Commission under the EC Merger Regulation and under Arts 81 and/or 82;

(vi)   the OFT's library, which keeps back issues of the trade press of various industries and independent market research reports; and

(vii) information gathered by other government departments.

The case officer will, at the same time, consult the OFT's legal division whenever there is uncertainty as to whether a merger qualifies for investigation under the Act, for example, if there are doubts as to whether the acquisition of an interest in a company is sufficient to enable the purchaser to exercise material influence over that company.[76] The case officer will also consult with the OFT's accountants[77] in mergers where there are potential competition concerns, in order to assess the profitability of the parties and the relationship between the earnings, assets and the purchase price of the business acquired. This information may be useful, for example, to test claims that the long term competitive significance of one of the parties may be overstated by its current market share, on the ground that its profits have been low or negative and that profits are unlikely to recover in the future. The OFT's accountants will also be involved when a merger involves the failing firm defence[78] or exceptionally raises gearing issues.

Where the case team identifies additional information needed from the parties, they will usually request it immediately; a short deadline for a response will usually be given. Where the parties consider that an information request or question will be particularly difficult or burdensome to answer, it is perfectly acceptable to speak to the case officer to explain the difficulties envisaged: indeed the OFT's *Procedural Guidance* encourages such a dialogue, although it emphasises that such issues should be raised promptly.[79] This sort of problem might arise, for example, where the OFT requests data which the parties do not systematically record or collect, or where the information requested will have to be collated from numerous different sources, which will cause delay. It is sensible, where requested information cannot reasonably be provided, to propose a "next best" alternative information response which comes as close as the parties can reasonably manage to the original request. Where such issues are raised and are considered reasonable, the OFT may adjust the question or information request (for example, accepting the suggested "next best" alternative), or may extend the deadline.

    3.045

Requests for additional information are often made over the phone or by email, although where the OFT's evaluation is being done against the statutory prenotification timetable, any information request made to the notifying party is likely to be framed in a statutory notice under s.99(2) of the Act.[80] Similarly, if the merger is already completed so that the OFT has four months within which to make any reference, it may request information

---

[76] For a discussion on qualifying mergers see Ch.2, above.

[77] There are no accountants or business analysts in the Mergers Branch itself, but the business analysts of the Markets and Policy Initiatives Division are consulted where necessary.

[78] See Ch.6 at paras 6.108 *et seq.*

[79] See para.5.4 of the OFT's *Procedural Guidance*.

[80] The required contents of any such notice are specified in s.99(3) of the Act.

from the merged parties using a formal notice under s.31(1) of the Act.[81] Where information is not received within the deadline specified in a s.99 notice or a s.31 notice, the OFT may extend the statutory deadline concerned.[82] Even where there is no statutory clock running, the OFT may consider that any delay by the parties in supplying requested information will stop the clock on its internal administrative timetable for considering the merger.[83] These "stop the clock" powers are considered further at para.3.052, below.

In any case which appears to raise competition issues, the OFT will meet with the parties once sufficient information has been gathered in order to probe various points of their submissions and to relay and discuss (generally on an unattributed basis) the validity of any concerns expressed by third parties.[84] Such meetings may raise fresh issues, resulting in the need for additional information to be supplied, and in complex cases it would not be uncommon for further meetings with the OFT to take place.

Third party comments

3.046   The OFT will invite comments on any public merger situation under review from interested third parties by means of an "invitation to comment" notice, which will be one of the first steps taken in the evaluation process.[85] The invitation to comment is published on the Regulatory News Service and the OFT's website. It is a very short, neutral statement, which simply states the names of the parties concerned, the relevant industry sector, whether the merger is proposed or has been completed, a deadline for submitting comments and the deadline for the OFT's consideration of the merger (if any), together with the name and contact details of the case officer to whom any comments should be addressed. The stated deadline is not absolute: the OFT is usually receptive to later submissions, although submissions are certainly more likely to influence the OFT's analysis if they are made early in the evaluation process and it may be difficult to take late submissions fully into account in the OFT's by then advanced analysis. The OFT may also receive unsolicited comments from third parties in relation to the effects of a merger, and in cases where a third party is actively seeking to oppose the merger, third party submissions can be as detailed and sophisticated in their arguments and analysis as those of the merging parties themselves.

In relation to mergers raising material competition concerns, the OFT will actively seek to explore issues with third parties. The parties' submission, whether or not it is in the format of a Merger Notice, should provide the OFT with names and full contact details for relevant customers, suppliers and/or competitors of both parties and the case officers will usually follow these contacts up in the first few days of their analysis, to facilitate the gathering of views as to the effects of the merger.[86]

---

[81] The contents of any such notice are specified in s.31(2) of the Act.
[82] In relation to a s.99(2) notice, see s.97(5) and (6); in relation to a s.31(1) notice, see ss.25(2) and (3).
[83] See para.5.2 of the OFT's *Procedural Guidance*.
[84] As to the OFT's obligations to maintain confidentiality, see paras 3.078 *et seq.*, below.
[85] See para.5.5 of the OFT's *Procedural Guidance*.
[86] See para.3.027, above which describes the content of submissions.

The OFT economist's views on product and geographical market definition and the intensity of existing competition within a market will draw
from customers' reactions to the merger, which will also be used to verify
the information provided by the parties. Similarly, the economist's views on
the magnitude of barriers to entry and expansion in the market in question
are strongly conditioned by the responses of competitors and, in particular,
any recent new entrants. Where the parties have argued that customers have
strong countervailing buyer power, the OFT case team will explore that
question with the parties' customer base.

The OFT is aware that there may be bias in the comments of competitors
and, to a lesser extent, customers. Competitors, for instance, may argue
against mergers which enhance competition in a market, whilst supporting
mergers which, by eliminating a competitor, may enable them to raise
prices, for example, without materially losing market share.[87] Similarly, in
hostile takeovers, the target company may attempt to use merger control as
a tactical weapon in its takeover defence and the OFT will have that factor
in mind when considering the arguments that are presented. Because of
these "hidden agenda" considerations, the OFT's *Procedural Guidance*
indicates that comments from customers will usually be given greater
weight than comments from competitors.[88] As a general comment, it is
thought that the OFT tends to take the view that an unsolicited comment
from a third party where a merger has been well publicised is likely to
reflect a more genuine concern as to the likely adverse effects of a merger
than one that is given only at the OFT's invitation although, equally, such
an unsolicited response may suggest that the respondent has a particular
"axe to grind". In cases which raise sufficient concerns to warrant a case
review meeting,[89] the views of competitors, customers and other interested
third parties summarised in the case review paper which the case officer
and the economist prepare for the case review meeting. A merger reference
will not, however, be made on the basis of concerns raised by competitors
and customers which have been found to be without foundation.

Although the Secretary of State for Trade and Industry is no longer   **3.047**
involved in the day-to-day decision-making process under the Act, the OFT
will also contact relevant government departments and sectoral regulators,
where appropriate for their views. The sectoral regulators may carry out
their own public consultation, assisted by their detailed knowledge of the
industry sector involved, before providing comments to the OFT.[90]

---

[87] Of course, if the merged company's dominance would be such that it would reduce the
ability of its rivals to compete effectively, these rivals would suffer from the merger.

[88] See para.5.6 of the OFT's *Procedural Guidance*.

[89] The case review meeting procedure is discussed at paras 3.060 *et seq.*, below.

[90] See, for example, OFGEM's contribution in relation to the proposed purchase by
International Power plc of an interest in AES Drax Holdings Limited (reference 115/03,
published on October 1, 2003, with a deadline for responses on October 7, 2003).
Following the public consultation, OFGEM reported its views to the OFT (ref 136/03),
which concluded that the merger did not raise significant competition concerns (and indeed
no third party views were received by OFGEM). The OFT noted this view in its decision to
clear the transaction (see the OFT's decision of October 27, 2003, *Anticipated acquisition
by International Power plc of AES Drax Holdings Ltd*). Not all the sectoral regulators
publish their views on a merger; see for example the OFT's decision of September 18, 2003,
Anticipated acquisition by Vodafone Group plc of Project Telecom plc, which notes
OFTEL's views, which do not appear to have been published by OFTEL itself.

Competing bids and contemporaneous mergers

3.048   In some circumstances, the extent to which the OFT will take other possible events in the market concerned into account may have a material effect on the analysis of the case. In a competing bid situation, for example, will the OFT look at each proposed bid in isolation, or will it consider them in a comparative manner? In public bid situations, timing issues can be particularly important and the question arises as to whether the OFT will co-ordinate the timeframe of its assessment of the competing bids. Alternatively, where there is more than one merger likely to take place in a market, will the OFT take the possible imminent changes in market conditions due to a first merger into account in its assessment of a second merger? If the second merger becomes public during the assessment of the first, will the OFT adjust its analysis? Although these types of question can appear a simple matter of procedure, the responses can fundamentally affect the competition analysis and therefore the level of risk of a reference; in essence they concern identifying the correct counter-factual[91] against which a particular merger should be assessed. These issues are considered in turn below.

Competing bids

3.049   The fact that there are a number of competing bidders does not mean that if one bid is referred to the Competition Commission, the others will be treated in the same way. The OFT's assessment is undertaken on competition grounds and the risk that avoiding a reference may give one bidder a strategic advantage in acquiring the target business is not relevant to the competition assessment; the OFT will consider each case on its merits. The question arises, however, as to the extent to which the OFT's analysis of the impact on competition of one bid must take into account the alternative offers. The OFT's *Procedural Guidance* states:

> "Where there are competing bids for the same company, the OFT tries to consider them simultaneously. This may not be possible when the bids have not been made at the same time, where the bids are notified to the OFT at materially different times, or where they raise different issues. Although the OFT may have the power to refer all bids to the [Competition Commission], it does not necessarily follow that, because one is referred, the other or others will be also. As in the case of a single bidder, each case must be considered on its own merits".[92]

Competing bids can affect the substantive analysis of a proposed merger because they add levels of complexity to the question of the counterfactual scenario against which the competing bid should be assessed. This issue is discussed in detail in Ch.6 below,[93] but the problem is essentially that merger analysis rests on a comparison of the conditions of competition if the merger were to proceed against the conditions of competition in the *absence* of the merger (not the conditions *before* the merger).

---

[91] See further paras 6.103 *et seq.* of Ch.6.
[92] See para.3.29 of the OFT's *Procedural Guidance*.
[93] See paras 6.103 *et seq.*

This issue was brought under the spotlight by the bidding war for the UK supermarket chain Safeway plc. Wm Morrison Supermarkets PLC, a regional supermarket chain, made a public offer for Safeway in January 2003. The offer was recommended by the Safeway board, but prompted a flurry of public announcements by other parties who expressed an interest in making competing offers. The competing bidders comprised three national UK supermarket chains, Tescos, Sainsburys, and Asda (owned by the US chain Wal-Mart) and a private investor, the entrepreneur Philip Green, through his investment vehicle Trackdean Investments. The various bids were assessed under the FTA regime, but consistent with the OFT's stated policy under the Act that each case is assessed on its merits, Trackdean's bid was cleared by the Secretary of State, following the advice of the Director General. Although Trackdean and its controlling share-holders had other retailing interests, no competition concerns arose.[94] The assessment does not appear to have been affected by the bidding war taking place, even though the unconditional clearance may have given Mr Green a strategic advantage.

It is, however, less clear whether Morrison's bid was treated as it might have been in the absence of the competing bids. There were horizontal over-laps between the Morrisons and Safeway stores, a fact acknowledged by Morrison's willingness from the outset to consider divestment undertakings to remove competition concerns at the local level. However the OFT's advice to the Secretary of State[95] stated that in order to arrive at acceptable undertakings in lieu of reference, it would be necessary to identify "both a clear-cut competition concern and a clear-cut remedy".[96] The difficulty in this case was that the methodology for identifying precisely the local over-laps in stores was very sensitive to the assumptions on which it was based. Morrisons and the competing supermarkets all proposed essentially the same methodology as to how local concentrations should be assessed but used different assumptions in their mapping software, thereby generating different outcomes. This made it difficult for the OFT to reach a clear-cut conclusion as to the precise areas of local concern, making undertakings in lieu of reference an unworkable proposal. If Morrison's methodology and assumptions had been the only model presented to the OFT, it is possible that a reference could have been avoided, because the technical complexi-ties arising from the differences in the assumptions used in the various soft-ware tools would arguably not have arisen. Ultimately, the Competition Commission recommended (and the Secretary of State decided) that Morrisons was the only one of the four supermarket bidders whose offer was not against the public interest[97] (provided that certain local divestments were made).

---

[94] See the Director General's advice of March 13, 2003, *Proposed acquisition by Trackdean Investments Ltd of Safeway plc.*

[95] See the Director General's advice on March 13, 2003, *Proposed acquisition by Wm Morrison Supermarkets PLC of Safeway plc.*

[96] See para.37 of the Director General's advice.

[97] *Safeway plc and Asda Group Limited (owned by Wal-Mart Stores Inc); Wm Morrison Supermarkets PLC; J Sainsbury plc; and Tesco plc,* Cm. 5950 (September 2003).

Contemporaneous mergers

3.050　Related questions arise where a number of contemporaneous or closely timed mergers take place in the same market. Where a market is already relatively concentrated, two mergers between existing competitors at a similar time can materially alter the conditions of competition in that market. A recent example occurred in the building products sector. On January 8, 2002, the Secretary of State cleared (on the OFT's recommendation) the proposed acquisition by Tarmac Ltd of the Durox building products business.[98] Durox's main product was aircrete blocks, which Tarmac also produced. Prior to this merger, there were four aircrete producers in the UK. At around the same time, the Mergers Branch considered a proposed merger between the other two producers, H+H Celcon Ltd and Marley Building Materials Limited, which was referred to the Competition Commission on February 13, 2002.[99] It is by no means clear that Celcon would have avoided a reference in the absence of the *Tarmac/Durox* acquisition, but it is always more difficult to justify a merger in a more concentrated market and the OFT treated the *Tarmac/Durox* merger as a *fait accompli* in its assessment of the *Celcon/Marley* merger. It is also not clear how far the *Tarmac/Durox* merger benefited from being a month or so ahead of the *Celcon/Marley* merger. Certainly the possibility of the *Celcon/Marley* merger is not mentioned in the Director General's advice in the Tarmac case, notwithstanding that the OFT was considering them contemporaneously. If the counterfactual scenario of the *Celcon/Marley* merger had been taken into account, it is possible that the *Tarmac/Durox* merger would also have been referred to the Competition Commission.

Tactical considerations

3.051　These cases highlight that where a number of mergers are being considered in the same economic market, it may be strategically important for the merging parties to move as quickly as possible in order to ensure that their case is the first to be considered, or (as was the case in the Safeway bidding war, discussed above) so that the first merger to be notified cannot be assessed in isolation from other proposed transactions. The degree to which the OFT can consider a case on its own merits or must take into account other notifications of mergers in the same sector is materially affected by timing, particularly where the first merger to come through the OFT's door is on a Merger Notice so that there is minimal flexibility to slow the timeframe of the analysis down to take competing or contemporaneous mergers into account.

---

[98] See the Director General's advice of December 21, 2001, *Proposed acquisition by Tarmac Ltd of the Durox Building Products business from RMC Group plc*, and DTI press release P/2002/008 of January 8, 2002.

[99] The recommendation was in line with the Director General's advice of February 5, 2002, *The proposed acquisition by H+H Celcon Ltd of Marley Building Materials Ltd (Thermalite)*. See also DTI press release P/2002/087 of February 13, 2002.

Enforcement powers of the OFT during the investigation of a merger situation

"Stop the clock" sanctions

Unlike the position of the Competition Commission under the Act or the European Commission under the EC Merger Regulation, the OFT does not have powers to fine parties or third parties in relation to the late or inadequate provision of information.[1] However, the OFT has powers to "stop the clock" which can be an effective incentive on the parties to act with due speed and diligence given the importance of timing considerations in the assessment of mergers, where the parties may have decided to delay completing their planned merger whilst competition clearances are obtained.[2]

3.052

As noted above, the OFT can make a formal request for information, in a prenotification Merger Notice case, using a statutory notice under s.99(2) of the Act.[3] The notice can only be issued to "the person who gave the merger notice". The notice will state the information which is required, impose a deadline for provision of the information and outline the consequences of failure to provide the information.[4] If the stated deadline is not met by the parties, then the OFT is able to stop the clock on the 20 (or 30, where extended) working day period for consideration of the Merger Notice from the point at which the deadline is missed until a full response is received[5], or can reject the Merger Notice altogether.[6] Since the fixed timeframe for the decision is one of the major advantages of the prenotification procedure, the parties risk diluting or even losing this advantage altogether if they fail to respond to an information request.

Similarly, if a merger has already been completed so that the clock is running towards the four month statutory longstop on making a reference, the OFT can request information using a formal notice under s.31(1) of the Act.[7] Such a notice will set out the information required, the deadline for providing it and the consequences of failure to provide it[8] and can be issued to any of the persons carrying on the enterprises which have ceased to be distinct. Where the parties fail to provide the required information by the stated deadline, the OFT may extend the statutory deadline for reference for the period of the delay in responding (*i.e.* from the point at which the

---

[1] The Competition Commission can impose fines for failure to comply with an information request notice: see s.110 of the Act and para.5.026 of Ch.5, below. The European Commission can impose fines and periodic penalties for the provision of incorrect, incomplete or misleading information, or failure to supply information within a required time limit: see Arts 14 and 15 of the EC Merger Regulation.

[2] In the UK, there is no requirement of prior clearance under the merger control regime, but for the reasons discussed above, the parties will often have agreed in the sale and purchase contract to make completion conditional on clearance, or prior clearance may be required because the acquisition is governed by the Takeover Code.

[3] See also para.5.3 of the OFT's *Procedural Guidance*.

[4] See s.99(3) of the Act.

[5] See ss.97(5) and (6) of the Act.

[6] See s.99(5)(c) of the Act.

[7] See also para.5.3 of the OFT's *Procedural Guidance*.

[8] See s.31(2) of the Act.

stated deadline has been missed)[9], or ultimately may refer the merger because its analysis cannot be concluded. This power enables the OFT to deal with situations where parties may be trying to use delaying tactics in the hope that the OFT will run up against the statutory deadline for reference and be unable to act to stop the merger. In fact, any such tactic would be highly risky and potentially costly in the absence of the stop the clock powers, as it is probably more likely that where the OFT was in danger of running out of time to reach a conclusion as to whether a merger is anti-competitive, it would err on the side of caution and refer the merger. In practice where the OFT finds that it is running up against the statutory deadline for reference of a completed merger, it is most likely to address this by seeking to reach an agreement with the parties to extend the deadline, pursuant to s.25(1). Such an extension may be for up to 20 working days.[9A]

Even where there is no statutory clock running, the OFT may consider that any delay by the parties in supplying requested information by a stated deadline will stop the clock on its internal administrative timetable of 40 working days for considering the merger.[10] The parties are usually anxious to obtain clearance as quickly as possible and will not welcome further delay to the expected eight week investigation process. Where the OFT fixes a deadline which the parties consider will be difficult to achieve, this should be raised with the OFT as soon as possible.[11]

3.053 Note that these timetable powers, statutory and administrative, do not apply to information requested from third parties.[12] This is logical as it prevents third parties from engaging in strategic delaying tactics, to the prejudice of the notifying parties.

The ability to issue questions or information requests to the parties, and so to keep the clock running on whether to refer the merger, appears widely drawn. The parties might try to challenge an information request which they believed was simply a stalling tactic, but demonstrating that that was the case might well be difficult to do, and it cannot be ruled out that the courts would give the OFT the benefit of any doubt in this respect.[13-14]

---

[9] See s.S25(2) and (3) of the Act.

[9A] s.32(4) specifies that for the purposes of s.25(1), no account is to be taken of Saturday, Sunday, Good Friday or Christmas Day, or a bank holiday in England and Wales—*i.e.* "days" means "working days".

[10] See also para.5.2 of the OFT's *Procedural Guidance*.

[11] See further paras 3.034 and 3.045.

[12] This contrasts with the position of the Competition Commission, which can require either the parties to the merger or third parties to appear as a witness before the Commission, or to produce documents, and may impose fixed or daily penalties for failure to do so (see further ss.109 to 116 of the Act. It also contrasts with the position of the European Commission which is able to impose fines on the parties and third parties to a merger for failure to provide information, or delays, at the first stage of its investigation (see Art.14 of the EC Merger Regulation).

[13-14] Judicial review of the decisions of the OFT and Competition Commission is dealt with in Ch.10, below. Note that it is possible that the issue of an information request may remain subject to judicial review by the High Court rather than review by the Competition Appeal Tribunal under s.120 of the Act: this jurisdictional question has not yet been considered by the CAT of the High Court. See further para.10.007 of Ch.10.

Offences related to information provided to the OFT

Under s.117 of the Act, it is an offence for "a person", *i.e.* one of the parties   3.054
to the merger, a third party, or any of their advisers knowingly or recklessly
to supply false or misleading information to the OFT (or the Competition
Commission or Secretary of State), or to give false or misleading information to someone knowingly or recklessly, in the knowledge that it will be
used to supply information to the OFT (or the Competition Commission or
Secretary of State). Both offences are punishable by two years in prison or
a fine, or both. It should be noted that the offences are wide enough to
apply to the parties' advisers. This provision reflects the wording of s.93B
of the FTA, which was also expressed by reference to "a person" and was
inserted by the Companies Act 1989. So far as the authors are aware, no
prosecutions were ever brought under the FTA.

"Hold separate" (or "initial") undertakings and orders

As noted above, the Act has given the OFT powers which were not avail-   3.055
able to it (or the Secretary of State) under the FTA to accept undertakings
(s.71 of the Act) or make orders (s.72 of the Act) in relation to completed
mergers to keep the merging entities separate, or prevent them from integrating further, or to prevent the parties from engaging in actions which
could otherwise undermine the effectiveness of remedies. Under the FTA,
the OFT's only option was to move as quickly as it could to recommend a
reference,[15] from which point steps could be taken to keep the businesses
separate. The new powers under the Act increase the flexibility with which
the OFT can act, at least as regards completed mergers.

The OFT's *Procedural Guidance* confirms that since there is no obligation
under the Act to notify mergers, even where they clearly give rise to a substantial lessening of competition, there is correspondingly no prohibition on
completing a merger or on proceeding to integrate the merged businesses
during the course of an OFT investigation.[16] The grant of the power to accept
"hold separate" or (in the terminology used in the Act) "initial" undertakings
or to make "hold separate" or "initial enforcement" orders has not altered
this basic precept, and indeed the power is not wide enough to allow the OFT
to require hold separate undertakings or make corresponding orders as a
matter of course where it is investigating a merger; in particular, the OFT
cannot require the parties not to complete a proposed merger. The OFT's
powers can be exercised only where a merger has been completed and only
for the purposes of preventing "pre-emptive action" (discussed below). This
underlines the fact that these powers could not become the platform for a *de
facto* moratorium on the completion of mergers pending clearance in the UK.

---

[15] For example, in the case of *AAH/Medicopharma*, the OFT took only thirteen working days
to recommend reference to the Secretary of State. A hold separate order was imposed at the
same time as the Secretary of State announced the reference of the merger to the MMC. (The
Merger Reference (Medicopharma NV and AAH Holdings plc) Order 1991, SI 1991/2648).
The completed transaction was found by the MMC to be against the public interest (*AAH
Holdings plc and Medicopharma NV*, Cm. 1950 (May 1992)) and initially required by the
Secretary of State to be unscrambled, although it was subsequently decided that this would
not be necessary (see DTI press release P/92/679 of October 23, 1992).
[16] See para.5.12 of the OFT's *Procedural Guidance*.

The OFT's hold separate powers may be used only where the OFT believes that a relevant merger situation has been created,[17] and before making an order, the OFT must further believe that pre-emptive action is in progress or being considered by the parties.[18] Undertakings can take such form as the OFT considers appropriate, but must be made for the purpose of preventing pre-emptive action.[19] The scope of orders is set out more precisely, but is nonetheless wide.[20] The central concept of "pre-emptive action" is defined as meaning:

> "action which might prejudice the reference concerned or impede the taking of any action [under the merger provisions of the Act] which may be justified by the [Competition] Commission's decisions on the reference".[21]

In other words, the hold separate powers are available to prevent the parties from seeking to integrate the merging entities to such a degree that any subsequent prohibition decision would be difficult or impossible to implement, or would otherwise alter the situation so that any remedies required by the Competition Commission would become impracticable or unworkable. For example, if employees were laid off, factory closures undertaken, plant and equipment sold or disposed of, or contractual arrangements altered as part of the process of integration between the merging enterprises, it might be very difficult subsequently to seek to restore the conditions of competition which prevailed before the merger took place by re-establishing two competing businesses.

3.056   In practice, it is likely that these powers will be used by the OFT in only a small proportion of the cases which it considers (and this certainly appeared to be the case at the time of writing). The s.72 order-making power is likely to be needed in an even smaller number of cases, because in the majority of cases, the parties are likely to prefer to negotiate the terms of undertakings rather than to have an order imposed on them. Whilst it is not a precondition to the exercise of the order-making power that the OFT should first have sought to obtain undertakings from the parties, the expectation is that an order would only be used where the parties will not co-operate.[22] It was certainly the case under the FTA that, following a reference, hold separate measures usually took the form of undertakings. Of the 87 qualifying mergers which had been considered by the OFT as at June 1, 2004, hold separate undertakings had been accepted by the OFT in

---

[17] See s.71(3) and s.72(3)(a) of the Act.
[18] See s.72(3)(b) of the Act.
[19] See s.71(2) of the Act.
[20] See s.72 of the Act. The types of order which may be made are specified in s.72(2) of the Act. The OFT may prohibit or restrict actions which it considers would constitute pre-emptive action (*i.e.* which could prejudice a reference or impede any remedies ultimately required by the Commission: see s.71(8)); impose on any persons concerned obligations as to the carrying on of any activities or the safeguarding of any assets; provide for the carrying on of any activities or the safeguarding of any assets, either by the appointment of a person to conduct or supervise such steps or in any other manner; or require the production and/or publication of certain information.
[21] See s.71(8) of the Act.
[22] This is consistent with the indications at para.5.13 of the OFT's *Procedural Guidance*.

only one case, with two further examples between June 1, 2004 and the time of writing (October 2004).[23] No orders had been made.

In *iSOFT/Torex*, the parties notified the merger before it was completed and were initially given unconditional clearance. However, the clearance decision was appealed by a third party, IBA Health, and overturned. The Court of Appeal confirmed the quashing of the decision, and the OFT was required to reconsider the case. In the interim, however, the parties decided to proceed to completion. In *Emap/ABI Building Data* and *Lenzing/Tencel*, the mergers had already been completed by the time the OFT came to consider them. In all three cases, the OFT required hold separate undertakings to be given by the purchaser.

Whilst each of the sets of undertakings is tailored to the particular parties and businesses, the following core provisions are found in all three sets of hold separate undertakings:

(i)   except with the prior written consent of the OFT, the purchaser is required not, during the "specified period",[24] to take any action which might:

- lead to the integration of the purchaser's business with the purchased business; or
- prejudice the reference to the Competition Commission or impede the taking of any action under the Act which may be justified by the Competition Commission's decisions on the reference;

(ii)   more specifically, except with the written prior consent of the OFT, the purchaser is required to procure that at all times:

- the purchased business is carried on separately and under a different name to the purchaser's business[24A];
- the purchased business is maintained as a going concern;
- except in the ordinary course of business, none of the assets of the purchased business are disposed of and no interest in the assets of the purchased business is created or disposed of;
- the nature, description, range and standard of products and services currently supplied in the UK by each of the purchaser's business and the purchased business are maintained preserved; and
- the assets of the purchased business are maintained and preserved, including facilities and goodwill.

---

[23] *Completed acquisition by iSOFT Group plc of Torex plc*; undertakings given by iSOFT plc to the Office of Fair Trading pursuant to s.71 of the Enterprise Act 2002, January 26, 2004. *Completed acquisition by Emap plc of ABI Building Data Ltd*; undertakings given by Emap plc to the Office of Fair Trading pursuant to s.71 of the Enterprise Act 2002, June 4, 2004. *Completed acquisition by Lenzing AG of Tencel Holding Limited*; Undertakings given by Lenzing AG to the Office of Fair Trading pursuant to s.71 of the Enterprise Act 2002, July 28, 2004.

[24] This period is simply defined as the period specified in ss.71(5) or (6), which are the statutory provisions governing when the undertakings will cease to have effect. These provisions are discussed below at para.3.057.

[24A] This provision was not included in the *Lenzing/Tencel* undertakings.

Essentially, the purchaser is prevented from integrating the businesses or doing anything which would make it difficult to re-establish the pre-merger position of two independent and self-standing competing businesses. To that extent, there are certain parallels between the situation where hold separate undertakings have been given and the blanket ban on pre-implementation which is imposed in many merger control regimes where prior notification and clearance is compulsory.

3.057   In public interest cases, initial undertakings and orders can also be accepted or made. Undertakings may be accepted by the Secretary of State, or he may adopt undertakings already accepted by the OFT under s.71 (*i.e.* before the intervention notice was served).[25] Either the OFT or the Secretary of State may make initial orders in relation to public interest cases, or the Secretary of State or OFT can adopt an order made by the OFT under s.72 prior to service of the intervention notice.[26]

The procedural requirements set out in Sch.10 of the Act for the acceptance of most types of undertakings do not apply to hold separate undertakings.[27] This means that the OFT is not required to publish draft undertakings under s.71 for consultation before they can be formally accepted. Given that the purpose of initial undertakings and orders is precisely to move quickly to stop the parties from undermining the merger control process, and that they are essentially a temporary measure to preserve the status quo whilst the OFT completes its analysis of whether a reference is warranted, the absence of third party consultation in the process would appear appropriate. Of course, this is not to say that a third party which is opposed to the merger and which believes that the parties are proceeding to integrate the merged business could not raise the need for initial undertakings with the OFT. Where the OFT accepts hold separate undertakings and orders, it is required to publish them[28] and to enter them in its Register of Undertakings and Orders.[29] All initial undertakings accepted to date are available on the OFT's website.

Hold separate undertakings accepted under s.71 remain in force until one of the following events occurs[30]:

(i)   the OFT makes a hold separate order in relation to the same reference;

(ii)   the merger is referred and the Competition Commission makes an interim order[31];

(iii) the Secretary of State, in a public interest case, makes a hold separate order to prevent pre-emptive action;

(iv)   where a reference is made, seven days after the date of the reference (although the Competition Commission is able to adopt the OFT's

---

[25] See para.1 of Sch.7 to the Act.
[26] See para.2 of Sch.7 to the Act.
[27] See para.1 of Sch.10 to the Act.
[28] See s.107(1)(d) and (e) of the Act.
[29] See s.91 of the Act.
[30] See ss.71(5) and (6) of the Act.
[31] See further para.[XX] of Ch. 5.

initial undertakings if they have not yet expired,[32] in which case they would not cease to have effect);

(v) on acceptance of undertakings in lieu of reference;

(vi) where an intervention notice is issued by the Secretary of State, seven days after the date of the notice (although as noted above, the OFT or Secretary of State can adopt the OFT's initial undertakings in such circumstances, if they have not yet expired,[33] in which case they would not cease to have effect);

(vii) where the OFT decides not to refer, on the making of that decision.

The OFT's decision-making process

Although much of the OFT's external procedure for handling merger cases is substantially the same as it was under the FTA, and although the substantive factual and economic analysis undertaken by the case team has not materially altered following the replacement of the public interest test by the substantial lessening of competition test, the OFT's internal procedures for arriving at the final decision whether to refer a merger to the Competition Commission have been revised and reworked, originally because of its change in role from adviser to decision-maker, and also to reflect comments received during consultation on the Act and then subsequently in light of the clarification of procedural issues which came out of the *IBA Health* litigation.[34] The decision-making process is described in paras 5.16 to 5.21 of the OFT's *Procedural Guidance*. 3.058

The major change, as far as the parties are concerned, is the removal of the Mergers Panel and the formal adoption of the "issues letter" procedure. With the exception of the interaction with third parties, the internal procedure under the Act is the same for confidential guidance cases, cases where clearance is sought through a traditional submission and cases using the statutory prenotification procedure using a Merger Notice. The OFT's procedure is also the same where the Secretary of State issues an intervention notice, triggering the public interest provisions of the Act[35], although the OFT's conclusions will take the form, as under the FTA, of advice to the Secretary of State rather than a definitive conclusion whether to refer the merger.

Cases which do not raise substantive competition concerns

Where a case is straightforward and raises no difficult issues[36] (which might be issues of jurisdiction as well as substantive competition concerns), once the investigation and information-gathering phase is complete the case 3.059

---

[32] See s.80(3) of the Act.

[33] See para.1(4) of Sch.7 to the Act.

[34] *OFT and others v IBA Health Ltd* [2004] EWCA Civ 142, (2004) 101(11) L.S.G. 33, (2004) 154 N.L.J. 352, on appeal from *IBA Health v OFT* [2003] CAT 27, [2004] Comp. A.R. 235, discussed further at paras 3.068 *et seq.*

[35] See further paras 2.025 *et seq.* of Ch.2.

[36] The OFT's *Procedural Guidance* estimates (pre-*IBA Health*) that 80 per cent of cases per year fall into this category (see para.5.16).

officer will draft a clearance decision (or an "unlikely to refer" paper in the case of a confidential guidance request, or clearance advice, in a public interest case) which will be agreed and signed off by the Director of the Mergers Branch or one of the Deputy Directors. The decision will then be passed to the Case Review Group, for comment within 48 hours. "Comment" essentially means making a request that a case review meeting be held, in which case the matter will follow the procedure for a merger which raises substantive concerns (see below). The Case Review Group is composed of the Chairman and the Executive Director from the OFT Board, together with the Director of the Competition Enforcement Division, a member of the Competition Policy Co-ordination Branch, the OFT Chief Economist (or a deputy), a representative of the OFT Legal Division, representatives of the Mergers Branch and, in some cases, the director of the relevant OFT Sector Branch.

If a case review meeting is not requested, the clearance decision will be announced on the Regulatory News Service. Such announcements are normally made at 11am, or (less frequently) at 3pm, and occasionally at other times. The parties (typically via their legal advisers) will be informed by the case officer around five minutes before it is made that the announcement is imminent but will not be told the contents of the announcement. Following announcement of the decision, the full version of the decision will be sent to the parties with a short deadline (typically 48 hours) to submit any requests for confidential treatment of information. The reasoned decision will then be published on the OFT's website once any necessary excisions have been made.[37]

Cases which raise substantive competition concerns

3.060   Where the economist's advice indicates potential substantive competition concerns in relation to a public case or a request for confidential guidance, the case officer will contact the parties to arrange an "issues meeting". Two or three days prior to the meeting, the parties will be sent an "issues" letter. The OFT's *Procedural Guidance* describes the issues letter as follows:

> "[it] will set out the core arguments and evidence in the case. It is intended that "issues" letters will set out the arguments in favour of a reference so that parties have an opportunity to respond to the reasons why a reference, if it follows, has been made. That is not to say that a reference will follow in all cases in which an 'issues' letter is sent".[38-39]

This procedure is an improvement in transparency over the FTA procedures, where there was no systematic disclosure of the case for reference, although it was possible to obtain an outline agenda of the OFT's concerns prior to a meeting with the case team.

The OFT's issues letters are not normally made public. However, the issues letter sent to iSOFT in relation to its proposed acquisition of Torex was published as a result of IBA Health's appeal against the OFT's initial

---

[37]   See further para.3.081 below.
[38-39]   See the OFT's *Procedural Guidance* at para.5.17

decision not to refer the proposed acquisition.[40] The description (quoted above) of an issues letter in the OFT's *Procedural Guidance* could be interpreted as indicating a rather fuller document than the text published in the *IBA Health* judgment.[41] In particular, the "core evidence" is not included: the issues letters as set out in the CAT's judgment appears to be unsubstantiated by reference to any documents or other evidence. It was also clear from the issues letter in iSOFT/Torex that the statements were hypothetical concerns, which is perhaps not necessarily the approach which might have been expected on the basis of the description in the OFT's *Procedural Guidance*.[42] The authors' experience in other cases indicates that the iSOFT/Torex issues letter followed a reasonably standard format.

However, it is doubtful that a fully reasoned and supported document such as a full statement of objections issued during the second stage of an EC Merger Regulation investigation could be produced during the limited timeframe of a first stage merger investigation (it certainly is not under EC Merger Regulation procedure). As a matter of good administration it is important that the first stage is not unduly costly or lengthy, either for the parties or the regulator itself.

The issues letter is written before the case review meeting and therefore **3.061** at a stage in the OFT's investigation before the competition concerns have fully crystallised. There is therefore a risk that the case officers will err on the side of including a possible issue, rather than find at the case review stage that material areas of concern have not been fully explored with the parties. It is also worth noting that the issues letter can be a way of seeking to draw out further assistance from the parties. Third parties may have raised concerns which the OFT do not believe to be material, but which it may have insufficient evidence to rebut; the issues letter can be used as a mechanism to obtain additional evidence from the parties to enable the OFT to rule out issues.

It is the authors' understanding that the issues letter procedure has not been altered following the *IBA Health* litigation. The conclusion of both the Competition Appeal Tribunal and the Court of Appeal in the *IBA Health* litigation was that the OFT's decision was inadequately reasoned, and it appears that this conclusion was strongly influenced by the fact that the OFT appeared to move from a fairly lengthy list of issues of potential concern to an unconditional clearance decision in around eight days.[43] The CAT commented that it considered that the OFT's clearance decision should have contained "a detailed point by point rebuttal of the matters set out in the issues letter demonstrating that the alternative view could not

---

[40] The text of the iSOFT issues letter is set out in the Competition Appeal Tribunal's judgment of December 3, 2003 in *IBA Health v OFT* [2003] CAT 27, [2004] Comp. A.R. 235 at para.89 and reproduced in App.5.

[41] See para.5.17 of the OFT's *Procedural Guidance*.

[42] The CAT described the issues letter as setting out the provisional reasons for a reference, suggesting that the document is analogous to a statement of objections which is perhaps an understandable interpretation in light of the comments in the OFT's *Procedural Guidance*: this is not however, the authors' understanding of the issues letter procedure as it is used in practice by the OFT, given its presentation of hypothetical and not actual concerns. See the CAT's *IBA Health* judgment (cited above) at para.175.

[43] See paras 57 and 71 of the Court of Appeal's judgment and paras 176 and 236 of the CAT's judgment.

reasonably be held, and the material relied on"[44] although as is discussed below, the comments of Carnwath L.J. suggest that this requirement went too far[45] and moreover, the CAT may have elevated the status of the issues letter to correspond to a statement of objections, which is not how it is seen by the OFT. The confidentiality of issues letters makes any comparison, post-*IBA Health*, of the concerns expressed in an issues letter with the arguments set out in the final decision difficult. However, in the authors' experience, the breadth and depth of the OFT's questioning at the fact and information-gathering stage of the investigation has increased since the *IBA Health* litigation and this is reflected in the issues letters; by contrast, the style and length of OFT decisions post-*IBA Health* does not appear to have materially changed.

The parties may respond to the issues letter either in writing or at a meeting (or more likely in practice, both). In most cases, the issues letter will lead to an issues meeting, at which the possibility of undertakings in lieu of a reference will be raised and discussed with the parties.

A further issue highlighted by the IBA Health litigation is the question of whether a complainant (or indeed any third party) should be given an opportunity to comment on the issues letter. This has not been the OFT's practice, a point noted by the CAT and the Court of Appeal in *IBA Health*[46-47], and the position has not changed subsequently. Of course, as the CAT noted, the OFT's "'first screen' procedure does not lend itself to the same degree of transparency [as the Competition Commission's procedures]",[48] primarily because of the necessary speed with which any effective and efficient first stage merger review must be conducted.[49] From the parties' perspective, more transparency in relation to the issues letter might have the advantage of increasing the robustness of the reasoning in the OFT's subsequent decision—in particular by enabling the OFT to focus on key areas of third party concern—thereby potentially reducing the risk of an appeal. On the other hand it is difficult to see how third parties could be involved without adding delay—not only for the third parties to review and consider the issues letter and the parties' response, but also for the

---

[44] See para.237.

[45] See paras 104 to 106, in particular of the Court of Appeal judgment, where Carnwath L.J. emphasised that "there is no statutory requirement for all the evidence to be set out in the decision letter". See further para.3.069, below.

[46-47] See para.90 of the CAT's judgment and para.3 of the Court of Appeal's judgment.

[48] See para.206 of the CAT's judgment.

[49] In relation to proceedings under the Competition Act 1998, where third party rights to participate in the OFT's investigation of an alleged infringement were very vague and not expressly set out either in the Competition Act itself or in the Director General's Rules (see Competition Act 1998 (Director's Rules) Order 2000 (SI 2000/293)), the CAT ruled in *Pernod Ricard SA and Campbell Distillers Limited v OFT* [2004] CAT 10 that third parties should be given an opportunity to comment on the Rule 14 Notice. However, a Rule 14 Notice is directly comparable to a statement of objections in an Art.81/82 investigation and an issues letter is probably not comparable to a statement of objections. Moreover, the CAT's conclusion that third parties had rights to participate in the investigation was based on the operation of s.60 of the Competition Act 1998, which requires the UK Competition Act 1998 to be interpreted so as to ensure no inconsistency with corresponding principles of Community law. There is no equivalent to s.60 under the merger regime laid down by the Act.

parties to reply in turn to the third parties' comments. It would certainly be undesirable and unnecessary, given its right to seek judicial review of a merger clearance, for a third party which is actively objecting to a merger to be given a "no-issues letter" setting out the (hypothetical) reasons why a reference should *not* be made, and giving the complainant an opportunity to respond.

Following the issues meeting, the case officer will circulate to the members of the Case Review Group an outline decision, summarising the arguments for and against reference, the internal economic analysis, the issues letter and any written response by the parties in advance of holding a case review meeting. The Case Review Group will then meet to discuss the case. The group will normally comprise the following individuals:

3.062

- Director of the Competition Enforcement Division (who will usually chair the meeting);
- Director of the Mergers Branch;
- the Senior Economist in the Mergers Branch; and
- the case team (including one of the Deputy Directors of the Mergers Branch, with the case economists and one or sometimes two case officers).

The following may also attend:

- OFT Board Members (this would be most likely to be the Chairman although the person taking the final decision whether to refer (usually the Chairman) will typically not attend the case review meeting and so a presence from the Board is rare);
- a representative of Competition Policy Co-ordination Branch;
- the OFT Chief Economist (or a deputy);
- officers from the relevant OFT sectoral branch if appropriate;
- a representative of the OFT's Legal Division;
- a representative of one of the sectoral regulators (OFCOM, OFGEM, OFWAT, etc.) if the merger concerns one of these industries.

In addition, an OFT official from outside the Mergers Branch will attend to act as "devil's advocate". The role of the devil's advocate is to ensure that the recommendation of the case team is properly challenged and examined and that all points raised in argument by the parties have been addressed. Case review meetings typically take place on a Wednesday morning. By scheduling the meetings for the same time every week, the OFT ensures that all of those required should always be available to attend.

Following the case review meeting, key personnel will reconvene for a decision meeting. This typically takes place on the afternoon of the day on which the case review meeting is held. The decision meeting will be chaired by the decision maker (usually this will be the Chairman or the Executive Director).

3.063   The following will also attend:

- the chairperson of the case review meeting;

- the attendees of the case review meeting from the Mergers Branch;

- the "devil's advocate";

- others from the case review meeting as appropriate, "where this would enhance the level of debate and scrutiny at the decision meeting".[50]

The decision meeting provides an occasion for the decision maker to hear the various views on the merger and any criticisms of the outline decision, and to reach his or her conclusion. The final decision will then be drawn up (by the case officer, in line with the decision maker's instructions) and will then be signed off by the decision-maker. Where the matter is public (*i.e.* in cases other than confidential guidance), the headline decision—whether to refer, clear, or seek undertakings in lieu—will be published in a press release. Typically such release will be issued on the Regulatory News Service (usually at either 11am or (less often) 3pm) and on the OFT's website.

The procedures for investigation and decision-making where the public interest regime is triggered

Investigation and decision-making as regards competition issues

3.064   Where an intervention notice has been served by the Secretary of State, triggering the public interest provisions under the Act, the OFT will still undertake an investigation of possible competition concerns arising out of the merger, in order to produce its report to the Secretary of State.[51] The Act specifically empowers the OFT to carry out "such investigations as it considers appropriate" in order to produce its report.[52]

The OFT's investigation and report will cover largely the same ground as for a merger in any other sector. Thus the OFT will consider and advise the Secretary of State on:

- whether a qualifying merger situation has been created or is in contemplation;

- whether the merger has resulted or may be expected to result in a substantial lessening of competition within any market(s) in the UK;

- whether the market(s) concerned would be of sufficient importance to justify a reference;

- where the merger is not yet completed, whether the arrangements are not sufficiently far advanced or not sufficiently likely to proceed to justify a reference;

---

[50] See para.5.20 of the OFT's *Procedural Guidance*.
[51] See s.44 of the Act.
[52] See s.44(7) of the Act.

- whether any relevant customer benefits arising out of the merger outweigh the substantial lessening of competition (or its adverse effects); and

- whether, disregarding any public interest considerations, the competition concerns could be dealt with through undertakings in lieu.[53]

It is understood that the OFT's procedure for public interest mergers will not differ from its procedure for investigating mergers in any other sector, although it may be that a greater degree of liaison with other relevant government departments is required. The timing of the OFT's investigation should not alter. Indeed, one of the pragmatic aspects of the public interest regime is that the basic analysis undertaken by the OFT does not alter and so need not be delayed, at least in theory: it remains to be seen whether this is the case in practice.

The key difference, of course, will be that the OFT will not take the decision whether to refer: the OFT's conclusions will take the form of advice to the Secretary of State to enable him to take the decision whether to refer. However, the Secretary of State must accept the advice of the OFT as regards the need to refer on competition grounds, and whether undertakings in lieu would be suitable. However, where the Secretary of State concludes that public interest considerations outweigh the competition issues on which the OFT has advised that a reference is appropriate, the Act allows the competition concerns to be overridden by the wider public interest considerations such that notwithstanding the OFT's advice that there are competition concerns, the Secretary of State can "trump" these in the light of the relevant public interest considerations and clear the merger.[54]

If the Secretary of State concludes that there are no public interest relevant issues, then he must put the OFT on notice of this, and the OFT's duty to refer is then reactivated.[55]   **3.065**

Investigation and decision-making as regards public interest issues

As well as advising on competition issues, the OFT's advice to the Secretary   **3.066** of State must include a summary of any representations which it has received in relation to the public interest issues other than newspaper and media considerations (which OFCOM will have dealt with, although the OFT may also summarise any such representations in its report).[56] The OFT is also permitted, under the Act, to make recommendations to the Secretary of State regarding the public interest issues which have been identified in the intervention notice[57]; the Act does not require the OFT to advise on the

---

[53] See s.44(4) of the Act. These various aspects of the OFT's analysis are discussed in detail in Ch.4.

[54] See further para.4.031 of Ch.4 and s.45(6) of the Act.

[55] See para.4.032 of Ch.4.

[56] See s.44(3)(b) and s.44(5A) of the Act. Note however that the OFT can omit from its report considerations which it believes the Secretary of State would consider immaterial in the context of the particular case: see s.57(1).

[57] See s.44(6) of the Act.

wider public interest issues, but gives it a discretion whether to do so. It remains to be seen how far the OFT chooses to become involved in this aspect of public interest cases. In his more recent advice under the FTA, the Director General saw his expertise as relating to the assessment of mergers by reference to competition law and economics and he typically declined to advise the Secretary of State on any wider public interest issues.[58] Under the Act (although under the public interest intervention regime in relation to the EC Merger Regulation and not UK merger control), the OFT's two reports as at the time of writing to the Secretary of State to date on national interest grounds advised the Secretary of State on jurisdictional issues but gave no advice itself on the public interest issues, simply stating:

"The OFT is not expert in national security matters and therefore does not go beyond summarising here representations made by the MoD and other third parties".[59]

Where an intervention notice has been served in relation to newspaper and media cases, OFCOM is expressly charged with preparing advice for the Secretary of State on public interest issues[60] (and it may therefore be that in relation to such cases, the OFT does not consider it necessary to duplicate or supplement this advice). As regards investigation by other bodies, OFCOM's *Guidance for the public interest test for media mergers* sets out its investigation processes and is discussed in detail in Ch.7. The approach of the DTI and Secretary of State in newspaper or media mergers is set out in its guidance *Public interest intervention in media mergers*, also discussed (as regards newspapers) in Ch.7.

In relation to national security mergers, the only other category of public interest considerations at the time of writing, there is no body designated to advise the Secretary of State, although in practice it can be expected that the Ministry of Defence will be closely involved (and this was certainly the case in the European intervention notice cases referred to above[61]). There is similarly no published guidance on the procedures to be followed by the DTI and Secretary of State (or MOD) in relation to mergers where an intervention notice is served on national security grounds. However, it is to be hoped that, broadly, the DTI would adopt a similar procedure as for newspaper and media mergers.

---

[58] See further para.4.030 of Ch.4.

[59] See the report of the OFT pursuant to Arts 4(2) to (5) of the Enterprise Act 2002 (Protection of Legitimate Interests) Order 2003 of May 20, 2004, *Anticipated acquisition by General Dynamics Corporation of Alvis plc*, published on the DTI's website at para.15. Very similar wording was used in the OFT's report to the Secretary of State under the same provisions, dated September 19, 2004 in *Anticipated acquisition by Finmeccanica Societa Per Azioni of Agustawestland NV*, at para.16.

[60] See further Ch.7.

[61] The report of the OFT pursuant to Arts 4(2) to (5) of the Enterprise Act 2002 (Protection of Legitimate Interests) Order 2003 of May 20, 2004, *Anticipated acquisition by General Dynamics Corporation of Alvis plc*, published on the DTI's website, makes it clear that the MOD was heavily involved and lead the consideration of the public interest issues, to the extent of proposed draft undertakings in lieu to address the national security concerns which it had identified. The MOD similarly led the public interest analysis (and proposed remedies) in relation to the *Finmeccanica/Agustawestland* transaction.

The Act provides that the Secretary of State can set a deadline by which the OFT[62] (and, in newspaper and media mergers, OFCOM[63]) must provide its report to the Secretary of State. In the case of mergers pre-notified on a Merger Notice, this will need to be in good time to allow the statutory deadline for the decision whether to refer to be met.

Once the Secretary of State has received advice from the OFT, OFCOM (in newspaper and media merger cases) and any other body, it is then for him to take his decision on whether the public interest considerations are relevant to the assessment of the case. As noted, where he decides that they are not, the case must be returned to the OFT,[64] who will take the decision whether to refer the merger on competition grounds alone, on the basis of the competition advice which it has already prepared for the Secretary of State.[65] Where the Secretary of State concludes that public interest issues are relevant and, moreover, warrant reference, he will also consider whether reference is also needed on competition grounds. As noted above, in this respect he is obliged to accept the advice of the OFT[66], although reference can be made by the Secretary of State on public interest grounds combined with competition grounds or on public interest grounds alone and where the Secretary of State considers that the public interest considerations override the competition concerns, he can clear the merger notwithstanding the OFT's advice that it should be referred.[67]

3.067

In terms of timing of the decision whether to refer, in cases which have been notified on a traditional written submission, the DTI's guidance "Public interest intervention in media mergers" indicates that the Secretary of State will seek to take [his] decision within 10 working days of receipt of the OFT's and OFCOM's advice,[68] although this is an administrative deadline only. There is no guidance in relation to procedure for national security mergers but it is to be hoped that the same administrative target will apply. In cases which have been pre-notified on a Merger Notice, the basic 20 working day statutory period for consideration of the Merger Notice can be extended by an additional 20 working days in public interest cases[69] and so the Secretary of State must take his decision whether to refer within a maximum of 40 working days from the date of notification (regardless of the point at which the intervention notice was served).

Contents of the decision whether to refer

The OFT's decision

Save in the case of confidential guidance requests and informal advice responses,[70] the OFT's decision to refer or clear a merger must be

3.068

---

[62] See s.44(2) of the Act.
[63] See s.44A(2) of the Act.
[64] See s.56 of the Act.
[65] See para.10.5 of the OFT's *Substantive Assessment Guidance*.
[66] See s.46(2) of the Act.
[67] See further para.4.031 of Ch.4 and s.45(6) of the Act.
[68] See para.4.11 of the DTI's guidance *Public interest intervention in media mergers*.
[69] See ss.97(1), (3) and (4) and s.98(3) of the Act.
[70] In confidential guidance cases, the OFT will send a letter to the parties indicating whether the OFT is able to give guidance on the case and if so, whether it would refer the merger in

published.[71] There is, moreover, an obligation on the OFT to give reasons for its decision,[72] although these do not need to be published at the same time as the decision is announced.[73] In early 2001, the OFT began to develop the practice of publishing the Director General's advice to the Secretary of State under the FTA on whether to refer the merger in question. Not all advice was published, only advice in more complex cases.[74] A broad comparison of the content of advice where reference was recommended and the content of reference decisions under the Act leads to the conclusion that, notwithstanding differences in the precise formats and subtitles, the content and style of the OFT's decisions under the Act are broadly the same as the advice it gave to the Secretary of State under the FTA.

The *IBA Health* litigation[74A] raised a certain amount of doubt in relation to the content and style of the OFT's decisions. It is clear that the market concerned in that case was complex: not only did the case concern a niche IT software market, but it was a market where major tender processes were held on a national basis, where the key purchaser was the NHS and where a major overhaul of the IT systems across the NHS hospitals network in England was being embarked on with a series of major international tenders. It remains to be seen, therefore, to what extent the concerns about the adequacy of the OFT's reasoning are of general application rather than a reflection of the complex facts of that particular case. That said, various observations were made by the courts which are undoubtedly of wider relevance.

The CAT, in its first instance review of the OFT's *iSOFT/Torex* decision, clearly considered that, given the obligation on the OFT to give reasons for its decision[75], "the material on which the decision maker relied will be apparent from the decision itself".[76] The CAT went on to comment that it would not necessarily be appropriate to allow "material gaps to be filled by affidavit evidence"[77] and that:

"If a material element is not set out in the decision, it is very difficult for the reviewing court or tribunal to be satisfied that the matter was properly investigated or that the supplementary reasons did in fact form part of the decision making process".[78]

---

question. Such a letter typically contains no reasoning or explanation of the OFT's thinking or concerns, although it may be possible to have a meeting with the case team to discuss any negative conclusions: see further para.3.006, above. Responses to informal advice are usually given orally: see para.3.014.

[71] See s.107(1)(a) of the Act.
[72] See s.107(4) of the Act.
[73] See s.107(5) of the Act.
[74] It is believed that advice was usually published in cases where a Mergers Panel had been called or where the OFT believed that publication would be useful or, sometimes, because publication was requested by a third party.
[74A] *IBA Health v OFT* [2003] CAT 27, [2004] Comp. A. R. 245 (the CAT's judgment) and on appeal, *OFT v IBA Health* [2004] EWCA Civ. 142, (2004) 101(11) L.S.G. 33 (the Court of Appeal's judgment).
[75] See s.107(4) of the Act.
[76] See para.209 of the CAT's judgment, which cites *R. v Westminster City Council Ex p. Ermakov* [1996] 2 All E.R. 302.
[77] See para.257 of the CAT's judgment.
[78] See para.258 of the CAT's judgment.

This approach resulted in part from the CAT's view that no significant   **3.069**
disclosure exercise would be possible:[79]

"... in practical terms, in a case such as the present, material that is not
referred to in the OFT's decision cannot easily be made available in the
course of the proceedings, at least in any systematic and comprehensive
way ...

If the Tribunal is called upon to review the legality of a decision such
as the present, without access to the material which underpins it, in our
view the effectiveness of any such review is weakened".[80]

The Court of Appeal's judgment, however, indicates that the CAT's view
that the decision should contain all relevant reasoning was not correct.
Although he did not give the leading judgment in the case, Carnwath L.J.
noted the CAT's "concern at having to consider material outside the
decision letter" and its criticisms of the "failure of the OFT to set out all the
underlying material", and commented as follows:

"With respect, I think this concern, and the associated criticisms, were
misplaced. The statutory duty to give reasons is an important one, but it
is not the same as a duty to give a 'judgment' (such as that of a court) or
a duty to make a 'report' (such as that of an inquiry inspector). .... The
numerous cases on the subject lay down no general test, other than the
requirement that reasons must be 'intelligible and must adequately meet
the substance of the arguments advanced' (see *Re Poyser and Mills
Arbitration* [1964] 2 Q.B. 467, 477–478; cited in de Smith para.9–049
as 'the most frequently cited judicial articulation of the test'; see also
Wade pp. 916–9).

In a case such as the present, where the subject-matter is complex and
the supporting material voluminous, there is no statutory requirement
for all the evidence to be set out in the decision letter. However when a
challenge is made, there is, as the Tribunal noted, an obligation on a
respondent public authority to put before the Court the material necessary to deal with the relevant issues; 'all the cards' should be 'face
upwards on the table' (see *R. v Lancashire County Council Ex p.
Huddleston* [1986] 2 All E.R. 941).

There is certainly nothing unusual, particularly in a case which has to
be dealt with in a relatively short timescale, for the stated reasons to be
amplified by evidence before the Court. While in some areas of the law,
the Court may need to be 'circumspect' to ensure that this is not used as
means of concealing or altering the true grounds of the decision, that

---

[79] This view was in some ways the inevitable consequence of the CAT's decision to review the
case extremely quickly. Whilst appropriate speed of review in the mergers context is
certainly desirable, the time pressure on all concerned in this case (the hearing took place a
week after the application was lodged, with judgment issued three working days later) effectively ruled out the possibility for any supplemental evidence of the basis for the OFT's
conclusions to be disclosed before the CAT. The Court of Appeal commended the CAT's
speed (see para.6 of the Court of Appeal's judgment), but it does seem, at least on one
analysis, to have been to some degree prejudicial to the OFT and those supporting the
decision under challenge because of the evidential difficulties which resulted.

[80] See paras 210 and 211 of the CAT's judgment.

does not arise in this case. As I understand it, no objection had been taken to any of the evidence being put before the Tribunal (or to the additional evidence adduced in the Court of Appeal). The question for the Tribunal was not whether the reasoning was adequately expressed in the decision, but whether the material ultimately before it, taken as a whole, disclosed grounds on which the Tribunal could reasonably have reached the decision it did".[81]

In the light of these observations, the CAT's expectation that the OFT's decision should contain all of the evidence relied on by the OFT in reaching its conclusions, and that the decision should include "a detailed point by point rebuttal of the matters set out in the issues letter"[82] would seem to be misplaced. The comments of the Vice Chancellor in the leading judgment in *IBA Health* contain further guidance as to what the decision should contain. In particular he noted that the OFT's decision "expresses its conclusions . . . in terms of likelihood"[83] but went on to observe that:

"None of these conclusions excludes a likelihood to the opposite effect so as reasonably to justify the belief that the anticipated merger 'may' result in a significant lessening of competition".[84]

Accordingly, it appears that even though the OFT's decision need not contain all of the reasoning and evidence relied on, it should include the key elements, in order adequately to meet the substance of the argument advanced against the merger. In a clearance decision, the reasoning should focus not only on the positive elements which indicate the absence of a substantial lessening of competition, but also why those positive factors outweigh or override the negative factors in the analysis which would point to a reference—and indeed the OFT typically highlights third party concerns in its decisions and briefly addresses whether it considers them to be well founded or not.[85]

3.070   OFT decisions issued post-*IBA Health* do not seem to take a particularly different approach from pre-*IBA Health* decisions; they are similar in style, content and length. However, as noted at para.3.061 above, there appears to have been an increase in both the number and the detail of questions put to the parties by the OFT and the scope and depth of the information-gathering process seems to have increased. It appears that the OFT has taken comfort from the Court of Appeal's judgment and has not altered the basic shape of its decisions, but has perhaps bolstered the underlying evidence so that, were there to be any challenge to the reasoning in a particular deci-

---

[81] See paras 104 to 106 of the Court of Appeal's judgment.
[82] See para.237 of the CAT's judgment. This expectation also appears to be tainted by the CAT's incorrect interpretation of s.33(1) of the Act.
[83] See para.72 of the Court of Appeal's judgment.
[84] See para.73 of the Court of Appeal's judgment.
[85] Even though there may be scope for argument about where the standard of "adequacy" lies, the point that the OFT's decision must be adequately reasoned is clear from the obligation in s.107(4) of the Act to give reasons. This point is reflected in the CAT's comments in *FWD v OFT* that a third party must be able to "assess the legality of the decision, a sufficiency of the reasons being of course a key element in reviews taking place under section 120 of the Act". See *Federation of Wholesale Distributors v Office of Fair Trading* [2004] CAT 11 at para.25.

sion, the OFT would have a greater arsenal of evidence with which to defend it. This would seem to be a more efficient allocation of effort (given that, at least at the time of writing, challenges to merger decisions remained relatively infrequent under the Act[86]) than the CAT's requirement of full reasoning and supporting evidence in the OFT's decision would have produced. The latter might have facilitated speedy judicial review, but it would have hampered efficient first stage merger case handling and decision-making. It remains to be seen whether the CAT gives the OFT greater scope for disclosure of additional evidence in future cases (at the time of writing, the only other application for review under s.120 had been withdrawn before any case management decisions had been taken by the CAT).[87–88]

The decision of the Secretary of State in public interest cases

The Secretary of State must publish his decision whether to refer[89], as well as the advice which he has received from the OFT[90] (and OFCOM, in newspaper or media merger cases[91]). In what appeared to be a material departure from the FTA regime, the reasons underlying the Secretary of State's decision must also be published.[92] At the time of writing, no cases had yet been considered under the public interest regime, and so there were no examples of such decisions, but in relation to the two cases which had, at the time of writing, been considered under the European intervention provisions (see para.2.050 of Ch.2), the press release seems to be all that is published as regards a statement of the reasons underlying the Secretary of State's decision; there is no more fully reasoned document.[93] **3.071**

Avoiding a reference by undertakings in lieu

Section 73 of the Act continues the possibility introduced under the FTA, where the competition concerns and the steps which could be taken to remedy them are clear cut, of avoiding a reference by giving the OFT undertakings in lieu of a reference to the Competition Commission. The circumstances in which undertakings in lieu might be appropriate and the tactical considerations in relation to whether and when to offer them, are discussed in Ch.4, below. The procedure followed by the OFT (or the Secretary of **3.072**

---

[86] There were only two challenges to the 87 OFT decisions taken under the Act in the period to June 1, 2004, one of which was withdrawn, *i.e.* the *IBA Health* case (cited above) and *Federation of Wholesale Distributors v OFT* (cited above). No other s.120 review cases had been brought as at the time of writing (October 2004). These were both lodged by third parties challenging a decision not to refer: at the time of writing there had been no challenges to OFT decisions by the merging parties themselves.

[87–88] See *Federation of Wholesale Distributors v OFT*, cited above [2004] CAT 11.

[89] See s.107(3)(c) of the Act.

[90] See s.107(3)(b) of the Act.

[91] See s.107(3)(ba) of the Act.

[92] See s.107(4) of the Act.

[93] In relation to *General Dynamics/Alvis*, the Competition Minister's announcement of his decision to seek undertakings in lieu of reference was made in a press release (see DTI press release P/2004/208 of June 3, 2004, *Proposed acquisition by General Dynamics Corporation of Alvis plc*). The reference on the DTI's website to "the Secretary of State's decision" simply links to the press release. A similar approach has been taken in relation to *Finmeccanica/Agustawestland*.

State in public interest cases) in negotiating and accepting undertakings in lieu is set out below.

Procedure for accepting undertakings in lieu

3.073   Schedule 10 of the Act sets out the procedure to be followed by the OFT in negotiating and accepting undertakings in lieu. Although the outline terms of an undertaking will have been discussed with the parties prior to the OFT announcing its decision on a reference, such discussions take place on a hypothetical basis (as was the case under the FTA) because at that stage the OFT will not have announced (and may not have reached) its decision on whether a substantial lessening of competition has resulted or may be expected to result. It is therefore not until the OFT's decision is announced that the OFT will start to discuss the detail of how the undertaking will be documented. The OFT will usually produce the first draft of the detailed terms and conditions of the undertakings, shortly after the decision to seek undertakings is announced. The parties will be able to comment on and negotiate the detail of the draft terms, which may go through a number of drafts before agreement is reached.

Once the parties and the OFT have arrived at an agreed draft, para.2(1)(a) of Sch.10 requires the OFT to give notice of the proposed undertakings and to give third parties an opportunity to comment on their terms. It is not until this point that undertakings in lieu will be "market tested" with third parties: in contrast to with the European Commission's procedure under the EC Merger Regulation as to whether to accept undertakings offered by the parties to enable a first stage clearance, there is no third party consultation leading up to the OFT's decision whether to accept undertakings in lieu in principle. Paragraphs 2 and 3 of Sch.10 to the Act set out the legal requirements for the notice and consultation process. In particular, the consultation period must be at least 15 days[94] and all such notices must be published[95]: in practice, this requirement is met by posting the notice on the OFT's website, attaching the draft undertakings. Where, following consultation, the draft undertakings are modified, the consultation process must be recommenced with notice being given of the revised draft, with a further period of not less than seven days for comments.[96]

The time between the announcement of the intention to seek undertakings and the issue of the notice and the draft undertakings usually takes several weeks, and can take six months or longer. The shortest timeframe

---

[94] See para.2(2)(f) of Sch.10 to the Act. It appears that "days" are not "working days" in the context of the Sch.10 requirements.

[95] See para.2(3)(b) of Sch.10 to the Act.

[96] See para.2(5)(c) of Sch.10 to the Act, although if the OFT does not consider that the modifications are material, the second round of consultation can be dispensed with (see para.5(1) of Sch.10). Where the second round of consultations results in further material modifications then a third round of consultation may be necessary (see para.5(2) of Sch.10: again subsequent consultation is only required if the OFT considers the modifications to be material). It should be noted, however, that where "special reasons" exist, the requirements of Sch.10 can be dispensed with altogether (see para.9 of Sch.10. It is not clear what "special reasons" might extend to, although one area where para.9 has been used is to justify the excision of confidential information from draft or finalised undertakings (such as the deadline for divestments)).

within which the OFT has negotiated and accepted undertakings in lieu so far is a little over one month, in the *iSOFT/Torex* case. The decision to seek undertakings in lieu was announced on March 24, 2004[97] and the finalised undertakings were published on April 29, 2004[98]—an impressively fast timeframe. Undertakings in lieu in relation to Ivax's proposed acquisition of 3M's distribution business for certain asthma drugs took from October 20, 2003[99] to January 9, 2004[1] to agree (about two and a half months). The announcement that undertakings in lieu were required in relation to Arriva plc's completed acquisition of the Wales and the Borders rail franchise was made on March 16, 2004[2] and the finalised undertakings were accepted by the OFT on July 9, 2004,[3] some four months later. The requirement imposed on Tesco to give undertakings in lieu in relation to the acquisition of the Slough Co-op store was announced on February 2, 2004[4] and at the time of writing, around six months later, draft undertakings had not yet been published and the consultation process had not yet commenced.

Where undertakings in lieu are being discussed in the context of a case that has been referred back to the UK under Art.9 of the EC Merger Regulation, there was previously a four month deadline within which the whole national procedure had to be completed.[5] However, the timeframe for a referral back has been amended under the 2004 reforms to the EC Merger Regulation and s.34A of the Act[5A] provides that the OFT must reach its decision on whether to refer or, pursuant to s.34A(3), announce that it is seeking undertakings in lieu of a reference within the EC Merger Regulation's deadline of 45 working days.[6] The remainder of the national investigation must be completed "without undue delay"[7]: no precise deadline is imposed. This removes the significant time pressure which previously existed (the OFT's *Procedural Guidance* considered that undertakings in lieu under the previous Art.9 referral back procedure would have to be agreed within two weeks of the referral back[8]).

3.074

Where the delay in agreeing undertakings becomes unreasonable, the OFT can still make a reference to the Competition Commission.[9] Indeed, the duty of the OFT to refer remains fully effective and in the absence of undertakings in lieu, a reference must be made: such undertakings, after all, cannot be sought *unless* that duty has been triggered.[10] In order to preserve

---

[97] OFT press release 56/04.

[98] OFT press release 78/04.

[99] OFT press release PN 132/03.

[1] OFT press release 04/04.

[2] OFT press release 44/04.

[3] [OFT press release 6925A, appearing on the Regulatory News Services.

[4] OFT press release 14/04.

[5] See Art.9 of Council Regulation (EEC) 4064/89 on the control of concentrations between undertakings.

[5A] Inserted by The EC Merger Control (Consequential Amendments) Regulations 2004 (SI 2004/1079).

[6] See Art.9(6), second para., of Council Regulation (EC) 139/2004 on the control of concentrations between undertakings.

[7] See Art.9(6), first para., of the 2004 EC Merger Regulation.

[8] See para.7.9 of the OFT's *Procedural Guidance* as originally written when first published (at the time of writing it had not yet been updated to reflect the new EC Merger Regulation provisions).

[9] Para.7.8 of the OFT's *Procedural Guidance* refers to this power.

[10] See s.73(1) of the Act and para.4.022 of Ch.4, above.

this alternative to agreeing undertakings in lieu (and the pressure to reach agreement which it creates over the parties), the normal statutory deadlines for considering the merger can be extended. This power applies to both the four month period within which a reference must be made[11] and the deadline which applies where notification has been made using a Merger Notice.[12] It is common practice for the OFT to extend the timetable in this way whilst undertakings in lieu are being negotiated, which is done by a letter from the case officer, giving notice to the parties that the OFT is extending the four month period. The end of the extension is governed by s.25(5) of the Act which provides that it will end with the earliest of the following events occurring:

(i)   the giving of the undertakings concerned;

(ii) the expiry of a period of 10 working days[12A] beginning with the day after receipt of notice from one of the persons due to give the undertakings that it is not prepared to do so;

(iii) the cancellation by the OFT of the extension.

On the other hand, if undertakings in lieu are agreed and accepted by the OFT (as is usually the case), this operates to bar the OFT[13] (or the Secretary of State, in public interest cases[14]) from making a reference. Nevertheless, a reference may still be made in relation to a *different* merger situation from the one in relation to which the undertakings were accepted,[15] or where material facts about relevant arrangements or transactions were not notified to the OFT or made public before the undertakings were accepted,[16] *i.e.* that the undertakings were accepted in relation to an incomplete or misleading understanding of the merger situation by the OFT. Under para.4 of Sch.10 to the Act, once agreed and accepted by the OFT, undertakings in lieu must be served on the person who gave them and any other person as specified in the undertakings, and must be published. They will also be entered in the Register of Orders and Undertakings maintained by the OFT pursuant to s.91 of the Act.[17] This register is a physical document in hard copy which is open to inspection by the public,[18] but the OFT also maintains an electronic version on its website (although there is sometimes a delay before the latest undertakings are entered on it).

---

[11] See s.24 of the Act for the four month deadline and ss. 25(4) and (5) for the power of the OFT to extend the s.24 deadline where it is seeking undertakings in lieu.

[12] See ss. 97(7) and (8) of the Act for the power of the OFT to extend the period for considering a Merger Notice. Again, the end of the extension is governed by s.97 (8) of the Act.

[12A] In this context, "days" are "working days": see s.32(a).

[13] See s.74(1) of and paras 3 and 4 of Sch.7 to the Act.

[14] See s.46(1) of the Act.

[15] See s.74(1)(b) of the Act.

[16] See s.74(2) of the Act.

[17] Note that the OFT also maintains a Register of Orders and Undertakings containing orders and undertakings accepted under the FTA and still in force.

[18] s.91(6) of the Act sets out the obligation to make the contents of the Register available to the public. The OFT Registers of Undertakings and Orders (Available Hours) Order 2003 SI 2003/1373 specifies that the Register must be available at least between 10.00am and 4.00pm on each working day.

Under the FTA, the full text of undertakings in lieu was published without any deletion of sensitive material or information. This included for example, the deadline for any required divestment, which potentially created material difficulties for the seller in seeking to achieve a sale at full value. It is notable that the undertakings in lieu given by iSOFT[18A] were published in full but that the confidentiality of the divestment deadline was preserved by defining the "Divestment Period" as "the period of time determined by the OFT and notified in writing to iSOFT by the OFT in confidence".[19] The extent to which this technique can be used to protect commercially sensitive material in the undertakings must, however, necessarily be limited by the fact that the undertakings must be capable of private enforcement through the High Court by third parties (see below) and this enforcement mechanism would be undermined if the key elements of the undertakings were not made public.[20-21]

Enforcement of undertakings in lieu

Section 75 of the Act gives the OFT power to take action where it becomes clear that an undertaking in lieu "has not been, is not being or will not be" complied with, or where the undertaking was accepted on the basis of information that was false or misleading in a material respect. The OFT may make an order containing anything permitted by Sch.8 to the Act, together with any supplementary, consequential or incidental provision which it considers appropriate,[22] for the purposes of remedying, mitigating or preventing the substantial lessening of competition or any adverse effect arising out of the merger situation.[23] In particular, there is no requirement that the content or scope of the order should correspond to the undertaking in lieu which it replaces. An order could therefore potentially be more (or alternatively less) onerous on the parties than the undertakings. The OFT also has powers to make an interim order to ensure that the effectiveness of an intended s.75 order is not prejudiced in the interim.[24] The OFT can also use civil proceedings to enforce an undertaking, which would, for example, enable it to seek an injunction from the High Court to enforce compliance.[25]

3.075

However, it is not only the OFT who can enforce an undertaking. Third parties are given a right in s.94 of the Act to bring an action for breach of statutory duty against a party to an undertaking who does not comply with it, where the third party has suffered loss or damage.[26] A corresponding provision existed under the FTA[27], although it proved to be more difficult

---

[18A] Undertakings dated April 29, 2004 given by iSOFT plc in relation to the completed acquisition of Torex plc.

[19] Note that para.8.7 of the OFT's *Substantive Assessment Guidance* states that "The sale should be completed within a stated period (usually a maximum of six months)", after which an independent trustee may be appointed to manage the divestment process.

[20-21] There is arguably a key difference here with procedure under the EC Merger Regulation, where key elements of undertakings are often kept confidential, but where there is no provision for private enforcement by third parties.

[22] See s.75(4) of the Act.

[23] See s.75(2) and s.73(2) of the Act.

[24] See s.76 of the Act.

[25] See s.94 of the Act.

[26] See s.94(4) of the Act.

[27] See s.93A of the FTA

for a third party to make use of than might have appeared on the face of the statutory wording.[28]

Undertakings in lieu where the public interest regime has been triggered

3.076 Where the Secretary of State has served an intervention notice so that the public interest regime applies, undertakings in lieu remain a possible way in which to avoid a reference. As the OFT's *Procedural Guidance* confirms,[29] the OFT's advice under s.44 will include advice on whether undertakings in lieu would be appropriate to address the competition concerns,[30] and if so, descriptions of the undertakings which the OFT believes would be appropriate.[31] The Secretary of State is required to accept the conclusions of the OFT in full in this respect (including the descriptions of appropriate undertakings)[32] and, unlike the position under the FTA, cannot for example accept the advice that undertakings in lieu would be appropriate but alter their scope. The OFT's advice on undertakings in lieu will be limited to the competition concerns only: the Act specifically requires the OFT to disregard the public interest considerations specified in the intervention notice in this regard.[33]

The power of the Secretary of State to accept undertakings in lieu is not limited to the competition concerns in a particular case: he may also accept undertakings in lieu which remedy the public interest concerns arising out of the merger.[34] The Act does not require the OFT to advise the Secretary of State in this regard. In relation to national security mergers, the OFT's *Procedural Guidance* expressly indicates that the Ministry of Defence will discuss any proposed undertakings in lieu with the parties on behalf of the Secretary of State[35] and this was certainly the case in *General Dynamics/ Alvis* and in *Finmeccanica/Agustawestland*, both considered under a s.67 European intervention notice.[36] As regards newspapers and media mergers, the advice which OFCOM is required to give to the Secretary of State on the public interest considerations does not expressly include advice on the possibility that any concerns could be dealt with through undertakings in lieu. OFCOM's *Guidance for the public interest test for media mergers* says very little about undertakings in lieu but does indicate that OFCOM can be requested to consider undertakings in lieu in confidential guidance requests[37], which in turn suggests that it may cover this question in its advice to the Secretary of State.

---

[28] See para.9.030 of Ch.9, below which discusses the interpretation of the private enforcement provisions of the FTA in *Mid Kent Holdings plc v General Utilities* [1997] 1 W.L.R. 14,[1996] 3 All E.R. 132.

[29] See para.7.20 of the OFT's *Procedural Guidance*.

[30] See s.44(4)(f) of the Act.

[31] See s.44(5) of the Act.

[32] See s.46(2) of the Act.

[33] See s.44(4)(f) of the Act.

[34] See para.3(2) of Sch.7 to the Act.

[35] See para.7.20 of the OFT's *Procedural Guidance*.

[36] The report of the OFT pursuant to Arts 4(2) to (5) of the Enterprise Act 2002 (Protection of Legitimate Interests) Order 2003 of May 20, 2004, "*Anticipated acquisition by General Dynamics Corporation of Alvis plc*", published on the DTI's website, states that draft undertakings in lieu were drawn up by the MOD, to remedy the national security concerns which it had identified. The same approach was taken in *Finmeccanica/Agustawestland*.

[37] See paras 24 and 37 of OFCOM's *Guidance for the public interest test for media mergers*.

A further area of uncertainty is whether the Secretary of State can decide to deal with the competition concerns through undertakings in lieu (where the OFT has so advised), but refer the public interest concerns. On the one hand, the ability to split the issues in this way would seem consistent with the fact that a reference can be made on public interest grounds alone[38] and with the rationale underlying the undertakings in lieu mechanisms, namely that it is preferable as a matter of efficiency and good public administration to avoid (or, in this case, limit) the cost of a reference where possible. On the other hand, if the merger is in principle expected to result in a substantial lessening of competition, and the Competition Commission is going to be asked to consider the public interest considerations in any case, it may be preferable to allow the Competition Commission to investigate both the competition and wider public interest issues in their entirety so as to give it maximum flexibility as regards remedies, without any possible constraints that undertakings in lieu might create. This is arguably part of the wider issue as to whether a reference under the Act is made in relation to a merger situation as a whole, or in relation to individual economic markets, or (as here) in relation to particular concerns, thus allowing a "split" reference which does not concern all aspects of the merger. This issue is discussed further in para.4.009 of Ch.4.

Where the Secretary of State decides to seek undertakings in lieu, the provisions of Sch.10 to the Act, described above, apply as regards the procedure to be followed. It is unclear at this stage whether undertakings in lieu would be negotiated by the DTI on behalf of the Secretary of State or whether this task would be delegated to the OFT (which would seem more likely). The Act certainly gives the Secretary of State power to require the assistance of the OFT in this regard.[39] In *General Dynamics/Alvis*, which (as noted above) was considered under a s.67 European intervention notice, it is clear that it was the MOD which drew up undertakings and confirmed with the parties that they would be acceptable, with the OFT reporting on this process to the Secretary of State.[40] The DTI simply ran the consultation process on the draft undertakings itself.[41]

As regards enforcement of undertakings in lieu given to the Secretary of State, the Secretary of State can make an order in similar circumstances to the OFT's order making power under s.75 of the Act.[42] The Secretary of State can also bring an action in the High Court to enforce undertakings in lieu.[43] Moreover, the right of a third party to whom loss is caused by contravention of undertakings in lieu to bring an action for breach of statutory duty for failure to comply with the terms of undertakings in lieu applies equally where they have been given to the Secretary of State.[44]

---

[38] See ss.45(3) and (5) of the Act.
[39] See s.93 of the Act.
[40] This is clear from the report of the OFT in this case, discussed in para.3.066, above.
[41] See the DTI press release of June 3, 2004, *Proposed acquisition by General Dynamics Corporation of Alvis plc*, which announced commencement of the consultation process and stated that comments should be sent to a named officer in the Consumer and Competition Policy Directorate of the DTI.
[42] See paras 5 and 6 of Sch.7 to the Act.
[43] See s.94(8) of the Act.
[44] See s.94(4) of the Act.

Ancillary restrictions

3.077   Ancillary restrictions are competition restrictions which are agreed in the contractual documentation drawn up to implement the merger. They are considered to be unobjectionable and "ancillary" in the strict legal sense where they are directly related to and necessary for the merger in question, taking into account issues such as their duration, subject matter and the geographical area affected. The basic concepts relating to ancillary restrictions are set out in para.2.054 and following of Ch.2 above.

As regards the procedure on the basis of which the OFT will consider ancillary restrictions, the OFT's *Procedural Guidance* states that it will consider them at the same time as its assessment of the merger to which it is claimed they are directly related and necessary.[45] The OFT sets out in its guidance that, should the parties require a view as to whether restrictions are ancillary, they should indicate this when lodging their merger submission. The OFT requests that, in order for it to give a view, the parties should provide:

"— details of each restriction which is considered to be ancillary and a copy of the relevant agreement(s)

— an explanation of why each restriction is directly related and necessary to the implementation of the merger, and

— an explanation of why each restriction may be subject to the prohibition in Chapter I of the Competition Act if it is not considered to be ancillary to the merger".[46]

The OFT may consult with third parties as to the ancillary aspects of arrangements as part of its merger assessment process and will deliver a written decision as to whether it considers the restrictions to be ancillary. The OFT states that it will give such a verdict even where the merger does not qualify for investigation, and aims to carry out the assessment within the administrative timetable for considering mergers. The OFT also states that it is willing to consider ancillary restrictions as part of a confidential guidance application[47], although it states that any opinion given in such an application will be the view of the Mergers Branch and will not form part of the confidential guidance.

In practice, the OFT's approach to ancillary restrictions in the few cases to date where they have been mentioned in its decisions has been low key.[48]

---

[45] The European Commission originally followed this approach under the EC Merger Regulation. However, the 2001 Ancillary Restraints notice announced the abandonment of the practice of individually assessing and formally addressing ancillary restraints in each merger decision. This change of approach was reinforced with the 2004 EC Merger Regulation reforms: the EC Merger Regulation now states expressly that a merger clearance decision is deemed to cover any ancillary restraints in the merger documentation (see Arts 6(1), final para., Art.8(1), second para., and Art.8(2), third para.) and the European Commission no longer considers each restriction individually.

[46] Para.B.19 of OFT's *Procedural Guidance*.

[47] See para.3.004, above.

[48] Ancillary restrictions were mentioned in four of the 87 cases considered by the OFT under the Act as at June 1, 2004. See further paras 2.055 *et seq.* of Ch.2, above.

Confidentiality in dealing with the OFT

Confidentiality under the Act—Part 9

It will have become evident from the discussion at paras 3.027 and 3.031 **3.078** above of the information to be included in a "traditional" notification and in a Merger Notice[49] that much of the information that is made available to the OFT in the course of the merger assessment process is likely to be unpublished and of a commercially sensitive nature. This realisation inevitably leads to questions relating to security within the OFT, the obligations imposed upon it to maintain confidentiality and its practice concerning the handling of confidential material.

The OFT's *Procedural Guidance* confirms that it is "strict OFT policy to observe confidentiality in all aspects of its operation", and experience in dealing with the OFT suggests that parties submitting material to it in connection with the evaluation of a merger situation (including third parties to whom enquiries have been addressed), need have little concern that information supplied by them, or views which they have expressed, will be "leaked" to the public.[50] On occasion the OFT will need to make use of information supplied to it in connection with the evaluation of a merger proposal. In doing so, however, the OFT is, like the Competition Commission, bound by the Act to maintain confidentiality.[51]

The statutory provisions governing confidentiality are set out in Pt 9 of the Act (ss.237 to 246). The basic rule is that information which the OFT obtains in connection with the exercise of its functions under Pt 3 of the Act—*i.e.* the merger control regime—and which relates to the affairs of an individual or any business of an undertaking, must not be disclosed during the lifetime of the individual or while the undertaking continues in existence.[52] This general restriction is subject only to disclosures which are permitted under the Act.

Section 239(1) permits disclosure where consent is obtained. The remainder of s.239 specifies which consents are required:

(i) where the information was obtained by the OFT from person who had the information lawfully and the OFT knows the identity of that person, the consent of that person is required for disclosure;

(ii) if the information relates to the affairs of an individual, the consent of the individual is required for disclosure;

(iii) if the information relates to the business of an undertaking, the consent of the person carrying on the business is required for disclosure. For these purposes, consent can be obtained , as appropriate, from a director, secretary or other officer of the company, a partner of the partnership, or someone concerned in the

---

[49] Reproduced at App.4.
[50] See para.5.9 of the OFT's *Procedural Guidance*. See also paras 5.023 and following which discuss Pt 9 of the Act as it applies to the Competition Commission.
[51] See Pt 9 of the Act.
[52] See ss.237 and 238.

management of the undertaking where it is unincorporated or an association of undertakings.[53]

3.079   The wording of the Act suggests that these required consents are potentially cumulative: for example, it is possible to envisage that the consents specified in paras (i) and (ii) above might both apply to a single piece of information which was lawfully in the possession of one party but relates to the business of a different party. The Act specifies that "*each* required consent" (emphasis added) must be obtained.[54]

Section 241 permits disclosure where it is for the purposes of facilitating the exercise by the authority (including the OFT) of any statutory function or to facilitate the exercise by any other authority of its statutory functions (in each case, whether under the Act or other legislation). In relation to any disclosure, however, s.244 requires the OFT to have regard to:

(i)   the need to exclude from disclosure so far as practicable, any information whose disclosure the OFT thinks is contrary to the public interest;

(ii)   the need to exclude from disclosure so far as practicable any commercial information whose disclosure the OFT thinks might harm the legitimate business interests of the undertaking to which it relates, or any information relating to the private affairs of an individual whose disclosure the OFT thinks might significantly harm the individual's interests; and

(iii)   the extent to which the disclosure of the information is necessary for the purpose for which the authority is permitted to make the disclosure.

It is the OFT which makes the decision about whether disclosure will significantly harm a party's interests: the party itself may make representations requesting confidential treatment of information but cannot demand it.

"Information" is not defined in Pt 9 of the Act, but in practice the confidentiality obligations are treated as covering more or less everything that comes into the OFT's files during the course of investigating a merger. Thus submissions made will be treated as confidential. A non-confidential version may be provided, although submissions are seldom passed directly to other parties for their comments: the OFT tends instead to extract issues in which it wishes to obtain comment or a view from a different party or third party. If a summary paper is prepared for this purpose, it will usually be passed to the party who made the original submission for comment before it is disclosed to the third party.

3.080   The apparent emphasis in Pt9 of the Act is on the obligation to maintain confidentiality. However, the permission noted above in s.241 which allows the OFT to disclose information "for the purposes of facilitating the exercise by the [OFT] of any function it has under or by virtue of this Act or any other enactment" is potentially very wide in its scope: "which would

---

[53] See s.239 of the Act.
[54] See s.239(1) of the Act.

facilitate" is a much lower threshold than, for example "which is necessary". In relation to the corresponding confidentiality provisions under the FTA, case law confirmed that the threshold of showing that disclosure is for the purposes of facilitating the performance of the functions of (on the facts in question) the Competition Commission was fairly low (see paras 5.024 and 5.025 of Ch.5, below).

There are, on occasion, situations where disclosure of confidential information may well be desirable in merger cases. For example, the OFT is under a duty to publish its decisions on whether to refer or clear a merger,[55] and such decisions must be reasoned.[56] Publication is important because of the interplay between transparency of decision-making and the ability of the parties and particularly third parties to seek review of the decision under s.120 of the Act.

Dealing with confidentiality in practice

As a general point, it is always good practice to identify for the benefit of the OFT those aspects of a submission that are regarded by the parties as commercially sensitive or any circumstances where identification of the source of certain information would be commercially prejudicial. If requested, the OFT will inform the party supplying the information of the intention to disclose it to third parties in advance of doing so. This may enable the party involved to suggest to the OFT how such disclosure might be achieved with the minimum damage to its interests.   3.081

Clearly the OFT may sometimes need to test with third parties, or with the other party to a contested takeover, propositions put forward supporting one view or another: usually, however, this can be done without revealing specific sensitive information or the identity of the party supplying the information (although this will sometimes be obvious). The standard approach where the OFT wishes to seek comments from another party about statements or data submitted to it by another party is to inform the party which submitted it that the OFT is proposing to disclose the information. The party concerned will be given an opportunity to prepare a non-confidential version of the information, or to request that certain excisions be made from the material to protect commercially sensitive material.

At the end of the OFT's inquiry, the full, reasoned decision will not be published contemporaneously with the announcement of the headline decision whether to refer. At that time, the parties (but not complainants or other third parties who may have been involved in the OFT's consultation process) will receive the full text of the decision, which is very likely to contain some information which is commercially sensitive. The parties will be given a short period[57] to identify business secrets[58] in the decision and to

---

[55] See s.107(1) of the Act.
[56] See s.107(4) of the Act.
[57] The length of time given for confidentiality requests is not fixed and seems to depend to some extent, on the level of interest in the case. Thus in the authors' experience, in a case where a reference was made, only two working days were given for the submission of confidentiality requests; in cases where clearance is given, a longer period may be allowed. That said, the parties should probably assume that as little as 48 hours may be given.
[58] The expression "business secrets" is adopted from EC competition law procedure. The European Commission's Notice on the internal rules for processing requests for access to the

request any excisions. The process of seeking "consent" for Pt 9 purposes is essentially done in a passive way: the OFT indicates what they propose to publish and it is for the parties to object. The OFT does not systematically obtain a consent for each piece of information which will be disclosed in the course of publishing the decision.

Where confidential treatment is accorded to a claimed business secret, it will be excised from the published, non-confidential version of the OFT's decision. There is always an indication in the document that something has been deleted and sometimes a guide as to the substance of the deleted information: for example, data such as market share information is usually replaced by a range, rather than a blank. The parties are not always consulted about any such excisions (or substitute information), although it is often sensible for the parties to make a suggestion when making the original business secrets request. It is also usually sensible to include a brief justification for each claim for confidentiality.

3.082   Finally, in relation to confidentiality, it is worth noting that the process of seeking review of a decision before the Competition Appeal Tribunal under s.120 of the Act can sometimes result in the disclosure of material which was previously treated as confidential.[59]

Fees for merger clearance

3.083   Section 121 of the Act gives the Secretary of State power to provide for fees to be payable in relation to merger clearance procedures. That power has been exercised and the provisions regarding merger fees are contained in the Enterprise Act 2002 (Merger Fees and Determination of Turnover) Order 2003[60] ("the Merger Fees Order").

---

file [1997] O.J. C23/3, lists the following categories of information as potentially constituting "business secrets": methods of assessing manufacturing and distribution costs, production secrets and processes, supply sources, quantities produced and sold, market shares, customer and distributor lists, marketing plans, cost price structure, sales policy and information on the internal organisation of the firm (see n.9 of the Notice). Budgets, financial plans and other financial and/or management strategy information will also typically be considered to constitute business secrets. See further Kerse, "EC Antitrust Procedure", 4th ed, Sweet and Maxwell, at 8.22 *et seq.*

[59] In its judgment in *IBA Health v Office of Fair Trading* [2003] CAT 27, [2004] Comp. A.R. 235, the CAT included the full text of the OFT's issues letter sent to the merging parties iSOFT and Torex. That document had previously been seen only by the parties and had not been published. Although not a merger case, it is perhaps instructive also to consider a judgment of the CAT at an interim stage in the appeals against the OFT's decision under the Chapter I prohibition in relation to price-fixing of replica football kit (see OFT decision No.CA98/06/2003 *Price-fixing of Replica Football Kit* of August 1, 2003). In its judgment of October 27, 2003 in *Umbro Holdings Ltd v Office of Fair Trading* [2003] CAT 26, [2004] Comp. A.R. 217, the CAT held that information concerning Umbro's leniency application, in respect of which confidentiality had been claimed by Umbro and granted at the OFT stage of the proceedings, had to be disclosed at the CAT stage of the proceedings. The CAT ruled that "there are insuperable difficulties in maintaining the confidentiality which Umbro claims", including writing the eventual judgement on Umbro's appeal, conducting the hearing, and because of the possible prejudice which maintaining confidentiality might cause to other appellants in the case. This case concerned proceedings under the Competition Act 1998 but it is possible that similar issues could arise in cases under s.120 of the Act.

[60] SI 2003/1370.

At the time of writing, a major review of merger fees was underway.[60A] The rationale behind merger fees has always been that the merger regime should, to some degree, be self-financing (with the intention being that the fee should cover not just the work of the OFT's Mergers Branch but also the costs generated by the work of the Competition Commission and, where applicable, the Secretary of State/DTI). However, merger fees had not been increased since 1990 (they were not initially increased under the Act and had not increased with inflation[60B]), and the change to the jurisdictional thresholds caused by the replacement of the assets test with the turnover test had the effect of reducing the number of mergers which fell under the jurisdiction of the UK merger regime. That point, together with the increasing cost of Competition Commission inquiries under the Act[61], had the consequence that merger fee income was falling far short of covering the cost of the regime. In 2002/2003, the OFT's Annual Report states that merger fees income was £2.1 million, which, compared to the costs incurred by the OFT, resulted in a deficit of £4.5 million (similar to the deficit in 2001/2002).[62] In 2003/2004, by contrast, the OFT's Annual Report states that merger fees income has fallen to just below £1 million, with a more than threefold increase in the deficit to £14.7 million.[63]

The DTI's consultation paper published in August 2004 raised questions of principle as to whether, and if so how, the fees structure should be changed. As at the time of writing, the consultation period was still open, so there was no draft statutory instrument outlining the planned changes and the outcome of the consultation process was unknown. Key questions raised in the paper included whether the purpose of charging merger fees should be to achieve full cost recovery or just greater cost recovery; how a phased approach to build up to full cost recovery might be achieved; whether (contrary to the then current position) fees should be charged for the acquisition of material influence; whether fees should be charged in relation to special merger situations and investigations under taken by the UK pursuant to Art.21(4) of the EC Merger Regulation[63A]; and the merits of various alternative fee structures. The last question included, in the context of identifying alternative fee structures for discussion, some very significant fee increases.[63B] It remains to be seen what basis the government

---

[60A] In August 2004, the DTI issued its *Consultation on possible changes to the system of charging firms for the costs of merger control*, available from the DTI website.

[60B] The DTI's consultation paper (cited below) calculated that if annual increases had been made for inflation, the fees would, by 2004, have been significantly higher: for example, the highest level fee of £15,000 (see below) would have grown to £22,115 (see para.2.13 of the paper).

[61] See para.4.011 of Ch.4 below.

[62] See the OFT's Annual Report for 2002/2003 at p.128.

[63] See the OFT's Annual Report for 2003/2004 at p.133. Note that the DTI's consultation paper also includes an analysis of the costs of the UK merger control regime: see para.2.2 of the paper.

[63A] See further paras 2.050 and following of Ch.2, above.

[63B] One of the most material proposed changes was to introduce a second fee where a merger is referred to the Competition Commission, ranging from £75,000 up to £300,000. Overall, the maximum proposal in the consultation paper was a fee of £30,000 for mergers concerning a target business with UK turnover greater than £200 million, plus a further fee of £300,000 if the matter is referred to the Competition Commission (see para 3.8 of the paper). Note that even by the time the paper was published, the cost estimates had been

decides to apply to fees, and how significant any increases are, although it seems inevitable that there will be increases. The remainder of this section discusses the fee structure as it stood at the time of writing (October 2004), but it should be borne in mind that the fee levels (although not other aspects of payment of fees, such as who should pay and the exceptions) was expected to change shortly.

3.084 Merger fees are payable in relation to all cases which are pre-notified by way of a Merger Notice,[64] and in relation to all other cases where the OFT (or the Secretary of State, in public interest cases[65]) concludes that the merger meets the jurisdictional thresholds for a qualifying merger (whether the turnover test or the share of supply test).[66] The obligation to pay the fee applies regardless of whether a reference is made. Fees are also payable on the making of a merger reference under the Water Industry Act 1991.[67]

There are a few exceptions to the obligation to pay the fee. First, in cases which are not pre-notified on a Merger Notice, the fee is only payable in relation to acquisitions of a controlling interest. It is not payable where *de facto* control or control amounting only to material influence are acquired.[68] Secondly, merger fees are not payable where the OFT concludes that although there is a qualifying merger situation in contemplation, the proposals are either not sufficiently advanced or not sufficiently likely to proceed to warrant reference.[69] Thirdly, there is an exception where the acquiring party qualifies as a small or medium sized enterprise.[70]

Where a Merger Notice is used to notify a proposed merger, the merger fee is payable by the person submitting the Merger Notice[71] at the time at which the Merger Notice is given.[72] In practice, payment is either made by cheque delivered with the Merger Notice to the OFT or can be arranged to be transferred directly to the OFT's accounts at a point in time close to when the Merger Notice is lodged (although it is sometimes considered simpler and more certain to use a cheque, which avoids in particular, any delay in starting the clock running on the statutory timeframe, because the payment is not immediately identified when it arrives in the accounts of the OFT). Payment of the fee in full and at the appropriate time is critical because the statutory timeframe for consideration of the Merger Notice does not commence until the day following payment of the fee.[73]

---

overtaken and the cost of the regime was believed to be greater than stated in the consultation paper—so the maximum proposal of a £300,000 fee for a Commission reference could be increased further if the government were to decide to base the fees on the principle of full cost recovery and to charge a separate fee for a reference to the Competition Commission.

[64] See Art.3(a) of the Merger Fees Order.

[65] See Art.3(c) of the Merger Fees Order.

[66] See Art.3(b) of the Merger Fees Order.

[67] See the Merger (Fees) Regulations 1990, SI 1990/1660.

[68] See Art.4(1)(b) of the Merger Fees Order. See also paras 2.006 *et seq.* for a discussion of these concepts of control. Note that as at the time of writing the DTI was consulting in relation to removing this exception in relation to the acquisition of material influence (and although it is not mentioned in the consultation paper, presumably if the exception in relation to material influence were to be withdrawn, the exception in relation to *de facto* control would also be lost).

[69] See Art.4(2) of the Merger Fees Order.

[70] See Art.7 of the Merger Fees Order.

[71] See Art.6(1) of the Merger Fees Order.

[72] See Art.9(1) of the Merger Fees Order. See further para.3.029 above.

[73] See s.97(1) of the Act.

Where notification of a merger (whether anticipated or completed) is made by way of a traditional written submission, or where no notification has been made but the OFT raises questions with the parties about the merger of its own initiative, the merger fee is payable by the acquirer.[74] Where there is more than one acquirer, the co-acquirers will be jointly and severally liable for the fee.[75] In either of these cases, the fee becomes payable when the OFT (or the Secretary of State, in public interest cases[76]) announces its decision that there is a qualifying merger situation (and whether a reference is being made).[77] In practice, the OFT will issue an invoice for the appropriate fee to the acquiring party at the time the decision is announced, which will be payable within 30 days of the invoice date.[78]

The levels of fees payable as at the time of writing (as noted above, reforms and increases are anticipated) are laid down in the Merger Fees Order[79] and vary according to the size of the acquisition. As at October 2004 they were as follows:

Value of the UK turnover of the enterprises being acquired	Fee
£20 million or less	£ 5,000
Greater than £20 million but less than or equal to £70 million	£10,000
Greater than £70 million	£15,000

Under the prenotification procedure, where the merger fee has been paid but it is subsequently established by the OFT either that the merger does not qualify for investigation or that the EC Merger Regulation applies, it is clear that a refund of the fees must be made.[80] However, where a merger subject to UK merger control is transferred to the European Commission pursuant to Art.22 of the EC Merger Regulation, the Merger Fees Order provides only that a refund *may* be made[81], apparently affording some discretion to the OFT as to whether or not to return the fee. Art. 22 references have, under the pre-reform EC Merger Regulation[82] been fairly rare occurrences. However, it is to be noted that where the OFT had a discretion whether to repay a merger fee under the FTA[83] it invariably repaid fees without question.

3.085

---

[74] See Art.6(2) of the Merger Fees Order.
[75] *i.e.* each of them individually is liable for the full amount. See Art.6(4) of the Merger Fees Order.
[76] See Art.9(3) of the Merger Fees Order.
[77] See Art.9(2) of the Merger Fees Order.
[78] See para.6.3 of the OFT's *Procedural Guidance*.
[79] See Art.5(1) of the Merger Fees Order.
[80] See Art.10(a) and (b) of the Merger Fees Order.
[81] See Art.10(c) of the Merger Fees Order.
[82] *i.e.* Council Regulation (EEC) 4064/89 on the control of concentrations.
[83] Under the previous provisions, the OFT had a discretion whether to repay merger fees where it emerged following notification on a Merger Notice either that no merger situation had arisen or that the acquisition was not a qualifying merger situation.

Where the parties withdraw a Merger Notice, the fee is not repayable.[84] It is open to debate whether it would become repayable should it subsequently emerge that there is no qualifying merger situation: arguably it should be as the Art.10 refund provisions do not expressly require that the Merger Notice must not have been withdrawn. On the other hand, there would not appear to be scope to demand a refund of the merger fee if a Merger Notice used to notify an acquisition of *de facto* control or of material influence was subsequently withdrawn.

Where a merger between two overseas enterprises qualifies for investigation but no substantial lessening of competition within a UK product or service market could conceivably arise, it is perhaps questionable whether it is appropriate for the OFT to demand the payment of fees. In practice, the OFT will not normally seek fees in the case of a foreign merger in these circumstances.[85] It should also be noted that there is scope for the OFT to seek information on mergers in respect of which no clearance has been sought and which raise no adverse competition concern, and thereafter issue clearance and demand the requisite fee (which has certainly occurred).

---

[84] As is expressly stated at para.6.2 of the OFT's *Procedural Guidance*.

[85] See Art.6(5) of the Merger Fees Order which provides for a limited exemption to paying fees for wholly foreign acquisitions where the merger situation in question does not arise either wholly or partially from something done by the acquirer in the UK.

CHAPTER 4

THE OFFICE OF FAIR TRADING'S DUTY TO REFER

Introduction

Having considered the legal basis on which the OFT may have jurisdiction   4.001
to consider a merger (Ch.2) and the procedure which will be followed in
relation to notification and the OFT's investigation (Ch.3), this chapter will
consider the meaning of the statutory duty which is imposed on the OFT to
refer a merger in respect of which it believes that it may be the case that it
has resulted or may be expected to result in a substantial lessening of
competition. In particular, the meaning of the duty, as considered by the
Competition Appeal Tribunal (the CAT) and the Court of Appeal in the
IBA Health case[1], will be discussed.

This chapter will go on to consider the circumstances in which that
duty is potentially overtaken by the OFT's discretion *not* to refer, and the
circumstances where the duty does not operate. There are three sets of
circumstances in which the Act gives the OFT a discretion *not* to refer a
merger, notwithstanding that the OFT has concluded that it can be
expected to result in a substantial lessening of competition. The discretion
will arise where the market in question is not of sufficient importance to
warrant reference: this is essentially a question of proportionality,
comparing the value of the potential reference market to the cost to the
public purse of a reference. The discretion will also arise where the parties
can show that "relevant customer benefits" will arise as a result of the
merger, such as lower prices, better quality or greater innovation. In such
circumstances, if the customer benefits outweigh the anti-competitive
effects of the merger, the OFT does not have to refer it. Finally, in the case
of anticipated mergers which have not yet been completed, the OFT does
not have to make a reference where it considers that the merger plans are
not sufficiently advanced or likely to proceed to warrant reference.

Finally, this chapter will consider the situations where the Act prevents a
reference being made even though the OFT's duty to refer has been triggered. Each of these situations will be highlighted below but two warrant
closer consideration. First, a reference cannot be made where the OFT is
considering whether to accept undertakings in lieu of reference, and then
subsequently once undertakings in lieu have been accepted. Secondly, the
OFT cannot make a reference where the Secretary of State has served an

---

[1] *IBA Health Limited v Office of Fair Trading* [2003] CAT 27, [2004] Comp. A.R. 235, *Office
of Fair Trading v IBA Health Limited* [2004] EWCA Civ.142, (2004) 101(11) L.S.G. 33,
(2004) 154 N.L.J. 352.

intervention notice, triggering the public interest regime under the Act, as discussed above in Ch.2.[2]

The meaning of the OFT's duty to refer

The initial understanding of the test for reference under the Act

4.002   Under the FTA, the basis upon which the Secretary of State should exercise his discretion to refer or clear a merger, having received the OFT's advice, was not specified: he had an absolute discretion in making the decision whether to refer. In practice, the public interest test laid down for the Secretary of State's final decision following a reference to the Competition Commission[3] was also applied to the question of whether to refer. In line with the "Tebbitt doctrine" and then Labour government policy,[4] the OFT drew up its advice on competition grounds and the Secretary of State, in the vast majority of cases, followed the Director General's recommendation to refer, clear, or seek undertakings in lieu of reference based on an analysis of the impact of the merger on competition.

Under the Act, the decision to clear a merger or make a reference to the Competition Commission has been taken away from the Secretary of State and given to the OFT, except in relation to a limited category of public interest cases.[5] The absolute discretion has been replaced by a duty to refer where certain conditions are met. The duty of the OFT to refer a merger to the Competition Commission is set out in s.22(1) of the Act for completed mergers, and s.33(1) for anticipated mergers. The essence of the two tests is the same: subject to a limited discretion and certain statutory exceptions,[6] the OFT has a duty to refer a merger (anticipated or completed):

"if the OFT believes that it is or may be the case that

(a)   a relevant merger situation has been [or will be] created; and
(b)   the creation of that situation has resulted, or may be expected to result, in a substantial lessening of competition within any market or markets in the United Kingdom for goods or services".[7]

Accordingly, the public interest test on which the decision whether to refer was based under the FTA has been replaced with the substantial lessening of competition test under the Act: a test which is expressly focussed on an analysis of the conditions of competition and how the merger will impact on them.

Notwithstanding these reforms and the procedural changes which they have brought about, the OFT's substantive analysis and methodological approach under the Act were not generally expected to change materially from those employed by the Director General of Fair Trading in advising

---

[2] See paras 2.025 *et seq.* of Ch.2.
[3] See s.84 of the FTA.
[4] See further para.1.001 of Ch.1, above.
[5] See paras 2.026 *et seq.* of Ch.2 for a discussion of the categories of public interest consideration which have been specified under the Act.
[6] Discussed below at paras 4.020 *et seq.*
[7] S.22(1) adjusted to reflect s.33(1) of the Act.

the Secretary of State under the FTA. As the then Director General (who became the first Chairman of the OFT under the Act) commented shortly before the Act received Royal Assent:

"The Enterprise Bill proposes major reform of the framework for UK merger control, but substantive policy will be largely unchanged. In many respects the reform will bring the law more sharply into line with existing policy.

At present, the test by which mergers are appraised is formally the 'public interest'; in practice a competition test is paramount in virtually all cases. This is entirely consistent with the public interest on the view that the best that merger control can do for the public interest is to safe-guard competitive conditions. But there is great advantage in focusing the legal test clearly and sharply on competition criteria.

The new test will be whether a merger has resulted, or may be expected to result, in a substantial lessening of competition [(SLC)] in a market in the UK. . . .

. . . At present the OFT's role is to advise the Secretary of State for Trade and Industry (SoS) whether to refer a merger for full investigation to the Competition Commission (CC). In the new framework we will have direct responsibility for references. I doubt this will make a practical difference, because reference advice is independently given—with SLC paramount—and invariably accepted as things stand now".[8]

As the quotation indicates, the public interest test had in practice been interpreted as a substantial lessening of competition test by the OFT for a number of years (wider public interest considerations being introduced by the Secretary of State, if at all). The fact that the OFT already analysed mergers under the FTA by reference to the substantial lessening of competition test is clear from the text of the advice given by the Director General to the Secretary of State under the FTA in a number of cases.[9] The same **4.003**

---

[8] See the speech of John Vickers *"Competition economics and policy—A speech on the occasion of the launch of the new social sciences building at Oxford University"*, October 3, 2002 (available on the OFT's website), at pp.7 to 8.

[9] See for example, the Director General's advice of October 18, 2000 in *Acquisition by GWR Group plc of the radio interests of the Daily Mail and General Trust plc* where the Director General concludes on horizontal issues that "any loss of actual competition arising from the merger is likely to be marginal and the loss of prospective competition is probably not substantial". See also the Director General's advice of December 21, 2001 in *Proposed acquisition by Lallemand UK Ltd of LHS (Finings) Ltd* in which the Director General refers expressly to the risk of a substantial lessening of competition. The wording of the conclusions of the advices given by the Director General in relation to the various competing bids for Safeway are very much in the language used for competition assessment under the Act: "We believe that there is a significant prospect that this merger may be expected to result in a substantial lessening of competition. The potential adverse effects we have identified do not appear to be outweighed by potential consumer benefits. Nor do we believe that undertak-ings in lieu of reference would be appropriate . . .". These words are taken from the Director General's advice in relation to Sainsbury's bid but the same or similar words were used in his advices regarding the Tesco, Asda and Morrison bid as well. See the Director General's advices, all dated March 13, 2003, in *Proposed acquisition by J Sainsbury plc of Safeway plc*, *Proposed acquisition by Tesco plc of Safeway plc*, *Proposed acquisition by Asda Stores Limited, a subsidiary of Wal-Mart Stores, Inc of Safeway plc* and *Proposed acquisition by Morrison Supermarkets plc of Safeway plc.*

point was made in the original wording of the OFT's *Substantive Assessment Guidance*: "The OFT considers that this threshold is the same as that against which FTA reference advices were prepared".[10] There was not therefore expected to be any interruption to on-going merger analysis[11] as the change of legal test was not in practice expected to alter the basis or methodology of the OFT's assessment.[12]

The first few months of the new regime proceeded on this basis. However, notwithstanding this widespread expectation by regulators and practitioners, the first application to the Competition Appeal Tribunal under s.120 of the Act for review of a merger control decision threw both the meaning of the test for reference and the role of the OFT under the Act into doubt.

No power to decide where there is room for two views?

4.004 In *IBA Health v OFT*,[13] the CAT was asked to consider the legality of a decision by the OFT not to refer the proposed acquisition of Torex plc by iSOFT plc.[14] The correct interpretation of s.33(1) was not in dispute between the parties and was not included in the written pleadings lodged with the CAT, but the CAT itself raised the issue with the parties and asked them to address it at the oral hearing, and went on to rule on its meaning. It is clear that the CAT was not of the view that the new test essentially ratified/codified existing practice.[15] The CAT held that the s.33(1) threshold essentially amounted to a two stage test:

> "In a case where real issues as to the substantial lessening of competition potentially arise, it seems to us that the words 'it may be the case' imply a two-part test. In our view, the decision maker(s) at the OFT must satisfy themselves (i) that as far as the OFT is concerned there is no significant prospect of a substantial lessening of competition and (ii) there is no significant prospect of an alternative view being taken in the context of a fuller investigation by the [Competition Commission]. These two elements may resemble two sides of the same coin, but in our view they are analytically distinct".[16]

---

[10] See para.3.2 of the original version of the OFT's *Substantive Assessment Guidance*. This has since been deleted.

[11] Indeed the transitional provisions for the replacement of the FTA regime with the regime introduced by the Act provided for the OFT to simply switch the legal basis of its review on June 20, 2003, potentially mid-way through its analysis (although this was not the case for Merger Notice cases). See paras 13 and 15 to 19 of Sch.24 to the Act.

[12] Even after the *IBA Health* litigation, there is a view that the regime under the Act is far from being a wholesale overhaul of the FTA regime. The DTI's *Peer Review of Competition Policy* of May 17, 2004 notes "Interviews suggest that the UK merger regime is the strongest part of its competition regime due to . . . the length of time it has been in place, *i.e.* more embedded than the non-merger regime and the more established processes this brought. This was true despite the recent changes which, whilst they enhanced the regime, did not change it fundamentally." (See para.1.3.1).

[13] *IBA Health v OFT* [2003] CAT 27, [2004] Comp. A.R. 235, ("the CAT's judgment").

[14] See the OFT's decision of November 6, 2003, "*Anticipated acquisition by iSOFT Group plc of Torex plc*".

[15] See in particular para.268 of the CAT's judgment.

[16] See para.197 of the CAT's judgment.

The CAT adopted a shorthand for this test as being whether there was "room for two views" about the merger, *i.e.* whether there is an alternative credible view to the OFT's view:

> "In our opinion, in such circumstances, the statutory duty of the OFT under section 33(1) is not to decide, definitively, which of those two views it, the OFT, prefers. Under the scheme of the Act, the definitive decision maker, in a case where there is room for two views, is not the OFT but the [Competition Commission]. If there is room for two views, the statutory duty of the OFT is to refer the matter to the [Competition Commission], whose duty is to *decide* on the question whether the merger may be expected to lead to a substantial lessening of competition, as section 36(1) expressly provides".[17]

On the basis of this interpretation of the s.33(1) test, the CAT ruled that the OFT had failed to apply the correct test in deciding whether to make a reference because it had not asked the second limb of the question, namely whether the Competition Commission might take an alternative view.[18] The judgment provoked concern in the merger control community, because it seemed to reduce the role of the OFT to clearing only wholly uncontentious mergers, where there was no credible alternative view about the impact of the merger on competition. The CAT appeared to have taken away any power of the OFT to make intelligent judgments in complex cases about the likely effects of a merger, particularly if an alternative view were credible. The ruling also appeared to increase the prospects for complainants (typically competitors) wishing to provoke a reference and thereby create regulatory difficulties for their competitors. General concern was expressed[19] that this lowering of the threshold for reference would inevitably increase the number of references[20] with adverse cost and timing implications, with possible ramifications for the level of merger activity in the UK as a whole.

---

[17] See para.192 of the CAT's judgment.

[18] See para.233 of the CAT's judgment.

[19] See for example the *Financial Times* on December 4, 2003, "*Key ruling sets stage for merger challenges*" which reported:

> "Mergers stand to cost more and take longer after a ground-breaking decision yesterday by the Competition Appeal Tribunal, which urged the [OFT] to refer more takeovers to the Competition Commission".

See also the *Financial Times* on December 8, 2004, "*Ill wind over health tie-up*", which reported:

> "Some lawyers were quick to warn that the likelihood of the OFT's being forced to refer more deals, which it otherwise might have been inclined to clear, to the Competition Commission for detailed scrutiny could have a "chilling effect" on the market at a time when merger and acquisition activity was showing signs of picking up".

See also the *Financial Times* on December 12, 2003, "*OFT to challenge ruling on mergers*" when it reported:

> "Lawyers said the judgment meant the [OFT] would be forced to refer many more bids to the Competition Commission for full scrutiny, increasing delays and costs for businesses. Mr Vickers [Chairman of the OFT] had always insisted the Enterprise Act would not bring a significant change to the way proposed mergers were assessed".

[20] Estimates of the potential increase in references ranged from a factor of two to as many as four times the number of references. On the most pessimistic interpretation, the CAT's ruling

Shortly after the judgment, the OFT issued a brief press release confirming that it would henceforth apply the CAT's interpretation of the statutory test for reference.[21-22] It also highlighted that confidential guidance and informal advice given prior to the *IBA Health* judgment might not be reliable given the new interpretation of the test. In fact, the CAT's interpretation of the reference test seemed to take away the utility of confidential guidance and informal advice altogether: since the two procedures were conducted in confidence without third party input, it was not clear that the OFT would ever be able to rule out the possibility of a credible alternative view emerging at the public consultation stage.

4.005   Inevitably, given the potentially fundamental change to the OFT's role, the case was appealed to the Court of Appeal by the OFT (as well as by iSOFT). The CAT gave fairly lengthy reasons for its decision to permit an appeal,[23] although these included a number of passages which appeared inconsistent with its original judgment of December 3, 2003.[24] The status of these "clarifications" of the CAT's original ruling was not entirely clear in light of the Practice Direction on the citation of authorities; in the end this issue fell away.[25]

---

seemed to require that any case which prompted an issues letter (see para.3.060 *et seq.*) was likely to be referred. In the end, in the eleven weeks between the CAT's judgment and the Court of Appeal's subsequent ruling, four mergers were referred (not including a reference made on the day of the CAT's judgment, which did not take the ruling into account). In relation to one of these, it is clear that the reference would not have been made had it not been for the CAT's new interpretation of the s.33(1) test (see the OFT's decision of January 13, 2004, *Anticipated acquisition by First Group plc of the ScotRail Franchise*, at para.34 in particular). The other three references in question were *Anticipated acquisition by Dräger Medical AG & Co. KGaA of the Air–Shields business of Hillenbrand Industries Inc*, OFT decision of December 18, 2003; *Anticipated acquisition by Carl Zeiss Jena GmbH of the microscopy business of Bio-Rad Laboratories Inc*, OFT decision of December 30, 2003; and *Anticipated acquisition by Convatec Limited of Acordis Speciality Fibres Limited*, OFT decision of February 12, 2004. It had certainly not been the government's expectation that the new regime would increase the number of references: the *Competition Reform—Regulatory Impact Assessment* published by the DTI to accompany the new Act envisaged that the new mergers regime (referred to in the document as "option 3(c)") "would be broadly neutral in terms of costs for business" and that any increased costs would come from "a more thorough CC investigation" (see p.20 of the paper).

[21-22] "*OFT to look again at merger*" (PN 164/03) of December 5, 2003.

[23] Decision on applications for permission to appeal, [2003] CAT 28, [2004] Comp. A.R. 294, "the CAT's permission decision".

[24] See, for example, paras 20, 34 and 42 of the CAT's permission decision, where the CAT seems to accept that the OFT is entitled to "exclude or discount any alternative credible view" (para.34). This is in contrast to the main judgment of December 3, 2003 which stated that it was not for the OFT to exercise its judgment in relation to any alternative view, as any such decision should be taken by the Competition Commission following a reference and full investigation as discussed at 4.004 above.

[25] See para.6.1 of the *Practice Direction (Citation of Authorities)* [2001] 1 W.L.R. 1001. The Court of Appeal in its subsequent judgment noted that there was an issue in relation to whether it should have regard to the CAT's "explanations". The Vice Chancellor stated that "I see no reason why we should not, but, as will be seen, I have not found it necessary to do so" (see para.20 of the Court of Appeal's judgment, cited above).

The Court of Appeal's interpretation of section 33(1) in IBA Health

On appeal, the Court of Appeal overturned the CAT's interpretation of s.33(1).[26-27] The Vice Chancellor noted ways in which the CAT's interpretation of s.33(1) would make other parts of the Act unworkable,[28] before turning to what it considered to be the correct interpretation of the test: **4.006**

> "The short (and correct) answer to the question is that the test to be applied is that stated in s.33(1). The words are ordinary English words; they should be applied in accordance with their ordinary meaning; the Court should not substitute other words for those used by Parliament nor paraphrase nor gloss them. Nevertheless in view of the evident importance of the test and the range of meaning the word 'may' can connote it may help to explain the statutory test by reference to a series of propositions."[29]

The Vice Chancellor then set out the following "propositions" to be taken into account:

> "First, it is apparent from s.33(1) and the contrast between belief and suspicion demonstrated in ss.42 and 131 that it is necessary for OFT to form the relevant belief. . . .
>
> Second, the belief must be reasonable and objectively justified by relevant facts. . . .
>
> Third, by themselves, the words 'may be expected to result' in paragraph (b) of both s.33(1) and 36(1) involve a degree of likelihood amounting to an expectation. . . .
>
> Fourth, however, the belief that must be held by OFT under s.33(1)(b) is 'that it is or may be the case that'. This introduces two alternatives, the certainty posed by the word 'is' and the possibility envisaged by the words 'may be' . . . [I]t is apparent that the degree of likelihood required by the word 'may' is less than that required by the answer to question (a) in s.36(1). The answer in accordance with s.36 will be that the anticipated merger 'will result in the creation of a relevant merger situation' or not as the case may be. The test for OFT is only whether the anticipated merger 'may result in a relevant merger situation' or not. This is consistent with the respective functions of OFT and the [Competition Commission]. The former is a first screen, the latter decides the matter. Accordingly, although the word 'may' appears in the opening phrase of s.33(1) and in paragraph (b) of both s.33(1) and 36(1) it is clear that the opening phrase 'believes that it . . . may be the case' imports a lower degree of likelihood than paragraph (b) in ss.33(1) or 36(1) would by itself involve. That lower degree of likelihood might, for example, exist in circumstances where the work done by the OFT did not justify any positive view, but left some uncertainty, and where OFT therefore

---

[26-27] See para.38 of the Court of Appeal's judgment in *OFT v IBA Health Ltd* [2004] EWCA Civ. 142, (2004) 101(11) L.S.G. 33, ("the Court of Appeal's judgment").

[28] See paras 39 and 40 of the Court of Appeal's judgment.

[29] See para.43 of the Court of Appeal's judgment.

believed that a substantial lessening of competition might prove to be likely on further and fuller examination of the position (which could only be undertaken by the Competition Commission).

At the other end of the scale it is clear that the words 'may be the case' exclude the purely fanciful because OFT acting reasonably is not going to believe that the fanciful may be the case. In between the fanciful and a degree of likelihood less than 50% there is a wide margin in which OFT is required to exercise its judgment. I do not consider that it is possible or appropriate to attempt any more exact mathematical formulation of the degree of likelihood which OFT acting reasonably must require."[30]

The Vice Chancellor also commented that the OFT's *Substantive Assessment Guidance*, which referred to the test for reference being met where there is a significant prospect that a merger may be expected to lessen competition,[31] probably set the bar too high. He noted that "the word 'significant' tends to put the requisite likelihood too far up the scale of probability".[32] In practice, however, it would seem highly unlikely that the OFT would *not* have referred a merger which it felt was more than 50 per cent likely (*i.e.* "more likely than not") to result in a substantial lessening of competition. The Vice Chancellor's criticism was understandable given the broad range of probability which is caught by the term "significant". However when this is assessed by reference to the OFT's case practice, the criticism was arguably unwarranted.

In his supporting judgment Carnwath L.J. commented that the CAT's identification of such a limited role for the OFT could not have been right given the scheme of the Act "combined with the undoubted expertise of the OFT".[33] One of the general concerns about the CAT's interpretation is that it would have risked emasculating a merger control enforcement body widely respected for the skill and sophistication of its analysis.[34]

It is worth highlighting that the pre-*IBA Health* status quo was not reinstated by the Court of Appeal. In particular, the Court of Appeal was clearly of the view that the Act introduced a new regime so that reference to FTA cases is not an appropriate source of guidance (at least in relation to the question of the reference test).[35] As has been noted above, this conclusion may not fully reflect the apparent continuity of approach of the OFT in practice to competition analysis under the FTA and under the Act.

---

[30] See paras 44 to 48 of the Court of Appeal's judgment.

[31] See the original version of the OFT's *Substantive Assessment Guidance*, at para.3.2. The wording has since been amended.

[32] See paras 49 and 86 of the Court of Appeal's judgment.

[33] See para.83 to 85 of the Court of Appeal's judgment.

[34] The DTI's *"Peer Review of Competition Policy"*, published on May 17, 2004, recorded that interviews had indicated that the UK merger regime was seen as the strongest part of the UK competition regime overall and gave the reasons for this as being the length of time that the regime has been in place (seeing the Act as enhancing the FTA rather than changing it fundamentally) which has enabled it to be more embedded with more established processes, and also noted that "the staff . . . are rated as being the most capable within the UK authorities". Overall, the merger regime was ranked as third in the world, behind the United States and Germany. See para.1.3.1 of the report.

[35] See paras 44 and 80 of the Court of Appeal's judgment.

The reference test post-IBA Health

The Court of Appeal's judgment was widely welcomed as putting UK   **4.007**
merger control back on a workable footing, and removing the risk of a
swathe of unnecessary references to the Competition Commission.[36] Given
that, under the FTA, the Competition Commission reached an adverse
finding in around 50 to 60 per cent of references, there is no reason to
assume that the reference test on the pre-*IBA Health* interpretation had
been either too lenient or too robust. The impact of a reference in terms
of time and cost is significant: in the authors' experience, the costs of a
full Competition Commission reference are up to ten times greater than
the cost of an OFT investigation, and the businesses under scrutiny will be
disrupted for as much as an additional six months, or even longer where
clearance is subject to the negotiation of satisfactory remedies.[37]

In terms purely of the threshold for triggering the duty of the OFT to
refer, the OFT has probably regained the discretion which it was previously
understood to have: it can exercise its judgment unfettered where the risk
of a merger resulting in a substantial lessening of competition is more than
fanciful but less than 50 per cent. This is not to say that mergers within
that zone will be cleared: the OFT's duty to refer might be engaged, for
example, where a sufficiently robust evaluation of the level of risk is in
itself difficult because of evidence, information or methodology issues or
because of timing constraints.[38] As to the evaluation of the risk of a
substantial lessening of competition, see Ch.6, below.

In overall terms, however, the *IBA Health* judgment may have slightly
increased the risk of the OFT making a reference to the Competition
Commission. Consistent with this view, the OFT's Annual Plan for
2004/2005[39] anticipated that 20 to 25 cases would be referred or closed
subject to undertakings in lieu out of an estimated 30 to 50 more complex
cases[40]: in its Annual Plan for 2003/2004,[41] by contrast, it anticipated only 10
to 20 references from the same number of complex cases (and in fact, 12 were
made[42]). The 2004/2005 Annual Plan expressly comments that the estimates
are based on "experience, and the Court of Appeal's clarification of the
substantive merger test".

---

[36] See para.4.004, above.

[37] The timeframe of a Competition Commission investigation is discussed in more detail in
Ch.5, below at para.5.004.

[38] For example, the Morrisons bid for Safeway was referred alongside the more obviously
potentially anti-competitive bids by Tesco, Sainsburys and Asda. Difficulties in identifying
the correct market definition methodology meant that in the time available, the OFT could
not advise the Secretary of State that local competition concerns could be ruled out by
undertakings in lieu of reference. See the Director General's advice of March 13, 2003,
Proposed acquisition by Wm Morrison Supermarkets PLC of Safeway plc. In *Anticipated
acquisition by FirstGroup plc of the Scotrail Franchise*, OFT decision of January 13, 2004,
the OFT was similarly unable to accept proposed undertakings in lieu because "The timeframe of the OFT investigation has not permitted clear identification of possible detriments
to competition" (para.35).

[39] See *The Office of Fair Trading Annual Plan 2004–2005*, March 2004, HC 460 at p.20.

[40] "More complex" cases were described as those requiring a case review meeting: see
para.3.060 of Ch.3.

[41] See *The Office of Fair Trading Annual Plan 2003–2004*, June 2003 at p.23.

[42] See Table 2 in App.2.

The increase in risk is primarily because of the emphasis in the case on the adequacy of reasoning.[43] As a consequence, there may be marginal cases where an overall view that the merger is not anti-competitive cannot be adequately substantiated by concrete facts and analysis to a sufficient degree, such that a reference is required. The *IBA Health* litigation has perhaps reduced the ability of the OFT to rely on its "professional instincts". Indeed in the *IBA Health* case itself, on its second review of the merger following the quashing by the CAT of its original decision, the OFT again found that there would be no substantial lessening of competition in relation to one market affected by the merger; in relation to the other affected market, however, the OFT found that a substantial lessening of competition would result from the merger but accepted undertakings in lieu to divest those parts of the acquired business active in the second market.[44] In the first decision, the merger had been cleared unconditionally in all respects.

4.008   Following the Court of Appeal's judgment in *IBA Health*, the OFT initially simply issued a brief statement welcoming the judgment and commenting that it provided "a good basis for the OFT's role in the UK merger assessment [sic] from now on".[45] The OFT has subsequently amended its *Substantive Assessment Guidance*. Paragraph 3.2, which attracted criticism from the CAT and the Court of Appeal, now reads [in draft form] as follows:

> "The test for reference will be met if the OFT has a reasonable belief, objectively justified by relevant facts, that there is a realistic prospect that the merger will lessen competition substantially.[45A] By the term 'realistic prospect', the OFT means not only a prospect that has more than a 50 per cent chance of occurring, but also a prospect that is not fanciful but has less than a 50 per cent chance of occurring.
>
> • This test differs from that used by the [Competition Commission] in its merger enquiries, reflecting the fact that the OFT is a first screen while the [Competition Commission] is determinative. Hence the threshold applied by the OFT for making a merger reference imports a lower degree of likelihood than the [Competition Commission's] threshold for *deciding* that a merger may be expected to lessen competition substantially.
> • The OFT's test will be met where the OFT believes that there is more than a 50 per cent chance of a merger resulting in a substantial lessening of competition, because the OFT's view of such a merger is that it is "more likely than not" to result in a substantial lessening of competition. In such cases, the degree of likelihood required for reference is necessarily met since the OFT believes that it <u>is</u> the case [that] the merger may be expected to result in a substantial lessening of competition.

---

[43] These aspects of the *IBA Health* litigation are discussed at paras 3.068 *et seq.* of Ch.3, above.

[44] See the OFT's decision of March 24, 2004, *Completed acquisition by iSOFT plc of Torex plc.*

[45] Press statement of February 19, 2004, *OFT statement on Court of Appeal merger law judgment.*

[45A] At this point the guidance cites the Court of Appeal's *IBA Health* judgment.

- The OFT's test may be met in other cases where the OFT believes that there is less than a 50 per cent chance of a merger resulting in a substantial lessening of competition. However, in such cases, there is no exact mathematical formulation of the degree of likelihood which the OFT acting reasonably must require in order to make a merger reference. Between the fanciful and a degree of likelihood less than 50 per cent there is a wide margin in which the OFT must exercise its judgment as to whether it <u>may be</u> the case that the merger may be expected to result in a substantial lessening of competition.
- Merger review involves assessment of uncertain future prospects, often on the basis of imperfect information and in a limited time frame. The degree of uncertainty may vary from case to case depending on the subject-matter of the merger and the nature and scope of evidence available to the OFT. Whilst the OFT will seek information of its own initiative, the more comprehensive the information available to the OFT, the more confident it will be as to the possible effect of the merger. So, where the information available to the OFT is full and extensive, the degree of likelihood that the OFT must require to believe that it may be the case that a merger may be expected to result in a substantial lessening of competition may be higher up the scale of probability (albeit less than 50 per cent) than compared to when there is less information available, particularly as regards central points in the analysis. Merging parties and third parties are therefore encouraged to provide relevant information on a timely basis, whether or not it is expressly sought by the OFT."

It is not clear that the first paragraph of the revised para.3.2 of the OFT's *Substantive Assessment Guidance* is an accurate reflection of the Court of Appeal's *IBA Health* judgment. It is certainly correct that the OFT's duty to refer will be triggered where there is a likelihood of greater than 50 per cent that the merger will result or has resulted in an substantial lessening of competition. However, where the degree of likelihood is more than fanciful but less than 50 per cent, it is not correct to state (as the first part of para.3.2 of the guidance does) that the duty to refer *will* be triggered: in such circumstances it *may* be triggered, depending on the OFT's assessment of the case. This key distinction is, however, recognised in the second and third of the explanatory bullet points which follow the initial part of para.3.2.

Other aspects of the test for reference

Although the *IBA Health* judgments considered the degree of likelihood   4.009
of a substantial lessening of competition that will trigger the s.33(1) duty to refer,[46] they did not consider the meaning of the phrase "substantial lessening of competition" itself, nor the question of what the reference should relate to.

---

[46] Given the very similar wording of s.22(1), the judgments can be applied by analogy to that section as well.

The main discussion of the meaning of this test is contained in Ch.6, but it is worth noting at this stage the relevance of the word "substantial". In a couple of cases under the Act, the OFT has found that a merger has resulted or can be expected to result in some lessening of competition, but not to a degree which is considered "substantial". In relation to a proposed joint venture between P&O and Stena Line created to acquire Cairnryan Port,[47] the OFT noted concerns of third parties that the merger might increase incentives for collusion between the parties in their downstream ferry businesses. However, the OFT observed that the conditions for co-ordination might exist already in the relevant market, and concluded:

". . . the structure of the JV, the limited nature of the common port facilities and the marginal increase in the similarity of services arising from the JV means that any increase in incentive and ability to co-ordinate cannot be characterised as substantial".

Similarly, in relation to FirstGroup plc's proposed acquisition of the Thames Trains franchise,[48] the OFT found that "any loss of competition arising from the merger is insubstantial".

By contrast, in National Express/Greater Anglia franchise,[49] it appears that the parties sought to argue that any loss of competition was not substantial. The OFT's decision to refer the case indicates that the parties argued that there should be little or no expectation of competition on the routes where the merging businesses overlapped (and therefore no loss due to the merger). The OFT, however, found that insufficient evidence had been presented to substantiate this claim and referred the merger on the basis that it was reasonable to expect a reduction of competition to result from the merger.[49A]

A further issue is the question of what the subject-matter of the reference should be: in particular, is the OFT able to refer only part of a merger to the Competition Commission? In *Sibelco/Tarmac*, the OFT identified a series of different relevant economic markets for minerals, namely, the supply of silica flour, dolomite, high purity silica sand and feldspar. In relation to dolomite and feldspar, the OFT concluded that no substantial lessening of competition was to be expected. In relation to high purity silica sand, the OFT concluded that although a substantial lessening of competition was to be expected at least in relation to some customers in this market, the market was too small to warrant reference. The reference made under s.22 therefore related only to the market for silica sand, a limitation which was reflected in the terms of reference. In contrast, in *Taminco/Air Products*, the OFT identified various alternative market definitions. The

---

[47] See the OFT's decision of August 22, 2003, *Anticipated joint venture between Stena and P&O to acquire Cairnryan Port*.

[48] See the OFT's decision of March 26, 2004, *Anticipated acquisition by FirstGroup plc of the Thames Trains Franchise*.

[49] See the OFT's decision of May 27, 2004, *Completed acquisition by National Express of the Greater Anglia Franchise*.

[49A] As at the time of writing, the Competition Commission's inquiry was continuing, but it had provisionally concluded that the merger would not lead to a substantial lessening of competition. See the Commission's provisional findings report on *The acquisition by National Express Group of Greater Anglia Franchise* of September 23, 2004.

widest market definition encompassed a group of chemicals known as methylamines and methylamine derivatives. Alternative market definitions essentially concerned sub-categories of chemicals within this group, namely dimethylformamide (DMF), alkylalkanolamines (AAA) and choline chloride. The OFT concluded that a substantial lessening of competition could only be expected in relation to AAA. However, a different approach was taken from that in *Sibelco/Tarmac* and the OFT referred the whole merger to the Competition Commission. In this case, the terms of reference mentioned AAA expressly but in a manner which was not intended to limit the scope of the reference.

On the one hand, it might be argued that it is inherent in the nature of the substantial lessening of competition test that the analysis of a particular merger will necessarily involve dividing the assessment between the various relevant markets which are affected, in order to identify whether the substantial lessening of competition test is met. On that basis, where a merger affects more than one market, there will not be a single answer to the question of whether a substantial lessening of competition may be expected to result or has resulted—a separate answer will need to be given for each relevant market (as it was in *Sibelco/Tarmac*), and the duty to refer will only be engaged in relation to those markets where there is a finding of a likelihood of a substantial lessening of competition. If that analysis is correct, then split references would appear to be inevitable in some cases.

On the other hand, however, this interpretation could render the Competition Commission's assessment of a merger very difficult if it is not able to view the merger as a whole but must limit itself to particular aspects of the markets in which the merged business will be active. For example, customer benefits may arise as a result of the merger but not necessarily in relation to the specific market where the substantial lessening of competition was identified by the OFT: must they then be ignored? Alternatively, in a case such as *Taminco/Air Products*, where the market definition was central to the competition assessment, it would arguably be undesirable if the Competition Commission were unable to review all alternative market definitions afresh (particularly given the OFT's role as a first stage "filter"). This issue has not yet been considered by the CAT, but it would appear that in overall terms, the approach taken by the OFT in *Taminco/Air Products* of referring the whole merger is more consistent with the overall framework of the Act.

49B See further para.4.011 below.
49C See the OFT's decision of August 14, 2003, *Anticipated acquisition by Sibelco Minerals & Chemicals Limited of the minerals and materials business of Tarmac Central Limited*. The reference was subsequently cancelled.
49D See the OFT's decision of July 16, 2004 *Anticipated acquisition by Taminco NV of the European Methylamines and Derivatives Business of Air Products and Chemicals Inc.* At the time of writing, the Competition Commission's inquiry was ongoing.
49E A related point arises in relation to the question of whether, in a case where a public interest intervention notice had been served, the Secretary of State could, for example, deal with competition concerns in a merger by accepting undertakings in lieu (in accordance with the OFT's competition analysis), but refer the aspects of the merger which give rise to public interest concerns: see further para.3.076.

Exceptions to the duty—a limited discretion not to refer

4.010   As noted above, the Secretary of State's absolute discretion under the FTA whether to refer a merger has been replaced under the Act by a duty on the OFT to make a reference where there is a qualifying merger situation in respect of which it believes that it may be the case that it has resulted or may be expected to result in a substantial lessening of competition. However, s.22(2) provides that the OFT may decide not to make a reference in either of two sets of circumstances, to which s.33(2) adds a third. The three situations where the OFT has such a discretion are:

(i)   where the market(s) concerned is/are not of sufficient importance to justify the making of a reference;

(ii)   where any relevant customer benefits in relation to the creation of the relevant merger situation concerned outweigh the substantial lessening of competition concerned or any resulting adverse effects; or

(iii) in relation to anticipated mergers only, where the arrangements in contemplation are not sufficiently advanced, or are not sufficiently likely to proceed, to justify a reference.

In practice, these considerations appear rarely to come into play; at least they are seldom referred to in the OFT's decisions. One obvious reason is that the discretions not to refer do not become relevant unless the OFT believes that its duty to refer has been triggered. It may therefore be that parties make submissions on these points fairly often, but that due to a more general absence of competition concerns which leads to the case being cleared by the OFT, those submissions do not need to be recounted in the final decision. It remains the case that even in relation to mergers which the OFT concludes do trigger its duty to refer, there is no systematic consideration in the OFT's decision of the extent to which its discretion not to refer might be relevant. In many cases where a reference was made, the decision is silent even as to whether such arguments were raised by the parties.[50] However, the discretions have been exercised in some cases to date (and there were relevant parallels under the FTA), and these are considered in turn below.

The markets concerned do not warrant reference

4.011   Both ss.22(2) and 33(2) give the OFT a discretion not to make a reference where the market(s) concerned are of insufficient importance to warrant a reference. The OFT's *Substantive Assessment Guidance* comments:

---

[50] See, for example, the OFT's decision of August 22, 2003, *Anticipated acquisition by Stena of certain assets operated by P&O on the Irish Sea*; the OFT's decision of October 31, 2003, *Proposed acquisition by Unum Limited of the employee benefits business of Swiss Life (UK) plc*; the OFT's decision of December 3, 2003, *Anticipated acquisition by AAH Pharmaceuticals Limited of East Anglian Pharmaceuticals Limited*; the OFT's decision of December 18, 2003, *Anticipated acquisition by Dräger Medical AG & Co. KGaA of the Air-Shields business from Hillenbrand Industries Inc*; the OFT's decision of January 13,

"The purpose of this provision is to avoid reference being made where the costs insured would be disproportionate to the size of the markets concerned. By way of guidance, at the time of writing the OFT would expect a [Competition Commission] inquiry to cost around £400,000. This exception is likely to apply only very rarely since in the majority of cases where a substantial lessening of competition is identified, it will be appropriate for the [Competition Commission] to investigate."[51]

The reference to the cost of a Competition Commission inquiry is the cost to the public purse, not to the parties. The DTI's regulatory impact assessment, issued to accompany publication of the Act, estimated that the impact of the new mergers regime would be to *increase* the cost of a merger inquiry by the Competition Commission by approximately £370,000.[52] This suggests that the figure of £400,000 in the OFT's *Substantive Assessment Guidance* is out of date, and that the current figure may be closer to £800,000 for each reference.

As at June 1, 2004, this exceptional discretion had been discussed in four of the OFT's decisions under the Act. In *Sibelco/Tarmac*,[53] the OFT considered various different markets. In relation to specialist high purity sand supplied to lead crystal manufacturers, the OFT concluded that a substantial lessening of competition would result from the merger, but went on to observe that "the scale of such effects (given that sand supplied to lead crystal manufacturers is valued at approximately £400,000 per year) would not appear to justify reference". Whilst a reference (subsequently cancelled) was made in relation to a different market, high purity sand for lead crystal manufacture was not included within the scope of the reference, despite the fact that the *incremental* cost of adding a further market to the scope of the Competition Commission's inquiry would presumably have been less than the basic inquiry cost of £400,000 (or more likely £800,000).[53A]

In *Tesco/Co-op store* in Slough,[54] on the other hand, the OFT concluded that the acquisition by Tesco of a single store in Slough with a very localised impact on competition was of sufficient importance to warrant a reference. Without giving any further detail or explanation in its decision, the OFT commented:

". . . while the affected area would be Slough and the surrounding area, the affected sector appears to be sufficient[ly] important to justify reference, given the total expenditure on groceries at the one-stop stores in this area".

2004, *Anticipated acquisition by FirstGroup plc of the Scotrail franchise*; the OFT's decision of February 12, 2004, *Anticipated acquisition by Convatec Limited of Acordis Speciality Fibres Limited*; and the OFT's decision of May 20, 2004, *Completed acquisition by DS Smith PLC of LINPAC Containers Limited*.

[51] See para.7.5 of the OFT's *Substantive Assessment Guidance*.

[52] See s.5.2 of the Overarching Regulatory Impact Assessment for the Enterprise Act.

[53] See the OFT's decision of August 14, 2003, *Anticipated acquisition by Sibelco Minerals & Chemicals Limited of the minerals and materials business of Tarmac Central Limited*.

[53A] Note that, as discussed at para.4.009, it cannot be assumed that the OFT will always split a merger in this way and refer some but not other affected markets.

[54] See the OFT's decision of February 2, 2004, *Completed acquisitions by Tesco plc of the Co-operative Group's stores in Uxbridge Road, Slough as well as Stapleford Lane, Toton, Nottingham and Towers Place, South Shields*.

The decision does not give any indication of the expenditure levels referred to, which inevitably limits the usefulness of this decision as a precedent for future cases. The case was cleared subject to undertakings in lieu which in fact comprised divestment of the acquired store.[55]

4.012   A much clearer indication of the level of revenues involved was given in relation to National Express' acquisition of the Greater Anglia franchise,[56] where amongst other revenue figures, the OFT noted that annual revenues from all stations on the train route where the competition concerns arose were £4 million, whilst revenues for the 52 coach routes which overlapped with all or part of the train route were at least £1.2 million. Accordingly, the OFT concluded that the markets at issue were of sufficient importance to warrant reference.

Finally, the exercise of this discretion was raised in *Archant/ London Regionals Division of Independent News & Media plc.*[57] The case concerned the acquisition of local newspaper titles in the London area. The OFT concluded that the markets concerned were of sufficient importance to warrant a reference noting, "The annual revenue of each of [the vendor's] North, East and Post Divisions alone exceeds [   ]" (the actual figure was excised for reasons of confidentiality).

Although the lack of any indication of the level of revenue which the OFT considered to justify the reference again makes it difficult to use this case as a benchmark, the decision is helpful in that it highlights that the question whether the market is of sufficient importance to warrant a reference is a distinct issue from the jurisdictional question as to whether the share of supply test is met in a "substantial part of the UK".[58] In considering whether the latter threshold was met in this case, the OFT took into account the number of residents in the relevant geographic area, as well as the percentage of the national population which they represented. It took into account the "international economic significance of both the City and the Docklands area", and the social significance of the distinct multicultural communities of East London. By contrast in considering whether the market was of sufficient importance to warrant a reference, the OFT simply considered the value in monetary terms of the market, presumably (although this is not stated) comparing it to the estimated cost to the public purse of a reference.

The question whether a market warrants reference would therefore appear to be essentially one of proportionality of the cost of the reference to the financial importance of the market in question. The Explanatory Notes to the Act confirm that this discretion not to refer "is designed primarily to avoid references being made where the costs involved would be disproportionate to the size of the markets concerned".[59]

4.013   In addition to these concrete examples of when the discretion not to refer a market of insufficient importance might be exercised, the OFT's

---

[55] At the time of writing the divestment undertakings were still being negotiated with the OFT. These undertakings are discussed further at para.4.025, below.

[56] See the OFT's decision of May 27, 2004, *Completed acquisition by National Express of the Greater Anglia Franchise.*

[57] See the OFT's decision of April 29, 2004, *Completed acquisition by Archant Limited of the London Regionals Division of Independent News & Media plc.*

[58] See s.23 of the Act, discussed at paras 2.018 *et seq.* of Ch.2.

[59] See the Explanatory Notes to the Act at para.97.

Substantive Assessment Guidance provides some theoretical examples of where a market which is very small might nevertheless warrant reference:

"● where the product concerned is an important input into a larger downstream market
● where the market is growing quickly, such that current market size is not a good reflection of the actual or potential importance of the market (particularly in new technology markets)
● where the goods or services are considered essential to vulnerable consumers, or
● where the market is one of many smaller or local markets (for the goods or services concerned) that are together of considerable significance."[60]

In relation to the first example, in 2002 under the FTA the Secretary of State referred to the Competition Commission the proposed acquisition by Lallemand UK Ltd of LHS (Finings) Ltd. The businesses overlapped in the supply of brewing process aids, *i.e.* products used in the brewing of cask ale to clear ("fine") and stabilise the beer. Concerns arose in relation to a particular product, isinglass finings made from the swim bladders of certain tropical fish, over which the merged entity would have a near monopoly. Although the Director General's advice to the Secretary to State[61] does not expressly mention this point, one of the reasons for making the reference may well have been the much larger size of the downstream beer market. A reference was therefore made[62] notwithstanding that the value of the UK isinglass finings market was estimated at some £2 million per annum. However, while the cost to the public purse may have been considered to be warranted, the potential cost of a reference to the parties themselves presumably proved prohibitive because the reference was cancelled.

A further example under the FTA (from December 2000) is the proposed **4.014** acquisition by City Technology Limited of the gas sensors business of Marconi Applied Technologies Limited.[63] In this case the market under consideration was the UK market for pellistors, a type of gas sensor device, which was valued at only £1.2 million per annum. However the Director General commented as follows, in advising the Secretary of State to refer the merger:

"Bearing in mind the possible extent and duration of the adverse effects, on balance I consider that the competition concerns in this case warrant further investigation."[64]

---

[60] See para.7.6 of the OFT's *Substantive Assessment Guidance*.
[61] See the Director General's advice of December 21, 2001, *Proposed acquisition by Lallemand UK Ltd of LHS (Finings) Ltd.*
[62] See DTI press release P/2002/018 of January 14, 2002.
[63] See the Direct General's advice of December 11, 2000, *Proposed acquisition by City Technology Limited of the gas sensors business of Marconi Applied Technologies Limited*, and DTI press release P/2000/858 of December 21, 2000. Again, the reference was cancelled.
[64] Regarding the comments about the "extent" and "duration" of the adverse effects of this merger, the Director General had found that the market was at least UK-wide but there is no mention in his advice of imports from the EU and by contrast the advice records

It is perhaps tempting to conclude from these cases and the *Sibelco/Tarmac* example discussed above that the threshold in monetary market value terms for warranting a reference lies somewhere between £400,000 (or perhaps £800,000, if the DTI's regulatory impact assessment cost increase estimates are taken into account[65]) where reference is not warranted, and £1.2 million, where it is. However in this respect it is worth noting the comments of the Director General in his advice in the isinglass finings case[66] where he observed:

". . . on general grounds it would be unfortunate if there were an actual or perceived market size threshold below which mergers escaped scrutiny. That might lead to a substantial lessening of competition in many small (*e.g.* local) markets which, in aggregate, account for a good deal of economic activity".

The substantial lessening of competition is outweighed by relevant customer benefits

4.015 Both ss.22(2) and 33(2) give the OFT a further discretion not to refer a merger where the substantial lessening of competition which the OFT has identified—or the adverse effects which it produces—are outweighed by "any relevant customer benefits in relation to the creation of the relevant merger situation." The possibility that efficiencies arising from a merger might justify clearance notwithstanding a substantial lessening of competition is relevant not only at the OFT stage of the proceedings but also to the assessment undertaken by the Competition Commission. The concept of countervailing customer benefits and the way in which they are analysed is discussed in detail in Ch.6.[67] This chapter will briefly consider the way in which this limb of the OFT's discretion not to refer a case has been exercised in recent cases.

In *Banque Centrale de Compensation/London Clearing House*[68] the OFT in fact concluded that the duty to refer was not triggered but nevertheless engaged in a discussion of customer benefits. In this case, which concerned the provision of central counterparty clearing bank services, there was an acknowledgement amongst many third parties that the merger would benefit customers because of the beneficial network externalities which would flow from the merger, including harmonised trading platforms and reduced fees. The OFT noted the existence of these benefits, but did not refer to them in its consideration of whether a substantial lessening of competition could be expected to result from the merger. The case high-

---

comments that supplies from the Far East were of inadequate quality. The Director General also found significant barriers to entry with a minimum of two and a half years to obtain the necessary regulatory approvals, as well as "not insubstantial" entry costs and other factors which would discourage new entry.

[65] See para.4.011, above. Of course it may be a pure coincidence that a market worth no more than the public cost of a reference was considered too small to incur that cost; if so, it would not be appropriate to raise the lower figure to £800,000.

[66] Cited above.

[67] See, in particular, paras 4.187 *et seq.*

[68] See the OFT's decision of August 11, 2003, *Anticipated merger of Banque Centrale de Compensation SA and the London Clearing House Ltd.*

lights the question of the stage at which the issue of customer benefits should be considered by the OFT:

(i) should it be, as the statutory framework suggests, only once it is established that there has been or can be expected to be a substantial lessening of competition? or

(ii) can the existence of customer benefits affect the assessment of whether there is a substantial lessening of competition in the first place?

The OFT addresses this question in paras 4.29 to 4.31 of its *Substantive Assessment Guidance*. It considers that some efficiencies/customer benefits flowing from a merger should be taken into account in the central assessment of whether the merger will result in a substantial lessening of competition, whilst others are taken into account only once the duty to refer has been triggered. Where a merger will increase rivalry, for example "where two of the smaller firms in a market gain such efficiencies through merger that they can exert greater competitive pressure on larger competitors",[69] this will go to the question of whether there is a substantial lessening of competition.[70] Other types of efficiency enter the analysis at the stage of deciding whether the discretion not to refer is available to the OFT:

"For example, if a merger would reduce rivalry in a market but proven efficiencies would be likely to result in lower prices to customers, the OFT would not take this into account in reaching a conclusion on the substantial lessening of competition test, but it might be a consideration under the customer benefits exception to the duty to refer."[71]

The statutory discretion not to refer where there are countervailing efficiencies must be applied in the light of s.30 of the Act which defines "relevant customer benefits". A benefit will constitute a relevant customer benefit where it takes the form of "lower prices, higher quality or greater choice of goods or services in any market in the UK . . . or greater innovation in relation to such goods or services." These categories of benefit are expanded upon with suggested examples at para.7.8 of the OFT's *Substantive Agreement Guidance*. As the Explanatory Notes to the Act observe, these are benefits that would normally be expected to be the result of a fully competitive market, rather than one which has experienced a

---

[69] See para.4.30 of the OFT's *Substantive Assessment Guidance*.
[70] In the OFT's decision of December 30, 2003, *Anticipated acquisition by Carl Zeiss Jena GmbH of the microscopy business of Bio-Rad Laboratories Inc*, Carl Zeiss argued that the proposed acquisition would strengthen its position as a competitor of Leica (both having market shares in the region of 30 to 40 per cent). Since Bio-Rad was not a strong competitive constraint (with a share of 0 to 10 per cent), Carl Zeiss argued that the merger would increase rivalry between it and Leica and benefit innovation. The OFT considered the argument plausible but found that there was insufficient evidence to conclude that the discretion not to refer could be exercised. Enhanced rivalry was also argued but rejected in the OFT's decision of April 29, 2004, *Completed acquisition by Archant Limited of the London Regionals Division of Independent News and Media plc*.
[71] See para.4.31 of the OFT's *Substantive Assessment Guidance*.

substantial lessening of competition, and accordingly relevant customer benefits "are not expected to arise very often".[72]

4.016 The OFT makes a similar comment in its *Substantive Assessment Guidance*:

> "To count as customer benefits, by definition, customers need to be better off with the merger, despite the fact that the OFT believes that the merger might lessen competition substantially. These will be rare cases since, ordinarily, the OFT would expect competition to deliver lower prices, higher quality and greater consumer choice".[73]

The Explanatory Notes to the Act give some concrete examples of where, exceptionally, customer benefits may arise,[74] including where the merger creates beneficial network effects; where large economies of scale reduce prices below their pre-merger level; or where the merger will create the critical mass necessary to enable research and development to boost innovation. However, a benefit which falls within one of the above categories will nevertheless not be a "relevant customer benefit" unless, in the case of a completed merger, the benefit has actually accrued as a result of the merger or, in the case of a completed or an anticipated merger, is expected to accrue "within a reasonable period", and moreover was or is unlikely to accrue without the merger "or a similar lessening of competition".[75] The OFT's *Substantive Assessment Guidance* gives no guidance as to what might constitute a "reasonable period"; the Explanatory Notes to the Act merely rephrase it as "a reasonable time-frame". The point has yet to be addressed in the OFT's decisions under the Act. The requirement that the benefits must arise out of the merger itself is discussed further at para.4.017 below.

Finally, s.30(4) of the Act specifies who "relevant customers" are and states that they are not limited to direct customers of the merged entity, but can be customers at the next level down in the chain of supply or at any other point in a chain of customers which begins with the merged entity's customers. Moreover, "relevant customers" includes future customers: the Explanatory Notes clarify that "in some circumstances a merger can lead to the development of new products or services and the creation of new markets".[76] Consistent with the inclusion of the whole chain of customers within the category of "relevant customers", the benefits of the merger can arise in a market other than that in which the substantial lessening of competition has or may have occurred.[77]

The OFT's *Substantive Assessment Guidance* lays down reasonably strict requirements to be fulfilled if arguments regarding countervailing customers benefits of the latter type are to override the duty to refer. These requirements go beyond the already limiting provisions of s.30 of the Act, because they add that claimed cost savings must be quantifiable:

---

[72] See para.122 of the Explanatory Notes to the Act.
[73] See para.7.10 of the OFT's *Substantive Assessment Guidance*.
[74] See para.124 of the Explanatory Notes to the Act.
[75] See ss.30(2) and (3) of the Act.
[76] See para.123 of the Explanatory Notes to the Act.
[77] See s.30(1)(a)(i) of the Act, and para.7.9 of the OFT's *Substantive Assessment Guidance*.

". . . the claimed customer benefits must be clear and, in the case of cost savings, quantifiable. In other words, the parties should be able to produce detailed and verifiable evidence of any anticipated price reductions or other benefits. Moreover, the OFT must believe that the claimed benefits will materialise within a reasonable period of time and must believe that such benefits would be unlikely to arise without the merger".[78]

The OFT goes on to emphasise that theoretical benefits are not enough: it must be shown that the parties will have incentives to pass the benefits on to customers. *Archant/London Regionals Division of Independent News & Media plc* provides an example of a case where the OFT concluded that the claimed customer benefits were not, on the evidence, shown to be clear, quantifiable and merger-specific.[79]   **4.017**

As explained above, a key requirement of s.30 of the Act is that the customer benefits must flow from the merger itself. In its consideration of National Express' acquisition of the Greater Anglia rail franchise,[80] the OFT considered that it was not clear on the basis of the evidence that the claimed customer benefits arose out of the merger rather than out of the creation of the new rail franchise, which combined routes formerly comprised in three separate rail franchises. The OFT therefore concluded that the claimed benefits were not merger-specific.

In *NMS/CIS*,[81] the parties both supplied milk recording services,[82] NMR mainly in England and Wales and CIS primarily in Scotland (reflecting their inheritance on deregulation of the businesses of the England and Wales Milk Marketing Board and Scottish Livestock Services, respectively). The parties planned to create a single combined database of milk recording information, to be run as a charity, and also to merge their corporate structures as well. The OFT noted that many third parties welcomed the merger, believing that it would "significantly benefit the dairy industry as it will remove duplication of information and increase efficiency, value and usability of data by all industry members". However, it was also clear that the creation of the single database was not dependent on the merger of the companies taking place: the two were complementary but not dependent on the other. As a result, the benefits arising out of the single database could not be said to arise out of the merger and therefore could not form the basis of an exception to the duty to refer in relation to the merger of the companies themselves. The OFT concluded that that duty was engaged, and referred the merger.[83] As the OFT commented, the formation of the database could of course itself constitute a qualifying merger: if such a case were

---

[78] See para.7.7 of the OFT's *Substantive Assessment Guidance*.
[79] See the OFT's decision of April 29, 2004, *Completed acquisition by Archant Limited of the London Regionals Division of Independent News & Media plc*.
[80] See the OFT's decision of May 27, 2004, *Completed acquisition by National Express plc of the Grater Anglia Franchise*.
[81] See the OFT's decision of March 3, 2004, *Anticipated acquisition by National Milk Records plc of The Cattle Information Service Limited*.
[82] Essentially, data for individual dairy cattle about milk samples and key events (such as calving and vaccinations).
[83] The reference was subsequently cancelled as the parties abandoned the merger.

to be considered by the OFT, the duty to refer might well turn out to be outweighed by the customer benefits.

It is interesting to consider the provisions of ss.30(2)(b) and 30(3)(b) of the Act (which require that customer benefits must have been unlikely to accrue without the merger or a similar lessening of competition) against this case. If NMS and CIS had agreed that structural merger of the corporate groups was a pre-condition to the operational merger of the databases, then these sections might have come into play. The OFT might then have had to consider whether combining the databases through a looser joint venture or licensing arrangements (thereby retaining NMS and CIS as independent companies) would have been a less anti-competitive way of achieving the customer benefits, or whether such structures would have brought about a "similar lessening of competition" as the full structural merger.[84] Essentially this aspect of the analysis of customer benefits requires the OFT to review, in the words of the Explanatory Notes, whether "the only other ways of realising the customer benefit would have a similar detrimental effect on competition".[85]

4.018   In practice, whilst the commercial rationale behind a merger will very often be to make cost savings and to increase the efficiency of the combined business, it is much less common that there is a demonstrable intention to pass those savings on to customers as is required by para.7.8 of the OFT's *Substantive Assessment Guidance*. Given that the OFT will usually request sight of the board papers and strategic analyses put together when contemplating the merger, parties need to take care that any claims of customer benefits are consistent with the commercial analysis documentation recording the rationale for the merger.[86]

The merger is not sufficiently advanced or sufficiently likely to proceed

4.019   Finally, s.33(2) of the Act, which deals with anticipated mergers, adds a third set of circumstances where the duty to refer is subject to a discretion of the OFT not to refer, namely in cases where the OFT believes that the merger plans are not significantly advanced or sufficiently likely to proceed to warrant reference. As the OFT's *Substantive Assessment Guidance* notes, this provision was primarily envisaged to allow the process of confidential guidance[87] to continue without the risk that such consultations would engage the duty to refer.[88] The *Substantive Assessment Guidance* comments that this discretion will *not* usually apply where a public announcement has

---

[84] In fact a full structural merger is often seen as preferable (in terms of its impact on competition) to a looser joint venture structure which might cause wider or "spill-over" co-ordination between the independent parent businesses, co-ordination which could itself be anti-competitive and contrary to the Chapter I prohibition under the Competition Act 1998 and/or Art.81 of the EC Treaty.

[85] See para.123 of the Explanatory Notes to the Act.

[86] Lloyds TSB Bank appears to have encountered a similar problem in seeking to claim that merger synergies from its proposed acquisition of Abbey National would create customer benefits. The Competition Commission considered Lloyds TSB's internal strategy documents and concluded that it was more likely to use any such synergies "to enhance profits rather than to compete more intensively". See paras 2.208 and 2.220 of *Lloyds TSB Group plc and Abbey National plc*, Cm. 5208 (July 2001).

[87] Discussed at para.3.004 of Ch.3, below.

[88] See para.7.2 of the OFT's *Substantive Assessment Guidance*.

been made about the intention to merge, or where a public announcement has been made about the intention to make a public offer, even though the bid may be subject to conditions or may prove to be hostile.[89-90] This clarification is useful but not surprising: it has never been the case that there must be a legally binding obligation to proceed with the merger before the UK merger control regime can apply.

Consistent with the latter point, the OFT will proceed with its competition analysis and may make a reference in situations where there are a number of competing potential purchasers. Under the FTA, this occurred on a number of occasions both in relation to competing public bid situations, where at the time of the OFT's assessment there is typically not yet any established intention to sell on the part of the shareholders[91], and in relation to private sales, where at least the vendor has clearly signalled an intention to sell.[92] Under the Act, no reference had yet been made in similar circumstances at the time of writing, but it appears that the OFT considered and analysed alternative purchasers for the "ASK" restaurant business. In each case the OFT found that no material competition concerns could be expected to arise and cleared the proposals.[93]

In its *Substantive Assessment Guidance*, the OFT states that it will take an early view on whether the merger is significantly advanced or likely to proceed to warrant reference and so whether any real competition analysis is required.[94] This is a slightly odd comment given the stated primary purpose of this discretion, which is to deal with confidential guidance cases: the whole point of seeking confidential guidance is to request the OFT to undertake "real competition analysis", albeit without third party input. Moreover, the discretion not to proceed with a reference is not available unless and until the OFT has concluded that its duty to refer has been engaged: again, it would require "real competition analysis" to reach such a conclusion. The comment perhaps suggests that the OFT sees the discretion rather more as an option to decline to accept jurisdiction at a particular point in time, an interpretation which would not fit clearly with the structure of the statutory regime.

Circumstances where a reference may not be made

Apart from the three situations where the OFT has a discretion whether to refer, ss.22(3) and 33(3) specify a number of situations where a reference *cannot* be made. The exceptions are discussed in turn below with brief comment where appropriate: where they warrant closer review, this will follow in the subsequent paragraphs.

4.020

[89-90] See para.7.3 of the OFT's *Substantive Assessment Guidance.*

[91] Most recently, four competing bids for Safeway were referred. See *Safeway plc and Asda Group Limited (owned by Wal-Mart Stores Inc); Wm Morrison Supermarkets PLC; J Sainsbury plc; and Tesco plc,* Cm. 5950 (September 2003).

[92] This has happened most frequently in the newspaper sector. See, for example the competing bids for Regional Independent Media: *Regional Independent Media Limited and Gannett UK Limited/Johnston Press plc/Guardian Media Group plc,* Cm. 4887 (November 2000).

[93] See the OFT's decision of January 19, 2004, *Proposed acquisition by City Centre Restaurants plc of ASK Central plc* and the OFT's decision of April 14, 2004, *Anticipated acquisition by Riposte Limited of ASK Central plc.*

[94] See para.7.4 of the OFT's *Substantive Assessment Guidance.*

(i)   No reference is possible where undertakings in lieu of reference have been accepted by the OFT[95] or the Secretary of State[96] or where the OFT is considering whether to accept them[97]: this exception will be considered in detail below.

(ii)   No reference is possible where a Merger Notice has been submitted in relation to the proposed merger and the statutory timeframe has expired without a reference being made.[98] Use of a Merger Notice triggers a statutory obligation on the OFT to make a reference by a fixed deadline.[99] Where a pre-notified merger is cleared, it can subsequently be referred only where it emerges that material information which was or should have been known to the notifying parties and which is material to the notified merger was disclosed to the OFT less than five working days before the end of the statutory period for consideration of the Merger Notice.[1] A reference can also be made following clearance of a pre-notified merger where information given in the Merger Notice or otherwise by the notifying party or connected persons, is false or misleading in any material respect.[2] Finally, a reference may be made, notwithstanding that the transaction was notified on a Merger Notice and the statutory deadline has expired without a reference being made, if that merger is subsequently treated as having occurred on the same day as one or more subsequent transactions, and in relation to the last of those, the s.96(3) protection against reference does not apply.[2A]

(iii)   No reference is possible where the relevant merger situation has been dealt with in connection with a reference made under s.33 (this prevents a reference under s.22)[3] or s.22 (this prevents a reference under s.33).[4]

(iv)   No reference is possible where a public interest intervention notice has been issued by the Secretary of State and remains in force, or the Secretary of State has himself made a reference.[5] This is dealt with in detail below.

(v)   No reference is possible where the European Commission is considering a request made by the UK[6] under Art.22 of the EC Merger Regulation for the European Commission to accept jurisdiction

---

[95] See s.22(3)(a) and 33(3)(a) and s.74(1) of the Act.
[96] See ss.22(3)(a) and 33(3)(a) and para.4 of Sch.7 to the Act.
[97] See ss.22(3)(b) and 33(3)(b) of the Act.
[98] See ss.22(3)(c), 33(3)(c) and 96(3) of the Act.
[99] This is discussed in detail in para.3.028 of Ch.3, above.
[1] See s.100(1)(c) of the Act and Reg.4 of the Enterprise Act 2002 (Merger Prenotification Regulations) 2003 (SI 2003/1369).
[2A] See further ss.100(2)–(5) of the Act and para.3.036 of Ch.3.
[2] See s.100(1)(g) of the Act.
[3] See s.22(3)(c) of the Act.
[4] See s. 33(3)(c) of the Act.
[5] See ss.22(3)(d) and 33(3)(d) of the Act.
[6] In practice, the OFT fulfils this function: see paras 12.3 and 12.6 to 12.7 of the OFT's *Substantive Assessment Guidance*, and para.9.2 of the OFT's *Procedural Guidance*.

over the case[7], notwithstanding that it does not qualify under the jurisdictional turnover thresholds of the EC Merger Regulation. No reference is possible either where a reasoned submission (known as "Form RS") from the parties is being considered by the European Commission, requesting that the European Commission accept jurisdiction over the case pursuant to Art.4(5) of the EC Merger Regulation, although this restriction will fall away if any Member State competent to review the merger in question has expressed its disagreement with the request to refer the merger up to the European Commission. The "corrective mechanisms" of the EC Merger Regulation which allow the transfer of a case falling under national merger control to the European Commission are considered in Ch.2 above.[8] In such situations, the OFT's investigation may have to be put "on hold" pending the decision of the European Commission whether to accept jurisdiction. Section 25(6) of the Act gives the OFT power to extend the four month statutory deadline for a reference[9] where an Art.22 request has been made, and ss.25(7) and (8) provide that the extension of time comes to an end when the OFT gives the parties notice that the European Commission has finished its consideration of the UK's request. Since the European Commission is itself required to inform the parties, as well as the UK government, of its decision regarding the Article 22 request,[10] the requirement that the UK should also give notice of the decision seems unnecessary, unless it is to give the OFT control of when the s.25(6) extension of time ceases. This would enable the OFT to give itself sufficient time to conclude its own investigation in circumstances where it had not already done so and the European Commission had declined to take the case. There is no comment on how these provisions will be used in the OFT's *Procedural Guidance*.

It should be noted that unless a merger has been notified on a Merger Notice,[11] the fact that a merger situation has been cleared by the OFT does not in itself prevent a subsequent reference: the Act is silent on this point. There is no requirement that the initial assessment must have been based on misleading or incomplete information if a merger investigation is to be reopened.[11A] Until the four month deadline for reference has expired,[12] the OFT is still theoretically free to make a reference. Of course any attempt to refer a merger which had previously been cleared, in the absence of material new facts or some other significant shift in the

---

[7] See ss.22(3)(e) and 33(3)(e) of the Act.
[7A] See ss.22(3)(f) and 33(3)(f), inserted into the Act by The EC Merger Control Consequential Amendments Regulations 2004 (SI 2004/1079).
[7B] See ss.22(3A) and 33(3A) of the Act.
[8] See paras 2.043 *et seq.*
[9] See s.24 of the Act.
[10] See Art.22(3), second paragraph of the EC Merger Regulation.
[11] See para.(ii) above and paras 3.028 *et seq.* of Ch.3 in this respect.
[11A] Correspondingly, the fact that a merger clearance is subsequently found to have been based on misleading or incomplete information does not entitle the OFT to revoke its decision, as would be the case under the EC Merger Regulation (see Arts 6(3) and 8(6)).
[12] See s.24 of the Act and Ch.2 at para.2.023.

grounds on which the earlier clearance had been based, would be very vulnerable to challenge by the parties, and for that reason this is largely a theoretical risk only.[12A]

Avoiding a reference by undertakings in lieu

Background

4.021 Since April 1990 merger control legislation has provided for the parties (usually the purchaser) to give undertakings to dispose of assets or shares to address competition concerns arising out of the merger which would otherwise warrant a reference to the Competition Commission (or formerly the MMC). Prior to 1990, it was not uncommon for a merger or proposed merger to be referred because of regulatory concerns arising as a result of the combination of an aspect of the target business with the purchaser's business activity which, to the purchaser, was peripheral to the commercial logic of the merger. The outcome of such a reference was often to require the purchaser to divest business or assets that it would in any event have been prepared to dispose of without a reference. During the mid 1980s, at a time of intense public bid activity, parties increasingly sought to avoid a reference by divesting certain businesses or assets giving rise to perceived competition detriments in advance of the main sale and purchase transaction, or making the latter conditional upon the agreed divestments, so that it could be shown that the possible detriments would never arise.[13]

However, such mechanisms as were developed were not easy to use (particularly in hostile bid situations) and relied on being able to second guess the OFT and/or MMC's analysis of the case.[14] It was, moreover, accepted that it was clearly in the interests of good administration to avoid the expense and delay inherent in a reference if at all possible.[15] The FTA was therefore amended by the Companies Act 1989 to provide for a power for the Secretary of State for Trade and Industry to accept undertakings in lieu of a reference.[16] Initially, the power was limited to allow only structural undertakings to be accepted,[17] but the scope of the power was extended by the Deregulation and Contracting Out Act 1994 to enable undertakings as

---

[12A] The authors understand that in one case under the FTA, the OFT cleared an anticipated merger unconditionally but then reviewed it again as a completed merger, following the emergence of material new information. It was ultimately cleared again following the second review.

[13] See the first edition of this book at pp.81 to 84 for a discussion of the techniques which developed to avoid a reference by putting in place contractual commitments to divest parts of the business which, if retained by the merged entity, might otherwise have given rise to competition concerns warranting a reference.

[14] The risks inherent in trying to second guess the regulators' analysis are discussed at para.3.018 and following in Ch.3 (albeit by reference to cases which took place at a time when undertakings in lieu had become possible).

[15] This point is still important and is reflected in para.226 of the Explanatory Notes to the Act, discussed below at para.4.022.

[16] See ss.75G to 75K of the FTA.

[17] The concept of "structural" undertakings as distinct to "behavioural" or "conduct" undertakings is discussed at para.4.024, below.

to future conduct (*i.e.* behavioural undertakings) to be accepted by the Secretary of State.[18]

Although undertakings in lieu remain statistically much less common than references,[19] there is no doubt that they represent an important weapon in the regulatory arsenal of remedies, not least because they allow significant savings in cost and time for all concerned. The main limitation on a greater use of undertakings in lieu is of course that the fact that a merger creates an aggregation of market share, or of buyer power, will often be precisely the rationale for the merger and so the parties prefer to undergo a reference than to concede part of the core value of the merger at the outset.

Undertakings in lieu under the Act

The utility of undertakings in lieu was recognised by their preservation in the overhauled regime introduced by the Act (ss.73 to 75 give the OFT power to accept them). Exercise of the power is subject to a number of conditions.   **4.022**

First, the power is not triggered unless the OFT has concluded that the merger under consideration should be referred under s.22 or 23 of the Act: *i.e.* the OFT must believe that it may be the case that the merger has resulted or may be expected to result in a substantial lessening of competition. Moreover, as the OFT emphasises in its *Substantive Assessment Guidance*, the power to accept undertakings in lieu is to allow concerns to be *remedied*.[20] It cannot therefore be used to strengthen, guarantee or "lock in" customer benefits which may have caused the OFT to conclude pursuant to ss.22(2)(b) or 33(2)(c) of the Act[21] that reference is not warranted: in such circumstances, undertakings are not available. On the other hand, where undertakings in lieu are used to remedy competition concerns, there is no objection if they also operate to secure any customer benefits arising from the merger. Indeed, the OFT has confirmed that it will "seek to agree undertakings that preserve any merger-specific customer benefits"[22] although this, as noted, cannot be the primary aim of the undertakings, only a subordinate one.

Secondly, in considering whether to accept undertakings in lieu, the OFT must have regard to "the need to achieve as comprehensive a solution as is reasonable and practicable" to the competition concerns.[23] The OFT has said

---

[18] See further the first edition of this book at pp.86 to 97.

[19] In the 87 cases reviewed under the Act from its coming into force until June 1, 2004, 12 references were made and undertakings in lieu were accepted (or were still being negotiated at the time of writing) in four cases. In the cases reviewed under the FTA in 2003, six references were made (four of which concerned the competing Safeway bids) but no cases were closed by undertakings in lieu. In 2002, 14 references were made and no cases were closed by undertakings in lieu. In 2001, ten references were made under the FTA, and undertakings in lieu were accepted in four cases.

[20] s.73(2) of the Act specified that undertakings in lieu are for the purpose of "remedying, mitigating or preventing the substantial lessening of competition concerned or any adverse effect [resulting from it]".

[21] See para.8.2 of the OFT's *Substantive Assessment Guidance*.

[22] See para.8.2 of the OFT's *Substantive Assessment Guidance*. The discretion to take this issue into account is expressly set out in s.73(4) of the Act.

[23] See s.73(3) of the Act. In the OFT's decision of May 27, 2004, *Completed acquisition by National Express of the Greater Anglia Franchise*, the OFT rejected a proposed price-cap

that it "will seek to achieve undertakings in lieu that are sufficient to address clearly the identified adverse competition effects and are proportionate to them".[24] As the Explanatory Notes to the Act state clearly:

"The purpose of accepting undertakings [in lieu] is to allow the OFT (where it is confident about the problem that needs to be addressed and the appropriate solution) to correct the competition problem the merger presents without recourse to a potentially time-consuming and costly investigation."[25]

The key point is perhaps the comment in parenthesis that the OFT must be "confident about the problem that needs to be addressed and the appropriate solution". The OFT typically uses the shorthand that the competition concerns and the remedies proposed to eliminate the concerns must be "clear-cut". The OFT's *Substantive Assessment Guidance* explains that:

"In order to accept undertakings in lieu of a reference, the OFT must be confident that the competition concerns identified can be resolved by means of undertakings without the need for further investigation. Undertakings in lieu of reference are therefore appropriate only where the competition concerns raised by the merger and the remedies proposed to address them are clear cut, and those remedies are capable of ready implementation. It is for this reason that undertakings in lieu have typically been used in merger cases in the past where a substantial lessening of competition arises from an overlap that is relatively small in the context of the merger (*e.g.* a few local markets affected by a national merger)".[26]

4.023   On a number of occasions under the Act, undertakings in lieu have been offered by the parties but found to be insufficiently "clear-cut".[27] A proposed undertaking can fail to be clear-cut either because the OFT's analysis has not identified a clear-cut area of concern, or because it is insufficiently clear that the proposed remedy will address and remove the concern. The former situation can occur because the OFT simply runs out of time to complete its analysis, or because the case is too complex for the analysis to be satisfactorily completed in a first phase merger investigation. In relation to FirstGroup's proposed acquisition of the ScotRail franchise, the parties offered undertakings in lieu but the OFT was unable to accept them:

---

undertaking in lieu because "it does not address concerns related to non-price competition", *i.e.* it was not a sufficiently comprehensive solution. This is a recurring problem with price cap commitments in the context of undertakings in lieu and is discussed further at para.4.025, below.

[24] See para.8.2 of the OFT's *Substantive Assessment Guidance*.

[25] See para.226 of the Explanatory Notes to the Act.

[26] Para.8.3 of the OFT's *Substantive Assessment Guidance*.

[27] See, for example, the OFT's decision of May 20, 2004 in *Completed acquisition by DS Smith PLC of LINPAC Containers Limited*, its decision of April 29, 2004 in *Completed acquisition by Archant Limited of the London Regionals Division of Independent News & Media plc* and the OFT's decision of December 18, 2003 in *Anticipated acquisition by Dräger Medical AG & Co. KGaA of the Air-Shields business of Hillenbrand Industries Inc.*

"The timeframe of the OFT investigation has not permitted clear identi-fication of possible detriments to competition. Although the parties have offered [details were excised for confidentiality], it would therefore not be appropriate to accept them at this stage".[28]

Under the FTA, Morrison's bid for Safeway (which was reviewed by the OFT alongside various competing bids) encountered similar problems. Morrison's bid raised some local competition concerns, but it might have been possible to resolve these by undertakings in lieu to divest stores in areas where there would otherwise have been a local aggregation of market share. Indeed, Morrison proposed such divestments. However, when other bidders joined the bidding war, the methodology for local market definition (which involved using specialist software to generate "isochrones", mapping drive times around various stores in order to identify where local competition occurred) became a highly contentious issue. A clear cut iden-tification of the areas of concern and therefore the appropriate divestment remedies could not be achieved where there was intense debate on precisely how to identify the local overlaps and which of these overlaps should be considered to raise concerns. A reference was therefore considered neces-sary because of the technical complexities of the arguments being made by the competing bidders on local market definition issues. The OFT observed:

"While Morrison has indicated a willingness to consider divestments in any area of overlap, there is potential for consumer harm by accepting divestments in areas where none might be required, just as there is in being too narrow in our assessment of where any divestment should be made".[29]

As the quotation makes clear, there was a further concern in relation to Morrison's bid that competition could be damaged if *too much* restructuring occurred through undertakings in lieu. The same point is raised in the OFT's *Substantive Assessment Guidance*, which states:

"In cases in which there is doubt over the precise identification of the substantial lessening of competition or in which the effectiveness *or proportionality* of the proposed undertakings in lieu may be questioned, the OFT considers it unlikely that the 'clear cut' criteria . . . would be met" (emphasis added).[30]

That said, the authors understand that the OFT has been focussing less on this issue in more recent cases and the risk that the divestments might go too far has been less of a concern.

---

[28] See the OFT's decision of January 13, 2004, *Anticipated acquisition by FirstGroup plc of the ScotRail franchise*. It is not expressly stated in the decision whether the parties had noti-fied using a Merger Notice, but the reference to time pressure suggests that they may well have done so.

[29] See para.39 of the OFT's advice to the Secretary of State of March 13, 2003, *Proposed acquisition by Wm Morrison Supermarkets PLC of Safeway plc.*

[30] See para.8.4 of the OFT's *Substantive Assessment Guidance*.

The provisions which may be included in undertakings in lieu are not specified in the Act, although s.89 clarifies that their scope is not limited to the matters set out in Sch.8 of the Act (which delimits the provisions which may be contained in enforcement orders). As was the case under the FTA,[31] the OFT may therefore accept both structural and behavioural undertakings.

Structural and behavioural undertakings in lieu

4.024   Structural undertakings involve a permanent change in the structure of the transaction so that the competition concerns are removed outright. The simplest example is where the substantial lessening of competition arises from an aggregation of market share, and this concern is removed by the divestment of one of the overlapping businesses. More complex examples can include long term intellectual property licences or supply arrangements which might, for example, operate to re-establish competition using a particular technology or trade-mark, or using particular input products.

Behavioural undertakings are those which do not remove the competition risk created by the merger altogether but put in place requirements regarding the future conduct of the merged entity and/or its parent companies, such that the risk of an adverse impact on competition is managed and rendered immaterial and the concern thereby falls away. This distinction is discussed at paras 8.6 to 8.10 of the OFT's *Substantive Assessment Guidance* and, in relation to remedies imposed after a Competition Commission reference, in Ch.9, below.

It should be noted that the aim of divestment undertakings (whether in this context or where they are given following a Competition Commission reference) is not simply to avoid an aggregation of market share, but to *preserve* competition. This means that the OFT will not be satisfied by, for example, a divestment of assets resulting in a reduction in output capacity, suppressing the merged entity's market share. The parties must be prepared to divest a going concern which will continue to compete in the market place under its new ownership. Thus where an acquisition concerned a single depot, the OFT concluded that divestment undertakings would not be appropriate.[32] This is emphasised in paras 8.7 and 8.8 of the OFT's *Substantive Assessment Guidance*:

> "Ideally [the divested business] should be a self-standing business, capable of being fully separated from the merging parties, and in most cases will be part of the acquired enterprise" (para.8.7).
>
> Before approving the sale of any business as a remedy, the OFT will approve the buyer. This is to ensure that the proposed buyer has the necessary expertise, resources and incentives to operate the divested business as an effective competitor in the market place. If that is not the case, it is unlikely that the proposed divestiture would be an effective remedy for the anti-competitive effects identified" (para.8.8).[33]

---

[31] See pp.85 to 87 of the first edition of this book for an account of the development in the permitted scope of undertakings in lieu.

[32] See the OFT's decision of December 3, 2003, *Anticipated acquisition by AAH Pharmaceuticals Limited of East Anglian Pharmaceuticals Limited.*

[33] Note that the approval process mentioned in this quotation is separate and potentially supplemental to any formal merger control clearance requirements (whether under the Act,

The OFT has indicated that since mergers cause a structural change to the market, a structural remedy "will often therefore be the most appropriate remedy".[34] Indeed, the OFT notes in its guidance that because structural remedies resolve the competition concerns outright, they are more likely to be appropriate as undertakings in lieu than behavioural remedies,[35] although behavioural remedies might be considered where divestment is impractical or disproportionate and/or where they might be needed to support a structural remedy.[36]

The OFT's *Substantive Assessment Guidance* comments at para.8.10:   4.025

"The OFT will consider behavioural undertakings where it considers that divestment would be impractical, or disproportionate to the nature of the concerns identified. However, given that structural undertakings are more likely to remedy any competition concerns identified since they address structural changes in the marketplace from which the competitive effects flow, the OFT is unlikely to consider generally that behavioural undertakings have sufficiently clear effects to address the identified competition concerns. Behavioural undertakings may sometimes also be necessary to support structural divestment".

The difficulties in presenting behavioural—and in particular price-related—undertakings as "clear-cut" solutions to the competition concerns have been demonstrated in a number of cases under the Act. In relation to Sibelco's proposed acquisition of Tarmac's minerals and materials business, the OFT commented:

"[Sibelco] has . . . indicated that it would be prepared to consider other alternative behavioural remedies in particular a price cap. However, the lack of any obvious benchmark against which to limit prices and the fact that [Sibelco] will shortly need to make a considerable investment—to meet new health and safety regulations—might suggest that devising a price cap that would adequately replicate the loss of competition arising from the merger would be difficult. Moreover, while any cap might limit prices it would not address concerns relating to the aspects of non-price competition, such as quality and service, the incentives for which might also be reduced by the merger. On balance, therefore, and in the absence of a divestment undertaking [refused by the parties for commercial

---

the EC Merger Regulation or foreign merger control legislation) which the divestment may trigger. In its decision regarding clearance under the Act of the acquisition by Waitrose of certain stores from Morrisons, a sale which formed part of the divestments required by the Secretary of State as the condition for clearance of Morrison's bid for Safeway in the preceding year, the OFT referred to the fact that it also had to be satisfied that the terms of the divestment undertakings had been met. The OFT's assessment of whether those terms had been met appears to have taken place in parallel to its competition assessment of the merger, since the decision on compliance with the undertakings is recorded in the OFT's s.33 decision on whether to make a reference as having been taken on the same date as the latter decision. See the OFT's decision of May 28, 2004 in *Anticipated acquisition by John Lewis Partnership plc of 19 one-stop stores from Wm Morrison Supermarkets plc.*

[34] See para.8.6 of the OFT's *Substantive Assessment Guidance.*
[35] See para.8.6 of the OFT's *Substantive Assessment Guidance.*
[36] See para.8.10 of the OFT's *Substantive Assessment Guidance.*

reasons], the OFT does not consider that the competition concerns identified in this case can be resolved by means of undertakings without the need for further investigation of the proposed merger by the [Competition Commission]. The OFT does not consider that behavioural undertakings, in particular a price cap, are sufficiently clear cut or capable of ready implementation in this case".[37]

That said, the difficulties with behavioural undertakings in lieu are not insurmountable. As at the time of writing (October 2004), undertakings in lieu had been required in five cases under the Act, of which four sets of undertakings had been finalised, signed and published[38] and one was in the process of negotiation.[39] In two of the five cases, the undertakings were behavioural (being a price control mechanism[40] and a commitment to extend an integrated transport ticket scheme to include competing transport providers[41]); in the other three, they were structural, selling the part of the acquired business which gave rise to competition concerns.[42] Statistically, this would appear to be a higher proportion of behavioural undertakings in lieu than is likely to be the case in future years, for the reasons just discussed.

For a discussion of the content and provisions typically included in undertakings generally, see Ch.9, below.

The decision whether to offer undertakings in lieu

4.026   The OFT does not usually take the initiative in proposing undertakings in lieu. It is for the parties to come up with proposed outline undertakings to

---

[37] See the OFT's decision of August 14, 2003 in *Anticipated acquisition by Sibelco Minerals & Chemicals Limited of the minerals and materials business of Tarmac Central Limited*. Similar problems were noted by the OFT in its decision of February 12, 2004, *Anticipated acquisition by Convatec Limited of Acordis Speciality Fibres Limited*, and in its decision of May 27, 2004, *Completed acquisition by National Express plc of the Greater Anglia Franchise*.

[38] Undertakings were given by IVAX International GmbH in relation to the completed acquisition of 3M Company's distribution business for certain asthma products on January 9, 2004. Undertakings dated April 29, 2004 were given by iSOFT Group plc in relation to the completed acquisition of Torex plc. Undertakings were given by Arriva plc in relation to its acquisition of the Wales and Borders rail franchise on July 9, 2004. Undertakings dated October 6, 2004 were given by *Greene King PLC* in relation to its completed acquisition of *Laurel Pub Holdings Limited*.

[39] Undertakings are being negotiated in relation to the completed acquisition by Tesco plc of the Co-op store in Uxbridge Road, Slough. See the OFT's decision of February 2, 2002, *Completed acquisition by Tesco plc of the Co-operatives Group's stores in Uxbridge Road, Slough as well as Stapleford Lane, Toton, Nottingham and Towers Place, South Shields*. At the time of writing, draft undertakings for consultation had not yet been issued.

[40] IVAX agreed not to increase the price of certain asthma products unless certain conditions were fulfilled.

[41] Arriva agreed to allow competing bus operators to participate in integrated train and bus ticketing schemes.

[42] Tesco was required to sell outright the Co-op store which it had purchased, effectively unscrambling the merger altogether. iSOFT agreed to divest the part of the acquired Torex business which gave rise to competition concerned. Greene King agreed to divest a number of pubs in the various petty sessional divisions (the geographical areas which are used to define the relevant geographic market for assessing local competition in relation to pubs) where the OFT had identified competition concerns that would otherwise have warranted reference.

remedy the OFT's concerns about a merger, although the OFT might invite the parties to consider whether they wish to put proposals forward, particularly where the competition concerns which it has identified "seem amenable to remedy by undertakings in lieu".[43] Discussions as to the shape of possible undertakings can commence very early on in the OFT's investigation, particularly where they concern a non-core part of the merged entity which the parties do not object to disposing of to remove competition concerns: indeed, proposals for undertakings can be made in the initial notification of the merger.[44] The last sensible point in the procedure at which they could be offered would be the issues meeting.[44A]

However, difficulties can arise in practice as it is not the policy of the OFT to indicate to the parties whether it believes its duty to refer is triggered by the merger prior to the announcement of its decision. The discussion regarding undertakings in lieu therefore takes place in circumstances where the parties do not yet know whether they will be required, which creates inevitable difficulties for the parties and their advisers in deciding whether to engage in discussions on suitable undertakings. In practice, discussions with the OFT may indicate (as the parties will ideally already have been advised) that a particular issue is giving rise to concern (this much can usually be gleaned by the OFT's requests for further information or an indication that various unidentified third parties have raised particular concerns). Moreover, the authors are aware of cases in which the OFT has raised the question as to whether the acquirer should contemplate offering undertakings; but that cannot be taken as necessarily indicating that a decision to refer is likely.[45] It is, therefore, difficult in some cases for the parties to be certain that they are not volunteering to remedy competition concerns that may ultimately prove not to warrant a reference. That said, the structure of the Act clearly requires the OFT to consider, first, whether the duty to refer has been engaged and, if so, secondly, whether any proposed undertakings would remedy the perceived adverse effects on competition. Accordingly, the situation should not arise that undertakings in lieu are accepted by the OFT where they are not necessary.

The decision whether to offer undertakings is one that can only be taken on a case by case basis in the light of all the relevant economic and market circumstances and the range of tactical considerations outlined above. For example, if the acquisition has already been made, or completion is not conditional upon clearance, the acquirer may decide that, although not the prime reason for entering into the transaction, the business area in question is sufficiently substantial to risk the management time and expense of a reference. On the other hand, in the context of a hostile public bid, the fear of the bid lapsing upon a reference being made, with the consequence that, even if ultimately cleared by the Competition Commission, a second bid may be impossible through changes of circumstances (with the target spending the interim time making itself less attractive to the bidder, or a

---

[43] See para.8.5 of the OFT's *Substantive Assessment Guidance*.
[44] As is noted in the OFT's *Procedural Guidance* at para.7.5.
[44A] See para.3.060 of Ch.3.
[45] In a case known to the authors where this occurred the parties resisted the "invitation" to offer undertakings in lieu in the context of a hostile public offer: in the end no reference was made.

"white knight" appearing, for example), may encourage the bidder to consider the possibility of offering to enter into undertakings in lieu of a reference at an early stage. However, such considerations may be outweighed by the fact that, in the context of a hostile bid, the bidder may not have access to sufficient information on the target company to form a reasonable judgment as to whether the undertakings required would be financially prudent in the interests of its shareholders.[46]

So far under the Act, although undertakings in lieu have been offered in most of the cases which were ultimately referred to the Competition Commission[47], in a number of cases it appears that the OFT may well have invited the parties to consider offering undertakings in lieu but the parties declined. In the case of Carl Zeiss' acquisition of the microscopy business of Bio-Rad Laboratories Inc, the OFT's decision makes it clear that the parties refused to offer undertakings in lieu.[48] This turned out to be the right decision tactically: although the parties had to go through the costly and time-consuming process of a reference, the Competition Commission ultimately decided that the merger would not result in a substantial lessening of competition, and it was cleared unconditionally.[49] In the case of Stena AB's proposed acquisition of certain Irish Sea ferry routes from P&O, again the parties did not offer undertakings in lieu.[50] In that case, the Competition Commission gave unconditional clearance to part of the planned acquisition, although the other part was blocked outright.[51]

4.027   Of course in many cases, the undertakings which might remedy the competition concerns and thereby avoid a reference are simply unacceptable to the parties from a commercial standpoint. In some cases, the commercial deal will be such that it is "all or nothing" and a merger restructured to remove the competition concerns will be unacceptable—in particular the financial logic of the deal may be critically affected. In relation to Sibelco's proposed acquisition of Tarmac's minerals and materials business, the OFT identified that if Sibelco were to undertake not to acquire Tarmac's silica flour business, the rest of the merger could proceed. However, the OFT's decision also records that "we have been told by [Sibelco] that such an undertaking would not be forthcoming. [Sibelco] regards the silica flour business as an essential part of the merger".[52] When the merger was subsequently referred, the parties abandoned their merger plans.

---

[46] Such difficulties are likely to be compounded in the context of a hostile bid, given that the target company's submission to the OFT may argue not only that the proposed merger should be referred to the Competition Commission, but also that any undertakings that might be offered in lieu of a reference would not remedy the competition detriments that arise.

[47] Of the 12 cases referred to the Competition Commission as at June 1, 2004, undertakings in lieu appear to have been offered in eight cases.

[48] See the OFT's decision of December 30, 2003, *Anticipated acquisition by Carl Zeiss Jena GmbH of the microscopy business of Bio-Rad Laboratories Inc.*

[49] *Carl Zeiss Jena GmbH and Bio-Rad Laboratories Inc* (May 2004).

[50] See the OFT's decision of August 22, 2003, *Anticipated acquisition by Stena of certain assets of operated by P&O on the Irish Sea.*

[51] *Stena AB/P&O* (February 2004).

[52] See the OFT's decision of August 14, 2003, *Anticipated acquisition by SibelCo Minerals & Chemicals Limited of the minerals and materials business of Tarmac Central Limited.*

The OFT's procedure for negotiating and accepting undertakings in lieu was discussed in detail in Ch.3 above,[53] followed by a discussion of the mechanisms available to the OFT and third parties for enforcing undertakings once they have been accepted. That Chapter also considers the acceptance of undertakings in lieu where the public interest regime has been triggered.

The public interest regime

Whilst one of the headline changes to the UK merger regime introduced by the Act was the removal of Ministerial involvement from the vast majority of cases, the Secretary of State for Trade and Industry retains power to take decisions on reference and on the final decision and any remedies following a Competition Commission investigation in prescribed categories of cases where wider public interest issues arise. The areas where the Secretary of State retains the final say over merger control have been discussed in detail in Ch.2[54] (and as regards newspaper and media mergers, are discussed in Ch.7 below), but essentially, they concern national security (including the defence sector) and the newspaper and media sectors. The Secretary of State has powers to prescribe new public interest categories,[55] although as discussed in Ch.2 the indication of the Government during the Parliamentary debates of the Enterprise Bill was that this power was not expected to be used in the near future.[56] The issue, however, is a political one, and to that extent is subject to changes in government policy.

4.028

Issue of an intervention notice and the OFT's report to the Secretary of State

The OFT is under a duty to inform the Secretary of State of cases where public interest issues (as prescribed under s.58 of the Act) may arise, so that the Secretary of State can consider whether to intervene.[57] This duty applies to all cases unless the OFT believes that the Secretary of State would consider the public interest consideration to be immaterial. Moreover, the OFT (and OFCOM and the Competition Commission) must also bring to the attention of the Secretary of State any representations which it receives to the effect that the Secretary of State should use his powers under s.58(3) to prescribe a new public interest consideration.[58] For example, in relation to the merger of the technical services divisions of Scottish Courage and Carlsberg Tetley Brewing, representations were made to the OFT by third parties and MPs that the Secretary of State should intervene to protect pension rights.[59] The OFT's decision records that these concerns were

4.029

---

[53] See paras 3.073 *et seq.*
[54] See para.2.025 of Ch.2.
[55] See s.58(3) of the Act. Note that the Secretary of State is empowered to prescribe new public interest considerations by statutory instrument: primary legislation is not needed (although it was used when the newspaper and media merger public interest considerations contained in ss.58(2A), (2B) and (2C) of the Act were introduced by the Communications Act 2003).
[56] See paras 2.030 *et seq.* of Ch.2.
[57] See s.57(1) of the Act.
[58] See s.57(2) of the Act.
[59] See the OFT's decision of March 24, 2004, *Anticipated merger of the Technical Services Divisions of Scottish Courage Limited and Carlsberg-Tetley Brewing Limited.*

passed on to the Secretary of State, although no action was taken in response.

Where the Secretary of State wishes to become involved in the consideration of a particular merger situation, he must serve an intervention notice.[60] As at the time of writing, no intervention notices under s.42 had yet been published,[61] although there had been two cases involving a proposed merger of newspaper businesses where the Secretary of State declined to intervene.[62]

From the point at which the Secretary of State serves an intervention notice, the role of the OFT essentially reverts to mirror its advisory role under the FTA. The duty to refer is suspended, pursuant to ss.22(3) and 33(3), as discussed above, and s.44 requires the OFT instead to investigate the merger and report its findings to the Secretary of State. The Act requires the OFT's report to contain the following:

(i)   advice from the OFT on whether the merger has or may be expected to result in a substantial lessening of competition; and

(ii)   a summary of the representations received by the OFT in relation to the public interest consideration as specified in the intervention notice.[63]

The procedure followed by the OFT in preparing its report under s.44 of the Act is set out in Ch.3: essentially, it follows its standard procedure for assessment of any merger under the Act.[64] The OFT's s.44 report will cover broadly the same scope as would a decision under ss.22 or 33 of the Act, including whether any of the circumstances which in a non-public interest case would trigger the OFT's discretion not to refer are present[65] and whether undertakings in lieu would be appropriate to remedy any competition

---

[60] See s.42 of the Act.

[61] No intervention notices had been served in relation to the UK merger regime, although a European intervention notice, under s.67 of the Act, had been served in relation to a merger being considered under the EC Merger Regulation by the European Commission, which raised national security issues. This is discussed further in para.2.050 of Ch.2.

[62] See the OFT's decision of April 29, 2004, *Completed acquisition by Archant Limited of the London Regionals Division of Independent News & Media plc*. This merger was referred to the Competition Commission by the OFT. This case was referred to the Competition Commission which subsequently cleared it unconditionally: *Archant Limited and the London newspapers of Independent News and Media Limited* (September 2004). The Secretary of State also did not intervene in relation to the sale of *The Daily Telegraph* and related titles: see the OFT's decision of October 11, 2004, *Completed acquisition by Press Acquisitions Limited of Telegraph Group Limited*. This case was not referred.

[63] See s.44(3) of the Act. Although where the OFT believes that the Secretary of State would consider any public interest consideration to be immaterial, the OFT is not obliged to bring it to his attention: s.57(1) of the Act.

[64] As confirmed in the OFT's *Substantive Assessment Guidance* at para.10.4.

[65] The three sets of circumstances are discussed above and briefly comprise where the market(s) concerned are not of sufficient importance to warrant a reference (considered in more detail at paras 4.011 *et seq.*, above); where there are countervailing customer benefits which outweigh the substantial lessening of competition or the adverse effects flowing from it (considered in more detail at paras 4.015 *et seq.*, above); and, in relation to mergers not yet completed, where the merger is not sufficiently far advanced or sufficiently likely to proceed to warrant reference (considered in more detail at paras 4.019 *et seq.*).

concerns which arise (and if so, a description of the type of undertakings which would be appropriate).[66]

Additionally, the OFT may, if it wishes, include advice and recommendations on the public interest considerations mentioned in the intervention notice,[67] although the OFT's *Substantive Assessment Guidance* comments:

4.030

> "The OFT will not usually make any recommendation on the public interest matter because comment on such issues lies outside its competition expertise".[68]

Towards the end of the FTA regime years, the Director General of Fair Trading similarly declined from expressing views or giving advice on issues other than competition concerns and simply passed on comments received on any wider public interest issues. For example, in relation to the acquisition of the Express newspaper[69] by a business controlled by Mr Richard Desmond, (which did not fall under the regime for newspaper mergers because the purchaser did not previously have any interests in the newspapers sector), the OFT reported third party concerns regarding the impact of the merger on employment; concerns that as a publisher of "adult magazines", Mr Desmond was not an appropriate purchaser of the Express; and that editorial or ethical standards might suffer. However, the Director General advised in his conclusions:

> "Overall, we consider this merger is unlikely to have an adverse impact on competition in any relevant economic market. We would therefore recommend that the merger should be cleared on competition grounds.
> The OFT is not well-placed, however, to assess the non-competition issues which have been raised in this case. These have been summarised above in order that Ministers can consider these concerns should they wish to do so."

Likewise in relation to the proposed rocket motors joint venture between MBDA and SNPE, the OFT noted in its advice to the Secretary of State that the Ministry of Defence considered that the case could raise national security issues relevant to the public interest but commented in its conclusions on national security considerations:

> "The OFT is not expert in national security matters and must therefore rely heavily on the representations made by the MOD."[69A]

Although the OFT's report in public interest cases under the Act is not required to include advice on the public interest considerations, it remains to be seen whether representations in this respect will simply be reported

---

[66] See ss.44(4) and 44(5) of the Act.
[67] See s.44(6) of the Act.
[68] See para.10.4 of the OFT's *Substantive Assessment Guidance*.
[69] See the Director General's advice of February 2, 2001, *Completed acquisition by Northern and Shell Group of the Express Newspaper Business*.
[69A] See the Director General's advice of November 21, 2002, *Proposed Rocket Motors joint venture between MBDA and SNPE*.

without comment. In the OFT's report to the Secretary of State in relation to the European intervention notice issued in relation to the *General Dynamics/Alvis* acquisition,[70] third party representations were simply reported without comment. By contrast, the Director General's advice in relation to purchase of the Express newspaper (discussed above) did not include express advice on the non-competition public interest issues, but did include comment on the extent of evidence presented to back up the concerns expressed, and on the extent to which they had taken into account other factors which the Director General appeared to consider relevant to the cogency of the concerns.

Following receipt of the OFT's report, the Secretary of State will then consider the case and decide whether to take action on the basis of the public interest issues. In cases concerning newspapers or media mergers, the Secretary of State will additionally receive a report from OFCOM[71], which will not consider the competition issues covered in the OFT's report but will advise the Secretary of State on the public interest considerations.

Where the Secretary of State concludes that the public interest consideration is relevant

4.031   Where the Secretary of State concludes that the public interest concerns are relevant to the outcome of the case (whether in a positive or negative sense), he is empowered to refer the merger and the OFT's duty to refer falls away pursuant to ss.22(3)(d) or 33(3)(d). The Secretary of State is obliged to accept the advice of the OFT regarding the possible anti-competitive effects of the merger and whether a reference should be made on competition grounds: unlike under the FTA, he cannot reach a different conclusion, including as to the appropriateness and description of any undertakings in lieu.[72] This obligation to accept the OFT's findings on competition issues is, of course, consistent with the scheme of the reforms to the UK regime in that the decision whether a merger may be expected to have an anti-competitive outcome and warrant a reference is essentially taken by the OFT. However, where the OFT concludes that no competition concerns arise, the Secretary of State can still refer a merger to the Competition Commission on public interest grounds alone.[73]

Moreover, public interest considerations can override the competition analysis in that the Act enables the Secretary of State to clear a merger on public interest grounds, notwithstanding that the OFT has advised that it believes that it may be the case that the merger may be expected to result, or has resulted, in a substantial lessening of competition (*i.e.* an anti-competitive outcome). Section 45(6) of the Act provides that "any anti-competitive outcome shall be treated as being adverse to the public interest

---

[70] See the report of the OFT pursuant to Arts 4(2) to (5) of the Enterprise Act 2002 (Protection of Legitimate Interests) Order 2003 (SI 2003/1592) of May 20, 2004, *Anticipated acquisition by General Dynamics Corporation of Alvis plc*, published on the DTI's website. As noted above, this case concerned intervention by the Secretary of State in a case being considered by the European Commission under the EC Merger Regulation but the Act provides for intervention mechanisms in this context which are broadly parallel to those in relation to the UK regime.

[71] See s.44A of the Act and Ch.7.

[72] See s.46(2) of the Act.

[73] See ss.45(3) and (5) of the Act.

unless it is justified by one or more than one public interest consideration"; in other words, public interest considerations in favour of clearance may "trump" the competition analysis which points to a reference. As the Explanatory Notes to the Act state, this provision "ensures that the Secretary of State will view a competition problem identified by the OFT as being adverse to the public interest unless [he] considers this to be outweighed in the overall assessment".[74] This is perhaps the key point of the public interest provisions: where a merger is in the public interest from the perspective of considerations of national security or relating to the media sector, the fact that a merger is expected to be anti-competitive may not be the end of the story in deciding whether it warrants reference.

Where the Secretary of State concludes that the public interest consideration is not relevant

Where the Secretary of State concludes that the public interest issues which were the subject of the intervention notice are not in fact relevant to consideration of the merger, the Secretary of State must serve notice on the OFT under s.56(1) and return the case to the OFT. The OFT's duty to refer is reactivated by s.56(2) and it will then take a decision on whether to refer the case. The OFT's *Substantive Assessment Guidance* confirms that in such circumstances, its decision will be consistent with the advice which it gave in its report to the Secretary of State.[75] Thus if the report concluded that the merger would not result in a substantial lessening of competition, or where the OFT's report to the Secretary of State considered that the circumstances which, under ss.22(2) and 33(2), would trigger its discretion not to refer were relevant,[76] the OFT will clear the merger. If conversely, the OFT advised the Secretary of State that there was a risk of a substantial lessening of competition then it will refer the case (or seek undertakings in lieu, etc.).

4.032

Where the Secretary of State decides to accept undertakings in lieu of reference

Paragraph 3 of Sch.7 of the Act gives the Secretary of State power to accept undertakings in lieu of making a reference. These can be accepted to remedy the competition concerns (in which case, as noted, the Secretary of State must accept the advice of the OFT on the appropriateness of undertakings in lieu and on their description[77]) or to remedy the public interest concerns, or both. In either case, the acceptance will remove the duty on the OFT to refer the merger.[78]

4.033

---

[74] See para.161 of the Explanatory Notes to the Act.

[75] See para.10.5 of the OFT's *Substantive Assessment Guidance*.

[76] As noted above, the three sets of circumstances are discussed above and briefly comprise where the market(s) concerned are not of sufficient importance to warrant a reference (considered in more detail at paras 4.011 *et seq.*, above); where there are countervailing customer benefits which outweigh the substantial lessening of competition or the adverse effects flowing from it (considered in more detail at paras 4.015 *et seq.*, above); and, in relation to mergers not yet completed, where the merger is not sufficiently far advanced or sufficiently likely to proceed to warrant reference (considered in more detail at paras 4.019 *et seq.*).

[77] See para.3(3)(a) of Sch.7 to the Act.

[78] See para.4.020 above, and ss.22(3)(a) and 33(3)(a) and para.4 of Sch.7 to the Act.

At the time of writing, there were no examples of such undertakings. However, undertakings in lieu had been required in two cases where European intervention notices had been issued in relation to mergers being considered by the European Commission under the EC Merger Regulation, and which gave rise to national security concerns in the UK. The OFT's report to the Secretary of State in those cases,[79] which reported the representations which it had received on the public interest considerations, also appended draft undertakings in lieu which, in both cases, were clearly drawn up by the Ministry of Defence (MOD).

---

[79] See the report of the OFT pursuant to Arts 4(2) to (5) of the Enterprise Act 2002 (Protection of Legitimate Interests) Order 2003 of May 20, 2004, *Anticipated acquisition by General Dynamics Corporation of Alvis plc*, published on the DTI's website. The merger was subsequently abandoned and the undertakings in lieu were accordingly never finalised. See also the report of the OFT in relation to the *Anticipated acquisition by Finmeccanica Societa Per Azioni of Agustawestland NV*. As at the time of writing, the draft undertakings required by the Secretary of State in that case were undergoing the consultation process and had not yet been finalised.

CHAPTER 5

COMMISSION PROCEDURE AND PRACTICE

Introduction

The immediate effect of a reference to the Competition Commission is to   5.001
introduce several months of uncertainty into the plans, aspirations and
future business management of the parties to the merger and those
connected with it. Reference also triggers provisions of the Enterprise Act
which give the Commission the power to prevent the carrying out of acts
which may render the imposition of remedies more difficult in the event
that the merger is found to result or have resulted in a substantial lessening
of competition.[1] In addition, the Act contains provisions to prevent contemplated mergers from proceeding[2]; proposed mergers which are subject to
the Takeover Code are required to lapse[3]; and, at a practical level, the
managements of the parties to the merger face a number of months' diversion from their normal business activities as they make submissions to,
respond to enquiries from, and attend hearings with the Commission, with
all the costs, in terms of management time and external advisers' fees,
which those tasks necessarily involve.

For some buyers and sellers, the combination of cost and uncertainty
represents too big a gamble, and the Act provides a means in the case of an
uncompleted merger to avoid that uncertainty by abandoning the proposal
and cancelling the reference. For those prepared to bear the cost and take
the risk, or having no choice but to do so, the procedures involved raise a
number of issues and practical considerations which are reviewed in this
Chapter.

Legislative background

The powers under which the reference is made

The reference to the Commission of a merger situation which already exists   5.002
(that is, where the enterprises concerned have already ceased to be distinct)
will be made by the OFT under s.22 of the Act, whilst the reference of a
proposed merger will be made under s.33. References cannot be made
under both although the Commission has the power to vary a reference so
as to treat it as having been made under s.22 of the Act when made under

---

[1] See ss.80 and 81 of the Act which provide for interim undertakings and orders.
[2] See s.78 of the Act.
[3] See Rule 12.1 of the City Code on Takeovers and Mergers and para.5.014, below.

s.33 and vice versa, if justified by the facts (and any subsequent events) relating to the initial reference.[4]

Where control is acquired in stages, s.29 of the Act gives the OFT (and, in certain public interest cases, the Secretary of State) the power to treat the acquisition of control by a series of transactions taking place over a two-year period as having occurred by means of a single transaction effected on the date of the latest of the transactions to occur.[4A] In the case of Archant's acquisition of Independent News and Media ("INM"), Archant acquired three divisions of newspaper titles from INM on December 11, 2003, and subsequently acquired two further divisions of titles on December 30, 2003. The OFT exercised its discretion under s.27(5) of the Act to treat the acquisitions of December 11 and 30 as having occurred simultaneously on December 30 giving it until April 29 to issue its decision in relation to both acquisitions.[4B]

The jurisdictional test

5.003   Section 35(1) of the Act requires the Commission to decide, upon a reference being made under s.22, whether a relevant merger situation has been created and, if so, whether it has resulted, or may be expected to result, in a substantial lessening of competition within any market or markets for goods or services in the United Kingdom; and s.36(1) of the Act sets out similar requirements in relation to mergers in contemplation.[5] Sections 35(6) and 36(5) of the Act then provide that the reference may be so framed as to require the Commission, in relation to the question of whether a merger situation qualifying for investigation has been created, to exclude from consideration one or other of subs.(1) or subs.(2) of s.23 (the turnover test and the share of supply test respectively[6]); or, more generally, to exclude one of such paragraphs upon their finding that the other is satisfied.

These provisions mirror precisely the terms of s.69(2) of the FTA. The instruction permitted by that section occasionally caused difficulties under the old regime in circumstances where the Commission had been required by the terms of the reference to exclude from consideration whether the share of supply test (then often referred to as the market share test) was satisfied and subsequently found that the gross assets acquired[7] fell short of the applicable threshold. This situation arose in relation to the reference of MAI plc's acquisition of London & Continental Advertising Holdings plc.[8]

---

[4] See s.37 of the Act.

[4A] Moreover, s.27(5) and (6) allow the OFT to treat successive events (for example transactions concerning different target enterprises but between the same vendor and purchaser) within a period of two years as having occurred on the date of the final one of them: see para.2.024 of Ch.2.

[4B] OFT's decision of April 29, 2004, *Completed acquisition by Archant Limited of the London Regionals Division of Independent News & Media plc.*

[5] In the case of a merger referred to the Commission by the Secretary of State on public interest or special public interest grounds, different or further requirements are placed on the Commission. See para.5.056, below.

[6] See paras 2.021 and 2.017 respectively of Ch.2, above.

[7] *i.e.* the alternative jurisdictional test under the FTA (s.64(1)(b)), now replaced by the turnover test.

[8] Cm. 258 (November 1987).

The reference was made on the basis that the gross assets acquired exceeded £30 million (the threshold level at that time), but the Monopolies and Mergers Commission (the predecessor to the Commission) found that the gross assets of LCAH were in fact only some £27.5 million.[9] However, the reference had not been framed so as to exclude the application of the share of supply test and accordingly, although the reference had been based only on the gross assets exceeding £30 million, the MMC concluded that it was not precluded from considering whether the market share test was satisfied as a means of establishing jurisdiction. As, following the merger, MAI's share of the roadside advertising market (a market definition used in an earlier monopoly enquiry[10]) amounted to approximately 27.5 per cent, the MMC was able to carry out its inquiry. Since that time the practice, when framing a reference, has usually been to specify that once the Commission has established that one of the jurisdictional tests has been satisfied it is not required to determine whether the other is also satisfied. This practice would appear to be preferable, leaving the jurisdictional issue free from doubt, and it appears surprising, therefore, that the Act has retained the option of a more restrictively framed reference.

Timing of the reference

Section 39(1) of the Act requires the Commission to prepare its report within 24 weeks of the date of a reference being made, although it is the Commission's stated aim to endeavour to complete its enquiries in advance of that deadline in normal circumstances.

5.004

Where the Commission subsequently considers that there are special reasons[11] for it not being able to prepare its report within that period, it may upon publication extend this deadline by a maximum period of up to eight further weeks (although such an extension may only be made once). The Commission may also extend the deadline for publication of its report where it considers that one of the merging parties has failed to comply with any requirement of a notice made pursuant to s.109 of the Act.[12] In either

---

[9] It appears that in advising the Secretary of State the OFT had taken the view that whilst the gross assets disclosed in LCAH's last available accounts, of 12 months previously, fell short of £30 million and the company had since sustained losses, the proceeds of a rights issue a few months previously had increased the assets so that the test was satisfied. However, MAI was able to demonstrate that the funds raised by the issue had all been used to repay loans and accordingly that the gross assets fell significantly short of £30 million.

[10] *The Supply of Roadside Advertising Services in the UK* HC 365 (July 1981).

[11] The Commission itself has not issued any guidance as to what might constitute "special reasons". However, in the Explanatory Notes accompanying the Act it is stated that "special reasons" are anticipated to include the illness or incapacity of a member of the Commission reporting group or unexpected events such as the merger of competitors (not the subject of the reference). An extension may also be considered if another bid is made for a target company following a reference in respect of a prior bid for the same target, as was the case when the Secretary of State, having earlier referred the proposed merger between Carlton Communications plc and United News & Media plc, subsequently referred Granada Group plc's proposals to acquire Carlton or United. The timetable for the United/Carlton reference was extended and the Commission reported its conclusions on all three proposals in a single report. (*United News & Media plc/Carlton Communications PLC/Granada Group PLC* Cm. 4781 (July 2000))

[12] See para.5.026, below. Note that the power to extend applies only in the case of delays by one of the main parties, and not where a third party has failed to comply with a s.109 notice.

case, however, the extension must be made during the initial 24 week period, (although a further extension could potentially be made during the period of the first extension, after the 24 week period has elapsed).[13]

The FTA provided that a merger reference could not exceed six months (unless the Secretary of State consented to an extension). Until 1987, it was customary for the MMC to be given the full six-month period within which to report, leading to criticisms, particularly in the context of public bids, that the delay resulting from a reference might interfere permanently with the bid, frustrating the intentions of the parties through the target becoming too expensive for the bidder as a result of share price movements, or by leaving the target, in the case of a recommended merger, exposed to an unfriendly bid. In order to address these concerns, the Secretary of State announced in 1987 that he proposed to accelerate the reference process[14] and it became, and remained until the enactment of the Act, the almost invariable practice to specify that the Commission deliver its report in three, or exceptionally, four months with requests for an extension unusual even for the most complex of cases. In those circumstances, it may seem a little surprising that the Act should now revert to provision for, in effect, a six month reference period, particularly in the context of the increasing adoption by the Commission of e-mail communication and other electronic aids that have speeded up its procedures. It remains to be seen whether the 24 week period specified in the Act becomes the norm, but in any event it should be noted that under the new regime the outcome of the reference will actually be published by the deadline specified (rather than at some considerable time thereafter following the Secretary of State's deliberations); and that the Commission is now required to undertake a number of further responsibilities—in particular, the publication of provisional findings and the consideration of remedies—which may be argued to extend the duration required for a reference. To some extent, the duration of a reference is now driven by the Commission's findings in the particular case in question. Where it reaches the provisional conclusion under the Act that a merger will not lead to a substantial lessening of competition, there is no need to consider the often complex issue of suitable remedies. By contrast, under the FTA a discussion of remedies would always take place on a hypothetical basis, regardless of whether the Commission expected to recommend to the Secretary of State that they were required.

The Commission's enhanced role

5.005   Of central importance amongst the Commission's new responsibilities under the Act are that in the majority of cases[15] its decision will be determinative of the outcome and that it is responsible for imposing remedies, formerly the role of the Secretary of State who was able under the FTA to

---

[13] These deadlines also apply where the Commission is required to prepare a report by virtue of a reference made in accordance with Art.9 of the EC Merger Regulation. Art.9 now provides that [the Commission] "shall decide upon the case without undue delay. See Council Regulation 139/2004.

[14] DTI press notice P/87/597, issued on October 8, 1987.

[15] That is, except where the Secretary of State has made a reference on public interest or special public interest grounds: see para.5.056, below.

decide whether or not to follow the Commission's recommendations as to remedies and could permit a merger to proceed which the Commission had identified as having adverse consequences.

In carrying out its inquiries under a reference, and investigating whether the merger has resulted or may be expected to result in a substantial lessening of competition, the Commission sets its own administrative timetable and procedures, subject to the requirement to consult as far as practicable all those parties who might be affected by the decisions it proposes to make, and to the need to ensure transparency.[16] Alongside these new responsibilities enhanced powers have been given to the Commission to enforce the provision of information.[17]

The Act also required the Chairman to develop and publish Rules of Procedure[18] and written guidance as to its approach to merger references so as to enhance predictability, transparency and accountability. The Commission's Rules, and a series of guidance notes, were published in final form, following a period of consultation, in June and July 2003.[19]

The reference

The making of a merger reference is announced by way of a press release **5.006** and simultaneously through the Regulatory News Service of the London Stock Exchange (even where the companies involved are not listed). The parties are generally notified by a telephone call from the OFT to the advisers who have represented them during the OFT stage, and this call is usually followed by a faxed or e-mailed confirmatory letter attaching a copy of the reference. References to the Commission are normally (although not invariably) announced at 11am.

Although the Act requires the OFT to publish its reasoned decisions in order to increase the transparency of its assessment procedure, the form of the reference itself does not disclose the reasoning behind the decision to make it. The wording of the reference merely states that the OFT believes it is or may be the case that a relevant merger situation has been created (or, in the case of an anticipated merger, that arrangements are in progress or contemplation which, if carried into effect will result in the creation of a relevant merger situation); and that that results, or may be expected to result, in a substantial lessening of competition within a market or markets in the United Kingdom for (as the case may be) goods or services.[19A] Section 107(5) permits the OFT to publish its reasons other than simultaneously

---

[16] See s.104 of the Act in relation to the duty to consult and ss.105 to 107 in relation to the duty to publish certain information.

[17] See para.5.026, below.

[18] Pursuant to para.19A of Sch.7 to the Competition Act 1998, which was inserted by s.187(3) of the Act.

[19] These are as follows:
Rules of Procedure (CCI); Merger References Competition Commission Guidelines (CC2); General Advice and Information (CC4); Statement of Policy on Penalties (CC5); Chairman's Guidance to Groups (CC6); Chairman's Guidance on Disclosure of Information in Merger and Market Inquiries (CC7).

[19A] See App.7 for the wording of the first reference made under the Act, that of the anticipated acquisition by Stena AB of the Irish Sea Ferry Services operated by the Peninsular & Oriental Steam Navigation Company.

with its headline decision and accordingly while the full reasoned decision will be sent to the parties to the merger on announcement of the decision, the OFT will publish it later, once a non-confidential version has been prepared in consultation with the parties.[20] However, the OFT's published decision will set out in reasonable detail the OFT's concerns and reasons for making the reference, which is of assistance to the parties in drafting their initial memorandum to the Commission in connection with the effects of the merger.

The immediate consequences of the announcement of a reference

5.007   The announcement of a reference has a number of immediate consequences. First, in relation to completed mergers, any initial "hold separate" undertakings accepted or orders adopted by the OFT under ss.71 or 72 of the Act cease to be in force at the end of the period of seven days beginning with the making of the reference, unless the Commission has, whilst they remain in force, adopted them as its own (pursuant to s.80(3) or s.81(3) respectively).[21] Notwithstanding any such adoption, the Commission is empowered under s.81 of the Act to make an interim order preventing the parties to the merger (whether completed or in contemplation) from taking any pre-emptive action (that is, action which might prejudice the reference or impede the implementation of the Commission's decisions[22]). Alternatively the Commission may accept from the party or parties concerned interim undertakings to the same effect.[23] Thirdly, in the case of completed mergers, s.77 of the Act automatically prohibits any "relevant person" (that is, the persons carrying on any enterprise to which the reference relates) from taking any further steps to integrate the merged businesses; and s.78, which applies to anticipated mergers, prevents the parties from acquiring interests (or further interests) in one another's shares. Finally, any proposed acquisition which is subject to the provisions of the Takeover Code[24] automatically lapses pending the outcome of the reference (although, as discussed below, certain rules of the Takeover Code continue to apply during the reference period).

---

[20] See paras 3.078–3.082 of Ch.3.

[21] See s.71(6)(a) in relation to the ceasing in effect of initial undertakings and s.72(6)(a) in relation to initial orders. As an example of adoption of initial undertakings, the Commission adopted the initial undertakings given by Emap plc relating to its acquisition of ABI Building Data Limited immediately following the reference to it of the merger and subsequently accepted interim undertakings from Emap thereupon releasing it from the adopted initial undertakings, pursuant to s.80(4) of the Act. As at the time of writing, interim undertakings had also been accepted from DS Smith in relation to its proposed acquisition of LINPAC Containers Limited and from Archant in relation to its proposed acquisition of certain titles of Independent News and Media plc. In all three cases, the merger was already completed at the time of the reference.

[22] As defined in s.80(10) of the Act.

[23] See s.80(2) of the Act.

[24] See para.5.014, below.

Interim orders and undertakings

Section 81(2)[25] provides that the Commission may by order for the purpose   5.008
of preventing pre-emptive action:

(i)   prohibit or restrict the doing of things which might prejudice or impede the taking of any action that might be warranted by the Commission's report;

(ii)   impose obligations as to the carrying on by the parties of any activities or the safeguarding of any assets, either by the appointment of a person to conduct and supervise the same, or in any other manner; and

(iii) prohibit or restrict the acquisition by a person of the whole or part of the undertaking or assets of another person's activities, or impose conditions thereon.

It is more likely, however, that the Commission will seek interim undertakings pursuant to s.80 for the purpose of preventing pre-emptive action (after having, in the first instance, adopted the OFT's initial undertakings).[25A] Recent Commission experience suggests that the acquiring party in completed mergers will often be keen to negotiate undertakings in order, as the Commission has stated in its note on interim measures[25B] to clarify precisely what action it may carry out pending final determination of the reference.[25C]

However, if undertakings cannot be agreed, the Commission may resort to an interim order under s.81.

Interim measures, whether orders or undertakings, can subsist until—and must cease to have effect upon—the time of expiry of the period allowed to the Commission for making a report without its having done so or, if earlier, the final determination by the Commission of the reference to which it relates (that is to say, including the finalisation of any remedies).

In the case of a completed merger, the purpose of the provision is to ensure that no pre-emptive action may be taken within the merged entity for the purpose or with the effect of making more difficult the imposition of any remedies by the Commission following an adverse finding. Although there are statutory restrictions on dealing in relation to completed mergers,[25D] there may be scope for pre-emptive action which falls outside

---

[25] It is understood that s.81(2) is intended to have the same meaning as s.74(1) of the FTA. Confusingly, s.81(2)(d) refers only to para.19 of Sch.8 to the Act whose equivalent is para.12A of Sch.8 to the FTA, whereas s.74(1)(d) of the FTA refers also to para.12 of that Schedule. The draftsman of the Act evidently considered, unlike his predecessor, that s.81(2)(a) sufficiently covered the provisions of para.12 of Sch.8 to the Act (which is the equivalent of the earlier para.12).

[25A] See para.5.008, below. For a discussion on s.71 undertakings, see paras 3.055–3.057 of Ch.3, above.

[25B] *Note on interim measures pending determination of merger references*, published on the Commission's website on October 14, 2004.

[25C] It is not invariably the case that the Commission will seek interim undertakings or impose interim orders; the need for interim measures is considered on a case by case basis.

[25D] s.77: see para.5.011, below.

these restrictions and which it is the purpose of interim measures to address. The Commission has adopted a template for interim undertakings[25E] which provides that the acquired business should be carried on separately and maintained as a going concern; but no substantive changes are made to its organisational structure or to the range and quality of its goods or services; that except in the ordinary course of business the assets of the acquired business should be maintained and that none should be disposed of; that there should be no integration of information technology or staff; that key staff in the acquired business should be encouraged to remain; and that no business secrets or sensitive or proprietary information should pass from the acquired business to the acquirers business.

In the case of a merger which remains to be completed, the principal aim is to ensure that following the reference no further steps are taken by the parties to carry the merger into effect following the announcement of a reference. In practice, the powers of the Commission under ss.80 and 81 are likely to apply mainly to completed mergers.[26] However, these powers may be appropriate in relation to contemplated mergers where the provisions of s.78[27] are inapplicable (for example, where the merger proposed involves the acquisition of assets rather than shares, or the creation of a joint venture).

5.009   In making interim orders (and negotiating interim undertakings) the Commission may act through its Standing Group, a group of at least five members of the Commission chaired by the Chairman or a Deputy Chairman established pursuant to the Rules of Procedure[28] to discharge any general functions of the Commission. Alternatively it may request the OFT to do so.[29] In practice, however, the involvement of the Standing Group is more likely to be limited to adopting any initial undertakings accepted by the OFT; thereafter, the inquiry group will consider what, if any, interim undertakings should be sought.[30]

Section 107(2) requires the Commission to publish undertakings and orders under ss.80 and 81 and these are reuqired to be entered in the OFT's Register of Orders and Undertakings,[31] and the Commission is required in both cases to consider as soon as it is reasonably able any representations as to variation and revocation.

Automatic restriction on share dealings

5.010   The effect of s.78 of the Act is to render it unlawful, during an inquiry into an anticipated merger, for an acquiring company or a subsidiary[32] of that

---

[25E] See Annex to the Commission's note on interim measures, *op. cit.*

[26] Since s.78 prohibits the acquisition of further shares once a reference has been made, unless made pursuant to a pre-existing obligation. It is notable that the Commission is given powers in relation to interim control of a merger which has not yet been completed: there is no corresponding power for the OFT (see para.3.055 of Ch.3).

[27] See para.5.010, below.

[28] Rule 5; see para.5.027, below.

[29] s.93 of the Act.

[30] See, for example, the procedure adopted in relation to Emap's acquisition of ABI Building Data Limited: see n.21, above.

[31] See s.91(3) read with s.86(6) (meaning of "enforcement order") and s.89(2) (meaning of "enforcement undertaking"): see para.5.013, below.

[32] s.78(6) provides that s.78 (and s.79) covers:

company to acquire, directly or indirectly, an interest in shares in a company which carries on a business to which the reference relates,[33] except with the consent of the Commission. The Act provides[34] that an acquisition of an interest in shares will arise where the acquirer conditionally or otherwise:

(i)   enters into a contract to acquire such shares (whether or not for cash);

(ii) acquires the right to exercise or control the exercise of any right conferred by the holding of the shares; or

(iii) acquires the right to call for delivery of the shares or assumes an obligation to acquire such an interest.[35]

It should, however, be noted that an acquisition made pursuant to an obligation existing before the reference was made is excluded. Thus, a contract to acquire shares of a target may be closed notwithstanding a reference being made if it was not expressed to be conditional on OFT clearance, and so long as closing has not been precluded following the reference by the terms of interim undertakings or interim orders.[35A]

The Commission's discretion to consent to the acquisition of shares or interests of shares may be by means of either a general consent (*i.e.* relating to all cases of a particular type) or a special consent (*i.e.* applying in specified cases).[36] Under the FTA regime the Secretary of State granted a general consent exempting intra-group transactions from the general prohibition, but no equivalent consent has yet been granted by the Commission. The power to grant special consent was exercised by the Secretary of State only very rarely, and even then not so as to permit a bidder to acquire shares in a target company in excess of those already owned at the time the reference was made. However, in 2000 the Minister gave consent to Nutreco Holding NV to acquire the non-UK seafood businesses of Norsk Hydro SA whilst the acquisition of the UK business which it had contracted to buy as a further element of the same agreement was the subject of a reference.[37] Further guidance as to when consent might be granted may perhaps be drawn from an instance known to the authors, where a pragmatic approach

---

(a)   any person carrying on an enterprise to which the reference relates or having control of any such enterprise;
(b)   any subsidiary of such person; and
(c)   any person associated with such person or any subsidiary of the person so associated.

Subsidiary has the meaning given by ss.736 and 736A of the Companies Act 1985 which sections are stated to apply to determine whether a company is a subsidiary of an individual or of a group of persons as well as a subsidiary of a company.

[33]   The restriction on acquiring shares applies equally to the vendor of the business.
[34]   s.79(3). s.79(6) refers to conditional rights and obligations.
[35]   See s.79(4).
[35A] It would be expected that the acquiring party in this situation would point out to the Commission the need to avoid being in breach of its contractual commitments but would agree to interim undertakings to hold separate, effective immediately upon closing.
[36]   s.78(3)(a).
[37]   *Nutreco Holding NV/Hydro Seafood GSP Ltd*, Cm. 5004 (December 2000). The terms of the reference had encapsulated all the enterprises being acquired, and not just those carried on in the United Kingdom.

was adopted by the Secretary of State in circumstances where Company "A", whose bid for Company "B" had been referred to the MMC, made a private acquisition of Company "C" during the course of the inquiry. Shortly thereafter it was discovered that amongst Company "C"'s assets was a small holding of shares in Company "B". Company "A" drew this to the attention of the Secretary of State who concluded that no action should be taken against Company "A", notwithstanding the technical contravention of the FTA, the implication being that it was the type of incidental acquisition that would have been permitted if consent had been sought at the appropriate time. It is probably unlikely that special consents granted by the Commission will be frequent occurrences.

Restrictions in the case of completed mergers

5.011   Section 77 of the Act creates a further protection of the integrity of a merger inquiry in the case of completed mergers, by providing that no relevant person[38] may take any further steps towards integration of the enterprises to which the reference relates without the Commission's consent, for example (as in the case of undertakings and orders under ss.80 and 81) by closing down production lines or integrating headquarters operations. Section 77(1)(b) specifies that this restriction is to apply where no undertakings under ss.71 or 80 or orders under ss.72 or 81 are in force in relation to the relevant merger situation.

It is not entirely clear from the wording of the Act whether the prohibition simply concerns technical steps to give effect to completion of the merger (which might, for example, include legal "post-completion" matters such as the registration of new directors, or changes of ownership of property, etc.), or catches any action taken in connection with integration of the merging businesses. However, the Explanatory Notes to the Act state that this section will "prevent [the parties] undertaking any further integration without the consent of the [Commission]". The Notes go on to comment that this is a new provision added in respect of completed mergers because "in almost all merger cases the authorities seek to prevent such further integration either by securing undertakings or making an interim order".[38A] The Commission's guidelines similarly refer to s.77 preventing "any further steps to integration".[39] Such an interpretation does raise a question mark over the purpose of the powers in ss.80 and 81 to accept interim undertakings and make interim orders, given that there is an automatic prohibition on further integration of completed mergers and, as noted, hold separate obligations are rarely imposed on mergers which have not yet been completed. As in relation to the prohibition on share dealings, s.77 provides that the Commission's consent may be general or specific. As with s.78, it is anticipated that such consents will be rare. Section 77(4) confirms that the section does not apply to anything which is required to be done by law. Finally, s.77(7) contains important limitations on the extent to which this prohibition applies to conduct outside the UK.

---

[38]   "Relevant person" is defined by s.77(8) of the Act as any person who carried on or has control of any enterprise to which the reference relates.

[38A]   See para.230 of the Explanatory Notes to the Act.

[39]   See para.7.13 of the Commission's *General Advice and Information*.

Enforcement of interim measures

Compliance with ss.77 or 78 of the Act or with undertakings accepted or orders made under ss.80 and 81 may be enforced in civil proceedings brought by the Commission seeking an injunction or any other appropriate relief.[40] The duty to comply with the statutory restrictions contained in of ss.77 and/or 78 of the Act or undertakings or orders under ss.80 and 81 of the Act is additionally owed to any person who may be affected by a contravention of the relevant statutory restriction, undertaking or order and such contravention is actionable by any such person who has sustained loss or damage.[41]

5.012

OFT Register of Orders and Undertakings

The OFT is required to keep a public register of all orders and undertakings including s.80 undertakings, s.81 orders and consents given pursuant to ss.77 and 78,[42] and the Commission (and where applicable, the Secretary of State) is required to inform the OFT of any matters that should be included in the register.

5.013

Lapse of the offer under the Takeover Code

As has been noted above[43] it must be a term of an offer to which the Takeover Code applies that the offer will lapse (that is, the bidder will not proceed to acquire control of the target under the terms of the offer) where the proposed merger is referred to the Commission before the first closing date of the offer[44] or the date on which the offer becomes or is declared unconditional as to acceptances, whichever is the later.[45] In addition, the bidder usually chooses to provide that the offer is conditional on the bid being cleared by the OFT on terms satisfactory to it.[46] Upon a reference being made, therefore, the offer automatically ceases to be capable of further acceptances, and the bidder and the shareholders are not bound by acceptances received prior to the reference.

5.014

During the course of the reference certain provisions of the Takeover Code continue to apply, particularly to the target.[47] In particular, Rule 21,

---

[40] ss.94(7) and 95(4). The OFT also has the power to enforce undertakings given to or orders made by the Commission and in practice it is probably more likely to be the OFT that exercises these enforcement powers.

[41] ss.94(4) and 95(2).

[42] s.91 of the Act. Note that the details disclosed on the register will be subject to the restrictions on disclosure contained in Pt 9 of the Act (redaction of commercially sensitive information: see para.5.024, below.

[43] See para.3.002 of Ch.3, above.

[44] Usually, the 21st day after the bidder's offer has been posted to shareholders in the target.

[45] Takeover Code, Rule 12(a) and (b), which also provides that the bid must lapse if, being subject to the EC Merger Regulation, the European Commission initiates proceedings under Art.6(1)(c) of the Regulation or makes a referral to a competent authority of the UK under Art.9(1).

[46] Rule 12(c) See para.3.002 of Ch.3, above. The right to make an offer conditional does not apply in the case of a mandatory offer (Takeover Code, Rule 9).

[47] See note 1 on Rule 12.2; General Principle 7; and Rule 21. In addition, Rule 19.8 provides that any statements made by the target to shareholders and others during a reference period (for example, relating to profits) and which during the course of the bid would be governed by Rule 19 should be capable of substantiation.

which provides that the target may not during the course of a bid take frustrating action without the approval of its shareholders (or the bidder or, in certain circumstances, the Takeover Panel), continues to restrict the target's ability to reorganise itself, for example by issuing further shares or making acquisitions or disposals, in order to put itself out of reach of or make itself unattractive to the bidder. Often, however, once a reference is in progress the Takeover Panel will permit actions to be taken by the target without recourse to shareholders which it would not be prepared to sanction during the course of the bid itself.[48]

If the Commission finds that the merger has resulted or might be expected to result in a substantial lessening of competition, and that the merger should be blocked, the Takeover Code will cease to apply upon the announcement of that fact. If, however, the bid is cleared by the Commission to proceed (subject where applicable to certain undertakings being given[49]) the bidder may, with the consent of the Takeover Panel,[50] decide to make a new offer for the target (following binding undertakings having been given where applicable), in which event the Takeover Code would continue to apply.[51]

Cancelling the reference

5.015   As discussed in Ch.3 above[52] the acquiring party may have decided to take the risk of the acquisition being referred to the Commission by completing the transaction prior to the OFT's decision; or it may have had no choice but to do so. However, it will often be the case that the contract between the parties is expressed to be conditional on the OFT not referring the transaction to the Commission, and, as discussed, a public offer which is subject to the Takeover Code will usually be subject to a condition to that effect. Alternatively, at the time the reference is made no contractual relationship may exist between the parties. In each of these circumstances the purchaser or the parties together may conclude that, faced with an uncertain outcome and the significant amount of management time and expense that a reference necessarily involves, it is preferable to abandon the transaction.

Where the purchaser no longer has any intention of acquiring the target, common sense would suggest that it would not be good administration for the Commission to continue to carry out its inquiry. Under the old regime, the Commission was not empowered to stand itself down and the FTA did not provide for the automatic abandonment of a reference once made but provided that the Secretary of State might lay aside a reference relating to a merger in contemplation on the application of the Commission where it appeared to the Commission that "the proposal to make arrangements such as are mentioned in the reference has been abandoned". This was a discretion exercised frequently: of the 20 prospective mergers referred to the

---

[48] Note 4 on Rule 21. Further provisions apply to mandatory offers under Rule 9; see the notes on Rule 9.4.
[49] See Ch.9, below.
[50] See the Takeover Code note on Rules 35.1 and 35.2.
[51] The position is different in the case of mandatory offers under Rule 9. The note on Rule 9.4 states that if the Secretary of State clears the merger, the offer *must* be reinstated as soon as practicable.
[52] See paras 3.016–3.020.

Commission between April 2001 and March 2003, for example, seven were subsequently laid aside.

Section 37(1) of the Act simplifies the process of laying aside (or cancellation, as the process is now called) by providing that the Commission shall cancel a reference made under s.33 if it considers that the proposal to make arrangements of the kind mentioned in the reference has been abandoned. Accordingly, if the Commission is satisfied that the proposed merger has been abandoned, it can reach a decision to cancel the reference and notify the parties accordingly.[53] A purchaser's decision to abandon a proposed transaction will generally be made shortly after a reference is announced. Accordingly a cancellation typically takes effect within one or two weeks of the decision to refer, with the consequence that the parties will not have made much, if any, progress in the preparation of their submissions to the Commission. In principle, however, there is no reason why the cancellation should not take place later, and sometimes much later, during the course of the reference.[54]

The Act does not provide for the procedure involved in the cancellation of a reference, other than that the Commission must publish any cancellation and give its reasons therefore.[55] In practice, as the Commission will have exclusive control over the reference at the relevant time, the first step to be taken if the parties to a proposed merger decide to abandon it is to make contact with the Commission, possibly seeking a meeting with the group selected to carry out the reference, or with the chairman of the Commission[56] if no group has been appointed at that time, as is sometimes the case where the decision to abandon the acquisition is made immediately following the announcement of a reference. A meeting is not always necessary: many references have been laid aside over the years on the basis only of a letter from the acquirer to the Commission confirming abandonment of the proposal. Where necessary, however, a meeting can normally be convened without delay. At the very least, however, the Commission will require a written explanation of the fact that the proposal has been abandoned.

The aim of the acquirer is to demonstrate to the Commission that it no **5.016** longer has any intention of acquiring the target. Depending upon the circumstances, the Commission may request further information or clarification, and if satisfied as to the accuracy and completeness of the acquirer's statements, will cancel the reference. In the first case of cancellation under the new regime, the reference of the proposed acquisition by Sibelco Minerals and Chemicals Limited of the minerals and materials businesses of Tarmac Central Limited, which was made on August 14, 2003, the Commission announced on September 23, 2003 that it had been cancelled, the Commission having "received assurances" from the parties that the proposed acquisition had been abandoned, resulting in the Chairman of the Commission being satisfied that Sibelco had abandoned the proposal.

---

[53] The Commission's decision to cancel must be published pursuant to s.107(2)(a) of the Act.
[54] For example, the reference of the proposed acquisition by Vishay Intertechnology Inc of Crystalate Holdings plc referred on July 26, 1990, was laid aside six weeks after being made on September 7.
[55] ss.107(2)(a) and 107(4) of the Act.
[56] As to the legal position of the chairman in this situation see n.60 to para.5.017, below.

In the vast majority of cases, abandonment and cancellation are essentially procedural events following on from the fact that the acquiring party's intention to merge with the target no longer stands. However, in 1986, the question of what constitutes an abandonment was considered by the courts in the context of the laying aside of the reference of Guinness plc's bid for The Distillers Company plc and its subsequent reconstructed (and ultimately successful) bid. Although decided under the old regime, the almost identical wording of s.37(1) of the Act and s.75(5) of the FTA suggests that the court's reasoning is likely to remain relevant.

The first Guinness bid for Distillers was referred to the MMC on February 13, 1986, a little more than a month after an earlier bid by Argyll Group plc, fiercely contested by the board of Distillers, had been cleared without a reference. The effect of the reference appeared to be to deliver control of Distillers to Argyll. However, Guinness and its advisers sought to avoid this result by developing a precedent which had been established a few weeks earlier: the abandonment and laying aside of the reference of Imperial Group's agreed bid for United Biscuits, followed by a reversal of the proposal, with United Biscuits making an agreed bid for Imperial and contemporaneously entering into a conditional agreement to sell its Golden Wonder subsidiary in order to avoid the concentration in snack foods which had prompted the initial reference. During the course of a sequence of meetings held on February 17, 18 and 19, Guinness and its advisers satisfied the then chairman of the MMC, Sir Godfrey le Quesne, Q.C., that the proposed changes in the arrangements relating to their proposed acquisition of Distillers, including the divestment, conditional only on the bid succeeding, of a number of whisky brands, constituted an abandonment within the meaning[57] of s.75(5) of the FTA. The Minister[57] consented on February 19, 1986, to the reference being laid aside, and the following day a reconstructed bid was announced.[58]

Argyll was granted leave to apply for judicial review of the MMC's recommendation and the Minister's consent to lay aside. Argyll argued that the "arrangements . . . mentioned in the reference" referred to any arrangements by Guinness which would result in a merger situation and therefore included the new proposals, such that it could not be said that the original proposal had been abandoned; that the new proposal was merely the original proposal in a modified form; and that the chairman of the MMC, in acting alone in considering Guinness' arguments (not having at that stage appointed a group of MMC members to undertake the reference), had acted *ultra vires*.

5.017   Macpherson J. dismissed Argyll's application, and their appeal was also dismissed by the Court of Appeal. Sir John Donaldson M.R. stated in his judgement that s.75(5) of the FTA was to be construed in the context of s.75 as a whole and in particular by reference to s.75(2), which gave the MMC

---

[57] The then Secretary of State, Paul Channon, took no part in the decision to refer or lay aside being a member of the Guinness family. The decisions were instead made by Geoffrey Pattie, a junior minister at the DTI.

[58] A number of authors have written accounts of Guinness' acquisition of Distillers and its aftermath describing what they consider took place in the period February 13 to 19, 1986: notably Nick Kochan and Hugh Pym, *The Guinness Affair: Anatomy of a Scandal*, (A&C Black (Publishers) Ltd, London, 1987), pp.116–118; and James Saunders, *Nightmare: Ernest Saunders and the Guinness Affair*, (Hutchinson, 1989), pp.158–162.

jurisdiction to proceed as if the arrangements in question had actually been made. Thus construed s.75(5) could only refer to the arrangements (*i.e.* the takeover bid), which were in progress or in contemplation at the time the Secretary of State made the reference and could not encompass arrangements which at that time had not been proposed. It followed that, if the arrangements originally proposed by a takeover bidder had been replaced by new arrangements proposed by the bidder which were significantly different from the original proposals, the MMC was entitled to find that the proposal to make arrangements, such as those mentioned in the reference, had been abandoned, and to exercise their power under s.75(5) to request the Secretary of State to lay the reference aside. It was a question of fact, to be determined by the MMC, whether an amended or revised bid amounted to new arrangements or merely an amended form of the existing arrangements. The Court of Appeal concluded[59] that on the facts, the chairman of the MMC had been entitled to find that Guinness had abandoned its original bid and replaced it with new arrangements when it proposed to make a new bid on revised terms.[60]

Following the Court of Appeal's decision in the Argyll application, it is clear that the question of whether a given proposal has been abandoned is a question of fact and degree for the Commission. Thus, when Lloyds Chemists plc's bid for Macarthy plc was referred to the MMC in 1991, Lloyds requested that the reference should be laid aside on the ground that because Macarthy's principal supplier of ethical pharmaceuticals had, subsequent to the reference being made, withdrawn from the United Kingdom market, a significant part of Macarthy's activities (namely the purchase of goods from that supplier) would not be acquired and alternative arrangements for supply would need to be put in place, with the result that the arrangements in progress or contemplation at the time of the reference had been abandoned. The MMC concluded, however, that on the facts there had been no abandonment by Lloyds, within the meaning of s.75(5).[61]

One interesting issue arose in relation to the reference of the proposed acquisition of Newcastle United plc by NTL Communications Corp.[62] NTL had acquired 6.3 per cent of the issued share capital of Newcastle United and had obtained an irrevocable undertaking from Newcastle United's majority shareholder to sell another 50.8 per cent in the event that it made

---

[59] [1986] 1 W.L.R. 763.

[60] The Court of Appeal also concluded that the chairman of the MMC had acted *ultra vires* in purporting to act on behalf of the MMC in the interregnum before a group of members had been appointed, although it was recognised that this had been a longstanding practice. In the circumstances, however, the Court considered that it was not appropriate to grant relief because the group would have reached the same conclusion as the chairman. The Secretary of State had consented to the laying aside, and Guinness, the shareholders of Distillers and the public at large had been entitled to rely and act upon the laying aside, and it would not be in the interests of good public administration to grant relief. The chairman's ability to lay a reference aside with the Secretary of State's consent but prior to the appointment of an MMC group was subsequently regularised by an amendment to the FTA and it is now provided for by para.10(8) of Sch.7 to the Competition Act 1998 (which was inserted by virtue of Sch.11 to the Act) that where no group has been appointed with respect to the investigation on a merger reference or a group has been appointed but has not yet held its first meeting, the chairman may perform the Commission's functions.

[61] Cm. 1845 (February 1992), para.6.6.

[62] Cm. 4411 (July 1999).

a formal bid for the company. Shortly after the announcement of these arrangements, the transaction was referred to the Commission under both s.64 and 75(1) of the FTA (completed and contemplated mergers respectively). After publication of the Commission's report on the proposed merger of BSkyB and Manchester United plc[63] a few days later, the parties wrote to the Commission notifying it of NTL's abandonment of the proposed transaction (including lapse of the irrevocable undertaking) and requesting that the reference be laid aside. Pursuant to s.75(5) of the FTA, the Secretary of State consented to the laying aside of the reference in respect of the merger in contemplation. However, that part of the reference which related to the completed merger could not be laid aside and the Commission therefore remained bound to consider whether in relation to NTL's acquisition of its 6.3 per cent shareholding, a merger situation qualifying for investigation had been created (and if so whether it might be expected to operate against the public interest). It appears that the reasoning behind the reference of the completed merger was that the shareholding, when considered alongside certain terms of the irrevocable undertaking, gave NTL a position of material influence over Newcastle United pursuant to s.65(3) of the FTA (now s.26(3) of the Act). In the shortest merger report ever published, the Commission concluded that even if a merger situation might have existed during the short period when NTL had the benefit of the irrevocable commitment, there was no indication that that situation might now operate against the public interest; and that following the termination of the commitment NTL was in no position to influence the policy of Newcastle, with the result that no merger situation qualifying for investigation now existed.

It is noteworthy that, as stated at para.5.002 above, a single reference can no longer be made in respect of both completed and contemplated mergers[64] so such an odd consequence as arose in relation to NTL should not arise in the future.

The purpose of the Commission's investigation

5.018   As described above[65] the terms of a merger reference require the Commission to report on whether a qualifying merger exists and, if so, whether that merger situation might be expected to result, or in the case of a completed merger may result or has resulted, in a substantial lessening of competition within any market or markets in the United Kingdom for goods or services. If such a substantial lessening of competition has been, or is expected to be, created (defined by s.35(2) of the Act as "an anti-competitive outcome"), then the Commission is also required to decide whether action should be taken by it or others for the purposes of remedying, mitigating or preventing the substantial lessening of competition or any adverse effect resulting or likely to result from it, and, if so, what that action should be.[66] In so deciding, the Commission is required to have regard to the need to achieve a comprehen-

---

[63] Cm. 4305 (April 1999). The Commission recommended that BSkyB's proposed acquisition of Manchester United should not be allowed to proceed, on grounds which suggested that NTL's proposed acquisition would also be blocked.

[64] See s.22(3)(c) of the Act.

[65] See para.5.003, above.

[66] ss.35(3) and 36(2).

sive solution which is both reasonable (*i.e.* proportionate) and practicable[67] and is entitled to take into account the effect that any contemplated action might have on customer benefits in relation to the creation of the relevant merger situation concerned.[68] These aspects of the Commission's responsibilities, and the nature of the substantive analysis which the Commission will undertake, are discussed in detail in Ch.6, and the Commission's responsibilities for consideration and implementation of remedies are discussed in Ch.9. The purpose of this chapter is to consider the general principles followed and the procedures adopted by the Commission in carrying out its investigation and reaching its conclusions.[69]

It should be noted at this point (as described above[70]) that the Secretary of State may exceptionally make a reference to the Commission under ss. 45 or 62 where a merger raises certain defined public interest issues. How the Commission's procedure differs in relation to such references is described at para.5.056, below. Except in para.5.056 the remainder of this chapter refers to the procedure adopted in the case of standard references under ss.22 or 33 by the OFT.

General principles

Burden of proof

In reaching an adverse decision in respect of a merger, the Commission must be satisfied that a substantial lessening of competition results, or may be expected to result, and not merely that it might do so. In its guidelines,[71] the Commission has stated that for it to reach an adverse decision, either the merger must have resulted in a substantial lessening of competition or the Commission must expect such a result. The Commission will usually have such an expectation, the guidelines state, where it considers it is more likely than not that a substantial lessening of competition will result. This statement of the level of proof required closely follows the Commission's approach under the FTA to public interest detriment, as explained in the report on the proposed merger between S.W. Berisford Limited and British Sugar Corporation Limited:

5.019

"The question we have to consider is not merely whether there is a possibility that the merger will operate against the public interest. If only a possibility were required, hardly any merger could ever be allowed to

---

[67] ss.35(4) and 36(3).
[68] ss.35(5) and 36(4).
[69] Sch.11 to the Act, enacted pursuant to s.185 of the Act sets out a number of amendments to Sch.7 to the Competition Act 1998 which governs performance of the Commission's functions. In addition, pursuant to para.19A of the Competition Act 1998 (as inserted by s.187(3) of the Act) the Chairman of the Commission must make and publish rules of procedure (in relation to which see para.5.005, above). The content of these rules is governed by Sch.7A to the Competition Act 1998 (as inserted by s.187(4) of the Act). However, the Commission's procedure on merger references is primarily discretionary and subject to the rules of procedure each merger reference group may determine its own procedure: s.187 of the Act.
[70] See further paras 4.028 *et seq.* of Ch.4, above.
[71] *Merger References: Competition Commission Guidelines*, CC2 at para.1.19.

proceed, for it is very rarely that such a possibility can be quite excluded. The question is whether the evidence creates an expectation that the merger will operate against the public interest. To put the matter colloquially, the required conclusion is not, 'This may happen', but 'We expect that this will happen'."[72]

This approach was further elaborated in the report into the acquisition by the Kuwait Investment Office of a substantial shareholding in British Petroleum, where it was stated that:

"In considering . . . what may be expected to happen . . . our approach should be based upon reasonableness; it should represent our reasonable expectation, having taken into account all the factors which we consider relevant, among them the risk of serious adverse consequences for the public interest. In so doing . . . we would think it right to have regard to the position where, although the risk of an event occurring might be relatively small, the adverse consequences to the public interest would be serious."[73]

Arguably this changed the test somewhat, suggesting that the Commission may reach adverse conclusions if a merger could give rise to significant adverse consequences even if it is unlikely that such an event would occur. A recent House of Lords judgement[74] which focused on the burden of proof required in relation to future events may be of relevance to merger references. The point in question was the standard of proof required to justify the Home Secretary deporting a foreign national on the grounds of national security.
According to Lord Hoffmann:

"The whole concept of standard of proof is not particularly helpful in a case such as the present . . . the question in the present case is not whether a given event happened but the extent of future risk. This depends upon an evaluation of the evidence of the appellant's conduct against a broad range of facts with which they may interact. The question of whether the risk to national security is sufficient to justify . . . deportation . . . is a question of evaluation and judgment, in which it is necessary to take into account not only the degree of probability of prejudice to national security but also the importance of the security interest at stake and the serious consequences of the deportation for the deportee."

Applying that principle, it might be argued that the question of whether the risk of a resulting substantial lessening of competition is sufficient to justify reaching an adverse decision involves taking into account not only

---

[72] S & W Berisford Limited/British Sugar Corporation Limited, HC 241 (March 1981) at para.9.40.

[73] The Government of Kuwait/The British Petroleum Company plc, Cm. 477 (October 1988), para.8.109.

[74] Secretary of State for the Home Department v Rehman [2002] 1 All E.R. 122 at para.56.

the probability of an anti-competitive outcome, but also the significance of that outcome. In practice, however, the consequences of an adverse decision on the parties is more likely to be addressed at the remedies stage.

The Court of Appeal in *IBA Health* commented that, as regards the meaning of "may be expected to result"[75]:

> "the words 'may be expected to result' in paragraph (b) of both s.33(1) and 36(1) involve a degree of likelihood amounting to an expectation. In paragraph 182 of its judgment CAT expressed the view that these words connoted more than a possibility and adopted what they described as a crude way of expressing the idea of an expectation as a more than 50% chance. No doubt this is right when applied to the single question which the Commission is required to answer under s.36(1)(b)".

No system of precedent

Unlike the United Kingdom courts, the Commission does not follow any strict adherence to precedent. To do so would, it is argued, be inconsistent with the Commission's statutory duty to investigate and report on the particular circumstances and issues raised by each case. The view often expressed by Sir Sydney Lipworth Q.C., chairman of the MMC between 1988 and 1993, was that companies involved in merger references would not welcome a dependence on past cases for decisions which affect their commercial future. At the same time, however, an inconsistent approach to inquiries would tend to undermine confidence in the Commission. The Commission has frequently returned to this theme in successive editions of its Annual Review and in public statements concerning its approach to its statutory duties, and has acknowledged the difficulties in establishing consistency given the increasing scope and volume of its workload, the reduced timescales within which it has been expected to report and the formulation of groups for specific references as discrete groups of members who have little opportunity to enter into wider discussions with members of other groups.

5.020

Recognising these difficulties, the Commission aims to adopt a pragmatic approach in striving to achieve a balance between the desirability of consistency and the need to avoid inappropriate reliance on earlier reports. In particular, it endeavours to:

(i)   pay attention to how similar issues have been approached in previous enquiries (acknowledging, however, that each reference presents its own unique mix of facts and circumstances);

(ii)   take into account general principles established in previous and, sometimes, concurrent cases: as, for example, in relation to the series of references in 1990 involving state control when, as noted in each of the relevant reports[76] the chairmen of different panels

---

[75] *Office of Fair Trading v IBA Health Ltd* [2004] EWCA Civ. 142, at para.46.
[76] *Credit Lyonnais SA/Woodchester Investments plc*, Cm. 1404 (January 1991); *Kemira Oy/ICI plc*, Cm. 1406 (January 1991); *British Aerospace plc/Thomson-CSF SA*, Cm. 1416 (January 1991); *Sligos SA/Signet Limited*, Cm. 1450 (February 1991); *Amoco Corporation/Elf Aquitaine*, Cm. 1521 (May 1991).

consulted with one another to ensure consistency of overall approach[77];

(iii) test its thinking on the facts of the specific case in hand against past treatment by the Commission of similar issues and, more particularly, the same industry.[78]

The practical application of some of these principles was demonstrated in the Commission's report into the proposed merger between Carlton Communications plc and Granada plc[79] in which, in one of the last decisions referred to the Commission under the FTA, it recommended that the Secretary of State clear the merger, effectively paving the way for a consolidated ITV, subject to the parties giving certain behavioural undertakings in relation to the sale of television advertising. Three years earlier the Commission had had referred to it a previous proposal by Granada to acquire Carlton or, alternatively, United News & Media plc, the third major operator of ITV franchises. Granada's proposals were set against the backdrop that United and Carlton had agreed, subject to regulatory approval, to merge; a proposal that had also been referred to the Commission.[80] The intended outcome of the earlier proposals was that the three major ITV companies would reduce to two, each with its own advertising sales house. The Commission concluded that neither of Granada's proposals would be expected to operate against the public interest, so long as the requirements of existing broadcasting legislation were complied with; whilst the merger between Carlton and United should be permitted only if they undertook to dispose of one major franchise, without which the Commission considered the combined entity would enjoy excessive power in the market for advertising airtime. In consequence, the Carlton/United merger did not proceed and United sold its ITV interests to Granada.

In support of their subsequent proposal to merge, Carlton and Granada argued that the market had changed substantially in the intervening period. The Commission concluded that, as the earlier group had found, television advertising should be seen as a separate market; but ITV advertising should no longer be regarded as a separate segment of the market, contrary to the views of the group considering the earlier proposals, there having been in the interim a decline in ITV in terms of its audience share and its revenue earned from television advertising. This conclusion opened the way for the creation of a single ITV, a result that would not have been contemplated three years earlier.

Independence and the duty to act fairly

5.021 As an independent public body, not involved in formulating merger policy or in the decision to refer individual cases, the Commission is in a position

---

[77] A similar procedure was adopted in relation to the various reference involving water company mergers.

[78] This may not always be desirable, as it may result in the Commission too readily making assumptions, as to market definition, for example, where they have access to previous reports.

[79] *Carlton Communications plc/Granada plc*, Cm. 5952 (October 2003).

[80] *Carlton Communications plc/Granada Group plc/United News & Media plc*, Cm. 4781 (July 2000). These three references were reported on in a single report.

to be wholly impartial and fair in its deliberations and proceedings. This is a feature to which the Commission itself has in the past attached particular significance. In the 1992 Annual Review, for example, the chairman wrote:

"Our independence needs to be stressed; we are not agents of government policy. We have no axe to grind: we bring an impartial view to bear based on the assessment of facts, not on presumption. We enter each inquiry with no preconception as to the outcome. It is natural that our findings sometimes disappoint those who are crusading for a different outcome. The system demands both fairness of approach, with procedures that are fair to all, and impartiality of view. Action taken to promote competition can fundamentally affect the prospects of companies and their employees. It has been a basic principle (which underlies most arrangements in British public life) that power should be limited by checks and balances. In keeping with that, the principle of separation of powers has governed the institutional arrangements for competition regulation since 1948."

Although the Commission has a duty to act in accordance with the powers and duties conferred upon it, many of those powers are discretionary and are not easily challenged. Under the FTA regime, the Commission's duty to act fairly was broadly interpreted with the question in any case being whether it had adopted a procedure so unfair that it could be said to have acted with manifest unfairness.[81] The courts did not lay down rules as to procedure, emphasising that the Commission had a broad discretion which should not be prescribed or inflexible,[82] and although there has at the date of writing been no application to the Competition Appeal Tribunal in respect of a Commission decision there is no reason to suppose that the Competition Appeal Tribunal will take any different view.[83]

Transparency

Fairness can more readily be demonstrated through the adoption of procedures which are transparent and open. In its guidelines[84] the Commission states that transparency facilitates inquiries because:

5.022

(i)   it is a means of achieving due process and of ensuring that by having a better understanding of the case against them, the main parties in an inquiry are treated fairly;

---

[81] See, *e.g.* *R. v Monopolies and Mergers Commission Ex p. Matthew Brown plc* [1987] 1 All E.R. 463 at 469e, *per* Macpherson J.

[82] The same conclusion on the question of fairness was reached in *R. v Monopolies and Mergers Commission Ex p. Elders IXL Limited* [1987] 1 All E.R. 451 at 461h, *per* Mann J. For a further discussion see generally Ch.10, below, which discusses the principles of review of merger decisions.

[83] However, the Competition Appeal Tribunal has been quite intrusive on OFT procedure under the Competition Act 1998. For a further discussion on the role of the Tribunal see generally Ch.10, below.

[84] Chairman's Guidance on Disclosure of Information in Mergers and Market Inquiries, CC7 at para.1.6.

(ii)   it enables other interested persons, such as consumers and their representative bodies, suppliers and customers and other persons who may be affected by the Commission's decision, to understand the issues that the Commission is considering and to participate effectively in the process;

(iii) it helps the main parties and other interested persons in providing the Commission with information, including identifying inaccuracies and incomplete or misleading information; and

(iv)   the effectiveness, efficiency and quality of Commission inquiries and decisions are improved.

The Commission has in recent years made a number of changes to its procedures in the name of transparency, the result of a consultation process undertaken in 1999, aimed at identifying the appropriate balance between openness on the one hand and, on the other, rigour in the context of the need, supported by statutory provision, for confidentiality. In particular, it introduced the practice of publishing issues statements which identified the key issues of concern arising in connection with the merger, and, where appropriate, additional information on its views as they evolved; it also began to publish statements of possible remedies and introduced the possibility of joint hearings involving opposing parties, hearings open to a broader spectrum of interested parties and hearings open to the public and the press. The former Chairman of the Commission, Sir Derek Morris, described the process as follows in the Commission's Annual Review of 2000/1:

"There are major challenges in this. There are legitimate confidentiality concerns which must be fully respected; greater transparency may lead parties to expect ongoing debate on any or every point, whereas the duties of the Competition Commission are to conduct an investigation and reach its own findings; and timescales may be put at risk, an issue of understandable concern to business."

These practices, along with the publication of provisional findings and the disclosure to the parties of the Commission's working papers and extracts of surveys, have now been enshrined in the procedures which have been adopted under the Act, as explained below. There is, however, no right for the main parties to have access to the Commission's file, which many practitioners had proposed during the consultation process which preceded the adoption of the Act as an obvious enhancement to transparency. This omission places obvious limitations on the ability of the main parties to respond to issues raised by third parties or to challenge the Commission's interpretation and use of market surveys and other material proposed to be relied upon by the inquiry group as well as the "weight" given to such evidence, and it is argued by some to be a matter of regret that the principle of transparency was not extended to include access to the file, which has worked well in EC Commission procedures for many years and has been adopted in the UK under the OFT's Competition Act 1998 procedures.[85]

---

[85] See also para.5.046, below. The Commission's Deputy Chairman, Peter Freeman, commented on this issue in his paper *"UK Merger Control – A year's experience of the*

240

Confidentiality

It is inevitable that during the course of an inquiry the Commission will   5.023
seek information which is, or may be regarded by the provider of such
information to be, commercially sensitive or otherwise confidential. It may
be the case, for example, that publication of certain information would or
might be of benefit to the competitors of the party supplying it or, in the
case of a hostile bid, of value to the target, or a competing bidder. A requirement of the Commission to provide confidential information will therefore
often be received with concern by the party that has been "requested" to
provide it. As noted below,[86] withholding such information is not an
option, and the parties will therefore wish for reassurance that, upon disclosure being made, it will not be disclosed to third parties or otherwise made
public, whether during the course of the Commission's inquiry or in its
subsequent report. There is thus an obvious tension between the desirability
for transparency described above and the need for confidentiality to ensure
thoroughness of inquiries.

Some reassurance to providers of confidential information is set out in the
Act, which imposes a general restriction on the disclosure by the Commission
of information which it has received in the course of carrying out its functions
under the Act[87]: information relating to the affairs of an individual may not
be disclosed during the lifetime of the individual, and information relating to
the business of an undertaking may not be disclosed while the undertaking
continues in existence, unless in either case the Act permits such a disclosure.
Sections 239 to 242 of the Act set out the circumstances in which the
Commission may disclose specified information. These are:-

(i)   if the Commission obtains consent from the party disclosing it[88];

(ii)   if the disclosure is required for the purpose of a Community
        obligation[89];

(iii)   in connection with the investigation of a criminal offence, or for
        the purpose of any criminal proceedings (including any decision as
        to whether to commence or terminate such an investigation or
        proceedings) provided that "the making of the disclosure is propor-
        tionate to what is sought to be achieved by it".[90]

More generally, the Commission is authorised by s.241 of the Act to
disclose information for the purpose of facilitating the exercise of its functions under the Act or to facilitate the exercise by any other person of that

---

Enterprise Act", delivered to the Third NERA Competition Policy Symposium (October 2,
2004), which may be found on the Commission's website. He stated that this is not a closed
issue, but that the Commission would need to be convinced that any alteration in its
practice fulfilled a real, rather than a formalistic, need, drawing distinctions between the
Commission's procedures and those of the European Commission.

[86] See para.5.026, below.
[87] The provisions of the Act on confidentiality and disclosure also apply to the OFT, see paras
3.078–3.080 of Ch.3, above.
[88] s.239 of the Act.
[89] s.240 of the Act.
[90] s.242 of the Act.

person's functions under the Act (for example, the OFT). Where information is disclosed by the Commission other than to the public, it may not be further disclosed by the recipient of the information except with the Commission's consent, or used by the recipient for any purpose other than in relation to its functions under the Act.

In practice, the Commission's powers of disclosure under s.241 are wide. However, s.244 provides that prior to publishing any information supplied to it, the Commission must have regard to:

(i) the need to exclude from disclosure so far as practicable (a) any information the disclosure of which the Commission considers to be contrary to the public interest; and (b) commercial information whose disclosure the Commission considers might significantly harm the business interests of the party to whom it relates, or information relating to an individual whose interests might be significantly harmed by such disclosure; and

(ii) the extent to which disclosure of the information referred to in paragraph (i)(b) above is necessary, notwithstanding the potential for significant harm, for the purpose for which the Commission is permitted to make the disclosure (*i.e.* to enable it to carry out its functions).[91]

5.024   The Commission has published guidance on the disclosure of information.[92] In that guidance, groups established to conduct a particular inquiry are required to have regard to:

(i) the need to make sufficient information available to parties which are the main subject of the inquiry, so that they have sufficient understanding of the arguments, are able to comment on information supplied by third parties and can identify and draw attention to any inaccuracies or incomplete or misleading information;

(ii) the desirability of making sufficient information available to the public who will then be in a more informed position to provide information for the purpose of the inquiry;

(iii) the need to disclose information so that interested parties may comment generally and on any inaccuracies or incomplete or misleading information; and

(iv) the need to conduct the investigation effectively and efficiently.[93]

The guidance advises that in respect of all information supplied, the parties should be required to identify those parts which are sensitive, and provide reasons, so that the Commission can apply the three considerations to which it is required to have regard in an informed manner. The intention

---

[91] s.244(4) of the Act.
[92] Chairman's guidance on Disclosure of Information in Merger and Market Inquiries, CC7. There is a useful checklist set out in this guidance note indicating the types of information that will be published or may be disclosed to the main or third parties.
[93] Para.3.1 of the Chairman's guidance.

is that parties to the inquiry should provide two versions of their submissions, one in complete form, the other excluding information claimed to be sensitive, and, in the case of the Main Submission, the Commission's best practice is to post the excised version on its website. It is worth highlighting that the restrictions on disclosure under the Act apply not just to the final report but at all stages of the Commission's procedures

The provision enabling the Commission to make disclosure for the purpose of facilitating the exercise of its functions under the Act is equivalent to the provision in s.133 of the FTA which permitted disclosure to be made "for the purpose of facilitating the performance of any functions of . . . the Commission", which was subject to judicial interpretation in *R. v Monopolies and Mergers Commission Ex p. Elders IXL Limited.*[94] The case concerned an application for judicial review of a decision of the MMC that certain information provided by the bidder to the MMC in the context of a reference of a hostile takeover bid should be disclosed to the target, Allied-Lyons plc. The information in question related to details of the financing of the new bid which Elders proposed to make if cleared to do so by the Secretary of State following the reference. The initial bid had been referred to the MMC because the Secretary of State considered that "the financing of the proposed acquisition" raised issues which deserved investigation, and the MMC concluded, after consulting both parties, that the information on the proposed new bid should be disclosed to the target on the grounds that:

(i)   the target's comments, which would be made with special knowledge and authority, were necessary for the MMC to be able to form an adequate view of whether the merger would operate against the public interest;

(ii)   the MMC's duty to conduct a full investigation into the proposed merger overrode any duty which it owed to the applicant company not to disclose confidential information; and

(iii)   natural justice required that the target be given an opportunity to make fully informed representations about the information provided by the applicant company.

Elders maintained that the MMC had not acted fairly towards it because its interest in non-disclosure had not been sufficiently taken into account, and that disclosure would not be for the purpose of facilitating the performance of the functions of the MMC. In declining to grant the application, the court held that in performing its inquisitorial function of determining whether the prospective results of a merger would or could be expected to be against the public interest the MMC was under a duty to act fairly to all parties which had a substantial interest in the subject matter of the reference. However, the concept of fairness was flexible and depended upon the particular situation under consideration and it therefore had to decide what was fair in each particular situation. The court held that in the circumstances, the MMC had been entitled to decide that the perceived detriment to the applicant, which disclosure would cause,

---

[94] [1987] 1 W.L.R. 1221.

should be subordinated to the MMC's judgment of how best to perform its statutory function (of carrying out an investigation as to what is or is not in the public interest) which in its view involved disclosing the applicant's information to the respondent.

5.025   Since s.133(2) of the Act permitted the MMC to disclose information obtained by it under the Act if the disclosure is for the purpose of facilitating the performance of its functions, the court simply had to determine whether the MMC had made the decision to disclose with the intention of facilitating its investigation. Since the MMC had reached its decision on this basis, it was entitled to disclose the information. Accordingly, the test the Commission has to apply is not an objective one: the question is whether it has made its decision rationally and in good faith, having regard to the need to balance the protection of confidentiality against its statutory duty to ensure the proper conduct of its investigation.

Investigatory powers

5.026   Under the FTA the Commission had the power to issue notices requiring any person, whether or not a main party to the reference, to provide oral or written evidence and to produce documents and other items of information; and, in the event of refusal, to institute contempt proceedings in the courts. In practice formal notices were rarely issued because parties have generally co-operated fully with the Commission's inquiries (and in the event of any failure or delay, a gentle reminder of the powers available to the Commission was generally sufficient); moreover, the impracticality of issuing contempt proceedings within the time constraints of a Commission inquiry meant that that power was never used.

Notwithstanding this spirit of co-operation, the Act has given the Commission new, more direct powers to enforce compliance with its requests. Section 109 of the Act sets out the Commission's powers by notice to require the attendance of witnesses to give evidence (including under oath), as well as the production of documents and the provision of information, following broadly the same format as s.85 of the FTA. Sections 110–112 confer on the Commission for the first time the power to impose direct monetary fines on a person who fails to supply information or supplies information which is incomplete; or who intentionally obstructs or delays the provision of any document which he has been required to produce by a notice issued under s.109. These fines may be up to £30,000 for each failure, and/or a daily penalty of up to £15,000 per day for each day of non-compliance, but are currently limited by statutory instrument to a maximum £20,000 fixed fine and £5,000 per day.[95] The Commission may be unlikely to impose the maximum penalty on every party that declines to provide information or is late in doing so, having indicated[96] that it will consider a variety of factors in deciding what penalty to impose, including repeated contravention, continuation of contravention after being notified of the Commission's concern, the absence of evidence of mechanisms or

---

[95] The Competition Commission (Penalties) Order 2003 (SI 2003/1371).
[96] Statement of Policy on Penalties, CC5.

procedures intended to prevent a contravention, the involvement of the party's senior management in any contravention, and any attempt to conceal contraventions. In addition, s.110 sets out a criminal offence which will be committed by any person who intentionally alters, suppresses or destroys any document which has been required to be produced by a notice issued under s.109. A person who commits this offence will be liable to imprisonment for up to two years, or to a fine, or both.

It should be noted that no penalties may be imposed until the Commission has issued a notice requiring information under s.109. Normally, as described above, the Commission would not, in the first instance, issue a notice on a party that had no record of refusing or delaying the provision of information in response to a request from the Commission and it may be anticipated that the spirit of co-operation which has served the Commission well in the past will continue to ensure that the new powers are invoked only occasionally.

Standing Group

The Rules of Procedure[97] authorise the chairman of the Commission to appoint a standing group comprising five or more Commission members for the purpose of carrying out any general functions of the Commission. Rule 5.6 identifies the functions of the standing group as including the acceptance, variation and release of undertakings and the making, variation and revocation of orders and final orders. The Remedies Standing Group, as it is known, held its first meeting on November 11, 2003 and is intended to meet in alternate months and, when necessary, at short notice. It is supported by a Director and Deputy Director from the Commission's staff, as well as representatives from the economic and legal divisions. The Group's principal functions are described on the Commission's website as being: 5.027

- to adopt initial undertakings and initial orders, within the seven day period following the reference (after which they lapse), on the basis that it is likely usually to take more than seven days to appoint an inquiry group[97A];

- to oversee the implementation of divestiture remedies, after the inquiry group has been stood down following its acceptance of final under-takings or its having made a final order[97B];

- to vary, release or revoke undertakings or orders[97C];

- to develop a policy on remedies.[97D]

---

[97] Rules of Procedure, para.5.
[97A] See paras 5.007 and 5.008 and n.21.
[97B] See para.9.030, below.
[97C] See para.9.033, below.
[97D] See paras 9.011 to 9.016, below.

The first few days

5.028 Upon a reference being made, the parties to the merger or proposed merger will be notified by telephone by the OFT, normally through their respective advisers. That will be followed by a faxed or emailed copy of the reference and accompanying press release, and, usually later the same day, the Commission's letter described in para.5.029, below will be received by the parties. At that point it will be necessary for the parties, if they have not already done so, to put in place a team of managers and advisers, charged with the primary responsibility of preparing the information requested by the Commission and the memoranda containing their arguments and supporting evidence as to why the merger should be approved (or, in the case of the target in a hostile bid, why it should be prevented). In practice, the need to supply the OFT with information and submissions means that the nucleus of a team is already likely to exist. However, the volume of work required to be undertaken at this stage—to gather and collate further information requested by the Commission, to prepare and debate propositions internally prior to presentation to the Commission, and generally to feel comfortable that no issue has been overlooked—is very significant.

It is not possible or appropriate to set out any specific requirements as to the composition of a working team; much depends upon the particular issues raised by the merger, the extent to which all the supporting material has already been collated and the calibre and experience of those involved. One general principle can, however, be applied: that the higher the quality of the submissions made to the Commission, the greater will be the likelihood of the Commission producing an accurate, complete and well-presented report. Accordingly it is likely to be in the parties' interests, faced with a reference, to treat it as a high priority, to devote high level and competent internal resources, and to enlist professional advisers: lawyers skilled and experienced in understanding the issues and presenting the arguments and, depending upon the issues raised, accountants, economists and sometimes lobbyists.[98] Whatever the nature of the reference, and regardless of the issues raised, the first three weeks following the reference are likely to be frenetic: there will be submissions to write, questionnaires to address, an early meeting with the Commission's staff, and all at a time when there is a business to run. The magnitude of the task should not be underestimated.

The initial "first day" letter

Introduction

5.029 The Commission will have been forewarned that a reference is likely to be made and will have received certain information about the merger from the OFT. This will have given the Commission sufficient opportunity to prepare an initial letter to each of the parties concerned in the merger (the so-called "first day" letter), which they may expect to receive usually no later than the day following the announcement of the reference. This letter, normally

---

[98] See Ch.8, below.

signed by the chairman of the Commission and addressed to the chairman, chief executive or secretary of the relevant party, or its legal adviser, follows a relatively standard form,[99] beginning with a preamble describing the statutory basis of the reference and the questions which the Commission is required to consider pursuant to ss.35 or 36 of the Act.

The composition of the group

The letter then notifies the recipient that a group of members is being or has been established to deal with the reference. If already set up, the letter will give their names and attach biographical details of each of them.[1] More usually, however, only the chairman of the group, and sometimes not even he/she, will have been appointed at that stage, and details will follow in a few days.

5.030

A group is required under the Rules of Procedure[2] to comprise at least three members. Typically, however, four or five members will be appointed to carry out an inquiry. Although the chairman of the group has a casting vote as regards deadlocked groups of four members,[2A] the Commission is unable to adopt any remedy unless two thirds of the group's members concur.[2B] (In the Scottish Milk report,[3] the group was split, two members finding that Wiseman had exploited its monopoly position and two that it had not. Although the chairman was one of those who considered that it had exploited its position, no remedies could be adopted since two thirds of the group had not so found.

One of the members of the group must be appointed as its chairman; that may be the Commission chairman, a deputy chairman or another member of the Commission. The chairman of the Commission takes some care to ensure first, that the composition of the group represents a broad range of skills, experience and background and secondly, that no member of the group could be thought to begin the inquiry other than with a totally open mind. In so doing, the chairman of the Commission is required to have regard to the Commission's Code of Practice for Reporting Panel Members and Specialist Panel Members and to the Commission's Guidance on Conflicts of Interest[4] and more generally to take into account any other factors which in his opinion might prejudice the group's independence and impartiality. Where a party involved in a reference believes there may be the possibility of some prejudice or conflict of interest which has not been recognised by the Commission, that concern should be notified to the Commission immediately. Very occasionally in the past such action has led to a change in the composition of the group, but the chairman of the

---

[99] An example of the Commission's first day letter appears at App.6.
[1] Biographical details of the members of the Commission are available on the website of the Competition Commission: see further App.1.
[2] Competition Commission: Rules of Procedure, at para.4.2, which repeats the earlier requirement set out in para.15 of Sch.7 to the Competition Act 1998.
[2A] See para.21 of Sch.7 to the Competition Act 1998 (as amended).
[2B] See para.20(2) of Sch.7 to the Competition Act 1998 (as amended).
[3] Scottish Milk, Cm. 5002 (December 2000).
[4] Both of these were published on July 31, 2002 and are accessible on the Commission's website.

Commission will wish to be wholly convinced by the party's arguments before agreeing to any change.[5]

Once appointed, the members of the group will work together throughout the period of the reference. It is expected that members will attend most meetings, although the absence from any meeting of the group or from any hearing with one of the parties to the merger or any third party, will neither disqualify the member nor prejudice the inquiry. In the event that a member is likely to be unable for a substantial period to perform his duties as a member of the group, typically through illness, or ceases to be a member of the Commission (which would happen during the course of a reference usually only if he died) or where it subsequently becomes apparent that a member has a conflict of interest that would render his continued membership of the group inappropriate, the chairman of the Commission has the power to appoint another member in the place of the absent member.[6] In practice, however, this power is rarely used, and would strictly only need to be if the absence reduced the number of members comprised in the group to less than three.

The staff

5.031 The letter will also name the member of the Commission's staff responsible for managing the team[7] designated to assist the group of members conducting the inquiry (the "inquiry director", of whom there were, at the time of writing, seven on the Commission's staff). It will also name the inquiry secretary, who is responsible for the day to day administration of the reference and is the principal point of contact with the parties and their advisers. It will request the names of those at the relevant party and/or its advisers who are to be nominated as the contact points with the Commission, and request an early meeting between the Commission staff and the parties to discuss administrative matters, notably the draft of the administrative timetable which the Commission is required to adopt.[8] The staff meeting also gives a party the opportunity to invite early consideration by the Commission of any novel, difficult or logistical issues raised by the reference.

Administrative timetable

5.032 As described above, the group appointed to conduct the inquiry is required to draw up an administrative timetable, making provision for the principal stages of the reference. In so doing, the group must have regard to representations from the main parties (as to the availability of key executives, for example); the Commission generally prefers not to make any significant variations to the deadlines it has proposed, having regard to its duty to comply with the statutory 24 week timetable, but will usually accommodate reasonable requests for minor variations and extensions. Once the

---

[5] The fact that a member has sat on a previous inquiry involving the same party is unlikely to be regarded as sufficient grounds.
[6] Rules of Procedure, para.4.10.
[7] *i.e.* the inquiry secretary, accounting adviser, economist, lawyer and other supporting officials.
[8] Rules of Procedure, para.6.2.

administrative timetable has been finalised, it is both notified to the parties and published, usually on the Commission's website. The Commission now has substantial powers under the Act to ensure that the timetable is complied with, notably the power to impose penalties for late or non-provision of information following a formal demand.[9] The Commission may also ignore information which has been submitted late without reasonable explanation,[10] although to do so might potentially raise questions as to the accuracy and completeness of the Commission's final report.

In practice it is unlikely that the Commission will be obliged to use its enforcement powers because parties have traditionally co-operated voluntarily with the Commission. Clearly, where a party anticipates difficulties as the inquiry proceeds in complying with any deadline, it is good practice to warn the inquiry secretary as early as possible in advance. Typically, once a working relationship between the staff and the relevant party's team has been established, this informal process works well.

The initial request for information

The principal purpose of the first day letter is to identify those areas in respect of which the Commission requires information and views from the recipient. This initial request for information comprises the party's "Main Submission"[11] and copies of certain off-the-shelf material.[12] About a week later these information requests are followed by two detailed questionnaires, one relating to the market (the Market Information Request[13]), and the other containing a series of detailed financial questions about the party and the transaction (the Financial Information Request[14]).

5.033

The request for the main submission follows a relatively standard form, as might be expected at such an early stage of the inquiry prior to the issues raised by the merger having been identified by the Commission with sufficient particularity, and as the letter itself states, the Commission will find it necessary to raise further issues and issue additional requests for information as the inquiry progresses. The generality and breadth of the request for the main submission enables the recipient of the letter to supply the basic information needed for an understanding of the issues, to identify for the Commission the points raised by the merger and to express views on them, thereby inviting the Commission to reach the conclusion that the merger may not be expected to result in a substantial lessening of competition (or, in the case of an unwilling target, that it may be so expected and should not therefore be permitted to proceed).

It should be noted that although the Commission will have received certain information from the OFT, the Commission's information gathering

---

[9] s.109 of the Act; the related enforcement powers are contained in ss.110 and 111: see para.5.026, above.

[10] Rules of Procedure, para.9.3. The Commission tends to include in its timetable two deadlines: one prior to publication of the provisional findings, the other prior to publication of the final report; these are intended to allow time for material to be fully considered by the group in time to meet the relevant publication date.

[11] See para.5.034, below.

[12] See para.5.035, below.

[13] See para.5.036, below.

[14] See para.5.037, below.

process will effectively start from scratch. Unlike EC Merger Regulation procedure where the European Commission moves seamlessly from Phase I into Phase II, the Commission's investigation does not pick up where the OFT left off, but investigates all issues itself. This procedure is understandable in light of the fact that the reason for the reference will often be that the complexity of the competition analysis—for example as regards market definition, remedies or the impact of claimed customer benefits—is such that the OFT has not been able to reach firm conclusions itself in the time available. Of course the parties themselves will be able to use the work done at the OFT stage as the foundations for their submissions to the Commission. In practice the experience of the OFT's investigation will typically have gone a long way to identifying the issues which the Commission is likely to concentrate on, and the parties may focus in particular on developing their case on those points before the Commission. Of course, any major shift in the arguments of the parties at this stage would be risky, not least as regards credibility.

Request for main submission

5.034 It is primarily through the main submission that the parties set out their principal arguments; and accordingly its preparation requires and deserves considerable effort on the part of the parties and their advisers. The submission will usually be required by the Commission's letter to contain:

(i) a brief history of the party and a summary of its organisation, financial structure and principal activities;

(ii) the main product and geographic markets in which the party operates;

(iii) the background to and reasons for the merger (together, where appropriate, with details of any previous relationships between the parties);

(iv) views on the expected consequences of the merger, in particular identifying its likely effects on:

- the relevant markets;
- competition within the relevant product and geographic markets;
- suppliers and customers and the effect of the merger on them;
- barriers to entry;
- levels of prices and variety and quality of products;
- research and development;
- capital structure and financing of the merger and of the merged concern.

The letter also invites the identification of, and discussion on, any other issues which may be thought to be relevant; and this request in particular enables the parties to set out the arguments to support the basic premise that the merger should, or should not, be allowed to proceed or remain in place.

Despite any implication contained in the first day letter, there is no requirement that the main submission containing the information and views requested by the Commission should follow any particular format. In practice the Commission expects the parties to produce their responses in the manner most suited to the conveyance of the views and arguments the parties wish the Commission to comprehend. The memorandum should, of course, comprise (or have appended to it) all the items of information specifically requested by the Commission. In the case of an agreed merger or joint venture, the parties may decide upon a joint submission, where applicable, accompanied perhaps by each party's individual annexes containing confidential information not yet disclosed to the other party. The Commission normally requests fifteen copies of the submission and its appendices; sufficient for each of the members of the group and the officials working on the inquiry to have a copy. It also requests an electronic copy, sent either by encrypted email, CD-rom or floppy disk.

The first day letter sets a deadline by which the main submission is to be provided. This is typically two to three weeks after the date of the letter. As described above[15] there is a small degree of flexibility here and the Commission will normally try to accommodate any reasonable requests for short extensions of time—but in practice the scope for flexibility is limited by the statutory deadline imposed on the Commission, with the result that any extension granted is likely to be of only a few days.

Off-the-shelf material

In a further Annex, the first day letter will request the provision of a number of specific documents required by the Commission's staff to carry out a preliminary investigation of the financial and structural implications of the merger. Some of the requested documents may be case-specific—copies of the shareholders' agreement in the case of a joint venture, for example—but most will be requested in every case; in particular, the party's latest annual report and accounts; copies of any documents issued to shareholders in relation to the merger and of any press releases (each of which is likely to give some explanation for the commercial logic of the merger and its financial implications); any legal agreements (or, if applicable, draft agreements) governing the merger; a group structure chart; any market research reports either publicly available or specifically commissioned; and copies of any documents prepared by the party or its advisers in relation to the merger, including consultants' reports, relevant board and committee presentations, minutes and board papers.

5.035

This last head of documentary information should be particularly noted: in essence, the Commission asks to be supplied with any papers containing information circulated at senior management and board levels in which the commercial logic and implications of the merger are discussed.[16] Information contained in such papers may, of course, be damaging to the party's arguments, sometimes significantly so; for example, papers presented to the board may purport to justify the merger on the basis that

---

[15] At para.5.032, above.
[16] As to the use the Commission may make of confidential information see para.5.023, above.

it will result in the creation or strengthening of a dominant position in the relevant market, and/or facilitate price increases.

Although the wording of the request for such documents is sufficiently wide to cover the production to the Commission of letters of advice written by the party's lawyers as to, for example, the likelihood of a reference and/or of an ultimately successful outcome, such documents would be privileged, to the extent that their purpose is to advise on the party's rights and liabilities, and not therefore subject to disclosure; but a board memorandum commenting on such advice might not be so protected.[17]

Other procedural points

5.036   The remainder of the first day letter comprises a brief explanation of the procedure the Commission proposes to adopt during its inquiry. In particular, it explains that:

(i)   the Commission will require the recipient to attend a hearing with members of the group as soon as practicable after the requested submission has been received, for the purpose of clarifying facts and discussing the expected consequences of the merger in the light of submissions received from the parties and from others,[18] with the Commission notifying the party in advance of the main areas likely to be discussed[19]; and

(ii)   during the course of the inquiry, the Commission will publish certain documents on its website: notably the statement of issues referred to in (i) above, the group's provisional findings[20] and, in the event of an adverse finding, a statement of possible remedies.

Market Information Request

5.037   As forewarned in the first day letter, the Commission supplements its request for the parties' main submission with a—frequently extensive—questionnaire prepared by the Commission's economists. This may normally be expected within about a week of the inquiry. It will have been prepared following an initial study by the economist of the material then available to him: principally published material and the OFT's papers. Understandably, it may sometimes disclose a somewhat superficial understanding of the facts and the issues. Almost inevitably, some of the questions raised will be among those which are intended to be addressed in the principal submission being prepared; and the limited knowledge available to the economist at that time may sometimes mean that further questions will need to be posed later, once the issues are more fully understood.

---

[17] The scope of legal privilege is currently uncertain, pending the decision of the House of Lords in the recent *Three Rivers* case (*Three Rivers District Council and OFS v The Governor and Company of the Bank of England.*

[18] As to the gathering of views of third parties, see para.5.046, below.

[19] As to the conduct of hearings, see para.5.043, below.

[20] As to provisional findings, see para.5.048, below.

The Market Information Request nonetheless represents an important part of the Commission's investigation and the responses must be prepared with considerable care. There is no standard format for answering the questionnaire, but a number of points should be borne in mind:

(i)   it is important to identify which questions may not be capable of complete answers (perhaps because the requested information is not available, or the requested data is not collected, or because in its current form, the request would be very onerous to meet) and to raise these with the Commission as quickly as possible: the Commission encourages early discussion of a party's difficulties in responding and will often be prepared to consider how, by alternative means, to obtain the information needed or some appropriate substitute for it;

(ii)   there is no purpose to be served in responding in detail to a particular question if a full response is being or has been given in the main submission. In such circumstances it is sufficient to cross refer to the section of the memorandum where the point is addressed. (In practice, it is often desirable, if deadlines permit, to submit the memorandum and response to the Market Information Request simultaneously, such that cross-reference is not only feasible but can be encouraged);

(iii) it is invariably sensible to spend time analysing the questions before attempting to answer them: such an exercise will not only identify the issues that need to be addressed but will often throw up the desirability—as a means of ensuring the Commission's full understanding—of answering a slightly different question, or answering it in a manner not obviously envisaged in the request;

(iv)   where a question or series of questions is likely to take a longer time to answer than the Commission has allowed, the inquiry secretary should be notified as soon as possible, in response to which the Commission may sometimes be able to indicate that the particular question is of lesser importance and a delay in response can therefore be accommodated.

Typically a two to three week deadline is set for the provision of responses to the Market Information Request.

Financial Information Request

At the same time as being required to respond to the Market Information Request, and usually with the same deadline, the parties will be requested to provide information on group structure and finance and on the financial aspects of the proposed transaction, including profitability, in response to questions prepared by the Commission's accounting adviser which are set out in the Financial Information Request. Inevitably there tends to be some duplication between this Request and the information required in response to the initial request for off-the-shelf material, and it is preferable to cross-refer to earlier material where appropriate. The information requested will typically include statutory accounts for several years (five or six) for the

5.038

parent company and any relevant subsidiaries, historic and current management accounts, budgets and forecasts, performance indicators and benchmarks used by the party (including a range of profitability measures) and miscellaneous supplementary financial information to the extent not apparent from the accounts; brokers reports; and pro forma accounts reflecting the effect of the merger and any consequent tax implications. Like the main submission, responses to these Information Requests are required to be supplied in both hard copy and electronic forms.

Further information requests

5.039   During the course of the inquiry, as envisaged in the first day letter, further requests for information will be made. There will be a need for expansion and clarification of points made in the main submission or in response to the market and financial information requests. In addition, points will be raised at the oral hearing which are not capable of immediate answers[21] and the investigations of the Commission's staff and their analysis of publicly available material and submissions of third parties will inevitably raise further questions. Such questions may be conveyed in writing or, less formally, may be raised over the telephone, either by the inquiry secretary to the nominated contact, or by the relevant member of the Commission's staff (for example, the accounting adviser working on the inquiry) to the appropriate representative, with whom direct contact will already have been made.

Oral hearings

Introduction

5.040   Oral hearings with the principal parties and certain interested third parties have always been an integral part of Commission inquiries. It was formerly the invariable practice of the Commission to hold two hearings with each of the principal parties: the first dealing principally with factual aspects and the second with issues raised by the merger and hypothetical remedies.[22] When in the late 1980s the reference duration was contracted it became more usual to hold only one hearing with each party, although there remained scope for the Commission to convene further hearings if it were considered to be desirable in light of the issues involved, and for the parties themselves to request another hearing if they felt that there were issues raised by the merger that had received insufficient attention.

The practice adopted by the Commission under the new regime is to convene a hearing once the main submission and responses to the market information and financial information requests have been received and the Commission has identified what it understands to be the main issues. In the context of fixing the administrative timetable, dates will have been pencilled in for further hearings. The second hearing will explore further

---

[21] See para.5.043, below.
[22] As to remedies, see para.5.049, below.

the issues raised once the Commission has completed its analysis of the facts and third party views, and another will focus on provisional findings and remedies if these subsequently prove necessary. There may also be a hearing before the provisional findings are published.

Hearings are held with each party separately unless, in the case of an agreed merger or joint venture, the parties and the Commission agree together that a joint hearing, perhaps with short separate sessions to deal with confidential aspects of the parties' submissions would be appropriate. The Rules of Procedure provide for joint hearings to be held purely at the instance of the Commission if, for example, it considers that such an approach would enable the parties to reach a better understanding of each others' positions.[23] So far as the authors are aware, no such joint hearing between the main parties has yet been held except where requested by the parties. There have been suggestions in the past that a more adversarial approach to hearings, with both parties being present, might promote further transparency. Such an approach, involving parties with widely divergent views, implies the imposition of greater formality, including the adoption of elementary rules of evidence, such that hearings would inevitably take longer and require greater preparation at greater cost and without any assurance of benefit to the parties, the Commission or the public, and has not been adopted under the new regime.[24] However, since 2001 the Commission has held public hearings where the group has considered it appropriate to do so. This procedure is described below.[25]

The statement of issues

The date for the hearing of each party will usually have been fixed at, or as a result of, discussions at the administrative meeting. About a week before the fixed date the Commission will provide to the party and publish on its website an Issues Statement, which sets out the principal points the Commission believes are raised by the merger, and which the Commission therefore wishes to discuss. These will typically cover the areas of market definition, the dynamics of the market including rivalry between competing suppliers, entry barriers, competitive effects of the merger, the likely development of the market in the absence of the merger, and customer benefits. The Commission emphasises that at this stage it has reached no conclusions on any matter. Although no further written submission commenting on the issues is normally required prior to the hearing, parties sometimes find it helpful or necessary to provide further information or argument in advance. In that event it is important to make it available to the Commission in enough time for the Commission staff to review it and brief the group accordingly. It is in any event usually wise for those who are to attend the

5.041

---

[23] Rules of Procedure, para.7.4.

[24] However, the Act (at s.109(5)) does provide for the Commission to take evidence on oath or by solemn affirmation, just as the FTA did, and the Rules of Procedure (at para.8.1) allow for cross-examination. It is not thought that either of these powers has ever been used, either under the old regime or the new regime. A joint hearing involving opposing parties was held in the context of the Commission's scale monopoly inquiry into the supply of Scottish Milk under the FTA, Cm. 5002 (December 2000).

[25] See para.5.047, below.

hearing to spend time beforehand preparing themselves for the likely questions.[26] After the hearing, parties and their advisers sometimes consider it to be helpful to their case to provide a written submission in response to the Issues Letter and the key points raised by the Commission at the hearing.

The hearing room

5.042   Most hearings with the principal parties take place in a designated hearing room in the Commission's offices.[27] Members of the group are seated at a table with the chairman of the group in the centre, the Commission's chief executive or the inquiry director at his side and other members of the group either side of them. At the far end is a stenographer who records the whole of the proceedings.[28] Behind the group's table are seated those members of the Commission's staff who are working on the inquiry. They are there to clarify any of the questions which may not be readily understood and, of course, to hear the responses given.

Representatives of the party being heard are seated in a row facing the Commission, each row being able to seat approximately eight people. Where there are eight or fewer representatives, it is customary for all to be seated in the front row; where there are a greater number, those who are to be principally involved in responding to the Commission's questions will be seated at the front, with supporting team members behind. Usually, one of the advisers will sit alongside or close to the principal representatives of the party, ready to answer questions of a legal, procedural or jurisdictional nature and to intervene if a question or a response appears to have been, or to be likely to be, misunderstood.[29] The precise seating plan is for the party being heard to propose: a member of the reference team will seek instructions on this a few days beforehand.

Conduct of the hearing

5.043   Hearings typically commence in the middle of the morning. The group customarily breaks for an hour at around 1pm and it is sensible for the party being heard to make its own arrangements for that period at a nearby location although a room for the parties' use can often be made available at the Commission. The length of hearings necessarily depends on the number of questions the Commission wishes to ask and the length of the answers but typically a hearing might be expected to be over by 5pm or a little later. It would be unusual, but not unheard of, for a hearing to run into a second day, but that would be likely to have been anticipated beforehand.

---

[26] It is advisable to hold a rehearsal a few days beforehand at which the party's advisers can take those who are to attend through the more difficult aspects of the "case" it is intended to present in response to the Commission's questions. This exercise enables previously unidentified gaps in individuals' understanding and presentation of the facts and issues to be filled and often helps those present to feel more at ease in the hearing itself.

[27] The Commission has recently moved to new premises in London's Southampton Row. There are five meeting rooms, three of which are capable of being transformed into a single room for larger hearings.

[28] The record is then transcribed: see para.5.044, below.

[29] Generally, however, advisers are not expected to take a leading role: the Commission will wish to hear from the parties themselves, and not their advisers.

At the opening of proceedings, after the chairman of the group has introduced himself and his fellow members and explained the procedure of the hearing, he will ask the senior representative of the party being heard whether he wishes to make an opening statement. Usually the decision as to whether to say anything at this stage will have been made beforehand, in discussion between the party's representatives and their advisers. That decision will depend on the circumstances; but unless there is anything specific and significant which it is thought the Commission should be made aware of immediately, it is often preferable to save any statement until the end of the hearing, when points that have arisen during questioning can be further addressed if necessary.

The Commission's questions will have been prepared beforehand by the staff in discussion with the group. Some will be purely for the purposes of clarification of points made in the party's written submissions and responses to information requests; others will test out propositions put to the group by third parties, and the Commission's own thoughts. The questions will be searching, but are not designed to "catch out" those responding. They will be directed to the senior executive of the party being heard.[30] Whether that individual executive responds himself or invites one of his colleagues to do so will, by preference, have been decided beforehand following receipt of the Issues Statement. Clearly no fixed rules can be set down here, but two general points should be kept in mind. First, those attending the hearing should maintain discipline in giving their responses and avoid the situation where two or more executives give similar (or, worse, conflicting) answers to the same question. Secondly, advisers should remember that the Commission generally wishes to hear from their clients and not themselves; contributions from advisers should normally be limited to avoiding misunderstandings arising from ambiguous questions or responses and addressing any legal or jurisdictional issues. The Commission can, ultimately require, by means of a s.109 notice, a person to attend and give evidence on oath, although it has not to date used this power.

There is no set form to the contribution made by group members; sometimes the chairman will pose most of the set questions, leaving other members to raise supplemental issues prompted by particular responses. On other occasions the members of the group will have been designated different sets of questions on which to lead the examination. But in all cases the style of the hearing is relatively informal. Almost inevitably, some of the factual questions will be incapable of immediate and complete response. In these circumstances it is acceptable to offer to respond to the Commission after the hearing, having checked the facts or collated the relevant information; and it is certainly preferable to respond in such manner, rather than to give an immediate but incorrect response. At the end of the hearing, the senior executive of the party will be asked whether he wishes to make a closing statement, and the legal adviser will usually be invited to do so too. This gives an opportunity for one or both of them to make any points in support of their views that may not have sufficiently come across in responding to the Commission's questions; to revert to questions which it is felt may not have

---

[30] The Commission expects that the hearing will usually be attended by senior executives of the party, typically the chairman and/or chief executive, finance director and other relevant members of senior management.

been fully answered; and generally to leave with the Commission a favourable impression of the merits of their case.

The transcript

5.044 As explained above, a transcript will be produced of the proceedings. A few days after the hearing, numbered copies of the transcript will be distributed for correction and comment. This gives the opportunity not only to read the record of the hearing for accuracy, but also to correct any responses that were wrong or may have been misunderstood, and by separate letter or memorandum to expand upon answers which, on reflection, may be thought to have been misleading or inadequate. The transcript is marked "Confidential". As in the case of written submissions, the Commission's general obligation is to maintain confidentiality[31] and, save to test out propositions on the other principal party or on third parties (where possible on a paraphrased and unattributable basis), the Commission will not disclose the content of the transcript to anyone (except where essential to do so in its report or, occasionally, in the other circumstances set out in ss.239, 240, 241 and 242 of the Act[32]) although it may, particularly in the case of hearings with third parties who have not provided a written submission, decide that certain points made orally ought to be disclosed for discussion with the main parties. The Commission will expect the parties to maintain the confidentiality of the proceedings at oral hearings, and the chairman has been known to rebuke a party which breaches this confidence.

Site visits

5.045 It used to be the almost invariable practice of the Commission to visit parts of the principal parties' business operations during the course of its inquiry. The advent of three-month references caused the Commission to review this, and site visits are no longer a constant feature of merger references, although the Commission will still wish to follow this practice in any inquiry in which it believes a visit will assist its understanding of the facts and issues involved and does so in most cases, usually during the first few weeks of an inquiry as part of the process of understanding the context of the merger. Typically a visit will be conducted by some, but not necessarily all, of the members of the group and the principal staff members involved. They will have indicated beforehand what specifically they are interested to see; nonetheless there is scope for the party to direct the group's attention to particular issues, whether through formal presentations or informal discussions, as the party tours the site or over lunch. The informality of the occasion may sometimes lead to misunderstandings: there have been instances when a staff member has formed an erroneous view on a particular issue following an informal conversation with a relatively junior employee of the party. Nonetheless, site visits may often be of benefit to the parties as well as to the Commission, affording them the opportunity of explaining their business and putting across points in a way not so easily

---

[31] s.237 of the Act.
[32] See para.5.023, above.

achieved either at oral hearings or in formal submissions. Accordingly such visits tend to be, to some extent, "stage-managed"; the Commission knows this and doubtless allows for it in its wider considerations.

Evidence from third parties

Although the Commission will rely heavily on the information and evidence   5.046
given by the principal parties to the reference, it will also wish to hear the often widely varying views of third parties. It achieves this by a variety of means. It will place a notice in national and trade newspapers and journals and on its website, informing the public of the reference and inviting comments and views; certain third parties will be specifically identified to give information, either generally or in response to a questionnaire; the principal parties may themselves—sometimes when invited, sometimes not—identify third parties from whom they believe the Commission should seek information; and some third parties will offer evidence to the Commission of their own initiative. It may in addition commission market surveys to be carried out as a means of assessing general consumer reaction to particular situations and issues or may seek expert advice or econometric analysis.

Those third parties considered by the Commission to have particular contributions to make to its understanding of the issues raised by the merger and its effects may be requested to attend an oral hearing; and some may in any event ask to do so. These hearings are usually conducted at an early stage of the reference, and there has been an increasing willingness on the part of the Commission to hold them outside London where this is more convenient to the parties to be heard.[32A] Although there is usually no shortage of third party views available to the Commission it may sometimes be difficult for the group to reach a balanced view as to the appropriate weight to place on them, particularly in the case of conflicting views. There is also the suspicion that the group may sometimes pay undue attention to third parties regarded in the market as insignificant or known to have an "axe to grind", and in consequence may misunderstand the significance of particular aspects of the merger (although it would be fair to add that the Commission will be alive to the possibility of third party bias).

In addition to hearings with third parties, the Commission will wish to question the OFT on the earlier investigation which led to the reference, as a means of giving a flavour to the inquiry and in order to understand the relevant market in outline. Usually, the meeting with those members of the OFT's staff responsible for the OFT's review of the merger will be the Commission's first hearing, held shortly after the OFT's reasons for reference have been published.

Public hearings

The Rules of Procedure specify that the group conducting a reference has a   5.047
duty to consider which, if any, of its hearings are to be held in public, having regard, *inter alia*, to the views of the main parties and others, the

---

[32A] In *P&O/Stena*, for example, hearings were held with third parties in Belfast and Dublin.

need for confidentiality, the extent to which a party might be inhibited from providing or encouraged to provide information in a public forum, and general considerations of administration and efficiency.[33] Such hearings, at which the main parties and other intended parties are invited to make presentations and members of the public and press are present, have been more prevalent in the case of market inquiries, but public hearings have been held in the course of a few merger inquiries usually dealing with consumer goods and services.[34] Although such hearings may be argued to demonstrate transparency in the Commission's proceedings, it is questionable whether they assist the Commission's inquiry in any material way. Indeed, Professor Paul Geroski, who became Chairman of the Commission in April 2004, has indicated that he will not normally favour such an approach, being quoted in an early interview as saying "One of the disadvantages is you never get confidential information and often that is what you really need to get into the issue. It is also not necessarily the right kind of forum to get the information you need".

Provisional findings

5.048   The Commission is required[35] to reach provisional findings on the statutory questions referred to it in the reference[36] and to issue a notice setting out its findings both to the parties and, via its website, to the public. The notice has attached to it the group's full provisional findings report, along with an executive summary. In the first instance only the main parties receive the report (usually on the day before publication and after close of business if one or more of the parties is listed). Copies of the notice and the executive summary, together with a press release, are published on the Commission's website by the opening of business the next day, and this is followed a few days later by the complete provisional findings report. This gap allows the parties to be given a short opportunity to request the excision of sensitive material from the published report.[37] The provisional findings report is a substantial document (as at the time of writing, such reports have mostly been between 55 and 80 pages long) and will typically set out details of the reference, the companies, the proposed transaction and jurisdiction, market definition and assessment of the competitive effects of the merger. There appears to be scope for flexibility in the contents, with the *Dräger Medical* provisional findings report also containing sections on the counter-factual and market entry.[38]

---

[33] At paras 7.1 and 7.2

[34] As at the time of writing, these had been public hearings in three merger inquiries: *News Communications & media plc and Newsquest (Investments) Limited/Johnston Press plc/Trinity Mirror plc*, Cm. 4680 (April 2000); *Lloyds TSB Group plc/Abbey National plc*, Cm. 5208 (July 2001); *Safeway plc/Asda Group Limited/Wm Morrison Supermarkets PLC/J. Sainsbury plc/Tesco plc*, Cm. 5950 (September 2003).

[35] Rules of Procedure, Rule 10.

[36] *i.e.* (a) whether a relevant merger situation has been created or arrangements are in progress or contemplation which if carried into effect will result in the creation of a relevant merger situation; and if so (b) whether the merger situation has resulted or may be expected to result in a substantial lessening of competition.

[37] See para.5.024, above.

[38] *Dräger Medical AG & Co KGaA and Hillenbrand Industries, Inc* (May 2004) at p.26.

The notice specifies a date, which para.10.5 of the Rules of Procedure states should be not less than 21 days after the date of the notice, by which the parties and third parties are required to provide in writing its reasons why the Commission's provisional findings should not become final or, as the case may be, should be varied. If the deadline is missed, the Commission is not obliged to take into account any reasons subsequently expressed. Paragraph 10.6 of the Rules specifies that the Commission is not required to hold a further oral hearing in the light of any response from a main party, but in practice a provisional date for a further hearing is likely to have been identified in the administrative timetable and it would be normal, in circumstances of an adverse finding having been reached, for a further hearing to take place. This is almost inevitable where the Commission is contemplating remedies.

Remedies

As described above, one of the most significant changes introduced by the Act is that if the group decides (by a majority of two thirds[39]) that the merger has or may be expected to have an anti-competitive outcome it is now required to consider whether action should be taken by the Commission or others[40] for the purposes of remedying, mitigating or preventing the substantial lessening of competition or any adverse effect arising from it; and, if so, what that action should be.

    5.049

If the provisional findings report concludes that the merger is not expected to result, or has not resulted, in a substantial lessening of competition, then the parties have effectively won the case and there is no need (or legal basis) to go on to consider the issue of remedies. The procedure under the Act represents a significant improvement on the approach under the FTA, where the Commission would engage in a discussion about "hypothetical remedies" in circumstances where the parties did not know whether they were in fact going to be required to give undertakings and where, even if that did turn out to be the case, it would not be the Commission which negotiated them with the parties.[40A]

The range of remedies available to the Commission, their implementation, proportionality, consumer benefits and certain policy issues are considered in Ch.9, below. This section considered the procedure adopted by the group, having reached an adverse finding.[41]

Pursuant to the Rules of Procedure (at para.11.1), the group is required to give as much notice to the parties as practicable of the remedial actions it considers might be taken and to publish such notice on the Commission's website. The notice may be included within the notice of provisional findings but is more likely to be published a little later. In *Stena/P&O*,[42] the provisional findings report was published on November 27, 2003, with the

---

[39] See para.20(2)0 of Sch.7 to the Competition Act 1998.

[40] *i.e.* government or other public authorities.

[40A] See para.9.001 of Ch. 9 below.

[41] As noted, the group must reach its decision that there is an anti-competitive outcome by a two thirds majority, otherwise the Commission will not have the power to impose remedies: see para.20(2) of Sch.7 to the Competition Act 1998.

[42] *Stena AB/The Peninsular & Oriental Steam Navigation Company* (February 2004).

remedies notice being published on December 1. In *Dräger Medical*[43] the dates were March 5, 2004 and March 10, 2004, respectively. There is a duty to consult with the main parties, which typically involves an oral hearing (usually the same hearing at which the relevant party gives its views as to the Commission's provisional findings).

As to the proposed remedies themselves, some will have been developed by the Commission itself while others may have been proposed by the parties or, occasionally, by third parties. They may range from the giving of undertakings to behave in relation to the merged business in a manner which the parties have already indicated they are doing and/or will be prepared to do in the future, to the prevention in its entirety of a contemplated merger or the complete divestment of the business, the earlier acquisition of which has resulted in the reference.[44] The purpose of consultation, therefore, is to obtain views as to what is practical and achievable, and the effects that any contemplated remedies may be expected to have, in order to eliminate the impractical, the ineffective and the disproportionate. In the course of these consultations the group may take into account any countervailing customer benefits arising from the merger[44A] and is also likely to have regard to any comments made by third parties.

5.050   Having assimilated the views expressed by the main parties and others it is the duty of the group to finalise its decision as to proposed remedies and to include these in the Commission's report on the merger, incorporating sufficient detail to support with clarity their implementation. The remedies which are to be imposed are ultimately decided by a simple majority of the members of the group.

The Commission's report

Statutory requirements

5.051   The basic provisions as to what a report by the Commission on a merger reference should contain are set out in s.38 of the Act. The Commission is required to include its decisions on the questions comprised in the reference,[45] together with its reasons for those decisions and such information as it considers appropriate for facilitating a proper understanding of those questions and of its reasons for its decisions.[46] Accordingly, when the Commission has found that a merger situation qualifying for investigation has been created and that the creation of that situation results or may be expected to result in a substantial lessening of competition, the report will also address the questions of whether, and if so what, action should be taken by the Commission or others for the purpose of remedying, mitigating or preventing the substantial lessening of competition or any adverse effect resulting or expected to result from it. Possible actions to be taken will of course have been discussed with the parties following the issue of the

---

[43] *Dräger Medical AG & Co KGaA and Hillenbrand Industries Inc* (May 2004).
[44] See Ch.9, below for a discussion of how remedies are arrived at and the Commission's policy in this respect.
[44A] See s.41(5).
[45] *i.e.* the questions it is required to answer by virtue of s.35 or (as the case may be) s.36.
[46] s.38(2).

remedies notice.[47] In preparing its report the Commission is required to have regard to the provisions of s.244 of the Act. Accordingly, it is required to exclude, so far as practicable, any information whose disclosure would in its view be contrary to the public interest or the publication of which might seriously and prejudicially affect the interests of an individual, corporate or other body, unless the inclusion of that matter is necessary for the purposes for which the Commission is permitted to make the disclosure (that is, for the purpose of facilitating a proper understanding of the reasons for its decisions on the statutory questions).[48]

Prior to commencement of the new regime and in anticipation of it, the Commission undertook a critical review of the format of its reports, with the aim in the future of producing a report appropriate for a determinative body (released from the requirement to explain all the background material necessary for the Minister to reach a decision); accommodating the shift in emphasis to accountability to the public; and making its reports more accessible. In the Commission's Annual Review and Accounts 2002/3 the former chairman stated that reports would, in the future, be as concise and clear as possible, tightly focused on the legislative requirements and making a transparent link between evidence received and conclusions reached. He anticipated that reports would be shorter in the future, structured around the competition and remedies decisions required to be contained in the report; resulting in something akin to the conclusions chapters contained in reports under the old regime, with such supporting material included as the group judges to be necessary. At the time of writing, four reports under the Act had been published[49] and it appears that the anticipation of shorter and more concise reports has so far been achieved. Just as under the old regime, a report may contain a statement written by a member of the group who disagrees with any decision of the Commission contained in the report, setting out his reasons for disagreeing.[50]

Fairness and consistency

The Commission will also have regard, in preparing the report, not only to its duty to act fairly[51] but to the need to be seen to be acting fairly and to remove, as far as practicable, any risk of its report becoming subject to an application to the Competition Appeal Tribunal for judicial review.[52] Thus the draftsmen will endeavour to ensure that there is no scope for the principal parties or any third party subsequently to argue that the Commission has failed to take into account any material piece of evidence.

It was well established under the FTA regime through applications to the court for judicial review that the weight that should be placed on any piece

5.052

---

[47] See para.5.049, above and Ch.9, below.
[48] As to how questions of disclosure are addressed by the Commission, see para.5.024, above and para.5.054, below.
[49] *Stena AB/The Peninsular & Oriental Steam Navigation Company* (February 2004); *Carl Zeiss Jena GmbH/Bio-Rad Laboratories Inc* (May 2004); *Dräger Medical AG & Co KGaA and Hillenbrand Industries Inc* (May 2004); and *First Group plc and the Scottish Passenger Rail Franchise* (June 2004).
[50] s.119 of the Act.
[51] See para.5.021, above.
[52] See Ch.10., below

of evidence was a matter for the Commission alone to decide. For example, in *R. v Monopolies & Mergers Commission Ex p. Ecando Systems* Simon Brown J. said that:

"It was for the Commission to judge the commercial realities of the situation and it is only for this court to interfere if satisfied that the Commission came to a perverse view of the matter . . ."[53];

and, further:

"But in my judgment it will be a rare case indeed when a report is appropriately quashed on the ground that it is simply not possible to gain from it a proper understanding of the Commission's conclusions upon the statutory questions, and when therefore it could properly be said that the reasons given were not capable of facilitating such understanding."[54]

As noted above,[55] the Commission does not follow any strict adherence to precedent, arguing that to do so would be contrary to its statutory duty to investigate the particular circumstances and issues caused by each case. As a consequence, it is sometimes criticised, perhaps unjustifiably, for inconsistency of approach. In practice, however, the Commission does take steps to achieve a reasonable level of consistency in its reports.

Put-back material

5.053   The timetable imposed by the Act necessitates that the Commission should begin drafting the factual parts of the report whilst still carrying out its investigations. It would normally expect by the end of the eighth week of the inquiry to have begun preparation of a series of working papers containing material which is likely to be used in its notice of provisional findings and, subsequently, in its report. Heavy reliance is placed on the material which the principal parties themselves have written, notably concerning themselves and their businesses, their descriptions of the relevant markets and their views on the merger, which often will be précised or, sometimes, transcribed verbatim. Nonetheless, in order to ensure that the factual parts of the provisional findings and the report are as accurate as possible, the Commission's practice is to request the parties to consider and comment upon the working papers and, in an ongoing process, any further material subsequently produced for potential inclusion in the report.

This procedure does afford the parties a further opportunity to ensure their views are presented accurately and clearly, and although the Commission will neither invite nor wish to receive substantial redrafts of its drafts, it is possible at this stage to suggest alterations to the Commission's proposed report.

Although intended simply to enable accuracy to be checked by those who have provided the information being summarised, the put-back procedure

---

[53] [1993] C.O.D. 89.
[54] See *Ecando Systems*, cited above, at p.38.
[55] See para.5.020, above.

can sometimes cause controversy where the material which a party is requested to check at a late stage contains new information on which that party has not previously been asked to comment. Where the relevant information is, in the party's opinion, wrong or misleading, it will be under considerable pressure to submit arguments and evidence to challenge and contradict the new information within the very tight timetables imposed for the put-back process. Clearly it is not the Commission's intention to catch a party out in this way and the hope must be that the chairman's Guidance on Disclosure of Information[56] will prompt groups to be as assiduous in disclosing to the main parties in a timely manner material supplied by third parties or commissioned specifically, as in withholding or sanitising information on the grounds of confidentiality.

Confidentiality

As part of the put-back procedure, the parties are requested to identify those parts of the draft material in respect of which they wish to claim confidentiality. Although the Commission's general duty under s.244 of the Act is to have regard to the need to exclude from its report matters relating to an individual, company or other body of persons where publication would seriously and prejudicially affect the interests thereof, it is recognised by that provision that exclusion might not be practicable, and that inclusion might be necessary, for the purposes of ensuring a proper understanding of the Commission's decisions. Accordingly, it is not always possible to present the report in such a way as to exclude commercially sensitive information; nonetheless the Commission considers carefully all representations for exclusion made to it and does endeavour to write the report in such a way as to avoid disclosure of such information. 5.054

If there is a disagreement between the Commission and a party who has requested non-disclosure of a piece of evidence, the aggrieved party is entitled to raise with the Commission's Chief Executive any concerns which it considers have not been fully taken into account. As at the time of writing, this opportunity had not so far been used.

Publication

Once the preparation of the report has been completed it is published, both on the Commission's website, the website of The Stationery Office and in printed form.[57] The main parties are e-mailed an embargoed copy the evening before publication, following close of business of the Stock Exchange. However, at that point, if the report makes an adverse finding, then the group's work is not complete. The group will not be discharged until the completion of negotiations on any undertakings which the Commission has required to be entered into by way of remedy and such 5.055

---

[56] Chairman's Guidance on Disclosure of Information in Mergers and Market Inquiries, CC7
[57] The printed hard copy report is no longer necessarily made available by The Stationery Office at the time of publication. In the case of the *Stena/P&O* report (cited above) the hard copy became available over two weeks after publication on the internet.

undertakings have been finalised and signed by the parties, or until orders have been imposed.[58]

Public interest references and special public interest references

5.056   The descriptions of the Commission's practice and procedures in handling merger references in this Chapter have related to standard references made by the OFT under ss.22 and 33, in respect of which the Commission's responsibility is to decide whether a merger situation exists which results or may be expected to result in a substantial lessening of competition; and if so, what actions should be taken to remedy the adverse consequences arising therefrom. Where a reference has been made by the Secretary of State on public interest grounds[59] or special public interest grounds[59A] there are two significant variations to the Commission's procedure. First, the Commission is required to consider whether the merger operates or may be expected to operate against the public interest as well as whether it has resulted or may be expected to result in a substantial lessening of competition (if the reference has also been made on that ground). Secondly, in the event that the Commission makes an adverse finding either as to a substantial lessening of competition, or the public interest, or both, it must decide what action should be taken by the Secretary of State and others (including the Commission itself) to remedy the adverse public interest effects it has identified as having arisen or likely to arise.

A number of different scenarios is possible. If a reference to the Commission is made only on public interest grounds (which will always be the case in relation to special public interest references and can also be the case in relation to public interest references[60]), the Commission's role is limited to considering that issue.[61] Its report does not reach final conclusions and is not published in accordance with the procedure described above but will contain the Commission's recommendations and is submitted to the Secretary of State who may make a public interest finding[62] (that is, conclude that the merger operates or may be expected to operate against the public interest). If he so decides, he will publish the Commission's report whilst announcing his decision and will instruct the OFT to consult on and negotiate remedies (which may or may not be those recommended by the Commission). The Minister may, however, decide not to make such a finding, in which event the report is simply published, whereafter the merger may proceed.

The position is more complicated where a reference is made on both public interest and competition grounds.[63] The questions the Commission

---

[58]   See Ch.9, below.

[59]   s.45. See paras 2.026 et seq. of Ch.2 in relation to the grounds on which the Secretary of State may issue an intervention notice and take over from the OFT the power to decide whether to make a reference.

[59A]   See s.62.

[60]   ss.45(3) and 45(5).

[61]   s.47(3).

[62]   s.54(2).

[63]   ss.45(2) and 45(5). Note that competition grounds are never considered in relation to a special public interest merger.

must answer are whether there is a relevant merger situation; whether the merger is expected to result in a substantial lessening of competition; and whether, taking into account the public interest issue identified in the intervention notice and any substantial lessening of competition, the merger is expected to operate against the public interest. As in the case of a uniquely public interest reference, the duty of the Commission is to submit its report to the Secretary of State, where conclusions have been reached on either or both grounds, together with recommendations as to remedies which will, as in the case of normal references, have been discussed with the main parties during the course of the inquiry. Where it is decided to make a public interest finding, the Minister will instruct the OFT to negotiate undertakings both in relation to public interest and, where applicable, competition grounds, and, as before, the Minister is responsible for publication. If, on the other hand, the Minister decides to make no adverse public interest finding, the matter reverts to the Commission once the report has been published by the Minister, so that the Commission may negotiate appropriate remedies with the parties if it has concluded that a substantial lessening of competition may be expected to result.

CHAPTER 6

THE ECONOMIC ANALYSIS OF SUBSTANTIAL LESSENING OF COMPETITION

Introduction

What is meant by "substantial lessening of competition"?

6.001   This Chapter considers the practical application of the OFT's and Competition Commission's merger assessment guidelines[1] with particular reference to the key economic principles underpinning them. It also considers by reference to individual cases the evidence which the decision-makers have relied on in reaching their conclusions.[2]

An obvious starting point for this Chapter is to consider what is meant by "substantial lessening of competition"[3] (which is referred to as the "SLC test"). Both the OFT's and the Commission's guidelines refer to assessing substantial lessening of competition in terms of whether, following a merger, "market power" would be created or enhanced.[4] It is generally

---

[1] *"Merger References: Competition Commission Guidelines"*, June 2003 (referred to as "the Commission's guidelines" in this chapter), and *"OFT Mergers—substantive assessment guidance"*, May 2003 (referred to as "the OFT's guidelines" in this chapter).

[2] This Chapter can only be a brief introduction to the subject of industrial economics. There are a number of books on the subject which are referred to throughout this Chapter. A useful introductory text which covers a very broad range of antitrust issues (not just mergers) is *"The Economics of EC Competition Law: Concepts, Application and Measurement"* by Bishop and Walker, Second Edition, 2002, Sweet & Maxwell ("Bishop and Walker"). As its title suggests, this book focuses on EC cases, but it is of general relevance. Another helpful text which covers a range of antitrust issues is *"Competition Policy Theory and Practice"*, (Motta, Cambridge University Press, 2004) ("Motta"). This book focuses on EU and US cases, but again is of general relevance.

[3] s.35(1)(b) (as regards completed mergers) and s.36(1)(b) (as regards anticipated mergers) of the Enterprise Act 2002 (see further Ch.2).

[4] See p.15 of the OFT's guidelines (cited above, para.6.001, n.1), and para.1.24 of the Commission's guidelines, (cited above, para.6.001, n.1). The US Horizontal Merger Guidelines similarly identify as their "unifying theme" that "mergers should not be permitted to create or enhance market power or to facilitate its exercise" (US Horizontal Merger Guidelines, issued by the Department of Justice ("DOJ") and Federal Trade Commission ("FTC") on April 2, 1992, at section 0.1). The European Commission's 2004 Horizontal Merger Guidelines on the assessment of horizontal mergers under the EC Merger Regulation ("the European Commission's Horizontal Merger Guidelines") emphasise that: "Effective competition brings benefits to consumers, such as low prices, high quality products, a wide selection of goods and services, and innovation. Through its control of mergers, the [European] Commission prevents mergers that would be likely to deprive customers of these benefits by significantly increasingthe market power of firms. By "increased market power" is meant the ability of one or more firms to profitably increase prices, reduce output, choice or quality of goods and services, diminish innovation, or otherwise influence parameters of competition" (para.8, [2004] O.J. C31/5). A consideration of the reasons why substantial

accepted by economists that market power is held by a firm, or jointly by a group of firms where their conduct is not fully constrained by their competitors, customers, and/or suppliers.[5] Firms with market power may, for example, be able to increase prices above the competitive level[6] for a significant period of time without their profits being eroded by the entry and expansion of competitors. Similarly, buyers with market power may have the ability to pay prices to suppliers which are below the competitive level.[7] There may also be scope for firms with market power to engage in anti-competitive conduct which raises barriers to entry and expansion, and thus increases or sustains their market power.

The term "substantial lessening of competition" is described by the OFT as follows:

"A merger may be expected to lead to a substantial lessening of competition when it is expected to weaken rivalry to such an extent that customers would be harmed. This may come about, for example, through reduced product choice, or because prices could be raised profitably, output could be reduced and/or product quality or innovation could be reduced."[8]

At the outset, it is appropriate to identify a number of points as to the breadth and scope of this interpretation. First, the test was adopted as a result of concerns that a test based solely on the creation or enhancement of a dominant position might not be sufficiently broad to capture all possible anti-competitive effects of mergers.[9] Secondly, a substantial lessening of

---

market power is generally perceived as being undesirable is outside the scope of this book. A good discussion of the relevant issues is set out in Scherer and Ross, "*Industrial market Structure and Economic Performance*", (Third Edition, Houghton Mifflin Company, 1990) Ch.2; and Motta, cited above, para.6.001, n.2, Ch.2.

[5] See, for example, the OFT's guideline under the Competition Act 1998 on the "*Assessment of Market Power*", OFT 415. It should be noted that at the time of writing the OFT was consulting on revised Competition Act guidelines.

[6] Market power may be defined in terms of the ability of firms to charge prices in excess of marginal costs, with marginal costs being the addition to total costs by producing one more unit of output. The Lerner index of market power considers the relationship between prices and marginal costs. This index is calculated as $m=(p-c)/p=1/e$. In this formula, m is the gross margin, p is price, c is marginal cost and e is the absolute value of the firm's own price elasticity of demand. However, this is arguably not a particularly helpful definition as economists have not found any perfectly competitive markets in which prices are set equal to marginal costs (*i.e.* the increase in total costs from selling one more unit of output), not least because if prices were equal to marginal costs they would not cover their fixed costs which do not vary with output (see further Motta, cited above, para.6.001, n.2, at p.41).

[7] The exercise of market power by buyers ("monopsony" in the case of a single buyer or "oligopsony" in the case of a number of buyers) to depress price below the competitive level and reduce output has similar adverse effects to the exercise of market power by sellers. The framework developed in this Chapter is also applicable to the assessment of monopsony, see paras 6.161 to 6.162.

[8] OFT's guidelines, cited above, para.6.001, n.1, at para.3.7. The Commission's guidelines make these points in analogous terms at para.1.24, cited above, para.6.001, n.1.

[9] See further John Vickers' (Chairman of the OFT) article on "*Merger Policy in Europe: Retrospect and Prospect*", [2004] E.C.L.R. 455. Since UK merger control does not have a dominance test and the EC Merger Regulation is no longer based purely on a dominance test, this issue is not discussed in detail in this Chapter. However, some brief comments are warranted. First, Vickers' view is that there is a "gap" in a dominance test in relation to mergers which do not create or enhance a single dominant firm or have co-ordinated effects, but otherwise have non-coordinated effects. However, the existence of a gap is debateable,

competition might still arise even if only some (as opposed to all) customers may be expected to suffer as a result of the merger. This may be the case if some (but not all) customers are able to safeguard their interests due, for example, to these customers possessing significant countervailing buyer power[10] or being more able to switch to alternatives. Thirdly, the competition concerns are not limited to price increases, but all dimensions of competition including impacts on innovation and product quality. Finally, the emphasis is on harm to customers, not competitors, or any other interest group. This point is reinforced by the fact that, in broad terms, UK authorities may clear a merger or allow it to proceed with less stringent remedies in circumstances where, notwithstanding a realised or expected substantial lessening of competition, they expect the merger to result in specific customer benefits.

6.002   In short, with a very broad economics based legal test, the OFT's and Competition Commission's task is to assess the facts of individual mergers in the light of a very wide variety of broad ranging economic theories of competitive harm.[11] In this regard, and in contrast to the position in 1994 when the first edition of this book was published, there is now considerable guidance available as to how mergers may lead to competitive harm, from regulators' own guidelines, research papers, and the OFT's advice under the FTA and decisions under the Enterprise Act (as well as many more reports by the Commission and its predecessor the MMC):

(i)   until Spring 2003, no substantive guidelines had been published in relation to economic assessment.[12] However, the Commission and

---

since dominance is arguably a sufficiently broad concept to cover non-co-ordinated effects which arise due to the merger of particularly close competitors, or otherwise in circumstances where rivals have little constraining effect despite them having a significant share of a broader market. See further Bishop and Walker, cited above, para.6.001, n.2, at pp.309–312. In addition, RBB observes in the context of EC merger control: "But regardless of whether the gap exists, one consequence of the introduction of the concept of non-coordinated effects is to open up a wide area of enforcement discretion beyond that envisaged by the proponents of the gap theory by reducing the market share threshold at which mergers might be considered to be problematic from the traditional 40% threshold to 25%" (see further RBB Brief 14, "*Assessing Unilateral Effects in Practice: Lessons from GE/Instrumentarium*", May 2004, and RBB Brief 07, "*Full Marks? The Draft EC Notice on the Appraisal of Horizontal Mergers*", January 2003).

[10] See further paras 6.072 to 6.079, below.

[11] One question which could be posed is whether the assessment of mergers has changed due to the Enterprise Act 2002. Notwithstanding the legal and institutional changes, it can be strongly argued that the substantive assessment of mergers has not changed due to the Enterprise Act 2002, although the various guidelines encourage a greater degree of consistency in approach. In particular, it is noteworthy that the OFT began to apply the "substantial lessening of competition" criterion in assessing mergers prior to the entry into force of the Enterprise Act 2002. In addition, the Commission and the MMC have focused for many years their assessment of the public interest effects of mergers on the effects on competition. Accordingly, this Chapter makes extensive reference to decisions of the UK competition authorities under the Fair Trading Act 1973. This is a separate issue to the question of whether the OFT's duty to refer applies at the same level as was typically applied in the exercise of discretion by the Secretary of State under the Fair Trading Act 1973 to make merger references, which is considered further in Ch.4. For the purposes of this Chapter, it is sufficient to note that there is a hierarchy of decision making with the Commission being responsible for detailed second stage investigations and the OFT being a first stage investigator.

[12] There were brief documents published by the OFT and MMC, but these could not be described as substantive guidelines.

OFT have now each published *different* guidelines. (Some of the substantive points of difference are discussed below);

(ii)   as at Spring 1994, only two economics research and discussion papers had been commissioned by the OFT and DTI (all of these papers make clear that the opinions expressed in them are those of the authors and not necessarily those of the OFT or the DTI), whereas as at October 2004 there were around 30 such papers; and

(iii)   up to Summer 2000, the Director General's advice on merger references or clearances was not published, except in the minority of cases where undertakings in lieu of reference were accepted. Since that time, the Director General's and OFT's advice has been published in a large number of cases, and since the entry into force of the Enterprise Act the OFT's decisions are always published. (In this regard, it should be noted that s.2 of the Enterprise Act transferred the functions of the Director General to the OFT with effect from April 1, 2003.)

In order to arrive at balanced decisions in merger cases there needs to be a thorough factual investigation based on the identification and evaluation of evidence, so that competing economic theories can be accepted or rejected to the requisite legal standard. This has been a theme of recent judgments by the European Court of First Instance overturning part or all of certain European Commission merger decisions; and can also be identified in the Competition Appeal Tribunal's and Court of Appeal's judgments in *IBA Health Limited v Office of Fair Trading.*[13]

The importance of the OFT's and Competition Commission's guidelines

The focus of this Chapter on the OFT's and Commission's merger assessment guidelines reflects the importance these authorities have ascribed to them. For example, John Vickers, the Chairman of the OFT, has stated that guidelines: 6.003

"... can be seen as the economics bridge between the law and the facts of cases. They say how the authorities will interpret and apply the law, particularly in respect of economic analysis, to case facts ...
        In a world of multiple sovereign jurisdictions there is no guarantee that all will adopt the same approaches. But guidelines help expose similarities

---

[13] *IBA Health Limited v Office of Fair Trading* [2003] CAT 27, [2004] Comp. A.R. 294; *Office of Fair Trading and others v IBA Health Limited* [2004] EWCA Civ. 142, (2004) 101(11) L.S.G. 33; Case T–342/99, *Airtours plc v Commission* [2002] E.C.R. II–2585; Case T–5/02, *Tetra Laval BV v Commission* [2002] E.C.R. II–4381; Case T–310/01, *Schneider Electric SA v Commission* [2002] E.C.R. II–4071. Many of the procedural innovations in UK merger control discussed elsewhere in this book should make a substantial contribution to the robustness of decisions, perhaps particularly by generally emphasising the importance of reliable economic evidence, the OFT providing the parties with an issues letter in advance of issues meetings, the OFT having a "devil's advocate" in case review meetings to take a contrary view, and the Commission publishing draft provisional findings (so the parties to the merger and third parties know the case and key supporting facts for or against the merger).

and differences—*e.g.* concerning approaches to market definition, entry conditions, analysis of co-ordinated and non-co-ordinated effects, and efficiencies—which it is healthy to have exposed ... Guidelines also assist the accountability of the authorities. Do we walk the talk? Without the talk it is hard to say. Guidelines provide the talk, and the language is economics."[14]

Nevertheless, the Commission has emphasised that it will not follow its guidelines slavishly, but will assess the specifics of individual cases according to their circumstances and may depart from its guidelines if appropriate.[15] Although it is important that cases should be judged on their merits, it would nevertheless be prudent for any authority departing from its guidelines to explain why it has done so.

The categorisation of mergers which may lead to a substantial lessening of competition

6.004   Following the approach taken by both the OFT's and Competition Commission's guidelines, mergers which may lead to a substantial lessening of competition may be categorised as either "horizontal", "vertical" or "conglomerate" mergers.[16]

Horizontal mergers are mergers between actual or potential competitors which operate at the same stage of production (such as manufacturing or retailing). Anti-competitive effects in these cases are described in terms of "unilateral effects" (or "non-co-ordinated effects") and "co-ordinated effects". Non-co-ordinated effects arise where a significant competitive constraint is eliminated by the merger, such that the merged entity could unilaterally and profitably increase prices (which may also lead to other firms increasing their prices without any co-ordination), or otherwise behave anti-competitively. Concerns about co-ordinated effects may arise where a merger may increase the likelihood, efficacy or stability of tacit or explicit co-ordination/collusion between all or some of those firms left in the market.

Vertical mergers are mergers between firms involved at different stages of production (for example, mergers between raw material suppliers and manufacturers, or between wholesalers and retailers). One key concern

---

[14] Cited above, para.6.001, n.9. As to the differences between different countries' merger guidelines, these should not be overstated, although various differences between the OFT's, Commission's, European Commission's and Federal Trade Commission/Department of Justice's guidelines are noted where relevant throughout this Chapter. Indeed, it is striking that the UK guidelines are very similar in many respects to the US merger guidelines, suggesting that the UK authorities owe a debt to the authors of the US Horizontal Merger Guidelines. One particular strength of the European Commission's guidelines is their footnote references to cases which illustrate various points. More generally, increasing co-operation between competition authorities should promote convergence in economic assessment (for example, co-operation between the European Commission and the US anti-trust authorities, and between national competition authorities which are part of the European Competition Authorities Network).

[15] Paragraph 1.4 of the Commission's guidelines, cited above, para.6.001, n.1.

[16] See the various sections of the Commission's guidelines which discuss the various categories of mergers (cited above, para.6.001, n.1); and para.3.8 of the OFT's guidelines (cited above, para.6.001, n.1).

with such mergers is the threat of foreclosure, whereby the merged firm may be able to deny competitors access to essential raw materials or to retailers/distributors.

Conglomerate mergers may be defined as mergers between firms active in different markets (excluding horizontal and vertical mergers). Typically these mergers would not be considered to raise appreciable competition concerns unless certain conditions apply, for example, if the merged entity is able to acquire or increase its market power, because it is able to offer common customers a "bundle" of goods or services by virtue of its strong market position across several markets—so called "portfolio power".

Before directly assessing whether any particular category of merger raises substantive issues (and mergers may, of course, fall into more than one category), it will generally be necessary to assess the various competitive constraints which firms face. The next section considers the extent to which firms may be constrained by alternative products and suppliers (*i.e.* market definition), with subsequent sections considering the additional constraints which may be imposed by the threat of entry and expansion by new and small suppliers, the exercise of buyer power, and/or the discipline that may be imposed by suppliers to these firms. The following sections consider the circumstances in which the various categories of merger outlined above may lead to a substantial lessening of competition, with the penultimate section considering the analysis of the possible effects on competition and customers that efficiencies brought about by the merger may have. The final section considers the relevance of the parties' motives, plans and internal documents, and of third parties views. **6.005**

Market definition

An overview of the hypothetical monopolist or SSNIP test

Both the OFT's and Competition Commission's guidelines start their economic analysis with a consideration of the role of market definition, whilst emphasising that the economic importance of market definition should not be overstated. The Commission's guidelines state that "the Commission does not regard market definition as an end in itself, but rather as a framework within which to analyse the effects of a merger on competition. The definition of the relevant market is a useful tool for analysing the competitive constraints faced by the parties to the merger from other firms supplying the market."[17] **6.006**

Both the OFT and Commission define markets by reference to the so called "hypothetical monopolist" or "SSNIP" test. This test takes into account both substitution by customers to alternative products and services ("demand-side substitution") and supplier substitution into supplying the relevant products or services in the area in question ("supply-side substitution").[18]

---

[17] Para.2.2 of the Commission's guidelines, cited above, para.6.001, n.1. The OFT's guidelines make similar points at para.3.11, cited above, para.6.001, n.1.

[18] This test is broadly applied by many competition authorities worldwide, including the European Commission, the US Department of Justice and the US Federal Trade Commission. (See further p.88 of Bishop and Walker, cited above, para.6.001, n.2.)

The test focuses on whether, in the context of the merger in question, a hypothetical monopoly supplier in a particular sector would find it profitable to impose a "small but significant non-transitory increase in price" (hence the abbreviation to "SSNIP test") without this being rendered unprofitable by demand or supply-side substitution. A relevant market comprises a particular sector in which such a price increase by a hypothetical monopolist would be profitable. This application of the SSNIP test may require a consideration of whether distinctions should be drawn between different products or services, whether the product/service market is local, national and/or international in its geographic scope, and whether further segmentation may be appropriate (for example, between supplies which are consumed in-house compared with sales to third parties, or between different customer types if discrimination against certain customers is feasible and profitable).

It is important that the various dimensions of market definition, such as product and geographic market definition, should be determined simultaneously rather than sequentially, in order to avoid the risk of the market being defined too narrowly.[19] For example, suppose that a local monopoly supplier would find it unprofitable to impose a SSNIP due only to the *combined* aggregate substitution that would occur to alternative products and non-local suppliers (as well as customers simply reducing their purchases), with substitution separately to alternative products or non-local suppliers being insufficient. In these circumstances, it would be incorrect to conclude that the local monopolist would be able to increase prices profitably, but such a conclusion might be reached if a separate product market were first to be defined and analysis conducted before the local geographic market is defined. The fact that various possible dimensions of market definition (product, geographic, etc.) are addressed separately below simply reflects that certain specific information is relevant to assessing substitution to alternative products, non-local suppliers and so on, rather than that each aspect of market definition should be assessed in isolation.

6.007 Before considering how supply and demand-side substitutability can be practically assessed, two introductory points on the limitations of market definition as an analytical tool should be noted. First, markets are defined not with a view to deciding whether certain firms' products are "in" or "out" of the market, but whether sufficient sales would, in aggregate, be lost to both close and distant competitors to render a hypothetical price increase unprofitable. This is an issue because there tends to be an (incorrect) implicit assumption that the relative competitive importance of all firms within a market is perfectly captured by their respective market shares, and that no customers would respond to small price increases by switching any sales to firms "outside" the market. However, an inherent problem is that in differentiated goods/services markets, or where firms are differentiated according to their geographical location or other factors, any market share calculation might well be a very imperfect measure of the competitive interaction between firms. Including only close competitors "in" the market may lead to important substitution to other firms being disregarded, whereas including a broader

---

[19] This point is made in "*Achilles uncovered: revisiting the European Commission's 1997 market definition notice*", Camesasca and Van Den Bergh, The Antitrust Bulletin, Spring 2002.

class of firms might be misleading as competition from certain differentiated rivals might be very poorly reflected by their respective market shares.

Secondly, in assessing the market power of firms which have a substantial, but not 100 per cent, share of the relevant market it is entirely possible that a unilateral price increase by such a firm could be rendered unprofitable by the combined impact of switching to alternative products/potential suppliers outside the defined market, *as well as* to competitors within the defined market. The substantive point here is that assessments of the market power of non-monopolists should not ignore substitution to alternative products and suppliers which would, coupled with competition from within the relevant market, act as a binding constraint on the firm(s) in question. For example, the relevant geographic market may be national in its scope (on the basis that a single national supplier could increase prices absent of other constraints), but in assessing the effects of the merger account should be taken of the aggregate impact of competition from other national suppliers in that country and imports.

Defining the relevant product market—demand-side substitutability

The most precise way of assessing whether different products are close   6.008
substitutes for one another from a demand perspective would be, if possible, to measure accurately "own price" and "cross-price elasticities" for the products in question. A firm's own price elasticity of demand measures the impact of small changes in its price for a particular product upon volume sales of that product. "Market own price elasticity" of demand measures the impact of small changes in the price of all supplies in a market upon total volume sales in that market. Cross-price elasticity of demand measures the effect of small changes in the price of one product upon the volume sales of another.[20]

The Competition Commission's guidelines identify a number of different categories of information that can be useful, when available, in the analysis of demand-side substitution.[21] These may be grouped under a number of headings:

---

[20] The own price elasticity of demand for a product is the percentage change in its volume sales divided by the small percentage change in its price that caused the change in sales. For example, if a 2% change in the price of a product led to a 10% reduction in the quantity purchased, own price elasticity of demand would be −5 (−10/2). (It is conventional for the minus sign on own price elasticities to be omitted.) If the elasticity is below 1, then demand is referred to as price inelastic. If elasticity is over 1, demand is price elastic. If it is equal to 1, demand is referred to as being of unitary price elasticity. If price elasticity of demand is below 1, then price increases will (by definition) be profitable since revenue will increase and there should be some cost savings. If price elasticity of demand is above 1, then the profitability of price increases depends on how costs vary as volumes fall (see further paras 6.035–6.036, below). Similarly, cross-price elasticity of demand is the percentage change in sales volume of a product divided by the small percentage change in the price of another product that caused the change in sales of the first product. For example, if a 0.5% change in the price of one product increased the quantity demanded of another by 5%, the cross-price elasticity of demand would be 10 (5/0.05). Cross-price elasticities of demand are positive for substitute products, and negative for complements (*i.e.* an increase in the price of one product will increase the volumes sold of a substitute product, and decrease the volumes sold of a complementary product).

[21] Para.2.16 of the Commission's guidelines, cited above, para.6.001, n.1. This part of the Commission's guidelines focus more on where the information may come from (*e.g.*

(i)   the relative prices, qualities and functions of alternative products. This is based on the assumption that the more "different" products are, the less likely they are to be close substitutes;

---

customers, competitors, board papers, etc.), rather than the nature of the economic evidence, which is the approach adopted in this Chapter.

A further issue which is relevant to demand-side substitution is whether, in response to a small but significant non-transitory price increase, a proportion of customers might be encouraged to re-use durable goods, for example by purchasing second-hand products, recycling such goods, or delaying the replacement of a product by spending more on maintenance. To the extent that a proportion of customers might choose to use second-hand products or re-condition existing products, this will have the result of reducing the sales of a supplier of new products, and therefore represents a further potential competitive constraint. The issue of whether the re-use of so-called "durable" products represents a competitive constraint has been considered in a number of cases. For example, the proposed merger between Sylvan and Locker concerned the supply of drums which were used for the packaging and transportation of cables and wires. One of the issues considered by the Commission was whether used drums should be regarded as being in the same market as new drums. The parties had argued that the re-use of drums should be included in the market definition because every time a drum was re-used, this equated to a lost sale of a new drum by suppliers. However, the Commission rejected this argument for a number of reasons. First, the Commission considered that the inclusion of the re-use of drums in the relevant market would have the effect of overstating the true value of the market. In particular, any attempt to attribute a value to every occasion in which a drum was re-used would, in the Commission's view, ignore the fact that customers who re-used drums a number of times would initially purchase those drums with the expectation that they would be re-usable, with this being reflected in the original purchase price. Second, the Commission did not find any evidence that the price of new drums in the market was being constrained by the availability of second-hand (traded) drums; no significant market existed for second-hand drums or for drum rental. Third, the Commission observed that a number of large customers had expressed an intention to develop further the re-use of drums, but considered that those customers which had developed a drum management system would be expected to maximise the number of times each drum was re-used. Accordingly, it did not appear to the Commission that the increased use of old drums would provide a significant, continuing price constraint on new drums, with customers switching between new and used drums in response to changes in relative costs. (*Sylvan International Limited/Locker Group plc*, Cm. 4883 (November 2000), at paras 4.45 to 4.48).

Similarly, in its 2000 report on the supply of new cars, one of the issues considered by the Commission was whether the supply of new cars was a separate market from the supply of used cars. The Commission concluded that on balance, new cars formed a separate market which was distinct from used cars of all ages (although the Commission considered there was some blurring of the market where pre-registered cars were concerned). In particular, the Commission noted that there existed different price trends for new and used cars, and a lack of evidence of consumers switching to used cars in response to divergences between the prices of new and used cars. Furthermore, suppliers appeared to have little regard for the prices of used cars when setting prices for their new cars. Other factors which pointed to a market consisting only of new cars included an apparent "emotional pull" of owning a brand new car which, for certain people would usually overcome the financial attraction of buying a nearly-new vehicle. There was also evidence that consumers attached weight to a car being new, perhaps due to their greater reliability. (*New Cars: A report on the supply of new motor cars within the UK*, Cm. 4660 (April 2000), at paras 2.71 to 2.81.)

Finally, in considering Duralay's proposed acquisition of Gates, which concerned the supply of carpet underlay, the Commission acknowledged that it was possible that a price increase in underlay would lead to some increase in the re-use of existing underlay. However, whilst the Commission considered that this would act as some form of competitive constraint in the underlay market, it did not go as far as concluding that the re-use of carpet underlay ought to be included in the same market as new underlay. (*Duralay International Holdings Limited/Gates Consumer and Industrial*, Cm. 5289 (November 2001), at para.2.77.)

(ii) the costs customers incur in switching products. Such switching costs reduce the willingness of customers to switch suppliers, but do not directly reveal how consumers respond to price increases;

(iii) information on how consumers respond to price increases; and

(iv) historical evidence on the variation in the prices of alternative products, or changes in the prices of the same product across different areas, and the impact of this variation on sales.

The relative prices, qualities and functions of alternative products

Whilst information on the relative prices, qualities and functions of various products is readily available and widely referred to by the OFT and Commission, distinguishing one product from another due to some differences in their attributes or prices reveals nothing about whether sales of the product in question are sensitive to the relative prices of alternative products. Similarly, observing that customers purchase a range of different products, or that their attributes or prices can in some way be described in similar terms, does not prove that these different products are close substitutes for one another.

6.009

Bishop and Walker make the following observations about using such information to define markets:

"The process is arbitrary and any market definition can be advanced simply by selectively appealing to product characteristics and intended end use. Too much importance is laid on physical differences since such a focus does not answer the main question—what is the extent of lost sales following a price rise?

Such logic may give the correct answer in some cases; in others it will not. In particular, defining relevant markets on the basis of differences in price will be flawed if price differences reflect (actual or perceived) quality differences. Wherever there are quality differences, consideration of absolute price levels will ignore the possibility of consumers making a trade-off between price and quality. If product A is universally considered to be "twice as good" as product B (perhaps because it lasts twice as long) then both products can co-exist in the market with product A priced exactly twice as high as product B (€10 for product A versus €5 for product B). If the manufacturer of product A tried to raise price to €15, it is clear that customers would switch to product B. If product A is only "twice as good", it is not worth paying three times as much for it . . ."[22]

---

[22] Cited above, para.6.001, n.2 at pp.107–110. The OFT's Research Paper on "*Market definition in UK competition policy*" is similarly critical of reliance on price and product characteristic differences as a means of delineating markets, given that ". . . the test for the relevant market does not require all products to be perfect substitutes or to be completely interchangeable for one another. It does require that there is sufficient switching between differentiated products to ensure the existence of a common pricing constraint. Would the hypothetical sole supplier of a certain sub-group of products lose sufficient sales in the event of a unilateral price rise to make that strategy commercially unattractive?" (OFT RP1, "*Market definition in UK competition policy*" (February 1992), prepared by National Economic Research Associates (NERA), at p.xi, and also see pp.83–87). In particular, the paper is critical of the emphasis placed by the MMC in a number of cases on such information.

Notwithstanding the above, the conclusion to draw is not that comparisons of different products and services are irrelevant (not least because such comparisons can be used to identify quickly the relevant empirical questions which should be asked), but simply that less weight should be attached to such information compared with evidence of substitution in response to price changes. This is in line with the Commission's general practice, although such information has been emphasised in certain cases.

For example, in relation to the acquisition by NV Verenigde Bedrijven Nutricia of certain businesses of Milupa AG, the MMC noted in deciding that manufactured baby meals were a separate market that[23]:

> "The fact that a baby is fed a variety of foods does not necessarily mean that the foods are all part of the same market. In distinguishing between manufactured baby meals and home-prepared meals, we noted that baby meals exhibit a distinctive degree of convenience, particularly for working parents or when the baby is being fed away from home."[24]

6.010   Similarly, in its report on the proposed merger between Johnston Press and Trinity Mirror, the Commission observed that evidence that advertising yields differed materially for local newspapers and "shopper"—type publications supported the view that these types of media were not close substitutes.[25]

However, the existence of significant price differences between differentiated products has not always led the Commission to conclude that such products do not nevertheless impose some kind of competitive constraint upon each other. For example, in its report on the acquisition by National Express Group PLC of Saltire Holdings Ltd, the MMC concluded that the price of coach tickets on the London-Scotland routes was directly constrained by competition from discounted leisure rail fares, despite differences in the price (around 30 per cent) and attributes of these two modes of transport.[26] Similarly, in its report on the proposed merger between P&O Princess Cruises PLC and Royal Caribbean Cruises Limited, although no definitive conclusions were drawn as to the scope of the relevant product market, the Commission emphasised that[27]:

> "If ... the [price] comparison suggests that premium cruises command a higher price than standard cruises, then all that can be inferred is that the quality of service offered differs. It does not necessarily follow that the two types of operators are in separate markets. Indeed, in many markets one finds an array of goods or services of differing quality and, associated with this, different prices."

---

[23] *NV Verenigde Bedrijven Nutricia and enterprises belonging to Milupa AG*, Cm. 3356 (August 1996), para.2.19.

[24] There was no consideration of whether a SSNIP for baby meals would lead to a significant decline in their sales due to switching to home prepared meals. However, it should be noted that market definition was not determinative in this case as the MMC did not consider that the acquisition raised any substantive competition concerns as regards baby meals.

[25] *Johnston Press plc and Trinity Mirror Press plc*, Cm. 5495 (May 2002), at paras 2.28–2.29.

[26] *National Express Group plc and Saltire Holdings Ltd*, Cm. 2468 (February 1994), paras 6.21–6.26.

[27] *P&O Princess Cruises PLC and Royal Caribbean Cruises Limited*, Cm. 5536 (June 2002), para. 5.45.

Moreover, when comparing prices, it may not be appropriate to compare the prices of different products on a one-to-one basis. For example, in the context of its inquiry into the acquisition by Universal Foods Corporation of Pointing Holdings Limited, the Commission wished to compare the prices of natural and synthetic colourings. The Commission noted that different colours had different colouring power and were sold at varying dye contents, and in these circumstances, the Commission considered that it was inappropriate to compare prices of natural and synthetic colours on a price per kilogram basis alone. In order to analyse the true relative cost of synthetic and natural colours the Commission looked at prices standardised on a per unit of dye content basis.[28] The Commission also recognised this point in the context of the proposed acquisition of the stone wool manufacturing business of Owens-Corning Building Products (UK) Limited by Rockwool Limited. In that case, the Commission observed that although glass wool cost around twice as much as stone wool to produce, tonne for tonne, glass wool provided an insulating performance equivalent to stone wool products with about twice the density. Accordingly for a given application, glass wool and stone wool were similar in price.[29]

Switching costs

A further consideration when assessing consumer behaviour is the extent to which there exist obstacles which might deter customers from switching between suppliers. The OFT's Economic Discussion Paper on Switching costs emphasises that such costs can take a variety of forms, ranging from inconvenience to monetary costs.[30] For example, switching costs will be incurred if machinery must be adapted following a change of raw materials, if there is uncertainty as to the suitability of an alternative product (or costs associated with testing whether the product is suitable), if there are training costs associated with learning to use a new product, costs associated with searching for a new supplier, or costs created by the existence of contractual penalties and so on. Where switching costs are significant, this is likely to reduce the willingness of customers to switch from one product to an alternative. This, of course, reveals nothing about actual levels of switching.

6.011

One example of a case in which switching costs were deemed to be significant is the Commission's report on the proposed merger between H+H Celcon Limited and Marley Building Materials Limited. The Commission emphasised that one of the reasons given by third parties as to why there would be a low degree of substitution in response to a 5 per cent price rise was that:

"... some builders said they would face significant one-off switching costs if they sought to substitute aggregate blocks for aircrete blocks. Builders, we were told, would need to alter their working designs which,

---

[28] *Universal Foods Corporation* and *Pointing Holdings Ltd*, Cm. 4544 (December 1999), paras 2.66 to 2.69.

[29] *Rockwool Limited/Owens-Corning Building Products (UK) Limited*, Cm. 4330 (May 1999), para.2.23.

[30] OFT 655, "*Switching Costs*", Economic discussion paper 5, April 2003, prepared by NERA. Chapter 2 of this paper summarises various different types of switching costs and Ch.7 considers the links between switching costs and competition policy.

for major housebuilders, can extend across many types of dwelling construction and a variety of construction sites; added to which are changes in labour costs, additional procurement costs, changes in bills of quantities, health and safety issues, and the need, as appropriate, to obtain technical approvals from professional bodies such as the National House-Building Council (NHBC)."[31]

In this regard, it should be noted that switching costs may well vary between customers, and in particular may be low or zero for new customers. Moreover, suppliers might offer substantial discounts to win new customers due to the stream of income from future sales which would be derived from such customers. Accordingly, the competitive assessment of the merger might need to take account of the possibility of price discrimination between new and existing customers (see further paras 6.121 to 6.122, below). Moreover, if price discrimination between new and existing customers is limited, smaller competitors seeking to grow their market share might be particularly important in such markets. This is because established suppliers with larger installed bases of customers who are captive to some degree to their existing supplier by virtue of the costs they would incur in switching supplier, may not compete vigorously for new customers if they are compelled to apply the lower prices offered across their entire installed base of customers who are not price sensitive.

Switching costs may lead to customers being reluctant to switch between products if a price increase for one product is not expected to be permanent. Customers may also respond to such switching costs by procuring supplies under long-term contracts which specify how prices are calculated, with such contracts being entered into when customers' investments (which commit them to one product rather than another) are initially made or come up for renewal. Longer contracts may also provide sufficient sales to permit a new supplier to compensate the customer for the switching costs they may incur. Such market characteristics may mean that a specific issue which needs to be explored is the competition which exists when long term contracts come up for renewal, with market shares based on annual sales from on-going contracts not necessarily being a good measure of this periodic competitive process (see further paras 6.091 to 6.092).

Consumer behaviour

Econometric estimates of price elasticities

6.012   Although econometric models have been used to estimate price elasticities of demand, econometric studies may not be sufficiently robust in their analysis, and are often inconclusive. They may also be unreliable due to data problems. As well as the need to obtain accurate price and quantity data as well as data on other variables which affect supply and demand conditions, a large number of "observations" (or pieces of data) are often required. Furthermore, some of the information required will be qualitative (such as changes in the relative quality of products since quality improve-

---

[31] *H+H Celcon Limited/Marley Building Materials Limited*, Cm. 5540 (June 2002), para.2.53.

ments will lead to consumer switching between products), and this may be very difficult to assess, with consequent adverse effects on the reliability of the study. There are also a number of technical econometric difficulties which may arise.[32] The difficulty of using econometrics does not mean that such approaches should not be used, but that such studies should be carried out carefully, be subject to critical review and those seeking to rely on such studies should be aware of their limitations.[33] In this regard, the Commission's guidelines state the following:

"Any econometric estimates submitted to the Commission should be supplemented by the full data set used, as well as a detailed description of each of the steps taken in the course of the estimation. This will help the Commission to understand fully the methodology used and allow it to replicate and assess the results."[34]

Regulators worldwide are increasingly referring to econometrics to define markets where suitable data is available. In the UK, elasticity estimates have tended not to be available in the vast majority of cases, but there are some exceptions. For example, in its report on the acquisition by National Express Group PLC of Midland Main Line Limited, the MMC commissioned a study which suggested that a 10 per cent price increase in rail fares would lead to a 3 per cent increase in demand for coach travel, whilst a 10 per cent increase in coach fares would lead to a 1.4 per cent increase in rail demand. The MMC also referred to a variety of other econometric studies on this issue[35]. Similarly, in its report on the merger involving Stagecoach Holdings plc and SB Holdings Limited, the MMC emphasised that studies had found that the market own price elasticity of demand for bus travel was price inelastic, with the consequence that a dominant operator could increase fares profitably since this would (by definition—see n.20, cited at para.6.008) increase revenue and potentially lead to some cost savings:

"A key question is the extent to which a dominant operator might be able to raise fares. This will depend on consumer sensitivity to price changes which is influenced by fundamental demand characteristics (such as journey purpose) and availability of substitutes (such as other modes of transport). In the case of the market for local bus services there is a substantial body of research which suggests that demand for bus services is relatively insensitive to fare changes. Thus if fares are increased (within bounds), while some traffic will be lost as some

---

[32] See Chs 9 and 10 of Bishop and Walker, cited above, para.6.001, n.2, which provide a useful introduction to econometrics and estimating elasticities. See also Chs 9, 14 and 15 of "*Quantitative techniques in competition analysis*", October 1999, prepared for the OFT by LECG, OFT Research Paper 17, OFT 266.

[33] It is with good reason that there are articles on econometrics with titles such as the article by Leamer "*Let's Take the Con Out of Econometrics*", American Economic Review (1983) 73, 31–43, 1983.

[34] Cited above, para.6.001, n.1, at para.2.17.

[35] *National Express Group PLC* and *Midland Main Line Limited*, Cm. 3495 (December 1996), paras 4.55–4.68.

customers switch to other modes or cease travelling, the net effect on revenue will be positive."[36]

Customer surveys[37]

6.013   The Competition Commission has considered evidence from sample surveys in a number of its recent merger inquiries,[38] and the Commission's guidelines emphasise the role of surveys as a method of obtaining economic evidence.[39] Sample surveys are generally recognised as an efficient and economical method of obtaining robust data from large populations.[40] In markets with a large number of customers (many hundreds or even thousands in some cases), surveys may be the only sensible way of obtaining a balanced and objective picture of customers' views. The alternative for the Commission would be to rely solely on the views of the minority of customers who make their views known. Experience suggests that such customers' views are often not representative of the whole set of customers

---

[36] *Stagecoach Holdings plc* and *SB Holdings Limited*, Cm. 2845 (April 1995), at para.4.61. Similarly, in the context of the Commission's report on the proposed acquisition by FirstGroup plc of the Scottish Passenger Rail Franchise, the Commission noted that, unlike in most of its inquiries, it had been able to draw on an extensive and complex array of evidence on the price elasticity of demand for different modes of transport (although they might differ between local areas) (*FirstGroup plc* and *Scottish Passenger Rail Franchise*, (June 2004), at para.4.2.)

[37] This brief section on surveys is introductory in nature—further general information on survey research can be found in textbooks such as, for example, Rea & Parker, *Designing and Conducting Survey Research*, (2nd ed., Jossey-Bass, 1997); Doyle, "Introduction to Survey Methodology and Design", in Handbook for IQP Advisors and Students (Woods, Worcester Polytechnic Institute) Ch.10; and in Ch.12 of the OFT Research Paper on "*Quantitative techniques in competition analysis*", cited above, para.6.012, n.32. Other practical points are made in various short publications of the American Statistical Association under its *What is a survey?* series (*www.amstat.org*) and, specifically in the context of US court cases, the US Federal Judicial Center (the education and research agency for the US Federal courts) has produced a practical "*Reference Manual on Scientific Evidence*" (2nd edn., 2000) for judges which includes a Chapter on survey research and its use as evidence in the US courts (available at *www.fjc.gov*).

[38] The Competition Commission has commissioned sample surveys in a number of recent merger inquiries including: *Eastman Kodak Company/ColourCare Limited*, Cm. 5339 (December 2001); *Johnston Press plc/Trinity Mirror plc*, Cm. 5495 (May 2002); *Scottish Radio Holdings plc and GWR Group plc/Galaxy Radio Wales and the West Limited*, Cm. 5811 (May 2003); *Newsquest (London) Limited* and *Independent News and Media (INM)*, Cm. 5951 (October 2003); *March UK Ltd and the home shopping and home delivery business of GUS plc*, Cm. 6102 (December 2003); and *Stena AB/The Peninsular and Oriental Steam Navigation Company* (February 2004). Reflecting its role as a first stage regulator, the OFT does not typically commission surveys in merger cases.

[39] The Commission guidance document: "*General Advice and Information*", June 2003, states that in some inquiries "surveys (for example, of consumers) are commissioned to provide evidence about a particular market" (para.6.13(d)). The Commission's guidelines expand on the above statement: "In merger cases, information may be limited and market surveys of various kinds are often used to provide information on the responsiveness of customers to price changes, sometimes, formally as estimates of demand elasticities. Surveys usually take the form of questionnaires to customers, competitors and interested and informed third parties" (cited above, para.6.001, n.1 at para.2.18). In some cases the Commission has relied particularly heavily on its interpretation of survey results in reaching its conclusions, for example, *Scottish Radio Holdings and GWR/Galaxy* and *Stena/P&O*, cited above, para.6.013, n.38.

[40] Where surveying each member of the population would be too costly or time-consuming to be worthwhile.

(as they may be biased towards those complaining about the merger, larger customers with greater administrative/legal resources, or those with specific interests such as disputes with one of the merging parties or those seeking to secure a concession to improve their positions).

In general terms, quantitative survey evidence can assist the Commission and OFT in assessing market definition (including customer sensitivity to price increases) and other matters such as the identification of firms which are close competitors and the factors which influence customers' choice of product and supplier.[41]

As with any piece of research, a survey needs to be very carefully planned, with specific objectives clearly in mind. Survey objectives should state clearly the aims of the survey in terms of the kinds of data sought, the relevance of that data to the issues under investigation and the use to which that data will be put. One of the clearest statements of the Commission's survey objectives was in relation to its March/GUS inquiry.[42] Publishing clear and measurable survey objectives has a number of beneficial effects on the practical use of the survey results. In particular, it can assist in ensuring that the quality of the data collected is optimal (or is in the most useful format) for determining the issues in the inquiry. Perhaps more importantly, it also reduces the possibility of interpretive bias at the analysis stage (either in the choice of which of the many survey results are analysed in detail, or in the types of analysis applied to those results). The more precisely the survey objectives can be identified, the stronger these positive effects are likely to be.

Once the survey objectives have been set, the practical issues can be divided under three broad headings: (a) the mode of data collection; (b) the choice of survey participants; and (c) the questions asked. Finally, there is the issue of how the results should be analysed in the light of how these practical issues have been resolved.

The collection of data may be carried out: in person, face to face; by telephone interviews; by postal questionnaires; or by internet questionnaires. Each of these different modes of data collection has its own potential positive and negative factors (*e.g.* in terms of costs, time taken and quality of data obtained) which will need to be considered in deciding which mode is the most appropriate. The Commission has often used telephone surveying to conduct its sample surveys.[43] However, face-to-face interviews may provide higher quality responses.[44] An issue with postal questionnaires is

6.014

---

[41] Qualitative surveys are also sometimes conducted. However, these cannot generally be used for drawing any quantitative conclusions (due to their sample size and the format of responses) since their results only represent the views of respondents and are unlikely to present a robust picture of the views of the entire population of customers. This point has been accepted by the Commission, see, *e.g. Stena/P&O*, App.H, para.16, cited above, para.6.013, n.38.

[42] *March/GUS*, App.4.1, para.1, cited above, para.6.013, n.38. Similarly, a relatively clear objective was specified in *Kodak/ColourCare*, App.5.1, para.1.

[43] Telephone surveys were conducted in *Johnston/Trinity*, *Vibe/Galaxy* and *Stena/P&O*; face-to-face interviews were the basis of the results in *Kodak/Colourcare* and *March/GUS* (although these were part of wider household surveys); and a postal questionnaire was used in *Newsquest/INM* (cited above, para.6.013, n.38).

[44] For example, one recent study has shown that the quality of responses obtained from telephone surveys is generally worse than that obtained in face to face interviews (Holbrook, Green & Krosnick, "*Telephone vs. Face-to-face Interviewing of National Probability Samples With Long Questionnaires: Comparisons of Respondent Satisficing and Social Desirability Response Bias*", Public Opinion Quarterly, 67, 79–125, 2003.

that these tend to achieve lower response rates[45] than face-to-face or tele-phone surveys, which can lead to very small sample sizes and increase the chances of the survey being biased due to disproportionately high non-response rates from particular groups within the population (referred to as "non-response bias"). For example, in *Newsquest/ INM*, the Commission sent a postal questionnaire to a total of 903 newspaper advertisers, but received only 129 responses.[46]

A further issue that must be considered is the means of selecting those sampled. Probability sampling is strongly recommended. This involves the survey sample being selected by a random mechanism from the whole popu-lation.[47] Unless the sample surveyed is randomly selected, the results cannot robustly be inferred to represent those of the whole population. Indeed, according to the American Statistical Association: "virtually all surveys that are taken seriously by social scientists and policy makers use some form of probability sampling. . . . One way to ruin an otherwise well-conceived survey is to use a convenience sample rather than one which is based on a probability design".[48]

---

[45] *i.e.* the proportion of those surveyed which answer the questionnaire.

[46] *Newsquest/INM*, App.5.3, para.6, cited above, para.6.013, n.38. The possibility of "non-response bias" is an important consideration in the analysis of survey results where the numbers of those not responding are significant. That is, it is necessary to consider whether the non-response was entirely random, or whether those not responding to a question (or the survey) are doing so for a particular reason which is linked to the question (or the purpose of the survey). If non-response is linked to the question or the purpose of the survey, then it is necessary to consider whether, if non-respondents had replied, a significant number of them would have responded to the question (or survey) in a particular way which would have changed the observed results. This is an important area of survey research which has generated a substantial amount of academic literature.

One question which could be posed is whether a potentially biased sample of the popu-lation "is better than nothing" for estimating the views of the population. Selzer has responded very negatively to such arguments in the context of surveys carried out and reported by certain US newspapers to advertisers as to the make-up of their readerships, which did not take any effort to ensure that the sample responding was an unbiased sample. The argument that was advanced in favour of such surveys was that any information which they could provide to newspaper advertisers about their readerships was better than nothing. Seltzer compared such a position to "asking if it was okay to gift-wrap a cockroach and give it to their advertisers, because at least it was a gift. And wasn't that better than nothing?" Selzer's concern was that "there is no way to calculate margin of error on unsci-entific samples. The principle does not apply. There are no confidence levels to decide upon, and no way to estimate how far from the attitudes of the target population the findings might vary. Because it isn't science; therefore no scientific principles apply . . . In short, the findings [of such surveys] may not be a true representation of the population to which the respondents belong" (Selzer, "*When Something isn't better than Nothing*" (2001), NAA Research Federation Newsletter, January 2001).

[47] Technically, at the very least, each person who may potentially be surveyed must have a known and non-zero probability of being selected to be part of the survey. See, *e.g.* Campanelli, notes from Centre for Applied Social Surveys course on "*Survey Sampling*" May 2004-and further, *inter alia*, Kish, "*Survey Sampling*" (Wiley-Interscience, 1995).

[48] Ferber, Sheatsley, Turner and Waksberg, "*What is a survey?*" (1980) American Statistical Association. In this regard, it is assumed that the Commission's aim in each case has been to conduct probability sampling based surveys. This appears to have been the stated inten-tion in *Kodak/ColourCare* (App.5.1, para.3), *Newsquest/INM* (App.5.3, para.5), *March/GUS* (App.4.1, para.2), and *Stena/P&O* (App. H, para.5) (cited above, para.6.013, n.38). However, it is unlikely that the survey conducted in the context of the *Johnston Press/Trinity Mirror* inquiry could be regarded as employing random sampling because only a selected group of customers (the highest spending) were surveyed (App. 5.4, paras 13 to 19, cited above, para.6.013, n.38).

The next issue is how many of the target audience should be surveyed (taking into consideration the possibility of some of those selected to be surveyed not responding) with a view to obtaining results that may be robustly generalised to the population. Specifically, for each of the various questions considered, the sample size needs to be large enough for the researcher to be confident that the likely result for the population is within a reasonably narrow range of that reported by the sample survey.[49] To give a trivial example, pulling, say, four black cards and one red card from a pack of playing cards would clearly not be a robust way of proving that 80 per cent of the playing cards were black. Accordingly, in general terms, the sample size needs to be sufficiently large if the researcher wishes to be confident that it is likely to be representative of the population. As to the range of likely accuracy, a researcher might wish to be 95 per cent confident[50] (this is referred to as a "confidence level") that the results of a sample survey are within ±5 percentage points of the likely population result (this is referred to as the "confidence interval").[51] Generally speaking, at a given confidence level and assuming a relatively small (in statistical terms) population,[52] the larger the sample size, the narrower the confidence interval within which the Commission can be confident that the population result would be likely to be.[53]

---

[49] This is clearly somewhat of a simplification for a subject that has generated a huge amount of academic literature. An introduction can be found, for example, in: Rea & Parker, *"Designing and Conducting Survey Research"* (2nd ed., Jossey-Bass, 1997).

[50] At a 95 *per* cent confidence level, the researcher may be confident that 19 times out of 20 the population result would be likely to fall within a specified confidence interval around the observed sample survey result.

[51] These are the confidence levels and confidence intervals generally aimed at in conducting research in the social sciences.

[52] As may often be the case in Commission merger inquiries.

[53] One expression of the standard formula for calculating the required sample size (corrected for population size) is:

$$n = \frac{N.p(1-p)}{(N-1)\left(\frac{MofE}{C}\right)^2 + p(1-p)}$$

where:

n—represents the required sample size;

p—represents the proportion of respondents giving a relevant response (a proportion of 50% has been chosen in the example given below, allowing for an equal split of responses within the sample—if this figure was known to be likely to be lower (for example, on the basis of previous research) then it might be legitimate to allow for a less balanced divergence of responses, which would translate into a lower required sample size);

N—represents the total population;

MofE—represents the allowable Margin of Error (that is, the acceptable confidence interval); and

C—represents the confidence level required and is the value of the distribution corresponding to that confidence level (*e.g.* with a large sample size, for a 95% confidence level the corresponding value of the t distribution is 1.96).

(See, *e.g.* Campanelli, notes from Centre for Applied Social Surveys course on *"Survey Sampling"* May 2004—and further, *inter alia*, Cochran, *"Sampling Techniques"*, (3rd edn., John Wiley & Sons, 1977). The basic formula generally used for calculating necessary sample sizes does not correct for population size. In the context of Commission merger inquiries where population sizes may be small (in statistical terms), such a correction may be necessary.)

It should be noted that the relationship between population size and sample size is not simply one of proportionality. In fact, the smaller the population size, the greater the

6.015   Returning to the *Newsquest/INM* survey mentioned above, the Commission received 129 responses to its postal questionnaire and used results from these to represent a total population of advertisers in excess of 15,750.[54] Using the standard formula set out in footnote 53, this total number of customers would have required a sample size of around 375 for robust and generalisable results (with a confidence interval of +/–5 percentage points at a 95 per cent confidence level).[55]

Where a range of different groups are identifiable within a population (*e.g.* large versus small customers, and customers with specific characteristics) and one of the aims of the survey is to compare the results between these groups, it is important that each group is properly represented in those surveyed by, for example, the use of stratified sampling. This involves ensuring that sufficient, randomly selected, numbers of each group are combined within the total sample for each group to be adequately represented at each level of analysis. In this regard, it should be emphasised that the relationship between population size and required sample size is not directly proportionate (see n.53, cited above at para.6.015). Accordingly, as population size decreases, it is necessary to use proportionately larger sample sizes of the remaining population to obtain equally reliable results. However, where initial sample sizes are small this may not be possible and the robustness and general applicability of the results will deteriorate with each further customer segmentation.[56]

The confidence interval and confidence level define the scope of the statistical uncertainty accompanying any survey results. They are crucial information to anyone analysing sample survey results, since they define the precision with which it may be possible to generalise the results to the population. Accordingly, the general advice given to all publishers of survey results is to include confidence levels and confidence intervals along with all relevant results, as these are the key statistics that are relevant to assessing whether the sample survey results may be robustly generalised.[57]

In appropriate circumstances, it is possible to use statistical significance testing procedures to test whether the answer to a question given by one group of respondents is "statistically significantly" different from the

---

proportion of the population are required to be included in the sample to achieve the same likely levels of statistical robustness. For example, for a population size of 1000, it would be necessary (applying the above formula and allowing for a proportion of 50% to respond in a particular way) to have a sample in excess of 278 in order to achieve results with a confidence interval of ±5 percentage points at a confidence level of 95%. However, for a population size of 100, the necessary sample size required to achieve equally reliable results would be 80.

[54] Para.5 of App.5.3 indicates that the total advertiser lists of both parties added up to about 31,500, cited above, para.6.013, n.38. However, some customers were customers of both parties and, accordingly, the list contained a number of duplicate entries.

[55] Assuming that extreme views were not anticipated in response to each question (*i.e.* a high proportion of those surveyed giving one answer).

[56] At various points in a number of other Commission inquiries the parties have raised issues regarding the sample sizes relied on by the Commission. See, for example: *Scottish Radio Holdings* and *GWR/Galaxy*, para.2.47 and App.6.2, paras 40 to 44; and *Stena/P&O*, App.H, paras 15 and 16 (cited above, para.6.014, n.38).

[57] The Commission has not generally published confidence levels or confidence intervals alongside the results of its surveys.

answer given by another group of respondents.[58] However, the advantage in the use of confidence intervals and confidence levels for comparing results is that "statistically" significant differences between answers do not necessarily represent practically significant differences and vice versa.[59] For example, it might be possible to conclude that one group of customers' response to a specific question is statistically significantly different from another-but if the actual difference were only to be, say, one percentage point different then (depending on the context of the question) the statistical difference might not be of any practical significance.

The questions asked in the survey must be very carefully put together and it is very important to ensure that they are presented in such a way as to be simple, unambiguous and free from bias. Simple questions require less cognitive effort to answer and so better results may be expected to be obtained from them. If questions are imprecise, this introduces a real risk that different respondents are responding to different personal interpretations of the questions and means that their responses may not be comparable. Clarity also requires the avoidance of specific terminology that may mean one thing to some respondents and a different thing to others. An example of this problem arose in the *Johnston Press/Trinity Mirror* survey that asked about differences between advertisers' expenditure on "classified advertising" and "display advertising". However, the distinction between the two was not clear to respondents and the Commission accepted this, stating that, accordingly, it would not use the answers to the relevant question in drawing any conclusions.[60]

In addition, even if a question is clear and unambiguous, the question phrasing may influence the answers given. For example, psychological research shows that respondents are unwilling to be confrontational in survey situations.[61] Accordingly, questions should avoid formulations such as "do you agree or disagree that . . .", because they can create a bias due to acquiescence (that is, the tendency to endorse an assertion made in a question).[62]

---

[58] This has been done by the Commission in a number of cases, *e.g. Scottish Radio Holdings and GWR/Galaxy*, Tables 5.27 and 5.27 (and accompanying text); *Stena/P&O*, App.H, paras 15 to 27; *Johnston Press/Trinity Mirror*, App.5.4, para.35; and *Newsquest/INM*, App.5.3, paras 22 to 49. In general, the academic debate on the usefulness of statistical significance tests, particularly in social science research, has been long and heated. See, *e.g.* Coe, *"The Significance of Significance"* (1998). See also Johnson, *"The Insignificance of Statistical Significance Testing"* (1999), Journal of Wildlife Management 63(3): 763-772, who reports that the American Psychological Association was, at one stage, seriously debating a ban on presenting the results of significance tests in its scientific journals, and the proposal was only rejected because of its appearance of censorship, not lack of merit. Another useful introduction to the problems in the use of statistical significance testing is provided in Thompson, *"The Concept of Statistical Significance Testing"* (1994), Practical Assessment, Research & Evaluation, 4(5).

[59] See, *e.g.* The Economist, "Signifying nothing?—Too many economists misuse statistics" (2004) Economics Focus, January 31, 2004, p.71.

[60] *Johnston Press/Trinity Mirror*, App.5.4, para.92, cited above, para.6.013, n.38.

[61] See, for example, Krosnick, *"Survey Research"* (1999), Annual Review of Psychology.

[62] This particular formulation is in eight of the twelve questions in the survey conducted in *Newsquest/INM* inquiry, cited above, para.6.013, n.38. Krosnick also includes "Yes/No" and "True/False" type questions in the same category: Krosnick, *"Survey Research"* (1999), Annual Review of Psychology.

6.016   Similarly, the formatting of response options can affect the results of a survey question. The basic response option choice is between open and closed questions. In quantitative surveys, however, closed questions are generally used for all key questions since it makes the categorisation and analysis of responses more manageable.[63] However, there is a wide range of answer formats for closed questions including: agree/disagree scales, rating scales (*e.g.* 1 to 5) and lists of types of behavioural responses from which one or more options can be picked.[64] In addition, there is the issue of whether a "don't know" option should be explicitly offered.[65] Finally, there is the question of whether the responses offered include the complete range of reasonable responses in a balanced way.[66]

In discussing the Commission's approach to survey questions, it is instructive to consider the variety of formulations of the survey questions it has used to obtain data for the application of the SSNIP test. For example, in *Kodak/ColourCare* the key question asked was:

"If the prices of the next day, 3 day and 6 day services were to increase by 76 pence, but the prices of same day and mail order remained the same, which would you choose?"[67]

There was no mention of the permanence of the price increase, the customer was not given the option of simply reducing the number of films processed per year, and the increase of 76 pence was a different proportionate increase for each of next day, 3 day and 6 day processing services.[68] Furthermore, there was an untested implicit assumption that next day, 3 day and 6 day services were in the same market.

---

[63] The responses to open questions generally require some form of classification before they can be quantitatively analysed (unless simply numerical). This may involve a considerable amount of work and may introduce the possibility of some form of analytical bias.

[64] In relation to such lists, the issue also arises of the order in which the responses should be offered. Research indicates that response order biases may be important. Where the options are presented visually (*e.g.* in a postal questionnaire) primacy effects are often observed (*i.e.* there is a tendency to pick from the first options), whereas, where the options are presented orally (*e.g.* by telephone) recency effects are often observed (*i.e.* there is a tendency to pick from the later options offered). See, for example, Krosnick, "*Survey Research*" (1999), Annual Review of Psychology.

[65] Including a "don't know" option may give a respondent who knows the answer to a question an easy way out of answering. However, excluding a "don't know" option may encourage a respondent who does not know the answer to the question to guess between the options he is presented with. Which type of error to avoid is something that will need to be decided in each case.

[66] An example of the kinds of problems this can cause, which is referred to by Creative Research Systems on their website (*www.surveysystem.com*), arises in relation to a number of recent US polls concerning the death penalty. In polls asking simply whether respondents support the death penalty between 70 and 75 per cent are generally in favour. However, polls that offer a choice between the death penalty and life in prison without parole only show support for the death penalty at between approximately 50 to 60 per cent. Moreover, when a third option of life in prison, without the possibility of parole, with inmates working in prison to pay restitution to their victims' families, is included, support for the death penalty has been recorded as low as 30 per cent.

[67] *Kodak/ColourCare*, App.5.1, Q.6, cited above, para.6.013, n.38.

[68] In any event, prices for each of the services were assumed at certain aggregate levels, and the actual prices paid by each customer were not considered.

In *Johnston Press/Trinity Mirror*, the question asked was:

"Finally, if all the local weekly papers in the area where you advertise were to put up their advertising rates by 10 per cent, what would you do?"[69]

Again, there was no mention of the duration of the price increase, or whether the price increase should have been imagined to be to all customers or to that individual customer alone. Furthermore, there was no reference to the price of other products remaining the same.   **6.017**

The *Scottish Radio Holdings and GWR/Galaxy* survey asked whether customers would keep to "exactly the same pattern of advertising" in response to a 5 per cent price increase.[70] Unfortunately, this question could have been interpreted by many respondents as maintaining the same expenditure on radio advertising (and buying fewer or cheaper advertising slots) rather than increasing expenditure on radio advertising (and keeping exactly the same advertising slots).[71]

In *Newsquest/INM*, the two relevant questions asked were:

"Do you agree or disagree that if there was an increase in the advertising rates following the proposed merger, you would respond by reducing your spend with the titles concerned?

Do you agree or disagree that if there was an increase in the advertising rates following the proposed merger, you would respond by switching your spend with the titles to other localities or other media?"[72]

Not only do these questions have the same failings as the other examples above, but they also do not even specify the level of price increase that the customer should be imagining. Furthermore, the questions also appear to suffer from question phrasing bias as described above at para.6.015.

These kinds of question relating to customers' willingness to pay are   **6.018**
clearly of significant importance to the Commission's analysis in any merger inquiry. In particular, in its application of the SSNIP test. One relevant academic study on the effect of question formulation as regards questions relating to customers' willingness to pay, conducted by Helmstetter & Murphy,[73] asked consumers about their willingness to pay extra for petrol

---

[69] *Johnston Press/Trinity Mirror*, App.5.4, Q36, cited above, para.6.013, n.38.
[70] *Scottish Radio Holdings and GWR/Galaxy*, App.5.1, para.7 (App.C), Question 33a, cited above, para.6.013, n.38.
[71] See para.2.7 of App.6.1, cited above, para.6.013, n.38. Although it should be noted that the Competition Commission stated that the survey in this case was not designed to allow it to conduct a formal SSNIP test, but merely to gather a "wide range of evidence" on price sensitivity of local radio advertising, see *Scottish Radio Holdings and GWR/Galaxy*, para.2.40.
[72] *Newsquest/INM*, App.5.3, Table 1, cited above, para.6.013, n.38.
[73] Helmstetter and Murphy, "*How much extra would you be willing to pay for gasoline? Depends on how you ask*" (2002), Survey Research Newsletter, Volume 33, No.3. This study is not without its problems, for example: the wording of the first part of the question in relation to price rises—"if you knew it would significantly improve the natural environment . . ."—is far from clear and could have meant different things to different respondents; the graduation of the prices in the closed-ended options appears arbitrary (and may cause bias) and although it claims that "the results show that . . . question format did not play a role in respondents' willingness to pay extra at the pump . . ." this is not shown, since

to improve the environment. This study investigated two different question response formats. First, they asked two groups of respondents the same initial "yes/no" question: "If you knew it would significantly improve the natural environment, would you be willing to pay extra for gasoline?"[74] Secondly, they asked one group of those who responded "yes" to the first question the open question: "How much extra would you be willing to pay per gallon of gasoline?" Those who responded "yes" to the first question from the other group were then asked the closed series of questions: "Would you be willing to pay an extra 20 cents (per gallon of gas)? Would you be willing to pay an extra 50 cents (per gallon of gas)? Would you be willing to pay an extra dollar (per gallon of gas)?"[75] Between the two groups the proportions responding "yes" to the first question were almost identical (60 per cent and 61 per cent). However, the amount that consumers said they would be willing to pay differed substantially between the two types of question. The mean and median responses of those responding to the open question were $0.23 and $0.10 respectively, whereas, the same figures for those responding to the series of closed questions were $0.13 and $0.05 respectively.[76] In the context of a Commission merger inquiry such differences between the mean prices (approximately 15 per cent and 8 per cent respectively of total average price per gallon) that customers state that they would be willing to pay could clearly be significant. In one case, the average customer would not switch in response to a 10 per cent price increase, in the other case the same customer would switch. This is just one example of how the phrasing of questions relating to customers' willingness to pay can be affected by seemingly neutral phrasing. This is something to which the Commission needs to be particularly sensitive, given the importance of this type of question.

An alternative approach to asking consumers how they would respond to hypothetical price increases is to use stated preference surveys. In stated preference surveys customers are asked how much of a good or service they would buy at various prices/qualities, and different customers can be asked

---

respondents were asked the same basic "yes/no" question about willingness to pay extra if it would significantly improve the natural environment. The level of positive response may also be overstated by a degree of social desirability bias (see, for example, Krosnick, "*Survey Research*" (1999) Annual Review of Psychology). However, the study does clearly demonstrate the potential effects of different question formats on customers' statements about their willingness to pay. A similar study was carried out by Green, Jakowitz, Kahneman and McFadden (1998), in relation to willingness to pay for action to be taken to protect sea birds from oil spills and is reported in summary in McFadden, "*Economic Choices*" (2000) Nobel Lecture.

[74] A "don't know" response was allowed, but accounted for only 2 per cent of each group.

[75] Average US Gasoline prices at the pump (including taxes) in July to September 2001 (when the study was conducted) were approximately $1.56 per gallon (based on the individual average monthly figures, from the US Government's Energy Information Administration website (*www.eia.doe.gov*), for July, August and September respectively of $1.565, $1.509 and $1.609).

[76] The "mean" being the sum of all the price increases customers would be willing to accept divided by the total number of customers (commonly referred to as the "average"). The "median" being the price increase at which half of customers would be willing to accept a lower price increase and half a higher price increase. The fact that the means are higher than the medians in both groups in this study shows that those who would be willing to pay more than the median figure, would be willing to pay significantly more than the median, whereas, those who would not be willing to pay the median figure were notably closer to it.

about their purchase decisions at different sets of prices. A model of consumer demand is then obtained by comparing how sales of the various products would vary at the different prices. An example of this approach can be seen in the survey carried out for Kodak in the context of the *Kodak/ColourCare* inquiry.[77] Whilst this approach is arguably superior to asking customers questions about how they might respond to hypothetical price increases, these techniques do not avoid many of the same problems as outlined above, and are not without their own difficulties.[78]

A further difficulty, perhaps particularly where responses to hypothetical situations are requested (*e.g.* future price increases), is that various other psychological factors may lead to respondents failing to provide optimal answers. In other words, the survey responses may accurately represent what the respondents said that they would do if faced with the relevant hypothetical situation, but, this is not always what respondents would actually do in such a situation,[79] particularly if a certain answer were deemed to be the appropriate or correct answer[80] or if the respondents have only given limited thought to their responses to the question.[81]

---

[77] See *Kodak/ColourCare*, App.5.2, cited above, para.6.013, n.38.

[78] This approach is advocated, for example, by Dubow, "*Understanding Consumers: The value of stated preferences in antitrust proceedings*", [2003] E.C.L.R. 141. A helpful introduction to the application of these techniques is contained in "*Stated Preference Methods in Transport Research*" (1988), Journal of Transport Economics and Policy, Vol.22(1). See also, on the subject of question format and consumer willingness to pay, Loomis, Brown, Thompson Lucero and Peterson, "*Evaluating the Validity of the Dichotomous Choice Question Format in Contingent Valuation*" (1997), Environmental and Resource Economics, p.109.

[79] See, for example, paras 12.8 to 12.9 the OFT Research Paper on "*Quantitative techniques in competition analysis*", cited above, para.6.012, n.32.

[80] The classic example of this is "LaPierre's study". In 1934 LaPierre (a Caucasian) travelled across North America with a young Asian couple. At the time there was widespread anti-Asian sentiment and there were no anti-discrimination laws. They visited around 200 hotels, motels and restaurants along the way. Only one refused to admit the Asian couple. After the journey, a letter was sent to each of the establishments asking if they would refuse to admit Asians. Around 90% of the responses received said that they would refuse to admit Asians (see further, *e.g.* R. Atkinson, *et al.*, "*Introduction to Psychology*" (12th ed., Harcourt College, 1996)). This kind of "virtuous" response (in the widest possible sense of responding in a way that might be expected by the majority of people), contrary to *actual* behaviour, is clearly something that people conducting surveys need to be particularly wary of. There are also wider issues of respondents failing to properly apply their minds to answering questions—see further, para.6.019, n.91 below. See also, for an overview of these issues in an economics context, McFadden, "*Economic Choices*" (2000) Nobel Lecture, which discusses a number of psychological factors that affect human decision-making.

[81] All of the technical survey design issues mentioned above should be seen against the substantial problem of getting respondents to make the effort to provide optimal answers to difficult questions. This issue goes further than simple unwillingness to disclose known information—for example, if it is regarded as confidential business information. It relates to a respondent's unwillingness to expend the necessary cognitive effort to understand the question, bring the relevant information that they have to mind, make a judgement based on that information and then translate that judgement into a response to a question by, for closed-ended questions, selecting one or more of the responses on offer. Psychological research has shown that each of these four steps can be complicated and require significant effort. The effect of the repeated effort required to answer questions can be for the respondent to begin to engage in what is termed "satisficing". That is, in these circumstances, taking a mental shortcut to responding to a question, rather than analysing it carefully on its own merits and providing an optimal response. Such mental shortcuts can include skipping the information retrieval and analysis stages of responding to a question and simply

These kinds of issues are clearly hard to pick up in the analysis of survey data. However, they may become apparent due to inconsistencies in the answers provided.[82]

It is also important that only respondents with appropriate knowledge answer questions, otherwise uninformed respondents may guess at what they believe to be a reasonable answer from a position of ignorance. Accordingly, a well-constructed sample survey should contain appropriate filter questions to ensure that this is the case.[83]

6.019   Finally, in the light of all the difficulties that might emerge, all advice on survey design strongly advocates pre-testing the survey on a small sub-section of the population on which the survey will be carried out.[84] This is to minimise the pitfalls relating to survey design and implementation described above. Failure to pre-test a survey, and adjust it if problems are observed, must be seen as a very risky strategy in the light of all of the potential problems that may arise.

The use to which the Commission has put the evidence it has obtained through conducting surveys also merits comment.

For example, two of the key questions in the *Scottish Radio Holdings and GWR/Galaxy* inquiry were: (a) whether advertising on local radio competed with other forms of advertising; and (b) whether advertising on one radio station competed with advertising on different local and regional radio stations serving similar and different localities. The evidence collected from the survey appeared to suggest that a significant proportion of radio advertisers would switch significant amounts of advertising spend to other media in response to a 5 per cent price increase in radio advertising—68 per cent[85] of advertisers would have changed their pattern of advertising in some way and, of these, 74 per cent would consider switching to other media.[86] This might be seen to indicate that other media ought to be considered in the same economic market as local radio. However, this was not the conclusion drawn by the Commission. It concluded that it was "difficult to draw conclusions from the survey in this respect",[87] because: (i) customers

---

picking one of the possible answers that appears reasonable. Satisficing may also involve respondents using decision rules such as picking what they believe are uncontroversial answers (*e.g.* mid-points on ratings scales) or "don't know" options. Satisficing by respondents can greatly compound any technical survey design problems, since it is in relation to poor survey design where satisficing would seem to be most likely to lead to unreliable responses being observed. These issues are set out in more detail in, for example, Krosnick, "*Survey Research*" (1999), Annual Review of Psychology, which also provides wider references on specific points.

[82] See, for example, the inconsistencies noted in *Scottish Radio Holdings and GWR/Galaxy*, App.6.2, para.42(b)(iii); *Newsquest/INM*, para.2.31; and *Stena/P&O*, App.H, paras 30 to 32 and 35 (cited above, para.6.013, n.38).

[83] See, for example, the US Federal Judicial Center, "*Reference Manual on Scientific Evidence*" (2nd ed., 2000), pp.249–251 (*www.fjc.gov*).

[84] For example, the OFT Research Paper on "*Quantitative techniques in competition analysis*" recommends that the questionnaire ". . . should be piloted on a small sub-sample to identify ambiguities and other problems with the draft questionnaire" (cited above, para.6.012, n.32, at para.12.3).

[85] 86% if weighted by value, *Scottish Radio Holdings and GWR/Galaxy*, Table 5.14, cited above, para.6.013, n.38.

[86] *Scottish Radio Holdings and GWR/Galaxy*, Table 5.13 and App. 5.1, para.4.32, cited above, para.6.013, n.38.

[87] *Scottish Radio Holdings and GWR/Galaxy*, para.2.43, cited above, para.6.013, n.38.

may have overstated their reaction to a price rise to discourage companies from raising prices or they might not have actually responded in that way[88]; (ii) there was other evidence from the survey that (according to the Commission) could be interpreted as suggesting that customers' response to a price increase may not have been so "dramatic"[89]; (iii) there may have been "'vulnerable' advertisers" whose alternatives were limited[90]; and (iv) only 8 per cent of advertisers stated that they would switch between radio stations in response to a 5 per cent price increase.[91] Accordingly, the Commission found that local radio was in a different market to other media. However, by way of contrast, and particularly given point (iv) above which may seem to indicate that local radio stations operate in separate markets (for example, if substitution between media is overstated due to factor (i) why would it not be similarly overstated as regards substitution between radio stations?), the Commission concluded for a number of reasons that different local radio stations should be considered in the same market. In this regard, the Commission stated: "We do not believe, . . . that substitution within radio would be less than substitution between radio and other media, suggesting that the degree of switching to other media was overstated in response to our survey". It is therefore important to note that although survey results may seemingly provide persuasive evidence in relation to certain points (and are often strongly relied on by the Commission), the Commission by no means always treats them as conclusive.

Examples of potentially imprecise terms being used in questions may be found in the Commission's *Scottish Radio Holdings and GWR/ Galaxy* survey, which asked respondents to consider whether local radio commercials were "complementary" to advertisements in other media or "individual, alternative advertisements", whether local radio commercials were "unique" or "substitutable", what the "practical alternatives" to advertising on certain local radio stations were, and whether certain alternative media were "attractive propositions or not attractive propositions." As pointed out by GWR, it is far from clear that all respondents were assessing these questions on the same bases (*i.e.* they were open to wide interpretation by respondents), which leads to the results obtained being difficult to rely on as part of any further analysis, and none of these types of question provided the Commission with meaningful information as regards customers' sensitivity to price increases since they contained no references to prices or price changes which would have made customers change their behaviour.[92] As regards the questions concerning the "uniqueness" and "complementarity" of radio as part of the mix of media used by advertisers, the Commission accepted that since half of the respondents to the survey interpreted these questions inconsistently they "may not provide a wholly reliable way of identifying advertisers liable to face higher prices" (which was the Commission's aim).[93]

6.020

---

[88] *Scottish Radio Holdings and GWR/Galaxy*, para.2.43, cited above, para.6.013, n.38.
[89] *Scottish Radio Holdings and GWR/Galaxy*, para.2.44, cited above, para.6.013, n.38.
[90] *Scottish Radio Holdings and GWR/Galaxy*, para.2.45, cited above, para.6.013, n.38.
[91] *Scottish Radio Holdings and GWR/Galaxy*, para.2.46, cited above, para.6.013, n.38.
[92] Cited above, para.6.013, n.38, App.5.1, App.C, Questions 27, 28, 37 and 38, and App.6.1, paras 2.9 to 2.11 and para.5.91.
[93] Cited above, para.6.013, n.38, para.5.65.

To sum up, surveys can provide very relevant economic evidence in merger cases. However, in order for survey results to be robust and reliable, standard survey research methods must be employed and any analysis must be carried out with due caution and awareness of to the inherent issues with survey data outlined above.

Price trends and the impact of "shocks"

6.021   As a general proposition, if two products are close substitutes for each other, then it would be expected that an increase in the price of one product would lead to material switching by consumers to the other. Similarly, if there is a high degree of supply-side substitution, and the relative prices of products change, producers can be expected to switch to supplying the product whose relative price has increased. Accordingly, it might expected that the prices of demand or supply-side substitute products move together over time.[94] However, there is no particular reason to expect perfect price correlations between competitors supplying close substitutes. This is because the competitive process may involve one firm seeking to secure a competitive advantage over others by cutting price, in order to win market share and profits at the expense of rivals, and changes in relative prices should thus trigger switching.

The pricing behaviour of suppliers, and the impact of changes in prices of different products (and other market shocks) on the relative sales of suppliers of different categories of products, have been used by the Competition Commission and the OFT in their analysis of market definition in a number of cases. However, it should be noted at the outset that such measures do not directly relate to the degree of demand or supply side substitutability.

There are a number of ways in which price trends for different products can be considered:

(i)   graphing the trends in prices (which is very easy if the data is available and permits the data to be easily observed). However, whilst this approach can be used to identify the specific times when price trends have diverged, it does not provide a statistical measure of the extent to which the prices of different goods are tracking one another;

(ii)   calculating correlation coefficients, which are a simple statistical measure of the extent to which one variable moves in line with another (in this circumstance, the prices of alternatives); and

---

[94] In *Nutreco Holding NV/Hydro Seafood GSP Ltd*, Cm. 5004 (December 2000), the Commission emphasised the general relevance of price correlations as follows: "One would expect that, apart from temporary shocks, prices within the same market would move together relatively closely over time. Where products are differentiated in some real or perceived way, they would not be expected to have the same prices, but their price movements would be expected to correlate closely with each other" (at para.4.112).

(iii)   using other econometric based tests focusing on the relationship between the prices of different products, namely speed of adjustment tests, the Granger causality test and cointegration analysis. These tests are not considered further in this Chapter; it should be noted that, arguably, their apparently greater sophistication may add little to simple price correlations.[95]

The calculation of correlation coefficients is described briefly in App.12.[96] The correlation coefficient ranges from $+1$ to -1, with a correlation coefficient of $+1$ on the prices of two products indicating that their prices move in a perfect linear fashion with one another. A zero price correlation coefficient would suggest that there is no linear correlation in their prices. A -1 pricing correlation coefficient would indicate that an increase in the price of one product is linearly correlated with a corresponding decline in the other.

To be useful, price correlation data normally requires accurate data on actual transaction prices (rather than list prices.)[97] It may also be necessary to adjust for changes in the relative qualities of the products in question, which may encourage consumers to switch to the improved product in the same way that they would respond to a decrease in its relative price. The importance of robust pricing data was emphasised by the MMC in its report on the proposed merger between Capital Radio plc and Virgin Radio Holdings Limited.[98] Capital sought to show that the prices of advertising on Capital's radio stations moved closely in line with the advertising prices of other media during a recent period of 33 months. In particular, Capital found pricing correlations between Capital FM's advertising price (expressed in cost per thousand audience ("CPT")) for six other radio stations between 0.8 and 0.6, and also found pricing correlations between Capital FM CPTs and those for some other media in the range 0.9 to 0.7.[99] These "high" price correlation coefficients were used to support the argument that the other media were close substitutes for radio. One of the three main reasons for the MMC deciding that Capital's data did not support these conclusions was that:

6.022

---

[95] Chapter 15 of Bishop and Walker sets out an overview of Granger causality and cointegration tests which concludes that: "Granger causality and cointegration analysis do not therefore, for all their apparent statistical sophistication and accuracy, provide better tests of market definition than standard price correlation analysis. While price correlation analysis is far from being a perfect test of the competitive constraints which exist between firms or groups of products, it can still offer useful insights into the competitive process. However, its weaknesses are not solved by burying the underlying intuition of the test (that the prices of products in the same market will tend to move together over time) under the guise of apparent sophistication" (cited above, para.6.001, n.2, at p.454). Also see LECG's Research Paper for the OFT on "*Quantitative techniques in competition analysis*", Chs 6, 7 and 8, cited above, para.6.012, n.32. As regards the speed of adjustment test, LECG succinctly observes that: "This technique has been hardly ever used, however, as it is fundamentally flawed" (para.6.1).

[96] Also, see Ch.11 of Bishop and Walker, cited above, para.6.001, n.2; and chapter 5 of LECG's report on "*Quantitative techniques in competition analysis*", para.6.012, n.32.

[97] For example, Bishop and Walker emphasise that price correlation analysis makes sense only when it is carried out using transactions prices, not list prices from which discounts may be granted, cited above, para.6.001, n.2 at p.386.

[98] *Capital Radio plc/Virgin Radio Holdings Limited*, Cm. 3817 (January 1998).

[99] Cited above, para.6.022, n.98, at para.4.93.

"We have serious doubts about the robustness of the data for the purpose of the study. It was based on prices provided by only one media agency and the sparseness of the data was reflected in the need frequently to impute data because there were no actual price observations in particular months."[1]

A further point is that the price correlation coefficients may be sensitive to the time period considered, and poor correlations over different time periods wholly undermine arguments that the prices of alternatives are correlated. For example, in the Capital Radio report referred to above the MMC observed that the price correlation coefficient collapsed when a slightly different time period was considered:

"Looking at the comparison of monthly changes in Capital FM CPTs with those for one particular medium for which [Capital's economic consultants] Case found a high correlation we found a correlation degree of 0.70; this result which might be regarded as a relatively high correlation was to a substantial degree due to the changes of 21.0 and 22.8 per cent recorded in their respective CPTs in December 1995 as compared with the previous month's CPTs; when the data set was limited to January 1996 to September 1997 the correlation was found to be only 0.3."[2]

In addition, it should be noted (for the reasons set out at App.12) that even a perfect price correlation coefficient of $+1$ is consistent with the relative prices of alternatives changing in percentage terms. Accordingly, even with a price correlation coefficient of 0.7 between Capital FM CPTs and the CPTs of another medium, the MMC found in the Capital Radio report that:

"Moreover, over the 33-month period as a whole, we found that for this particular medium the ratio for its CPT compared with that for Capital FM moved from 1.08 in January 1995 to 1.32 in September 1997 (or when expressed in absolute terms the average CPT for Capital FM in Case's data was only 14p lower (at 179p) than the other medium's average CPT in January 1995, but the difference had risen to 76p (at 236p) in September 1997). This divergence appears to be inconsistent with the argument that there is close competition between the two media."[3]

Spurious correlations may arise if there are common costs or influences on prices (*e.g.* if both of the relevant products are manufactured using a common raw material, or are affected by common seasonal cost changes),[4] and data should be adjusted to take account of these factors. Another reason for spurious price correlations is that the price series might be "non-

---

[1] Cited above, para.6.022, n.98, at para.2.69(b).
[2] Cited above, para.6.022, n.98, at para.4.94(e).
[3] Cited above, para.6.022, n.98, at para.4.94(e).
[4] This point is recognised in the OFT's Research Paper on "*Market definition in UK competition policy*", cited above, para.6.009, n.22, at p.37. Also see p.390 of Bishop and Walker, cited above, para.6.001, n.2.

stationary"[5] in that they are subject to trends over time. Bishop and Walker observe that if high correlations are found as regards price levels, the analysis should also be checked by considering correlations on the basis of the changes in price levels from one period to the next, for both the products in question and alternative products.[6] If there are material differences between price correlations calculated using price levels as opposed to price changes, then this casts doubt on the validity of the analysis. A striking example of this point is provided by the Capital Radio inquiry, in which the MMC found that apparently high levels of correlations in the level of prices collapsed when correlations of price *changes* were considered:

"The relatively high degree of correlation found by Case [economic consultants] was based on a method that, in our view, is inappropriate. Simply comparing price levels fails to distinguish possible responses of one set of prices to another from the influence of trends such as inflation. When we carried out similar correlation analysis ourselves using the same basic data but using the more appropriate method of comparing price changes (instead of price levels), we found a much lower level of correlation."[7]

A further issue is that the degree of price correlation necessary for products to be regarded as close substitutes cannot be objectively defined,[8] which is unsurprising given that it is not directly related to the SSNIP test. One potential partial solution that is advocated is to adopt as a benchmark the correlation coefficient between the various products which are clearly within the market (although this may involve a subjective assessment), and then observe for other products whether the correlation is higher or lower.[9]

6.023

Pricing correlations might also emerge even if there is very limited demand-side substitutability. For example, if alternative products are in fixed supply because of capacity constraints or other reasons, then the price of the product in question would be bid up even if there was only a slight increase in its sales following an increase in the price of an alternative. Although there may be a high degree of price correlation between the

---

[5] This is a technical term. In simple terms, the mean and/or variance of a "non-stationary" series do not remain constant over time. The mean price is the sum of prices over time divided by the number of units of time considered and the variance is a measure of the extent to which actual prices differ from the average price.

[6] This is recommended, for example, by Bishop and Walker cited above para.6.001, n.2, at pp.390–391. This is commonly referred to as calculating correlations in "first differences" (*i.e.* calculating whether there is a correlation between the changes in the price of one product from one period to the next with the corresponding change in the price of the alternative product over the same period).

[7] Cited above, para.6.022, n.98, at para.2.69(a).

[8] See further Werden and Froeb, "Correlation, Causality, and All that Jazz: The Inherent Shortcomings of Price Tests for Antitrust Market Definition", *Review of Industrial Organisation* 8: 329–353, 1993. A point reiterated by Werden and Froeb (originally noted in Werden, "Market Definition and the Justice Department's Merger Guidelines" (1983), Duke Law Journal, 514–579) is that if a product has many partial substitutes, an increase in its price might well lead to customers switching to a diverse range of alternatives. This may well mean price correlations are limited between the product in question and the alternatives, even if aggregate switching to the various alternatives is substantial.

[9] See *e.g.* Sherwin, cited below, n.26; and Bishop and Walker, cited above, para.6.001, n.2 at pp.392 to 394.

alternative products in such circumstances, treating them as being within the same market would understate the market power of the merged company.[10]

In addition to price correlations, the scope of the relevant market may be revealed by suppliers' and customers' behaviour following significant changes in the relative prices or quality of products over time, or other market shocks. For example, in considering the extent of competition between coach and rail services, the MMC observed in the context of the merger between National Express Group PLC and ScotRail Railways Limited that:

> "A study of the effects of coach deregulation in the early 1980s showed that, when coach fares were cut, about half the newly-generated demand on some services in the East Midlands was from passengers transferring from rail. BRB's main response was to introduce lower fares aimed at leisure travellers, and another study suggested that the introduction of Saver tickets had attracted passengers primarily from the coach rather than the car. When BRB introduced APEX fares in the early 1990s, the number of coach passengers between London and Scotland fell sharply . . . We believe that the findings of these studies are likely to be broadly relevant to the situation within Scotland."[11]

Similarly, in relation to the proposed acquisition by FirstGroup plc of the Scottish Passenger Rail franchise, the Commission identified various evidence of a direct impact on competition and substitution between bus and rail:

> ". . . we were told that an increase in competition between bus operators on services between Cumbernauld and Glasgow had led to a 45 per cent reduction in the number of passengers on rail services between these two places. The SPTE had responded to this competition by introducing a number of discounted rail fares. The route between Cumbernauld and Glasgow, however, is not necessarily typical of most bus and rail services in the areas we are considering. Express bus services between Cumbernauld and Glasgow use a motorway for most of the journey. Journey times for bus are therefore similar to those by train."[12]

---

[10] In this regard, the Commission's guidelines state that in assessing the scope for substitutability between products the Commission takes into account the ability of producers of substitute products to meet increased demand; cited above, para.6.001, n.1, at para.2.23. This specific issue is discussed at some length by Werden and Froeb, cited above at para.6.023. Sherwin made a number of points in reply by Werden and Froeb, "*Comments on Werden and Froeb—Correlation, Causality, and all the Jazz*", (1993) Review of Industrial Organisations: pp.385–358. He observes that Werden and Froeb's main criticism is that price correlations will be lower where the elasticity of supply of alternative products outside of the candidate market is high. Sherwin first argues that very high short term supply elasticities of close substitutes will be quite rare. Moreover, if supply is very elastic, substantial switching will be observed in response to price changes, indicating a broader market.

[11] *National Express Group PLC/ScotRail Railways Limited*, Cm. 3773 (December 1997), at para.2.52. Similar evidence was referred to in the context of the merger between *National Express Group PLC and Midland Main Line Limited*, cited above, para.6.012, n.35, at para.4.71.

[12] Cited above, para.6.012, n.36, at paras 4.20–4.22.

Defining the relevant product market—supply-side substitutability

In order for supply-side considerations to be taken into account at the market definition stage as opposed to the subsequent assessment of barriers to entry and expansion,[13] any re-configuration of production and supply should be able to occur within a relatively short period of time and without incurring significant sunk costs (*i.e.* costs which could not be recovered should a firm exit the market). The Competition Commission's guidelines state that:

6.024

> "In order to consider a competitor's response as supply-side substitution . . . the response should, normally, be likely to occur within a year of the price rise (although the exact time period will depend on the nature of the market considered) and should not involve significant investment in plant, equipment, skills or marketing."[14]

---

[13] Motta addresses succinctly the question of why supply-side substitutability should be addressed at the market definition stage, not in the subsequent assessment of barriers to entry. He observes that: "One can then wonder why it is necessary to consider supply substitutability at the market definition stage as well. The answer is that there is no reason to delay the moment at which substitutes on the supply side are considered. Immediate consideration of the existing competitive constraints will save time and help the investigation. Drawing the borders of the market in a narrower way than supply considerations would authorise might force an anti-trust agency to spend time and energy in justifying why a firm with a considerable market share does not actually have considerable market power. In contrast, if immediate consideration of supply substitutability arguments leads to a correct wider market, and accordingly a low market share, there will be an immediate presumption of absence of market power" (cited above, para.6.001, n.2, at pp.104–105). Similarly, Bishop and Walker state that: "There is a sense in which it does not much matter whether or not supply-side substitution is taken into account in defining the relevant market. Provided the competitive constraints provided by the possibility of supply-side substitution are taken into account at some point of the competitive analysis, the appropriate conclusions on market power should be reached. However, there is a sense in which taking account of supply-side substitution at the market definition stage is important. If market shares are to provide as meaningful an indicator of market power as possible then supply-side substitutability should be taken into account at the market definition stage" (cited above, para.6.001, n.2, at p.94).

[14] Cited above, para.6.001, n.1, at para.2.21. Similarly, the US Horizontal Merger Guidelines draw a distinction between supply side substitutes and new entry, in that supply side substitutes do not face significant barriers to entry and would become available on the market within a year, whereas this is not the case for potential entrants (cited above, para.6.001, n.4, at s.1.32). The Guidelines state that:

> "[a] firm is viewed as a participant, if, in response to a 'small but significant and non-transitory' price increase, it likely would enter rapidly into production or sale of a market product in the market's area, without incurring significant sunk costs of entry and exit. Firms likely to make any of these supply responses are considered to be 'uncommitted' entrants because their supply response would create new production or sale in the relevant market and because that production or sale could be quickly terminated without significant loss."

The Guidelines note that: "[p]robable supply responses that require the entrant to incur significant sunk costs of entry and exit are not part of market measurement, but are included in the analysis of the significance of entry. . . Entrants that must commit substantial sunk costs are regarded as "committed" entrants because those sunk costs make entry irreversible in the short term without foregoing that investment; thus the likelihood of their entry must be evaluated with regard to their long-term profitability" (cited above, para.6.001, n.4, s.1.0). The Guidelines go on to state that: "In measuring a firm's market share, the Agency

The OFT research paper on market definition in UK competition policy outlines the key issues which will affect any consideration of supply side substitution. These will include an assessment of technical feasibility and also other commercial factors which might affect a supplier's ability to switch production. In particular, there may be barriers to supply-side substitution if time needs to be spent establishing a brand or presence in the market through advertising or other marketing activities. Equally there may be barriers associated with the need to establish a supply chain, for example a distribution network.

The OFT's guidelines on market definition under the Competition Act 1998 indicate that evidence from some or all of the following sources would be considered in assessing supply-side substitution by the UK authorities:

"(i) potential suppliers might be asked whether substitution was technically possible, and about the costs of switching production between products, and the time it would take to switch production. The key question is whether it would be economic to switch production given a small (*i.e.* 5–10 per cent) price increase;

(ii) undertakings might be asked whether they had spare capacity or were free to switch production. Undertakings may be prevented from switching production because all their existing capacity was tied up—they may be committed to long-term contracts. There might also be difficulties obtaining necessary inputs or finding distribution outlets;

(iii) although new undertakings may be able to supply the market, there may be reasons why customers would not use their products, so the views of customers might be sought."[15]

6.025 The Commission's guidelines also highlight the following relevant types of information[16]:

- "information on past supply-side substitution (for example, information on the extent to which supply-side substitution has resulted from variations in price differentials over time);
- information on the willingness of customers to switch to new suppliers following a SSNIP;
- information on the size of adjustment costs[17] for potential suppliers;
- information on the production processes involved;
- the extent of spare capacity within the industry;
- the business plans of potential suppliers and the assessment of their competitive threat by firms in the market;

---

will not include its sales or capacity to the extent that the firm's capacity is committed or so profitably employed outside the relevant market that it would not be available to respond to an increase in price in the market" (s.1.41).

[15] OFT 403 "*Market Definition*", OFT guidelines under the Competition Act 1998, at para.3.20. As at the time of writing these guidelines were in the process of being updated.

[16] Cited above, para.6.001, n.1, at para.2.23.

[17] Adjustment costs are costs incurred in adjusting to the supply of the new product. For instance, they might include the costs of altering the production process or establishing the distribution of the product.

- assessment by independent technical consultants and interested third parties of the likelihood and feasibility of supply-side substitution; and
- information on supply-side substitution in similar markets in other countries."

The Commission and the Director General/OFT have considered the possibility of defining markets by reference to supply-side considerations in many cases. For example:

(i)   in relation to the proposed merger between Tomkins plc and Kerry Group plc, both leading suppliers of milled flour in the UK, the Commission took into account supply side considerations in reaching a decision as to whether distinct markets existed for "hard" flour (used for breadmaking) and "soft" flour (used for products such as biscuits). The Commission concluded that although these products were non-substitutable from the consumer's point of view, they did not constitute separate markets since most mills can produce both types of flour, and can switch production quickly and with little cost[18];

(ii)   in the case of the merger between Rockwool Ltd and Owens-Corner Building Products Ltd, the production of stone wool was defined as the relevant market. The Commission found that in order to manufacture stone wool a high level of specialist equipment was needed such that ". . . there is no possibility of even a manufacturer of glass wool, the nearest equivalent, switching to the production of stone wool without making substantial capital investment."[19] For this reason, the Commission considered that the question of supply-side switching should be more appropriately investigated in the context of entry into the market rather than as part of market definition;

(iii) in relation to the proposed merger between Alanod Aluminium—Veredlung GmbH and Co and Metalloxyd Ano-Coil Ltd, each of the merging parties was a supplier of various types and grades of anodised aluminium coil/strip. The Commission noted that while those types of coil with similar properties might be demand substitutes, others—particularly those with different finishes (*e.g.* matt, ridged and reflective)—may not be direct substitutes. However, the Commission considered that the relevant market should be all grades of conventional anodised aluminium coil on the basis that ". . . existing producers of anodized material are generally able to switch production from one grade to another in response to market signals . . ."[20]; and

---

[18] *Tomkins plc/Kerry Group plc*, Cm. 4031 (September 1998), para.2.23.
[19] *Rockwool Ltd/Owens-Corner Building Products (UK) Ltd*, Cm. 4330 (April 1999), para.4.89.
[20] *Alanod Aluminium-Veredlung GmbH and Co/Metalloxyd Ano-Coil Ltd*, Cm. 4545 (January 2000), para.4.52.

(iv)   in relation to the proposed acquisition by RCG Holdings Limited of Doncasters plc, the Director General advised that: "On the supply side the manufacturing process is very specialised and normally requires licensing by OEMs [original equipment manufacturers]. Switching into the manufacture of vacuum melted superalloys by other metal producers would require significant capital investment and probably take at least a year. Supply side substitutability is therefore limited . . .."[21]

Defining the relevant geographic market

6.026   The relevant market will also have a geographical dimension. Geographic market definition raises issues analogous to product market definition, and the test is essentially the same—the relevant geographic market is the smallest area within which a hypothetical monopoly supplier could unilaterally raise prices above the competitive level.[22] Assessments of geographic market definition may be informed by evidence as to whether:

(i)   various barriers to trade place "distant" suppliers at a significant cost disadvantage to local suppliers, *e.g.* transport costs, the perishability of the product, differences in product standards;

(ii)   suppliers in one area price their products with reference to those of their competitors based outside the area in question; and

(iii)   the volume of trade is sensitive to changes in the relative prices of products between different areas.

Barriers to trade

6.027   Key barriers to trade between two different geographic areas are non-local suppliers facing high additional transport and tariff costs (compared with the costs incurred by local suppliers) and the rapid perishability of products. In a number of reports the MMC and Competition Commission has found that transport costs of under about 5 per cent of the price of a product will not deter trade between areas. For example, in their report on the proposed merger between Robert Wiseman Dairies plc and Scottish Pride Holdings plc, the MMC referred to average total costs of transporting raw milk at 1p per litre, equating to approximately 4 per cent of the realised sales price. This finding contributed to the MMC's conclusion that ". . . the market for raw milk is markedly less regional than was the case in 1992."[23]

However, the extent to which transport costs act as a barrier to trade depends more upon their magnitude relative to profit margins than ex-manufactured prices, with non-local suppliers potentially enjoying a cost

---

[21] Director General's advice of June 13, 2001, *The proposed acquisition by RCG Holdings Limited of Doncasters plc.*

[22] This is the approach taken by, for example, the Commission's guidelines (para.2.25, cited above, para.6.001, n.1); the OFT's guideline on *Market Definition* under the Competition Act 1998, at para.4.3, cited above, para.6.024, n.15; and the US Horizontal Merger Guidelines, cited above, para.6.001, n.4.

[23] *Robert Wiseman Dairies plc/Scottish Pride Holdings plc*, Cm. 3504 (December 1996), at paras 2.33, 2.40 and 2.44.

advantage which offsets transport costs. For example, in his advice on the proposed acquisition by Tessenderlo Chemie of the Widnes Plant and business of Atofina, the Director General observed that:

"I understand that non-EU producers (*i.e.* from China and India) are subject to import duties as well as transport costs which together add some 10–11% to product cost. Against this, the parties claim that Chinese and Indian producers benefit from very low production costs due, in the main, to lower labour and investment costs, lower raw material costs and less demanding environmental regulations. Thus any additional costs incurred as a result of importation are largely, if not wholly, countered by lower production costs."[24]

The geographical area that it will be economic for a firm to supply in the long run will generally depend upon the interaction between economies of scale and transport costs. If a firm's potential customers are dispersed geographically then it may be possible for the firm to increase manufacturing output only by selling to more distant customers. If there are substantial economies of scale that cannot be reaped by purely local sales, then it may be profitable to supply the products to distant customers *despite* incurring significant additional transport costs.

In retailing markets, transport costs may well be borne by consumers (rather than retailers) in the sense that it is costly (whether in financial terms, time or inconvenience) for them to procure from distant retailers.[25] In such circumstances, local markets may be very narrow in their scope (*e.g.* a short distance from a specific retailer, or from a population centre, or a single shopping centre/area). Appendix 13 provides a detailed analysis of the Commission's analysis of local markets in relation to the various contested bids for Safeway in 2003.[26]

Even if transport costs are low relative to profit margins, other factors may create barriers to trade. For example, in relation to the merger between Interbrew SA and Bass plc, the Commission concluded that one barrier to imports would be the need for new suppliers (including overseas suppliers) to develop a brand. The Commission noted that a small-scale importer might utilise its reputation or may develop awareness through niche strategies, but that entry on a significant scale would require expenditure on advertising and promotion which would represent an irrecoverable outlay should entry prove unsuccessful.[27]

---

[24] Director General's advice of July 24, 2001, *The proposed acquisition by Tessenderlo Chemie SA of the Widnes Plant and business of Atofina UK Limited.* It is, of course, the case that low cost suppliers in China and India might face little competition from non-local suppliers and a merger between Chinese suppliers might be assessed primarily on the basis of local/national competition in China. This is one example of why market definition may well depend on the market power issue at hand (*e.g.* can a merger of UK suppliers lead to price increases versus whether a merger of Chinese suppliers can lead to higher prices).

[25] Clearly, the development of the Internet has the prospect of facilitating the ability of consumers to procure from distant suppliers and of such suppliers to market their products and services to non-local customers.

[26] *Safeway plc and Asda Group Ltd (owned by Wal-Mart Stores Inc.); WM Morrison Supermarkets PLC; J Sainsbury PLC; and Tesco plc*, Cm. 5950 (September 2003).

[27] *Interbrew SA/Bass plc*, Cm. 5014 (January 2001), at para.2.36. See further paras 6.061 to 6.063.

Other factors may constitute barriers to trade for "distant" suppliers including differences in product standards, restrictions created by the existence of patents and trademarks, nationalistic procurement policies and/or other government regulations. For example when advising on the proposed acquisition by Fernco Inc of Flex-Seal Couplings Limited, the Director General found that:

"The relevant geographic market for flexible rubber couplings is considered to be no wider than national at present. This is largely due to the UK-specific standard for flexible rubber couplings for public sector use set by the water companies and is higher than specifications used in other European countries . . . This means that, at present, European suppliers cannot supply the UK as they do not have the necessary certification, which can take up to one year to acquire."[28]

In assessing the acquisition by Coloplast A/S of the continence care business of SSL International plc, the Commission stated that:

". . . our attention was drawn to a number of factors that constrain parallel imports. These include the existence of exclusive distribution arrangements for particular territories, as in the case for Mentor sheaths, and restrictions arising from differences in patent protection. For instance, the Coloplast one-piece synthetic adhesive sheaths as sold in Europe cannot be sold in the UK without infringing Mentor's UK patent . . . Other factors are variations in packaging, instructions in different languages, trademarks and sometimes the use of different names for the same products in different European markets . . ."[29]

Import penetration

6.028 In a number of its reports, the Commission has emphasised that high and/or rising levels of import penetration may reflect the fact that there is effective competition from suppliers in other territories. For example, in its 2002 report on the proposed acquisition by Cargill Inc of Cerestar SA, the Commission concluded that the relevant market for glucose syrups and blends was wider than the UK. In particular, imports represented 17 per cent of UK sales in 2001, they had been growing over the preceding decade, and had not been brought about purely by exchange rate factors.[30]

However, there is no particular correlation between the level of import penetration and geographical market definition for a number of reasons. First, whilst high and/or rising levels of import penetration or exports tend to suggest that transport costs are not a barrier to trade, foreign suppliers not currently supplying the geographical area in question may still face other barriers to entry, such as the costs of establishing a new brand, or the sunk costs of obtaining national regulatory approvals and so on. For example, in relation to the proposed merger between Alanod Aluminium-

---

[28] Director General's advice of June 21, 2002, *The proposed acquisition by Fernco Inc of Flex-Seal Couplings Limited.*

[29] *Coloplast A/S/SSL International plc*, Cm. 5522 (June 2002), at para.2.48.

[30] *Cargill Inc/Cerestar SA*, Cm. 5521 (May 2002), paras 2.49—2.60.

Veredlung GmbH and Metalloxyd Ano-Coil Ltd, the Commission favoured a UK market definition despite the fact that around 60 per cent of anodised aluminium sold in the UK was imported. The Commission reached this view on the basis that while products may be manufactured overseas, the service-oriented market in the UK required suppliers to establish a presence in the UK in order to meet tight delivery requirements (typically within one, two or three days) and service functions.[31]

Secondly, whilst competition from imports may be vigorous at the time of the merger, it is necessary to consider whether such competition is likely to persist (it might be more appropriate in such circumstances to define the market more broadly, and then assess whether existing competition from non-local suppliers is likely to diminish materially). Competition from imports is unlikely to subsist in the medium to long term if it occurs as a result of temporary excess capacity which makes it economic for suppliers based in other areas or territories to export their products for a short period in order to make some contribution to their fixed costs. As local demand recovers or excess capacity is reduced through plant closures or other ratio-nalisations, firms may find it more profitable to supply only their more local customers. The same will be true if foreign suppliers are likely to face cost increases in the future (such as increases in the cost of locally supplied raw materials), which will further increase the competitive disadvantages they face in supplying the United Kingdom.

For example, in its 1991 report on the proposed acquisition by Kemira Oy of Imperial Chemical Industries plc's fertiliser business, the Commission considered that competition from imports in Western Europe and the United Kingdom would diminish for a number of reasons including, *inter alia*, the fact that Eastern European countries would have to pay more for their oil and gas feedstocks which could render some capacity obsolete, and Western European excess capacity was being cut.[32]

---

[31] Cited above, para.6.025, n.20, para.2.55. Similarly, in *Dräger Medical AG & Co KGaA/Hillenbrand Industries, Inc*, the Commission rejected the parties' arguments that the market was global despite the fact that at least one-third of neo-natal warming therapy prod-ucts sold in the EC were manufactured in the USA, virtually all the products sold in the UK were manufactured outside the UK, and transport costs represented no more than 3 per cent of the selling cost of the equipment. The Commission nevertheless concluded that there was a separate UK market, because the availability of UK-based support and the track record of suppliers in UK hospitals were important to hospitals in buying this equipment (*Dräger Medical AG & Co KGaA/Hillenbrand Industries, Inc* (May 2004), at paras 5 and 4.17). These cases can be contrasted with the Commission's report on *Carl Zeiss Jena GmbH/Bio-Rod Laboratories Inc* (May 2004), which noted that customers had a preference for local support and suppliers had different strengths in different parts of the world, but nevertheless concluded that the relevant market was global due to global R&D, production generally being concentrated in one country, UK and worldwide market shares were broadly similar, and customers and sale processes being broadly similar throughout the world (at paras 4.33 to 4.36).

[32] *Kemira Oy/Imperial Chemical Industries PLC*, Cm. 1406 (January 1991), at para.6.40. The OFT's Research Paper on "*Market definition in UK competition policy*", cited above, para.6.009, n.22 is critical of the Commission's approach to market definition in this case as the Commission identified that there were high and growing trade flows, and as UK prices had been driven down by changes in international prices—suggesting that high transport costs were not a barrier to trade (see pp.80–81). Whilst such criticisms would appear to be valid, it is conceivable that markets might become less international in their scope and UK suppliers would have greater market power if, as the Commission expected, European excess capacity were to reduce and competition from non-EC suppliers were to diminish as their raw material costs rose.

6.029   Thirdly, a lack of entry by foreign companies may reflect effective competition among existing suppliers, with the resulting level of prices being too low to generate a sufficient level of profits that would serve to attract new entrants. Indeed, as noted in the Commission guidelines: "Even when imports account for a small proportion of UK consumption, it might be relatively easy for the proportion to increase in response to a SSNIP . . .".[33] For example, in its report on the acquisition of Icopal by Icopal Holding A/S, the Commission noted only a very limited increase in the value of imports of roofing felt material between 1994 and 1999. However the Commission stated that:

> "[The] limited increase in the level of penetration does not, in itself, prove that imports are not a constraint on the UK market. They may pose a threat in the sense that local manufacturers keep prices low to constrain their entry, or it may also be that excess capacity at home has kept prices low and, hence, imports down—and, indeed, the parties told us that imports are a source of concern for them."[34]

Similarly, in his advice on the proposed joint venture between the Mayflower Corporation and Henlys Group, the Director General concluded that despite low imports into the UK of single deck bus bodies, there appeared to be few barriers to overseas manufacturers wishing to supply the UK. The Director General therefore concluded that the market was at least European in its scope.[35]

Producers' pricing policies and the impact on trade of changes in prices in different areas

6.030   The willingness of customers to seek supplies and quotes from firms based in other areas is likely to be an important indicator of the intensity of competition from such suppliers. If suppliers in other areas are effective competitors, this should ensure that common prices apply in different territories (allowing for differences in local supply costs), otherwise customers would switch to cheaper suppliers based in other areas. Accordingly, for a finding of a single geographic market to be made between suppliers in different locations, it may be expected that prices in different geographical areas would be strongly correlated, particularly at the ex-manufacturer level (bearing in mind the comments made in relation to price correlation in paras 6.022 to 6.023, above). For example, in its report on the proposed acquisition by BASF AG of certain assets of Takeda Chemical Ltd, the Commission reviewed whether prices moved independently in different geographic areas on the basis that different prices in the US, Europe and UK might suggest a degree of market separation. The Commission concluded that:

> "The data on UK and world prices . . . appear to show similar price behaviour, if slightly different pricing levels. BASF was able to provide a

---

[33] Cited above, para.6.001, n.1, at para.2.27.
[34] *Icopal Holding A/S/Icopal a/s*, Cm. 5089 (April 2001), at para.2.83.
[35] Director General's advice of November 24, 2000, *The proposed joint venture between the Mayflower Corporation plc and Henlys Group plc.*

continuous price data series for vitamin B2 feed grade showing the UK, Europe and the USA ... This appears to show similar pricing patterns with some temporary divergences."[36]

This contributed to the view that the geographic markets for the supply of vitamins in question were global.

Similarly, in the context of its report on the *Nutreco Holding BV/Norsk Hydro ASA* merger, the Commission considered the degree of correlation between Norwegian and Scottish gutted salmon prices in the UK, after adjustment for duties, marketing fees and transport costs. The Commission observed that the two price series appeared to be closely linked with a correlation coefficient of 0.67, which was higher than the correlation in UK prices between adjacent classes of salmon. The Commission also noted that the ratio of Norwegian and Scottish salmon prices was stationary in that a statistical test indicated that it tended to deviate from a stable relationship and return rapidly to a constant average after any deviations. In addition, the Commission noted arguments that salmon prices did not appear simply to reflect the costs of salmon feed, which represented some 50 per cent of salmon costs, as feed prices had displayed different trends over the time period considered. These facts contributed to the Commission's view that the relevant geographic market for gutted farmed salmon was the EEA.[37]

However, this approach can be problematic, not least where manufacturers' prices are not easily observable. Even where prices are observable, price comparisons may be complicated due to various factors affecting prices such as different product specifications between countries, different tax and subsidy regimes and trends in exchange rates.[38] There may also be problems in comparing retail prices due to differences in distribution channels, the strength of retail competition and value added and other sales taxes in different countries.

As in the case of product market definition, geographic price correlations can be misleading where a product is sold within two separate geographic markets, and the price of the product is heavily influenced by the price of a single raw material. Although the two markets are entirely distinct, the prices of the goods in each region will be highly correlated. However the price of the good in the first region neither affects, nor is affected by, the price of the good in the second region. The MMC commented on this problem in its report on the merger between Robert Wiseman Dairies and Scottish Pride Holdings: 6.031

"We start from the position that different geographical markets do not automatically generate different price trends. In particular where demand is of a similar nature and the two areas also share major elements of cost and have similar cost structures, the existence of competitive conditions in each region is likely to lead to similar price levels and trends. To

---

[36] *BASF AG/Takeda Chemical Industries Limited*, Cm. 5209 (July 2001), at para.4.123. This conclusion was based on charts comparing prices, rather than calculations of correlation coefficients.

[37] Cited above, para.6.021, n.94, at para.2.56–2.65.

[38] In this regard, Bishop and Walker observe that exchange rate conversions can introduce common trends, affecting price correlations, and they conclude that price correlation analyses across exchange rate areas are not in general valid (cited above, para.6.001, n.2, at pp.394–402).

observe no major price difference in this situation does not constitute evidence that there is (in economic terms) a single market: one is simply observing two markets behaving in a similar way."[39]

In addition, competition may also occur primarily at a national level notwithstanding the existence of local suppliers and customers' choices being limited to local suppliers, for a number of reasons.[40] First, it may be more cost effective for firms facing local competition in a number of areas to promote the prices of their products nationally, rather than to purchase local advertising in a number of separate locations. In addition, the cost of implementing and administering local pricing (including reputation issues if consumers discover that certain stores are high price stores) may outweigh its benefits if the conditions of competition are materially different only in a few separate locations. The existence of such conditions may imply that the costs of employing a local pricing system may exceed the benefits of any increase in profits that could be achieved by raising prices in local areas where suppliers face less competition. However, following a merger that materially reduces competition in a number of local areas, it might become profitable for the merged company to abandon national pricing and exercise market power at the local level. Alternatively, a reduction in local competition in a significant number of localities might render it profitable for a firm to increase prices or otherwise reduce competitiveness nationally. More generally, it should be noted that product/service markets may well have both local elements (*e.g.* certain prices may be set locally and consumers may choose between local stores) and national elements (*e.g.* other aspects of competitive strategy, such as branding, retail share quality, opening hours, may be determined nationally).

For example, in the context of the various competing bids for Safeway, the Commission concluded that "the geographical scope of the one-stop-shopping market is essentially local but that there are national dimensions of competition" (*e.g.* in terms of national pricing strategy, national price levels, strategic decisions on stores, overall marketing and so on).[41] The Commission added that national prices are set according to the overall competition faced by a firm across all the local markets in which it is active.[42] It also noted that, notwithstanding the administrative costs of

---

[39] Cited above, para.6.027, n.20, at para.2.58.

[40] A number of UK cases have considered the impact of mergers on local and national competition. For example, in *Connells/Sequence* (OFT decision of January 27, 2003), the OFT examined local markets for estate agency services based on particular radii; whilst in *Punch Taverns/Pubmaster* (OFT decision of February 25, 2004), the OFT considered local markets for the on-licence trade based on Petty Sessional Divisions (PSDs). In this latter case, the OFT acknowledged that PSDs were only a proxy for local markets. In *Whitbread/Premier Lodge* (OFT decision of March 11, 2004), the OFT observed that there were both local and national dimensions to competition in the supply of branded budget accommodation. Similarly, in *Kingfisher/Dixons*, the MMC observed that whilst the purchase of electrical goods remained an essentially local activity, the pricing of electrical goods in the UK was substantially influenced by the rivalry and price strategies of national chains (*Kingfisher plc and Dixons Group plc*, MMC, CM1079 (May 1990), at paras 6.23–6.31).

[41] Cited above, para.6.027, n.23, at paras 2.57, 2.62 and 2.65.

[42] Cited above, para.6.027, n.23, at para.2.111.

store-by-store pricing and reputation issues raised by different store prices, retailers might vary prices regionally or locally if this were to be more profitable.[43]

The Commission is also interested in the parties' internal analyses of the market in assessing whether there are national elements to competition as well as local elements. In *Ladbroke/Coral*, Ladbroke had sought to argue that competition took place primarily at the local level rather than the national level.[44] The MMC observed, in relation to national price competition between bookmakers, that: "Ladbroke said that the importance of price competition at national level was negligible ... However, we noted statements in Ladbroke's internal strategy document which indicated that Ladbroke recognized an element of price competition at the national level and attached some importance to it."[45] The document stated, *inter alia*, that: "... competition has been reasonably well restrained in terms of discounts, bonuses and betting percentages ... After the Lottery hit the industry in 1995 intense competition was replaced to a considerable extent by increased co-operation between the major companies. Ladbrokes have led the way with the removal of an array of uneconomic [ ] customer offers."[46] In addition, presumably in relation to questioning based on the document, the MMC reported that: "Ladbroke agreed with our suggestion that in taking this stance it was seeking to mobilize its leadership role and encourage others to follow it. Our interpretation of these passages is that they show Ladbroke seeking to use its national influence in order to dampen these forms of price competition."[47] The MMC went on to conclude that national price competition was a significant industry factor. The same document was also used by the MMC to support its conclusion that non-price competition was also relevant at a national level.[48]

The OFT's Research Paper on market definition raises the theoretical issue as to whether separate markets may exist for the same product where, for example, national customers wish to deal only with national suppliers due to the advantages of having a single national supplier, although local/regional customers may be able to deal with local/regional suppliers. In these circumstances, national suppliers may be able to discriminate against national customers on non-cost related grounds. This will not be the case where national customers can easily use a network of local suppliers, or national suppliers cannot engage in price discrimination between local and national customers for the reasons given at paras 6.039 to 6.043, below.[49]

6.032

Finally, it should be noted that firms' local competitiveness might well depend on their national/international scale (*e.g.* due to national/international economics of scale in procurement, distribution or advertising).

---

[43] Cited above, para.6.027, n.23, at paras 2.97–2.98.
[44] *Ladbroke Group PLC/the Coral betting business*, Cm. 4030 (September 1998).
[45] Cited above, para.6.031, n.44, at paras 2.125–6.
[46] Cited above, para.6.031, n.44, App.6.1, at pp.20 and 23.
[47] Cited above, para.6.031, n.44, at para.2.126.
[48] Cited above, para.6.031, n.44, at para.2.139.
[49] Cited above, para.6.009, n.22, pp.101–102.

In-house supplies

6.033   In some markets a number of firms are vertically integrated inasmuch as they both produce and consume the relevant product, or supply it to another member of the same group of companies. For example, in advising on the proposed acquisition by Tessenderlo Chemie of the Widnes Plant and business of Atofina, the Director General noted that "All producers of Benzyl Chloride are vertically integrated in the manufacture of one of the several downstream products. Thus much of their production is dedicated for internal use. In terms of external sales, the parties' combined EU-wide share is between 35%–55%."[50]

In defining the relevant market it is important to identify whether such vertically integrated firms have the *ability* and the *incentive* to expand their sales to third parties if the prices paid by such customers were to increase above the competitive level. The OFT's guidance states that:

"In some cases, a supplier may be using some of its capacity or production to meet its own internal needs. In the event of a rise in price on the open market, the supplier may decide to divert some or all of its 'captive' capacity or production to the open market if it is profitable to do so, taking into account effects on its downstream business that is now deprived of the captive supply. The extent to which 'captive' capacity or production is likely to be released onto the open market will be taken into account in assessing the competitive constraint."[51]

In practice, a number of constraints may limit the ability and incentives of in-house suppliers to commence or expand their sales to third parties. These include barriers such as material sunk investments in facilities that may have to be made in order to supply third parties as well as in-house consumption or simply in order to expand production. Moreover, in certain circumstances commercial interests may discourage the expansion of sales by in-house suppliers to third parties. For example, in-house suppliers may not wish to assist direct competitors to their own downstream business by providing access to inputs on competitive terms. Equally, third parties may not wish to purchase inputs from the upstream business of their rivals, particularly if this would create a position of dependency or lead to valuable information being provided to these firms. For example, it may be possible for competitors to use purchases of inputs as a way of calculating rivals' market shares, or the precise combination of inputs may be a trade secret.

The MMC considered this issue as part of its investigation into the acquisition by Tomkins plc of enterprises previously under the control of Kerry Group plc, both leading suppliers of milled flour in the UK. The MMC noted that although complete substitution was possible on the demand-side, such that flour used in-house could equally be used by third parties in the free market, substitution between in-house and free supplies was likely to be more limited. The MMC made the following remarks on this:

---

[50] Cited above, para.6.027, n.21.
[51] Cited above, para.6.001, n.1, at para.3.21.

"We were told by several companies that vertical integration was the result of a clear policy to ensure supply of flour to their bakeries or, vice versa, to ensure some customer base for their milling operations. The first call on the company flour production is likely to be for its own use. Prices in the free market may have to rise quite significantly before production is diverted from in-house use to the free market. All the considerations noted above lead us to view the free market for flour as a separate market."[52]

In considering the likely strength of competition from in-house supplies, the OFT's Research paper on market definition states the following:

6.034

"This constraint is more likely to be effective if it is the current practice of the vertically integrated firm to supply the semi-finished product to third parties, and provided it does so on a competitive arms-length basis. The best assurance that this is so is if the firm is dependent on the sales volumes it achieves through such third party sales to maintain the viability of its operations."[53]

How much substitution is necessary?[54]

An introduction to critical loss analysis

The discussion above focussed on assessing the extent of demand and supply-side substitution, but without considering how much substitution is enough to render a SSNIP unprofitable, which is at the heart of the test. The Competition Commission's guidelines indicate that calculations of critical losses and elasticities may help it to assess how likely it is that a SSNIP would be profitable:

6.035

"(i)   estimates of the sales that must be lost before a given price increase would be unprofitable (sometimes referred to as 'critical loss'). This would then have to be judged against the likelihood of such a loss occurring; and

(ii)   estimates of the maximum own-price elasticity of demand that would still make an increase in price profitable (sometimes referred to as 'critical elasticity'.)"[55]

---

[52] Cited above, para.6.025, n.18, at paras 4.45–4.46.

[53] Cited above, para.6.009, n.22, at p.96.

[54] To paraphrase the title of Harris' and Simons' article *"Focusing Market Definition: How Much Substitution Is Necessary?"*, 12 Research in Law and Economics 207 (Richard O. Zerbe, Jr. ed, 1989).

[55] Critical losses and elasticities are closely related. For example, the breakeven "critical" market own price elasticity (for the profits of the hypothetical monopolist not to increase) can be approximated by the critical percentage sales loss divided by the percentage price increase envisaged. This critical breakeven elasticity figure would then be compared with any estimates of the actual own-price elasticity of market demand for the relevant product in the area in question. Paragraph 2.16 of the Commission's guidelines (cited above, para.6.001, n.1), refers only to whether the degree of demand-side substitution observed is sufficient to render a price increase unprofitable, but substitution to supply-side alternatives should also be taken into account when assessing the aggregate degree of substitution.

If the actual loss which a hypothetical monopolist would experience following a SSNIP is greater than the critical loss, then it may be inferred that the market should be defined more broadly (and vice versa).[56] More generally, even within a market, critical loss and elasticity calculations are relevant to the assessment of whether a firm would find it profitable to increase prices unilaterally.[57] The analysis below is based on the assumption that the hypothetical monopolist would impose an "across the board" standard price increase, rather than targeting specific customers for discriminatory price increases. The issue of price discrimination and how this potentially impacts on critical loss calculations is considered further in paras 6.039 to 6.043, below.

Critical losses and elasticities depend on gross margins[58] prior to the price increase (*i.e.* the contribution made at prevailing prices to fixed costs, with such costs, by definition, not varying with output). The higher the gross margin prior to the price increase, the lower the critical loss and elasticity and vice versa. That is, with high gross margins the loss of a few customers will have a significant impact on profitability, whereas, with low gross margins more customers will need to be lost for the same impact on profitability. Price increases have two opposing effects (which both depend on gross margins):

(i) the profits derived from retained sales at higher prices will increase; and

(ii) profits will be lost from sales volumes loss.

Appendix 14 provides a simple example of how the breakeven critical loss can be calculated (*i.e.* the minimum percentage decline in sales necessary for a price increase not to be profitable).

6.036   Critical loss analysis has been considered in a number of the Commission reports. For example, in its report on the proposed merger between P&O Princess Cruises plc and Royal Caribbean Cruises Ltd, the Commission used financial information from the parties to estimate the proportion of

---

[56] Critical losses and elasticities can be calculated on two different bases. First, break-even critical losses and elasticities can be estimated for price increases not to increase profits (*i.e.* for the price increase to break-even). Secondly, profit maximising critical losses and elasticities can be estimated for the price increase envisaged to be profit maximising. For example, a 5% price increase might break-even, whereas a, say, 4% price increase might be profit maximising. These distinctions may be relevant if the degree of substitution expected in the event of a price increase by a hypothetical monopolist is close to the break-even critical loss for a given percentage price increase.

[57] There are a number of interesting articles on the subject of critical losses and elasticities e.g. Ch.10 on Critical Loss Analysis of the OFT research paper on "*Quantitative techniques in competition analysis*", cited above, para.6.012, n.32; "*Demand Elasticities in Antitrust Analysis*", Werden, (1998) 66 Antitrust Law Journal 363; Langenfield and Li, "*Critical loss analysis in evaluating mergers*", The Antitrust Bulletin, Summer 2001; Danger and Freech "*Critical thinking about 'critical loss' in antitrust*", The Antitrust Bulletin, Summer 2001; Katz and Shapiro, "*Critical Loss: Let's Tell the Whole Story*", Antitrust magazine, Spring 2003: O'Brien and Wickelgren, "*A Critical Analysis of Critical Loss Analysis*", May 23, 2003, Federal Trade Commission working paper; and Scheffman and Simons, "*The State of Critical Loss Analysis: Let's Make Sure We Understand the Whole Story*", *www.antitrustsource.com*, November 2003.

[58] *i.e.* price less marginal cost.

customers an individual cruise operator would be able to lose after a 5 to 10 per cent price increase and still remain as profitable (*i.e.* breakeven critical losses). The Commission estimated this break-even critical loss in passenger numbers to be around 9.5 to 11.5 per cent if prices were raised by 5 per cent, and to be around 17.0 to 21.0 per cent for a hypothesised 10 per cent price increase (with the range depending on the exact categorisation of costs as fixed and variable). The Commission stated that: "Though fully aware of its limitation, we found this estimate a useful benchmark against which to compare views on customers' likely responsiveness to price changes, and thereby assess the profitability of a 5 to 10 per cent price rise."[59]

In relation to the proposed acquisition by FirstGroup plc of the Scottish Passenger Rail franchise, the Commission carried out critical loss-type analysis which sought to simulate the increase in profitability on rail and bus services in aggregate of a reduction in bus service frequency and higher fares, assuming that there would be no constraints on FirstGroup taking such actions. This analysis was based on estimates of own and cross-price demand elasticities and costs.[60] This suggested that reducing bus service frequency would not be particularly profitable, but that fare increases might be profitable.[61] This analysis did not directly factor in all the constraints (*e.g.* existing price controls), and suggested that price increases were already profitable regardless of the merger. The later point might suggest that the constraints on price increases were understated by the Commission's modelling.

What do critical losses and critical elasticities reveal about actual elasticities and the likelihood of price increases?

Suppose that on the basis of a firm's gross margins pre-merger, the critical loss analysis indicates that a 10 per cent price increase would be rendered unprofitable by, say, a 40 per cent volume loss. Does this mean that a post-merger price increase is *prima facie* likely in the absence of any consideration of actual price elasticity of market demand for the product in the relevant geographic area? The answer to this question is an emphatic no.

6.037

In this regard, in its report on the proposed merger between Duralay International Holdings Ltd and Gates Consumer & Industrial (part of the Tomkins PLC group), the Commission noted that Duralay's carpet underlay business had relatively low fixed costs, and the Commission stated that from Duralay's financial information it had calculated that a 10 per cent price increase would be rendered unprofitable only if there were a substantial decline in sales volumes. The Commission nevertheless did not seek to rely on this point, and it noted Duralay's arguments that observing such a break-even critical loss did not prove that Duralay would have market power post-merger for a number of reasons. First, a high critical loss simply reflected. Duralay's cost structure (*i.e.* that only low gross margins are

---

[59] *P&O Princess Cruises plc/Royal Caribbean Cruises Ltd*, Cm. 5536 (June 2002), at para.5.6 and App.5.1.
[60] Cited above, para.6.012, n.36, at para.5.42 and App.I
[61] This analysis did not directly factor in all the constraints (*e.g.* existing price controls), and suggested that price increases were already profitable regardless of the merger. The latter point might suggest that the constraints on price increases were understated by the Commission's modelling.

required to cover low fixed costs and thus generate profits). This also meant that the merged business would not enjoy any appreciable cost advantages due to its scale, and that small-scale entry was a real threat as new suppliers would be viable on a small scale. Secondly, Duralay argued that a substantially greater sales loss would arise in practice were it to seek to increase prices in this way.[62]

6.038   Similarly, in its report on the merger between Littlewoods Organisation PLC and Freemans PLC (a subsidiary of Sears plc) the parties' economic advisers constructed a critical loss-type model which, on the basis of information gross margins and various assumptions as to the customers which would be lost and retained, suggested that a 10 price increase would not be profitable. Whilst the Commission found that the exercise was helpful, it did not find it conclusive, as small changes in the assumptions would have led to price increases being profitable.[63]

Critical loss analysis yields the "topsy turvey" result emphasised by Danger and Freech that if a market is highly competitive and gross margins are low, critical loss analysis may define the market narrowly in the sense that a substantial sales volume loss may be necessary to render a hypothetical price increase unprofitable: "Thus, the parties' argument that the market is exceptionally competitive may be at odds with a broad market definition."[64]

Similarly, if the critical loss is "low" (with gross margins being correspondingly high), Danger and Freech, O'Brien and Wickelgren, Katz and Shapiro, and Langenfield and Li all emphasise that in such circumstances a merger between two close competitors might render unilateral price increases profitable (or even potentially not particularly close competitors), because customers previously lost if prices were to be increased unilaterally by one firm to the other party would now be retained by the merged group (see further para.6.115).

The key point to appreciate is that market definition, and the market power of firms, cannot be assessed solely on the basis of critical loss and elasticity analysis—it is necessary to have this evidence, together with evidence as to actual substitution to alternatives.

A more complex issue is that Katz and Shapiro and O'Brien and Wickelgren argue that if the critical loss is low, then the actual loss that the merged firm would experience if it raised prices would be similarly low.[65] This is based on the premise that simple economic theory suggests that if gross margins are high this is evidence that a firm's own price elasticity is

---

[62] Cited above, para.6.008, n.21, at paras 3.37 to 3.38. Barriers to entry and expansion are addressed later in the Chapter, but is perhaps helpful to note a number of points briefly. If a high proportion of costs are fixed, this is also relevant to the assessment of barriers to entry and expansion. This is because: (i) it might mean that a new entrant needs to win a sizeable market share in order to break-even, which may make entry costly and risky; (ii) incumbent firms' profits will also be sensitive to the loss of relatively small sales volumes, and incumbent firms may therefore find it profitable to cut prices substantially in response to entry or expansion, which may in itself deter entry by making it harder for new or expanding rivals to achieve a return on their investment.

[63] *The Littlewoods Organisation PLC/Freemans PLC* (a subsidiary of Sears plc), Cm. 3761 (November 1997), at paras 2.99 to 2.102.

[64] Cited above, para.6.035, n.57. High gross margins will, however, not translate into high profits if fixed costs are also high.

[65] Cited above, para.6.035, n.57.

low—*i.e.* gross margins are high because if a firm decided to cut the standard price per unit, it would not generate sufficient additional sales to increase profits despite the large contribution to fixed costs and profits that winning new sales would achieve. However, Scheffman and Simons argue strongly that this simple economic theory might not be valid in all markets and that the actual loss may therefore exceed the critical loss.[66] In particular, they emphasise that this simple theory may be invalid under certain circumstances, such as if price elasticities were to be higher for price increases than decreases (*i.e.* even if cutting prices would not have much impact on sales volumes, raising prices would have a large impact). In addition, it might be invalid if prices are negotiated with customers (with the prices agreed not depending on simple elasticities, but bargaining leverage, relationships and so on). More generally, real market complexities are often not captured by the simple theory.

Price discrimination

In the above paragraphs it was emphasised that although a hypothetical monopolist would retain some sales following a price increase (referred to as "infra-marginal" sales), such a price increase could be rendered unprofitable due to the "marginal" sales which would be lost. However, this result may be radically different if instead of increasing prices to *all* customers, the hypothetical monopolist could increase prices selectively to so-called "vulnerable" or "captive" customers, since they would not reduce their purchase volumes sufficiently to render such a price increase unprofitable.

6.039

Accordingly, it is possible that a separate market should be defined for these captive customers, and this possibility is raised briefly in the OFT's guidelines on market definition under the Competition Act 1998 and the Competition Commission's guidelines.[67] Both sets of guidelines refer to the example of rail fares being higher on peak-time commuter services reflecting the fact that the own price elasticity of demand for peak rail travel is lower than for leisure travel, either because peak-time commuters do not view coach services as close substitutes (whereas off-peak leisure passengers do), or (rather more plausibly) due to differences in the willingness of commuter and leisure passengers to travel at non-peak times or to pay high fares. The key issue is whether profitable price discrimination is feasible.[68]

---

[66] Cited above, para.6.035, n.57.

[67] OFT guidelines on market definition under the Competition Act 1998, cited above, para.6.024, n.15, at paras 3.7–3.8, and Commission guidelines, cited above, para.6.001, n.1 at paras 2.33–2.34. It is also raised in the European Commission's "*Notice on the definition of the relevant market for the purposes of Community competition law*", (1997) O.J. C372, at p.9. A similar approach is adopted by the US Horizontal Merger Guidelines (cited above, para.6.001, n.4, s.1.12).

[68] Scherer and Ross state that: "No simple, all inclusive definition of price discrimination is possible. Succinctly, price discrimination is the sale (or purchase) of different units of a good or service at price differentials not directly corresponding to differences in supply cost" (cited above, para.6.001, n.4, at p.489).

Price discrimination may be categorised under three main headings:

(i)   "first degree" or "perfect price" discrimination, which requires firms to know the various maximum prices each of their customers is willing to pay and then to charge the maximum price to each customer. Obviously, customers have every interest in

The feasibility of profitable price discrimination

6.040   In order for it to be feasible for a supplier to discriminate against particular individual customers, or categories of customers, certain conditions must be satisfied.[69] First, the supplier in question must enjoy "some" degree of market power.[70] In the absence of market power, any attempt to seek to charge prices above marginal costs[71] would lead to customers switching to rivals offering lower prices. However, as pointed out by Motta[72] and others[73] this is arguably not a particularly helpful criterion as it is unlikely that real world firms operate in perfectly competitive markets and thus lack any market power (in the sense of setting prices equal to marginal costs), not least because if prices were equal to marginal costs they would not cover suppliers' fixed costs. Indeed, Motta rejects market power as a criterion to identify whether price discrimination is feasible.

The second condition for profitable discrimination is that those customers who are less price sensitive can be identified by reference to objective characteristics and thus charged higher prices.

The third condition that must be satisfied is that, in order successfully to discriminate between customers, it must be possible for the supplier to minimise or eliminate re-trading (or arbitrage) between low price and high price customers. To give an example, sweet shops would not offer lower prices to children because such a policy could easily be circumvented by children buying sweets on behalf of adults, whereas transport operators such as railways and airlines may offer discounts to children and students by requiring proof of their status to be shown prior to travelling. Similarly, train operators are able to discriminate between off-peak and peak

---

(ii)   "second degree" price discrimination, which involves firms offering products under different terms of supply with the objective of allowing consumers with different willingness to pay to self-select the product and terms of supply they prefer. For example, customers might be offered quantity discounts, with only larger purchasers who are more price sensitive qualifying for the higher quantity discounts. Lower prices might also be offered by an airline for staying a Saturday night as a means of discriminating against business travellers whose business trips do not usually end on a Sunday; and

(iii)   "third degree" price discrimination involves different prices being charged to different customers on the basis of some observable characteristic of the customer, again with the objective of identifying consumers with different price sensitivities. For example, students and the elderly might be given discounts at cinemas if it is believed that they are more price sensitive, or consumers based in a poorer country might face lower prices than consumers in a richer country, or customers using products for different end uses might be identified.

[69] These conditions are summarised in many textbooks (see, for example, the OFT's Research Paper on *"Market definition in UK competition policy"*, cited above, para.6.009, n.22, at pp.71–73; and Motta, cited above, para.6.001, n.2, at pp.491–493).

[70] See, for example, Scherer and Ross, cited above, para.6.001, n.4, at p.489, and the OFT's Research Paper on *"Market definition in UK competition policy"*, cited above, para.6.009, n.22, at p.71.

[71] In other words, the increase in total costs in the short run from selling one more unit of output.

[72] Cited above, para.6.001, n.2, at n.107 at pp.497 to 499.

[73] Muysert, *"Price Discrimination—an Unreliable Indicator of Market Power"*, [2004] E.C.L.R. 3500.

customers, with no risk of arbitrage between different categories of customers.

The existence of wholesalers, purchasing agents or other resellers may **6.041** facilitate arbitrage by selling to customers who might otherwise face high prices if they were to buy directly from the supplier (*e.g.* if a particular product is expensive in one country and cheaper in another, then resellers might well seek to parallel import the product depending on the cost and viability of such trade). In addition, resellers may make it very difficult for suppliers to gain detailed knowledge as to the identities of the customers supplied by resellers, and thus to charge a higher price to those customers deemed to be less price sensitive.

However, Hausman *et al.*[74] argue that the feasibility of profitable price discrimination should be carefully analysed with reference to the particular facts of any case, with the question of the existence of current price discrimination being an obvious starting point. As Hausman *et al* point out, identifying whether prices to customers reflect different price-to-cost ratios for the same product is often a difficult task. In particular, it is important to take into account differences in any marginal costs, such as transportation costs, differences in product costs if customers are not supplied with identical products, the existence of contracts including other bundled products and services (*e.g.* after-sales advice, warranties, etc.) and so on. In addition, in markets in which long term contracts are important, prices might well differ between customers due to differences in economic conditions at the time they entered into their supply contracts.

In addition, Hausman *et al.* argue that even if price discrimination is not **6.042** being practised *currently* in the proposed market, discrimination may become feasible once the proposed market is under the control of the hypothetical monopolist if the necessary conditions for price discrimination become met following the merger.

A particular issue considered by Hausman *et al.* is, assuming arbitrage between customers is impossible, how accurate a monopoly supplier must be in its identification of infra-marginal customers for targeted price increases to be profitable. As with the critical loss analysis set out above, the price increase to the targeted consumers has two effects:

(i)   for the fraction of customers within the target group whom the hypothetical monopolist has identified "correctly" as being infra-marginal, the monopolist gains additional revenues from the price increase; but

(ii) for the remainder of customers within the target group, which have not been correctly identified as "marginal", the monopolist loses the entire gross profit margin since these volumes are lost.

Hausman *et al.* present two different models to consider how accurately vulnerable customers need to be identified for price discrimination to be profitable: a model in which there are no repeat sales (so that customers incorrectly identified as vulnerable are effectively lost forever); and a model

---

[74] Hausman, Leonard and Vellturo, "*Market definition under price discrimination*", Antitrust Law Journal, issue 2, winter 1996.

in which vulnerable customers behave myopically (so that the only customers lost in the first period are those incorrectly identified, and they can be won back by offering them low prices in the next period). The first model indicates that very accurate identification of vulnerable customers is required for price discrimination to be profitable,[75] whereas much less accurate identification is required in the second model since the only consequence is that customers incorrectly identified are lost in only one period.[76]

However, it may not be realistic to assume that customers behave myopically. In particular, in a repeated-sales situation, customers with a high valuation of a product (*i.e. infra*-marginal customers) would not wish to be identified as such, as this would render them vulnerable to targeted price increases in the future. Accordingly, such customers have an incentive to "bluff", disguising themselves as marginal customers by foregoing or reducing purchases of the product for a finite period of time.[77] Hausman *et al.* refer to studies by Hart, Tirole and Schmidt, which ultimately conclude that price discrimination is less likely to be profitable in the repeated-sales situation than in the single-sale situation, if customers are allowed to act strategically. The authors warn that:

> "extreme caution is warranted when attempting to define relevant markets based on the possibility of price discrimination. This conclusion applies particularly strongly when no price discrimination is currently occurring in the industry under scrutiny. With no currently existing price discrimination, the assumption that a hypothetical monopolist could price discriminate is all the more speculative."

6.043   A further issue is that price increases targeted against certain customers or categories of customers could lead to alternative suppliers with spare capacity increasing their sales to these customers, thereby rendering the

---

[75] In the first model, a 5 per cent price increase is imposed on targeted customers and there are no repeated sales from one period to the next. Under this model, Hausman et al show that if the ratio of price to marginal cost is 2, then at least some 91 per cent of those customers targeted must be retained following the price increase for the price discrimination attempt to be profitable. Accordingly, very accurate identification of vulnerable customers is required. For higher price-to-cost ratios, the losses associated with guessing incorrectly increase, with the result that the hypothetical monopolist must guess correctly with even greater frequency to make a price increase profitable.

[76] In the second model, the assumption is made that targeted customers behave myopically so that the only consequence of incorrectly targeting marginal customers is the lost profit on sales to these customers for one period before they are won back at the old low price. In these circumstances, the accuracy with which infra-marginal customers must be correctly targeted falls sharply. For example, with the monopolist facing a cost of capital of 10 per cent. Hausman *et al* show that with a price/marginal cost ratio of 2, the monopolist would need to guess correctly whether targeted customers were infra-marginal only 48 per cent of the time for price discrimination to be profitable, compared with over 91 per cent of customers in the simple static model presented above. (The OFT Economic Discussion paper on "*Assessing profitability in competition policy analysis*" indicates that: "Broadly speaking, the cost of capital reflects the return required by investors to invest in the company's activities rather than elsewhere" (Economic Discussion paper 6, (July 2003), prepared by OXERA, OFT657, at para.7.5)).

[77] It may also be difficult for suppliers to identify whether a customer is buying less of their product due to lower requirements or due to the supplier charging high prices.

price increase unprofitable.[78] The so-called "capacity-diversion" defence, whereby outside capacity could be diverted into the market where price discrimination was occurring, has been examined in further detail by Glasner, and he makes a number of important points.[79] Taken at its simplest level, the capacity-diversion defence would suggest that price discrimination cannot occur if there are more than, say, two firms or a dominant firm facing a competitive fringe of smaller firms. Glasner concludes that such a result has not been adequately justified.[80]

Glasner also considers that the role of elasticity of demand within the narrow price discrimination market has ambiguous effects under the capacity-diversion argument. He argues that if there is a group of customers which can be discriminated against, then such customers would be relatively price insensitive, such that they would not materially reduce their purchases in response to a discriminatory price increase. This implies, on the one hand, that non-collusive suppliers would not need to divert a significant amount of production capacity into the narrow market in order to defeat such a discriminatory price increase, because customers' purchases would have fallen only slightly following the price rise. However, on the other hand, for those collusive suppliers within the narrow market, inelastic demand increases the gains from collusion (because prices can be increased without demand falling materially). Furthermore, with a low elasticity of demand, collusive suppliers within the narrow market would not need to divert a significant amount of production capacity out of that market in order to sustain a collusive price increase.

A further issue is that whilst a merger increasing market shares might lead to price increases to vulnerable customers who already pay higher prices that do not reflect differences in supply costs, this may equally not be the case. For example, difficulties in identifying customers to whom prices can be profitably increased further and/or increasing arbitrage between high and low priced customers as price differentials increase (*e.g.* due to the consequential development of purchasing agents and intermediaries), may preclude further price increases.

Finally, it is important to note that the anti-competitive effects of price discrimination are often identified by comparing a market structure characterised by monopoly with that of perfect competition. Froeb and O'Brien have raised questions as to whether these insights survive when considering

---

[78] Indeed, more generally the ability of rivals to increase sales is a factor recognised by both the OFT's and Commission's guidelines as a factor preventing non-co-ordinated (or unilateral) price increases, because a merged company contemplating increasing prices would face losing substantial sales to rivals which can readily expand their sales (see the fifth bullet point of para.4.8 of the OFT's guidelines, cited above, para.6.001, n.1 and the fifth bullet point of para.3.29 of the Commission's guidelines, cited above, para.6.001, n.1).

[79] Glasner, *"The capacity-diversion defense in Owens-Illinois and Donnelley"*, The Antitrust Bulletin, Vol. XLII, Number 1, Spring 1997.

[80] In particular, he observes that the capacity-diversion argument focuses exclusively on the ease of non-colluding firms to undermine a discriminatory price increase in the narrow market by shifting capacity into that market. However, ease of capacity diversion also allows the colluding firms within the narrow market more readily to support a price increase by shifting capacity out of that targeted market. Accordingly, he argues that there are two opposing forces at work, one tending to undermine collusion and one tending to stabilise it.

an oligopolisitic market structure.[81] Indeed, they identify circumstances where price discrimination may increase competition by allowing firms to compete for all customers (rather than exclusively marginal customers) by offering selective discounts to certain customers (*i.e.* those in the market area closer to a rival or those loyal to a rival's brand).

Case studies

Johnston Press/Trinity Mirror

6.044   There have been a number of cases where the possibility of price discrimination against certain customers has been assessed in the context of market definition. In *Johnston Press/Trinity Mirror*,[82] the Commission sought to assess whether advertising in local newspapers constituted a distinct economic market, or whether it constituted a sector within a wider advertising market which incorporated other media. The Commission found in this case that the closest substitutes for local newspapers were advertising-only publications, and, to a lesser extent, other forms of printed media. The Commission considered that radio and television were less direct competitors and may be seen by advertisers as complements to, rather than substitutes for, local newspapers. The Commission went on to indicate that for many advertisers, other media wer not close substitutes for advertising in local newspapers. The Commission observed that "These advertisers are likely to have to use several alternative media at the same time in order to achieve an effect similar to advertising in a local newspaper, and this may not be practicable at all for small advertisers."[83]

     The Commission then went on to consider different categories of advertisers, and the alternatives available to them. The Commission considered that advertisers such as estate agents and motor dealers were more likely than others to have good alternatives available to them, in particular because of the availability of advertising-only publications specialising in those categories, and the relative ease with which such publications could be launched. This could also be true to some extent of recruitment. The Commission considered that for retailers (the main source of display advertising), the most likely alternative to local newspapers was leaflets delivered to homes. Providers of home services (such as builders and plumbers) and of local entertainment and leisure services, could use directories and direct marketing for some purposes but were unlikely to find these as wholly adequate substitutes for local newspapers. Public sector bodies and private individuals, though not without other possibilities for some purposes, were considered least likely to have good substitutes to local newspaper advertising.[84] The Commission found that these latter categories of advertising customers already paid, on average, much higher prices than estate agents and motor dealers. The Commission concluded that it expected that a significant number of advertisers, and particularly providers of leisure and consumer

---

[81] "Price Discrimination & Competition: Implications for Antitrust", speech by Luke Froeb (Federal Trade Commission) before American Bar Association's Fall Forum, National Press Club, 529 14th Street, N.W., Washington, DC, November 19, 2003.

[82] *Johnston Press plc/Trinity Mirror Press plc*, Cm. 5495 (May 2002).

[83] Cited above, para.6.044, n.82, at para.2.31.

[84] Cited above, para.6.044, n.82, at para.2.32.

services, recruitment agencies and local government, would experience price increases following the proposed transaction.[85]

Scottish Radio Holdings and GWR/Galaxy

In the context of *Scottish Radio Holdings and GWR/Galaxy*,[86] the **6.045** Commission sought to assess whether radio advertising ought to be regarded as a separate market, or whether radio advertising was part of a wider advertising market which also included advertising in other media. The Commission concluded, having considered a variety of evidence, for a significant number of advertisers, that radio advertising was complementary to (rather than substitutable by) other media. In particular, the majority of respondents to a survey conducted by the Commission described radio commercials as unique and/or complementary to other forms of advertising. Furthermore, only 15 per cent of respondents to the survey (eight per cent weighted by value) referred to newspaper advertising as a practical alternative to the use of one of GWR's radio stations. Significantly fewer respondents referred to other media as being practical alternatives to radio advertising generally. Almost one half of local businesses (as opposed to agency buyers on behalf of businesses) surveyed by the Commission regarded other media as unattractive *vis-à-vis* advertising on GWR's radio stations, and most of the advertising customers that had switched away from Galaxy had switched to other radio stations, rather than to other media.[87]
The Commission concluded that:

"We regard local radio advertising as a separate market . . . This does not, however, necessarily imply that we believe that there is no price competition between local radio advertising and advertising on other media. There may be some price sensitivity caused by the availability of other media, which may constrain the pricing of advertising on radio, but we believe that it is likely to be significant only for certain advertisers and at certain times, and is not large enough in total to justify a definition of a market wider than that of radio advertising. Rather than regarding local radio advertising as part of a wider market, we feel it more appropriate to consider the effects of the availability of other media on the price sensitivity of certain advertisers when evaluating the effect of the merger on competition . . .."[88]

The Commission concluded that the merger may be expected to result in higher prices to at least some local advertisers in particular local areas, although the Commission emphasised that the extent of any price increase might vary between advertisers. The Commission believed that the most vulnerable advertisers on whom such price increases were likely to be focussed were local advertisers not using agencies.[89]

---

[85] Cited above, para.6.044, n.82, at para.2.121.
[86] *Scottish Radio Holdings plc and GWR Group plc/Galaxy Radio Wales and the West Ltd*, Cm. 5811 (May 2003).
[87] Cited above, para.6.045, n.86, at para.2.52.
[88] Cited above, para.6.045, n.86, at para.2.55.
[89] Cited above, para.6.045, n.86, at para.2.126.

The Commission concluded that GWR would be able to target price increases at a significant proportion of local advertisers (who did not purchase advertising through an agency) because prices were individually negotiated and this gave (according to the Commission) GWR sufficient knowledge of its customers to be able to identify vulnerable advertisers and price accordingly so that GWR could "increase prices without losing business." GWR argued that given its large customer base such individual customer analysis would be ineffective and that local advertisers could operate through agencies if they wanted to (and many did). The Commission did not accept these arguments, stating in particular that the number of vulnerable customers probably exceeded those estimated because the Commission had decided that survey respondents had a tendency to exaggerate responsiveness to price increases, and because "GWR provided no evidence on how readily available and cost-effective such an option [i.e. using agents] would be for local advertisers."[90] However, no evidence was provided by the Commission on how individual vulnerable customers (as opposed to the vague group categorised as local non-agency customers) could be identified by GWR or the extent to which it believed prices could be raised to those individual customers or how the acquisition of Galaxy would worsen their position. Arguably, if such customers were sophisticated enough to play off a local radio station against a regional one in order to secure discounts, why could they not disguise their vulnerability or buy through an agency?

Stena/P&O

6.046   In *Stena/P&O*,[91] the Commission concluded that accompanied and (with the distinction between the two being whether or not the driver travels with the freight on the vessel) unaccompanied freight services should be treated as a single market. However, the Commission noted that "due to the different nature of accompanied and unaccompanied operations, there may be some differences in the reaction of ferry operators and their customers in each of these segments to market events."[92] In this case, the Commission found that whilst the accompanied and unaccompanied freight sectors imposed a strong competitive constraint upon one another, different prices were charged for accompanied and unaccompanied traffic, and according to the time of crossing. The Commission found there to be a high degree of variation in prices paid by individual customers, and noted that the opaque nature of the market meant that ferry operators had the potential to discriminate between customers as regards pricing. The Commission concluded that:

> "whether or not there was a reduction in capacity on the central corridor, there would be scope for Stena post-merger to exercise market power by increasing prices to certain customers. Such price discrimination would be possible given the lack of pricing transparency in the market, and the knowledge gained over time of individual customer preferences through

---

[90] Cited above, para.6.045, n.86, paras 2.107 to 2.111.
[91] *Stena AB/The Peninsular and Oriental Steam Navigation Company* (February 2004).
[92] Cited above, para.6.046, n.91, at para.4.17.

close working relationships and the regular bargaining process. We considered that Stena would be able to focus price increases on certain customers and may also be able to increase prices to other customers, albeit to a lesser extent."[93]

Other issues in market definition

Chains of substitutes

A further complication in seeking to define markets from the perspective of demand substitutability arises where there are continuous chains of substitutes within a market. For example, product "A" may be a close substitute for product "B" and product "B" may be a close substitute for product "C", but consumers and producers may perceive that products "A" and "C" are poor substitutes. The Commission's guidelines observe that:

> "Despite not being direct substitutes, A and C may, in some instances, be considered to be in the same market if they are constrained by their common relationship with B."[94]

The concept of chains of substitution was briefly described by the Commission in the context of its inquiry into the supply of *New Cars*.[95] The Commission stated that:

> "Chains of products (such as small, medium-sized and large cars) and of ages of car (new, nearly-new and used) should be seen as part of the same market as long as each link of the chain is strong enough to ensure that all products in the chain are affected by a common price constraint."

In relation to the proposed acquisition by Duralay International Holdings of the Gates Consumer & Industrial business of Tomkins, the Commission found that different types of carpet underlay (*i.e.* sponge, crumb, foam, felt and polyurethane) were seen by the industry as a broad continuum in terms of quality and price. Although crumb underlay tended to be, on average, a higher quality and more expensive product than sponge underlay, and whilst foam and felt underlays were generally seen as being lower quality and lower priced products, there was a substantial overlap between the price ranges of these different materials. The Commission noted that this suggested that a material price increase in one of these types would be likely to prompt a switch to an alternative type. The Commission therefore concluded that sponge, crumb, polyurethane, felt and foam underlay belonged to the same market.[96]

In its guidelines, the Commission warns that:

> "In the presence of chains of substitution in the product market, consideration will be given to the extent to which there are breaks in the chain

6.047

---

[93] Cited above, para.6.046, n.91, summary para.13.
[94] Paragraph 2.30 of the Commission's guidelines, cited above, para.6.001, n.1.
[95] Cited above, para.6.008, n.21, at para.2.66.
[96] Cited above, para.6.008, n.21, at paras 2.22–2.24.

of substitution. Where . . . breaks . . . are identified, it might be appropriate to define separate markets on either side of the break."[97]

6.048   Similarly, there may be geographical chains of substitutes, and as with product markets, there may well be breaks in the chain of geographic substitutes.[98] As set out in App.13, in its report on the various bids for Safeway, the Commission rejected arguments that there might be a geographical chain of substitutes, largely on the basis that the links between the various chains were not sufficiently strong.[99] In addition, in relation to the proposed merger between Arla Foods amba and Express Dairies plc, the Commission observed that:

> ". . . when prices are not transparent and suppliers can price differentiate, the chain of substitution can break down. That is, those customers who can only be supplied by one firm will most likely be charged a higher price than those customers for whom A and B both compete to serve, even if it costs the same to supply both types of customers."[1]

Moreover, the existence of a chain of substitution might not necessarily define the scope of the relevant market. For example, in the case of a geographic chain of substitutes such as retailers located along a straight road (or equally a chain of products), A to Z, E might well be constrained by competition from the adjacent retailers D and F. However, if stores (or products) D, E and F were in common ownership, there might well be scope for prices at E to be increased, since those customers lost to D and F would be retained within the group company. This point is made by the OFT's guideline on Market Definition under the Competition Act 1998.[2]

Should the SSNIP be 10 per cent, 5 to 10 per cent, 5 per cent or some other number?

6.049   The Commission's guidelines state that it will normally use a 5 per cent price increase when applying the SSNIP test, assuming that all other prices remain unchanged, on the grounds that this will significantly impact on consumers' expenditures and firm's profit margins:

> "Whilst the absolute size of the price rise used will depend on the circumstances of the merger, the Commission will normally hypothesise an increase of around 5 per cent, whilst assuming all other prices remain unchanged. This price rise is assumed to last for the foreseeable future and the Commission will typically consider the extent of response which is likely to occur within a year of the price rise (although the exact time period will depend on the nature of the market considered).
> "The Commission will normally use 5 per cent for the SSNIP test, rather than the more common 5–10 per cent, because in many instances

---

[97] Cited above, para.6.001, n.1, at para.2.31.
[98] See para.2.32 of the Commission's guidelines, cited above, para.6.001, n.1.
[99] Cited above, para.6.027, n.26, at para.5.319.
[1] *Arla Foods amba/Express Dairies plc*, Cm. 5983 (October 2003), at para.5.56.
[2] Cited above, para.6.024, n.15, at paras 3.12 and 4.5.

an increase in the price of a product of around 5 per cent (with all other prices unchanged) might reasonably be judged to have a significant effect on customers' expenditure on that product and so provides an appropriate level at which to consider the test. In addition, a 5 per cent increase in price might be expected to have an appreciable effect on a firm's profit margin, the main issue then being whether demand would be reduced to such an extent as to offset the effects of the higher margin."[3]

This does not seem to be a particularly convincing case for the use of a 5 per cent increase in price (rather than, say, 10 per cent). This is because the impact on consumers of such an increase will depend on their overall expenditure on the product and their sensitivity to price changes, and the impact on suppliers' profits of such an increase will depend on the gross margin being earned prior to the increase (as noted above).[4] Indeed, the OFT has a more flexible approach to this issue. Its guidelines refer to a "five to ten per cent" price increase[5], whilst its guidance on market definition under the Competition Act 1998 refers to the 5 to 10 per cent test as "a rough guide rather than a rule."[6]

In many circumstances, it may make very little or no difference whether the SSNIP test is based on a 5 per cent price increase, a 10 per cent price increase or some other number. However, if the own price elasticity of demand increases as prices rise (which is a common assumption), then estimates of substitution at prevailing pre-merger prices might well understate the substitution that might occur at higher hypothetical monopoly prices. Werden notes that this can give rise to a "reverse" Cellophane fallacy (the Cellophane fallacy is considered in the next sub-section):

---

[3] Cited above, para.6.001, n.1, at paras 2.7–2.8. It should be noted that the Commission has considered a variety of price increases for the purpose of applying the SSNIP test. For example, in *Eastman Kodak Company/ColourCare Limited*, the Commission expressly considered a 10 per cent price increase (see, for example, paras 5.12 and 5.17 and App.5.1 from para.21 relating to a survey of consumers' responses to a 10 per cent price increases, cited above, para.6.013 n.38). On the other hand, the Commission's report on *Scottish Radio Holdings plc and GWR Group plc/Galaxy Radio Wales and West Limited*, considered the SSNIP test with reference to a 5 per cent price increase and the survey commissioned by the Commission considered responses to a 5 per cent price increase (see, for example, paras 5.50 and 5.51, cited above, para.6.013, n.38). The Commission's report on the proposed merger between *P&O Princess Cruises plc and Royal Caribbean Cruises Ltd*, considered the SSNIP test with reference to a price increase of 5 to 10 per cent (see paras 5.5 and 5.6, cited above, para.6.036, n.59).

[4] For example, if a firm is earning a gross margin equivalent to 5 per cent of price, then a price increase of 5 per cent would lead to a doubling of gross margins. However, if a firm was earning a gross margin equivalent to 40 per cent of price, then a 5 per cent price increase would have a much smaller impact on gross margins.

[5] Cited above, para.6.001, n.1, at para.3.17.

[6] "*Market Definition*", OFT guidelines under The Competition Act 1998, cited above, para.6.024, n.15, at para.3.2. Similarly, the US Horizontal Merger Guidelines take a flexible approach as to whether the SSNIP should be 5 per cent or some other number:

> "In attempting to determine objectively the effect of a 'small but significant and non transitory' increase in price, the Agency, in most contexts, will use a price increase of five percent lasting for the foreseeable future. However, what constitutes a 'small but significant and non transitory' increase in price will depend on the nature of the industry, and the Agency at times may use a price increase that is larger or smaller than five percent". (Cited above, para.6.001, n.4, para.1.11.)

"For any given demand elasticity and prevailing price, the higher the rate at which the elasticity of demand increases as price is increased, the smaller the price increase that would be imposed by a hypothetical profit-maximizing monopolist. Using estimated demand elasticities to delineate markets in merger cases, therefore, requires an assumption about the shape of the demand curve between the monopoly and premerger prices."[7]

Moreover, price elasticities of demand might not vary in a simple uniform fashion with price, and Danger and Freech, and Langenfield and Li[8] envisage a number of circumstances in which this might be the case. For some products, it is entirely possible that there might be zero or very low demand for the product or service if its price were to increase above (or perhaps even become close to) a superior quality alternative. Another possibility is that there might be a relatively small set of price-sensitive customers who would switch in response to a price increase (*e.g.* due to them being located in between two factories so that sources of supply from either factory are equally convenient or costly, taking into account transport times and costs) or some finite substitution to alternatives is possible (*e.g.* because pipeline infrastructure can import from non-local suppliers only strictly limited volumes of the relevant material).

In these latter circumstances, it is entirely possible that a 5 per cent price increase would be rendered unprofitable by the price sensitive customers switching to alternatives, but that a larger price increase might be profitable as a large customer base would be retained following the larger price increase (the price sensitive customers/ volumes having already switched at a lower price increase). In this regard, it should be noted that the critical loss calculated depends on the size of the price increase (see further App.14).

Pre-existing market power (the Cellophane fallacy), and related fallacies

6.050   A firm with pre-existing market power will raise prices until further price increase are no longer profitable, which may arise at the point that alternative products, which would not be considered substitutable at competitive prices, may become close substitutes. Accordingly, one question is whether existing market prices are the most appropriate basis upon which to apply the SSNIP test where there is significant pre-existing market power. This problem is generally known as the "Cellophane fallacy" after the Du Pont case in the US.[9]

On this subject, the Commission's guidelines state that:

"... where the Commission's subsequent understanding of the market leads it to believe that prices are substantially above the competitive level, the Commission recognises that prices more indicative of the competitive level might be more appropriate in its analysis of market definition ...

---

[7] Werden describes this as a "reverse" Cellophane fallacy (the Cellophane fallacy is considered in the next subsection) (cited above, para.6.035, n.57).

[8] Cited above, para.6.035, n.57.

[9] *US v El Du Pont de Nemours & Co* [1956] 351 US 377.

"Suppose that at a competitive price level, product A is in a different market from products B and C, but co-ordinated behaviour (see paragraphs 3.32 to 3.43) between the firms producing B and C has raised the prices of B and C to the point where A becomes a substitute. Therefore, the SSNIP test at current prices places all three products in the same market.

"In this instance, considering a merger of firms producing B and C, the Commission would tend to rely on the SSNIP test at competitive price levels; otherwise a merger which might increase market power could appear benign simply because the firms concerned had already been able to exercise a degree of market power. Although, necessarily in this example, the existence of product A would prevent more than a 5 per cent price increase, the merger would eliminate rivalry between the similar products B and C."[10]

The Commission's solution in assessing a merger between B and C, the two firms which are jointly exercising market power, is to apply the SSNIP test at "competitive" prices.[11] This raises two issues. The first is a practical issue as it assumes that competitive prices can be determined accurately. This is questionable, particularly in the context of a time limited merger reference, which would, by definition, not be a general industry investigation. As observed in the OFT research paper on "The role of market definition in monopoly and dominance inquiries", in the context of abuse of dominance investigations under EC and UK competition law:

"If one could identify the competitive price level then all Article 82 and Chapter II investigations would be trivial. One would simply identify the competitive price level and then compare it with the observed price level. If the observed price level were significantly above the competitive price level then the firm can be deemed to hold a dominant position (*i.e.* the ability to charge prices significantly in excess of the competitive level). There would be no need even to consider the definition of the relevant market, other than to satisfy strict legal requirements to do so.

"But in practice it is extremely difficult and in most cases impossible to determine the competitive price level."[12]

The second difficulty is that the test is in UK merger control "substantial lessening of competition", not whether there is pre-existing market power,   **6.051**

---

[10] Commission guidelines, cited above, para.6.001, n.1, at para.2.10.
[11] The Commission's position is also adopted by the US Department of Justice and Federal Trade Commission in their joint Horizontal Merger Guidelines, cited above, para.6.001, n.4, at s.1.11. The position taken in the European Commission's market definition notice is somewhat ambiguous, but it does draw a clear distinction between merger cases and cases relating to abuse of a dominant position: "Generally, and in particular for the analysis of merger cases, the price to take into account will be the prevailing market price. This may not be the case where the prevailing price has been determined in the absence of sufficient competition. In particular for investigation of abuses of dominant positions, the fact that the prevailing price might already have been substantially increased will be taken into account" (cited above, para.6.039, n.67, at para.19).
[12] Paras 3.7 and 3.8 of OFT 342, "*The role of market definition in monopoly and dominance inquiries*" (July 2001), OFT Economic Discussion Paper 2, prepared by National Economic Research Associates (NERA).

which may be termed the "Cellophane Fallacy Fallacy" (*i.e.* the Cellophane Fallacy has no practical relevance in merger cases).[13] Interestingly, the OFT's guidelines essentially take the same view as the research paper and thus the opposite view to that taken by the Commission:

"Where the OFT is able to use quantitative price data as a basis for the hypothetical monopolist test, it will generally use prevailing market price data. This is because a merger investigation focuses on whether prices could be raised above current levels, rather than whether current prices are too high."[14]

One example of the application of the Commission's approach is potentially provided by its report on the proposed merger between H+H Celcon Limited and Marley Building Materials Limited in which the Commission stated that it had:

"... concluded that aircrete block suppliers have nonetheless to some extent been able to sustain prices in recent years above the level that would be expected in fully competitive conditions. While the extent to which fully competitive conditions have or have not existed in recent years is not directly relevant to assessment of the merger, it is relevant to

---

[13] The Cellophane Fallacy Fallacy is a phrase coined by one of the authors, Dr Nigel Parr. The OFT research paper on "The role of market definition in monopoly and dominance inquiries" makes the point clearly that abuse of dominance investigations are very different from merger investigations:

"In merger inquiries, the competitive concern is whether the merger will create or strengthen a dominant position—or to put it in economic terms—will the merger result in an increase in prices above the *prevailing level*? This is likely to be the case where a merger results in the elimination of an important competitive constraint on the current pricing behavior of the merging parties. Hence, merger inquiries are *forward-looking* and are concerned with the identification of the competitive constraints that exist at *current prices*. In this context, market definition provides an appropriate framework within which the most important competitive constraints can be identified in a systematic manner.

In marked contrast to the forward-looking focus of merger inquiries, dominance inquiries are concerned with the current competitiveness of the markets in question. In such inquiries, the issue is whether the firm under investigation possesses the ability to act independently of competitors—or in economic terms—whether the firm already possesses market power. In making this assessment, one is interested in assessing whether the prevailing price is excessive and not with whether the firm is prevented from raising prices still further." Cited above, para.6.050, n.12, at paras 2.26 and 2.27.

[14] Cited above, para.6.001, n.1, at para.3.19. The OFT further emphasises the difference between merger inquiries and investigations as to abuse of a dominant position under c.II of the Competition Act 1998 in a footnote to this para.:

"In Chapter II investigations under the Competition Act 1998, for example, the competitive prices version of the SSNIP test is used. An important aspect of these investigations is whether firms have market power. Where market power is being exercised, prices may be higher than they would be under competitive conditions, and rival products may appear to be closer substitutes than they actually are (the 'cellophane fallacy'...). In such a situation, if the SSNIP test were based on prevailing prices, one might erroneously conclude that the firm under investigation did not have market power. In other words, the fact that the firm under investigation had used its market power to raise prices above competitive levels might, in certain circumstances, lead to the conclusion that it did not in fact have market power."

the SSNIP test, and therefore to the question of market definition. Specifically, to the extent that prices have been above fully competitive levels, the SSNIP test has been applied to price levels above the competitive level. This will bias the results to indicate more substitutability than would have been the case at competitive levels. There is, therefore, some evidence to suggest that the extent of substitutability revealed in the responses to our questionnaire overstates the degree of substitutability relevant to defining the product market."[15]

The Commission did not define how much lower prices should have been or the economic evidence for its conclusion that profits should have been lower if the market had been more competitive (against a background of low and negative historical profits and efficiency improvements). Nor did it indicate in its subsequent analysis how this observation should be taken into account for the purpose of assessing the risk of future price increases.

After indicating that it will generally consider prevailing prices, the OFT's guidelines add that: "There may however be cases in which the OFT will use other than prevailing prices, for example where future market prices can be accurately predicted on the basis of, say, changes in an industry's price regulation."[16] What the OFT is referring to as regards price regulation is not precisely defined, but if, for example, the products sold by the merged firm were to be subject to price controls, this could act as a constraint on price increases (*e.g.* in mergers involving regulated utilities or rail operators).

Why should the price of substitutes remain constant?

As noted above, the version of the SSNIP test applied by the Commission assumes that whilst there is a small but significant increase in the price of the set of products under consideration, the prices of all other (potentially competing) products remain constant. This assumption might well be wrong if, for example, suppliers of alternative products cannot readily expand (*e.g.* because they have little or no spare capacity, and capacity expansions would be slow or non-economic), or because of co-ordinated effects (such that other firms would also increase their prices).[17] In such circumstances, assuming that the prices of alternatives remain constant might lead to markets being defined too widely in the sense that market shares might understate the market power of the firms in question.[18]

6.052

---

[15] Cited above, para.6.011, n.31, at para.2.51.

[16] Cited above, para.6.001, n.1, at para.3.19.

[17] In particular, the existence of a close substitute for a specific product will not constrain suppliers of this product unless the supplier(s) of the substitute product would readily increase their sales to meet any additional demand. If suppliers of the substitute product cannot or will not increase their sales, this will lead to the price of the substitute product also being bid up. Such factors might well lead to the prices of two products being closely correlated, without the substitute materially constraining the price of the product in question (see further paras 6.021 to 6.023 on the commentary on price correlations).

[18] In this regard, a distinction may be drawn between a firm's own price elasticity of demand for its products (which is calculated assuming that the prices of alternatives remain constant) and its residual own price elasticity of demand (which takes into account the supply responses of other firms, i.e. whether they increase prices if one firm increases its prices). Simons and Williams argue that "it seems inefficient to ignore supply-side responses in market definition, and delay their consideration until the competitive effects portions of the

Danger and Freech, and Langenfield and Li[19] emphasise that critical loss and elasticity calculations should take account of rivals' likely responses to price increases by the merged firm.

However, the presumption that the price of alternatives would remain constant may also lead to artificially narrow markets being defined. For example, going back to the example given in relation to chains of substitutes, suppose now that retail outlets A and C merge. Ordover and Willig pose the question of whether A and C can now profitably raise price:

"Assume now that A and C, who are located on either side of B, want to merge. Can they profitably raise their price by 5%? The answer is 'No' if B does not go along. The reason is that if A raises his price, some of his customers will leave for B, but none of his customers will venture to C. His merging partner C faces the same predicament . . . The analyst must inquire whether B is likely to maintain his price, or whether he is likely to take advantage of A's and C's efforts and raise his price as well. If the latter is true, then according to this inquiry, the merger can lead to a price increase, even though a more simple-minded approach might produce a different conclusion . . . [*i.e.* that A and C are not competing in the same local market as they share no common customers]."[20]

Both of the above points have merit, but the key point to appreciate is that such factors need to be considered as part of the competitive assessment if they are not considered in the context of market definition (*i.e.* so that the market definition decision does not lead to an incorrect competitive assessment). It is suggested that in each case the market should be defined widely, and then the risks of non-co-ordinated or co-ordinated effects should be considered within such a market.

---

analysis. Ignoring supply responses during market definition is very likely to result in including firms that will not have sufficient constraining influence on a potential price increase, whether through collusive [i.e. coordinated] or unilateral mechanisms. As a result, the definition of such broader markets would either understate the dangers of particular mergers or require that the firms exercising insufficient influence somehow be removed from the analysis of competitive effects" ("The renaissance of market definition", The Antitrust Bulletin/Winter 1993.) The alternative view is to recognise, as does the OFT Research paper on market definition, that this is part of a wider problem that a literal interpretation of the SSNIP test means that any firm with the ability to raise prices above the competitive level would be defined as being a relevant market on its own (cited above, para.6.009, n.22, at pp.24 and 25). Factors which mean that certain rival firms included in the market do not exercise sufficient competitive influence can be taken into account in subsequent competitive analysis (see further below the various factors which influence the risk of a merger leading to anti-competitive non-coordinated or coordinated effects).

[19] Cited above, para.6.035, n.57.

[20] Ordover and Willig, "*The 1982 Department of Justice Merger Guidelines: An economic assessment*", California Law Review (1983), at Port 1, s.3. See, in particular, the Commission's approach to assessing local concentration in the context of the various bids for Safeway (cited above, para.6.027, n.26) which is set out at App.13. In particular, the Commission also identified local competition concerns in relation to mergers of non-competing stores (*i.e.* A and C merging) if they reduced the number of local independently owned supermarket competitors to supermarket chains which were not the merging parties.

Wider competitive constraints

Apart from competition from demand-side and supply-side substitutes, a **6.053** supplier of goods or services may face two wider competitive constraints. These will arise in markets in which consumers are unwilling to pay more for a product either because they place a low valuation upon it,[21] or because they face active competition in a "downstream" final product market, with the consequence that they are unable to pass on any increases in the cost of components to their customers in the form of higher prices.[22] The extent to which the price sensitivity of consumers acts as a competitive constraint has been considered in a number of cases. For example, the Director General's advice on the proposed acquisition by easyjet plc of NewGo 1 Limited stated that:

> "First, for leisure travellers, who are the bulk of the parties' customers, there will continue to be a wide range of competitive choice available. This includes choice among destinations and among rival carriers. Price sensitive leisure travellers might also decide not to travel by air at all in the event of a price increase."[23]

Similarly, competition in the market for the finished products may put pressure upon customers to resist price rises for specific raw materials and semi-finished products, which would make them uncompetitive. For example, in relation to the proposed acquisition by Tessenderlo Chemie SA of the Widnes Plant and business of Atofina UK Ltd, the OFT observed that a further competitive constraint in relation to one of the overlapping products related to competition in downstream markets:

> "There are further constraints on manufacturers of Phenylacetic Acid [used in the manufacture of penicillin] from the competitive downstream industry. The market for the downstream penicillin products was the subject of an EC merger investigation in 1998 (Case No. IV/M.1143—DSM/Gist Brocades). In that case, the EC concluded that the geographic market for the end product could be considered to be worldwide. Given that this downstream product market is competitive, any action by the parties to increase the price of Phenylacetic Acid would probably result in European penicillin manufacturers losing market share to non-EU producers, thus resulting in a loss of business for the intermediate good suppliers. Hence the competitive global downstream market will act as a constraint against the EU producers of Phenylacetic Acid."[24]

---

[21] Consumer price sensitivity is just as much a competitive constraint as consumers diverting expenditure to substitute products.

[22] The US Merger Guidelines state that in considering the likely reaction of buyers to a price increase the Agency will take into account "the influence of downstream competition faced by buyers in their output markets" (cited above, para.6.001, n.4, s.1.21).

[23] Director General's advice of July 10, 2002 *The proposed acquisition by easyJet plc of NewGo 1 Limited*.

[24] Cited above, para.6.027, n.24.

Conclusion: Key points as regards market definition

6.054 It is apparent from the preceding discussion that a range of factors is likely to be relevant to determining the scope of the relevant market in merger cases.

The Commission's guidelines note that: "Occasionally this process may not give a clear-cut or unique answer".[25] The Commission also correctly emphasises that the issue is whether or not there will be an SLC, rather than market definition *per se*:

"Whilst in most instances, the Commission will want to be clear as to its preferred market definition, its duty is to decide whether a merger will result in an SLC or not and, as a result, it will not devote disproportionate resources to determining exactly whether a particular competitive constraint results from within the market (and so should be included in the market definition) or from outside the market. As a result, the Commission may need to consider several alternative market definitions as part of its investigation, or may choose to identify particular sections of whatever market is considered."

These difficulties are likely to be substantially greater for individual suppliers, who will typically have substantially less information and less reliable information than the authority, particularly in relation to:

(i)   the views of customers;

(ii)   the views of other firms that are potential supply-side substitutes;

(iii)   how other actual and potential competitors view the market and their resulting pricing policies; and

(iv)   trends in the relative prices of alternative products and similar products supplied in different areas; and so on.

Nevertheless, a good place to start such an analysis is a consideration of how the suppliers in question set their prices in practice, drawing on internal documents.[26] For example, in the context of FirstGroup's proposed acquisition of the Scottish Passenger Rail Franchise the Commission referred to FirstGroup's business plans in reaching its conclusion that there was competition between bus and rail services:

"A degree of competition between bus and rail was also implied by some background material provided by FirstGroup. The First in Glasgow 2003/04 five-year business plan for its bus operations states that 'a signif-

---

[25] Cited above, para.6.001, n.1, at para.2.6.

[26] Certainly, the Commission is likely to request such documents and the OFT is increasingly asking for internal documents relating to competitive analysis. It should be noted in this connection that internal documents will often be prepared for purposes other than to undertake the type of economic assessment advocated by regulators. They will often be open to interpretation, and will be heavily influenced by business people's perceptions of the markets in which they operate, such perceptions not necessarily being fully informed or based on the SSNIP test.

icant proportion of the operating area experiences major competition from many modes including rail' (while also referring to long-established competition from other bus operators)."[27]

Similarly, in the context of the proposed merger between Stena AB and the Peninsular and Oriental Steam Navigation Company, the Commission stated that there were various other arguments consistent with its view that there was a central corridor freight market, including: Stena's own management papers which identified it as being in competition with a range of other central corridor operators (and not just the other operator on the same route it served); Stena's financial modelling of a route's closure on this corridor which assumed that the business would be redistributed to a number of central corridor services; and the parties' submissions to the OFT, which made a similar assumption.[28] **6.055**

In many cases, therefore, it may be difficult for the parties to a merger to define the relevant market accurately. In these circumstances, the parties' arguments in favour of the merger should not rest upon a contention that the merged company will enjoy a relatively low share of a more widely defined market, but should focus on the strength of the remaining competitors, and the magnitude of barriers to entry and expansion, even if a narrow market definition were to be adopted.

Previous investigations by competition authorities may also provide useful information, and are likely to be particularly influential at the OFT stage. In particular, the OFT's guidelines note that:

"In defining markets, the OFT will have regard to previous OFT, [Commission] and EC decisions concerning the same industry sectors and take due account of them, but does not consider itself bound by those precedents in particular because markets may change over time. Where appropriate, the OFT will also have regard to decisions of other competition authorities that concern the scope of the market(s) at issue."[29]

---

[27] Cited above, para.6.012, n.36, at paras 4.20–4.23.

[28] Cited above, para.6.012, n.36, at para.4.25(a) and (b). Reliance on internal documents may be ill advised if they have plausible alternative interpretations, or are based on incomplete or inaccurate information, or if they do not reflect business decision making.

[29] OFT guidelines, cited above, para.6.001, n.1, at para.3.16. Similarly, the OFT guidelines on market definition under the Competition Act 1998 indicate that although precedents in market definition can provide a useful reference point, previous conclusions may not always be the correct ones to use in future cases. In particular, the OFT notes that "innovation may make substitution between products easier, or more difficult, and therefore change the market definition" (cited above, para.6.024, n.31, at para. 5.15). More generally, demand and cost conditions might change over time and vary between member states (for example, consumer loyalty to established brands might be high in one member state impeding supply side substitutability from other member states, whereas retailers' own-label brands might account for the vast bulk of sales in other member states, thereby facilitating imports as non-local suppliers do not need to incur the costs and risks of establishing their own brand names). Equally important, market definition may well vary according to the economic issue at stake. For example, a merger between two bus operators might lead to price increases, but so might a merger between a monopoly local bus operator and a monopoly rail operator if pre-merger rail fares were preventing the bus monopoly operator from increasing its bus fares yet further (see further the OFT Research Paper on market definition, cited above, para.6.009, n.22, p.23).

Barriers to entry and expansion

6.056 The Competition Commission's guidelines define barriers to entry and expansion as:

"... features that may prevent or restrict firms from exploiting profitable opportunities in a market and hence might enable a merged firm to raise price above costs persistently without significant loss of market share to other firms."[30]

Both the OFT's and Commission's guidelines emphasise that low barriers to entry and expansion prevent the exercise of significant market power.[31]

The assessment of barriers to entry and expansion requires the consideration of three broad issues[32], namely whether new entry and expansion:

(i)   is likely on normal commercial terms;

(ii)   would be timely, reflecting the fact that it may take time for new entrants or small firms to establish themselves as significant rivals. The OFT's guidelines indicate that: "Entry within less than two years will generally be timely, but this must be assessed on a case by case basis. . ."[33];

---

[30] The Commission's guidelines, cited above, para.6.001, n.1, at para.3.49. The OFT's guidelines adopt a similar definition, cited above, para.6.001, n.1, at para.4.21. This approach follows the definition proposed by Bain, as it focuses on the ability of incumbent firms to make excess profits, with Gilbert's version of this definition emphasising that these excess profits are being earned while other equally or more efficient firms are excluded (see further pp.62–64 of Bishop and Walker, cited above, para.6.001, n.2). Under this definition the low profits or losses of incumbent firms are not deemed a barrier to entry or expansion, although they obviously impede entry and expansion. (As noted by Bishop and Walker, there are other potential definitions of barriers to entry and expansion.) The OFT's Research Paper on "*Barriers to Entry and Exit in UK Competition Policy*", by London Economics, March 1994, OFT 117 has a good review of barriers to entry and expansion. The OFT's September 2004 research paper, "*Empirical indicators for market investigations*", which was prepared by NERA, observes that "high levels of entry barriers in an industry . . . have been found to be associated with high levels of industry concentration" (at para.2.9).

[31] See para.3.51 of the Commission's guidelines (cited above, para.6.001, n.1); and paras 4.18 and 4.26 of the OFT's guidelines (cited above, para.6.001, n.1),

[32] This is the approach taken by: the OFT's guidelines (cited above, para.6.001, n.1, at paras 4.19–4.23); the Commission's guidelines (cited above, para.6.001, n.1, at paras 3.51–3.52); the European Commission's Horizontal Merger Guidelines (paras 69–75, cited above, para.6.001, n.4); and the US Horizontal Merger Guidelines (cited above, para.6.001, n.4, at ss.3.0–3.4).

[33] Cited above, para.6.001, n.1, at paras 4.22–4.23. It should be noted that unlike the OFT, the European Commission, and the US Department of Justice/Federal Trade Commission, the Competition Commission does not refer to an indicative two year period within which entry would be deemed likely. A longer period might be appropriate if such delayed entry might nevertheless be an important constraint on existing firms prior to such entry occurring. This might be the case if, due to switching costs or the importance of long term relationships, successful entry would have a very serious impact on the long term profitability of the firm, as once customers were lost they would be hard to regain (although such switching costs may be a barrier to entry and expansion, see further para.6.065). Similarly, if customers are supplied under long term contracts which specify prices, then the issue is whether there could be additional suppliers when these contracts come up for renewal. The US Horizontal Merger Guidelines also indicate that a period longer than two years might be

(iii) would be sufficient to constrain any attempt to exploit market power, with small scale or niche entry potentially not achieving this.[34]

Absolute advantages

Absolute advantages arise where a firm is able to enjoy lower costs (or alternatively a superior quality product commanding higher prices) at each level of output compared with its competitors.[35] If potential entrants face higher costs or must offer, temporarily or permanently, lower prices to offset perceived quality advantages enjoyed by an established competitor, they are less likely to enter the market.

6.057

As described below, absolute cost advantages may arise for a number of reasons including, *inter alia*, regulation, access to scarce input resources or resources of superior quality, access to superior technology through research and development, the ownership of intellectual property rights or a superior brand.[36]

Regulatory and legal barriers

Regulatory and legal barriers to entry and expansion include a wide range of factors such as restrictive licensing laws, planning constraints, regulatory approvals and disposal/pollution controls, and have been considered in a number of cases.[37]

6.058

---

considered in the context of a durable good market, if consumers, in response to a significant commitment to entry, would delay new purchases (e.g. by increasing maintenance of existing equipment, rather than replacing it with new equipment) thereby preventing the exercise of market power before entry occurs (see s.3.2, cited above, para.6.001, n.4).

[34] A number of caveats should nevertheless be noted. First, a number of small scale entrants could have a major impact, even if one would not. Secondly, small scale entry might still be a major constraint. For example, as set out at paras 6.035 to 6.036, above, critical loss analysis might indicate that a small volume loss could substantially depress profits. In addition, if the competition concern raised by a merger relates to discrimination against a minority of customers, then a new small supplier targeting these customers might represent a major competitive constraint.

[35] This Chapter adopts the approach that absolute cost advantages differ from economies of scale, with the latter arising where increases in output reduce average unit costs.

[36] It should be noted that both research and development and brands/advertising can also confer strategic advantages.

[37] In considering the extent to which regulation may affect barriers to entry, the Director General notes that there is a distinction between regulation which sets objective standards, and that which places a limit on the number of competitors in the market. His guidelines on the assessment of market power under the Competition Act 1998 state that:

"Objective standards which apply equally to all undertakings, such as health and safety regulations, should not, in general, be an absolute barrier to entry, although the position may be different if they were drawn up largely under the influence of incumbents with a view to making entry more difficult. Conversely, some regulation may limit the number of undertakings which can operate in a market—through the granting of licences, for example. When the numbers of licences are restricted, there may be an absolute limit to the number of undertakings that can operate in the market. This will act as an entry barrier unless licences are tradeable in a competitive market, in which case a potential entrant could purchase a licence and enter the market if a profitable opportunity arose." (Cited above, para.6.001, n.5, at para.5.5.)

For example, in *Coloplast/SSL International*, the Commission identified as a barrier to entry the need for medical products to be included on the UK Drug Tariff in order for pharmacies and contract dispensers to supply these products on NHS prescription. This was because the controls:

(i)   materially increased the time required to obtain a listing;

(ii) distorted prices by allowing products that were similar to products already on the Drug Tariff to be listed only at prices equal to, or more usually below, the prices of the products already listed; and

(iii) prevented new suppliers using a low promotional price to enter the market in order to gain market share with a view to raising prices once the product had been established. This was because the controls prevented price increases in the absence of negotiation with the Association of British Healthcare Industries.[38]

Similarly, in *London Clubs International/Capital Corporation*, the MMC found that as a consequence of the regulatory regime, barriers to entry into the market for "upper segment" casinos in London were high. The major barrier to entry identified by the MMC was the need for a potential entrant to demonstrate the existence of "unsatisfied demand" for gaming in the area, although other important barriers to entry included, *inter alia*, the need to obtain planning permission at suitable premises, and restrictions on advertising which limited any new casino's scope to market itself. Potential new entrants also faced the hurdle of having to obtain a Gaming Board certificate of consent before they could get an operating licence, which could take a number of years.[39]

Access to scarce input resources or superior technologies

6.059   Incumbent suppliers may enjoy an absolute advantage over new entrants as regards access to scarce input resources or superior technologies, if new entrants either cannot gain access at all to these resources, or they can gain access only at a cost which is substantially higher than that faced by the incumbents. As noted in the Director General notes in his guidelines on the assessment of market power:

"In some cases, entry to a market might require the use of an essential facility, an asset or facility with two key characteristics. First, access to it must be indispensable in order to compete on the market and, secondly, duplication of the facility is impossible or extremely difficult owing to physical, geographic or legal constraints, or is highly undesirable for reasons of public policy."[40]

However, as regards the trading of licences, the Commission's guidelines on market investigation references emphasise that a relevant factor is how often opportunities for new entrants to purchase licences would be expected to arise in practice ("*Market Investigation References: Competition Commission Guidelines*", June 2003, at para.3.30).

[38] Cited above, para.6.028, n.30, at paras 2.74–2.75.

[39] *London Clubs International PLC/Capital Corporation PLC*, Cm. 3721 (August 1997), at paras 2.43–2.49.

[40] Cited above, para.6.005, n.5, at para.5.6.

The guidelines note, however, that there may be circumstances in which difficulties accessing assets or resources will constitute an entry barrier, without those assets or resources meeting the strict criteria required to be defined as "essential facilities."

In the context of its inquiry into the acquisition of Fife Silica Sands and Fife Resources by SCR-Sibelco, the Commission found that:

"We think that there are also severe constraints on new entry . . . into the glass-sand market. These constraints are mainly attributable to Sibelco's control of most of the known, economically-workable reserves of glass sand in Great Britain. Given this market strength of Sibelco, the incentives for another company to surmount the hurdles of exploring for new sources of sand, obtaining the required planning permission and committing the necessary investment, are likely to be very limited. We therefore think that new entry is most unlikely and we would not expect Sibelco to be deterred from increasing prices by the threat of it."[41]

Intellectual property rights

Whether intellectual property rights such as patents, copyright and know-how constitute material barriers to entry depends upon the magnitude of the advantages they yield to their holders in particular cases. If they can be easily circumvented, or if alternative unprotected technologies and processes are available which are equally effective, they will not act as material barriers to entry. For example, in the context of its inquiry into the acquisition by McKechnie Paxton Holdings of Linpac Group, the Commission noted that: **6.060**

"Most [returnable transit packaging] manufacturers . . . patent new designs or innovative features in their product range. In theory, this should act as a barrier to other manufacturers producing similar products, but it does not appear to do so in practice, or at least not to any significant extent . . . we were told that patents could be circumvented by relatively small changes in a design . . . So while patenting certainly exists in the [returnable transit packaging] business we did not find evidence that it constituted a significant barrier to competition, or to the entry of new players . . . ."[42]

Brand loyalty

In general terms, brand loyalty,[43] as reinforced by advertising, may create barriers to entry if: **6.061**

---

[41] *SCR—Sibelco SA/Fife Silica Sands Ltd and Fife Resources Ltd*, Cm. 5139 (July 2001), at para.2.108.

[42] *Linpac Group Limited/McKechnie Paxton Holdings Limited*, Cm. 5496 (May 2002), at para.2.46.

[43] It should be emphasised that this section is a brief summary. For a more detailed discussion on this subject see: Parr and Hughes, "*The Relevance of Consumer Brands and Advertising in Competition Inquiries*", European Competition Law Review (1993), Vol. 14, Issue 4; Clarke, "Industrial Economics", Basil Blackwell Ltd, 1985, pp. 119–142; and Scherer and Ross, cited above, para.6.001, n.4, pp.130–135 and 571–600. The OFT Research Paper on "*Barriers to Entry and Expansion in UK Competition Policy*" contains a good discussion of these issues, cited above, para.6.056, n.29, at s.2.3.2.

(i)   "strong" brands are able to command a price premium amongst consumers relative to new or minor brands, without their market shares being significantly eroded by alternative brands; and

(ii) attempts to enhance consumers' acceptance of new or minor brands through advertising would place suppliers of such brands at a competitive disadvantage compared with the major suppliers of "strong" brands.

There are two main reasons why consumers are likely to be loyal to established strong brands. First, consumers may have entrenched preferences for established brands because of their "image", which may be created or reinforced by advertising, and they may therefore consider that competitors' brands are poor substitutes even if they are physically very similar. Secondly, for some goods it may be difficult for consumers to assess product quality without a trial purchase or even after purchase. Examples of goods of this nature would include products such as instant coffee and health related products, such as contact lens solutions. In this situation, branded suppliers' established reputation for product quality may be valuable to consumers if the low cost and infrequency of purchase means that it is not worthwhile for consumers to try competing brands which may not perform adequately, even if these alternative products are significantly cheaper.[44]

The advantages conferred by a strong brand in the context of a market where there existed customer uncertainty as to product quality were illustrated in *Coloplast/SSL International*. In that case, the Commission found that for urobags and catheters:

"Whether or not names such as Clear Advantage are brand names within the commonly accepted meaning of that term, it is clear to us that possession of such a widely recognized name is helpful for marketing purposes and confers a significant advantage upon its holder. We were not convinced by Coloplast's argument that all continence care professionals are likely to be so well informed on the relative functional characteristics of all available products as to remove the value of reputational factors relating to particular products or suppliers."[45]

Similarly, in *Alanod Aluminium-Veredlung/Metalloxyd Ano-Coil*, the Commission found that:

"Another possible barrier to a new entrant is the reluctance of end-users to switch from their established supplier without strong reason. Customers in this market require a high level of reliability, both in product quality and delivery time, and may be unwilling to switch to a supplier with no reputation in the market . . . .."[46]

---

[44] This effect has been modelled by a number of economists. See for example, Schmalensee, "*Product Differentiation Advantages of Pioneering Brands*", American Economic Review (1982), pp.349–365.

[45] Cited above, para.6.027, n.29, at para.2.71. Nevertheless, the Commission concluded that this barrier could be surmounted through the distribution of free samples and services to continence advisers.

[46] Cited above, para.6.025, n.18, at para.2.64.

Suppliers of new or minor brands may attempt to secure consumer **6.062** acceptance by engaging in advertising and promotion. Such a decision may be risky, as investment in advertising to build up a level of acceptance (or a stock of consumer goodwill) comparable to that enjoyed by suppliers of major brands can be regarded as being "sunk" as it will have no value if entry fails, thereby making entry risky, with the consequence that entry may be deterred. For example, in its report on the proposed merger between Cendant Corporation and RAC Holdings, the MMC stated that:

"... it appears to us that the main obstacle to entry and growth in [the motor vehicle breakdown services market] is the relatively large sunk costs required to establish a brand name able to compete with the longstanding and trusted AA and RAC brands. Green Flag's advertising and promotional expenditure has been considerable ... yet even with these levels of expenditure, public awareness of the Green Flag brand had reached only about 35 per cent nationally by December 1997 ... Even Direct Line, already well known as a motor insurer, felt the need for what it termed significant advertising expenditure in support of its own breakdown service which it launched in May 1998 ...."[47]

However, it may be more meaningful to treat advertising as an ongoing fixed cost, rather than as a sunk investment (although any start-up losses are irrecoverable), because most empirical studies suggest that the benefits of advertising typically depreciate rapidly, in the sense that past advertising has a minimal impact on current sales.[48] Accordingly, the advantages enjoyed by suppliers of major brands may be more attributable to the existence of a first mover advantage and/or cost advantages in advertising, rather than to the cumulative effect of sunk advertising expenditure. In particular, suppliers of major established brands may enjoy a competitive advantage, at least initially because, *inter alia*:

(i) there may be economies of scale in advertising above certain threshold levels of expenditure (so that doubling advertising expenditure will have a more than proportionate impact on sales) which is likely to favour established brands[49]; and

(ii) the effectiveness of advertising may be greatest when a new product category is first launched, as consumer loyalty to individual products may be weak or absent (that is, a first mover advantage may arise).[50]

---

[47] *Cendant Corporation/RAC Holdings Ltd*, Cm. 4196 (February 1999), at para.4.127.

[48] See, for example, Schmalensee "*Sunk Costs and Market Structure: A Review Article*", The Journal of Industrial Economics (June 1992), pp.125–134. Schmalensee cited as support Ch.6 of Berndt, "*The Practice of Econometrics: Classic and Contemporary Reading*" (Addison-Wesley, 1991). See Landes and Rosenfield in "*Durability of Advertising Revisited*", Journal of Industrial Economics, September 1994, p.263.

[49] This effect may be particularly pronounced if it is cost effective only for suppliers of major brands to advertise on television. In addition, at least initially (until sales are built up), new entrants will have to amortise their advertising expenditure over a lower volume of sales.

[50] The successful launch of a new brand may therefore require a higher level of advertising expenditure relative to that necessary to support established brands, which consumers have tried and with which they are familiar.

For these and related reasons, small firms may operate at a cost disadvantage relative to larger established firms as they may need to spend more on advertising in relation to their sales. If they spend less on advertising, they may face a demand disadvantage in the sense that their products may be less attractive to consumers. For example, in the context of its inquiry into the proposed merger between Rockwool and Owens-Corning Building Products, the Commission noted that:

> "Although stone wool is largely a commodity product, Rockwool is the world market leader and has succeeded in establishing its brand name as the generic term for stone wool . . . Rockwool has an established reputation for product quality and support and often succeeds in getting specifications written by reference to its brand . . . there is reason to believe that an entrant would not only have to spend significant amounts on marketing in order to establish itself in competition with Rockwool but also to price at a discount to it."[51]

A further indication of the difficulties faced by new entrants and small existing companies can be obtained by comparing the advertising/sales ratios of such companies with those of their larger established competitors. However, a comparison of large and small firms' advertising/sales ratios independently of other factors may give a misleading indication of relative competitive advantages in advertising. This is because even if small firms spend a comparable (or higher) proportion of their sales revenue on advertising, their products may still be less attractive to consumers than the major brands. Alternatively, if small firms were to spend a lower proportion of their sales revenue on advertising this could reflect a belief that it is not worthwhile for them to advertise, as they do not believe that it would appreciably improve the attractiveness of their products compared with those sold under established brand names.

6.063   One way for new and small firms to reduce consumer uncertainty as to the quality of their products is to market them under retailers' own-labels, which are increasingly recognised by consumers as quality brands in their own right. This development has facilitated the entry and expansion of new and small firms, by enabling them to signal the quality of their products to consumers in circumstances where having to develop their own reputable brand names through advertising would place them at a significant competitive disadvantage compared with established firms. For example, in its report on *Duralay/Gates*, the Commission stated that:

> "The main parties discounted the importance of brands in underlay and gripper. They said that consumers were not concerned what underlay was laid under carpet. They also told us that, in their estimate, some 65 per cent of the underlay they sold was wholesaler or retailer own label. This, together with the importance attached by some buyers to price above other considerations, suggests that underlay is not a strongly-branded product. Provided an entrant could provide underlay of the required material, spec-

---

[51] Cited above, para.6.010, n.29, at para.2.54.

ification and weight, therefore, the presence of established brands need not, in our view, represent a significant barrier to entry."[52]

Similarly, in its report on the merger between Arla and Express, the Commission observed that whilst milk was a very important product for the national multiples to carry, nearly all milk was sold under retailers' own labels. The Commission concluded that this lack of brand loyalty increased the power of the multiples *vis-à-vis* suppliers.[53]

Strategic advantages

The Director General's guidelines on the assessment of market power refer to a number of possible strategic advantages which might constitute barriers to entry. These include first mover advantages, sunk costs, economies of scale, information constraints, time lags, and access to finance.

6.064

First mover advantages

A first mover advantage arises when there is an advantage to a company in being the first to enter the market—perhaps because this offers the company an ability to shape the way the market develops, possibly deterring further entry into the market. This may be particularly relevant in markets where network effects are important. Network effects arise when the value of the product to a customer increases with the number of other customers consuming the same product, and might arise particularly in hi-tech markets. An example of this was the emergence of VHS, developed by JVC as the standard video technology over Sony's Betamax at the beginning of the 1980s. In these circumstances, incumbents with an existing customer base have an automatic advantage over new entrants. However, when demand is growing fast, or innovation is rapid, the barrier associated with network effects might not be as high as when demand or technological change is more static.[54]

6.065

As noted in para.6.011, switching costs can limit the scope of the relevant market by deterring customer switching to new suppliers, which may also act as a barrier to entry. For example, in the context of Lloyds TSB Group plc's proposed acquisition of Abbey National plc, the Commission observed that as regards the personal current account ("PCA") market:

"Switching barriers may also raise the costs of entry and expansion: entrants will tend to incur large sunk costs of customer acquisition (generous terms have to be offered to attract customers and costs are incurred in providing a switcher service to deal with originators of direct debits and others). Furthermore, by constraining the rate of expansion, a low rate of switching makes it more difficult to take advantage of economies of scale. In this context PCA entrants face both a low rate of switching and a low natural rate of account opening and closure

---

[52] Cited above, para.6.008, n.21, at para.2.55.
[53] Cited above, para.6.048, n.1, at para.2.80.
[54] Commission guidelines on market investigation references, cited above, para.6.058, n.37, at para.3.29.

compared with some other products such as mortgages (a mortgage attaches to a property and thus is redeemed whenever the customer moves house)."[55]

Alternatively, a first mover advantage through superior access to scarce resources may arise simply because incumbent companies were first into the market. For example, in its report on the merger between P&O Princess Cruises and Royal Caribbean Cruises, the Commission found that the allocation of slots at two sea ports (Bermuda and Glacier Bay in Alaska) were controlled (either by government-imposed limits or by a finite number of licences), and that incumbency was a major factor in deciding which companies would have access to these ports.[56]

Similarly, in its report on the merger between Bond Helicopters Ltd. and British International Helicopters Ltd, the MMC concluded that access to on-shore bases may amount to a barrier to entry as all the "existing helicopter facilities at the bases most favoured by oil and gas companies would be either owned or leased by the two established suppliers."[57] However, in its subsequent report on the proposed merger between CHC Helicopter Corporation and Helicopter Services Group, the Commission found that Aberdeen Airport would be able to make appropriate facilities available to any potential new entrant, with the consequence that the availability of such facilities did not constitute a barrier to entry.[58]

It should be noted, however, that in certain markets there may be advantages to new entrants which are not enjoyed by incumbent operators. For example, in industries where production technologies evolve over time, it may be the case that new entrants to such markets are able to establish highly efficient production facilities using the latest technologies, whereas incumbent operators' existing production facilities may be less efficient. For example, in the Commission's inquiry into the merger between Air Canada and Canadian Airlines, the European Commission noted that under Council Regulation (EEC) No.95/93 (1993), when airport take-off/landing slots become available, preference is given to new entrants rather than to existing airlines wishing to begin to operate new services.[59]

Sunk costs and economies of scale

6.066　　Sunk or irretrievable entry or exit costs may constitute barriers to entry by making entry a risky proposition as such costs would be irrecoverable on market exit, with the consequence that entry may be deterred. Irretrievable entry costs include long lasting investments in specialist machinery that cannot be recovered by selling the equipment second-hand or switching its

---

[55] *Lloyds TSB Group plc/Abbey National plc*, Cm. 5208 (July 2001), at para.4.62.
[56] Cited above, para.6.010, n.27, at para.2.73.
[57] *Bond Helicopters Ltd/British International Helicopters Ltd*, Cm. 2060 (September 1992), paras 6.32–6.34. The MMC concluded that new entrants might be able to find some suitable facilities, although they would face a period of uncertainty and the alternative arrangements could involve some additional cost, which they would find difficult to pass on to their customers.
[58] *CHC Helicopter Corporation/Helicopter Services Group ASA*, Cm. 4556 (January 2000), at paras 2.44–2.49.
[59] *Air Canada/Canadian Airlines Corporation*, Cm. 4838 (August 2000), at para.2.76.

use to the production of other products.[60] Clearly, sunk costs may be low if, for example, specialist machinery can be leased, or if it is viable to contract-out production.

Sunk costs may be of direct relevance to the issue of first mover advantage. As the Director General states in his guidelines on the assessment of market power:

"First, to the extent that an incumbent has already made its sunk investments it may not need to earn as high a rate of return as a potential entrant, because the potential entrant still has a choice not to enter and so could avoid incurring all costs if it stayed out of the market. Secondly, an incumbent may decide to use its own sunk costs strategically in a way that raises entry barriers. An incumbent may, for example, be able to sink costs in a way that sends a credible signal as to how it would behave if another undertaking decided to enter a market: it might "over-invest" in sunk assets so that when it operated as the only undertaking in the market, it had significant spare capacity. From the potential entrant's point of view, the mere existence of that capacity might imply that the incumbent could adopt an 'aggressive' stance and manufacture large quantities of product at a very low unit cost. The entrant might decide not to enter if it believed that the incumbent was likely to respond to entry aggressively by pushing down the price to such a low level that the entrant would earn insufficient revenue to cover its sunk costs."[61]

Economies of scale arise where the unit average costs fall as output increases (*e.g.* because fixed costs which do not vary with output are spread over greater sales volumes). They can constitute barriers to entry as they increase the market share a new entrant must win in order to break even, and if entry were attempted on a smaller scale the potential entrant would operate at a cost disadvantage compared with the major established firms.[62] This was a particular consideration in the Commission's inquiry into the merger between Cargill and Cerestar. In that case, the Competition Commission found that:

---

[60] If the value of the investment depreciates rapidly in the sense that the benefits of expenditure are reaped soon after it is made, such expenditure should be regarded as a fixed cost which in a durable asset must be "renewed" constantly as opposed to a sunk investment.

[61] Cited above, para.6.001, n.5, at para.5.13.

[62] The US Horizontal Merger Guidelines state that entry:

". . . is likely if it would be profitable at premerger prices, and if such prices could be secured by the entrant. The committed entrant will be unable to secure prices at premerger levels if its output is too large for the market to absorb without depressing prices further. Thus, entry is unlikely if the minimum viable scale is larger than the likely sales opportunity available to entrants. Minimum viable scale is the smallest average annual level of sales that the committed entrant must persistently achieve for profitability at premerger prices".

The Guidelines add that:

"The minimum viable scale of an entry alternative will be relatively large when the fixed costs of entry are large, when the fixed costs of entry are largely sunk, when the marginal costs of production are high at low levels of output, and when a plant is underutilized for a long time because of delays in achieving market acceptance". (Cited above, para.6.001, n.4, s.3.3.)

". . . new entry by building a plant to serve the UK would be risky, particularly in view of the fact that . . . the production of glucose syrups and blends is a scale business that requires high capacity utilization to break even. A new entrant would have to contemplate possibly sustained losses until significant market share could be achieved."[63]

The existence of economies of scale in conjunction with sunk costs raises barriers to entry by:

(i)   increasing the magnitude of potential losses should entry prove unsuccessful; and

(ii)   committing incumbent firms to maintaining high levels of output in the face of entry, so that new large scale entry may lead to prices collapsing, thereby reducing the profitability of the new entrant even if, prior to entry, prices were above the competitive level.[64]

6.067   In the presence of such market conditions there may be scope for incumbent firms to increase prices significantly above the competitive level without entry occurring. Economies of scale combined with high sunk costs were regarded by the Commission as a particular barrier to entry in *Alanod Aluminium-Veredlung/Metalloxyd Ano-Coil*:

"A potential new entrant would also face a range of economic barriers. The first of these is the capital expenditure required for entry at a cost-efficient level of output. As far as we are able to ascertain, a new anodizing line comparable to that currently operated at Milton Keynes by Ano-Coil would cost at least £10 million. These costs would be largely irrecoverable if the venture failed, thus adding to its risk. Because of the capital-intensive nature of the production process, the new entrant would need to achieve a high level of output . . . in order to be cost-effective."[65]

Sunk costs and economies of scale will constitute less significant barriers to entry in a number of circumstances, including, *inter alia*:

(i)   where new entrants are able to insulate themselves from incumbent firms' responses to entry by, for example, entering into long term contracts with purchasers, which increases entrants' ability to recover their sunk costs profitably;

(ii)   if total demand in the market is increasing, then new entrants could expect incumbent firms to be more willing to accommodate their entry by not substantially cutting their prices if the growth in

---

[63] Cited above, para.6.028, n.30, at para.2.114.

[64] In technical terms, the existence of sunk costs may make it credible for incumbent firms to threaten to "fight" new entrants, as maintaining output at high levels is their short-run profit maximising response to such entry. Such a response maximises the contribution incumbent firms make to their unavoidable sunk fixed costs. In other words, there is an asymmetry in the competitive positions of potential entrants and existing firms. New entrants will enter only if they expect to achieve a return on their full costs (*i.e.* including sunk fixed costs).

[65] Cited above, para.6.025, n.20, at para.2.61.

market demand is sufficient to allow them to maintain sales at a high level;

(iii) if the new entrants enjoy an absolute cost advantage (for the reasons described above), so that they could continue to make profits even if market prices were to fall (a similar advantage would also exist if the new entrant were able to launch a more attractive product); and/or

(iv) where entry occurs via a popular, new "niche" product which is not a particularly close substitute for existing products. This is because any decline in the price of the existing products will have a less damaging effect upon the new entrant's sales. It should be noted that such entry may only moderate price increases due to the merger, rather than prevent them.[66]

Typically markets exhibiting high levels of innovation require significant sunk fixed costs in the form of R&D in order for new entrants to enter the market successfully, and are likely to lead to the market exhibiting economies of scale. (This is in addition to any intellectual property rights barriers which are considered above.) Furthermore, many innovation markets are characterised by the presence of "network effects" which may also constitute significant barriers to entry (for example, software markets often exhibit network effects if the exchange of data/documents between the users is facilitated the more prevalent the software is amongst users).[67]

Information constraints and time lags

The Director General's guidelines on the assessment of market power state that:

6.068

"An incumbent is likely to have more information on the existing costs of production than an entrant and this, in conjunction with sunk costs, may constitute a barrier to entry. Lack of information itself may deter entry when production technology is complex: obtaining the information may involve large sunk expenditures in R&D or in 'learning by doing'. The incumbent may seek to exploit its information advantage to deter entry by, for example, over-investing in sunk costs in an attempt to signal that the industry is one characterised by high sunk costs, when in reality it is not. Even when entry is not fully deterred, entrants may take time in acquiring the relevant information, raising capital and building the necessary plant and machinery. Thus, the incumbent may attract entry but retain market power for a substantial amount of time.

---

[66] Barriers to entry may be high where the opposite circumstances apply. For example, the US Merger Guidelines note that the sales opportunities available to new entrants will be reduced by a number of factors, including, *inter alia*, "the exclusion of an entrant from a portion of the market . . . because of vertical integration or forward contracting by incumbents", and "the prospect that an entrant will share in a reasonably expected decline in market demand" (cited above, para.6.001, n.4, s.3.3).
[67] See, *e.g.* OFT 377, "*Innovation and competition policy*" (March 2002), OFT Economic Discussion Paper 3, prepared by Charles River Associates, paras 1.4 to 1.10.

This may be particularly relevant where there are economies of scale, so that time-consuming and expensive large scale entry is necessary."[68]

Information asymmetries were considered by the Director General in his advice on the proposed acquisition by Group 4 Falck of Wackenhut Corporation, where he noted that "Given Group 4's and Premier's already detailed knowledge of the Home Office's custodial and transportation requirements, the merger may discourage entry by concentrating this informational advantage in the hands of one bidder."[69]

The time lags associated with new entry were considered in the Commission's inquiry into the merger between Cargill and Cerestar. In that case, the Commission found that glucose syrups and blends for the food industry, and in particular confectionery, underwent extensive testing by potential customers (which could take up to two years) before the product was finally accepted by potential customers.[70] Similarly, in advising on the proposed joint venture between Hilton and British Sky Broadcasting, the Director General noted that:

"A pay TV competitor wishing to launch a new premium sports channel would need to outbid other broadcasters and acquire a portfolio of rights sufficient to offer a credible channel. Since these rights are available at different times, and contracts may last from 3–5 years, it can take some time, and entail a significant investment, to assemble a portfolio. Given the uncertainty of demand for a new sports channel, such an investment entails a significant commercial risk both for the broadcaster and, potentially, for those rights holders with whom the company deals".[71]

Access to finance

6.069 New entrants may lack the same access to finance as an incumbent for a variety of reasons. For example, a new entrant's inability to demonstrate a "proven track record" in a particular market may make it more difficult for them to gain access to finance. Inferior access to market data may also put a potential entrant at a disadvantage *vis-à-vis* an incumbent supplier which is able to compile a more convincing business case. In addition, to the extent that there are fixed costs associated with raising finance, these would

---

[68] Cited above, para.6.001, n.5, at para.5.17.

[69] Director General's advice of May 1, 2002, *The proposed acquisition by Group 4 Falck a/s of the Wackenhut Corporation.* The conclusion that information on the Home Office's requirements was a substantial advantage would be more persuasive if it was explained why this information was so valuable (*e.g.* surely such requirements would be set out in tender documents and contracts?), why another bidder could not readily acquire the knowledge (*e.g.* by poaching knowledgeable employees from existing suppliers or recruiting a civil servant), and why the Home Office would not have an incentive to promote competition by explaining its requirements to would be bidders. Nevertheless, the Commission also observed in its report on the merger that: "Incumbents also have the advantage of knowing how to set out bids which, in substance and presentation, would give confidence to the purchaser". (*Group 4 Falck A/S and The Wackenhut Corporation*, Cm. 5624 (October 2002), at para.2.88).

[70] Cited above, para.6.028, n.30, at para.2.114.

[71] Director General's advice of September 27, 2001, *The proposed joint venture between Hilton Group plc and British Sky Broadcasting Group plc.*

bear disproportionately on smaller potential entrants.[72] For example, in *Johnston Press/Trinity Mirror*, the Commission found that entrepreneurs wishing to launch new newspaper titles would face certain difficulties in competing with major groups, including their inability to raise finance on the same terms as larger groups.[73] However, it is generally recognised by economists and regulators that capital entry costs per *se* do not create significant barriers to entry where potential entrants are large established firms that should be equally able to finance such entry costs as are incumbent firms.

Anti-competitive and exclusionary behaviour

Depending upon market conditions, there are a wide range of practices that firms gaining market power through merger may adopt, and which, may increase barriers to entry and expansion. It was explained above that existing firms' sunk costs may commit them to maintaining output at high levels in the face of new market entry, with the consequence that they may respond aggressively to such entry in the short term by cutting their prices. In this context, existing firms may be able to deter future entry by acquiring a reputation for aggressive or even "predatory" pricing in response to entry. In essence, the regulatory concern with predatory pricing is that short run losses will be financed by higher profits in the future once the unprofitable low prices have forced the new entrant to exit the market.[74]

6.070

The risk of aggressive responses deterring new entry has been considered in a number of cases. For example:

(i)   in the context of the proposed acquisition by Johnston Press of eight free weekly newspapers published by Trinity Mirror, the Commission considered that entrepreneurs attempting to launch a new title might "be vulnerable to a robust response by an incumbent publisher, who may, for example, cut advertising rates or cross-sell in a way which lowers prices for [advertising] space in publications that compete head-on with the entrant; launch an additional title as a 'spoiler'; or strengthen the editorial content of its existing titles in response to entry . . ."[75];

(ii)   in the context of its 1996 investigation of the proposed acquisition by Robert Wiseman Dairies of Scottish Pride Holdings, the MMC noted that there would be a very large disparity in size between the merged company and the next biggest dairy company in Scotland. The merged company would be responsible for around 80 per cent of supplies of fresh processed milk to non-major multiple retailers in Scotland. Aside from one competitor which operated only in the

---

[72] See further p.67 of Bishop and Walker, cited above, para.6.001, n.2.

[73] Cited above, para.6.013, n.38, at para.2.61(b). In this connection, the Commission noted that although investment costs were low, a new entrant was likely to have to fund losses over an initial period of perhaps two years before the new title would become profitable.

[74] The issue of predation is dealt with in some detail in the OFT's research paper "*Predatory Behaviour in UK Competition Policy*" (November 1994), by Geoffrey Myers and in the Director General's guidelines on the assessment of individual agreements and conduct under the Competition Act 1998, OFT 414, at s.4.

[75] Cited above, para.6.013, n.38, at para.2.61(e).

north of Scotland, the next biggest suppliers of fresh processed milk would have only around 2 per cent of the market each. Against this background, the MMC expressed the concern that if Scottish Pride were to be removed as an independent competitor, many of the remaining small dairies would be likely to opt for a "relatively passive stance . . . rather than to challenge Wiseman and risk retaliation"[76];

(iii)   in *Alanod Aluminium-Veredlung/Metalloxyd Ano-Coil*, the Commission noted that: "A potential entrant might also fear that, given the high level of post-merger market concentration in the UK, the incumbent supplier would react vigorously to any new entry in order to protect its sales and market share"[77];

(iv)   in its report on the merger between ARRIVA and Lutonian Buses, the MMC observed that: "We have moreover noted . . . the possibility that a merger brought about directly as a result of the aggressive operation of Challenger [an ARRIVA bus operation] could generate a reputational effect, and so create or reinforce a barrier to entry. In relation to the bus market in Luton, we think this is likely, since a successful merger which eliminated competition to ARRIVA the Shires in Luton would leave potential entrants in no doubt that it would be likely to take similar action against any new entrant in that market. We therefore think that in relation to Luton the merger is likely to have reinforced the barriers to entry we have identified . . ."[78]; and

(v)   in the proposed acquisition of Dräger Medical AG & Co. KGaA of certain assets representing the Air-Shields business of Hill-Rom Inc (Hill-Rom), a subsidiary of Hillenbrand Industries, the Commission concluded that:

> "We consider that predatory pricing to encourage exit is unlikely, for two reasons. First, for this to be successful the barriers to re-entry must be high. We think that in this market they are low—a market reputation would not immediately disappear with a company exiting the UK market; re-entry as prices rise would be relatively easy for a company with such a reputation. Second, the same parties compete with one another in several different markets; any predatory practices in one market would be likely to attract retaliation in another. It has been suggested to us that Ohmeda and the merged entity might lower prices to the extent that it would be difficult for smaller players to compete profitably, and we think that action of this kind short of predation is possible. However, we have seen no firm evidence that this type of pricing behaviour is likely, and we do not believe there is a sufficient basis to consider it a risk."[79]

---

[76] Cited above, para.6.037, at paras 2.88 and 2.90.
[77] Cited above, para.6.025, n.20, at para.2.64.
[78] *ARRIVA plc/Lutonian Buses Limited*, Cm. 4074 (November 1998), at para.2.72.
[79] Cited above, para.6.028, n.31, at para.7.12.

Other aspects of firms' conduct may create barriers to entry, such as refusing to allow competitors access to scarce raw materials or distribution facilities (*i.e.* to seek to raise rivals' cost or to foreclose competition altogether). For example, in its report on the proposed merger between CHC Helicopter Corporation and Helicopter Services Group, the Commission stated that:

"We think that there would be a temptation for existing Northern Zone helicopter operators to behave strategically over the leasing of their helicopters and the licensing of their designs in order to signal to potential entrants that they would not find it easy to obtain North Sea-modified Super Pumas were they to win a contract in the Northern Zone."[80]

Nevertheless, the Commission doubted whether the need to obtain suitable helicopters would amount to a major entry barrier since such helicopters could be obtained elsewhere.[81] This possible risk of foreclosure is considered more generally below in paras 6.165 to 6.166 below on vertical mergers.

It might also be possible for incumbent suppliers to create switching costs in the market. As the OFT's guidelines indicate: "The costs faced by customers in switching to a new supplier are also important in determining whether new entry would be an effective and timely competitive constraint."[82] One means of creating switching costs would be to offer loyalty discounts. These may have the effect of imposing a requirement on any new/small suppliers wishing to win business from incumbent suppliers to offer even greater discounts which may make entry/expansion unprofitable. Incumbent suppliers might also seek to "tie" or "bundle" together the sale of complementary goods, making it more difficult for new entrants with only one product to compete effectively. This latter issue is considered further in paras 6.183 to 6.186 below which discusses conglomerate mergers.

New entry, exit and variations in market shares

A degree of variability in the market shares of individual firms within a market may provide evidence of competition between them and a willingness on the part of consumers to switch suppliers. In particular, the introduction and growth of smaller suppliers in a market may suggest that new entrants are able to compete effectively with major established suppliers. For example, in their report on the proposed merger between P&O Princess Cruises and Royal Caribbean Cruises, the Commission observed that there had been a number of successful new entrants in recent years into the cruise market. Many of these new entrants had been existing travel companies which had diversified into the supply of cruise holidays, whilst others were wholly new entrants. The Commission concluded that "the speed with which a number of recent arrivals have won acceptance

6.071

---

[80] Cited above, para.6.065, n.58, at para.2.54
[81] Cited above, para.6.065, n.58, at para.2.54.
[82] Cited above, para.6.001, n.1, at para.4.21.

leads us to believe that the obstacles that new entrants are likely to face are not insuperable."[83]

Similarly, the Director General's advice on the proposed joint venture between BBC Resources and Granada Media Group referred to evidence of a large number of studios having been opened over the preceding five years in order to support his conclusion that barriers to entry into the provision of TV studio facilities were low.[84] He also referred to examples of recent market entry in his advice on the proposed formation of a joint venture between Schlumberger and Baker Hughes, which would operate in the market for the acquisition of seismic data in the marine environment.[85] However, historical evidence of new entry might be discounted if this depended on particular special circumstances which are not generally applicable or if barriers to entry and expansion had subsequently increased.

In some cases, evidence that there has been a lack of major new entry is used by the Commission to support its view that barriers to entry and expansion are high. For example, in *H&H Celcon/MBM*, the Commission pointed to the fact that the only entrant into the market in the preceding six years, Thomas Armstrong, would be of only limited scale (it could supply only 3.4 per cent of UK aerated concrete) and would take three years to reach that output level. In this case, the Commission concluded that:

"there is little likelihood of prospective new entry exerting more than a marginal constraint on the merged company for a significant period of time."[86]

In this connection, it is important to note that the OFT and the Commission generally take the view that in order to be a material competitive constraint, new entry ought to consist of the introduction of new capacity to a market, rather than merely the acquisition of existing companies within the market. In his guidelines on the assessment of market power, the Director General notes that:

"New entry into an industry requires that both a new undertaking is established in the industry and that new productive capacity is set up in that industry."[87]

For example, in its report on the *Tomkins/Kerry Group* merger, the MMC observed that whilst there had been some new entry into the milling industry, this had been by acquisition of existing businesses rather than through the creation of additional production capacity. The Commission concluded that there was little prospect of significant new entry other than

---

[83] Cited above, para.6.010, n.27, at paras 2.66–2.82.
[84] Director General's advice of December 21, 2000, *The proposed joint venture between BBC Resources Ltd and Granada Media Group Ltd.*
[85] Director General's advice of December 21, 2000. *Completed merger of the surface seismic acquisition and data processing interests of Schlumberger Limited and Baker Hughes Incorporated.*
[86] Cited above, para.6.011, n.31, paras 2.105–2.111.
[87] Cited above, para.6.001, n.5, at n.6.

by acquisition, and that entry by acquisition would not change the degree of concentration in the industry, nor would it necessarily lead to more competitive behaviour.[88] However, the Commission's guidelines observe that new entry may take the form of the acquisition by a new firm of existing capacity provided that the capacity will be used "in new, or more productive, ways."[89]

It is not the case that the absence of successful new entry and expansion will establish conclusively that barriers to entry are high. In this connection, the Commission has observed that a lack of entry may reflect effective competition among existing suppliers, with the resulting level of prices being too low to generate excessive profits which would serve to attract new entrants. For example, in *CHC Helicopter Corporation/Helicopter Services Group*, the Commission did not find that the fact that the same three helicopter operators had won all of the contracts in the Northern Zone[90] throughout the period 1992 to 1999 constituted evidence of high barriers to entry. Instead, the Commission concluded that this was "likely to be an indication of the unattractiveness of the market in terms of its profitability . . . ."[91] In such circumstances, it is essential to assess the degree of competition between existing firms as well as the magnitude of barriers to entry; otherwise the inference that a lack of market entry reflects high barriers to entry may be incorrect.

Even if there has been little new entry into the relevant market, the entry and expansion of smaller firms in other geographical markets may provide an insight as to the competitive position of established firms. In *CHC/Helicopter Services Group*, the Commission observed that entry had taken place into the Southern Zone of the UK Continental Shelf (south of latitude 56°N), and considered that this provided evidence that entry could similarly occur in the Northern Zone.[92] However, some caution needs to be exercised in assessing the viability of entry by reference to the history of entry in other markets, as different geographical markets may be characterised by differences in supply and demand conditions, such as, for example, differences in the effectiveness of advertising as a result of variations in culture and taste, the number and size of competitors, distribution and retail structures (and therefore countervailing purchasing power) and so on.

---

[88] Cited above, para.6.025, n.18, at paras 2.48–2.51.

[89] Cited above, para.6.001, n.1, at para.3.46.

[90] *i.e.* that part of the UK Continental Shelf lying north of latitude 56°N.

[91] Cited above, para.6.065, n.58, at para.2.61.

[92] Cited above, para.6.065, n.58, at para.2.61. This conclusion is to be contrasted with the Commission's earlier report on the same market in the context of the proposed merger between Bond Helicopters and British International Helicopters. In this earlier report, the Commission concluded that competitive conditions in the UK sector of the North Sea were such that successful entry, on a scale likely to provide effective competition, was unlikely within a reasonable period and that prices could therefore rise, possibly substantially, despite the recent new entry that had occurred in the Dutch and Norwegian sectors (cited above, para.6.065, n.57, paras 6.24, 6.37 and 1.6–1.7). The Commission did not attempt to explain why entry had been successful in the Norwegian and Dutch sectors. However, the Commission noted that they had been told that prices in these markets were significantly higher than in the UK (at para.6.35), which is consistent with their proposition that entry would only be viable if prices increased.

Countervailing buyer power

6.072   In certain circumstances, the buyer power of customers may impose a constraint on the market power of sellers. In his guidelines on the assessment of market power, the Director General provides some guidance on the circumstances in which buyer power might impose a constraint within a market:

> "It requires that a buyer should be large in relation to the relevant market, well informed about alternative sources of supply and that the buyer could readily, and at little cost to itself, switch from one supplier to another, or even commence production of the item himself."[93]

This was echoed by the Commission in its report on *Sylvan International/Locker Group*:

> "We consider that whether or not a customer has buyer power depends on a number of factors. The most important is its share of drum sales. Other factors are the availability of offers from other suppliers, the market knowledge of the customer (particularly in respect to possible alternative sources of supply), and the customer's preparedness in the last resort to manufacture drums itself."[94]

Powerful purchasers may be able to prevent or constrain suppliers from exercising market power in a number of ways. As highlighted in the quotes above, customers may refuse to accept price increases by threatening to switch to alternative suppliers, or alternatively, they may threaten to produce the products themselves. However, a third possibility is that they may be able to foster new entry/expansion by, for example, offering new/small suppliers a long-term contract. This would insulate such new suppliers to a certain extent from incumbent firms responding aggressively to their entry by cutting prices, and would guarantee that they will recover at least some of their sunk costs. In addition, buyers might well be able to "punish" sellers if they seek to raise prices by various other means.[95] The various ways in which customers might be able to exert countervailing buyer power are described below. Before considering these factors, it is important to note that the issue of buyer power does not rest solely on the size of customers. First, procurement practices may have a major bearing on whether buyer power can be exercised in practice. For example, in its report on *Coloplast/SSL International*, the Commission noted that:

> "The NHS might be expected to have considerable purchasing power. However, the role of clinical choice, the freedom of healthcare profes-

---

[93] Cited above, para.6.001, n.5, at para.6.1.

[94] Cited above, para.6.008, n.21, at para.2.64. See also the Commission's guidelines, cited above, para.6.001, n.1, at para.3.59.

[95] The various ways in which buyer power may be exercised are briefly outlined at para.3.59 of the Commission's guidelines, cited above, para.6.001, n.1. The key point is, referring to the themes set out in the section on critical losses and elasticities, that the exercise of buyer power can render attempted price increases unprofitable, with this depending on how costs change as well as the volume of sales lost.

sionals to determine products to be used in each case primarily on clinical grounds, and the way in which prices are set under the Drug Tariff, serve as a major inhibition on any attempt to exercise that power by making it more difficult for the NHS to negotiate lower prices by buying particular products in bulk."[96]

Similarly, in relation to the proposed merger between GE and VSEL **6.073** (which would have entailed a reduction from three to two in the number of possible bidders for prospective warship orders), the Ministry of Defence accepted that it did not have sufficient buyer power or other means to fully replace the competitive pressures that would be lost as a result of the merger to reduce prices and to innovate.[97]

In addition, when advising on the proposed acquisition by Group 4 Falck of Wackenhut Corporation, the Director General observed that:

"The Home Office is the only purchaser of transportation and custodial services for prisoners, immigration detainees and juveniles. However, despite an apparently strong bargaining position, its ability to utilise that buying power depends on the degree of competition between bidders and its ability to play off bidders against each other".[98]

---

[96] Cited above, para.6.027, n.29, at para.2.80. Similarly, in its report on the merger between *Dräger Medical AG & Co. KGaA and Hillenbrand Industries, Inc*, the Commission stated that:

> "It might seem possible for the NHS to exercise some countervailing buyer power in the market because of its scale and its status as a virtual monopsonist. However, there are no plans for the NHS to exercise power as a single buyer in this area. Moreover, we heard from hospitals that they were very reluctant to give up any freedom to exercise clinical choice in which products to buy, which inhibited the development of joint purchasing even with neighbouring hospitals. The importance of clinical choice in the selection of products to buy imposes limits on the development of joint purchasing of equipment in the NHS." (Cited above, para.6.028, n.31, at para.14).

A similar conclusion was reached in the MMC's report on the merger between Nutricia Holdings and Valio International even where there were price ceilings in place, where the MMC concluded that:

> "The countervailing power of the [Department of Health], . . . appears on the face of it strong . . . However, the effectiveness of the [Department of Health] is, in our view limited, regarding pricing at the present time. Its current price limits tend to be above those of many of the products being supplied, with scope for manufacturers to increase prices before the limits become effective. Even at that point—or if it should try to lower the price ceilings—it can resist price increases only by delisting or threatening to delist particular products. Its ability to judge the justification for any price increase is likely to be weaker, the smaller the number of suppliers there are in the industry and the more concentrated the market. Its ability to delist products is similarly likely to be weaker, the fewer the number of products from competing companies that are available for users. Its position therefore is likely to be weakened by the merger of the two main suppliers in the market". (*Nutricia Holdings Ltd/Valio International UK Ltd*, Cm. 3064 (December 1995), at para.2.48.)

[97] *The General Electric Company plc/VSEL plc*, Cm. 2852 (May 1995), at para.1.8.

[98] Cited above, para.6.068, n.69. In its report on this merger, the majority of the Commission panel concluded that in certain markets:

> ". . . whilst the Home Office and the Scottish Executive, as monopsony purchasers of these services, had sufficient countervailing buyer power to induce new entry or revert to 'self-supply', there was not sufficient evidence [that they would]" (cited above, para.6.068, n.69, at para.1.11).

In contrast, the Commission concluded that the proposed acquisition of McKechnie Paxton Holdings Ltd by the Linpac Group Limited did not operate against the public interest for a number of reasons including:

"the extreme price sensitivity of . . . large customers who operate in sectors—such as supermarkets or automotive manufacturing—where procurement and cost control techniques are very highly developed."[99]

Switching to alternative suppliers

6.074 The ability of customers to exercise countervailing buyer power by switching to alternative suppliers has been noted in a number of cases. For example, in its inquiry into the merger between Linpac Group and McKechnie Paxton Holdings, the Commission noted that there were a number of alternative available sources of supply of the types of packaging materials supplied by the parties. These included: a number of existing UK firms which, in the Commission's view, could expand and extend their output over a short period of time; a number of non-UK suppliers that either already had a manufacturing presence in the UK or an existing business importing into the UK; and a number of plastic producers in the UK that could switch to producing the relevant types of packaging in response to consumer demand. Given that customers in this industry had demonstrated historically that they were not prepared to accept price rises, and had introduced a number of initiatives in order to streamline and to increase the efficiency of their procurement processes, the Commission was satisfied that large customers would exercise buyer power by switching (or threatening to switch) to these alternative sources of supply.[1]

Countervailing buyer power was also recognised by the Director General as an important constraint in his advice on *Longulf/Golden Wonder*, where he stated that ". . . the segment is characterised by large customers periodically tendering large orders. The most significant constraint within the supply of private label snacks appears to be the ease of switching from one manufacturer to another."[2] Similarly, when advising on *E.I. Dupont De Nemours/Kappler Safety Group*, he noted that: "In addition, distributors can exercise significant countervailing buying power by switching suppliers or selling competing 'private label' garments."[3]

More generally, in circumstances where there exists bilateral market power, in the sense that a supplier with significant market power is bargaining with a customer with significant purchasing power, the actual price that will eventually be reached will typically, *i.e.* somewhere between the monopoly price and the monopsony price even if there are no alternative suppliers, in-house production is infeasible and there is no scope for punishment in other markets. The actual price level which is eventually agreed will depend upon the bargaining process between the supplier and customer. Rubinstein, in seeking to resolve this issue, assumes that the bargaining process is one in which parties make alternating offers/counteroffers and both are impatient to settle. Then with complete information regarding each other's preferences, etc, the parties will agree on an outcome which reflects their relative eagerness to settle the deal. (See Rubinstein, "*Perfect Equilibrium in a Bargaining Model*", Econometrica, Vol.50, pp.97–109 (1982).)
[99] Cited above, para.6.060, n.42, at para.1.8.
[1] Cited above, para.6.060, n.42, at paras 2.82–2.85.
[2] Director General's advice of June 21, 2002, Longulf Trading/brands of Golden Wonder.
[3] Director General's advice of April 29, 2002, *The acquisition by E.I. Dupont De Nemours and Company of assets of Kappler Safety Group Inc, namely its protective clothing business.*

In contrast, in *SCR-Sibelco/Fife Silica Sands & Fife Resources*, the Commission found that the position of customers within the glass industry had been dependent upon competition between a number of suppliers of glass sand for their business. The Commission considered that the merger between glass sand suppliers therefore weakened the bargaining position of glass manufacturer customers as Sibelco faced insufficient competitive constraints.[4]

In-house production

In certain circumstances, customers may be able to exercise countervailing buyer power by establishing, or increasing, in-house production. This possibility was recognised by the Commission in its report on *Eastman Kodak/ColourCare*. In that case, the Commission concluded that retailers which bought photographic development and printing services from the parties would have the option to install mini-labs within their stores, or to increase their reliance on mini-labs, as a means of reducing or eliminating the outsourcing of the development and printing activities.[5]

6.075

Purchasers encouraging market entry/expansion

The scope for larger customers to foster the new entry and expansion of smaller suppliers was recognised by the Commission in its report on *Duralay/Gates Consumer & Industrial*. In that report, the Commission observed that:

6.076

"If faced with the real likelihood of unjustified price increases, we would expect large customers of the merged company to be prepared to take the risk of offering alternative suppliers long-term contracts for substantial volumes. This could well involve a high level of commitment and resources on the part of buyers, to ensure that the product was of the right quality. However, such commitment would at the same time provide suppliers with the incentive and the security to risk increasing their existing capacity or, as necessary, investing in new capacity."[6]

The fostering of new entry/expansion as a means of exercising buyer power was also a relevant factor in *CHC Helicopter Corporation/ Helicopter Services Group*, where the Commission stated that:

"It seems likely to us that oil companies could encourage new entry without undue difficulty and would do so if they felt that existing operators were charging too much or otherwise offering an unsatisfactory service . . . because new entry promoted by oil companies is a credible threat it may be expected to influence the behaviour of the existing [helicopter] operators, making them less inclined to take advantage of any reduction in competition arising from the merger, even in the absence of any actual new entry."[7]

---

[4] Cited above, para.6.059, n.41, at para.2.107.
[5] Cited above, para.6.013, n.38, at paras 2.90–2.92.
[6] Cited above, para.6.008, n.21, at para.2.40.
[7] Cited above, para.6.065, n.58, at para.2.82. Although, in its September 1992 report between the same parties, cited above, para.6.065 n.57, it had found the opposite.

Similarly, his advice on *Longulf/Golden Wonder*, the Director General observed that: "Supermarkets can award large contracts and through this sponsor the growth of the smaller manufacturers of snacks or encourage new entry."[8]

The viability of fostering new entry would depend very much on the nature and magnitude of barriers to entry into the industry generally. In this connection, the OFT's guidelines state that:

"As such threats to change the market structure often involve making investments and incurring sunk costs, it may be possible for incumbent suppliers to raise prices to some extent before such threats become credible. Thus where the sunk costs of sponsoring entry are large, countervailing buyer power is unlikely to act as a strong competitive constraint. Buyers may also have a limited incentive to sponsor entry because the benefit of their investment is shared with their rivals and customers."[9]

"Punishment" in related markets

6.077   The OFT's guidelines observe that:

"Even where a customer has (or customers have) no choice but to take the supplier's products, they may still be able to constrain prices if they are able to impose substantial costs on the supplier, *e.g.* by refusing to buy other products produced by the supplier or by delaying purchases.[10]

Retailers may also be able to impose costs on the supplier through their own retail practices, *e.g.* by positioning the supplier's products in less favourable parts of the shop."[11]

There are certain instances where the Commission and OFT have found that one means available to customers to exercise buyer power is to "punish" suppliers in related markets where such suppliers may not enjoy market power.

For example, in the context of the proposed joint venture between Mayflower Corporation and Henlys Group, the Director General advised that, ". . . the parties' customers are sophisticated purchasers with buyer power and will be seeking a range of single and double deck bodies. It is possible that they will be able to use their buyer power in the more competitive (and considerably larger) single deck market to ensure that Transbus is not able to exploit its large share in the supply of double deck bodies."[12]

---

[8] Cited above, para.6.074, n.2.

[9] Cited above, para.6.001, n.1, at n.26. Similarly, the European Commission states that: "it may be important to pay particular attention to the incentives of buyers to utilise their buyer power. For example, a downstream firm may not wish to make an investment in sponsoring new entry if the benefits of such entry in terms of lower input costs could also be reaped by its competitors." (Cited above, para.6.001, n.4, at para.66): this is an example of a phenomena called a "coordination problem" in that investments that one customer makes in securing a competitive alternative source of supply (*e.g.* by entering into a long term contract) may be reaped by other customers if that supplier were also to supply them.

[10] Cited above, para.6.001, n.1, at para.4.27.

[11] Cited above, para.6.001, n.1, at para.4.27.

[12] Cited above, para.6.029, n.35.

Similarly, in the context of the proposed joint venture between the Northern Ireland milk and cream businesses of Express Dairies and Golden Vale, the Director General advised that, ". . . Express is also a major supplier to these same supermarket groups over the rest of the United Kingdom. It is possible, therefore, that if Express sought to exploit its position in Northern Ireland, itself a relatively small market, then it might risk the loss of some business elsewhere."[13]

In addition, in relation to the proposed merger between Arla Foods amba and Express Dairies plc, the Commission stated that:

    6.078

". . . the national multiples may be able to exert pressure in respect of the price they pay for milk because of their discretion over whether to stock other products from the processor. Of course, in theory, this dynamic can benefit the processor if it has strongly branded products. However, in this instance we believe that the balance of power lies with the national multiples" [reflecting, *inter alia*, the importance of retailers' own label products].[14]

The effectiveness of such a punishment mechanism would depend on the contribution to fixed costs and profits earned in the competitive market(s) and the increase in profits which the supplier would otherwise enjoy in the market in which it possess substantial market power. For example, if a supplier enjoys significant market power in Market A, but does not have market power in Market B, then that supplier may wish to raise its prices above competitive levels in Market A in order to generate additional profits. To the extent that there are customers purchasing products in both Market A and Market B, they might choose to punish such behaviour by ceasing to purchase from the supplier in question in relation to Market B. This may be a particularly credible threat for the purchaser in question, if it can be carried out at no cost to the purchaser (*i.e.* where there are alternative sources of supply available at equally low prices as were offered by the supplier in question). This punishment will lead to the supplier losing the contribution to fixed costs and profits it was making in Market B. However, in certain circumstances, it should be noted that the additional profits from exploiting market power in Market A might still be greater than the contribution to fixed costs and profits at risk in Market B.

Not all customers may possess buyer power

The OFT guidelines note that, even if some customers possess buyer power, smaller customers lacking buyer power might be discriminated against.[15] For

    6.079

---

[13] Director General's advice of February 5, 2001, *The proposed joint venture between the Northern Ireland liquid milk and cream businesses of Express Dairies plc and Golden Vale plc.*

[14] Cited above, para.6.063, n.53, at paras 5.95, 5.96, and 5.101.

[15] OFT guidelines, cited above, para.6.001, n.1, at para.4.28, see further paras 6.039 to 6.043 above. In this regard, it may be the case that large intermediate customers for a product (*e.g.* retailers buying a consumer good or manufacturers buying a raw material they process into a finished product) may be less concerned about the absolute level of prices they face, than ensuring that their terms of supply are superior to those of their rivals. For example, if large customers expect that their terms of supply will deteriorate following a merger of two of

example, in assessing the proposed acquisition by Nutreco Holding NV of Hydro Seafood GSP Ltd, the Commission, commenting on the potential response of retailers to any attempt to pass through increased salmon feed costs by means of higher prices for salmon, stated that:

> "We expect the powerful retailers to resist higher prices for Scottish salmon and to pass the extra costs back up the supply chain to the secondary processors and the farmers, but smaller retailers may be unable to do so, and so the price of Scottish salmon for some consumers will rise."[16]

Nevertheless, the exercise of buyer power by certain customers can have broader market impacts. For example, in the context of the merger between Icopal Holdings A/S and Icopal a/s, the Commission emphasised the buyer power of large national distributors/chains and stated that:

> ". . . the combination of the buying power of the larger distributors, and of the coincidence of market pressures on them to have keenly priced felts to sell, and the belief of the manufacturers that they need to keep their multi-product production lines fully utilized creates a strong constraint on price increases. This is evidenced, we believe, by the success of some large buyers in resisting attempts by producers, over the last year or so, to pass on substantial rises in the cost of raw bitumen; and in the need for Ruberoid, in the recent past, and Icopal Ltd at the moment, to rationalize its production capacity in order to reduce costs."[17]

However, there were also many substantially smaller purchasers. Nevertheless, the Commission concluded that the buyer power of these large distributors would act as a discipline in the wider market in a number of ways. The Commission emphasised that "the existence of larger suppliers (i.e. outlets) offering keen prices means that the smaller outlets face competitive pressures to offer comparable prices too." It also added that there was some merit in the argument that this factor also puts pressure on the manufacturers to continue to supply their products to the smaller distributors at prices that make it possible for them to compete with the large chains.[18]

Similarly, in the context of the merger between Universal Foods Corporation and Pointing Holdings, the Commission observed that there were smaller customers which do not have buyer power and are thus dependent on the availability of competitors to the merged business. However, the Commission observed that: "These customers could, if they do not do so already, purchase via distributors, which are in turn are large customers with a degree of buying power."[19]

---

their suppliers they might well not complain to the regulator if they expect their rivals to be adversely affected to a greater degree.

[16] Cited above, para.6.021, n.94, at para.1.10.
[17] Cited above, para.6.029, n.34, at paras 2.139–2.143.
[18] Cited above, para.6.029, n.34, at paras 2.144–2.146.
[19] Cited above, para.6.010, n.28, at para.1.14.

Finally, in assessing the credibility of the various threats which buyers may make in order to discipline their suppliers (as outlined above), an obvious starting point is to consider how customers presently procure products and how they seek to secure competitive terms.

Supplier power

The Commission's guidelines envisage that there are circumstances in which upstream suppliers may be able to constrain downstream firms, in an analogous way to the exercise of buyer power by large purchasers.[20] For example, if wholesalers increase their margins by raising their selling prices to their customers, these higher prices will reduce manufacturers' sales, which might prompt manufactures to develop their own distribution channels direct to customers in order to prevent their sales from being compromised.

6.080

Horizontal mergers

This section considers the assessment of mergers between actual and potential competitors. It starts by considering the importance of market shares, before considering specific difficulties with the calculation of market shares and forward looking assessments as to future market shares (specifically what would happen to market shares if the merger were not to proceed— *i.e.* the counterfactual to the merger). It then considers separately the non-co-ordinated (or unilateral) and co-ordinated effects of a merger between competitors. This separate consideration of non-co-ordinated and co-ordinated effects is merely for ease of presentation—there is no reason why both categories of effects might not be observed in relation to a particular merger.[21]

6.081

The relevance of market shares and measures of market concentration

Market shares

The market share of a firm within a market may provide some indication of its competitive position relative to rival firms. As the Commission's guidelines state:

6.082

"a firm with a large market share relative to other firms in the same market may have the ability to raise its price independently of other firms, at least to some extent. Further, a large market share may confer substantial advantages in bargaining with suppliers upstream or buyers downstream, and a firm may be able to control prices in its favour or impose unreasonable restraints in the negotiation process."[22]

---

[20] See para.3.60 of the Commission's guidelines (cited above, para.6.001, n.1).
[21] This point is expressly made in the OFT's Guidelines, cited above, para.6.001 n.1, at para.4.6.
[22] Cited above, para.6.001, n.1, at para.3.3. It is, of course, the case that the purchasing market affected may well be narrower or wider than the supply market. For example, a national retailer of clothes might well be a very minor purchaser of clothes in a global clothing market, but have a high market in national and local clothing retailing markets.

However, the Commission goes on to state that:

"... a firm with a large market share will not always be able to exert market power. Other features of a market will affect a firm's ability to exercise its market power, such as the extent of switching costs, threats of entry and countervailing buyer power."[23]

Despite this, the Commission endeavours to provide some guidance on the relevance of market shares:

"There is no particular market share threshold that will denote the likelihood of the Commission deciding that the merger has resulted in or is expected to result in a [substantial lessening of competition]. However, a combined market share of 25 per cent or above ... would normally be sufficient to raise potential concerns regarding the effect of the merger on competition. Mergers which result in a market share below 25 per cent are less likely to raise such concerns although the possibility, depending on how the market operates, cannot be ruled out."[24]

In this regard, it should be noted that the European Commission's Horizontal Merger Guidelines[25] suggest that substantive concerns are less likely to arise at such low market share levels. The European Commission's Horizontal Merger Guidelines refer to very high market shares of 50 per cent or more as "in themselves" potentially being evidence of a dominant market position (albeit this might not be the case if, for example, smaller suppliers have the ability and incentive to expand). However, the Guidelines add that the creation or strengthening of a dominant position has been found in some cases with market shares below 40 per cent, but indicate that a concentration is not liable to impede effective competition where the market share of the undertakings concerned does not exceed 25 per cent[26] (reflecting recital 32 of the EC Merger Regulation (ECMR) which also makes this point).

6.083   In practice, few adverse findings have been reached in the UK in relation to mergers between actual competitors (*i.e.* disregarding issues in relation to the loss of potential competition) where the combined market share has been under 30 per cent. However, adverse findings have been reached by the MMC and Competition Commission despite relatively low combined market shares in a number of inquiries such as:

(i)   Lloyds TSB's proposed acquisition of Abbey National, which would have increased the parties' share of personal current

---

[23] Cited above, para.6.001, n.1, at para.3.3.

[24] Cited above, para.6.001, n.1, at para.3.4.

[25] The European Commission's Horizontal Merger Guidelines, cited above, para.6.001, n.4, at paras 17 and 18.

[26] Similarly, in markets where products are relatively undifferentiated and firms' production capacities are the main factors distinguishing them and determining competition, the US Horizontal Merger Guidelines indicate that where the merged firm has a market share of at least 35 per cent it may find it profitable to increase prices unilaterally (cited above, para.6.001, n.4, at s.2.22).

accounts in the UK by 5 per cent to around 27 per cent (this case also raised potential competition concerns)[27];

(ii)   Asda's proposed acquisition of Safeway, which would have increased its share of GB grocery sales from large stores to 32 per cent[28];

(iii)   Elders' proposed acquisition of the brewing interests of Grand Metropolitan, which would have increased the parties' share of United Kingdom beer sales by 9 per cent to 20 per cent (with their combined share of lager sales being slightly higher at 23 per cent)[29]; and

(iv)   the proposed merger between Allied Lyons and Carlsberg, where the merged undertaking had only 21 per cent of lager sales and 16 per cent of all beer sales.[30]

Measures of industry concentration

The OFT and the Competition Commission use measures of market 6.084 concentration as broad indicators of the competitive pressures within a particular market. Both the OFT and the Commission in their guidelines on the assessment of mergers refer to concentration ratios, and the Hirschman-Herfindahl Index ("HHI"). The concentration ratio of a market measures the aggregate market share of a small number of the leading firms within a market (*e.g.* CR4 is the combined market share of the largest four firms in a market). Both the OFT's and Commission's guidelines emphasise that concentration ratios take no account of differences in the relative size of firms that make up the leading group within the market.[31]

The HHI is calculated by aggregating the squares of the market shares of all of the firms within the market, with the consequence that firms with low market shares are accorded considerably less weight than large firms.[32] As well as calculating the HHI for a market, it is also possible to calculate the increase in the HHI (or "delta") that would arise as a result of a merger.[33] The OFT's guidelines state that:

"The OFT is likely to regard any market with a post merger HHI in excess of 1800 as highly concentrated, and any market with a post merger HHI in excess of 1000 as concentrated. In a highly concentrated market, a merger with a delta in excess of 50 may give rise to potential

---

[27] Cited above, para.6.065, n.55, at para.1.6.

[28] Cited above, para.6.027, n.23.

[29] *Elders IXL Ltd/Grand Metropolitan PLC*, Cm. 1227 (October 1990), para.1.3.

[30] *Allied-Lyons PLC/Carlsberg A/S*, Cm. 2029 (July 1992), at para.1.6.

[31] Cited above, para.6.001, n.1, of the OFT's guidelines at para.4.3; and cited above, para.6.001, n.1, at para.3.9 of the Commission's guidelines.

[32] So, for example, if there are two firms within a market with a 30 per cent market share each, and another firm with a 40 per cent market share, then the HHI for that market will be $30^2 + 30^2 + 40^2 = 3,400$.

[33] Since the HHI is the sum of the squared market shares of the firms in the market place, the change in the HHI (delta) can easily be calculated. If firms a and b merge, then their contribution to the HHI will increase from $(a^2 + b^2)$ to $(a^2 + 2ab + b^2)$, with the change in the HHI thus being 2ab.

competition concerns. In a concentrated market, a merger with a delta in excess of 100 may give rise to potential competition concerns."[34]

The Competition Commission's guidelines similarly state that the increment to market share is important:

"Generally speaking, the smaller the increment in market share brought about by the merger, the smaller the threat to the effectiveness of competition. However, a small increment to an already large market share may be regarded as a sufficiently significant change to the structure of a market for the merger to lead to a [substantial lessening of competition]."[35]

Interestingly, the European Commission's Horizontal Merger Guidelines specify higher HHI thresholds than the OFT, below which the European Commission is unlikely to identify horizontal competition concerns, namely:

- if the post-merger HHI is between 1000 and 2000 and the delta is under 250; and

- if the post-merger HHI is over 2000 and a delta of under 150 (albeit that a number of caveats are attached to these generalisations).[36]

6.085   To put the difference between a post-merger HHI of 1800 and 2000 in context, a market would have an HHI of 1800 if it were supplied by 7 firms with the following market shares: 30 per cent; 20 per cent; and five firms with 10 per cent each. The market would have an HHI of just over 2000 if market shares were instead: 34 per cent; 21 per cent; and 5 firms with 9 per cent each.

The OFT's statement suggests that *prima facie* competition concerns can arise with very small increments in market share. For example, 1 per cent, 2 per cent and 3 per cent additions to the market share of a firm with an existing 25 per cent share would lead to deltas of 50, 100, and 150 respectively, with even a 1 per cent increment in market share thus being outside the threshold indicated by the OFT (although, in this instance a 3 per cent increment in market share would be within the thresholds indicated by the European Commission). In practice, there are very few (if any) published

---

[34] Cited above, para.6.001, n.1, at para.4.3. The European Commission also indicates that: "Market shares and concentration levels provide useful first indications of the market structure and of the competitive importance of both the merging parties and their competitors ..." "The Commission is unlikely to identify horizontal competition concerns in a market with a post-merger HHI below 1000. Such markets normally do not require extensive analysis." (Cited above, para.6.001, n.4, at para.16.)

[35] Cited above, para.6.001, n.1, at paras 14 and 19.

[36] The European Commission's Horizontal Merger Guidelines, cited above, para.6.001, n.4, at para.20. The Guidelines refer to a number of special circumstances in which this generalisation will not apply, namely: "(a) a merger involves a potential entrant or a recent entrant with a small market share; (b) one or more merging parties are important innovators in ways not reflected in market shares; (c) there are significant cross-shareholdings among the market participants; (d) one of the merging firms is a maverick firm with a high likelihood of disrupting co-ordinated conduct; (e) indications of past or ongoing co-ordination, or facilitating practices, are present; (f) one of the merging parties has a pre-merger market share of 50% or more."

Competition Commission reports where market share increments of this level appear to have triggered a reference decision or an adverse finding in the absence of other factors.[37] Accordingly, either this statement is over cautious or this is an important policy change.

Both the OFT and the Competition Commission in their guidelines indicate that market shares, concentration ratios and HHIs will not be used alone to support a presumption of a substantial lessening of competition. The OFT's guidelines state that:

"Each of these measures may be used as an initial indicator of potential competition concerns, but will not give rise to a presumption that a merger may be expected to lessen competition substantially."[38]

The Commission's guidelines state that:

"Where it uses the HHI, the Commission will have regard to the threshold levels . . . [used by the OFT], but only as one factor in its wider assessment of competition."[39]

---

[37] One case in which a relatively low market share increment appeared to trigger a reference to the Commission was *BUPA/CHG* (see para.6.174, above). *BUPA and CHG* were both suppliers of private medical services, with respective market shares of 17.4 per cent and 5.1 per cent respectively. The post-merger HHI in this market was 1,130, with the change in the HHI being 180. However, in this case, the increase in concentration in the private medical services market was aggravated by BUPA's 40 per cent share of the supply of private medical insurance (a highly concentrated market with an HHI of 2,795), see paras 2.168–2.189 of the Commission's report, cited above at n.38 to para.6.174. This merger was ultimately prohibited.

In *National Power PLC/Southern Electric plc* (Cm. 3230, April 25, 1996), *National Power* was responsible for 32.6 per cent of electricity generation and *Southern Electric* had interests in three independent power producers, which together had a 3 per cent share of generation. The post-merger HHI was 2,518, with an increase of 196. In this case, a key concern was that in acquiring *Southern Electric's* interests in the independent power producers, *National Power* would gain influence over and information about the operation and development of these producers. This was expected to lead to a reduction in competition in generation, against a background of the two leading generators (*National Power and PowerGen*) having a strong market position but progressively losing market share to such independent producers. Furthermore, *National Power* would gain influence over and information about these independent power producers through *Southern Electric's* power purchase agreements with these producers, also leading to a reduction in competition. See paras 1.9 and 5.17 of the MMC's report.

Finally, in *Lloyds Chemists plc/Macarthy PLC* (C, 1845, February, 26 1992), Lloyds was responsible for 5.7 per cent of retail sales of ethical pharmaceuticals in the UK, with Macarthy being responsible for 1.5 per cent. Perhaps one reason why this transaction was referred to the MMC was concern over the merged company's buyer power-following the transaction, Lloyds would remain the second largest retailer, behind Boots with 11 per cent. Furthermore, there may have been potential concerns as regards local competition in areas where both parties were active. Aside from pharmaceuticals, the parties would together be responsible for 20 per cent of sales of health foods through specialist stores, and were the two largest such suppliers. In this regard, both also had activities in the wholesaling of health foods, and these vertical relationships may have been an additional source of concern at the OFT stage. See paras 6.10 and 6.73–6.98 of the MMC's report, with the MMC ultimately concluding that the proposed merger would not be anti-competitive or otherwise contrary to the public interest.

[38] Cited above, para.6.001, n.1, at para.4.4.

[39] Cited above, para.6.001, n.1, at para.3.10.

6.086   These caveats in relation to market shares, concentration ratios and the HHI are important for a number of reasons. First, as discussed in para.6.007, any such measures implicitly involve a "zero/one" type approach to assessing competition from alternative suppliers in that all alternatives outside the "market" are deemed to be completely irrelevant (which may not be the case) and all firms within the market are treated as being equally close competitors in line with their respective market shares (which also may not be the case).

Secondly, reliance on HHIs implicitly treats a lower HHI as indicative of a more competitive market structure than a higher HHI, but this may not be the case for a variety of reasons. For example:

(i)   the HHI does not measure the number of significant competitors, which may be relevant to competitive assessment. For example, the Chairman of the FTC has emphasised in the context of a review of the US Horizontal Merger Guidelines, that "The number of significant competitors is certainly important—4 to 3 gets our attention quicker than 6 to 5."[40] However, a given HHI level may correspond with the market having many significant competitors or only a few. For example, consider the following market structures which both have a HHI of 1800:

  • one firm with a 30 per cent share, one with 20 per cent, and five firms with 10 per cent each; and
  • one firm with a 40 per cent share, one with 10 per cent, with the remainder of the market being supplied by 25 firms with only a 2 per cent share each.

In the first market, there are seven significant competitors with a market share of at least 10 per cent; but in the second market there are only two significant competitors, with the first competitor being many times larger than its next largest rival; and;

(ii)   an asymmetric market structure (*i.e.* where individual firms' market shares vary) may be more competitive than one in which the main competitors have similar market shares, because differences in firms' market shares may lead to their interests diverging which may increase competition (see further para.6.140 below). However, for a given number of competitors, the HHI is lower the more similar are firms' market shares.

Thirdly, and more generally, market share statistics do not take any account of differences in: the cost structures of competing firms; their competitive strategies (*e.g.* certain firms may be "maverick" aggressive competitors); their price/quality offer; their product ranges; innovation; their levels of vertical integration; spare capacity or any of a large number of factors which influence the risks of co-ordinated or non-co-ordinated

---

[40] Prepared Remarks of Timothy J. Muris, Chairman of The Federal Trade Commission, Workshop on Horizontal Merger Guidelines, Federal Trade Commission/Department of Justice, Washington, DC, February 17, 2004.

effects. All of these factors may affect the competitive process, and will determine the relative importance of competitors.

Fourthly, they take no account of the fact that the counterfactual to the merger (*i.e.* what may happen in the absence of the merger) may not be the competitive status quo, with no change in individual firms' relative competitive positions.

Finally, they are entirely based upon a "snapshot" of market shares at a **6.087** point in time. It therefore follows that they cannot provide meaningful information on the dynamics of competition in a market (*i.e.* barriers to entry and expansion, countervailing buyer power, the impact of the merger on the merged parties' efficiency, etc.).

In light of the above, it is uncontraversial that concentration indices should be used only as a "sieve" to establish where "safe harbours" might lie (without there being any absolute presumption either way), and this seems to be the suggestion in the OFT's and the Commission's guidelines.

Since the HHI thresholds specified in the OFT guidelines are the same as those specified in the US Horizontal Merger Guidelines[41], it is noteworthy that the US Guidelines emphasise that:

"Although the resulting regions [*i.e.* the thresholds outlined above] provide a useful framework for merger analysis, the numerical divisions suggest greater precision than is possible with the available economic tools and information."[42]

There have been a number of mergers which have been cleared at the first stage despite the existence of high HHIs. For example, in *Clear Channel*

---

[41] See the US Horizontal Merger Guidelines, cited above, para.6.001, n.4, at s.1.51.

[42] Cited above, para.6.001, n.4, at para.1.5. The US FTC published in February 2004 a review of 151 mergers from fiscal years 1996–2003 where it had issued second stage requests due to competition concerns relating to the elimination of actual horizontal competition between rivals (excluding minority shareholdings) (see *www.ftc.gov/opa/2004/01/ horizmerger.htm.*). These cases are then sub-divided into those cases which were subsequently closed and those where relief was sought, with the various cases being broken down further including according to post merger HHI, changes in HHI (delta), the number of significant competitors, customer complaints, and the merging parties having "hot" documents (*e.g.* envisaging price increases post merger). This sample is clearly biased in the sense that it does not cover the population of cases which were notified to the FTC, and the size of the sample is small in various of the sub-categories. However, it is striking that in over 75 per cent of cases, second stage investigations were undertaken in relation to markets where the number of significant competitors fell to three or less. In these cases, relief was sought in approximately 86 per cent of cases. In addition, in the fewer markets subject to second stage investigation where at least four competitors remain, these were subject to case closure decisions in relation to some 55 per cent of cases.

The FTC data characterises significant competitors according to the competitive effects theory being considered. If the primary issue is that there would be co-ordination between the remaining competitors, significant competitors have been defined "as required participants in the collusive group". If the issue is non-coordinated effects, then significant competitors includes firms identified as "close rivals" as well as those that might reposition or otherwise affect the likelihood of an anti-competitive price increase. The FTC adds that significant competitors would usually have a market share in excess of 10 per cent, but might include smaller competitors which would constrain the merged entity (*e.g.* if they had recently entered the market with an innovative new product or can readily expand output). There is obviously at least some subjectivity in any such identification of significant competitors, but this is arguably more meaningful than relying on "raw" HHI data.

UK/Score Outdoor, the pre-merger HHI of 2486 increased to 2869 (an increment of 383).[43] In addition, in *Adastra Software/Owl Software*, the HHI of the two merging firms prior to the merger was 2473, and the HHI of the merged company alone would be 3721 (an increment of 1,248).[44] Finally, in the context of *Longulf Trading/brands of Golden Wonder*, the Director General recommended clearance despite a pre-merger HHI of 1580, increasing to 2716 post-merger, with an increment of 1136.[45] It remains to be seen how the *IBA Health* case will influence the OFT's willingness to clear mergers unconditionally which create high market shares.[46]

6.088   Similarly, the Commission has permitted mergers to proceed despite the merged undertaking possessing a high market share in a concentrated market:

(i)   in the case of the proposed acquisition by Duralay International Holdings Ltd of Gates Consumer and Industrial, the Commission noted the high market share of the merged entity[47] which, unless constrained, would allow it to exploit its position by attempting to gain share at the expense of competitors or by raising prices. However, the Commission concluded that the acquisition would not be expected to operate against the public interest due to a number of constraints which would prevent the merged entity from exploiting its market position. These included countervailing purchasing power on the part of large wholesale and retail customers who could switch or threaten to switch to other suppliers (either UK suppliers or imports), and who could foster entry by new suppliers or expansion by existing ones[48];

(ii)   no adverse finding was reached in relation to *Icopal Holdings A/S/Icopal a/s* despite the merged business increasing its UK market share in glass felt by 16.0 per cent to 59.9 per cent. In this case the Commission emphasised the partial overlap in the parties' coverage of distribution channels, competition from rivals and the market wide importance of the exercise of buyer power by large customers[49];

(iii)   in relation to the merger between Linpac Group Limited and McKechnie Paxton Holdings Limited, the Commission identified a number of relevant product markets in which high market shares would be created or enhanced. In particular, it was estimated that

---

[43] Director General's advice of July 16, 2002, *Proposed Acquisition of Clear Channel UK Ltd of Score Outdoor Ltd.*

[44] Director General's advice of August 29, 2002, *Completed Acquisition by Adastra Software Limited of Owl Software Limited.*

[45] Cited above, para.5.074, n.15.

[46] Cited above, para.6.002, n.13.

[47] The market share figure was redacted from the Commission report for reasons of commercial sensitivity. The Director General's advice reported that the merged undertaking's share of carpet underlay would be in the range of 55–75 per cent (Director General's advice of May 24, 2001, proposed acquisition by Duralay International Holdings Ltd of Gates Consumer and Industrial).

[48] Cited above, para.6.008, n.21, at para.1.8.

[49] Cited above, para.6.029, n.34, at paras 2.156–2.157.

the merged undertaking would have increased its share by 4 per cent to 71 per cent as regards plastic baking trays in the UK.[50] The Commission, nevertheless, did not reach an adverse finding, emphasising (*inter alia*) the buyer power of customers, the strength of competition from existing competitors and the ease of entry[51];

(iv) the MMC concluded that the proposed merger between Technicolour Limited and Metrocolour London Limited would not operate against the public interest despite the fact that in the six sectors of film processing in which both parties were active, the market share for the merged entity would range between 42 per cent and 76.5 per cent. The Commission reached this view on the basis that competition in each of the six sectors would remain from current suppliers in the UK, laboratories in mainland Europe or new entrants given that barriers to entry were considered to be low[52]; and

(v) in the case of the acquisition of Cerestar SA by Cargill Incorporated, the market share of the merged entity would be 48.1 per cent of UK production and 38 per cent of the EC-wide production of glucose syrups and blends. The Commission concluded, however, that the merger may be expected not to operate against the public interest because, *inter alia*, it considered there to be barriers to co-ordinated action and the possibility of new entry given growing demand and strong buyers capable of switching to new entrants or sponsoring new entry.[53]

These examples serve to illustrate the importance of looking beyond market share figures and examining the wide variety of factors which will affect the intensity of competition within a market. Indeed, the significance of market share figures and market concentration *per se* is summed up by Williams who has stated that:

". . . the industrial organization literature now recognizes that the connections between market structure and concentration on the one hand and market power on the other are not very strong and may even not exist at all, so there is nothing economically significant about 25 per cent."[54]

Nevertheless, the process of defining the relevant market and calculating market shares provides an important basis for such an analysis.

Calculating market shares

As described in paras 6.006 to 6.055, regulators will consider a wide **6.089** variety of information in order to reach a view on the scope of the relevant market. Once the relevant market has been defined, market shares

---

[50] Cited above, para.6.073, at para.5.84.
[51] Cited above, para.6.073, at para.1.8.
[52] *Technicolour Limited/Metrocolour London Limited*, Cm. 3720 (July 1997), para.1.4.
[53] Cited above, para.6.028, n.30, para.1.10.
[54] Williams, *"The Effectiveness of Competition Policy in the United Kingdom"*, Oxford Review of Economic Policy (Summer 1993), Vol.9, No.2.

are allocated to the various market participants. The calculation and allocation of market shares can raise a number of practical issues, and the OFT's and Competition Commission's guidelines provide almost no advice on how these practical issues may be overcome, although the OFT's guidelines indicate some preference for calculating market shares by sales revenue and possibly by capacity in relation to traded commodities.[55] This section considers some of these issues in further detail.

An obvious starting point is to consider what one might be seeking to assess by considering market shares, bearing in mind that market shares are a poor measure of market power. In this regard, Werden provides the followings advice:

". . . because market shares never come close to telling the whole market power story, the goal in assigning them should be merely to accurately and usefully indicate the relative sizes of competitors in a market place."[56]

Market shares by sales volume/value—finding a "common denominator"

6.090   When calculating market shares, a "common denominator" needs to be found so that different suppliers' sales of products can be aggregated and shares allocated. This is straightforward if the products sold by various suppliers are identical or nearly so. However, once some form of product heterogeneity arises, it can be more difficult to calculate market shares. For example, how should the regulator add together a large loaf of bread with a small loaf of bread, or a product that lasts twice as long as another with

---

[55] The Commission's guidelines merely indicate that: "Market shares can be measured in terms of revenues, volumes, production capacities or inputs, depending on the markets concerned and the information available" (at para.3.6, cited above, para.6.001, n.1). Similarly, the OFT's guidelines indicate that although shares by sales revenue are generally preferred, other measures such as production volumes, sales volumes, capacity or reserves, may be used as appropriate. The OFT's guidelines give the example of a market where a product is a traded commodity and where production capacity may therefore represent the best indication of competitive strength (at para.4.3, cited above, para.6.001, n.1). The OFT's Guidelines on the Assessment of Market Power under the Competition Act 1998 state that:

"market share is determined by an undertaking's sales to customers. The Director General will therefore normally measure market share using the value of sales to direct customers rather than the value of an undertaking's production (which can vary from sales when stocks increase or decrease)" (cited above, para.6.001, n.5, at para.4.6).

As regards the OFT's general preference for sales revenue data rather than sales volume data, its Guidelines on the Assessment of Market Power indicate that:

"The Director General will use whichever available method of calculating market share data is most appropriate for the case in hand. If sales data by value and by volume are both available for a market where goods are differentiated, for example, data by value may provide a better proxy of market share, although both measures may provide useful information. Sales data by value will not always be the preferred measure, however—data on passenger volumes may be preferred when looking at the transport sector, for example." (cited above, para.6.001, n.5 at para.4.5).

[56] Werden, *"Assigning Market Shares"* Antitrust Law Journal, vol.70, issue 1 2002. Similarly, the US Horizontal Merger Guidelines state that "Market shares will be calculated using the best indicator of a firms' future competitive significance" (cited above, para.6.001, n.4, at s.1.41).

the less durable alternative, or a higher priced product/service with another? In certain cases, it may be possible to construct a common denominator that accurately reflects usage and how consumers trade off one product against another[57] (*e.g.* £ per use).

One means of seeking to address some of these issues is to use sales revenues as a basis for calculating market shares. The theory behind the use of revenues is that differences in the efficiency, quality and durability of different products ought in some way to be reflected by differences in their prices. Consequently, less efficient, lower quality, less durable products would be expected to have lower prices than more efficient, higher quality, more durable products, such that using revenues for a basis of market shares ought to allocate weightings to different types of products which reflect superior quality or performance. This point was recognised by the Commission in *SCR-Sibelco/Fife*, which indicated that "[m]easuring market shares by sales value is often our preferred approach because product value inherently encompasses variations in product prices."[58] Similarly, in *BUPA/ Community Hospitals Group/Salomon International*, the Commission considered market shares in the market for private medical services at the national level on a number of different bases, including numbers of hospitals, numbers of beds and revenues. The Commission indicated that "[i]n our view revenue is to be preferred as the basis for measuring market shares, because it reflects physical capacity, its utilization, and variations in the mix of procedures and services."[59]

However, Werden sets out a number of difficulties with this approach. For example, price differences between different products may be solely due to brands rather than product performance (for example, own-label brands are often priced more cheaply than premium brands, whilst not objectively being of an inferior quality).[60] He adds that there may be a significant variation in the relative prices of products over time, whilst the rates at which the products are traded off against one another by consumers remains

---

[57] Werden gives the illustrative example of a market for bread. He indicates that loaves of bread are sold in the United States in standard-size loaves weighing 1, 1.25 and 1.5 pounds, with some packages containing two or even three such loaves. He indicates that in this situation weight is an obvious choice of common denominator, although slices might also be used (recognising that two slices may be considered as a standard serving), but he emphasises here the need to recognise that slices vary in thickness (cited above, para.6.089, n.56). Also see para.6.010, above.

[58] Cited above, para.6.059, n.41, at para.4.52. Similarly, the US Horizontal Merger Guidelines state that "Dollar sales or shipments generally will be used if firms are distinguished primarily by differentiation of their products" (cited above, para.6.001, n.4, at s.1.41).

[59] *BUPA Ltd and Community Hospitals Group Plc; BUPA Ltd, Salomon International LLC and Community Hospitals Group plc; and Salomon International LLC and Community Hospitals Group plc*, Cm. 5003 (December 2000), at para.4.130. However, it is unclear why revenue provides a better reflection of physical capacity than numbers of hospitals or beds.

[60] In addition, products may be sold either separately or as part of an integrated unit. Werden (cited above, para.6.089, n.56) gives the example of a product which may come both integrated with an essential complement and separate from it. If revenues were to be used in this case, then the integrated product would be given a greater weight than the single product, even though any purchaser of the single product would also need to purchase the separate complementary product, thereby paying the same overall price as a consumer buying the integrated product. Using revenues in this case would therefore give undue weight to the integrated product.

constant. In this type of situation, revenue-based market shares could paint a false picture of market share volatility.

Issues raised by the use of current sales revenues/volumes to calculate market shares

6.091 For the purpose of assessing the current and future competitiveness of suppliers, it is generally the case that current market shares over, say, the last year are more relevant than historical shares (although changes in market shares may well be revealing as to the dynamic competitiveness of the market and the magnitude of barriers to entry and expansion). In this regard, there is no particular need to consider recent new contract awards or orders separately from repeat sales or sales under established contracts with existing customers. However, there are a number of potential exceptions to this position.

In circumstances where long-term contracts are used, it may be more appropriate to assign market shares on the basis of recent contract awards (since historical contract awards reflect competitiveness at that time, rather than current competitiveness). However, to the extent that past contract awards may "tie up" productive capacity, this may influence the ability of a supplier to win new contracts going forward. In such circumstances, the capacity of suppliers to compete for future contracts[61] may be of greater importance than either current sales volumes under all contracts or share of new orders. (Paragraphs 6.093 to 6.094 and 6.121 to 6.122 below respectively consider market shares by capacity[62] and the importance of considering market shares of new business in markets where switching costs are important).

In addition, market shares at a specific point in time can be affected by factors such as errors in data samples or various extraordinary events (such as temporary production line closures due to product quality or delivery issues). In such circumstances, market shares over a longer period of time may be preferable to those over a shorter period. However, the further back in time one goes, the more the data may reflect demand and supply conditions which are significantly different from those existing today. The nature of this trade-off varies with the frequency of transactions in the market and the rate of change of market conditions. Werden suggests that a time period of one year should generally be used for assessing market shares, with two years probably being a maximum ideal length of time, unless transactions are very infrequent[63] (for example, some bidding markets such as major defence procurements).

---

[61] Whether these future contracts are new contracts or customers putting their existing requirements out to tender.

[62] See further Werden, cited above, para.6.089, n.56. Similarly, in markets where there is a delay between products being ordered and delivered, recent orders reflect the current competition in the market, while deliveries under existing contracts reflect conditions at some point in the past, possibly in the distant past. In this situation, Werden argues that a good case can be made for assigning shares on the basis of orders, provided that they are likely to translate to eventual deliveries. However, if cancellation penalties are relatively low, then cancellations may be common, and actual shipments may become more appropriate than orders as a basis for assigning market shares.

[63] Similarly, the US Horizontal Merger Guidelines state that "Typically, annual data are used, but where individual sales are large and infrequent so that annual data may be unrepresen-

The Competition Commission's guidelines recognise that in bidding markets, which tend not to have multiple buyers and multiple sellers over a continuous time period, competition for contracts occurs only at particular times. In these circumstances, the application of the SSNIP test might lead the Commission to consider each contract as a market in itself. However, this would not be helpful in understanding the dimensions of the market within which rivalry between firms occurs. The Commission suggests that in these circumstances, it will be necessary to consider other factors relevant to market definition, such as information on the firms bidding for contracts, how they bid, and their track record in bidding for contracts. The Commission states that this type of information may be more informative as to the significance of firms in the market than, for example, their market shares at any specific point in time.[64]

For example, in its report on *Compass Group/Rail Gourmet Holding/ Restorama/Gourmet Nova*, the Commission stated that: 6.092

"As the supply of on-train food services to [train operating companies] operates through a series of contracts, which are let at different times by the [train operating companies], it would not matter for the purposes of competition if one company held all the contracts at any point in time, as long as this or other factors did not restrain or prevent the possible entry of a competitor, each time one of those contracts was tendered, or else act to restrain or prevent the regular tendering of the contracts."[65]

In its report on the acquisition by CHC Helicopter Corporation of Helicopter Services Group ASA, the Commission noted that: "Market shares reflect helicopter operators' past success in winning contracts. Consequently the gain or loss of a major contract can have a significant effect on an operator's market share."[66] For this reason, the Commission examined shares over the period 1994 to 1999 in conjunction with information on the distribution and movement of major contracts between the operators.[67]

---

tative, the Agency may measure market shares over a longer period of time" (Cited above, para.6.001, n.4, at s.1.41).

[64] Cited above, para.6.001, n.1, at para.2.29. In this regard, the OFT comments on this issue in its guideline on how to assess market power under the Competition Act 1998. It states that: "The Director General will usually look at the history of the market shares of all undertakings within the relevant market. . . . This is more informative than considering market shares at a single point in time, partly because such a snapshot might hide the dynamic nature of the market. In aerospace or defence products markets, for example, there are large, often long-term, irregularly-timed contracts. In these instances, the Director General might look at shares over a period of perhaps five years, as well as at how they have changed during the recent history of the market as part of the assessment of market power." (cited above, para.6.001, n.5, at para.4.2.)

[65] *Compass Group PLC/Rail Gourmet Holding AG*, Restorama AG and Gourmet Nova AG, Cm. 5562 (July 2002), at para.2.15.

[66] Cited above, para.6.065, n.58, para.4.40.

[67] Cited above, para.6.089, n.56. Similarly, in the context of the proposed acquisition of Dräger Medical AG & Co. KGaA of certain assets representing the Air-Shields business of Hill-Rom Inc (Hill-Rom), a subsidiary of Hillenbrand Industries, Inc, the Commission observed that:

"Market shares tend to fluctuate from year to year because of the nature of the market— a few large tender wins or losses can have an impact on the overall position. We have shown

Market shares based on capacity

6.093   In process industries that produce homogenous products (*e.g.* traded commodities) using equipment for which there is a rated capacity, it may be appropriate to use capacity-based market shares. Werden envisages the following scenario to illustrate the point:

"If two producers of a homogeneous product proposed to merge, there could be a concern that the merged firm would restrict output to drive up the market price. The merged firm's ability to restrict output would be indicated by the merging firms' pre-merger outputs, but its ability to drive up price by restricting output will be determined by the elasticity of its rivals' supply at prices near those prevailing pre-merger. Even if the merging firms accounted for a very large portion of pre-merger industry output, the merged firm would have little market power if rivals' supply were highly elastic, and it would have no market power at all if rivals' supply were perfectly elastic."[68]

In other words, if rivals could readily increase supplies should a profitable opportunity arise, then an attempt on the part of the merging firms to restrict output would fail to increase prices to any degree as rivals could readily expand their own production. In this scenario, market shares based on production capacity would reveal the ability of smaller suppliers to expand sales in response to a profitable opportunity. In contrast, market shares based on sales pre-merger (*i.e.* performance based market shares) may suggest that the merging firms would together enjoy market power.[69] However, a number of caveats should be noted. First, in many cases certain high-cost capacity should be ignored in assigning market shares. For example, Werden indicates that "[t]he clearest case is that in which an industry has sufficient modern, low-cost capacity to satisfy the entire anticipated demand, even in the event of an exercise of market power. High-cost capacity that never would be used ought not to be considered in assigning market shares."[70]

---

three- and five-year cumulative market shares as well as annual figures . . . in order to smooth some of these effects and to give a sense of the different suppliers' shares of the base of installed equipment, which is relevant given the discussion of switching costs above."

However, the Commission added that it recognised that three year cumulative market shares do not provide a complete picture, "notably understating the position of Ohmeda, whose market share has been growing throughout the period in the closed care market, and concealing important developments in the phototherapy market" (cited above, para.6.028, n.31, at paras 5.23 and 5.25).

[68] Cited above, para.6.089, n.56.

[69] In this connection, the US Horizontal Merger Guidelines state that:

"Market shares will be calculated using the best indicator of firms' future competitive significance. Dollar sales or shipments generally will be used if firms are distinguished primarily by differentiation of their products. Unit sales generally will be used if firms are distinguished primarily on the basis of their relative advantages in serving different buyers or groups of buyers. Physical capacity or reserves generally will be used if it is these measures that most effectively distinguish firms." (Cited above, para.6.001, n.4, s.1.41)

[70] Cited above, para.6.090, n.57.

Specific complexities may, however, arise. For example, in relation to electricity generation, demand is highly variable by time of day, week and seasonally, and the costs of the generating plants are highly variable. The complexities of assessing market power in the electricity generating industry are discussed in the Commission's report into proposed modifications to the operating licences of AES and British Energy groups.[71] In its *Centrica/Dynegy* inquiry, which related to the market for gas storage (where similar demand variability issues arose), in considering whether it might be profitable for the merged firm to restrict output in an attempt to raise market prices, the Commission calculated market shares on the basis of both capacity and recent annual capacity utilisation.[72]

Finally, Werden suggests that it is normally best not to create capacity measures for industries which are not commonly used, because it may be difficult and time consuming to construct consistent capacity measures, not least because industry participants may not carefully and accurately respond to requests for information on capacity that is not readily available.

6.094

Market shares based on assets held

In certain markets, the true "bottleneck" faced by suppliers may not relate to the processing stage of the manufacturing process, but access to a key raw material in scarce supply. For example, certain industries are based heavily on the extraction of limited natural resources (oil, gas, minerals, etc.) and there may be a bottleneck as regards these reserves, although this will not always be the case. In these circumstances, current production may not be the best measure of competition, given that current production will typically be based on contracts/business won in the past, and may not reflect the potential of suppliers to win future business. Whilst recent contracts awarded may be a good predictor of future contract awards in some industries, they may not be a good predictor in exhaustible resources industries, since each contract awarded makes a block of resources unavailable for future contracts.[73] Accordingly, in this type of industry, shares of ownership of resources could well be a more appropriate basis for market shares.

6.095

Nevertheless, assigning market shares on the basis of resource ownership may be very difficult in practice, because there may be no reliable figure for the "universe" of the reserves in the relevant market which are economically extractable.

---

[71] *AES and British Energy: A report on references made under section 12 of the Electricity Act 1989*, CC. 453, (January 2001), see Ch.Two.

[72] *Centrica plc/Dynegy Storage Ltd and Dynegy Onshore Processing UK Limited*, Cm. 5885 (August 2003), at paras 2.53 to 2.57.

[73] This point is recognised in the US Horizontal Merger Guidelines, which indicate that:

"In measuring a firm's market share, the Agency will not include its sales or capacity to the extent that the firm's capacity is committed or so profitably employed outside the relevant market that it would not be available to respond to an increase in price in the market." (cited above, para.6.001, n.4, s.1.41).

The Guidelines also state that: "Physical capacity or reserves generally will be used if it is these measures that most effectively distinguish firms."

Market shares based on intangible assets

6.096   Werden argues that there is essentially only one scenario whereby market shares are commonly assigned on the basis of intangible assets. He refers to this scenario as a "one over N market". He indicates that such markets have two essential characteristics:

(i)   a finite number of entities possessing a readily identifiable set of assets essential for successful competition; and

(ii)   the extent of ownership or control over the essential assets does not distinguish among these entities in any important way.

Werden explains that in the clearest case, all competitors have the same costs, and each can supply the entire market demand. In markets with these two characteristics, each competitor is assigned the same market share. So with N competitors in a market, their shares are $\frac{1}{N}$. The categories of markets that are suitable for this type of market share allocation include technology markets and innovation markets, and those markets where competition essentially takes place "for the market" rather than "in the market" (for example, where competition occurs largely through the introduction of new products or technologies). In markets where the above conditions are met, it would be reasonable to assume that all competitors possessing the same assets would have a reasonable prospect of market success, such that there will be no sound basis for assigning asymmetric market shares.[74] However, in such markets a small number of competitors might be sufficient for effective competition, and rather contrived market share measures might well be uninformative.

Assigning market shares to individual competitors

6.097   This section considers the assignment of market shares to individual firms themselves.

Own label/contract manufacture

6.098   Attribution issues can arise when different assets associated with the production and distribution of a single product have different owners. For example, suppliers of grocery products may well supply both under their own brands and under retailers' own label brands.

Often market shares are attributed to firms according to the market power concern. For example, the main concern with a merger of branded suppliers may be that the merged firm would unilaterally exercise market power, raising prices for its brands as it internalises the competition between them. In assessing these issues it can be strongly argued that the market shares assigned to retailers' own labels should be attributed to the retail chains that own those labels, even if they contract out their manufacture, assuming that there are many actual or potential competing own label suppliers. The retailers are the strategic decision makers for pricing

---

[74] Cited above, para.6.089, n.56.

the private/own label and how they competitively interact with branded products.[75]

If, by contrast, a potential concern was the exercise of market power by contract manufacturers, then it can be argued that market shares assigned to own labels should be attributed to the manufacturers.[76]

Licensing of brands

Licensed trademarks present different issues as regards market share allocation, depending on the nature of the licence. In the simplest case, where a licence is paid up and perpetual, it is equivalent to an assignment and therefore amounts to brand ownership and should be treated as such (*i.e.* the market share would be assigned to the firm with the perpetual licence). However, where licences may be transferred and there may be no assurance that the current licensee will control a brand for long, it may be appropriate to attribute a licensed brand's share to the brand's owner rather than to its licensee. Nevertheless, in certain circumstances the termination, or even transfer, of a licence may lead to some of the market share previously held by a brand being transferred to the other brands of the licensee (*e.g.* due to its established relationships with customers such as retailers). Accordingly, it is important to understand the exact nature of the licence and the conditions attached to it.[77]

6.099

In this regard, in the context of the merger between Interbrew SA and Bass PLC the Commission calculated Interbrew's market share excluding the Heineken brands (reflecting the termination of agreements relating to the use of these brands) *and* including these brands (noting that Interbrew would have an incentive to encourage on-trade retailers to replace Heineken's brands with Interbrew's brands).[78]

Minority shareholdings, minority financial interest, and the degree of control

Chapter 2 describes s.26 and 27 of the Enterprise Act 2002, which deal with the circumstances in which enterprises must be treated as being under common control. The Enterprise Act defines control to include the acquisition of material influence over policy, as well as control of policy (*de facto* control) and a controlling interest (*de jure* control). As is clear from Ch.2, there is often no simple correlation between the financial interest (*i.e.* its entitlement to a share in the profits) held by a firm in another and the degree of control exercised by the acquiring firm in question. However, the OFT's and the Commission's guidelines do not seek to address how minority stakes and the degree of control affect the competitive analysis of mergers. It can be strongly argued that simply adding together the market

6.100

---

[75] See further Werden, cited above, para.6.089, n.56.
[76] Similarly, "integrators" which combine purchased components into final products may be in an analogous position to contract manufacturers. If integrators alone possess the technology or other assets essential to the production of the final product (*e.g.* important brands names), then market shares associated with the final products should be attributed to the integrators. However, if the integrators' task could just as easily be performed by the component manufacturers or the final customers, then the final product shares should be attributed to the component manufacturers.
[77] See further Werden, cited above, para.6.089, n.56.
[78] Cited above, para.6.027, n.27, at para.4.56.

shares of a firm and all firms in which it has a minority shareholding does not adequately reflect the effects of minority shareholdings.

Focusing on the risks of unilateral (non-co-ordinated) effects, firms' incentives to compete will be affected by[79]:

(i) "financial interest", or the right to receive a share of the profits generated by the firm in which a minority interest is held ("the acquired firm"). In particular, prior to the acquisition of a share-holding in a competitor, a firm may have found it unprofitable to increase prices due to the loss in sales revenue it would have suffered. However, following the acquisition, the shareholding firm might well find it profitable to increase prices because some of the sales lost would be recaptured by increased sales of the acquired firm, which would enjoy additional profits as a consequence, with the share-holding firm gaining a share in these profits in line with its financial interest. This affects the incentives of the acquiring firm (but not the acquired firm) to alter its competitive behaviour; and

(ii) "corporate control", or the acquiring firm's ability to control or influence the minority-owned firm. This affects the competitive deci-sions of the acquired firm, with possible outcomes varying depending on the level of shareholding and the governance structure. Control can be held to varying degrees, and for a given financial interest and everything else being equal, the least anti-competitive is a silent financial interest, because it is assumed that the acquisition of a passive stake has no effect on the competitive decisions of the acquired firm.[80] The anti-competitive effects generally increase as the financial stake in the acquired firm increases (but see further below), because the acquiring firm gains a greater share of any increase in the profits of the acquired firm due to the acquiring firm's customers switching to this firm if the acquiring firm increases its prices.

---

[79] See, for example, O'Brien and Salop, "*Competitive effects of partial ownership: financial interest and corporate control*", Antitrust Law Journal, Vol.67 issue 3 (2000). See also Dubrow, "Challenging the economic incentives analysis of competitive effects in acquisitions of passive minority equity interests", Antitrust Law Journal, Vol.69, issue 1(2001); and O'Brien and Salop, "*The competitive effects of passive minority equity interests: reply*", Antitrust Law Journal 69, issue 2 (2001).

[80] O'Brien and Salop present two economic models which seek to analyse and quantify the potential for anti competitive unilateral effects that may result from holding a minority equity interest in a competitor (cited above, para.6.100, n.79). The first economic model is known as the "modified HHI analysis" ("MHHI"), and is a variant of the HHI. However, O'Brien and Salop emphasise that in a differentiated products model, a different economic analysis should be applied. This is especially the case if the products supplied by the merging firms are particularly close substitutes. The reason why an HHI-type calculation would not be appropriate in this case is that HHI's fail to capture which firms are the closest competi-tors to each other (or "head to head" competitors). O'Brien and Salop apply what is called a "price pressure index" ("PPI") model, which they claim provides a more refined analysis based on the closeness of the products of the firms involved. The PPI analysis is based on gross profit margins and diversion ratios (which are used to calculate the proportion of sales that would be lost to a particular competitor should a firm raise its prices) and can also take into account efficiency benefits (such as cost synergies).

The most potentially anti-competitive control scenario is the total control scenario, in which the shareholding firm has total unconstrained control over the acquired firm (without regard to the best interests of the acquired firm or any of its minority shareholders). In this situation, the anti-competitive effects increase the *smaller* the acquiring firm's stake in the acquired firm. This is because there is a "free rider" issue in that if the acquiring firm can increase the acquired firm's prices it will lose only a share of the acquired firm's profits, but it will gain 100 per cent of the profits from additional customers that switch to it. Accordingly, it can be pro-competitive in this scenario for a firm with total control to increase its financial interest in the acquired firm, since with a higher shareholding, greater profits would be foregone by the acquiring firm if the acquired firm raised its prices and lost customers. In other words, the "free rider" effect would be reduced.

Chapter 2 describes a number of cases in which material influence has been found to arise due to minority shareholdings and other factors, but most cases provide little guidance as to how the potential anti-competitive effects identified differ from those that would arise in relation to full mergers.

In the context of its report in relation to the merger between Icopal **6.101** Holdings A/S and Icopal a/s the Commission considered the effects on competition of IKO effectively increasing its shareholding in Icopal from 10.2 per cent to 25 per cent. The Commission noted, *inter alia*, that a 25 per cent share confers no legal rights not already available to the holder of a 10.2 per cent share, that there were three other shareholders each with a 25 per cent stake, there was a confidentiality agreement in place limiting IKO's access to confidential information, and it had observed no co-ordination between IKO and Icopal to date. Notwithstanding the above, the Commission concluded that:

". . . although the acquisition is not a full merger creating a single pricing unit in the UK, the shareholding arrangement and the information flows that naturally spring from it create a relationship that could be used to encourage a degree of common interest that might lead to a different attitude by the parties to mutual competition. They also provide a mechanism by which decisions made among shareholders about Icopal's strategy could be transmitted to the operating subsidiaries in the UK; and (although we have found no evidence of this happening to date) there are grounds for a reasonable expectation that this relationship would be likely to lead to such a development, if the parties were so minded.

"Were this to happen, then IKO would be likely to receive the lion's share of any profits that might arise as a consequence, because it would obtain all of the benefit that came to Ruberoid [owned by IKO] as a result of any market cooperation and 25 per cent of that accruing to Icopal. The other shareholders would receive only 25 per cent each of the gains to Icopal. Given these circumstances we would expect IKO to have the greater interest in making use of the relationship to generate opportunities for cooperative behaviour. Nevertheless, all the parties have a positive incentive to engage in behaviour that would maximize the profits of Icopal."[81]

---

[81]Cited above, para.6.029, n.34, at paras 2.116–2.132.

As considered in para.6.139, information flows may due to cross-shareholdings well increase transparency and facilitate co-ordination, but in this case were strictly limited. Information on Icopal's quarterly sales and profits would be exchanged, but the Commission emphasised that prices paid by individual customers were not transparent which raises the question as to how useful for co-ordination this information would be in facilitating co-ordination. Moreover, any explicit co-ordination between IKO and Icopal (*e.g.* IKO providing corresponding information to Icopal on its UK sales), as separate undertakings for the purpose of EC and UK competition law, would presumably fall for consideration under Art.81 and the analogous prohibition on anti-competitive agreements under Chapter I of the Competition Act 1998.

As to the incentives created due to the shareholding, as set out above, IKO's incentives to increase its prices might be increased somewhat as it would receive a 25 per cent stake in any increase in profits generated by Icopal due to those customers IKO would lose as a result switching to Icopal. However, the other shareholders in Icopal (with a combined stake of 75 per cent) have no interest whatsoever in increasing Icopal's prices if this would not be profitable for Icopal alone—customers lost to IKO would simply lead to lost profits for Icopal. Rival suppliers generally have an interest in higher prices, absent other competitive constraints, but the other shareholders' interests in higher prices are not increased by the shareholding agreement *per se*.

A contrasting case related to Scottish Radio Holdings ("SRH") acquiring a 22.5 per cent shareholding in Kingdom FM.[82] The OFT noted that SRH currently had no entitlement to appoint a director to the board nor any special voting rights, and that SRH had stated that it was not involved in the day-to-day running of Kingdom FM and was not currently selling any radio airtime on its behalf. The advice stated that:

> "Were a single company to control both Kingdom FM and Forth it might well find it profitable to raise Kingdom's prices somewhat given that some of the lost revenue caused by Kingdom's customers switching away would be reclaimed by Forth.
>
> While SRH appears to have acquired material influence over Kingdom FM, it is not in a strong position to seek to control or determine the price of Kingdom's radio advertising or its commercial policies. This, together with the relatively small size of the local radio advertising market in the Fife area, lead me to conclude that the effect of this merger is unlikely to result in a substantial lessening of competition."

6.102   A distinction can be drawn between these two cases in that SRH would not have any board representation (which might remove the information issue raised in the previous case), but it is striking that the OFT emphasised that minority shareholdings reduce firms' unilateral incentives to increase price compared with full mergers.

---

[82] Director General's advice of March 11, 2002, *The completed acquisition by Scottish Radio Holdings plc of 22.5% shareholding in Kingdom FM Radio Limited.*

These issues may well arise in other contexts. For example, in the context of the merger between National Express Group PLC and Central Trains Limited, the Commission observed that National Express could not increase fares or reduce service levels on Centro-supported rail services due to the terms of the franchise agreement. However, National Express had an interest in the incremental revenues of such rail services, and the MMC considered whether this might create incentives for National Express to take action as regards its overlapping bus services to divert bus passengers to rail. The MMC rejected such a possibility on the basis that this revenue sharing arrangement only gave National Express a small and uncertain incentive to act in such a way, any such action would give opportunities to rival bus operators, and could also breach separate assurances given by National Express regarding bus services.[83]

The counterfactual to the merger

An overview

The analysis in merger cases is "forward looking", in the sense that the relevant question is how competition will develop going forward. In this regard, the OFT's guidelines emphasise that a core issue in relation to the assessment of a substantial lessening of competition is a comparison between competition if the merger proceeds to the competitive situation without the merger (with this later scenario being referred to as "the counterfactual"). The OFT's guidelines states that: **6.103**

> "In most cases, the best guide to the appropriate counterfactual will be prevailing conditions of competition. However, the OFT may need to take into account likely and imminent changes in the structure of competition in order to reflect as accurately as possible the nature of rivalry without the merger. Examples of such circumstances may include the following:
>
> • where a firm is about to enter or exit the market. Similarly, the OFT may also take account of committed expansion plans by existing competitors
> • where changes to the regulatory structure of the market, such as market liberalisation, or tighter environmental constraints, will change the nature of competition."[84]

Accordingly, considering the counterfactual requires an assessment of a broad range of factors.

The loss of potential competition

One possibility which could be considered as part of the assessment of a   **6.104**
merger is whether it might lead to a loss of potential competition between the

---

[83] *National Express Group plc/Central Trains Limited*, Cm. 3774 (December 1997), at paras 2.56–2.59.
[84] OFT guidelines, cited above, para.6.001, n.1, at para.3.24.

parties and in turn, amount to a substantial lessening of competition. This might be the case even if there is no direct overlap in the products or customers supplied by the parties to a merger, because their existence as potential suppliers of the product in question in the relevant area may act as an important competitive constraint upon pricing (hence the rationale for including supply side substitutes within the relevant market).[85] The fact that mergers between potential competitors might reduce or eliminate the competitive constraint represented by new entry is emphasised by the OFT's guidelines which state that:

"This might arise, for example, where the acquired entity was one of the most likely entrants or was genuinely perceived as such by those already in the market: in other words, the merger would substantially lessen pressure from potential competitors."[86]

The Commission's guidelines also make the very different point that the target company might be acquired by another firm as a means of this other firm entering the market:

"The merger may directly prevent entry by a new firm (or expansion by an incumbent) by eliminating an entity which might provide an effective means of access to the market to other firms. Therefore the merger itself might be an act aimed at preventing entry or expansion."[87]

The acquisition of an existing competitor by a non-competitor does not, however, alter competition in itself and is not normally characterised as new entry. It is possible that the new owners of an existing supplier might increase its competitiveness. However, this cannot be assumed to be the counterfactual, without clear evidence that in the absence of the merger in question it may be expected that another firm would have acquired the target business *and* the competitiveness of the target business would have improved.

Clearly, such a merger involving a potential competitor would only be anti-competitive if, following the merger, competition would be substantially less effective, taking into account actual competition between the remaining existing suppliers and the scope for new entry from other potential suppliers. In its Horizontal Merger Guidelines, the European Commission observes that:

"For a merger with a potential competitor to have significant anti-competitive effects, two basic conditions must be fulfilled. First, the potential competitor must already exert a significant constraining influence or there must be a significant likelihood that it would grow into an effective competitive force. Evidence that a potential competitor has plans to enter a market in a significant way could help the Commission to reach such a conclusion. Second, there must not be a sufficient

---

[85] See further paras 6.024 to 6.025.
[86] OFT guidelines, cited above, para.6.001, n.1, at para.4.25
[87] Commission guidelines, cited above, para.6.001, n.1, at para.3.53.

number of other potential competitors, which could maintain sufficient competitive pressure after the merger."[88]

In this regard, in the context of Stena AB's proposed acquisition of the   6.105
Peninsular and Oriental Steam Navigation Company's Fleetwood/Larne service (which operated on the "diagonal" Irish Sea freight routes), the Commission observed that although Stena did not operate on those routes it was a potential entrant. However, it concluded that:

"Whilst the appropriate counterfactual, set out in paragraph 5.25, was that Stena was one of several potential entrants on the diagonal routes, we did not receive evidence to suggest that Stena's threat of entry has had much impact on the competitiveness of the market. Further, we were unable to form an expectation that Stena would have entered a diagonal route with a new service in the next two to three years, not least because of its clearly stated preference for entry by acquisition. Finally, we found no evidence to form an expectation that the merger would reduce capacity on this route. We conclude, therefore, that the transfer of the Fleetwood-Larne route from P&O to Stena could not be expected to result in an SLC."[89]

One circumstance in which a merger may lead to a substantial lessening of competition due to the elimination of potential competition would be in relation to "local" markets (e.g. possibly individual public transport routes between certain locations, or local retailing markets, or where firms offer partially overlapping product ranges covering many different product variants). In relation to such "localised" markets, it may be the case that there is limited existing competition in relation to certain such markets and the only credible potential entrants (which may also find entry relatively easy) are rivals which are already active in "nearby" markets or are large scale suppliers across a range of such markets (for example, national retailers which compete in different local product markets might be the most viable potential entrants in specific local markets).[90]

In this regard, in the context of the proposed merger between ARRIVA and Lutonian Buses, the Commission found that Lutonian had a record of establishing new bus routes for previously unserved areas, and an objective of introducing one new route every year. In addition to concluding that the proposed merger would lead to a loss of actual competition on bus routes in Luton where both parties were operating services, the Commission also found that the merger would result in a loss of *potential* competition elsewhere in Luton. The Commission stated that:

---

[88] Cited above, para.6.001, n.4, at para.60. Paragraph 59 also refers to the potential entrant constraining existing competitors if it could enter the market without incurring significant sunk costs (in which case it may already be included in the market as this may indicate that there is a high degree of supply-side substitutability, see further paras 6.024 to 6.025) or it is very likely that the firm would incur the necessary sunk costs in a relatively short period of time.

[89] Cited above, para.6.013, n.38, at para.5.35.

[90] See para.3.55 of the Commission's guidelines, cited above, para.6.001, n.1.

"We believe . . . that the loss of competition and potential competition on commercial services in Luton may be expected to result in higher fares, and/or lower choice, and/or less innovation on routes and services and poorer levels of service. These effects are likely to arise not only on those routes on which Lutonian operated where previous competition has been largely eliminated, but also on other routes operated by ARRIVA the Shires in Luton where potential competition has been lost as a result of the merger."[91]

In contrast, in its inquiry into the proposed merger between Cowie Group and British Bus Group, the MMC found that outside London, although the operations of Cowie and British Bus overlapped or were contiguous with each other in several areas, there would be only a limited loss of potential competition, which was mitigated by the proximity of other significant operators in these areas. The Commission did not, therefore, expect the merger to operate against the public interest.[92]

6.106   A reduction in potential competition will not have any adverse effects if existing competitive constraints remain effective. For example, in its report on the proposed acquisition by Compass Group PLC of Rail Gourmet Holding AG, Restorama AG and part of Gourmet Nova AG, the Commission considered whether the merger increased barriers to entry by removing a potential competitor from the market. In this regard, the Commission observed that Compass was a bidder for the First Great Western Ltd contract won by Sodexho UK, and might have been expected to bid for future contracts. However, regardless of whether this was the case, the Commission concluded that:

". . . the removal of Compass from the list of bidders would not in any case significantly reduce competition. In a bidding market of this kind it may only be necessary for one genuine and serious competitor to remain for competition to be maintained. The possibility that the TOC [train operating company] could bring the service in-house also acts further to maintain competitive pressure."[93]

In its inquiry into the proposed acquisition by Lloyds TSB of Abbey National, the Commission first expressed concerns about the competitiveness of the market for personal current accounts ("PCAs") as it observed that:

"The merger would increase the PCA share of Lloyds TSB, already the market leader, from 22 to 27 per cent and would raise the combined share of the big four banks from 72 to 77 per cent.
    We considered the merger's effects not only on Lloyds TSB but also on the merged firm's rivals, particularly the other members of the big four. There are several features of the PCA market—homogeneity of products, many small customers lacking buyer power, transparent prices, stable demand, similarity of size and cost structure among the main suppliers, and suppliers' past behaviour—which make the market vulnerable to

---

[91] Cited above, para.6.070, n.78, at para.2.83.
[92] Cowie Group plc/British Bus Group Limited, Cm. 3578 (March 1997), at para.1.11.
[93] Cited above, para.6.092, n.65, at para.2.32.

tacit collusion in pricing, that is, parallel pricing by rival firms, without any overt agreement between them, in ways which serve their common commercial interest. These features would tend to exacerbate any adverse effects on competition arising from the loss of a significant player."[94]

The Commission found that Abbey National was one of the two most successful branch-based suppliers of personal current accounts. It had shown the capability and staying power to win a significant share of the personal current account market from the major banks, despite the existence of barriers to growth. Abbey National offered a distinct alternative to the big four banks, it had been reasonably innovative, and it had to compete actively to maintain its market position. Given Abbey National's financial performance, the Commission considered that it was capable of maintaining its independence and, furthermore, that there was a possibility of Abbey National merging with another player to form an enlarged group which would maintain or increase competitive pressure on the big four banks. Against this background, the Commission concluded that the acquisition of Abbey National by Lloyds TSB would reduce the incentives to compete of:

(i)   Lloyds TSB individually, by increasing its customer base and thereby encouraging it to attach more weight to increasing its margins than to the growth of shares (see further paras 6.132 to 6.133 for further explanation of this effect); and

(ii)   the big four banks, by removing one of the two main sources of actual and potential competition they faced in the market for personal current accounts.[95]

Similar conclusions were reached as regards banking services to small and medium sized enterprises, despite the fact that Abbey National only offered a restricted range of products and had less than 1 per cent of supply.[96]

Competing bidders

Where there are competing bidders for a business, assessing the counterfac-   **6.107**
tual to the merger may require a view to be taken as to whether an acquisition by one of these competing bidders would lead to lesser or greater competition concerns. For example, in its report on FirstGroup's plc proposed acquisition of the Scottish Passenger Rail Franchise[97] the Commission observed that in the absence of the FirstGroup merger either of the other two remaining bidders—National Express or Arriva—would obtain the franchise. The Commission concluded that since National Express was the incumbent operator, there would be no change in the current situation if it were to win the new franchise. If Arriva were to

---

[94] Cited above, para.6.065, n.55, at paras 1.6–1.7.
[95] Cited above, para.6.065, n.55, at paras 1.9–1.10.
[96] Cited above, para.6.065, n.55, at paras 1.13–1.15.
[97] Cited above, para.6.012, n.36, at para.5.2.

acquire the franchise, then overlaps would be substantially smaller than if FirstGroup acquired the franchise.

The failing firm defence

6.108 In brief, the so-called "failing firm defence" maintains that a merger that may give rise to anti-competitive consequences may nevertheless be permitted if the company being acquired (and its assets) would have exited the market in any event, on the basis that the merger itself will not result in a loss of competition.[98] The Competition Commission's guidelines state that:

> "Where the Commission considers that one of the firms would fail then the situation in the market without the merger may be similar to that which would result from the merger, and thus the merger itself may not lead to any significant changes in the extent of competition in the market."[99]

The OFT's guidelines state that:

"In order to satisfy the failing firm defence against a finding of an expected substantial lessening of competition, the following conditions need to be met.

---

[98] For example, the US Horizontal Merger Guidelines state that:

". . . a merger is not likely to create or enhance market power or to facilitate its exercise, if imminent failure . . . of one of the merging firms would cause the assets of that firm to exit the relevant market. In such circumstances, post-merger performance in the relevant market may be no worse than market performance had the merger been blocked and the assets left the market. . . . A merger is not likely to create or enhance market power or facilitate its exercise if the following circumstances are met:

(1) the allegedly failing firm would be unable to meet its financial obligations in the near future;

(2) it would not be able to reorganize successfully under Chapter 11 of the Bankruptcy Act;

(3) it has made unsuccessful good-faith efforts to elicit reasonable alternative offers of acquisition of the assets of the failing firm that would both keep its tangible and intangible assets in the relevant market and pose a less severe danger to competition than does the proposed merger; and

(4) absent the acquisition, the assets of the failing firm would exit the relevant market."

Cited above, para.6.001, n.4, ss.5.0–5.1. One question that may arise which is related to the failing firm defence is whether a decision by one of the parties to exit a particular market or cease producing a particular product is a consequence of an announced merger. In the context of the proposed acquisition of Dräger Medical AG & Co KGaA of certain assets representing the Air-Shields business of Hill-Rom Inc (Hill-Rom), a subsidiary of Hillenbrand Industries, the Commission concluded that it was not persuaded that a decision by Dräger to withdraw its transport incubator from the UK was wholly unrelated to the merger. It noted that the product continued to be offered elsewhere in Europe, Dräger's evidence suggested that the merger might hasten the planned withdrawal of the product internationally, and the Commission would otherwise have expected the introduction of a successor transport incubator in the absence of the merger (cited above, para.6.028, n.31, at paras 6.7–6.8).

[99] Cited above, para.6.001, n.1, at para.3.61.

First, in order to rely on a failing firm defence, the firm must be in such a parlous situation that without the merger it and its assets would exit the market and that this would occur in the near future. Firms on the verge of administration may not meet these criteria, whereas firms in liquidation will usually do so. Decisions by profitable parent companies to close down loss-making subsidiaries are unlikely to meet this criteria.[1]

Second, there must be no serious prospect of re-organising the business. Identifying the appropriate counterfactual in these types of situation is often very difficult. For example, even companies in receivership often survive and recover.

Third, there should be no less anti-competitive alternative to the merger. Even if a sale is inevitable, there may be other realistic buyers whose acquisition of the plant/assets would produce a better outcome for competition. These buyers may be interested in obtaining the plant/assets should the merger not proceed: that could indeed be a means by which new entry can come into the market. It may also be better for competition that the firm fails and the remaining players compete for its share and assets than that the failing firm's share and assets are transferred wholesale to a single purchaser."[2]

These factors are considered in turn below.[3]

The financial position of the company

The OFT and the Commission are often sceptical of arguments that the financial position of the business in question is so precarious that it is likely to fail. For example, in *Sibelco/Fife*, Sibelco had argued that Fife Silica Sands had been a failing firm on the basis that: **6.109**

(i)   Fife had incurred significant trading losses for four years prior to its acquisition by Sibelco, and it was able to continue in business only through the support of its then parent company, Anglo Pacific; if the sale to Sibelco had not proceeded, then Anglo Pacific would have soon withdrawn financial support from Fife;

(ii)   Anglo Pacific under-invested in Fife, leading to quality problems. Any significant expenditure aimed at remedying these problems could have tipped Fife "over the edge"; and

---

[1] A comment is warranted in relation to the OFT's statement that failing divisions of profitable firms will not be deemed failing firms. Profitable parent companies can be expected to close down unprofitable business. For example, the US Horizontal Merger Guidelines accept that the failing firm defence can apply to failing divisions as well (see s.5.2, cited above, para.6.001, n.4). See also, for a UK example of a failing division, *VNU Entertainment Media UK Limited/Book Data Limited*, Cm. 5779 (March 2003), which is discussed at paras 6.109 to 6.110, below.

[2] Cited above, para.6.001, n.1, at para.4.37.

[3] Whilst not determinative to the application of the failing firm defence, the acquisition of a failing firm may also yield customers benefits. For example, the OFT's guidelines refer to examples of possible customer benefits as including ". . . ensuring that customers will continue to be supplied during the process of change or through commitments to honour existing warranties." (cited above, para.6.001, n.1, at para.4.38).

(iii)   an extensive sales process for the business had failed to elicit any serious interest other than from Sibelco itself.

Significantly, however, Anglo Pacific indicated to the Commission that whilst Fife had experienced profitability difficulties, and that it had had limited funds for investment in Fife, Fife's poor performance was mainly due to management problems which had been resolved just prior to the sale of the business to Sibelco. Furthermore, whilst Anglo Pacific had been disappointed at the lack of success of the auction of Fife, it told the Commission that had the sale to Sibelco not taken place Anglo Pacific would have continued to operate the business. Key customers of Fife also confirmed that the product quality problems referred to by Sibelco were being resolved.

In that case, the Commission concluded that there had been mismanagement of the Fife business in the past, and this had resulted in certain product quality problems and loss of customers. Whilst there had been certain deficiencies in the operational and health and safety aspects at Fife, none were fundamental to the viability of the operation. As regards the profitability of the business, Anglo Pacific had made management charges to Fife in the three years preceding the acquisition and a different accounting treatment of these charges would have led to an operating profit being earned. As regards the auction process for the business, the Commission found that there would have been a number of potential purchasers had the asking price for the business been lower. The Commission therefore concluded that these points were insufficient to support a finding that Fife was a failing firm.[4]

One case in which the financial position of an acquiring subsidiary (VNU) was such that its market exit might have otherwise occurred (and also raising issues in relation to competing bidders) is the Competition Commission's inquiry into the acquisition by VNU Entertainment of Book Data. The Commission stated that:

> "It is unusual for the [Commission] to clear a merger which has brought about a significant reduction in competition compared with the situation that pertained beforehand. As we have said, however, in determining whether the merger has adverse effects for the public interest we have to compare the situation with the merger with what would have been the situation without the merger (. . .). On that footing, once we have reached the view that the counterfactual is unlikely to have been materially different from the post-merger situation, we have no option but to conclude that the merger is not against the public interest."[5]

6.110   According to the Commission, VNU and Book Data were in competition only as regards the supply of commercial bibliographic data services in the UK and were the only two competitors in this market. The Commission found that the prospects for VNU in the market absent its acquisition of Book Data were such that VNU would have been expected to have exited

---

[4] Cited above, para.6.059, n.41, at paras 2.66–2.89.
[5] Cited above, para.6.108, n.1, para.2.130.

the market in the very near future despite significant exit costs. It also considered that had VNU not acquired Book Data then Book Data would have been likely to have been acquired by Bowker, a firm which provided a worldwide English language commercial bibliographic data service, but not one which was specific to the UK (and which was therefore not in direct competition with those of VNU and Book Data). The Commission concluded that an acquisition of Book Data by VNU was preferable to one by Bowker because it considered that at least the acquisition by VNU preserved Bowker as a potential competitor (a limited constraint which would have been lost had Bowker acquired Book Data).[6] The Commission did, however, add that it appeared to it that the merged entity would be in a dominant position and would therefore be subject to the Chapter II prohibition of the Competition Act 1998 (which prohibits the abuse of a dominant position).[7]

In *Air Canada/Canadian Airlines*,[8] the MMC concluded that an alternative bid for Canadian Airlines could not be regarded as likely. In particular, Onex Corporation had attempted to launch a takeover bid for Air Canada, with a view to combining Air Canada with Canadian Airlines. However, the bid had been rejected by Air Canada, and was withdrawn in November 1999.[9] Following this, Canadian Airlines had investigated whether other members of the Oneworld Alliance would be prepared to provide financial support, but Canadian Airlines had been unable to prepare any business plan which demonstrated its future viability. In late November 1999, British Airways had made an offer to acquire Canadian Airlines' operations between London and Toronto and the associated airport slots. However, the terms of the offer could not be met in practice. As a result of these various failed initiatives, the MMC could not foresee an alternative bid for Canadian Airlines.

The existence of alternative purchasers

If there are alternative purchasers available for the business, it is possible **6.111** that competition between the businesses in question might be sustained in the absence of the merger. In this connection the Director General indicates that in assessing this issue the OFT will request evidence that there are no other credible bidders in the market, and that all possible options have been explored.[10] In the context of *Rockwool/Owens Corning*, the Commission had been told by Owens Corning that if the merger with Rockwool were to be prohibited, then Owens Corning would rapidly rationalise the business' product lines, cutting out loss-making lines and reducing overall output. Owens Corning also told the Commission that it would quickly look for another buyer for the business, although it was unlikely that an acceptable buyer could be found.

---

[6] Cited above, para.6.108, n.1, paras 2.109 to 2.113. This is also relevant to the points made above in paras 6.104 to 6.106 in relation to the loss of potential competition.

[7] Cited above, para.6.108, n.1, para.2.131(c).

[8] Cited above at para.6.065, n.59, at paras 2.13 to 2.19.

[9] This followed a ruling by the Quebec Superior Court that the offer violated the terms of the Air Canada Public Participation Act, which prevented any one shareholder in Air Canada from holding more than 10 per cent of the company's shares.

[10] Cited above, para.6.001, n.1, at para.4.39.

However, the Commission was not persuaded by these statements. The Commission believed that there were potential buyers who would be prepared to offer Owens Corning a worthwhile price for the business. Some expressions of interest had already been received from third parties, and the Commission considered that there were other stone wool producers in continental Europe which might see the acquisition of the business as a good means of entering the UK market. The Commission believed that, faced with a choice between a worthwhile offer for the business and incurring the cost of closure, Owens Corning would sell the business. The Commission stated that it could not rule out the possibility of there being no buyers for the business, but they believed that a buyer could be found. It is perhaps noteworthy that although Owens Corning had argued that it was unlikely that an acceptable buyer could be found, Owens Corning acknowledged that it had not carried out extensive research into the question as to whether there would be another buyer for the business.[11]

The mitigation of competition concerns

6.112 The Commission and the OFT will consider whether the imminent failure of one of the parties to the merger would mitigate the competition concerns that would otherwise arise. In particular, the OFT's guidelines (quoted above) emphasise that a key issue is whether, even if the firm in question exits the market, its assets might be acquired by new or existing competitors.[12] In this connection, the OFT's guidelines indicate that in such cases, the OFT will seek information on how the acquiring firm proposes using the failing firm's assets post-merger,[13] which is presumably a reference to the question of whether or not the firm intends to use the assets in the market.

This issue very much depends on the facts of the case and asserting a possibility that the assets might remain in the market (and be acquired by smaller rivals or used by a new entrant) does not render this a likelihood. For example, in a market where many firms have excess capacity, additional productive assets might have little or no value in that market. Similarly, certain assets which are not market specific might expect to be redeployed in other more profitable markets (for example, the site of the asset might be more valuable if it were to be used to build houses on or to open a retail outlet).

A further issue raised in both the Commission's and OFT's guidelines is what would happen to market shares in the absence of the merger. The Commission's guidelines express the issue as follows:

"A further consideration is how the sales of the failing firm, should it exit the market, will be redistributed among the firms remaining in the market. If without merger they are likely to be dispersed across a number

---

[11] Cited above, para.6.025, n.19, at paras 2.143–2.149.
[12] Indeed, Bishop and Walker emphasise that: "If other firms will buy the assets after a firm has failed, then the failing firm defence of a merger is not valid. Only if productive assets would otherwise exit the market does the failing firm argument provide a legitimate defence" (cited above, para.6.001, n.2, at p.307).
[13] Cited above, para.6.001, n.1, at para.4.39.

of other firms, then the merger, by transferring most or all sales of the failing firm to the acquirer, may well have a significant impact on competition in the market. In other cases the great majority of sales may be expected to switch to the acquiring firm anyway, in which case the merger may have little effect on competition."[14]

For example, in *Air Canada/Canadian Airlines*, the Commission concluded that:

". . . in assessing the effects of this merger, we have to consider what would have happened in the absence of the merger. The only meaningful scenario against which to judge the effects of the merger is the financial failure of Canadian Airlines and its break-up, an alternative regarded as unacceptable by the Canadian Government. Within such a scenario, we see little evidence that other operators would have been able or willing to take on Canadian Airlines' services on the Heathrow-Calgary or Heathrow-Ottawa routes, or to any significant extent the domestic services in Canada which provide flights connecting to the Heathrow-Canada routes. The possible detriments arising from such a lack of competition . . . arise as a result of the failure of Canadian Airlines to sustain competition in the Canadian market and on the Canada-UK routes, and irrespective of the merger situations we have to consider."[15]

Future competitive developments

A further issue is whether competitive conditions would change in the future even in the absence of the merger. Perhaps the most obvious possible developments in this regard are changes in the competitive positions of the parties and their rivals.

6.113

In this regard, the Commission has concluded that current (and historical) market shares may not reflect the long-term competitive strengths of the merged company and its competitors. This issue was considered by the Commission in its report on the proposed merger between Neopost and Ascom (AMS) Holding. The Commission observed that:

"In assessing the impact of the loss of AMS as a separate competitive force it is important that we take into account the prospective weakening of AMS's position in the absence of the merger. Because of the high proportion of its UK customers whose machines require replacement . . . its lack of proven digital products and the smallness of its sales force, AMS would in these circumstances be at risk of losing a sizeable part of its UK installed base within the next few months. Nor are there grounds to expect its fortunes to be improved by a new generation of products: because of the comparative failure of its joint development programme with Secap . . . its digital machines are, at best, late in reaching the market and will not offer innovative features compared with products already available from other suppliers."[16]

---

[14] Cited above, para.6.001, n.1, at para.3.63.
[15] Cited above, para.6.065, n.59, at para.1.9.
[16] *Neopost SA/Ascom Holding AG*, Cm. 5518 (May 2002), at para.2.141. Similarly, in relation to the merger between Express Dairies plc and Arla Foods amba, the Commission

Similarly, in *Compass Group/Rail Gourmet Holding/Restorama/ Gourmet Nova*, the Commission noted that:

". . . RGUK has inherited the logistics supply system and many of the staff from . . . the successor to the original nationalized monopoly supplier [of on-train food services]. It understands the business thoroughly, and is used to dealing with all the [train operating companies]. This gives it an apparently strong market position in relation to any competitor as contracts are tendered. However, if the contract were not awarded to RGUK, the staff and basic facilities would be transferred to the successful bidder, so this apparent advantage does not rest on any very strong foundations."[17]

However, it is possible that competition between the parties might well have increased in the absence of the merger. For example, in the context of National Express Group PLC's merger with ScotRail Railways Limited, the Commission concluded that rail/coach competition would otherwise increase:

". . . our perception is that the competition which Citylink has encountered in practice from ScotRail in recent years has been relatively weak. The Saltire report noted that ScotRail made less use of price competition than InterCity and the evidence we received suggests that that situation has continued. Following the franchising of ScotRail's service we would expect to see a much more commercial approach by the management given that, on the one hand, subsidy levels are now determined for seven years in real terms and, on the other hand, the amount of subsidy will decline, putting NEG under pressure to boost revenues. If NEG did not also own Citylink, we would have expected—given the evidence of substitutability between rail and coach which we have cited—that ScotRail would see the winning of passengers from the coach network as a significant part of its strategy, and that the coach company would respond vigorously to defend its market, with a resulting downward pressure on fares and a stimulus to innovation and improved quality of service on both rail and coach. Given the common ownership, however, we do not expect vigorous competition to develop in this way and these potential benefits will be lost. There will still be incentives on NEG to offer attractive fares and improve services on ScotRail because of the pressures arising from the franchise agreement (see paragraph 2.84) but our concern is that the incentives will be diminished by the common ownership of rail and coach."[18]

---

concluded that: "Although the merger would reduce the number of suppliers to the national multiples from four to three, this may overstate the risk to competition which the merger would represent since, . . . absent the merger, we consider that one of the four will be weakened, potentially severely." (cited above, para.6.048, n.1, at paras 2.65–2.72 and 2.79). However, the Commission did not appear to treat Safeway's poor competitive performance as a mitigating factor in its competitive assessment, emphasising that its position could recover and that it was a target for price cutting by rivals (cited above, para.6.027, n.26, at paras 2.181 to 2.192).

[17] Cited above, para.6.092, n.65, at para.2.20.
[18] Cited above, para.6.023, n.11, at para.2.85.

In addition, in *Cargill/Cerestar*, the Commission took the view that the **6.114** market shares of two smaller suppliers of glucose syrup and blends were likely to understate their true competitive influence:

> "We consider, moreover, that despite their relatively small market shares to date, Syral and Pfeifer & Langen are likely to be important in checking the behaviour of their larger competitors. In our view, they will exert an important indirect effect on prices by ensuring that the major producers cannot bring about artificial capacity shortages of product in the reference market . . . Both companies have grown significantly in a relatively short time and we think it likely that they will see their interests as lying in the continued pursuit of that growth . . .."[19]

However, market conditions may change in other ways, such as the manner in which products are procured and the exercise of buyer power, or the magnitude of barriers to entry and expansion (*e.g.* due to new government regulations). For example, in connection with the acquisition by iSOFT of Torex the OFT concluded that the relevant counterfactual was one in which the National Programme for IT (a programme to modernise the role of IT in the provision of NHS healthcare services in the UK) was implemented as planned. This was important to the OFT's assessment of the merger due to the resulting rationalisation of suppliers and increasing degree of competition "for" the market (rather than "in" the market).[20]

Non-co-ordinated effects

Non-co-ordinated effects are described succinctly in the OFT guidelines as **6.115** follows:

> "Non-co-ordinated effects, also referred to as unilateral effects, may arise where, as a result of a merger, the merged firm finds it profitable to raise prices (or reduce output or quality) as a result of the loss of competition between the merged entities. This is because, pre-merger, any increase in the price of the acquiring firm's products would have led to a reduction in sales. However, post merger, any sales lost as a result of a price increase will be partially recaptured by increased sales of the acquired enterprise. So sales lost will no longer be foregone. In addition, the firm may find it profitable to raise also the price of the acquired products, since it will recapture some of the lost sales through higher sales of its original products."[21]

The OFT guidelines emphasise that non-co-ordinated effects include the impact of the merged firm's price changes on its rivals. In particular, the OFT guidelines state that:

---

[19] Cited above, para.6.028, n.30, at para.2.112.
[20] See the OFT's decision of March 24, 2004, *Completed acquisition by iSOFT Group plc of Torex plc.*
[21] OFT guidelines, cited above, para.6.001, n.1, at para.4.7.

"Other firms in the market may also find it profitable to raise their prices because the higher prices of the merged firm's products will cause some customers to want to switch to rival products thereby increasing rivals' demand." [22]

Whether or not a price increase by the merged firm would be profitable will clearly depend upon:

(i)   the degree of competition between the parties;

(ii)   the aggregate degree of existing competition that the parties face from other sources (including alternative products and suppliers, existing rivals, or customer price sensitivity);

(iii)   the impact of the sales loss on costs (factors all emphasised in paras 6.035 to 6.036); and

(iv)   whether such a price increase would be constrained by the entry or expansion of rivals or the exercise of buyer power (factors emphasised in paras 6.056 to 6.071 and paras 6.072 to 6.079 respectively, above).

The focus of this section is the extent to which a merger between competitors may render a non-co-ordinated price increase profitable, given competition between the parties and their rivals. Both the OFT's and Commission's guidelines list a similar set of factors which are relevant to competition between the parties and their rivals, whilst also emphasising the importance of entry, expansion and buyer power.[23]

The parties' market shares

6.116   The OFT's guidelines refer to non-co-ordinated effects arising where there are "few firms in the affected market(s)"[24] and the Commission's guidelines refer to mergers which result "in a firm with a large market share."[25] This is based on the premise that firms with high market shares have greater market power and that the competitive constraint imposed by any firm prior to the merger is in line with its market share (*i.e.* a firm contemplating increasing prices will lose more sales the higher the market share of its rivals, and sales will be lost to each of its rivals in line with their respective market shares).[26] The other points considered by both the OFT and the Commission relate to circumstances when market share is not a reliable indicator of the market power of a firm or the relative competitive importance of individual rivals.

---

[22] OFT guidelines, cited above, para.6.001, n.1, at para.4.7.

[23] The importance of potential new entry and expansion and buyer power as constraints against the exercise of market power, whether by the merged firm or a number of firms coordinating their competitive conduct, is not repeated below. These factors are emphasised in the Commission's and OFT's guidelines, and are considered in detail in paras 6.056 to 6.071 and paras 6.072 to 6.079 respectively, above (see also, for example, the final two bullet points of para.3.29 of the Commission's guidelines, cited above, para.6.001, n.1).

[24] Cited above, para.6.001, n.1, at para.4.8 (first bullet point).

[25] Cited above, para.6.001, n.1, at para.3.29 (first bullet point).

[26] See further paras 6.086 to 6.087, above.

The loss of competition between the merging companies

Market shares may provide a poor measure of the degree of competition **6.117** between the parties for a number of reasons. First, in markets where firms are differentiated due to differences in the products they offer or their geographical location, market shares are not meaningful indicators of the relative competitive importance of individual firms (as emphasised in para.6.086 above). For example, a report prepared for the OFT on merger appraisal in oligopolistic markets emphasises in the context of assessing non-co-ordinated effects, that:

"Merger models whose results are largely based on an analysis of market shares and market concentration have value when the competitive influence of a product in a market is proportional to its share of the market. However, in differentiated products markets it does not necessarily follow that a product which enjoys a large share of the market necessarily provides a stronger competitive constraint on others' pricing than a product with a lower share of the market. Crucially, in a differentiated product setting it will often be those products that are closest in product or geographic space to the product of concern that provide the most immediate competitive constraint rather than the largest alternative product within the market."[27]

The key point to appreciate is that if two firms are particularly "close competitors" it may be the case that the main factor constraining their prices is the loss of sales that would occur to each other if one firm were to increase its prices.[28] However, even if customers' first two choices were to be under common ownership, they still might be able to switch sufficient volumes to other alternatives to render a price increase unprofitable. In addition, mergers between firms which are *not* "close" competitors may still lead to non-co-ordinated effects if there is limited scope for substitution to other rivals. The OFT's guidelines describe "close competitors" as:

"representing for a substantial number of customers the 'next best alternative' to each other's products, so a merger between the two will prevent those customers from switching to the best rival product in the event of a post merger price increase."[29]

---

[27] "*Merger appraisal in oligopolistic markets*", prepared for the OFT by NERA, November 1999, Research paper 19, OFT267, at p.40.

[28] The US Horizontal Merger Guidelines discuss this issue in terms of whether the parties to the merger are perceived by a high proportion of common customers to be their first and second choice suppliers; cited above, para.6.001, n.4, paras 2.21 and 2.211. The Commission's guidelines express this point in the same terms (cited above, para.6.001, n.1, at para.3.29 (sixth bullet point). Similarly, the European Commission's Horizontal Merger Guidelines indicate that: "The higher the degree of substitutability between the merging firms' products, the more likely it is that the merging firms will raise prices significantly. For example, a merger between two producers offering products which a significant number of customers regard as their first and second choices could generate a significant price increase. Thus, the fact that rivalry between the parties has been an important source of competition on the market may be a central factor in the analysis." (cited above, para.6.001, n.4, at para.28).

[29] Cited above, para.6.001, n.1, at para.4.8.

In assessing the completed acquisition by Coloplast A/S of the continence care business of SSL International plc, the Commission identified a detriment arising from an agreement between the parties, which, together with the merger, "has the effect of concentrating in Coloplast's hands control, at least until 2007, of the two market-leading brands of non-latex sheaths in the UK. These had previously been in head to head competition."[30] Similarly, in his advice on the proposed acquisition by Bidvest of Brake Bros, the Director General observed that "The parties are the two largest companies in food delivery/wholesaling in the UK. Indeed, third parties have suggested that the parties are the only real national providers and are the only providers covering all temperature regimes. As such, they are each other's closest competitors."[31]

In many cases it may be difficult to assess whether firms are close competitors simply by comparing their products and/or locations, and indeed this may give the wrong indication (see further below). The closeness of competition between the parties may in certain circumstances be assessed using various techniques, such as econometrics, to calculate cross-price elasticities of demand[32] or "diversion ratios" (*i.e.* the proportion of sales that may be lost to another product in the event of a price increase), or assessments of customers' preferences using surveys, etc. (see further para.6.013).[33]

6.118   In bidding markets, the closeness of competitors may be assessed by the extent to which they have won/lost contracts from one another. For example, in the context of the merger between Express and Arla (two processors of fresh liquid milk with similar coverage of England by virtue of their network of depots and dairies), the Commission observed that:

> "The parties submitted that although they were clearly competitors, they were not each other's closest competitor. The evidence supports this claim. Since 2000, Express has lost/gained [_] supply arrangements for fresh processed milk to the national multiples—Arla UK has lost/gained [_]. However, only one has involved a national multiple switching supply to a group of stores directly between Arla UK and Express. Rather, it seems to us that, of the four major processors, Wiseman has been the most dynamic in gaining market share. As a result of a lack of investment

---

[30] Cited above, para.6.027, n.29, at para.2.126.

[31] Director General's advice of June 20, 2002, *The proposed acquisition by Bidvest plc of Brake Bros plc.*

[32] *i.e.* the proportionate increase in demand for one good following a small increase in the price of another (see further paras 6.008 and n.20 cited at para.6.008).

[33] These possibilities are outlined at n.23 on p.25 of the OFT guidelines, cited above, para.6.001, n.1. In this regard, Coleman and Scheffman advise that:

> ". . . in our opinion, demand estimates must be supplemented by evidence bearing directly on competition between the parties in order for estimates of market structure to be given much weight. For example, suppose the estimates of "diversion ratios" indicate two companies are "close" competitors, but evidence from [customer and competitor] interview, [suppliers'] documents [describing competitive conditions], and empirical analyses do not support that conclusion. In such a situation, in our view, the estimates of "diversion ratios" should not be given weight" (Coleman and Scheffman, "*Quantitative Analyses of Potential Competitive Effects from a Merger*", chapter three of "*Global Competition Policy: Economic Issues & Impacts*", edited by Evans and Padilla, LECG, 2004).

in new processing infrastructure by both the merger parties (although particularly by Express), they have fallen behind their two main rivals in being able to compete aggressively."[34]

Coleman and Scheffman indicate that in bidding markets it may be possible to assess whether the parties to the merger "often" have the lowest two bids, which would suggest that they are close competitors. They also suggest that the analysis of transaction price data may be revealing as to whether the parties to the merger are particularly close competitors. For example, it could be considered whether the merging parties' prices with customers are more closely correlated with one another than they are with other rivals' prices (extending the premise considered in para.6.021 regarding price correlations; that competitors will have close regard to their rivals' prices—and, therefore, that close competitors will have closer price correlations).[35]

In markets subject to substantial innovation, historical market shares may have little meaning. For example, in the context of its report on the merger between Carl Zeiss Jena GmbH and Bio-Rad Laboratories Inc, the Commission rejected any conclusions that the merged business would have a dominant position despite its historical market share of 65–75 per cent due to the importance of innovation and the nature of the bidding market in which the parties competed:

"The reason we reject this line of argument is that in these particular markets, it is possible for firms with small market shares to compete for customers with players with larger historic market shares. This is because each sale is substantially independent of others, including those to the same customer that has preceded it. Customers are well informed and choose suppliers through a detailed search process that establishes what product best satisfies their specific research needs. Specifications are varied and reflect those needs. Innovation plays a key role in determining product performance in the customers' eyes, and so in a firm's success. Past sales to that customer and historic market share both play minor roles. This is consistent with the evidence and submissions we have received, describing both customer needs and behaviour, and how market shares can change significantly following a successful innovation."[36]

Maverick competitors

The OFT's guidelines emphasise that an important factor which may lead to non-co-ordinated effects is if one of the parties to the merger is a "maverick", *i.e.*: **6.119**

---

[34] Cited above, para.6.048, n.1, at para.5.120. See also, *"Assessing Unilateral Effects in Practice: Lessons from GE/Instrumentarium"*, RBB Brief 14, May 2004. This article has a helpful discussion of the econometric studies employed in that case, considering how the presence or absence of one of the parties from a specific tender influences prices/discounts, with the econometric modelling also allowing for other factors which influence bid pries (thus isolating the impact on price of whether the merging parties were both bidding or not).

[35] Cited above, para.6.117, n.33.

[36] *Carl Zeiss Jena GmbH/Bio-Rad Laboratories Inc*, (May 2004), at paras 5.11–5.12.

". . . an important rivalrous force in the market representing a competitive constraint greater than its market share indicates, whose elimination may thus be an important change in competitive dynamics."[37]

Competition from the maverick does not necessarily impact solely on one firm (*e.g.* a close competitor) but may impact more broadly on many competitors in the market, causing them to compete more actively, thereby enhancing overall market competitiveness. Coleman and Scheffman describe the role of a maverick as follows:

". . . the 'maverick' may have been very disruptive by attempting to expand market share-lowering prices, trying to win customers from competitors and/or expanding capacity—and this behaviour has caused other competitors to compete more aggressively and may have undermined their ability to co-ordinate. A merger that removes this maverick may, as a result, significantly change the nature and intensity of competition, and high prices may result as all firms compete less aggressively. For this theory to be applicable, one must show that one of the firms has behaved as a maverick competitor and that its incentives will change post-merger."[38]

Mavericks can also prevent or destabilise co-ordination, because other competitors might be very reluctant to co-ordinate tacitly (*e.g.* to increase prices and reduce output) if they consider it likely that the maverick would respond by increasing its sales and thus undermining any attempt to increase prices. Obviously non-merging firms might also be maverick competitors as well, and this may be a constraint on the merged parties' ability to increase prices post-merger.

Coleman and Scheffman suggest that there are a number of ways in which maverick firms might be identified. For example, a maverick firm might have won a higher proportion of its sales from new customers, might bid for more customers than other firms (depressing prices even if it does not win business), or might win a higher share than rivals of the aggregate volume of business "lost" by suppliers in the market over a period of time.[39]

The loss of potential competition

6.120   Both the Commission's and OFT's guidelines emphasise that non-co-ordinated effects may arise if the merger eliminates a recent new entrant or potential entrant which may be expected to be or become an important competitive threat.[40] This issue is addressed at paras 6.104 to 6.106 above, but it should be noted that assessing future competitive threats can be highly speculative (*e.g.* many new products fail), and the competitive importance of other existing competitors and potential entrants must be limited for the loss of potential competition to be a substantive issue.

---

[37] Cited above, para.6.001, n.1, at para.4.8 (seventh bullet point). There is no explicit reference to maverick competitors in the Commission's guidelines.
[38] Cited above, para.6.117, n.33.
[39] Cited above, para.6.117, n.33.
[40] OFT guidelines, cited above, para.6.001, n.1, at para.4.8 (eight bullet point); and Commission guidelines, cited above, para.6.001, n.1, at para.3.29 (third bullet point).

For example, one area where such issues may arise is in the context of mergers in markets that are characterised by rapid innovation. This is because, in such markets, new entrants or potential entrants may well be considered as important competitive threats. As indicated in the OFT Economic Discussion Paper on *Innovation and Competition Policy*, this will particularly be the case where competition is "for" the market, rather than "in" the market as may be the case in innovation markets.[41] One of the problems with analysing non-co-ordinated effects in such markets is that future market conditions (including the products available and prices—even those of the merged firm) are considerably harder to predict than in more stable markets.[42]

Competition from rivals

Both the Commission's and OFT's guidelines emphasise that whether or not **6.121** non-co-ordinated effects arise depends on the ability of customers to switch to rivals.[43] The ability to switch may not be revealed by the market share of those rivals. The competitiveness of smaller rivals will be influenced by factors such as the competitiveness of their cost base and product offering.

If rival firms have efficient spare capacity, then they may have substantial scope to increase their sales and thus defeat any attempt by the merged undertaking to increase prices. In a homogenous goods industry (which is not differentiated by the location of suppliers), customers may be expected to be very willing to switch to such firms. This provides the rationale for calculating market shares on the basis of capacity in such markets (see further para.6.093, above). This may not be the case where firms are differentiated (whether by product or location). In its report on the merger between Express

---

[41] Cited above, para.6.067, n.67, paras 7.4 and 7.5. This paper highlights that when competition is "in" the market in dynamically competitive industries, it is likely to be based on a combination of continuous innovation and price competition. However, where competition is "for" the market it is more likely to be based on innovation (with less emphasis on price). Many high-tech markets (for example, computers, software, etc.) exhibit network effects which occur when the value of a product or service to a buyer increases with the number of other users. The value of the network increases if others own or use the same software programme or operating system (indirect network effects); synergies can be achieved through sharing of expertise and a larger customer base supports a greater variety of complementary hardware and software by allowing fixed cost recovery. The OFT's Economic Discussion paper discusses in detail network effects and in particular demand-side network effects, concluding that "large networks offer more value to users than small networks, and as a result, there is the potential to create a 'winner-take-all' situation'". A "winner-takes-all" situation occurs when "network and systems effects are present , there is a tendency for markets to 'tip' to a single dominant vendor or technology."

[42] "In dynamically competitive markets [assessing whether a firm has an incentive to increase prices post-merger] this is a very difficult calculation to make using logit models or any other form of model because today's products will not in general be the same as those in the near future. It is almost certain that many of the critical relationships among those products relative to [there] being a unilateral effect will have changed. Therefore, attempts to estimate unilateral effects based upon current products are doomed to significant inaccuracy". Cited above, para.6.067, n.67, para.7.11.

[43] OFT guidelines, cited above, para.6.001, n.1, at para.4.8 (third, fourth, and fifth bullet points); and Commission guidelines, cited above, para.6.001, n.1, at para.3.29 (second, fifth, and sixth bullet points). The ability to swtich suppliers may well vary between customers, hence the reference in the OFT's guidelines to the ability of suppliers to price discriminate against those customers with narrower choices. OFT guidelines, cited above, para.6.001, n.1, at para.4.8 (third bullet point).

and Arla, in the context of its assessment of the impact of the merger of two large processors of fresh processed milk selling to large national multiple supermarket chains (largely under these retailers' own-label brands), the Commission noted the substantial spare capacity of the parties' rivals and concluded that notwithstanding possible demand growth:

> "Although it is difficult to determine the exact level of post-merger capacity, it appears that there will be sufficient overcapacity to enable the national multiples to continue to move considerable volumes of business between the major processors. This will be an important source of competitive pressure on the major processors."[44]

Switching costs[45] may limit the ability of customers to switch to rivals. In this regard, in the Commission's report on the merger between Dräger Medical AG & Co. KGaA and Hillenbrand Industries, Inc, it rejected arguments that the market was most appropriately characterised as a bidding market, in which having a high market share does not confer market power because market share can easily be lost in the next bidding round. This was because:

> "While the direct costs of switching supplier do not appear to be high, we identified some psychological and practical barriers to switching supplier which give rise to 'stickiness' in customer behaviour. Having an installed base in the hospital seems to confer advantage in tender processes (though not to the extent that customers are effectively locked in). Also, while it is important to customers that prices are not greatly out of line with suitable alternatives, it is clear that clinical preference is generally more important than price in the ultimate selection of a product to buy. Taken together, the existence of barriers to switching and the low level of price sensitivity among customers give us reason to suppose that market shares are a relevant indicator of potential market power."[46]

In addition, switching costs may have other broader and more complex effects on competition. The OFT and DTI Economic Discussion Paper on Switching Costs emphasises that "Switching costs do affect how competition works in a market but they do not necessarily make markets less competitive." In particular:

---

[44] Cited above, para.6.048, n.1, at paras 5.69–5.74.

[45] OFT 655, "*Switching Costs*", (April 2003), OFT Economic discussion paper 5, prepared by NERA. This report defines switching costs as covering all costs incurred by customers in changing supplier that are not incurred if the customer chooses to remain with their existing supplier. These costs include, *inter alia*, the fact that the customer has made some supplier specific investment (*e.g.* in associated equipment which can only be used with one supplier's products, or in costly testing that a supplier's product meets their precise requirements, or if products differ and the customer needs to learn how to use different products), there is uncertainty and risk in switching to alternatives which are not tried and tested, and there may be transaction costs in changing suppliers (see Ch.2).

[46] Cited above, para.6.028, n.31, at para.9.

(i)   "switching costs intensify competition in growing markets with large numbers of uncommitted new customers". This is because winning a new customer will also generate a stream of profits from future sales to that customer, due to the reduced likelihood of that customer switching to a new supplier as a result of the costs of doing so;

(ii)   "Furthermore, their softening effect in more mature markets may be compensated by aggressive *ex-ante* competition (so that consumers have been 'refunded in advance' for later high prices) and by competition from small competitors who price low, even below cost, to attract customers from established firms"; and

(iii)   "What's more, switching costs can sometimes be an important spur to competition". The paper describes switching costs as potentially having analogous effects to a patent by being an impediment to imitation and increasing the future sales and profits of innovative new products.[47]

It also emphasises that in markets where switching costs are important **6.122** this has an important bearing on the assessment of non-co-ordinated effects[48], as in such markets competitive constraints are likely to come disproportionately from two related sources:

(i)   ex-ante competition for customers' business, that is competition to win the custom of new purchasers or those which are not yet committed to a supplier[49]; and

(ii)   competition from smaller firms, which can be more important than their overall share of total sales to all customers suggests where large incumbent firms cannot price discriminate between new and old customers (or can do so only imperfectly). This is because firms with ". . . a large customer base have an incentive to passively harvest the rewards from their current customer base rather than competing aggressively to win new business. By contrast, the main competitive dynamic is likely to be provided by those firms who do not have a large customer base to exploit and so can afford to compete aggressively. As a result, these small firms may have an importance for the competitive process that is not reflected by their share of the whole market."[50]

The paper emphasises that "These two factors mean that market shares based on total stock (as opposed to shares based on new business) may not be a good reflection of the intensity and importance of competitors in the

---

[47] Cited above, para.6.121, n.45 at paras 7.1–7.2.
[48] Cited above, para.6.121, n.45 at paras 7.102 to 7.118.
[49] The OFT Discussion Paper observes that "low prices to attract new customers can (at least in part) compensate customers for high prices when they are locked-in. Moreover, if firms' abilities to price discriminate are limited, then the desire to attract new customers will, at least partially, protect older 'locked in' customers." (cited above, para.6.121, n.54, para.7.104).
[50] Cited above, para.6.121, n.45, at para.7.105.

market." Indeed, in the extreme case where two firms with large existing customer bases were to merge and were not acquiring any new customers, there might be no loss of competition at all because the competitive constraint they face comes entirely from other small firms. In this regard, the Commission has noted that switching costs may well have mixed effects. In the context of Lloyds TSB Group plc's proposed acquisition of Abbey National plc the Commission stated that:

> "The existence of such switching barriers may have a number of effects. It may give existing providers some market power over their existing customers, enabling prices to be increased to the 'back book'. It may on the other hand also lead to stronger competition and lower prices for new customers, both switchers and first-time customers such as students."[51]

In that case, the Commission observed that one factor which concerned it was "back-book pricing", whereby established personal current account ("PCA") customers are left with worse terms than those offered to customers when new products are introduced. The Commission added that:

> "Although the 'back book' is less important in the PCA market than in some other personal finance markets, its existence brings out the point that incumbent suppliers with sizeable market shares have to take account of the effect of price initiatives on the profitability of their existing customer base. If a market is characterized by switching costs and/or customer inertia, suppliers can focus on new customers when competing through price, assured that cutting prices to new customers is likely to have little impact on retaining existing customers. Abbey National submitted that, in markets with switching costs, firms with low market share tended to grow (or 'sow') their share by competing aggressively and through price, while those with high market share tended to exploit (or 'harvest') theirs by preserving or increasing margins on the existing customer base. The merger, it argued, would replace a firm in sowing phase with one in harvesting phase, to the detriment of consumers and competition."[52]

Theoretical modelling—merger simulation

6.123   In certain cases, it may be possible to model the likelihood of non-co-ordinated effects and likely price increases. In particular, (computer based) simulations use economic models based on industrial organisation theory to predict the effect of mergers on prices and output in relevant markets. This is achieved by inputting estimates of elasticities of demand (derived from econometric modelling and other sources) and other variables such as marginal costs, prices and quantity, into a simplified economic model of how firms compete with one another and, in particular, how they respond to their rivals' competitive decisions.[53] An appropriate model in any partic-

---

[51] Cited above, para.6.065, n.55, at para.4.61.
[52] Cited above, para.6.065, n.55, at paras 2.78–2.79.
[53] See, for example, Epstein & Rubinfeld (2001), "*Merger simulation: A simplified approach with new applications*", 69 Antitrust Law Journal 883–019; Werden and Froeb, (2002),

ular case should thus reflect both the significance of individual competitors and the essence of the competitive process in the industry. According to Epstein and Rubinfeld:

"Merger simulation models predict post-merger prices based on information about a set of premerger market conditions and certain assumptions about the behaviour of the firms in the relevant market. Simulation models typically assume that firms' behavior is consistent with the [differentiated] Bertrand model of pricing, both pre- and post-merger. According to this theory, each firm sets the prices of its brands to maximize its profits, while accounting for possible strategic, noncollusive [*i.e.* non-co-ordinated] interactions with competitors. An equilibrium results when no firm can increase its profit by unilaterally changing the prices of its brands."

In this regard, Werden, Froeb, and Scheffman observe that merger simulation has often been applied in the context of US branded consumer good mergers, with the differentiated Bertrand model being applied (n.63). However, they caution that:

"Whether the Bertrand model is appropriate in any particular case may depend on many considerations, three of which are of general application: First, the role of non-price competition should be evaluated. Aspects

---

"*Calibrated economic models add focus, accuracy, and persuasiveness to merger analysis*" in The pros and Cons of Merger Control, The 10th anniversary of the Swedish Competition Authority; Werden and Froeb (1996), "*Simulation as an alternative to structural merger policy in differentiated product industries*", in The Economics of the Antitrust Process, edited by Malcolm Coate and Andrew Kleit, Kluwer Academic Publishers 1996; Motta, cited above, para.6.001, n. 2, at pp. 124–134, and Bishop and Walker, cited above, n.2, at pp.132–168. It is outside the scope of this Chapter to describe in any detail traditional non-coordinated static oligopoly models, with useful descriptions being set out in Chapter Three of the OFT's research paper on "*Merger appraisal in oligopolistic markets*", cited above, para.6.117, n. 27, and Chapters Two and Three of The European Commission's paper on "*Assessment criteria for distinguishing between competitive and dominant oligopolies in merger control*", Enterprise Papers No.6—2001, European Commission Enterprise Directorate-General. However, some points should be noted. First, the traditional Cournot and Bertrand models are static in the sense that they are generally conceptualised either on the basis that:

- each firm sets its output (Cournot)/price (Bertrand) simultaneously once and for all, and that there is no competitive interaction between firms thereafter; or
- that equilibrium is reached on the basis of specific assumptions as to how each firm believes its rivals will respond (or more accurately not respond) to changes in its output or price decisions. These assumptions about how rivals will respond are exogenously determined, rather than being determined endogenously by the models.

These give rise to the powerful and long standing criticism that static models cannot explain how firms' dynamic competitive responses to their rivals' competitive initiatives are determined (e.g. that their decisions trigger competitive responses from rivals which influence their decisions). Secondly, the Cournot model yields the result that firms' price-cost margins increase as industry concentration increases for a given price elasticity of market demand, whereas the simple Bertrand model with undifferentiated goods and no capacity constraints leads to prices equal to marginal costs even if there are only two competitors. This later extreme result is avoided if firms' products are differentiated or there are capacity constraints, and in such circumstances higher concentration leads to higher price-cost margins.

of marketing strategy may interact in important ways with the choice of price or be affected by the merger in ways that would cause the price-increase predictions to be a seriously misleading description of the merger's effects. Second, responses in the recent past to any significant cost changes, new product introductions, or other 'shocks' should be evaluated, asking how well the Bertrand model would have predicted them. Finally, the observed price-cost margins for the merging products and close substitutes should be compared to the margins predicted by the Bertrand model."[54]

More generally, the sensible theme of this article is that its authors "propose that every modelling choice in a merger simulation apt to matter significantly be accompanied either by some sort of justification or by a sensitivity analysis indicating its impact."

There are a number of other important issues raised by the use of simulation models. For example, the Cournot model or differentiated goods Bertrand model conclude that any reduction in the number of competitors automatically leads to higher prices and lower output.[55] It can be strongly argued that such a general conclusion is fundamentally wrong, and results in an exaggerated role for efficiency defences in the merger context (otherwise all mergers between competitors automatically lead to price increases in these models unless efficiencies are realised). In addition, as emphasised by RBB Economics:

"slavish use of merger simulation models will give rise to policy that is out of line with economic reality, since such models (and those who advocate their use without due regard for their limitations) systematically underestimate the resilience of markets to change."[56]

6.124   They go on to say:

"The main ingredient that is missing from the simulation models . . . is market dynamics in the form of active customers and responses by rivals. Simulation models uniformly assume essentially passive customers who, although they switch demand away from brands whose price has increased, take no active steps beyond this to prevent the merger from inflicting harm on them."

Making simplistic assumptions as to the nature of the competitive process has the merit of being convenient and simple to model, though it is often inconsistent with the way in which competition and markets actually operate. When an element of customer action and reaction, buyer power and/or supply-side responses (e.g. the entry or expansion of new or existing competitors) is added to the mix, the simple predictions from such models may no longer be robust. For example, in a merger involving the supply of

---

[54] Werden, Froeb and Scheffman, Draft of February 16, 2004, "A Daubert Discipline for Merger Simulation", available at www.ftc.gov.
[55] See the second point under para.6.123, n.53.
[56] RBB Economics, "The Emperor's New clothes?—the role of merger simulation models", January 2004.

specific grocery products, supermarket scanner data might provide good information on how consumers respond to increases in prices for specific brands and product ranges. Unfortunately, it fails to capture supermarkets buyers' responses to such price changes in terms of the ranges of brands/products stocked, where these brands are positioned in terms of shelf space, and how retailers' promotion and development of their own label brands are impacted. Similarly, it fails to capture the fact that supermarkets might respond to price increases by certain suppliers by encouraging the entry and expansion of rivals, and that other suppliers might take the opportunity to launch new brands, or increase the promotion of existing brands.

The comments set out above should not be interpreted as arguing that merger simulation is always inappropriate and of little value in a mergers context. However, very good and extensive information may be required to yield robust results, and results may be very sensitive to modelling assumptions.

"Natural experiments"—bidding studies and price-concentration studies

There are a number of other quantitative techniques which may be used to   6.125
seek to quantify the non-co-ordinated and co-ordinated effects of merger, and which may also address market definition questions. The key feature of these techniques is that they seek to make comparative assessments of markets on the basis of the historical impact of entry/exit of competitors on prices and profit margins, comparisons of prices and profit margins between different geographical markets which are more or less concentrated, or in bidding markets where the number of bids made varies between tenders or over time. These approaches are commonly referred to as "natural experiments", since they provide a measure of how the number of competitors, and perhaps specifically the presence of both parties in a market or bid, impacts on prices and profit margins.

In particular, Coleman and Scheffman refer to evidence being collated as to whether the entry of one party either generally or in specific geographic markets led to the other party lowering prices and/or losing sales.[57] Similarly, prices could be compared between different geographic markets or bids to assess whether prices are lower where both parties are present, compared with those where only one is present. Coleman and Scheffman emphasise that it is important for the econometric analysis to take account of other factors which vary over time and/or across areas. For example, the parties' prices may be lower in those areas or bids where they are both active because their costs coincidently tend to be lower. This can generate spurious relationships, as discussed in the context of price correlations in paras 6.022 to 6.023. Equally, if variables other than price are not taken into account, this may lead to a failure to discern the true price-depressing impact of competition between suppliers.

For example, in *SCI/Plantsbrook*, SCI carried out a regression analysis to try to explain the differences in funeral prices by differences in six other variables—the level of concentration in the local area, the number of

---

[57] Cited above, para.6.117, n.33. This could be akin to the impact studies which might be carried out for market definition purposes, as discussed in para.6.023.

different firms, the type of coffin, "extras" bought for the funeral, funeral costs and average local wages. The analysis concluded that the only significant variable was that relating to "extras", such that price was not sensitive to the other variables—in particular, it was not sensitive to the number of competitors in the local area. The MMC reviewed the study and the data used in the study. It concluded that the study itself was flawed (in particular as concentration was not measured by market shares but the number of firms in the local area, with the latter not being a good measure of local competitive pressures) and the explanatory power of the model nearly all came from the variables for coffin type and "extras." Furthermore, standard econometric testing indicated that the results of the study could not be relied upon. In addition, the economic consultancy instructed by the MMC concluded that a robust model could not be created on the basis of the data provided.[58]

Similarly, in *Newsquest/INM*[59], the Commission investigated the possibility of a link between newspaper market share and newspaper yields. To do this it carried out separate regression analyses for Newsquest's and INM's newspapers. In each case, the results appeared to the Commission to indicate a positive relationship between newspaper market share in different localities and yield (*i.e.* newspaper advertising prices) based (apparently) on the slope of the fitted regression line to the data (that is, in simple terms, the "best" straight line which could be drawn through the various plotted data points on the graph)—although the Commission noted that, in relation to the Newsquest titles, "the relationship was. . . positive, but less marked and the regression model explained only a low proportion of the variation."[60] A key statistic reported in relation to the Commission's model was "R^2" which measures the "goodness of fit" of the regression line to the data, or, to put it another way, the proportion of the total variation in the relevant variable which can be explained by the estimated regression model. R^2 lies between zero and one—with an R^2 of zero suggesting that there is no relationship between the variables in question, and an R^2 of one suggesting that the estimated regression model perfectly describes the relationship between the variables. In this case, the Commission reported R^2 values of 0.35 for its regression related to the INM titles and 0.05 for the Newsquest titles.[61] An R^2 of 0.35 is, by any standard, on the low side, and an R^2 of 0.05 is extremely low. This raises a serious concern that the results derived by the simplistic regressions carried out were distorted by omitted variables, (which is commonly referred to as omitted variable bias and tends to lead to biased coefficient estimates). These results would seem to raise serious concerns that the results of the regression were not robust. Accordingly, the Commission's conclusion that there was a positive relationship between yields and concentration is surprising, especially as regards the Newsquest titles where the regression model explained only 5 per cent of the variation in yields.

---

[58] *Service Corporation International/Plantsbrook Group plc*, Cm. 2880 (May 1995), at para.2.34 and App.2.1. See also, the OFT Research Paper on "*Quantitative Techniques in Competition Analysis*", cited above, para.6.012, n.32, paras 13.14 to 13.18.
[59] *Newsquest (London) Limited/Independent News & Media PLC*, Cm. 5951 (October 2003).
[60] Cited above, para.6.125, n.59, para.5.59.
[61] Cited above, para.6.125, n.59, Figures 5.6 and 5.7.

In relation to the proposed merger between Arla Foods amba and Express **6.126**
Dairies plc, one of the issues considered by the Commission was the
geographical scope of the market for the supply of fresh processed milk to
large national multiple retailers, since in certain regions of Great Britain the
number of such suppliers varied from two to four, with Wiseman being the
largest supplier by a substantial margin in Scotland.[62] This suggested that an
obvious issue to consider was whether prices were higher where there were
fewer suppliers, particularly in Scotland due to Wiseman's position.
However, the Commission made a number of important points in relation to
the interpretation of price information in such circumstances.

In support of their claim that wholesale fresh milk prices were not higher
in Scotland than elsewhere, the parties provided data on retail prices for
various national multiples in a number of regions throughout Great
Britain.[63] The Commission concluded that this data showed no discernible
difference between the price in Scotland, and England and Wales. The
Commission first observed that it was not clear whether this is because
wholesale prices are the same in all regions, or that the national multiples
have a policy of charging the same retail price. Nevertheless, the national
multiples contacted by the Commission all said that they generally paid a
single price for fresh processed milk from each of their suppliers throughout
Great Britain. More importantly, the Commission observed that a supplier
with market power in one region may be able to set a somewhat higher
average price nationally (with this price being the average price for all the
local stores supplied):

". . . even though the national multiples pay a single price for milk from
each processor, it may be the case that this price factors in the actual
nature of competition within a particular region. That is, if there were
only one or two suppliers capable of servicing a set of stores located in a
particular region, then this may result in a higher average price for supply
to all stores, given the policy of the national multiples of paying a single
price for all milk delivered by any one supplier."[64]

Nevertheless, given the potential for the other major processors to
expand their national coverage (bar possibly Scotland) and also the
national buying practices of the national multiples, the Commission
concluded that the geographic scope of the market to supply the national
multiples generally incorporated all of Great Britain.[65]

In some cases, the analysis of how prices vary with the number of
competitors might be very straightforward. For example, in the context of
the completed acquisition by Arla Foods UK plc of milk supply businesses
in Quinton, Birmingham from Midlands Co-operative Society Limited, the
OFT noted that doorstep milk prices were no higher where there were no
other local doorstep providers: "The parties have stressed that their pricing
does not differ between areas in which there are other doorstep providers

---

[62] Cited above, para.6.049, n.1, at para.5.34.
[63] Cited above, para.6.049, n.1, at para.5.41.
[64] Cited above, para.6.049, n.1, at paras 5.42–5.43.
[65] Cited above, para.6.049, n.1, at para.5.44.

and those in which there are not, suggesting that they are constrained by other forms of milk supply."[66]

6.127   In the context of its report on the merger between Carl Zeiss Jena GmbH and Bio-Rad Laboratories Inc, the Commission sought to assess whether the presence of competition between the parties or the number of competitors depressed prices. It concluded that:

"We analysed the relevant contract awards over a sample period. In this regression analysis we could identify no statistically significant relationship between the price of Bio-Rad's winning bid and either the number of competing bidders or the presence of Zeiss as a competing bidder. This is possibly because negotiations between suppliers and customers take place over product specification as well as price, and also because the available data allowed us only partially to control for differences in product specifications. Nonetheless, this result is also consistent with Zeiss not imposing a strong competitive constraint on Bio-Rad in the tender process. This analysis also suggested that neither the procurement process nor the source of funding were significantly related to Bio-Rad's prices. This suggests that customers have similar incentives to bargain whether or not they are using formal tendering procedures."[67]

Co-ordinated effects

Overview and a brief introduction to game theory

6.128   The OFT's guidelines state that:

"A merger situation may also lessen competition substantially by increasing the probability that, post merger, firms in the same market may tacitly (or explicitly) co-ordinate their behaviour to raise prices, reduce quality or curtail output. This does not necessarily mean express collusion (which is generally an infringement of the Chapter I prohibition of the Competition Act 1998). Given certain market conditions, and without any express agreement, tacit collusion arises merely from an understanding that it will be in the firms' mutual interests to co-ordinate their decisions. Co-ordinated effects may arise where a merger situation reduces competitive constraints in a market, thus increasing the probability that competitors will collude or strengthening a tendency to do so."[68]

Co-ordinated effects are defined by Coleman and Scheffman in terms of how such effects can render price increases profitable as follows:

"A coordinated effects theory occurs when one or more other significant competitors *also restrict their output* when the merged entity restricts its output. A co-ordinated effects theory exists when a unilateral price

---

[66] The OFT's decision of May 10, 2004, *The completed acquisition by Arla Foods UK plc of milk business in Quinton, Birmingham from Midlands Co-operative Society Limited.*
[67] Cited above, para.6.118, n.34, at para.5.25.
[68] Cited above, para.6.001, n.1, at para.4.11.

increase of a particular amount . . . is not profitable *unless there are accommodating responses (i.e. output restrictions) by other significant competitors, and the evidence indicates that there will be sufficient accommodating responses.*"[69]

The issue for firms in an oligopolistic market[70] is that they would like to produce less output and sell it for a higher price, and could do so if all others in the industry would do the same. However, they might be unable to do so because, if they were to raise prices or reduce quantities, others would not follow them and they would lose market share and profits.[71]

The first potential co-ordination difficulty is the need for consensus to be reached between a sufficient number of competitors to ensure that their accommodating conduct is profitable. This entails firms reaching consensus on the type of accommodating conduct they will jointly adopt (*e.g.* raising prices directly, customer allocation, or cutting capacity), and the outcome of this co-ordination (*e.g.* how high prices should be, how customers should be allocated, and/or what amount of capacity should be withdrawn or not added). This issue is considered further below, but at this stage it is sufficient to note that the existence of some common interest between firms (*e.g.* higher industry profits) is in many circumstances insufficient for a consensus if: the degree of consensus required is too complex (*e.g.* due to the complexity of product offerings); the terms of co-ordination cannot be observed (*e.g.* due to a lack of market transparency as to prices); or there are conflicts of interest (*e.g.* differences in market shares, costs and capacities, etc. leading to different firms having very different incentives as to their desired prices and sales levels).

In particular, those conditions will not often be met in markets charac-   **6.129**
terised by innovation, where the likelihood of co-ordination is generally perceived to be low. As set out in the OFT Economics Discussion Paper on "*Innovation and competition policy*"[72] in such markets there are often only a few players in the market reflecting cost conditions (high fixed costs, low marginal costs), but the paper suggests that this should not be interpreted as an indication of a high likeliness of co-ordination problems. On the contrary, according to the paper, the combination of few players facing similar cost conditions also implies that "the players in the market will have both the means and incentive to compete strongly", particularly as successful innovation may yield the prospect of substantial competitive advantages and profits. The incidence of co-ordination is considered even less likely in innovation markets where products are differentiated.

---

[69] Cited above, para.6.117, n.31. This approach mirrors that adopted in the US Horizontal Merger Guidelines which state that: "Coordinated interaction is comprised of actions by a group of firms that are profitable for each of them only as a result of the accommodating reactions of the others" (cited above, para.6.001, n.4, at s.2.1).

[70] The key feature of oligopolistic markets—with oligopoly literally meaning few sellers—is that firms are strategically interdependent in the sense that the profitability of a competitive initiative (*e.g.* a price cut) depends on how rivals will respond (*e.g.* by cutting their own prices).

[71] This section only briefly summarises some of the key points. For introductory texts on oligopoly theory see further, for example, Chs 5 and 6 of Carlton and Perloff, "*Modern Industrial Organisation*", Third Edition, Addison-Wesley, 1999; Chs 6 to 8 of Scherer and Ross cited above, para.6.001, n.4; and Coleman and Scheffman, cited above, para.6.117, n.31.

[72] Cited above, para.6.067, n.67, at paras 7.13–7.14.

Given that cartels are generally illegal, an obvious question is how consensus can be reached tacitly (*i.e.* without any direct communication between firms as to, for example, the prices they should charge). Scherer and Ross argue that insight into how a tacit agreement on co-ordination as to prices and other aspects of competitive conduct may be reached is provided by Schelling's theory of focal points.[73] Schelling poses the following problem of two people wishing to meet in New York city, but without knowing the time and place, without any prior understanding, and without any ability to communicate with the other person. Schelling found that the majority of the people asked chose the information booth at Grand Central Station, and nearly all chose to meet at twelve noon. The explanation given by Schelling for this is that Grand Central Station (at least for New Yorkers in 1960) and noon have a certain compelling prominence: they are focal points. When behaviour must be co-ordinated *without direct communication*, choices (*e.g.* the level of prices or the structure of discounts, etc.) may converge on some focal point where such a focal point exists. More generally, firms may well be able to signal their competitive intentions without any express communication.

The second potential difficulty is the need to sustain adherence to the consensus outcome. Possibly the most illuminating hypothetical situation in game theory, the "prisoners' dilemma", is directly relevant to this problem. The key elements of the prisoners' dilemma are generally set out in the following manner:

> "Two prisoners have been accused of collaborating in a crime. They are in separate jail cells and cannot communicate with each other. Each has been asked to confess to the crime. If both prisoners confess, each will receive a prison term of five years. If neither confesses, the prosecution's case will be difficult to make, so the prisoners can expect to plea bargain and receive a term of two years. On the other hand, if one prisoner confesses and the other does not, the one who confesses will receive a term of only one year, while the other will go to prison for ten years."[74]

The dominant strategy for each prisoner is to confess, even though the aggregate time spent in jail would be shorter if neither confessed (four years in total, two years each).[75] This is because confession yields the shortest sentence for the individual regardless of the actions taken by the other prisoner (one year in prison if the other prisoner does not confess, and five years if he does).

6.130   This dilemma is analogous to that faced by firms in oligopolistic markets, because they must decide whether to lower their prices in an attempt to capture market share at the expense of the other firms in the market and

---

[73] See further Scherer and Ross, cited above, para.6.001, n.4, Ch.7.

[74] Taken from Pindyck & Rubinfeld, "*Microeconomics*", (4th ed., Prentice Hall, 1998) p.455.

[75] One of the key concepts of game theory is the "Nash equilibrium". In this context, a Nash equilibrium is where each firm adopts a strategy that gives it the highest possible profit, given the actions of its competitors. This leads to another important concept—the "dominant" strategy. That is a strategy that is the best for a firm regardless of the strategies of the other firms in the market. A basic introduction to these concepts is given in *e.g.* Pindyck & Rubinfeld, cited above, para.6.129, n.74.

risk the same reaction from the other firms in the market (equivalent to "confess"), or to keep prices high and trust that the other firms in the market will do the same (equivalent to "not confessing"). While the former is the "dominant strategy", it leads to lower profits for all firms involved, whereas, the latter is less stable but leads to higher profits all round, provided no firms cut prices. This dilemma provides the intuition for the incentive for firms to "cheat" (*e.g.* charge lower prices) in order to capture greater market share for themselves.

The oligopoly dilemma of cheating is not necessarily removed by there being an explicit agreement between firms (*i.e.* a cartel which would infringe the Chapter I prohibition of the Competition Act 1998 or Art.81 of the EC Treaty), although an agreement may provide a mechanism for reaching consensus. Both prisoners may well have agreed not to confess if caught (equivalent to firms agreeing to adhere to co-ordinated prices), but after being caught each individually has incentives to cheat on this agreement since the agreement will not be legally enforceable.[76]

However, this outcome may not apply when the "game" is repeated, in the sense that firms can regularly change their prices or increase capacity from one period to the next. In such circumstances, a dynamic approach is required. The key point is that firms' incentives to deviate depend on their profits from adhering to the consensus compared with the possible (temporary) gains to cheating followed by the lower profits that they may then experience once rivals detect and punish such cheating.[77]

---

[76] In addition, Motta observes that with tacit coordination mistakes might be made in the sense that prices might not be set at a jointly optimal level and might be difficult to change:

- if a firm considers that prices are too high, signalling this by cutting prices might by interpreted as a deviation and trigger a costly price war; and
- if a firm considers that prices are too low, signalling this by increasing prices might lead to lost market share and profits at least during the adjustment period.

On the other hand, "under explicit collusion . . . firms can talk to each other and coordinate on their jointly preferred equilibrium", thus enabling prices to be changed (*e.g.* in response to cost and demand shocks) without costly mistakes and adjustment periods (cited above, para.6.001, n.2, at p.141).

[77] In order to understand the (possibly conflicting) incentives faced by oligopolists, suppose that there are "n" identical firms in a market and that a collusive agreement can be reached which will permit the achievement of supernormal profits (ps) of which they will each receive an equal share (ps/n). If a firm cheats on this agreement by offering slightly lower prices it can achieve higher profits for a while (pcheat exceeds ps/n), until its competitors respond by cutting prices and then its profits will fall to a lower level (these lower future profits are effectively a "punishment" for cheating, ppunish is less than ps/n).

Whether or not it is more profitable to cheat will depend upon whether the discounted present value (PV) of a firm's share of supernormal profits exceeds the discounted present value of the total profits if they cheat (*i.e.* pcheat for a while, followed by ppunish). The higher the opportunity cost of capital (*i.e.* the discount rate), the greater the weight attached to each £1 of additional current profit achieved through cheating now compared with the profits foregone in the future after rivals cut their own prices (*i.e.* future profits foregone are ps/n less ppunish). In simple terms, it will be profitable to cheat if:

$$PVp_s/n \quad < \quad PVp_{cheat} + PVp_{punish}$$

Or:

$$PVp_{cheat} \quad > \quad PVps/n - PVp_{punish}$$

(Temporary profits after cheating) (Future profits foregone after rivals detect and punish cheating)

Given the difficulties inherent in maintaining co-ordinated higher prices, it is well recognised that oligopolistic market structures do not necessarily lead to uncompetitive outcomes. For example, Salop states that:

"It is now well established in both the economic and legal literature that successful price co-ordination (either express or tacit) is not inevitable— even in highly concentrated industries protected by insurmountable barriers to entry."[78]

6.131   The final issue is that any co-ordination may be rendered practically impossible due to the threat of new entry and expansion or the exercise of buyer power (see further below).

For lengthier discussions see Tirole, "*The Theory of Industrial Organization*", The MIT Press, 1990, s.6.3, at pp.245 to 253; and Rees, "*Tacit Collusion*", (Summer 1993) Oxford Review of Economic Policy, Vol.9, No.2.

In the above simple example the temporary profits from not adhering to the agreement last for a single period of undefined length. If competitors cannot readily detect cheating (*i.e.* there are detection lags), or there are delays before they can respond (*i.e.* there are punishment lags), then this may increase the profitability of cheating and thereby reduce the sustainability of collusion. "Cheating" may be detected by competitors in a number of different ways, for example, if a firm can observe directly a rival cutting its prices (or engaging in other types of competitive initiative), or increasing its sales/output (or the rival installing new additional capacity), or indirectly if there is an otherwise unexplainable fall in its own sales (as customers switch to buying from the cheating firm). It is also important that any punishment mechanism is viable and credible, so that firms believe that their rivals would punish independent competition after it is detected.

One problem with such repeated games models is that they generally do not result in a single possible equilibrium. This is known as the "folk theorem", which states broadly that any price/output level can be an equilibrium provided that profits are at least as much as could be earned in a single period game. That is, any result between "confessing" in all rounds (price equals marginal cost) and "not confessing" (price at the level that an absolute monopolist might charge) in any round is a possible equilibrium. This, naturally, is not a particularly helpful result in attempting to predict the behaviour of firms in oligopolistic markets and/or industry prices and outputs. A further issue is how firms move from one equilibrium to another (e.g. following a merger).

The Commission's guidelines refer to one factor which may be relevant to its assessment of non-coordinated effects as "short-term financial pressures on firms, which may encourage them to depart from any common pattern of long-term behaviour" (see the twelfth bullet point of para.3.41, cited above, para.6.001, n.1). Such pressures would be equivalent to the loss of future profits being given less weight (*i.e.* discounted at a high rate) than the gain in current profits which would be derived from "cheating". The Commission's guidelines also refer to it considering "evidence of a long-term commitment to the market by firms" (see the third bullet point of para.3.41, cited above, para.6.001, n.1). In the Safeway merger inquiry, the Commission explained this in terms of firms without any long-term market commitment having a greater incentive to cheat for analogous reasons:

"In some cases, firms without a long-term stake in a market may choose not to respond to competitive price behaviour, instead making as much short-term profit as possible and then phasing out of the market. In these circumstances, coordinated effects may not emerge. Conversely, a long-term commitment to the market suggests that firms are likely to respond to competitive actions of their rivals in order to stay in business. Moreover, if firms intend to stay in the market over the long term, a deviation from a coordinated situation could involve a long-term loss in profits, such that coordination is more likely." (cited above, para.6.027, n.26, at para.2.152.).

[78] Salop (1986), "*Practices that (Credibly) Facilitate Oligopoly Co-ordination*", Ch.9 in J. Stiglitz and Mathewson, "*New Developments in the Analysis of Market Structure*", (Macmillan, 1986).

The OFT's guidelines are consistent with the above analysis[79] and state that:

"In order for tacit co-ordination to be successful or to become more likely, the OFT considers that three conditions must be met or be created by a merger:

(i) the participants must have an ability to align their behaviour in the market;

(ii) the firms must have incentives to maintain the co-ordinated behaviour, which means detection of deviation from tacit co-ordination and perhaps also credible 'punishment' of deviating firms through retaliatory behaviour by others; and

(iii) the co-ordinated behaviour should be sustainable in the face of other competitive constraints in the market."[80]

Similarly, in *BASF/Takeda Chemical*, the Commission observed that ". . . the maintenance of tacit collusion requires clear signalling within the market, common interests in collusion for all major players, and a strong credible punishment for any 'cheating' on other members."[81]

There are a range of factors which can affect the feasibility of co-ordination, in terms of the ability of firms to reach consensus, and to detect and then punish cheating. These are commonly referred to as a "check list", with there being some debate as to whether certain factors hinder or facilitate co-ordination. Various factors are addressed in this sub-section, but the substantive issue, as emphasised by the Commission,[82] is how the merger

---

[79] As well as the approach taken by the European Court of First Instance in *Airtours plc v Commission*, cited above, para.6.002, n.13.

[80] Cited above, para.6.001, n. 1, at para.4.12. The Commission's guidelines describe similar conditions; cited above, para.6.001, n.1, paras 3.37–3.39. Similarly, the European Commission's Horizontal Merger Guidelines state that: "three conditions are necessary for coordination to be sustainable. First, the coordinating firms must be able to monitor to a sufficient degree whether the terms of coordination are being adhered to. Second, discipline requires that there is some form of credible deterrent mechanism that can be activated if deviation is detected. Third, the reactions of outsiders, such as current and future competitors not participating in the coordination, as well as customers, should not be able to jeopardise the results expected from the coordination" (cited above, para.6.001, n.4, at para.41). The US Horizontal Merger Guidelines adopt a similar approach (see ss.2.1–2.12, cited above, para.6.001, n.4).

[81] Cited above, para.6.030, n.36, at para.2.101. Analogous comments have been made in a number of other reports. For example, in relation to the proposed merger between Arla Foods amba and Express Dairies plc, the Commission stated that:

"There are three conditions necessary for coordinated behaviour to occur and be sustainable through time. First, firms must be able to observe if there is significant deviation from the prevailing behaviour. A high level of concentration facilitates this. Second, it must be in each firm's interest to go along with the coordinated arrangement rather than deviate from it. Third, there must be relatively weak competitive constraints, otherwise the prevailing behaviour will not be sustained." (cited above, para.6.048, n.1 at para.5.109).

[82] Para.3.42, cited above, para.6.001, n.1. Where coordinated effects already exist prior to the merger, the Commission refers to it assessing whether a merger is likely to "maintain" or "exacerbate" such effects. It is assumed that the word "maintain" refers to the possibility that a merger might increase the stability of coordination, rather than suggesting that the Commission might reach an adverse finding in relation to a merger which did not lead to a substantial lessening of competition.

changes competitive dynamics. Unfortunately, the substantive influence of a merger on many of the "check list" factors in specific cases is potentially far from obvious at first sight.[83] Coleman and Scheffman state that: "We believe that the Check List is inadequate and largely unnecessary" and instead advocate a detailed empirical analysis of the relevant markets "rather than relying on "30,000 foot" industry structural factors."[84]

6.132   Some economists, such as Coleman and Scheffman, argue that if co-ordination is already occurring, there should be a rebuttable presumption that it is likely that a merger between competitors would render co-ordination more effective or durable.[85] They make the point that it is not necessary in this situation to assess whether conditions exist which make consensus, detection and punishment feasible, but rather whether there is convincing evidence of existing co-ordination. In certain circumstances, they suggest that this presumption might be refuted if on the facts of the case the merger might have very little impact or merger efficiencies would create an aggressive competitor undermining co-ordination. In addition, as discussed below, it is possible that a merger could increase asymmetries between firms, and this may be a factor reducing the viability of co-ordination. Any such presumption, however, is highly controversial, with such a proposal being included in the draft European Commission Horizontal Merger Guidelines but deleted from the final version. For example, presumptions may be inconsistent with legal standards, proving that existing co-ordination is occurring may be difficult, forming a cartel might be easier than tacit co-ordination, and historical cartels might have occurred in different economic environments.[86]

Perhaps the most obvious way in which a merger may render co-ordination viable is if it eliminates a maverick competitor.[87] This is because it may be impossible to reach any consensus with such a firm due to conflicts of interests arising from such firms' different strategies, which may arise due to differences in costs, capacities, ability to cheat with lower risk of detection[88] and/or market share aspirations.[89] In addition, maverick competitors may prevent or destabilise co-ordination, because other competitors might be very reluctant to co-ordinate tacitly (e.g. to increase

---

[83] The Commission's guidelines set out a variety of check list type factors, many of which offer no explanation of why the factor is relevant, or how these factors interact with one another, or whether more or less weight should be afforded to particular factors (cited above, para.6.001, n.1, at para.3.41). The following subsection discusses the relevance of all of the factors outlined following similar headings to those adopted in the European Commission's Horizontal Merger Guidelines (cited above, para.6.001, n.4, at paras 39–57), which is consistent with the approach adopted by the OFT (cited above, para.6.001, n.1, at paras 4.11–4.16).

[84] Cited above, para.6.117, n.33.

[85] Cited above, para.6.117, n.33.

[86] See further Robert and Hudson, "Past Co-ordination and the Commission Notice on the Appraisal of Horizontal Mergers" (2004) E.C.L.R., Vol.25: Issue 3.

[87] Maverick competitors are considered generally, and in the context of potential non-coordinated merger effects, at para.6.119.

[88] In this regard, the US Horizontal Merger Guidelines indicate that: "A firm also may be a maverick if it has an unusual ability secretly to expand its sales in relation to the sales it would obtain if it adhered to the terms of coordination. This ability might arise from opportunities to expand captive production for a downstream affiliate" (s.2.12, cited above, para.6.001, n.4).

[89] See further, Scherer and Ross, cited above, para.6.001s, n.4, at pp.277 to 279.

prices and reduce output) if they consider it likely that the maverick would respond by increasing its sales and thus undermining any attempt to increase prices. For example, in relation to the proposed merger between Arla Foods amba and Express Dairies plc, the Commission stated that:

"... at present at least one company is following an aggressive growth strategy, which is inconsistent with stable co-ordinated outcomes. For example, Wiseman has expanded its business with new large-scale dairies at Manchester and more recently Droitwich, at which it has had to try to fill capacity. Dairy Crest has also now followed suit."[90]

It can be argued in general terms that concentration facilitates co-ordination, and this factor is noted in the OFT's research paper entitled *"Merger appraisal in oligopolistic markets"*:

"Market shares and the extent of post-merger concentration are highly relevant to an assessment of the risk of greater post-merger collusion. Concentrated markets are more amenable to collusion because the profitability of competing on the fringe of a tacit or explicit cartel rises as the number of firms in the market rises. Concentration also aids the effective policing of cartels by making cheating easier to detect. This in turn may make a cartel more likely or an existing cartel more stable at higher prices."[91]

All other things being equal, economic theory suggests that co-ordination is less likely the larger the number of firms in an industry. This is because the profits derived by individual small firms from adhering to the consensus will be only a small share of co-ordinated profits, whereas the temporary gains from cheating (*i.e.* a high share of industry profits) will be correspondingly greater.[92]

The opposite applies as regards large firms particularly in more concen-   **6.133**
trated markets. In this regard, in the Safeway mergers inquiries, the Commission observed that:

"... with a sufficient degree of concentration, and provided that the right conditions exist, the pursuit of profitability will create incentives for firms to avoid competitive strategies (primarily in the shape of lower prices) that would be unavoidable in a less concentrated market structure."[93]

It is important to note that there is no particular number of firms which is particularly conducive to tacit collusion. As the Commission observed in *BASF/Takeda Chemical*:

"... it is the degree of competitive pressure in the market which determines whether firms are able to form or to enforce a cartel, not simply the number of companies involved in the industry."[94]

---

[90] Cited above, para.6.048, n.1, at para.5.115.
[91] Cited above, para.6.117, n.27, at p.7.
[92] See further Tirole, cited above, para.6.130, n.86, at s.6.3.2.1, pp.247 to 248.
[93] Cited above, para.6.027, n.33, at para.2.121.
[94] Cited above, para.6.030, n.36, at para.2.100.

Nevertheless, there may be circumstances in which mergers which increase concentration can also increase competition due to the creation or enhancement of asymmetries between firms in their capacities, market shares, costs or product range or due to efficiencies creating a more aggressive competitor (see further below). In addition, external competitive constraints due to low barriers to entry and expansion and/or the effective exercise of buyer power can render co-ordination unsustainable (see further below).

Finally, the potential maximum gains to co-ordination will be smaller the higher the market price elasticity of demand, since even a monopolist would set lower prices than if market elasticity were low.[95]

Reaching consensus

6.134   As indicated above, the first key issue potentially undermining co-ordination is the difficulty of reaching consensus as to the form and outcome of the co-ordination. As emphasised by the US Horizontal Merger Guidelines, the substantive concern is not just complete co-ordination which would lead to the same prices and output levels as would be observed if there was a monopoly—lesser co-ordination may still lead to substantial competitive harm.[96]

Product differentiation

6.135   It is often argued that when products are complex or differentiated the problem of coordinating on a common price structure is much more complex than it is with homogenous products.[97] This is because focal points and consensus have to be reached as to the prices of a number of different products or a wide variety of product specifications, rather than merely the price of one homogeneous product. For example, the OFT's research paper on *Merger Appraisal in Oligopolistic Markets* states that:

> ". . .fears of collusive activity are, by and large, confined to industries in which the products are relatively homogenous, with little differentiation or customisation. This is because it is easier to fix a schedule of collusive prices when products are similar than when they all have different characteristics, sell at very different prices and can be modified for specific customer needs."[98]

---

[95] See further para.6.053, above. However, beyond this it is difficult to draw any firm conclusions. In particular, if firm own price elasticity of demand is also high, then a price cut will both increase the gains from deviating and the sales loss experienced when rivals punish price cuts. Nevertheless, it may be easier for firms to detect (and therefore respond to) secret price cutting in markets where the price elasticity of demand is low, because the growth in sales achieved by the undercutting firm will be observed by its rivals experiencing a corresponding fall in sales (rather than low prices also leading to market sales volumes being expanded by existing customers increasing their purchases, or new customers starting to buy the product in question).

[96] Cited above, para.6.001, n.1, at s.2.11.

[97] See, for example, Scherer and Ross, cited above, para.6.001, n.4, at pp.279 to 282.

[98] Cited above, para.6.117, n.27, at p.78. In this regard, the Commission's guidelines refer to a high degree of homogeneity of firms' products as a relevant factor to assess coordinated effects, although they do not explain why (see para.3.41 (the fourth bullet point), cited above, para.6.001, n.1).

In this regard, the European Commission's Horizontal Merger Guidelines indicate that: ". . . It is also easier to co-ordinate on a price for a single, homogeneous product, than on hundreds of prices in a market with many differentiated products."[99]

Product homogeneity was also considered by the Commission to be a relevant factor in its assessment of the proposed acquisition by H+H Celcon of Marley Buildings Materials. The Commission noted that:

". . . given the relatively homogenous nature of aircrete blocks, Tarmac [the merged entity's largest competitor] could largely or completely follow the price rise. This assumes that price information would generally disseminate through the market. In the absence of any special factors it appears that . . . Tarmac might well have a much stronger profit incentive to [follow a price rise], given that prices and profit margins would be higher without necessarily any significant impact on volumes. If so, the duopoly structure of the aircrete market could generate a substantial dampening effect on inter-firm price competition."[1]

Market transparency

Transparency also assists the reaching of consensus. For example, if the prices charged by different firms within an industry are publicly available it is likely to be easier for firms to reach a consensus over what price to charge, as there may be observable focal points to prices (*i.e.* without any explicit exchange of information firms may be able to observe prevailing market prices, see further below). On the other hand, tacit co-ordination on prices may be harder to achieve if prices are highly opaque, for example, if they are individually negotiated with customers, and secret discounts are given. **6.136**

In addition, in the context of the merger between Interbrew SA and Bass PLC, the Commission stated that:

"While we accept that the market is not completely transparent in terms of prices (see [ ]), we are not persuaded by Interbrew's argument that there is no market price in the on-trade and therefore successful price co-ordination would be impossible (see [ ]). We recognize that contract terms vary from customer to customer, depending on the outcome of negotiations, as they do in most markets. Parties to any negotiation summarize these complex contract terms down into a single net price per barrel; in our view, this is a focal point around which tacit understandings can occur."[2]

In his advice on the proposed acquisition by Clear Channel UK of Score Outdoor, the Director General said that "Factors that would contribute towards a propensity tacitly to collude do not appear to be strongly evident . . . There is little or no price transparency as actual prices are often individually negotiated and not reflected on the published rate cards."[3]

---

[99] Cited above, para.6.001, n.4, at para.45.
[1] Cited above, para.6.011, n.31, at para.2.87.
[2] Cited above, para.6.027, n.34, at para.2.116.
[3] Cited above, para.6.087, n.43.

Non-price competition

6.137   In addition, when firms compete not only on price but also on factors such as terms of supply, product quality, innovation and/or advertising, reaching consensus may be highly complex as consensus may need to be reached on all of these factors. Similarly, if sellers are located at varying distances from buyers and transportation costs are relatively high, a very complex price structure for delivered goods may be required.

In this regard, the Commission noted in the Safeway inquiry that:

"Where a marked degree of homogeneity of goods or services exists in a market, it will be easier to compare prices and other aspects of the product or service and co-ordinated behaviour will be more easily achieved. It follows that the more heterogeneous the products or services, the more difficult it will be for other firms to detect changes in others' behaviour."[4]

Product innovation

6.138   If product qualities are dynamically unstable, as in fashion goods industries and fields subject to rapid technological change, each product change alters the relative competitive position of every producer. This requires either a new set of pricing decisions or the acceptance of a rigid, historically based price structure not likely to maximise profits.[5] In this regard, the European Commission points out that:

"In markets where innovation is important, co-ordination may be more difficult since innovations, particularly significant ones, may allow one firm to gain a major advantage over its rivals."[6]

The Commission noted in the Safeway inquiry that:

"Innovation in markets can cause disruption to established patterns and this disruptive effect can make co-ordination more difficult and hence discourage such behaviour."[7]

In this regard, in the context of the merger between Interbrew SA and Bass PLC, the Commission stated that:

"We accept that beer is not a completely homogeneous product, that brewers seek differentiation through developing distinctive brands and that there is some degree of product innovation (see [   ]). However, the main brands in each main product segment are similar and prices are directly comparable (see [   ]). Moreover, the fact that seven of the top ten brands in 1999 appeared in the 1989 top ten and the other three

---

[4] Cited above, para.6.027, n.34, at para.2.134.
[5] In this regard, Coleman and Scheffman recommend that the number and importance of product innovations be assessed, considering, for example, the proportion of sales accounted for by new products recently launched (cited above, para.6.117, n.34).
[6] Cited above, para.6.001, n.4, at para.45.
[7] Cited above, para.6.027, n.33, at para.2.145.

(Stella Artois, John Smiths, Budweiser) were all available in 1989 (see [ ]) indicates that the leading brands have been able to maintain their position despite product innovation. Innovation, in our view, mainly occurs at the margins of the beer industry, and in the development of other alcoholic beverages, such as FABs [flavoured alcoholic beverages]. We note Interbrew's evidence that it could take up to 20 years to establish a leading brand (see paragraph 4.34)."[8]

Market stability

It may be easier to reach consensus if the terms of the consensus do not need to be revisited frequently due to volatile demand or supply conditions.[9] Apart from general volatility in market demand (*e.g.* due to the business cycle) or costs (*e.g.* due to volatile input prices), there may be volatility in individual firms' demands and costs (*e.g.* due to differences in the production technologies they employ).

6.139

However, the European Commission's Horizontal Merger Guidelines emphasise that:

"Coordinating firms may, however, find other ways to overcome problems stemming from complex economic environments short of market division. They may, for instance, establish simple pricing rules that reduce the complexity of coordinating on a large number of prices. One example of such a rule is establishing a small number of pricing points, thus reducing the co-ordination problem. Another example is having a fixed relationship between certain base prices and a number of other prices, such that prices basically move in parallel. Publicly available key information, exchange of information through trade associations, or information received through cross-shareholdings or participation in joint ventures may also help firms reach terms of co-ordination."[10]

In assessing this issue it is important to appreciate that the form of the co-ordination can vary and, if one form of consensus cannot be reached or is not sustainable (*e.g.* price), another form might meet both of these requirements (*e.g.* customer allocations or capacity co-ordination). The European Commission's horizontal merger guidelines suggest that co-ordination "by market division" (*i.e.* customer allocations) may be feasible if customers have

---

[8] Cited above, para.6.027, n.34, at para.2.110.

[9] In this regard, the European Commission's Horizontal Merger Guidelines state that ". . . it is easier to coordinate on a price when demand and supply conditions are relatively stable than when they are continuously changing" (cited above, para.6.001, n.4, at para.45). Historical volatility in demand and costs should be relatively simple to measure.

[10] Cited above, para.6.001, n.4, at para.47. In this regard, one of the factors referred to in the Commission's guidelines which is relevant to assessment of coordinated effects is ". . . the existence of institutions and practices that may aid coordination, for example information sharing agreements, trade associations, regulations etc." (cited above, para.6.001, n.1, at para.3.41 (seventh bullet point)). See further pp.151–156 of Motta for a further discussion of information sharing agreements, and public and private announcements (cited above, para.6.001, n.2). Motta also observes that if a firm has a director on the board of a rival it will be easier to coordinate pricing and marketing policies and to monitor its conduct. He also observes that minority stakes in the profits of firms can reduce their incentives to compete with one another (see further paras 6.100 to 6.102, above).

simple characteristics which provide a basis for allocation to suppliers (*e.g.* customer type, location, or the identity of their existing supplier) and it is easy to identify which competitor serves which customer.[11] Motta suggests that co-ordination on customer allocations might be viable in the face of variable cost and demand conditions because this allows prices to individual customers served by different suppliers to be adjusted in the light of cost or demand shocks without triggering price wars.[12] However, this assumes that such shocks are consistent across the customers served by different suppliers, so that one firm does not disproportionately gain or suffer which might prompt them to wish to revisit the terms of the co-ordination.

Co-ordination on customer allocations or capacities may or may not be beset with similar complexity and transparency issues as co-ordination on prices. For example, if a customer base is made up of a large number of purchasers with volatile volume requirements and a large turnover of customers, it may be too complex to co-ordinate on customer allocations and the identity of the suppliers of different customers may not be sufficiently transparent. Similarly, consensus as to capacity increases may be too complex in the face of unstable demand or costs, and observing firms' capacities may be difficult (perhaps particularly if capacity can readily be increased by "de-bottlenecking" or running additional shifts, or if this depends on unobservable product mix).

Asymmetry of competitors

6.140   Consensus may be difficult to reach wherever firms' interests are materially different, with this potentially impacting on the form of the co-ordination and its outcome in terms of the level of prices and individual firms' market shares.[13] For example, if one firm has lower costs (or lower rates of capacity utilisation) its profit maximising co-ordinated price will be lower than that preferred by its higher cost competitors, and accordingly they may find it difficult to reach consensus over what price to charge, customer allocations, capacities or firms' market shares. Similarly, if some firms are vertically integrated and others are not, their marginal production costs may differ considerably.

In this regard, in the context of the merger between Interbrew SA and Bass PLC and assessing the risk of anti-competitive duopoly emerging between Interbrew and S&N, the Commission stated that:

"We are not persuaded by Interbrew's arguments as to why it has a completely different commercial strategy from that of S&N [by virtue of S&N being vertically integrated by having its own tied estate of pubs,

---

[11] Cited above, para.6.001, n.4, at para.46.

[12] Cited above, para.6.001, n.2, at p.141.

[13] In this regard, the Commission's guidelines indicate that one factor which is relevant to the assessment of co-ordinated effects is whether there is "a high degree of homogeneity of firms (*i.e.* the extent to which firms are similar, for instance, with respect to their size, market shares, cost structures, business strategies and attitudes to risk)" (cited above, para.6.001, n.1, at para.3.41 (fifth bullet point)). The European Commission's guidelines also make the point that it is easier to reach consensus if firms are symmetric, especially in terms of cost structures, market shares, capacity levels and levels of vertical integration (para.48, cited above, para.6.001, n.4).

whereas Interbrew owned no pubs] (see [ ]). In our view, Interbrew and S&N both share a common interest in raising margins and a long-term commitment to the market. These factors are not offset by S&N's retail interests. We note that S&N has only about 2 per cent of fully licensed on-trade outlets, including clubs, and a slightly higher percentage of sales, but as a brewer it has 26 per cent of the beer market (see [ ]). This indicates that only a small proportion of sales of S&N's brands are through its own estate, certainly not enough to have the effects claimed by Interbrew. Moreover, S&N's pubs would benefit if net wholesale prices for rival pubs were to rise."[14]

In short, consensus may be difficult to reach due to product differentiation, lack of market transparency, high degree of non-price competition, high degree of innovation in the market, instability of market conditions, and asymmetry of competitors.

Detection

Market transparency

As emphasised above, a credible punishment mechanism first requires that cheating is detected, which requires the market to be sufficiently transparent.[15] As suggested in the preceding subsection, transparency can vary considerably between markets according to the precise market conditions. In this regard, the OFT's research paper on *Merger Appraisal in Oligopolistic Markets* states that "Transparent pricing makes cheating easier to spot and so deters it making collusion more stable."[16]

6.141

This point was made by the Commission in the Safeway inquiry:

"Markets in which prices and other aspects of the product or service are transparent tend to be favourable to co-ordinated behaviour since any significant divergence from the prevailing behaviour will readily be detected by the other participating firms."[17]

Concentration may increase the transparency of the market, and deviations by a large firm may be more likely to be noticed (since they have a greater impact on market sales), and a larger firm may be more likely to detect unexplained variations in its sales due to rivals' deviations.[18]

In this regard, in the context of its inquiry into the proposed merger between Neopost and Ascom, the Commission observed that "The number of rival firms in an industry is one factor, and a duopolistic market structure may be particularly vulnerable to the development of tacit co-ordination because of the relative ease with which two major suppliers can monitor each

---

[14] Cited above, para.6.027, n.34, at para.2.117.
[15] In this regard, the Commission's guidelines refer to the market needing to be sufficiently concentrated for deviations from prevailing behaviour to be observed, and price cutting by rivals potentially being observed where prices are transparent or one firm's sales fall (see paras 3.37 and 3.41 (the sixth bullet point), cited above, para.6.001, n.1).
[16] Cited above, para.6.117, n.27, at p.86.
[17] Cited above, para.6.027, n.26, at para.2.133.
[18] See further Bishop and Walker, cited above, para.6.001, n.2, at p.278.

other's activities." Nevertheless, in that case the Commission considered that competition from two smaller competing suppliers, actively looking to win customers from the two leading suppliers, would help to destabilise any tacit collusion.[19]

6.142   In the context of its inquiry into the merger between Cargill and Cerestar, the Commission observed that:

> "We have already noted that glucose syrups are purchased following individual negotiation between producer and customer, often following a tender or auction process. Prices are not transparent. We think that in this sort of market it would be more difficult for co-ordinated action to succeed in engineering price rises than in other markets (such as retailing) where prices are visible and known . . . By the same token, the lack of transparency in the market would in our view also make it difficult for the co-ordinating firms to discipline any deviant member that attempted to depart from the agreed line in order to pursue its own interests."[20]

In this regard, the presence of vertical integration can also have an effect on market transparency and detection. On the one hand, the competitors of vertically integrated firms may be able to observe only the final product price and not any internal transfer price which might be lower than the tacitly "agreed" price for the semi-finished product. On the other hand, a vertically integrated firm whose downstream operation also procures from competing suppliers might have better knowledge of the prices charged by rivals, although this would not reveal secret discounting by these suppliers to other customers.

Market stability

6.143   Demand and cost shocks may make it difficult to monitor competitors' activities. Green and Porter present a model which considers how co-ordination may be sustainable where firms are unable to distinguish between a decline in sales which may be attributable to an unobservable recession or secret price cutting by competitors. In this model firms retaliate with a price war when prices fall below a "trigger price", even though they believe (but do not know) that this is due to low demand, as otherwise this would undermine cheating deterrence at times of high demand. Accordingly, uncertainty undermines the ability of firms to sustain full co-ordination throughout the business cycle.[21] The conclusions to be drawn from this model are that co-ordination may be difficult to sustain in markets which are prone to

---

[19] Cited above, para.6.113, n.16, at paras 2.146 and 2.151. Similarly, in relation to the proposed merger between Arla Foods amba and Express Dairies plc, the Commission observed that: "When markets are sufficiently concentrated, firms recognize their interdependence since the actions of any individual firm can have identifiable effects on its competitors. Given the already high level of concentration in this case, the reduction in the number of competitors may, but will not necessarily, facilitate coordinated behaviour." (cited above, para.6.048, n.1, at para.5.106.)

[20] Cited above, para.6.028, n.30, at para.2.111. Similarly, in *Icopal Holdings A/S/Icopal a/s* the Commission emphasised "the undisclosed ways in which prices are set, which make it difficult for any manufacturer to know another manufacturer's prices" (cited above, para.6.029, n.34, at para.2.156(d)).

[21] See further Tirole, cited above, para.6.130, n.77, at s.6.3.2, pp.247 to 251.

demand shocks, and that temporary price wars are not unambiguous proof of effective competition (as opposed to temporary phenomena necessary to maintain cartel/tacit co-ordination discipline). In this regard, the Commission's guidelines indicate that:

". . . unpredictable changes in demand or costs might make it more diffi-cult for firms to decipher whether a change in volume sold, for instance, is due to the actions of another firm or due to demand changes in the market as a whole . . ."[22]

In the Safeway mergers inquiry, the Commission maintained that:

"Stability of demand and costs in a market will tend to favour co-ordination of activity, as they enable firms more easily to identify changes, for example, in volumes sold, and so can enable those firms more readily to gauge whether such changes emanate from the behaviour of a competitor who decides to adopt a new strategy, or from broader demand changes in the market as a whole."[23]

Product differentiation and switching costs

It was noted above that with homogenous products it may be easier to reach consensus. On the other hand, Levy and Reitzes argue that differentiated markets may also be subject to co-ordination.[24] A merger between suppliers which are the "closest" competitors to a would-be cheater, might enable them to monitor the conduct of this firm and also ensures that the costs of any punishment are shared between the two parts of the merged firm. **6.144**

The OFT's and DTI's report on Switching costs suggests that switching costs may facilitate detection in a mature market as large price reductions might be required in order to persuade the majority of locked-in customers to switch suppliers due to the switching costs that customers face.[25]

Contractual supply provisions

As discussed above, the European Commission observes that there are a number of practices which might increase transparency and thus facilitate the detection of deviations from the terms of any co-ordination. The European Commission also refers to various clauses in supply agreements which increase transparency and facilitate detection.[26] In particular, "meeting the competition" clauses[27] commit the existing supplier of a customer to match the price offered by a rival, which renders the deviator's **6.145**

---

[22] Cited above, para.6.001, n.1, at para.3.41. The European Commission makes the point in analogous terms and also adds that ". . . when overall demand or cost conditions fluctuate, it may be difficult to interpret whether a competitor is lowering its prices because it expects the coordinated prices to fall or because it is deviating" (cited above, para.6.001, n.4, at para.50).

[23] Cited above, para.6.027, n.33, at para.2.144.

[24] See s.3.4.3 of the OFT Research paper on "*Merger appraisal in oligopolistic markets*", cited above, para.6.117, n.27.

[25] Cited above, para.6.121, n.45 at paras 7.28–7.30.

[26] Cited above, para.6.001, n.4, at para.51.

[27] Also known as "English clauses".

prices highly transparent, thereby facilitating detection, and potentially removes the incentive to deviate in the first place if the alternative supplier cannot win new customers. Salop also emphasises that meeting the competition clauses without release provisions contractually commit suppliers to behave aggressively in the face of new entry, thus rendering such responses a credible threat which is likely to deter new entry. "Most favoured nation" clauses commit the supplier to not offering lower prices to other customers, thereby reducing the gains to deviating (since the lower prices must be offered to all customers). However, Motta observes that most favoured nation clauses would appear to have an ambiguous effect because they also increase the costs of punishment as price cuts must be offered to all customers.[28]

Punishment

6.146   As observed in para.6.0131 above, one of the conditions for sustainable co-ordination is that there is a credible punishment mechanism, which renders deviations from the terms of the consensus reached unprofitable. In this regard, it is important to be clear that the discounted future profits foregone after rivals detect and respond to cheating only need to be sufficient to offset the gains to cheating. Accordingly, any discussion of punishment also needs to consider the gains to cheating.

Frequency of contracts and buyer power

6.147   The regularity and frequency of orders can influence the sustainability of any co-ordination. "Lumpy" markets are markets in which contracts are large and awarded infrequently. Profitable co-ordination is least likely when requests for price quotations on large orders are received infrequently and at irregular intervals. When a large order is at stake, or a major customer offers a supplier a high proportion of its business for a material period of time, the gains of cutting price are likely to outweigh the profits foregone even if this undercutting triggers a price war on the next order (which may be some time in the future).[29] Buyer power can thus be a major destabilising factor.

For example, the Commission's guidelines state that: "[i]f prices can be adjusted quickly then such a [retaliatory] response is very likely, but in markets where prices can only be set infrequently, the short-term gains from lower prices until a response is possible could outweigh the long-term gains of higher oligopolistic prices. If price setting is very infrequent then the

---

[28] Cited above, para.6.001, n.2, at pp.156–158. Motta also emphasises that such clauses might also have efficiency justifications. First, such clauses might provide insurance to risk averse buyers that lower prices would not be offered to other purchasers either by their incumbent supplier (in the case of the most favoured nation clause) or other suppliers (in the case of the meeting the competition clause). Secondly, they might speed up the conclusion of supply arrangements by providing the buyer comfort that he is not missing out on better deals. Thirdly, in long-term contracts they can provide a mechanism for ensuring that prices are in line with market prices. Also see Salop, cited above, para.6.130, n.78.

[29] See further Tirole, cited above, para.6.130, n.77, at s. 6.3.2.2, p. 248. The OFT's research paper on "*Merger appraisal in oligopolistic markets*" notes that "It is easier to sustain collusion with many small buyers rather than a few large ones", cited above, para.6.117, n.27, at p.86.

basic perception of interdependence may cease to hold at all."[30] This was a particular consideration in *CHC Helicopter Corporation/Helicopter Services Group*, where the Commission noted that:

"Prices are set in contract negotiations which are relatively infrequent events. Once a contract has been lost, it is lost for a period of years and the loser cannot make good the damage by a quick readjustment of prices. In the absence of [explicit] collusion the duopolists will therefore have an incentive to bid their best price for each contract. . .."[31]

Similarly, in relation to the proposed merger between Arla Foods amba and Express Dairies plc, the Commission stated that:

". . . although the market for the supply of fresh processed milk to national multiples exhibits some of the factors that would give rise to an environment that facilitates co-ordinated behaviour (for example, homogeneous product and ability to co-ordinate on allocations to a small number of customers), other characteristics of this market are not conducive to co-ordinated behaviour. In particular, prices are negotiated confidentially between the processors and the multiples, with the latter likely to be able to disrupt any co-ordinated outcome through their buyer power, control over the tender process and ultimately their ability to encourage expansion/entry."[32]

The importance of buyer power was emphasised further by the Commission:

". . . a co-ordinated outcome will not be sustainable if there is potential for disruption by new competitors or by customers themselves. In general, co-ordination is more difficult in bidding markets when individual tenders are large relative to the size of the market, and when transactions take place infrequently. In both instances, this is because it raises the incentive for one of the firms to deviate unilaterally from the co-ordinated outcome. In the case at hand, the national multiples determine the number of suppliers from whom they will procure milk, the timing of tenders/reviews, and the number of stores that will be made contestable at any time. It thus appears that the national multiples will be able to organize their procurement in such a way that each of the processors is likely to have sufficient incentive to bid aggressively to capture a large volume of business in a single tender process."[33]

---

[30] Cited above, para.6.001, n.1, at para.3.38.

[31] Cited above, para.6.065, n.58, at para.2.72.

[32] Cited above, para.6.048, n.1, at para.5.119.

[33] Cited above, para.6.048, n.1, at para.5.117. Similarly, in the context of the proposed acquisition of Dräger Medical AG & Co. KGaA of certain assets representing the Air-Shields business of Hill-Rom Inc. (Hill-Rom), a subsidiary of Hillenbrand Industries, the Commission considered that the bidding nature of the market, a lack of price transparency, and the smaller market shares of rivals rendered co-ordination unlikely, despite the market being highly concentrated following the merger:

"The incentives to undercut a prevailing level of prices to win a high-value tender would be high and, due to the lack of transparency in the market and the infrequency of

6.148   On the other hand, in the Safeway inquiry, the Commission emphasised that:

> "In many cases, the mere fact of the interdependence between firms and hence the strong likelihood of a matching price cut will be enough to create a disincentive to depart from prevailing pricing norms. Timing will, however, be significant here and if prices can be adjusted quickly, then any volume gains from a price cut are likely to be relatively small."[34]

Similarly, if firms compete in a number of separate markets, this may increase the sustainability of collusion where markets and firms are asymmetrical (*e.g.* the number of firms or their market shares differ between markets). The intuition behind this result is that in some markets (say market A) the gains from cheating may be substantially less than the future profits foregone once cheating is detected and punished, thus rendering consensus highly sustainable. In other markets (say market B), consensus might not be sustainable because the gains from cheating might be higher than the future profits foregone. Where there is multi-market contact, the comparison of the gains to cheating and the future profits foregone may be "pooled" across the two markets, and cheating in one market can be punished in all the markets in which the firms in question both operate. In such circumstances, firms considering cheating find it most profitable to cheat in all the markets in question. If cheating is highly unattractive in one market but attractive in another, then multi-market contact may increase the sustainability of co-ordination.[35]

Asymmetry of competitors

6.149   In addition, substantial cost asymmetries may render collusion unsustainable. The intuition behind this result is that the gains to collusion may be modest for the low cost firm (its profit maximising price may be lower than the cartel price) and the punishment which rivals can inflict for cheating may be lower (as its rivals may not wish to cut prices below their higher costs).[36] For example, the OFT's research paper on "*Merger Appraisal in Oligopolistic Markets*" states that "Differences in cost structure or size may

---

purchases, the threat of retaliation low. Moreover, the fact that the merged party would have such a large market share even by comparison with its nearest competitor leads us to believe that the risk of this type of coordination of pricing is not high." (cited above, para.6.028, n.31, at para.7.13).

The Commission also referred to the multi-market contact between firms (i.e. that they compete together in many countries) as a factor discouraging predation as it would be likely to lead to retaliation in other countries (see para.7.12). However, the Commission did not consider whether this multi-market contact might facilitate co-ordination.

[34] Cited above, para.6.027, n.33, at para.2.147.

[35] See further Tirole, cited above, para.6.130, n.77, at s.6.3.2.5, p.251; Motta, cited above, para.6.001, n.2, at pp.148–149; and the OFT's research paper, "Empirical indicators for market investigations", at paras 5.5 to 5.8 (cited above at para.6.056 at n.43).

[36] See further Tirole, cited above, para.6.130, n.77, at s.6.3.2.4, pp.250–251, and Exercise 6.5, pp.272–273 .

give firms different incentives to cut prices making the collusion less stable."[37]

For example, in the context of the effect of the proposed joint venture between *P&O/Stena* in the provision of tourist passenger services on the Short Sea routes, the MMC stated that:

"We take the view that, in general, such duopolies [between the joint venture and Le Shuttle] tend to settle down into a pattern of parallel behaviour, particularly on pricing policies. Had the operating costs of Le Shuttle been significantly lower than the joint venture then we believe that a pattern of parallel behaviour between them would be less likely, but this is not the case."[38]

Asymmetries in capacities can also hinder co-ordination. In this regard, Compte, Jenny and Rey,[39] present a model where firms produce homogeneous goods and have identical costs, but have different capacities. They point out that the firm with the largest capacity has the greatest incentive to deviate from a co-ordinated arrangement, since it could win the highest market share by competing independently. This model was applied by Express and Arla in the context of their proposed merger which would reduce the number of large processors supplying fresh milk to national multiples from four to three, and the Commission reported that:

"The parties said the key point was that before the merger any combination of three firms was able to supply the entire market and therefore (in the event of co-ordinated behaviour) inflict the strongest punishment on any firm that competed independently and failed to adhere to the co-ordinated terms. After the merger, however, the remaining competitors (Wiseman and Dairy Crest) would not be able to supply the entire market on their own, so the punishment they could inflict on Arla/Express would be weaker and co-ordination would be less likely."[40]

---

[37] Cited above, para.6.117, n.27, at p.86. Similarly, the European Commission indicates that: "Firms may find it easier to reach a common understanding on the terms of coordination if they are relatively symmetric, especially in terms of cost structures, market shares, capacity levels and levels of vertical integration." (cited above, para.6.001, n.4, at para.48).

[38] *The Peninsular and Oriental Steam Navigation Company/Stena Line A/B*, Cm. 3664 (November 1997), at para.1.13. In this regard, it should be noted that the European Commission reached the opposite view in relation to its decision to grant a three-year exemption to the joint venture under Art.85 (now Art.81):

"When the combined variable and semi-variable costs are considered, Le Shuttle's 1996 per unit operating costs at GBP [XX] remain lower than those of P&O at GBP [XX] and significantly lower than those of Stena at GBP [XX]. Given the differences in variable and semi-variable costs, Eurotunnel may have more room to manoeuvre than the ferries when it comes to sustaining periods of low pricing. In addition, the composition of costs is quite different between Eurotunnel and the ferries, in particular with regard to the port due which are paid by the ferries. There is also scope for further divergence in cost structures in the future, as the market evolves. Eurotunnel may therefore be tempted to try to increase market share by underpricing the ferries as it did from May 1996". (European Commission Decision, Case IV/36.253—P&O Stena Line, O.J. (1999) L 163/61 at para.106.)

[39] Compte, Jenny and Rey, "*Capacity constraints, mergers, and collusion*", European Economic Review 46 (2002), 1–29.

[40] Cited above, para.6.048, n.1, at para.7.85.

Kuhn and Motta present a very different model in which multi-product firms sell a number of different product variants. The larger the firm and the higher the number of product variants it offers, the lower its incentives to deviate (since price cutting reduces the profitability of its large existing sales of the various product varieties it offers). On the other hand, smaller firms that sell one or a few varieties have a stronger incentive to deviate as they would capture a greater volume of sales from rivals.[41]

Notwithstanding the above, in its consideration of the proposed acquisition by H+H Celcon of Marley Building Materials, the Commission stated that it remained ". . . agnostic on the issue whether competitiveness as between companies of equal size is greater than in situations where their shares are asymmetrical."[42]

Market stability

6.150   There are a number of models in which fluctuations in market demand (*e.g.* over the course of the business cycle) may undermine the sustainability of tacit or explicit collusion. For example, Rotemberg and Saloner[43] present a model in which price wars may arise in temporary booms. This model assumes that there is an observed, random demand shock and then firms choose their prices simultaneously. When demand is high, the gains to undercutting are high (as industry profits are high). In addition, the punishment for cheating entails only the loss of a share of lower *average* profits (covering future periods when demand is low and high). As a consequence, the degree of collusion which is sustainable during temporary booms may be reduced.

When market growth is predicted, firms' incentives to cheat are reduced. This is because the short-run gains to cheating will be smaller relative to the future share of co-ordinated profits foregone in the growing market. The opposite applies if market demand is predicted to decline.[44] However, barriers to entry and expansion may tend to be lower in growing markets (see further para.6.067, above), so that co-ordination may be destabilised by the threat of entry or expansion.

Product homogeneity

6.151   The previous sub-section indicated that detection and punishment might be facilitated in a differentiated goods industry. In addition, it might be argued that by supplying differentiated products and intensive advertising, firms may be able to build strong brand loyalty. This may make it difficult for one supplier to win customers from another supplier, and in such circumstances, competition between suppliers may be limited. For example, Martin presents a model in which the greater the degree of product differentiation the greater the sustainability of co-ordination, because the gain in business due

---

[41] See further Motta, cited above, para.6.001, n.2, at pp.147–148. This is analogous to the point made in paras 6.132 to 6.133, above that the larger the firm, the smaller its incentives to deviate.
[42] Cited above, para.6.011, n.31, at para.2.99.
[43] See further Tirole, cited above, para.6.130, n.77, at s.6.3.2.3, pp.248 to 250.
[44] See further Tirole, cited above, para.6.130, n.77, Exercise 6.4 on p.272.

to a price cut is progressively reduced as differentiation increases.[45] Motta argues that more generally product homogeneity does not unambiguously increase the scope for co-ordination because product differentiation both reduces the gains to deviating and the losses which can be inflicted by a punishment mechanism (since some customers may still be retained by the deviating firm in such circumstances).[46]

Switching costs

In the OFT and DTI papers on Switching costs it is noted that switching costs may both reduce the gains to cheating (*i.e.* deviating from the terms of co-ordination) and also the severity of punishment, because in a mature market it is both harder for a deviator to win new customers and for its customers to be lost in a punishment phase.[47]

6.152

Capacity constraints

Generally, decreasing returns to scale (*i.e.* unit costs increasing as output increases) or capacity constraints reduce the short-run gains to undercutting. However, they also weaken the strength of future retaliations. Accordingly, the effects of returns to scale and capacity constraints/spare capacity are generally ambiguous.[48] In this regard, the Commission's guidelines note that:

6.153

"... for instance a high level of excess capacity will make co-ordinated effects more difficult if some firms have a strong incentive to utilise their excess capacity ... However, in other instances, excess capacity may make co-ordination easier because firms could use the spare capacity as a credible threat to other firms thinking of deviating from the prevailing behaviour."[49]

This ambiguity was highlighted by the Commission in its consideration of the proposed acquisition by H+H Celcon of Marley Building Materials. In relation to H+H Celcon's recent investment in new capacity, the Commission observed that:

"To the extent that it is relevant, three considerations arise. First, it clearly provides no new alternative supply for any customer who wished to switch away from the merged company. Second, it will increase the competitive pressure on H+H Celcon to lower prices, in order to utilise the new capacity. Third, it will increase the threat that any price reduction by Tarmac or, indeed, a new entrant seeking an increase in market share can be countered by the merged company. As

---

[45] Martin, *Advanced Industrial Economics* (Blackwell, 1993) at pp.116 to 117.
[46] Cited above, para.6.001, n.2, at pp.146–147.
[47] Cited above, para.6.011, n.30 at paras 7.20–7.38. The Commission's guidelines refer to one factor relevant to the assessment of co-ordinated effects as "the existence of switching costs" but add that "however, in some instances, switching costs might increase competitive pressure so destabilising any coordination" (cited above, para.6.001, n.1, at para. 3.41 (eighth bullet point)).
[48] See further Tirole, cited above, para.6.130, n.77, at s.6.1.4, pp.242 to 243; and Motta, cited above, para.6.001, n.2, at pp.149.
[49] Cited above, para.6.001, n.1, at para.3.41 (ninth bullet point).

a result, to the extent that such capacity is relevant to our evaluation of inter-firm rivalry for aircrete blocks, it is unclear what overall impact this new plant will have."[50]

Barriers to entry and expansion—the strength of potential and actual competition

6.154 The risk of oligopolistic co-ordination is increased if barriers to entry and expansion are high. This is because existing suppliers are able to co-ordinate in order to set high prices, in the knowledge that new entry will not occur if they earn high profits. Whilst firms *within* the market have to weigh up the short terms gains of a price cut against their share of monopoly profits which will be foregone as a consequence, this opportunity cost does not apply to new entrants. In addition, as noted above, the profits derived by individual small firms from adhering to the consensus will be only a small share of co-ordinated profits, whereas the temporary gains from cheating (*i.e.* a high share of industry profits) will be correspondingly greater.

As regards the scope for, and incentives of, smaller "fringe" firms to compete with core oligopolists in a market, the Commission's guidelines state the following:

"The extent to which fringe firms act as a competitive constraint will in part depend on the number, and size, of such fringe companies and their cost and profit margins. It will also depend critically on their scope to expand output, first in relation to their current levels, and secondly in relation to the output of the core oligopolists. To the extent that fringe firms can significantly expand their own output, their existence will provide a threat to firms considering pricing above competitive levels. If, however, capacity is limited, then pricing up to the 'umbrella' price set by the core oligopoly may be more profitable. Even if a lower price strategy for the fringe firms is preferable (to pricing up to the 'umbrella' price) this will only tend to undermine the prevailing price level if the loss of output by core companies to the fringe is sufficiently large in relation to the output of the core oligopolists."[51]

In this regard, the Commission stated in the Safeway inquiry that:

"Co-ordination and unilateral behaviour can only be sustained in markets where there are relatively weak external constraints. If barriers to entry are low, then actual entry or the threat of entry will tend to undermine such conduct. Alternatively, if there is a fringe of other firms already in a market outside the core firms, and if the fringe firms have both the incentive to undercut and the scope to attract significant volume away from the core firms, then an uncompetitive price level is less likely to be sustainable."[52]

For example, in its inquiry into the proposed merger between CHC Helicopter Corporation and Helicopter Services Group, the Commission

---

[50] Cited above, para.6.011, n.31, at para.2.104.
[51] Cited above, para.6.001, n.1, at para.3.40.
[52] Cited above, para.6.027, n.33, at para.2.156.

noted that, in the context of its assessment of the risk of tacit collusion ". . . such behaviour by duopolists will be more likely when entry to the market is difficult . . ."[53]

Similarly, in the context of the proposed joint venture between **6.155** *P&O/Stena* on the Short Sea routes, the MMC did not have any concerns as to the effects of the merger on competition in the provision of tourist transportation services on these routes (which were held to be a relevant product and geographical market) prior to the abolition of duty-free. This was despite the fact that the parties to the joint venture had a market share of 46 per cent, Le Shuttle 39 per cent, and three smaller competitors would have an aggregate market share of 15 per cent.[54] This was primarily because until this time the MMC expected that the joint venture and Eurotunnel would face effective competition from three other competitors, and by undercutting prices or introducing innovative services these competitors could deter or undermine any parallel behaviour between the joint venture and Le Shuttle.[55]

A further issue for smaller competitors in such circumstances is their expectations as to how market leading rivals would respond to their expansion (as considered further in para.6.070, above).

Conclusions in relation to the risk of oligopolistic co-ordination and the assessment of whether co-ordination is presently occurring

The above analysis indicates that, although firms in oligopolistic markets **6.156** face a basic dilemma as to whether it is better for them to co-ordinate or to "cheat", there are a wide variety of factors which will affect individual firms' decisions and many of these factors have ambiguous effects depending on precise market circumstances. Economic theory highlights these factors, and indicates what might happen, *but* it is not definitive[56] *and* there are a wide range of devices that firms may adopt in order to facilitate co-ordination (*e.g.* publishing prices or information sharing agreements to

---

[53] Cited above, para.6.065, n.58, at para.2.70. Similarly, in the context of the merger between Interbrew SA and Bass PLC, the Commission stated that:

"We are not persuaded by the argument that were S&N and Interbrew to seek to engage in any form of tacit collusion, with a view to increasing wholesale prices, their competitors would have no difficulty in increasing their output to satisfy demand, thereby defeating such attempted collusion (see para.2.96). No competitor has a brand portfolio that can compete for the full range of customers' beer requirements (see para.2.106). Furthermore, although new entrants might be willing to make use of whatever spare capacity was available, we have not seen any persuasive evidence to suggest that the available excess capacity would necessarily be suited to high-volume, efficient production of the sort that would be required to compete effectively with Interbrew and S&N. Finally, entrants that wished to take advantage of higher prices would find it difficult to gain access to the market as a result of the control that Interbrew and S&N would have in wholesaling and distribution (see paras 2.142 to 2.149)." (cited above, para.6.027, n.34, at para.2.110.)

[54] *The Peninsular and Oriental Steam Navigation Company/Stena Line A/B*, Cm. 3664 (November 1997), at para.1.12.

[55] Cited above, para.6.155, n.54, at paras 2.162 and 2.163.

[56] For example, Scherer and Ross conclude their analysis of oligopoly theory by stating that: "None of these links is strictly deterministic; all reflect central tendencies subject to random deviation. It is in part because of this complexity and randomness that oligopoly poses such difficult problems for the economic analyst". (cited above, para.6.001, n.4, at p.315.)

make markets more transparent). Low barriers to entry and expansion and/or substantial buyer power may be determinative in precluding anti-competitive co-ordination, but in many cases the analysis may be more complicated.

Coleman and Scheffman strongly advocate carrying out empirical analysis to assess whether co-ordination is presently occurring, what factors in practice make co-ordination difficult, and how the merger might change matters. In this regard, the Commission's guidelines refer to a variety of information that might be collated in order to assess whether there is existing co-ordination. In particular, the Commission suggests that: "If profits are excessive then this may be an indicator of existing oligopoly pricing."[57]

It is beyond the scope of this Chapter to address all the complexities of assessing profitability, but it is important to appreciate that there are a number of complexities.[58] First, it may be difficult to assess accurately the profitability of a specific activity (e.g. due to issues relating to the allocation of costs to that activity which are common to a number of activities, or valuing a firm's intangible assets, or valuing a firm's assets on a replacement cost basis).

Secondly, a view needs to be taken as to what is the competitive benchmark level of profitability. A range of accounting and economic measures may be used in order to compare the undertaking's actual profits with those of other firms/sectors.[59] In addition, the company's cost of capital (which captures the return required by investors and lenders to fund in the company's activities rather than investing elsewhere and which, thereby, takes account of the level of risk normally associated with the investment) may be compared with the firm's actual return on capital employed. Using the cost of capital as a benchmark of the market-based competitive return may be problematic, however, since there are a myriad of reasons why profits may exceed the cost of capital in a competitive industry. For example:

(i)   some firms may be expected to earn more than their cost of capital due to superior efficiency;

(ii)   high profits can occur at certain times as a result of the business cycle or where there are capacity constraints in a growing market;

(iii)   profits may be high in markets where there is innovation. Firms should be able to earn a fair return on the cost of innovation given the risks of their investment; and

(iv)   more generally, profits may reflect a successful gamble whether due to innovation or other risk taking. Moreover, returns may be generally higher than the cost of capital due to "survivor bias"—i.e. because the firms which earn returns in excess of their cost of

---

[57] Cited above, para.6.001, n.1, at para.3.43.

[58] OFT 657, "*Assessing profitability in competition policy analysis*" Economic discussion paper 6, (prepared by OXERA) (July 2003); and Bishop and Walker, cited above, para.6.001, n.2, at ss.3.58–3.69 at pp.74–79. Also see an article by Lind and Walker, "*The Mis(use) of Profitability Analysis in Competition Law Cases*" (2004) E.C.L.R., Vol.25: Issue 7.

[59] Comparisons with other firms/sectors can be fraught with difficulty, not least because the approach requires the identification of suitably comparable benchmark firms/sectors, which is often difficult due to different market conditions and accounting policies.

capital will tend to be those which survive. In this case, the average returns of firms in the industry may be expected to be above the cost of capital.

Thirdly, high profits might be wholly or mainly attributable to non-co-ordinated effects.[60] This is potentially important because errors in economic assessment as to the effects of the merger might otherwise be made, with potentially different factors being relevant to the assessment of co-ordinated and non-co-ordinated effects. None of the above should be interpreted as indicating that profitability information should be wholly disregarded, but rather that care should be applied in interpreting such information.

6.157

The Commission has considered profitability in a number of merger inquiries. For example, in the context of considering the merger between Express Dairies and Arla, the Commission observed that: "Pre-merger profit margins can provide an indication as to the current level of competition in the market", and "although it can be difficult to form firm conclusions from reported profit levels, we note that there does not appear to be any evidence to suggest that the processors have earned excessive profits on the fresh processed milk supplied to the national multiples."[61]

The Commission's guidelines also refer to prices being more stable in response to cost or demand changes if there is "oligopoly pricing":

"A second indicator might be that prices in competitive conditions, though tending to the same level, are, over time, likely to exhibit significant variation as they respond to changing supply and demand conditions. This is less likely to be the case with oligopoly pricing, because the incentive not to depart from an established level of high prices will to some extent dampen the responsiveness of prices to cost and demand changes."[62]

Unfortunately, this may not provide a workable indication of the existence or degree of co-ordination. For example: cost and demand changes will vary between markets (so greater price stability in one market compared with another might be attributable to less variation in costs and demand); cost and demand changes may not impact on all firms equally, which will also dampen the responsiveness of prices to such changes even in competitive markets; as noted above, cost and demand instability may itself make it difficult to reach and sustain co-ordination; firms which are very effective at coordinating may

---

[60] This may, for example, occur due to switching costs. In this regard, the OFT/DTI report on "Switching costs" observes that: "Switching costs create a unilateral incentive for firms with large customer bases to focus on harvesting the rewards of this base, rather than competing aggressively for new customers. The outcome—less aggressive competition—can resemble the outcome from co-ordination between firms, even though no co-ordination, whether tacit or explicit, has occurred. That is, the observance of firms concentrating on their own customer bases and not actively competing for a competitor's customers, should not necessarily be interpreted as evidence of collusion (*i.e.* market splitting) in a market with switching costs" (cited above, para.6.011, n.30, at para.7.20).
[61] Cited above, para.6.048, n.1, at para.5.76–5.81.
[62] Cited above, para.6.001, n.1, at para.3.43.

be very successful at adapting prices quickly in response to cost and demand changes; and certain forms of co-ordination, such as co-ordination on customer allocations, might facilitate the adjustment of prices in response to demand and cost changes.

6.158   The Commission also envisages assessing trends in competitors' prices, although the Commission notes that similar or identical prices can also result from intense competition.[63] Coleman and Scheffman also observe that parallel pricing may be expected to result from common cost and demand changes,[64] as observed more generally in para.6.022, above in the context of considering pricing correlations to assist with market definition. However, they observe that a finding that prices are not very correlated is inconsistent with existing price co-ordination, and also suggests that there are significant complexities in individual firms' pricing decisions that would make price co-ordination and detecting deviations difficult. They also suggest that it would be interesting to assess whether over time firms are consistently ranked in terms of their competitiveness on price, with changes in firms' relative price competitiveness also being inconsistent with co-ordination and suggesting that reaching consensus would be difficult (e.g. co-ordination on price is inconsistent with observing firms under cutting one another on price over time, thereby changing their relative competitive positions).

Coleman and Scheffman also suggest that analysing the parties' prices to individual customers may be revealing. For example, different pricing for common customers and variations in changes in prices (controlling for differences between customers such as purchase volume and location) suggests that co-ordination is not occurring and would be difficult. Lack of variation, on the other hand, does not imply co-ordination, because (as noted above) some parallelism would be expected in competitive market conditions.[65]

Coleman and Scheffman advise that the relationship between published list prices and transaction prices be considered, since this may permit an assessment of whether "signalling" is occurring through price announcements. Again, parallelism is not proof of co-ordination, but the absence of such a relationship is suggestive that co-ordination is not occurring and is not facilitated by price lists. In addition, they suggest that whether price leadership is occurring may be assessed by considering factors such as whether price changes are announced (e.g. via published price lists), which supplier initiates price changes, whether this varies over time, and whether competitors follow price changes. The relationship between transaction prices and announced prices may also be revealing.[66]

Since transparency or lack of transparency is easy to assert, Coleman and Scheffman make a very sensible suggestion that the regulator should compare firms' internal documents covering rivals' prices to individual customers, capacities, sales and so on with rivals' actual data. If estimates are significantly different from reality this would suggest a lack of transparency, thus making consensus and detection of deviations more difficult.[67]

---

[63] Cited above, para.6.001, n.1, at para.3.43.
[64] Cited above, para.6.027, n.34.
[65] Cited above, para.6.027, n.34.
[66] Cited above, para.6.027, n.34.
[67] Cited above, para.6.027, n.34.

Coleman and Scheffman also emphasise that maintaining fairly high **6.159** capacity utilisation is often important to profitability. As a result, effective co-ordination may require capacity co-ordination since otherwise capacity additions will depress prices. They observe that considering historical capacity changes may be revealing, because large and frequent capacity changes can destabilise co-ordination, particularly if firms add capacity at different times.[68]

The Commission's guidelines also very briefly refer to "the stability of market shares over time" as a factor relevant to the assessment of co-ordinated effects.[69] Stability of market shares is arguably the key feature of co-ordination—*i.e.* firms do not compete with one another to win customers off one another (although dominant firms and those in fierce competition with one another may also enjoy stable market shares). Accordingly, in the context of assessing whether customer allocation is occurring, Coleman and Scheffman suggest assessing the extent to which customers switch suppliers over time, with the greater degree of customer turnover the less likely co-ordination is occurring. Such customer turnover is also indicative that co-ordination on price is not occurring.[70] However, as the Commission observes "high and static market shares do not always indicate that a firm has market power: the firm may simply have competed successfully on a continuing basis."[71] Coleman and Scheffman also correctly observe that customers may well be able to secure competitive terms of supply by threatening to switch even if actual switching between suppliers is limited.[72]

In this regard, in relation to the proposed merger between Arla Foods amba and Express Dairies plc, the Commission stated that:

"Addressing first the issue of whether or not there is evidence of co-ordination in the supply of fresh milk to national multiples to date, we note that the European Commission said in its EC Article 9 Decision: 'The past shift in market shares, modest margins in the industry and expansion in geographical reach of Wiseman does not in itself point towards a market situation that historically has been characterized by co-ordinated behaviour by members of the oligopoly.'"[73]

On the other hand, in reaching its conclusion that the market for personal current accounts ("PCA") was vulnerable to tacit co-ordination in pricing in the context of Lloyds TSB Group plc's proposed acquisition of Abbey National plc, the Commission conclude that there was little evidence that the big four have competed keenly on price for the bulk of customers. In particular, the Commission referred to Lloyds TSB's internal strategy document of September 2000 which commented that the previous year's plan had been prepared against the background of a favourable economic

---

[68] Cited above, para.6.027, n.34.
[69] Cited above, para.6.001, n.1, at para.3.41 (eleventh bullet point).
[70] Considering individual customer data, as well as overall market shares, may be revealing as the winning and losing of individual customers may be masked by considering only net changes in market shares.
[71] Cited above, para.6.001, n.1, at para.3.5.
[72] Cited above, para.6.027, n.34.
[73] Cited above, para.6.048, n.1 at para.5.108.

environment and "limited impact from competitors", contrasting this with the more competitive situation which the company now faced in 2000. The document also commented: "Historically, customer inertia for banks has been high. With little difference between the offers of the major banks, the perceived rewards to moving bank were seen as small." The document added that market research indicated that "so far customers remain relatively price-insensitive for core banking services (*i.e.* current account), except for what are perceived as hidden charges, with service seemingly much more important."[74]

6.160   Finally, evidence of recent collusion in the past or in other geographic markets with similar characteristics might be informative as to the risks of co-ordination.[75] Past history of collusion/cartels was a particular consideration for the Commission in its inquiry into *BASF/Takeda Chemical*, which concerned the vitamins industry. In that case, the Commission nevertheless emphasised that the question it had to address was whether the merger would change the economic environment in such a way as to make it easier for firms to form and/or enforce a cartel or to collude tacitly in the market for vitamins.[76] The Commission concluded that:

> "We expect that there would be a considerable degree of competitive pressure after the merger, particularly because of the presence of Chinese producers. We also believe that, while it is possible for tacit collusion to exist, any such situation would exist independently of, and would not be affected by, the merger."[77]

Mergers creating excessive buyer power

6.161   A merger might create excessive buyer power, with this having analogous effects to excessive supplier market power. However, as noted in para.6.072 above, buyer power may well offset supplier market power, with customers potentially benefiting from lower prices as a result.

In September 1998 the OFT published a paper prepared by Dobson, Waterson and Chu concerning buyer power.[78] Whilst acknowledging that buyer power can act as an effective constraint on the exercise of market power by suppliers, the OFT research paper also outlines a range of detrimental effects which may result from excessive buyer power. One potential concern is that where customers enjoy excessive buyer power, prices may be driven to a level which is below the competitive price and would not enable

---

[74] Cited above, para.6.065, n.55, at paras 2.63 and 2.73.

[75] The OFT's guidelines indicate that in its assessment of whether conditions are favourable to co-ordination it will review "any history of coordination in the market concerned" (cited above, para.6.001, n.1, at para.4.13). The US Horizontal Merger Guidelines indicate that it is likely that conditions conducive to co-ordination exist when there has been past explicit collusion and the key characteristics of the market have not changed since this time, and collusion in other geographic markets will have the same weight when the markets are comparable to the market in question (s.2.11, cited above, para.6.001, n.4). The European Commission's Horizontal Merger Guidelines make the same points (para.42, cited above, para.6.001, n.4). The Commission, however, makes no reference to past collusion in the same market or another comparable geographic market as a relevant factor.

[76] Cited above, para.6.030, n.36, at paras 1.13, 2.99–2.101.

[78] OFT 239, "*The Welfare Consequences of the Exercise of Buyer Power*", Research Paper 16, (September 1998), (prepared by Dobson, Waterson and Chu).

suppliers to earn a reasonable return. Another potential concern arises where buyer power is asymmetrically distributed between customers (for example due to firm size differences). In these circumstances, those customers with greater bargaining power may be able to negotiate substantial discounts from suppliers compared to other less significant customers. This, in turn, can lead to a virtuous circle whereby a cost advantage enjoyed by a particular supplier can be used to increase its market share advantage, which can in turn be used to gain an even larger cost advantage over rivals, etc. This can distort retail competition by creating economies of scale in purchasing which smaller retailers do not benefit from.

Alternatively, customers enjoying buyer power may seek to impose a variety of vertical restraints on suppliers which may have anti competitive effects (possibly foreclosing markets or dampening competition between existing rival suppliers), as well as, or alternatively, offering them possible efficiency benefits. These might include exclusive supply arrangements, which retailers might seek to place on suppliers of own-label products, and "slotting allowances", whereby producers pay retailers an up front fee to obtain store shelf space for their products.[79] Against this background, any merger situation which is expected to lead to an increase in buyer power on the part of the merging companies may run the risk of distorting competition in procurement markets.

One of the key issues raised in the context of the various bids for Safeway in 2003 was whether any of the proposed mergers might be expected to result in an increase in buyer power in relation to suppliers; and if so, whether any such increase might be expected to have adverse affects on the public interest.[80] In particular, the Commission observed that each of the proposed bidders expected to reap cost savings from the acquisition of Safeway through lower prices from their suppliers. The Commission noted that to the extent that such savings were made and passed on to consumers, then this would be a benefit of the merger. However, if such cost savings also resulted in adverse effects on suppliers, and hence on the quality, range or diversity of their products, then those benefits might be partially or wholly off-set. In this connection, the Commission had concluded in its 2000 report on supermarkets that certain supermarkets, including Asda, Safeway, Sainsbury and Tesco, possessed buyer power and identified a number of practices which were against the public interest. The Commission had recommended at that time a code of conduct to which these supermarkets should adhere when dealing with their suppliers in order to ensure that their buyer power was not exploited.[81]

In its report on the various bids for Safeway, the Commission concluded that an acquisition of Safeway by Asda, Sainsbury or Tesco would be expected to aggravate further the imbalance in the respective bargaining positions of these parties and their suppliers (as identified in the 2000 report). The Commission noted that "We would in broad terms expect competitive prices to emerge where there was a reasonable balance of

6.162

---

[79] This Chapter does not seek to consider all of the possible adverse effects of excessive buyer power, as discussed in the OFT Research Paper, cited above, para.6.161, n.78.

[80] Cited above, para.6.027, n.33, at paras 2.216 to 2.258.

[81] *Supermarkets: A report on the supply of groceries from multiple stores in the UK*, Cm.4842 (October 2000).

bargaining power as between competitive suppliers and competitive buyers; but would not expect them to emerge with such a degree of imbalance as exists in the one-stop grocery market."[82]

Possible consequences of the proposed acquisitions by Asda, Sainsbury and Tesco included, in the Commission's view, a general weakening of the bargaining position of some suppliers, and also a possible "waterbed effect", whereby suppliers might need to charge higher prices to smaller retailer customers if larger retailers forced through price reductions which would otherwise leave suppliers insufficiently profitable. The Commission also considered that an acquisition of Safeway by Morrisons would have similar effects, albeit to a lesser degree, because suppliers would face four large grocery retailers (and not three) and, as it would not expect price and non-price competition to be reduced due to the Morrisons acquisition, the Commission expected cost savings to be passed on to consumers in the form of lower prices.[83]

In the context of the proposed merger between Arla Foods and Express Dairies, one of the OFT's concerns in its Art.9 request to the European Commission was whether the combined group would have excessive buyer power in relation to the procurement of raw milk. However, the European Commission noted that a combined share of procurement of between 15 and 25 per cent,[84] was "unlikely to raise any concerns of single dominance." In addition, one supplier of raw milk had raised a concern that there may be a situation of "collective dominance"[85] on the buyer side following the proposed merger. This would entail the large purchasers of raw milk for the production of fresh processed milk jointly reducing their demand in order to generate an oversupply of raw milk, thereby triggering price decreases. The European Commission observed that a number of factors would serve to undermine any such co-ordination amongst purchasers. First, the purchase of raw milk was fragmented. Secondly, buyers were very heterogeneous in that they used raw milk for a variety of different end-uses, including not only the production of fresh processed milk and cream but also the production of flavoured milk drinks and yellow fats. This would make it more difficult for purchasers to collude in relation to the purchase of raw milk. Thirdly, the larger purchasers differed with respect to their levels of vertical integration, with certain larger milk processors having in-house supplies of raw milk through their own farmer groups. This would make it more difficult for purchasers to reach and agree terms of co-ordination. Fourthly, if the large purchasers were to co-ordinate a decrease in their demand, then prices for raw milk might become depressed, and demand for raw milk for other end uses would be likely to increase. Alternatively, the level of over capacity would adjust, thereby cancelling the over-supply that could generate a price decrease. The Commission therefore concluded that the proposed merger would not threaten to create or strengthen a dominant position as a result

---

[82] Cited above, para.6.027, n.33, at para.2.257.

[83] Cited above, para.6.027, n.33, at paras 1.20–1.21.

[84] The merged entity's exact share of raw milk procurement in Great Britain was excised from the European Commission's decision on grounds of confidentiality.

[85] Issues of collective dominance/coordinated effects are discussed earlier in this Chapter in paras 6.128 to 6.160.

of which effective competition would be significantly impeded in the market for the procurement of raw milk in Great Britain.[86]

Assessing the effects of vertical mergers

Overview

A merger may create "vertical links" between a firm and its customers, or with the firm's suppliers of raw materials or other inputs. That is, the merger may create a vertically integrated firm. The competition implications of vertical integration and vertical restraints (imposed by manufacturers upon retailers and distributors as to the terms and conditions of sale[87]) have been investigated by the Commission in a number of monopoly and merger inquiries.[88] The literature on this subject is vast and controversial, and this section will therefore provide only a brief overview of the relevant issues.[89]

6.163

---

[86] European Commission's decision, Case COMP/M.3130 *Arla Foods/Express Dairies*, (June 10, 2003).

[87] There are a number of different forms of vertical restraints, which may be categorised under three main headings:

(i) dealing restrictions. These arise if one firm undertakes not to deal with competitors, or certain competitors, of the other. If the firm agreeing not to deal with competitors is the "upstream" manufacturing firm, then such a restriction is usually called "exclusive or selective distribution". Exclusivity is generally granted with respect to a certain territory (*e.g.* a single distributor/retailer might be granted an exclusive territory), whereas selectivity can be conditional on various factors such as location or quality (*e.g.* only retailers making particular commitments as to the quality and types of service they provide will be supplied). If the firm agreeing not to deal with competitors is the "downstream" distributing/retailing firm, then this restraint is typically referred to as "exclusive purchasing". In some cases, exclusivity can also be limited to a particular customer base, type of service or product provided;

(ii) non-linear pricing. Non-linear pricing describes all pricing terms other than the sale of customer specified volumes at a fixed per unit price. Such pricing alters the cost structure of the downstream firm. Examples include, *inter alia*, fixed fees (which are often termed "franchise fees" even if the purchaser is not a franchisee), volume discounts, loyalty discounts, slotting allowances, full line forcing, quantity forcing, or the practice of tying/bundling; and

(iii) price restrictions such as resale price maintenance and the recommendation of a resale price.

[88] Monopoly inquiries which have focused on such issues include, *inter alia*, the 2000 reports on *Supermarkets* (cited above, n.81), *New Cars* (cited above, para.6.008, n.21) and *Impulse Ice Cream (The supply of Impulse Ice Cream: A report on the supply in the UK of ice cream purchased for immediate consumption*, Cm. 4510 (January 2000)), the 1999 report on *Milk: a report on the supply in Great Britain of raw cows' milk*, Cm. 4286 (July 1999)) and the 1997 report on Domestic Electrical Goods (*Domestic Electrical Goods: A report on the supply in the UK of televisions, video cassette recorders, hi-fi systems and camcorders*, Cm. 3675 (July 1997)).

[89] A more detailed treatment of these issues is given in a series of publications: Carlton and Perloff, cited above, para.6.128, n.71, at Ch.12; Scherer and Ross, cited above, para.6.001, n.4, at Ch.15; Rey and Tirole, "*The Logic of Vertical Restraints*", American Economic Review Vol.76 No.5, December 1996; Comanor, "*Vertical Price-Fixing, Vertical Market Restrictions, and the New Antitrust Policy*", Harvard Law Review, Vol.98, 1985; Kay, "*Vertical Integration: The Regulatory Issues*", Lectures on Regulation, London Business School, 1991; Tirole, cited above, para.6.130, n.77, Ch.4; Bishop and Walker, para.6.001, n.2, Ch.5 and pp.288–290; Hughes, Foss and Ross, "*The Economic Assessment of Vertical Restraints under UK and EC Competition Law*", E.C.L.R. 2001, 22(10), 424–433; Motta, cited above, para.6.001, n.2, at Ch.6; see also:

Whilst current mainstream economics rejects the so-called "Chicago School" arguments that vertical restraints and vertical mergers are always pro-competitive, it is helpful first to outline the nature of some of these arguments. A key insight of the Chicago School is that vertical restraints/mergers are between producers of "complementary" goods or services (*e.g.* manufacturers and retailers) rather than competing suppliers of substitutes (*e.g.* competing manufacturers). In general suppliers of complementary goods/services have no interest in raising the price of a complementary product, because (by definition) this will depress the demand for their own product (*e.g.* higher retail margins reduce manufacturers' sales and profits).[90] The Chicago School emphasises the efficiency motivations of vertical restraints and mergers.[91] For example, Bork maintains that a:

"[v]ertical merger does not create or increase the firm's power to restrict output [and thereby raise prices above the competitive level]. The ability to restrict output depends on the share of the market occupied by the firm. Horizontal mergers increase market share, but vertical mergers do not."[92]

Whilst the Chicago School has a number of useful insights, it substantially disregards the adverse effects that vertical restraints can have on third party competitors (*e.g.* by reducing inter-brand competition, see further below).[93]

Generally, vertical mergers can raise competition concerns if the merged business has market power at any stage of the production or distribution of the product in question. However, detrimental effects on competition are unlikely in cases where a significant number of competitors would still

---

OFT 414, "*Assessment of Individual Agreements and Conduct*", paras 6.22 and 6.31; OFT 177, "*Vertical Restraints and Competition Policy*", (December 1996), Research paper 12, by Dobson and Waterson; "*European Commission Notice: Guidelines on Vertical Restraints*", (2000) O.J. C 291/1.

[90] Contrastingly, competing suppliers of substitute products have in general a common interest in raising prices, as rivals' high prices increase their own sales.

[91] The OFT's Research Paper on *Vertical Restraints and Competition Policy* identifies a wide range of potentially beneficial effects to vertical restraints, many of which relate to various "externalities" which lead to the interests of distributors/retailers diverging from those of the manufacturer. In these circumstances, vertical restraints provide a way of aligning distributors'/retailers' interests with those of the manufacturer. In these circumstances, the Chicago School would argue that if a manufacturer chooses to accept a vertical restraint which limits retail competition, then there must be some offsetting efficiency justification, cited above, para.6.163, n.89.

[92] Bork, "*The Antitrust Paradox*", New York: Basic Books (1978).

[93] According to Whinston, the Chicago School considers whether vertical integration and restraints are profitable given the prices and qualities of competitors' products (Whinston, "*Tying, Foreclosure, and Exclusion*", American Economic Review, September 1990). However, other economists emphasise that such practices may change market structure, thereby enabling prices and profits to rise. Salop and Scheffman argue that if economies of scale exist in retail distribution or there are other barriers to entry at the retail level, retailers' exclusive dealing arrangements with manufacturers could raise small manufacturers' distribution costs—possibly to the extent that rival manufacturers' continued operation would be unprofitable. In addition, reduced sales could also lead to the loss of economies of scale at other stages of production, such as in manufacturing and purchasing. This could enable integrated firms to raise their prices and profits; Salop and Scheffman, "*Raising Rivals' Costs*", AEA Papers and Proceedings (May 1983).

remain in both the "upstream" and the "downstream" markets linked by the merger. The OFT's guidelines note that the risk of anti-competitive effects "is . . . unlikely to arise except in the presence of existing market power at one level in the supply chain at least, or in markets where there is already significant vertical integration/restraints."[94]

For example, in the context of the proposed acquisition by RCG Holdings of Doncasters, the Director General advised that:

6.164

"The acquisition raises a vertical issue because the parties are involved in the manufacture of superalloys, which is upstream to investment casting of components. However, given the low market shares in both investment casting and superalloy production, there is unlikely to be any foreclosure of supply of superalloy to non-vertically integrated investment casters. Therefore this vertical link raises no significant competition concerns."[95]

Similarly, the Commission's guidelines state that:

"Generally, a vertical merger will only raise competition concerns when the firms involved are able to exercise a substantial level of market power in one or more markets along the supply chain."[96]

In *Fresenius/Caremark*[97], for example, the Commission considered a proposed merger between, *inter alia*, a producer of parenteral nutrition ("PN") products (Fresenius) and a supplier of homecare services in relation to those products (Caremark). One of the adverse effects on competition identified by the Commission was the effect of the creation of vertical links in relation to these products due to Caremark's dominant position as a homecare provider. In particular, the Commission was concerned that Caremark could be "use[d] as a vehicle to promote the sale of Fresenius [PN] products"[98] to the exclusion of products of other competitors.

However, it is important to note that an examination of market shares alone is insufficient to determine whether competition concerns might be raised by a vertical merger. Other considerations should include existing supply relationships and levels of spare capacity held by competing firms. This is discussed further in the next section. Vertical links between suppliers and purchasers may also raise a number of other potential competition concerns, a number of which are described further below.

The risk of market foreclosure and raising rivals' costs

One potential concern is that vertical mergers may adversely affect competition by raising a competitor's costs or wholly foreclosing the market to an actual or potential competitor. The former may occur where access to a scarce input (*e.g.* essential raw materials or distribution facilities) is

6.165

---

[94] Cited above, para.6.001, n.1, at para.3.8.
[95] Director General's advice of June 13, 2001, *The proposed acquisition by RCG Holdings Limited of Doncasters plc.*
[96] Cited above, para.6.001, n.1, at para.3.64.
[97] *Fresenius AG/Caremark Limited*, Cm. 3925 (April 1998).
[98] Cited above, para.6.164, n.97, para.2.157.

restricted by the merged business acquiring a supplier of such facilities with substantial market power, with the consequence that rivals are forced to use more expensive supplies, thereby reducing the ability of such rivals to compete[99] (*i.e.* the merged business may discriminate between its own downstream or upstream operations and those of its competitors). If access to an asset is not just restricted but denied, and if this asset is not replicable (*e.g.* due to the prohibitive cost of replicating a physical distribution network), then market foreclosure will result.[1]

The Commission's guidelines emphasise that vertical integration can increase barriers to entry and expansion:

> "Vertical mergers can raise barriers to entry or expansion by limiting or foreclosing altogether the access to essential inputs or means of distribution. They can also increase the difficulty and risk of entry if it means that entry has to occur at more than one level in the supply chain."[2]

As noted above, an examination of market shares alone is insufficient to determine whether competition concerns might be raised by a vertical merger. In particular, if the merging upstream firm does not currently supply the rivals of the downstream merging firm, then the merger would not afford the upstream firm scope to discriminate against rival purchasers of the raw material. Similarly, if the merging upstream firm currently supplies rival purchasers of the raw material, but other suppliers of the raw material have substantial spare capacity, then it may be straightforward for rival purchasers of the raw material to avoid purchasing from the merged company (subject to the existence of switching costs),[3] again denying the merged company the opportunity for discrimination.[4]

In addition, a particular complexity of competition assessments in vertical mergers is understanding not just the potential for the merged entity to act anti-competitively post merger but its incentives to do so in practice. For example, returning to the above example of a merger between an input supplier and a manufacturer, discriminating against rival manufacturers may reduce the profitability of the merged input business—with this needing to be weighed up against any resulting increase in profits enjoyed by its downstream manufacturing business.

Where market foreclosure by the upstream firm is a concern, it would be helpful to demonstrate that:

(i)   the merged entity would have a low share of supply of the raw material(s) in question to rivals;

(ii)   the raw material(s) account(s) for a small proportion of the costs associated with the manufacture of the final product, such that

---

[99] See, for example, Salop and Scheffman, "*Cost-raising Strategies*", (1983) Journal of Industrial Economics, Vol.36, pp.19–34.

[1] See, for example, Whinston (1990), cited above, para.6.163 at n.93 and Ordover, Saloner and Salop, "*Equilibrium Vertical Foreclosure*", American Economic Review, Vol.80(1) (1990).

[2] Cited above, para.6.001, n.1, at para. 3.68.

[3] Switching costs are considered further in paras 6.011 and 6.121 to 6.122.

[4] See further NERA, "*Analysing the Effects of Vertical Mergers: Incentives Matter, But Market Shares Do Not*", Antitrust Insights September/October 2002.

even if certain customers had to pay more for the raw material this would not render them unable to compete effectively in the market for supply of the manufactured product;

(iii) other suppliers of the raw material could readily expand production (*e.g.* due to spare capacity);

(iv) purchasers of the raw material would not face significant costs in switching to alternative suppliers; and

(v) the merged company would continue to be dependent on other purchasers of the raw material for a high proportion of its sales, such that it would have little incentive to seek to worsen the terms of supply to these customers.

Another potential competition concern is that the merged undertaking with a high downstream market share could acquire or strengthen a dominant position in the supply of the raw material by foreclosing a substantial part of the market to competing independent suppliers of that raw material following the transaction. In these circumstances, it would be helpful to demonstrate that: **6.166**

(i) the merged company would account for only a small proportion of purchases of the raw material(s), such that even if it were to stop purchasing the raw material from third parties, the viability of other suppliers of the raw material would not be prejudiced (*i.e.* they would be excluded from only a small part of the market);

(ii) the merged company would have strong incentives to continue sourcing part of their raw material requirements from third parties (*e.g.* to ensure security of supply); and

(iii) even if certain third party suppliers of the raw material(s) were no longer able to supply the merged company, the reduction in their sales volumes would not have a material impact on their manufacturing costs such that they would not be rendered less effective competitors.

The potential foreclosure effects of vertical mergers were considered by the Commission in its report on *Nutreco Holding/Hydro Seafood GSP*.[5] This case concerned the proposed merger between Nutreco (which was engaged in salmon farming and the supply of fish feed) and Norsk Hydro (which was engaged in salmon farming). Through their various subsidiaries, the parties were the largest salmon farmers in the UK, and Nutreco was the UK's largest manufacturer of feeds for salmon and trout. Following the merger, Nutreco would be responsible for the supply of 46 per cent of farmed Scottish salmon (which was regarded as a distinct "premium" segment within a wider EEA farmed salmon market) and 48 per cent of UK supplies of salmon feed. Furthermore, Nutreco was the largest UK purchaser of salmon feed, and following the merger it would be

---

[5] Cited above, para.6.021, n.94.

responsible for the procurement of at least 38 per cent of salmon feed in the UK (with its purchases expected to increase in the future).[6]

The Commission found that salmon feed represented a very significant cost to salmon farmers, representing over half of their total cost of sales. Accordingly, the cost effectiveness of salmon farmers in downstream markets depended on them being able to obtain food supplies at competitive prices. The Commission also found that there were significant barriers to entry into the production and supply of salmon feed, including the need for a "proven track record", and a significant minimum efficient scale of production. Furthermore, there was already excess production capacity for salmon feed within the UK (with the majority of the excess capacity being held by the merged entity).[7]

Against this background, the Commission concluded that:

". . . Because of the enlarged customer base to which [Nutreco's feed business] would have access following the merger, its position would be strengthened. This would enable it to enjoy significant economies of scale through spreading its overhead costs over a greater volume of production . . . We expect the competitive position of [competing feed suppliers] to be weakened as a result . . .

[Nutreco] might be expected to take advantage of its relative economies in the feed market to undercut [its rivals]. The loss of [the parties] as customers would be expected to push up [its rivals'] relative costs to the extent that their effectiveness as competitors would be seriously diminished . . . In the longer run, we would expect that the feed market would become less competitive and prices would rise.

The merger would discourage new entry either by existing feed importers setting up a base in the UK, or by salmon farmers or other new entrants. As a result of the enhanced position of Nutreco, we expect that the feed market would become less competitive and that feed prices would rise. We would expect Nutreco to charge different customers different prices for similar products and levels of service and that as a result the costs of some salmon farmers would rise. Finally, we expect that, as the cost base for salmon farmers rose, smaller or financially weaker farmers would become more dependent on Nutreco, for example through subcontracting their production or by receiving extended credit. Some would leave the industry. All this would further increase Nutreco's market power."[8]

An interesting case in relation to vertical effects related to the merger between Carl Zeiss Jena GmbH and Bio-Rad Laboratories Inc. In that report, the Commission noted that apart from Bio-Rad all the main suppliers provided their own microscope stands, with the bulk of these being supplied by Nikon. These stands could also be purchased separately.[9]

---

[6] Cited above, para.6.021, n.94, at paras 1.1–1.3,1.5 and 1.8.
[7] Cited above, para.6.021, n.94, at paras 1.7–1.8 and 2.11.
[8] Cited above, para.6.021, n.94, at paras 2.112–2.113 and 2.123. However, the exit of Nutreco's customers does not increase its market power as a feed supplier, and the Commission held that there was an EEA market in farmed salmon so that a higher share of Scottish farmed salmon for Nutreco may not confer substantial market power.
[9] Cited above, para.6.118, n.36, at para.2.31.

The Commission noted that if Zeiss were to supply only its own microscope stands as part of its systems, this would affect other suppliers of stands, particularly Nikon. Nevertheless, the Commission concluded that:

"However, in our view any such effect would be felt primarily in the supply of microscope stands rather than in the markets for confocal and multi-photon systems. Given the strength of Nikon as a supplier of microscope stands, we consider this effect to be marginal. Also, Nikon would still be able to compete to supply confocal systems using its own microscope stands as part of integrated systems."[10]

Market "tipping"

The potential foreclosure effects of vertical mergers may be strengthened in circumstances where market "tipping" is possible. The Commission's guidelines describe markets prone to tipping as follows:

6.167

"Certain markets are characterised by network effects. Such effects arise when the value of a product to a customer increases with the number of other customers consuming the same good. As a result, incumbents with an existing customer base have an automatic advantage over entrants. Markets characterised by network effects may be prone to 'tipping'. That is, as one firm, or technology, gains an advantage in the market, in effect the balance of power in the market 'tips' in its direction leaving it as the prevalent firm, or technology."[11]

In these markets, competition takes place *for* the market as opposed to *within* the market, and vertical mergers provide an effective means for upstream firms to secure a customer base by acquiring a downstream firm.

Access to confidential information

A further issue potentially raised by vertical integration is whether one of the merging firms has access to, confidential information which would enable the other firm to gain a competitive advantage over its rivals. For example, the upstream firm may be aware that supplies of an essential raw material may become limited at some point, and this would enable the downstream firm to purchase additional supplies in advance. Other purchasers of the raw material would not have access to similar information and would not be able to make any such provision. Alternatively, a vertical merger may enable the merged company to gain confidential information about its upstream or downstream rivals' businesses.

6.168

Access to confidential information about rivals' businesses was a particular concern in the Commission's inquiry into the acquisition by Thomas Cook of Interpayment Services.[12] Both Thomas Cook and Interpayment Services were major issuers of travellers cheques, together accounting for 49 per cent in the

---

[10] Cited above, para.6.118, n.36, at para.5.86.
[11] Cited above, para.6.001, n.1, at para.3.13.
[12] *Thomas Cook Group Limited/Interpayment Services Limited*, Cm. 2789 (March 1995).

UK versus American Express' 40 per cent.[13] However, the Commission concluded that for the majority of sales agents—banks and building societies—there would continue to be vigorous competition between American Express and Thomas Cook.[14]

Nevertheless, the Commission had other concerns as Thomas Cook was also active in the travel agency business. Competitors to Thomas Cook's retail operations (*i.e.* travel agencies and bureaux de change) had expressed fears that in supplying Thomas Cook's travellers cheques, information about their clients or the state of their businesses might be passed to Thomas Cook's retail business. One major travel business had described the situation as akin to handing over its customer list to a close competitor. The Commission observed that if at any time certain sales agents became unwilling to do business with Thomas Cook due to concerns over the information they would need to supply, this would have the effect of reducing competition amongst travellers cheque issuers. They would then effectively have a choice between sourcing travellers cheques from American Express (with a UK share of 40 per cent) or Citicorp (with 1 per cent), potentially affording American Express scope to worsen its terms of supply.[15] The Commission recommended certain safeguards including, *inter alia*, maintaining Interpayment Services Limited as the sole issuer's name on *VISA* cheques designed to prevent customer information being passed to Thomas Cook's retail business.[16]

"Toe-hold" effects in auction markets

6.169 Vertical integration might also lead to a substantial lessening of competition in circumstances where the upstream merging company participates in auctions for the purchase of key inputs, and where the downstream merging company supplies such inputs via the auction. This is particularly the case where factors such as access to confidential information can improve yet further the position of the bidder in such an auction.

These factors were an important consideration in the context of BSkyB's proposed acquisition of Manchester United.[17] In that case, the Commission had found that BSkyB had market power in the sports premium channel market. It also had advantages from being the incumbent broadcaster of Premier League football. The Commission considered that both of these factors would put BSkyB in a strong position in any future auction to obtain Premier League TV rights. One of the issues the Commission had to consider was whether the proposed acquisition of Manchester United would give BSkyB further significant advantages in the competition for rights, under the existing rights selling arrangements, and assuming that no other broadcasters were to hold interests in Premier League clubs.

---

[13] Cited above, para.6.168, n.12, at para.1.2.
[14] Cited above, para.6.168, n.12, at para.2.46.
[15] Cited above, para.6.168, n.12, at paras 2.51, 2.55–2.57 and 2.70.
[16] Cited above, para.6.168, n.12, at para.2.79. It might have been expected that Thomas Cook would have put such measures in place itself so as to avoid losing market share to American Express if this were a serious concern with many customers.
[17] *British Sky Broadcasting Group plc/Manchester United PLC*, Cm. 4305 (April 1999), at paras 1.5–1.8.

The Commission observed that auction theory predicts that when a bidder in an auction has an ownership stake in the asset being sold, even if only a small stake, it will be more likely to win the auction than competitors without such a "toehold."[18] There are two reasons for this effect:

(i)   first, because part of the value of any bid will return to the bidder with the ownership stake[19]; and

(ii)   second, this small initial advantage may be multiplied by the operation of the so-called "winner's curse". This occurs when there is uncertainty about the value of an asset. Bidders then face the risk of paying too much for it. In an auction in which one bidder has an ownership stake in the asset, all the other bidders will know that it can afford to pay a little more for the asset than they can (for the reason set out above). Therefore if a bidder without an ownership stake wins the auction, it may find that it has paid more for the asset than it is worth to it. The theory suggests that the existence of the winner's curse will make bidders without an ownership stake more cautious in their bidding, with the result that the bidder with the ownership stake is more likely to win the auction than any other bidder and the price paid for the asset is likely to be lower than it would be in the absence of a bidder with an ownership stake. The winner's curse operates particularly strongly in an ascending price auction (i.e. where prices are bid up) when each bidder can observe the behaviour of others in the auction process.

In the case of *Manchester United/BSkyB*, the Commission did not consider that the toe-hold effects described above would, alone, give BSkyB a major advantage over competing broadcasters.[20] In particular, the auction process could be designed such that the importance of toe-hold effects would be minimised and, furthermore, previous rights-selling processes had revealed that the bids made by broadcasters were not identical as regards their terms and conditions, such that it was not possible to readily compare different bids on the basis of price.[21]

However, the Commission expected BSkyB to gain some benefits in the overall rights-selling process from its ownership of Manchester United, particularly since it would gain access to confidential information concerning the bidding process that was not available to other broadcasters, and because

6.170

---

[18] Cited above, para.6.169, n.17, at paras 2.106–2.117.

[19] For example, if a bidder owns 5 per cent of an asset and bids £100 million for that asset, it will receive its share of the bid price as an owner (£5 million) so that the net cost of its bid would be only £95 million. However, to some extent, this advantage may be negated by the opportunity cost of winning the auction—i.e. the share of proceeds foregone by the downstream firm had another, non-vertically integrated bidder won the auction. To give the example presented by the Commission, if Bidder A had a toehold of 5 per cent, then if its bid of £100 million won, it would gain back proceeds of £5 million. But if, instead, Bidder B had won the auction with a bid of £95 million, then the vertically integrated Bidder A would have received a 5 per cent share of that £95 million (i.e. £4.75 million). When the opportunity cost of winning is taken into account, the net gain from winning (£0.25m) is smaller than would first appear. Cited above, para.6.169, n.26, at para.2.112.

[20] Cited above, para.6.169, n.17, at para.2.117.

[21] Cited above, para.6.169, n.17, at para.2.115.

Manchester United (as a powerful club in terms of its financial performance, fan base, and sporting successes) would enjoy an influential position during the rights-selling process. This, together with the toe-hold effects BSkyB would enjoy, and "fall-back" strategies available to BSkyB (such as using its ownership of Manchester United to secure it an opportunity to outbid any winning bid by another broadcaster) would, cumulatively, be expected to improve BSkyB's chances of securing the Premier League rights. In turn, this could make other broadcasters more cautious in their bidding behaviour, perhaps deterring others from bidding at all (given the costs involved in preparing bids), thus reinforcing further BSkyB's advantages. The Commission considered that as a result, there was likely to be less competition for Premier League rights, leading to less choice for the Premier League of alternative broadcasting packages, and less scope for innovation in the broadcasting of Premier League football, any or all of which might be expected to operate against the public interest.[22]

The Commission also concluded that since the merger might be expected to reduce the chances of anyone other than BSkyB winning the Premier League rights in the foreseeable future, the barriers to entry to the sports channel market may be expected to be even greater as result of the merger. In turn, reduced opportunities for entry would mean that consumers were less likely to be given a choice between different sports packages. The Commission therefore concluded that the foreclosure of entry to the sports premium channel market would have the additional adverse effect of reducing the pressure to innovate and to offer new choices to consumers.[23]

Price discrimination

6.171 A further potential concern with vertical integration is that it may facilitate price discrimination and possibly output reduction. This was a concern in the Commission's inquiry into the supply of milk in 1999.[24] Milk Marque was responsible for around 50 per cent of raw milk supplies in Great Britain, and its customers included a variety of different dairy processors, which purchased raw milk via an auction system and had different requirements for their raw milk supplies. For example, fresh liquid milk processors required reliable and broadly stable supplies of raw milk, and were prepared to pay higher prices for such supplies. In contrast, processors of less perishable dairy products (such as cheese and skimmed milk powder) were able to cope with more fluctuating raw milk supplies and were only prepared to pay lower prices than those paid by fresh liquid milk processors, since the former were competing downstream in internationally traded commodity markets.[25]

The Commission found that Milk Marque had been able to price discriminate and to raise the average price of raw milk above competitive levels by engaging in a variety of practices. These included (*inter alia*):

---

[22] Cited above, para.6.169, n.17, at paras 2.140–2.144.
[23] Cited above, para.6.169, n.17, at paras 2.172–2.177.
[24] Cited above, para.6.163, n.88.
[25] Cited above, para.6.163, n.88, at paras 1.3 and 2.34–2.36.

(i)   altering the terms and conditions of its contracts to a greater degree than was justified;

(ii)   widening the price differentials between its different contract types;

(iii) forcing smaller processor customers to pay higher average prices for their milk than Milk Marque's larger customers to an unjustified extent;

(iv)   imposing restrictions on the use of milk supplied through its lowest-priced contracts, therefore obliging some processors to purchase milk at higher prices than they would otherwise have had to pay; and

(v)   entering into individually negotiated contracts with certain large processors on terms that were not disclosed to the remainder of its customers.[26]

In order to facilitate this price discrimination, Milk Marque had had to ensure that it would not be easy for processors to engage in secondary trading of raw milk, for example by purchasing raw milk under the cheaper contracts and on-selling the milk to those customers prepared to pay higher prices for milk (such as the fresh liquid milk processors). Milk Marque therefore adopted strategies which would inhibit secondary trading in milk between processors, and would reduce overall milk supplies. For example, it had arranged for certain volumes of raw milk to be contract processed outside the market in Great Britain. In doing so, Milk Marque had been able to constrain the volumes of milk on offer to its usual customers in the face of largely unchanged demand, thereby raising the marginal price of milk.[27]

In addition, Milk Marque owned two cheese making companies at the time of the inquiry. At that time, the two businesses consumed only small volumes of raw milk, such that the Commission did not find that Milk Marque was exploiting its monopoly position in respect of its existing vertically integrated processing activities. However, Milk Marque had expressed an intention to materially increase its vertically integrated processing capacity, having stated that there was no reason why it could not be processing 15 per cent of its daily raw milk throughput by the end of 2000, and 50 per cent a few years later. This significant scaling-up of vertically integrated processing capacity was expected by the Commission to operate against the public interest.[28]

These strategies had the effect of reducing supplies of raw milk, particularly at the low-end of the market where milk supplies would otherwise be available at low prices to customers with less stringent supply requirements (such as processors of internationally traded commodity products), thus removing arbitrage opportunities for processors.

---

[26] Cited above, para.6.163, n.88, at para.1.9.
[27] Cited above, para.6.163, n.88, at paras 2.207–2.220.
[28] Cited above, para.6.163, n.88, at paras 2.205–2.206.

Case studies

Centrica/Dynegy

6.172 The Competition Commission's inquiry into the acquisition by Centrica of certain assets of Dynegy (in particular, the "Rough" gas storage facility) involved the consideration of a number of vertical issues.[29] Centrica operated at both the retail and wholesale supply levels of the gas market in Great Britain. Centrica's share of the overall supply of gas to end-users in total was 36 per cent, including 20 per cent of supplies to non-domestic customers and 63 per cent of supplies to domestic customers.[30] In terms of maximum daily flexibility, Centrica's share would increase from 24 per cent to 34 per cent (attributing the whole of Rough to Centrica). Taking capacity over the December–March period would raise Centrica's share from 34 per cent to 46 per cent.[31] Centrica's downstream competitors in the retail sales of gas were not generally vertically integrated into gas storage (although most were involved in upstream electricity markets).

The Commission found that as a result of the transaction, Centrica could be expected[32]:

(a) "to discriminate between customers in giving access to capacity at Rough" (*i.e.* between its own downstream retail operations and those of third parties);

(b) "to use to its advantage sensitive information gained from the operation of Rough" to its advantage at the downstream (retail) level of the gas supply market;

(c) "to withhold information about the operation of Rough" from third party competitors;

(d) "to be less innovative in marketing Rough products than another owner" to the detriment of its downstream competitors; and

(e) "to invest less in expanding Rough's capacity than another owner", again, to the detriment of its downstream competitors.[33]

The Commission then said that it believed that the merger would increase the uncertainty faced by other (downstream) industry participants leading to a likely reduction in entry into the gas storage, trading and supply markets, a reduction in the willingness of other downstream operators to compete vigorously with Centrica, and a distortion in investment in storage.

---

[29] *Centrica plc and Dynegy Storage Ltd/Dynegy Onshore Processing UK Ltd*, Cm. 5885 (August 2003).

[30] Cited above, para.6.172, n.29, at paras 2.69–2.72.

[31] Cited above, para.6.172, n.29, para.2.54. Gas suppliers require flexibility in their supplies to meet variations in gas demand and supplies, with flexibility being provided by storage facilities, variations in gas production, as inter-connector, and customers' supplies being interrupted.

[32] The Commission noted that it interpreted the word "expected" "as meaning a more than 50 per cent likelihood of something happening", cited above, para.6.172, n.29, para. 2.86(c).

[33] Cited above, para.6.172, n.29, para.2.171.

According to the Commission, all of these consequences would have the effect of weakening competition in gas supply markets (with the likely consequence of higher prices than in the absence of the merger) and lessening innovation and investment at Rough.[34] Despite the range of adverse effects identified, the Commission proposed that they could be remedied by the adoption of a broad range of undertakings.[35]

The profitability of Centrica withholding flexible gas supplies from the market was also considered by the Commission, with flexibility being provided by gas storage, variations in UK gas production (known as beach swing), supplies via inter-connectors and interruptible gas supply contracts. In this regard, in particular, it considered a detailed study submitted on behalf of Centrica which concluded that it would not be profitable for Centrica to withhold supplies of flexible gas from the market at times of high demand in order to increase the price of gas. However, the conclusions of this study were questioned by the Commission and the Office of Gas and Electricity Markets ("OFGEM"). The Commission made its own (simpler) projections as to the profitability for Centrica of withholding gas supplies which concluded that the profitability of withholding gas supplies was highly sensitive to assumptions about domestic pass-through (*i.e.* the extent to which higher prices to downstream gas retailers would be passed on to final customers). OFGEM's comments highlighted the limitations of Centrica's study, pointing out a number of significant simplifications that could have impacted on the final results.[36] In the light of these issues, and various other complicating industry factors, the Commission concluded that it did not have a sufficient basis for concluding that Centrica might be expected to withhold capacity in order to increase wholesale gas prices.[37]

6.173

BUPA/CHG

Another example of the vertical aspects of a merger raising competition issues is provided by the Commission's inquiry into the proposed merger between BUPA and CHG.[38] BUPA was the largest provider of Private Medical Insurance ("PMI"—with a market share of around 40 per cent by value) and the second largest provider of Private Medical Services ("PMS") in the UK. CHG was the fourth largest provider of PMS, but did not provide PMI.[39] Private medical insurers rely on the services of PMS providers in order to be able to provide a service to their clients. BUPA was, by far, the largest vertically integrated firm in the supply of PMS and PMI, and the merger would have led to BUPA owning two of the top four national PMS providers.

6.174

---

[34] Cited above, para.6.172, n.29, paras 2.171 and 2.172.
[35] Cited above, para.6.172, n.29, para.2.225.
[36] Cited above, para.6.172, n.29, paras 5.71 to 5.81, paras 8.36 to 8.43 and Apps 5.5, 5.6 and 5.7.
[37] Cited above, para.6.172, n.29, paras 2.85 to 2.125, but see para.6.172, n.32 above, as to the Commission's interpretation of the word "expected".
[38] *British United Provident Association Limited/Community Hospitals Group plc; British United Provident Association Limited/Salomon International LLC/Community Hospitals Group plc; and Salomon International LLC/Community Hospitals Group plc*, Cm. 5003 (December 2000).
[39] Cited above, para.6.174, n.38, at para.2.57 and Table 2.1.

In addition to the horizontal issues identified by the Commission in the PMS market,[40] the Commission also highlighted a range of vertical competition concerns with the merger. This was despite the fact that BUPA told the Commission that it operated its PMI and PMS interests as two entirely separate businesses operating "at arm's length". However, the Commission disregarded this, quoting the MMC monopoly report on Milk which had commented that "wherever the commercial interests of a company conflict with the demands of arm's length trading, there is a strong likelihood that the commercial interests will prevail."[41]

The Commission concluded that the strengthening of BUPA's PMS offering also strengthened its (already strong) position on the PMI market, giving it a "unique position among PMI and PMS providers."[42] In particular, it said that the main effects would be:

(a)   to increase BUPA PMS's bargaining power *vis-à-vis* other PMI providers, leading to higher prices to other PMI providers (and thereby creating pressures for higher prices generally in the PMI market (including those offered by BUPA PMI);

(b)   to increase BUPA PMI's bargaining power *vis-à-vis* PMS providers, leading to lower prices for BUPA PMI than other PMI providers from these PMS providers and (again) pressures on other PMI providers to increase prices; and

(c)   a reduction in the scope for other PMS providers to be included in BUPA PMI's network of PMS providers.

BUPA had argued that the lower prices it may be able to secure from other PMS providers would be passed on in the PMI market due to the competitive nature of that market. However, the Commission observed that BUPA PMI's forecasts required premiums to rise in order for them to be achieved (based on BUPA PMI's predicted numbers of subscribers).[43]

BA/CityFlyer Express

6.175   Another example is the Commission's analysis of the proposed merger between British Airways and CityFlyer Express. CityFlyer (which operated out of Gatwick airport) was a small competitor of BA (in relation to seven of its routes operating out of Heathrow airport), although CityFlyer did not compete with BA on any of its Gatwick based flights. The Commission did not find any adverse effects related to the loss of competition on those routes as a result of the transaction. However, the Commission did have concerns about BA's acquisition of CityFlyer's slots at Gatwick airport. CityFlyer had around 12 per cent of take-off and landing slots at Gatwick airport, compared with BA's 41 per cent (no other airline having more than 4 per cent).[44] In this connection, the Commission concluded that BA's acquisition of CityFlyer's slots (and ground services) would:

---

[40] Cited above, para.6.174, n.38, for example, para.2.174.
[41] Cited above, para.6.174, n.38, para.2.176. The Commission's concerns in this regard are considered further at paras 2.155 to 2.161.
[42] Cited above, para.6.174, n.38, paras 2.177 and 2.178.
[43] Cited above, para.6.174, n.38, para.2.180.
[44] *British Airways PLC/CityFlyer Express Limited*, Cm. 4346 (July 1999), at Table 2.2.

(i) "give it extra flexibility that would strengthen further its competitive position relative to other airlines." The Commission found that the increase in the number and variety of slots available to BA would amount to a limited enhancement of BA's ability to respond more quickly to new opportunities or competitive threats than other airlines by reallocating its slots between this increased number of routes. Furthermore, the Commission stated that "in circumstances where slots are difficult to obtain and there is such a large gap between the size of BA's slot portfolio and that of the next largest competitor (. . .), it is in our view likely that the erosion of BA's advantage by its competitors will be even more difficult as a result of the merger and we would expect this to lead ultimately to a loss of effective competition"[45]; and

(ii) foreclose "the competition that other airlines could provide using CityFlyer's slots." In this regard, the Commission observed that potential competition for BA at Gatwick was already restricted by slot constraints, and would be further restrained if BA were to take control over CityFlyer's slots, in particular, as regards time-sensitive passengers who may not be able to benefit from competition from low-cost airlines operating from other London airports.[46]

The Commission therefore concluded that the merger "may be expected to operate against the public interest in that there would be a reduction of potential competition for BA which might be expected to lead ultimately to higher prices and a poorer quality of service than would otherwise be the case."[47]

The risk of co-ordinated effects

The assessment of oligopolistic co-ordination is considered in detail in paras 6.128 to 6.160, in the context of horizontal mergers. One way in which vertical integration might facilitate co-ordination is if it leads to a firm obtaining access to information about upstream and downstream prices which it would not otherwise have had, and this may increase market transparency and therefore the scope for tacit co-ordination. **6.176**

The OFT's guidelines state that:

"In rare cases, vertical integration may facilitate collusion by increasing market transparency between firms. Such concerns may arise, for example, where vertical integration affords the merged entity better knowledge of selling prices in another market, which facilitates tacit collusion in that market."[48]

---

[45] Cited above, para.6.175, n.44, at para.2.192.
[46] Cited above, para.6.175, n.44, para.2.193.
[47] Cited above, para.6.175, n.44, para. 2.197.
[48] Cited above, para.6.001, n.1, at para.5.5. Similarly, the Commission's guidelines state that:
  "Vertical mergers may change the conditions of competition such that coordinated effects are more likely. For example, wholesale prices in upstream markets tend to be less transparent than retail prices. When manufacturers are vertically integrated with retailers, they are more likely to be informed about the final prices and thus coordinated effects may be more likely to occur." (cited above, para.6.001, n.1, at para.3.67.)

This theoretical possibility needs to be assessed with reference to a number of specific points. First, does vertical integration increase transparency as a matter of fact? As noted above in para.6.142, the existence of vertical integration can also undermine the sustainability of collusion by hindering market transparency. This is because competitors of vertically integrated firms will be able to observe only the final product price and not any internal transfer price which might be lower than the tacitly "agreed" price for the semi-finished product. In addition, the vertically related firm might not buy any or much of its requirements from competing suppliers, and thus gain little knowledge of their prices. Moreover, whilst a supply relationship with competing suppliers might yield some knowledge of their prices, this would not reveal secret discounting by these suppliers to other customers.

Secondly, vertical integration might well impede co-ordination in other ways, such as by permitting various efficiencies to be achieved (thus creating a downward pressure on prices or improving quality), and/or otherwise lead to greater asymmetries in cost structures.[49]

Thirdly, there are a myriad of other factors which influence the assessment of co-ordinated effects. These are considered in detail in paras 6.128 to 6.160, above.

Assessing the effects of conglomerate mergers

Overview

6.177   The Commission's and OFT's guidelines agree that only in a small number of instances will substantive issues arise in relation to conglomerate mergers.[50] However, neither the OFT's nor the Commission's guidelines provide a clear definition of conglomerate mergers. Both indicate that conglomerate mergers refer to mergers between firms active in different markets, and these sections of the guidelines do not refer to vertical mergers. However, the two different guidelines raise a number of quite different competition issues in relation to conglomerate mergers.

---

[49] The marginal costs of vertically integrated firms might well be materially lower than those of non-integrated firms, because the prices paid for raw materials or distribution to its suppliers by a non-integrated firm will include a mark-up on the marginal costs of supply. This is in fact one of the rationales for vertical restraints and vertical mergers. More generally, one fundamental problem faced by manufacturers discussed by the OFT research paper on Vertical Restraints and Competition Policy is that for each additional unit sold by the retailer by it cutting its prices or through other demand-boosting activities (e.g. advertising, pre-sale advice, etc.), the manufacturer's profit increases by the difference between its marginal cost of production and the wholesale price (cited above, para.6.163, n.89). However, other things being equal, retailers will not take these beneficial effects on the manufacturer into account, with the result that the retailer will set its retail prices too high and engage in too little of the demand boosting activities from the manufacturer's perspective. For example, Spengler (1950) observes that the successive addition of margins by the manufacturer and the retailer ("double marginalisation") leads to retail prices being set at too high a level, and output being set at too low a level, than would maximise their joint profits. This would also be to the detriment of customers.

[50] OFT guidelines, cited above, para.6.001, n.1, at para.6.1; and Commission guidelines, cited above, para.6.001, n.1, at para.3.60.

The OFT's guidelines make clear that mergers involving potential competitors (*e.g.* suppliers of the same products which are active in other geographic markets) are regarded as horizontal mergers.[51]

The Commission's guidelines state that one example of a conglomerate merger which may raise competition issues involves suppliers of substitutes:

"[An] example of where a conglomerate merger might raise competition concerns is where it involves a merger of two firms operating in what, on the basis of the SSNIP test considered at competitive price levels, are separate markets but which are nonetheless the closest substitutes to each other. Each may then act as a constraint on the extent to which the other raises prices. If so, a merger would permit a further increase in prices. This is one reason why it is sometimes necessary to consider the SSNIP test at existing prices in a merger."[52]

A different section of the Commission's guidelines indicate that in such relevant circumstances the relevant market would be defined using current rather than competitive price levels. On this basis, the market may be defined to include both the firms in question (*i.e.* it would be a horizontal merger and assessed as such).[53] The Commission's intention to use competitive price levels in defining markets is addressed in paras 6.150 to 6.151.

The OFT's guidelines, however, refer to conglomerate mergers which **6.178** increase multi-market contact between firms as possibly facilitating co-ordination[54] if the markets are otherwise susceptible to co-ordination. As discussed in para.6.148, this can be one factor amongst many which contributes to the sustainability of tacit co-ordination, with the key concern being that such a conglomerate merger may render co-ordination sustainable in additional markets (*i.e.* where there is not presently co-ordination). Without compelling factual evidence that this is a likelihood on the specific facts of a case (*e.g.* that prices are higher or have increased due to multi-market conduct), it may be strongly argued that this is too speculative a concern on its own to sustain a finding that a substantial lessening of competition may be expected.

The OFT's guidelines also refer to conglomerate mergers as possibly increasing the feasibility of predation. The mechanism by which this is achieved is not described. The usual explanation advanced is that the profitability of predatory behaviour (involving the deliberate sacrifice of profits with no other business rationale than reducing competition) would be increased if it enables the predator to deter entry by enabling it to develop a reputation for such behaviour both in the market in question and in other markets where it is active. Again, without compelling factual evidence in a particular case, this seems a rather speculative concern.

---

[51] See n.30 on p.40 of the OFT's guidelines, cited above, para.6.001, n.1. In this regard, it should be noted that in certain markets buyers may be viable potential entrants (see para.6.075, above), as many suppliers in other related markets.

[52] Cited above, para.6.001, n.1, at para.3.72.

[53] Commission guidelines, cited above, para.6.001, n.1, at para.2.10, and the boxed example below para.2.10.

[54] The Commission's guidelines make no reference at all to multi-market contact as a factor influencing coordination.

Both sets of guidelines refer to bundling, tying and portfolio effects as potentially raising competition concerns. In this regard, in February 2003, the DTI published a paper covering the issues raised by bundling, tying and portfolio effects,[55] which provides a useful review of the issues.

In his advice on the acquisition by SMG of a 29.5 per cent shareholding of Scottish Radio Holdings, the Director General explained that:

> "Portfolio power is said to exist when the market power derived from a combined portfolio of brands ... exceeds the sum of its parts so that power could be created or strengthened over and above the consequences of any increase in market share in individual markets. Such power could potentially be increased where: (1) the firm's offerings are more attractive because they offer a wider range of products; (2) economies of scale and scope are realised; (3) there is greater potential for tying products; and (4) the threat of refusal to supply is more potent."[56]

These four factors provide a basis for assessing the issues. A further factor may be added as well, which is the incentive of a merged firm of two suppliers of complementary goods to set lower prices.

Improved product offering and lower costs

6.179   The Commission's guidelines indicate that:

> "The concept of portfolio power is that a firm may be able to exercise more market power from owning a range of products in separate markets than it could from each of the markets separately. Such instances are likely to arise only when customers have a strong incentive to purchase from a single source rather than from many suppliers."[57]

The Commission's guidelines give the example of a complex product with a need for on-going service, and where contracts are incomplete (e.g. they do not cover every eventuality as to who is responsible for the repair

---

[55] DTI Economics Paper Number 1 *"Bundling, Tying, and Portfolio Effects"* (February 2003), Professor Barry Nalebuff, Yale University, assisted by Charles River Associates. This section does not seek to summarise all of the issues discussed in the DTI paper, but rather it refers to some of its main conclusions. The DTI paper states that "Bundling is the practice of selling two (or more) products together; the products may be available only as a bundle or, if available separately, are offered at a discount relative to their individual prices." (See s.1.1 of the DTI paper.) Meanwhile, "Tying is the practice of requiring the purchaser of one product to also purchase a second product" (*i.e.* there would be a refusal to supply one product separately from another) (see s.1.1 of the DTI paper.) The assessment of conglomerate mergers has been actively debated, particularly in two important EC cases namely *Tetra Laval/Sidel* (cited above, para.6.002, n.13) and *GE/Honeywell* (Case COMP/M.2220 General *Electric/Honeywell*, Commission's decision of July 3, 2001, (2004) O.J. L48/1, on appeal to the European Court of First Instance with judgment pending at the time of writing). There are many commentaries on these cases, with Bishop and Walker having a good description of the issues (cited above, para.6.001, n.2, at pp.293–296). Motta has a good description of the broader range of horizontal, vertical and conglomerate issues raised in GE/Honeywell (cited above, para.6.001, n.2, at pp.379–391).

[56] Director General's advice of June 21, 2001, *The completed acquisition by SMG plc of 29.5% shareholding of Scottish Radio Holdings plc.*

[57] Cited above, para.6.001, n.1, at para.3.69.

of the product).[58] In such circumstances, it is easy to envisage that customers may expect preferential treatment if they buy a range of products. For example, the DTI paper considers the example of a printer and a computer which do not work together correctly. If the products are purchased from one supplier, then such an issue could be addressed by contacting that single supplier, without disputes between suppliers at the customer's expense as to who is responsible for the fault. There could also be quality improvements in the sense that, for example, the printers and the computer could be configured to interface in an optimal way. This could make the products more appealing to the customers.[59]

The OFT guidelines give another example of a customer benefit from purchasing a range of products from one supplier in that it can reduce customers' transaction costs.[60] For example, with a single supplier the customer can arrange a single contract, a single delivery, and a single invoice for the range of products.

There may also be broader economies of scale and scope which lower costs. For example, there may also be economies of scale and scope as regards raw material purchasing (if the different products are made using some common materials), production (if there are some commonalities in production), marketing and advertising (for example, in jointly promoting certain products), and distribution (costs savings may be achieved in delivering a greater volume of a range of products to customers' premises).

All of these factors may be described as pro-competitive, and the possibility that competition may be enhanced is noted by the Commission. However, the Commission adds that customers' preference for buying from a single supplier: **6.180**

> ". . . may, in some circumstances, enhance competition, but in others may lessen it, for example if it inhibits effective competition from others or progressively leads to a small number of multi-product firms, each operating in a number of highly concentrated markets."[61]

It is important to appreciate that the above line of argument would also apply to any economy of scale and scope derived from a merger—including those arising in the context of a horizontal or vertical merger, notwithstanding the fact that the Commission's guidelines make no reference to such "detriments" from horizontal or vertical mergers. It should also be noted that the concerns have been expressed in published reports about merged firms achieving such efficiencies.

For example, in the context of the proposed merger between Capital Radio plc and Virgin Radio Holdings Limited, the MMC expressed concerns about Capital's plans to increase Virgin's supply of advertising (which would be expected to depress prices) and to make Virgin a more effective competitor:

---

[58] Cited above, para.6.001, n.1, at para.3.70.
[59] Cited above, para.6.178, n.55, at p.32.
[60] Cited above, para.6.001, n.1, at para.6.3.
[61] Cited above, para.6.001, n.1, at para.3.70.

"We look first at the effect of the proposed merger on the supply of radio advertising in London, and the ability of other stations to compete for business. Capital has proposed that following the merger the maximum amount of London-specific advertising time available on Virgin FM will increase from two to nine minutes an hour. It also plans to stop the daytime simulcasting of Virgin AM and Virgin FM and to reprogramme the output of Virgin FM to make it more relevant to the London audience. These actions will have the effect of making Virgin FM a much more focused competitor in the London market than it is at the moment. Given that Capital currently enjoys a very substantial share of the London market (60.9 per cent for 1996 and 58.1 per cent for the first half of 1997) and that post-merger it is seeking to grow Virgin FM's share vigorously, we can well understand the concerns of the smaller stations. Advertising revenue is the lifeblood of a station and if the merger reduces the ability of the smaller stations to compete for revenue, then this would weaken them."[62]

6.181   The DTI paper observes that:

"It is possible to argue that such cost savings or quality improvements can create an antitrust issue. A firm might gain a large advantage over its rivals by putting such a package together, and this might well force rivals out of the market. However, we reject such arguments. The idea that cost savings or quality improvements should lead to antitrust problems—the efficiency offence argument—runs counter to basic economics. This is no different from saying that a firm should not invest in cost-saving technology or quality improvement. Antitrust policy should not be used to shackle competition."[63]

Motta acknowledges that it is theoretically possible that two merging firms might have such important cost savings or demand efficiencies that rivals would be unable to compete on an equal footing with them, and that in the future the exit of these rivals might lead to higher prices. However, if the efficiencies are sufficiently strong to force rivals to exit, then consumers could still be better off after the merger, even if some rivals are forced to exit (indeed the closure of higher cost rivals might increase efficiency by lowering total industry costs and depressing prices). Moreover, rivals can be expected to react to maintain their competitiveness through a combination of efficiency drives, mergers, or co-operation agreements. Finally, greater weight should be given to the current immediate benefits of the merger than to the future detriments, not just because the latter may be speculative or uncertain, but also because each £1 of current benefits is more valuable to customers than discounted future benefits.[64]

---

[62] Cited above, para.6.022, n.98, at para.2.103.
[63] Cited above, para.6.178, n.55, at s.4.3.1 at p.33.
[64] Cited above, para.6.001, n.2, at pp.261–263, 275–276, and 388–89. For example, if a discount rate of 10 per cent is applied, a benefit of £1 in (say) three years time would have a present value of about £0.75 (1/1.13). See further the OFT Economic Discussion paper on "Assessing profitability in competition policy analysis" which describes further the importance of discounted cashflows (cited above, n.90 at para.6.076).

Incentives to set lower prices

The Commission's guidelines further observe that a: 6.182

"... conglomerate merger might also involve the bringing together of products that are complements. In general, the merger should then increase the incentive to lower prices."[65]

Complements are products whose sales increase when the price of the other complementary good falls. A simple example given by Cournot is copper and zinc which are used to produce brass, but there are a wide range of other examples such as hardware and software. The simple intuition behind the result that a merger of suppliers of complements can create incentives for them to depress prices of a "bundle" combining both products is given very succinctly in the DTI paper. It states that the customer is interested only in the combined price of the two complementary products, and bases his purchasing decision on this combined price. However, two independent suppliers of complementary products take into account only the impact of a price increase on their own sales, not the adverse effects of such an increase on the sales of complementary products.[66]

Nevertheless, the profitability of price cuts for the merged entity become ambiguous if the merged firm faces rivals which also cut their prices, since rivals' price cutting responses will reduce the profitability of the price cuts, offsetting to some degree the market expansion effect of lower prices. The DTI paper also envisages that there may be circumstances in which such conduct may have predation-type effects on rivals.[67]

As regards the incentives of a merged supplier of complementary products to set lower prices, the Commission's guidelines state that:

"This is likely to be advantageous to competition, provided that it does not threaten to drive out existing firms or raise entry barriers to such an extent that long-term competition is substantially reduced. In addition, such a merger might increase the possibility of tying or bundling, which might, in some instances, result in competition concerns, for instance, if it is difficult for competitors, or potential entrants, to offer competing bundles."[68]

In this regard, the DTI paper outlines a detailed test advocated by Shapiro and the US Department of Justice which focuses on whether there

---

[65] Cited above, para.6.001, n.1, at para.3.71.
[66] Double marginalisation may occur at a vertical level where a manufacturer has an element of market power in that its product prices exceed marginal cost, and the product is then sold by a wholesaler or retailer who applies a further mark-up to the manufacturer's (already inflated) price. Double marginalisation may also occur at a horizontal level, where two complementary products are sold by two separate firms. When each firm sets prices, it does not take into account the impact that its own price has on sales of the other firm's product. If, instead, the two products were to be sold as a bundle, the bundle price could be set at less than the sum of the individual prices, and additional custom might be generated as a result (through market expansion and/or the gain of market share from rivals).
[67] See ss.4.3.2.2 and 4.4.1 of the DTI paper, cited above, para.6.178, n.58.
[68] Cited above, para.6.001, n.1, at para.3.71.

is an incentive to bundle, the immediate gains to consumers, the impact on competitors, how long lower prices can be expected to last, and what harm is expected if rivals exit.[69] Motta expresses scepticism that such effects are any more of a competition issue than general cost savings or demand efficiencies from mergers.[70]

Bundling/tying and refusal to supply

6.183   There are a variety of ways in which bundling and tying may be used to increase barriers to entry and lessen competition, a number of which are considered further below.[71]

The DTI paper indicates that bundling can be used to increase entry barriers, and thus protect market power. It envisages circumstances where a firm has market power in two markets, A and B, but faces entry in only market A. In these circumstances, a bundled price for A and B which means that the incremental cost of A is very low, is likely to lead to the new entrant in market A having relatively few customers which may be insufficient for its entry to be profitable. Such bundling can also be thought of as artificially increasing economies of scope, in that to compete effectively the firm needs to enter both markets A and B.

Another related possibility is that a firm may use bundling/tying as a means of denying a competitor or potential entrant access to a complementary product market. A typical example here is a market for a product where there also exists a service or after-care market. If a firm is able to use bundling/tying as a means of eliminating an independent service market, then a potential entrant would have to enter with both a product and a service network thus raising such rivals' costs.

Rather than raising rivals' costs, certain bundling/tying strategies may enable firms to gain a competitive advantage by lowering the benefits that consumers anticipate from rivals' products. Examples here are frequent flyer programmes or unlimited cinema passes. The key point is that if customers wish to purchase a variety of products or services, the best way to do is to purchase the bundle.

6.184   In relation to the proposed acquisition by FirstGroup plc of the Scottish Passenger Rail franchise, the Commission expressed concerns that, by combining the operations of the main operator of rail services in Scotland with those of the leading bus operator in Scotland, and in Glasgow in particular, there could be broader adverse effects on competition than those identified on the overlapping rail/bus flows. These adverse effects may be categorised as a combination of conglomerate and vertical effects, with the vertical effects relating to the possible reduced availability of information at Scottish railway stations on competing bus operators' services. The conglomerate effects in this case related to travelcards, which in a public transport context may be valuable to consumers wishing to travel on a number of operators' services. In this case, the Commission concluded that there would be a substantial lessening of competition in wider public transport network markets with regards to travelcards on the grounds that:

---

[69] Cited above, para.6.178, n.58 at pp.64–65.
[70] Also see pp.273–276 of Bishop and Walker, cited above, para.6.001, n.2.
[71] See further DTI paper, Ch.4, cited above, para.6.178, n.58.

"FirstGroup could introduce a multi-modal ticket scheme, confined to its own services, to its own commercial benefit and to the detriment of any schemes open to other bus operators. This could be expected to distort competition between FirstGroup and other operators, and that effect could extend to areas where it does not currently operate, but where it could leverage its control of the rail franchise to extend its bus operation. But even in the case of multi-operator schemes, FirstGroup would be in a strong position to influence the setting of fares on the relevant travelcards, in particular the SPTE ZoneCard [an existing all operator multi-modal travelcard], to its own commercial benefit and to the disadvantage of other operators, and it may be expected to do so."[72]

Apart from contractual bundling/tying, a firm may be able to engage in technical bundling by rendering its products incompatible with complementary products supplied by rivals.

The DTI paper adds that should entry occur, bundling may also reduce the impact of this competition. The intuition behind this is that the firm offering the bundled product and the firm offering just one product may be devices for the two firms to focus on different categories of customers and/or divide up the market between them. However, it should be noted that firms offering packages of products, or bundling in additional value added features, could use this as a device to offer secret discounts and this may generally make it more difficult to reach consensus. Accordingly, there are ambiguous effects on the risk of co-ordination.

The DTI paper discusses certain merger cases where portfolio/bundling/tying issues were raised. One of these was *Interbrew/ Bass*.[73] Interbrew brewed and distributed (under licence) Stella Artois in the UK, as well as owning a number of beer brands. Bass also owned a number of brands. Following the merger, Interbrew would have a 33–38 per cent share of beer brands in Great Britain, and a 33 per cent share of distribution, together with a strong brand portfolio.

6.185

The DTI paper states that one question the merger raised was whether Interbrew might be able to engage in an entry-deterrence strategy by gaining control of a significant proportion of the distribution market, as well as the brewing market. However, there appeared still to be plenty of opportunities for new entrant brewers to gain access to third party distribution, such that a new entrant brewer would not need to also establish its own distribution network.

The DTI paper also states that another question raised was whether Interbrew would be able to offer bundled discounts across its brand portfolio, which might encourage pubs not to purchase competitors' brands. However, the merged entity's shares of brewing and distribution were not so high as to suggest that competitors could be excluded from *all* pubs in local areas (even if they might be excluded from particular pubs). This did not, therefore, appear to be a material concern.[74]

---

[72] Cited above, para.6.012, n.36, at para.12.
[73] Cited above, para.6.027, n.27.
[74] See s.IX of Part 2—Case Studies of the DTI paper, cited above, para.6.178, n.55.

The question of portfolio concerns also arose in the OFT's consideration of *SMG/Scottish Radio Holdings*.[75] The merger had combined the leading television and radio stations in central Scotland, as well as three newspaper titles.[76] The OFT considered the possibility that the parties would have bundled advertising packages across all of its media interests. The OFT was sceptical that the parties could gain economies of scale or scope through such bundling given that there were disparate production, distribution and marketing processes for the different media. There was also no evidence that customers preferred to purchase all of their advertising requirements from one source. The ITV television licence also prevented cross-selling of advertising. The OFT concluded in this case that the merger was unlikely to result in anti-competitive bundling of products.

The hypothesis that appeared to be advanced in the MMC's report on the proposed merger between Capital Radio plc and Virgin Radio Holdings Limited was that Virgin was a complementary station to other radio stations in London in that by combining Virgin and other stations a credible alternative to advertising on Capital could be constructed. Thus if Capital could engage in bundling/tying such that advertisers would be incentivised not to purchase advertising on Virgin on its own, they could be deterred from using other radio stations. The Commission expressed concerns about Capital adopting such practices as follows:

> "We believe one result of the merger would be to increase the relative attractiveness of the Capital/Virgin group of stations to advertisers. The three stations Capital FM, Capital Gold and Virgin FM would, between them, provide by far the greatest access to important audience groups in London and thus it would be virtually essential for an advertiser seeking good radio coverage throughout London to use the Capital/Virgin stations. By contrast, the remaining non-Capital/Virgin stations will become of more marginal usefulness for major campaigns.
>
> At present, advertisers have told us, it is possible to construct alternative advertising packages to Capital FM using combinations of Virgin FM, Kiss 100 FM, Heart and Melody. The ability to construct effective alternatives would be greatly reduced by the removal of an independent Virgin FM from the equation, since Capital would be in a position to offer combinations of stations covering particular types of audience which its competitors would be unable to match. We therefore consider that the change in the relative positions of the companies, if the merger were to go ahead, with Virgin FM moving from the non-Capital group of stations to the Capital group, would immediately put Capital in a dominant position for the supply of radio advertising."[77]

6.186   Unfortunately, this hypothesis was not supported by any factual evidence in the Commission's report.

---

[75] *Completed acquisition by SMG plc of a 29.5 per cent shareholding in Scottish Radio Holdings plc*, cleared by the Secretary of State on July 9, 2001 in line with the Director General's advice.

[76] Cited above, para.6.185, n.75.

[77] Cited above, para.6.022, n.98, at paras 2.104–2.105.

The issue of bundling/tie-in sales was also considered by the Commission in its inquiry into the proposed merger between Duralay and Gates Consumer & Industrial. In that case, the Commission considered whether the merged company could use its strong market position in the supply of carpet underlay and carpet gripper to make the purchase of one of these products dependent on the purchase of the other, thus protecting its market power in these markets. However, the Commission concluded that[78]:

(i)   if the merged company were to attempt to tie sales of underlay to its gripper sales, thus extending market power from the gripper market to the underlay market, then customers could resist such an attempt by turning to imports of gripper. Barriers to entry into the gripper market were deemed to be low, such that a bundling strategy on the part of the merged entity might also encourage new entry into the supply of gripper; and

(ii)   as regards the risk of the merged company attempting to tie sales of gripper to its underlay sales, thus extending market power from the underlay market to the gripper market, the Commission noted that the UK gripper market was of low-value (only £6.5 million). In these circumstances, it was unlikely that the merged company would regard any attempt to tie gripper to its underlay sales as worthwhile given the potential loss of much more valuable underlay contracts.

In certain cases, concerns as to bundling/tying can be ruled out by the customers' procurement practices and/or if rivals also offer ranges of equipment. Such concerns were rejected by the Commission on this basis in the context of the proposed acquisition of Dräger Medical AG & Co. KGaA of certain assets representing the Air-Shields business of Hill-Rom Inc (Hill-Rom), a subsidiary of Hillenbrand Industries:

"It has been argued that the ability of the parties to offer a full range of neonatal warming therapy products might enable them to exercise port-folio power, by offering preferential terms to tie in customers to buying a broad range of equipment (possibly extending beyond neonatal warming therapy products). This seems unlikely, since customers always appear to specify the particular types of equipment required at any given time, and we have seen no evidence that clinicians would accept equipment with which they are not wholly satisfied solely because there was a better price on offer. We note that although Dräger, Hill-Rom and GE are all already in a position to offer a wide range of equipment within and beyond the neonatal care field, only a small percentage of respondents to our questionnaire had experienced such behaviour."[79]

In addition, in *iSOFT/Torex* the OFT rejected concerns that the merged business would be able to exercise "portfolio power" and leverage its strength in secondary healthcare IT products into other parts of the NHS

---

[78] Cited above, para.6.008, n.21, at paras 2.97–2.99.
[79] Cited above, para.6.028, n.31, at para.7.10.

461

system, particularly as the various products are procured separately, customers have not chosen to purchase full product ranges from the parties, and there are requirements for inter-operability:

> "We do not believe that this transaction raises any conglomerate competition issues. First, we have not been provided with any evidence to support the assertion that it would. The fact that a firm's products may be inter-operable or form part of a broader portfolio of products is not of itself evidence of anti-competitive effects: on the contrary, this may well be a sound customer benefit of the transaction. Second, many of the contracts for these products may well be purchased separately. In these circumstances, the parties would appear to have no material ability or incentive to engage in anti-competitive leveraging conduct. Third, the fact that both Torex and iSOFT in the NPfIT [National Programme for IT] have been successful with some individual products but not with others suggests that LSPs [Local Service Providers] want to buy the best product in a class, rather than looking for a one-stop shop. The NPfIT's emphasis on interoperability will reinforce this purchasing pattern."[80]

The role of efficiencies in merger control

Introduction

6.187   As explained in Ch.4, the main provisions of Pt 3 of the Enterprise Act provide for the competition authorities to be given discretion to clear a merger, or allow it to proceed with less stringent competition remedies, in circumstances where, notwithstanding an expected substantial lessening of competition, they expect it to result in defined types of customer benefits.

It was also explained in Ch.5 that the main provisions of Pt 3 of the Enterprise Act provide that if a merger is referred to the Commission, the Commission is required to determine whether the merger will result in a substantial lessening of competition. If the Commission makes such a determination, it will have a duty to apply remedies, and at that stage, the Enterprise Act gives it scope to have regard to customer benefits. If such benefits are found to be expected to result from the merger, the Commission will have scope to apply lesser competition remedies than would otherwise be the case. This scope extends, at one extreme, to clearing a merger unconditionally if the customer benefits are of sufficient importance and competition concerns cannot be allayed without eliminating the relevant customer benefits that the Commission wishes to recognise.[81]

---

[80] Cited above, para.6.114, n.20.

[81] Under the US Horizontal Merger Guidelines, the assessment of efficiency savings constitutes a distinct stage in the analysis. Under the Guidelines, a merging party must establish that the efficiencies resulting from the merger clearly outweigh any increase in market power and that comparable savings could not reasonably be achieved through other (less anti-competitive) means (cited above, para.6.001, n.4, at s.4). The European Commission's Horizontal Merger Guidelines take a similar approach in that the efficiencies must benefit consumers, be merger specific and be verifiable (cited above at para.6.001, n.4, at paras 76–88). Taking efficiencies into account in this way is open to criticism on a number of grounds. Leibenstein and others have argued that a lack of competitive pressure may reduce firms' incentives to manage and control their costs, which may therefore increase (Leibenstein, *"Allocative*

Analysis of efficiencies assuming a consumer welfare standard

Focusing on consumer welfare, efficiencies are assessed on the basis of   **6.188**
whether the nature and size of the proposed gains is sufficient to ensure that
consumers are not worse off given a potential reduction in competition. The
difficulty with the approach is that it requires an analysis of the dynamics
of a market pre-and post-merger, which may be subject to uncertainty. For
example, the analysis would require investigation of the following effects:

(i)   the effect of the merger on competition (assuming that there are no
      cost savings);

(ii) any interaction between efficiencies and competitive effects such that
      competition is made more difficult for non-merging competitors or
      entry is blocked as a result of the efficiencies—the so called
      "efficiency offence"; and

(iii) the size and nature of the claimed efficiencies, together with a
      consideration of the extent to which efficiencies are passed on to
      consumers.

This is not a simple task, as emphasised by Röller, Stennek, and Verboven
who state that:

"The calculation of minimum required efficiencies [*i.e.* efficiencies required
to compensate for market power effects] requires essentially an assessment
of the likely expected market power (or anti-competitive) effects. The difficult task for the merger authorities is to obtain a good idea of the nature
of competitive interaction before and after the merger. This is not an
obvious task, given the various possible models of competition . . ."[82]

In addition to understanding the potential effects of market power in the
absence of cost savings (*i.e.* in order to establish the "cost" benchmark
against which the "benefits" of efficiencies may be weighed), competition
authorities need to understand whether the cost savings themselves may have
anti-competitive effects. For example, a merger may have the effect of
reducing or eliminating competition if the merged entity passes through lower
marginal costs resulting in lower prices such that some rival firms are forced

---

efficiency vs 'X-efficiency' ", American Economic Review (1966), pp.392–415). Such scepticism may be well placed, given that most research on the subject indicates that mergers yield
few private benefits in terms of higher profits and distributions to shareholders (which may
understate their adverse effects on the public interest if some mergers increase market
power). Scherer and Ross suggest, *inter alia*, that where a merger is permitted to proceed
because of the efficiency gains it is expected to yield, the regulatory authorities could audit
the merged company's business following the merger and, if it has failed to achieve the cost
savings envisaged it could be forced to divest (cited above, para.6.001, n.4, at Ch.5). Clarke
suggests that a better solution to anti-competitive mergers that are likely to yield offsetting
social benefits might be to impose behavioural or conduct undertakings upon the merged
company, such as price controls (cited above, para.6.061, n.43, at pp.265–267). These
points suggest that a strong case can be made that the burden of proof should be on the
parties to prove that efficiency gains will benefit consumers, not least because the parties are
bound to have greater information than the regulator on such matters.
[82] Röller, Stennek, and Verboven, "*Efficiency Gains from Mergers*", Working Paper No.543,
2000, The Research Institute of Industrial Economics.

to exit the market. The implication of this is that the analysis of anti-competitive effects must be performed in conjunction with an analysis of a merger's effects on costs. This is the so-called "efficiency offence".

At present, the inherent tension between efficiencies which are pro-competitive and those which result in potential market power has not been clearly addressed by competition authorities. For example in the EU, despite statements by the European Commission that there is no "*efficiency offence*",[83] there is a widespread perception that these considerations do have a significant bearing on merger decisions.[84] As noted at paras 6.179 to 6.182 above, the Commission's guidelines certainly suggest that there is an efficiency offence as regards conglomerate mergers. The difficulty for competition authorities is to distinguish between situations where there is a realistic chance that the merged entity could force competitors to exit the market and subsequently raise prices without a threat of re-entry (or entirely new entry), and situations where the efficiency stimulates competition such that competitors have strong incentives to match cost reductions in order to retain or recapture market share and margins. A commentator on the *General Electric/Honeywell* merger, which was prohibited by the European Commission, states:

"... deciding to block a merger on grounds that it will lead to lower prices and eventually exit means giving up the predicted immediate benefit of lower prices in favour of the speculative, long term possibility of price rises. A competition authority needs to be confident about the risk of exit, and conclude that it outweighs the short-term benefit of lower prices ..."[85]

6.189   In addition, competition authorities need to investigate the extent to which efficiencies are passed through to the benefit of consumers. Again this can be framed in terms of economic models of competitive behaviour. Stennek and Verboven[86] provide a detailed discussion of the determinants of pass-on, drawing on the theoretical literature on competition and monopoly and adding generalisations on oligopoly market structures. An important distinction is made between pass-on of industry wide cost savings (*i.e.* cost savings realised by all firms in the industry) and firm-

---

[83] See, for example the comments of the Commissioner responsible for Competition, Mario Monti: "I have said this before, but let me clarify it once and for all: there is no such thing as a so-called 'efficiency offence' in EU merger control law and practice" and "the Commission does not rely on the fact that efficiencies resulting from a merger are likely to have the effect of reducing or eliminating competition in the relevant market (for example by enabling lower prices to be charged to customers) as a ground for opposing a proposed transaction." Speech by Commissioner Mario Monti to a Conference on Reform of European Merger Control, Brussels, June 4, 2002.

[84] For example, in the case of the proposed merger between General Electric and Honeywell, one of the main concerns of the European Commission was that the merged entity would be able to offer package discounts to customers who bought both GE engines and Honeywell products, and that this would present a major competitive hurdle to rival firms offering a narrower product range.

[85] Lexecon, "*The Economics of GE/Honeywell—Part 1: Mixed Bundling*", August 31, 2001.

[86] Stennek and Verboven, "*Merger Control and Enterprise Competitiveness—Empirical Analysis and Policy Recommendations*", Report for EC Contract III/99/065, February 20, 2001.

specific pass-on. With respect to the industry level, the degree of pass-on depends on the consumer's response to price reductions (*i.e.* price elasticity of demand) and the firm's ability to expand and the costs associated with expansion. For example, consider the circumstances in which pass-on might be incomplete in a competitive industry. A reduction in marginal costs, as a result of the merger inducing firms to lower their price, would cause consumers to increase their purchases (the extent of this effect will depend on consumers' elasticity of demand). However, if firms face increasing marginal costs as output rises, because, for example, they face capacity constraints, prices will not reduce by the full amount of the decrease in marginal costs as a result of the merger. Thus pass-on will be more complete if consumers respond less to price reductions and if producers can expand production more easily without raising their marginal costs too much.

In the case of monopoly and oligopoly market structures, there may be incomplete pass through of savings even where marginal costs are constant such that there are no capacity constraints to expansion. This is because firms with market power charge a mark up over costs, where the size of the mark up depends on the sensitivity of consumer demand to price increases (*i.e.* price elasticity). In the most likely case, where consumers are less sensitive to price (demand is price inelastic) at lower price levels, firms will increase mark ups by passing on only a part of the cost reductions. Stennek and Verboven state that:

> ". . . it is worth stressing that even in the monopoly case (or the dominant firm case) firms pass on at least part of the cost savings onto customers. As the number of firms increases, pass on of industry wide cost savings generally becomes more complete."[87]

Although an industry-level analysis provides a useful starting point, it is important to understand how firm-specific cost savings are passed through to consumer prices, given that cost savings arising from mergers are typically realised at the firm rather than the industry level. Stennek and Verboven investigate this question using specific oligopoly models assuming homogenous and differentiated goods. Their findings suggest that the market share of the firm realising the cost savings is a key factor influencing the degree of pass-on. Indeed pass-on is limited when the market share of the firm is very small or very large, with intermediate market shares leading to the greatest pass-on. Intuitively, pass-on is low where market shares are small in line with the finding that, in competitive markets, where firms act as price takers, there are few incentives to pass-on any cost changes.[88]

---

[87] Cited above, para.6.189, n.86, p.61.
[88] To illustrate this point, consider the case described by Yde and Vita ". . . suppose two adjacent wheat farms merge to reduce their per-unit irrigation costs by more efficiently exploiting an underground reservoir bordering the two properties. Because the combined output of these farmers is trivial relative to the total market output of wheat, they act as price takers in this market both before and after the merger—that is, they can sell their entire output of wheat at the market price. It is therefore unnecessary for them to reduce price in order to sell additional output. In this situation their profit-maximizing response to the cost reduction is to expand their output because, with their now-lower marginal costs, they can cultivate more acreage and still earn a profit on the additional units. They will expand their output up to the point where the market price of wheat equals the now-lower marginal cost. They continue to receive the

Where market shares are high, firms' incentives are similar to those described for the oligopoly and monopoly industry models above.

Economic theory is less well developed in analysing the effect of efficiencies on the price level in a market where there are co-ordinated effects. This is because cost savings may or may not facilitate the circumstances required for consensus to be sustainable. For example, the US Horizontal Merger Guidelines state that:

> "In a co-ordinated interaction context, marginal cost reductions may make co-ordination less likely or effective by enhancing the incentive of a maverick to lower price or by creating a new maverick firm."[89]

In other words, the suggestion is that changes in relative costs may disturb the alignment between firms which had previously enabled them to co-ordinate their behaviour. As described above, the analytical framework for assessing the net effects of a merger, taking into account the potential anti-competitive effects due to a change in market power, and the efficiencies expected from the merger, is highly complex. Given the challenge this represents for competition authorities, a number of studies have considered how efficiency considerations can practically be addressed as part of merger analysis. The remainder of this section considers these procedures, and then discusses the qualitative and quantitative evidence which will be required to implement an efficiency defence, taking into account the OFT and Commission guidelines on this subject.

Implementing an efficiency defence

6.190   The analysis described above reflects a situation in which efficiency benefits must be, in some sense, "weighed up" against potentially anti-competitive effects. The Enterprise Act allows for this analysis at two stages in the merger control process, as described in the guidelines of the OFT and the Commission[90]:

---

same price as they did pre-merger, and thus earn greater profits (efficiency rents) owing to their improved productive efficiency". Yde and Vita, "*Merger Efficiencies: Reconsidering the "Passing-On Requirement*", (1996) Antitrust Law Journal, 64.

[89] Cited above, para.6.001, n.4, at para.4. For example, Motta observes that efficiency improvements should generally be looked at positively as they should depress prices. However, with coordinated effects, the effects become more ambiguous. On the one hand, creating a low cost rival or high capacity rival might disrupt coordination by giving such a firm a greater incentive to deviate from the terms of coordination. However, a merger could create a more symmetric cost structure by lowering the costs of high cost rivals, but Motta expects that this effect will be outweighed by the efficiency gains, particularly if the counterfactual is single firm dominance by a single low cost rival (cited above, para.6.001, n.2, at p.252).

[90] The OFT's guidelines also indicate that efficiencies will be considered "where they increase rivalry in the market so that no substantial lessening of competition would result from the merger" (cited above, para.6.001, n.1, para.4.30). They then go on to cite an example where two smaller firms merge, and as a result of efficiency gains, are able to exert greater competitive pressure on larger companies. The implication of this provision is that efficiencies may be considered as the pro-competitive rationale for deals which do not raise issues of unilateral or co-ordinated effects. However, it is not clear why efficiencies should be relevant in this context since a finding that there is no substantial lessening of competition should be sufficient to allow the OFT to reach a decision not to refer. Efficiencies are only relevant

First, the OFT states in its guidelines on mergers assessment that "efficiencies might . . . be taken into account where they do not avert a substantial lessening of competition, but will nonetheless be passed on after the merger in the form of customer benefits. For example, if a merger would reduce rivalry in a market but proven efficiencies would be likely to result in lower prices to customers, the OFT would not take this into account in reaching a conclusion on the substantial lessening of competition test, but it might be a consideration under the customer benefits exception to the duty to refer."[91]

The Commission is required (under s.34(4) of the Enterprise Act) to have regard to customer benefits in deciding the question of remedies. Specifically "[i]f the Commission is satisfied that relevant customer benefits would result from a merger that also led to a SLC, it will consider whether to modify the remedy that it would otherwise put in place."[92]

A number of commentators have considered how competition authorities might best implement the "weighing up" of efficiencies against anticompetitive effects given the complexity of the analysis described above. For example, Roller, Stennek, and Verboven suggest a methodology based on the calculation of "minimum required efficiencies" ("MRE") (*i.e.* efficiencies required to compensate for market power effects) which may then be compared with actual expected efficiencies involved in the merger. In order to reduce the information burden associated with this assessment, Roller *et al.* propose an assumption-based approach for calculating MRE. They assume a "worst case scenario" consisting of an increase in price of 5 to 10 per cent (assuming no changes in efficiency).[93] The MRE (*i.e.* the required drop in marginal cost to compensate for the price increase) is calculated by dividing the worst case scenario price increase (5 to 10 per cent) by the pass-on rate (*i.e.* the proportion of any cost-saving which will be passed on to consumers given the prevailing market structure and price elasticity of demand). For example if the pass on rate is 50 per cent, the minimum required cost reduction will be in the range 10 to 20 per cent. Actual expected efficiencies are then compared to this benchmark in order to evaluate whether they would be sufficient to compensate for anti competitive effects.

This approach has been criticised on the basis that an assumed pass on **6.191** rate is likely to be economically inaccurate. In particular, Ilzkovitz and Meiklejohn state that:

". . . the extent of the firm pass on depends on several factors, including the presence of capacity constraints, the price elasticity of demand, the degree of market power, and the market share of the merging firms and the pass-on rate must be consistent with the assumed or estimated price increase in the absence of efficiencies."[94]

---

where a consideration of customer benefits might be weighed against a finding that a merger is likely to result in a substantial lessening of competition.

[91] Cited above, para.6.001, n.1, at para.4.31.

[92] Cited above, para.6.001, n.1, at para.4.45.

[93] This postulated price increase is linked to the principles of market definition, specifically the "SSNIP test", as discussed in para.6.049.

[94] Ilzkovitz and Meiklejohn (2001), "*European Merger Control: Do We Need an Efficiency Defence?*", Paper prepared for the 5th Annual EUNIP Conference.

The authors go on to recommend a sequential approach which involves three stages:

(i)   a screening test to identify those merger cases where an efficiency analysis is appropriate, thereby economising on information costs;

(ii)   a qualitative investigation of the possible merger synergies involving a consideration of whether they are merger specific, the possible effects on costs, prices, quality of product and innovation, and the period over which the effects are expected to be realised; and

(iii)   a quantitative assessment (if the qualitative evidence is deemed insufficient) to identify whether the net effects of a merger are beneficial. In particular, a simulation analysis is described involving the simultaneous estimation of the price increase in the absence of the efficiencies and the degree of pass-on. In this way, the complex economic analysis which was described above is only undertaken in a small number of cases where qualitative evidence has not been sufficiently convincing.

The OFT's and Commission's guidelines on efficiencies

6.192   The key questions for competition authorities in evaluating efficiencies in practice are as follows:

(i)   what types of efficiencies are most likely to be beneficial to customers?[95]; and

(ii)   can the efficiencies be created through alternative means or are they "merger specific"?

Types of efficiencies

6.193   Assessing the likely impact of proposed efficiency gains on consumers raises a number of questions for competition authorities, namely:

(i)   whether benefits should be limited to price reductions or whether wider (and possibly less immediate) benefits to customers may be considered;

(ii)   whether the transfer is required to be immediate;

(iii)   whether the types of efficiencies proposed are likely to be passed on to customers; and

(iv)   whether gains must be passed on to consumers in the same market as that where a substantial lessening of competition has been iden-

---

[95] One question which might be posed is "who is a customer?" In this regard, in its report on *FirstGroup plc/Scottish Passenger Rail Franchise*, the Commission indicated that it regarded public sector bodies who procure the provision of public transportation services as customers (cited above, para.6.012, n.36, at para.6.4).

tified, or whether gain and harm to different groups of consumers can be weighed against each other.

The 1997 revision of the US Horizontal Merger Guidelines suggests flexibility in the consideration of which efficiencies may be considered as beneficial to customers. These guidelines allow for the possibility that efficiencies may be considered where there are no direct short-term effects on prices, but customers may benefit in the longer term (although these are to be given less weight).[96] This is an important consideration since certain efficiencies will tend to have longer term effects such that they will outweigh anti-competitive effects where they are evaluated on a present value basis, if not in the years immediately following the merger.

The discussion of possible relevant customer benefits in the OFT and Commission guidelines highlights productive efficiencies (*e.g.* economies of scale in production or distribution) where these result in lower prices to customers. The OFT guidelines indicate that price reductions of this nature are considered to be "rare" and that the "key question is whether the claimed efficiency will enhance rivalry among the remaining players in the market."[97] This may be questionable in the context of a significant lessening of competition. The Director General has expressed scepticism on the extent of pass-on in his advice on the proposed acquisition by Orbital Marketing Services of Surridge Dawson:

"The presence of substantial economies of scope suggests that the merger might reduce costs. But if so, there can be no certainty that they would be passed on to consumers. As this is essentially a bidding market, the parties are likely to set their price in relation to the cost of their closest competitors. There is thus no compelling reason why cost savings would be passed on to customers post-merger, particularly as potential new entrants are likely to have significantly higher costs, at least initially, than the parties."[98]

---

[96] "The Agency also will consider the effect of cognizable efficiencies with no short-term, direct effect on prices in the relevant market. Delayed benefits from efficiencies (due to delay in the achievement of, or the realization of consumer benefits from, the efficiencies) will be given less weight because they are less proximate and more difficult to predict." (cited above, para.6.001, n.4, at n.37.) However, the application of these guidelines, particularly in the context of court determinations, has tended to favour a requirement that benefits are directly passed on to consumers. In the *Heinz/Beech-Nut* case, for example, the FTC stated that "even if an efficiencies defense can be entertained, defendants must show that the "proven" efficiencies will be passed on and that they overwhelm any possible anti-competitive effects of the merger." (*FTC v HJ Heinz Company*, on appeal from the United States District Court for the District of Columbia, Brief for Plaintiff-Appellant FTC, *FTC v H.J Heinz Company et al.*, Reply Brief for the Plaintiff-Appellant FTC No.00-5362 (November 29, 2000), at 43 (citing Cardinal Health and Staples), cited in the Propane Tribunal Redetermination Decision, at para.127. This case is discussed in Venit, "The Role of Efficiencies in Merger Control", Conference Paper given at 2002 EC Merger Control conference organised by the European Commission and the International Bar Association. This paper provides a useful overview of the economic theory and policy considerations.) Under this approach, efficiencies must "reverse" the potential harmful effects on consumers.
[97] Cited above, para.6.001, n.1, at para.4.32.
[98] Director General's advice of July 5, 2002, *The proposed acquisition by Orbital Marketing Services Group Limited of certain assets of Surridge Dawson Limited.*

The guidelines also indicate that efficiencies are most likely to be taken into account where they impact on marginal or variable costs as opposed to fixed cost savings such as the avoidance of a duplication of overheads or administrative costs. This is because reductions in marginal cost will directly affect short term pricing decisions and thus are more likely to be passed on to customers. Although the OFT acknowledges that fixed cost savings can be important in the longer run (since over a longer period they become variable), and in the context of competition via auctions and bidding procedures where prices will tend to reflect fixed and variable costs, the OFT will give less weight to savings of this nature.[99]

6.194   The guidelines also specifically allow for certain benefits other than immediate lower prices to be weighed against an identified loss of competition. In particular, the scope for greater innovation (*i.e.* where R&D is made possible by the achievement of a "certain critical mass" as a result of the merger) and greater product choice or higher product quality.[1] The Commission acknowledges potential enhancements to innovation "through economies of scale, specialisation in R&D and/or the pooling of risks".[2] However, the Commission raises a question as to whether incentives to innovate may be blunted by the reduction of competition resulting from the merger.[3]

The Commission also describes potential customer benefits which might arise in markets which are characterised by network effects. The Commission's guidelines state that:

"Where services are provided over an infrastructure network, the larger the number of customers with access to, or connected with, the network, the more highly customers value the network. Network benefits of this type may be enhanced by a merger. In passenger road transport, for example, mergers might lead to improved services to customers such as a wider choice of routes, service times and frequencies, or extended through-ticketing over previously competing networks. In telecommunications, customers could benefit from a merger that improved connections between networks as a result of greater service reliability and speedier connections."[4]

---

[99] Cited above, para.6.001, n.1, at n.27.

[1] Cited above, para.6.001, n.1, at para.7.8.

[2] Cited above, para.6.001, n.1, at para.4.42.

[3] The economics literature on this question provides different results. One finding (d'Aspremont and Jacquemin, American Economic Review, Vol.78(5), 1988) is that, due to the fact that R&D is not completely proprietary (given the scope for imitation or information spill-overs) a concentration can increase incentives because it allow parties to internalise the benefits of R&D. Ignoring spill-over effects, economists have considered the impact of different market structures on R&D incentives. The incentives for a large firm may be described in terms of two effects. Firstly, the so-called "efficiency effect" is based on the principle that a dominant firm will have an incentive to retain its competitive advantage and associated monopoly rents, provided the investment is sufficiently low risk. For higher risk investments, the firm would rather enjoy the current monopoly rents and accept the risk of being displaced by a rival—the so-called "replacement effect". Reinganum (Amercian Economic Review, Vol.73(4), (1983) analyses the role of uncertainty in the R&D outcome to assess the relative importance of these effects.

[4] Cited above, para.6.001, n.1, at para.4.43.

Finally, the Commission's guidelines note that vertical mergers may generate efficiencies as a result of, for example, improved co-ordination (for instance in product design and marketing between firms at different stages of the supply chain), lower transaction and inventory costs and removal of the "double marginalisation" that occurs when two non-integrated firms both have significant market power.[5]

As to the question of whether customer benefits should accrue in the same market as that in which a substantial lessening of competition would occur, the OFT's guidelines indicate that:

"The claimed customer benefits must accrue to customers of the merging parties (or to customers in a chain beginning with those customers), but need not necessarily arise in the market(s) where the substantial lessening of competition concerns have arisen. It is therefore conceivable that sufficient customer benefits might accrue in one market as a result of the merger that would outweigh a finding of substantial lessening of competition in another market(s). That said, the OFT's normal expectation is that these customer benefits will arise in the market where the competition concerns have been identified. To show that benefits in one market outweigh an expected substantial lessening of competition in another will require clear and compelling evidence."[6]

Are the customer benefits merger-specific?

The OFT and Commission will also need to consider whether the benefits are unlikely to arise without the merger (unless the only other ways of realising the customer benefits would have a similarly detrimental effect on competition). In this connection, the OFT's guidelines indicate that the key issue is that the analysis is incremental, so that the efficiencies must be judged relative to what would have happened without the merger.[7] Similarly, the Commission emphasises that:

"... the benefits must clearly result from the merger and be unlikely to have come about without the merger or a similar lessening of competition."[8]

The burden of proof on the parties to the merger

Both the OFT's and the Commission's guidelines emphasise that the burden is on the merging parties to provide evidence that any claimed benefit falls within the meaning of a relevant customer benefit for the purposes of the Enterprise Act. The OFT's guidelines indicate that:

6.195

6.196

---

[5] Cited above, para.6.001, n.1, at para.4.44. Double marginalisation may occur because, in the absence of price discrimination, each non-integrated firm has the incentive to raise prices above cost without taking account of the fact that this lowers the output of the other. The result is lower output and profits (and higher prices) than if the two firms pursued a policy of joint profit maximisation.

[6] Cited above, para.6.001, n.1, at para.7.9.

[7] Cited above, para.6.001, n.1, at para.4.34.

[8] Cited above, para.6.001, n.1, at para.4.36.

". . . the evidence presented by the parties on efficiencies and their likely impact on rivalry must indeed be compelling. This is moreover the case because of the information asymmetries between the OFT and the merging parties in respect of efficiency claims. All of the information relating to such claims is in the hands of the merging parties so it is for them to demonstrate their case on the [basis] of the information available to them. Such evidence might, for example, include estimates and origin of likely cost-savings as evidence in pre-merger planning and strategy documents, coupled with objective factual and accounting information needed to verify proposed cost saving claims. External consultancy reports pre-dating the merger might also be helpful in this context."[9]

In assessing whether customer benefits are so significant as to justify a less harsh remedy, the Commission's guidelines emphasise that:

"When deciding whether to modify a remedy the Commission will consider a number of factors including the size and nature of the expected benefit and how long the benefit is expected to be sustained, taking into account whether as a result of the reduction of competitive pressure in the market, any immediate benefit to customers will be eroded in future. The Commission will also consider the differing impacts of the merger on different customers."[10]

Case studies

6.197 It is noteworthy that between the entry into force of the Enterprise Act and August 2004, none of the OFT's published decisions have contained a detailed analysis of efficiencies/customer benefits. Furthermore, only six published decisions mention the possibility of customer benefits in their conclusions.[11]

Carl Zeiss Jena/Bio-Rad

6.198 Since the Enterprise Act came into force, the first published decision to mention benefits in its conclusions was the OFT's decision of December 30, 2003 concerning the proposed acquisition by Carl Zeiss Jena GmbH of the microscope business of Bio-Rad Laboratories Inc. This briefly raised the issue of benefits in terms of increased rivalry within the market place and increased innovation. Carl Zeiss had argued that its acquisition of Bio-Rad

---

[9] Cited above, para.6.001, n.1, at para.4.35.
[10] Cited above, para.6.001, n.1, at para. 4.45.
[11] The six OFT decisions which briefly mentioned the possibility of customer benefits in their conclusions were: (i) anticipated acquisition by National Milk Records Plc of The Cattle Information Service Ltd (March 3, 2004); (ii) completed acquisition by Archant Ltd of the London Regionals Division of Independent News and Media Plc (April 29, 2004); (iii) completed acquisition by National Express of the Greater Anglia Franchise (May 27, 2004); (iv) anticipated acquisition by Knauf Insulation Ltd of Superglass Insulation Ltd (June 17, 2004); (v) completed acquisition by Emap Plc of ABI Building Data Ltd (July 1, 2004); and (vi) anticipated acquisition by Carl Zeiss Jena GmbH of the microscope business of Bio-Rad Laboratories Inc. (December 30, 2003).

would be pro-competitive since it would strengthen Carl Zeiss as a direct competitor to Leica (a principal competing supplier of microscopes). Carl Zeiss had argued that increased rivalry between the enlarged Carl Zeiss and Leica would benefit innovation, particularly as both companies were recognised as leading innovative companies in this area. However, the OFT concluded that whilst Carl Zeiss's argument appeared plausible, there was insufficient evidence that rivalry and innovation would increase as a consequence of the proposed transaction.[12] No detailed analysis of the issue of customer benefits was presented in the OFT's decision.

As regards the remaining five OFT decisions, possible customer benefits were dismissed on the basis that they could not be shown to be merger-specific, were not clear nor verifiable, and/or would not be expected to be passed on to customers. Benefits have been considered in a number of Commission reports (including reports under the Fair Trading Act 1973). However, again, the parties' arguments in this regard have often been rejected on the basis that claimed benefits are too speculative, not merger-specific and/or insufficient to outweigh identified detriments.

H+H Celcon/MBM

For example, in *H+H Celcon/MBM*, the Commission concluded that whilst the parties had claimed certain cost reductions as a result of the merger, with a 66 per cent market share, the Commission considered that the parties would have little pressure or incentive to pass such cost savings onto customers in the form of lower prices. The Commission also observed in this connection that the valuation of the bid by H+H had assumed that all of the savings arising from the merger would accrue to shareholders.　6.199

H+H had also argued that product innovation and development was one of its main objectives, and that the merger would provide the new firm with enhanced R&D capacity. However, the Commission observed that overall, the concrete block industry was not characterised by heavy spending on R&D and innovation, although certain product developments had been made. The Commission remained of the view that it continued to be very speculative as to whether it would be necessary for the company to maintain or improve its past record of innovation given its high market share going forward.[13]

Sylvan/Locker

Similarly, in the context of *Sylvan/Locker*, the Commission noted that the parties' business plan suggested that they hoped to retain many of the bene-fits accrued by forming a joint venture, rather than passing such benefits onto customers. With an expectation that the merger would damage competition, the Commission concluded that any customer benefit would at best be only small.[14]　6.200

---

[12] See the OFT's decision of December 30, 2003, *Anticipated acquisition by Carl Zeiss Jena GmbH of the microscopy business of Bio-Rad Laboratories Inc* at paras 37 and 38.
[13] Cited above, para.6.011, n.31, at paras 2.37 and 2.123 to 2.125.
[14] Cited above at para.6.008 n.21, at paras 2.127—2.128. Similarly, in the context of Lloyds TSB Group plc's proposed acquisition of Abbey National plc, the Commission stated that it expected that the proposed merger would lead to "substantial" cost savings. However, the Commission noted that in estimating the revenue synergies, Lloyds TSB assumed that very

SCR-Sibelco/Fife

6.201   Similarly, in the context of *SCR-Sibelco/Fife*,[15] Sibelco had argued that a number of countervailing public interest benefits would result from the merger, and would outweigh any actual or potential loss of competition. First, Sibelco argued that in the context of the Fife companies experiencing financial difficulties, Sibelco offered the most realistic prospect of the company's scarce resources and mining reserves being exploited. Had the Fife companies fallen into liquidation, or had some other arrangement been made with creditors, mineral extraction rights associated with leased land may have been lost. Secondly, Sibelco argued that since it was a responsible manager of high-quality reinstatement programmes, and had a reputation and track record of dealing with environmental concerns, the merger would remove any potential environmental concerns. Thirdly, Sibelco indicated that its willingness to take a long term view as regards the extraction of silica sand had saved direct and indirect employment in an area suffering from significant unemployment.

However, the Commission did not consider the Fife companies to be failing firms, in the sense that in the absence of the proposed transaction the companies would fall into liquidation and cease to trade. In particular, the Commission considered that a shift of focus of the Fife businesses could improve the companies' financial position. Given that the Commission did not accept that the Fife companies would be likely to fall into liquidation in the

---

few Abbey National customers would be lost to competitors following the merger. Accordingly, the Commission concluded that: "The assumption clearly indicates that Lloyds TSB expects that there will still be a low level of switching of customers between banks in the next few years." The Commission also observed that Lloyds TSB's internal papers dealing with the planned bid for Abbey National made clear that the benefits of the cost savings and revenue increases were expected to accrue to shareholders. The Commission concluded by stating that:

"To the extent that the markets are competitive, Lloyds TSB would be obliged to cut prices and margins regardless of the merger. The synergies it gained from the merger would simply put it in a better position to make those cuts without damaging profitability. But in our view Lloyds TSB's current profitability is such that it does not need the merger synergies in order to be able to cut prices: the September 2000 strategy document . . . stated that 'we still expect to make acceptable returns from [the retail banking] sector in the medium term. . . .' We therefore do not believe that consumers would benefit from the merger synergies in terms of lower prices than they would otherwise pay." (cited above, para.6.065, n.55, at paras 2.216 to 2.220).

In this regard, in the context of the merger between Interbrew SA and Bass PLC the Commission rejected Interbrew's arguments as to the benefits of the merger on the grounds that:

"We note that Interbrew paid £[!] million more for Bass Brewers than its own estimate of fair value and considered this a reasonable premium to pay in order to achieve the synergistic savings, which have a net present value of £[!] million. The payment of this premium limits any beneficial effects that consumers would experience from those synergies even if Interbrew realized all the synergies that it claims are available.

"In any case, the merger is likely to lead to Interbrew increasing prices and hence to raising rather than maintaining margins." (cited above, para.6.027, n.27, at paras 2.189–2.190.)

There was no specific analysis in either of these cases of whether marginal costs would fall or how cost savings might create incentives for price cuts.

[15] Cited above, para.6.059, n.41, at paras 2.112 to 2.123.

absence of the proposed transaction, it followed that the mineral extraction rights would not necessarily be terminated.

As regards Sibelco's argument that the merger had removed potential environmental concerns, the Commission indicated that they had no reason to suppose that another owner of the Fife companies, particularly if this were a large, reputable company with experience of mineral extraction, would not also do so. All companies in the industry were subject to the same environmental and planning legislation.

As regards Sibelco's third argument that it was willing, unlike other potential purchasers, to take a long-term view of the business, the Commission rejected this argument. Sibelco had argued that aggregates companies such as Tarmac or Hanson would have been primarily interested, had they acquired the Fife companies, in exploiting the company's quarries for construction sand, with silica sand extraction as a secondary by-product. However, the Commission considered that any rational and commercially minded purchaser of the Fife companies would be expected to exploit the silica sand resources at Fife if they could, since this would represent a higher value product. It did not seem to the Commission that Sibelco could provide any greater security of employment than any other company running the Fife companies.

The Commission therefore concluded that there were no benefits arising from the merger.

Coloplast/SSL International

In the context of *Coloplast/SSL International*[16], the Commission concluded that the proposed acquisition would lead to a negative impact on competition, resulting in the cost of non-latex sheaths to NHS hospitals in the UK being higher than they would have otherwise been. In this case, the Commission did not believe that this detriment could be outweighed by any benefits to the public interest. **6.202**

In particular, Coloplast had argued that it would devote 4 per cent of its increased turnover to R&D, leading to greater innovation driven by improved understanding of patient needs. Coloplast argued that this was a benefit to the public interest because this level of R&D spending would be greater than that which was devoted to R&D by Coloplast and SSL separately. However, the Commission concluded that whilst overall expenditure on R&D would be likely to rise as a consequence of the transaction, and some benefits could be expected to result from this, any incremental effect was likely to be modest, especially in relation to the scale of R&D that was undertaken internationally by Coloplast and other manufacturers.

The Commission expected that in the absence of the acquisition, Coloplast would be one of the companies developing new products or improving its existing products in order to compete more effectively with SSL's market-leading products. However, instead, as part of the proposed transaction, Coloplast had entered into an exclusive distribution agreement with a third party supplier (Mentor) which required it to purchase substantial minimum volumes of sheaths. This reduced Coloplast's incentive to develop its own new and competitive offerings.

---

[16] Cited above, para.6.027, n.29, at paras 2.113 to 2.120.

Notwithstanding this, Coloplast argued, and the Commission accepted, that Coloplast was in head to head competition with Mentor in other parts of the world, and Coloplast stressed that it was strongly committed to innovation, which it saw as key to competition, and had an explicit goal of achieving at least 20 per cent of turnover of sales of products introduced within the last four years. Coloplast therefore argued, and the Commission accepted, that the majority of R&D on Coloplast's products took place overseas with a view to supplying the products in many different countries, such that the merger within the UK (and therefore the agreement with Mentor) would not have a significant adverse impact upon innovation generally.

6.203   Because of the key role of a relatively limited number of advisers in determining the sheaths used and the emphasis on clinical performance, a product's reputation for quality was central to its success. Against this background, Coloplast would need to maintain or improve the quality of its sheaths in other markets if its products were to remain competitive, and the Commission did not believe that it would make sense for Coloplast to manufacture different lower-quality sheaths for supply to the UK.

Accordingly, the Commission believed that the commercial incentive on Coloplast to maintain and improve quality would imply that the proposed transaction would not have any adverse effects on product quality. Against this background, an increase in R&D spend would not constitute a merger-specific benefit so great as to outweigh expected detriments to price competition.

Scottish Radio Holdings and GWR/Galaxy

6.204   In addition, in *Scottish Radio Holdings and GWR/Galaxy*,[17] the Commission concluded that the proposed merger would operate against the public interest, and the Commission did not believe that there were any merger-specific benefits that would off-set the adverse effects the Commission had identified. The parties had claimed that as a result of the acquisition and cost savings from integration of operations, Vibe 101 (a radio station operated by Galaxy) would be able to focus more effectively on the 15–24 year-old market, increasing diversity of output. The parties claimed that this would result in real benefits for advertisers and listeners. However, the Commission had concluded that the merger would be likely to reduce competition for advertisers, and against this background, the Commission did not believe that lower costs would be passed on in the form of lower prices to advertisers.

As regards any benefit to advertisers from improved performance of the radio station, including its improved focus on a younger, regional (or "lifestyle") market, the Commission did not believe that the merger was necessary for such a strategy to be pursued. Any new owner of the station could try to reposition it in this way. Accordingly, this benefit would not be merger-specific.

Furthermore, any benefits to listeners associated with a repositioning of the station would be diminished in some localities by the weakening position of other local commercial radio stations. This was because the

---

[17] Cited above, para.6.013, n.38, at paras 2.121 to 2.125.

Commission had concluded that a result of the merger would be to weaken the competitive position of other radio stations competing for local advertising in the area, thereby reducing their ability to invest.

GWR had also argued that cost savings resulting from the merger would help it to finance the development of digital radio, although the Commission found that such an investment would be made if profitable, irrespective of the merger.

Stena/P&O

In the context of a proposed merger of certain of the ferry businesses of Stena and P&O on the Irish Sea, the Commission rejected Stena's argument that as a consequence of the proposed transaction there would be benefits to the freight community. Stena had argued that it had a good record of commitment and investment, and was a strong long-term player on the Irish Sea. It had brought significant innovation and investment to the Irish Sea in recent years, including the introduction of new craft and investment in a new berth and other facilities. Stena had argued that a beneficial effect of the merger would be that it would be replacing P&O, which was no longer committed to operating the ferry routes in question. However, the Commission concluded that should the proposed transaction not proceed, P&O or any other purchaser of the business would be expected to maintain service quality and customer goodwill. Accordingly, any benefits to customers arising following the transaction could not be defined as merger-specific.[18]

6.205

Safeway

Nevertheless, arguments with regard to benefits have been accepted in certain cases. In the context of Morrisons' bid for Safeway, Morrisons had argued that it expected to achieve significant cost reductions and synergies as a consequence of the proposed transaction, and that it would thereby be able to reduce prices to consumers.[19] Morrisons' business plan was predicated upon Morrisons introducing its own product/price offer into most Safeway stores with prices within these stores falling to Morrisons' level. In smaller stores (below 1400 square metres), the stores would continue to be branded as Safeway, although they would offer Morrisons' own-brand products, and prices would not fall by as much as in larger stores in order to off-set the higher costs of running smaller stores. As a result of this re-branding exercise, Morrisons had estimated that overall, the prices charged in Safeway stores would fall on average.[20]

6.206

As a consequence of the price reduction, Morrisons anticipated that sales densities (*i.e.* sales per square foot) would increase from their current levels. Increased sales densities would lead to an increase in gross profits, although such an increase in gross profit would be insufficient to offset the loss in gross profit resulting from the price reduction on current sales volumes. Nevertheless, Morrisons argued that this net reduction in gross profit

---

[18] Cited above, para.6.012, n.36, at para. 6.6–6.7.
[19] Cited above, para.6.027, n.27, at paras 2.356–2.361.
[20] The percentage price fall was excised from the published version of the Commission's report on confidentiality grounds.

would be offset by synergies achieved through savings on procurement and central costs, as well as additional profits from Morrisons' vertically integrated processing plants.

In this case, the Commission emphasised that:

"In order to assess the extent to which any adverse effects of the merger might be offset by benefits accruing to consumers in price cuts, we need to assess the likelihood of the claimed cost savings being achieved. Moreover, the cost savings must be attributable to the merger if they are to be weighed against any adverse effects arising from the merger."[21]

The Commission accepted that buying synergies would be likely to be achievable, and that to the extent that they resulted in increased efficiency (for example, from larger production runs of own-brand products), there would be a benefit arising from the merger. However, the Commission expected certain buying synergies to result from an increased level of buyer power for Morrisons *vis-à-vis* suppliers. The Commission accepted that the synergies Morrisons anticipated as regards central costs, and additional profits from its vertically integrated processing plants, appeared to be reasonable and would be unlikely to be achieved in the absence of the merger. As regards the increase in sales densities that Morrisons anticipated, and expected resulting reductions in unit costs, the Commission concluded that this benefit was more speculative than the other synergies anticipated. In particular, it depended upon the successful implementation of Morrisons' sales strategy into Safeway stores, and in this connection, Safeway had indicated that Morrisons' proposals were not based on how the Safeway stores might be improved but on how its own stores, of comparable size and in comparable locations, performed.

6.207   In summary, the Commission concluded that overall there would be some adverse effects on suppliers due to Morrisons' increased buyer power. However, the merger would generate some reductions in central costs, whilst other anticipated cost savings were too speculative. The Commission expected that the likely merger-specific cost savings would be passed on to customers given that the Commission had found that price and non-price competition would not be expected to be reduced following the merger. The Commission concluded that on balance, the benefits to consumers would broadly offset the detriments to suppliers.[22]

In contrast, as regards the proposed bids by Sainsbury, Asda and Tesco, the Commission concluded that whilst some genuine cost savings could be expected to arise from the proposed mergers, the Commission did not expect such cost savings to be passed on to consumers in the form of, for example, lower prices, and such cost savings were insufficient to outweigh the detriments to competition that the Commission had identified in relation to the other bids.[23]

---

[21] Cited above, para.6.027, n.27, at para.2.362.
[22] Cited above, para.6.027, n.27, at paras 2.361 to 2.366.
[23] Cited above, para.6.027, n.27, at paras 2.306–2.307, 2.429–2.430 and 2.488–2.489.

The relevance of the parties' motives, plans and internal documents, and third parties' views

It is standard practice for the Commission to seek internal documentation **6.208** (such as board minutes and management reports and working papers) in order to gain some idea as to the motives behind the acquisition or merger.[24] Such information is also increasingly being requested by the OFT. One issue that is generally of interest to the Commission is how the purchase price was determined. The rationale behind this line of inquiry is based on the proposition that instead of making the acquisition in question, the acquirer could have purchased similar assets at their net replacement cost, and that any substantial premium paid above the net asset value may suggest that the merger will enhance the merged company's profitability, by increasing its market power and thereby enabling it to raise prices. For example, in *H+H Celcon/Marley Building Materials*, the Commission considered the valuation which H+H Celcon had placed on MBM, and concluded that:

". . . we think the more likely explanation for the apparent discrepancy between the stand-alone value placed on MBM by H+H Celcon and MBM's depreciated replacement cost of capital employed is the existence of sustainable excess profits, arising from a lack of competition."[25]

However, a significant price premium above net asset value might reflect the fact that:

(i)   net asset values shown in the target company's accounts do not reflect their current economic replacement cost. This may arise if asset values exclude intangible investments such as amortised research and development expenditure which will yield benefits in the future, or if assets are valued at their depreciated historical cost rather than their true economic replacement cost; and/or

(ii)   the merger will enable the merged company materially to lower its costs by facilitating economies of scale or scope.

Alternatively, exit price/earnings ratios for the business being sold may be considered, as these provide a means of assessing whether the merger is likely to generate sufficient profits at prevailing market prices to provide an adequate return on the purchase price. (Exit price/earnings ratios may be a more appropriate measure in industries in which accounting net assets are low, such as services industries.) A high price/earnings ratio may reflect the low level of commercial risk faced by the business, and/or the expectation that profits will rise in the future due to the achievement of cost savings or an increase in market power.[26]

---

[24] This may particularly be the case where there is perceived to be scope for anti-competitive behaviour.

[25] Cited above, para.6.011, n.31, at para.2.94.

[26] It should be noted that the converse is not necessarily true. A "low" purchase price may merely reflect the fact that the vendor needs to sell the business (for example, to finance debt repayments) and the absence of alternative purchasers. In other words, the vendor may not be in a position to appropriate a share of the additional profits the merger is expected to

Finally, a key factor in how a merger will be viewed by competition authorities is the extent to which third parties corroborate or reject the parties' economic evidence, and whether credible complaints are received. The parties may have informed views as to the likelihood, nature and strength of any customer and competitor complaints, and any issues likely to be raised by sector regulators (*e.g.* OFGEM, OFCOM, etc.). Regulators' views on competition issues will also be given weight, but the OFT has from time-to-time taken a different view. Competition authorities' general approach is to give greater weight to the complaints of customers, on the grounds that competitors might well complain about mergers that depress prices. However, the substantive issue is the quality of the information provided and the credibility of any complaints, rather than necessarily their source.

---

bring. Information on the purchase price relative to current and future earnings is perhaps most appropriately viewed as circumstantial evidence of the parties' expectations. The Commission will also assess whether any expectation of higher prices is realistic given the strength of remaining competitors, barriers to entry, the extent of buyer power and so on.

CHAPTER 7

THE CONTROL OF NEWSPAPER MERGERS

Introduction

Special provisions relating to newspaper mergers in the United Kingdom have applied since 1965.[1] Prior to December 29, 2003, these provisions were contained in the Fair Trading Act 1973.[2] Under this regime:

7.001

- the prior consent of the Secretary of State for Trade and Industry was mandatory, except in certain limited circumstances;

- a reference to the Commission was compulsory except in certain specified circumstances; and

- the system of control was administered by the Secretary of State and the Department of Trade and Industry rather than the OFT.

Where consent was required and not obtained, the resulting "merger" was unlawful and void[3] and any person who was "knowingly concerned in, or privy to" such a purported unlawful transaction was guilty of a criminal offence. [4]

The newspaper provisions of the FTA were replaced as from December 29, 2003 by new provisions contained in the Enterprise Act 2002, as amended by the Communications Act 2003 ("the Communications Act"). The Communications Act heralds a more general reform of the media ownership rules covering TV ownership, radio ownership and cross-media ownership, as well as newspaper ownership. The Government made clear that it wanted the Communications Act to deregulate the media industry, adopting a new "light touch" approach.[5] The key provisions relating to TV, radio and cross-media ownership are considered in Ch.2, above.

---

[1] The control of newspaper mergers was introduced at the same time as the general merger control provisions contained in the Monopolies and Mergers Act 1965, the objective being to regulate and control the concentration of newspaper ownership in order to safeguard freedom of expression and variety of opinion. (*Report of the Royal Commission on the Press*, Cmnd. 1811 (1962)).

[2] FTA, ss.57–62.

[3] s.58(1) of the Act.

[4] s.62(1); by virtue of s.62(3), a person guilty of an offence under s.62 was liable, on conviction, to imprisonment for a term of up to two years, or to a fine, or both. However, so far as the authors are aware, there were no prosecutions in respect of unlawful transfers under the previous regime.

[5] See, for example, the Summary to the joint Department of Trade and Industry/Department of Culture Media and Sport Consultation Paper: *Draft Communications Bill—A new Future for Communications*, May 2002, which stated, *inter alia*, that the Government would "simplify and liberalise the rules on media ownership" and "reform the newspaper merger regime to make it less onerous and less pervasive."

The new newspaper rules are much more closely aligned to the general merger regime under the Enterprise Act. In particular, notification is voluntary as for general mergers (with the consequence that there are no longer criminal offences for failure to notify); the requirement for compulsory references to the Competition Commission has been removed; and the regime is primarily (but not entirely) administered by the OFT.

The new regime under the Communications Act

7.002   As from December 29, 2003, there is no longer an entirely separate regime for the control of newspaper mergers in the UK. Instead, the general Enterprise Act regime applies, so that a transaction involving newspapers will be a qualifying merger if the share of supply test or UK turnover test is met,[6] and will be assessed by the OFT by reference to the substantial lessening of competition test. However, the Communications Act inserts into the Enterprise Act additional "public interest" grounds relating to newspapers in relation to which the Secretary of State may serve an intervention notice under s.42(2) of the Act, or a special intervention notice under s.59(2) of the Act. The distinction between an intervention notice and a special intervention notice is explained in Ch.2, above.

So far as newspaper mergers are concerned, the additional specified public interest considerations have been inserted as ss.58(2A) and 58(2B) of the Enterprise Act.[7] They are:

"(2A) The need for—

    (a)   accurate presentation of news; and
    (b)   free expression of opinion;

in newspapers . . . [and]

(2B)   The need for, to the extent that it is reasonable and practicable, a sufficient plurality of views in newspapers in each market for newspapers in the United Kingdom or a part of the United Kingdom".

The considerations specified in s.58(2A) (accurate presentation of news and free expression of opinion) are the same as those which the Competition Commission was required to take into account on a reference under the FTA,[8] and the issues which the Commission considered in that context are likely to remain relevant. Indeed, the DTI has confirmed that this should be the case in its guidance, *Enterprise Act 2002: Public Interest Intervention in Media Mergers*, published in May 2004, in which it emphasises the continuity of assessment of newspaper mergers on public interest

---

[6] These jurisdictional tests are considered in detail in Ch.2, above. The previous regime under which the average circulation/distribution of the acquirer's titles and the target titles had to be considered (see s.58 of the FTA), is therefore no longer relevant.

[7] The additional public interest considerations relating to broadcasting and cross-media mergers contained in s.58(2C) are considered briefly in Ch.2, above.

[8] See s.59(3).

grounds between the previous regime and the new regime.[9] The approach of the Commission in past cases is therefore considered below in the section dealing with the evaluation of newspaper mergers. The plurality of views consideration specified in s.58(2B) was not specifically referred to in the FTA but, as is explained below, similar issues were considered in newspaper merger cases arising under the FTA. This is also evident from the DTI's guidance on the new regime.[10]

The Communications Act[11] introduces the public interest considerations specifically relating to newspapers in the context of a more general section entitled "media public interest considerations". Section 58(2C) of the Enterprise Act introduces three additional media-related public interest considerations which relate to broadcasting (principally, radio and television) mergers, although certain of the provisions are of potential relevance to cross-media transactions involving newspapers. Since this is primarily a cross-media issue, it is considered briefly in Ch.2, above.

The addition of the further public interest considerations in s.58 of the Enterprise Act enables the Secretary of State to serve an intervention notice under s.42(2) on any of the specified grounds. In addition, s.378 of the Communications Act adds provisions to s.59 of the Enterprise Act, relating to the circumstances where a special intervention notice can be given. The additional condition relevant to newspapers is contained in s.59(3C) of the Enterprise Act:

7.003

"The condition mentioned in this sub-section is that, in relation to the supply of newspapers of any description, at least one-quarter of all the newspapers of that description which were supplied in the United Kingdom, or in a substantial part of the United Kingdom, were supplied by the person or persons by whom one of the enterprises concerned was carried on."

The effect of this provision is that the Secretary of State may intervene in respect of a merger even where the standard merger thresholds are not met, provided at least one of the parties has a 25 per cent share of the supply of newspapers of a particular description, either in the whole of the UK or a substantial part of the UK. The meaning of substantial part of the UK is discussed in Ch.2.[12] Accordingly, if an existing newspaper proprietor has a

---

[9] See for example, the Executive Summary. The guidance is considered further below. The full title of the guidance is *Enterprise Act 2002: Public Interest Intervention in Media Mergers, Guidance on the operation of the public interest merger provisions relating to newspaper and other media mergers*. A copy of the guidance is available on the DTI's website, *www.dti.gov.uk*.

[10] See, for example, paras 5.11 *et seq*.

[11] s.375.

[12] It remains to be seen how the "substantial part of the UK" test will be applied to very small, local newspaper transactions, in particular whether the OFT will take jurisdiction even though the transaction only materially affects one small area, on the basis that this area forms part of a wider area which can be regarded as a substantial part of the UK. The Competition Commission suggested that this may be inappropriate by stating in its *Report on the acquisition by Archant Limited of the London newspapers of Independent News and Media Limited* (September 2004) that: "It is the essence of a local newspaper that it is circulated or distributed only locally. In itself, in many cases that area will not be significant and will not be a substantial part of the UK" (at App.C, para.29). However, that statement was

market share of 25 per cent or more either in the whole of the UK, or in a substantial part of the UK (bearing in mind that the Secretary of State may focus on particular types of newspaper only), *any* acquisition by such a publisher would potentially be subject to a special intervention notice, even when there is no product or geographic overlap with the target's business activities. The same applies to *any* acquisition, for example, by a non-newspaper proprietor, of newspapers which have a 25 per cent market share either in the whole of the UK or a substantial part of the UK. Given that (as discussed further below) geographic markets for local newspapers are local in scope, this has given rise to concerns that the Secretary of State could theoretically intervene in respect of any acquisition by the substantial publishers of local/regional newspapers, since they are likely to have a 25 per cent share of supply in some part of the UK which may be regarded as substantial. However, it is assumed that the Secretary of State will exercise his intervention rights in such circumstances sparingly. The DTI's guidance on the new regime indicates that a special intervention notice may be considered, for example, where conflicts of interests might arise with other businesses owned by the acquirer,[13] and where there are concerns regarding the identity of the proposed proprietor (the "contentious acquirer" type of case).[14]

Meaning of "newspaper"

7.004   A "newspaper" is defined by s.44(10) of the Enterprise Act (as amended) as "a daily, Sunday or local (other than daily or Sunday) newspaper circulating wholly or mainly in the United Kingdom or in a part of the United Kingdom". This is the same definition as applied under the FTA regime, with the consequence that decisions and guidance issued under the FTA on the meaning of "newspaper" should remain relevant. For example, the question has arisen in the past whether magazines, journals and periodicals, as well as free newspapers (or "free-sheets") come within the definition of a "newspaper", and the Commission has indicated that magazines, journals and periodicals do not constitute newspapers.[15] The Commission has also

---

made in the context of an acquisition of a considerable number of local newspapers distributed over a relatively wide area of Greater London which the Commission found exceeded the substantial part of the UK threshold, on the basis of population, area (as compared to the whole of the Greater London) and the gross value added of the relevant areas. It is therefore rather differnet from an acquisition of one local title.

[13] Such an issue was considered to be relevant when a company forming part of the Lonrho group sought to acquire *The Observer*, see *The Observer and George Outram & Company Limited*, HC 378 (June 1981).

[14] See paras 5.9 and 6.10.

[15] In *United Newspapers plc/Fleet Holdings plc*, Cm. 9610 (July 1985), both United Newspapers and Fleet Holdings published magazines as well as newspapers, and despite arguments by Fleet Holdings that if the merger were permitted to proceed, United Newspapers would enjoy a dominant position in farming periodicals, the MMC (as it then was) concluded that "we do not think that the merging of the farming magazines of the two companies is a matter of any real consequence" (at para.8.54). Similarly, in *Regional Independent Media Limited and Gannett UK Limited/Johnston Press plc/Guardian Media Group plc*, Cm. 4887 (November 2000), the transfer involved a number of magazines and specialist publications such as *Biker, Farming in the North, the Yeller, Writing Magazines, North West Business Insider, Lancashire Style, the Rugby Leader and Trials and Motorcross News*, as well as various newspapers. Regional Independent Media submitted that these

stated that "[p]ublications which appear only six or twelve times a year may be considered more akin to periodicals than newspapers".[16]

The DTI guidance on the new regime indicates that the DTI considers that the transfer of free-sheets may be subject to the newspaper regime provided the titles contain some news content. "Publications consisting wholly or almost wholly of advertising are not, in the Secretary of State's view, newspapers."[17] In view of this, it is clear that most "advertising only" publications will not be newspapers. The guidance goes on to add:

"In considering whether or not a publication is a "newspaper" for the purposes of the newspaper public interest considerations, the following questions are in the opinion of the Secretary of State relevant:

- Is there any real attempt at news coverage? News coverage is not limited to actual reporting of events but includes editorials and articles of interest.
- Does it contain advertisements that should properly appear in a newspaper? For instance certain statutes require matters to be advertised in a newspaper and not in an advertising free sheet.
- What is the proportion of the publication that contains advertisements or advertorials as compared with news content?"[18]

Acquisition of control

It should be noted that the FTA newspaper merger regime applied only to direct or indirect acquisitions of a 25 per cent voting interest.[19] Under the new regime, the standard Enterprise Act test applies, namely, whether two or more enterprises come under common ownership or control. As discussed in Ch.2, an acquisition of control includes an acquisition of material influence, which will frequently arise with a shareholding of less than 25 per cent.

7.005

---

titles were not newspapers for the purposes of the FTA. The Commission stated (in App.3.1) that "their specialist nature alone does not exempt them from being newspapers for the purposes of the [FTA]". However, the Commission's analysis essentially took no account of these titles. The issue of a potential competition concern in the supply of magazines arising in connection with a newspaper transfer raised interesting jurisdictional questions under the FTA regime. s.59(3) of the FTA required the Commission to report to the Secretary of State whether "the *transfer in question* may be expected to operate against the public interest". It is thought that if a public interest issue were identified in relation to magazines or other media interests, the Commission would have only been able to recommend against that particular aspect of the transaction (and, more importantly, the Secretary of State prohibit the transfer) if a reference had been made to the Commission under the general merger provisions of the FTA. The issue does not arise in the same way under the new regime, although clearly the Secretary of State could only intervene in relation to the newspaper and/or broadcasting aspects of the transaction.

[16] *Northcliffe Newspapers Group Limited/Aberdeen Journals Limited*, Cm. 3174 (February 1996). However, the Commission declined to determine that three such publications, which only contained editorial in relation to their specific subject matter, were not newspapers, merely that there was "considerable doubt" as to whether they were.

[17] *Enterprise Acto 2002 Public Interest Intervention in media mergers*, cited above, at para.3.12. Similar comments were made in the DTI guidance on the previous regime: *Guidance on DTI procedures for handling Newspaper Mergers* (February 1997), p.3.

[18] DTI guideance, para.3.13.

[19] See s.57 of the FTA.

Role of OFT and OFCOM *in newspaper merger cases*

7.006   To the extent that the newspaper public interest considerations are not considered to be relevant (and therefore an intervention notice is not served), the OFT's role will be to carry out a competition assessment in the usual way.

     The OFT has a duty under s.119B of the Act to ensure that the Secretary of State is aware of cases where he might wish to consider giving a special intervention notice. This is broadly equivalent to the OFT's obligations in relation to "standard" public interest cases under s.57 of the Act. It is clear from the DTI's guidance on the new regime that the DTI expects the OFT to draw to the Secretary of State's attention any cases which may raise newspaper public interest considerations.[20] Once an intervention notice or a special intervention notice has been given, the OFT will provide a report to the Secretary of State on competition issues (in the case of "ordinary" intervention notices only), and may include in its report a summary of representations received by the OFT relating to the public interest considerations specified in the intervention notice.[21]

     The Office of Communications ("OFCOM") is a new regulator for the media and communications sector which, as from December 29, 2003, replaced five pre-existing regulators, the Broadcasting Standards Commission, the Independent Television Commission, OFTEL (the Office of Telecommunications), the Radio Authority and the Radio Communications Agency. The role of OFCOM in respect of newspaper mergers is to advise the Secretary of State in connection with newspaper public interest considerations (it has a similar role in respect of other media mergers). In particular, where an intervention notice or a special intervention notice has been given by the Secretary of State and the intervention notice mentions any media public interest consideration, OFCOM has to provide the Secretary of State with a report on the effect of the relevant consideration on the case, including its advice and recommendations on such consideration.[22] For the purpose of providing such a report, OFCOM is required to carry out a public consultation process.[23] OFCOM is also obliged to give the Commission or the OFT information in its possession which may reasonably be required by the OFT or the Commission or which it would otherwise be appropriate to give to the OFT or the Commission (similar obligations are also imposed on the OFT and the Commission).[24] In cases where an intervention notice or a special intervention notice has been given, and a reference is subsequently made to the Commission, OFCOM has the power to provide such advice as it considers appropriate to the Secretary of State in relation to the Commission's report and the taking by the Secretary of State of any enforcement action. It also has a more general power to

---

[20] See para.4.2.

[21] See ss.44 and 61 of the Act, as amended. Note that in non-media public interest cases (*i.e.* currently, those relating to national security/defence contractors), the OFT is obliged to include such a summary in its report as opposed to merely having the power to do so. The difference in approach is presumably due to the involvement of OFCOM in media public interest cases.

[22] See ss.44A and 61A of the Act.

[23] s.105(1A) of the Act.

[24] ss.105(3A) and (4A) of the Act. The OFT is subject to a similar obligation in connection with the competition aspects of a newspaper merger.

provide any other advice which it considers appropriate to the Secretary of State in connection with media public interest cases. Any such advice is to be published.[25]

The involvement of OFCOM in newspaper mergers has been a source of concern for some newspaper publishers, bearing in mind that none of the five regulators which OFCOM replaced has any history of involvement in the newspaper sector. However, it should be noted that OFCOM's role is merely advisory and relates solely to public interest issues. In addtion, OFCOM has indicated that it will draw upon a panel of experts in the newspaper industry to provide analysis and advice in each case.[26] In addition, OFCOM does not advise the Secretary of State as to whether an intervention notice should be issued; its role essentially begins after an intervention notice has been served.[26A] Nevertheless, it is clear that OFCOM will have a key role in the clearance process.

Applications for clearance

As indicated above, the newspaper merger provisions will be primarily administered by the OFT and notifications for clearance should therefore be made to the OFT in the usual way. As with general mergers, a notification for clearance may be made by means of a merger notice or an informal submission; alternatively, the parties may decide not to make a notification at all. The DTI's guidance and OFCOM's guidance contradict each other to some extent as to whether copies of notifications should also be provided to the DTI and OFCOM. The DTI guidance indicates that merger notices should be copied to OFCOM (but not the DTI), and that informal submissions may be copied to OFCOM and the DTI if the parties think that media public interest issues may arise.[27] On the other hand, the OFCOM guidance suggests that all submissions should be sent to the DTI as well as the OFT, and that the parties may choose to copy their submission to OFCOM.[28] In practice, copying all submissions to the DTI and OFCOM is likely to be prudent.

7.007

As regards the content of notifications, the DTI's guidance indicates that, in addition to the matters discussed in the OFT's general procedural guidance, the information should be supplemented with such details as are required by OFCOM.[29] OFCOM's guidance states clearly that there is no requirement to provide specified information with respect to public interest issues prior to the issue of an intervention notice, adding that it is not essential to send any submission to OFCOM, merely that the parties may consider doing so in order to assist and expedite the process in the event

---

[25] s.106B of the Act.
[26] OFCOM *guidance for the public interest test for media mergers*, para.63. The guidance is available on OFCOM's website, *www.ofcom.org.uk*.
[26A] Although it should be noted that the DTI's guidance states at para.4.13 that the Secretary of State may nevertheless receive and/or seek information from OFCOM in order to inform his decision as to whether or not to intervene, which suggests that OFCOM may provide unsolicited information to the Secretary of State.
[27] DTI guidance, paras 4.9 and 4.11.
[28] OFCOM guidance, paras 48 to 49.
[29] DTI guidance, para.4.9.

that an intervention notice is issued.[30] Nevertheless, OFCOM requests in App.1a to its guidance that certain information should be provided in all submissions, and encourages merging parties to discuss OFCOM'S information requirements with it before making any submissions.

Appendix 1a to OFCOM's guidance sets out the information which OFCOM will request in relation to all public interest cases, and App.1b sets out the information that OFCOM may request in assessing the public interest issues arising from a merger, although it is not envisaged that all this information will be required in every case. Appendix 1c consists of information required in exceptional circumstances, although there is no express indication of what those circumstances might be. The entirety of App.1 to OFCOM's guidance is reproduced in App.8.

The information to be required in all public interest newspaper cases[31] is relatively uncontroversial and includes full details of the parties, details of existing media businesses (both in the UK and overseas), circulation/average sales information for UK newspapers, details of circulation area for local/regional titles (*e.g.* maps) and details of any complaints about accuracy of news made to the parties or the Press Complaints Commission (or similar overseas bodies) in the last five years.

7.008 The App.1b information (which may be required in certain cases) with respect to newspapers includes: readership demographics; current policies on editorial independence; plans for the titles if the transaction proceeds (for example, whether newspapers will continue as separate newspapers); sample copies; and statements as to general plans and type of market usually targeted by the acquiring owner.

Appendix 1c (information required in exceptional cases) includes an assessment of the proportion of content dedicated to news, advertising and general features in each title, together with an assessment of the likely impact of the merger and an indication of likely post-merger changes (the guidance refers to the David Sullivan case considered further below, suggesting that this sort of information may only be requested in "contentious proprietor" type cases where there is a concern that quality of content may be affected); and details of the employment history of the acquiring owner (the members of the Board in the case of a plc).[32]

OFCOM's approach to the information that should be provided in notifications altered considerably during the consultation process on its guidance. The draft guidance had seemed to suggest that a large amount of information should be provided in all cases. The approach of the final guidance is considerably more "user friendly", recognising that much information will be unnecessary in some cases, and also the fact that, formally at least, public interest issues only became relevant once an intervention notice has been served. As noted above, OFCOM invites parties to discuss its information requirements with it before making any submissions. The authors expect that OFCOM will request much of the information referred to in Apps 1a and 1b in most cases where public interest issues may arise. However, given the Government's desire for a "light touch" approach, which suggests that the number of interventions ought to be relatively small

---

[30] OFCOM guidance, para.48.
[31] Each part of App.1 includes a similar list with respect to broadcasting mergers.
[32] Again, the guidance refers to the *David Sullivan* case.

(this is backed up by the DTI guidance on the new regime), acquirers may take the view in uncomplicated cases which should not raise any material public interest issues that the provision of much of the information referred to in App.1 to OFCOM's guidance is unnecessary.

The standard time periods apply in relation to submissions made on merger notices, save that the assessment period can be further extended to 40 working days where an intervention notice has been served.[33] In relation to informal submissions, the OFCOM guidance indicates that the parties can expect a decision within 50 working days,[34] which represents an extension of 10 working days to the OFT's standard 40 working day period.   **7.009**

Applications for confidential guidance or informal advice

The DTI and OFCOM guidance indicate that both confidential guidance and informal advice will be available in respect of newspaper transactions. The application should be sent to the OFT with a copy being provided to OFCOM and the DTI. The OFT will advise on competition issues in the usual way, the DTI/Secretary of State will advise on the likelihood of intervention[35] and OFCOM will advise as to whether it would be likely to recommend a reference on public interest grounds if an intervention notice were to be issued.[35A] No guidance is available from the DTI/Secretary of State as to whether a reference is likely. Joint meetings with the OFT, DTI and OFCOM will be held in the context of informal advice (and confidential guidance if requested by the parties following receipt of the guidance). The OFCOM guidance clarifies that OFCOM will only provide informal advice/confidential guidance with respect to the media public interest issues if the DTI/Secretary of State indicates that intervention would be likely. Advice/guidance with respect to the media public interest issues must also be specifically requested.[36] The DTI guidance indicates that in the case of informal advice, a paper should be submitted to the OFT and copied to OFCOM and the DTI at least 48 hours in advance[37]; essentially the same period as applies for informal advice in connection with general mergers under the OFT's procedural guidance.[38]   **7.010**

Informal advice was not available from the DTI under the former FTA newspaper regime and its introduction is to be welcomed. Given that the Secretary of State rather than OFCOM is the final decision-maker as to whether a reference is made, it is perhaps unfortunate that the advice/

---

[33] The same applies to all public interest cases; see ss.97(3) and 97(4) of the Enterprise Act.

[34] OFCOM guidance, para.57.

[35] DTI officials provide the advice in the context of informal advice, whereas the advice is from the Secretary of State in the context of confidential guidance.

[35A] The precise wording used in OFCOM's guidance in the context of informal advice is that advice will be given "on the likely public interest considerations arising out of a prospective media merger situation". This mirrors the wording used in relation to informal advice applications at para.3.4 of the OFT's *Procedural Guidance*. It is understood that, like the OFT, OFCOM will seek to go beyond merely commenting on the likely issues and will provide its non-binding view on whether it would be likely to recommend reference on the basis of the information received, even in informal advice cases.

[36] OFCOM guidance, paras 29 and 36.

[37] Para.4.6. The OFCOM guidance refers to "at least two to three days", see para.31.

[38] See para.3.6 of the OFT publication, *Mergers: Procedural Guidance*, published in May 2003. The actual wording used in this context is "two to three days".

guidance which is available from the DTI/Secretary of State relates only to the likelihood of intervention on public interest grounds, rather than the likelihood of reference on such grounds, with the latter advice/guidance being provided only by OFCOM. Nevertheless, the present position is at least an improvement on the original proposal under which neither the DTI nor the Secretary of State would have been involved in the informal advice or confidential guidance processes at all.

It is assumed that the Secretary of State will follow the advice of OFCOM in most cases, but this will not become clear until the new regime has been operating for some time, and in any event, it would appear to be inevitable that there will be some cases where the Secretary of State will take a different view.

OFCOM indicates that it will respond to complete confidential guidance requests within 30 working days.[39] As indicated in Ch.3 above, this is the same timetable which the OFT is now working to. It is assumed that the Secretary of State's guidance will be available within the same time period.

Procedure following the service of an intervention notice or a special intervention notice

7.011   Apart from the involvement of OFCOM, the procedure followed after the service of an intervention notice or a special intervention notice will essentially be the same as in other public interest cases (discussed in Ch.2, above). Accordingly, the Secretary of State will consider whether a reference to the Commission should be made on the basis of the specified newspaper public interest consideration, together with any competition issues raised by the OFT, and may also direct the OFT to seek undertakings in lieu of a reference. The Secretary of State will be advised by the OFT and OFCOM, and OFCOM will carry out a consultation of third party views with respect to the specified newspaper public interest consideration (whilst the OFT will consult on any competition aspects of the transaction). If the Secretary of State decides that the newspaper public interest consideration is not relevant to the transaction, the case reverts to the OFT to be considered in the usual way (or in the case of a special intervention notice, the procedure comes to an end).

As with other public interest cases, the Secretary of State will not be able to dispute the OFT's competition assessment. Accordingly, if no competition concerns are identified by the OFT, a reference can be made only in respect of the public interest considerations. Nevertheless, the Secretary of State may decide not to make a reference even where the OFT has concluded on competition grounds that a reference should follow on the basis that public interest considerations outweigh the competition concerns. One (arguably extreme) example of where this might occur is set out in the DTI's response to the consultation on its draft guidance issued in April 2004.[40] The response document puts forward a situation where the competition authorities have concluded that a merger should be blocked on

---

[39] OFCOM guidance, para.43.
[40] *Result of DTI's consultation on Draft Guidance: "Enterprise Act 2002: Public Interest Intervention in Media Mergers"*, available on the Consultations page of the Consumer and Competition Policy section of the DTI's website, *www.dti.gov.uk.*

competition grounds despite the fact it would result in the relevant title going out of business, because the competitive conditions following such failure would still be better than if the transfer were permitted. The Secretary of State may decline to make a reference on the basis that there are strong public interest grounds in favour of the title remaining in business despite the competition concerns.[41]

Competition Commission procedures

Following a reference on newspaper public interest grounds, the Commission's procedures are essentially the same as in other public interest cases (as discussed in Ch.4, above). Accordingly, the Commission will: assess jurisdiction; consider whether the merger may be expected to result in a substantial lessening of competition (assuming the reference is made partly on competition grounds); consider whether the transfer operates or may be expected to operate against the public interest; and propose remedies to any competition detriments and any overall adverse public interest findings.[42]

    7.012

One difference from other public interest cases is that in media public interest cases, the Commission has a specific obligation to have regard to the need to consult the public, so far as practicable.[43] The Communications Act does not affect the arrangements whereby there is a panel of Commission members, generally referred to as the newspaper panel, available for selection in connection with newspaper merger references.[44] The chairman of the Commission must appoint at least one member from the newspaper panel to the group constituted to deal with newspaper references.[45] The current members of the panel may be viewed on the website of the Competition Commission.

The Secretary of State's decision and remedies

As in other public interest cases, the Secretary of State must publish a decision as to whether he has reached an adverse public interest finding within 30 days of receipt of the report from the Commission.[46] The Secretary of State must accept the Commission's conclusions on competition issues and must take the Commission's recommendations in relation to public interest issues into account (but is not bound by them) in determining what remedial action (including prohibition), if any, should be taken.[47]

    7.013

The Communications Act introduces a number of additional remedies in the context of newspaper mergers to those which are available in the context of general mergers.[48] These additional provisions, which apply only

---

[41] These comments are made in the context of what was para.4.16 of the draft DTI guidance, which became para.4.23 in the final guidance. Interestingly, this example is not repeated in the actual guidance.

[42] See ss.47 and 63 of the Act.

[43] See s.104A of the Act.

[44] See para.22 of Sch.7 to the Competition Act 1998, as amended.

[45] Para.15(5) of Sch.7 to the Competition Act 1998, as amended. It is possible for the whole group to consist of members of the newspaper panel.

[46] ss.54(5) and 66(3) of the Act.

[47] See s.55 of the Act.

[48] New para.20A of Sch.8 to the Act.

where a newspaper public interest consideration is relevant to the adverse determination are:

- the possibility of altering the constitution of a company (*e.g.* to establish an editorial board)[49];

- requiring the consent of a particular person before taking certain actions, including the appointment or dismissal of editors, journalists or directors;

- attaching conditions to the operation of a newspaper; and

- prohibiting consultation or co-operation between subsidiaries.

These remedies are potentially very far reaching; for example, the authors are not aware of any past case where controls were put on the publisher of a newspaper as regards the appointment or dismissal of journalists. However, it is assumed that the circumstances where such a remedy would be appropriate will be very rare.

Secretary of State policy on intervention

7.014 The DTI's guidance on the new regime makes clear that the parties will be informed and invited to submit their views if the Secretary of State is going to take a view on whether or not to intervene. In taking such a view, the guidance states that the Secretary of State will have regard to all available information, which may include complaints made to and judgments of the Press Complaints Commission; any previous regulatory decisions; published articles; and third party representations. However, the Secretary of State will not receive advice from OFCOM (although he may seek or receive information from OFCOM in order to inform his decision).[50]

The Secretary of State will aim (but is not obliged) to take an initial decision on whether to intervene within 10 working days of the transaction being notified to the OFT, or the transaction otherwise being brought to his attention, whichever is later. In view of this timescale, the parties will only generally be given 3–4 working days to provide any written representations. The guidance indicates that the Secretary of State will not normally conduct a formal consultation exercise, but that any representations received will be taken into account and that the views of a few interested parties may be sought.[51]

If an intervention notice is to be served, a press notice to this effect will be released, along with the notice. No announcement will be made if the decision is not to intervene, although the parties will be informed.[52]

On the Secretary of State's likely policy towards intervention, the DTI guidance explains that each case will need to be considered on its own facts and merits.[53] However, it observes that:

---

[49] Such a remedy was used in the *T Bailey Forman* case discussed further below.
[50] DTI guidance, para.4.13.
[51] DTI guidance, para.4.14.
[52] DTI guidance, para.4.15.
[53] DTI guidance, para.6.1.

"The small number of cases that have resulted in adverse public interest findings other than on competition grounds under the FTA newspaper merger regime suggests that the number of cases in which the Secretary of State will find it necessary to intervene on the basis of newspaper public interest considerations under the new regime is likely to be small."[54]

Nevertheless, the guidance also states that fewer newspaper mergers will be referred to the Commission than are initially reported on by OFCOM.[55] There is also an indication that the Secretary of State may consider intervening where there are market overlaps on the basis that "there is a recognisable correlation between high levels of concentration and the potential for newspaper ownership concerns to arise".[56] Intervention would of course be on the basis of plurality concerns, rather than competition concerns, which are the exclusive preserve of the OFT (and the Competition Commission). The guidance clarifies that such intervention would only be likely in the context of local newspaper transfers at a level above that at which a potential competition issue would commonly be identified. However, for acquisitions of national newspapers by existing proprietors, the guidance states that intervention may be appropriate at a lower threshold.[57]

The guidance acknowledges that a special intervention notice may be served where an existing newspaper owner acquires a non-newspaper business, but indicates that intervention in such cases would be extremely rare (for example, where for corporate structuring or tax reasons the form of a transaction does not reflect the reality of the situation (*i.e.* in reality, the transaction involves an acquisition of a newspaper), or cases where the transaction has unusual features raising particular plurality issues).[58] As regards third party comments, the DTI indicates that the Secretary of State will consider intervening where there is a "significant volume of adverse third party comments regarding the impact or potential impact of the transaction on newspaper public interest considerations", and notes that unsubstantiated allegations should not automatically lead to intervention. The guidance states that intervention is more likely where the comments received raise and substantiate a specific public interest concern relating to newspapers.[59]

7.015

The Secretary of State may consider intervening in cases where the acquirer of a newspaper already owns other non-newspaper media in the same geographic area.[60] Clearly, the cross-media ownership rules and the cross-media plurality public interest consideration will be relevant in such circumstances[61]; however, the Secretary of State might also wish to serve a special intervention notice under s.59 of the Act in respect of one of the newspaper public interest considerations, for example, because the acquirer's existing

---

[54] DTI guidance, para.6.3.
[55] DTI guidance, para.6.4. However, the Secretary of State has yet to issue an intervention notice under the newspaper merger provisions, see further para.7.015 below.
[56] DTI guidance, para.6.7. No supporting evidence is provided for this statement.
[57] DTI guidance, para.6.7.
[58] DTI guidance, para.6.5.
[59] DTI guidance, para.6.6.
[60] DTI guidance, para.6.8.
[61] These are briefly considered in Ch.2, above.

media interests may provide an indication of the likely editorial policy in relation to the newspapers to be acquired. The DTI guidance states that the Secretary of State may consider intervention on the basis of a newspaper public interest concern in such circumstances where the relevant newspaper has a significant market share.

In respect of acquisitions by persons with no existing newspaper (or other media) interests, the DTI guidance indicates that such acquisitions are likely to raise public interest concerns only in exceptional circumstances where the identity of the acquirer gives rise to concerns. In such cases, the guidance suggests that there will need to be a "significant volume" of adverse third party comment in relation to the newspaper public interest considerations, or evidence of previous undesirable conduct (such as prior editorial interference in non-newspaper publications), before the Secretary of State is likely to intervene in relation to acquisitions of local newspapers. In relation to national newspapers, the guidance states that intervention might occur even in the absence of a significant volume of third party comments in cases involving "contentious acquirers" or where the purchaser is present in other media in the same geographic area,[62] indicating that a lower threshold is likely to apply in national newspaper cases.[63]

The authors believe that, at the time of writing, only three newspaper cases have been considered by the OFT so far under the new newspaper regime. The first related to Archant Limited's acquisition of certain local London titles from Independent News & Media plc, which was referred to (and subsequently cleared by) the Competition Commission.[63A] The second related to Tindle Newspapers' acquisition of *Y Cmyro*,[63B] which the OFT found not to be a qualifying merger. The third relates to Press Acquisitions Limited's purchase of The Telegraph Group Limited (primarily comprising *The Daily Telegraph* and *Sunday Telegraph* newspapers) which the OFT cleared in October 2004.[63C] (Press Acquisitions is ultimately controlled by Sir David and Sir Frederick Barclay). The Secretary of State did not intervene on public interest grounds in any of these cases.

7.016   Finally, it should be noted that no express statements of policy have yet been published by OFCOM. Its guidance on the new regime (discussed above) is largely procedural and confines itself to stating that substantive guidance on how the tests will be applied can be found in the DTI guidance.[64]

The evaluation of newspaper mergers

7.017   There are essentially two broad categories of issues which may be relevant in assessing newspaper mergers:

---

[62] Presumably this simply means in the UK given that national newspapers are being discussed.

[63] DTI guidance, para.6.10.

[63A] The Commission's report is considered further below.

[63B] Tindle also purchased Radio Ceredigion.

[63C] Completed acquisition by Press Acquisitions Limited of Telegraph Group Limited, October 11, 2004.

[64] OFCOM guidance, para.58.

(i)   the accurate presentation of news, the free expression of opinion
       and the need for a plurality of views (that is, the "newspaper public
       interest considerations" on the basis of which a public interest
       reference may be made by the Secretary of State); and

(ii)   issues associated with concentration of ownership and competition
       for readers and advertisers (in other words, the "normal" competition
       issues which are relevant to newspapers).

The issues connected with (i) above will be decided upon by the
Secretary of State, subject to advice from OFCOM and, following a reference on public interest grounds, the Commission. The competition issues
relating to the second category of issues identified above are assessed by
the OFT and the Competition Commission (although where both competition issues and public interest considerations are present, the Secretary of
State may prohibit a transaction or require remedies on public interest
grounds even where the Commission or the OFT have decided that the
merger should not be prohibited on competition grounds). The economic
assessment of mergers is discussed in detail in Ch.6 above, and the analysis
of the competition assessment of newspaper mergers summarised below
should be read in conjunction with that analysis.

The accurate presentation of news, the free expression of opinion and the need for a sufficient plurality of views

These expressions are not defined in the Enterprise Act (as amended by the   7.018
Communications Act). The meaning of "accurate presentation of news" is
reasonably self-explanatory; recent Commission reports under the FTA
regime have not considered the issue in any detail as it has not been
regarded as a concern in the absence of evidence that the proposed
acquirers had engaged in inaccurate reporting.[65] However, it was referred
to in the David Sullivan case discussed further below.

The main issues which have been considered in the context of free
expression of opinion in Commission reports under the FTA are the degree
of editorial independence/freedom granted by newspaper owners to their
editors, and the diversity of news and opinion expressed by the media. The
diversity of opinion issue appears to be similar to the public interest consideration set out in s.58(2B) of the Act relating to a sufficient plurality of
views and it is likely that a similar approach will be adopted by the
Secretary of State and OFCOM in applying the concept.

Although these issues are not wholly divorced from competition issues
(for example, the elimination of rivalry between competing titles may
reduce diversity[65A] as well as switching opportunities for advertisers), they
are substantially wider than "pure" competition issues, which might be

---

[65]   See, for example, *Gannett UK Limited and SMG plc* Cm. 5782 (March 2003), para.2.40;
       and *Portsmouth & Sunderland Newspapers plc and Johnston Press plc/Newsquest
       (Investments) Limited/News Communications and Media plc*, Cm. 4358 (June 1999),
       para.1.6.
[65A] Although this would not necessarily follow as diversity of views does not require diversity
       of ownership.

defined as an elimination of rivalry leading to reductions in quality, choice or innovation or price increases.

The DTI's guidance on the new regime comments on plurality issues as follows:

> "The test of a sufficient plurality of views is intended to enable regard to be had not only to the need for a sufficient number of views to be expressed, but also to the need for variety in those views and for there to be a variety of outlets and publications in which they can be expressed. There is a qualitative element to the plurality assessment that requires account to be taken of the context in which titles circulate and the nature of those titles—for example, one title in a particular area may be of greater significance for plurality purposes than another".[66]

7.019　　The plurality consideration, unlike accurate presentation of news and free expression of opinion, is qualified in s.58(2B) of the Enterprise Act by reference to the reasonableness and practicality of achieving a "sufficient plurality of views" in each newspaper market. The DTI's guidance on the new regime states that whilst plurality of views in all markets is the ideal goal of the regime, "it may not be reasonable to require this in relation to a particular part of the market, for example, because of associated costs". The guidance also recognises that a higher level of plurality may be achievable in large urban areas than small rural communities.[67]

Previous Commission analysis of the newspaper public interest considerations

7.020　　In 21 out of the 25 newspaper reports published between January 1988 and October 2003, the Commission concluded that the proposed transfers would not have any adverse effects on the accurate presentation of news or the free expression of opinion.[67A] Such conclusions have been reached primarily on the basis of the reputations and existing policies of the acquiring companies of allowing a high degree of editorial independence and the fact that it is in their commercial interests to do so. For example, in their reports on the proposed acquisitions by Newsquest (Investments) Limited ("Newsquest"), Johnston Press plc ("Johnston") and Trinity Mirror plc ("Trinity Mirror") of News Communications & Media plc ("NewsComm"), the Commission stated:

> "At no time have we received any evidence that casts doubt on [the] commitment [of the bidders] to accurate reporting or editorial freedom. Nor have we found any suggestion that any of them has, or is intending to introduce, a standardized editorial product. We did not find anything

---

[66] DTI guidance, para.5.11.
[66A] For example, certain markets may only support one title.
[67] DTI guidance, para.5.12.
[67A] The issue was not considered in the Commission's *Report on the acquisition by Archant Limited of the London newspapers of Independent News and Media Limited* (September 2004) ("the *Archant/INM* report"), the first newspaper report under the new regime, as no intervention notice was served by the Secretary of State.

to sustain the concerns put to us that the proposed transfers threatened a loss of local independence for editors, or would lead to remoteness from local communities, lower journalistic and production standards, or a reduction in journalists' jobs. All three of the groups interested in acquiring Newscom stressed the importance of their titles remaining close to their readerships' communities if they were to continue to be successful commercially. This meant giving editors on the spot the freedom to decide what stories to cover, and what line to take on controversial issues ... The commercial logic of their argument, that newspapers need to be edited in a way which reflects local issues and concerns if they are to survive and prosper, is one we find compelling. For any of these groups to seek to impose a uniform content or style on their titles would not only harm the accurate presentation of news and free expression of opinion it would also be bad for business".[68]

In one of the four reports in which the Commission reached adverse conclusions, Century Newspapers and Thomson Regional Newspapers (TRN), the Commission concluded in its 1989 Report that diversity of opinion[69] would be adversely affected by the transfer of *The News Letter*, a daily regional newspaper in Northern Ireland which represented Unionist opinion, to TRN, which owned the *Belfast Telegraph*. In reaching this conclusion the Commission emphasised that the three regional papers published in Northern Ireland expressed different political opinions and had different readerships, and that it was particularly important to maintain the diversity of opinion in Northern Ireland. This conclusion was reached despite TRN's arguments that commercial imperatives would require it to maintain the paper's political stance in order to retain readers, and despite TRN's policy of allowing its regional newspapers to have a high degree of local autonomy and editorial freedom.[70]

A similar view was reached 10 years later when Trinity plc sought the Secretary of State's consent to acquire Mirror Group plc.[71] The Commission concluded that, whilst the transaction would have no adverse effects, including in relation to diversity, in Great Britain, this was not the case in Northern Ireland. In line with earlier reports, the Commission accepted that diversity would generally be adequately protected by editorial independence,[72] but that this was not the case in Northern Ireland. It concluded that there was a risk that the combination of Trinity's broadly Unionist, but "middle of the road" *Belfast Telegraph* and Mirror Group's more radically

---

[68] *News Communications and Media plc and Newsquest (Investments) Limited/Johnston Press plc/Trinity Mirror plc*, Cm. 4680 (April 2000), para.2.33. Similar views have also been expressed in a number of other cases, including *Portsmouth & Sunderland Newspapers plc and Johnston Press plc/Newsquest (Investments) Limited/News Communication and Media plc*, Cm. 4358 (June 1999), para.1.6; *Regional Independent Media Limited and Gannett UK Limited/Johnston Press plc/Guardian Media Group plc*, Cm. 4887 (November 2000), para.2.49; and *Gannett UK Limited and SMG plc*, Cm. 5782 (March 2003), para.2.59.
[69] The DTI guidance on the new regime specifically discusses *Century/TRN* in the context of plurality of views; see para.5.13
[70] *Century Newspapers Ltd/ Thomson Regional Newspapers Ltd*, Cm. 677 (April 1989), paras 6.26–6.28 and 6.30.
[71] *Trinity plc/Mirror Group plc and Regional Independent Media Holdings Limited/Mirror Group plc*, Cm. 4393 (July 1999).
[72] *ibid.*, para.1.4.

Unionist, *The News Letter,* whether deliberately or not, was likely to lead over time, to a softening of the stance of *The News Letter*, to bring it into line with the more commercially successful *Belfast Telegraph*. The Commission stated that it was "vital to the public interest that there should be as much opportunity as possible for the expression of a wide variety of political views in Northern Ireland".[73] In view of these concerns (together with the fact that the combined Trinity/Mirror Group would have had a 67 per cent share of advertising in regional and local newspapers in Northern Ireland), the Commission recommended that Trinity should be required to divest *The News Letter* (and Mirror Group's other Northern Ireland titles) as a condition to consent being granted. Whilst the Secretary of State agreed that there was a problem, he decided on a different solution, having concluded that the combination of Trinity's Northern Irish titles, in particular the *Belfast Telegraph*, and the Mirror Group's national titles (in particular *The Mirror*), posed a real risk that a third party title, *The Irish News*, which was the main nationalist title in Northern Ireland, would be unable to obtain sufficient advertising revenue to remain viable. The Commission had considered this risk, but on balance, decided that it was not a likely outcome. However, the Secretary of State disagreed and required Trinity to divest its own Northern Irish titles (*i.e.* including the *Belfast Telegraph*), rather than those of the Mirror Group.[74]

It is clear from these cases that transactions involving regional titles in Northern Ireland will be considered very carefully to ensure that there is no adverse effect on the plurality of views expressed in Northern Ireland, and there is no reason to suppose that a different approach will be adopted following the Communications Act. To a lesser extent, similar issues may arise with respect to Scottish and Welsh regional titles, as was seen in connection with the acquisition by Gannett UK Limited of *The Herald, The Sunday Herald* and *The Glasgow Evening News* from SMG plc,[75] where the Commission recommended clearance but only after examining closely the likely impact of the transaction on the "Scottishness" of the target titles (in particular, *The Herald* and *The Sunday Herald*), despite the fact that Gannett had no pre-existing newspaper interests in Scotland.

7.021   The second adverse finding on non-competition grounds was reached in relation to the proposed acquisition by Mr David Sullivan of a controlling interest in The Bristol Evening Post plc (BEP),[76] notwithstanding the Commission's conclusion that the different readership of newspapers already owned by Mr Sullivan and those of BEP implied that the acquisition would not raise any significant competition concerns. Mr Sullivan owned 50 per cent of Sport Newspapers Ltd, publisher of the *Sunday Sport* and *The Sport*, which the Commission described as having a limited news content and being heavily sex-orientated. In reaching this conclusion the Commission expressed three main concerns. First, it concluded that despite Mr Sullivan's present intention not to change the character and content of the BEP newspapers, or to restrict editorial freedom, he could be expected

---

[73] *Trinity plc/Mirror Group plc and Regional Independent Media Holdings Limited/Mirror Group plc*, para.2.70.
[74] See DTI press release P/99/639, July 23, 1999.
[75] *Gannett UK Limited and SMG plc*, Cm. 5782 (March 2003).
[76] *Mr David Sullivan/The Bristol Evening Post plc*, Cm. 1083 (May 1990).

to do so and that this would harm both the accurate presentation of news and the free expression of opinion. This view was based on his active involvement with the editors of the *Sport* newspapers and his previous involvement with the *Daily Star*. In addition, editors of the BEP papers were likely to give weight to any suggestions made by Mr Sullivan if he were to become a major shareholder. Secondly, the Commission stated that Mr Sullivan had no experience in the responsibilities of organising a news service for a regional newspaper, and his association with the *Daily Star* in the past had accelerated its loss of readers and advertisers.[77] The Commission added that any adverse effects would be particularly serious as the absence of other local or regional papers meant that BEP's newspapers were the only printed source of local news in the majority of their circulation areas, and some 56 per cent of the readers of the *Western Daily Press* (owned by BEP) took no other newspaper at all. Finally, the Commission emphasised that the public's perception of Mr Sullivan's business activities, whether justified or not, was such that the standing of the papers would be adversely affected, and this would be detrimental to the ability of the papers to hold readers and advertisers and thus would adversely affect their profitability.[78] The Sullivan case is an illustration of the "contentious proprietor" issue which was raised as an issue in the 1977 report of the Royal Commission on the Press[79] and has also been mentioned in subsequent Commission reports.[80]

The third adverse finding on non-competition grounds was reached by the Commission in 1994 in relation to the proposed transfer to Daily Mail and General Trust plc (DMGT) of the local newspapers published by T. Bailey Forman Limited (TBF) in the Nottingham area, in particular the *Nottingham Evening Post*. The transaction would have resulted in DMGT owning all the daily local/regional newspapers in Derbyshire, Leicestershire, Nottinghamshire, Lincolnshire, Humberside and the northern part of Staffordshire. The Commission concluded that the significant increase in the concentration of ownership of local newspapers in the East Midlands triangle (Nottinghamshire, Derbyshire and Leicestershire) would pose real risks to the maintenance of diversity of opinion, as it was possible that editors within the group would adopt similar positions on some issues as a result of close contact with each other and the uniform standards set by the group. This would be accentuated because of the degree of operational

---

[77] However, in the reverse situation, the Commission concluded that the lack of experience of the proposed acquirers of Mirror Group (Trinity plc and Regional Independent Media Holdings Limited) in the management of national newspapers was unlikely to have any adverse effects in view of the substantial (regional) newspaper management experience of the proposed acquirers (see *Trinity plc/Mirror Group plc and Regional Independent Media Holdings Limited/Mirror Group plc*, Cm. 4393 (July 1999) at para.2.28).

[78] *Mr David Sullivan and the Bristol Evening Post plc* (cited above), at paras 6.8 to 6.15 and 1.5.

[79] Royal Commission on the Press 1974–1977, Cmnd. 6810.

[80] See for example, *Trinity International Holdings plc and Thomson Regional Newspapers Limited*, Cm. 3033 (November 1995), para.2.17; and *Daily Mail and General Trust plc and T Bailey Forman Limited*, Cm. 2693 (October 1994), para.2.20. The issue was also raised by some when a company controlled by Richard Desmond acquired Express Newspapers in 2000, although that transaction was not subject to the newspaper provisions of the FTA since Mr Desmond had not previously owned any newspapers. As indicated above, a similar acquisition in the future would potentially be subject to public interest intervention by the Secretary of State.

integration that would be likely, notwithstanding the existing degree of editorial freedom, which could change at some time in the future.[81]

This was despite the fact there was very little overlap between the circulation areas of TBF's newspapers and the local/regional newspapers of DMGT. The Commission concluded that public debate on important regional issues was more likely to be fully informed if neighbouring newspapers were forming their views with the maximum degree of independence from each other,[82] and therefore recommended that the transaction should not be permitted (this was also partly as a result of the "dominant commercial position" which DMGT would obtain in the Midlands, but the Commission felt that this in turn would increase the risks to diversity of opinion in the region[83]). However, the Secretary of State ultimately decided to grant consent to the transaction subject to various conditions including: the appointment of a new editorial board responsible for maintaining editorial independence at the *Nottingham Evening Post* (the majority of the members of the board had to be approved by the Secretary of State); the divestment of two of TBF's paid-for weekly titles; and a requirement not to re-enter the paid-for weekly sector in the East Midlands (so as to protect the position of competing weeklies and thereby further protect against the erosion of diversity of opinion).[84]

7.022   The cases considered above suggest that plurality and editorial freedom issues are more likely to arise in cases involving regional daily titles, rather than those involving local weekly titles, particularly free weekly titles, since the former tend to have a wider circulation area, will frequently have a higher news content, have the capacity to exert a greater influence as a result of their daily publication, and may well adopt more defined positions on issues of relevance to their readers. Clearly, plurality issues are also likely to arise in connection with mergers involving national titles, although there have been no Commission reports relating to the acquisition of national newspapers in recent years.[85] As noted above, the acquisition by Press Acquisitions Limited of The Telegraph Group Limited was cleared by the OFT in October 2004 without an intervention notice being served. Given that the previous newspaper interests of the Barclay brothers are understood to have been limited to *The Scotsman, Scotland on Sunday, The Business* and some local newspapers in Scotland, and that the brothers are thought to have a record as "hands-off" proprietors, the Secretary of State clearly took the view that the acquisition raised no material public interest issues. It is likely that an acquisition by a proprietor of one of the other UK general interest national titles would have been reviewed much more carefully.

Despite the comments above, it is clear that newspaper public interest considerations might on occasion arise in connection with weekly titles. For example, in its report on the proposed acquisition by Johnston of eight

---

[81] *Daily Mail and General Trust plc/T Bailey Forman Limited*, Cm. 2693 (October 1994).
[82] Para.2.30.
[83] See para.2.50.
[84] P/94/730.
[85] The Commission has accepted that it is difficult for local newspapers to adopt political viewpoints in most instances, due to the commercial necessity of reflecting the interests and viewpoints of their local communities. See *Mirror Group plc and Midland Independent Newspapers plc*, Cm. 3762 (October 1997), para.2.48.

free weekly titles owned by Trinity Mirror,[86] the Commission considered in detail an allegation that Johnston had put pressure on the editor of one of its paid-for weekly titles to drop a campaign to overturn the conviction for murder of a local man.[87] Ultimately, the Commission concluded that the allegations had not been established and accepted that Johnston was committed to a policy of editorial freedom. However, the Commission observed that "the situation in practice is often not as absolute and clear-cut as publishers sometimes imply" with respect to editorial freedom, since editors operate within the framework of commercial businesses and face financial and other constraints as a consequence.[88]

In the same report, the Commission considered whether head-to-head competition between different publishers in a particular area provided a spur which caused even free newspapers to be of higher quality than equiv-alent titles published by monopoly publishers (the transaction would have given Johnston ownership of all the local newspapers in Northampton and Peterborough, for example). The Commission suspected that, in general, readers were likely to be better served as regards quality of editorial mate-rial if two or more local newspapers were under separate ownership in the relevant area.[89] However, on the facts of the case, the Commission felt there was insufficient evidence of likely adverse effects on diversity of views and quality of editorial material, mainly because of the existing weakness of the target titles. Nevertheless, the Commission has clearly identified the potential relevance of this issue.

The suggestion that the Commission has recently become more sceptical of newspaper publishers' claims that they actively pursue a policy of edito-rial freedom is supported by reference to the *Gannett/SMG* report in which the Commission set out a detailed list of criteria relating to editorial freedom which it regarded as necessary, if not sufficient, conditions for ensuring that such freedom is maintained.[90] The full list of criteria is set out in App.9, below. The key points included:

- that editors be assured of their basic rights including the right to reject material provided by management, the right to determine the contents of the paper and to reject advice on editorial policy, the right to criticise the paper's own group, the right to change position on specific issues and the right to appoint or dismiss journalists;

- that each title should have a competent editor of integrity whose standards include accurate reporting of news and free expression of opinion and that mechanisms are in place to defend editorial inde-pendence and to protect editors from pressure from proprietors, advisers or anyone else; and

- that newspapers should be operationally independent from their proprietors in terms of organisation (for example editor has mana-gerial control of editorial staff), finance (that is, sufficient resources

---

[86] *Johnston Press plc and Trinity Mirror plc*, Cm. 5495 (May 2002).
[87] See paras 2.127 *et seq.*
[88] Para.2.126.
[89] Para.2.88.
[90] *Gannett UK Limited and SMG plc*, para.2.55

to engage in full and accurate reporting) and personnel (for example, freedom to join a union).

7.023   Nevertheless, in its last report under the FTA regime, which related to Newsquest's proposed acquisition of 23 local newspapers in the London area[91] the Commission found no evidence that Gannett (the owner of Newsquest) did not follow a policy of editorial independence and also noted, as it had done in the *Gannett/SMG* report, the risk to Gannett's reputation should it fail to follow such practices given that its conduct with respect to editorial independence would be assessed in the context of future acquisitions.[92] The Commission also accepted that Newsquest would wish to maintain or enhance the diversity of its existing titles and the titles it planned to acquire within the same areas, to ensure that they continued to attract readers and advertisers, and to reduce the scope for new entrants successfully to enter a niche in the market.[93] Accordingly, the Commission concluded that editorial diversity would not be put at risk.[94]

It remains to be seen how frequently references will be made under the new regime in relation to the newspaper public interest considerations. It is likely that more intervention notices will be issued than references are made to the Commission. The Government has expressed a desire for a "light touch" approach,[95] and the early indications, in particular the lack of an intervention notice in respect of the acquisition of The Telegraph Group Limited, are that it is following this approach in practice. Accordingly, it is likely to remain the case that most cases will be decided on competition grounds, as was the case in relation to the majority of newspaper cases under the FTA regime.

Concentration of ownership and competition for readers and advertisers

7.024   As explained above, under the Communications Act regime, the assessment of competition issues is conducted by the OFT and (if necessary) the Commission. Newspaper mergers may affect competition in two separate (but related) markets, the market for advertising and the market for readers. As explained in Ch.6 above, the starting point for assessing the competition implications of a horizontal merger is identifying the number and relative size of suppliers, which in turn requires the relevant product and geographical markets to be defined. Market definition has been an important consideration in a number of Commission newspaper inquiries under the FTA and was also an important consideration in the first report under the new regime, the *Archant/INM* report.[95A] Reaching a definitive

---

[91] *Newsquest (London) Limited and Independent News & Media PLC*, Cm. 5951 (October 2003) ("the Newsquest/INM report").

[92] See the *Newsquest/INM* report, para.2.135.

[93] See the *Newsquest/INM* report, para.2.139.

[94] However, the transaction was partially blocked on competition grounds.

[95] See, for example, the Summary to the joint DTI/DCMS Consultation Paper: Draft Communications Bill—A new Future for Communications, May 2002, which stated, *inter alia*, that the Government would "simplify and liberalise the rules on media ownership" and "reform the newspaper merger regime to make it less onerous and less pervasive."

[95A] Although it should be noted that in this report, the Commission focused exclusively on competition for advertisers.

view on market definition involves addressing a number of questions including, *inter alia*:

(i)   is there a wider market in the provision of news including all newspapers, radio, and television?

(ii) do paid-for/free, daily/weekly, morning/evening, national, regional, or local newspapers compete with each other for readers and/or advertisers? and

(iii) is there a wider advertising market including television, radio, posters, directories, the Internet, direct mail, specialised advertising magazines and so on? To what extent is advertising in one type of newspaper a close substitute for advertising in another?

Product market definition—competition for readers

The Commission has generally reached the view in cases under the FTA that other news media are complementary to newspapers from the perspective of readers, and that national newspapers are unlikely to compete directly with local/regional newspapers. In their 1993 monopoly report on the supply of national newspapers, the Commission stated that: 7.025

"Looking at the wider market issue first, we note that regional newspapers and television/radio are themselves rather different types of products and they therefore compete with national newspapers in different ways. Television and radio stations, for example, often offer more rapid coverage of the day's major news events than can newspapers, though the latter generally provide a far wider range of news stories and each story is often dealt with in much greater depth. . . . By and large, therefore, we take television/radio more as a complement to newspapers than a substitute product, at least for the majority of consumers. Regional newspapers, particularly morning editions perhaps, represent more of a direct substitute and we are aware of both the competition for advertising between regional and national newspapers (see the Sadler Report), and also the publishers' moves to produce regionalized versions of national newspapers. For the most part, however, the regionalized elements of the content of national newspapers are limited to sports coverage and television listings. Moreover, regional newspapers by their nature focus on news which is primarily of local and regional interest and most consumers wanting national and international news will usually purchase a national newspaper. On parallel grounds of differing content, we would not regard magazines and periodicals as being in the same market. For these reasons, we do not believe that regional newspapers, magazines and television/radio are sufficiently close substitutes for national newspapers that many consumers would switch away from these and buy more national newspapers were the latter to decrease significantly in price."[96]

---

[96] *National Newspapers*, Cm. 2422 (December 1993), para.3.5.

Similarly, in their 1989 report on Century Newspapers and Thomson Regional Newspapers, the Commission concluded that:

"We have seen no indication that national titles are ever likely to provide an adequate substitute for the regional news coverage of Century's titles."[97]

Similar views have been expressed in more recent reports[98] although the position may be to some degree different in Scotland, where some of the national titles have introduced increasingly regionalised Scottish editions.[99] Indeed, in its recent clearance decision relating to the acquisition by Press Acquisitions of The Telegraph Group (referred to above), in light of the Barclay brothers' existing ownership of *The Scotsman* newspapers (as well as *The Business*), the OFT considered the position (without distinguishing in detail between readers and advertisers) both by reference to the UK as a whole, and by reference to Scotland only. In relation to Scotland, the OFT also considered the position more narrowly by reference to Scottish broadsheet circulation (that is, including both the Scottish national titles, and the Scottish editions of the UK-wide titles). However the transaction was analysed, the transaction was not thought to raise material competition concerns and therefore the OFT did not reach any firm conclusions on market definition.

In its monopoly report on the supply of national newspapers, the Commission concluded that the national newspaper market was a unitary one, notwithstanding the differences in the prices and readership of the tabloids and the quality newspapers. This conclusion was reached on the ground that the rather modest price differences between mid-market papers and those in the quality and tabloid segments suggested that there was a "chain of substitutes" from the tabloids to the mid-market papers to the quality papers, so that prices in any particular segment could not be increased independently. In addition, the Commission found that there was some scope for supply-side substitutability between the various market segments.[1] If the Commission were to revisit this issue, it would no doubt wish to consider whether there had been any evidence of switching between broadsheet and tabloid readers in response to the tabloid price wars of the last five years.

7.026   As regards competition for readers between different types of local/ regional newspaper, the Commission has generally concluded (as it has done in relation to competition for advertisers) that weekly newspapers (whether paid or free) compete more directly with each other than daily (or Sunday) titles, on the basis that daily titles offer regional news (and advertising) and tend to have more editorial content, whereas weeklies tend to be far more local in their content and area of circulation/distribution.[2]

---

[97] *Century Newspapers Ltd/Thomson Regional Newspapers Ltd*, Cm. 677 (April 1989), para.6.24.

[98] See, for example, *Mirror Group plc and Midland Independent Newspapers plc*, Cm. 3762 (October 1997), para.2.36 (re national v regional newspapers); and *Johnston Press plc and Trinity Mirror plc*, Cm. 5495 (May 2002), paras 2.18 and 5.4.

[99] See *Gannett UK Limited and SMG plc*, cited above, para.5.6

[1] *National Newspapers*, Cm. 2422 (December 1993), paras 3.3 and 3.7.

[2] See, for example, *News Communications and Media plc and Newsquest (Investments) Limited/Johnston Press plc/Trinity Mirror plc*, Cm. 4680 (April 2000), para.4.51; *Trinity*

Product market definition—competition for advertisers

The Commission's analysis in relation to advertisers has been broadly   7.027
similar to that for readers, except that in some cases the Commission has
been more willing to accept that other media may compete for advertising.
For example, the Commission stated in 1991 that:

> "As far as advertisers are concerned, we have shown in Chapter 3
> (para.3.10) that on average some 85 to 90 per cent of advertisements
> placed in the newspapers of the five companies involved in our inquiry
> are of a local character, the remainder being regional or national in
> varying proportions. By their very nature, regional newspapers are not
> well placed to compete for national advertising. Regional advertising
> appears to constitute a small part of the overall advertising market.
> National and regional advertisers have a number of alternatives to
> regional newspapers, notably television, radio and, increasingly, regional
> editions of national newspapers."[3]
>
> "As far as competition from other media is concerned, commercial radio
> and television compete for some kinds of local advertising though they
> cannot do so for much classified advertising. We were told, further, that
> there were several other potential sources of competition with local news-
> papers. These included publications devoted solely to particular categories
> of advertising such as house property and motor vehicles; the development
> of paid-for publications which carried free advertising but no editorial
> content; directories, which were taking a growing share of the advertising
> market; direct mail; and shop and supermarket notice-boards. We agree
> that these are strong and, in some cases, growing sources of competition."[4]

Nevertheless, throughout most of the 1990s, the Commission tended to
regard alternative advertising media as indirect, rather than direct substitutes.
For example, in its review of Newsquest's proposed acquisition of
Westminster Press in 1996, the Commission accepted that local radio and
advertising-only publications competed for local advertising, but considered
that they did not present powerful constraints and that "there is still a recog-
nizable market in which the publishers of regional and local newspapers
compete largely with each other."[5] Similarly, the Commission stated in the
Johnston Press/Home Counties report in 1998 that:

> "in our view there remains a very substantial area of advertising, not
> least by individuals and small businesses which, because it is too general
> for specialist publications, too local for radio, television or regional
> guides or too short term for directories . . . is essentially the preserve of

plc/Mirror Group plc and Regional Independent Media Holdings Limited/Mirror Group plc,
Cm. 4393 (July 1999), para.4.33; and *Johnston Press plc and Trinity Mirror plc*, Cm. 5495
(May 2002), paras 5.7 and 5.11.
[3] *Southern Newspapers plc/EMAP plc/Pearson plc/Reed International plc/Trinity International
Holdings plc*, Cm. 1772 (November 1991), at para.6.19.
[4] *Southern Newspapers plc/EMAP plc/Pearson plc/Reed International plc/Trinity International
Holdings plc* (cited above) at para.6.63.
[5] *Newsquest Media Group Limited and Westminster Press Limited*, Cm. 3485 (November
1996), para.2.16.

local newspapers. We do not therefore regard the availability of other media as, by itself, an adequate substitute for competition from a local newspaper."[6]

7.028   However, in 1999 and early 2000, the Commission appeared to accept that the advertising market had begun to extend beyond local newspapers, covering advertising-only publications (such as *Auto Trader* and *Loot*) in particular, and also potentially the internet. Thus, the Commission came to a favourable view of Johnston Press' proposed acquisition of Portsmouth & Sunderland Newspapers plc (PSN), partially as a result of competition from advertising-only publications such as *Friday-Ad* in the relevant areas, but also from other media.[7] In the NewsComm report,[8] the Commission went so far as to state:

"it is the advertising-only publications that provide the sharpest competition to local and regional newspapers at the moment, while the Internet and the emerging digital media represent a growing threat. . . . Our view therefore is that the market for regional and local advertising remains competitive, and now extends beyond newspapers. The local and regional press competes with the nationals, and with radio and television, for large-scale display advertising, and is being increasingly challenged by a growing range of advertising-only publications in the classified sector. The new electronic means of communication are already beginning to establish themselves as credible advertising media, and the signs are that they will grow as a competitive force."[9]

However, in most subsequent newspaper reports, whilst the Commission has accepted that in respect of certain categories of advertising, such as property, motors, and to a lesser extent recruitment, the constraints from other media (in particular, other printed media such as advertising-only publications) are relatively strong, the Commission has generally concluded that other "more vulnerable" categories of advertisers, such as individuals, small businesses, and public sector bodies have less choices. As a consequence, the Commission has been reluctant to accept that these alternative media should be regarded as forming part of the same market.[10] In the *Johnston Press/Trinity Mirror* report, the Commission concluded that newspaper publishers were in a position to discriminate against vulnerable advertisers due to the fact that rates were typically determined by negotia-

---

[6] *Johnston Press plc and Home Counties Newspapers Holdings plc*, Cm. 3962 (June 1998), para.2.74.

[7] *Portsmouth & Sunderland Newspapers plc and Johnston Press plc/Newsquest (Investments) Limited/News Communications and Media plc*, Cm. 4358 (June 1999), para.2.84.

[8] *News Communications & Media plc and Newsquest (Investments) Limited/Johnston Press plc/Trinity Mirror plc*, Cm. 4680 (April 2000).

[9] *News Communications & Media plc and Newsquest (Investments) Limited/Johnston Press plc/Trinity Mirror plc*, paras 2.26 and 2.28

[10] See *Regional Independent Media Limited and Gannett UK Limited/Johnston Press plc/Guardian Media Group plc*, Cm. 4887 (November 2000), para.2.22; *Johnston Press plc and Trinity Mirror plc*, Cm. 5495 (May 2002), paras 2.31 to 2.32; *Gannett UK Limited and SMG plc*, Cm. 5782 (March 2003), paras 5.13 to 5.14; and *Newsquest (London) Limited and Independent News & Media PLC* Cm. 5951 (October 2003), para.5.9 ("Newsquest/INM").

tion, with the consequence that these vulnerable advertisers would not be protected by switching by less vulnerable advertisers who may have more choices.[11] This was one of the factors which led the Commission to recommend blocking parts of the proposed merger. A similar view was reached by the OFT in its first newspaper case under the Enterprise Act which related to an acquisition by Archant of certain London titles of Independent News & Media plc.[12]

However, in its approval in September 2003 of Guardian Media Group's acquisition of the approximately 50 per cent stake in Trader Media Group (the publisher of *Auto Trader* and other, mainly motor, advertising publications) which it did not already own, the Office of Fair Trading concluded that the relevant market was print advertising for the sale of vehicles in local areas; that is, including both local newspapers and advertising-only publications. This did not lead the OFT to adopt a different approach to market definition in its *Archant/INM* reference decision of April 2004 than had hitherto been adopted by the Commission in newspaper cases. However, in the recent *Archant/INM* report, whilst the Commission did not conclude that there were separate product markets for the different advertising categories, primarily due to supply-side considerations,[12A] it did conclude that the relevant product market "could also extend to some other publications such as advertising-only publications".[12B] The Commission then took into account the constraint exercised by advertising-only publications (and indeed, other media such as the internet), as well as its survey of advertisers, in arriving at its ultimate conclusion that the transaction would not result in a substantial lessening of competition.[12C] The Commission also reached the view, on the basis of its survey evidence, that there was insufficient evidence to justify a conclusion that Archant could price discriminate between customers in order to render a five per cent price increase profitable.[12D] Whilst the Commission was at pains to point out that its conclusions were based on an analysis of newspaper advertising in areas of London and that "[n]o presumption should be made as to the applicability of our findings to newspaper mergers in other parts of the UK",[12E] it seems to be clear that the Commission does not have a settled position on product market definition with respect to local newspapers at this time.

As regards competition for advertising between different types of newspaper, the Commission's conclusions have generally been similar to those it

---

[11] *Johnston Press plc and Trinity Mirror plc*, Cm. 5495 (May 2002), para.2.104.
[12] *Completed acquisition by Archant Limited of the London Regionals Division of Independent News and Media plc*, April 29, 2004. This case related to the same titles which Newsquest had sought consent to purchase under the FTA and which led to the Newsquest/INM report of October 2003 (Cm. 5951).
[12A] Such as the ability to increase the advertising pages in a title (with or without decreasing the non-advertising space) and/or to increase the share of advertising taken by one category of advertising. See *Archant/INM* report, para.4.18 and App.E, paras 6 to 8.
[12B] *ibid.*, para.4.34.
[12C] *ibid.*, paras 5.21, 5.23, 5.29 and 5.31.
[12D] *ibid.*, paras 4.26 to 4.30. The relevant evidence included the fact that all categories of advertisers appeared to be similarly price sensitive (*i.e.* including the "vulnerable" categories which had been identified in previous reports).
[12E] *ibid.*, Executive Summary, para.6. For example, it may be the case that there are significantly more advertising-only publications in London than other parts of the UK.

has reached in relation to readers. Accordingly, national newspapers have been found to compete only to a limited extent for advertising with local/regional newspapers,[13] and in relation to local/regional newspapers, the Commission has consistently concluded that daily newspapers (whether morning or evening) compete more directly with each other than with weekly newspapers (whether paid for or free).[14] This conclusion seems to have been based primarily on their similarity of circulation area and frequency of publication[14A] rather than any detailed economic analysis, and despite the parties to transactions frequently arguing that evening titles at least, do compete for advertising with weekly titles, on the basis that both categories of title are focused on local content, including local advertising and evening titles often have a weekly advertising focus or supplement in relation to particular categories of advertising such as property, motors or recruitment.

In its Aberdeen Journals decision under the Competition Act 1998, the OFT concluded that the local weekly titles in Aberdeen *did* form part of the same market as the evening title, and referred to the fact that advertising in the major classified categories tended to be placed in a weekly supplement in evening titles, such that the frequency of advertising was the same as in weekly titles.[15] This finding was supported by the Competition Appeal Tribunal on appeal.[15A] The Commission noted this decision in its *Gannett/ SMG report*[16] but did not state whether it was inclined to depart from its previously stated view that daily newspapers were in a separate market from weekly newspapers (as no weekly titles were being acquired in that

---

[13] See, for example, *Mirror Group plc and Midland Independent Newspapers plc*, Cm. 3762 (October 1997), para. 2.40; *News Communications & Media plc and Newsquest (Investments) Limited/Johnston Press plc/Trinity Mirror plc*, Cm. 4680 (April 2000), para.4.48; and *Gannett UK Limited and SMG plc*, (cited above), para.5.5. This latter report indicates that the position may be a little different in Scotland, and the approach taken by the OFT in its recent Press Acquisitions/Telegraph Group decision is consistent with this. Genuinely regional newspapers, such as *Metro*, the London *Evening Standard* and the *Yorkshire Post* are also likely to be considered separately from purely local titles. See, for example, *Regional Independent Media Limited and Gannett UK Limited/Johnston Press plc/ Guardian Media Group plc* (cited above), para.4.33; the *Newsquest/INM* report, para.2.45; and the *Archant/INM* report, para.4.21.

[14] See, for example *Trinity plc/Mirror Group plc and Regional Independent Media Holdings Limited/Mirror Group plc*, Cm. 4393 (July 1999), para.4.31; and *Johnston Press plc and Trinity Mirror plc*, Cm. 5495 (May 2002), para.5.7. Despite reaching broadly the same conclusion on this issue in *Newsquest/INM* (see para.2.43), the Commission also rather inconsistently indicated that Archant's existing paid-for title would be unlikely to compete with a free title (see para.2.93).

[14A] In the *Regional Independent Media Limited and Gannett UK Limited/Johnston Press plc/Guardian Media Group plc* report (cited above), the Commission also based this view on the fact that daily titles allowed advertising to be placed or changed more frequently, and asserted that weekly newspapers tended to be retained for several days for reference, whilst dailies had a more short-lived impact, which the Commission felt suggested advertisers would regard them as complements rather than substitutes (see para.4.34).

[15] *Predation by Aberdeen Journals Limited* (Remitted case), September 16, 2002, Case CE/1217–02, paras 83 *et seq.*

[15A] Case No.1009/1/1/02, *Aberdeen Journals Limited v The Office of Fair Trading*, June 23, 2003, at para.256.

[16] *Gannett UK Limited and SMG plc*, Cm. 5782 (March 2003), para.5.9.

case, the issue was not of direct relevance).[17] It should be noted that having apparently reached the view that daily titles do not compete directly with weekly titles in most of its recent reports, the Commission has nevertheless taken the presence of evening titles into account in assessing the impact of transactions primarily concerning weekly titles, for example, by including daily titles in market share calculations. (In this respect, it should be noted that market shares have typically been calculated on the basis of average circulation/distribution per issue rather than per week, with the result that the competitive strength of weekly titles is likely to have been overstated *vis-à-vis* daily titles.)[18] As will be implicit from the above commentary, the Commission has consistently regarded free and paid-for weekly titles as competing directly for advertising.

Geographical market definition

In recent years the Commission's newspaper merger reports have primarily involved mergers of regional/local newspapers, rather than national titles.[18A] Transactions involving local newspapers have been assessed primarily (but not entirely) at the local level. As the Commission stated in one report: "as local newspapers compete primarily for local readership and the custom of local advertisers, it is the analysis of competitive effects at the local level that is particularly germane".[19] However, concentration at the national and regional levels has also been discussed and these issues are considered briefly below.

7.029

Prior to the *Archant/INM* report, the question of the precise geographical level at which local market concentration should be analysed had generally not been addressed directly by the Commission, and there was little analysis of what determined the geographic scope of local advertising markets. Instead, partly due to the limited data which is readily available, rather than rely on advertising value and volume data (which is likely to be a better measure of market power), the Commission has tended to rely on circulation and distribution data produced by the Joint Industry Committee for Regional Press Research (JICREG) for the particular localities within the UK which are relevant to its inquiry.[20] Clearly, this information is only a proxy for the strength of individual publishers in particular advertising

---

[17] The Commission also declined to comment on this issue in its *Newsquest/INM* report on the basis that the transaction only involved weekly publications, Cm. 5951, para.2.44. The Commission also concluded that the relevant product market covered free and paid-for weekly local newspapers (*i.e.* not daily newspapers) in the *Archant/INM* report (cited above), at para.4.12.

[18] See, for example, *Johnston Press plc and Trinity Mirror plc*, Cm. 5495 (May 2002), paras 5.31 *et seq.*

[18A] Although, as noted above, in its recent clearance decision relating to the acquisition by Press Acquisitions of The Telegraph Group, the OFT considered the position both by reference to the UK as a whole and Scotland alone.

[19] *Regional Independent Media Limited and Gannett UK Limited/Johnston Press plc/Guardian Media Group plc*, Cm. 4887 (November 2000), para.4.56.

[20] The Commission stated in the Newsquest/INM report that: "it is not possible to derive accurate measures of shares of revenue, which will to a large extent depend on how revenues from advertisements included in several newspapers are allocated between those newspapers". Cm. 5951, n.1, p.18.

markets.[21] In its earlier reports, the Commission analysed the effect of the proposed merger on particular local areas without it being clear precisely why those specific areas had been selected (for example, the Commission sometimes analysed individual JICREG areas, and on other occasions analysed combinations of a number of JICREG areas, typically with little attempt to establish whether they constituted a relevant economic market).[22]

In its report into the proposed acquisition by Johnston Press of eight free weekly titles from Trinity Mirror,[23] the Commission adopted a slightly different approach. Here, the Commission essentially analysed the impact of the transaction by reference to the main distribution areas of each individual title being acquired, adding together individual JICREG areas where the relevant title achieved a reasonably high household penetration rate,[24] and which accounted for a relatively significant proportion of the distribution volume of the title concerned.[25] The Commission stated that this gave "a more complete and coherent assessment of the relevant geographic market"; although in reality, a properly defined geographic market may bear little relation to the area in which the product of one of the merging parties is actually sold.

7.030   The relevance of penetration rates is that, as highlighted in previous reports,[26] where a title does not reach a significant proportion of households (10 per cent is the threshold usually adopted) in a particular locality, it is unlikely to be regarded by advertisers as an effective means of reaching consumers in that area.[26A] Similarly, if an area accounts for a small proportion of a title's total distribution/circulation (say below 20 per cent), that area is unlikely to be important in the determination of advertising rates (or editorial policy) for the relevant title, since the publisher will be more concerned with the price in the "core" area for its titles. Accordingly, it is the "core" areas which should form the focus of the analysis.

However, in October 2003 the Commission further amended its approach in the *Newsquest/INM* report by largely discarding the penetration rate and core area criteria and including all circulation/distribution areas of each title being acquired, including areas where the title had very little presence. (It also analysed market shares by reference to individual

---

[21] As the Commission partially recognised in the Newquest/INM report (cited above), para.2.60 and fully recognised in the *Archant/INM* report (cited above), at App.D, paras 19–20. For example, JICREG data will tend to overstate the strength of free titles as compared to paid-for titles.

[22] See, for example, *Portsmouth & Sunderland Newspapers plc and Johnston Press plc/Newsquest (Investments) Limited/News Communications and Media plc*, Cm. 4358 (June 1999), paras 4.28 to 4.49; *News Communications & Media plc and Newsquest (Investments) Limited/Johnston Press plc/Trinity Mirror plc*, Cm. 4680 (April 2000) paras 4.61 to 4.97; and *Regional Independent Media Limited and Gannett UK Limited/Johnston Press plc/Guardian Media Group plc*, Cm. 4887 (November 2000), paras 4.56 to 4.90.

[23] *Johnston Press plc and Trinity Mirror plc*, Cm. 5495 (May 2002).

[24] *i.e.* the percentage of households in a particular locality which receive/purchase a title.

[25] Cited above, at paras 5.24 to 5.30.

[26] See, for example, *News Communications & Media plc and Newsquest (Investments) Limited/Johnston Press plc/Trinity Mirror plc*, Cm. 4680 (April 2000), paras 4.61 to 4.63; and *Regional Independent Media Limited and Gannett UK Limited/Johnston Press plc/Guardian Media Group plc*, Cm. 4887 (November 2000), paras 4.57 to 4.60.

[26A] However, as noted in the *Johnston Press plc and Trinity Mirror plc* report, penetration rates are likely to be "more pertinent" for paid-for titles than free titles since the publisher effectively decides the distribution area of a free title (see para.5.14).

JICREG areas, but seemed to put less emphasis on this.) However, this may have at least partly related to the fact that the relevant markets were in London, where the Commission felt that the notion of "core" areas was of limited relevance due to the close proximity of different communities and the overlaps between them[27]: "many people may live in one area, but work in a different area and possibly do their shopping in a third area. As a consequence, local market boundaries are far from clear or unambiguous in economic terms".[28]

In the *Archant/INM* report of September 2004, the Commission focused closely on the appropriate geographic market definition.[28A] By analysing hypothetical advertiser switching behaviour in response to its survey of advertisers and by carrying out price-concentration analysis, the Commission concluded that, on the facts of the case, the relevant geographic market was wider than the "footprint" (*i.e.* distribution/circulation area) of any individual title, but was local, extending no wider than the areas covered by the former INM-publishing units (each publishing unit consisted of a number (generally three or four) of different titles/series covering a mixture of overlapping and neighbouring areas).[28B] The Commission therefore assessed the position primarily by reference to the areas of the former INM-publishing units. It is worth noting that, in its assessment, the Commission also took the view that in any area where the combined share of circulation was below 50 per cent and/or the increment in share of circulation was below 10 per cent, the potential for competition concerns would not generally arise.[28C] This would be considered a rather generous threshold in most non-newspaper markets.

National and regional concentration issues

As noted above, when considering transactions involving local/regional newspapers, the Commission has focused primarily on the impact of the transaction at the local level, but has also considered concentration at the national and regional levels. In relation to national concentration, the Commission has noted the shares of circulation at the national level which would result from particular transactions, and has commented that "the structure of the local newspaper market in the UK could be of concern in future, particularly if further consolidation increases concentration and the degree of regional clustering".[29] However, the principal issues raised in connection with high national shares have related to issues which would now be considered under the newspaper public interest considerations. Accordingly, in connection with Trinity's and Regional Independent Media's proposed acquisition of the Mirror Group, the Commission stated:

7.031

---

[27] See n.1, p.81, *Newsquest/INM* report, Cm. 5951 (October 2003).
[28] *Newsquest/INM* report, para.5.25.
[28A] *Archant/INM* report (cited above), paras 4.3 to 4.11 and App.D.
[28B] *ibid.*, para.4.3.
[28C] *ibid.*, para.4.5, read in conjunction with, inter alia, para.5.20.
[29] *Newsquest/INM* report, para.2.51. This issue of clustering is considered further below.

"The real issues raised by an increase in concentration at the UK level are a possible reduction in the diversity of the press and the risk that a large number of titles might fall into the hands of an unsuitable proprietor."[30]

These issues have been considered above. In assessing local newspaper mergers the Commission has not focused closely on the issue of regional concentration primarily on the basis that the vast majority of advertising carried by local newspapers is of a local rather than regional nature, and therefore the ability to offer region-wide packages to drive competitors out of business is likely to be limited.[31] Clearly, where the newspapers concerned are more regional in nature, and therefore more likely to carry more regional advertising, the position may be different. For example, in relation to the proposed acquisitions of Mirror Group in 1999, the Commission concluded that the fact that a combined Trinity/Mirror Group would have a 67 per cent share of advertising in regional and local newspapers in Northern Ireland would reduce competition, leading to higher costs for advertising in Northern Ireland than would otherwise be the case. Together with the diversity of opinion issues considered above, this led the Commission to recommend that Trinity should be required to dispose of certain titles as a condition to consent being granted.

In its report into the proposed acquisitions of Regional Independent Media Limited,[32] the Commission considered the

"risk that high levels of concentration of ownership across geographically proximate newspaper markets might:

(a) enable multi-market operators in new areas to exploit their market position, damage independent local rivals and raise barriers to entry if they were so minded;

(b) increase the market power of newspaper owners, enabling them to raise rates for at least some types of local advertiser for whom alternative media are not, or are not yet, a realistic alternative; and

(c) reduce the drive to maintain and improve quality that comes from editorial competition and comparison between independently managed titles, and increase the potential for sharing of editorial and other resources, in ways that could lead to a less diverse and innovative local press."[33]

This led the Commission to conclude that in general it would be desirable for all local newspaper markets to be within easy geographical reach of at least two major publishers of local newspapers to enable them to use

---

[30] *Trinity plc/Mirror Group plc and Regional Independent Media Holdings Limited/Mirror Group plc*, Cm. 4393 (July 1999), para.2.42.

[31] See, for example, *Trinity International Holdings plc and Thomson Regional Newspapers Limited*, Cm. 3033 (November 1995), paras 2.42–2.44; *Newsquest Media Group Limited and Westminster Press Limited*, Cm. 3485 (November 1996), para.2.27; and *Johnston Press plc and Home Counties Newspapers Holdings plc*, Cm. 3962 (June 1998), para.2.25.

[32] *Regional Independent Media Limited and Gannett UK Limited/Johnston Press plc/ Guardian Media Group plc*, Cm. 4887 (November 2000).

[33] *Regional Independent Media Limited and Gannett UK Limited/Johnston Press plc/ Guardian Media Group plc*, para.2.15.

their existing infrastructure to support the launch of new titles into those markets.[34] The fact that there were at least two other major publishers "within striking distance" in each of the regions which were considered to be relevant in that report was one of the factors which led the Commission to clear each of the proposed transactions, which in a number of instances (particularly an acquisition by Gannett), would have led to the acquirer owning 100 per cent of the local newspapers in a number of localities.

However, 18 months later in the context of its report into the proposed   7.032
acquisition by Johnston Press of eight free weekly titles from Trinity Mirror, the Commission was not so convinced that the proximity of other major publishers would act as a competitive constraint on Johnston Press following the acquisition, and concluded that the major publishers were unlikely to challenge each other in their "heartlands". This issue is considered further below in the context of an analysis of barriers to entry. However, it is worth noting at this stage that in the *Johnston Press/Trinity Mirror* report and the *Newsquest/INM* report, the Commission has expressed concerns in relation to what it has described as the development of regional "clusters" of titles by the major publishers.[34A] The Commission has stated that the development of geographically concentrated clusters of complementary publications (*i.e.* paid/free combinations) could be "symptomatic of a mutual desire among major publishers to 'live and let live', sharing the market on a geographical basis and avoiding head-to-head competition in the same local areas".[35] This led the Commission to recommend in the *Johnston Press/Trinity Mirror* report that the OFT should carry out a wider market investigation into local newspaper markets on this issue. The OFT carried out a review in 2002, but decided not to launch such an investigation, although it stated that it would keep the market under review.

Nevertheless, the Commission raised this issue again in the *Newsquest/INM* report, where it considered whether the strengthening of Newquest's "cluster" of titles in the London area might give rise to concerns in connection with the reduction of potential competition even in areas where there was no overlap between the parties' titles. This was based on the Commission's view that competition with the other major publisher in the London market, Trinity Mirror, would be limited, due to the supposed "live and let live" attitude of the major publishers. However, the Commission concluded that there were insufficient reasons to conclude that adverse consequences could be expected as a result of the expansion of Newsquest's cluster of titles in the London area in this instance. First, any loss of potential competition could be expected to be minimal as Newsquest and INM had not frequently entered each other's markets. Entry by other publishers was also limited. Secondly, most other publishers did not raise any concerns as to the strengthening of Newsquest's position (and the position of Newsquest and Trinity Mirror combined) in the London area despite Newsquest's greater financial strength as compared to INM. Thirdly, whilst small new entrants might have greater difficulty entering against Newsquest as opposed to INM due to the latter's greater financial strength, it was a

---

[34] Para.2.16.
[34A] The Commission did not really focus on this issue in the *Archant/INM* report of September 2004, perhaps because Archant is not one of the largest four publishers.
[35] *Newsquest/INM* report, para.2.129.

matter of speculation whether entrepreneurial entry would occur in the absence of the transfer, and whether such entry would be less likely following the transfer. It was equally possible that the transaction might be pro-competitive in items of increasing competition with Trinity Mirror and Archant.[36]

Barriers to entry and expansion

7.033   In recent years newspaper merger inquiries have involved publishers of regional/local newspapers rather than publishers of competing national newspapers.[36A] Accordingly, it is unsurprising that there has been no detailed analysis of entry conditions in the supply of national newspapers. The issue was discussed at some length in the 1993 Commission monopoly report on the supply of national newspapers, in which the Commission concluded that significant economies of scale, coupled with high launch costs in the order of £10 million (a high proportion of which are sunk) reduced the number of possible new entrants in the supply of national newspapers. Nevertheless, the Commission noted that there had been six new entrants since the mid–1980s, of which three had survived (one with a change of ownership).[37]

As regards regional/local newspapers, the Commission has generally concluded in its recent reports that in principle, barriers to entry for free newspapers are relatively low, but that they are higher in relation to paid-for titles. For example, in its report on the proposed acquisition by Mirror Group of Midland Independent Newspapers, the Commission stated:

"In the case of free newspapers, market entry can be comparatively cheap using desktop publishing and contract printing. Successful launches suggest that a strongly targeted local weekly free newspaper can gain reader and advertiser acceptability quickly. On the face of it, the initial requirements for setting up such a newspaper are small, all the more so as "desk-top publishing" hardware and software becomes more readily available and less expensive. Many publishing activities can be contracted out, notably the printing and physical distribution of the newspaper. . . . Entry into the paid-for newspaper market is more difficult. For example, during an earlier inquiry we were told by one newspaper publisher that it took about 12 months for a newly launched paid-for title to gain credibility with readers, and a further 12 months for it to become an accepted regional or local title by advertisers."[38]

---

[36] *Newsquest/INM* report, paras 2.132–2.133.

[36A] In its October 2004 Press Acquisitions/Telegraph Group clearance decision (referred to above), the OFT did not find it necessary to take a determinative view on the issue of barriers to entry given its conclusion that the transaction raised no substantive competition concerns.

[37] *National newspapers*, Cm. 2422 (December 1993), paras 3.52 –3.56 and 11.4–11.5. The Commission reiterated its earlier conclusions in the *Trinity plc/Mirror Group plc and Regional Independent Media Holdings Limited/Mirror Group plc* report (cited above) in 1999, at para.4.111.

[38] *Mirror Group plc and Midland Independent Newspapers plc*, Cm. 3762 (October 1997), paras 4.59–4.60. Similar conclusions were reached in *Trinity International Holdings plc and Thomson Regional Newspapers Limited*, Cm. 3033 (November 1995), paras 2.38–2.40;

However, most of the recent Commission reports have also highlighted 7.034
that whilst, in principle, barriers to entry for free local newspapers may be
relatively low, it is often difficult to establish a credible challenge to a
powerful incumbent. For example, in relation to Johnston Press' proposed
acquisition of Home Counties Newspapers, the Commission commented:

"There are a number of potential problems for new entrants. First, there
is a need to finance initial losses [the Commission was informed that a
new entrant could often expect to make losses for four or five years]. . .
. Secondly, as editorial content of existing free titles improves and reader
loyalty increases entry might become more difficult. Both credibility and
acceptability are important because without them advertisers, the only
source of revenue for free titles, are more reluctant to buy advertising
space. . . . Thirdly, it can be difficult and time consuming to establish a
distribution network. . . . The behaviour and reputation of the incumbent
will influence the ease of entry. Established newspaper publishers can
respond to new entrants in a variety of ways, for example by cutting their
advertising yields or launching new titles. The expectation of the
incumbent's response could deter potential entrants and, if entry does
take place, could reduce the entrant's chances of being successful."[39]

As a result of these difficulties the Commission concluded that major
publishers were more likely to provide an effective challenge to an incumbent, since their resources would allow them to cope with teething problems and to bear initial operating losses for an extended period.[40] However,
the Commission noted that major publishers were in fact unlikely to launch
new titles in areas already dominated by other major publishers, save
through acquisition (see further the comments on the *Johnston Press/Trinity
Mirror* report below). This led the Commission to conclude that the general
threat of entry could not be regarded as an adequate substitute for actual
competition.[41]

However, in the *NewsComm* report, the Commission did conclude that
the threat of new entry, most plausibly by a free newspaper or an advertising-
only publication, represented a competitive constraint on the commercial
activities of incumbent newspaper proprietors.[42] It will be recalled that the
NewsComm report was also the first time that the Commission accepted
that other advertising media formed part of the same market as local newspaper advertising.[43] The Commission was not prepared to go so far in the

---

*Portsmouth & Sunderland Newspapers plc and Johnston Press plc/Newsquest (Investments)
Limited/News Communications & Media plc*, Cm. 4358 (June 1999), paras 4.68 and 4.71;
and *News Communications and Media plc and Newsquest (Investments) Limited/Johnston
Press plc/Trinity Mirror plc*, Cm. 4680 (April 2000), paras 2.21–2.22.
[39] *Johnston Press plc and Home Counties Newspapers Holdings plc*, Cm. 3962 (June 1998),
paras 4.62–4.63.
[40] Para.2.73.
[41] Para.2.73. Similar conclusions were reached in the *Portsmouth & Sunderland Newspapers*
report at para.2.28.
[42] *News Communications and Media plc and Newsquest (Investments) Limited/Johnston
Press plc/Trinity Mirror plc*, Cm. 4680 (April 2000), at para.2.23. A similar conclusion was
reached in the *Independent News and Media plc and Trinity Mirror plc* report, Cm. 4770
(July 2000), para.2.20.
[43] See the section on product market definition above.

report into the proposed acquisitions of Regional Independent Media, but as we have noted above, it did conclude that there was a credible threat of new entry from other major publishers of local newspapers with titles in nearby areas.[44] The Commission did not consider that the threat of new entry from small new entrants was a sufficient constraint bearing in mind the difficulties they faced (including lack of economies of scale, limitations in access to high quality printing, inability to offer advertising packages, and inability to obtain finance at the same rates as large newspaper groups).[45]

The Commission was much more cautious on the issue of the threat posed by new entry in its report into the proposed acquisition by Johnston Press of eight free titles belonging to Trinity Mirror.[46] As noted above, in this report, the Commission reached the view that there was an increasing tendency for publishers to publish clusters of titles in particular locations. The Commission also noted that major publishers tended not to launch titles at a distance from their existing areas of operation (although they might make substantial acquisitions in new areas which could then form the basis of additional clusters of new titles). As mentioned above, the Commission was concerned that the development of clusters of titles might be symptomatic of a mutual desire among major publishers to "live and let live", in other words, to avoid competing with each other head to head in the same local areas.[47] In light of these factors, whilst the Commission had no doubt about the ability of major publishers to launch new titles in areas adjacent to those where their existing titles circulated, it was doubtful that they would actually be willing to do so.[48] Accordingly, the Commission abandoned the position it had reached in the RIM report 18 months earlier that the presence of two major publishers in close proximity would act as a competitive constraint on the incumbent publisher. It also confirmed the conclusions it had reached in earlier reports that small scale entrants face significant difficulties in competing with major groups,[49] and stated that "the launching of new local newspapers, by publishers not already present in the area concerned, is now rather less likely than it was. In particular, . . . the prospects for entry into the territory of a strong and efficient publisher with a monopoly of existing titles are highly uncertain, and . . . in these circumstances local monopolies may have scope to raise prices, or reduce service levels, at least to some of their customers, without inducing entry."[50]

Similar conclusions were reached in the *Newsquest/INM* report, in which the Commission noted that despite the limited fixed and working capital requirements associated with the Newsquest and INM operations in London, profitability was high, suggesting that barriers to entry were

---

[44] *Regional Independent Media Limited and Gannett UK Limited/Johnston Press plc/Guardian Media Group plc*, Cm. 4887 (November 2000), para.2.27.

[45] *Regional Independent Media Limited and Gannett UK Limited/Johnston Press plc/Guardian Media Group plc* (cited above) at para.2.24.

[46] *Johnston Press plc and Trinity Mirror plc*, Cm. 5495 (May 2002).

[47] *Johnston Press plc and Trinity Mirror plc* (cited above) at para.2.43.

[48] *ibid.*, at para.2.56.

[49] *ibid.*, para.2.61.

[50] *ibid.*, para.2.67.

also high.[51] The Commission found further evidence suggesting high barriers to entry in the fact that publishers were prepared to pay what it regarded as high prices for established titles and the fact that the major publishers preferred to expand through acquisition rather than launches into new areas where they might face significant competition. The Commission also referred to the fact that major publishers tended to have portfolios of titles in particular areas so as to minimise any "gaps" for new entry and observed that advertising packages would make it more difficult for new entrants to compete. Due to the "live and let live" attitude which the Commission felt existed, the prospects of new entry from the major publishers were limited and insufficient to offset the adverse effects on existing competition of the transaction in certain areas. Again, the Commission did not accept that entry from smaller publishers was a significant threat to the major publishers due to the various disadvantages they operated under.[52]

The analysis of barriers to entry did not form a significant part of the Commission's analysis in the *Archant/INM* report, due to its conclusion that the transaction did not in any event raise substantial competition concerns. Nevertheless, the Commission did arrive at a conclusion similar to those of its most recent reports, namely that "incumbents retained significant advantages, and new entrants faced considerable risks if they attempted to overcome them".[52A]

In summary, the current position of the Commission would appear to mean that the parties to a newspaper merger are unlikely to be able to rely successfully on the threat of new entry as a competitive constraint in circumstances where little direct newspaper competition would remain in the local markets in question.[53]

Failing firm defence

The failing firm defence (discussed in Ch.6, above) or variations of it, have been relied on in two recent newspaper merger cases. First, Johnston Press' proposed acquisition of Home Counties Newspapers would have led to little or no effective local newspaper competition to the merged group in Luton, Dunstable and Milton Keynes, and as noted above, the threat of new entry was not considered by the Commission to be a sufficient competitive constraint. However, the relevant Home Counties titles were making substantial losses and there was a significant risk that they would be closed if they were not sold. The Commission did not consider it to be likely that another publisher (other than Johnston Press) would be prepared to acquire the titles and return them to profitability and accordingly, the Commission did not expect that any publisher other than Johnston Press would maintain the relevant titles. The Commission therefore concluded that the situation resulting from the transfer would not be materially different from the

7.035

---

[51] *Newsquest/INM* report (cited above), para.2.110.
[52] *Newsquest/INM* report (cited above), paras 2.120 *et seq.*
[52A] *Archant/INM* report, para.5.35. A more detailed analysis of market entry is included in App.I to the report.
[53] In its reference decision in *Archant/INM*, the OFT also concluded that the likelihood of entry or expansion could not be relied on as an effective competitive constraint.

situation if the transaction did not occur, and recommended that the transfer should be permitted.[54]

Secondly, in the *Newsquest/INM* report, the Commission concluded that the transfer of 10 of the 23 relevant titles could be expected to operate against the public interest. However, in respect of two of these titles, the *Hornsey Journal* series and the *North London Weekly Herald* series, the Commission noted their considerable interdependence with other titles of INM's North London Newspapers division, through significant levels of shared content, in particular advertising, and shared employees. Because of these business links, the Commission acknowledged the serious difficulties that would arise in splitting the two titles from the other North London titles including the possible absence of willing buyers for the two titles alone, and concluded that there was a real risk (but not an expectation) that the two titles would eventually cease to be viable if separated from the other titles of the division. If the titles were to weaken or go out of business, this would in itself be adverse to the public interest, and indeed possibly more so than a transfer to Newsquest.[55] For these reasons, the Secretary of State ultimately decided to permit the transfer of these two titles to Newsquest despite the competition concerns identified by the Commission.[56]

Competition among existing firms

7.036   The Commission has not directly addressed the issue of oligopoly or duopoly in its assessment of regional/local newspaper mergers. For example, in its report on the proposed acquisition of a controlling interest in Southern Newspapers by EMAP and others, the Commission dismissed the resulting substantial increase in market shares of all weekly newspapers (including free and paid for newspapers) from 46 to 73 per cent in four local areas on the ground that there would be at least two competing newspapers in these locations.[57] No doubt, this reflects the reality that, so far as local newspapers are concerned, the majority of localities will not support more than two or three local newspapers, at most. However, as noted above, in recent reports the Commission has expressed the view that there may be a "live and let live" attitude between the major publishers of local newspapers, as a result of which, the Commission contends, they do not compete head on. In view of this concern, the Commission raised the question in its issues statement in the *Newsquest/INM* report whether the creation of a strengthened duopoly in the London area between Newsquest and Trinity Mirror would emerge and whether the duopolists would "display a conscious parallelism that would dampen competition for readers and/or advertisers between them". However, the Commission

---

[54] *Johnston Press plc and Home Counties Newspaper Holdings plc*, Cm. 3962, paras 2.76–2.92.

[55] See *Newsquest/INM* report (cited above), paras 2.154 –2.155.

[56] DTI News Release, November 21, 2003.

[57] *Southern Newspapers plc and EMAP plc/Pearson plc/Reed International plc and Trinity International plc*, Cm. 1772 (November 1991), paras 6.50–6.69. Other factors, such as the ease of entry, were discussed in relation to different areas where the *prima facie* competition concerns raised by the transfers were greater.

concluded that the London region as a whole should not be the focus of its inquiries, as the relevant titles were more local in scope,[58] and in any event reached the view that competition between Newsquest and Trinity Mirror was already limited and therefore not likely to be further reduced by the transaction.[59]

---

[58] A similar view was reached by the Commission in its *Archant/INM* report of September 2004, at para.5.9.
[59] *Newsquest/INM* report (cited above), paras 2.54–2.58.

CHAPTER 8

LOBBYING

Introduction

8.001 In a speech to the London Stock Exchange in October 1988, Lord Young, the then Secretary of State for Trade and Industry, declared that lobbying him in relation to merger cases, either directly or through the media, was not an exercise worth pursuing.[1] Other holders of that office have from time to time expressed similar views. With the Enterprise Act now having removed the political element from the decision making process, except in the case of public interest mergers, it may seem even less likely that lobbying has any part to play; and yet professional lobbyists, strategy consultants and policy analysts continue to play a role in merger activity. The purpose of this chapter, therefore, is to consider what constitutes lobbying, and in what circumstances, and to whom, lobbying efforts might be aimed to good effect. It is not intended here to discuss how in any particular situation the lobbying process should be organised and carried out; that is better left to specialist public affairs consultants.

What is lobbying?

8.002 The term lobbying in the context of merger control under the FTA was sometimes understood to connote the use of pressure on and influence over the DTI as a means of achieving an outcome which would not have been likely without such effort. So understood, it is not difficult on the facts to agree with Lord Young's declaration: prior to the Enterprise Act entering into force, the Secretary of State followed the Director General of Fair Trading's advice in all but a very small number of cases (under one per cent), most of which may be attributed to the application by him of wider public interest policies than the OFT had thought appropriate to take into

---

[1] Lord Young stated that:

"There seems to be a belief that references are sometimes used as a kind of political bolt-hole, and that decisions on whether or not to refer can be influenced by extensive—and expensive—campaigns involving lobbying and advertising. I have even known cases where parties to a bid have published open letters addressed to me in full page advertisements in the national press, although, heaven knows, if they did want to write postage would be cheaper. This is not how the system works.

The decision [as to whether to refer] is mine: but I would need very strong reasons to reject the Director General's advice. On only 9 occasions, out of a total of over 2,000 cases since 1979, has that advice not been followed by the Secretary of State of the day. So the message to companies involved in controversial takeovers who want to influence referral is—don't advertise, don't talk to me, talk to [the OFT]."

account.[2] More broadly defined, however, as the art of educating the decision makers—of seeking to ensure that the OFT, the Competition Commission and, where applicable, the Secretary of State together have available as much relevant information as possible to enable them to reach an informed view on the issues raised by a merger—it is clear that lobbying sometimes has an important role in the regulatory evaluation process, for purchasers, vendors, target enterprises and interested third parties alike.

The provision by the parties to a merger of closely argued submissions to the OFT and, following a reference, to the Competition Commission is an essential and well-understood part of that education process. But in a difficult or controversial case particularly in markets raising potential public interest issues such as newspapers, media, and defence, the parties may see a need to widen their efforts to ensure that, directly or indirectly, the regulatory authorities are fully briefed on all the angles of, and implications raised by, the merger.

The opportunities for lobbying

The role of lobbying in the merger process needs to be put in context. As described above, it was rare, even prior to the removal by the Enterprise Act of ministerial involvement in most mergers, for lobbying of ministers to have any effect whatsoever. The Secretary of State only very rarely took a different view from the OFT as to whether a merger should be referred to the Competition Commission or disagreed materially with the Commission as to whether a merger operated against the public interest and, if so, as to what remedies should be adopted. Moreover, since the tenure of Stephen Byers as Secretary of State from 1998 to 2000, it was government policy not to deviate from the advice of the Director General or Competition Commission. So the removal from the process of the Secretary of State in the vast majority of cases will not make a major difference; and the minister's continued involvement in public interest and special public interest cases is unlikely to represent a major opportunity for lobbying.

8.003

Potential lobbying targets

The Secretary of State for Trade and Industry

Although the Secretary of State was (and in the case of a public interest case remains) unlikely to be susceptible to lobbying efforts either during the OFT's evaluation of a merger or during the course of a Commission reference it was thought that upon receipt of the OFT's advice, or the

8.004

---

[2] For example, in *Credit Lyonnais SA/Woodchester Investments plc; Sligos SA/Signet Limited*, Cm.1450 (February 1991); and *Societé Nationale Elf Acquitaine*, Cm.1521 (May 1991), *Amoco Corporation* Cm.1404 (January 1991); the relevant consideration was the degree of foreign state ownership by the acquiring enterprises. The double reference made by Nicholas Ridley contrary to the Director General's advice concerning lawnmowers (*Ransomes plc/Westwood Engineering and Laser Lawnmowers Limited*, Cm.1128 (July 1990)) was widely attributed by the media, in the absence of any obvious development in government policy, to the Secretary of State's interest in gardening. Whatever may have been the justification, there is no suggestion that lobbying of the DTI played any role in the decision.

Commission's recommendations following a reference, there might be a window of opportunity to make representations. If there was, that window has now been closed, except where he retains power over public interest and special public interest cases. Even in those infrequent cases, DTI policy remains clear, that the Secretary of State is not susceptible to lobbying, but so long as the legislation and procedure permit him to take into account issues beyond those considered by the OFT and the Commission, there will remain the suspicion that in difficult or controversial cases, endeavours to make direct representations to the Secretary of State may be justified.

Other government departments and regulators

8.005 Government departments other than the DTI may still have a role to play in merger regulation, and any lobbying efforts should involve considering which departments are likely to be interested in the outcome and implications of a merger, or would be if their involvement were sought. For example, a merger involving suppliers to the armed forces would interest the Ministry of Defence; and a merger between pharmaceutical wholesalers would be of relevance to the Department of Health. The role of such departments is not that of an interested bystander: in many mergers, the views of government departments may be of significance to the outcome, in two distinct ways. First, a government department may have a view as a customer of one or both of the parties to a merger. The opposition of the Ministry of Defence to a change of control of a supplier to the armed forces, for example, might well be influential on the OFT and the Commission (as well as being relevant in the assessment of public interest or special public interest issues relating to national security)[3], as would the views of the Department of Health on a merger between two suppliers of drugs to the National Health Service.[4] Indeed, in relation to the analysis of issues other than competition, the OFT tends to defer to those with greater expertise: in relation to the analysis of national security in the two cases at the time of writing where a European intervention notice had been issued, the OFT simply reported the views of the Ministry of Defence to the Secretary of State, commenting that as it was not expert in this field, it did not go beyond summarising the representations received, and noting that it had no reason to doubt them.[5] Secondly, although the OFT does not typically invite

---

[3] In the two cases at the time of writing where the Secretary of State had issued a European intervention notice in respect of national security issues, although the OFT was responsible for reporting to the Secretary of State, the content of the report was extensively made up of the analysis of the Ministry of Defence and in both cases, the MOD took the initiative in drafting undertakings in lieu of reference to deal with the security concerns which it identified. See the OFT's report to the Secretary of State of May 20, 2004, *Anticipated acquisition by General Dynamics Corporation of Alvis PLC* and its report to the Secretary of State of September 29, 2004, *Anticipated acquisition by Finmeccanica SpA of AgustaWestland NV* (both available on the DTI's website). In UK or EC cases where national security issues are raised, therefore, it is to be expected that the MOD will drive or at least significantly influence the analysis. See also para.6.073 of Ch.6 in relation to the MMC's report *The General Electric Company plc/VSEL plc*, Cm. 2852 (May 1995).

[4] See para.5.072 of ch.6, above, which discusses cases concerning the NHS/Department of Health in the context of countervailing buyer power.

[5] See the OFT's reports to the Secretary of State in *General Dynamics/Alvis* and *Finmeccanica/AgustaWestland*, cited above.

representatives of interested departments to case review meetings in difficult cases, the input of these departments in writing may still be sought by the OFT, and the Competition Commission too may seek departmental views in certain cases. Educating interested departments may, therefore, be of considerable importance; if a department is likely to express views it is desirable that those views should be based upon a full understanding of all relevant issues. Even if a government department's wholehearted support for a merger cannot be assured, it may often be possible, through educating the civil servants, to neutralise their potential opposition.

Care must be taken to ensure that contact with a department is made at the appropriate level. Whilst a meeting between the chairman of a merging company and a junior minister may give the chairman some comfort, it is not the minister, but his civil servants, who have the appropriate detailed knowledge of the relevant sector and issues and whose input may ultimately find its way to the regulatory bodies. It is they, therefore, who should normally be contacted in the first instance; and it is generally better to do this through existing contacts with the department, with persons already known to them making the initial approach.

The role of OFCOM in public interest and special public interest cases relating to the newspaper and media sectors is examined in detail above.[6] In addition, they and other regulators such as OFGEM, ORR and Postcom may be expected to submit their views to the OFT and the Competition Commission in connection with merger activity in their sectors, and their officials are generally receptive to receiving submissions prepared by the parties and third parties and, where convenient, willing to meet with them; indeed some regulators will actively solicit views in relation to mergers in their sector by issuing consultation papers.[7]

Members of Parliament

It has often been assumed in the past that backbench MPs have a significant role to play in the regulatory process; that their influence in the corridors and tearooms of the House of Commons will bring pressure to bear on the Secretary of State in cases in which he continues to have a role to play; and that the OFT and the Commission will be influenced by their representations. As a result, parties to difficult or controversial mergers, especially contested public bids, will sometimes orchestrate a campaign involving letters to, and meetings with, interested MPs, notably those whose constituencies contain a business affected by the merger. Moreover, the shift from a general public interest test under the FTA to a competition-based test under the Enterprise Act, and the heavy emphasis on industrial economics techniques in modern merger analysis arguably means that the types of issues that an MP might be concerned about (for example, the impact of the merger on local employment) and the local knowledge that he or she can bring to the analysis, are perhaps of reduced relevance and thus of less influence than they might have been in the past.

8.006

---

[6] See paras 2.060–2.065 of Ch.2 and Ch.7.
[7] See Ch.2 at paras 2.068–2.069.

523

It was MPs who prompted Lord Cockfield, the then Secretary of State, in 1982, to refer Knoll International's bid for Sothebys to the MMC[8] but that is thought to have been the only occasion when a concerted campaign involving MPs had that effect. In practice, MPs have little influence or locus in the regulatory process, the exceptions being those backbenchers who are known and respected for their particular knowledge and expertise on issues and subjects that are relevant to the merger in question, or who are members of parliamentary committees whose view might be taken note of by the OFT or the Commission. Moreover, the shift from a general public interest test under the FTA to a competiton-based test under the Enterprise Act, and the heavy emphasis on industrial economics techniques in modern merger analysis arguably means that the types of issues that an MP might be concerned about (for example, the impact of the merger on local employment) and the local knowledge that he or she can bring to the analysis, are perhaps of reduced relevance and thus of less influence than they might have been in the past.

Third parties and representative groups

8.007 As a matter of routine, parties to mergers which are being evaluated by the OFT or investigated by the Competition Commission should consider which of their customers, suppliers, competitors and trade bodies and where relevant representative groups such as the Consumers' Association[9] are likely to support their arguments and which are likely to object; and to seek to encourage those whose support can be relied upon to make their own representations. As has been described earlier, the regulatory authorities will ask the parties to provide contact details for customers and competitors which they will approach to give evidence[10], and it is not unusual where there is an element of discretion in the contact details given, to offer names of contacts who are likely to support the merger (or, in the case of a target in a contested bid, are likely to express adverse views). But, in practice, greater relevance may be placed on the opinions of an organisation that has made representations without being requested to do so. Hence efforts can be made by the parties to a merger to motivate third parties to submit supporting evidence. Equally importantly, efforts may need to be made to neutralise potential opposition through educating such third parties as to the merits of the case. Accordingly, where a merger raises potentially difficult regulatory issues, the parties should consider identifying and enlisting the help of supporting third parties and should seek to ensure that adverse comment is not inadvertently expressed to the OFT and Commission.

---

[8] The bid was subsequently abandoned and the reference laid aside.
[9] The Consumers Association is arguably the most sophisticated and active of the consumer representative bodies in making submissions in merger cases which are likely to have a direct impact on consumers, as is the case in relation to mergers in the retail sector, for example.
[10] See para.3.046 of Ch.3.

The Media

Although considerable efforts are often made by an acquirer's public rela-   8.008
tions advisers to enlist the support of the media through the publication of
informative or supportive material, it is highly unlikely that the OFT, or the
Commission (or, in public interest cases, the Secretary of State) will be
persuaded or influenced by it. Media coverage might influence the City and
shareholders generally, which can be relevant, for example, in the context
of a takeover bid (although, as both parties may be seeking to enlist media
help in broadly equal proportions, the extent of such influence may be very
limited), but it will not persuade those who must advise or decide upon the
making of a reference or its outcome.

Conclusion

Examples of references being made as a direct result of lobbying efforts were   8.009
extremely rare under the FTA and are likely to be more so under the new
regime. The proposed acquisition of Sotheby's by Knoll International,
referred to above, was one of the very few.[11] Clearances ensuing as a result of
lobbying are rarer still. Nevertheless a carefully constructed and appropriately focussed and targeted lobbying campaign may sometimes have the effect
of influencing the OFT's decision as well as ensuring that on a reference, all
the Commission's conclusions are based upon a full understanding of all the
relevant facts.

---

[11] A further illustration is afforded by Imperial Group's proposed acquisition of Permaflex
Limited in 1985: the proposed acquisition for an insignificant consideration of a snuff
blender was referred to the MMC following a campaign mounted by two snuff-grinding
companies whose sales might have been adversely affected by the merger, following an
informal indication by the OFT that the transaction was too insignificant to be likely to
concern the Secretary of State. The campaign involved significant press coverage, the
lobbying of influential backbench MPs and the mobilization of tobacconists throughout the
country who encouraged all their customers to complain to the OFT. The proposed merger
was subsequently abandoned and the reference laid aside.

REMEDIES

Introduction

9.001   Under the merger provisions of the Fair Trading Act, it was the duty of the Competition Commission, if it found that the merger operated, or might be expected to operate, against the public interest, to make recommendations to the Secretary of State as to how (if at all) the identified detriments might be remedied.[1] It was then for the Secretary of State to decide whether to accept the Commission's findings as to detriment and, in that event, whether to adopt its proposed remedies or to substitute remedies of his own,[2] or indeed to clear the merger unconditionally.

Accordingly, as part of the hearing (or second hearing) with the acquiring party, and prior to the Commission having reached (or at least expressed) any conclusions as to the existence or otherwise of adverse effects arising from the merger, the practice was to raise the question of hypothetical remedies, as a means of assessing what remedies might address any adverse effects that might hypothetically be found to arise; how these remedies might be implemented; and their effect on the merged entity. In the event of it subsequently concluding that the merger might be expected to operate against the public interest, the Commission would formulate its recommendations on the basis of discussions with the parties and, where appropriate, third parties.

There was something inherently artificial and defective about a system that required a party to comment on remedies which might have a fundamental effect on its future business and strategy at a time when the Commission had not, officially at least, concluded that the merger was detrimental to the public interest, and to restrict the party to that premature opportunity to comment. The procedure at times caused the Commission to make recommendations that were unworkable; it was also inefficient, prompting the parties to respond strategically on the basis of speculation as to what the Commission might be thinking, avoiding any concessions, rather than offering the honest and practical appraisal that would be appropriate once the outcome of the reference became known: since the parties were clearly reluctant to engage in any detailed discussion of the efficacy and practicality of individual remedies whilst maintaining that no remedy at all was necessary. At the same time, the OFT, whose role it was to negotiate any undertakings required in consequence of the Secretary of State's decision, was often placed in the difficult position of having to interpret the Commission's recommendations and consider objections to them without having been party to the

---

[1] s.72(2), Fair Trading Act 1973.
[2] ss.73(2) and (3), Fair Trading Act 1973.

arguments made before the Commission or to the Commission's due reasoning and deliberations.

These difficulties have been addressed by the Enterprise Act. In removing the role of the Secretary of State (except in the case of mergers affecting the public interest[3]) and granting to the Commission the final decision whether to clear a merger, prohibit it or approve it subject to remedies in the form of undertakings or an order, the Act has cleared the way for a practical discussion on remedies. The Commission must now publish its provisional findings,[4] such that the parties (and also third parties) know the potential outcome well in advance and are afforded the opportunity for a meaningful dialogue with the Commission about remedies. The Competition Commission's Rules of Procedure, moreover, now require that the Commission should publish a notice of proposed remedies (to the extent that they were not included in the provisional findings), enabling not only the parties to the merger but also third parties to be fully aware of the remedies which are being considered.[4A] Publication of this notice is the starting point for the consideration of remedies.

The legal principles underlying the selection of remedies

If the Commission concludes that a merger results, or may be expected to result, in a substantial lessening of competition within any market(s) in the UK, then it must consider three further questions. Section 35(3) of the Act (in the case of completed mergers) and s.36(2) (in relation to anticipated mergers) state that the Commission must consider: **9.002**

(i) whether action should be taken by it, for the purpose of remedying, mitigating or preventing the substantial lessening of competition concerned or adverse effect which has resulted from, or may be expected to result from, the substantial lessening of competition;

(ii) alternatively, whether it should recommend the taking of action by others for the same purpose; and

(iii) in either case, if action should be taken, what that action should be taken and what is to be remedied, mitigated or prevented.

Under the FTA, s.73 gave power to the Secretary of State to make an order to remedy the anti-competitive effects of a merger "as he may consider it requisite . . . for the purpose of remedying or preventing the adverse effects specified in the [Competition Commission's] report".[5] The meaning of the corresponding wording in s.56(2) of the FTA (which concerned the power of the Secretary of State to make an order to implement remedies following a reference to and report by the Competition Commission in relation to a monopoly situation) was considered by the

---

[3] See Ch.2 at paras 2.025–2.033.
[4] See para.5.048 of Ch.5, above.
[4A] See Rule 11 of the *Competition Commission: Rules of Procedure* CC1.
[5] See s.73(2) of the FTA.

Court of Appeal in 1999 in the *Thomson Holidays* case.[6] Following a monopoly reference into foreign package holidays, the Secretary of State had issued the Foreign Package Holidays (Tour Operators and Travel Agents) Order 1998,[7] intended to implement the remedies recommended by the MMC in its report. However, the order was challenged by Thomson Holidays, on the basis that the scope of the order went further than the areas where the MMC had identified adverse effects on the public interest. Laws L.J., giving the leading judgment in the case, considered the meaning of s.56(2) and commented:

"... it needs to be borne in mind that the terms of the MMC's report will set the reach of the Secretary of State's powers under the subsection; and for this reason there is a particular public interest in having the 'adverse effects', and the s.49 facts,[8] identified with conspicuous clarity."[9]

Laws L.J. went on to conclude that certain provisions in the order went beyond the scope of facts which the MMC had found to operate against the public interest, and quashed the offending parts of the order.

It is suggested that the Enterprise Act retains the same critical linkage between the remedies which may be imposed and the Competition Commission's findings of fact regarding the substantial lessening of competition and any adverse effects arising out of it. Sections 35(1) and 36(1) require the Commission to identify whether a substantial lessening of competition has resulted or may be expected to result from the merger. If so, s.35(2) defines such a situation as an anti-competitive outcome and ss.35(3) and 36(2) require the Commission to consider whether action should be taken to remedy the substantial lessening of competition or any adverse effects resulting or expected to result from it. There is therefore a corresponding chain of analysis under the Act which starts with the findings of fact as to whether the merger will have an anti-competitive outcome and ends with the identification of remedies. It will therefore continue to be necessary for the Competition Commission to identify "with conspicuous clarity" the findings of fact which it considers constitute the substantial lessening of competition and any consequent adverse findings, and to tailor its remedies precisely to correspond to those conclusions.

The requirement of proportionality is not expressly set out in the Act, which instead requires the Competition Commission to take into account "the need to achieve as comprehensive a solution as is reasonable and practicable to the substantial lessening of competition and any adverse effects resulting from it."[10] It is not clear that this wording is aimed specifically at ensuring proportionality; certainly the reference to comprehensiveness might create a risk that the Competition Commission would err on the side of a

---

[6] *R. v Secretary of State for Trade & Industry Ex p. Thomson Holidays*, Times Law Reports, January 12, 2000, [2000] U.K.C.L.R. 189, transcript available from Lawtel.

[7] SI 1998/1945.

[8] "S49 facts" was Laws L.J.'s shorthand for "the facts which in the MMC's concluded view operate, or may be expected to operate, against the public interest". See the *Thomson Holidays* case, cited above, at p.14 of the transcript.

[9] See the *Thomson Holidays* case, cited above, at p.19.

[10] See ss.35(4) and 35(3) of the Act.

"safety first" approach in constructing its remedies rather than seeking to balance the benefits in competition terms of a particular remedy against the burden it would impose. Moreover, the Explanatory Notes to the Act suggest that the wording is intended to point to structural rather than behavioural remedies as being more appropriate[11]; again, this interpretation is not necessarily consistent with imposing an obligation of proportionality. However, the Competition Commission itself expressly states that proportionality will be one of the factors which drives its consideration of appropriate remedies:

> "The Commission will aim to ensure that no remedy is disproportionate in relation to the [substantial lessening of competition] or other adverse effect. If the Commission is choosing between two remedies which it considers would be equally effective, it will choose the remedy that imposes the least cost or that is least restrictive."[12]

In any case, it is arguable that administrative law and human rights considerations might impose a requirement of proportionality on the Competition Commission's remedies, regardless of whether it is expressly stated in the Act.[12A] Indeed, the ruling in *Thomson Holidays* discussed above can be interpreted as essentially concerning issues of proportionality.   **9.003**

Other considerations which the Competition Commission states will bear on its identification of suitable remedies are cost (linked closely to proportionality) and effectiveness.[13]

Once the Commission has decided that a merger results, or may be expected to result, in a substantial lessening of competition, it is unlikely that it will decide that there is no case for remedial action[14] but the Commission has suggested that such exceptional circumstances might arise where, for example, the costs of implementing any practical remedy may seem disproportionate in the light of the size of the relevant market or where the only appropriate remedial action would fall outside the UK's jurisdiction. In those circumstances, the Commission may still recommend action by others—for example, the government, other regulators or other public bodies—to change the regulations governing an industry, to increase market transparency, to encourage market entry in order to increase competition in a market, or to prevent or limit potentially anti-competitive behaviour.[15] The Commission has acknowledged that where it falls to others to make a decision on the recommendation, there will be uncertainty as to whether the recommendation will be accepted and, if so, as to the time period before which it will be implemented. In those circumstances, the

---

[11] See further para.9.009, below.
[12] *Merger References: Competition Commission Guidelines*, CC2 at para.4.9.
[12A] But see n.82 cited above at para.10.016.
[13] See further paras 4.10 to 4.16 of *Merger Guidelines*.
[14] *Merger Guidelines*, at para.4.6.
[15] For example, in *Dräger Medical AG & Co. KGaA/Hillenbrand Industries, Inc* (May 2004) the Commission indicated that it considered that there was scope for buyer power latent in the NHS to be exercised more effectively, and that the Department of Health and other similar bodies could promote market entry. Accordingly, in addition to concluding that certain undertakings should be given by the merged entity, the Commission made various recommendations to the medical authorities to encourage market entry and to increase the exercise of buyer power by NHS trusts.

Commission is likely to take this inherent uncertainty into account when deciding whether to make such a recommendation.[16]

The choice between action by way of undertakings or an order

9.004   In the majority of cases where the Commission concludes that the merger may be expected to lead to a substantial lessening of competition, the Commission will take action itself and may do so either by way of an order or by way of undertakings.[17] The Commission's guidance[18] indicates that various considerations will dictate whether the Commission decides to seek undertakings from the party or parties, or to make an order: first, the parties' willingness to negotiate and agree undertakings in the light of the Commission's report; secondly, the scope of the Commission's powers and whether the remedy that it considers appropriate falls within those powers[19]; and thirdly, issues of practicality such as the need to take speedy action, which may necessitate the making of an order to avoid the delay likely while undertakings are negotiated.

In practice, undertakings rather than orders have been used in all cases to date where remedies have been sought under the Act, and this was by far the more common outcome under the FTA where remedies were required. It is to be expected that undertakings will remain the primary way of imposing remedies, except in cases where the parties are not co-operating so that a more aggressive approach is needed by the Competition Commission.

The negotiation and implementation of undertakings and orders

9.005   It was noted in para.9.001 above that having reached an adverse finding, the Commission will publish a notice of the proposed remedies[20] and will consult the parties to the merger, as well as interested third parties, on a range of possible remedies. The remedies which the group ultimately decide (by simple majority) to impose will be set out in the Commission's final

---

[16] *Merger Guidelines*, at para.4.20. The Commission's guidance also records that the Government has indicated that it would consider any Commission recommendation and give a public response within ninety days of publication of the Commission's report, setting out options on which it proposes to consult, or changes that it proposes to make, in the light of the Commission's report, cross-referring to the DTI's White Paper, *A World Class Competition Regime*, July 2001, at para.4.15. In fact it is not expressly confirmed (although neither is it ruled out) in the White Paper that that commitment will extend to recommendations made in relation to merger references and the comment appears in the context of the general review of legislation to ensure that it does not have a detrimental impact on competition. It is also worth noting in this context that, as noted, recommendations were made to the government in *Dräger Medical AG & Co KGaA/Hillenbrand Industries, Inc* in May 2004 (cited above) but, as far as the authors are aware, no such public response from the government had been made at the time of writing, some five months later.

[17] ss.82 and 84 of the Act.

[18] *Merger Guidelines* at paras 4.46 to 4.49.

[19] The Enterprise Act limits the content of any orders made by the Commission, whilst the subject matter of an undertaking is not similarly limited (except by the facts underlying the anti-competitive outcome finding, as discussed at para.9.002, above). As regards orders, s.84(2) limits the contents of the order to anything contained in Sch.8 to the Act. There is no corresponding limitation in s.80 regarding undertakings and s.89(1) expressly confirms that Sch.8 does not apply in relation to undertakings.

[20] See Rule 11 of the *Rules of Procedure*.

report, in sufficient detail to support the implementation of the under-takings or order.[21] The Commission's report may also specify the timescale within which undertakings should be agreed, before the Commission will consider imposing an order as an alternative (although this has not been normal practice to date). The group is discharged *only* when negotiations have been completed and suitable undertakings have been received or orders imposed.

After the publication of the Commission's report, the Commission will therefore seek to negotiate undertakings, or impose an order, which is consis-tent with the Commission's report (unless there has been a material change of circumstances since the preparation of the report or other special reason). Section 93 of the Act allows the Commission to require the OFT to negotiate undertakings, but with the Commission retaining the final decision on whether undertakings should be accepted. However, the Commission has indicated that it has decided in practice that it will take responsibility for negotiating and implementing undertakings with support from the OFT[22] and has established a specialist remedies unit headed by a Director of Remedies, and as at the time of writing had handled the negotiations of remedies itself.

The remedial action decided upon by the Commission will depend on the circumstances of the case and the nature and extent of the substantial less-ening of competition that has been identified. As described above,[23] Sch.8 to the Act limits the Commission's order-making powers but its ability to negotiate undertakings is not similarly restricted by the Act.[24] In practice, therefore, the options available to the Commission once a substantial less-ening of competition has been identified are limited only by its obligation to have regard to the underlying facts of the anti-competitive outcome[25] proportionality, cost and the expected effectiveness of any proposed remedy, and within those confines it enjoys broad scope to consider the proposals of the affected parties and third parties as well as its own ideas as to remedies.

The choice of remedies in practice

Types of remedies available

A wide range of remedies is available to the Commission aimed at countering the adverse effects of a merger. The Commission's guidelines categorise the potential scope for remedies as follows: 9.006

(i)   Remedies that are intended to restore all or part of the status quo ante market structure; for example:

   • prohibition of an anticipated merger;
   • divestment of a completed acquisition;
   • partial prohibition or divestment.

---

[21] *General Advice and Information*, CC4 at para.6.25.
[22] *General Advice and Information*, at para.7.7.
[23] See n.9, above.
[24] s.89(1) of the Act.
[25] See para.9.002, above.

(ii)   Remedies that are intended to increase the competition that will be faced by the merged firm (whether from existing competitors or new entrants); for example:

- requiring access to essential inputs/facilities;
- licensing know-how or intellectual property rights;
- dismantling exclusive distributions arrangements;
- removing no-competition clauses in customer contracts.

(iii)   Remedies aimed at excluding or limiting the possibility that the merged firm will take advantage of the increased market power resulting from the merger to behave anti-competitively or to exploit its customer or suppliers; for example:

- a price cap or other restraint on prices;
- a commitment to non-discriminatory behaviour;
- an obligation to increase the transparency of prices;
- an obligation to refrain from conduct, the main purpose or effect of which is to inhibit entry.[26]

Effectiveness

9.007   The Commission announced in April 2004 that it had embarked upon a study of remedies imposed in relation to previous mergers, with a view to creating solutions that are more customised and tailored. In the words of the Commission's Chairman, "we are trying to provide a way for the members to see what's available, what typically works and what doesn't, early on in the remedies phase so that we can focus our attentions."[27] For now, the Commission's merger guidelines[28] reflect three yardsticks as to effectiveness: clarity; ease of implementation and compliance; and the timescale taken by the remedy to achieve the restoration of competition or to eradicate the adverse consequences of the merger:

(i)   clarity: a remedy must be clear to the parties who must implement it, to the OFT and/or other regulators who must monitor compliance, and to competitors, suppliers and customers (who can have an important role to play in monitoring compliance);

(ii)   ease of implementation and compliance: one-off remedies that change the structure of the market are likely to be more acceptable, as they are likely to be relatively straightforward and, after implementation, to require little monitoring or enforcement; and

(iii)   timescale: generally the Commission will tend to favour a remedy which can be expected to be effective within a relatively short timescale as against one which would take time to implement or, after being put in place, to produce the hoped-for beneficial effect on competition.

---

[26] *Merger Guidelines*, at para.4.17.
[27] Professor Geroski, quoted in the *Financial Times*, "Competition Regulator to review merger remedies", April 12, 2004.
[28] *Merger Guidelines*, at paras 4.13 to 4.16.

Proportionality and cost

As noted, the Commission has indicated that it will also have regard to the 9.008
principle of proportionality. It will seek to ensure that no remedy is disproportionate to the substantial lessening of competition or other adverse
effects of a merger. Accordingly, if the Commission is choosing between two
remedies which it considers would be equally effective, it will generally
choose that which imposes the lower cost or which is the less restrictive.[29]
For example, in its 1999 report on *Rockwool/Owens-Corning*, the
Commission observed that:

> "The areas which we identified as likely to be subject to increased prices
> represent a minority of Rockwool's sales. We have therefore considered
> whether a behavioural remedy could be found which would satisfactorily
> deal with this adverse effect and enable us to recommend that the merger
> be allowed to proceed on a conditional basis so that the benefits we
> foresee from the merger could be realised."[30];

and in its report on *Dräger Medical/Hillenbrand*, the Commission "began by
considering the least cost, least intrusive remedy, adding to that where necessary in order comprehensively the SLC and its adverse effects."[31] The
Commission may therefore include in its consideration the costs to the parties
of implementing the remedy. However, its guidelines emphasise that in relation to completed mergers, the Commission will not normally consider the
actual costs of divestment, on the basis that it was open to the parties to make
their merger proposals conditional upon competition authorities' approval: it
is for the parties to assess whether there is a risk that a completed merger
would be prohibited subsequently, and in the Commission's view that risk
would normally be expected to be reflected already in the acquisition price.[32]

Neither will certain other costs, such as environmental costs or the
social costs of unemployment, be assessed by the Commission in its
consideration of remedies. It will, however, endeavour to minimise any
ongoing compliance costs to the parties, subject to the effectiveness of the
remedy not being reduced, and will have regard to the costs to the OFT
in monitoring compliance with any remedies that the Commission may put
in place.[33]

A preference for structural over behavioural remedies?

The considerations of proportionality and cost discussed above would tend to 9.009
imply that the Commission will generally favour so called structural remedies
(that is, divestments of assets which will change the structure of the market)
over so-called behavioural remedies (which seek to control the future
conduct of the merged company).

---

[29] *Merger Guidelines* CC2, at para.4.49.
[30] *Rockwool Limited/Owens-Corning Building Products (UK) Limited*, Cm. 4330 (May
1999), at para.2.173.
[31] *Dräger Medical AG & Co. KgaA Hillenbrand Industries Inc*, May 2004 at para.10.14.
[32] *Merger Guidelines* CC2, at para.4.10.
[33] *Merger Guidelines* CC2, at paras 4.11 to 4.12.

In 1991, the then Secretary of State, Peter Lilley, stated that "clean structural remedies" are preferable to "behavioural remedies which require long term monitoring by the Office of Fair Trading."[34] Some relaxation of this policy stance could perhaps have been inferred from subsequent changes introduced by the Deregulation and Contracting Out Act 1994, which allowed the Secretary of State for the first time to accept behavioural undertakings in lieu of making a merger reference to the Commission. Nevertheless, the Commission's guidelines indicate that it remains the case that structural remedies are likely to be preferable to behavioural remedies as they address the effect of the merger directly and will require comparatively little, if any, monitoring or enforcement of compliance.[35]

In relation to the requirement in ss.35(4) and 36(3) of the Act that the Competition Commission must take into account "the need to achieve as comprehensive a solution as is reasonable and practicable to the substantial lessening of competition and any adverse effects resulting from it", the Explanatory Notes to the Act comment:

> "The reference to a 'comprehensive solution' will require the [Commission] to consider remedies that address the substantial lessening of competition itself (*e.g.* the features arising from the merger that give rise to the creation of market power) because it is generally more effective to tackle the cause of any problems at their source rather than by tackling the symptoms or adverse effects."[36]

This comment could again be interpreted as suggesting that structural remedies, which typically eliminate the competition concern at source, are more appropriate than behavioural remedies, which instead leave the risk of anti-competitive behaviour in place but seek to manage it by controlling the conduct of the undertaking—*i.e.* by tackling the symptoms rather than the cause.

9.010   The Chairman of the Commission, Professor Paul Geroski, has, on the other hand, emphasised that the Commission has an open mind as regards the type of remedies which may be appropriate to address competition concerns in a particular case, and has predicted that there could be greater use of "behavioural" remedies as the Commission gains experience. In April 2004, discussing the Commission's newly launched remedies study[37] he told the *Financial Times* that:

> "If we can find ways of doing things using [behavioural] remedies that work, that are not too expensive to monitor and relatively effective, then

---

[34] Speech to Law Society Groups on June 12, 1991.
[35] *Merger Guidelines*, at para.4.15. Similarly the OFT's Substantive Assessment Guidance, at para.8.6, states that: "A merger involves a structural change to a market. A structural solution will therefore often be the most appropriate remedy if the OFT believes that it is or may be the case that a merger may (or may be expected to) result in a substantial lessening competition. The OFT considers that structural undertakings are more likely to be accepted as undertakings in lieu than behavioural undertakings because they clearly address the market structure issues that give rise to the competition problems."
[36] See the Explanatory Notes to the Act at para.134.
[37] See para.9.007, above.

the answer is yes [we will use them more often], because with those remedies we do stand a chance of fine tuning and getting it absolutely right."[38]

As noted below, in the five cases under the Act which had been concluded at the time of writing, two were cleared subject to conditions, and in both cases, behavioural undertakings were sought.[38A] That said, it is too early to interpret this as signalling a change of approach and for the time being it must continue to be the expectation that structural remedies will be the preferred option.

Structural remedies

Despite the recent interest in behavioural remedies, structural remedies are nonetheless likely to remain the principal instrument used by the Commission in addressing findings of a substantial lessening of competition. In order to be effective, a divestment should create a new source of competition (via divestment to a *new* market participant) or strengthen an existing source of competition (via divestment to an *existing* market participant). In June 2004 the Commission published draft guidelines on divestiture remedies for consultation which, if implemented in substantially their current form following the consultation, indicates the Commission's thinking for the future with regard to the effectiveness of structural remedies.[39] In these draft guidelines, the Commission recognises that to be effective divestment should involve the sale of an appropriate divestiture package to a suitable purchaser through an effective process. Acknowledging the uncertainty of all remedies as to their ultimate impact, the Commission identifies in the draft guidelines three categories of risk arising out of the divestiture process:

9.011

(i)   Composition risks: that the scope of the package divested may be too constrained or inappropriately configured to attract suitable purchasers or enable the buyer to operate effectively in the market;

(ii)   Purchaser risks: that a suitable purchaser may not be available or that the parties may dispose to an ineffective purchaser;

(iii) Asset risks: that the viability of a divestment package will deteriorate prior to completion of the divestment.

Each of these issues is considered below.

---

[38] "*Competition Chief not yet at home with new powers*", *Financial Times*, April 12, 2004. However, as the *Financial Times* observed, whilst greater use of behavioural remedies will be welcomed by business, Prof Geroski warned that such sanctions would not be a soft option. He has said that "it's a mixed blessing because a behavioural remedy does mean that the regulators are watching you."

[38A] Of the other three cases, one was prohibited in part and clearly unconditionally as to the remainder and the other two were cleared unconditionally.

[39] *Application of Divestiture Remedies in Merger Inquiries: Competition Commission Guidelines*, Draft for consultation (June 2004). At the time of writing the consultation period had closed but the outcome of the consultation process was not yet known.

The scope of the divestment package

9.012 The draft guidelines indicate that the starting point for defining the scope of a divestment package is identifying the minimum package of assets or substantive business which, if successfully divested, would be expected to remedy the substantial lessening of competition. Other assets or business segments may then need to be added to the package to ensure an ongoing ability to compete. The Commission will generally prefer the divestment of an existing, stand-alone business to the divestment of part of a business or a collection of assets. In this connection, the Commission's guidelines on merger references indicate that a key question that will determine whether partial divestment can be an effective remedy is "whether the assets to be divested provide the basis of a viable business that can operate independently of the merging firms and, in a reasonably short time, say within one year, can be expected to provide effective and sustained competition to the other firms in the market . . ."[40]

This was an issue in *Lloyds TSB/Abbey National*. The Commission had concluded that the proposed merger would have adverse effects in both the personal current account ("PCA") market and in relation to the supply of services to small and medium enterprises ("SME"). In considering possible remedies, the Commission examined whether the divestment of Cheltenham & Gloucester (part of Lloyds TSB and a supplier of mortgages and savings accounts) might remedy the adverse effects the Commission had identified in relation to PCAs and in the SME market. The Commission observed that Cheltenham & Gloucester's activities in relation to these two markets were either very small or non-existent, and moreover the divestment of Cheltenham & Gloucester was not necessary to remedy any adverse effects in those markets in which it was primarily active. However, the Commission considered whether, given that its concerns in respect of the PCA and SME markets surrounded the loss of a branch-based competitor, the divestment of Cheltenham & Gloucester would provide a ready-made branch network which might enable a new player to enter the PCA and SME markets, or an existing player to expand within those markets. The Commission concluded, however, that the divestment of Cheltenham & Gloucester branches would not in itself achieve a great deal, because anyone interested in using the branches to supply PCAs and products for SMEs would need suitable IT systems, staff trained to handle those products and, above all, customers. A party acquiring Cheltenham & Gloucester would do so primarily for its existing businesses in mortgages and savings accounts, and given that Cheltenham & Gloucester was not active to any great degree in PCAs and services for SME customers, it was unlikely to be seen as an attractive platform for entry or expansion within those markets. The Commission therefore eliminated the divestment of Cheltenham & Gloucester as a possible remedy.[41]

The Commission will generally prefer the divestment of an existing stand-alone business to divestment of a specially constructed group of assets; but if a divestment of a set of assets or part of a business is proposed

---

[40] *Merger Guidelines* CC2, at para.4.27(a).
[41] *Lloyds TSB Group/Abbey National plc*, Cm. 5208 (July 2001), at paras 2.245 to 2.248.

rather than of a complete business,[42] the Commission will normally prefer that all the assets to be sold be provided by one of the merging parties, since the divestment of a mixture of assets from both the merging parties may create additional risks that the divestment package will not function effectively.[43]

Perhaps the most controversial of the Commission's proposals is that which states that:

"In order to incentivise parties to complete an agreed divestiture, a broader, more valuable group of assets may be defined (*i.e.* 'crown jewels') which the [Commission] would require the parties to sell if a proposed divestiture is not completed within a specified period. The [Commission] will generally only consider use of such crown jewels packages in circumstances where other effective options are not available. The [Commission] would wish to be satisfied that the purchaser of a crown jewels package was committed to operate the core assets necessary to remedy the SLC and not primarily attracted by the ancillary assets."[44]

The Commission's thought is, presumably, that the threat of such a remedy will ensure timely compliance. It remains to be seen whether the Commission sees fit to adopt such a proposal and, if adopted, in what circumstances it might be invoked; but there must be concern that in adopting such a remedy as a fall back, the Commission would exceed its powers.[45] The proposal also raises the question of proportionality: if the Commission has concluded that the divestment of a particular business would be proportionate to the adverse effects identified, then the forced divestment of the "crown jewel" assets could arguably be disproportionate, being beyond what was necessary to remedy the anti-competitive outcome. Nor is it clear how this proposal would fulfil the requirement on the Commission to have regard to "the need to achieve as comprehensive a solution as is reasonable and practicable to the substantial lessening of competition".[46] The proposal also potentially increases the risk that competition clearance divestments become "fire sales" under which it is difficult

9.013

---

[42] This may be the case, for example, if a partial divestment would be considered more proportionate to identified adverse effects.

[43] Commission's consultation paper at para.3.5.

[44] Consultation paper, para.3.6.

[45] For example, suppose that a merger party owns multiple production plants, and that the divestment of just one plant would be sufficient to remedy an expected substantial lessening of competition. In these circumstances, the firm in question might undertake to sell one of its older plants, as opposed to its newest, hi-tech plant. If, however, it fails to sell the older plant within a specified period, it is conceivable that the Commission would be acting within its powers to force the sale of the newer plant, since this would also remedy the substantial lessening of competition. However, suppose instead that the market in which the substantial lessening of competition is expected is a regional market, such that only the divestment of one, local production plant would remedy the competition concerns identified. In this case, the forced sale of an alternative plant in a different regional market may fail to address the expected substantial lessening of competition. There would, moreover, be serious questions as to the legality of any remedy which did not relate closely to the underlying facts which lead to the finding of a substantial lessening of competition, as is discussed in para.9.003, above.

[46] ss.35(4) and 36(3) of the Act.

for the vendor to achieve an acceptable sale price in light of the threat of the potential need to make further divestments. It may also encourage "game playing" by potential purchasers, deliberately slowing down divestment in order to become entitled to acquire the enhanced "crown jewel" assets. As noted, at the time of writing these proposals were undergoing the consultation process. Many of the concerns identified above were raised as part of the consultation and it remains to be seen how the Commission will address them in the finalised guidance.

The need for a suitable purchaser

9.014   The second risk factor highlighted by the Commission is that a suitable purchaser for the business to be divested may not be available, or that the merging parties may seek to dispose of the divested business to a weak or otherwise inappropriate purchaser. The Commission's guidelines on merger references indicate that a key question is "whether a purchaser of the assets will be capable of operating the assets and running a viable, competitive business, and have the incentive to compete with the merged firm."[47-48]

Accordingly, the Commission will generally require the subsequent purchaser to be approved by it so as to ensure that it is capable of running the divested business in such a way that it provides effective competition in the market, imposing a competitive constraint on the merged company. This will require that the purchaser be independent of the merging parties, and that it has the necessary resources and expertise. Note, however, than any process of approving the purchaser of a business to be divested does not correspond to a full assessment of the impact on competition of that acquisition. The approval for the purposes of the divestment will essentially involve verifying that the purchaser will be able to operate the divestment package effectively going forward. It will be a separate issue whether that change of control also requires review and clearance under merger control provisions, whether under the Enterprise Act, the EC Merger Regulation, or in other jurisdictions.

The Commission's consultation paper on divestment remedies further commented that where it is not clear that a divestment package will be viable or sufficiently attractive to purchasers, or where the number of potential purchasers is small, the Commission may require the merging parties to enter into a contractual commitment with a suitable purchaser, *before* the proposed merger may proceed, a so-called "fix it first" remedy. The Commission may also require that the identified buyer completes the acquisition of the divested business before the original merger may proceed, if the Commission is concerned that the competitive capability of the business to be divested may deteriorate pending the divestiture or that completion of the divestiture may be prolonged.[49]

Protection of the divestiture business in the interim

9.015   The third risk highlighted by the Commission is that the competitive capability of a divestiture package may deteriorate prior to completion of the

---

[47-48] *Merger Guidelines*, at para.4.27.
[49]   See para.4.4 of the Commission's consultative paper.

divestment, for example, through loss of customers or key members of staff. The Commission's aim is therefore to establish a divestment process that will protect the competitive potential of the divestment package prior to disposal, and will enable a suitable purchaser to be secured in an acceptable timescale. In particular, the Commission observes that the parties to a merger may have significant incentives to "run down" or neglect the business or assets to be divested in order to reduce its future competitive impact. The Commission will therefore generally seek undertakings imposing a general "duty of care" to maintain the divestment package in good order and not to undermine its competitive position. This may involve undertakings on the part of the merging parties to hold the divested business separate, under separate management, until it can be disposed of. Of course these comments in the Commission's consultation paper can be balanced to some degree by the fact that where a party is being obliged to sell a business or bundle of assets, it will want to achieve the best sale price possible. This consideration will incentivise the parties *not* to "run down" the business to be divested.

In terms of the timescale for divestment, the Commission will, on the one hand, prefer a shorter timescale in order to ensure a swift resolution of the competition problem(s) identified, as well as to minimise any possible reduction in the commercial value and effectiveness of the business to be divested. However, on the other hand, a longer timescale may be preferred where it is necessary to canvass a sufficient selection of suitable purchasers and to facilitate adequate due diligence.

Implementation of divestment remedies

To facilitate an efficient and effective divestiture process in which the value and viability of the package are preserved, the Commission's draft guidelines on divestment remedies envisages that it will usually require the appointment of an independent trustee to oversee the parties' compliance with the divestment undertakings and any requirements placed upon them pending divestment to hold the package to be divested separately from the remainder of the business.[50] The role of the trustee is to oversee the management of the process. It is not, however, intended that the trustee should himself take steps to make the required divestment unless the parties fail to do so themselves within the required timeframe; in that event, a divestiture trustee, who may, but will not necessarily be the same person as the monitoring trustee, will be mandated by the Commission to effect the divestment at the best available price. 9.016

Behavioural remedies

The Commission has stated in its draft guidelines on remedies that: 9.017

"behavioural remedies may be considered more suitable in some circumstances, for example, where the effectiveness of structural remedies is constrained (for example, through the absence of suitable buyers for a

---

[50] The practice of appointing a trustee to administer the implementation of undertakings following a merger investigation is well established under EU procedures and appears to work well.

proposed divestiture). It may also be necessary to add behavioural remedies to a structural remedy in order to provide an effective and comprehensive solution. For example, a divestiture may need to be supported by a commitment from the merged firm to supply inputs for a limited period at agreed prices."[51]

Behavioural remedies may be used in order to increase competition in a market, and/or to control the behaviour of the merged entity. As regards remedies aimed at increasing competition in a market, the Commission's merger guidelines indicate that:

"There may be circumstances where the Commission concludes that other remedies would increase the competitive constraints on the merged firm and that the constraints would be both sufficient and timely enough for the merger to be allowed without any divestment or prohibition. Such remedies might for example facilitate the entry of newcomers to the market through a commitment by the merged firm to supply inputs that they would control after the merger, or might enable existing competitors to compete more effectively through the licensing by the merging parties of know-how or intellectual property rights; or the removal of restrictions in contracts that tie customers to the merged firm."[52]

Where the Commission has concerns that, following a merger, the merged company would have scope to behave anti-competitively, behavioural undertakings may provide a means of moderating that scope for anti-competitive behaviour. Despite their various shortcomings, behavioural remedies may in particular be useful as a supplement to structural remedies; for example where the Commission imposes a partial divestment remedy, a commitment by the merged business not to approach former customers of the divested business for a limited period of time may increase the Commission's confidence that the acquirer of the divested business will prove a viable and effective competitor.[53]

Behavioural remedies are relatively rare: between April 1999 and October 2003, 45 Commission merger reports were published under the FTA.[54] As the table below shows, behavioural remedies were recommended in only six cases during this period:

	Mergers	% of all Mergers
Not against the public interest	27	54
Against the public interest	23	46
— (partial) prohibition/divestment alone	17	34
— behavioural remedies	6	12

---

[51] See the Commission's consultative paper, para.1.9
[52] *Merger Guidelines* CC2, at para.4.29
[53] *Merger Guidelines*, at para.4.33.
[54] These 45 reports dealt with 50 merger situations, since certain reports covered more than one proposed merger.

Of the five cases which had been completed under Enterprise Act as at **9.018** July 1, 2004, the Commission had decided to seek behavioural under-takings in two. This, however, would appear a disproportionately high percentage of cases, and it is too early to assume that any change in approach by the Commission can be expected.

The reports under the FTA which recommended behavioural remedies related to a variety of industries: two cases related to industrial products, one to healthcare products, one to the airline industry, one to the gas industry and one to a media market. Under the Act, the two reports which recommend behavioural remedies concerned healthcare products and local/regional transport services. When choosing to recommend behavioural remedies the Commission has given a number of reasons for its approach. For example:

(i) divestment would not be commercially realistic or would be in-effective in restoring competition. This is particularly the case where there are unlikely to be alternative purchasers for the business (for example, because loss-making businesses are concerned), or where the relevant business assets are outside the UK[55];

(ii) to impose structural remedies would be disproportionate to the adverse effects identified, with other remedies being sufficient to remove those effects; and

(iii) behavioural remedies would be effective in removing or attenuating the adverse effects of the merger, whilst preserving some or all of its benefits.

The behavioural remedies that have been recommended in past cases by the Commission can be considered as falling within the following categories:

(i) direct controls to protect customers;

(ii) measures aimed at lowering barriers to entry and expansion, in particular by reducing the scope for the merged company to engage in anti-competitive behaviour;

(iii) measures aimed at improving the accountability of the merged company, for example, by requiring it to provide information to the OFT or to publish information on profitability generally; and

(iv) restrictions or prohibitions on further acquisitions.

However, the relatively low number of examples of behavioural remedies reflects the difficulties associated with this category of remedy. The Commission has identified a number of shortcomings with behavioural remedies:

"They can involve detailed prescription of behavioural rules, for example to prevent discriminatory or predatory behaviour or to restrain price increases, with the danger of restraining legitimate competitive behav-iour. They may not be fully effective in dealing with a merger in a market

---

[55] This was the case in the Commission's consideration of *Dräger Medical AG & Co. KGaA and Hillenbrand Industries Inc* (May 2004), at para.10.10.

where coordinated behaviour is a concern; it is not realistic to expect that a remedy requiring firms to ignore their rivals in their own decision-making could be effective. Behavioural remedies will usually require continual monitoring by the OFT. Notwithstanding the ability to vary subsequently any remedy imposed, behavioural remedies can also be difficult to keep in tune with current market conditions and may therefore introduce their own distortions to competition."[56]

The various categories of behavioural remedies which have been considered suitable in past cases are considered below, together with a discussion of the associated problems.

Direct controls to protect customers

9.019   The clearest control to protect customers is a price cap. However these types of undertaking are difficult to construct and to enforce.[57] Perhaps unsurprisingly, given such difficulties, the Commission has rarely recommended the imposition of direct price controls in order to remedy the adverse effects of mergers. One of the few cases in which such a recommendation was made was the 2000 report on *Alanod Aluminium/Metalloxyd*. In that case, the Commission recommended that a price cap (equal to the prices paid by customers prior to the merger) be imposed for a period of five years. This could be raised in order to take partial account of raw material cost increases.[58] Even in this case, however, the Commission acknowledged that price control remedies can be difficult to design, implement and monitor.

The complexity of the merged entity's pricing structure can add to the difficulties in devising an effective price cap. In relation to the proposed ferry services joint venture between P&O and Stena Line,[59] the Secretary of State permitted the merger subject to a price cap on future prices of the joint venture.[60] In this case, the price cap was based on published prices for passenger ferry services, as set out in the brochures which were regularly published. There were various different ticket categories, and the seasonality of the business meant that even within each ticket category, there were a variety of different price bandings, depending on the time of year and of travel. The cap was therefore based on a "basket" of actual published prices in each category, rather than capping each price in the matrix of ticket categories and bands. The complexity of the price cap undertakings in this case provides a good example of the practical difficulties associated with this type of remedy, particularly where pricing structures are complex. It is perhaps relevant to note that the Commission had not recommended a price cap in this case: a majority of the Commission recommended that the merger should be permitted to proceed subject to a package of behavioural remedies but they did not include price controls in the package. However,

---

[56] *Merger Guidelines* CC2, at para.4.32.
[57] See para.9.018, above.
[58] *Alanod Aluminium-Veredlung GmbH & Co/Metalloxyd Ano-Coil Ltd*, Cm. 4545 (January 2000), at paras 2.110–2.115.
[59] *The Peninsular and Oriental Steam Navigation Company and Stena Line AB*, Cm. 3664 (November 1997).
[60] See DTI press release P/98/153 of February 27, 1998 *Undertakings from P&O and Stena accepted in follow-up to MMC Report*.

the Director General advised the Secretary of State that the package of proposed remedies recommended by the Commission could in fact stifle competition and harm the consumer and so the price cap mechanism was devised as an alternative remedy.

Another way to protect customers is to preserve to some degree the pre-merger situation for them so that they are not affected by a lack of choice. Countervailing customer power and the ability of customers to walk away from an unattractive offer by a supplier is, as discussed in Ch.6, a key constraint on the exercise of market power. The Commission's 2003 inquiry into *Carlton/ Granada* led to the recommendation of an undertaking governing contract terms for the merged company's sale of advertising slots to advertisers and media buyers. The ITV television network consisted of 15 regional broadcasting licences, of which Granada controlled seven and Carlton controlled four. The parties also controlled the only two sales houses for advertising on the ITV network. The Commission considered that whilst ITV's position as a provider of advertising airtime had continued to decline, it still had certain unique advantages, such as its ability to deliver mass-peak time audiences to advertisers. The Commission concluded that, following the merger, the combined group would be able to raise advertising prices.

One of a number of remedies considered involved the formulation of a "contract rights renewal" mechanism. This would give customers the option of renewing the terms of their 2003 (pre-merger) contracts, such that whilst they would be free to negotiate other deals, this would represent a "fall-back" option for them.[61] Four of the five panel members considered that this remedy could be potentially effective, whilst placing a lesser burden on the parties than the divestment of the parties' sales houses.[62] The Commission commented that:

"Behavioural remedies often raise problems associated with monitoring and enforcement. Television is, however, a highly regulated sector, and, when supplemented by a properly resourced adjudicator, the ITC should provide a regulatory structure to alleviate the worst of these problems."

The Commission went on to indicate that the ITC[63] and Ofcom[64] **9.020** favoured this remedy, which in the Commission's view was an important point in its favour.[65]

Returning to price cap mechanisms, a further difficulty is the limitations which they can place on the merged business from developing its product range or pricing structure. Price caps intended to apply for an indeterminate duration can be undesirable for this reason. In Dräger Medical/Hillenbrand

---

[61] However, any contract renegotiated on the basis of the 2003 contract terms would not include a share of broadcast commitment, but instead would include a share which varied in direct proportion to ITV's share of commercial viewing, subject to a cap.

[62] *Carlton Communications plc and Granada plc*, Cm. 5952 (October 2003), at paras 2.154–2.170.

[63] The Independent Television Commission was the statutory body which licensed and regulated all independent television services in the UK, operating under the Broadcasting Acts 1990 and 1996. On December 18, 2003, its functions were transferred to OFCOM and it was disbanded.

[64] The Office of Communications regulates various aspects of television, radio and telecoms.

[65] At para.2.167.

Industries[66], which concerned markets in which the NHS was the main customer, the Commission decided to impose a price cap but made it temporary only. The Commission had also recommended in its conclusions that competition could be improved if the NHS were to take certain steps to strengthen its procurement practices, in order to increase the extent to which it exercised buyer power and to increase the prospects for market entry. The benefits of such steps would not be felt immediately, however, but protection could be provided in the interim by a three-year price cap. The Commission commented that: "imposing a longer time period would become increasingly restrictive on the merged entity's ability to withdraw outdated products and replace them with new ones . . . and create increasing difficulties in applying to new products a price control regime based on historic price lists."[67]

The positive impact of price caps or other direct controls on a merged company's behaviour is that they constrain the exercise of market power, and such controls have been applied in the United Kingdom utility industries (telecommunications, water, gas and electricity). However, as noted, they are often difficult and costly to implement and monitor, and would be likely to fail to remedy the adverse effects on competition of the merger in question. A number of reasons have been forwarded by the Commission as to why price caps are inappropriate, some of which have already been touched upon:

(i)   complex price structures may exist in a market, necessitating a complex price cap;

(ii)   different prices may be negotiated with individual customers (*i.e.* there may be no commonly used list prices which are adhered to and which could be controlled);

(iii)   non-price competition may also be important (for example, quality, innovation and service levels);

(iv)   it may be difficult to extend price caps to future product developments;

(v)   it may be difficult to monitor adherence to price controls;

(vi)   it may be difficult to find a competitive "benchmark" level at which to set prices;

(vii)   some view would need to be taken on the duration of any control;

(viii) a price "freeze", or even reductions in prices, may deter new entry into a market by reducing the likely profits available to a new entrant;

(ix)   cost changes may need to be factored into any price control; and

(x)   if a cap were set on *average* prices, certain customers could still be discriminated against.

For example, in its report on *Johnston Press/Trinity Mirror Press* the Commission observed that:

---

[66] *Dräger Medical AG & Co. KGaA and Hillenbrand Industries Inc*, May 2004.
[67] See para.10.38 of the report.

"Johnston said that it could not see how a behavioural remedy in the advertising sphere could be made workable. Given the extent of discounting, a control on rates would be very complex and difficult to operate. It was not clear how a behavioural remedy of this kind would apply, for example, if Johnston desired to extend the distribution of a title or launch new titles. Behavioural remedies would also limit Johnston's ability to respond to rivals' competitive initiatives, to carry out product developments, and to respond to advertisers' requirements... We agree that any behavioural remedy concerning advertisers would be unworkable."[68]

Similarly, in the context of *H+H Celcon/Marley Building Materials*, the Commission identified a number of potential problems with imposing some form of price control on the merged company in relation to the supply of aerated concrete:

9.021

"we considered two main variants of a price cap. The first was based on an 'RPI minus X' formula. The second variant was price cap based, not on the RPI or another external index, but on a weighted basket of aircrete production costs, presuming appropriate indices could be determined. A key question with the first variant was what value should be attached to 'X' in order to secure an outcome in which the price of aircrete after the merger rose by no more than it might have done in the absence of the merger. Without appropriate cost and demand estimates, it was not clear how this could be assessed. In theory the second approach, if it were based on a cost plus formula, could eliminate exploitation of the market power of the merged company in the form of extra profit. But we consider that there is a significant risk that it would in effect, provide a cover for the passing on of costs which might have otherwise have been absorbed in a fully competitive environment... Moreover, under either approach, measuring and monitoring prices would be complex, given that there are nine main aircrete products and different prices, discounts and rebates for different customers... More generally, to introduce price controls into a non-utility industry such as construction might in any case be an undesirable extension of regulation to be adopted only if more pro-competitive remedies are not available... There are also problems with the duration of any such control: whether it should be for a fixed period, or linked to market developments, for example... We agree that an indefinite regulatory regime is to be avoided if at all possible."[69]

The Commission's 2004 report on *Stena/P&O*,[70] highlighted further difficulties associated with price caps:

---

[68] *Johnston Press plc /Trinity Mirror plc*, Cm. 5495 (May 2002), at paras 2.161 to 2.162
[69] *H+H Celcon Limited and Marley Building Materials Limited*, Cm. 5540 (June 2002), at paras 2.136 to 2.138.
[70] *Stena AB and The Peninsular & Oriental Steam Navigation Company*, (February 2004), at para. 6.18(c). Note that in contrast to the 1997 report discussed above, which concerned passenger ferry services, the 2004 report concerned freight services, which had a much lower degree of price transparency.

"We did not believe that a price cap was likely to be effective in a market of this nature. There is a lack of transparency in the market, as well as a lack of formal contracts between ferry operators and customers. . . . In addition, since price is not the only relevant factor—availability on peak crossings, for example, may also be important . . . a cap on price was unlikely to be effective in limiting Stena's market power. Any remedy would by necessity be very intrusive, and enforcement and monitoring would be very difficult, making it less likely that such a remedy would be effective. Even if the price freeze could be made to work, there was a danger that such a freeze would discourage entry by limiting the likely revenue that a new entrant could achieve."

In *Newsquest/INM* the Commission observed that controls over advertising rates following the merger would be "highly complex and intrusive given the extent to which advertising rates are negotiated and the influences on them"[71]; and in *SCR-Sibelco/Fife*, the Commission observed that "effective monitoring of Sibelco's prices pre-supposes the existence of meaningful benchmarks by which the DGFT could judge whether prices were excessive. In the absence of an indicator of competitive price levels such as would be provided by an organized glass sand market, it is difficult to see what benchmark could be used."[72]

In *Fresenius/Caremark*, the Commission rejected the idea of a price regulation regime on the basis that the services provided by the parties in the medical home care market were not homogeneous but tailored to the needs of the individual patient. "The reduction in competition would take place within a context in which contracts to serve new patients are bid for, whether by formal tender or otherwise. It would be impracticable to devise a regime of price regulation which could be adapted to each situation. Furthermore, any constraint on price increases would have to allow for developments in medical technology, including the introduction of new products. . . ".[73]

Finally, in *Coloplast/SSL International* in 2002, the Commission considered a price cap in the relevant market (non-latex sheaths) as one potential remedy, but concluded that the competitive tendering for inclusion in the contracts to supply non-latex sheaths to NHS hospitals was the one area in which price competition had played a significant role in the supply of continence care products, and against this background, the introduction of price controls for Coloplast sheaths would reduce the role of price competition and might further inhibit new competitive entry.[74]

Lowering barriers to entry and expansion—preventing anti-competitive behaviour

9.022   As has been noted, the benefit of price caps (and other mechanisms to protect customers) is that they prevent the exercise of market power

---

[71] *Newsquest (London) Limited and Independent News & Media plc*, Cm. 5951 (October 2003), at para.2.151.

[72] *SCR-Sibelco SA/Fife Silica Sands Ltd and Fife Resources Ltd*, Cm. 5139 (July 2001), at para.2.129.

[73] *Fresenius AG/Caremark Limited*, Cm. 3925 (April 1998), at para.2.177.

[74] *Coloplast A/S/SSL International plc*, Cm. 5522 (June 2002), at para.2.131.

through excessive pricing. Another way to ensure that prices remain competitive is to devise remedies which will operate the increase to contestability of the market, so that market power is more difficult to achieve or maintain and prices can accordingly be subject to normal competitive pressure in the market. A further category of behavioural remedies is therefore those which seek to ensure that the merged entity does not act to maintain or increase barriers to entry.

In *IMS Health/Pharmaceutical Marketing Services* in 1999, which concerned the market for the provision of specialised pharmaceutical data services[75], the Commission found that the merger would be expected to operate against the public interest. In particular, it was expected to result in higher prices to pharmaceutical companies, weaker incentives to improve quality of data and service, and less innovation and choice in the supply of specialised pharmaceutical data services. One of the Commission's recommendations was a behavioural remedy which would serve to lower barriers to entry into the market. The Commission recommended that:

(i) IMS should not sell UK specialised pharmaceutical data service products only as a package or apply discounts to the same effect, nor should it make the sale of any UK specialised pharmaceutical data service products (or the terms on which they were sold) dependent on the sale of any other UK data service or product. The Commission noted that the prospect of such bundling or discounts was one of the main deterrents to entry into the market, and a means by which IMS could abuse its position; and

(ii) IMS should not enter into contracts with its sources of UK specialised pharmaceutical data that contained a provision that restricted the source's right to supply any data to a third party. The Commission observed that such exclusivity had in the past been a further significant barrier to entry into the market, and the continuing perception of exclusivity remained, in the Commission's view, a barrier to entry which would be addressed by such a requirement.[76]

Another case in which behavioural remedies were recommended by the Commission as a means of lowering barriers to enter into a market was *British Airways/CityFlyer Express* in 1999. In that case, the Commission recommended that a cap be imposed on the share of airport slots operated by British Airways and its subsidiaries. The Commission observed that:

"A cap would provide BA's competitors with greater access to new slots than would otherwise be the case and, if set at the right level, would address the detriment we have identified in three ways. First, it would limit BA's ability to exploit the advantage it gains from being able to absorb less desirable slots into its large portfolio of services. . . Secondly,

---

[75] Used by pharmaceutical companies to monitor their competitive positions, identify areas of product development, etc.

[76] *IMS Health Inc/Pharmaceutical Marketing Services Inc*, Cm. 4261 (February 1999), at para.2.90.

those of BA's competitors who wish to establish a stronger presence at Gatwick will have a better opportunity to develop their own portfolio of slots thereby eroding BA's competitive advantage. . . thirdly, the scope for direct competition for BA. . . would be increased."[77]

Similarly the Commission recommended in *Sylvan/Locker* in 2000 on a majority view that, should the merged company offer low prices to selected customers, it should be prevented from subsequently raising prices for a period of time. This remedy was intended to address the concern that the merged company might seek to damage competitors by pursuing selected important customers with non-cost-related low prices. This remedy would make such a strategy more expensive for the merged company to implement.[78]

The provision of accountancy information—increasing accountability

9.023   Where market power is being exercised, this will often start to show in the accounts, for example through increased profits or increased profit margins. Monitoring financial performance is therefore a common adjunct to other behavioural remedies, and may be seen as a control on conduct in itself. In some merger reports, the Commission has accordingly recommended various supplementary remedies to improve the accountability of the merged company, which would require it to provide certain information to the OFT, to make it easier for the OFT to determine whether the company was abusing its monopoly position or engaging in anti-competitive practices, and by the same token to discourage abuse.

For example, in *Wiseman/Scottish Pride*, the Commission recommended a remedy whereby Wiseman would be required to provide certain categories of information to the OFT on a quarterly basis. This comprised data on its average prices to different categories of customers in Scotland, so that the OFT could identify whether any categories of customers were being discriminated against. The Commission assessed that this remedy would be practical and would involve limited administration. The Commission further recommended that Wiseman should provide its customer lists in Scotland to the OFT, so that the OFT could carry out any random sampling of actual prices paid that it considered necessary, and it could scrutinise prices in a particular geographical area.[79]

Similarly, in *Sylvan/Locker*, the majority of the Commission's panel members recommended (*inter alia*) that independently audited financial information be provided to the OFT.[80]

---

[77] *British Airways plc /CityFlyer Express Limited*, Cm. 4346 (July 1999), at para.2.213.
[78] *Sylvan International Ltd/Locker Group plc*, Cm. 4883 (November 2000), at para.2.136. However, the chairman of the group considered that behavioural remedies would not be sufficient to remedy the adverse effects and only a structural remedy would suffice.
[79] *Robert Wiseman Dairies plc/Scottish Pride Holdings plc*, Cm. 3504 (December 1996), at paras 2.116 to 2.117.
[80] *Sylvan International Ltd and Locker Group* plc, cited above, at para.2.138.

Restrictions on further acquisitions

A final category of behavioural remedies which has been deemed to be workable and effective in some cases is a control on future acquisitions. Such
controls are additional to the normal mechanisms of legislative merger
control which operate through the Act and the EC Merger Regulation and
can result in a merger being considered by the OFT which does not fall under
the normal jurisdictional thresholds. In *Wiseman/Scottish Pride*, the
Commission observed that if Wiseman were to make further acquisitions of
operators in the Scottish milk market, it would be less likely that a better-
balanced supply structure in Scotland would emerge. The Commission therefore recommended that in addition to the provision of information
undertakings described above, Wiseman should obtain consent from the
OFT, seperate from normal merger clearance, before acquiring *any* other
supplier of fresh processed milk in Scotland (whether a processor, wholesaler
or retailer).[81] A similar remedy was recommended in *Sylvan/Locker*.[82]

9.024

Other behavioural remedies which have been deemed "inadequate"

The Commission has rejected other types of behavioural remedies on the
ground that they would be inadequate. For example, in the context of *SCR-
Sibelco/Fife*,[83] the Commission was concerned that a requirement on the
merged company to publish and adhere to price lists could in fact encourage
collusion.[84] As the Commission noted "So far as price transparency is
concerned, while this is in principle desirable, it would not address the basic
problem of the increase in Sibelco's market power resulting from the merger.
Moreover, in a market such as glass sand with a relatively small number of
players, the requirement for transparency could encourage collusion".[85]

9.025

In *Scottish Radio Holdings/GWR/Galaxy* which concerned the acquisition by Vibe (a joint venture company owned by SRH and GWR) of
Galaxy, a local radio station in the West Country, it was found that GWR's
already high share of local radio advertising within certain localities would
be enhanced, reducing options for local radio advertisers. There was little
prospect of sufficient new entry into the area given the need to obtain a
radio authority licence, and competition was further reduced by the superior ability of GWR to negotiate prices, bundle advertising packages across
stations and cross-sell between different stations. One possible remedy was
an undertaking by GWR not to bundle advertising rates between different
stations and areas. However, the Commission considered that this would be
very difficult, would involve excessive regulatory intrusion, and would
fail to address the weakening of the competitive position of other local
radio stations as a result of GWR's sales house being uniquely able to sell
advertising on a greater range of stations.[86]

---

[81] *Robert Wiseman Dairies plc/Scottish Pride Holdings plc*, cited above, at para.2.120.
[82] *Sylvan International Ltd/Locker Group* plc, cited above, at para.2.139.
[83] *SCR-Sibelco SA/Fife Silica Sands Ltd and Fife Resources Ltd*, cited above.
[84] The issues raised by tacit collusion are discussed in Ch.6.
[85] *SCR-Sibelco SA/Fife Silica Sands Ltd and Fife Resources Ltd*, cited above, at para.2.133.
[86] *Scottish Radio Holdings plc and GWR Group plc/Galaxy Radio Wales and the West Ltd*,
Cm. 5811 (May 2003), at paras 2.131–2.132.

In *Fresenius/Caremark*, one of the adverse effects identified by the Commission was that Fresenius (as a supplier of both products and services in the healthcare industry) would seek to use the acquisition of Caremark (a supplier of healthcare services) to increase sales of its own products, thereby reducing the freedom of purchasers to choose the products and services best suited to their needs. The Commission considered a remedy whereby Fresenius should supply Caremark on non-preferential terms but concluded that such a remedy would be unlikely to be effective, as "it would still be open to Fresenius to charge a higher price than otherwise for its product . . . to *all* service providers, including its own subsidiary, Caremark, with Caremark under-recovering its own costs by an equivalent amount. In such a situation, given the vertical integration between Caremark and Fresenius, only Caremark would be able to offer a reasonably priced overall package involving Fresenius products; nor would such a remedy bear upon any tendency for Fresenius's competitors to charge more for products supplied to Caremark, where the latter was a purchaser's preferred service provider. A non-discrimination requirement would not therefore preclude an undesirable distortion in the working of the market."[87]

One of the issues raised during the Commission's inquiry into Stena/P&O in 2004 was whether an undertaking on the part of Stena to facilitate access to berths by other existing or potential ferry operators, would reduce barriers to entry on the "central corridor" of the Irish Sea and thus remedy a substantial lessening of competition on that corridor. The Commission rejected this remedy on the basis that it would be insufficient to ensure entry of a nature and scale which could constrain Stena. In particular, access to berths was not the only potential barrier to entry. Furthermore, the Commission indicated that "the creation of an opportunity for entry does not ensure that entry—or a credible threat of entry—will actually occur." The Commission considered that the most likely source of entry in this case would be a low-cost, non-time-sensitive, unaccompanied freight operator, which would be insufficient to constrain Stena.[88]

Behavioural remedies which could be detrimental to competition

9.026   As well as being inadequate, some behavioural constraints have been regarded by the Commission as being positively detrimental. In the *SRH/GWR/Galaxy* case referred to above, a potential remedy involving the discontinuation of an arrangement whereby GWR's sales house sold advertising airtime on behalf of Classic Gold 1260 AM was rejected, in part because it could be detrimental to Classic Gold (GWR was a minority shareholder in Classic Gold). In particular, it would force Classic Gold to establish its own sales house in the face of significant economies of scale, Classic Gold would face a possible loss of custom due to certain customers preferring to retain links with the GWR sales house, and there could be a distraction on management effort if it had to operate advertising sales, etc. All of these factors could reduce Classic Gold's ability to compete effectively.[89]

---

[87] *Fresenius AG/Caremark Limited*, cited above, at para.2.182.
[88] *Stena AB/The Peninsular & Oriental Steam Navigation Company*, February 2004, at para.6.14.
[89] *Scottish Radio Holdings plc and GWR Group plc/Galaxy Radio Wales and the West Ltd*, cited above, at paras 2.133–2.135.

In *Lloyds TSB/Abbey National*, the Commission expressed the belief that undertakings concerning the prices or other conditions on which products and services were supplied ". . . would represent a significant interference in the operation of market forces. This is a particular problem in a merger situation inasmuch as the undertakings would apply to only one supplier in the market. Since Lloyds TSB would be by some margin the biggest supplier of PCAs, it is to be expected that other suppliers would have to respond, but the nature of their response is unpredictable. It seems likely to us that the overall result would be less attractive terms for customers than would be produced by the operation of the market in the absence of the merger."[90]

It is too soon to say whether behavioural remedies will become more prevalent in the future, but it may probably be assumed that in the case of many mergers structural remedies will still be regarded as more appropriate.

The relevance of customer benefits

The Enterprise Act enables the Commission to take into account any rele-   **9.027**
vant customer benefits that arise from the merger when deciding whether, and if so what, action should be taken. If the Commission is satisfied that relevant customer benefits would result from a merger that also led to a substantial lessening of competition, it will consider modifying the remedy it would otherwise put in place in light of those benefits.

However, relevant customer benefits are limited to benefits to "relevant customers" in the form of:

(a)   "lower prices, higher quality or greater choice of goods or services in any market in the United Kingdom (whether or not the market or markets in which the substantial lessening of competition concerned has, or may have, occurred or (as the case may be) may occur); or

(b)   greater innovation in relation to such goods or services."[91]

"Relevant customers" are defined widely for the purposes of Pt 3 of the Act to be, broadly, any customer at a lower point in the chain of supply than the point at which the merger occurs.[91A] Moreover, the Act provides that a benefit is only a "relevant customer benefit" if the Commission believes that:

(a)   "the benefit has accrued as a result of the creation of the relevant merger situation concerned or may be expected to accrue within a reasonable period as a result of the creation of that situation; and

(b)   the benefit was, or is, unlikely to accrue without the creation of that situation or a similar lessening of competition."[92]

---

[90] *Lloyds TSB Group plc/Abbey National plc*, cited above, at para.2.267.
[91] s.30(1)(a) of the Act.
[91A] See further para.4.016 of Ch.4, above.
[92] s.30(2), which relates to completed mergers. Section 30(3) relating to anticipated mergers, contains similar wording.

Thus, for example, the Commission acknowledges in its guidelines that economies of scale in production or distribution may result in benefits to the merged firm, but even if the Commission is satisfied that such economies are attributable to the merger, it also must satisfy itself that such cost economies would be translated into lower prices, to the benefit of customers, than if the merger had not taken place. The guidelines state that "This must be the case notwithstanding the scope to charge higher prices because of the reduction in competitive pressures in the market."[93] The Commission's guidelines also emphasise that where the benefit claimed is that innovation would be enhanced by a merger (for example through economies of scale, specialisation in R&D and/or the pooling of risks), incentives to innovate may be blunted by the reduction in competition resulting from the merger.

These potential benefits were considered in *Dräger Medical/ Hillenbrand*. First, the parties anticipated price reductions as a result of economies of scale (primarily in relation to production) which would be achievable through the merger. However, whilst the Commission accepted that there might be economies of scale achievable through the merger, neither the parties nor the Commission were able to quantify them. Furthermore, the Commission did not expect any reduced costs to be passed on to UK consumers in the form of lower prices. This was because following the merger, the merged entity would have less incentive to pass on such cost reductions. The Commission therefore excluded price reductions from its analysis of customer benefits and remedies. The second category of customer benefits that the parties identified was innovation improvements. In its analysis of the effects of the merger, the Commission had considered that it was *possible* that the merger might have the effect of removing a source of innovation and of reducing the incentive on the remaining competitors to innovate. On the other hand, increased economies of scale in manufacturing and development might assist the merged company in increasing the effectiveness of its product development programme. The Commission concluded that the evidence it had seen did not lead it to expect any increase in innovation as a consequence of the merger. Accordingly, the remedies considered by the Commission were not limited in any way in order to take account of any customer benefits. That said, the Commission noted that it took care in considering remedies to avoid any remedy which might restrict the parties' ability to invest in product development or to introduce new products in the UK.[94]

9.028   It is clear that the Commission will not easily be convinced of the benefits that are argued to arise as a consequence of the merger. Thus, in *Stena/P&O*, the Commission rejected Stena's argument that as a consequence of the proposed transaction there would be benefits to the freight community. Stena had argued that it had a good record of commitment and investment, and was a strong long-term player on the Irish Sea. It had brought significant innovation and investment to the Irish Sea in recent years, including the introduction of new craft and investment in a new berth and other facilities. Stena had argued that a beneficial effect of the merger would be that it would be replacing P&O, which was no longer committed

---

[93] *Merger Guidelines* CC2, at para.4.41.
[94] *Dräger Medical AG & Co. KGaA/Hillenbrand Industries Inc*, cited above at paras 10.4 to 10.6.

to operating the ferry routes in question. However, the Commission concluded that should the proposed transaction not proceed, P&O or any other purchaser of the business would be expected to maintain service quality and customer goodwill. Accordingly, any benefits to customers arising following the transaction could not be defined as merger-specific.[95]

Where the Commission is faced with a merger that would result in a substantial lessening of competition, but where it is also satisfied that relevant customer benefits would result, it will consider whether to modify the remedy that it would have otherwise put in place. Its consideration of whether to modify a remedy will take into account a number of factors, notably the size and nature of the expected customer benefit and how long the benefit is expected to be sustained, taking into account whether as a result of the reduction of competitive pressure in the market, any immediate benefit to customers will be eroded in the future. Moreover, the Commission will consider the impact of the alleged benefits on different categories of customer.[95A] Even where it is satisfied that the expected relevant customer benefits are significant, it may nonetheless not allow the merger to proceed without intervention, and may require remedies, short of prohibition or complete divestment, that are intended to reduce the detrimental effects of the merger while preserving all or most of the customer benefits.

Procedure and enforcement

The procedural framework applicable when the Commission is accepting undertakings and making orders following a finding of a substantial lessening of competition is provided for in Sch.10 of the Enterprise Act.[96] Under para.2 of Sch.10, the Commission must, prior to accepting an undertaking or making an order, publish a notice setting out its proposal. The Commission must also consider any representations made in relation to the notice which have not been withdrawn. Paragraph 2(2) of Sch.10 sets out the information that must be contained within the notice. In particular, the notice must set out the purpose and effect of the undertaking or order, the situation that the undertaking or order is seeking to address, and any other facts which the Commission considers justifies the acceptance of the under-taking or order. The notice must also refer to a means by which interested parties can gain access to an accurate version of the proposed undertaking or order at all reasonable times (in practice normally via the Commission's website[97]), and must stipulate the period within which representations may be made in relation to the proposed undertaking or order, which may not be less than 15 days from the date of publication of the notice in the case of an undertaking, and not less than 30 days from the date of publication in

9.029

---

[95] *Stena AB/the Peninsular and Oriental Steam Navigation Company*, (2004) cited above, at paras 6.6–6.7.

[95A] See para.4.45 of the *Merger Guidelines*.

[96] Para.9 of Sch.10 permits the Commission, in special circumstances, to dispense with the procedures normally followed. However, the Commission guidelines indicate that the Commission will only accelerate the procedure with good reason and that it will explain its reasons to the parties and the public. See the Commission's General Advice and Information, CC4, at para.7.23.

[97] *www.competition-commission.org.uk*.

the case of an order. In addition, in the case of an order, a copy of the proposed order must also be served on any person identified in the order as a person on whom a copy of the order should be served.

If the Commission wishes to make any material modification to a proposed undertaking or order following the publication of the notice, para.2(4) of Sch.10 states that it may not do so unless it has given notice of the proposed modifications and considered any representations made in accordance with the notice and not withdrawn. In this case, a notice must be published setting out the proposed modifications, the reasons for them, and a period within which representations may be made in relation to the proposed modifications (not less than seven days from the date of publication of the notice setting out the modifications).[98] Again, in the case of a proposed order, a copy should also be served on any person identified in the order as a person on whom a copy of the order should be served. Effectively, a second consultation process is required where the proposed undertakings or order are amended in the light of the first consultation process. Note, however, that the Commission is give complete discretion to waive any or all of the procedural requirements where it considers there are "special reasons" to do so.[98A]

If, after this process, the Commission decides not to accept the proposed undertaking or make the proposed order concerned, it must give notice of that decision.[99] If the Commission decides to accept the proposed undertaking or order concerned, it must then serve a copy of the undertaking on any person by whom it is given, or serve a copy of the order on any person identified in it as a person on whom a copy of the order should be served as soon as is practicable thereafter. It must also publish the undertaking or order.[1]

An undertaking will come into force on the date on which it is accepted by both the Commission, having been signed by the relevant parties.[2] An order will come into force at the time it is determined to do so according to its terms.[3]

9.030 Section 94(2) of the Act places a statutory duty on a person to whom an undertaking accepted by the Commission or an order relates to comply with such undertaking or order. Section 94(3) provides that such duty is owed to any person who may be affected by a contravention of the undertaking or order, and a breach of the duty which causes a person loss or damage is actionable under s.94(4). Section 94(5) provides that it is a defence for the person against whom the breach is alleged to prove that "he took all reasonable steps and exercised all due diligence to avoid contravening the undertaking or (as the case may be) order". Sections 94(6) and 94(7) further provide that the Commission and the OFT may also bring proceedings for the enforcement of undertakings and orders accepted or made by the Commission (in practice it is understood that the OFT is likely to take the lead in any enforcement process).

---

[98] Pursuant to para.2(5) of Sch.10.
[98A] See para.9 of Sch.10 to the Act.
[99] Pursuant to para.3 of Sch.10.
[1] Pursuant to para.4 of Sch.10.
[2] s.82(2) of the Act
[3] s.84((3) of the Act.

The Explanatory Notes to the Act do not add particularly to the legislative wording on enforcement, stating simply that:

"This section ensures that orders and undertakings can be enforced through the courts. Any person who sustains loss or damage as a result of the contravention of an order or undertaking may bring action before the courts. The OFT may bring civil proceedings to enforce compliance with orders or undertakings. The Competition Commission and Secretary of State may also bring civil proceedings in respect of orders or undertakings for which they are responsible."[4]

Under the FTA, ss.93(2) and 93A similarly appeared to give a right to third parties suffering loss as a result of a breach of an order or undertakings respectively to bring an enforcement action in the courts. However, in *Mid Kent v General Utilities*[5], Knox J. held that:

"(1) It is not enough for a plaintiff to show a breach of statutory public duty and damage thereby caused to the plaintiff, whether the claim is for damages, injunction or declaration.

(2) It is always necessary, where a private claim is brought in respect of a breach of statutory public duty, to investigate how far the statutory provisions in question were intended to confer a private right of action.

(3) Where a procedural remedy is provided by the statute, whether by way of criminal sanction or other particular procedure (such as a civil action only to be brought by a minister or other public officer) that constitutes an indication that it is that procedural remedy alone that is intended by Parliament to be available as a sanction.

(4) There are two exceptions to the last mentioned principle. The first of them arises where statutory provisions are enacted in order to provide protection for a class of persons, such as mine workers or factory workers, and the breach of duty in question is one which would be likely to cause to a member of the class intended to be protected, injury either to their property, or person or economic loss. The second exception arises where a public right is created by the statute to be enjoyed generally by persons wishing to avail themselves of it and damage peculiar to the plaintiff is suffered as a result of interference with the public right in question. A statutory prohibition of otherwise lawful conduct cannot amount to the creation of such a public right."[6]

In this case, Knox J. concluded that the FTA wording was not sufficient to give Mid Kent Holdings a right to seek to enforce certain undertakings given by General Utilities to the Secretary of State. The undertakings in question provided that General Utilities would reduce its stake in Mid Kent Holdings to below 20 per cent and that neither it nor any associated person

---

[4] See para.252 of the Explanatory Notes to the Act.
[5] *Mid Kent Holdings plc v General Utilities plc* [1996] 3 All E.R. 132.
[6] See *Mid Kent Holdings*, cited above, at 153.

would acquire any greater interest in Mid Kent subsequently. Mid Kent alleged that General Utilities had breached the undertakings through actions taken to form a joint venture with another Mid Kent shareholder, in the preparatory stages of a joint bid for Mid Kent itself.

9.031   At the time of writing, the new enforcement provisions under the Act had yet to be tested in the courts. However, the wording in the Act is drafted in a very different manner from the wording in the enforcement provisions in the FTA, which simply stated:

> "Any person may bring civil proceedings in respect of any failure, or apprehended failure, of the responsible person to fulfil the undertaking, as if the obligations imposed by the undertaking on the responsible person had been imposed by an order to which section 90 of this Act applies."

The wording of the Enterprise Act creates a statutory duty which is expressly owed to individuals who may suffer loss or damage as a consequence of its breach. Arguably, therefore, the new wording creates a *private* right of action for breach of statutory duty. If this is correct, it could operate to distinguish the new enforcement provisions from the restrictive interpretation placed on the FTA enforcement provisions, which were categorised by Knox J. as concerning breach of a statutory *public* duty.

Moreover, the FTA provisions focussed essentially on enforcement being primarily an issue for the Crown.[7] Under s.94 of the Act, this does not appear to be the case: the enforcement rights of individuals are set out first, followed by those of the regulatory authorities and the Secretary of State. Indeed, the Act was drawn up at a time when there was a strong push in relation to both UK and EC competition law, towards developing the private enforcement of competition law. Indeed, during the passage of the Act through Parliament, the then Minister of E-Commerce and Competitiveness, Douglas Alexander, confirmed that s.94 had been drafted having regard to the impact of the *Mid Kent* judgment and that an intentionally different approach had been taken under the Act.[7A]

Persons against whom an order may be made or from whom undertakings may be accepted

9.032   Generally, orders made by the Commission pursuant to ss.83 and 84 of the Act (and by implication pursuant to Schs 8 and 10 of the Act) are expressed in the Act as capable of being applicable to "any person" in the context of the terms of a given order. Similarly, s.82 of the Act entitles the Commission to accept undertakings from "such persons as it considers appropriate."

However, jurisdictional issues can arise in that s.86 of the Act provides that an enforcement order in respect of either an undertaking or an order may only extend to a person's conduct outside the United Kingdom only if that person is:

---

[7] See s.93(2) and *Mid Kent Holdings*, cited above, at 144.
[7A] Hansard, House of Commons Standing Committee B, May 1, 2002, Column 388.

(i)   a United Kingdom national;

(ii)   a body incorporated under the law of the United Kingdom or any part of the United Kingdom; or

(iii) a person carrying on business in the United Kingdom.

Similar provisions were contained in s.90(3) of the FTA, and in a number of reports, the MMC recommended that action should be taken against non-United Kingdom companies where a merger involving non-United Kingdom companies had threatened to have an adverse effect on the United Kingdom public interest.[8]

Review of undertakings/orders

Once undertakings or orders have been implemented, s.92 of the Enterprise Act imposes a monitoring duty on the OFT which is required to recommend to the Commission their variation or release if appropriate. In particular, the OFT will monitor compliance and will also consider from time to time whether, as a result of any change in circumstances, an enforcement undertaking or order in its current form is no longer appropriate. In these circumstances, the OFT may recommend either that one or more of the parties should be released from the undertaking, or that the undertaking needs to be varied or to be superseded by a new enforcement undertaking; or in the case of an order, that it is no longer appropriate and may require variation or revocation.[9]

9.033

The OFT's recommendations in the circumstances will be made to the Commission's Remedies Standing Group[10], which is required by s.82(5) of the Act to consider any representations received by it in relation to varying or releasing an undertaking under this section as soon as is reasonably practicable. Any decision taken by the Standing Group on the basis of the OFT's recommendations is to be taken by a simple majority with the chairman of the Group having a casting vote on any question to be decided.[11]

Paragraphs 6–8 of Sch.10 of the Act set out the Commission's duties in the event that it wishes to release an undertaking or revoke an order. In these circumstances, the Commission must give notice of the proposed release or revocation, setting out the reasons therefor and the period within

---

[8] See, *e.g. Mitek Industries Inc/Gang Nail Systems Inc*, Cm. 429 (July 1988) in which the MMC recommended that a US company, Mitek Industries Inc., should divest itself of the UK subsidiary of another US company that it had acquired, Gang Nail Systems Limited, because of competition concerns in the supply of punched metal connector plates and related machinery. Similarly, in *Government of Kuwait/The British Petroleum Company plc*, Cm. 477 (October 1988), the MMC recommended that the Government of Kuwait's 21.6 per cent. shareholding in BP should be reduced to a level at which it would be unable to exercise material influence over BP. In *Stora Kopparbergs Bergslags AB/Swedish Match NV/The Gillette Company*, Cm. 1473 (March 1991), the MMC recommended that the UK subsidiary of the US Gillette Company should divest itself of its holding of non-convertible loan stock in a Dutch company (Swedish Match NV) which had recently acquired the competing wet shaving business of Wilkinson Sword.
[9] Pursuant to s.92(2) of the Act.
[10] See para.5.027 of Ch.5.
[11] Rules of Procedure, CC1, para.5.

which representations may be made. This must be not less than 15 days from the date of publication of the notice in the case of an undertaking, and not less than 30 days from the date of publication in the case of an order. If, following publication of this notice, the Commission decides not to proceed with the proposed release/revocation, it must give notice of that decision. Notice will be given by serving a notice on the person who gave the undertaking that was to be released, or on the person identified in the order that was to be revoked as a person on whom a copy of the order should be served. It must also publish the notice. In the event that the Commission proceeds with the release/revocation, it must serve a copy of the release of the undertaking on the person who gave the undertaking, or serve a copy of the order on any person identified in the order being revoked as a person on whom a copy of the order should be served as soon as is practicable thereafter. It must also publish the termination/revocation decision. Again, however, the Commission is empowered to dispense with any or all of these procedural requirements where it considers "special reasons" apply.[11A]

Undertakings and orders following a reference made under the public interest regime

9.034   Where a reference is made by the Secretary of State under s.45 of the Act, following the issue of an intervention notice, the Competition Commission is required to consider the issue of remedies first as regards any competition concerns which have been identified and secondly as regards any public interest concerns which have been identified. The Act requires the consideration of remedies to be undertaken separately for the public interest issues on the one hand and the competition issues on the other.[11B] Accordingly, the Commission will include in its report recommendations as to appropriate remedies for any public interest concerns which it has identified and also, or alternatively, recommendations as to suitable remedies for any competition concerns which it has identified.[12] Essentially the factors which it must take into account mirror those where it is acting in relation to a reference by the OFT under ss.22 or 33.

In the event that the Secretary of State decides not to take action because the public interest issues do not warrant it[13], s.56(6) of the Act requires the Competition Commission to proceed as if it had been acting under a reference under ss.22 or 33. With this possible outcome presumably in mind, the Competition Commission's guidelines confirm that the advice which it gives to the Secretary of State concerning remedies for any competition concerns will be given assuming that the Commission will be required to take action if the Secretary of State himself decides not to make a finding.[14] This rein-

---

[11A] See para.9 of Sch.10 to the Act.
[11B] See ss.46(7) and (8) of the Act. S.46(8) expressly requires the question of remedies to the competition concerns to be considered "separately". This appears to be so that, in the event the Secretary of State ultimately decides not to take action in relation to the public interest issues, the competition remedies do not need to be reconsidered by the Commission.
[12] See s.47(7) of the Act.
[13] As set out in s.54(4) of the Act, the Secretary of State can only make no finding where he concludes that there is no relevant public interest consideration.
[14] See *Merger Guidelines*, CC4, at para.5.7.

forces the point that the Competition Commission's advice in relation to remedies in a public interest case will follow the principles and procedure discussed in the rest of this chapter.

The Secretary of State is not bound by the recommendations of the Competition Commission in relation to remedies in relation to either the competition or the wider public interest issues; he must merely "have regard" to the Competition Commission's report.[15] Section 55(2) of the Act provides for the Secretary of State to take such action as he considers reasonable and practicable to remedy, mitigate or prevent any of the effects adverse to the public interest which have resulted or are expected to result from the merger. To this end, para.9 of Sch.7 to the Act gives the Secretary of State power to accept undertakings and para.11 gives him power to make an order. The procedural provisions of Sch.10, discussed above, must be followed.

---

[15] See s.55(3) of the Act and the Commission's General Advice and Information, CC4, at para.3.12.

CHAPTER 10

REVIEW BY THE COMPETITION
APPEAL TRIBUNAL

Introduction

10.001 Under the FTA merger regime those parties and third parties seeking to challenge decisions of the OFT, Competition Commission or Secretary of State had to do so by way of an application for judicial review to the High Court. The very low rate of success of judicial review applications under the FTA regime meant that tactically, recourse was not often had to this type of challenge.[1] Section 120 of the Enterprise Act has introduced a new statutory review procedure whereby persons aggrieved by a decision of the OFT, the Competition Commission or the Secretary of State made in connection with the merger control regime may apply to the Competition Appeal Tribunal (CAT) for a review of that decision.[2] These review powers were considered in detail by the CAT and the Court of Appeal in the *IBA Health* case,[3] and it is instructive to consider the case in some detail before engaging in a discussion of the key substantive and procedural elements of an application for review.

---

[1] The case of *Interbrew SA and Interbrew UK Holdings Ltd v Competition Commission and Secretary of State for Trade and Industry* [2001] EWHC Admin 367 (judgment of May 23, 2001) [2001] U.K.C.L.R. 954 is the only example under the FTA merger regime of a successful review where the challenged decision was quashed, in that case due to a procedural failure to put a proposed remedy to the merging parties.

[2] Following the decision of the Court of Appeal in *Davies v The Financial Services Authority* (judgment of the Court of Appeal, July 30, 2003) [2004] 1 W.L.R. 185, it arguably follows that save in exceptional circumstances, an applicant seeking review is obliged to make an application to the specialist CAT rather than the Administrative Court. In concluding that there was no right to seek judicial review from a decision of the Financial Services Authority in light of the scheme for statutory review set out in the Financial Services and Markets Act 2000, Mummery L.J. held that "the legislative purpose evident from the detailed statutory scheme was that those aggrieved by the decisions and actions of the Authority should have recourse to the special procedures and to the specialist tribunal rather than to the general jurisdiction of the Administrative Court. Only in the most exceptional cases should the Administrative Court entertain applications for judicial review of the actions and decisions of the Authority, which are amenable to the procedures for making representations to the Authority, for referring matters to the tribunal and for appealing direct from the tribunal to the Court of Appeal", at para.31.

[3] *IBA Health Limited v Office of Fair Trading, supported by iSOFT PLC and Torex PLC* [2003] CAT 27; [2004] Comp. A.R. 235 (in the CAT); and EWCA Civ. 142 (in the Court of Appeal).

The *IBA Health* case

The first application to the CAT under the new regime was made in   **10.002**
November 2003 by a third party competitor seeking to challenge the OFT's
decision not to refer the proposed acquisition by iSOFT Group plc of Torex
plc to the Competition Commission. The case arose out of the public offer by
iSOFT for the entire issued share capital of Torex which was announced on
July 23, 2003, and notified to the OFT for merger clearance on August 1,
2003. Both iSOFT and Torex were engaged in the supply of software and IT
systems to the healthcare industry. The principal software systems supplied by
iSOFT and Torex to hospitals were electronic patient records ("EPRs") and
laboratory information management systems ("LIMS"). The OFT found that
the combined share of iSOFT and Torex would be 44 per cent of EPRs and
56 per cent of LIMS and described the merging parties in its clearance decision as "clearly the two leading suppliers of IT software to the healthcare
sector in the UK." On August 15, IBA Health Limited, an Australian company
that was active in the same market, complained to the OFT about the effect
of the proposed merger. In its decision of November 6, 2003, the OFT decided
not to refer the merger to the Competition Commission for a detailed investigation pursuant to s.33(1) of the Act. The OFT concluded that whilst the
strong base of installed systems enjoyed by the parties (so-called "legacy
contracts") gave the parties a large market presence, it was unlikely, in itself,
to confer significant market power on the merged entity in view of the changes
being brought about by a Government led overhaul of healthcare IT systems
known as the National Programme for IT ("NPFIT"). The OFT considered
that the introduction of the NPFIT fundamentally altered the future competitive landscape with the consequence that competitive constraints would be
enhanced by the creation of a new bidding market which would attract from
international competitors. For these reasons the OFT did not believe that the
test for a reference to the Competition Commission under s.33 of the
Enterprise Act was met, namely "that it is or may be the case that, if carried
into effect, the creation of this relevant merger situation may be expected to
result in a substantial lessening of competition. . .[4]"

On November 21, 2003 IBA Health applied to the CAT under s.120 of the
Act for review of the OFT's clearance decision. Following an expedited
hearing conducted on November 28, the CAT gave judgment in favour of IBA
Health, quashing the OFT's decision and referring the matter back to the
OFT with a direction for it to reconsider the matter.[5] The CAT summarised
its concerns in the following way:

"we are not satisfied that the OFT applied the right test, or that the OFT
reached a conclusion that was reasonably open to them. We are not satisfied that the facts are sufficiently found in the decision or that all material considerations have been taken into account. We are unable to verify
whether there was material on which the OFT could reasonably base
important findings in the decision."[6]

---

[4] OFT decision dated November 6, 2003 at para.33.
[5] *IBA Health Limited v Office of Fair Trading supported by iSOFT PLC and Torex PLC*
  [2003] CAT 27; [2004] Comp. A.R. 235.
[6] The CAT's *IBA Health* judgment at para.266.

The CAT's conclusions rested upon two principal findings. First, the CAT held that the OFT had misdirected itself as to the meaning of the statutory test under s.33 of the Act which governs when the OFT's duty to refer a merger to the Commission will arise. In particular, the CAT found that a duty to refer arose not only when the OFT itself considered that the transaction raised a significant prospect of a substantial lessening of competition (SLC), but whenever the OFT was obliged to refer when faced with a credible alternative view that an SLC would arise, even if the OFT did not share that view itself.[7] Secondly, the CAT considered the scope of its statutory review powers in light of the requirement in s.120(4) of the Act that such a review is to be carried out on the basis of judicial review principles. In this regard, whilst the CAT took care to state that its task was not to take the decision itself, it nevertheless adopted a broad interpretation of its review powers, finding that "as a matter of general approach, the broad question we ask ourselves is whether we are satisfied that the OFT's decision was not erroneous in law, and was one which it was reasonably open to the OFT to take, giving the word "reasonably" its ordinary and natural meaning."[8]

10.003   The CAT's judgment was appealed to the Court of Appeal on the grounds that the CAT had erred in its interpretation of the s.33 reference test and had interpreted the scope of its judicial review powers too widely. In its judgment, the Court of Appeal rejected the CAT's interpretation of the s.33 test, partially accepted the Appellants' arguments in respect of the scope of the review under s.120 of the Act, but dismissed the appeal on the basis that the CAT was correct (notwithstanding its error in respect of the s.33 test) to have quashed the OFT's decision on the grounds that "a decision such as the present should in our view clearly set out the OFT's reasoning on issues such as these, together with sufficient material to show that the conclusion can be supported and that the matter has been properly investigated. The Tribunal has been unable to satisfy itself that such is the case here."[9]

In the leading judgment, the Vice-Chancellor clarified the question of the appropriate scope of review under s.120 of the Act. First, irrespective of the CAT's specialist expertise, s.120(4) required the application of the ordinary principles of judicial review as would be applied by a court.[10] Secondly, if the CAT had been seeking to examine whether the decision was reasonable on the basis of the ordinary and natural meaning of that word, in contrast to the narrower concept of *Wednesbury* unreasonableness, it would have been wrong to do so.[11] To the extent that the CAT had wrongly applied this broader test, the Vice-Chancellor found it was of no consequence to the facts of the particular case as this application had been limited to the CAT's consideration of its flawed s.33 test.[12] Thirdly, when applying the s.33 test, it was beholden upon the OFT in forming its belief that it is or may be the case that the merger may be expected to result in an SLC that "the belief must be reasonable and objectively justified by relevant facts".[13] Fourthly,

---

[7] The CAT's *IBA Health* judgment at para.190.
[8] The CAT's *IBA Health* judgment at para.225.
[9] *Office of Fair Trading and IBA Health Limited* [2004] EWCA Civ. 142 at para.69.
[10] The Court of Appeal's *IBA Heath* judgment at para.53.
[11] The Court of Appeal's *IBA Health* judgment at para.61.
[12] The Court of Appeal's *IBA Health* judgment at para.64.
[13] The Court of Appeal's *IBA Health* judgment at para.75.

the Vice-Chancellor considered the issue of the adequacy of the OFT's reasons, referring to *Education Secretary v Tameside BC*[14] together with the judgment of Lord Upjohn in *Padfield v Minister of Agriculture, Fisheries and Food* (see further below).[15] Finally, the Vice-Chancellor concluded that in his judgment it was appropriate to quash the OFT's decision not to refer because "either [the] OFT applied too high a test of likelihood when forming their belief or they failed adequately to justify the belief [as to the risk of an SLC arising] they formed in accordance with the proper test."[16] The tentative nature of this conclusion presumably reflects the lack of clarity (and consequent inadequacy) present in the OFT's reasoning. Nevertheless, it indicates the willingness of the Court of Appeal to criticise not only the OFT's reasons in failing adequately to justify their belief in respect of whether or not an SLC may be expected to result, but also to examine the factual analysis upon which the reasoning was based.

In the second judgment, Carnwath L.J. set out the judicial review principles that should guide the CAT's statutory review function. He emphasised the flexibility of the legal concept of reasonableness and stated that this may involve a narrow review when examining a decision dependent upon policy or political considerations best considered by the decision maker, but went on to observe that ordinary judicial review principles will permit the court to interfere more intensively where the question turns upon the fairness of the procedure adopted. In the context of the case, which involved an issue for the OFT that was essentially one of factual judgment, Carnwath L.J. agreed with the Vice Chancellor that the CAT is entitled to enquire whether there was adequate material to support the OFT's decision. With regard to adequacy of reasons, Carnwath L.J. noted that the case law did not lay down a principle of general application other than the requirement that the reasons must be "intelligible and adequately meet the substance of the arguments advanced." However, there should be no objection, subject to the usual caution against "post-rationalisation", where the OFT sought to supplement the reasons provided in the original decision with further material before the CAT. In this regard, the question for the CAT was not whether the reasoning was adequately expressed in the decision, but whether the material before it, taken as a whole, disclosed grounds on which the OFT could reasonably have reached the decision it did.

Following the judgment in *IBA Health*, the CAT has retained considerable scope to review merger control decisions, whether by the OFT or the Commission, even though its role is limited to applying judicial review principles. In particular, the CAT may scrutinise the factual basis of the decision in order to ascertain whether the regulator's conclusion was inconsistent with the only reasonable conclusion that was open to the regulator to have reached. Moreover, there is arguably a greater obligation upon the regulator to ensure that the underlying rationale for the decision is capable of objective justification by reference to those facts and, ultimately, is capable of expression in the reasons put forward in support of the decision. This is likely to place a greater burden on the OFT than the Competition Commission due to the time constraints under which the former invariably operates. Whether

---

[14] *Education Secretary v Tameside MBC* [1977] A.C. 1014 *per* Wilberforce L.J. at 1047.
[15] *Padfield v Minister of Agriculture, Fisheries and Food* [1968] A.C. 997 at 1058.
[16] *Padfield* at para.75.

more cases will be referred to the Competition Commission than before as a result of the threat of challenge, remains to be seen. However, most practitioners would acknowledge that the risk of challenge in borderline mergers has increased, and that the OFT is now seeking more information and asking more questions in all but the most straightforward cases.

The remainder of this chapter sets out the statutory review procedure and examines the types of decisions which may be subject to review. The chapter also provides an outline of the primary grounds of judicial review which may be relied upon by parties seeking to challenge merger control decisions and whose relevance has been confirmed by the decision of the Court of Appeal in *IBA Health*.

Making an application for statutory review

10.004   In order to commence statutory review proceedings it is necessary to establish that the applicant is a "person aggrieved" and that the relevant time limits have not expired. In addition, the decision must have been "made in connection with a merger reference or possible reference", and there must be relevant grounds for review.

Persons aggrieved

10.005   In the absence of a definition in the Act, it will be necessary for the CAT to decide who is a person aggrieved. In other statutory appeal regimes which employ the "person aggrieved" test, the category has been limited to parties who have suffered a legal grievance and whose legal rights have been infringed.[17] However, recent cases under such regimes have tended to adopt a more liberal interpretation of who or what is a person aggrieved and which is perhaps closer to the "sufficient interest" test applied in judicial review proceedings. In this regard, the courts have permitted third parties to bring statutory appeals where their interests have been prejudicially affected or where they are able to demonstrate a direct personal interest in the outcome of the claim.[18]

In the context of merger control, the parties to a proposed merger will almost certainly be aggrieved persons. However, different considerations may arise in the case of challenges brought by third parties such as a disgruntled competitor or customer. In *IBA Health*, none of the parties contested IBA's status as a person aggrieved. This may have reflected the fact that IBA had a direct financial interest in the merger as it was party to a distribution agreement with one of the merging parties, Torex, under which the latter had the exclusive right to sell IBA's products in the UK. In

---

[17] *Buxton v Minister of Housing and Local Government* [1960] 3 W.L.R. 866.

[18] These decisions include *Cook v Southend on Sea Borough Council* [1990] 2 Q.B. 1 (local authority appeal against the decision of magistrates overturning the authority's original rejection of the licence); *R. (Nicholl) v Belfast Recorder* [1965] N.I. 7 (persons objecting to the grant of a licence to a third party); and *Berkeley v Secretary of State for the Environment* [2001] 2 A.C. 603 (the right of a local resident environmental activist to challenge a grant of planning permission on grounds of potential harm to the River Thames). For a general discussion of the meaning of "person aggrieved", see *Wade and Forsyth on Administrative Law*, 9th ed., at pp.736–739.

Federation of Wholesale Distributors v OFT,[19] no objection was made to the application by the FWD for review of the OFT's decision not to refer to the Competition Commission the acquisition by Tesco plc of 45 convenience stores owned by Adminstore Ltd. A further consideration is that, whilst the rules upon standing are not equivalent, the European Court of First Instance has permitted challenges to Commission merger decisions brought by third parties.[20] Accordingly, a third party should have a reasonable argument that it is a person aggrieved where it can demonstrate that its own financial interests will be affected by the merger and, in particular, where it has played an active role in the consideration of the transaction by the regulator whether through the consultation process or otherwise; indeed the CAT may accept that any competition or customer active within the relevant market and thereby affected by a potential SLC would be a person aggrieved.

Time limits

Although the time limit for judicial review before the High Court requires that an application must be brought without unreasonable delay and in any event within three months of the date of the decision subject to challenge,[21] Rule 26 of the CAT's Rules[22] requires statutory review proceedings to be commenced within four weeks of the date on which the applicant was notified of the disputed decision, or the date of its publication, whichever is earlier. The CAT confirmed in the *FWD* case[23] that the date of publication of the decision within the meaning of Rule 26 is the date of the publication of the reasons for the decision and not the date of the announcement by the OFT of the fact of the decision. In that case the OFT took the contested clearance decision and published a short press release on March 5, 2004. The detailed reasons for the OFT's decision, which ran to some eight pages in length, were published in the decision itself on March 19. The CAT's reasoning was based on the fact that it is only when a potential applicant is in possession of the reasons for the OFT's decision that it can reasonably assess whether it should apply for review; to oblige applicants to apply for review at a time when they merely know that there has been a decision, but do not know the reasons for it, would be both an inefficient and an inequitable result.[24]

10.006

---

[19] *Federation of Wholesale Distributors v Office of Fair Trading* [2004] CAT 11.
[20] See for example Case T–114/02, *Babyliss v Commission* [2003] E.C.R. II-1279.
[21] In the consultation draft of the CAT's Rules, the time limit corresponded to this three month long stop. However the possibility of a four week deadline was raised as an alternative proposal and only two of the fifteen respondents to the consultation process considered that the time period should correspond to the usual three months. The government concluded that "merger cases should be treated differently" and in the final version of the CAT's Rules, the four week deadline was implemented. See DTI publication *The Government's Response to its Consultation on the Competition Appeal Tribunal Rules,* March 2003.
[22] The Competition Appeal Tribunal Rules 2003 (SI 2003/1372).
[23] *Federation of Wholesale Distributors v Office of Fair Trading* [2004] CAT 11.
[24] *Federation of Wholesale Distributors* at para.23. Such an approach would be inefficient as the applicant may have to seek leave to amend its application when the reasons for the decision became known, which would disrupt the preparation of the defence. It could also lead to a number of appeals being lodged on a precautionary basis, brought by applicants before they knew whether they had grounds for appealing. The CAT observed that to adopt such

The restrictive timeframe imposed by Rule 26 reflects the need for expedition in every aspect of merger control review. The DTI commented in its response to consultation on the CAT's Rules[25] that mergers "involve time-critical transactions that risk collapsing in the face of any undue delay". It also reflects the fact that the merger investigation process may be on-going and should not be held up any further than is strictly necessary by a review application. Accordingly, whilst the CAT has discretion under Rule 8(2)[26] to extend the time limit for an application in exceptional circumstances, it is likely to be rarely exercised,[27] particularly where the difficulty which has prompted the application for extension could be addressed in an alternative manner.[28] Indeed, the CAT has stated that a deadline will rarely be extended unless "*force majeure* in the strict sense*" is involved,[29] and that:

> ". . . respect for the deadline in commencing proceedings is, in many ways, the keystone of the whole procedure. In my judgment, therefore, derogations can be granted only exceptionally under Rule 6(3) [now Rule 8(2) of the CAT's Rules]. That principle, important as it is under the Competition Act [1998], is likely to be even more important when the Tribunal assumes its various new jurisdictions under the Enterprise Act later this year."[30]

This sentiment was applied with vigour in *IBA Health*, as is evident from the timescale within which that case was heard. The OFT decided not to refer the proposed public bid by iSOFT of Torex to the Competition Commission on November 6, 2003[31] and IBA Health lodged its application under s.120 of the Act against this decision on Friday November 21, 2003. The following Monday, the President of the CAT issued an order permitting iSOFT and Torex to intervene and reduced the time period for lodging a request to intervene from three weeks to three days, expiring on Wednesday November 26. The CAT dispensed with the need for a preliminary case management conference and the OFT and intervener were required to lodge skeleton arguments

---

a course would be inequitable as it would require an applicant to appeal before it was in the position to assess the legality of the decision in circumstances where the sufficiency of the reasons was a key element of review under s.120 of the Act (at paras 24 and 25).

[25] Cited above.

[26] Read with Rule 28(1) of the CAT's Rules.

[27] By contrast, under CPR Pt 3.1(2)(a), the High Court has discretion to extend the three month deadline for a review application where there are good reasons to do so and where it would not cause substantial prejudice or hardship or be detrimental to good administration. It seems highly unlikely that such an extension would be granted by the CAT in this context.

[28] See Rule 11 of the CAT Rules, read with Rule 28(1). In proceedings under the Competition Act 1998, the CAT refused an application to extend the deadline for submitting an appeal in circumstances where difficulties were identified by the appellant in drafting its notice of appeal against a first infringement decision in the absence of knowledge of the contents of an anticipated second infringement decision against it. The President ruled that such difficulties could adequately be addressed by issuing a "protective appeal" within the deadline and then applying for it to be amended or amplified as necessary once the second decision had been issued. *Hasbro UK Limited v Director General of Fair Trading* [2003] CAT 1; [2003] Comp. A.R. 47.

[29] *Hasbro*, cited above, at p.5.

[30] *Hasbro*, cited above, at p.5.

[31] See OFT's decision of November 6, 2003: *Anticipated acquisition by iSOFT Group plc of Torex plc.*

and any evidence in support of the OFT's decision by 12pm Thursday November 27, despite a request from the OFT to extend that deadline. The case was then heard on Friday November 28, within a week of receiving the application, whilst judgment was handed down on Wednesday December 3, only 12 days after the application was lodged. The speed with which this matter was handled contrasts with the delay associated with judicial review challenges to public bids where the disruption involved was perceived by the High Court as a reason in itself why it should entertain such challenges reluctantly.[32]

The Act provides that the merger inquiry or inquiry decision itself is not suspended by the fact that an application for review has been made, unless the CAT rules to the contrary.[33] This raises the possibility that a merger may be subject to a CAT challenge and a concurrent Commission inquiry, or the merging parties are faced with CAT proceedings challenging a merger that has otherwise been cleared. In the case of a merger involving a UK public company, additional complications will arise due to the impact of any delay engendered by the statutory review process on the bid timetable prescribed by the Takeover Code.[34] In circumstances where a challenge will cause significant delay to a decision as to whether a reference to the Competition Commission is required, it should be open to the parties to request the Takeover Panel to suspend the timetable pending resolution of the issue.[35] However, the risk that such a challenge will result in a reference and the offer lapsing, will remain.[36] In this regard, it may well be preferable to declare the offer unconditional as to acceptances (subject to an assessment of the risk of divestment ultimately being required) before the application for review has been determined, although this may require the involvement of the OFT and/or the CAT and the provision of suitable undertakings.[37]

With regard to the availability of interim measures, in the *IBA Health* case the applicant requested that if the CAT were unable to hear the case with sufficient expedition, it should give the following directions: that the merging parties should not seek shareholder approval for the merger offer; that if the merger took place a direction should be given that the businesses be kept separate; and that the OFT's decision not to refer should otherwise be suspended.[38] In the event, the CAT disposed of the case so quickly that the interim measures application was not pursued and the issue of the scope of the CAT's jurisdiction in respect of the wide ranging nature of the inter-locutory remedies sought was not explored. Nevertheless, the interim measures process provides a clear indication of the potential for the statutory review process to interfere with the merger timetable. It is also important to note that even where the CAT proceeds with expedition, delay may still

---

[32] *R. v Monopolies and Mergers Commission Ex p. Argyll Group plc* [1986] 1 W.L.R. 763; [1986] 2 All E.R. 257.
[33] s.120(3) of the Act.
[34] The City Code on Takeovers and Mergers; for a general discussion of the application of the Code to the merger control regime see Ch.3 above.
[35] See n.3 to Rule 31.6 of the Code.
[36] Pursuant to Rule 12.1 of the Code.
[37] For example, in the IBA Health case the parties chose to declare the bid unconditional as to acceptances prior to the determination of the appeal by the Court of Appeal but subject to the provision of "hold separate" undertakings given to the OFT under s.71 of the Act.
[38] In reliance upon rule 61 of the Competition Appeal Tribunal Rules 2003, (SI 2003/1372).

arise as a result of an appeal to the Court of Appeal on a point of law. This, of course, occurred in the *IBA Health* case where, following the CAT's judgment on December 3, 2003, written permission to appeal was given by the CAT on December 12, 2003 and judgment was handed down by the Court of Appeal on February 19, 2004.

Decisions subject to statutory review

10.007   Any decision of the OFT, the Competition Commission or the Secretary of State is potentially subject to review where it is taken pursuant to their merger control powers in connection with a reference or possible reference in relation to a merger situation or special merger situation. This wide category of potential decisions is expressly stated to include a *failure* to take a decision.[39] The only identified exception is in respect of penalties imposed upon parties who obstruct investigations which are subject to their own distinct appeal procedure.[40] Otherwise, the right to review is likely to apply to any other decision taken in connection with a possible reference under Pt 3 of the Act. This will include decisions by the OFT to refer (or not to refer) a merger to the Commission, decisions to accept or refuse undertakings in lieu of a reference, decisions taken by the Commission as to whether a merger may result in a substantial lessening of competition, decisions to accept or reject particular remedies and all similar decisions taken by the Secretary of State under the public interest provisions. However, purely procedural matters such as time limits, confidentiality and possibly initial (hold separate) undertakings may remain subject to the judicial review jurisdiction of the High Court unless they are broadly construed by the CAT as relating to merger reference decisions.

Available remedies

10.008   In contrast to the wide range of powers available when hearing appeals under the Competition Act 1998, the CAT has recourse to a relatively limited arsenal of remedies in the context of statutory review proceedings. In this regard, the Act empowers the CAT to dismiss an application or to quash the decision challenged (either in its entirety or in part) and refer the matter back to the original decision maker.[41] These are arguably more limited than the powers available to the Administrative Court in judicial review proceedings.[42] They also differ from the remedies that may be obtained on the very rare occasions when a private law action may be contemplated against the regulator concerned.[43] However, the CAT may

---

[39] s.120(2) of the Act.
[40] s.114 of the Act.
[41] s.120(5) of the Act.
[42] Where the Administrative Court may not only make "prohibiting" and "mandatory" orders but also grant an injunction and, in exceptional cases, make an award of damages.
[43] A private law right of action may arise in limited circumstances where, exceptionally, it is possible to show the existence of a duty of care between undertaking and regulator (such as where the latter has not been exercising a statutory discretion with regard to public policy considerations) (see *Lonrho plc v Tebbit*, *The Times*, June 10, 1992; [1992] 4 All E.R. 280; see also *Lonrho v Tebbit* [1991] 4 All E.R. 973 at 981).

also give a direction that the regulator reconsider and make a new decision in accordance with the CAT's ruling.[44] In the *IBA Health* case, the CAT contented itself with merely remitting the decision to the OFT with a direction that it be reconsidered (following the Court of Appeal's decision in *IBA Health*, the OFT cleared iSoft's acquisition of Torex, having accepted certain divestment undertakings in lieu of reference). However, the track record of the CAT under the Competition Act suggests the possibility that it might take a more active role in giving directions to the regulator in appropriate circumstances when decisions are remitted.[45]

It is also important to note that remedies granted pursuant to judicial review proceedings are discretionary. This has important implications as a court may, exceptionally, refuse to grant relief even where the grounds of challenge have been made out. An example is where the court is of the view that the public body would have reached the same decision irrespective of the error and that to grant the remedy sought would be contrary to the public interest.[46]

Grounds for review

Forum of the case

When determining a statutory review application, the CAT is required to "apply the same principles as would be applied by a court on an application for judicial review."[47] "Court" is defined as meaning the Court of Appeal (of England and Wales or Northern Ireland) or the Court of Session in Scotland.[48] This reflects the fact that the CAT has UK-wide jurisdiction and can hear English, Scottish and Northern Irish cases. Rule 18 of the CAT

10.009

---

[44] s.120(5)(b).

[45] In the context of appeal proceedings under the Competition Act 1998, the CAT has assumed power to set detailed requirements where a quashed matter has been referred back to the OFT (or a sectoral regulator) for reconsideration. Despite the absence of a clear statutory power to do more than simply remit an issue, the CAT has, on a number of occasions, laid down a detailed timeframe for reconsideration by the decision-maker, with any extensions of time requiring a reasoned application to the CAT, and in one case has required a progress report to be submitted. See, for example *Aberdeen Journals Limited v Director General of Fair Trading* [2002] CAT 4; [2002] Comp. A.R. 167 at para.198 where a deadline of two months was set for the issue of a further Rule 14 notice on the matter remitted to the OFT, with any decision to be issued within two months of the end of the administrative procedure. In *Freeserve.com plc v Director General of Telecommunications* [2003] CAT 6; [2003] Comp. A.R. 280, the Director General of Telecommunications gave an undertaking to reconsider the part of his decision which had been set aside by the CAT, so that it was not formally remitted. Nevertheless, the CAT set a timetable for the reconsideration process and in a subsequent decision following a request for an extension of time, the CAT added a requirement that a progress report should be submitted to it (see [2003] CAT 15; [2003] Comp. A.R. 75 at para.20). See also *Argos Limited and Littlewoods Limited v Office of Fair Trading* [2003] CAT 16; [2003] Comp. A.R. 329 which fixed a detailed timetable for the reissue of a Rule 14 notice, the response to that notice, any oral hearing and any amended version of the remitted decision.

[46] See *R. v Monopolies and Mergers Commission Ex p. Argyll Group plc* [1986] 1 W.L.R. 763; see also *Interbrew SA and Interbrew UK Holdings Ltd v Competition Commission and Secretary of State for Trade and Industry* [2001] EWHC Admin 367; [2001] U.K.C.L.R. 954 where Moses J. drew attention to the fact that neither party had made submissions in respect of the court's discretion to refuse relief.

[47] s.120(4) of the Act.

[48] s.120(8) of the Act.

Rules governs the decision as to the forum of the proceedings. Rule 18(3)[49] states that in deciding whether the case is to be treated as proceedings in England and Wales, in Scotland or in Northern Ireland, the CAT may take into account all relevant matters, in particular the place where any party to the agreement is habitually resident or has its head office or principal place of business; the place where the majority of the parties to the agreement are resident or have their head office or principal place of business; the place where any agreement is to be or was implemented; and the place where any relevant conduct took place.

In the context of Competition Act proceedings, the question of forum will not usually affect the CAT's substantive assessment of the appeal, because the Competition Act provisions are consistently interpreted and applied across the UK.[50] In relation to judicial review however, the principles of review have developed separately in the three UK jurisdictions and the issue of forum is therefore potentially of greater significance. That said, two counter-observations are relevant. First, the procedural provisions for reviews under s.120 of the Enterprise Act have eliminated one of the most significant differences, at least between English and Scottish judicial review procedure. Under Scottish judicial review procedures, there is no preliminary requirement to seek leave to apply, as there is in England and Wales. The CAT's Rules have, however, dispensed with a leave stage, whichever forum the case is heard in: Rule 26 requires an application for the review of a decision to be lodged within four weeks of the date of notification or publication of the decision, and makes no provision that leave must first have been granted.[51] Secondly, the vast majority of cases concerning the judicial review of decisions by the merger regulators have been dealt with to date by the English High Court. The following discussion therefore focuses on the principles of judicial review as they have been applied by the courts of England and Wales.

Legal basis of judicial review in England and Wales

10.010 Judicial review proceedings in the English courts are not a full appeal on the facts but rather a review on the basis of long established administrative law principles. Accordingly, by virtue of s.120(4) of the Act which requires the CAT to apply judicial review principles, the CAT will be concerned with the legality of the decision-making process rather than the merits of the regulator's decision. In the *IBA Health* case, the Vice-Chancellor observed that the relevant legal principles to be applied by the CAT under s.120 of the Act are the ordinary principles of judicial review notwithstanding the fact that the CAT is a specialist tribunal.[52] The body of legal authority developed as a result of previous applications for judicial review in the context of merger control is therefore likely to continue to be of some relevance, although it

---

[49] Rule 18 applies to review proceedings by virtue of Rule 25 of the CAT Rules.
[50] It is primarily significant in relation to the forum for any appeal from the CAT's judgment. It may also affect the assessment of costs: see *Aberdeen Journals Limited v Office of Fair Trading* [2003] CAT 21; [2004] Comp. A.R. 189, where costs were subject to Scottish law.
[51] Compare CPR Pt 54.4.
[52] The Court of Appeal's *IBA Health* judgment, cited above, at para.53.

should not be forgotten that the Act introduces a materially different regime by replacing political discretion with statutory duties.

The grounds under which the courts have been willing to grant judicial review have traditionally fallen under three principal headings:

(i)   illegality (the decision maker has exceeded or misapplied its powers);

(ii)   procedural impropriety (the procedure used by the decision maker has violated the rules of natural justice or resulted in manifest unfairness);

(iii)   irrationality (the decision maker has reached a decision that no rational person could have made or, alternatively, has taken account of irrelevant matters or failed to take account of relevant matters).

These headings should not be considered as exhaustive or definitive, as this area of law continues to develop.[53] In particular, grounds of review may arise under heads such as error of fact, proportionality and inadequacy of reasons. Some of these grounds are acknowledged as stand alone heads of challenge, others are more often better raised as sub-species of the traditional categories noted above.[54]

---

[53] In recent years the Courts have considered the application of a wider head of challenge which may be described as "abuse of power". This category has included complaints such as Wednesbury unreasonableness and procedural abuses (see *R. v IRC Ex p. Unilever plc* [1996] S.T.C. 681) whilst complaints have also been brought within the categories of procedural and substantive "fairness" (see *R. v North and East Devon Health Authority Ex p. Coughlan* [2000] 2 W.L.R. 622). The ultimate question for the court in judicial review proceedings, as identified by Richards J. in *R. v National Lottery Commission Ex p. Camelot* [2000] All E.R. (D) 1205 with reference to *R. v Takeover Panel Ex p. Guinness plc* [1990] 1 Q.B. 146 at 160, is perhaps: "whether something had gone wrong of a nature and degree which required the intervention of the court". Further developments include the ability of the court to quash a decision on the grounds of misunderstanding or ignorance of an established or relevant fact: Slynn L.J. in *R. v Criminal Injuries Compensation Board Ex p. A* [1999] 2 A.C. 330 at 344 to 345; *R (Alconbury Ltd) v Environment Secretary* HL(E) [2001] 2 W.L.R. 1389 at 1407 para.53. The court may also quash a decision, at least in cases where rights under the European Convention on Human Rights are engaged, on the ground of proportionality: *R. (Daly) v Secretary of State for the Home Department* [2001] 2 A.C. 532; Hoffman L.J. in *Runa Begum* [2003] 2 W.L.R. 388 at 404, para.48. The question of proportionality of the remedy under review was also relevant in *Interbrew SA and Interbrew UK Holdings Ltd v Competition Commission and Secretary of State for Trade and Industry* [2001] EWHC Admin 367 (judgment of May 23, 2001) [2001] U.K.C.L.R. 954; because the reference to the Competition Commission was made following a reference back under Art.9 of the EC Merger Regulation of the UK aspects of Interbrew's acquisition of Bass PLC, having originally been notified to the European Commission. Art.9(8) of the EC Merger Regulation limits the Member State authority considering a reference back to taking only "measures strictly necessary to safeguard or restore effective competition on the market concerned." Moses J. concluded that this provision imposed a clear duty on the Commission and the Secretary of State to act in a proportionate manner and noted that this was reinforced by Art.1 of the First Protocol to the European Convention on Human Rights, which enshrines the right to peaceful enjoyment of possessions. In that case, however, there was no need to apply a balancing assessment between different remedies because there was only one which was feasible.

[54] For example, see Demetriou and Houseman "*Review for Error of Fact—a Brief Guide*" J.R. 1997, 2(1) 27–32 for a discussion of the circumstances in which a court will entertain

The remainder of this chapter considers each of the grounds for judicial review and examines some of the circumstances when they have been used to challenge merger control decisions in the past, before commenting on their potential application to the regime for statutory review introduced by the Act.

Illegality

10.011 This ground of review will arise where the public body in question has exceeded the powers granted to it by Parliament (or otherwise misdirected itself in law). In the context of merger control, an illegal (or *ultra vires*) act is likely to arise where the determining authority has exceeded or misinterpreted its powers arising under Pt 3 of the Enterprise Act.

Historically, the courts have been reluctant to find that either the Secretary of State (when that role carried the primary decision-making power in relation to merger control) or the Competition Commission (or, under its previous name, the Monopolies and Mergers Commission—the MMC) has acted illegally when exercising its merger control functions. For example, in *R. v MMC Ex p. Air Europe*,[55] Air Europe sought to challenge the MMC's conclusions on the ground that the regulator had acted unlawfully in taking account of certain undertakings given on behalf of British Airways during the course of the reference. Air Europe argued that under s.72(2) of the FTA the MMC was only empowered to report upon the original merger proposal at the time of the reference and lacked jurisdiction to consider and report on proposals that were developed during the course of its inquiry. Although the FTA did not give the MMC express powers to take account of variations to a proposal, the Divisional Court rejected the argument as artificial, perhaps even pedantic, in requiring the MMC to report on the original proposals and to ignore any developments, particularly where they rendered the original proposals academic.[56] Lloyd L.J. stated that:

"The Commission is . . . entitled to take account of the developing situation. It must not shut its eyes to what is going on. But this does not mean that it should allow itself to be placed in the position of negotiating with the parties . . . Its obligation is to investigate and report. It may not bargain or haggle . . . Nobody suggests there was any haggling here. Of course the Commission must be sensitive to the arguments and objections put forward by other interested parties. This is what they were."[57]

The case of *R. v MMC Ex p. Argyll* arose in connection with the contested take-over bid for Distillers by Guinness and Argyll. Argyll sought

---

a challenge on such a ground. See also the judgment of Carnwath C.J. in *IBA Health* at paras 88–101, cited above.

[55] *R. v MMC Ex p. Air Europe* [1988] 4 B.C.C. 182.

[56] Under s.37 of the Enterprise Act, the Commission similarly cannot vary its terms of reference, although there is express provision to enable it to request the OFT to vary the terms of reference. The Commission is, by contrast, able to treat a reference of an anticipated merger as one of a completed merger, or vice versa, without the terms of reference needing to be formally varied by the OFT.

[57] *Air Europe*, cited above, at 187.

judicial review of the decision of the Chairman of the MMC to lay the reference of Guinness's bid for Distillers aside in the light of an alternative bid for the company by Guinness. Although the Court of Appeal concluded that the power to lay a reference aside was vested in the MMC and that the Chairman had no such power acting alone,[58] in exercising the court's discretion to refuse a remedy, Sir John Donaldson M.R. refused to grant the relief requested on the grounds that to do so would be contrary to good administration:

"Good public administration is concerned with substance rather than form. Difficult although the decision on the fact of abandonment may or may not have been, I have little doubt that the Commission, or a group of members charged with the conduct of the reference, would have reached and would now reach the same conclusion as did their experienced chairman".[59]

An example of a more recent case (albeit a monopoly inquiry) in which a challenge on the grounds of illegality succeeded is provided by *R. v Secretary of State for Trade and Industry Ex p. Thomson Holidays Ltd.*[60] The Court of Appeal held that the Secretary of State had misdirected herself with regard to the scope of her powers to make an order under s.56 of the FTA on the basis of a Competition Commission report. Overturning the judge at first instance, the Court of Appeal found that the order making power under s.56 was circumscribed in that it might only seek to remedy adverse effects arising from findings of fact made by the Commission, rather than on the basis of findings of fact made by the Secretary of State herself. Whilst the appeal succeeded upon *vires* grounds, it is important to note that the manner in which the Secretary of State had proceeded also resulted in an underlying procedural lack of fairness, whereby Thomson had been able to put its case in respect of findings of fact made by the Commission but not those made by the Secretary of State upon her own initiative.

Whilst the number of overall challenges have been few, the majority of successful judicial review applications in the competition field have been founded upon an error of law.[61] Absent a glaring procedural irregularity, an error of law was perhaps considered a prerequisite if the case concerned

---

[58] Similarly, under s.37(1) of the Act, the power to cancel a reference is expressed to be a power of the Commission.

[59] *R. v MMC Ex p. Argyll*, cited above, at 266. In his judgment, Neil L.J. stated that even though the chairman had no power under s.75(5) to lay the reference aside: ". . . I am quite satisfied that the court in the exercise of its discretion, should not grant any relief to these applicants. The purpose of the legislation, the fact that the Secretary of State has and has had the power to refuse his consent to the laying aside or to make a further reference, and the fact Guinness and other third parties have acted in reliance on the announcement of the laying aside of the reference, point inevitably to this conclusion"; at 272.

[60] Times Law Reports, January 12, 2000; [2000] U.K.C.L.R. 189.

[61] See Robertson "*Judicial Review of Competition Law Decisions*" J.R. 2001, 6(2) 84–92 with reference to *R. v DGFT Ex p. Southdown Motor Services Ltd* (1993) 12 Tr. Law 90; Case C–392/93 *R. v HM Treasury Ex p. British Telecommunications plc* [1996] E.C.R. I–1631; *R. v Secretary of State for Trade & Industry Ex p. Thomson Holidays Ltd* [2000] U.K.C.L.R. 189; and *R. v Secretary of State for Trade & Industry Ex p. Orange Personal Communications Ltd* [2001] 3 C.M.L.R. 36.

was to avoid the risk of appearing somewhat speculative in character. It remains the case that a party able to identify an error of law which has had material effects will perhaps have greater prospects of success than applicants relying upon other grounds. However, there are good arguments that following the introduction of the scheme for statutory review under the Enterprise Act (as interpreted in the *IBA Health* judgment), some of the other potential grounds of challenge noted below are likely to assume increasing importance.

Procedural impropriety

10.012 In determining issues that affect a party's rights, a regulator is usually required to observe what are somewhat loosely referred to as the "rules of natural justice" and to ensure that the process employed complies with the requirements of "procedural fairness."[62] This is an area of administrative law that has been much affected by developments in the fields of European Community and human rights law and, in particular, the principle that where rights under the European Convention of Human Rights ("ECHR") are at stake, those adversely affected are entitled to an appropriate degree of involvement in the decision-making process and to receive prior notice of issues that are of concern (see further below).[63]

Natural justice is a flexible concept that will include the right to a fair hearing, the rule against bias and a variety of other common law principles such as the need to base any decision upon evidence that has some probative value.[64] Its underlying principles were extensively reviewed in *Wiseman v Borneman*[65] where Lord Morris stated that:

"...We often speak of the rules of natural justice. But there is nothing rigid or mechanical about them ... The principles and procedures are to be applied which, in any particular situation or set of circumstances, are right and just and fair. Natural justice, it has been said, is only fair play in action."

The question of whether the procedure adopted is a fair one will depend upon all the circumstances of the case, with particular regard to provisions of the governing statutory regime:

"The principles of fairness are not to be applied by rote identically in every situation. What fairness demands is dependent on the context of the decision, and this is to be taken into account in all its aspects. An essential feature of the context is the statute which creates the discretion,

---

[62] The principle of procedural fairness was summarised by Bridge L.J. in *Lloyd v McMahon* [1987] A.C. 625 as: "when a statute has conferred on any body the power to make decisions affecting individuals, the courts will not only require the procedure prescribed by the statute to be followed, but will readily imply so much and no more to be introduced by way of additional procedural safeguards as will ensure the attainment of fairness."

[63] *R. v Home Secretary Ex p. Fayed* [1998] 1 W.L.R. 763 at 773H.

[64] *R. v Monopolies and Mergers Commission Ex p. Matthew Brown plc* [1987] 1 W.L.R. 1235 at 1239.

[65] [1971] A.C. 297 at 308.

as regards both its language and the shape of the legal and administrative system within which the decision is taken."[66]

Alleged breaches of the rules of natural justice have been raised in a number of judicial review applications following the publication of Competition Commission reports. In these cases, the High Court has tended to confer a wide discretion upon the Commission with regard to the procedures it has chosen to employ. In *Elders IXL Ltd*,[67] which related to the hostile bid by Elders for Allied Lyons, Elders sought judicial review of the MMC's decision to disclose to Allied Lyons certain confidential information provided by Elders to the MMC during the course of their inquiry. The purpose of the disclosure was to enable Allied to comment on the likely effect of the proposed financing of the acquisition on Allied's business if the merger were permitted to proceed. Elders attacked the MMC's decision to disclose the information, *inter alia*, on the ground that the decision was unfair to Elders in that its interest in non-disclosure of the information was not sufficiently taken into account by the MMC. After noting the statement of Sachs L.J. in *R. v Pergamon Press Ltd*[68] that fairness is a flexible concept and the formulation of a precise set of rules may unduly hamper or frustrate an investigating body, Mann J. held that Elders' claim that the MMC's decision, although fair to Allied, inflicted disproportionate unfairness on Elders, had to be considered in the context of the MMC's statutory investigation to determine whether the merger was in the public interest. In dismissing the application he concluded:

"I am satisfied... that the Commission's intention is to facilitate the performance of its functions. It was not suggested that the formation of that intention was either irrational or made in bad faith. I reach my conclusion without regret because it seems to me that it would be most unfortunate if the Commission were to be in peril of exercises in objectivity by this court ... during the course of discharging the difficult functions put on the Commission by the 1973 Act."[69]

An equally generous approach to the lawfulness of the MMC's chosen procedure was adopted in *Ex p. Matthew Brown*. In that case, Macpherson J. rejected a charge that the MMC had acted unfairly in not giving Matthew Brown an opportunity to comment on further evidence submitted by Scottish & Newcastle: **10.013**

"Provided each party has its mind brought to bear upon the relevant issues it is not in my judgment for the court to lay down rules as to how each group should act in any particular inquiry. Of course neither side must be faced with a bolt from the blue and no party may be kept in the dark and prevented from putting its case. But I am wholly unable to say

---

[66] *R. v Home Secretary Ex p. Doody* [1994] 1 A.C. 531 at p.560. This decision was referred to by the CAT in *Pernod Record S.A. v OFT* [2004] CAT 10 at para.235.
[67] *R v Monopolies and Mergers Commission Ex p. Elders IXL Ltd* [1987] 1 All E.R. 451
[68] [1970] 3 All E.R. 535 at 542.
[69] *Elders IXL Ltd*, cited above, at 462.

that this happened in the present case or that I can detect unfairness which approaches that which might undermine this report."[70]

In *Ex p. Stagecoach Holdings plc*, the High Court confirmed that it would be reluctant to intervene in cases where the MMC considered that the procedure that it had adopted was fair[71]:

"I entirely accept that the Court will be slow to intervene [in procedural matters]. This is because regard must be had to the nature of the MMC and the knowledge that, having directed itself properly on the requirements of fairness, it will be unlikely that nonetheless it has been unfair. As Lloyd LJ said at page 184D (R v Take-over Panel *Ex p.* Guinness PLC [1991] QB 146) the court will give great weight to the tribunal's own view of what is fair. No doubt, this will mean that in the vast majority of cases the court will be unlikely to regard what the MMC has reasonably believed to be fair as unfair so that in practice the adoption of a Wednesbury test would make little difference."

Collins J. also distinguished between cases where a speedy decision was needed because the decision would be acted upon immediately by the market, and those cases where a decision resulted only in findings and recommendations.

In two more recent high profile decisions, the High Court has granted relief on the grounds that the procedure adopted failed to meet the requisite standard of "fairness".[72] In the *Interbrew* case,[73] the applicant challenged the recommendation given by the Competition Commission that if the merger were to be approved, Interbrew should be required to divest itself of the entire UK operations of Bass. The unfairness relied upon was that Interbrew was not given the opportunity to make representations to the Commission in respect of this proposed divestment before it was put forward and accepted by the Secretary of State as the appropriate remedy. Having rejected the other grounds of challenge, the High Court found in favour of Interbrew on the basis that the Commission owed Interbrew "a duty of fairness" when conducting its investigation into the merger. In particular, this duty required the Commission to have identified areas of concern with Interbrew and, on the facts of the case, given Interbrew a fair opportunity to address the issues

---

[70] *Ex p. Matthew Brown*, cited above, at 469.

[71] See *R v Monopolies and Mergers Commission Ex p. Stagecoach Holdings plc, The Times*, July 23, 1996. However, Collins J. confirmed that the guiding principle was that it is not what the MMC believed to have been fair that should prevail, but what was in fact fair. See also the comments of Richards J. in *R. v National Lottery Commission Ex p. Camelot* [2000] All E.R. (D) 1205 at para.69 where the court expressly confirmed the relevance of the regulator's own view of the appropriate procedure: "Indeed, in reaching my own conclusion on the issue of fairness I must take into account, and give weight to, the Commission's own view that exclusive negotiation with TPL would be a fair way of taking the matter forward, as well as the way best calculated to lead to the discharge of its statutory duties in relation to the grant of a new licence."

[72] See *Interbrew SA and Interbrew UK Holdings Ltd v Competition Commission and Secretary of State for Trade and Industry* [2001] EWHC Admin 367; [2001] U.K.C.L.R. 954; see also *R. v National Lottery Commission Ex p. Camelot Group plc* [2000] All E.R. (D) 1205.

[73] *Interbrew SA and Interbrew UK Holdings Ltd v Competition Commission and Secretary of State for Trade and Industry* [2001] EWHC Admin 367; [2001] U.K.C.L.R. 954.

associated with the specific remedy eventually proposed by the Secretary of State. In granting the application, the Court quashed both the Commission's decision to recommend the divestment of Bass and the decision of the Secretary of State to have required such a remedy:

"I do not believe it ever occurred to Interbrew that this would be a matter of concern to the Commission. . ... The Commission's argument seems to be that Interbrew ought reasonably to have been expected not only to deal with the question of the viability and independence of Whitbread with Stella Artois but also to have volunteered reasons why any expressed concerns that the Commission may have had as to that viability were unfounded. That seems to me to be going a step too far. Had the Commission had concerns flowing from that dual capacity at the time of either of the two hearings on 15 November or 20 November I am confident that they would have been put to Interbrew. I suspect that the issue between the members of the Group arose only later. But I can see no reason why the simple and, as it seems to me, clear point should not have been put to Interbrew:- 'do you accept that your capacity as owner of Bass and licensor of Stella Artois will inhibit the competitiveness of Whitbread with Stella Artois?'"

The *Interbrew* decision marks an important development in this area of judicial control. In particular, it demonstrates that the courts will be prepared to intervene on procedural grounds even where the views of the regulator as to the fairness of the process employed continue to have currency and the relevance of the time pressures affecting such procedures are also acknowledged. From the regulator's view point, great care will have to be taken to ensure that affected parties are given appropriate opportunities to give their views on material issues likely to affect the outcome of the determination concerned. In this regard, the Act imposes a duty to consult upon the regulator although this is qualified and need only be exercised "so far as practicable."[74] It remains to be seen whether the terms of this statutory duty are sufficiently strict to comply with common-law obligations of the sort relied upon in *Interbrew* or the wider obligations in respect of decisions affecting human rights which are discussed further below.

10.014

Similarly, in *R. v National Lottery Commission Ex p. Camelot Group plc*,[75] the Administrative Court upheld a challenge on the ground that the procedure adopted was unfair as the decision of the Lottery Commission to negotiate with only one of the parties following a competitive tender under which neither bid had emerged as a clear winner, showed a lack of even handedness that required the most compelling justification. Whilst the case arose outside the context of merger control, it reinforces the obligation to which all authorities are increasingly subject to adopt procedures that are essentially "fair" to those who stand to win or lose by them.

The Enterprise Act has codified many of the informal procedural practices that had evolved under the FTA regime, and the areas where the OFT or Commission is given a wide "discretion to regulate its own procedure"[76] are

---

[74] s.104 of the Act.
[75] [2000] All E.R. (D) 1205.
[76] See *Ex p. Matthew Brown plc*, cited above.

now more limited. The OFT and the Commission have issued their own assessment guidelines and the Commission has issued its Rules of Procedure to govern the conduct of its proceedings, which inevitably narrows the discretion of the Commission in the conduct of an inquiry. The Commission (and where relevant the OFT and Secretary of State) should therefore be more susceptible to challenge where they fail to observe the procedural requirements of the Act and/or their own rules and guidelines.

Legitimate Expectation

10.015   A ground of challenge closely related to that of "fairness" arises on the basis that a decision maker has breached a legitimate expectation that it will deal with a matter in a certain way.[77] For a legitimate expectation to arise, it is usually necessary for it to have been founded upon a clear and unambiguous representation which, in some circumstances, the aggrieved party may also need to demonstrate that it has relied upon.[78] Such an argument is more likely to succeed where the expectation has arisen in respect of the particular form of procedure to be followed[79] rather than in respect of the substantive decision itself.

Irrationality

10.016   This ground of review concerns the situation where the decision maker concerned has failed to take account of relevant considerations (or has taken account of irrelevant considerations) and thereby (or for other reasons) reached a conclusion that was so unreasonable that no reasonable decision maker could ever have come to it—so-called "Wednesbury unreasonableness."[80] This last category will only be satisfied where the decision in question is:

> "so outrageous in its defiance of logic or of accepted moral standards that no sensible person who had applied his mind to the question to be decided could have arrived at it."[81]

---

[77] National authorities responsible for applying European Community law, which will include the OFT and Competition Commission when they exercise powers under the EC Merger Regulation, are also subject to the general Community law principle of legitimate expectations: see Case T–571/93, *Lefebvre Freres et Soeurs v Commission* [1995] E.C.R. II–2379 at para.74.

[78] *R. v Jockey Club Ex p. RAM Racecourses* [1993] 2 All E.R. 225; although in exceptional circumstances a legitimate expectation may arise by virtue of the regulator's conduct.

[79] See *Claymore Dairies v DGFT* (admissibility) [2003] CAT 3; [2004] Comp. A.R. 1 for an example of where the CAT appears to have accepted an argument based upon the existence of a legitimate expectation in relation to procedure adopted by the OFT in connection with the exercise of their powers under the Competition Act.

[80] *Associated Provincial Picture Houses Limited v Wednesbury Corporation* [1948] 1 K.B. 223.

[81] See *CCSU v Minister for the Civil Service* [1985] A.C. 374 at p.410. Conceptually, to the extent that proportionality exists as a ground for review outside the application of the EC Merger Regulation (see n.88 below), it arguably constitutes an element of irrationality. In support of this view see the decision of the Court of Appeal in *R (Association of British Civilian Internees: Far East Region) v Secretary of State for Defence* [2003] Q.B. 1397 at 1412.

An application made on these grounds often amounts to an indirect challenge to the exercise of the discretion afforded to the decision maker. As the role of the courts in judicial review proceedings is not to substitute their decision for that of the decision-making body, relief is usually only granted under this head in exceptional circumstances. This difficulty is reflected in the limited number of challenges on this ground that arose under the FTA merger control regime. In *R. v MMC Ex p. Matthew Brown plc*,[82] which arose following the MMC's conclusion that the hostile bid by Scottish & Newcastle Breweries for Matthew Brown could not be expected to operate against the public interest, Matthew Brown sought judicial review of the MMC's report on the grounds, *inter alia*, that the MMC had taken irrelevant factors into account whilst failing to take into account relevant factors in deciding that the proposed merger would not have an adverse effect on beer prices in the north west of England. In particular, Matthew Brown argued that the MMC had attached insufficient weight to a price survey they had carried out and had failed to ensure that Scottish & Newcastle carried out a similar exercise. In response to this contention, Macpherson J. stated that:

"In those circumstances it seems to me that, provided the Commission had proper regard to such evidence as the parties did put before it as to prices, it was a matter for the Commission to decide what weight, if any, or what reliance it should place on the arguments and method of comparison contended for by Matthew Brown."[83]

He concluded that he was unable to detect a failure to consider relevant matters on the part of the MMC or that they had placed reliance upon irrelevant matters.

Similarly, in *Lonrho plc v Secretary of State for Trade and Industry*,[84] the House of Lords rejected a challenge alleging that the Secretary of State had acted irrationally in deciding not to refer the acquisition of House of Fraser by the Fayed Brothers to the MMC after new facts had arisen. Rejecting the approach adopted by the Divisional Court, the House of Lords found that:

"[the] absence of reasons for a decision where there is no duty to give them cannot of itself provide any support for the suggested irrationality of the decision. The only significance of the absence of reasons is that if all other known facts and circumstances appear to point overwhelmingly in favour of a different decision, the decision-maker who has given no reasons cannot complain if the court draws the inference that he has no rational reason for his decision."[85]

---

[82] [1987] 1 W.L.R. 1235.
[83] *Ex p. Matthew Brown*, cited above, at 1246.
[84] *Lonrho plc v Secretary of State for Trade and Industry* [1989] 2 All E.R. 609.
[85] *Lonrho*, cited above, at 620. Note that under the Enterprise Act, the OFT and/or Commission are now required to give reasons for the majority of their decisions.

Adequacy of reasons

10.017   Some "reasons" challenges seek to assert that the reasons are inadequate because they disclose an error of law or approach. In this sense, they are a variant of an irrationality challenge of the type considered above. Other "reasons" challenges are advanced because the reasons given do not allow the person affected by the decision to determine whether there has been, for example, an error of law or whether all relevant considerations have been taken into account and irrelevant ones omitted. Viewed in this light such challenges are a species of procedural impropriety. In the *Interbrew* decision,[86] Moses J. rejected a challenge to the Competition Commission's reasoning (which was subsequently adopted by the Secretary of State), whereby the minister determined that, due to the anti-competitive effects of the acquisition, Interbrew should be required to divest itself of Bass. In the context of its "reasons" challenge, Interbrew claimed first, that the reasoning lacked cogency (that is, it did not "stack up"), and secondly, that the reasons provided demonstrated that the Commission had failed to consider whether the divestment recommended to the Secretary of State as a precondition for approval for the merger was disproportionate in its effects (the "*balance*" argument).

With regard to the "*cogency*" point, Moses J. declined to interfere with the Commission's recommendation on the ground that, in his view, it was lawfully entitled to reject an alternative remedy on the basis of its inherent expertise in an area that was essentially a matter of commercial and economic judgment:

> "In my judgment these reasons do "stack-up". I do not think that the reasoning lacks cogency. It was a matter of commercial and economic judgment as to whether Whitbread with Stella Artois would lack sufficient viability and independence to eliminate the consequences of the duopoly. The Commission was entitled to take the view that the dual capacity of Interbrew would inhibit competition of sufficient vigour to eliminate the evils following from the duopoly. Whether Whitbread would be a viable business and a strong competitor was a matter upon which more than one view could be held. Mr Richmond took the opposite view. But the majority was entitled to take the view that the undertakings to which Mr Richmond referred (see 2.211) would be insufficient. After all, it had already rejected behavioural remedies as being insufficient and difficult, if not impossible, to enforce."[87]

Moses J. also rejected the "balance" argument on the ground that, in the Commission's view, the required divestiture was the only effective and available remedy. As such, it did not offend the test of proportionality that the restriction employed should be no more than is necessary to accomplish the objective.[88]

---

[86] *Interbrew*, cited above.

[87] *Interbrew*, cited above, at p.22.

[88] This requirement of "proportionality" of the remedy is in some respects a specificity of this case. The merger was subject to the EC Merger Regulation but was referred to the Commission following a reference back from the EC Commission under Art.9 of the EC

Another broad category of reasons challenges rests upon the starker proposition that the reasoning is inadequate due to the failure of the relevant authority to give proper reasons at all. In a departure from the previous regime, the Enterprise Act introduced a requirement for the OFT, the Commission and the Secretary of State to publish reasons for the majority of the decisions that they make under the merger control regime.[89] It is also likely that these bodies are subject to an obligation under common law, in addition to this new statutory duty, to provide reasons on the grounds of fairness in respect of the majority of the decisions they make.

In the *IBA Health* case, the Court of Appeal was careful to draw a distinction between the level of reasoning required in the OFT's decision letter and that which might ultimately be put before the CAT in order to permit it to exercise its power of review:

10.018

> "The question for the Tribunal was not whether the reasoning was adequately expressed in the decision, but whether the material ultimately before it, taken as a whole, disclosed grounds on which the Tribunal could reasonably have reached the decision it did."[90]

With regard to the case law governing the adequacy of reasons generally, it is suggested that where the Enterprise Act imposes a duty to give reasons, the decision maker should ensure that the decision letter contains sufficient reasoning to enable any would-be applicant to understand why the principal issues in dispute have been determined in the way they have.[91] However, when the matter comes before the CAT, it will be beholden upon the regulator to provide a standard of reasoning that is adequate to satisfy the CAT that any discretion that was exercised was reasonable and objectively justified by the relevant facts.[92] It follows that unnecessary challenges may be avoided if the level of explanation provided in the initial decision letter is sufficiently high to meet that latter standard.

Error of Fact

Error of fact is a controversial category which, whilst arguably yet to comprise an independent ground for review in its own right, underpins challenges advanced on other bases.[93] A helpful indication of the scope and

10.019

Merger Regulation. In such circumstances, Art.9(8) imposes a requirement only to take those measures that are strictly necessary to safeguard or restore effective competition. That said, the requirement of proportionality can also arise because of human rights considerations: see further paras 10.020 *et seq.*, below.

[89] For example, see s.107(4) of the Enterprise Act.

[90] The Court of Appeal's *IBA Health* judgment, cited above, at para.106 as per Carnwath L.J.

[91] *Bolton Metropolitan Borough Council v Secretary of State for the Environment* [1995] 3 P.L.R. 37 at 43 C as *per* Lloyd L.J. at 48 D; see also *R. v Brent Borough Council Ex p. Baruwa* (1997) 29 H.L.R. 915 as *per* Schiemann L.J. at 929 who held that the authority "is required to give reasons which are proper, adequate and intelligible and enable the person affected to know why they have won or lost".

[92] The Court of Appeal's judgment in *IBA Health*, cited above, at para.45.

[93] A particular exception to the proposition that error of fact is not an independent head of challenge is where the establishment of the fact concerned bears upon the jurisdiction of the subject authority.

application of this head of challenge in the context of merger control was given by the Vice-Chancellor in the *IBA Health* judgment, who referred to the House of Lord's judgment in *Education Secretary v Thameside BC*[94]:

> "If a judgment requires, before it can be made, the existence of some facts, then, although the evaluation of those facts is for the Secretary of State alone, the court must inquire whether those facts exist, and have been taken into account, whether the judgment has been made upon a proper self-direction as to those facts, whether the judgment has not been made upon other facts which ought not to have been taken into account."

Similarly, in *IBA Health* Carnwath L.J. emphasised that the intensity of review would depend upon the circumstances of the case but that, with regard to the distinction between issues of law and fact as considered in *Edwards v Bairstow*, it was not beholden upon the Competition Appeal Tribunal to avoid dealing with issues that turned upon questions of fact[95]:

> "But there is no reason to make a mystery about the subjects that commissioners deal with or to invite the courts to impose any exceptional restraints upon themselves because they are dealing with cases that arise out of facts found by commissioners. Their duty is no more than to examine those facts with a decent respect for the tribunal appealed from and if they think that the only reasonable conclusion on the facts found is inconsistent with the determination come to, to say so without more ado."

It is suggested that the CAT is likely to draw authority from such passages to permit it to examine the factual basis of merger decisions, in particular, whether the relevant facts are sufficiently found, whether they have been taken into account and/or disregarded as appropriate and, ultimately, whether they are consistent with the decision reached. Moreover, as a specialist tribunal[96] whose role is expressly envisaged by Parliament as an integral part of the merger review process, the CAT will be inclined to undertake such analysis, in contrast to the Administrative Court which gave every indication that in its view such matters were best left to the realm of the expert regulators save in the face of glaring legal or procedural error. In this connection, the CAT observed in its *IBA Health (costs)* judgment in response to the OFT's submission that a large part of IBA Health's costs should not be recoverable as it "impermissibly approached the case as a challenge to the OFT's decision rather than an application for a review"[97] that:

---

[94] See the Court of Appeal's judgment in *IBA Health*, cited above, at para.45 with reference to *Education Secretary v Tameside MBC* [1977] A.C. 1014 at 1047 *per* Wilberforce L.J.

[95] See the Court of Appeal's judgment in *IBA Health*, cited above, at para.96 with reference to *Edwards v Bairstow* [1956] A.C. 14.

[96] The Court of Appeal has characterised the Tribunal as "an expert and specialist tribunal, specifically constituted by Parliament to make judgments in an area in which judges have no expertise", *Napp Pharmaceutical Holdings Limited v Director General of Fair Trading* [2002] EWCA Civ. 796; [2002] 4 All E.R. 376; judgment of May 8, 2002 (Times Law Reports, June 26, 2002) *per* Buxton L.J. at para.34.

[97] *IBA Health Limited v Office of Fair Trading* [2004] CAT 6 at para.50.

"It is trite law that applications for judicial review are not principally concerned with disputes of fact but rather with issues of law and process. That said, applications for judicial review arise in a wide variety of statutory contexts. In the particular statutory context of the 2002 Act cases are likely to arise in which the underlying 'factual matrix' of the case is complicated, as was the case here.

When the Tribunal is called upon to consider whether there was material on which the OFT could reach the views that it did, whether material considerations have been left out and so on, it is important that it has been provided with, and understands, the facts."[97A]

Human Rights

The OFT, Competition Commission and Secretary of State are public authorities for the purposes of the Human Rights Act 1998 ("HRA") and are therefore obliged to act in a manner that is compatible with rights arising under the European Convention of Human Rights ("ECHR").[98] The victim[99] of a breach of such an obligation may rely upon it as a head of challenge for a statutory review under s.120 of the Enterprise Act.[1] As a relevant court for the purposes of the HRA, the CAT is required to have regard to (but not necessarily follow) the jurisprudence of the European Court of Human Rights when determining matters that have arisen in connection with a right arising under the Convention.[2] Moreover, the CAT will be required to construe Pt 3 of the Enterprise Act (and any other relevant legislation that governs the powers of relevant decision-makers in the mergers sphere) in a manner that is compatible with Convention rights in so far as it is possible to do so.[3]

There are a number of Convention rights that are potentially relevant to the merger control process, including the right to the peaceful enjoyment of possessions (Art.1 of Protocol 1); the right to a fair trial (Art.6); and the right to respect for one's private life (Art.8). It is important to note at the outset that, whilst all the rights recognised in the Convention may be described as fundamental rights, not all are equal in their status. The practical effect of this is that some rights (including Art.8[4]) are "qual-

10.020

[97A] *IBA Health (Costs)* (cited above), at paras 51–52.
[98] It is also almost certainly the case that the merger control procedures of the OFT and the Commission are required to comply with human rights legislation. It is questionable whether many of these procedures, as they stand, are fully compliant. In particular, the absence of a right of access to the Commission's file seems to fall short of the requirements of Art.6 of the European Convention on Human Rights. However, such failures may well be "cured" by the availability of appeal rights. Against that background the need for active involvement by the Tribunal where questions of human rights are at stake, for instance because the Commission has relied on third party evidence which the parties had no knowledge of, would seem all the more imperative and inherent to the structure of the merger regime.
[99] A corporate body may qualify as a victim (*Autronic AG v Switzerland* [1990] 12 E.H.R.R. 485).
[1] See s.7(1)(b) of the HRA.
[2] See s.2(1) of the HRA 1998.
[3] See s.3(1) of the HRA 1998.
[4] Whilst the matter is not settled, the English courts are of the view that the right to a fair hearing under Art.6 has more in common with those rights which are "absolute" than those which may be qualified: see *Brown v Stott* (PC) [2001] 2 W.L.R. 817 at 825.

ified rights" and the protection they afford may be restricted, although any such restriction must be legitimate, necessary, proportionate and refrain from engendering discriminatory effects. In particular, Art. 8 is expressly stated to apply subject to a wider consideration of where the overall balance of the public interest lies. In practice, this means that regulators and practitioners will have to carry out a careful assessment with regard to the circumstances of each case as to whether guaranteed Convention rights have in fact been infringed.

The right to peaceful enjoyment of possessions

10.021 The principal manifestation of this right is generally to limit any interference by a public authority in the exercise of its statutory powers with private property to measures that are connected to the statutory objective and which are no greater than necessary to accomplish that objective (the so called "proportionality principle").[5] The Administrative Court accepted the relevance of proportionality in principle in the *Interbrew* case although, as noted above, it is perhaps more appropriately seen as an aspect of irrationality.[5A] The CAT has also noted its potential application to the statutory review process in the *IBA Health* case without determining the matter.[6]

The right to a fair trial

10.022 Article 6(1) of the Convention includes the requirement that a determination of a party's civil rights and obligations should be subject to a fair and public hearing, held within a reasonable time and before an independent and impartial tribunal established by law. The courts have yet to determine whether regulatory decisions in connection with merger control may properly be considered to involve the determination of a party's "*civil rights*" and that Art.6(1) will apply.[7] However, it is questionable whether (in the absence of the right to statutory review under s.120) the procedures of the OFT and the Commission would comply with Art.6(1). In this connection, particular areas of concern would be the fact that the Commission (whilst not instigating an inquiry) both investigates and adjudicates upon the competitive impact of a merger, the parties do not have a right of access to the Commission's file[8] and

---

[5] See the analysis of Moses J. in *Interbrew SA and Interbrew UK Holdings Ltd v Competition Commission and Secretary of State for Trade and Industry* [2001] EWHC Admin 367 at pp. 10 to 12; [2001] U.K.C.L.R. 954.

[5A] See nn.83 and 89 above.

[6] See *Interbrew*, cited above; see also *IBA Health* at para.222.

[7] See *Ringeisen v Austria (No.1)* [1970] 1 E.H.R.R. 455 at para.91 where the European Court of Human Rights confirmed that Art.6(1) will include "all proceedings the result of which is decisive for private rights and obligations" and that the character of the "authority which is invested with jurisdiction in the matter (ordinary court, administrative body, etc.) [is] therefore of little consequence"). The extent to which decisions by the OFT to refer a matter to the Commission are subject to Art.6(1) is less clear as, in procedural terms, a decision to refer is not determinative of the matter in issue, although conversely a decision not to refer is determinative.

[8] In contrast to merger proceedings under the EC Merger Regulation, and proceedings under the Competition Act 1998, the parties under investigation have no right to review evidence and submissions collected or received by the decision-maker in the course of its investigation, but must rely on the Commission's discretion to pass relevant material (or extracts or summaries of such material) to them for comment.

the Enterprise Act merely requires the OFT and Commission where practicable to "consult" relevant parties[9] rather than afford a full hearing in which the regulator's arguments might be fully tested.[10] Finally, the Commission's practice in holding hearings is to put questions to and elicit responses from the business representatives who are present rather than permit their legal representatives to take a leading role in answering questions on their clients' behalf.[11]

Areas of concern such as these prompt the question as to whether the availability of overriding judicial control in the form of a statutory review, even where this does not involve a full re-hearing, is capable of curing an administrative procedure that in itself does not comply with Art.6(1).[12] The answer will depend upon the details of the procedure employed in each case and the issues at stake (for example disputes of primary fact as opposed to disputes relating to the assessment of such facts), but relevant case law suggests that the regulators should take particular care to ensure that, in so far as practicable, the initial phases of the decision-making process satisfy the requirements of Art.6. This is particularly the case given the restatement by the Court of Appeal in *IBA Health* that the CAT's statutory review procedure is restricted to judicial review and does not afford it discretion to reconsider the merits of the case.[13] Particular issues will arise in connection with the need to give the parties an opportunity to test objections that have been raised by the regulator or third parties, particularly where there is no access to the regulator's file, as this is an important aspect of the Art.6 right to equality of arms.[14]

---

[9] Relevant parties are those who control the undertakings subject to the reference. A relevant decision includes both a decision by the OFT whether or not to make a reference and a decision by the Commission as to whether or not a relevant merger situation has arisen and, if it has, whether it results in a substantial lessening of competition (see s.104 of the Act).

[10] However, Sch.12 to the Act allows the Commission to make rules to make provision for interested parties to be heard, cross-examine witnesses or otherwise take part in hearings before the Commission.

[11] See Ch.5, above at para.5.043.

[12] See *Albert and Le Compte v Belgium* [1983] 5 E.H.R.R. 533 at para.9 where the Court stated that it is necessary that "either the jurisdictional organs themselves comply with the requirements of Art. 6(1), or they do not so comply but are subject to subsequent control by a judicial body that has full jurisdiction and does provide the guarantees of Art. 6(1)"; see also *R. v Environment Secretary Ex p. Alconbury Limited* (HL (E)) [2001] 2 W.L.R. at 1416 *per* Hoffman L.J. at para.87. See also *Runa Begum v Tower Hamlets LBC* (HL (E)) [2003] 2 W.L.R. 388 *per* Bingham L.J. at para.5.

[13] This conclusion would appear to be consistent with *Alconbury* where the House of Lords appeared to place considerable weight upon the fact that the administrative stage of the system of planning control paid due regard to (and observed in substance if not in form) many of the Art.6(1) rights themselves.

[14] See the surprise expressed by the Vice-Chancellor at para.72 of the Court of Appeal's judgment in *IBA Health* (cited above) that the complainant was not given the opportunity to comment upon the issues letter produced by the OFT. The "equality of arms" principle is derived from Art.6(1) which, broadly, requires a party whose civil rights are to be determined:

   (a)   to be afforded equal access to evidence before the court (see *McMichael v UK* [1995] 20 E.H.R.R. 205);

   (b)   to have a "reasonable opportunity of presenting his case to the court under conditions which do not place him at substantial disadvantage *vis-à-vis* his opponent" (see, *e.g. De Haes and Gijsels v Belgium* [1998] 25 E.H.R.R. 1 para.53);

An additional obligation arises when the regulator is responsible for applying Community law, for example, when it is given jurisdiction to consider a merger following a reference back to the UK by the European Commission under Art.9 of the EC Merger Regulation, it will be required to observe the various fundamental rights which form part of the body of general principles of European law. These will include the "rights of the defence" which, following their application by the European courts, have done much to define the merger control procedure of the European Commission.[15] In contrast, when the Competition Commission or the OFT are applying the national merger control regime, it remains unclear whether they are bound to observe these "general principles" of European law although, at the time of writing, the CAT has indicated that they may be of potential relevance.[16]

The right to respect for one's private life (Article 8)

10.023   Under the Enterprise Act, both the OFT and the Competition Commission are given wide powers to investigate markets and require parties to the merger (and relevant third parties) to produce information for the purposes of that investigation. However, the extent to which Art.8 is likely materially to affect the investigative powers of the UK's merger regulators is questionable.[17] As noted above, Art.8 is a qualified right and its scope therefore falls to be balanced against wider public interest considerations. Accordingly, it would be reasonable to anticipate that the

---

(c)   to be afforded access to the records and documents which are relied on by the court (*Lynas v Switzerland* [1977] 10 Y.B. 412, 445–446); and

(d)   to have the opportunity to make copies of the relevant documents from the court file. (see P van Dijk and G van Hoof, *Theory and Practice of the European Convention of Human Rights* (3rd ed., Kluwer, 1998) pp.430–431; relying on *Schüler-Zgraggen v Switzerland* [1993] 16 E.H.R.R. 405).

[15] In Case 322/81, *Michelin v Commission* [1983] E.C.R. 3461, the rights of the defence were recognised as a fundamental principle of European Community law. The rights of the defence ensure that parties have the right to respond to a statement of objections prepared by the European Commission and have access to the European Commission's file. In the context of proceedings under Arts 81 and 82 of the EC Treaty, the ECJ has confirmed the right of access to all documents save for documents containing business secrets and internal Commission documents: see Case C–310/93P *BPB Industries plc and British Gypsum Ltd v Commission* [1995] E.C.R. I–865 para.25; see also *BASF v Commission* (Case T–305/94) [1999] E.C.R. II–931.

[16] See the CAT's judgment in *IBA Health*, cited above, at para.222; see also the comments of Laws J. in *R. v Ministry of Agriculture, Fisheries and Food Ex p. First City Trading Limited* [1997] 1 C.M.L.R. 250.

[17] See Case C–94/2000 *Roquette Freres* [2002] E.C.R. I-9011 at para.52 where, in the context of a European Commission investigation under Art.14(3) of Reg.17/62, the ECJ restated the obligation upon the national court to ensure that any interference with private property rights pursuant to the exercise by the competition authority of coercive investigative powers was not disproportionate or arbitrary with regard to the subject matter of the investigation. The potential for investigations to conflict with human rights law has already arisen in other contexts, notably in the case of *Societe Colas Est v France* (2004) 39 E.H.R.R. 17. In that case, agents of the French National Investigation Office had seized documents from the applicant companies' offices. The European Court of Human Rights held that Art.8 may under certain circumstances be construed as conferring on companies the right to respect for their business premises, and that it was therefore necessary to determine whether the National Investigation Office's interference with this right was justified under Art.8(2).

primary effect of Art.8 in the realm of merger control will be to ensure that the OFT and Commission exercise their powers of investigation in a manner that is necessary, reasonable and proportionate to the objectives concerned. In addition, once the relevant regulator has obtained the information, the Convention will re-enforce the obligation upon it to ensure that the requisite standards of confidentiality are observed.[18]

Costs

Rule 55(2) of the Tribunal's Rules provides: **10.024**

> "The Tribunal may, at its discretion, at any stage of the proceedings make any order it thinks fit in relation to the payment of costs by one party to another in respect of the whole or part of the proceedings. In determining how much the parties are required to pay, the Tribunal may take account of the conduct of all parties in relation to the proceedings."

In decisions under the Competition Act 1998 the CAT has held that Rule 55(2):

> ". . . gives the Tribunal a wide discretion on the question of costs to be exercised in the particular circumstances of the case. There is no explicit rule before the Tribunal that costs follow the event, nor is there any rule that costs are payable only when a party has behaved unreasonably. All will depend on the particular circumstances of the case."[19]

In *FWD v OFT* the CAT stated that:

> "In broad terms, some of the considerations that have emerged in the Tribunal's previous case law apply, in our judgment, to applications under section 120 of the 2002 Act. It is important in our view that we should not frustrate the objectives of the 2002 Act by making orders for costs in a way that might deter appellants or would have a chilling effect on the development of this jurisdiction."[20]

The CAT went on to decide that, in the circumstances of that case (in which the FWD sought permission to withdraw its application) the FWD should bear 25 per cent of the OFT's costs which the CAT calculated to be approximately equivalent to the OFT's external disbursements, leaving the OFT bear its own internal costs, and that the FWD (the applicant) and Tesco (the intevener) should bear their own costs. The CAT observed that "to some extent, in a case such as this and in the early stages of this new regime, we regard the internal costs incurred by the OFT as part of the general costs of the system."[21]

---

[18] Under the Act the OFT and Commission are under a duty to ensure that information relating to the affairs of an individual or the business of an undertaking is not disclosed without permission save, in particular, where such disclosure is required for facilitating their statutory functions (see ss.237 to 245 of the Act and paras 3.078 *et seq.* of Ch.3, above).

[19] *Federation of Wholesale Distributors v OFT*, cited above, at para.36.

[20] *Federation of Wholesale Distributors v OFT*, cited above, at para.38.

[21] *Federation of Wholesale Distributors v OFT*, cited above, at para.49.

In its judgment on costs in the *IBA Health case*,[22] the CAT set out a number of important principles that should be applied in determining costs applications under the Enterprise Act:

(i)   as is the case under the Competition Act 1998, there is no presumption under Rule 55 that costs should be borne by the losing party; Parliament had created no such presumption; and in the case of applications for review in respect of a decision by the OFT to clear a merger, such a rule would run the serious risk of frustrating the objectives of the 2002 Act by deterring potential applicants who may be much smaller than the merging parties;

(ii)   "different considerations are likely to apply where an unfounded application is brought by a corporate appellant with significant financial resources at its disposal"[23];

(iii)   where the OFT is unsuccessful, there should be no general principle that it should be liable to pay costs only if it has been guilty of manifest error or unreasonable behaviour, although the OFT should not be discouraged from standing by apparently sound administrative decisions made in the public interest by "fear of exposure to undue financial prejudice"[24] if the decision is successfully challenged. By the same token, in light of the high costs of litigation, it would be unsatisfactory if the risk of having to pay large orders for costs for having defended an application under s.120(4) were to adversely affect the performance by the OFT of its statutory functions;

(iv)   a range of factors may be relevant to the question of what, if any, order for costs should be made including: "whether the applicant has succeeded to a significant extent on the basis of new material introduced after the OFT's decision, whether resources have been devoted to particular issues on which the appellant has not succeeded, or which were not germane to the solution of the case, whether there is unnecessary duplication or prolixity, whether evidence adduced is of peripheral relevance, or whether, in whatever respect, the conduct of the successful party has been unreasonable . . ."[25]; and

(v)   generally the costs of an intervention should lie where they fall, with the costs of the intervention being borne by the intervener. However, where a large and well-resourced intervener has unsuccessfully intervened, the CAT may, where appropriate, order such interveners to pay the additional costs incurred by an applicant in addressing the issues raised by that intervention.

The CAT expressed the hope that ". . . applications for review under the 2002 Act may, in general, be expected to generate somewhat less expense

---

[22] See *IBA Health (Costs)* (cited above), which related to the cost of proceedings before the CAT. In relation to the proceedings before the Court of Appeal, the Court of Appeal ordered the OFT and iSOFT to pay 75 per cent of IBA's costs: see [2004] EWCA Civ. 142.
[23] *IBA Health (Costs)* (cited above), at para.38.
[24] *IBA Health (Costs)* (cited above), at para.40.
[25] *IBA Health (Costs)* (cited above), at para.42.

than penalty appeals under the 1998 Act, which may by their nature require a full investigation of the merits of the OFT's decision, including substantial evidential issues."[26] On the facts of the case, the CAT ordered the OFT to pay 82.5 per cent of IBA's costs, and iSOFT and Torex to pay 15 per cent and 2.5 per cent respectively.

Conclusion

Both the statutory review procedure and the wider field of human rights law **10.025**
introduce increasing opportunities for the courts to monitor and, where necessary, intervene in the UK merger control process. Whilst these opportunities are properly seen as recent legal developments, it is the case that the underlying principles governing both forms of judicial supervision have, in many instances, been present for a number of years. In this regard, the High Court has for many years had the power to strike down decisions of the Competition Commission where it has been found to have acted unlawfully. Similarly, many of the elements of the right to a fair hearing, such as the requirement for the parties not to be "faced with a bolt from the blue", have impressive English common law pedigrees.[27]

However, the introduction of the specialist CAT and the statutory review process under s.120 of the Enterprise Act, together with the crystallisation and development of fundamental rights under the HRA 1998, should lead to more pro-active judicial control of the UK merger control process. This is not to anticipate a flood of challenges to decisions of the OFT or the Commission; nevertheless, the ability to test the regulators' decisions in such a manner is likely to be an increasingly important factor in any modern mergers practice, whether it arises in the context of a substantive challenge, regulatory negotiation or the determination of procedural fairness.

---

[26] *IBA Health (Costs)* (cited above), at para.43.
[27] *Ex p. Matthew Brown*, cited above, *per* Macpherson J. at 469.

CHAPTER 11

CONCLUSIONS

11.001   When the first edition of this book was published in 1995, the FTA regime had been in place for some 20 years and there was a large body of MMC reports and established OFT practice (with some judicial guidance) upon which day-to-day merger practice and regulatory decision-making were based. By contrast, at the time of writing this second edition, the Enterprise Act had been in force for a little over a year and although in many ways it is "business as usual" for the regulators and practitioners involved in this field, there are some key areas of the law and practice which are new and as yet untested.

The changes introduced by the Act which caught the headlines were perhaps not those which practitioners in the field regarded as being the most radical. The removal of ministerial involvement in all but a few cases was an important reform in principle, and is certainly to be welcomed, but in practice ministers followed the advice and recommendations of the competition authorities in the vast majority of cases under the FTA. The change from a public interest test to a competition-based test was, again, a major reform in principle, but in practice the OFT had been advising the Secretary of State on the basis of whether a merger would be expected to lead to a substantial lessening of competition for a number of years. The residual role of the Secretary of State to intervene in mergers raising media plurality and defence/national security issues is uncontroversial, and is consistent with the ability of Member States to protect their legitimate interests under Art.21 of the EC Merger Regulation. It is to be hoped that these powers will be used sparingly and in clear cut cases. Perhaps the two areas which practitioners were watching most closely were the significant changes to the Competition Commission's role and procedures—in particular the introduction of published provisional findings prior to a review of potential remedies—and the approach to be adopted by the CAT in reviewing the decisions of the OFT and Competition Commission, in light of the detailed forensic approach it has taken in hearing appeals under the Competition Act 1998.

As events have unfolded, the focus on the role of the CAT was particularly appropriate. *IBA Health*[1] was the most important case in the UK merger field for many years and put under the spotlight both the role of the OFT in filtering cases for a second stage review by the Competition Commission and the role of the CAT itself in exercising its new power to review merger decisions under the Act. The general view of practitioners

---

[1] *IBA Health Limited v Office of Fair Trading, supported by iSOFT PLC and Torex PLC* [2003] CAT 27 (CAT judgment); *Office of Fair Trading v IBA Health Limited* [2004] EWCA Civ. 142 (Court of Appeal judgment).

of the CAT's judgment in *IBA Health* was that it risked emasculating the OFT by rendering it a first stage filter whose role was simply to distinguish between those cases that very clearly raised no issues at all and those cases which, even if the OFT did not perceive them to merit a reference, could be the subject of a credible counter view. In this connection, it was widely thought that the CAT's approach could lead to a chilling of merger activity in the UK compared with other merger regimes in Europe and the USA. The Court of Appeal's judgment, which did not overturn the outcome reached by the CAT but crucially overruled the CAT's reasoning on the substantive test for reference, is generally regarded as having put the regime back onto a workable footing but also raised important questions about evidence, reasoning and the depth of the OFT's investigation. Experience suggests that following the Court of Appeal's judgment, the speed of the OFT's review of merger cases has reduced. This has had the consequence that the OFT will generally be the slowest regulator to grant clearance in a complex case requiring multi-jurisdictional filings, where similar issues are raised in the various countries where notification and clearance is required. Most importantly though, the question remains whether, post-*IBA Health*, the OFT is more likely to make a reference to the Commission in circumstances where previously it would have weighed potentially conflicting evidence and decided on balance to clear a merger. It is suggested that in such borderline cases a reference is now more likely to be made, particularly where there is conflicting evidence.[2]

The key outstanding question in relation to the CAT's role under the Act is whether it will develop a body of procedural law to be applied by the Competition Commission in merger cases as it has done for the OFT in relation to its decisions under the Competition Act. There is no access to the file during the Competition Commission's investigation and in the absence of clear procedural failings, for example, consultation on remedies, the concern most often expressed by parties that have been through the Competition Commission's processes and have had their transaction prohibited is that they disagreed with the weighting that was given to the evidence relied upon by the Commission. The question of the standard of proof is an important one, and is inevitably more difficult in relation to proposed mergers where the Commission is engaging in a prospective analysis as to what is likely to occur, compared with the role of the OFT under the Competition Act which is obliged to establish on the basis of clear and compelling evidence that an infringement has occurred.[3] Under the FTA, the High Court showed little willingness to engage in a process of reviewing the weighing of conflicting evidence by the Commission in its merger reports, provided that the investigative process was fair. If the CAT adopts a similar approach to its review of Competition Commission decisions under the Enterprise Act, its main focus in merger cases may well be

---

[2] The OFT's Annual Plan 2004/2005 would appear to support this view: see para.4.007 of Ch.4.

[3] *Napp Pharmaceutical Holdings Limited v Director General of Fair Trading* [2002] CAT 1; [2002] Comp. A. R. 13 at para.109. The question of standard of proof under the Competition Act 1998 has most recently been considered by the CAT in *JJB Sports plc and Allsports Limited v Office of Fair Trading* [2004] CAT 17 (judgment of October 1, 2004), not yet reported.

the decision making of the OFT in deciding to clear or refer a merger or accept undertakings in lieu of reference. It is suggested that such an outcome would be unfortunate, as it would have the effect of increasing uncertainty for the merging parties at the OFT stage, for example, as a result of a judicial review application by a disgruntled competitor, whilst removing the incentive imposed by robust judicial scrutiny for vigorous evidential evaluation by the Commission.

11.002   To some extent the criticism of the OFT by the CAT in the *IBA Health* case was a consequence of the very rapid timetable adopted by the CAT in reviewing the OFT's clearance decision. In that case the CAT concluded as a matter of case management that significant disclosure was not possible because of the urgency of the case. It therefore focussed primarily on the reasoning contained in the OFT's clearance decision which it considered to be inadequate in light of the OFT's issues letter. It is likely that the OFT's reasoning, as revealed by its case file had disclosure been permitted, would have been much more detailed. It is not clear that if the CAT had adopted a slower timetable which provided for the possibility of disclosure by the OFT, the parties would have objected. The CAT's approach in *IBA Health* may be contrasted with its approach under the Competition Act where it has required disclosure and/or encouraged voluntary disclosure to be made[4] and was concerned to take "small steps" with the consequence that in the *Claymore* case[5] the OFT's non-infringement decision was effectively written during the course of the proceedings before the CAT. Fast tracking merger review cases also raises important questions of priority and of the appropriate allocation of public resources, particularly where the CAT's caseload is high; although merger cases are often important commercially and are generally subject to short commercial timetables, it is appropriate to raise the question as to whether they have any greater inherent importance than other competition cases, particularly those by complainants who may face a threat of potentially irreversible eviction from a market in the face of allegedly abusive behaviour by a dominant undertaking. A further question for the future in relation to the CAT will be to see how the Chancery Judges, who have been appointed to the panel of Chairmen of the CAT, approach judicial review in merger cases and in particular whether they continue the traditional "hands-off" approach of the High Court in judicial review applications under the FTA.

Many of the procedural innovations adopted by the OFT and the Competition Commission in light of the Enterprise Act should make a valuable contribution to the robustness of decisions. These include the OFT providing the merging parties with an issues letter in advance of the issues meeting and inviting an unconnected OFT official from another branch to play the role of "devil's advocate" in case review meetings. It is also welcome that the OFT now publishes all decisions (having started the process of publishing some decisions in 2001), including cases where a

---

[4] See, for example *Aquavitae (UK) Limited v The Director General of the Office Of Water Services* [2003] CAT 4; [2003] Comp. A.R. 197 (judgment on disclosure), which discusses the CAT's general approach to disclosure as well as the approach taken in earlier proceedings between *Freeserve v Director General of Telecommunications*.

[5] See the Chapter II appeal proceedings between *Claymore Dairies Limited and Arla Foods UK plc v Office of Fair Trading*, Case 1008/2/1/02, not yet decided.

merger is found not to qualify (which helps to increase transparency as to jurisdictional issues). Similarly, it is helpful that the Commission now publishes draft provisional findings, so the parties to the merger and third parties know the case and key supporting facts for or against the merger, although this falls short of full access to the file. The practice of publishing provisional findings also has the benefit of ensuring that remedies are no longer discussed on a wholly hypothetical basis, as was the situation under the FTA, where the parties did not know whether an adverse finding had been reached, or indeed the precise adverse effects (if any) that the hypothetical remedies were intended to address. The OFT's and Commission's substantive assessment guidelines are also a welcome development, although it would be helpful if the inconsistencies between the two sets of guidelines could be addressed when they are next revised, and references to relevant cases are introduced to illustrate how issues have been dealt with in practice, as is the case for many of the European Commission's notices adopted under the EC Merger Regulation.

Another area that is of particular interest in relation to the development of the new UK merger control regime is the approach the Competition Commission will adopt in connection with remedies. The anticipated greater use of behavioural remedies suggested by the current Chairman, Professor Paul Geroski, is likely to be generally welcomed, particularly if it results in proportionate steps being taken to remedy adverse effects so that transactions may be permitted to proceed. However, as explained in Ch.9, the Commission's approach to date in connection with behavioural remedies has not been entirely consistent.[6] A central question in connection with the suitability of behavioural remedies compared with prohibition will be the approach taken by the Commission, and by the CAT in its review of Commission decisions, to proportionality. It is likely to be the case that arguments as to proportionality will form a central part of applications for review of prohibition decisions of the Commission or indeed adversely affected third parties who perceive the Commission as having been too lenient in adopting behavioural remedies. A similar issue arises in connection with the proposed introduction of "crown jewels" provisions and in particular whether such a remedy would go beyond the identification of the adverse effects on competition with the consequence that they would run the risk of infringing the principle set out in the *Thomson Holidays* case.[7]

An issue that is likely to become the focus of considerable attention is the decision to review merger fees. Merger fees have been static since 1990 and the number of mergers subject to investigation following the changes in the jurisdictional thresholds introduced by the Enterprise Act has fallen. It is therefore not surprising that the DTI and Treasury are considering changing the fee regime. However, it is suggested that it would be a mistake to seek to recover the cost of Competition Commission investigations in full from

---

[6] Compare the rejection of behavioural remedies in the *Scottish Radio Holdings plc and GWR Group plc/Galaxy Radio Wales and the West Limited*, Cm. 5811 (May 2003) with their acceptance in *Carlton Communications plc and Granada plc*, Cm. 5952 (October 2003); see Ch.9.

[7] *R. v Secretary of State for Trade and Industry Ex p. Thomson Holidays* [2000] U.K.C.L.R. 189, *The Times*, January 12, 2000.

the parties; statutory fees of £300,000[8] or more for a Commission inquiry, as are proposed in the DTI's August 2004 consultation document,[9] are likely to be prohibitive except in relation to the largest transactions. In this connection, if statutory fees are to be imposed for the second stage of a merger review in the UK, the need for the OFT to overhaul its procedures in connection with undertakings in lieu of reference becomes even more important; it is suggested that a weakness in the current regime is the fact that there is no real opportunity for the parties at the OFT stage to have a full and frank discussion with the OFT in light of the OFT's decision to refer a merger to the Competition Commission, a lacuna which stands in stark contrast to the approach now adopted by the Commission of publishing its provisional findings before discussing remedies with the parties.

The recent "peer review" conducted by the DTI[10] to evaluate the relative standing of the UK competition regime indicated that it was placed third behind the USA and Germany. Prior to the *IBA Health* case, practitioners generally perceived the Mergers Branch of the OFT to be the "jewel in the crown", which is not surprising given that it has been long established under the FTA compared with the very recent creation of the various branches which handle cases under the Competition Act 1998. The peer review showed that effective decision making (*i.e.* "getting it right") was given a particularly high weighting by respondents, and it is inevitable that there is some conflict between that objective and the aims of speed and low cost. There is also a clear difficulty in comparing different regimes. In Germany the jurisdictional thresholds for merger control are purely financial and notification is mandatory so that a very large number of mergers which raise no competition issues are caught each year; many of these mergers would not have been notified under the UK regime either because they would not have qualified for investigation or because the parties would have decided to proceed to completion without seeking clearance. The efficiency with which these uncontroversial cases were reviewed and cleared has no parallel in the UK. In Germany in 2003, 1,341 mergers were reviewed by the Bundeskartellamt, of which 35 or 2.6 per cent required a second stage investigation. In the UK, the OFT reviewed 117 cases in 2003/2004, of which 12 or 10.2 per cent were referred to the Competition Commission.[11] In the USA, the first stage of the merger review process is generally regarded as imposing a minimal burden on the parties in terms of submissions, but second stage investigations impose very onerous disclosure requirements and significant costs on the parties, together with potentially very long delays before clearance is achieved. It is not clear that this system is preferable to the UK framework in terms of costs and efficiency.

11.003   By way of summary, it is suggested that the decision making framework adopted by the Enterprise Act, with an independent second-stage review conducted by the Competition Commission subject to specialist judicial

---

[8] See para.4.011 of Ch.4 for a discussion of the cost to the public purse of a reference to the Competition Commission.
[9] *Merger Fees: Consultation on possible changes to the system of charging firms for the costs of merger control*; August 2004, URN04/1419.
[10] DTI's *Peer Review of Competition Policy*, May 17, 2004.
[11] See Table 2 of App.2.

review by the CAT and the absence of Ministerial involvement except in national security and media plurality cases is essentially robust and difficult to improve upon. The key questions arise in connection with how judgments are made by each of these bodies and the procedures which they adopt. There is inevitably a tension in merger cases between speed and thoroughness at all stages of the process, including before the CAT. Ultimately the quality of decision making will reflect the skill and experience of those involved and any prescription at this stage would be relatively mild. It would include simply encouragement to the OFT to apply its undoubted skill and expertise in reaching decisions in borderline cases, and to investigate whether the procedure for accepting undertakings in lieu of a reference to the Competition Commission can be improved upon; that the Competition Commission should continue to develop its procedures to a stage where it is effectively giving access to the file to the parties and there is a greater emphasis on empirical evidence to complement and reinforce clearly set out economic theory[12]; and that the CAT should not be deterred, subject to the limits of the generally applicable principles of judicial review, from reviewing thoroughly the Commission's decision-making including the evidential robustness of its decisions. Finally, the existence of a flexible economy and a dynamic market for corporate control that merger activity entails should not be threatened by the imposition of punitive costs (in the form of merger fees) on those that are considering pursuing their corporate strategies through acquisitions or mergers.

---

[12] The provisional findings of the Commission in the *Archant/INM* inquiry published on July 29, 2004 are encouraging in this regard. In concluding that the merger would not be expected to result in a substantial lessening of competition the Commission stated at para.4.30 that ". . . we did not find sufficient evidence to justify a conclusion that a price increase of 5 per cent by Archant would be profitable, or to find that Archant could price discriminate between customers to bring this about."

NAVIGATING THE WEBSITES OF THE OFT, COMPETITION COMMISSION, COMPETITION APPEAL TRIBUNAL AND DTI

A1.001   Note: the description which follows describes the layout of, and how to navigate around, the websites of the OFT, Competition Commission, Competition Appeal Tribunal and Department of Trade and Industry, based on how those websites were structured at the time of writing (October 2004). It is possible that they will be restructured in the future, in which case the descriptions set out below may no longer be accurate.

THE WEBSITE OF THE OFT

Address: *www.oft.gov.uk*

A1.002   The main navigation bar, at the top of the page, below the OFT banner, outlines the main areas of the OFT's website:

- Consumer information
- Business information
- News and publications
- Adviser resources
- About the OFT

Consumer information

This section deals with the consumer protection work of the OFT and is outside the scope of this book.

Business information

This section essentially covers the competition law-related work of the OFT, including merger control cases under the Enterprise Act 2002 (and also the Fair Trading Act 1973). The main navigation options are set out in a menu which appears when the mouse hovers over "Business information" in the main menu bar. The main menu bar remains visible and the drop down menu for "Business information" therefore remains accessible wherever you are in the OFT's website.

For mergers-related matters, the most important of the options in the drop-down menu are the third and fourth options:

- **Mergers EA02**—Click on "Mergers EA02" from the drop down menu options which appear when you hover on "Business information" in the main menu bar. This will take you to the home page and main menu options for this topic. In addition to the options which are set out below, the main page in this section has links to OFT mergers publications (which may be difficult to locate through the "News and Publications" section of the website, described below). The "Mergers—publications" page lists all publications relevant to merger control, including the OFT's *Procedural Guidance*, its *Substantive Assessment Guidance*, the Merger Notice and accompanying notes, and the OFT's leaflets on merger fees, turnover and use of the prenotifications procedures.

  - **Invitations to comment**—this page contains the most recent invitations to comment which have been issued by the OFT. The list is split between prenotified Merger Notice cases, which are listed first, and other cases, which follow below. At the top of the page is a link to view all current invitations to comment. Invitations to comment whose deadline has passed are not usually displayed on the website.
  - **Decisions**—this page lists the most recent decisions taken by the OFT in relation to merger cases being considered under the Enterprise Act 2002. The list is split between, on the one hand, clearances and referrals to the Competition Commission (which also includes cases where the OFT concluded that the merger was not a qualifying merger under the Act) and, on the other hand, cases where assurances have been given, in partic-ular, undertakings in lieu cases, which follow. At the top of the page is a link to view all cases considered by the OFT to date, in date order starting which the most recent. Again, cases closed with undertakings in lieu are listed separately, at the end of the main list. Each case name is given, together with the date on which a decision was taken, the essence of the decision (*i.e.* cleared; referred; found not to qualify) and a link to the text of the non-confidential version of the reasoned decision (not the announcement of clearance or referral). At the time of writing, all cases were included in a single long list, although it may be in the future that more classification (*e.g.* by year, or by outcome) is introduced to break the list up.
  - **Case lists**—this section lists all cases, divided by year and then listed alphabetically. Choose the year and then the initial letter of one of the parties to the case you are searching for. You will be taken to the list of cases with that initial letter. Click on the one you are searching for. You will be taken to a page summarising key information about in that case (name, date of the decision, nature of the decision including a link to the non-confidential version of the reasoned decision, affected market and SIC code)
  - **EA02 Register of undertakings and orders**—this section reproduces the hard copy public register on-screen and also gives details of how to inspect the public hard copy. The first page in the section shows the cate-gories of undertakings and orders included in the register: initial under-takings; undertakings in lieu of reference, final undertakings, initial orders, orders in lieu of reference, final orders, and a companies index. The latter allows the register to be searched by reference to the party which gave the undertakings or is subject to the order, rather than searching by category of undertaking or order.

- **Mergers FTA**—Click on "Mergers FTA" from the drop down menu options which appear when you hover on "Business information" in the main menu bar. This will take you to the home page and main menu options for this topic. This part of the website contains information about mergers which were handled under the Fair Trading Act 1973. Past advices of the Director

General of Fair Trading to the Secretary of State can be accessed here. The section is divided into sub-sections which broadly mirror the sub-sections of the Mergers EA02 section, with the difference that in addition to "Decisions" (which contains the decisions of the Secretary of State, which are not reasoned) there is a sub-section titled "Advice" which contains the non-confidential version of the reasoned advice of the Director General to the Secretary of State, to the extent that these have been made public (publication was not obligatory).

News and publications

This section covers all of the OFT's work and is a central location from which to find all publications (NB this includes general publications relating to the OFT's mergers work but does not include the OFT's merger decisions which are located, as indicated above, through the "Business information" part of the website).

The main navigation options are set out in a menu which appears when the mouse hovers over "News and publications" in the main menu bar. The main menu bar remains visible and the drop down menu for "News and publications" therefore remains accessible wherever you are in the OFT's website.

For mergers-related matters, the most important of the options in the drop-down menu are the second and third options:

- **Press releases**—this section, as the name indicates, links to all press releases issued by the OFT. They are classified by year and then simply listed for each year (title, date and reference number). Note that "Statements" are listed separately to press releases, and again are classified by year and then listed for each year (title and date).

- **Publications**—the Publications section includes documents which can be downloaded from the internet, as well as details of how to order hard copies. A list of types of publications is set out on the first page of this section. Documents relevant to mergers are classified as "Business leaflets". From the list of categories within this section, choose "Enterprise Act". This will bring up a list of publications related to the Enterprise Act (not simply those relevant to merger control), including *Mergers—Procedural Guidance* and *Mergers—Substantive Assessment Guidance*. Note that other publications relating to mergers are not available in this section of the website—see "Business information" above.

In addition, copies of the OFT's Annual Report can be located in this section, as well as speeches and articles issued by OFT personnel including the Chairman and board members.

Adviser resources

This part of the website seldom contains material relevant to mergers and is not considered further.

About the OFT

The information available in this part of the website includes the following:

- **Who to contact**—this section lists key personnel at the OFT, including under "Competition Enforcement Division", Division CE2 Mergers, which is the Mergers Division. Names and direct telephone numbers are given for senior personnel in this section, as well as for the economists and for general merger inquiries.

- **OFT Board**—this section contains names and biographical details of the OFT Board Members (executive and non-executive), as well as links to minutes of Board meetings, Rules of Procedure for the Board and the Register of Interests.

Searching the OFT's website

At the top left hand of every page of the OFT's website, above the main menu bar, is a link to the search option. There is a also a "Quick search" facility on the top right hand of every page, again above the main menu bar.

Email alerts of new material

An automated email alert system is provided by the OFT, which anyone can subscribe to. It can be accessed through the link "email alerts" at the top left of every page.

THE WEBSITE OF THE COMPETITION COMMISSION

Address: *www.competition-commission.org.uk* A1.003

The main menu to navigate the Competition Commission's website is set out along the top of the page, beneath the Competition Commission's name:

- Home
- Inquiries
- Reports and publications
- Our role
- Our people
- Press releases

Inquiries

This section sets out information about current and past inquiries, including not only merger inquiries (under both the Enterprise Act and the FTA) but also market and any other inquiries (*e.g.* under communications or civil aviation legislation as well). The main division in this section is between "Current inquiries" and "Completed inquiries". "Completed inquiries" are classified by year: note that they are classified according to the date on which the inquiry was completed, not the reference date.

For each inquiry, whether current or completed, clicking on its name links to the homepage for that inquiry. The homepage contains links to all relevant documents for that inquiry, classified as:

- **Core inquiry documents**—key documents issued by the OFT/Competition Commission, including the terms of reference, issues statement, provisional conclusions, notice of possible remedies, the report and any undertakings.

Links to these documents also appear in the menu on the left of the screen on each inquiry's home page.

- **Announcements**—press releases from the Competition Commission about the various stages of the inquiry

- **Evidence**—non-confidential versions of key submissions and evidence from the parties and third parties, including responses to the provisional conclusions document and to proposed remedies.

Note that the description above applies to inquiries under the Enterprise Act 2002. Less information is published in relation to inquiries under the Fair Trading Act, and prior to 2003, inquiries were not given their own homepage.

Reports and publications

This section provides access to the following:

- **Reports**—reports are classified according to the year in which they were published. They are not classified according to the type of inquiry (*i.e.* merger, market investigation (or monopoly), etc.). At the time of writing, on-line copies of reports were available for all reports back to 1989, and titles and publication dates and references for earlier reports were available back to 1950.

- **Competition Commission notices, actions and decisions (including remedies)**—this section lists in chronological order all formal documents issued by the Competition Commission on any inquiry (including *e.g.* cancellation of a reference, notices adopting initial undertakings given by the parties to the OFT, issues letters, provisional findings, notices of possible remedies, acceptance of undertakings, etc.). At the time of writing, these documents were simply listed and were not classified by year or inquiry name.

- **Rules and guidance documents**—this section provides links to download the procedural documents and guidelines issued by the Competition Commission.

- **Consultations**—this section comprises information about current and past consultations.

- **Freedom of information—our publication scheme**—this section provides links to the Competition Commission's policy on publication.

- **Annual Review archive**—this section provides links to past Annual Reviews of the Competition Commission. At the time of writing, these were available back to 1998/1999.

- **Obtaining copies of a publication**—this section provides information on obtaining hard copies of Competition Commission reports and other publications.

Our role

This section provides information on the Competition Commission's role and practices, including links to its Mission Statement and frequently asked questions (FAQs).

Our people

This section provides information about the Members of the Competition Commission, including biographical details about the Chairman, Deputy Chairmen, and all Members. It also lists the members of the various panels and specialist groups (the Utilities Panel, the Newspaper Panel, the Telecommunication Panel, the Water Panel and the Remedies Standing Group). Links are available to the Register of Interests and to the Competition Commission's policy on conflicts of interest and the acceptance of gifts and hospitality. Links are also available to speeches made by the Chairman. Limited information is also available about senior Competition Commission staff.

Press releases

This section provides links the recent and archived Competition Commission press releases. An automated email alert system is also provided in this section, which anyone is able to subscribe to.

Searching the Competition Commission's website

A search bar (coloured green) is located at the top of every page immediately below the main menu.

Email alerts of new material

An automated email alert system is provided by the Competition Commission, which anyone can subscribe to. It can be accessed through the "join our mailing list" link in the menu on the left hand side of the "Press Releases" section of the website.

THE WEBSITE OF THE COMPETITION APPEAL TRIBUNAL

Address: *www.catribunal.org.uk*

The main navigation index, on the left hand side of the page, outlines the main areas of the Competition Appeal Tribunal's website:　　　　**A1.004**

- Home
- About the Tribunal
- Current cases
- Archived cases
- Judgments
- Rules and Guidance
- Other publications
- Useful links
- Sitemap
- Contact us

About the Tribunal

This section sets out information about how the Tribunal deals with cases, appeals under the Competition Act 1998, proceedings under the Enterprise Act 2002, appeals under the EC Competition Law (Articles 84 and 85) Enforcement Regulations 2001, appeals under the Communications Act 2003 and appeals from the Tribunal's decisions.

It also has sections with information and biographical data about the personnel of the Tribunal (*i.e.* the President, the members of the Panel of Chairmen, the Members, the Registrar and staff of the Tribunal), about the Competition Service, a link to an e-mail update service and frequently asked questions (FAQs).

Current cases

This section contains information about all current cases. Note that at the time of writing, these were simply presented in chronological order, starting with the most recently lodged case, and showing only two cases per page. There is no list of all case titles by which to navigate this part of the site and to find a particular case it is necessary either to click through the various pages or to enter the name of the case in the search box above the case summaries.

For each case, the case name and number are set out, with a statement of the status of the case, the names of the chairman and members hearing the case, and links to key documents issued by the Tribunal in relation to the case in question (including orders, transcripts of case management conferences and hearings, and judgments in that case.

Archived cases

This section contains essentially the same information as "Current cases", but for cases which have run their course in the Tribunal and been archived. The same points apply regarding how to find a particular case.

Judgments

This section lists all judgments handed down by the Tribunal (including decisions on interim measures, on preliminary issues, on the main issues, on costs and on applications for leave to appeal the Tribunal's judgment to the Court of Appeal). Judgments are listed in chronological order, with only two showing on any one page. Again, there is no list of all judgments so to locate a particular judgment, it is necessary to click through the various pages of this site, or to enter the name and year of a judgment in the search box above the judgment summaries.

Rules and guidance

This section contains links to the Tribunal's Rules of Procedure, Practice Directions which the Tribunal has issued, and to the Guidance on Appeals under the Competition Act 1998. At the time of writing, the latter document had not yet been updated to cover the other areas of jurisdiction of the Tribunal: the revised document was stated to be due to be published shortly.

Other publications

This section contains links to other documents issued by the Tribunal (note that it does not issue press releases). At the time of writing, the two categories of "Other publications" were "Notices" and "Annual Reviews".

Useful links

This section contains links to various other sites relevant to the work of the Tribunal.

Sitemap

This section sets out a plan of the Tribunal's website.

Contact us

This section contains contact details for the Registrar of the Tribunal and a form for email enquiries.

Searching the Competition Appeal Tribunal's website

At the bottom of the main menu list on the left of the screen is a search option. The search results are grouped by reference to the section of the website in which a "hit" has been found, which can assist in identifying which are the relevant hits for your search.

Email alerts of new material

An automated email alert system is provided by the Competition Appeal Tribunal, which anyone can subscribe to. It can be accessed from the "Register" box on the bottom right of the Tribunal's homepage, or through the "Register" option in the sub-menu to the "About the Tribunal" section.

THE WEBSITE OF THE DEPARTMENT OF TRADE AND INDUSTRY

Address: *www.dti.gov.uk*   A1.005

Consumer and Competition Policy Directorate

Information concerning competition issues on the DTI website is contained in the section relating to the Consumer and Competition Policy Directorate (CCP). To access this part of the website, go to the main DTI website home page. Below the main titles, there is a grey/beige bar with three option boxes. From the option box on the left, "Select a DTI site", click on the drop-down menu, scroll down and choose "Competition Policy". Click "Go". This will take you to the home page for Consumer and Competition Policy.

On the right hand of the page is a "What's new" box which lists recent activities and launches by the CCP.

The main menu for this part of the site is on the left hand side of the page.

- To access general information about mergers, choose "A–Z Index" from the menu, and choose "Mergers" from the alphabetical listings. The Mergers page contains general information about UK and European merger control rules.

- For information about consultations, choose "Consultations" from the menu. This will take you to a page with all current and recent past consultations listed. Note that the consultations are in a long list with no indexing. Scroll through (or use the "Find" function on your internet browser) to find what you are searching for.

- Regarding intervention notices, choose "A–Z Index" from the menu and choose "Mergers" from the alphabetical listings. Scroll down and click one of the links called "public interest considerations" or "public interest cases". This will move you down to the part of the page titled "Public interest mergers". In the third paragraph of the text below the title "Public interest cases" is a link ("available here") which takes you to a page where it is possible to access copies of OFT and OFCOM advice in relation to public interest cases, as well as copies of the DTI press releases announcing Ministers' decision in this context, and copies of intervention notices. These various documents are grouped together by reference to the case in question and the cases are divided into three categories, "Newspaper Cases", "Broadcasting and Cross-media Cases" and "National Security Cases". UK intervention notices are expected to appear alongside European intervention notices on this page (at the time of writing no UK intervention notices had yet been issued).

Press releases

DTI press notices are accessed via the Government News Network site. To access this, start at the DTI home page. From the right hand option box in the grey/beige bar below the main titles, "DTI quicklinks", click on the drop-down menu, scroll down and choose "Press Notices". Click "Go".

Recent DTI press releases are listed, and on the left hand side of the page is a search box. Searches can be done by keywords, any words, or by a date range.

Searching the DTI's website

At the top right of the main DTI home page is a search box. Once the initial results list has been generated, there are options to refine or expand the search. To search press releases, see the "Press releases" section above.

Email alerts of new material

An automated email alert system is provided by the DTI via the Government News Network, which anyone can subscribe to. It can be accessed from the GNN's DTI page, which is accessed as explained in "Press releases" above. On the left hand side of the page below the search box is a reference to email notifications. Click as indicated and this will take you to a registration form to be completed as appropriate. Note that the email alert service covers much more than competition/mergers and it is necessary to add key words to limit the information which you receive. The key words are not specified, but "competition" and "merger" might be appropriate, for example.

STATISTICS ON CASES CONSIDERED BY THE OFT AND COMPETITION COMMISSION

Table 1: Merger activity in the UK   A2.001

Year	Qualifying mergers	First Release data on acquisitions of UK companies (2)	Qualifying mergers as % of First Release cases
1998	269	887	30%
1999	254	714	36%
2000	192	765	25%
2001	200	554	36%
2002 (1)	194	502	39%
2002/2003 (1)	190	531	36%
2003/2004	117	642	18%

Source: OFT annual reports for 2000, 2001, 2002/2003 and 2003/2004

Notes:

1. Report for 2002/2003 covers 15 months from Jan 2002 to March 2003: data is shown for full year 2002 and for 12 months from April 2002 to March 2003

2. "First Release" is an Office for National Statistics publication giving data for the number of acquisitions of UK companies

A2.002

Table 2: Mergers examined by OFT and references to Competition Commission

Year	Number of cases examined by OFT	Found not to qualify, proposals abandoned and informal advice cases	Qualifying cases	Change	Confidential guidance cases	Pre-notified cases	Qualifying cases less confidential guidance	Total references	Total references as a percentage of	
									Qualifying cases	Qualifying cases less conf guidance
1998	425	156	269		45	45	224	8	3.0%	3.8%
1999	415	161	254	−5.2%	35	62	219	10	3.9%	4.9%
2000	315	123	192	−24.4%	21	60	171	14	7.3%	8.2%
2001	356	156	200	24%	27	40	173	10	5.0%	5.8%
2002 (1)	355	161	194	−3.0%	30	52	164	14	7.2%	8.5%
2002/2003 (1)	318	128	190		28	51	162	13	6.8%	8.0%
2003/2004	270	153	117	−38.4%	13	29	104	12	10.3%	11.5%

Source: OFT annual reports for 2000, 2001, 2002/2003 and 2003/2004

Notes:

1. Report for 2002/2003 covers 15 months from Jan 2002 to March 2003: data is shown for full year 2002 and for 12 months from April 2002 to March 2003

A2.003

Table 3: Cases handled under the Enterprise Act 2003 to July 1, 2004 (inclusive)

	OFT stage						Competition Commission stage				
Cases reviewed by OFT (1)	Completed acquisitions	Anticipated acquisitions	Found not to qualify	Cleared without conditions by OFT	Cleared subject to undertakings in lieu	Referred	Found no SLC (2)	Prohibited (2)	Cleared subject to conditions	Abandoned	Pending
156.0	78.0	78.0	61.0	77.0	4.0	14.0	1.5	0.5	2.0	5.0	5.0
As a percentage of all cases reviewed by OFT	50.00%	50.00%	39.10%	49.36%	2.56%	8.97%					
As a percentage of all qualifying cases				81.05%	4.21%	14.74%					
As a percentage of all references							10.71%	3.57%	14.29%	35.71%	35.71%

Source: OFT and CC websites

Notes:

1. This figure does not include informal advice and confidential guidance cases. The iSOFT/Torex case is counted only once.

2. In the *Stena/P&O/Irish Sea* inquiry, the Competition Commission found that one of the proposed route acquisitions did not give rise to an SLC but the other did and was prohibited.

607

EXAMPLE OF (NEGATIVE) CONFIDENTIAL GUIDANCE LETTER FROM THE OFT

A3.001 **[HEADED NOTEPAPER OF OFT]**

RESTRICTED — MARKET SENSITIVE

[Addressee—typically the party's advisers]

[References]

Dear [Addressee]

[Case name]

I refer to [party's name]'s request for confidential guidance on the above proposal that we received on [date].

As you will understand, while a proposed merger remains confidential, we cannot take account of the views of those other than the parties involved who may have an interest in the proposal. We are only able, therefore, to express a decision on the basis of the information available to us and not able to take a formal view on the question of reference to the Competition Commission at this stage.

I can tell you that on the basis of the information available at present, the OFT considers that there appears to be a significant prospect[1] that the merger may be expected to result in a substantial lessening of competition. As a result, the transaction is likely to be referred to the Competition Commission. Furthermore, the OFT is not confident at this stage, that acceptable undertakings in lieu of reference could be obtained.

Please be advised that this guidance is provided only on the understanding that the information remains strictly confidential to [party's name]. This decision is also provided without prejudice to any final decision and may be altered if new informa-

---

[1] This wording reflects the original drafting of the OFT's *Substantive Assessment Guidance* which was amended following the *IBA Health* litigation, and is expected to change further following consultation on the initial amendments. The wording of confidential guidance letters may similarly change.

tion comes to light about the structure of the merger or any other matter relevant to it.

[Party's name] may request a meeting for an explanation of the basis of our guidance decision if they wish. They should know, however, that the aim of the meeting would be to provide feedback and would not be an opportunity for [party's name] to dispute or challenge the outcome of the OFT's deliberations in this matter.

If [party's name] decides to proceed with this transaction, please inform the OFT as soon as this becomes public knowledge, giving us a copy of the press release and details of any changes following the confidential guidance, so that a decision on the question of reference can be made. Please note that if the proposed merger is considered at a public stage, a fee may be payable.

Yours sincerely

[Case officer name]

THE MERGER NOTICE FOR PRENOTIFICATION OF AN ANTICIPATED MERGER

Merger notice under section 96 of the Enterprise Act 2002

June 2003

Ref No: (Office use only)

A4.001   Use this Merger notice only for notifying the OFT of proposed mergers which will not be completed before expiry of the consideration period and which you wish to be subject to the statutory time limit for decision. Do not use it for notifying completed mergers or for submitting requests for confidential guidance or proposed mergers which will be subject to [an] administrative timetable. If you need any help or further information contact the Mergers Branch at the address at the end of Part Three.

The Guidance Notes form part of the Notice. Read them in full before answering any of the questions.

Please complete Parts One and Three of the notice in typescript or block letters. Give your answers to Part Two in typescript on separate sheets.

PART ONE—GENERAL INFORMATION

1.   Who is the authorised person giving this notice?

See Guidance Note 1.1

Name:
Position:
Company/firm:

2.   Have you authorised any representative to act on your behalf?

See Guidance Note 1.2

Name:
Position:
Company/firm:

3.   To which person and address should the OFT send any correspondence?

See Guidance Note 1.3

Name:
UK address:
Postcode:
Telephone No:
Fax No:
E-mail address:

4.   Briefly describe the merger proposal being notified stating:

- The names of the acquiring company and target;
- The type of transaction (for example, whether it is an agreed bid, a full takeover or the acquisition of assets or of a minority shareholding giving material influence, or a joint venture);
- How the transaction qualifies as a relevant merger situation (for example through UK turnover or combined share of supply);
- A brief description of the business or businesses being acquired;
- The areas of overlap between the acquirer and target;
- The reasons for the acquisition; and
- Any other countries where the transaction has been notified.

See Guidance Note 1.4 and Chapter 4 of *Mergers—Procedural guidance*

5.   Briefly describe the steps taken to publicise the proposal and enclose a copy of any press release or report (including those in specialist or trade journals) and details of any notifications to listing authorities, e.g. for admission to the UK Listing Authority Official List and for admission to trading on the London Stock Exchange.

See Guidance Note 1.5

PART TWO—MERGER DETAILS

Now give a full description of the merger proposal, on separate sheets, by replying to the following questions. Some of the questions are complex, and they may not all be relevant in every case. If in doubt, you should consider seeking legal advice. Please provide copies of documents referred to in this notice where possible.

The merger situation

See Guidance Note 2.1 and Chapter 2 of *Mergers—Substantive assessment guidance*

1.   Give details of the proposed arrangements by which the main enterprises will cease to be distinct ('the merging enterprises'). Include share acquisitions, changes of directorships etc, and any factors upon which completion of the merger is conditional.

2.   Give details of the ownership and control of the merging enterprises:

    (a)   before the merger; and

    (b)   following the merger.

3.   What other enterprises may cease to be distinct as a result of the notified arrangements? Give details of the proposed change in shareholdings or in other relationships by which they might cease to be distinct.

Jurisdiction

See paragraphs 2.3 to 2.25 of *Mergers—Substantive assessment guidance*

4.   What is the UK turnover associated with the enterprise being acquired?

Guidance Note 2.2

5.   Briefly describe the main products and services supplied by each of the merging enterprises. Give an estimate of their share of supply for any product or service of any description where any of the merging businesses (and/or any members of the same corporate group) have a share of supply in the UK, or in a substantial part of the UK, by value or volume, of 25 per cent or more.

Financial information

See Guidance Note 2.3

6.   Supply, for each of the merging enterprises, two copies of the most recent annual report and accounts. If annual reports are not available, give, for each of the merging enterprises, a profit and loss account and proforma balance sheet showing: total turnover (excluding VAT); and profit before tax.

7.   What is the UK turnover associated with the acquirer?

8.   What is the value of the consideration being offered? What form will it take?

Timing

See Guidance Note 2.4

9.   What is the expected time scale for: exchange of contracts; and completion of the merger?

City code on takeovers and mergers

See Guidance Note 2.5

10.   If the offer is subject to the City Code on Takeovers and Mergers, please supply two copies of the Offer Document and Listing Particulars. If these are not yet available, provide copies of the latest drafts and supply the final versions as soon as they are issued.

11. What is the effective closing date likely to be?

12. Has the offer been recommended by the board of directors of the target company?

Plans and motives

13. What are the reasons for the merger and the plans for the merged businesses?

14. Please provide copies of analyses, reports, studies and surveys submitted to or prepared for any member(s) of the board of directors, the supervisory board, or the shareholders' meeting, for the purpose of assessing or analysing the proposed transaction with respect to competitive conditions, competitors (actual and potential), and market conditions and indicate (if not contained in the document itself) the date of preparation.

Markets

See Chapter 3 paragraphs 3.11 to 3.22 of *Mergers—Substantive assessment guidance*

Horizontal links

See Chapter 4 of *Mergers—Substantive assessment guidance*

15. Please provide:

   (a) a brief description of each product or service, including the extent to which it is served at a regional, national or wider level and a brief description of the relevant product or geographic markets, referring where appropriate to any independent sources of information (such as MINTEL, trade publications, independent commissioned research etc.). (OFT publication 403—*Market definition* may assist in this latter task); and

   (b) a brief description, in terms of characteristics/price differences, of any product(s) or service(s) that might be considered close substitutes, on the demand or supply side, to the goods or services produced by the merged companies;

16. For the markets identified at 15 and where the merger will create combined market shares for the merged businesses of 10 per cent or more, by value or volume, in any product or service of any description, in the UK as a whole, or in any region, give the following information. Refer to industry data where available. Use the most recent figures available and specify the period they cover.

   (a) an estimate of the merged companies' market share plus attributed shares arising from any affiliated companies for these markets. Where this differs from the merging companies' market share as put forward in answer to 15a, provide an estimate of the merging companies' market share and that of the affiliated companies;

   (b) an estimate of the value and volume of goods or services supplied within the UK as a whole (i.e. UK output less exports, plus imports);

   (c) an estimate of the value and volume of imports and exports for the UK as a whole;

   (d) an estimate of the value and volume of UK sales for each business;

(e)   the names, contact details and market shares of both parties' top five competitors (including overseas companies/importers) for each product or service provided by both parties to the merger. Contact details to include contact name, address, e-mail address, fax and telephone numbers;

(f)   the names and contact details (to include contact names, addresses, e-mail addresses, fax and telephone numbers) and estimated share of the party's business of both parties' top five customers (including overseas customers if appropriate);

Where there are marked differences in the size of your customers, such that some customers may purchase goods or services by different means or in significantly different quantities, please provide these same details for five medium and five small customers.

(g)   a description of how competition works in the market(s) identified at 15(a) and (b);

(h)   details of any bids made by the parties in the last 3 years to win business in the overlapping markets, indicate whether these bids were won or lost and if known the reasons why;

(i)   details of any shareholding, agreement or joint ventures with other suppliers;

(j)   an estimate of the capital expenditure required to enter the market on a scale necessary to gain a 5 per cent market share, both as a new entrant, and as a company which already has the necessary technology and expertise (e.g. a company located overseas) and estimate to what extent this cost is recoverable should the firm decide to exit the market; See paragraphs 4.17 to 4.26 of *Mergers—Substantive assessment guidance*

(k)   an estimate of the scale of annual expenditure on advertising/promotion relative to sales required to achieve a market share of 5 per cent;

(l)   details of any other factors affecting entry, e.g. planning restraints, technology or R&D requirements, availability of raw materials, length of contract etc including, where possible, an estimate of the time and resources necessary to overcome these factors;

(m)   an assessment of the extent to which imports provide actual competition in the UK market, and the extent of potential competition from imports. (Cover factors such as transport costs, tariffs, quotas, standards, government regulations etc);

(n)   an assessment of the ease of exit from the market. Indicate any entry and exit over the past five years;

(o)   an assessment of any effects the merger may have at local level. Describe the nature of local competition and give details of any localities where competition may be reduced as a result of the merger;

(p)   a description of any efficiencies or customer benefits that you believe the merger will bring (attach any appropriate supporting documentation); See paragraphs 4.29 to 4.35 and 7.7 to 7.10 of *Mergers— Substantive assessment guidance*

(q)   a brief assessment of any other features of the industry that the OFT should take into account in considering the effect of the merger; and

Combined purchases

17.   Identify any product(s) (including raw materials) or service(s) for which the combined purchases of the merged businesses will account for more than 10 per cent of the total UK sales of that product or service.

Vertical links

See Chapter 5 of *Mergers—Substantive assessment guidance*

18. Where either of the parties has greater than 15 per cent of the share of supply of any inputs or outputs in a vertical supply chain, please provide details of:

    (a) the share of supply of these goods or services;
    (b) the extent of pre-merger vertical integration;
    (c) any long-term existing supply agreements; and
    (d) the impact of the merger, if any, on the vertical supply chain.

PART THREE—DECLARATION

Please return Parts One and Three of the Notice, with your answers to Part Two, to:

Office of Fair Trading, Mergers Branch, 2–6 Salisbury Square, London EC4Y 8JX
Telephone No. 020 7211 8915/8917/8452/8586
Fax No. 020 7211 8916 or Email mergers@oft.gsi.gov.uk

Declaration

The OFT will not accept a Merger Notice unless the Declaration has been signed by the authorised person. (See Guidance Notes 3.1 and 3.2).
I understand that:

- It is a criminal offence for a person to supply information in a Merger Notice which he knows to be false or misleading in any material respect.

- The OFT may reject any Merger Notice if it is suspected that it contains information which is false or misleading in any material respect.

- The OFT may bring the existence of the merger proposal described in this Notice, and the fact that the Notice has been given, to the attention of interested parties.

Signed:

Name:

Position:

Date:

I confirm that the person named in reply to question 1.2 (if any) is authorised to act on my behalf for the purposes of this Notice.

Signed:

Have you attached (as appropriate):
Press release
Two copies of the most recent annual report and accounts or appropriate profit and loss accounts and pro-forma balance sheets
Two copies of the Offer Document and Listing Particulars
Relevant Board documents
The appropriate fee—payable to the OFT

GUIDANCE NOTES TO MERGER NOTICE

Part One—General Information

Guidance Note 1.1

Only an authorised person can give a Merger Notice. An authorised person is defined by Regulations as any person carrying on an enterprise to which the notified arrangements relate.

Guidance Note 1.2

An authorised person can appoint a representative, *e.g.* a firm of solicitors, to complete the Notice on his behalf and to act for him in further correspondence with the OFT. If you do authorise someone to act in this way you must sign the authorisation at Part Three of the Notice.

You can withdraw or change the authorisation at any time but if you do so you must give immediate notice to the OFT in writing.

Guidance Note 1.3

You must give a full address to which the OFT can send all correspondence. If you have appointed a representative and wish correspondence to be sent to them, give their address here. Otherwise give details of the person within your company who will deal with the correspondence, and the address to which the OFT should write.

Wherever possible, give a UK address, fax number and email address and ensure that the OFT can make contact between 9.00am and 5.00pm on weekdays. If your address changes, you must notify the OFT immediately in writing.

Guidance Note 1.4

Part Two of the Notice seeks a full description of the proposed merger. Give a short description here on the following lines:

'AB Holdings Limited announced on June 3 that it was to acquire the whole of the assets and business of CD Co Plc (which is a wholly owned subsidiary of XY Group Plc) by share issue, for a consideration of £25 million. The overlap of products/services is in business computers and office equipment. . .'

If there are any changes in the circumstances of the merger after you have submitted the Notice, tell the OFT immediately.

Guidance Note 1.5

Use this Notice to notify the OFT of proposals which have already been made public. The OFT will issue a statement on the lines that: 'the proposed acquisition by A of B was notified to the OFT on [X date]. The period for considering the merger will end on [Y date].

Part Two—Merger Details

THE MERGER SITUATION
Guidance Note 2.1

Questions 1–3 will enable the Office to identify each of the merger situations which may arise from the transaction being notified. This is important because if the period for considering the Notice expires without the notified merger being referred to the Competition Commission (CC), there are restrictions on the OFT referring any of the relevant merger situations which might arise from completion of the notified merger. (This does not affect the OFT's powers to make a reference where material information was withheld or where the information given was false or misleading).

JURISDICTION
Guidance Note 2.2
UK Turnover is determined in accordance with The Enterprise Act 2002 (Determination of Turnover) Order 2003. Guidance is also available in the OFT's supplementary guidance note on the calculation of turnover for the purposes of Part 3 of the Enterprise Act 2002.

FINANCIAL INFORMATION
Guidance Note 2.3
The OFT will usually need only the most recent annual report and accounts of the main parties to the merger. However, where the acquiring company is part of a larger group, the OFT will normally also need the most recent group annual report and accounts. It will not need group accounts for the target's parent company where the target is a subsidiary or associate company and separate accounts are prepared for that company. It is important that the target's UK turnover for the preceding business year is provided. If no annual report or accounts are available, provide separate figures (audited if possible) on turnover (including UK turnover), profits and assets. On turnover, the OFT needs details of sales before VAT and duty. On profits it requires details of operating profit before tax and interest.

If a merger gives rise to a significant increase in market share, the OFT may subsequently wish to review profits, sales and capital employed in the relevant businesses.

Ensure that this information is available, or could be estimated if required, for both the acquiring and target company.

TIMING
Guidance Note 2.4
Section 100(1)(b) of the Enterprise Act provides that if any of the enterprises to which the Notice relates cease to be distinct from each other at any time during the consideration period, the pre-notified merger could remain liable for reference to the CC for four months from the date of its completion. You should bear this in mind when considering the timing of completion of a merger or submission of a Notice.

CITY CODE ON TAKEOVERS AND MERGERS
Guidance Note 2.5
To allow for submission of a Notice before the posting of an offer, you can supply the Offer Document and Listing Particulars in draft form. The consideration period will run from submission of the drafts, although the OFT will still need copies of the final versions as soon as these are published.

The OFT does not envisage that the pre-notification timetable will raise significant difficulties in relation to the timing of public offers. You should however bear in mind the need to reconcile submission of the Notice with the requirements of City Code on Takeovers and Mergers. If you are seeking a decision by the first closing date of an offer, the OFT will need to receive the Notice before the posting of the Offer Document. This will assist the OFT in reaching a decision by the first closing date. The OFT cannot be bound by the first closing date however, and where it is not in a position to reach a decision by then, the consideration period will need to be extended.

MARKETS
See Chapters 3, 4 and 5 of *Mergers—Substantive assessment guidance*

Part Three—Declaration

Guidance Note 3.1

The Declaration must be signed by the authorised person. It draws your attention to two important provisions of the Enterprise Act. The first relates to the provision of false or misleading information. Under section 117 of the Enterprise Act it is an offence to intentionally or recklessly [give] false or misleading information. In relation to pre-notification, it is an offence:

- knowingly or recklessly to give false or misleading information to the OFT, either in response to the Notice, or in reply to any additional questions raised by the OFT during the consideration period; or

- knowingly or recklessly to furnish false or misleading information to a third party, for example your authorised representative or legal adviser, in the knowledge that they will then supply it to the OFT.

The penalties for breach of this provision are severe: a fine of up to the current statutory maximum, or a maximum of two years imprisonment, or both.

The OFT also has powers to reject the Notice, at any time before the period for considering it expires, where it suspects that any information given in the Notice, or in response to further enquiries, is false or misleading. The effect of rejection is that the proposal which has been notified will remain liable for reference to the CC for a period of four months after the date of its completion.

Secondly, the Declaration reminds you that the OFT will publicise the existence of the merger proposal as notified. It will also draw it to the attention of third parties in order to seek their views (Guidance Note 1.5). The OFT will have regard to the provisions of the Act in relation to disclosure of information. Its aim in publicising the merger proposal is solely to ensure that those with an interest in the merger are given an opportunity to comment.

Guidance Note 3.2

The Declaration also confirms the authorisation of any representative named in reply [to question 1.2] to act on behalf of a company. [T]he Declaration must be signed by a director or other officer of that company.

EXAMPLE OF OFT ISSUES LETTER

Note: Issues letters are usually confidential to the parties to a merger but excep-   A5.001
tionally the issues letter sent by the OFT to the parties to the proposed acquisition by
iSOFT plc of Torex plc was published in the Competition Appeal Tribunal's judgment
in *IBA Health v OFT* [2003] CAT 27 at para.89. The letter is reproduced below as
it was set out in the Tribunal's judgment.

"Main background assumptions:
    Electronic patient records (EPRs) may be simple (level 1) patient administration
systems (PAS) which are systems to which the departmental modules are
connected, usually by means of an interface engine, or they may have been built
as an integrated system, a level 6 EPR, which includes departmental modules and
a Clinical Information System. The degree of complexity ranges from levels 1 to
6, with the NHS focused on implementing level 3 EPRs in the short term.
    Laboratory Information Management Systems (LIMS) consist of a patient
related database that can cover all diagnostic laboratory disciplines. Its main
function is the management of samples and analysis.
    The argument has been made that supply side substitutability is largely a ques-
tion of programming skills. However, this is undermined by the fact that companies
are highly specialised in a particular facet of programming and acquisition is used
in the industry as a means of expansion.

Key Potential Competition Concerns
    The following are hypothesis at this stage, which we are still evaluating in the
light of the evidence put to us by the parties and third parties. They do not
necessarily represent OFT's final view on these issues.

1.   The merger will result in loss of direct bidding competition between iSOFT
      and Torex, in particular for EPR systems and LIMS, as well as other
      departmental systems.
      The pattern of OJEC bidding competition shows iSOFT and Torex have
      bid against each other on 21 of 39 EPR contracts and 16 of 31 LIMS
      contracts since 1998, suggesting they are regular and direct competitors.
2.   The parties maintain that since Torex has not won an OJEC contract in
      the last 3 years it is no longer an effective competitor or constraint on
      iSOFT—however Torex has strengthened its portfolio of products by a
      number of acquisitions including for example Inhealth when it acquired
      the rights to IBA PAS/EPR systems. The up-dating and extension of its
      product range together with its strong position of the installed base
      suggests it is well placed to actively compete and mitigates against its lack
      of success in winning recent contracts.
      Competition takes place in bidding and being short-listed, not just in
      winning the contract.

619

3. iSOFT and Torex will hold a combined share of supply in excess of 50% of the installed base of both EPR/PAS systems, and LIMS systems, showing that on a historic basis they are the two leading suppliers in the UK. This will result in a significant structural change in the market where the presence/size of the next competitor is significantly smaller, and likely to result in a substantial lessening of competition.

The merger will give the combined company significant market coverage and potential incumbency advantages.

4. There appear to be high barriers to entry—systems are UK specific with high conversion costs for systems developed overseas. The broad portfolio of products offered by the merged company may also raise costs and deter potential entry.

5. It is not clear whether either Cerner or IDX (or other providers) are capable of providing a significant competitive constraint to the merged business given their current low level of success in winning contracts.

6. Hospitals buying IT systems on an individual basis are unlikely to have buyer power. The LSP programme will (for England) increase the size of contracts although the requirement on the consortia to specify a preferred partner may make it difficult for the LSP to exercise any buyer power (particularly if competing suppliers exit the market or do not continue to invest in product development).

7. Portfolio power—the merged company will be able to offer a broad portfolio of "leading" products/modules and may encourage more "one-stop" shopping by NHS hospitals. This may also have the effect of preventing smaller specialist providers of individual systems from competing and, in effect, freezing them out.

8. The likely effect of the NPfIT in terms of future changes and timing is uncertain. The proposed system of LSPs cover only England. This will not directly impact on procurement in Wales, Scotland and Northern Ireland, and in addition hospitals in England will continue to be able to purchase IT systems outside the NPfIT programme. It is not appropriate therefore to judge the effects of the merger solely in relation to the proposed NPfIT programme.

9. The parties are two key suppliers of PAS/EPR and LIMS system to the NHS. As such, they have a good understanding of existing IT systems and are well placed to deliver new and improved systems to meet increased standards. Absent the merger, the parties will continue to invest and innovate and develop new products to compete with each other. The merger reduces such incentives.

The parties are invited to put forward any evidence they wish to submit on the above issues and to consider appropriate undertakings to remedy the potential competition concerns outlined in the above in lieu of reference to the Competition Commission."

EXAMPLE OF FIRST DAY LETTER FROM THE COMPETITION COMMISSION

Note: the example below concerns a merger which has been completed at the time   **A6.001**
of the reference. Where the referred merger has not yet been completed, some of the
contents of the first day letter will change.

[HEADED PAPER OF THE COMPETITION COMMISSION]

[Addressee's name]	From:	Professor Paul Geroski, Chairman
[Addressee's address]	Direct line:	020 7271 0115

[Date]

Dear [name]

[Name of inquiry: Company 1/Company 2]

Terms of reference

1.   As you know, the Office of Fair Trading (OFT) has referred to the
Competition Commission (CC) the acquisition by [Company 1] of
[Company 2] for investigation and report. Copies of the terms of reference
and accompanying OFT press release are enclosed.

Appointment of Members

2.   I shall be appointing a group of members of the CC (the Group) to carry
out the inquiry and you will be informed of their names as soon as possible.
[Name] will be the chairman.

Relevant statutory questions

3.   Section 35 of the Enterprise Act 2002 (the Act) requires the CC to decide a
number of questions, as summarized below:

- whether a relevant merger situation has been created; and
- if so, whether the creation of that situation has resulted, or may be
expected to result, in a substantial lessening of competition within any
market or markets in the UK for goods or services.

621

If the CC decides that such a merger situation has been created which has had, or is expected to have, such an effect on competition, there is an 'anti-competitive outcome' and we must then also decide:

- whether action should be taken by it for the purpose of remedying, mitigating or preventing the substantial lessening of competition concerned or any adverse effect which has resulted from, or may be expected to result from, the substantial lessening of competition;

- whether it should recommend the taking of action by others for such purposes; and

- in either case, what action should be taken and what is to be remedied.

Relevant CC publications

4. More information about the statutory questions and our approach to inquiries is contained in the following publications, enclosed with this letter:

- Competition Commission: Rules of Procedure (CC1)

- Merger References: Competition Commission Guidelines (CC2)

- General Advice and Information (CC4)

- Statement of Policy on Penalties (CC5)

- Chairman's Guidance to Groups (CC6)

- Chairman's Guidance on Disclosure of Information in Merger and Market Inquiries (CC7)

Timetable and administrative arrangements

5. In due course, a copy of the administrative timetable will be published on our web site. We are required to report on the reference by [date], but we expect to be able to publish our report earlier. Our staff would like an early meeting with you and/or your advisers to discuss administrative matters, including the administrative timetable. They will send you a draft timetable as soon as possible. It would be helpful if, before the meeting, you could check if there are likely to be any availability problems for you, your colleagues and/or your advisers during the inquiry.

6. It would be useful if we could discuss any points in relation to the market at that meeting.

7. The staff team supporting the inquiry will be led by [name and full contact details of Inquiry Director]. Your main point of contact throughout the inquiry is the Inquiry Secretary, [name and tel, fax and email contact details].

8. Please contact [name of Inquiry Secretary] as soon as possible to arrange the administrative meeting with staff. Please also let him/her have the name and full contact details, including telephone and fax numbers and email address, of the person you are nominating as the main contact point for our staff for the duration of the inquiry.

9. The Act requires and authorises us to serve certain documents on you. The Companies Act 1985 enables us to effect service of a document by leaving

it at or sending by post to your registered office. However, section 126 of the Act enables us to serve documents on your company in other ways. If you specify another address within the UK as the one at which the company or someone on its behalf will accept service, the section enables us to effect service of a document by leaving it at or sending it by post to that address. If you wish to specify an address for service other that your registered office, please let us know. The section also enables documents to be served by transmission using a telecommunications system. We recommend that you ensure that arrangements are in place so that any document duly served is brought to the notice of the appropriate persons within your company as soon as possible after it is received.

10. Throughout the inquiry we shall be sending you a large number of documents that do not require formal service under the legislation. With these documents, if the contact name or the communication details identified in response to paragraph 8 is different from your formal address for service our staff will generally send them to the main contact.

Restrictions on certain dealings for completed mergers

11. As you may be aware, now that the reference has been made to the CC, you and your subsidiaries and associated persons are prohibited under the Act (section 77) from the following activities without first obtaining the consent of the CC:

- completing outstanding matters in connection with any arrangements which have resulted in the enterprise concerned ceasing to be distinct;

- making any further arrangements in consequence of that result (other than arrangements which reverse that result);

- transferring the ownership or control of any enterprises to which the reference relates; and

- assisting with any of the above.

12. The CC wishes to ensure that no action is taken which might prejudice the reference concerned or impede the taking of any action under the Act which may be justified by the CC's decisions on the reference. The CC will therefore need to understand what steps, if any, were taken prior to the reference to integrate the business of [company 2] into your own business, and what your proposals are going forward pending final determination of the reference by the CC.

13. In particular, at our initial staff meeting, it would be helpful to discuss whether, pending final determination, you intend to:

- retain a separate management structure for [company 2];

- sell any of [company 2]'s assets, move any of its staff and/or make any staff redundant;

- ensure that [company 2] continues to supply the same range of products to the same customers (as appropriate); and/or

- implement any arrangements to ensure that the [company 2] business is maintained as a going concern and that its assets are maintained and preserved.

Requests for information and disclosure

14. During the course of the inquiry, we will ask you to provide information and documents, sometimes at short notice. Compliance with the deadlines we set will greatly assist us and help to ensure that the timetable is met. Please therefore treat the dates by which we request information (including dates set out in this letter) as strict deadlines. If, however, there is likely to be a difficulty over supplying the information by the date requested, you should contact [name of Inquiry Secretary] as soon as possible, to discuss when the information can be provided. You should be aware that the Group may ignore information that is submitted late (see Rule 9 of Competition Commission: Rules of Procedure (CC1)) and that the CC has power to impose penalties for late or non-provision of information requested by notice under section 109 of the Act and the power to extend the period in which it must report. There is more on the CC's powers to gather, handle and disclose information in Annex A to this letter.

Main submission: deadline [date]

15. Your company should provide a written submission, as specified in Annex B to this letter, as soon as possible, and no later than the date set out above. You are also requested to provide a non-sensitive version for publication—see paragraph 10 of Annex A.

Questionnaires

16. In addition we shall shortly send you a series of detailed market-related and financial questions, which we aim to prepare within the next [seven] days.

Off-the-shelf material: deadline [date]

17. In the meantime please send us, by the date set out above, an electronic copy and one hard copy of the material listed in Annex C to this letter.

Hearings

18. The Group of members conducting this inquiry will wish to meet you (and any colleagues and advisers whom you may wish to accompany you) for a hearing after the submission has been received. The date and time will be arranged as soon as possible and it would be helpful if you or your advisers could discuss possible dates at the administrative meeting with staff. At this hearing the Group will raise the main issues as they see them in the light of your submissions and those received from other parties. The issues will be set out in the issues statement sent to you, and published on our web site, in advance of the hearing. You and your advisers will of course be free, at the hearing, to make any statement or raise any matters which you consider to be relevant. In discussing the administrative timetable with you, our staff will also suggest approximate timings for any further hearings, including a hearing on remedies at a later stage, as appropriate.

Checklist

19. A checklist of the information requested in this letter is enclosed for your assistance.

20. [We are copying this letter to [name of party's legal representatives].]

Yours sincerely

CHAIRMAN

Encs:

Checklist of information requested

Annex A   Information gathering, handling and disclosure

Annex B   Request for main submission

Annex C   Off-the-shelf material requested

CHECKLIST OF INFORMATION REQUESTED IN THIS LETTER

We seek information in electronic form plus one hard copy for checking purposes. Responses should be sent to [name of Inquiry Secretary and contact details]. Please contact [him/her] to make arrangements to set up encrypted email facilities for secure email exchange between you and the CC, which the CC is happy to do. Alternatively you could provide information on CD-ROM or floppy disc (which must, however, be compatible with Microsoft Office 2002 programmes, including Word and Excel). If you have any questions about the submission of your evidence, please contact [Inquiry Secretary].

1. Details of any problems with your availability or that of your colleagues or advisers during the inquiry period (see paragraph 5 of the letter).

2. Contact details (including email address, fax number and telephone number) for your nominated representative (see paragraph 8).

3. Details of your [client company's] registered office and Company Secretary. Contact details for any other person on whom you wish any documents under section 126 of the Act to be served (if different from the person nominated in point 2 above) (see paragraph 9).

4. Main submission (paragraph 11 and Annex B).

5. Off-the-shelf information (paragraph 13 and Annex C).

ANNEX A

THE COMPETITION COMMISSION'S PROCEDURES AND POWERS TO GATHER INFORMATION AND THE HANDLING AND DISCLOSURE BY THE COMPETITION COMMISSION OF INFORMATION

1.   Information about the CC's procedures and role is contained in the series of publications set out in paragraph 5 of this letter.

Information-gathering powers

2.   The CC's information-gathering powers under section 109 of the Enterprise Act 2002 (the Act) include the power to require persons to give evidence to it or to produce specified or described documents that are within that person's custody or under his control. In the event of late provision or non-provision of information requested by notice under section 109 of the Act, the CC has the power to impose a penalty. (In merger cases, if the person who has failed to comply with the notice is a main party, the CC may also have the power to extend the period in which it must publish its report.)

3.   Usually requests for information are made without formally exercising the CC's section 109 powers. However, in the event of delay or failure to respond to the CC's requests, the group of CC members appointed to conduct the inquiry (the Group) might decide to issue formal notices under section 109, this being the first necessary step towards the imposition of a penalty.

4.   For more information about these powers, please see the Statement of Policy on Penalties (CC5).

5.   The Group may ignore information submitted late (see Rule 9 of the Competition Commission: Rules of Procedure—CC1).

Disclosure of information

6.   The CC aims to be open and transparent in its work while maintaining the confidentiality of information that it obtains during its inquiries. Transparency is a means of achieving due process and of ensuring that, by having a better understanding of the case against them, the main parties in an inquiry are treated fairly. It also enables other interested persons to understand the issues that the CC is considering and thereby make an effective contribution to the process. In addition, an open and transparent approach assists parties when providing information and improves the effectiveness, efficiency and quality of the CC's decisions.

7.   The Act imposes a general restriction on the disclosure of information that the CC has obtained in connection with the exercise of its functions, including the investigation of merger and market references. However, the Act also sets out the circumstances in which the CC may disclose information, including when disclosure is made for the purpose of facilitating the CC's functions. Dependent upon the circumstances of any disclosure by the CC, restrictions may apply to any further use or disclosure of the information. Please note that if information is disclosed for the purpose of facilitating the CC's functions but is not made available to the public, the person to whom the disclosure is made may not further disclose the information other than with the agreement of the CC and for the purpose of facilitating the functions of the CC. Any person who does further disclose such information commits an offence unless disclosure is permitted under Part 9 of

the Act. For more information, see paragraphs 2.1 to 2.5 of the Chairman's Guidance on Disclosure of Information in Merger and Market Inquiries.

8. During the course of the inquiry, the CC will publish a number of its documents on its web site. These include a statement of issues, and, later, the CC provisional findings on the statutory competition questions. If the CC makes an adverse finding, it will publish a statement of possible remedies, either at the same time as publication of the provisional findings or later. The CC will also consider whether or not to disclose other information to the other main parties or selected third parties, or to publish information on the web site, having regard to the Chairman's Guidance on Disclosure of Information in Merger and Market Inquiries. For example, paragraph 3.5(c) of that document says that certain key arguments and views of third parties should be published, or, where the information is sensitive, made known to main and selected third parties, subject to the considerations set out in the following paragraph.

9. Whenever the CC is considering whether to disclose information, it must have regard to three considerations set out in section 244 of the Act:

(a) the need to exclude from disclosure (so far as practicable) any information whose disclosure the CC thinks is contrary to the public interest;

(b) the need to exclude from disclosure (so far as practicable):

(i) commercial information whose disclosure the CC thinks might significantly harm the legitimate business interests of the undertaking to which it relates; or

(ii) information relating to the private affairs of an individual whose disclosure the CC thinks might significantly harm the individual's interests; and

the extent to which the disclosure of the information mentioned in paragraphs (b)(i) or (ii) is necessary for the purpose for which the CC is permitted to make disclosure.

Non-sensitive version of submission

10. When providing views and comments (including your initial submission), you are requested to provide a non-sensitive version of your evidence for publication on our web site or for disclosure, which omits anything that you consider to be sensitive. Anything excluded from this non-sensitive version should be drawn to the attention of the CC. It is also to your advantage to explain why you regard the material that has been omitted as sensitive so that the CC may take this into account when it is considering the possible disclosure of your evidence. If you would like additional time in which to provide the non-sensitive version or have any queries concerning this request, please contact [the Inquiry Secretary].

11. Whenever you supply information (whether or not it appears likely that we will wish to disclose the information to others), you should indicate to the CC which parts are sensitive, and why, so that the CC may take this information into account when having regard to the three statutory considerations (see paragraph 9). It may not always be practicable to discuss any proposed disclosure with you, so an indication at the outset of what you regard as sensitive, and why, will enable us to take account of your concerns and, when time permits, explore those concerns with you. In general, the CC will take the view that a party has failed to give sufficient explanation

about the nature of the sensitivity if the information is marked 'sensitive' without further narrative.

12. The CC aims to be sensitive to requests for confidentiality. For example, it has often been possible for submission to be anonymized. If you do have any concerns as to the possible disclosure of information, you should make your concerns known to the Inquiry Secretary. In the event of a dispute with the group of members undertaking the inquiry, you may make representations to the Chief Executive. The Chief Executive will liaise with the group, though the decision whether or not to disclose will remain that of the CC.

13. For further information please see paragraphs 4.1 to 4.6 of the Chairman's Guidance on Disclosure of Information in Merger and Market Inquiries (CC7) and paragraphs 6.27 to 6.30 of the General Advice and Information (CC4).

Checking accuracy of information supplied

14. The CC may, for the purpose of preparing its report, send any material which it has produced based upon your submission back to you so that its accuracy can be verified. When doing so, you will be asked to identify any matter which you wish to have excluded from the report. When considering whether publication of the matter would be inappropriate, the Group will have regard to the considerations mentioned in paragraph 9. For further information about exclusions see Part V of the Competition Commission Rules of Procedure and paragraphs 6.27 to 6.30 of the General Advice and Information.

15. Please also note that it is a criminal offence to give false or misleading information to the CC.

ANNEX B

REQUEST FOR MAIN SUBMISSION FROM [NAME OF COMPANY]

Content of submission

Please provide the CC with a written submission by [date as paragraph 11] covering the following issues:

(a) Your company: Its brief history, together with the details of its organization, financial structure and principal activities.

(b) The relevant markets: An explanation of the product and geographic markets in which your company operates, dealing separately with the UK, the EC, and other international markets.

(c) The acquisition: A statement of the circumstances leading up to the acquisition, the acquisition itself and copies of any relevant agreements, together with the history of the previous relationship between the companies (if any) including relevant legal or financial issues.

(d) Your views on the purpose and effect of the acquisition: A statement of the purpose and expected consequences of the acquisition on competition.

On these points, among the considerations which may prove relevant in examining the effects of the merger on competition and on which you may like to comment in your submission are:

(i)   the relevant market [any particular areas relevant to this inquiry];

(ii)   information on [customers/suppliers];

(iii)   competition within the product and geographic markets identified in the terms of reference, and any other market definition you may consider relevant;

(iv)   barriers to entry to such markets;

(v)   the effect of the acquisition on [customers/suppliers];

(vi)   level of prices and variety and quality of products;

(vii)   capital structure and financing; and

(viii) any other issues which you consider relevant.

Non-sensitive version of submission

You should also provide a non-sensitive version of this submission indicating clearly the information that has been excluded by providing, for example, an annotated version of the full submission or by accompanying commentary provided the latter is sufficiently detailed. You should also give sufficient explanation of the nature of the sensitivity. For further information about the preparation of non-sensitive versions of submissions and the disclosure of information, please see paragraphs 10 to 13 of Annex A.

Delivery of submission

Please submit your response electronically—see Checklist of information for procedures—together with one hard copy for checking purposes.

ANNEX C

OFF-THE-SHELF MATERIAL REQUESTED FROM [NAME OF COMPANY]

Please send the following by [deadline as in paragraph 13] in electronic form plus one hard copy.

If this material is not genuinely easily available, please send what is. Do not delay your reply in order to fill any gaps, as we can return to the issues in the questionnaires.

1. The most recent annual report of the parent company 1: and the management accounts of any key subsidiaries that can be identified.

2. Any press notices issued, or other public announcements made, about the [proposed] acquisition.

3. Any circular issued to [Company 1] and/or [Company 2] shareholders concerning the acquisition(s).

4. [The legal agreement(s)]/[Any legal agreement(s) or drafts of such agreement(s)] governing the [proposed] acquisition(s).

5. [Company 1's [and possibly Company 2's]] internal appraisal, covering financial and other aspects, of the acquisitions. This should include any due diligence and valuation reports prepared by external advisers.

6. Extracts from the minutes of board meetings of any of the above companies, [and of any of the companies in the group of [name of company]] and/or of any executive committee, concerning the acquisitions, and any relevant presentations made to meetings of those bodies.

7. Latest version, including updates, of any business plan or other strategy document which you have prepared covering the operations in the areas of the acquisitions.

8. Any market research reports or consumer surveys on the [appropriate industry] sector that you have commissioned or are aware of in the last three years—but contact us if that request requires the production of an unreasonably large volume of data.

9. Any external assessments or commentaries and any broker/analyst reports that you are aware of concerning the [proposed] merger(s).

10. Names and contact points of those companies that you regard as actual and potential competitors in the reference area indicating their total size and size in the reference area.

11. Names and contact points of your most important suppliers and customers for [the reference product/service] including value of sales/purchases, length of the relationship and the contact details.

12. A corporate diagram showing names of companies in the group of Company 1 and Company 2 including relevant joint venture companies. If you think it would assist the CC's understanding, supply a diagram of the post-merger situation. Identify the companies by company number and indicate any other significant shareholdings that may be relevant to the inquiry. If it seems preferable to provide a simplified version of the group structure for the purpose of identifying those parts of the group that are most relevant to the inquiry, do so and indicate where omissions are made.

EXAMPLE OF TERMS OF REFERENCE MADE UNDER THE ENTERPRISE ACT

ANTICIPATED ACQUISITION BY STENA AB OF CERTAIN ASSETS OPERATED BY THE PENINSULAR AND ORIENTAL STEAM NAVIGATION COMPANY ON THE IRISH SEA   A7.001

Terms of reference

1. Whereas in exercise of its duty under section 33(1) of the Enterprise Act 2002 ('the Act') the Office of Fair Trading ('the OFT') believes that it is or may be the case that—

    (a) arrangements are in progress or in contemplation which, if carried into effect, will result in the creation of a relevant merger situation in that:

    (i) Stena AB ('Stena') will acquire certain assets currently used by The Peninsular and Oriental Steam Navigation Company (a body incorporated by Royal Charter in the United Kingdom) ('P&O') to supply ferry services on the Irish Sea between Liverpool and Dublin and between Fleetwood and Larne such that enterprises carried on by or under the control of P&O will cease to be distinct from enterprises carried on by or under the control of Stena; and

    (ii) as a result, the condition specified in section 23(4) of the Act will prevail to a greater extent; and

    (b) the creation of that situation may be expected to result in a substantial lessening of competition within a market or markets in the United Kingdom for services;

    now, therefore, the OFT, in exercise of its duty under section 33 of the Act and its power under section 36(5) of the Act, hereby makes a reference to the Competition Commission ('the Commission').

2. In relation to the question whether a relevant merger situation will be created, the Commission shall exclude from consideration one of subsections (1) and (2) of section 23 of the Act if they find that the other is satisfied.

Pat Edwards

Director of Legal Division

22 August 2003

APPENDIX 1 TO OFCOM GUIDANCE FOR THE PUBLIC INTEREST TEST FOR MEDIA MERGERS

APPENDIX 1—CONTENT OF SUBMISSIONS   A8.001

Some information from the merging parties will be requested by Ofcom in all public interest test cases, while other information will only be requested in certain circumstances and some information will only be required in exceptional circumstances. We recommend that all merging parties discuss Ofcom's information requirements with Ofcom before putting together any submission, to avoid unnecessary work and to expedite the process.

Appendix 1a—Information required in all cases

70. There is a certain amount of information that Ofcom would request that merging parties provide in their submission in all cases:

- Ownership

    — The full legal name of the parties involved, if they are parts of a corporate group(s), their position in the group and the name of relevant related companies. Any parts of the acquiring group, other than the acquiring company, that carry on business which overlaps with that of the target or which have a vertical relationship with that business should be identified

    — Name, address, contact telephone and fax numbers and email address for main contact for the merging parties

    — Details of the ultimate owner(s)/controller(s) and the ownership structure of the merged entity, including a breakdown of the shareholdings in the merging parties' and where possible, an assessment of any anticipated changes to the shareholding composition post-merger.

- Activities

    — Details of the parties' existing media businesses and the markets in which they operate, both in the UK and overseas:

        — List of newspaper titles
        — List of broadcasting services
        — Other media interests, held by those controlling the merging parties, the duration and size of interest, and details of any plans to increase or decrease such media interests post-merger.

- Share of "audience"

    — Audience reach, share and demographics of any broadcasting services in the UK and the likely impact of the merger on these numbers, together with revenues of the merging enterprises by source (e.g. advertising, subscription),

    — Circulation figures and average sales per issue for paid-for UK newspaper titles and free-sheets of both the acquirer and the acquired company,

    — Details (e.g. maps) of newspaper circulation area for local or regional papers.

- Complaints/Compliance in Broadcasting

    — For broadcasting services, details of complaints made directly against the acquiring owner, either in the UK or overseas, complaints made against broadcasting enterprises (for example, governing matters of accuracy, impartiality, harm, offence, fairness and privacy in broadcasting) to Ofcom or its predecessors, the outcome of complaints and details of any policy to apologise or publish corrections.

- Complaints in newspapers

    — For newspapers, details of complaints about the accuracy of news reporting made directly to the merging enterprises, complaints made about the merging newspapers to the PCC or other bodies, either in the UK or overseas in the past five years, and the outcome of complaints and details of any policy to apologise or publish corrections. Although Ofcom fully understands that the PCC process was not set up for this purpose, is not statutory and is non-binding we will take any relevant findings into account as one indicator of accuracy.

Appendix 1b -Additional information required in certain cases

71. In addition to the above list, Ofcom may request other information in assessing the public interest issues arising from a merger. It is not envisaged that all of this information will be required in every case.

72. The merging parties are recommended to discuss with Ofcom what information they may be requested to provide on a case by case basis. Information requests will be limited to that required to discharge Ofcom's statutory duties.

73. The list below gives the sort of information Ofcom may request. It is based upon information requested in previous cases by the Competition Commission and other regulators and is neither prescriptive nor exhaustive, and parties should also refer to the OFT guidance when compiling informal submissions, which sets out the background information that will be required in most cases.*

74. **Newspaper enterprises**

- **Readership** demographics and other information pertaining to the readership of the merging newspapers (e.g. relevant internal market research data) as well as an indication of the likely demographics of the readership(s) post-merger.

---

* See Chapter 4, OFT Mergers Procedural Guidance.

- **Current Policies on Editorial Independence.** Existing policies relating to reporting and journalistic standards and the accurate presentation of news. Information about the current level of contact between the owner and the editor/other senior management staff (relevant questions previously identified in the examination of issues raised by Johnston Press plc/Trinity Mirror, 2002).

- **Future Plans.** What will happen if the transfer is allowed to proceed

  — In the case of a merger between newspapers, whether it is intended that the newspaper(s) to be acquired should continue as separate newspapers and whether the transfer will lead to a concentration of ownership in a local area or region.

  — Arrangements envisaged for ensuring the accurate presentation of news in newspapers post-merger.

  — Arrangements for ensuring the policies of editorial independence of newspapers are maintained post-merger.

  — Details of whether the existing editor and reporting staff [are] likely to be maintained

  — What is the likely level of involvement of proprietors in editorial decisions, with evidence of track record from acquiring enterprise

- **Samples** of the newspaper where not already held by Ofcom (e.g. regional titles). A copy of the newspaper should be provided for each day of the most recent week in the case of daily newspapers and for each week of the most recent month in the case of weekly newspapers.

- **Personal statement** (in the case of acquisition by an individual) outlining any general plans for the newspapers post-merger, the type of market usually targeted by the acquiring owner, and details of personal editorial contributions to newspapers. In the case of a company we may look for a similar statement from the Board of that company.

75. Broadcasting enterprises

- **Content.** Data from each broadcasting operation controlled by each of the acquiring and the acquired enterprises as follows:

  — **For Television:** Data for the most recent calendar year and actual and planned for the current calendar year on:

    - Range of output measured by volume and cost by genre (standard Ofcom definitions) for the broadcasting enterprise being taken over (and if relevant the acquirer's broadcasting enterprises).
    - Data should be split into peak (18.00—22.30) and non-peak, with data for each of these day-parts further split into

      - In-house originations
      - Independent commissions
      - Acquired programming
      - Repeats

    - If relevant, information should also be provided on regional output by region (i.e. produced specifically for transmission in each region), split into:

      - news,
      - current affairs
      - other

    again split between peak and non-peak transmission.

- Data should also be provided on performance against each of the broadcaster's license commitments.

— **For Radio:** For both the acquired broadcaster and, if relevant, the acquiring broadcaster, data for the most recent calendar year and actual and planned for the current calendar year on:

- the location of each station,
- TSA coverage area and population,
- format,
- hours of locally produced programming,
- hours of automated programming,
- hours of syndicated programming (i.e. shared with other stations),
- the output of local news (hours per week and the number of journalists employed).
- Data should also be provided on performance against each of the broadcaster's license commitments

- Plans—Details of the planned output of the merged enterprise, including the acquirer's plans to ensure continued commitment to the existing range and quality of output, including:

— Broadcasting a wide range of subjects
— Meeting the needs/interests of as many different audiences as possible
— High general standards

- Originality and innovation
- High production values
- Ambitious programme making
- Acceptable standards of taste and decency

In particular, for mergers involving the Channel 3 licence holder or the Channel 5 licence holder:

— Details should be provided of any changes planned to the broadcasting service by reference to

- the type and content of the services
- the target audiences of the service
- the amount of original productions/commissions to be included
- the amount of first-run programmes to be included
- (as appropriate) the amounts of regional and sub-regional programmes broken down into news, current affairs and other types of programmes
- the proportion and range of programmes made in the UK that are made outside the M25 and the proportion of expenditure on programmes made in the UK which is referable to a range of production centres outside the M25
- the scheduling of programmes with particular reference to the amounts of original productions, news, current affairs and regional programmes in peak time (6pm to 10.30pm)

— Details of how the Channel 3 or Channel 5 licensee will in the future achieve the public service remit for the channel in Section 265 of the Communications Act 2003 and in . . . particular the requirement to provide a range of high quality programming and (in the case of Channel 3) high quality regional programmes. If any changes are planned to the organisation and staffing of the company, or to the

sources of supply for programmes to be included in the service, which might have a bearing on the ability of the licensee to achieve the above, give details.
— Details should be provided of . . . how the Channel 3 or Channel 5 licensee will contribute to the fulfilment of the purposes of public service broadcasting set out in Section 264 of the Communications Act 2003. Supporting information should be provided related to any changes planned as indicated above.
— In the case of Channel 3, details should be provided of any changes which are planned which would have the effect of reducing:

- The amount, quality and range of programmes to be offered to the network
- The proportion of regional (or sub-regional) programmes to be made in the region (or sub-region)
- The use in connection with the service of the services of persons employed (whether by the licensee or any other person) within the region (or sub-region)
- The extent to which managerial and editorial decisions relation to programmes are to be taken by persons employed within the region (or sub-region).

- Broadcasting obligations.

  — Merging parties past performance against the licence obligations specific to each service. Past investment in meeting broadcasting obligations and planned future investment.
  — Performance against published obligations to provide broadcasting services (e.g. enshrined in the statement of programme policy for TV broadcasters or in the format requirements for radio broadcasters). The past performance of the media enterprise against these obligations.
  — Merging parties' history of compliance with the various quotas applicable to broadcasters where relevant (e.g. origination, independent, European, regional) and the plans of the merged entity to comply with these quotas going forward.

- **For radio stations, samples** of the station's news output. The main news bulletin for each day (or the 8am bulletin if no special news programme is produced) broadcast over the most recent week should be recorded on to CD.

- **Personal statement** by the acquiring owner, or by the Board of the acquiring company, outlining any general plans for the broadcasting enterprise post-merger.

Appendix 1c—Information required in exceptional cases

76. Information in this Appendix will only be asked for in exceptional circumstances.

- **Content of Newspapers.** Ofcom may request an assessment of the proportion of content dedicated to news, advertising/advertorials and general features (e.g. sport, human-interest stories) in each relevant newspaper title together with an assessment of the likely impact of the merger and an indication of likely changes post-merger (relevant questions previously identified in the examination of issues raised by David Sullivan and the Bristol Evening Post, 1990).

- **Employment history** of the acquiring owner (either the acquiring individual or, in the case of a plc, the members of the Board) including newspaper and media-related employment, outlining length of service and position (relevant questions previously identified in the examination of issues raised by David Sullivan and the Bristol Evening Post, 1990).

EXTRACT FROM THE COMMISSION'S REPORT INTO THE PROPOSED ACQUISITION BY GANNETT UK LIMITED OF THREE TITLES OF SMG PLC[1]

Annex to public interest letter to SMG and Gannett　　　　　　　　A9.001

Criteria relevant to consideration of editorial freedom

1.　A useful if now historic discussion of this subject was included in the 1981 Observer: Outram report (Outram was then the owner of *The Herald*, and subsidiary of Lonrho). Of particular interest are the eight criteria set out in paragraph 8.37 of that report based on the suggestion of the 1974–1977 Royal Commission on the Press, namely that if editors were to be independent they should be assured of their basic rights, such as:

　(a)　the right to reject material provided by central management or editorial services;

　(b)　the right to determine the contents of the paper (within the bounds of reasonable economic consideration and the established policy of the publication);

　(c)　the right to allocate expenditure within a budget;

　(d)　the right to carry out investigative journalism;

　(e)　the right to reject advice on editorial policy;

　(f)　the right to criticise the paper's own group or other parts of the same corporate organisation;

　(g)　the right to change the alignment or views of the paper on specific issues within its agreed editorial policy; and

　(h)　the right to appoint or dismiss journalists and to decide the terms of their contract of employment within the established policy of the organisation, and the right to assign journalists to stories.

The Commission accepted those views as a useful description of the authority which the editor of a newspaper ought to possess but bearing in mind that presentation of news and expression of opinion depended on other journalists as well as the editor.

2.　In considering editorial freedom, however, it may be appropriate to consider supplementary criteria:

　(a)　that each title should have an editor and editorial team;

　(b)　that the editor should be a competent person of integrity who observes good professional standards;

---

[1] See *Gannett UK Limited and SMG plc*, Cm. 5782 (March 2003), Appendix 2.2

(c)   that those standards include accurate reporting of news relevant to the readership;

(d)   that those standards include free expression of opinion by the editor, the editor's team, invited columnists and feature writers, and members of the public by invitation and through letters;

(e)   that the editor be provided with resources to allow those professional standards to be achieved;

(f)   that the editor and editorial team is not exposed to (undue) pressure from proprietors, advertisers, politicians, businesses or managers in pursuit of financial objectives;

(g)   that there are mechanisms in place to defend editorial independence (such as policy statements, codes of conduct, appeal mechanisms).

3.   As well as freedom *from* such pressure, editorial freedom could be regarded as independence *to pursue* various courses of action, e.g.:

(a)   editorials—statements of views from the editorial team;

(b)   full news coverage from named reporters, including a willingness to criticize (and praise) politicians and other notables;

(c)   wide ranging feature articles with a good proportion of campaigning or critical content;

(d)   guest columnists, again with a critical as well as entertaining edge;

(e)   campaigns, which challenge government agencies, businesses, and established centres of power;

(f)   good election coverage with political views and preferences expressed openly;

(g)   vehicles for reader's and community views, traditionally a letters page, nowadays also web site vehicles?

4.   To this may be associated *operational independence*, in the development of expectations about aspects of the operations of newspaper companies. Three areas of immediate relevance may be:

(a)   Organisational. For example, the structure and hierarchy of the organisation—to whom does the editor report? Does he/she have managerial control of the editorial staff including hire and fire? Are there regional subsidiaries with prominent non-executives who could police independence (as proposed by Independent News and Media in the context of the Belfast Telegraph transfer in the recent INM/Trinity report).

(b)   Financial, as again in the INM/Trinity report, 'a threat to the accurate presentation of news and free expression of opinion could also arise from financial pressures leading to the closure of titles or to cost cutting so severe as to reduce the ability to engage in full and accurate reporting'.

(c)   Personnel. The contractual position of editors has been examined in previous inquiries, including hiring and dismissals. Freedom to join a Union might also be a factor.

OVERVIEW OF SUMMARIES OF MMC AND COMPETITION COMMISSION REPORTS (JANUARY 1986 TO JUNE 2004)

Note: under the FTA, where the Competition Commission or MMC concluded **A10.001** that a merger was not against the public interest, the Secretary of State was required to clear the merger unconditionally, with no discretion to do otherwise. In cases where this was the conclusion of the Competition Commission/MMC below, no entry is therefore made for the decision of the Secretary of State unless part of the merger was found to be against the public interest.

Key:

EA 2002	Enterprise Act 2002
ECMR	EC Merger Regulation
FTA	Fair Trading Act 1973
SLC	substantial lessening of competition

Date of report	Parties	Market activity	Relevant geographic market	Legal basis of jurisdiction	SLC/negative public interest finding?	MMC/CC recommendation (where applicable)	Sec of State/CC decision
28.06.04	FirstGroup plc and the Scottish Passenger Rail franchise	Operation of passenger rail services and local and regional bus services	Regional and local	EA 2002	SLC	N/A	Cleared subject to behavioural undertakings
19.05.04	Dräger Medical AG & Co KGaA and Hillenbrand Industries Inc	Various neonatal warming therapy products to UK hospitals	National	EA 2002	SLC	N/A	Cleared subject to behavioural undertakings
17.05.04	Carl Zeiss Jena GmbH and Bio-Rad Laboratories Inc	3D light microscope systems for biological research	Global	EA 2002	No SLC	N/A	Cleared unconditionally
06.02.04	Stena AB and The Peninsular and Oriental Steam Navigation Company	Maritime transportation by ferries of roll-on/roll-off and lift-on/lift-off freight	Regional	EA 2002	No SLC in northern corridor; SLC in central corridor	N/A	Part prohibited; part cleared unconditionally
22.01.04	March UK Ltd and the home shopping and home delivery businesses of GUS plc	Home shopping and home delivery services	National	FTA	Not against public interest		

Date of report	Parties	Market activity	Relevant geographic market	Legal basis of jurisdiction	SLC/negative public interest finding?	MMC/CC recommendation (where applicable)	Sec of State/CC decision
21.10.03	Newsquest (London) Limited and Independent News & Media PLC	Free and paid-for local newspapers	Local	FTA (newspaper reference)	Not against public interest in part; against public interest in other parts	Part should be cleared; part should be prohibited	Part cleared unconditionally; part prohibited
15.10.03	Arla Foods amba and Express Dairies plc	Fresh processed milk	Local, regional and national	Art.9 ECMR; FTA	Not against public interest		
07.10.03	Carlton Communications Plc and Granada plc	Commercial broadcasting, and sale of TV advertising airtime	National and regional	FTA	Not against public interest in part; against public interest in other parts	Clearance subject to behavioural remedies	Cleared subject to behavioural undertakings
18.08.03	Safeway plc and Asda Group Limited (owned by Wal-Mart Stores Inc); Wm Morrison Supermarkets PLC; J Sainsbury plc; and Tesco plc	One-stop supermarket shopping	National and local	FTA	Acquisition by Asda, Sainsbury's or Tesco against public interest at national and local level; acquisition by Morrisons against public interest at local level only	Acquisition by Asda, Sainsbury's or Tesco should be prohibited; acquisition by Morrisons should be cleared subject to structural divestments	Acquisition by Asda, Sainsbury's or Tesco prohibited; acquisition by Morrisons cleared conditional on structural divestments

Date of report	Parties	Market activity	Relevant geographic market	Legal basis of jurisdiction	SLC/negative public interest finding?	MMC/CC recommendation (where applicable)	Sec of State/CC decision
01.08.03	Centrica plc and Dynegy Storage Ltd and Dynegy Onshore Processing UK Limited	Retail gas supply and the operation of gas storage facilities and associated assets	National	FTA	Against public interest	Should be cleared subject to behavioural undertakings (failing which, structural divestments)	Cleared, conditional on behavioural undertakings (failing which, structural divestments)
16.05.03	Scottish Radio Holdings plc and GWR Group plc and Galaxy Radio Wales and The West Limited	Commercial radio broadcasting; sale of radio advertising airtime	Local	FTA	Against public interest	Any clearance should be subject to structural undertakings	Cleared, conditional on structural undertakings
28.03.03	Gannett UK Limited and SMG plc	Regional and local newspapers	Regional and local	FTA (newspaper reference)	Not against public interest		
07.03.03	VNU Entertainment Media UK Limited and Book Data Limited	Commercial bibliographic data services and electronic transaction services to the book industry	National	FTA	Not against public interest		

Date of report	Parties	Market activity	Relevant geographic market	Legal basis of jurisdiction	SLC/negative public interest finding?	MMC/CC recommendation (where applicable)	Sec of State/CC decision
08.11.02	Vivendi Water UK plc and First Aqua Limited	Supply of water and sewage services	Regional	Art.21 ECMR; Water Industry Act 1991	Against public interest	Should be cleared subject to structural undertakings	Cleared subject to structural and behavioural remedies
22.10.02	Group 4 Falck a/s and the Wackenhut Corporation	Out-sourced facility management services for public sector (including prison/ detention facilities, prisoner transport), security and safety services.	National	FTA	Not against public interest		
05.07.02	Compass Group plc and Rail Gourmet Holding AG, Restorama AG and Gourmet Nova AG	Supply of on-train food services	National	Art.9 EMCR; FTA	Not against public interest		
26.06.02	H+H Celcon Limited and Marley Building Materials Limited	Manufacture and supply of aerated concrete blocks for the construction industry.	National	FTA	Against public interest	Should be prohibited	Cleared, conditional on structural undertakings

Date of report	Parties	Market activity	Relevant geographic market	Legal basis of jurisdiction	SLC/negative public interest finding?	MMC/CC recommendation (where applicable)	Sec of State/CC decision
19.06.02	P&O Princess Cruises plc and Royal Caribbean Cruises Ltd	Operation of cruise lines	National (i.e. UK customers)	FTA	Not against public interest		
14.06.02	Coloplast A/S and SSL International	Manufacture and supply of continence care products	National	FTA	Against public interest	Should be cleared subject to structural undertakings, with possible additional behavioural remedy	Cleared subject to structural undertakings
30.05.02	Cargill Incorporated and Cerestar	Production of glucose syrups and blends for food applications and as fermentation agents	National and EU	Art.9 ECMR; FTA	Not against public interest		
23.05.02	Neopost SA and Ascom Holding AG	Supply of franking machines (and after-sales service) and folding and inserting machines (including maintenance and repair services)	National and global	FTA	Not against public interest but review of operation of market in 3–5 years also recommended		

Date of report	Parties	Market activity	Relevant geographic market	Legal basis of jurisdiction	SLC/negative public interest finding?	MMC/CC recommendation (where applicable)	Sec of State/CC decision
13.05.02	Linpac Group Limited and McKechnie Paxton Holdings Limited	Manufacture and supply of returnable transit packaging (plastic containers) for retail and food sectors	National	FTA	Not against public interest		
03.05.02	Johnston Press plc and Trinity Mirror Plc	Publication of weekly newspapers	Local	FTA (newspaper reference)	Not against public interest in part; against public interest in other parts	Part should be cleared; part should be prohibited	Part cleared unconditionally; part prohibited
21.12.01	Eastman Kodak Company and Colourcare	Wholesale photo-processing services to retailers	National	FTA	Not against public interest		
09.11.01	Duralay International Holding Ltd and Gates Consumer & Industrial	Carpet underlay and accessories (primarily gripper)	National	FTA	Not against public interest		
06.09.01	Octagon Motorsports Limited and British Racing Drivers Club Limited	Motorsports circuit operations	National	FTA	Not against public interest		

Date of report	Parties	Market activity	Relevant geographic market	Legal basis of jurisdiction	SLC/negative public interest finding?	MMC/CC recommendation (where applicable)	Sec of State/CC decision
10.07.01	Lloyds TSB Group plc and Abbey National plc	Sale of financial and banking products to personal customers, small and medium-sized enterprises and larger firms, and wholesale banking	National, global	FTA	Against public interest	Should be prohibited	Prohibited
05.07.01	Reed Elsevier plc and Harcourt General Inc.	Scientific, technical and medical publishing, sub-divided into books and journals	National	FTA	Not against public interest, but wider review of pricing in this market also recommended		
04.07.01	BASF AG and Takeda Chemical Industries Ltd	Supply of vitamins (in particular C and B2)	Global	FTA	Not against public interest		
04.07.01	SCR-Sibelco SA and Fife Silica Sands Ltd and Fife Resources Ltd	Sand for glass manufacture	National	FTA	Against public interest	Should be prohibited	Prohibited

Date of report	Parties	Market activity	Relevant geographic market	Legal basis of jurisdiction	SLC/negative public interest finding?	MMC/CC recommendation (where applicable)	Sec of State/CC decision
13.03.01	Icopal Holding A/S and Icopal A/S	Bituminous flat-roof coverings (roofing felts), pitched roof underslatings and damp proof courses	National	FTA	Not against public interest		
03.01.01	Interbrew SA and Bass plc	Brewing, wholesaling and distribution of beer	National	Art.9 ECMR; FTA	Against public interest	Should be prohibited	Prohibited
22.12.00	Nutreco Holding NV and Hydro Seafood GSP	Atlantic farmed and gutted salmon, including Scottish salmon; salmon feed manufacture	EEA, regional, national	FTA	Against public interest	Should be prohibited	Prohibited
07.12.00	British United Provident Association Ltd and Community Hospitals Group plc, Salomon International LLC and Community Hospitals Group plc	Private medical insurance, private medical services	National	FTA	Against public interest	Should be prohibited	Prohibited

Date of report	Parties	Market activity	Relevant geographic market	Legal basis of jurisdiction	SLC/negative public interest finding?	MMC/CC recommendation (where applicable)	Sec of State/CC decision
02.11.00	Sylvan International Limited and Locker Group plc	Small steel, timber, plywood and cardboard drums for the package and transport of cables and wires; timber drum management services	National	FTA	Against public interest	Should be cleared subject to behavioural undertakings	Prohibited
01.11.00	Regional Independent Media Limited and Gannett UK Limited/ Johnston Press plc/ Guardian Media Group plc	Publication of newspapers	Local, regional	FTA (newspaper reference)	Not against public interest		
31.08.00	Air Canada and Canadian Airlines Corporation	Airline passenger routes between the UK and Canada	Global	FTA	Not against public interest		
17.07.00	Independent News & Media plc and Belfast Telegraph	Publication of daily and weekly newspapers, and sale of advertising space in newspapers	Regional and local	FTA	Not against public interest		

Date of report	Parties	Market activity	Relevant geographic market	Legal basis of jurisdiction	SLC/negative public interest finding?	MMC/CC recommendation (where applicable)	Sec of State/CC decision
16.06.00	Carlton Communications plc/ United News and Media plc/Granada Group	Production and broadcasting of TV programmes, sale of advertising time	National	FTA	One of the three merger proposals against public interest; other two proposals not against public interest	Anti-competitive merger should be cleared subject to structural undertakings. Other two mergers needed divestments to comply with media ownership rules.	Anti-competitive merger cleared subject to structural undertakings (different to those recommended). Other two mergers cleared with necessary divestments.
18.04.00	Vivendi SA and BSkyB Group plc	Pay TV services	National	FTA	Not against public interest		
04.04.00	News Communications & Media plc and Newsquest Ltd/ Johnston Press Ltd/ Trinity Mirror plc	Daily and weekly newspapers	National and local	FTA (newspaper reference)	Not against public interest		
22.03.00	NTL Incorporated and Cable and Wireless Communications plc	Pay TV services, cable telecommunications services	National	FTA	Not against public interest		

Date of report	Parties	Market activity	Relevant geographic market	Legal basis of jurisdiction	SLC/negative public interest finding?	MMC/CC recommendation (where applicable)	Sec of State/CC decision
19.01.00	CHC Helicopter Corporation and Helicopter Services Group SA	Helicopter support services	Regional	FTA	Not against public interest		
19.01.00	Alanod Aluminium-Veredlung GmbH & Co and Metalloxyd Ano-Coil Ltd	Specular anodized aluminium coil for use in lighting	Global	FTA	Against public interest	Should be cleared subject to a package of behavioural undertakings	Cleared, conditional on behavioural undertakings
21.12.99	Universal Foods Corporation and Pointings Holdings Limited	Flavours, natural colours and synthetic colours for the food	National	FTA	Not against public interest		
23.07.99	Trinity plc/Mirror Group plc and Regional Independent Media Holdings Limited/Mirror Group plc	Publication of newspapers	Regional, local	FTA (newspaper reference)	Not against public interest, except, in the case of the Trinity/Mirror, in relation to Northern Ireland	Trinity/Mirror transaction should be cleared in part but in relation to Northern Ireland, subject to structural undertakings.	Cleared but, in relation to Trinity/Mirror transaction, conditional on structural undertakings (different to those recommended).

Date of report	Parties	Market activity	Relevant geographic market	Legal basis of jurisdiction	SLC/negative public interest finding?	MMC/CC recommendation (where applicable)	Sec of State/CC decision
20.07.99	British Airways plc and Cityflyer Express Limited	International passenger air services	Global, regional	FTA	Against public interest	Should be cleared subject to behavioural undertaking capping BA's share of landing slots at Gatwick	Cleared, conditional on behavioural undertaking capping BA's share of landing slots at Gatwick
16.06.99	Portsmouth & Sunderland Newspapers plc and Johnston Press plc/ Newquest (Investments) Limited/News Communications and Media plc	Publication and circulation of newspapers	Local, regional, national	FTA (newspaper reference)	Not against public interest		
07.05.99	Rockwool Ltd and Owens-Corning Building Products (UK) Ltd	Stone wool	National	FTA	Against public interest	Should be prohibited	Prohibited
09.04.99	British Sky Broadcasting Group plc and Manchester United plc	TV broadcasting, sale of TV rights for sporting events, premium sports channels	National	FTA	Against public interest	Should be prohibited	Prohibited

Date of report	Parties	Market activity	Relevant geographic market	Legal basis of jurisdiction	SLC/negative public interest finding?	MMC/CC recommendation (where applicable)	Sec of State/CC decision
25.02.99	IMS Health Inc and Pharmaceutical Marketing Services Inc.	Pharmaceutical business information services	National	FTA	Against public interest	Should be cleared subject to structural and behavioural undertakings	Cleared, conditional on structural and behavioural undertakings
04.02.99	Cendant Corporation and RAC Holdings Limited	Insured breakdown services for light vehicles	National	FTA	Against public interest	Should be cleared subject to structural undertakings	Cleared, conditional on structural undertakings required in short timeframe
18.11.98	Arriva plc and Lutonian Buses Ltd	Bus services	Local	FTA	Against public interest	Should be prohibited	Prohibited
25.09.98	Tomkins plc and Kerry Group plc	Production and supply of milled flour	National	FTA	Against public interest	Should be cleared subject to structural undertakings	Cleared, conditional on structural undertakings
24.09.98	Ladbroke Group PLC and the Coral betting business	Off-course betting through licensed betting offices and telephone betting	National	FTA	Against public interest	Should be prohibited	Prohibited

654

Date of report	Parties	Market activity	Relevant geographic market	Legal basis of jurisdiction	SLC/negative public interest finding?	MMC/CC recommendation (where applicable)	Sec of State/CC decision
10.06.98	Johnston Press plc & Home Counties Newspapers Holdings plc	Publication of weekly newspaper	Local	FTA (newspaper reference)	Not against public interest		
30.04.98	Fresenius AG and Caremark Limited	Contracted services procured by health authorities for patients at home	National	FTA	Against public interest	Should be prohibited	Prohibited
13.01.98	Capital Radio plc and Virgin Radio Holdings Limited	Commercial radio broadcasting and sale of radio advertising airtime	Local and national	FTA	Against public interest	Should be prohibited or cleared subject to structural undertakings	Merger abandoned
19.12.97	Pacificorp and The Energy Group plc	Supply of electricity	National	FTA	Not against public interest		
16.12.97	National Express Group plc and Central Trains Limited	Coach services and passenger rail services	Regional	FTA	Not against public interest		
16.12.97	National Express Group plc and Scotrail Railways Limited	Long distance coach services and passenger train services	Regional	FTA	Against public interest	Should be cleared subject to structural undertakings	Cleared, conditional on structural undertakings

Date of report	Parties	Market activity	Relevant geographic market	Legal basis of jurisdiction	SLC/negative public interest finding?	MMC/CC recommendation (where applicable)	Sec of State/CC decision
19.11.97	Peninsular & Oriental Steam Navigation Company and Stena Line AB	Cross channel ferry services for passengers and freight	National and cross-border	FTA	Against public interest	Should be cleared subject to behavioural undertakings	Cleared, conditional on behavioural undertakings
18.11.97	The Littlewoods Organisation plc and Freemans plc	Catalogue mail order business in home shopping sector of non-food retailing	National and regional	FTA	Against public interest	Should be prohibited	Prohibited
21.10.97	Mirror Group plc and Midland Independent Newspapers	Publication and distribution of newspapers	Regional and local	FTA (newspaper reference)	Not against public interest		
05.08.97	London Clubs International and Capital Corporation plc	Operation of London casinos	Local	FTA	Against public interest	Should be prohibited	Prohibited
24.07.97	Technicolour Limited and Metrocolour London Limited	Film processing for television and cinema	National and EU	FTA	Not against public interest		

Date of report	Parties	Market activity	Relevant geographic market	Legal basis of jurisdiction	SLC/negative public interest finding?	MMC/CC recommendation (where applicable)	Sec of State/CC decision
27.06.97	Bass PLC, Calsberg A/S and Carlsberg-Tetley PLC	Brewing of beer	National	FTA	Against public interest	Should be cleared subject to structural undertakings	Prohibited
13.06.97	Klaus J Jacobs Holding AG and Société Centrale d'Investissements et Associés	Supply of couverture (industrial chocolate)	National	FTA	Not against public interest		
18.03.97	Cowie Group plc and British Bus Group Limited	Vehicle leasing and financing, motor retailing, bus distribution and bus service operations	Regional and national	FTA	Not against public interest		
24.01.97	Firstbus and SB Holdings Limited	Provision of local bus services	Local and regional	FTA	Against public interest	Should be cleared subject to structural undertakings	Cleared, conditional on structural undertakings
21.01.97	Mid Kent Holdings plc and General Utilities plc and Saur Water Services plc	Supply of water	Regional	Water Industry Act 1991	Against public interest	Should be prohibited	Prohibited

Date of report	Parties	Market activity	Relevant geographic market	Legal basis of jurisdiction	SLC/negative public interest finding?	MMC/CC recommendation (where applicable)	Sec of State/CC decision
24.12.96	Robert Wiseman Dairies plc and Scottish Pride Holdings plc	Supply of fresh processed milk and cream, ultra heat treated milk, cream and cheese and procurement of raw milk	Regional and national	FTA	Against public interest	Should be cleared subject to structural and behavioural undertakings	Cleared, conditional on structural and behavioural undertakings
20.12.96	National Express Group plc and Midland Main Line Limited	Long distance coach services and passenger train operating services	Regional	FTA	Against public interest	Should be cleared subject to behavioural undertakings	Cleared, conditional on behavioural undertakings
28.11.96	Newsquest Media Group Limited and Westminster Press Limited	Publication of daily and weekly, paid for and free local and regional newspapers	Local, regional and national	FTA (newspaper reference)	Not against public interest		
25.10.96	Wessex Water plc and South West Water plc	Water and sewerage businesses	Regional	Water Industry Act 1991 and FTA	Against public interest	Merger should be prohibited	Prohibited
25.10.96	Severn Trent plc and South West Water	Water and sewerage businesses	Regional	Water Industry Act 1991	Against public interest	Merger should be prohibited	Prohibited

Date of report	Parties	Market activity	Relevant geographic market	Legal basis of jurisdiction	SLC/negative public interest finding?	MMC/CC recommendation (where applicable)	Sec of State/CC decision
09.08.96	NV Verenigde Bedrijven Nutricia and Enterprises belonging to Milupa AG	Enteral clinical nutrition products, baby drinks, baby meals and baby milk products	National	FTA	Not against public interest but recommended keeping market under review		
19.07.96	Unichem plc/Lloyds Chemists plc and Gehe AG and Lloyd's Chemists plc	Pharmaceutical wholesaling and retail pharmacies	Regional	Art.9 ECMR; FTA	Both mergers against public interest	Both mergers should be cleared subject to structural undertakings	Both mergers cleared, conditional on structural undertakings
25.04.96	PowerGen plc and Midlands Electric plc	Generation, distribution and supply of electricity	National and regional	FTA	Against public interest	Should be cleared subject to structural and behavioural undertakings	Prohibited
25.04.96	National Power plc and Southern Electricity plc	Generation, distribution and supply of electricity	Regional and national	FTA	Against public interest	Should be cleared subject to structural and behavioural undertakings	Prohibited
08.03.96	British Bus plc and Arrowline (Travel) Limited	Bus services	National	FTA	Not against public interest		

Date of report	Parties	Market activity	Relevant geographic market	Legal basis of jurisdiction	SLC/negative public interest finding?	MMC/CC recommendation (where applicable)	Sec of State/CC decision
27.02.96	Northcliffe Newspapers Group Limited and Aberdeen Journals Limited	Daily, weekly, monthly and bi-monthly publication of newspapers	Local and regional	FTA (newspaper reference)	Not against public interest		
02.02.96	The Go-Ahead Group plc and OK Motor Services Limited	Bus services	Regional	FTA	Not against public interest		
18.01.96	Stagecoach Holdings plc and Chesterfield Transport (1989) Limited	Bus services	Local	FTA	Not against public interest		
09.01.96	Belfast International Airport Limited and Belfast City Airport Limited	Airport services	Regional	FTA	Against public interest	Merger should be prohibited	Prohibited
21.12.95	Nutricia Holdings Limited and Valio International UK Limited	Supply of enteral clinical nutrition products, production and sale of specialist gluten-free and low protein foods	National	FTA	Against public interest	Should be cleared subject to behavioural undertakings	Cleared, conditional on behavioural undertakings

Date of report	Parties	Market activity	Relevant geographic market	Legal basis of jurisdiction	SLC/negative public interest finding?	MMC/CC recommendation (where applicable)	Sec of State/CC decision
10.11.95	Trinity International Holdings plc and Thomson Regional Newspapers Limited	Publication, sale and distribution of newspapers	Local and regional	FTA (newspaper reference)	Not against public interest		
03.11.95	Stagecoach Holdings plc and Ayrshire Bus Owners (A1 Service) Limited	Bus services	Regional	FTA	Against public interest	Should be cleared, subject to behavioural undertakings	Cleared, conditional on behavioural undertakings
28.07.95	Lyonnaise des Eaux and Northumbrian Water Group plc	Supply of water and sewerage services	Regional	Art.21 ECMR; Water Industry Act 1991	Against public interest	Should be cleared, subject to behavioural undertakings	Cleared, conditional on behavioural undertakings
25.05.95	Service Corporation International and Plantsbrook Group plc	Supply of funeral directing services, prepaid funerals and crematoria.	Local, regional and national	FTA	Against public interest	Should be cleared subject to structural and behavioural undertakings	Cleared subject to structural and behavioural undertakings
23.05.95	General Electric Company plc and VSEL plc	Military activities including supply of submarines, warships and warship equipment.	National	Art.223 EC Treaty; ECMR; FTA	Against public interest	Should be prohibited	Cleared unconditionally

Date of report	Parties	Market activity	Relevant geographic market	Legal basis of jurisdiction	SLC/negative public interest finding?	MMC/CC recommendation (where applicable)	Sec of State/CC decision
23.05.95	British Aerospace plc and VSEL plc	Military activities including supply of warships, armaments and prime contracting services.	National	Art.223 EC Treaty; ECMR; FTA	Not against public interest		
27.04.95	SB Holdings Ltd and Kelvin Central Buses Limited	Operation of bus services (other local transport considered)	Regional	FTA	Not against public interest		
27.04.95	Stagecoach Holdings plc and SB Holdings Ltd	Operation of bus services	Regional	FTA	Against public interest	Should be prohibited	Prohibited
23.03.95	Thomas Cook and Interpayment Services Limited	Issue of travellers cheques	National and global	FTA	Against public interest	Should be cleared subject to behavioural undertakings	Cleared, conditional on behavioural undertakings
09.03.95	Stagecoach Holdings plc and Mainline Partnership Limited	Operation of bus services	Regional and local	FTA	Against public interest	Clearance should be subject to structural undertaking limiting shareholding	Prohibited

Date of report	Parties	Market activity	Relevant geographic market	Legal basis of jurisdiction	SLC/negative public interest finding?	MMC/CC recommendation (where applicable)	Sec of State/CC decision
31.10.94	Daily Mail and General Trust PLC/ T Bailey Forman Limited	Publication of local newspapers	Local	FTA (newspaper reference)	Against public interest	Should be prohibited	Cleared, conditional on structural and behavioural undertakings
17.06.94	Johnston Press PLC/ Halifax Courier Holdings Limited	Publication of regional and local newspapers	Local and regional	FTA (newspaper reference)	Not against public interest		
24.02.94	Alcatel Cable SA and STC Limited	Supply of long and short haul submarine cable telecommunications systems	Global	FTA	Not against public interest		
17.02.94	National Express Group PLC/Saltire Holdings Ltd.	Scheduled coach services	National	FTA	Not against public interest, but recommended keeping market under review		
22.12.93	The Guardian & Manchester Evening News plc/Thames Valley Newspapers	Publication of regional and local newspapers	Regional and local	FTA (newspaper reference	Not against public interest		

Date of report	Parties	Market activity	Relevant geographic market	Legal basis of jurisdiction	SLC/negative public interest finding?	MMC/CC recommendation (where applicable)	Sec of State/CC decision
26.10.93	Trinity International Holdings plc/Joseph Woodhead & Sons Limited	Publication of regional and local newspapers	Regional and local	FTA (newspaper reference)	Not against public interest		
26.10.93	Argus Press Ltd/ Trinity International Holdings plc	Publication of regional and local newspapers	Regional and local	FTA (newspaper reference)	Not against public interest		
01.12.93	Stagecoach Holdings plc/Lancaster City Transport Limited	Local bus services	Local	FTA	Against public interest	Should be cleared subject to behavioural undertakings	Cleared subject to behavioural undertakings
10.02.93	The Gillette Company/Parker Pen Holdings Limited	Supply of refillable writing instruments	National	FTA	Not against public interest but certain consumer protection issues should be kept under review		
08.12.92	Scottish Milk Marketing Board/ Co-operative Wholesale Society Ltd	Processing and wholesale supply of fresh milk and production of dairy products	Regional	FTA	Against public interest	Should be prohibited unless restructured	Prohibited

Date of report	Parties	Market activity	Relevant geographic market	Legal basis of jurisdiction	SLC/negative public interest finding?	MMC/CC recommendation (where applicable)	Sec of State/CC decision
13.10.92	EMAP plc/United Newspapers plc	Publication of regional and local newspapers	Regional and local	FTA (newspaper reference)	Not against public interest		
16.09.92	Bond Helicopters Ltd/ British International Helicopters Ltd	Helicopter support services	Regional	FTA	Against public interest	Should be prohibited	Prohibited
13.08.92	Sara Lee Corporation/ Reckitt & Colman plc	Supply of shoe polish and related products	National	FTA	Against public interest	Should be cleared subject to structural undertakings	Cleared, conditional on structural undertakings
28.07.92	Allied-Lyons plc/ Carlsberg A/S	Brewing and related wholesaling activities	National	FTA	Against public interest	Should be cleared subject to behavioural undertakings	Cleared subject to modified behavioural undertakings
10.07.92	Trinity International Holdings plc/Scottish & Universal Newspapers Ltd	Publication of daily and weekly regional newspapers	Regional	FTA (newspaper reference)	Not against public interest		
07.07.92	Hillsdown Holdings PLC and enterprises belonging to Associated British Foods plc	Canning of fruit and vegetables, and production of ambient stored meals	National	FTA	Not against public interest		

Date of report	Parties	Market activity	Relevant geographic market	Legal basis of jurisdiction	SLC/negative public interest finding?	MMC/CC recommendation (where applicable)	Sec of State/CC decision
07.05.92	AAH Holdings plc/ Medicopharma NV	The supply of pharmaceuticals	National and regional	FTA	Against public interest	Should be prohibited	Cleared, subject to behavioural undertakings
26.02.92	UniChem plc/ Macarthy plc and Lloyds Chemists plc/Macarthy plc	Wholesaling and retailing of pharmaceuticals and health food	National	FTA	Neither merger against public interest but monitoring of pharmaceuticals sector recommended		
27.11.91	Southern Newspapers plc and EMAP plc, Pearson plc, Reed International plc and Trinity International Holdings plc	Publishing of local newspapers	National and local	FTA (newspaper reference)	Not against public interest		
22.11.91	Avenir Havas Media SA/ Brunton Curtis Outdoor Advertising Ltd	Supply of roadside poster advertising services	National	FTA	Against public interest	Should be cleared subject to structural undertakings	Cleared, conditional on structural undertakings
13.08.91	The enterprises of Alan J Lewis/Jarmain & Son Ltd	Supply of wool scouring services to third parties	National	FTA	Against public interest	Should be cleared subject to structural undertakings	Cleared, conditional on structural undertakings

Date of report	Parties	Market activity	Relevant geographic market	Legal basis of jurisdiction	SLC/negative public interest finding?	MMC/CC recommendation (where applicable)	Sec of State/CC decision
01.08.91	Prosper De Mulder Ltd/Croda International plc	Animal waste rendering	Regional	FTA	Not against public interest		
29.05.91	The Morgan Crucible Company plc/ Manville Corporation	Supply of refractory ceramic fibre	National and European	FTA	Not against public interest		
03.05.91	Amoco Corporation/ Société Nationale Elf Acquitaine	Refining, wholesaling and retailing of oil and petroleum products	National	FTA	Not against public interest		
20.03.91	Stora Kopparbergs Bergslags AB/Swedish Match NV, and Stora Kopparbergs Bergslags AB/The Gillette Company	Supply of razors and razor blades	National	FTA	Against public interest	Should be prohibited	Formal prohibition rendered unnecessary by unconditional sale, prompting revocation of interim order
26.02.91	Sligos SA/Signet Ltd	Processing of payment card transactions	National	FTA	Not against public interest		

Date of report	Parties	Market activity	Relevant geographic market	Legal basis of jurisdiction	SLC/negative public interest finding?	MMC/CC recommendation (where applicable)	Sec of State/CC decision
06.02.91	Tate & Lyle plc/ British Sugar plc	Refining of British sugar beet and imported raw cane sugar and production of related products	National	FTA	Against public interest	Should be prohibited	Prohibited
30.01.91	British Aerospace plc Thomson–CSF SA	Manufacture and sale of guided weapons systems	National	FTA	Not against public interest		
30.01.91	Caldaire Holdings Ltd/Bluebird Securities Ltd	Supply of bus services	Local	FTA	Against public interest	Should be cleared subject to behavioural undertakings	Cleared subject to modified behavioural undertakings
23.01.91	Crédit Lyonnais SA/Woodchester Investment plc	Provision of financial services, including equipment leasing, instalment credit, mortgage and trade finance	National	FTA	Not against public interest		
23.01.91	Kemira Oy/Imperial Chemical Industries plc	Manufacture and sale of solid and liquid chemical agricultural fertilisers	National	FTA	Against public interest	Should be prohibited	Prohibited

Date of report	Parties	Market activity	Relevant geographic market	Legal basis of jurisdiction	SLC/negative public interest finding?	MMC/CC recommendation (where applicable)	Sec of State/CC decision
09.01.91	Valhi Inc/Akzo NV	Sale of organoclays, organics and organic pastes for the manufacture of solvent-based paints and production of oil-based drilling fluids.	National	FTA	Against public interest	Should be prohibited	Prohibited
20.12.90	Stagecoach (Holdings) Ltd/Formia Ltd	Supply of bus services	Local	FTA	Against public interest	Should be cleared subject to behavioural undertakings	Cleared subject to behavioural undertakings
19.12.90	Trelleborg AB/ McKechnie Extruded Products Ltd	Production of semi-finished extruded brass	National	FTA	Not against public interest		
16.10.90	Elders IXL Ltd/Grand Metropolitan plc	Brewing and supply (through non-licensed premises) of beer	National	FTA	Against the public interest	Should be cleared subject to structural undertakings	Cleared subject to modified structural undertakings
04.10.90	Western Travel Ltd/ G & G Coaches (Leamington) Ltd	Supply of bus services	Local	FTA	Not against public interest		

Date of report	Parties	Market activity	Relevant geographic market	Legal basis of jurisdiction	SLC/negative public interest finding?	MMC/CC recommendation (where applicable)	Sec of State/CC decision
30.8.90	William Cook plc acquisitions	Supply of steel castings	National	FTA	Not against the public interest		
01.08.90	South Yorkshire Transport Ltd acquisitions	Supply of bus services	Local	FTA	Against public interest	Should be prohibited	Cleared subject to behavioural undertakings
25.07.90	British Airways plc/ Sabena SA	Provision of air transport services	UK/ Belgium routes	FTA	Not against public interest		
13.07.90	BICC plc/Sterling Greengate Cable Company Ltd	Manufacture and supply of cables	National	FTA	Not against public interest		
13.07.90	Ransomes plc/ Cushman Inc, Brouwer Equipment Inc and Brouwer Turf Equipment Ltd	Manufacture and distribution of commercial grass-care equipment	National	FTA	Not against public interest		
13.07.90	Ransomes plc/ Westwood Engineering Ltd and Laser Lawnmowers Ltd	Manufacture and sale of domestic lawn mowers	National	FTA	Not against public interest		

Date of report	Parties	Market activity	Relevant geographic market	Legal basis of jurisdiction	SLC/negative public interest finding?	MMC/CC recommendation (where applicable)	Sec of State/CC decision
12.07.90	Stagecoach (Holdings) Ltd/Portsmouth Citybus Ltd undertakings	Operation of bus services	Local	FTA	Against public interest	Should be cleared subject to behavioural	Prohibited
04.07.90	General Utilities plc/The Mid Kent Water Company	Supply of water and sewerage services	Regional	Water Act 1989	Against public interest	Should be cleared subject to behavioural undertakings	Cleared subject to behavioural and structural undertakings
04.07.90	Southern Water plc/Mid-Sussex Water Company	Supply of water and sewerage services	Regional	Water Act 1989	Not against public interest		
31.05.90	Mr David Sullivan/The Bristol Evening Post plc	Publication of newspapers	Regional	FTA (newspaper reference)	Against public interest	Should be prohibited	Prohibited
23.05.90	Kingfisher plc/Dixons Group plc	Retail of electrical appliances and photographic equipment	National	FTA	Against public interest	Should be prohibited	Prohibited
02.05.90	Tiphook plc/Trailerent Ltd	Trailer rental	National	FTA	Not against public interest		

Date of report	Parties	Market activity	Relevant geographic market	Legal basis of jurisdiction	SLC/negative public interest finding?	MMC/CC recommendation (where applicable)	Sec of State/CC decision
27.04.90	General Utilities plc/The Colne Valley Water Company/ Rickmansworth Water Company	Supply of water and sewerage services	Regional	Water Act 1989	Against public interest	Should be cleared subject to behavioural undertakings	Cleared subject to behavioural undertakings
04.04.90	British Steel plc/ C Walker & Son (Holdings) Ltd	Stockholding of steel products	National	FTA	Not against public interest		
21.03.90	The British United Provident Association Ltd/HCA United Kingdom Ltd	Private hospital services	National	FTA	Not against public interest		
07.03.90	Michelin Tyre plc/ National Tyre Service Ltd	Supply and distribution of tyres	National	FTA	Not against public interest for distribution of car tyres but against public interest for distribution of replacement truck tyres	Part should be cleared unconditionally; part should be cleared subject to structural undertakings	Part cleared unconditionally, part cleared subject to structural undertakings

Date of report	Parties	Market activity	Relevant geographic market	Legal basis of jurisdiction	SLC/negative public interest finding?	MMC/CC recommendation (where applicable)	Sec of State/CC decision
25.01.90	Atlas Copco AB/ Desoutter Brothers (Holdings) plc	Supply of industrial pneumatic power tools	National	FTA	Not against public interest		
21.12.89	Blue Circle Industries plc/ Myson Group plc	Manufacture of domestic gas central heating boilers	National	FTA	Not against public interest		
21.12.89	Yale & Valor plc/ Myson Group plc	Manufacture and sale of domestic gas fires	National	FTA	Not against public interest		
26.10.89	Coats Viyella plc/ Tootal Group plc	Textiles and clothing	Global, and national	FTA	Against public interest	Should be cleared subject to structural undertakings	Cleared subject to structural undertakings
18.10.89	Monsanto Company/ Rhone-Poulenc SA	Supply of analgesic chemicals, including salicylic acid, methyl salicylate and bulk aspirin	National	FTA	Not against public interest		
30.08.89	Glynwed International plc/ JB&S Lees Ltd	Supply of hardened and tempered steel strip	National	FTA	Not against public interest		

Date of report	Parties	Market activity	Relevant geographic market	Legal basis of jurisdiction	SLC/negative public interest finding?	MMC/CC recommendation (where applicable)	Sec of State/CC decision
23.08.89	Grand Metropolitan Plc/William Hill Organisation Ltd	Off-course bookmaking services	National	FTA	Against public interest	Should be cleared subject to structural undertakings	Cleared subject to structural undertakings
27.04.89	Century Newspapers Ltd/Thomson Regional Newspapers Ltd	Publication of regional newspapers	Regional	FTA (newspaper reference)	Against public interest	Should be prohibited	Prohibited
21.04.89	The General Electric Company plc/Siemens AG/The Plessy Company plc	Defence electronics, telecommunications, electronics components and traffic control equipment	National	FTA	Against public interest	Should be cleared subject to structural and behavioural undertakings	Cleared subject to structural and behavioural undertakings
11.04.89	Hillsdown Holdings plc/Pittard Garnar plc	Purchase of raw lamb and sheep skins	National	FTA	Not against public interest		
11.04.89	Strong & Fisher (Holdings) plc/Pittard Garnar plc	Purchase of raw lamb and sheep skins	National	FTA	Not against public interest		
21.03.89	Elders IXL Ltd/Scottish & Newcastle Breweries plc	Supply of beer	National	FTA	Against public interest	Should be prohibited	Prohibited (although low shareholding

674

Date of report	Parties	Market activity	Relevant geographic market	Legal basis of jurisdiction	SLC/negative public interest finding?	MMC/CC recommendation (where applicable)	Sec of State/CC decision
							permitted)
08.03.89	Badgerline Holdings Ltd/Midland Red West Holdings Ltd	Supply of bus services	Local	FTA	Against public interest	Should be cleared subject to behavioural undertakings	Cleared subject to behavioural undertakings
22.02.89	TR Beckett Ltd/ EMAP plc	Printing and publishing of newspapers	Local	FTA (newspaper reference)	Against public interest	Should be cleared subject to structural undertakings	Cleared subject to structural undertakings
02.02.89	Minorco/ Consolidated Gold Fields plc	High value minerals and metals	Global	FTA	Not against public interest		
11.01.89	Thomson Travel Group/Horizon Travel Ltd	Supply of foreign air inclusive tours, operation of charter airlines and retail travel agents	National	FTA	Not against public interest		
04.10.88	The Government of Kuwait/The British Petroleum Company plc	Upstream and downstream oil industry	N/A	FTA	Against public interest	Should be prohibited	Prohibited (although low shareholding permitted)
17.08.88	Parrett & Neves Ltd/ EMAP plc	Production and distribution of local newspapers	Local	FTA (newspaper reference)	Not against public interest		

Date of report	Parties	Market activity	Relevant geographic market	Legal basis of jurisdiction	SLC/negative public interest finding?	MMC/CC recommendation (where applicable)	Sec of State/CC decision
20.07.88	Mitek Industries Inc/ Gang-Nail Systems Inc	Supply of punched metal connector plates and related machinery	National	FTA	Against public interest	Should be cleared subject to structural undertakings	Cleared subject to structural undertakings
28.01.88	Warner Communications Inc/ Enterprises belonging to Chappell & Co. Inc	Publication and recording of music	National	FTA	Not against public interest		
22.01.88	Book Club Associates/ Leisure Circle	Sale of books through book clubs	National	FTA	Against public interest	Should be cleared subject to behavioural undertakings	Prohibited
25.11.87	MAI plc/London and Continental Advertising Holdings plc	Supply of roadside posters	National	FTA	Against public interest	Should be cleared subject to structural undertakings	Cleared subject to structural undertakings
01.11.87	British Airways plc/ British Caledonian Group plc	Supply of airline passenger services	National	FTA	Not against public interest following commitments made at MMC stage		

Date of report	Parties	Market activity	Relevant geographic market	Legal basis of jurisdiction	SLC/negative public interest finding?	MMC/CC recommendation (where applicable)	Sec of State/CC decision
21.10.87	Co-operative Wholesale Society Limited/House of Fraser plc	Supply of funeral undertaking services	Regional	FTA	Against public interest	Should be cleared subject to structural undertakings	Cleared subject to structural undertakings
01.10.87	Swedish Match AB/ Enterprises belonging to Allegheny International Inc	Manufacture of matches and distribution of lighters	National	FTA	Not against public interest		
16.04.87	Courier Press (Holdings) Ltd/ EMAP Plc	Publication of newspapers	Regional and local	FTA (newspaper reference)	Not against public interest		
04.03.87	Trusthouse Forte plc/ Enterprises belonging to Hanson Trust plc	Operation of hotels, motorway service areas and roadside catering	National	FTA	Not against public interest		
25.02.87	Tate & Lyle plc/ Ferruzzi Finanziaria SpA/S&W Berisford plc	The refining and distribution of sugar	National	FTA	Three mergers all against public interest	Should all be subject to structural undertakings	All made subject to structural and behavioural undertakings

Date of report	Parties	Market activity	Relevant geographic market	Legal basis of jurisdiction	SLC/negative public interest finding?	MMC/CC recommendation (where applicable)	Sec of State/CC decision
03.12.86	The Peninsular and Oriental Steam Navigation Company/ European Ferries Group plc	Ferry services	Regional	FTA	Not against public interest		
24.09.86	Norton Opax plc/ McCorquodale plc	Supply of cheques, lottery tickets and related products	National	FTA	Not against public interest		
03.09.86	Elders IXL Ltd/ Allied Lyons	Supply of beer, wines and spirits, tea and coffee	National	FTA	Not against public interest		
06.08.86	The General Electric Company plc/The Plessey Company plc	Supply of telecommunications equipment and defence electronic systems	National	FTA	Against public interest	Should be prohibited	Prohibited
16.05.86	BET Public Limited Company/SGB Group plc	Access equipment for construction or maintenance	National	FTA	Not against the public interest		
27.01.86	British Telecommuncations plc/ Mitel Corporation	Supply of private exchange equipment	National	FTA	Against the public interest	Should be cleared subject to behavioural	Cleared subject to behavioural undertakings

SUMMARY OF
COMPETITION COMMISSION/MONOPOLIES
& MERGERS COMMISSION MERGER REPORTS
(JANUARY 1995 TO JUNE 2004)

FIRSTGROUP PLC AND THE SCOTTISH
PASSENGER RAIL FRANCHISE 28.06.04

Proposed acquisition by FirstGroup plc of the Scottish Passenger Rail franchise   **A11.001**
currently operated by ScotRail Railways Ltd.

Activity

Operation of passenger rail services and local and regional bus services

Market Share

FirstGroup was the leading supplier of bus travel in the UK with around 22 per
cent of turnover of local bus services in 2003, and 35 per cent of all bus route
mileage in Scotland, with over half of those services in the Glasgow area. As at April
2004, it also operated five passenger train operating companies.
The Scottish rail franchise accounted for 95 per cent of railways services in
Scotland (including night sleeper services to London).

Assessment

FirstGroup had tendered for the Scottish rail franchise. If successful, the merger
would combine the largest operator of rail services in Scotland with the leading
operator of bus services in Scotland and in Glasgow in particular.
The Competition Commission found that bus and rail services were potentially
substitutable for certain people and at certain times of day. It found that the relevant markets were not only point-to-point routes, but the wider networks which
FirstGroup and others operated over wider market areas as well. It identified a
number of bus routes where there was a possibility of adverse effects on competition arising from the merger. Taking into account a survey of public transport users
which it had commissioned, the Commission concluded that enough passengers
would switch from bus to train to make a strategy of diverting passengers from bus
to train potentially profitable. The possibility of new entry or expansion in response
to any attempt by FirstGroup to increase fares or reduce frequency of service was
not expected to be a sufficiently effective source of competition to offset the loss of

competition on the specified routes. The Commission concluded that FirstGroup could be expected to seek to move passengers from bus to rail by increasing fares, and reducing frequency or rerouting services and/or by reconfiguring routes.

Competition Commission's Decision

The merger was be expected to give rise to a substantial lessening of competition on overlap flows on the identified routes, although they would affect only a minority of passengers on a minority of routes. The merger would also result in a substantial lessenin of competition in wider transport network markets, particularly through multi-modal tickets usable on FirstGroup services only, and by favouring its own bus services in information provided at railway stations.

The adverse effects were required to be remedied by behavioural remedies, namely FirstGroup would be required to agree undertakings related to fares, frequencies and other aspects of services on the affected routes, as well as undertakings related to multi-modal tickets and the provision of information at rail stations on the services of other bus operators.

Chairman and Panel Members

Professor Paul Geroski, Robert Bertram, Christopher Goodall, Charles Henderson

DRÄGER MEDICAL AG & CO KGAA AND HILLENBRAND INDUSTRIES INC 19.05.04

A11.002   Acquisition by Dräger Medical AG & Co KGaA of certain assets representing the Air-Shields business of Hill-Rom Inc "Hill Rom", a subsidiary of Hillenbrand Industries Inc.

Activity
Supply of neonatal warming therapy products to UK hospitals ("neonates"), used in the care of newborn and premature babies.

Market Share

It was found that although similarities existed between the four different types of neonatal warming therapy products (closed care incubators, open care warming beds, transport incubators and phototherapy products), they should still be regarded as separate product markets for the purposes of the inquiry. In addition, aftercare and product specific accessories were also to be regarded as the same market as the original purchase of a product. Whilst the vast majority of products sold in the UK were imported, the availability of UK-based support, and the track records of suppliers to UK hospitals were important. The UK was therefore the relevant market.

In the closed care, open care and transport incubator markets, the merged entity would have a market share in excess of 60 per cent based on three-year averages (in transport incubators almost 100 per cent), with no more than one significant competitor in each market. (The market for phototherapy was not thought to give rise to concern, particularly as the merged entity's share had declined significantly in recent years).

Assessment

Three competitors (Ohmeda, Fisher & Paykel and Atom) were identified as selling one or more of the different types of neonatal warming therapy product. Almost all neonatal warming therapy products supplied in the UK were bought by NHS hospital trusts. The purchase usually followed a formal or informal tender process, with the choice of product revolving largely around the product best suited to achieve the desired operational requirements and cost issues. Trusts sought to standardize equipment in order to reduce clinical error caused by unfamiliarity with the equipment and although the average effective life of a product was 10 years, new products appeared more frequently than this. In practice, many hospitals had more than one model of any type of equipment.

The markets displayed the characteristics of a bidding market and a high market share did not necessarily confer high market power, because market shares could easily be lost in the next bidding round. However, the Commission identified a "stickiness" in customer behaviour and although the direct costs of switching suppliers were not high, an installed base in the hospital seemed to provide an advantage to the tender processes. In addition, clinical preference appeared to be ultimately more important in the selection of a particular product than price. Therefore, the existence of barriers to switching coupled with the low level of price sensitivity, led the Commission to believe that market shares were a relevant indicator of potential market power.

The fact that the merging parties were close competitors was a cause for concern. In the absence of the merger, whilst one or both parties might decline as a competitive force, both would continue to provide a competitive constraint for the foreseeable future. No significant intrinsic barriers to entry were thought to exist. However, the need to build a reputation posed a significant barrier to expansion. Ultimately, the Commission did not believe that the prospect of entry or expansion would present a significant competitive constraint on the merged entity.

Although the NHS could potentially exercise some countervailing buyer power in the market (due to its size and status as a virtual monopsonist), it was not anticipated that the NHS would exercise its power as a single buyer in this area. Hospitals were very reluctant to give up their freedom regarding the choice of products they bought, which in turn imposed limits on the development of joint purchasing of equipment in the NHS. Real countervailing buyer power was not expected to operate in any of the markets.

Competition Commission's Decision

The merger may be expected to give rise to a substantial lessening of competition in the markets for closed care incubators, open care warming beds and transport incubators, but not in the market for phototherapy products. The merged entity could price discriminate against certain hospitals, and product choice could decline.

The Commission had grounds to believe that the substantial market power of the merged entity may provide an incentive to raise prices. Furthermore, the loss of an independent competitor and rationalization of product lines would be likely to give rise to a reduction in choice of products for hospitals. Innovation and the development of new products at a global level were thought to continue following the merger. No evidence was found to suggest that predatory pricing or other detrimental effects may occur.

Prohibition of the merger was considered impractical, even if it were found to be an appropriate remedy. In the long term, recommendations were made to the UK Health Departments and their procurement agencies to encourage market entry from overseas and increase the exercise of buyer power by trusts. In the short term, the merged entity was required to give time-limited undertakings to continue to supply a full range of products, accessories and aftercare in the relevant markets, as well as time-limited price retail price control on products, accessories and aftercare in the relevant markets.

Chairman and Panel Members

Derek Morris, Laurence Elks, Graham Hadley, Stephen Wilks

CARL ZEISS JENA GMBH AND BIO-RAD LABORATORIES INC 17.05.04

A11.003   The acquisition by Carl Zeiss Jena GmbH, "Zeiss" of the microscope business of Bio-Rad Laboratories Inc "Bio-Rad" (carried out by Bio-Rad's Cell Science Division).

Market

The supply of advanced 3D light microscope systems for biological research, and more specifically, "optical sectioning" systems. Within optical sectioning systems, there existed a separate worldwide market for "multiphoton" systems, and a separate worldwide market for "confocal" systems. Both parties supplied confocal and multiphoton systems.

Assessment

Product innovation, functionality, the use of leading-edge technology and investment in R&D were all important in assessing the operation of the market. The advanced 3D microscope systems industry displayed features of a bidding market, with highly differentiated products and varying prices. Barriers to entry were surmountable, except where restricted by patent rights. Firms spent a high proportion of their income on R&D and would compete using their R&D programmes to win market power. No evidence could be found to suggest that these markets were conducive to collusive behaviour.

There was competition between several large suppliers, and smaller "niche" suppliers. It remained uncertain whether a new supplier would be able to maintain a high market share by exploitation of an innovation. It may well need to be vertically integrated in order for it to operate profitably (for example, by supplying its own optics). It was found that the advanced 3D microscopy industry (as distinct from classical microscopes) was growing and was characterised by effective competition within the limits set by patent protection.

As regards confocal systems, these were developed commercially by Bio-Rad and had become standard equipment for advanced biological research. They were supplied by all of the main suppliers of advanced microscopes. Following completion of the merger the Commission did not believe that competition would be reduced in the markets for confocal and other optical sectioning systems (other than multiphoton systems), due to the strong number of competitors remaining and continuing competitive pressure from smaller suppliers.

As regards multiphoton systems, there were two main techniques. The technique using subpicosecond pulse durations was exclusively licensed to Bio-Rad, and an alternative multiphoton technique (using piosecond pulse durations) was exclusively licensed to a competing supplier, Leica. The Commission expected that Leica would continue to compete with Zeiss following the merger, incentives to innovate would remain and no evidence could be seen that the market was conducive to collusive behaviour.

The Commission considered that the loss of Bio-Rad as an independent supplier would occur regardless of whether or not the merger took place. The merger would not lead to a situation which created less competition than if Bio-Rad's business were sold to another purchaser.

Competition Commission's Decision

No substantial lessening of competition was expected to result from the merger.

Chairman and Panel Members

Peter Freeman, Nigel Macdonald, David Parker, Richard Rawlinson

STENA AB AND THE PENINSULAR AND ORIENTAL STEAM NAVIGATION COMPANY ("P&O") 06.02.04

The proposed acquisition by Stena AB "Stena" of certain assets operated by P&O on the Irish Sea between Liverpool-Dublin and Fleetwood-Larne. A11.004

Market

The transportation of roll-on/roll-off (ro/ro) and lift-on/lift-off (lo/lo) freight between Great Britain and Ireland, in the northern corridor (in relation to P&O's Fleetwood-Larne route) and in the central corridor (in relation to P&O's Liverpool-Dublin route).

Assessment

Capacity utilisation was found to be generally higher for long-sea as opposed to short-sea crossings and for the most part, services tended to be fully booked or even overbooked. Pricing in the freight ferry market was opaque, based on bilateral negotiations between specific customers and ferry companies, whereby terms would be agreed for different routes. Also relevant were the importance of particular customers to the company as a whole and as a consequence ferry operators were able to price discriminate between customers. Due to the strong relationships established between customers and ferry operators, switching was not commonplace, as customers did not possess a sufficient degree of buyer power.

The three significant ferry operators in the market for freight traffic on the northern corridor were highlighted as: P&O, Norse Merchant Ferries and Stena. The transfer of P&O's Fleetwood-Larne route would approximately double Stena's market share in the Northern corridor. Three significant ferry operators would remain, but Stena would replace P&O as the largest ferry operator on the northern corridor and market concentration would be reduced. The Commission did not anticipate a substantial lessening of competition on the northern corridor.

With regard to the central corridor, post merger, the number of competitors would reduce to three. Stena's market share would more than double and market concentration would be significantly increased. As a result, Stena's market share would be significantly larger than its nearest rival and it would also have a route on both the short and long central corridor crossings. Stena would have enhanced market power which it might exercise in relation to decisions on capacity, pricing or its unique ability to offer a "one stop shop" of short and long central corridor crossings.

Regardless of the merger, the Mostyn-Dublin route was expected to close. The Commission expected that in the absence of the merger, P&O, or an alternative purchaser of the Liverpool-Dublin route would have a greater incentive to add capacity to capture more of the displaced Mostyn traffic than would Stena if it were to acquire the route. Against this counter factual, the merger would lead to a reduction in capacity on the central corridor.

Post merger, regardless of there being a reduction in capacity in the central corridor, it would still be open to Stena to selectively increase prices (partly due to the opaque pricing trends previously referred to). Although potential entrants existed, access to suitable berths and sufficient surrounding land available at peak times would be necessary. Furthermore, an entrant would need to attract and retain an economically viable customer base. The threat of entry was therefore unlikely to offset the possible substantial lessening of competition in the central corridor.

Competition Commission's decision

The proposed merger was not expected to lessen competition substantially on the northern corridor. However, the Commission did expect there to be a substantial lessening of competition on the central corridor and no relevant customer benefits were anticipated. A number of remedies were put forward for the purpose of remedying, mitigating or preventing the loss of competition. The prohibition of the transfer of the assets used on the Liverpool-Dublin route from P&O to Stena was considered to be the most effective remedy, as this would serve as a preventative measure to the anti-competitive effects described.

Chairman and Panel

Paul Geroski, John Baillie, Barbara Mills, Jeremy Seddon, Peter Stoddart

MARCH UK LTD AND THE HOME SHOPPING AND HOME DELIVERY BUSINESSES OF GUS PLC 22.01.04

A11.005   An investigation into the acquisition of the home shopping and home delivery businesses of GUS plc "GUS" by March UK Ltd "March".

Markets and Market Shares

Both GUS and March were active in home shopping (particularly agency mail order, "AMO", and direct mail order, "DMO"), as well as the provision of home delivery services to their own businesses and to third parties.

The Commission concluded that with regard to home shopping, the relevant market was wide, as the companies were constrained by competition from other forms of home shopping and high street retailing. For home delivery, the Commission concluded that the economic market was all UK-wide "business-to-consumer" ("B2C") services delivering parcels with a weight range between 350g and 32kg. However, it was noted that the degree of competition might vary at different levels within that range. Both markets were UK-wide.

The parties had a combined share of 38 per cent in the AMO/DMO sector (an increase of 16 per cent) and 34 per cent in home delivery (an increase of 12 per cent).

Assessment

All the evidence appeared to point to a growing demand for home shopping as a whole, with regular new entry, but a decline in demand for AMO and an absence of new entrants in this sector. Over the past decade, AMO market shares demonstrated a high degree of stability, and there had been little innovation as regards products and services offered. Conversely, the DMO sector was characterised by regular entry of both companies and products, with much more variation in the terms on offer and also the number of providers and type of players. In addition, the nature of competition on the high street was considered to be more varied as regards prices and choice.

One of the most important developments in home delivery was the withdrawal from parts of the business by Parcelforce, which had been the largest service provider. The parties were now considered to be each other's major competitors, although they had failed to win a number of contracts and there were many sizeable delivery companies offering competition. Long-term prospects for new entry were expected to improve as demand for home delivery services grew and access to Royal Mail facilities improved.

Consumers were expected to benefit from cost savings arising from the merger.

Recommendations

Not against the public interest.

Chairman and Panel members

Mr P J Freeman, Professor A Gregory, Professor B Lyons, Mr R Turgoose, Mr A M Young

NEWSQUEST (LONDON) LIMITED ("NEWSQUEST") AND INDEPENDENT NEWS & MEDIA PLC ("INM") 21.10.03

The transfer to Newsquest of 23 newspaper titles of INM, circulating in London and north-west Kent.   A11.006

Market

Free and paid-for local newspapers (with limited substitution between these and other media).

Market Share and Increment

Newsquest's share of regional and local newspapers in the UK would increase from 15.4 per cent to 16.4 per cent. Newsquest's share of weekly local newspapers in the UK would increase from 20.2 to 22.5 per cent. Newsquest's share of local newspapers in Greater London would also be increased from 35 to 49 per cent, and the share of the two largest publishers, Trinity Mirror and Newsquest from 79 to 93 per cent.

Assessment

Further consolidation, increased concentration and regional clustering in the UK local newspaper market were seen as potential concerns, although the transfers were not expected to have adverse effects on a national level. Only a minority of advertising in London local newspapers was aimed at a regional market (*i.e.* London), rather than local, so local markets were the main focus of the inquiry.

The transfers would lead to multiple titles under the same ownership having very large local market shares, reducing the options available to local advertisers, with potentially adverse effects on advertising rates and quality of service. Furthermore, Newsquest could exercise cross-selling (across free and paid for newspapers), and potentially weaken the competitive position of smaller rivals or new entrants.

The Commission could see no evidence to suggest that the transfer would put at risk editorial independence or the accurate presentation of news and freedom of expression.

Recommendation

The transfer of 13 titles was found not to be against the public interest. However, the Commission recommended that the transfer of eight titles of the Kentish Times division should not be permitted. As regards the two remaining titles, whilst their transfer was expected to operate against the public interest, the Commission believed that in the absence of the proposed transfer they might go out of business. The Commission urged the Secretary of State to bear this in mind in considering remedies.

Secretary of State's Decision

The Secretary of State accepted the recommendations of the Commission and gave consent for the transfer of the two titles which might otherwise have gone out of business.

Chairman and Panel Members

Professor P A Geroski, Mr P J Freeman, Mr R Holroyd, Mr M R Webster

ARLA FOODS AMBA ("ARLA") AND EXPRESS DAIRIES PLC ("EXPRESS") 15.10.03

A11.007   Proposed merger between Arla and Express, both major fresh milk producers in Great Britain.

Market

Fresh processed milk, as distinct from UHT, sterilized and flavoured milk. The Commission identified three following customer segments:

- national multiples (Asda, Marks & Spencer, Morrisons, Safeway, Sainsbury's, Somerfield, Tesco and Waitrose);
- middle ground customers (including retailers other than the national multiples, public sector bodies, catering customers, bottled milk buyers and other wholesalers); and
- doorstep customers.

A different geographic market existed for each of the three market segments. The national multiples market was no wider than Great Britain, middle ground had a number of overlapping geographic markets and doorstep supply was local.

Assessment

The merger was not expected to substantially lessen competition in any of the market segments identified:

- where the national multiples were concerned, in the absence of the merger, Express' competitive position was expected to be severely weakened. Over-capacity would continue to exist, giving customers flexibility to switch between processors. This was particularly as there was strong competition between processors and a lack of brand loyalty. The buyer power of national multiples would be adequate to counter increased concentration of suppliers to this segment;

- there would continue to be a significant number of alternative suppliers to middle ground customers, exerting competitive constraints on the merged entity; and

- in the doorstep sector, the merger was expected to have little impact on competition.

Although the merger would reduce the number of competitors, there was no expectation that coordinated behaviour (either tacit or explicit collusion) would occur as a result.

Recommendation

The merger was not expected to operate against the public interest, nor lead to a substantial lessening of competition in the supply of fresh processed milk.

Chairman and Panel Members

Mrs D P B Kingsmill CBE, Mr G H Hadley, Mr C R Smallwood, Professor C Waddams, Professor S R M Wilkes

CARLTON COMMUNICATIONS PLC ("CARLTON") AND GRANADA PLC ("GRANADA") 07.10.03

Market

Commercial broadcasting, primarily focussing on television advertising in the UK.

A11.008

Assessment

The merger was not expected to operate against the public interest in the areas of programme production, the availability of studio facilities in the North of England, or the future competition for ITV licences.

In relation to other ITV regional licensees two issues were considered: the ITV networking arrangements and the arrangements for the sale of their airtime. It was concluded that without additional safeguards (which were at that time under negotiation between Carlton, Granada, other licensees and the ITC) networking arrangements might be expected to operate against the public interest.

In relation to the sale of advertising airtime, a merger that resulted in a single ITV sales house would reduce the other regional licensees' choice and were they not offered the choice to sell their airtime through the merged company's sales house on terms similar to those they currently enjoyed, the merger was expected to have an adverse effect and operate against the public interest.

London was considered to be the primary focus of competition within ITV (although competition existed between other regions). Competition between Carlton and Granada had the effect of limiting what advertisers or media buyers could be charged by, in particular, limiting the advertising budget commitment that could be demanded for a given level of discount.

Competition was reviewed in the context of the further decline in ITV post 2000, but this had not yet materially reduced the importance of Carlton and Granada. There was still a lack of available channel substitutes, and difficulty in purchasing enough slots to achieve the required coverage. ITV's own unique features (such as its ability to attract large audience numbers and high proportion of prestigious programmes) were also referred to.

In terms of advertising sales and the lessening of competition, following a merger the parties would have been expected to:

(a) insist on terms that were generally less attractive to advertisers/media buyers;

(b) enhance the degree of price discrimination; and/or

(c) change the system under which television advertising airtime was sold to the advantage of the merged entity.

These adverse effects were expected to allow the entity to achieve higher revenue to the detriment of advertisers and other commercial broadcasters.

The Commission considered a number of possible remedies as alternatives to outright prohibition of the merger. The Commission recommended that as regards ITV networking arrangements, the appropriate remedy was for Carlton and Granada to agree a package of safeguards proposed by the ITC, accepting any change in licence conditions that followed from them.

As regards the sale of national advertising airtime, Carlton and Granada should give an undertaking that the other ITV licensees should have the option to carry forward, for the duration of the companies' respective licences, the terms currently in effect between each of them and Carlton's and Granada's sales houses.

Secretary of State's Decision

The Secretary of State accepted the recommendations of the Commission.

Chairman and Panel Members

Professor P A Geroski, Mrs S E Brown, Mrs D Guy, Mr C E Henderson CB, Professor P Moizer

SAFEWAY PLC AND ASDA GROUP LIMITED (OWNED BY WAL-MART STORES INC); WM MORRISON SUPERMARKETS PLC; J SAINSBURY PLC; AND TESCO PLC 26.09.03

The proposed acquisition of Safeway by each of Asda, Morrisons, Sainsbury's and Tesco.   A11.009

Market

One-stop shopping in grocery stores of 1,400 sq metres or more. One-stop shopping was local, as most consumers were prepared to travel only a limited distance for their main grocery shop, but certain aspects of competition were determined at the national level. The effect of the merger on convenience stores (those below 280 sq metres) and on stores between 280 and 1,400 sq metres ("secondary" or "top-up" shopping) were also considered. The Commission decided to look at issues relating to buyer power in the context of the supply of groceries to supermarkets with a share of 8 per cent or more of groceries purchased for resale in the UK.

Assessment

Safeway was a potentially weak competitor, performing relatively poorly. However, it was not regarded as a failing firm, and its loss would have a significant bearing on the market for one-stop shopping. Significant barriers to entry existed for one-stop shopping, arising from the scale economies obtained by the four existing national players and the planning regime's effect on new store development.

An acquisition by Morrisons was not expected to reduce the number of national players, or effective price and non-price competition. Morrisons was expected to challenge its three main rivals on both price and non-price aspects of competition. Morrisons was also considered to be a stronger entry threat in new regions throughout the UK, with more incentive to expand and bid for sites, following the anticipated acquisition by Safeway.

The proposed acquisitions by Asda, Sainsbury's and Tesco would all reduce the number of effective national competitors to three. The Commission noted certain market conditions could be conducive to coordinated behaviour and/ or unilateral effects:

1.   high levels of market concentration;

2.   high degree of comparability between individual grocery products (enabling multiple grocery retailers to make price comparisons between their own and competitors' grocery baskets) and high levels of monitoring (both price and non-price factors);

3.   stable demand and cost conditions (making it easier to detect "cheating" on any tacit collusive agreement). Innovation was not important;

4.   the parties had the ability to change price quickly in response to each other, and had long-term financial commitments to the sector;

5.   high barriers to entry, associated with scale and the planning regime; and

6.   the lack of effective competition from grocery retailers outside the main parties.

At a national level, an acquisition by any retailer other than Morrisons would reduce the number of national players and would facilitate coordinated behaviour, lessening competition.

Any acquisition would have anti-competitive effects at a local level, where both parties had stores of 1,400 sq metres or above, and where insufficient fascias would remain post the merger. Adverse effects would be expected in areas where there would be a reduction in the number of fascias, and where 3 or less would remain.

An acquisition by any of Asda, Morrisons, Sainsbury's or Tesco was expected to exacerbate the imbalance in the bargaining positions of the respective parties and their suppliers; thus competitive prices were not expected to emerge, which could in turn lead to "waterbed" bed effects (where suppliers seek to recoup the lower prices they receive from large retailers through higher prices to smaller retailers). Furthermore, the cost savings derived from increased buyer power were not expected to result in lower prices for consumers.

In the case of Morrisons, any shift in bargaining power between it and suppliers would be less. Suppliers would benefit from having four relatively equal-sized grocery retailers, as these could be more readily played off against each other than three even larger ones. Furthermore, as price and non-price competition was not expected to be reduced following the merger, cost savings were expected to be passed on to consumers in the form of lower prices.

Recommendations

The Commission concluded that an acquisition by any of Asda, Sainsbury's or Tesco would lead to a substantial lessening of competition at the national level, leading to increased prices, a reduction in consumer choice, a reduction in competition for new sites and reduced threat of new entry. This would further intensify the conditions favourable to coordinated effects. Finally, there would be a general weakening of some suppliers' positions. An acquisition by Morrisons was not expected to lead to a substantial lessening of competition at the national level.

Any acquisition may have adverse effects on competition in particular local areas, in terms of reduction in numbers of stores and choice, resulting in rising prices over time.

The cost savings following an acquisition by Asda, Sainsbury's or Tesco were not considered sufficient to outweigh the adverse effects identified. An acquisition by Morrisons would not have adverse effect on competition in the market and costs savings would be passed on to consumers.

The Commission therefore recommended that the bid by Morrisons should be allowed to proceed, subject to Morrisons agreeing to divest one-stop grocery stores in 48 localities in which adverse effects had been identified. Furthermore, it was required to divest 5 smaller stores where adverse effects would result. Asda, Sainsbury's and Tesco should be prohibited from acquiring the whole or any part of Safeway, other than those stores specified to be divested by Morrisons and subject to certain conditions.

Secretary of State's Decision

Accepted Commission's recommendations.

Chairman and Panel Members

Sir Derek Morris, Professor J Baillie, Mr C Goodall, Professor P Klemperer, Mr J B K Rickford CBE, Mr J D S Stark

CENTRICA PLC AND DYNEGY STORAGE LTD AND DYNEGY ONSHORE PROCESSING UK LIMITED ("DYNEGY") 01.08.03

Activity

Retail gas supply and the operation of gas storage facilities and associated assets. Centrica had acquired from Dynegy two companies which owned and operated the Rough gas storage facility and associated assets.

A11.009A

Market Share and Increment

Centrica had 34 per cent of maximum flexible gas supplies in the UK, increasing to 46 per cent post-merger. Its share of flexible gas supplies actually used increased from around 40—51 per cent to around 59—70 per cent. Centrica also owned a high proportion of the share of gas supply to domestic customers (around 63 per cent). The Commission noted that supply to domestic gas and electricity customers appeared to be converging towards a single market. In this connection, Centrica was a joint leader in the electricity supply market with about 22 per cent of domestic customer accounts.

Assessment

Dynegy had acquired Rough in 2001, and it had given undertakings in lieu of a reference to the Commission. These included the following:

— it would offer Rough's full capacity to potential users on non-discriminatory terms;

— it would sell at least half the capacity for periods of not less than 5 years, and the remainder for periods of not less than 1 year;

— it would facilitate the development of a secondary market in storage services; and

— it would maintain full separation between its storage and other activities.

The Commission identified that gas storage was used to help deal with fluctuations in supply and demand (particularly in relation to domestic users) and changes in gas prices. Rough was used primarily for storage, as it was capable of providing a substantial amount of gas. A large volume of gas was supplied to Rough in the summer (when prices were low) and then withdrawn in the winter when prices were high. Rough was therefore used primarily as a source of seasonal (rather than short-term) supply. Flexibility within the industry was also gained from varying UK production, using supplies from mainland Europe and interruptible supply contracts.

A major issue for the inquiry was whether following the merger Centrica would potentially withhold sources of flexible gas in order to force up wholesale prices which would be passed on to domestic customers. However, the Commission concluded that the reputational risk and adverse regulatory consequences arising from such actions, coupled with the costs of doing so and Centrica's pricing policy in previous years, meant that it was unlikely that Centrica would withhold capacity as a result of the merger.

The Commission went on to note that Centrica may be expected to discriminate between customers in giving access to capacity at Rough, to use to its advantage sensitive information gained from the operation of Rough and to withhold such information. It may also be less inclined to market and invest in Rough. As a result, competition in the markets for flexible gas and domestic gas supply would be weakened and other industry participants would face uncertainty. It was likely that prices would rise and that innovation and investment at Rough would be lower than under another owner.

Recommendation

Against the public interest. The adverse affects identified could be remedied by Centrica giving various undertakings regarding its ownership of Rough. Centrica should:

(a) sell Rough's full capacity on non-discriminatory terms, retaining the existing licence;

(b) auction all capacity remaining unsold no less than 30 days before the start of each storage year, with no reserve price;

(c) not participate in the primary sale but reserve no more than 20 per cent of Rough's existing nominal capacity for the first year (2004/5) falling to 15 per cent over five years and remaining at that level thereafter;

(d) maintain legal, financial and physical separation between its storage business and all other parts of the group (including ensuring no commercially sensitive information was passed from Rough to other parts of Centrica);

(e) facilitate the efficient operation and development of the secondary market in Rough capacity;

(f) offer at least 20 per cent of Rough's capacity on annual contracts; capacity should also be offered on other durations with a possibility of fixed or indexed pricing; and

(g) arrange for Centrica's Audit Committee to undergo an independent review of compliance with all undertakings, with annual reports compiled for the OFT and the Office of Gas and Electricity Markets.

Divestment of assets acquired stood as a possible remedy if Centrica was not prepared to give all the undertakings recommended.

Secretary of State's Decision

The Secretary of State accepted the conclusions and recommendations of the Commission. In the event that the undertakings could not be effectively implemented, the Secretary of State invited the Commission to provide further advice on alternative behavioural or structural remedies, or a combination of the two, to address the public interest issues.

Chairman and Members of the Panel

Mrs D P B Kingsmill, Mr N C L Macdonald, Dr J Collings, Professor B Lyons

SCOTTISH RADIO HOLDINGS PLC ("SRH") AND GWR GROUP PLC ("GWR") AND GALAXY RADIO WALES AND THE WEST LIMITED ("GALAXY") 16.05.03

Activity

Commercial radio broadcasting. SRH and GWR, through the joint venture company Vibe, had acquired Galaxy.

A11.010

Jurisdiction

The Commission considered whether GWR had the ability materially to influence Galaxy and Vibe Radio Services Limited ("VRSL"), a joint venture company owned by SRH (51 per cent) and GWR (49 per cent). In concluding that GWR had material influence over VRSL and Galaxy the Commission took into consideration that GWR had a 49 per cent shareholding in VRSL, a right to appoint a minority of directors and a right to consent or not on such matters as sales, merger or winding up of the business or a material variation from the periodically agreed business plan. Other factors which the Commission considered seemed to undermine the independence of VRSL include: the terms on which VRSL is operated with a fixed return guaranteed to SRH (as long as one of its subsidiaries, Vibe 101, is profitable); the integration of Vibe 101 in GWR's activities, including physical facilities and administrative overheads; the relatively restricted role of the Managing Director of Vibe (having control over brand and content but not cost or revenues); the fact that there are no 'Chinese Walls' between the two organisations; and the fact that GWR acknowledged that it did exert material influence over VRSL and, therefore Vibe 101.

The Commission considered Galaxy, GWR and SHR to be associated persons under section 77 of the Act.

Market Share and Increment

Following the merger, GWR accounted for three quarters of advertising revenue from local advertisers and almost all advertising revenue from national advertisers in the Bristol and Bath area; and for over 90 per cent of advertising revenue from local advertisers and all revenue from national advertisers in the Taunton and Yeovil area.

Assessment

The Commission concluded that local radio advertising was a market distinct from other media. It had different characteristics, and was complementary to other forms of advertising. The Commission also noted that it was not easy for advertisers to compare the prices and assess the effectiveness of advertising using different media. There also existed sufficient overlap of listeners and advertisers between stations that they could not be regarded as operating in separate markets.

Before the merger Galaxy's share of advertisers (particularly local advertisers) had declined in the Bristol and Bath and Taunton and Yeovil areas. However, in the Commission's opinion, it was likely that had GWR not acquired Galaxy it would have reversed the previous decline in market share under its existing ownership or would have been acquired by another radio group. Therefore, the merger had increased the already high market share of local radio advertising held by the GWR stations in Bristol and Bath and Taunton and Yeovil areas. The merger had reduced the overlap of listeners and advertisers and options open to companies and had, therefore, reduced competition for local radio advertisers.

The Commission did not consider there to be a sufficient prospect of entry given the need to obtain a Radio Authority licence. Although other stations provided competition to GWR this was only in specialised localities. Competition was further reduced by the superior ability of GWR to negotiate prices, bundle advertising packages and cross-sell between different stations.

The Commission also noted the importance of using advertising agencies to safeguard the position of national advertisers. National advertisers could also switch advertising between regions to reach a particular number of listeners. However, local advertisers who did not use agencies were vulnerable to price increases and it was expected that rates to these advertisers would rise post-merger.

Recommendation

Against the public interest. The benefits the parties claimed would arise as a result of the merger (i.e. increasing diversity) would, in the Commission's opinion, arise irrespective of the merger. The Commission recommended the following undertakings:

— that GWR be required to reduce its interest in Vibe 101;

— if GWR maintains an interest in Vibe 101 it should satisfy the OFT that it has no material influence over Vibe 101; and

— GWR should be required to discontinue the arrangement whereby GWR's sales house sold advertising airtime for Vibe 101.

Secretary of State's Opinion

The Secretary of State agreed with the Commission's conclusions and recommendations.

Chairman and Panel Members

Professor PA Geroski, Mr R A Rawlinson, Mr E J Seddon, Mr R Turgoose, Mr S Walzer

GANNETT UK LIMITED AND SMG PLC 28.03.03

Activity

A11.011   The publication of regional and local newspapers.

Assessment

The Commission was required to investigate the transfer to Gannet of SMG plc's three titles (The Herald, the Sunday Herald and the Evening Times). The majority of the sales of the SMG titles were in Strathclyde and Glasgow and were regarded as playing an important role in the Scottish newspaper market. Gannett did not operate in Scotland and so the transfer did not alter the structure of the Scottish market, nor, did the Commission believe, that the transfer was likely in any other way to adversely affect competition between newspapers in Scotland.

Concerns were raised with the Commission regarding editorial independence and stance and content and quality under the ownership of Gannett. The Commission noted Gannett had a reputation for the preservation of editorial freedom and not interfering on a day-to-day basis in the editorial content of titles. Gannett advocated its commitment to the autonomy of local editors and a locally based management structure. The Commission also stressed that commercial considerations, fierce competition within Scotland and the risk of damaging Gannett's reputation were factors which would serve to deter Gannett from adopting a different approach to these titles.

Recommendation

Not against the public interest.

Chairman and Panel Members

Professor P A Geroski, Ms E Pollard, Miss J C Hanratty OBE, Professor S Wilks, Mr A M Young

VNU ENTERTAINMENT MEDIA UK LIMITED ("VNU") AND BOOK DATA LIMITED ("BOOK DATA") 07.03.03

Activity

The supply in the UK of commercial bibliographic data services (to identify, locate and order books, and to assist with purchasing and stock management) and the supply of electronic transaction services to the book industry.

A11.012

Market Share

Following the merger VNU would have a 100 per cent share of the commercial bibliographic data services market. In relation to transaction services, the Commission decided that the electronic order-routing service provided by VNU's TeleOrdering operation was in a separate market from other transaction services, including the electronic data interchange services provided by Book Data.

Assessment

Information was supplied by publishers to VNU and Book Data for editing and collation, in standardized form, in their respective databases. The parties had been in strong and direct competition with each other prior to the merger. VNU submitted that if it were not to acquire Book Data, a US bibliographic agency, R R Bowker LLc, would have done so instead. This would have left VNU no option but to leave the market as it would have had no prospect of trading profitably.

In considering VNU's argument the Commission took into account; VNU's declining bibliographic business, future loss estimations, factors that pointed toward there being no indication of a recovery in financial performance in the foreseeable future and the unsuitability of the market to maintain two profitable operations. The Commission also considered that although VNU would incur substantial closure costs should it leave the bibliographic market, this was a more preferential solution than to keep the business operating. The substantial cost savings due to the merger explained why two competing suppliers would have difficulty in earning an adequate return in this market.

The Commission believed that in the absence of the merger, Book Data would have been acquired by Bowker and would have become the only worldwide supplier of commercial bibliographic data for English language books. Alternatively, were the merger to go ahead, although there would have been some lessening of potential competition, two commercial bibliographic agencies for English Books worldwide would exist—VNU and Bowker.

Recommendation

Not against the public interest.

Chairman and Panel Members

Professor D Parker, Professor J Baillie. Mr C Darke, Professor C Graham, Dame Helena Shovelton DBE

GROUP 4 FALCK A/S ("G4F") AND THE WACKENHUT CORPORATION ("TWC") 22.10.02

Activity

A11.013   The provision of out-sourced facility management services for the public sector (including prison and detention facilities and the transport of prisoners), security services and safety services.

Assessment

The Commission conducted an analysis of whether the enlarged G4F would have an effect on competition in the markets relating to manned guarding, alarm and CCTV installation and monitoring and aviation security. It concluded that G4F would not gain market power in any of these markets, such that no competition issues arose.

The Commission then considered the overlap which would potentially exist in relation to the provision of prisoner and immigrant detainee transport, and four further categories of custodial market:

— the provision of services to Design, Construct, Manage and Finance (DCM.F) prisons;

— management only (MO) services for prisons;

— MO services for immigration detention centres (IDCs); and

— DCM.F services for Secure Training Centres (STCs).

As a result of the acquisition, the merged company would hold the majority of the relevant custodial and prisoner and immigrant detainee transport contacts and could potentially exercise market power in relation to this area.

In respect of the prisoner and immigrant detainee transport services and MO services for IDC's, the Commission concluded that the existence of competitive restraints (strong inter-firm rivalry, the threat of new entry and the potential use of countervailing buyer power by the monopsony public sector purchasers) meant that no competition issues were likely to arise.

A majority expressed concerns that the competitive constraints in the DCM.F prison market, the MO prison market and the DCM.F STC market would not be sufficient to prevent the merged entity from exercising its market power. Furthermore, there was not sufficient evidence that the Home Office and Scottish Executive would in practice, exercise sufficient power to induce new entry or revert to 'self-supply'.

In relation to Premier (a joint venture company which carried out the operations of WCC, which was partially owned by TWC) the Commission considered whether it would be likely to compete with GSL (the UK subsidiary of G4F) as Premier was a company within the enlarged G4F group. The Commission obtained reassurances that Premier would continue to act independently from, and in competition with G4F. The provisions of the Competition Act 1998 and Articles 81 and 82 of the EC Treaty would act to deter any anti-competitive conduct. Premier was considered to be an independent competitor having the necessary resources to compete effectively in the relevant markets.

Recommendation

Not against the public interest.

Chairman and Panel Members

Mr E J Seddon, Professor J Baillie, Mr R D D Bertram, Professor C Waddams, Mr A M Young

VIVENDI WATER UK PLC ("VWUK") AND FIRST AQUA ("JVCO") LIMITED 08.11.02

Activity

JVCo owned Southern Water Services Limited (Southern), a regulated provider of water and sewerage services in south-east England. VWUK owned a number of regulated water providers, including Folkestone & Dover Water Services Ltd (F&D), Three Valleys Water Plc and South Staffs Group.

A11.014

Assessment

The transaction qualified under the EC Merger Regulation; however, the EC Commission recognised that the UK authorities had a legitimate interest in examining the merger's implications for the regulatory regime under the Water Industry Act 1991.

In considering whether a water merger may be expected to operate against the public interest, the ability of the Director General of Water Services (DGWS) to make comparisons between different water enterprises should not be prejudiced, bearing in mind that the water industry is a natural monopoly, with the level of product market competition being very low.

The DGWS in his econometric analysis is concerned with setting price limits, enabling prices to customers to be low consistent with enabling companies to provide high standards of service whilst earning adequate return on capital. In his opinion the success of the regime depends on diversity of independent ownership. The loss of Southern's and F&D's independence would weaken the comparative system by undermining the DGWS' econometric modelling.

There would be no loss of a comparator in sewerage as VWUK had no sewerage interests. As regards water services, the Commission agreed with the DGWS that the merger would prejudice the DGWS' ability to make comparisons. However, the

Commission considered that the detriment could be mitigated if the DGWS were to use additional methods of comparison in his price reviews. The Commission also considered there would be a slight detriment as a result of the closer association of F&D with Southern, although the complete disappearance of F&D would not necessarily be a consequence of the merger.

The Commission also considered the financial structure envisaged by VWUK for Southern and a majority (4/5) decided that there was insufficient evidence that the structure would be prejudicial to the regulatory regime. In addition VWUK would have an incentive to ensure Southern performed well in both financial and service terms.

The benefits brought to the parties as a consequence of the merger were not of 'substantially greater significance' for the public interest than the detriment that the merger would cause to the DGWS' ability to make comparisons between companies.

Recommendations

Against public interest, as the merger would prejudice the DGWS' ability to make comparisons between different water enterprises.

A majority reached the view that the detriment identified was not sufficient to justify the prohibition nor require VWUK to divest its Three Valleys Water Plc business or require that Southern's operation in the Isle of Wight be sold off in order to create a new competitor. The majority recommended that VWUK be required to divest its 31.4 per cent stake in South Staffs Group, thereby securing the independence of that company as a comparator.

Secretary of State's Decision

The Secretary of State took into consideration the conflicting views of the Commission and those of the DGWS and concluded that the Commission's findings were not sufficient and asked that the DGWS discuss with Vivendi the terms of two other possible remedies. Following this the Office of Water Services set out its advice on the Commission's findings. Ultimately, undertakings were accepted requiring Vivendi to limit its voting shares in JVCo to no more than 25 per cent and to restrict the number of directors which it could appoint. Royal Bank of Scotland also undertook, upon taking a share of at least 75 per cent in JVCo, to appoint at least one director with substantial relevant industry experience.

Chairman and Panel Members

Mr P Mackay, Mr A Hadfield, Mr C F W Goodall, Profesor D Parker, Mr P Stoddart

COMPASS GROUP PLC ("COMPASS") AND RAIL GOURMET HOLDING AG, RESTORAMA AG AND GOURMET NOVA AG ("RAIL GOURMET") 05.07.02

Activity

A11.015   The supply of on train food services in the UK.

Market Share and Increment

The share of supply of the merged entity would be increased from 80 to 83 per cent.

Assessment

The Commission considered whether the acquisition would create any barriers to entry for a competitor wishing to provide on train food services. This was essentially a bidding market, in which any increase in share of supply would not be the critical factor in determining the effect on competition. Rather, the key issue was whether the merger would lead to any increase in market power in relation to competitors and to the train operating companies letting the contracts.

There had been a number of new entrants to provide trolley services, however less competition existed for the larger contracts to provide logistics, which made up the bulk of the market value. There was little interest among potential competitors in bidding for these contracts, although in principle there were a large number of suppliers of general food and logistics services who could be in a position to provide these services. In addition, train operating companies exercised tight control over the conditions under which on-train food was supplied, which could also discourage potential new entry.

The Commission considered whether the acquisition created further barriers to entry but concluded that the acquisition by Compass would not in itself discourage other potential competitors from bidding for the on train food service contracts, or give rise to opportunities for the combined entity to exercise market power in a way which would be detrimental to competition. Whilst Rail Gourmet had some competitive advantages as the experienced incumbent, it did not enjoy intrinsic market power.

Furthermore, although Compass Group had a substantial presence in on-station catering services, due to competition, its presence had diminished. The Commission did not believe that Compass' position in the on-station sector could be used to affect competitive conditions as regards on-train catering and did not give it any notable advantage in the market for on-train catering services.

Recommendation

Not against the public interest. As a side issue the Commission noted their concerns regarding the way train operating companies controlled their catering service contracts and suggested that the Strategic Rail Authority look at encouraging competition and creativity in relation to consumers.

Chairman and Panel Members

Mrs D P B Kingsmill CBE, Mr C R Smallwood, Mr R Turgoose, Mr M R Webster, Professor S Wilkes

H+H CELCON LIMITED ("CELCON") AND MARLEY BUILDING MATERIALS LIMITED ("MARLEY") 26.06.02

Activity

Manufacture and supply of aerated concrete blocks ("aircrete") for use in the construction industry.

A11.016

Market Share

Each party supplied around one third of aircrete blocks sold in Great Britain. Virtually all the remaining third was supplied by Tarmac Limited.

Assessment

The Commission spent considerable time examining the definition of the relevant product market, and whether this comprised aircrete blocks only or all concrete blocks. Taking all the evidence into account the Commission concluded that the relevant market was aircrete alone.

In particular:

— there seemed to be a reluctance amongst housebuilders to switch to other types of concrete blocks in response to a small (5 per cent) relative price change;

— there were grounds for believing that prevailing aircrete prices were above competitive levels, suggesting little demand-side substitution with other concrete blocks.

It was noted also that other suppliers of aircrete blocks had only limited capacity for the parties' customers to turn to and that little new capacity was likely to become available in the industry (apart from that being introduced by Celcon itself). Other manufacturers would not accordingly be in a position to act as a competitive constraint on the new firm. It was probable that the concentrated duopoly resulting from the merger would have the opportunity and incentive to raise and maintain prices above levels that would otherwise be expected.

In terms of new entry, the Commission concluded that the currently planned entry by one firm was not likely to be of a scale that would provide a significant competitive constraint on the activities of the merged firm. Additionally there was not the possibility of imports on a sufficient scale to act as a check on the behaviour of the merged firm.

Finally there was insufficient buyer power to offset the market power of the merged company, and such buyer power as did exist would be likely to be reduced as a result of the merger.

Recommendation

Against the public interest. The Commission was unable to identify an appropriate structural remedy, nor did it consider that a price control would be satisfactory. It therefore recommended that the merger be prohibited.

Secretary of State's Decision

The Secretary of State initially agreed with the Commission's recommendations that the proposed merger was expected to operate against the public interest, and should be prohibited. Subsequently, following representations made by Celcon to the OFT during the process of negotiating undertakings and in accordance with advice received from the DGFT, the Competition Minister decided to vary the instructions to the DGFT to seek undertakings from Celcon. The revised undertakings would prohibit Celcon from acquiring the entire Marley business, but would allow it to acquire one production plant (subject to assessment by the OFT and, if required, referral to the Commission).

Chairman and Panel Members

Dr D J Morris, Dr J Collings, Mr C Goodall, Professor C Graham, Mr M R Webster

P&O PRINCESS CRUISES PLC ("POPC") AND ROYAL CARIBBEAN CRUISES LTD ("RCL") 19.06.02

Activity

Operation of cruise lines. A11.017

Market Share and Increment

The Commission examined the variety of cruise holidays that were provided to customers in the UK by operators from a wide range of countries. It did not reach an appropriate product market definition for the inquiry; however it did find that the existence of a wider holiday market, and the availability of cruises of types other than those operated by the parties, both constrained these companies' actions and limited commercial freedom, whether or not they were regarded as being in the same market. The Commission also found that there were clear distinctions between the levels of quality and the national styles provided by different types of cruises, whether or not they constituted different markets.

The Commission concluded that the geographic market for the inquiry was the UK (i.e. cruises taken by passengers from the UK).

POPC accounted for 23 per cent of all cruises taken by UK customers, RCL for 6 per cent.

Assessment

The overall conclusion drawn by the Commission was that the market for UK cruise customers was characterised by growth, variety and new entry, and that this would continue. Furthermore, between one-third and one-quarter of UK passengers chose ships that were focused mainly on North American or mainland European customers. Given the diversity, choice and the widespread view among the industry that cruising capacity would continue, the Commission did not consider that the proposed merger was likely to have a significant impact on competition.

Recommendation

Not against the public interest.

Chairman and Panel Members

Mrs D P B Kingsmill, Mr A T Clothier, Mr P F Hazell, Professor P Klemperer, Mr E J Seddon

COLOPLAST A/S ("COLOPLAST") AND SSL INTERNATIONAL ("SSL") 14.06.02

Activity

A11.018   The manufacture and supply of continence care products.

Market Share and Increment

The Commission concluded that there were separate markets for intermittent catheters, sheaths and urobags. As a result of the acquisition the market share in the UK of Coloplast rose from 34 to 92 per cent for sheaths, from 6 to 58 per cent for urobags and from 19 to 26 per cent for intermittent catheters.

Assessment

The Commission took the view that the greatest effect on competition was in the market for sheaths, where in addition to giving Coloplast a very high market share, the acquisition had resulted in the elimination of its main competitor, thereby giving it control of the market leading brands. All other suppliers had small market shares, which they had failed to grow over several years, and there was no evidence to suggest that these would become large players in the future. New entrants faced manufacturing, marketing and regulatory barriers. There was no such combination of factors in the markets for urobags and intermittent catheters.

The Commission considered the effects on the public interest in relation to the supply of sheaths both to hospitals and to the community. While it expected the acquisition to result in higher prices of sheaths to NHS hospitals than they would otherwise have been, it did not expect the acquisition to lead to higher prices for sheaths in the community. This was because prices to the community were controlled by the Drug Tariff in England and Wales, and under equivalent arrangements in Scotland and Northern Ireland

Recommendation

Against the public interest. As part of the transaction an agreement giving SSL exclusive distribution rights in the UK for sheaths provided by the Mentor Corporation was novated in favour of Coloplast. This included exclusive distribution rights in the UK for Mentor's market-leading silicon Clear Advantage sheath. The Commission considered that an appropriate remedy might be:

(i)   the divestment of the Clear Advantage brand, leaving Coloplast with the right to source the silicon sheaths but market them under a different name; or

(ii)   the divestment of the Clear Advantage brand and product, which would involve terminating the Mentor Agreement with respect to silicon sheaths.

Any such arrangement would need to be in place within six months. An option which would remain available as a "last resort" would be a price control remedy together with an undertaking not to renew the Mentor Agreement.

Secretary of State's Decision

The Secretary of State accepted the recommendations of the Commission, and decided that Coloplast should be required to divest the Clear Advantage brand by amending the exclusive distribution agreement with Mentor Corporation, the owner of this brand.

Chairman and Panel Members

Mr A J Pryor CB, Professor J Baillie, Professor D Parker, Mr S Walzer, Mr A M Young

CARGILL INCORPORATED ("CARGILL") AND CERESTAR ("CERESTAR") 30.05.02

Activity

The production of glucose syrups and blends used in a variety of food applications and as fermentation agents.

A11.019

Market Share and Increment

Prior to the merger, Cargill had about 21 per cent and Cerestar 28 per cent of UK production and sales. They together had around 38 per cent of EC wide production.

Assessment

There were three other companies, as well as the merging parties, who produced the reference products in the UK; Amylum, Roquette and Grants. Two other companies, without UK manufacturing facilities, Syral and Pfeifer, produced glucose syrups and blends on the Continent and had begun to import into the UK. Overall, imports of standard glucose syrups represented around 17 per cent of UK sales, whilst exports represented around 13 per cent of UK production.

The Commission concluded that the relevant market was wider than the UK, extending at least to northern France and the Benelux countries. In particular, international trade was significant and growing, customers wishing to import did not face reliability/predictability of supply problems, and price trends in the UK broadly tracked those in Continental Europe.

There was evidence that the market had been competitive: market shares had been fluctuating, prices falling, EC-wide capacity expanding, demand growing and trade between the UK and Continental Europe increasing.

As regards the ability of the merged entity unilaterally to raise prices directly in the UK, or by way of capacity reduction, the Commission took the view that the two remaining strong competitors, both with UK and Continental plants, were sufficient to constrain the merged entity.

In considering the scope for co-ordinated action by the major producers, although the merger would bring about increased concentration, it was noted that the production of glucose syrup and blends was characterised by high fixed and raw materials costs, and that high capacity utilisation rates increased profitability. This made co-ordinated behaviour to restrict production a risky strategy. Prices were not transparent, and whilst new entry would be costly, demand was growing throughout the EC. This would make it more difficult for co-ordinated action to succeed in bringing about price rises. Finally, customers were large and powerful, capable of switching to a new entrant or even sponsoring new entry if they were in danger of becoming too dependent on their existing suppliers.

Recommendation

Not against the public interest.

Chairman and Panel Members

Mr P Mackay, Dr D Coyle, Mr C Darke, Professor C Graham, Mr P Stoddart

NEOPOST SA ("NEOPOST") AND ASCOM HOLDING AG ("ASCOM") 23.05.02

Activity

A11.020   The supply of franking machines (including their after sales service and certain related products) and folding and inserting machines (including maintenance and repair services).

Market Share and Increment

Neopost supplied 26 per cent of UK franking machines and Ascom's subsidiary 10 per cent. The market leader, Pitney Bowes, had 52 per cent, with two other suppliers having 6 per cent and 4.5 per cent. In the supply of smaller folding and inserting machines in the UK, Neopost had 48 per cent of sales and Ascom's subsidiary 3 per cent. Worldwide their shares were 56 per cent and 2 per cent respectively.

Assessment

In relation to the UK franking machines market, the Commission considered that the merger had three structural consequences for this market:

— it reduced the number of suppliers from five to four, and removed Ascom as an independent source of competition;

— it created a market structure in which the top two suppliers had over 85 per cent of this market between them; and

— it strengthened the number two supplier, Neopost, in relation to the market leader.

The Commission found that Ascom's subsidiary would be in fact a declining force in the UK market unless it merged with another franking machine supplier. However, whilst at a global level the Commission believed that the new market structure might be more competitive following the merger, the Commission had concerns that in the longer term UK price competition might be muted. Against this, the Commission believed that the merger would create a strong global competitor to Pitney Bowes, which currently dominated the supply of franking machines worldwide and had great technological strength through an extensive portfolio of patents. The UK would be likely to benefit from the resulting effect on product development and there might be a wider benefit from increased competition in the licensing of technology to smaller suppliers.

In relation to the supply of smaller folding and inserting machines, Ascom's subsidiary did not manufacture folders/ inserters, but sourced such machines for onward supply from PFE International Ltd ("PFE") under its own name. The Commission concluded that the merger would not significantly lessen competition in the folders/ inserters market.

Recommendation

The Commission did not consider, on balance, that the merger situation would operate against the public interest. However, because the supply side of the UK franking machines market was highly concentrated and the demand side highly fragmented, there was a risk stemming from the inherent characteristics of the market, and not from the merger itself, that competition among suppliers would become muted. Due to the switch to digital technology and the liberalisation of the postal services market, the market was undergoing a period of change. Accordingly the Commission proposed that the DGFT should review the operation of the market within three to five years.

Chairman and Panel Members

Dr G F Owen, Dame Barbara Mills QC, Professor D M G Newbery, Mr R A Rawlinson, Professor A Steele

LINPAC GROUP LIMITED ("LINPAC") AND MCKECHNIE PAXTON HOLDINGS LIMITED ("MCKECHNIE") 13.05.02

Activity

The manufacture and supply of returnable transit packaging ("RTP") (a wide range of plastic based containers, in many shapes and sizes, used for the retail and food sectors).

A11.021

Market Share

Linpac/McKechnie's combined market share for all types of RTP exceeded 30 per cent.

Assessment

The relevant product markets were five specific types of plastic RTP; bakery trays, deep nesting stack-nest containers, stack nest containers in general, securable stack nest containers and stacking containers. The Commission concluded that the relevant geographic markets were the UK for bakery trays and deep nesting stack nest containers and Europe for the remaining three markets.
The Commission did not identify any public interest concerns due to:

— the significant share of the UK market for these products that was controlled by large national and international companies with considerable buyer power;

— the extreme price sensitivity of these large customers who operated in sectors, such as supermarkets or automotive manufacturing, where procurement and cost control techniques were very highly developed;

- constraints on prices caused by the presence of existing competitors, both domestic and European in all these product ranges, and the relative ease in entering such markets;

- the expectation of competition being maintained, as large buyers acted to ensure that they would continue to have a choice by developing other producers, through dual sourcing, and by inviting companies from outside the UK or not currently manufacturing RTP, to tender for orders;

- the lack of any expectation of a reduction in either the quality of service to customers or the technical quality of these products; and

- the fact that no loss of UK capacity was expected to result from the merger.

Recommendation

Not against the public interest.

Chairman and Panel Members

Mrs D P B Kingsmill, Mr C Clarke, Dame Helena Shovelton DBE, Professor C Waddams, Mr M R Webster

JOHNSTON PRESS PLC ("JOHNSTON") AND TRINITY MIRROR PLC ("TRINITY") 03.05.02

Activity

A11.022   The publication of newspapers.

Market Share and Increment

The proposed transaction concerned the transfer of eight free weekly newspapers to Johnston. The newspapers were supplied in parts of the East Midlands and the transfers would give Johnston over 80 per cent of the local newspaper market in seven cases, and in four cases in and around Northampton and Peterborough, virtually 100 per cent.

Assessment

Free newspapers derived nearly all of their revenue from advertising, and accordingly, a key issue for the Commission was the degree of competition provided by other advertising media. The Commission concluded that the closest substitutes were advertising only publications, and to a lesser extent other printed media such as directories and direct mail. For many advertisers, none of these were close substitutes for local newspapers.

The regional and local newspaper sector had experienced such a wave of consolidation in recent years that the top five publishers now held 72 per cent of the total market between them. Publishers had also continued to develop clusters of titles in particular locations. While it was clear that growth in ownership concentration at a local level could bring benefits (i.e. through economies of scale to provide better products and services), the Commission believed that the loss of competition could have harmful effects for advertisers and/or readers.

New entry had become less likely as publishers established strongholds in particular areas. The Commission believed that local monopolists might therefore have scope to raise prices, or reduce service levels, to some of their customers without inducing entry.

Given the small size of the transaction, the transfers would not materially affect national concentration. Nor were there concerns over regional concentration, since nearly all of the advertising carried in Trinity's titles was of a local, rather than regional, nature.

As regards the four titles whose transfer would give Johnston a share of over 80 per cent, in each of the areas of distribution another major publisher had a significant presence which was expected to constrain Johnston's behaviour. As regards the four titles where virtual monopolies would be created, four of the panel believed that due to the lack of close substitutes for advertising, at least a significant minority of advertisers in the Trinity Mirror titles, and a proportion of advertisers in the Johnston titles which currently competed with them, would be vulnerable to price increases. Johnston would have the scope to raise prices to varying degrees to these advertisers, without attracting entry into the local markets concerned.

Recommendation

Four members of the panel recommended that the merger situation would operate against the public interest in relation to the four titles that would create virtual monopolies.

Secretary of State's Decision

Accepted the Commission's conclusions and prohibited the transfers of these four titles. The transfers of the other four titles were permitted to proceed.

Chairman and Panel Members

Professor PA Geroski, Miss L I Christmas, Mr W Gibson, Mr A T Clothier, Dr G F Owen

EASTMAN KODAK COMPANY ("KODAK") AND COLOUR-CARE ("COLOURCARE") 21.12.01

Activity

The provision of wholesale photoprocessing services to retailers.   A11.023

Jurisdiction

The Commission used different markets when considering the share of supply test for the purposes of jurisdiction and the market share test for substantive issues (see below). This discrepancy resulted in the parties having a combined share of 78 per cent based on the share of supply test and 51 per cent based on the market share test. Where goods or services are supplied in different ways, the Commission explained that, for the purposes of the share of supply test in a jurisdictional context it can consider those forms of supply either separately, together or in groups as appears appropriate to it. Different forms of supply occur where the transactions in question differ as to their nature, parties, terms or surrounding circumstances and the difference is one that in the Commission's opinion ought to be treated as material. The

Commission clearly stated that *"this is not the same as defining the relevant economic market for this inquiry. . .".*

Market Share and Increment

Taken together, Kodak and Colourcare would account for about half the wholesale processing market in Great Britain. This included overnight, next day or longer developing and printing services, supplied by either wholesalers (such as the parties) or by autonomous retailers carrying out developing and printing on-site.

Assessment

The Competition Commission did not consider that the barriers to entering the wholesale photoprocessing business were high, and had received strong indications that the number of mini labs, and their rate of utilisation would continue to increase. The Commission also considered that the merger would create opportunities for the smaller wholesale processors from retailers who had not previously given them much consideration. This was because retailers would no longer have two national photofinishers competing for their business, and so would be keen to seek quotes from the smaller providers.

The Commission also found that a significant share of the retailer customer base for wholesale photoprocessing was controlled by large national chains with considerable buyer power.

In addition, final consumers had a number of options available to them, including not only the types of photoprocessing services that the parties supplied to retailers, but also retail services from mini-labs, mail-order providers and retail stores vertically integrated into processing.

Recommendation

Not against the public interest.

Chairman and Panel Members

Professor P A Geroski, Mrs S E Brown, Miss J C Hanratty, Mr T S Richmond MBE, Mr E J Seddon

DURALAY INTERNATIONAL HOLDINGS LTD ("DURALAY") AND GATES CONSUMER & INDUSTRIAL ("GATES") 09.11.01

Activity

A11.024   The supply of carpet underlay and accessories (primarily gripper).

Market Share and Increment

Not provided in the published decision.

Assessment

In relation to the supply of underlay, the Commission considered that there were several constraints which would represent a powerful curb on the merged company, sufficient to prevent it from attempting significant price increases. It was expected that large wholesale and retail customers of the merged company would use their countervailing purchaser power to pre-empt price increases for underlay above the competitive level, either by switching or threatening to switch their custom to other suppliers, or by fostering the entry of new suppliers or the expansion of existing ones. It was also not considered that there were high barriers to entry to the underlay market, and that the threat of imports of underlay would be a factor inhibiting the merged company from pursuing an aggressive pricing policy.

At the retail level the Commission did not expect increases in underlay prices to be passed on to consumers, because retailers would find ways to offer underlay of similar quality (if differing specifications) to consumers, without increasing prices.

In relation to the supply of gripper, the Commission considered that the most likely constraint on attempted price increases were low entry barriers and the threat of increased imports.

Recommendation

Not against the public interest.

Chairman and Panel Members

Mrs D P B Kingsmill CBE, Mr A J Pryor CB, Professor A Steele, Mr A M Young

OCTAGON MOTORSPORTS LIMITED ("OCTAGON") AND BRITISH RACING DRIVERS CLUB LIMITED ("BRITISH RACING") 06.09.01

Activity

Three markets were affected: A11.025

(i) the supply to final consumers of motorsport activities based at licensed circuits (including spectator events, and participatory events for consumers in either their own vehicles or in supplied vehicles);

(ii) the supply of track time to organisations offering motorsport activities to final consumers; and

(iii) the promotion of motorsport events at licensed circuits.

Market Share and Increment

As a result of the merger, Octagon's share of turnover from circuit operations increased from 28 to 72 per cent. It controlled five of the 18 licensed circuits in the UK.

Assessment

The Competition Commission observed that as a sizeable proportion of spectators at major motor racing events were likely to see other sporting and leisure activities as acceptable substitutes for motorsport, the ability of circuit operators to raise prices for major events was constrained. Similarly, Octagon could not raise prices at Silverstone above market rates because of the competition it would face from other circuits in the Midlands. Given that the catchment areas of Silverstone and Brands Hatch overlapped, the constraint on prices at Brands Hatch would remain largely unchanged.

As regards customers for participatory activities, the Commission considered that motor racing clubs, track day organisers and teams wanting to carry out testing had sufficient choice of venues to prevent Octagon acquiring significant market power in the supply of circuits to these categories of customer.

While Octagon was vertically integrated in the supply of track days (whereby circuits are opened to members of the public to drive their own vehicles through On Track, its in house track day organiser ("TDO")), On Track organised only one fifth of the track days held at Octagon circuits, and Octagon did not exclude other TDO's from its circuits. There was therefore only a small difference made to the share of demand taken by Octagon controlled circuits as a result of the merger. Similarly, Octagon was vertically integrated in the promotion of motorsport events through its involvement with British Motorsport Promoters Limited ("BMP"). BMP was jointly owned by operators of licensed circuits, and the ownership of voting shares reflected the number of rounds of the three championships which were held at each shareholder circuit. Whilst the merger resulted in Octagon having a majority of the voting shares and formal control of the company, the Commission took the view that Octagon was already in effective control of BMP before the merger.

Recommendation

Not against the public interest.

Chairman and Panel Members

Professor P A Geroski, Mr P Mackay, Dr G F Owen, Mr G H Stacy CBE

LLOYDS TSB GROUP PLC ("LLOYDS") AND ABBEY NATIONAL PLC ("ABBEY NATIONAL") 10.07.01

Activity

A11.026   The sale of financial products to personal customers (in particular personal current accounts ("PCA"), mortgages and savings accounts), small and medium-sized enterprises ("SME") and larger firms, and wholesale banking.

Market Share and Increment

PCAs were the core product in personal banking. Lloyds's market share in PCAs would increase from 22 to 27 per cent, and the merger would raise the combined share of the four leading banks in the UK from 72 to 77 per cent.

The market for the supply of banking services to SME's was highly concentrated, and dominated by the traditional banks. The four leading banks in the UK had an existing 85 per cent of the total market (Lloyds itself had around 16 per cent) pre-merger. Abbey National had less than 1 per cent of total supply to the UK market.

Assessment

Wholesale banking and markets for financial products sold to larger firms were characterised by the presence of global competitors and strong buyers. The Commission had no concerns in these areas.

The Commission considered that there were several features of the PCA market which made it vulnerable to tacit collusion in pricing: product homogeneity, many small customers lacking buyer power, transparent prices, stable demand, similarity of size and cost structure among the main suppliers and suppliers' past behaviour. Whilst the market had been one, historically, in which change was slow, there were now signs of more rapid development and some strengthening of competition, although such development was still considerably constrained by the entrenched positions of the top four competitors, low rates of switching between banks by customers and low market entry by operators not related to the incumbent banks.

Abbey National had been able to win a significant share of the PCA market despite barriers to growth. It offered a distinct alternative to the big four banks, it had been reasonably innovative, and had competed actively. Given its financial performance, it would be capable of maintaining its independence, or of merging with another player to provide enhanced competition to the big four. In these circumstances, its acquisition by Lloyds would reduce incentives to compete. Lloyds would increase its customers base, thereby encouraging it to attach more weight to the enhancement of margins than to the growth of market share. Meanwhile, the big four banks collectively would have lower incentives to compete due to the removal of one of the two main sources of actual and potential competition. Such a reduction in competition could be expected to lead to higher prices, and a loss of innovation.

As regards the mortgages and savings accounts markets, the Commission considered that although the merger would significantly increase concentration on the supply side, these markets were already competitive and that the merger would not be damaging to competition or to consumers of these products. They also did not have concerns about the effects on the other personal product markets where the parties overlapped.

With regard to the supply of banking services to SMEs, this market was highly concentrated and dominated by the traditional banks. The market was characterised by high barriers to entry and there had been little change historically in suppliers' market shares. The structure and levels of prices charged by the banks were similar and the market therefore raised significant competition concerns. The Commission considered that the merger would therefore reduce competition in the supply of banking services to SMEs, where there was a particular need for increased competition, because it would eliminate one of the very few players outside the big four banks which were able to contest this market. As a result of the merger prices for SMEs banking services would be higher, and innovation lower than would be expected in the absence of the merger.

Recommendation

Against the public interest. No suitable remedy was identified.

Secretary of State's Decision

Accepted the Commission's recommendation and prohibited the merger.

Chairman and Panel Members

Mrs D P B Kingsmill CBE, Mr G H Hadley, Mr D J Jenkins MBE, Professor D Parker

REED ELSEVIER PLC ("REED") AND HARCOURT GENERAL INC. ("HARCOURT") 05.07.01

Activity

A11.027   Scientific, technical and medical publishing ("STM"), which divided into two separate segments, books and journals.

Market Share and Increment

In the market for STM books, Harcourt had a 7.6 per cent UK market share, and Reed 3.4 per cent. In the market for STM journal publishing, however, both parties had significant presence, with Reed having about one quarter of the UK market—both print and electronic (by value)—and Harcourt having around 7 per cent.

Assessment

The Commission considered that a single leading title could be regarded as constituting a unique product market. The relevant geographic market was regarded to be global on the basis that international STM journals published in Europe would sell about one third of their subscriptions in their home market, another third in North America and the remaining third elsewhere. STM journals were also offered at a global price with little variation for local conditions. Within the STM publishing world, there were three broad categories of STM publishers: commercial publishers; learned societies; and university presses.

There were differing views about how difficult it was to enter the market. While new titles appeared frequently, it took a long time for a journal to become established and secure a strong reputation. It was rare for a new journal to be launched successfully in a subject where established journals already existed. Demand for STM journals was also inelastic (i.e. non price-sensitive). Academics working in specialised fields covered by individual journals regarded easy access to key publications as a central element in keeping up with what was happening in their research community.

The Commission identified potential public interest concerns arising from the proposed merger in two areas, electronic delivery and pricing. Reed had spent considerable time developing an online publication, ScienceDirect, which had the potential to entrench further its already powerful position in the STM journal market. Adding a further range of 320 titles from Harcourt to this portfolio would make ScienceDirect an even more powerful offering. The Commission was concerned that the merger would create a corpus of STM material which would enable Reed to exploit its market strength, e.g. through refusing to link any of the ScienceDirect content to other formats for electronic access to STM material currently in existence or being developed, or through insisting that libraries take all the ScienceDirect package and not be able to select individual titles or groups of titles within it. However, based on industry responses, the Commission did not find any evidence of Reed denying its competitors links with ScienceDirect. It therefore concluded that it did not expect any increase in the number of titles that it would control post merger to lead to any adverse change in Reed's behaviour.

On pricing, the Commission did not consider that the merger would lead to an increase in the price of Harcourt's journals above levels which might otherwise have occurred. Reed was not the only STM publisher to charge high prices, and it did not consider that it would raise Harcourt's prices more steeply than any other publisher that might take over its journals.

Recommendation

Not against the public interest. The Commission did however note that the DGFT might wish to consider whether a wider review of pricing in the market for STM journals might be necessary, although this was outside the terms of reference.

Chairman and Panel Members

Mr A T Clothier, Mr A J Pryor CB, Dame Helena Shovelton DBE, Mr J D S Stark

BASF AG ("BASF") AND TAKEDA CHEMICAL INDUSTRIES LTD ("TAKEDA") 05.07.01

Activity

The supply of vitamins and particularly C and B2.   A11.028

Market Share and Increment

As a result of the merger the global market shares of the enlarged BASF would be 20 per cent for standard Vitamin C (an increment of 16 per cent), 38 per cent for direct compression grade vitamin C (no increment in market share), 30 per cent for Vitamin B2 food/pharmaceutical grade (an increment of 21 per cent) and 33 per cent for Vitamin B2 animal feed grade (an increment of 21 per cent). BASF would, as a result be the second largest supplier of Vitamins C and B2, behind Roche.

Assessment

The Commission noted that the vitamins industry had a long history of collusion and cartelization, and that a combination of cartel break-ups and increased competition (primarily from Chinese producers) had led to significant price reductions over the preceding 5 years.

The Commission concluded that competition between suppliers of vitamins was primarily on price and it had no reason to believe that this would change in the foreseeable future. However there was overcapacity in the production of Vitamin C, and producers were switching to new and more efficient technologies. While the Commission believed that demand would continue to increase, it was likely that production capacity would exceed demand for the foreseeable future. The Commission expected a considerable degree of competitive pressure after the merger, particularly because of Chinese production of vitamins.

The Commission observed that whilst industry conditions had been favourable for cartel formation in the past, such conditions would not be affected by the merger.

A further issue was that a BASF subsidiary produced animal feed premixes which included vitamins. The Commission was satisfied that neither Takeda's 96 per cent pure nor its 90 per cent pure vitamin B2 animal feed grade products competed *directly* with BASF's 80 per cent pure Vitamin B2 in the UK. Nevertheless, Takeda's products could have had an effect on Vitamin B2 animal feed prices in the UK because they competed with 80 per cent pure products in other markets, and because the geographic market for the supply of vitamins was global. However the Commission did not consider that the merger would impact adversely on the supply of Vitamin B2 to customers in the animal premix market or other markets for three reasons:

(a) there were alternative sources of Vitamin B2 feed grade product to BASF post merger;

(b) the Commission expected that there would be excess production capacity; and

(c) global demand for 96 per cent and 90 per cent pure products was declining.

Recommendation

Not against the public interest.

Chairman and Panel Members

Mrs D P B Kingsmill CBE, Professor D Parker, Professor J A Rees

SCR-SIBELCO SA ("SCR") AND FIFE SILICA SANDS LTD AND FIFE RESOURCES LTD ("FIFE") 04.07.01

Activity

A11.029   The production and supply of sand for glass manufacture.

Jurisdiction

The Commission considered that the enterprises ceased to be distinct at the date that the agreement became unconditionally binding, in this case when shareholder approval was given.

Market Share and Increment

The three main types of glass for which sand is used are clear container glass, float or flat glass and coloured container glass. The Commission found that due to demand-side substitutability, there was a single market for all glass sand. SCR, through its newly acquired company, Hepworth Minerals & Chemicals Ltd ("HMC"), had a 71 per cent share by volume of glass sand supplied to third parties in the UK in 1999/2000. The acquisition of Fife increased this share to 86 per cent.

Assessment

Sibelco wished to acquire the Fife companies primarily to secure sand reserves and extraction rights. The Commission found that despite experiencing quality problems and losing a number of important contracts, Fife had nevertheless acted as a constraint on HMC's prices. The Commission did not accept that Fife was a failing firm.

Prices for glass sand in the UK were agreed by individual negotiation. There were no price lists available. There was also no likelihood in the short term of glass sand prices being constrained by imports and there were severe constraints on new entry. Following the merger, with the competitive constraint of Fife removed, the Commission concluded that glass sand prices might be higher than they would otherwise be expected to be.

No benefits were expected to flow from the merger.

Recommendation

Against the public interest. SCR should be required to divest Fife to a purchaser approved by the DGFT, within 6 months of the publication of the report.

Secretary of State's Decision

Accepted the Commission's recommendations. Accepted undertakings from SCR on the divestment of Fife.

Chairman and Panel Members

Dr G F Owen, Mr C Darke, Mr R A Rawlinson, Mr M R Webster

ICOPAL HOLDING A/S ("ICOPAL HOLDING") AND ICOPAL A/S ("ICOPAL") 13.03.01

Activity

The manufacture and supply of roofing materials.   A11.030

Jurisdiction

CAIK (the former name of Icopal Holdings) was a consortium formed by IKO Sales Ltd (IKO), Carlisle Companies Inc., Kirkbi A/S and Axcel IndustriInvestor A/S). The commission considered whether CAIK's four shareholders, who had acquired Icopal, were "associated persons". The shareholders argued that as a matter of law they *"ceased to be capable of being regarded as **acting** together to secure control from the moment when the control was actually obtained"*. However, the Commission found that in the context of Section 77 of the Fair Trading Act 1973, "to secure" does not only mean "to obtain" but also "to safeguard".

The main factors which led the Commission to conclude that the four shareholders were "associated persons" acting together to obtain control and that they were still to be regarded as acting together to safeguard their control of Icopal were that: both before and after the acquisition, the relationship of the four shareholders was governed by a shareholders' agreement and the Articles of Association of CAIK; the parties continued to operate under the agreement and Articles; the agreement prohibited share transfers for 3 years and by doing so prevented control passing to a third party; and even after the 3 years, any shareholder wishing to dispose of its shares had to offer them to the other shareholders before they could be offered to a third party.

Both IKO and Icopal manufactured roofing materials and each had a significant share of sales in the markets for bituminous flat-roof coverings (roofing felts), pitched roof underslatings and damp proof courses in the UK. The Commission did not consider IKO's ability materially to influence the policy of Icopal in the jurisdiction section of its report because they considered that the *"associated persons"* links which caused the transaction to be referred were different in kind from *"a merger case where one party acquires control of another's enterprise"*. The Commission did however consider the issue of influence later in the conclusions section of its report.

Assessment

Only one other major UK manufacturer supplied products into all three of these markets, although there were two medium-sized manufacturers producing roofing felts and underslatings, and one large scale producer of damp proof courses. There were also significant imports of several types of roofing felts and underslatings.

The Commission had a reasonable expectation that IKO and Icopal would encourage the mutual cooperation of their respective UK subsidiaries. The question was therefore whether the parties might cooperate in order to seek to raise or otherwise manipulate prices.

Recommendation

A majority of panel members concluded that the structure and character of the UK markets for the relevant products was likely, in the absence of fundamental changes, to preclude any detriment to the public interest. In particular:

(a) over a quarter of all sales of these produces was controlled by large national distributors with considerable buyer power, and extensive chains of outlets throughout the country;

(b) this imposed a certain amount of price discipline, both on the manufacturers in selling to smaller distributors in these markets, and also on those distributors in selling to their customers;

(c) there existed effective current and potential competitors, domestic and/or foreign in all these product ranges;

(d) prices were non-transparent, which made it difficult for any manufacturer to know another manufacturer's prices; and

(e) there was only partial overlap of the parties' coverage of the channels of distribution, and they faced at least one significant competitor wherever they did meet.

The majority thus concluded that the merger did not, and was not expected to, operate against the public interest.

Chairman and Panel Members

Professor Geroski, Mr R D D Bertram, Mr N Garthwaite

INTERBREW SA ("INTERBREW") AND BASS PLC ("BASS") 03.01.01

Activity

A11.031   The brewing, wholesaling and distribution of beer.

Market Share and Increment

Following the merger, Interbrew would be the largest brewer in Great Britain, with an overall market share of between 33 and 38 per cent and a portfolio of leading brands. In terms of wholesaling and distribution, Interbrew would have a market share of approximately 33 per cent.

Assessment

The Commission considered that the merger would create a duopoly between Interbrew and Scottish & Newcastle plc ("S&N"). Interbrew and S&N would between them have the largest and most efficient wholesaling and distribution operations in Great Britain and would be able to control the route to market to multiple retailers. The Commission concluded that Interbrew and S&N would have a common interest in raising operating margins and that the conditions of the market would work to facilitate this. Retailers would pass on higher wholesale prices to consumers, for whom brand loyalty was important.

Furthermore, the Commission expected there to be a greater focus on non-price competition (e.g. advertising and marketing), which would raise barriers to entry and expansion for competing brands.

Additionally, the Commission noted that Interbrew charged different prices according to the type of customer with whom it was dealing, with those differences being only in part explained by differences in costs incurred. The Commission believed that the merger would enhance Interbrew's ability to price discriminate.

The Commission considered a number of behavioural remedies, but did not believe that any would address the adverse effects of the merger, and that they would be difficult, if not impossible to enforce. Similarly a number of possible structural remedies would either not address the adverse effects or they would be impracticable. The Commission did however consider two structural remedies, which involved divestment:

(i)   the divestment of Whitbread Beer Company (WBC) from Interbrew, with or without the divestment of the licence rights to Stella Artois; and

(ii)   the divestment of the UK business of Bass Brewers to a buyer approved by the DGFT.

A majority of the panel believed that the divestment of WBC, even with the licence rights to Stella Artois, would not be a sufficient remedy, since Interbrew would still own, and earn royalties from the Stella Artois brand, and could not therefore be expected to develop a brand in competition with Stella.

A majority of the panel believed that Bass Brewers was a viable business that could be disposed of without complications and that a number of international brewers would find it an attractive vehicle for entry or expansion in the UK. This option would leave Interbrew with a strong brand, making it a stronger competitor than it would be on a stand-alone basis.

Recommendation

The majority recommended that Interbrew should be required to divest the UK business of Bass Brewers to a buyer approved by the DGFT.

Secretary of State's Decision

Accepted the Commission's conclusions and decided that Interbrew should be required to dispose of either Bass Brewers or Carling Brewers.

Chairman and Panel Members

Professor Geroski, Mr T S Richmond MBE, Dame Helena Shovelton DBE, Mr J D S Stark

NUTRECO HOLDING NV ("NUTRECO") AND HYDRO SEAFOOD GSP LIMITED ("HYDRO") 22.12.00

Activity

A11.032   Salmon farming and fish feed manufacture.

Market Share and Increment

The Commission considered that the relevant market was that for Atlantic farmed and gutted salmon in the EEA. Within this wider market, the Commission found that there was a small market segment that regarded Scottish salmon as a differentiated premium product.

Following the merger, Nutreco's share of Scottish salmon production would have been 46 per cent, whilst its share in the wider Atlantic farmed and gutted salmon market would have been only 15.5 per cent.

As regards salmon feed in the UK, Nutreco's share of UK production capacity was 53 per cent. As a result of the merger, its share as a UK purchaser of salmon feed would increase from 26 per cent to over 38.3 per cent. There was significant over capacity in the fish feed market in the UK.

Assessment

The UK feed market was concentrated, with only three large players which together accounted for well over 90 per cent of UK sales.

The Commission considered that Nutreco's enhanced position as a feed purchaser in Scotland which would arise from the merger, when added to an already high share of the salmon feed supply market, would bring about a reduction in the supply of feed. This was because following the merger, the merged entity would purchase all or most of its salmon feed from Trouw (UK) Limited ("Trouw") (a subsidiary of Nutreco and the UK's largest manufacturer of fish feeds for salmon and trout and other farmed species). The other two main feed suppliers would therefore have reduced demand for their feed, resulting in a reduction in their capacity utilisation and an increase in their unit costs, while Trouw would enjoy greater economies of scale, increasing output and capacity utilisation.

With regard to Scottish salmon, Trouw would have had the scope to raise feed prices resulting in higher prices for Scottish salmon which most retailers (although not the more powerful retailers) would not be able to resist. The Commission expected the merger to have detrimental effects on employment in the medium to longer term and that the prospect of any benefits would not be sufficient to offset the adverse effects of the merger.

Recommendation

Against the public interest. As the adverse effects would be brought about by the loss of an independent customer to Nutreco's two feed competitors rather than to any accretion in Nutreco's feed capacity, divestment of feed capacity would not be an effective remedy against the adverse effects of the merger. As regards divestment of salmon capacity, such remedies would not be effective unless capacity at least equivalent to that of the target company were divested. The Commission therefore recommended that the merger should be prohibited.

Secretary of State's Decision

The merger was blocked by the Secretary of State.

Chairman and Panel Members

Dr G F Owen, Mr G H Hadley, Miss J C Hanratty, Professor A Steele

BRITISH UNITED PROVIDENT ASSOCIATION LIMITED ("BUPA") AND COMMUNITY HOSPITALS GROUP PLC ("CHG") SALOMON INTERNATIONAL LLC ("SIL") AND COMMUNITY HOSPITALS GROUP PLC 07.12.00

Activity

Provision of private medical insurance and private medical services.   A11.033

Jurisdiction

BUPA and Salomon Brothers UK Equity Limited ("SBUKE") agreed to put special arrangements in place so that SBUKE could assist BUPA in acquiring CHG once BUPA had been released from undertakings not to acquire CHG during a defined period. In light of those arrangements, SBUKE had a 26.8 per cent shareholding in CHG but argued that although such a holding would normally confer material influence (over 25 per cent) it should not be considered to do so in this instance because it was unlikely that SBUKE would use its ability to block a special resolution. In the alternative it suggested that the Commission should use its discretion not to treat the material influence as control in this case. The Commission found that the ability materially to influence rather than the likelihood that a company will use its influence is relevant in determining material influence. It emphasised that it would use its discretion only in "very special" circumstances.

On the question of whether BUPA and SBUKE should be regarded as "associated persons" under Section 77 of the Fair Trading Act 1973, the parties argued that they shouldn't because: the arrangements were intended to assist a possible future acquisition of CHG once BUPA was released from its undertakings; it was normal practice for a bidder to attempt to acquire a blocking stake and had it not been for the undertakings BUPA would have done so itself; there would be no "continuing cooperation" between BUPA and SBUKE regarding how the voting rights attached to the shares were exercised; and the fact that they were considered "concert parties" under the City Code was irrelevant to the question of whether they were associated persons for the purposes of the Act. The Commission found that the parties should be regarded as "associated persons" because, among other things, SBUKE would not have acquired the shares without the involvement of BUPA and SBUKE was unlikely to sell the shares, making the merger less likely to come about. Moreover, the Commission concluded that BUPA and SBUKE should be regarded as *"continuing to act together to secure control of CHG"* as a loan from BUPA to SBUKE for the purchase of the shares was still in place and SBUKE was still holding the shares.

Market Share and Increments

The report dealt with 2 acquisitions; the acquisition by BUPA of CHG, and the acquisition by SIL through its subsidiary SBUKE, of 26.8 per cent of the ordinary share capital of CHG. The first proposed merger raised concerns in respect of both private medical services ("PMS") and private medical insurance ("PMI"). In particular, the Commission was concerned that the reinforcement of BUPA's seller power in the PMS market and the vertical linkages between its PMS and PMI businesses would lead to a reduction of competition in the PMS market and higher prices for PMS and PMI. A secondary concern was that the Commission had identified some areas where local competition would be adversely affected.

The Commission concluded that the PMS and PMI businesses should be put under separate ownership and control, but BUPA was not prepared to proceed with the merger on that basis.

Whilst the boards of BUPA and CHG had announced that they had reached agreement in relation to the first proposed merger, BUPA learned that there were potential rival bidders and itself could not buy any CHG shares before a previous undertaking was lifted. Under an agreement with a BUPA subsidiary SBUKE acquired 26.8 per cent of CHG ordinary shares, (met wholly by a BUPA loan) creating a merger situation between SIL and CHG. The SIL/CHG and SIL/CHG/BUPA merger situations would allow BUPA to exercise material influence over CHG despite the previous undertaking.

Recommendation

The BUPA/CHG merger was against the public interest and the Commission recommended its prohibition.

In relation to the SIL/CHG/BUPA merger situation, the Commission recommended that SBUKE disposed fully of its CHG shareholding and be prohibited from exercising its rights to vote on any matter without the consent of the DGFT during the period it still held such shares.

Secretary of State's Decision

The merger was blocked by the Secretary of State.

Chairman and Panel Members

Professor J A Rees, Miss K M H Mortimer, Mr A J Pryor CB

SYLVAN INTERNATIONAL LIMITED AND LOCKER GROUP PLC 02.11.00

Activities

A11.034   The supply of small steel, timber, plywood and cardboard drums used for the package and transport of cables and wires, and timber drum management services. Each of these constituted a separate, UK-wide market.

Market Share and Increment

The already completed joint venture had an 80 per cent UK share of the supply of steel, timber, plywood and cardboard drums, and a 39 per cent UK share of timber drum management services.

Assessment

The Commission did not expect the merger to have any adverse effects on the market for timber drum management services. Barriers to entry were particularly low. However with regard to the markets for small steel, timber, plywood and cardboard drums, the joint venture's market share ranged from 84–93 per cent in the UK. The Commission considered whether this position could be constrained by customers dual sourcing, countervailing buyer power or the scope for new entry and expansion, and concluded that in the markets for timber, plywood and cardboard drums the merger might be expected to have an adverse effect on competition.

These adverse effects arose from the inability of small UK suppliers to survive if Pentre Askern made selective low price offers to the main customers of those suppliers and from the lack of information available to small customers to enable them to make informed purchasing decisions.

Recommendation

Against the public interest. A panel majority concluded that a package of behavioural remedies was the most appropriate means to alleviate the detriment to the public interest. These remedies should be confined only to the markets for timber, plywood and cardboard drums and should last for only three years. The Commission recommended to the DGFT that undertakings should be obtained from the joint venture covering:

—   information on a web site to improve price transparency;

—   restrictions on subsequent reversal of selective price cuts;

—   independently audited information for the DGFT;

—   prior clearance of further acquisitions in these three markets; and

—   notification to customers and potential customers of these undertakings.

The Commission Panel Chairman concluded, however, that a structural remedy would be more appropriate to a structural problem.

Secretary of State's Decision

The merger was blocked by the Secretary of State who asked the DGFT to seek an undertaking from the parties that they would return the businesses of the joint venture to the separate ownership of Sylvan and Locker.

Chairman and Panel Members

Mrs D P B Kingsmill, Mrs S E Brown, Mr P Mackay CB, Professor A Steele

REGIONAL INDEPENDENT MEDIA LIMITED ("RIM") AND GANNETT UK LIMITED ("GANNETT")/JOHNSTON PRESS PLC ("JOHNSTON")/ GUARDIAN MEDIA GROUP PLC ("GUARDIAN") 01.11.00

Activities

A11.035   Publication of regional and local newspapers in the UK

Market Share and Increment

The report examined whether any of the proposed transfers of newspaper titles and related assets of RIM to Gannett, Johnston and Guardian may be expected to operate against the public interest. The Commission noted that if any of the potential bidders were to acquire RIM then its share of the total circulation and distribution of regional and local newspapers in the UK would rise by around 4.8 per cent. This would have the effect of increasing Gannett's share to 19 per cent, Johnston's 13.3 per cent and GMG's to 8.5 per cent.

Assessment

The degree of national concentration among local and regional newspapers to which any of the proposed transfers would give rise was unlikely to operate against the public interest.

The areas most affected by the proposed transfers were Yorkshire and Humberside, and the North West. The market share increments would have been as follows:

	Yorkshire/Humberside		NorthWest	
	Current mkt share	Mkt share as a result of transaction	Current mkt share	Mkt share as a result of transaction
Gannett	14.1 per cent	45.7 per cent	29.2 per cent	43.0 per cent
Johnston	26.6 per cent	58.2 per cent	0.2 per cent	14.1 per cent
GMG	0 per cent	31.6 per cent	27.2 per cent	41.1 per cent

Any of the transfers would leave at least three major publishers with 10 per cent or more of the market in each region. The levels of regional concentration and common ownership of clusters of geographically proximate local titles that would result were not such as might be expected to operate against the public interest. The Commission also examined effects on market shares at a more local level, but did not identify substantive competition concerns.

Recommendation

Not against the public interest.

Chairman and Panel Members

Professor P A Geroski, Mrs J Hopkirk, Mr C Wilson, Mr CE Henderson CB

AIR CANADA AND CANADIAN AIRLINES
CORPORATION ("CAC") 31.08.00

Activities

Operation of domestic air services within Canada and international air services to A11.036
and from Canada.

Market Share and Increment

The Commission analysed the markets affected by reference to whether passengers were "time sensitive" or "price sensitive". A further distinction was made between passengers with origins in the UK and Canada, those with other origins and destinations, and those with origins at particular airports in the UK and Canada. The major route of concern was that between London and Toronto.

Following the merger Air Canada would account for 40 per cent of London-Toronto origin-destination passengers and would account for some 71 per cent of time sensitive passengers between Heathrow and Toronto.

Concentration had also increased significantly on the London/Calgary route. Competition had been eliminated for "time sensitive passengers" between Heathrow and Calgary. Likewise on the London/Ottawa route, Air Canada had an almost 90 per cent share of origin and destination passengers and competition had been almost eliminated for time sensitive passengers. Given the limited number of passengers on those routes, prospects of entry in the market for time sensitive passengers were poor.

Assessment

With regard to the London/Toronto route, the Commission decided that although there was less competition for "time sensitive" passengers, it believed that there were few constraints on BA expanding its services at Heathrow and that it was able to provide effective competition. There was already effective competition for price sensitive passengers.

In assessing the effects of the merger, the Commission considered what would have happened in the absence of the merger. Prior to the merger, CAC had been making substantial losses, and the Canadian government saw little prospect of CAC's future viability. The Commission found little evidence that other operators would have been able or willing to take on CAC's services on the Heathrow/Calgary or Heathrow/Ottawa routes, or to any significant extent, the domestic services in Canada which provide the flights connecting to the Heathrow/Canada routes. It concluded that the possible detriments which arose as a result of the lack of competition arose as a result of the failure of CAC to sustain competition in the Canadian market and on the Canada/UK routes, irrespective of the merger situation in issue.

Recommendation

Not against the public interest.

Chairman and Panel Members

Mr D Jenkins, Mr N Garthwaite, Miss J C Hanratty, Mr G H Stacy CBE

INDEPENDENT NEWS & MEDIA PLC ("INM") AND BELFAST TELEGRAPH 17.07.00

Activities

A11.037 Publication of national, regional and local newspapers.

Market Share and Increment

INM would have a 59 per cent share of sales of regional daily newspapers in Northern Ireland. With regard to Sunday newspapers, INM would have 37.4 per cent of sales post merger. As regards advertising, INM would have a 61.9 per cent share of sales of advertising space in Northern Ireland regional daily newspapers plus the Sunday Life.

Assessment

The Commission considered whether and to what extent there was single market in Ireland. As the titles transferred were regional and local titles which were circulated almost exclusively in Northern Ireland, it found that there was minimal competition between Northern Ireland regional daily newspapers and Republic of Ireland daily newspapers. The same conclusion applied to Sunday papers. If all regional and national daily newspapers in Northern Ireland were treated as a single market the Commission found that the effect of the transfers to INM would be to increase its market share to 28.5 per cent (from 3.4 per cent) and to reduce that of Trinity Mirror to 22.5 per cent. from 47.67 per cent.

As regards newspaper advertising, the Commission found that there were differences between the Republic of Ireland and Northern Ireland resulting in two distinct markets for newspaper advertising.

Recommendation

Not against the public interest.

Chairman and Panel Members

Mrs D P B Kingsmill CBE, Miss L I Christmas, Mr G L Holbrook, Mr P Mackay CB, Mr T S Richmond MBE

CARLTON COMMUNICATIONS PLC ("CARLTON")/ UNITED NEWS AND MEDIA PLC ("UNM")/ GRANADA GROUP ("GRANADA") 16.06.00

Activities

A11.038 Production and broadcasting of TV programmes, sale of advertising airtime.

Market Share and Increment

The Commission considered the implications of the proposed merger between Carlton and UNM and the potential merger between Granada and either Carlton or UNM. The three merger proposals would each result in a company with a share of the

TV audience greater than the 15 per cent permitted by the broadcasting legislation. The legislation also precluded any company from holding two London licences.

Assessment

The main concern was that any of the mergers would materially enhance the market power of the merged entities in relation to their advertising customers. A further concern was whether any of the mergers might give the merged company the ability to influence the ITV network to favour its own production interests over the wider interests of ITV. Additionally, a merger involving Granada could make ITV over-dependent on Granada as the dominant provider of programmes to the network.

The Commission concluded that it would have concerns regarding the advertising and production markets if the proposals were to result in one dominant TV company significantly larger than the next largest company within ITV. The Commission believed that without obligatory divestments each merger would materially enhance the power of a merged entity in the advertising market as the merged entity would be manifestly indispensable to major advertisers and would be able therefore to raise its advertising prices.

However it did not believe that the merger would have similarly adverse effects on the programme production market because entry was relatively easy and certain protections were built into the ITV network to hinder the ability of companies to favour their own production businesses.

Recommendation

The Commission found and recommended as follows:

—   in the case of a merger between Carlton and UNM, the merger would be against the public interest. However it could proceed on the basis that one leading licence should be divested and further divestment needed to comply with the audience share limit of 15 per cent (which could be achieved by disposal of a holding in GMTV Limited);

—   in the case of a merger between Carlton and Granada, the merger would not be against the public interest. However, to comply with diversity of media ownership rules, one London licence should be divested, and, in order to avoid a resulting market share of the TV audience in excess of 15 per cent a divestment of Tyne Tees Television would be required;

—   in the case of a merger between Granada and UNM, the merger would not be against the public interest. However, to comply with diversity of media ownership rules, the divestment of a UNM holding in Channel 5, a Granada holding in GMTV and the further divestment of HTV Group plc would meet the requirements to retain a less than 15 per cent share of the TV audience.

The DGFT considered that Carlton/United would require divestment of a significant franchise if it were not to operate against the public interest.

Secretary of State's Decision

The Secretary of State accepted the Commission's conclusions as regards the mergers involving Granada. However the Commission found that a merger of Carlton and UNM might be expected to operate against the public interest. In accordance with the recommendations of the Commission and the advice of the DGFT, the Secretary of State allowed the merger of Carlton and UNM to proceed on the condition that the parties gave an undertaking to divest the Meridian licence within a period of six months from the date of the completion of the merger.

Chairman and Panel Members

Mr P G Corbett CBE, Mr R D D Bertrain, Mr C E Henderson CB, Miss K M H Mortimer

VIVENDI SA & BSKYB GROUP PLC ("BSKYB") 18.04.00

Activities

A11.039   Pay TV services in the UK.

Market Share and Increment

BSkyB had a market share of about 50 per cent of pay TV subscribers in the UK and also had a strong position in the supply of content, having acquired rights to premium sport and films. Vivendi had interests in pay-TV services in France and other EC countries, as well as digital conditional access technology in the UK.

Assessment

The main concerns expressed to the Commission related to the acquisition of broadcasting rights for sports and films and the supply of conditional access technology (which allows programmes to be unscrambled only for subscribers). The availability of programme rights, particularly for sports and films was of great importance to the ability of other providers to compete, whilst conditional access systems were essential for the operation of pay-TV systems.

The merger situation was unlikely to result in any significant enhancement of the already strong position of BSkyB and would not have an adverse effect on the acquisition of sports rights in the UK or on competition between pay TV operators. Nor was the merger situation expected to have an adverse effect on the acquisition of film rights. The Commission did not expect that there would be adverse effects of the merger situation on the supply of conditional access technology.

Recommendation

Not against the public interest. However, the pay TV market would merit continued scrutiny by the regulatory authorities as a result of technological developments.

Chairman and Panel Members

Mrs D P B Kingsmill, Professor J Beatson QC, Professor J A Rees, Mr T S Richmond MBE

NEWS COMMUNICATIONS & MEDIA PLC ("NEWSCOM") AND NEWSQUEST LIMITED/JOHNSTON PRESS PLC/TRINITY MIRROR PLC ("TRINITY MIRROR") 04.04.00

Activities

Publication of daily and weekly national and local newspapers. **A11.040**

Market Share and Increment

The Commission found that if any of the "would be" bidders were to acquire Newscom then its share of the total circulation and distribution of local and regional newspapers would increase by about 4 per cent, which would lift Trinity Mirror's market share to over 25 per cent.

Assessment

The Commission did not believe that the proposed mergers would adversely affect national advertisers. Nor would they affect cover prices given the importance of maximising readership. The local/regional press market was competitive, with low barriers to entry.

At the local level, the Commission found no significant overlaps between daily newspapers or Sunday newspapers, only between weeklies (both paid for, and free newspapers). The Commission concluded, based on the small scale and insignificance of each of the overlaps, that the proposed transfers might be expected not to operate against the public interest as a result of the concentrations at a local level.

Recommendation

Not against the public interest.

Chairman and Panel Members

Mr P G Corbett, Mr G L Holbrook, Mr R Lyons, Mr P Mackay CB

NTL INCORPORATED ("NTL") AND CABLE AND WIRELESS COMMUNICATIONS PLC ("CWC") 22.03.00

Activities

Operation of cable telephone and pay TV services in the UK. **A11.041**

Market share and Increment

The combined company would account for 27 per cent of all subscribers to pay TV in the UK, the leading supplier of which was BSkyB with a 50 per cent share using satellite transmission.

Assessment

The parties operated in different geographical areas, and did not directly compete. The main Commission concern was whether the merger could increase or enhance the market power of the merged entity in relation to that of pay TV channel or programme providers, arising, for example, from NTL's potential ability (following the merger) to threaten (in contract negotiations) to deny content providers access to two or three of the substantial cable companies. However, the Commission did not believe that the merger would substantially affect the market power of NTL relative to content providers (since the attractiveness of its services depended on a wide variety of content) and that the content providers themselves would have countervailing power to some degree. The Commission also concluded that NTL's intention to acquire broadcasting rights would not distort competition in the market for the acquisition of such rights.

The Commission did not believe that the merger would adversely affect competition between pay-TV platforms (such as cable and satellite), rather that it might enhance the efficiency with which the technological advantages of cable could be deployed. Nor did it find any adverse effects on competition in communications given the low market shares of both NTL and CWC compared with British Telecommunications plc.

Recommendation

Not against the public interest. However, there was considerable uncertainty about how the relevant markets would develop given that there could be a significant increase in competition from other platforms, including new use of the ordinary telephone network to transmit pay TV services.

Chairman and Panel Members

Mrs D P B Kingsmill CBE, Mr R D D Bertram, Mr C Darke, Professor A Steele

CHC HELICOPTER CORPORATION ("CHC") AND HELICOPTER SERVICES GROUP SA ("HSG") 19.01.00

Activities

A11.042   Helicopter services.

Market Share and Increment

Both parties supplied oil and gas installations on the UK Continental Shelf. The Commission considered that the northern and southern zones of the UK Continental Shelf constituted distinct markets, with both parties being active in each. Market shares were 'lumpy', depending on the loss or gain of large contracts. In 1999, the parties together supplied 38 per cent of helicopter services in the northern zone and 64 per cent in the southern zone. There was only one competitor, Bristow.

Assessment

The Commission considered the following:-

— whether Brintel (the UK subsidiary of CHC) would have remained in the market for helicopter services in the absence of the merger. Despite a reduction in demand for helicopter services since 1990, and Brintel's loss of a large contract with Shell, Brintel had won an important contract in Denmark and the Commission were not convinced that it would have exited the market in the absence of the merger;

— whether entry barriers were sufficiently high that entry by another operator would be unlikely even if prices were to rise after the merger. The Commission found that access to on-shore facilities would not present a problem in either the northern or southern zone, and that it would not be difficult for a new entrant to obtain suitable helicopters provided that oil companies let their contracts in a way which assisted new entrants;

— whether the merger, by creating a duopoly, would materially reduce the level of competition. The Commission could find no reason to believe that the two remaining entities in the market would not engage in independent pricing, although there would be some loss of competition resulting from the reduction in the number of competitors; and

— whether countervailing purchaser power was enough to prevent any reduction in competition from leading to higher prices or other adverse effects. The Commission found this to be the case.

Recommendation

Not against the public interest.

Chairman and Panel Members

Mr P G Corbett, Professor P A Geroski, Mr M R Prosser, Mr A J Pryor CB

ALANOD ALUMINIUM-VEREDLUNG GMBH & CO ("ALANOD") AND METALLOXYD ANO-COIL LTD ("ANO-COIL") 19.01.00

Activities

The supply of specular anodized aluminium coil for use in lighting.   A11.043

Market Share and Increment

Prior to the acquisition, Alanod had a worldwide market share of 31 per cent, making it the largest supplier in the world. In the UK, Alanod's share of sales was around 35 per cent, whilst Ano-coil had around 40 per cent.

Assessment

Ano-Coil had been an effective competitor to Alanod in the UK and the Commission believed it would have remained a viable competitor for at least a reasonable period. The fact that the largest supplier in the UK was being acquired by the second largest supplier inevitably meant that there would be a significant loss of competition.

The Commission also considered the agreement which Alanod and Von Ardenne Anlagentechnik GmbH ("Von Ardenne") had entered into following the joint development of the vacuum deposition process (called the MIRO process) by Alanod and Von Ardenne which enabled high levels of reflectivity to be achieved in the anodizing process. In order to recognise Alanod's contribution in know how to the development of the MIRO production technology, it had been agreed that a substantial one off sum (DM 3 million) would be payable to Alanod if Von Ardenne installed a plant for any other company before 1 May 2001. The Commission considered that the payment could be expected to increase the costs faced by an entrant wishing to purchase a MIRO plant from Von Ardenne. The agreement therefore constituted a technical and commercial barrier to entry and would deter a newcomer from entering the market (which had, in fact, seen no new entrant in the preceding 10 years). Although the Commission doubted whether any other producer would wish on commercial grounds to invest in a MIRO plant in the next year or two, this agreement remained an additional hurdle and it considered that if the barrier were removed, it would be somewhat easier for others in the market to develop the capacity for producing material of the highest reflectivity and thereby become more effective competitors.

While there were no substantial technical barriers to entry, the commercial barriers were sufficient so as to deter any newcomer from entering the market. The Commission concluded that the merger had the result of diminishing competition and producing a dominant supplier which could have both the incentive and means to exploit market power by charging higher prices than they would be had the merger not taken place, and to tie in sales of MIRO vacuum deposition products (of which the merged company would be the sole source) with sales of anodised aluminium.

Recommendation

Against the public interest. The Commission recommended a package of behavioural remedies covering:

—   maximum prices;

—   continuing supply of existing grades;

—   not linking sales of MIRO to sales of anodised aluminium;

—   supplying MIRO products to competitors;

—   cancelling its agreement with Von Ardenne;

—   not giving retrospective rebates; and

—   maintaining arm's length business relationships with Jordan, part of the Alonod group which manufactured lighting louvres.

Secretary of State's Decision

The Secretary of State agreed with the Commission's conclusions.

Chairman and Panel Members

Mr R H F Croft CB, Mr C Darke, Miss J C Hanratty, Mr G H Stacy CBE

UNIVERSAL FOODS CORPORATION ("UFC")
& POINTINGS HOLDINGS LIMITED
("POINTING") 21.12.99

Activities

Manufacture and distribution of flavours and colours for the food, pharmaceuticals   A11.044
and cosmetics industries.

Market Share and Increment

In the flavours market, the market shares of UFC and Pointing in the UK were approximately 6.5 per cent and 1 per cent respectively The Commission considered that no public interest issues arose in the flavours market.

In respect of natural colours in the UK, Pointing had a market share of under 3 per cent, while Warner-Jenkinson Europe Limited ("WJE") (the entity running UFC's European colour business) had a market share of 12.4 per cent. As there were other manufacturers and distributors, the largest of which had a market share of just over 25 per cent, there were no public interest issues arising in this market.

In terms of synthetic food colours to the UK food industry, WJE had a market share of approximately 51 per cent prior to the merger and Pointing had a market share of approximately 23 per cent. The parties competed directly in the supply of basic unblended colours.

Assessment

The Commission examined the competitors of the merged entity, each of which had acquired a relatively small but significant market share, in some cases over a relatively short period of time. It was expected that competitors would continue to compete vigorously with WJE and that WJE would not be in a position to raise prices in the basic colours segment of the market. Customers (many of which were large food manufacturing companies) would be suspicious of any attempt by WJE to raise prices. The Commission did not therefore regard either the costs of switching or reluctance to switch as significant barriers to entry.

Equally the Commission did not believe that, post merger, WJE would be in a position to price discriminate or to refuse to supply distributors (which, in turn, competed with the parties). Nor would WJE be able to engage in predatory pricing given the cost advantages enjoyed by overseas suppliers.

As regards value-added synthetic colours (where Pointing was a potential, rather than actual, competitor), the Commission concluded that WJE would be unable to exploit its already high market share since customers would have the ability to blend colours themselves or to source them from alternative suppliers.

Recommendation

A panel majority concluded that the merger was not against the public interest.

Chairman and Panel Members

Dr G F Owen, Mrs K M H Mortimer, Dame Helena Shovelton DBE, Professor A Steele

TRINITY PLC ("TRINITY") / MIRROR GROUP PLC ("MIRROR") AND REGIONAL INDEPENDENT MEDIA HOLDINGS LIMITED ("RIM") / MIRROR GROUP PLC ("MIRROR") 23.07.99

Activities

A11.045   Publication of national, regional and local newspapers.

Market Share and Increment

Overlaps arose in relation to the supply of regional/local titles. At the UK level the following market shares would result from the proposed mergers: Trinity/Mirror (24 per cent); and RIM/Mirror (17 per cent).

Assessment

Neither merger would create significant overlaps of regional or local titles in Great Britain. In Northern Ireland, whilst RIM had no titles, Trinity had the Belfast Telegraph, Sunday Life and a free weekly series. Mirror owned the News Letter, the Derry Journal and some free weeklies. The Commission concluded that the increased concentration of ownership that would result from the transfer to Trinity of Mirror's Northern Ireland titles would have the following public interest detriments:

(i)   if the Belfast Telegraph and the News Letter were owned by Trinity, convergence between the two titles would be likely to occur, leading to the loss of the distinctive voice in the News Letter in representing unionist opinion; and

(ii)   Trinity/ Mirror would have a 67 per cent share of advertising in regional and local newspapers in Northern Ireland. This was expected to lead to higher advertising prices.

Recommendation

Not against the public interest, except, in the case of a transfer to Trinity, in Northern Ireland.

The Commission recommended that Trinity should be required to give undertakings to dispose of the News Letter, Derry Journal, the Belfast News, the North Down News, the Journal Extra and their related newspaper assets within six months of the completion of any transfer to Trinity.

Secretary of State's Decision

In relation to the proposed transfer to Trinity, the Secretary of State said that in order to protect diversity of the press and competition in newspaper advertising in Northern Ireland, he would give consent for the proposed transfer to Trinity on the condition that Trinity divested its four Northern Ireland titles—the Belfast Telegraph, Sunday Life, Community Telegraph and Farm Trader (N.B. The Commission had recommended the divestment of a different set of titles in Northern Ireland).

Chairman and Panel Members

Mrs D P B Kingsmill, Professor D G Trelford, Mr C E Henderson CB, Dame Helena Shovelton DBE

BRITISH AIRWAYS PLC ("BA") AND CITYFLYER EXPRESS LIMITED ("CITY FLYER") 20.07.99

Activities

Carriage of passengers on international air services. Within London, BA operated flights from Heathrow, Gatwick and Stansted, whilst City Flyer operated from Gatwick.

A11.046

Jurisdiction

BA would acquire a controlling interest in CityFlyer, so that the enterprises would cease to be distinct for the purposes of the Fair Trading Act 1973. The share of supply test would be satisfied regarding scheduled air services to and from south-east England. Even though the share of supply of air services could be measured in a number of ways (such as revenue or aircraft movement), the Commission considered it was more practicable to measure shares by reference to the number of passengers carried. BA's share of supply would accordingly increase from 40 to 41 per cent. The Commission rejected the parties' argument that this figure overstated the true share because it took into account passengers who were travelling *through* the south-east rather than to and from it.

Assessment

The Commission considered whether services from Heathrow, Stansted, Luton and London City Airports were substitutable for those from Gatwick. They concluded that this was generally not the case as far as passengers transferring between flights at Gatwick were concerned, with Gatwick facing competition from major hubs in Europe and further afield. However, for point to point travellers starting or finishing their air journeys in London, Gatwick services were subject to substantial competition from Heathrow (although more so in the leisure, rather than business sector).

The Commission considered the consequences of the merger in terms of the loss of competition between City Flyer and BA on the routes served by both airlines ("the overlap routes"). They also considered the wider effects of BA's acquisition of CityFlyer's substantial holding of take off and landing slots, together with third party concerns put to them that the merger would reduce other airlines' access to the noise and night movement quotas that govern night time activity at Gatwick.

The Commission concluded that the merger would have little effect on the level of competition on the overlap routes. The effect of BA's acquisition of CityFlyer's slots was more significant as BA's competitive position would be strengthened by increasing its flexibility to reorganise its schedules and services. This in turn would enable BA to respond more rapidly than its competitors to new opportunities. The merger would also preclude competition for BA at Gatwick that might be expected to arise in the absence of the merger.

Recommendation

Against the public interest.

The Commission considered that ring-fencing or divestment would not be appropriate remedies and went on to consider capping. It recommended that in order to remedy the competition issues posed by the proposed merger, the share of slots at Gatwick used by BA should be capped at a level of 41 per cent of available slots. To ensure that the appropriate capacity remained available to BA's competitors in the peak operating periods, they recommended that there should be a cap of 70 per cent in the share of slots available in any one hour held by BA, and a cap of 65 per cent on their share of slots in any two hour period.

Secretary of State's Decision

The Secretary of State approved the acquisition subject to BA limiting its holding of take off and landing slots at Gatwick.

Chairman and Panel Members

Dr D J Morris, Mr R D D Bertram, Mr A T Clothier, Mr A J Pryor CB

PORTSMOUTH & SUNDERLAND NEWSPAPERS PLC ("PORTSMOUTH") AND JOHNSTON PRESS PLC/NEWSQUEST (INVESTMENTS) LIMITED/NEWS COMMUNICATIONS AND MEDIA PLC: REPORT ON THE PROPOSED TRANSFERS OF THE NEWSPAPERS OF PORTSMOUTH & SUNDERLAND NEWSPAPERS PLC TO JOHNSTON PRESS PLC, NEWSQUEST (INVESTMENTS) LIMITED AND NEWS COMMUNICATIONS AND MEDIA PLC 16.06.99

Activities

A11.047   Publication and circulation of local, regional and national newspapers.

Market Share

If any of the bidders were to acquire PSN, its share of total circulation and distribution of regional and local newspapers in the UK would increase by around 3 per cent.

Assessment

The Commission concluded that any concentration at the national level would neither adversely affect powerful national advertisers, nor would it affect cover prices, given the importance of retaining readers in order to maximise revenues.

None of the proposed transfers involved the overlap of regional newspapers, and at the local level no material concerns were expected to arise.

Recommendation

Not against the public interest.

Chairman and Panel Members

Mr P G Corbett, Mr R Kernohan, Miss J C Hanratty, Mr M R Prosser

ROCKWOOL LTD ("ROCKWOOL") AND OWENS-CORNING BUILDING PRODUCTS (UK) LTD ("OCBP") 07.05.99

Activities

Manufacture of stone wool.   A11.048

Market Share and Increment

Rockwool had 78 per cent of all UK sales of stone wool. As a result of the transaction, 12 per cent of OCBP's overall 18 per cent share would be brought under common ownership or control with Rockwool.

Assessment

The Commission identified a number of areas where the merger would give Rockwool scope to raise prices; flat roofing, industrial process applications and supplies to fabricators. Internal evidence from Rockwool indicated to the Commission that it might be expected to raise prices in some areas as a result of the merger.

In addition the Commission concluded that OCBP's customers would face less favourable terms from Rockwool and would either incur higher costs or pay higher prices because they would have to buy through distributors. Such effects, and the loss of customers' ability to choose between two UK producers of stone wool would, in the Commission's view, have impaired competition in the distribution and fabrication sectors.

Recommendation

Against the public interest. The Commission could find no appropriate structural solution to remedy the adverse effects of the proposed transaction. It also considered at some length the possibility of behavioural remedies. It concluded that price controls would not be a suitable remedy since:

- the wide variety of discounts, quantity rebates and individually negotiated prices would make such a measure very hard to monitor;

- it would not be possible to define which products would be affected;

- it would be possible for Rockwell to introduce new products at higher prices to replace the price-controlled products; and

- such a measure would have a distorting effect in the market.

The Commission also rejected a remedy of price reporting for similar reasons, and it rejected a remedy easing prohibitions in the sale agreement so that OCBP could supply a wider range of products and sell to small customers which were not already included on the "compete" list. Accordingly, the Commission was unable to identify any appropriate remedies, and recommended that the merger be prohibited.

Secretary of State's Decision

The Secretary of State accepted the Commission's recommendation and prohibited the merger.

Chairman and Panel Members

Mr D P B Kingsmill, Mr P Mackay CB, Mrs K M H Mortimer, Mr T S Richmond MBE, Mr J D S Stark

BRITISH SKY BROADCASTING GROUP PLC ("BSKYB") AND MANCHESTER UNITED PLC 09.04.99

Activities

A11.049   BSkyB was active in TV broadcasting; programme production; distribution and retail of TV channels to subscribers using BSkyB's direct to home satellite platform and wholesale to other retailers using other distribution platforms. Manchester United's football related activities included the supply of TV rights for its matches.

Market Share and Increment

The MMC concluded that the relevant market for the purposes of examining the proposed merger was sports premium TV channels. In this market BSkyB was the only large provider.

The MMC considered that entry to the relevant market depended crucially on the ability of a provider to obtain the appropriate live sports rights, and it was unlikely that there were enough rights to sustain many sports premium channels, of which BSkyB currently provided three. Accordingly, the MMC concluded that BSkyB's very high market share and the barriers to entry in the market led BSkyB to have market power in the sports premium TV channel market.

Assessment

The MMC concluded that the merger might be expected to reduce competition for Premier League rights with the consequential adverse effects of restricting entry into the sports premium channel market by new channel providers, causing the prices of BSkyB's sports channels to be higher and, consequentially, choice and innovation lower. Reduced entry by sports premium channel providers would feed through into reduced competition in the wider pay TV market.

In addition the MMC concluded that the merger would adversely affect football in two ways, first by reinforcing the existing trend towards greater inequality of wealth between clubs, thus weakening the small ones and second, giving BSkyB additional influence over Premier League decisions relating to the organisation of football, leading potentially to some decisions which did not reflect the long term interests of football.

Recommendation

Against the public interest. Undertakings would not be effective. The MMC considered as unfeasible various methods whereby Chinese Walls would be inserted between the two companies. They also rejected a remedy whereby the Premier League would cease to sell all the rights to a single broadcaster, as well as a proposal relating to individual selling. The MMC concluded that prohibition of the merger was both an appropriate and proportionate remedy.

Secretary of State's Decision

The Secretary of State blocked the proposed acquisition.

Chairman and Panel Members

Dr D J Morris, Mr N H Finney OBE, Mr D J Jenkins MBE, Mr R J Munson, Dr G F Owen

IMS HEALTH INC ("IMS") AND PHARMACEUTICAL MARKETING SERVICES INC. ("PMSI") 25.02.99

Activities

The provision of pharmaceutical business information services. IMS and PMSI   A11.050
were global providers of market information to pharmaceutical manufacturers and healthcare companies.

Market Share and Increment

The relevant market was defined as the market for specialised pharmaceutical data services, based primarily on data from wholesalers and from prescriptions processed at pharmacies. IMS accounted for 85 per cent and PMSI for 8 per cent of this market.

Assessment

The MMC had received considerable evidence of objections by IMS's customers to the merger. It concluded that prospects of effective entry into the UK market were limited given existing barriers to entry and were insufficient to offset the loss of competition resulting from the merger. There were no other significant suppliers of such information. Although customers for IMS's services were major global pharmaceutical companies, their countervailing power was not sufficient to offset the loss of competition resulting from the merger.

The merger would result in higher prices to pharmaceutical companies, less innovation and weaker incentives to improve quality of data and service. The merger would have adverse effects on the efficiency and effectiveness and costs of the management and marketing of pharmaceutical companies and, as a knock on effect, might be expected to result in higher costs to the NHS and prices of non prescription (i.e. over the counter) products.

Recommendation

The MMC proposed a series of measures to encourage competition in the market and therefore to remedy the adverse effects of the merger.
The MMC recommended that IMS should undertake:

— to divest PMSI's former business based on wholesale data;

— to license prescription data on reasonable terms to other parties;

— to price all its UK specialised pharmaceutical data services according to transparent price lists and discounts;

— not to sell specialised pharmaceutical data services in the UK as a package or discount to the same effect; and

— not to enter into, maintain or enforce exclusive contracts with its data providers.

Secretary of State's Decision

The Secretary of State accepted the findings of the MMC, and the advice of the DGFT that the merger might be expected to operate against the public interest, and requested the DGFT to seek undertakings from IMS in the terms of the proposed remedies above.

Chairman and Panel Members

Sir Archibald Forster, Mr H G C Aldons, Ms P A Hodgson CBE, Mr M R Prosser, Professor A Steele

CENDANT CORPORATION ("CENDANT") AND RAC HOLDINGS LIMITED ("RAC") 04.02.99

Activities

A11.051   The supply of insured breakdown services for light vehicles in the UK.

Market Share and Increment

1998 estimates of market shares by sales revenue showed that the Automobile Association ("AA") was the biggest supplier with 48 per cent, RAC with 28 per cent and Green Flag (owned by Cendant) with 12 per cent. No other supplier had more than 3.5 per cent.

Assessment

The MMC took the view that the overall effect of the merger would be on balance to weaken competition and that this would have adverse effects in the medium to long term. The benefits were unlikely to be passed on to consumers. The merger would be against the public interest as prices would be higher, service quality lower and innovation reduced.

Recommendation

There were no behavioural undertakings which could remedy the loss of the dynamic benefits of competition.

The MMC recommended that before acquiring RAC's insured breakdown business, Cendant should undertake to divest Green Flag in a manner and to a party approved by the DGFT within six months of the undertaking being given. If Cendant were not prepared to give such an undertaking, the merger should be prohibited as being against the public interest.

Secretary of State's Decision

The Secretary of State agreed with the above analysis that if satisfactory undertakings could not be obtained by three months from publication of the MMC report, he would prohibit the merger.

Chairman and Panel Members

Mr P G Corbett, Professor J A Rees, Dr A Robinson, Mr J K Roe, Mr J D S Stark

ARRIVA PLC ("ARRIVA") AND LUTONIAN BUSES LTD ("LUTONIAN") 18.11.98

Activities

Operation of bus services.

Jurisdiction

The CC considered whether the share of supply test would be satisfied in a substantial part of the UK. It defined Bedfordshire and Hertfordshire as the "reference area", which included Luton. Arriva submitted that the merger had no effect outside Luton and referred to the House of Lords decision in *South Yorkshire Transport Limited* to suggest that Luton could not be regarded as a substantial part of the UK. The CC noted that it was for itself, in establishing its jurisdiction, to ascertain *inter alia* whether the reference area or another area could be regarded as a substantial part of the UK. The CC noted that the reference area had 2.7 per cent of the total population of the UK and covered 1.2 per cent of the UK land area, being larger than areas in other cases it had previously concluded represented a substantial part of the UK. The CC concluded that the reference area accounted for a sizeable proportion of the population of the UK, included a number of important towns and was of economic and social significance containing industries of national importance. In the specific context of the bus industry, even though use of bus services in Bedfordshire and Hertfordshire was relatively low, in Luton it was similar to the national average and a significant proportion of households remained dependent on bus travel. Accordingly, the reference area was of such size, character and importance to amount to "a substantial part of the UK".

A11.052

Market Share and Increment

The effect of the merger would be to increase Arriva's market share of bus services in Bedfordshire and Hertfordshire from about 52 per cent to about 54 per cent.

Arriva's service operations accounted for 82 per cent of the market in the borough of Luton whilst Lutonian accounted for 13 per cent.

Assessment

The MMC found that Lutonian had been an effective competitor, and that the merger had resulted in the removal of the only independent competitor to Arriva on intra-urban bus services in Luton.

The MMC concluded that there was insufficient prospect of competition from new entry to provide a sufficient constraint to discourage Arriva from taking advantage of its enhanced market power in Luton following the merger. The main barrier to entry would be the prospect of retaliation by Arriva. There were no benefits as a result of the merger to offset the adverse effects identified.

Recommendation

Against the public interest. The detriments identified could only be effectively remedied by requiring Arriva to divest Lutonian. Such divestment would also need to be linked to behavioural controls such as Arriva taking no action to hinder the ability of the divested business to establish a financially viable operation in competition with Arriva. In the longer term, appropriate measures would need to be taken to protect the divested business from predatory or unduly aggressive conduct. In implementing such behavioural controls, attention might need to be given to matters such as fare levels, the timing, introduction and frequency of services and other competitive relationships between operators.

Secretary of State's Decision

The Secretary of State was in agreement with the recommendations of the MMC.

Chairman and Panel Members

Professor J F Pickering, Mrs S E Brown, Sir Ronald Halstead CBE, Mr A J Pryor CB, Mr J B K Rickford

TOMKINS PLC ("TOMKINS") AND KERRY GROUP PLC ("KERRY") 25.09.98

Activities

A11.053   Production and supply of milled flour in the UK.

Market Share and Increment

Before the merger Tomkins (through its subsidiary Rank Hovis Ltd) produced 24 per cent of flour milled in the UK, over half of which Rank Hovis used in-house. The assets acquired from Kerry were primarily those of Spillers Milling which produced approximately 11 per cent of flour milled in the UK all of which was supplied to the free market. After the merger Rank Hovis Ltd would account for about 39 per cent of the supply of milled flour to the free market.

Following the merger the two leading suppliers would account for about 60 per cent of the output of flour in the UK and also for 55 per cent of production of bread.

Assessment

Spillers Milling had been an effective competitor in the free flour market, and the reduction in competition might be expected to result in higher prices for free flour than would otherwise be the case.

Spillers Milling had been the largest non-vertically-integrated supplier of flour, and the only such supplier with national coverage. The MMC considered that the merger had increased the dependence of the non-vertically-intergrated bakers on the major integrated millers, weakening the position of the non-vertically-integrated bakers, and adversely affecting competition in the supply of flour-using products.

Recommendation

Against the public interest.

The MMC took the view that only structural remedies, i.e. divestment of capacity, would be appropriate. The MMC recommended that Tomkins should be required to divest four of the six mills acquired as a result of the merger, which at the time produced hard flour for breadmaking. It also recommended that Tomkins should undertake not to increase production of hard flour at the Spiller Milling Cambridge mill, for a period of one year after the date of divestment, above the level of the 12 months to April 1998.

Secretary of State's Decision

The Secretary of State accepted the MMC's recommendations, and ordered that Tomkins should be required to divest four flour mills.

Chairman and Panel Members

Mrs D P B Kingsmill, Mr H G C Aldons, Dr G F Owen, Dr A Robinson, Mr J K Roe

LADBROKE GROUP PLC ("LADBROKE") AND THE CORAL BETTING BUSINESS ("CORAL") 24.09.98

Activities

UK off-course betting through chains of licensed betting offices ("LBOs") and telephone betting.

A11.054

Market Share and Increment

At a national level, the merger would increase Ladbroke's share of licensed betting offices from 21 per cent to 30 per cent and its share of off course betting turnover from 26 to 38 per cent. Coral was the third largest firm in the UK, with William Hill Organisation Limited being the only other national chain of licensed betting offices.

Assessment

Ladbroke had markedly increased its lead in the national retail betting market. The merger also had the effect of removing Coral which had been an important third national competitive force in the market. The effect of the merger would be to lead to a weakening of price competition at a national level. There would also be a dampening effect on innovation and a reduction of consumers' choice of major licensed betting office chains. The merger would have significant adverse effects in reducing local choice.

Recommendation

Against the public interest. The MMC believed it was likely that the merger would result either in dominance by Ladbroke or the existence of a comfortable duopoly between Ladbroke and William Hill, both of which were undesirable. It considered that partial divestment (including the divestment of a further 176 LBOs, in addition to the 134 conditionally sold to Tote Bookmakers) would not alleviate its concerns. While the acquisition of all 301 LBOs would allow Tote Bookmakers to become the third largest competitor in the market, it would not address the concerns raised by the removal of Coral as a separate competitor. Accordingly, the MMC recommended that Ladbroke be required to divest Coral's UK business. It also required that the 134 LBOs which, in anticipation of competition concerns at a local level, Ladbroke had already entered into a conditional agreement to sell to Tote Bookmakers also be divested with the Coral business. The divestments should take place within 6 months of the publication of the report.

Secretary of State's Decision

The Secretary of State accepted the findings of the MMC and announced that the merger might be expected to operate against the public interest. He prohibited the merger and asked the DGFT to seek undertakings from Ladbroke that within six months they would divest the whole of Coral's UK betting business.

Chairman and Panel Members

Mr P G Corbett CBE, Mr R D D Bertram, Mr N H Finney OBE, Professor J F Pickering, Mrs Shovelton

JOHNSTON PRESS PLC ("JOHNSTON") AND HOME COUNTIES NEWSPAPERS HOLDINGS PLC ("HOME COUNTIES") 10.06.98

Activities

A11.055   Publication of weekly newspapers.

Market Share and Increment

In terms of share of circulation and distribution, Johnston was the fifth largest publisher of regional and local newspapers in the UK with a share of around 7 per cent. The transfer of Home Counties to Johnston would make it the fourth largest with a market share of about 8 per cent. Johnston's share of weekly newspapers was 10 per cent with Home Counties' share being 2 per cent. However the transfer would not have changed Johnston's position as the second largest publisher of weekly newspapers.

Assessment

Although the transfer would increase overall concentration in Hertfordshire, Buckinghamshire and Bedfordshire, these did not comprise a coherent or self contained market.

The operations of the two groups overlapped in the six areas: Bedford, mid-Bedfordshire, Leighton Buzzard, Luton, Dunstable and Milton Keynes. Johnston's share of total circulation and distribution of weekly newspapers in these areas would increase to between 51 and 72 per cent. In each of these six areas the MMC believed that there would be some competition from free Sunday newspapers distributed by one other publisher. In Bedford, mid-Bedfordshire and Leighton Buzzard, the MMC was satisfied that these free papers would provide effective competition to Johnston's titles. Whilst Sunday newspapers were not sufficiently well established in Luton, Dunstable and Milton Keynes to provide effective competition to Johnston's titles, the MMC concluded that, if the titles were not transferred to Johnston, they would close, producing competitive conditions almost identical to those arising from the transfer to Johnston.

Recommendation

Not against the public interest.

Chairman and Panel Members

Dr D J Morris, Mr M Kersen, Mr T R C Willis, Mrs S E Brown, Mr M R Prosser

FRESENIUS AG ("FRESENIUS") AND CAREMARK LIMITED ("CAREMARK") 30.04.98

Activities

Caremark provided services to patients who suffer from serious medical conditions which were treated at home, including the delivery of drugs or artificial feeds and equipment required to administer them. Fresenius was a German healthcare company and a leading supplier of products and services for kidney dialysis. Its Pharma division provided infusion therapy, enteral nutrition and related homecare services.

A11.056

Jurisdiction

PN homecare treatment was provided to patients in three different manners; the Trust providing the homecare itself, or by a private sector company under a contract, or by another Trust under an NHS contract. The MMC considered that the latter two methods comprised a distinct service that was specifically required to be provided under a contract. In addition, even though it could apply various criteria to establish whether the test was satisfied within this service market, it concluded that the test would be satisfied regardless of the applicable criterion.

Market Share and Increment

In the contracted services market (comprising services procured by health authorities), Caremark had 69 per cent of private sector supply measured by sales revenue, Fresenius's share was 6 per cent.

Among prescribed services (services provided in response to GP prescriptions), Caremark had approximately a one third share of services for patients on immuno-globin treatment and effectively 100 per cent of the other prescribed services.

In the supply of services for patients on parenteral nutrition, which was the main area of overlap between the parties, Caremark's market share was 75 per cent, and Fresenius's share 8 per cent.

Assessment

In the market for contracted services, Fresenius was one of only three private sector suppliers (other than Caremark). In the absence of the merger, it was likely to become more active in the other contracted services. There was therefore a clear loss of competition from the merger. Barriers to entry were also significant.

Besides the effect which the merger would have on competition, the transaction would entail an element of vertical integration. Fresenius could use the acquisition of Caremark to increase sales of its products, and in the contracted services market the merger would reduce purchasers' freedom to choose the products and services best suited to their needs.

Recommendation

Against the public interest. The MMC considered the following undertakings:

— the merged entity to reduce or not increase its prices. However, this would not be practicable since PN services were not homogeneous, contracts to serve new patients were bid for, and constraints on price did not allow for any developments in medical technology;

— the merged entity would give up some of its PN services or refrain from entering into new contracts. This would be an unacceptable interference which would lead to disruption and possibly higher costs;

— Fresenius to divest parts of Caremark where there were overlaps. However, Caremark's business was not organised in separate departments to allow this, and reputation was a key competition factor, so that a part of the assets without the name would be of limited value;

— Fresenius not to direct Caremark's pricing policy, nor supply Caremark on better terms. This too was rejected as the first would be difficult to enforce, while the latter would be unlikely to be effective since Fresenius could charge its higher prices to all service providers.

Accordingly, the MMC concluded that there were no behavioural or structural remedies which would be practicable and effective, short of prohibiting the merger. The MMC recommended that the merger be prohibited.

Secretary of State's Decision

The Secretary of State accepted the findings and recommendations of the MMC that the merger might be expected to operate against the public interest and that it should be prohibited.

Chairman and Panel Members

Dr D J Morris, Professor J Beatson, Mr P Mackay CB, Professor J A Rees, Professor A Steele

CAPITAL RADIO PLC ("CAPITAL RADIO") AND VIRGIN RADIO HOLDINGS LIMITED ("VIRGIN RADIO") 13.01.98

Activities

Commercial radio broadcasting and the sale of radio advertising.   A11.057

Market Share and Increment

Based on 1996 data, the MMC concluded that the merger would result in Capital's share of the London market increasing from 60.9 per cent to 68.8 per cent, and Capital's share of the UK market increasing from 36.8 per cent to 46.0 per cent.

Assessment

Capital was engaged in operating local commercial radio stations and Virgin in operating one national commercial radio station and one local commercial radio station. The MMC regarded radio advertising as a separate economic market from other display advertising. It also found that there were two separate geographical radio advertising markets: that for local and national advertisers targeting a London audience; and that for national advertisers targeting the UK as a whole.

In relation to the London market, the MMC found that Capital's resulting dominance in the London market would enable it to offer wide ranging packages of advertising which would strengthen its position in the UK radio advertising market, thereby reducing the ability of advertisers to buy around Capital. As a result prices might be expected to rise.

There were three benefits stemming from the merger: first, the development of Virgin AM as a UK-wide station and of Virgin FM as a London-focussed station; second, the increased professionalism and financial strength in the management of Virgin; and third, a greater commitment by Capital to the development of digital audio broadcasting. The benefits were not sufficient to outweigh the detriments specified.

Recommendation

Against the public interest. The merger should be allowed only if either:

- Capital divested its Capital Gold activities in such a way that the divested business could continue to operate effectively in its present form. Such a divestment should take place prior to completion of the merger to a buyer unconnected with Capital and approved by the OFT and the Radio Authority; or

- Capital was prohibited from acquiring Virgin FM.

Secretary of State's Decision

The Secretary of State published the report at a time when there was no prospect of the merger being pursued. She stated however that, were the merger to be re-activated, she would want to consider further what action (if any) should be taken.

Chairman and Panel Members

Sir Graeme Odgers, Sir Archibald Forster, Dr G F Owen, Mr G H Stacy CBE

PACIFICORP ("PACIFICORP") AND THE ENERGY GROUP PLC 19.12.97

Activities

A11.058   The supply of electricity in the UK by The Energy Group through its subsidiary Eastern Electricity, and in western USA and Victoria, Australia by Pacificorp.

Jurisdiction, Market Share and Increment

Eastern Electricity was the fourth largest generator of electricity in the UK. PacifiCorp had no activities in the UK. There was therefore no increment in market share as a result of the merger and the merger did not have any direct effect on competition in the UK. However, the MMC considered the proposed merger on public interest considerations:

— the impact of the acquisition on the availability of information necessary for effective regulation of the licensed activities of Eastern Electricity;

— whether the US ownership of PacifiCorp may have affected these activities;

— the consequences of the financial structure of the acquisition; and

— any effects of the acquisition on the management strategy of Eastern Electricity.

Assessment

The MMC's main concern was the effect of the intended financial arrangements for the acquisition, which was to be financed largely by borrowing. Although the MMC did not expect financial difficulties to arise, they believed that in the absence of adequate controls, the high level of gearing resulting from the merger would give rise to a significant risk of financial pressure on the holding companies of Eastern Electricity, which potentially might lead to a requirement for higher cash flows from Eastern Electricity than would otherwise have been the case, and also to under-investment, poorer service standards and/ or higher prices for electricity in the longer term.

Recommendation

Not against the public interest. Eastern Electricity's existing licence conditions included terms which were intended to "ring fence" its licensed activities from those of the rest of the group, and the MMC took the view that adequate controls were in place and would be sufficient to address the risk that Eastern Electricity would be adversely affected by any such financial pressures.

Secretary of State's Decision

The Secretary of State accepted the MMC's findings, but indicated that she expected Pacificorp to honour assurances it had agreed with the DGES.

Chairman and Panel Members

Dr D J Morris, Professor M Cave, Mr A T Clothier, Mr D J Jenkins MBE, Mr R J Munson

NATIONAL EXPRESS GROUP PLC ("NEG") AND CENTRAL TRAINS LIMITED ("CENTRAL TRAINS") 16.12.97

Activities

Coach services and passenger rail services.   A11.059

Market Share and Increment

NEG's share in *"the supply of public transport passenger services involving journeys carried out wholly within the West Midlands"* was 78 per cent, while Central Trains' share was 7 per cent (within which Centro-supported services accounted for 6.8 per cent). The MMC noted that the Centro-supported services should be counted as part of NEG's supply; the MMC had a wide discretion in the application of the share of supply test, including over whether different forms of supply should be considered together or separately and how to identify different forms of supply. Further, the supply of services included both the rendering of services to order and the provision of services by making them available to potential users, so that a supplier's share (NEG) can include services supplied where another person (Centro) is able to determine the conditions under which those services are supplied.

Assessment

NEG owned National Express Limited ("NEL") and the leading bus company in the West Midlands, West Midlands Travel Limited ("WMT").

The MMC examined two sets out of issues. The first stemmed from the common ownership of Central Trains and WMT. WMT had a very strong position in the West Midlands market for bus services and would become the operator of the new Midland Metro light rail service between Birmingham and Wolverhampton which was due to start operating in 1998. The extent of competition between bus services and the rail services of Central Trains was quite limited. The same would be true of competition between the Midland Metro and Central Trains' rail services. Moreover, the West Midlands Passenger Transport Executive had sought various assurances from NEG in order to prevent abuses. As a result, the MMC did not expect NEG to wield any additional market power in the West Midlands passenger transport market as a result of the merger.

The second issue related to the combination of ownership of Central Trains and NEL, and two other train companies owned by NEG affecting areas largely outside the West Midlands. There were 12 journeys on which there were significant overlaps between the services of Central Trains and the other NEG subsidiaries. On the basis of the evidence available to the MMC, it decided that there was an element of competition for leisure passengers between coach and rail services. However, because of competition from other train operating companies which were not owned by NEG, and bus operators, the merger did not give NEG opportunities to exploit its market position.

Some benefits would result from the merger in the form of initiatives to promote transport integration in the West Midlands.

Recommendation

Not against the public interest.

Chairman and Panel Members

Sir Graeme Odgers, Mrs D P B Kingsmill, Mr D J Jenkins MBE, Professor J F Pickering

NATIONAL EXPRESS GROUP PLC ("NEG") AND SCOTRAIL RAILWAYS LIMITED ("SCOTRAIL") 16.12.97

Activities

A11.060   Long distance coach services and passenger train services.

Market Share and Increment

NEG's share in the supply of public transport passenger services, including bus services, on routes wholly within Scotland which exceeded 50 km in length, was 8 per cent, while ScotRail's share was 55 per cent. Within this, Scottish Passenger Transport Executive ("SPTE") supported services accounted for 20 per cent. Scotland comprised a substantial part of the UK in terms of its size, character and importance.

Assessment

NEG's subsidiary, Scottish Citylink Coaches Limited ("Citylink") was the leading provider of long distance coach services in Scotland. ScotRail was the principal operator of passenger transport in Scotland.

The majority of Citylink's coach routes overlapped with ScotRail routes. The MMC concluded that there had been an element of competition between coach and rail services, principally for leisure (price-sensitive) passengers, and that this had been lost as result of the merger.

Competition from other rail and bus operators, and regulatory restrictions on ScotRail's service and fare levels, were not sufficient to prevent an increase in coach fares nor a loss of more vigorous competition which might have been expected had Citylink and ScotRail remained separate entities.

The MMC concluded that the merger might have been expected to lead to higher coach fares, leading to higher rail fares, and a loss of innovation and service quality on both coach and rail services on nine overlapping routes.

Recommendation

Against the public interest. Behavioural undertakings were not an adequate remedy since their implementation would be too complicated in the context of the relevant market. Divestment of ScotRail would be both undesirable and disproportionate to the adverse effects of the merger. The MMC recommended that NEG should be required to divest Citylink within six months to purchasers approved by the Director General of Fair Trading. It was also recommended that NEG should be prevented from increasing its scheduled coach services within Scotland unless given consent to do so by the DGFT for the period of the ScotRail franchise agreement.

Secretary of State's Decision

The Secretary of State found that the merger might be expected to operate against the public interest, and considered that NEG should be required to divest Citylink to a buyer or buyers approved by the DGFT within six months of the date of publication of the report; and to undertake not to increase NEG's scheduled coach services within Scotland unless given consent to do so by the DGFT, for the period of the current ScotRail franchise agreement.

Chairman and Panel Members

Sir Graeme Odgers, Mrs D P B Kingsmill, Mr D J Jenkins MBE, Professor J F Pickering

PENINSULAR & ORIENTAL STEAM NAVIGATION COMPANY ("P&O") AND STENA LINE AB ("STENA") 19.11.97

Activities

Operation of cross channel ferry services for both passengers and freight.   A11.061

Market Share

The MMC considered that the markets relevant to the investigation were different for passengers and freight.

P&O and Stena carried 46 per cent of passenger vehicle traffic on the cross-Channel "Short Sea" routes, including services between Newhaven, Folkestone, Dover and Ramsgate in the UK and Dieppe, Boulogne, Calais, Dunkirk, Ostend and Zeebrugge in north east France and Belgium, Le Shuttle carried 39 per cent.

Within the Anglo-Continental unitized freight market, the joint venture would hold 24 per cent and the Tunnel 15 per cent.

Assessment

The MMC believed that competition in the relevant passenger market would remain effective until duty-free concessions were abolished in mid 1999. However, thereafter the expectation was that market conditions would become much tougher, and that one or more of the other ferry operators would exit. New entry onto the market would be costly, risky and only likely on a seasonal basis. The reduction of competition would create an effective duopoly between Le Shuttle and the

P&O/Stena joint venture, which would then carry the danger of settling down into a pattern of parallel behaviour.

By contrast, in the freight market, the MMC believed that competition would continue to be effective even after 1999. There were a number of other competitors providing the freight transport industry on both sides of the Channel with a number of alternative options.

Recommendation

The joint venture was against the public interest. However, adjustments of cross Channel capacity were necessary as a result of the opening of the Tunnel and the MMC concluded that the joint venture could bring other benefits to the public interest given a sufficiently competitive environment. The majority of the group therefore recommended that P&O and Stena should be required to give the following undertakings before completing or implementing the agreement to set up the joint venture:

— the joint venture would not introduce services using fast craft on any Short Sea route except Newhaven-Dieppe, although this restriction should be subject to DGFT review after five years;

— the joint venture would introduce interlining arrangements for full fare tickets on the Dover Calais route, where requested to do so by other ferry operators;

— the joint venture would provide the DGFT with an appropriate range of financial and other information to enable monitoring;

— P&O, Stena and the joint venture would not negotiate arrangements with travel agents jointly or aggregate incomes for the purpose of calculating commission;

— the joint venture would not enter into any exclusive arrangements with travel agents;

— P&O and Stena would not advertise the joint venture's services in promotional publications, brochures or advertisements which they had produced or commissioned; and

— P&O and Stena would give up any existing rights to one of the ticket desks at that time operated by P&O and Stena at Dover and to not less than four vehicle ticketing booths at Dover.

Secretary of State's Decision

The Secretary of State decided that the parties should be required to give undertakings in respect of passenger fares for the proposed joint venture.

Chairman and Panel Members

Mr D G Goyder CBE, Professor M Cave, Mr A T Clothier, Mr P Mackay CB

THE LITTLEWOODS ORGANISATION PLC AND FREEMANS PLC ("FREEMANS") 18.11.97

Activities

Catalogue mail order businesses in the home shopping sector of non-food retailing. A11.062

Market Share and Increment

In 1996 there were five firms operating in the agency mail order sector in the UK: The Great Universal Stores PLC (GUS) had 41 per cent market share, Littlewoods Home Shopping Group Ltd (LHSG) had 28 per cent, Freemans had 13 per cent, Grattan Plc had 10 per cent and Empire Stores Group plc (Empire) had 8 per cent. Each of these agency mail order companies also operated direct mail order businesses.

Assessment

The MMC found that agency and direct mail order were distinct markets: direct mail order did not use agents to sell goods, prices were not bundled (i.e. they did not include delivery charges etc) and were broadly comparable with high street prices; interest free credit was not normally offered; the range of goods was far narrower and more upmarket in direct mail catalogues. Additionally, agency mail order users came from lower-income socio-economic groups and were unlikely to have alternative sources of credit. The high street also was a distinct market but represented a general, though not tight, constraint on pricing.

The agency mail order market was static and highly concentrated and the proposed merger would raise concentration further: GUS and the merged entity would have over 80 per cent of agency sales, which would reduce the level of existing competition significantly and would deter new entry.

Recommendation

Against the public interest. Behavioural remedies, were not considered adequate to remedy the adverse effects identified and the MMC considered that, while only a structural solution would be appropriate, no form of divestment would be appropriate. The MMC recommended that the merger should be prohibited.

Secretary of State's Decision

The Secretary of State agreed with these findings.

Chairman and Panel Members

Dr D J Morris, Mrs D P B Kingsmill, Ms P A Hodgson CBE, Mr M R Prosser

APPENDIX 11

MIRROR GROUP PLC ("MIRROR GROUP") AND MIDLAND INDEPENDENT NEWSPAPERS PLC ("MIN") 21.10.97

Activities

A11.063   Publication and distribution of national and regional/local newspapers.

Market Share and Increment

Measured by shares of circulation and distribution, Mirror Group was the second largest publisher of newspapers in the UK and the transfer would not have affected this. Since MIN did not supply national newspapers, there would be no market share aggregation in this sector. Mirror Group's ranking in regional and local newspapers depended on the classification of its Scottish titles which shared some of the characteristics of national newspapers. If regarded as national titles, the proposed transfer would raise Mirror Group's share to 7 per cent; if regarded as regional titles, the Mirror Group would become the largest publisher of regional and local newspapers in the UK with a 13.3 per cent share.

In the region served by MIN's titles, Mirror Group's share of newspaper circulation and distribution would increase from around 12 per cent to 29 per cent. In MIN's core area around Birmingham and Coventry, the combined group would have a 48 per cent share.

Assessment

The regional editions of Mirror Group's and MIN's titles differed in terms of readership profiles, times of publication and the level of regional/local content. The degree of competition between them was very limited. The transfers would not, therefore, have an adverse effect on competition and choice as far as readers and advertisers were concerned.

In the MMC 's view, any unduly low cover prices or advertising rates resulting from economies of scale would not be substantial enough to pose a competition threat. Additionally, common ownership of the newspapers would not reduce diversity of opinion in the UK as a whole.

Recommendation

Not against the public interest.

Chairman and Panel Members

Mr P G Corbett, Mr G H C Copeman, Mr T R C Willis, Professor D M G Newbery

LONDON CLUBS INTERNATIONAL PLC ("LCI") AND CAPITAL CORPORATION PLC 05.08.97

Activities

A11.064   Operation of casinos.

Market Share and Increment

The MMC concluded that the relevant market consisted of the "upper segment" of London casinos. The merger would increase LCI's share from 49 to 79 per cent.

Assessment

The British casino market was highly regulated. Barriers to entry to the relevant market were high, the main barrier being the need to demonstrate the existence of unsatisfied, unstimulated demand. There had been very little entry to the upper segment of London casinos since 1983, particularly because of constraints on location. Nevertheless, competition was vigorous on matters such as quality of premises, services, maximum and minimum staking limits and the waive of ancillary charges.

The MMC found that the merger would increase the already high barriers to entry and would substantially reduce competition by removing LCI's largest competitor from the relevant market. The enlarged LCI would be able to absorb any small increases in demand and to ensure that there were no gaps in the market. If the merger were to proceed, the limited level of domestic competition would be the only commercial constraint on LCI's freedom of action to reduce quality or raise charges for its London based customers (as opposed to internationally mobile players). Innovation would also be reduced.

Recommendation

Against the public interest. Undertakings by LCI not to oppose licence applications by competitors and not itself to make any further applications would not prevent the creation of a company with an 80 per cent share likely to prevent potential competition. The divestment of casinos not in the upper segment would not remedy the adverse effect on competition in that segment, while the divestment of one or more casinos in the upper segment would be inadequate to deal with the loss. Undertakings not to increase ancillary charges for London-based customers or not to reduce the quality of service would be difficult to monitor and enforce. The MMC were unable to identify any suitable remedies, and recommended that the merger be prohibited.

Secretary of State's Decision

The Secretary of State decided not to permit the proposed acquisition.

Chairman and Panel Members

Mr P G Corbett CBE, Professor M Cave, Mr A T Clothier, Mr J Evans CBE

TECHNICOLOUR LIMITED/ METROCOLOR LONDON LIMITED 24.07.97

Activities

Film processing for television and cinema usage.   A11.065

Market Share and Increment

Film processing could be divided into six sectors, of which 35 mm feature release printing was by far the largest. The parties had significant shares in all six sectors and their combined shares as a result of the merger would range from 41.6 per cent to 76.5 per cent. There were other significant players in the market.

Assessment

The MMC concluded that sufficient competition would remain in all six sectors following the merger. Customers had considerable buying power, there were other significant players both in the UK and in Europe, and there were low barriers to entry.

Recommendation

Not against the public interest.

Chairman and Panel Members

Mr P H Dean CBE, Miss J C Hanratty, Mr R Lyons, Mr P Mackay CB, Mr C R Smallwood

BASS PLC ("BASS"), CARLSBERG A/S AND CARLSBERG-TETLEY PLC ("CT") 27.06.97

Activities

A11.066   Brewing of beer.

Jurisdiction

This was a complex transaction. The MMC considered that Bass had already obtained control of Allied Domecq's ("AD") 50 per cent interest in CT, as well as AD's brands licensed to CT, and that these would be examined as a single merger situation. Even though Bass had no seat on the board of CT, it could block ordinary and special resolutions by virtue of its shareholding, and could thus materially influence the policy of the company.

In addition, the MMC considered the joint venture between Bass, Carlsberg and CT ("BCT"). Bass would have had a controlling interest in BCT through its 80 per cent shareholding and its right to appoint 80 per cent of BCT's board. However, the MMC also held that Carlsberg would control BCT through its remaining 20 per cent shareholding. The MMC believed that Carlsberg would have the ability materially to influence BCT's policy since it was a powerful and active player in the international markets, it would have had board directors and it would have held a 20 per cent share in the business. Even though it would have had only shareholder minority protection rights, these rights and the fact that the companies would have an incentive to co-operate in order to ensure the long-term success of the joint venture would have conferred to it the ability materially to influence the policy of BCT.

Market Share and Increment

Bass was the UK's second largest brewer, having 23 per cent of the beer market and owning about 4,400 tied houses. CT had about 14 per cent of the market but no tied estate. The merged business would become the UK's largest brewer, ahead of Scottish Courage (the beer division of Scottish & Newcastle) which had 28 per cent of the market. The fourth largest brewer, Whitbread, had a 13 per cent market share.

Assessment

The proposed merger would lead to a reduction in the number of major brewers and would give Bass a significant increase in market power. This would have the effect of increasing wholesale and on trade retail prices of beer. On-trade retailers and consumers would suffer. The parties' anticipated efficiency gains would not outweigh the adverse effects identified.

Recommendation

Against the public interest. The MMC did, however, recommend undertakings which included a reduction of Bass's tied houses to a maximum of 2,500.

Secretary of State's Decision

The Secretary of State rejected the MMC's recommendations and decided to prohibit the merger.

Chairman and Panel Members

Mr P H Dean CBE, Sir Archibald Forster, Professor D M G Newbery

KLAUS J JACOBS HOLDING AG ("KJJH") AND SOCIÉTÉ CENTRALE D'INVESTISSEMENTS ET ASSOCIES ("SCIA") 13.06.97

Activities

Supply of couverture (industrial chocolate).   A11.067

Market Share and Increment

Producers fell within two categories: vertically integrated groups which made couverture and used it in-house (producer-users); and producers which supplied couverture to third parties (open-market suppliers). Producer-users accounted for 80 per cent of the overall supply of couverture. Callebaut and Barry (subsidiaries of KJJH and SCIA respectively) each had operating subsidiaries in the UK which had between them about 15 per cent of the UK's overall supply of couverture, but nearly three quarters of the supply to the open market.

Assessment

The MMC found that the distinction between producer-users and open-market suppliers was blurred. There was potential competition from imports but these only accounted for 4 per cent of UK consumption, and there were objective reasons for users to prefer to buy from UK suppliers.

Callebaut and Barry provided each other's main source of competition in the open market. However, the MMC concluded that following the merger there would be strong competition from independent producers, and from two producer-users which had significant spare capacity and had indicated an interest in expanding their sales in the open market. Additionally, customers had significant bargaining power and the merger was likely to lead to some cost savings which would, in part, be passed on to customers.

Recommendation

Not against the public interest.

Chairman and Panel Members

Sir Graeme Odgers, Mr P G Corbett CBE, Mr M R Prosser

COWIE GROUP PLC ("COWIE") AND BRITISH BUS GROUP LIMITED ("BRITISH BUS") 18.03.97

Activities

A11.068   Vehicle leasing and financing, motor retailing, bus distribution and bus service operations.

Market Share and Increment

As a result of the merger, Cowie had become third largest bus operator in the UK, with an estimated 14.9 per cent share of the national market. FirstBus plc remained the market leader with 19.8 per cent, and Stagecoach Holdings plc had 16.1 per cent.

In London as a whole, Cowie's share increased from 18 per cent to 25 per cent. In Croydon and Lambeth, Cowie's share increased from 34 per cent to 42.6 per cent.

Assessment

Cowie and British Bus' operations overlapped in North London but especially in south London, where Cowie's subsidiary, South London Transport Limited (SLT) and British Bus's subsidiary, London Links Buses Limited (Londonlinks) both operated services in the boroughs of Croydon and Lambeth. However there were two other large companies operating services in south London, the Go Ahead Group Plc and Stagecoach. Future competition in this part of the capital was not dependent solely upon continuing competition between Cowie and British Bus.

The MMC considered the London market and found that there were deterrents to entry to the market, particular for small operators and new entrants. These barriers included the large number of buses required to run some routes, advantages to incumbents deriving from the operation of a network of buses based on a single depot, the additional risks to the operator associated with net cost tendered contracts and the problems of acquiring suitable garaging facilities. However, some small operators, including two new entrants, had recently won routes. There was also an increasing volume of routes of all sizes coming up for tender over the next two years, many of which would require ten buses or fewer, which might provide opportunities for a wide range of operator to secure routes.

Where the operations of the parties overlapped outside London, or were contiguous with each other in several parts of the unregulated market, there was no loss of actual competition, only a limited loss of potential competition.

Recommendation

Not against the public interest.

Chairman and Panel Members

Mr D G Goyder CBE, Mr J Evans CBE, Mr P Mackay CB, Professor J F Pickering

FIRSTBUS PLC ("FIRSTBUS") AND S B HOLDINGS LIMITED ("SBH") 24.01.97

Activities

Provision of local bus services.   A11.069

Jurisdiction and Market Shares

FirstBus was the largest UK provider of local bus services with over 19 per cent of the market. In the reference area, which included Greater Glasgow, SBH had a 53 per cent share while FirstBus had a 1 per cent share. However, the MMC decided to consider the merger in the context of the wider area of central Scotland, Edinburgh and the Borders (the "designated area") since the Act did not require that the area chosen for the share of supply test should be relevant in an economic sense. The MMC considered that where it found there was such an area, it was under a duty to consider whether the merger would have an adverse effect on the public interest, and in this respect it was not confined to considering the consequences of the increase in the share of supply in the area concerned. In the designated area SBH had a 40 per cent share while FirstBus had a 21 per cent share.

Assessment

The merger situation had eliminated actual and potential competition between FirstBus and SBH. The scale and dominance of the merged entity in Central and South East Scotland was likely to deter actual and potential competition from the two other large adjacent operators, Stagecoach Holdings Plc and Cowie Group Plc. It would also deter entry by others. There would not be sufficient pressure on FirstBus to ensure that fares and subsidies were kept down and the frequency of services maintained.

Recommendation

Against the public interest. Behavioural remedies were inadequate to remedy the adverse effects identified, as was the divestment of FirstBus's Midland Bluebird subsidiary. The MMC recommended that FirstBus should be required to divest:

— the enlarged Midland Bluebird;

— part of the business of SBH including, as a minimum:

— one of the four central Glasgow depots and associated assets;
— a network of routes spread reasonably over Glasgow representing 20 per cent of SBH's turnover; and
— a bus fleet appropriate to service those routes,

to a single buyer approved by the Secretary of State. If such divestment proved to be impractical the MMC could recommend that FirstBus be required to divest SBH in its entirety, without divestment of any of Midland Bluebird's operations.

Secretary of State's Decision

The MMC's findings were accepted by the Secretary of State.

Chairman and Panel Members

Mr P H Dean CBE, Sir Archibald Forster, Professor D M G Newbury, Professor J A Rees

MID KENT HOLDINGS PLC ("MIDKENT") AND GENERAL UTILITIES PLC ("GU") AND SAUR WATER SERVICES PLC ("SAUR") 21.01.97

Activities

A11.070   The supply of water in most of Kent and East Sussex, and part of West Sussex.

Jurisdiction

GU and SAUR, at the time of reference, had voting shareholdings of 19.45 per cent and 19.39 per cent respectively in Mid Kent. GU had shares in a number of other water companies, including Folkestone & Dover Water Services Limited whose area adjoined that of Mid Kent and where GU had a 74.1 per cent shareholding. In turn, SAUR had two water subsidiaries in the UK, South East Water Services plc, which also adjoined MidKent's area and was wholly owned, and Mid Southern Water plc in which SAUR had a 99.5 per cent shareholding.

First, the MMC found that there was no existing merger regarding Mid Kent. GU and SAUR had not been acting together to exercise control of MidKent. Even though they had successfully blocked three resolutions, the MMC was satisfied they had not acted in a co-ordinated manner in order to do so, but that they had been through a separate independent management process to decide how to vote. The MMC then considered that even though by virtue of their joint 39 per cent holding in MidKent, GU and SAUR together had the ability to materially influence its policy, there were very special circumstances which indicated that they did not in fact have control over it, not least since the MMC had concluded that they had not been

758

acting together to exercise control. In addition, even though the proposed joint venture agreement would have conferred control to them, the companies would not have had control until a successful bid, GU was prohibited from seeking board representation, and the bid was conditional on the grant of regulatory approval. Finally, the MMC concluded that neither GU nor SAUR individually had the ability materially to influence the policy of MidKent; they had not been acting together to exercise control over it, GU was prohibited from seeking board representation, and for either to have such material influence, it needed either the backing of the other party or another shareholder, or it needed to be sure that the other would abstain. While there was some commonality of interest in relation to the proposed merger, their commercial interests did not necessarily coincide.

The MMC then considered the proposed merger. The proposals were complex but they involved, in the first stage, the setting up of a 50–50 joint venture between GU and SAUR to acquire the entire share capital of MidKent. In the second stage, the assets of MKH would have been split into two separate water supply businesses, one to be ultimately acquired by GU and the other by SAUR and a non-operational water resource company. After some deliberation, the MMC concluded that the second stage would give rise to a single merger situation.

The MMC considered whether the proposed joint venture arrangements might be expected to operate against the public interest.

Assessment

The proposed arrangements would lead to reduced prospects for competition within the region and would prejudice the ability of the DGWS to make comparisons between different water enterprises, which was a substantial detriment. Although GU and SAUR argued that there would be no major detriment to comparative competition and that price cuts were an inappropriate remedy in view of the amount they were proposing to spend to achieve the benefits of the merger, the efficiency gains achievable by the proposed arrangements were small.

Recommendation

Against the public interest.

The MMC considered that since the efficiency gains through the proposed merger were small, large price reductions would not be sustainable beyond an initial short-term period, and this would not be of benefit to the comparator regime which would suffer permanent damage. The MMC also concluded that the loss of visibility would not be sufficiently remedied by listing any majority-owned subsidiaries, and that the proposed measures relating to leakage and metering only went part of the way to remedying the loss of a comparator. Accordingly, any gain to water consumers arising from the proposed remedies would be temporary, while the comparator system would suffer permanent damage.

The MMC recommended that the merger be prohibited.

Secretary of State's Decision

The Secretary of State accepted the MMC's findings and blocked the merger.

Chairman and Panel Members

Mr D G Goyder CBE, Mr N F Matthews, Mrs K M H Mortimer, Mr M R Prosser, Mr G H Stacy CBE

ROBERT WISEMAN DAIRIES PLC ("WISEMAN") AND SCOTTISH PRIDE HOLDINGS PLC ("SCOTTISH PRIDE") 24.12.96

Activities

A11.071   The supply of fresh processed milk and cream, ultra heat treated milk ("UHT milk"), cream and cheese, and the procurement of raw milk.

Market Shares

Wiseman and Scottish Pride together accounted for about 5 per cent of all raw milk bought by processors in the UK, and for 10 per cent of wholesale sales of fresh processed milk. In Scotland, together they accounted for nearly half of raw milk purchases by processors and nearly 80 per cent of wholesale sales of fresh processed milk.

Assessment

The MMC considered whether the markets for raw milk and fresh processed milk in Scotland were separate from those in the rest of the UK.

The market for raw milk had become markedly less regional and there was sufficient scope for raw milk to be traded between southern Scotland and northern England to ensure that the market in Scotland was part of a continuous chain of substitution linking it with the markets in England.

As regards fresh processed milk, the market in Scotland had become less distinct from that in England and Wales (particularly in the supermarket sector). However, there was still relatively little trade between Scotland and the rest of Great Britain. The MMC concluded that the market still had some regional characteristics.

It was unlikely that Wiseman would be able to exert any monopsony power in the raw milk market. In addition, Wiseman would not be able to exercise dominance in the supply of fresh processed milk to the national supermarket groups.

The merger could, however, harm competition in the supply of fresh processed milk to other customers in Scotland, and could be expected to lead to higher wholesale prices and, potentially, higher retail prices than otherwise. The merger's effect on efficiency and employment did not offset this detriment to competition.

Recommendation

The best solution to this problem was to maintain two substantial fresh milk processors in Scotland. However, the MMC did not believe that Scottish Pride could continue as an independent company and the prospects of Scottish Pride finding an alternative buyer for its fresh processed milk business were remote.

The MMC considered that the divestment of one or more dairies would not be a practicable structural remedy and it then considered behavioural remedies. The MMC recommended that Wiseman should submit regular audited accounts to the DGFT on its prices to the different categories of customer in Scotland. The DGFT would therefore have early warning of any attempt by Wiseman to abuse its market position in relation to customers other than national supermarket groups. Wiseman would also provide its customer lists in Scotland so that the DGFT would be able to carry out random sampling of prices paid or scrutinise prices. The MMC also recommended that Wiseman should not acquire any other supplier of fresh processed milk in Scotland without the DGFT's prior consent.

Secretary of State's Decision

The Secretary of State agreed with the MMC's findings.

Chairman and Panel Members

Dr D J Morris, Professor M Cave, Mr A T Clothier, Mr D J Jenkins MBE, Mr P Mackay CB

NATIONAL EXPRESS GROUP PLC AND MIDLAND MAIN LINE LIMITED ("MML") 20.12.96

Activities

Long distance coach services and passenger train operating services.   A11.072

Jurisdiction

The share of supply test was met in relation to the supply of public transport between London and, respectively, Derby, Sheffield, Chesterfield, Nottingham and Leicester. It was also met in relation to the supply of long-distance public transport services in the area comprising Greater London in the south, the five areas mentioned to the north, and bounded by the MML route to the east and the M1 to the West. In answer to concerns raised by National Express, the OFT suggested that the Act did not restrict the authorities' ability to describe goods or services in any way they thought fit (by reference to geographical criteria or otherwise); the authorities were prevented from adopting unreasonably narrow descriptions simply by the general principle to act reasonably. The MMC also did not accept that any area it selected for the purpose of the share of supply test needed to be "relevant" in an economic sense.

Assessment

Five coach services operated by National Express Limited ("NEL") overlapped with MML's rail services between central London and, respectively, Sheffield, Chesterfield, Derby, Nottingham and Leicester. Coach services were less frequent than rail services, but fares were cheaper and journey times longer. About 90 per cent of NEL's passengers were travelling for leisure purposes. Most of MML's passengers were travelling for business or commuting, with only 40 per cent travelling for leisure purposes. The MMC considered that there was an element of competition between NEL's coach services and MML's rail services for the leisure passenger and that this had been lost as a result of the merger. Because of the absence of other strong constraints on fares or services, the merger might be expected to lead (over time) to higher coach fares or higher fares on both coach and rail services, and/or a lower quality of coach services or a lower quality of both coach and rail services, than would have been the case had the merger not occurred.

Recommendation

The MMC concluded that it would not be appropriate to require structural undertakings, in the form of divestment of NEL's contracts for the operation of coach services between central London and the five specified places, or divestment combined with undertakings to require NEL to provide the benefit of its network to other operators of the service. The MMC also rejected the possibility of divestment analogous to franchising, and the divestment of the relevant coach services. Instead, the MMC recommended a set of behavioural undertakings primarily relating to coach fares, the maintenance of the existing availability of categories of tickets, the provision of adequate capacity and the provision of a high level of service. These undertakings were expected to address the adverse effects of the merger in relation to both coach and rail.

Secretary of State's Decision

The Secretary of State accepted the MMC's findings and recommendations and asked the DGFT to seek undertakings from National Express Group.

Chairman and Panel Members

Mr P H Dean CBE, Professor J Beatson, Sir Archibald Forster, Sir Ronald Halstead CBE, Professor J S Metcalfe CBE

NEWSQUEST MEDIA GROUP LIMITED ("NEWSQUEST") AND WESTMINSTER PRESS LIMITED ("WESTMINSTER") 28.11.96

Activities

A11.073   Publication of daily and weekly, paid-for and free newspapers.

Market Shares

Newsquest was the fifth largest publisher of regional and local newspapers in the UK and Westminster was the eighth largest. As a result of the merger the combined group would be the third largest group with 11 per cent of the total market for regional and local newspapers.

Assessment

The MMC were satisfied that the increase in concentration at the national level would not operate against the public interest.

The two groups' operations adjoined and, to a small extent, overlapped in three geographical areas. The most significant area was Essex, where Newsquest's share of the total circulation and distribution of regional and local newspapers would double from 27 per cent to 54 per cent. However, the MMC found that there was virtually no competition between the newspapers of the two groups, which catered for separate local markets, and that there were other publishing groups with substantial presence in the county. The degree of regional concentration would not harm the public interest. Nor would the merger harm the public interest in the other two areas, central England and Lancashire. The proposed transfer would not threaten the accurate presentation of news and free expression of opinion. Nor did the MMC consider that the consequences for the transfer for efficiency and employment would be against the public interest.

Recommendation

Not against the public interest.

Chairman and Panel Members

Mr D J Morris, Mr G H C Copernam, Mr M Kersen, Mr L Priestley, Mr M R Prosser

WESSEX WATER PLC ("WW") AND
SOUTHWEST WATER PLC ("SWWS") 25.10.96

Activities

Water and sewerage businesses.   A11.074

Assessment

Under the Water Industry Act 1991, the MMC were obliged to have regard to the desirability of the Director General of Water Services's ("DGWS") ability to make comparisons between different water enterprises. The system of comparative competition by which the water industry is regulated depends upon the DGWS's ability to make such comparisons. The MMC did not accept WW's argument that while SWWS would be lost as a comparator, this loss would be more than offset by the emergence of an "exemplary comparator", and a comparator more representative of the industry as a whole in terms of size and other characteristics. The loss of SWWS as a comparator would weaken the comparative system across the range of uses to which comparisons are put, which would seriously prejudice the DGWS's ability to make comparisons between different water enterprises.

The MMC also found that the merger would reduce the scope for future cross-border competition between water enterprises.

Recommendation

Against the public interest. The MMC believed that the substantial detriment brought about by the proposed merger would have been of a different magnitude from previous cases, since it would have involved the loss, for the first time, of one of the ten Water and Sewerage Companies as a comparator. The MMC did not believe that any remedy in the form of price cuts would have adequately compensated such a permanent loss. In any event, the MMC was not convinced that WW would have been able to deliver sufficient efficiency savings to produce price cuts of the order proposed by the DGWS (between 15 to 20 per cent). Accordingly, the MMC concluded that the loss of one of the WaSCs would have caused substantial damage to the system of comparative competition that no remedy would have been sufficient to compensate.

Secretary of State's Decision

The Secretary of State accepted the MMC's findings and blocked the merger.

Chairman and Panel Members

Mr D G Goyder CBE, Professor J F Pickering, Dr A Robinson, Professor G Whittington

SEVERN TRENT PLC ("ST") AND SOUTH WEST WATER ("SWW") 25.10.96

Activities

A11.075   Water and sewerage businesses.

Assessment

A key concern of the MMC was whether the Director General of Water Service's ability to make comparisons between water and sewerage companies would be prejudiced by the merger.

Despite ST's arguments that it intended to maintain Severn Trent Water Ltd STW and South West Water ("SWW") as two separate water and sewerage companies, so that SWW would remain as valuable as it had previously been for comparative purposes, the MMC were not satisfied that this was correct. The MMC considered that companies which were not independently owned were not adequate substitutes as comparators, since differences in management style and priorities might well be significant factors in determining performance. In the MMC's view, SWW would have been lost as a comparator if the merger had proceeded.

Recommendation

Against the public interest. The MMC believed that the substantial detriment brought about by the proposed merger would have been of a different magnitude from previous cases, since it would have involved the loss, for the first time, of one of the ten WaSCs as a comparator. The MMC did not believe that any remedy in the form of price cuts would have adequately compensated such a permanent loss. In any event, the MMC was not convinced that ST would have been able to deliver sufficient efficiency savings to produce price cuts of the order proposed by the DGWS (between 15 to 20 per cent). Accordingly, the MMC concluded that the loss of one of the WaSCs would have caused substantial damage to the system of comparative competition that no remedy would have been sufficient to compensate.

Secretary of State's Decision

The Secretary of State accepted the MMC's findings and blocked the merger.

Chairman and Panel Members

Mr D G Goyder CBE, Professor J F Pickering, Dr A Robinson, Professor G Whittington

NV VERENIGDE BEDRIJVEN NUTRICIA ("NUTRICIA") AND ENTERPRISES BELONGING TO MILUPA AG ("MILUPA") 09.08.96

Activities

The supply of enteral clinical nutrition products ("ECN"), baby drinks, baby meals and baby milk products.

A11.076

Market Shares

The overlap in ECN products and baby drinks which both parties supplied was very limited.

As regards baby meals, the merged parties would have 28 per cent of the baby meals market in the UK, with Heinz/Farley as the market leader with 53 per cent. Boots The Chemists Ltd ("Boots") as part of the own label sector had a 13 per cent market share.

As regards baby milks, CGN (a subsidiary of Nutricia) had a 37.5 per cent share, whilst Milupa had 7.6 per cent. The market was highly concentrated prior to the merger, with the two market leaders, SMA Nutrition ("SMA") (with 44.4 per cent) and CGN holding a combined share of 81.9 per cent. Following the merger, the two market leaders (SMA and CGN/Milupa) would have a combined share of 89.5 per cent.

Assessment

In the baby meals market there were virtually no constraints on entry by established food manufacturers. There had been new entry and there was a growing own-label sector. Consumers also had the option of switching to home-prepared meals. The MMC did not expect the merger to have effects adverse to the public interest in the market for baby meals.

The baby milks market was already highly concentrated before the merger. Despite significant entry by Heinz, Boots and Sainsbury in the past four years, the MMC considered that further entry was unlikely.

The MMC considered that, without the merger, the continuation of the Milupa brand in the UK would have been in doubt over the longer term because of Milupa's continuing losses despite a subsidy from its parent company. The merger would help to preserve parents' choice. There was a risk of reduction in the diversity of research leading to less innovation, but this was balanced by the likelihood of more effective research.

In the retail sector, the underlying weakness of Milupa prior to the merger was likely to require price increases (without the merger) if viability and continuity of the brand were to be ensured. The merger, which would overcome the excessive cost problems associated with the brand, reduced these pressures for price increases.

In the Welfare Food Scheme ("WFS")/NHS, of which the NHSSA was the largest and most powerful purchaser of baby milks, the MMC did not feel that the merger was likely to lead to faster increases in prices. The MMC therefore took the view that in both the retail and WFS/NHS sectors of the baby milk market the merger would be unlikely to have adverse effects on prices.

Recommendation

Not against the public interest. The DGFT however informed the principal companies in the market that he would be keeping the matter under review, and it was therefore likely that any action by the market leaders (SMA and Nutricia) to raise prices unjustifiably would quickly be brought to his attention.

Chairman and Panel Members

Mr G D W Odgers, Professor S Eilon, Sir Archibald Forster, Mrs K M H Mortimer, Mr J K Roe

UNICHEM PLC ("UNICHEM") / LLOYDS CHEMISTS PLC ("LLOYDS") AND GEHE AG ("GEHE") AND LLOYDS CHEMISTS PLC 19.07.96

Activities

A11.077   Pharmaceutical wholesaling and retail pharmacies.

Market Shares

Unichem was responsible for 37 per cent of the wholesale supply of prescription medicines, Lloyds 14 per cent and Gehe 32 per cent, including sales to group retail pharmacies. As regards supply to external customers only, Unichem had 39 per cent, Lloyds 7 per cent and Gehe 34 per cent. As regards pharmacy retailing, UniChem had 3.4 per cent, Lloyds 7.8 per cent, and Gehe 2.8 per cent.

Assessment

General

The pharmaceutical market was subject to a great deal of regulation, with the pricing of branded prescription medicines at both wholesale and retail levels being constrained by a voluntary scheme agreed by the manufacturers and the Department of Health. Over the counter medicines (accounting for 20 per cent of pharmaceutical sales) were subject to resale price maintenance. The normal competitive pressures did not apply in many respects, as for example, the Department of Health determined the payment to retail pharmacies for dispensing NHS prescriptions.

There had been a trend in recent years towards concentration in both the wholesale and retail sectors. UniChem and AAH had increased their shares of the wholesale market, while regional wholesalers, taken together had declined in number and market share, mainly as a result of acquisition by Lloyds, and to a lesser extent by UniChem. There was however still evidence that the regional wholesalers which remained had on average been increasing their sales and profits more quickly than nationals. In terms of retailing, the proportion of outlets owned by chains of over 50 stores had risen from 20 per cent in 1991 to 28 *per* cent in 1995.

In terms of geographic market, the wholesale market was sub-national, essentially because it was not economically possible for full line wholesalers to provide a twice daily delivery service to pharmacies.

UniChem/Lloyds

The MMC considered that the increased concentration at the wholesale level would lead to a significant loss of competition in six areas, although the concentration at the retailer level would not raise concerns. The MMC also considered whether the enlargement of UniChem's retailing activities would enhance its position as a wholesaler, but found that the merger would not increase the number of retail outlets foreclosed to competition from other wholesalers, nor materially strengthen UniChem's buyer power.

GEHE/Lloyds

The MMC considered that the merger would lead to a significant loss of competition in seven areas, but did not identify any adverse effects arising from the increase in concentration at the retail level. The MMC did not consider that the enlargement of Gehe's retailing activities would enhance its position as a wholesaler for similar reasons to those applicable in the case of UniChem/Lloyds.

Recommendation

Both mergers were found to be against the public interest because of the adverse effects at the wholesale level. In the case of a UniChem/Lloyds merger, the MMC recommended the divestment of six of Lloyds's depots and the full line wholesaling business operated therefrom. In the case of a GEHE/Lloyds merger, the MMC recommended the divestment of seven of Lloyds's depots and the full line wholesaling businesses operated therefrom.

NB: Two members of the Group, while agreeing with the conclusions reached by the MMC, identified further adverse effects and believed that both mergers should be prohibited.

Secretary of State's Decision

The Secretary of State accepted the MMC's findings and the proposed undertakings should either UniChem or GEHE acquire Lloyds Chemists plc.

Chairman and Panel Members

Mr P H Dean CBE, Mr I S Barter, Mr J Evans CBE, Mr R J Munson, Professor J F Pickering

POWERGEN PLC ("POWERGEN") AND MIDLANDS ELECTRIC PLC ("MEB") 25.04.96

Activities

Generation, distribution and supply of electricity.   A11.078

Market Shares

Powergen was the second largest electricity generation company in England and Wales with a market share by output of 24 per cent. It was also the largest supplier of electricity in that part of the market which had been opened to competition (i.e. supply to customers with demands exceeding 100KW), with its share in this sector being 16 per cent.

MEB was one of the 12 Regional Electricity Companies, each of which had a local monopoly in the supply of the under 100 kW market. In addition it had a 6 per cent share of the competitive supply market of over 100kW in England and Wales, and limited generation interests as a minority shareholder in two independent power producers ("IPPs").

Assessment

The generation market had recently become increasingly less concentrated, with the shares of the two largest generators, PG and National Power PLC ("NP"), having dropped to 57 per cent. This was largely because of new entrant IPPs and this trend was expected to continue. PG's and NP's share was expected to further drop to 38 per cent over the next few years. As regards 'non-baseload' generation (i.e. that part of electricity generation which is turned on and off to meet variations in demand and which set prices in the Electricity Pool), PG's share was 41 per cent but was expected to fall to between 27 and 30 per cent. As a result of its share, PG historically set pool prices for a large proportion of the time, but its ability to do so was expected to become small as a result of its drop in market share.

The acquisition by PG of MEB's equity interest in IPPs, together with access to MEB's power purchase agreements with IPPs, would give it influence over, and information about, competing IPPs, leading to a reduction in competition and higher prices.

It was also argued that the merger would reduce the size of the "Contracts for Differences" ("CfD") market (hedging contracts), making entry by independent generators and independent suppliers difficult. The MMC believed the CfD market would be larger in the future and the merged company would continue to contract with third parties.

The merger would reduce the number of major players in the over 100 kW supply market from 16 to 15, but this market was highly competitive and would continue to be so. The MMC rejected the argument that competition in the under 100kW supply market would be reduced. It also rejected the notion that vertical integration would have adverse effects or would allow the integrated company to charge higher prices to customers than an independent supplier.

The Director General of Electricity Supply ("DGES") would, however, find it more difficult to monitor and enforce licence conditions, such as prohibitions on cross-subsidy and discrimination and the requirement for economic purchasing. The merger would give rise to uncertainty about the ability of the DGES to prevent PG from jeopardising the ability of MEB to finance its activities. Some customers might also lose rights deriving from the Electricity Act and the Public Electricity Supply licence.

Recommendation

Against the public interest. The MMC recommended the following undertakings:

— that MEB's equity interests in IPPs be disposed of within 18 months;

— that information arising from MEB's power purchase agreements with IPPs be ring fenced within the merged organisation; and

— that licence amendments be agreed to assist the DGES effectively to monitor and enforce licence conditions, to ensure that businesses carried on by MEB under its PES licence be kept separate, and to require the merged company to inform tariff customers in MEB's area that they would no longer have certain rights as a consequence of them being supplied under a different licence.

Secretary of State's Decision

The Secretary of State considered that the acquisition would operate against the public interest, but did not agree that the adverse effects arising from the merger could be remedied, and prohibited the merger.

Chairman and Panel Members

Mr G Odgers, Mr R O Davies, Ms P A Hodgson CBE, Mr D J Jenkins MBE, Professor J S Metcalfe CBE

NATIONAL POWER PLC ("NP") AND SOUTHERN ELECTRIC PLC ("SE") 25.04.96

Activities

Generation, distribution and supply of electricity.   A11.079

Market Shares

NP was the largest electricity generation company in England and Wales with a market share (by output) of 33 per cent. It was also the second largest supplier of electricity in the part of the market which had been opened to competition (i.e. supply to customers with demands exceeding 100KW), with its share in this sector being 14 per cent.

SE was one of the 12 Regional Electricity Companies, each of which had a local monopoly in the supply of the under 100kW market. In addition, it had a 7 per cent share of the competitive supply market of over 100kW in England and Wales, and limited generation interests as a minority shareholder in three independent power producers ("IPPs").

Assessment

The generation market had become increasingly less concentrated, with the shares of the two largest generators Powergen and NP, having dropped to 57 per cent. This was largely because of new entrant IPPs, and this trend was expected to continue. NP's market share was expected to reduce to around 21 per cent and NP and PG's combined market share to reduce to 38 per cent over the next few years. As regards 'non-baseload' generation (i.e. that part of electricity generation which is turned on and off to meet variations in demand and which sets prices in the Electricity Pool), NP's share was 57 per cent but was expected to fall to between 31 and 35 per cent by 2000/01.

The acquisition by NP of SE's equity interest in IPPs would give it influence over, and information about, their operation leading to a reduction in competition and causing higher prices.

It was also argued that the merger would reduce the size of the "Contracts for Differences" ("CfD") market (hedging contracts), making entry by independent generators and independent suppliers difficult. The MMC believed the CfD market would be larger in the future and the merged company would continue to contract with third parties.

The merger would reduce the number of major players in the over 100 kW supply market from 16 to 15, but this market was highly competitive and would continue to be so. The MMC rejected the argument that competition in the under 100kW supply market would be reduced, together with the notion that vertical integration would have adverse effects or would allow the integrated company to charge higher prices to customers than an independent supplier.

The Director General of Electricity Supply ("DGES") would, however, find it more difficult to monitor and enforce licence conditions, such as prohibitions on cross subsidy and discrimination and the requirement for economic purchasing. The merger would give rise to uncertainty about the ability of the DGES to prevent NP from jeopardising the ability of SE to finance its activities. Some customers might also lose rights deriving from the Electricity Act and Public Supply Licence.

Recommendation

Against the public interest. The MMC recommended the following:

— that SE's equity interests in IPPs be disposed of within 18 months;

— that information arising from SE's power purchase agreements with IPPs be ring fenced within the merged organisation; and

— that licence amendments be agreed to assist the DGES effectively to monitor and enforce licence conditions, to ensure that businesses carried on by SE under it PES licence be kept separate, to require the merged company to inform tariff customers in SE's area, that they would no longer have certain rights as a consequence of them being supplied under a different licence.

Secretary of State's Decision

The Secretary of State considered that the acquisition would operate against the public interest, but he did not agree with the MMC that the adverse effects arising from the merger could be remedied, and prohibited the merger.

Chairman and Panel Members

Mr G Odgers, Mr R O Davies, Ms P A Hodgson CBE, Mr D J Jenkins MBE, Professor J S Metcalfe CBE

BRITISH BUS PLC ("BRITISHBUS") AND ARROWLINE (TRAVEL) LTD ("ARROWLINE") 08.03.96

Activities

A11.080   Bus services.

Jurisdiction

The MMC concluded that the share of supply test was not satisfied in the area specified in the terms of reference.[1] However, it was met in a narrower "designated area", comprising Macclesfield, Vale Royal, Congleton, Crewe & Nantwich and Trafford. In this regard, British Bus had argued that Crewe & Nantwich should not be included in the designated area since Arrowline did not operate there, but the MMC noted that the Act did not require that the relevant part of the UK should only comprise of areas in which both the relevant enterprises operated.

Market Shares and Increment

British Bus was the third largest bus operator in the UK, supplying 29.9 per cent of bus services (measured by turnover) in the four districts of Vale Royal, Congleton, Macclesfield and Crewe & Nantwich in Cheshire and Trafford in Greater Manchester ("the designated area"). Arrowline had 11.8 per cent in that area.

---

[1] Namely Macclesfield, Vale Royal, Congleton, Crew & Nantwich, Trafford, Stockport and Manchester.

Assessment

The merger had brought some benefits, including efficiency gains for Arrowline and incentives to its drivers to deliver a better quality of service. There was increased scope for expansion of Arrowline's business and the potential for it to be a stronger competitor in Trafford.

The merger also led to a loss of actual competition in the supply of commercial bus services in Macclesfield and of tendered services in most of the designated area. However, the number of bids for tendered work in Trafford, Vale Royal, Congleton and Crewe & Nantwich had, historically, been greater than in the other districts of Cheshire and Greater Manchester, which led the MMC to believe that the loss of competition here was not significant. In relation to those districts there were several other operators both within and outside the designated area which were capable of providing competition.

The greatest problem lay in Macclesfield where there were fewer bidders for tenders and also less competition for commercial services than in the rest of the designated area. However, commercially, the district could only sustain one sizeable operator providing the full network of services, and there remained a number of smaller operators who were potential bidders for tendered services. Any detriment caused as a result of the merger was therefore limited to the loss of competition on a relatively small number of individual routes.

Recommendation

Not against the public interest.

Chairman and Panel Members

Dr D J Morris, Mr I S Barter, Mr R H F Croft CB, Professor S Eilon, Mr M R Prosser

NORTHCLIFFE NEWSPAPERS GROUP LIMITED ("NORTHCLIFFE") AND ABERDEEN JOURNALS LIMITED ("AJL") 27.02.96

Activities

Daily, weekly, monthly and bi-monthly publication of local and regional newspapers.   A11.081

Assessment

AJL's titles faced strong competition in the north of Scotland, while Northcliffe, wholly owned by The Daily Mail and General Trust Plc ("DMGT"), published local and regional newspapers in several areas. So far as increased concentration was concerned, at the UK level, Northcliffe's current 9.7 per cent share of the local and regional newspaper market would increase to 11.3 per cent if Northcliffe acquired AJL's titles. There was, therefore, no cause for concern in competition terms.

DMGT's share of the total market for newspapers would increase both in Scotland as a whole and in AJL's marketing area (the north of Scotland) if it acquired AJL's titles since its subsidiary, Associated Newspapers Limited ("Associated Newspapers"), already owned the *Scottish Daily Mail.* However as the *Scottish Daily Mail* was not a close substitute for *The Press and Journal,* AJL's flagship newspaper (the two newspapers were aimed at different markets), the MMC were satisfied that the increase in concentration would have no adverse effects.

The MMC concluded that there would be no risk to the accurate presentation of news or free expression of opinion if AJL's titles were transferred to Northcliffe

Recommendation

Not against the public interest.

Chairman and Panel Members

Mr D G Goyder CBE, Mr R D Kernohan OBE, Mr T R C Willis, Mrs C M Blight, Professor A P L Minford CBE

THE GO-AHEAD GROUP PLC ("GO-AHEAD") AND OK MOTOR SERVICES LIMITED ("OK") 02.02.96

Activities

A11.082   Operation of bus services.

Market Shares and Increment

In the reference area, Go-Ahead had a 29.2 per cent share of total turnover by bus operators, whilst OK had 5.4 per cent.

The bus market in the reference area was dominated by four large national operators, Go-Ahead, Stagecoach Holdings plc, National Express Group plc and British Bus plc. Following the merger, these four operators would have a 95 per cent market share in the reference area.

Assessment

Each operator was dominant within a core territory. However the territories overlapped and there was competition on the main corridors served by Go-Ahead. Within Tyne & Wear, competition was also provided by the Metro and Newcastle/Sunderland railway.

The merger resulted in (i) a slight loss of competition for commercial bus services, and (ii) a loss of competition for tendered services. However as regards (i), the competition which Go-Ahead continued to face from other bus operators and, on parts of its network, from other modes of transport such as the Metro, would be sufficient to prevent this loss of competition with OK from producing adverse consequences for bus users. The MMC also expected an increase in competition in the future as a consequence of reduced opportunities to expand by acquisition. As regards (ii), the number of potential competitors for tendered services remained sufficiently large that it would not be right to conclude that the loss of OK would, in itself, have a direct impact on tender prices.

Recommendation

Not against the public interest.

Chairman and Panel Members

Mr D G Goyder, Mr I S Barter, Mr J Evans CBE, Professor J F Pickering, Mr M R Prosser

STAGECOACH HOLDINGS PLC ("STAGECOACH") AND CHESTERFIELD TRANSPORT (1989) LIMITED ("CT89") 18.01.96

Activities

Operation of bus services.   A11.083

Jurisdiction

Within the area of reference, (seven local authority districts in north Derbyshire and north Nottinghamshire), CT89 supplied 20 per cent of bus services, measured by registered vehicle mileage and East Midland Motor Service ("EMMS"), 43 per cent.

In establishing whether the share of supply test would be satisfied, the MMC considered whether the designated area constituted "a substantial part of the UK". It had a population of 645,000 comprising 1.1 per cent of the total UK population and covering 1.1 per cent of the UK land area; the MMC noted that it would have been unreasonable to argue that the merger's effects on the inhabitants of a number of medium-sized towns would not have been worth consideration under the Act. Accordingly, the share of supply test was satisfied.

Assessment

The merger had brought several benefits: the continuation of the CTL service, increased efficiency in its operation, an improved fleet, quality of service and a more innovative approach to developing the market. The loss of actual competition was relatively small and the extent of overlap between the parties was minor. There had been a loss of competition between the parties for tendered services which might affect prices in one district but CTL's activities in that area were not sustainable in any case.

As to loss of potential competition, this was a possibility but the MMC did not regard this as a problem in the short to medium term. CTL would probably not have continued as an independent operator and they doubted that anyone else could have been able to make CTL an effective competitor.

The assessment of long term effects was problematic. There was no guarantee that Stagecoach would continue to maintain a low fare strategy. However, the MMC was "reasonably confident" that if Stagecoach's services were to deteriorate, other operators would see this as an opportunity to encroach on Stagecoach's area of operations.

Recommendation

Not against the public interest.

Chairman and Panel Members

Dr D J Morris, Mrs C M Blight, Mr J Evans CBE, Sir Ronald Halstead CBE, Mr J K Roe

BELFAST INTERNATIONAL AIRPORT LIMITED ("BIA") AND BELFAST CITY AIRPORT LIMITED 09.01.96

Activities

A11.084   Airport services.

Market Share and Increment

As a result of the merger BIA would have increased its share of airport services in Northern Ireland from 63 per cent to about 89 per cent.

Assessment

The overlap between the International Airport and the City Airport was almost wholly on domestic scheduled flights, which accounted for about 80 per cent of total Northern Ireland airport passenger services. Six domestic routes were presently served by both airports. Both the Belfast airports had sought to compete vigorously with one another and the airlines were influenced in their choice of airport by such competition. Competing airports encouraged competition between airlines. The MMC found that they could not expect competition to continue under joint ownership.

Higher airport charges were likely to result from the loss of competition. There would be a reduction in competition between airlines, and, as a result, there was a likelihood of a reduction in routes and services offered by airlines and/or an increase in fares.

Recommendation

Against the public interest. The merger should be prohibited.

Secretary of State's Decision

The Secretary of State agreed with the MMC's findings.

Chairman and Panel Members

Mr P H Dean CBE, Mr P Brenan, Mr D J Jenkins MBE, Dr A Robinson

NUTRICIA HOLDINGS LTD AND VALIO INTERNATIONAL UK LTD 21.12.95

Activities

A11.085   Supply of enteral clinical nutrition products ("ECN"), production and sale of specialist gluten-free and low protein food products.

Market Share and Increment

The merger increased Nutricia's market share in ECN products from 27 per cent to 37 per cent, it increased Nutricia's market share in specialist gluten-free and low-protein products from 44 to 88 per cent, and it increased Nutricia's market share from 30 to 46 per cent of all those products together.

Assessment

As regards ECN products, there were five particular product areas in which both parties operated. These accounted for only £3.5 million of the two companies' sales (i.e. about 15 per cent of total ECN sales). In these overlapping areas, combined market shares ranged from between 37 to 91 per cent. However, the market was highly specialised, largely dominated by knowledgeable and sophisticated buyers, mainly hospitals, who were themselves in a position to evaluate and consider alternative sources. There was also at least one other international supplier in each of the product areas affected, and few patents or significant barriers to entry. There was also a degree of control over prices exercised by the Advisory Committee on Borderline Substances ("ACBS")

The MMC recognised that the bulk of gluten-free products were supplied on prescription, so that consumer choice was not based on the prices charged. Prices were subject to approval by the ACBS which ensured that such substances were provided as economically as possible under the NHS. Despite the fact that, post merger, the combined company would supply over 80 per cent. of gluten-free and low protein products in the UK, given the importance of variety and quality of products as factors affecting consumer demand, the MMC did not share concerns that the merged company would wish to reduce the range of products available.

The increase in market share would, however, strengthen the company's ability to increase prices within the constraint of the present price cap and would remove a source of comparative price information between major competing companies. Finally, in the event of dispute and possible delisting of products, it would reduce the effectiveness of the ACBS in ensuring adequate alternative product suppliers, and in controlling prices.

Recommendation

Against the public interest. Structural remedies in the form of divestment would have been disproportionate. The MMC considered that the adverse effects of the merger would have been effectively remedied by requiring Nutricia to undertake, for a period of four years, to set prices of gluten-free and low protein bread, rolls and flour mixes at levels which were no higher than the prices at the time of its decision plus the annual change in the retail price index (less two percentage points). By the end of the four year period, a more competitive market situation would have been re-established and the ACBS price control arrangements would have had time to develop.

Secretary of State's Decision

The Secretary of State accepted the MMC's findings that undertakings should be given. However he did not agree that it was certain that a price control would be necessary after a four year period. He therefore asked the DGFT to seek undertakings for continuing price controls, subject to review after four years.

Chairman and Panel Members

Mr G D W Odgers, Mr P Brenan, Professor S Eilon, Mr D J Jenkins MBE, Mr J K Roe

TRINITY INTERNATIONAL HOLDINGS PLC "TRINITY" AND THOMSON REGIONAL NEWSPAPERS LIMITED "TRN" 10.11.95

A11.086   The proposed transfer to Trinity of newspapers published by TRN and associated assets.

Market

The publication, sale and distribution of regional and local newspapers within the UK.

Market Share and Increment

Following the transfer, Trinity's share would increase from 5.5 per cent to 12.3 per cent.

Assessment

The MMC drew particular attention to the increased concentration of ownership of regional and local newspapers and whether such increases would benefit diversity of opinion by securing a healthier newspaper industry, or, conversely, whether they may be harmful to diversity.

The market share post-transfer was not considered to be unduly high. The regional and local newspaper market had other strong newspaper groups within the UK, which would limit Trinity's prospective market power.

Following the transfer Trinity would have a 51 per cent share of regional and local newspapers in Wales. However, TRN was dominant in south Wales, and Trinity in north Wales. Due to poor communications and little cross-selling of newspapers between north and south Wales, the Commission was satisfied that Wales was not a single market and the subsequent transfer was not expected to have an effect on the concentration of ownership.

The transfer was considered to have a negligible impact on readers' choice in the Merseyside, Cheshire and North Wales region. Trinity informed the Commission that it was its intention to continue to publish TRN's existing titles and would continue with their policy on editorial freedom. Furthermore, local competition was not expected to be greatly affected (although Trinity's dominance in the region as a whole would be reinforced). It was observed that barriers to entry were low, other available substitutes existed and any attempt by Trinity to undermine its competitors by, for example, cutting advertising rates, would be limited, due to the fact that most advertising in local newspapers is local in scope. Advertisers had other media to which they could turn should rates increase, and since most advertising in local papers was very local in its scope, Trinity would not be able to benefit from offering geographical "packages" of advertising.

Recommendations

Not expected to operate against the public interest.

Chairman and Panel Members

Mr D G Goyder, Mr R D Kernohan, Mr M Kersen, Sir Ronald Halstead CBE, Mr M R Prosser, Professor G Whittington

STAGECOACH HOLDINGS PLC ("STAGECOACH") AND AYRSHIRE BUS OWNERS (A1 SERVICE) LIMITED ("A1") 03.11.95

Activities

Bus services. A11.087

Jurisdiction

In considering the size of the reference area, the MMC agreed that the area of overlap was very small. However, bus operators are not restricted to the areas where they operate at any given time and can profitably run services at a range of 20 miles or more from their depots. The MMC therefore found that it was appropriate for the reference area to be wider than the overlap area and that the MMC could determine the most appropriate area, having regard to what is sensible in the context of the business concerned.

Market Share and Increment

Western Scottish (owned by Stagecoach) supplied 26 per cent of bus services (measured by turnover) and A1 supplied 6.5 per cent in the reference area (which comprised eight districts of the Strathclyde region). Most of the overlap of the companies' operations was in two Ayrshire districts, Cunninghame (where A1 had 18 per cent and Western Scottish 10 per cent) and Kilmarnock & Loudoun (where A1 had 11 per cent and Western Scottish 70 *per* cent).

Assessment

The merger had led to a modest loss of actual competition between the two companies in the supply of commercial services and schools transport. There was also a more significant loss of potential competition; Western Scottish might have initiated more vigorous competition with A1 had the merger not taken place, or A1 (which was unlikely, by itself, to pose a significant competitive threat) might have been acquired by another operator. The merger formed part of Stagecoach's strategy to increase Western Scottish's already high share of bus services in Ayrshire which would have the effect of diminishing competition from existing operators yet further and raising barriers to entry from small entrants.

Although the merger brought benefits (including an improvement in A1's fleet of buses, innovative services being introduced and short term freezing of fares) the MMC considered that competition would be weakened as the scope for Stagecoach to grow by acquisition diminished. Stagecoach could be expected, in the longer term, to increase profits by raising fares and reducing levels of service.

Recommendation

On balance the merger was against the public interest. The MMC recommended several behavioural remedies with the aim of restricting Stagecoach's ability to exploit its position.

Secretary of State's Decision

The Secretary of State accepted the MMC's recommendations and asked the DGFT to seek undertakings from Stagecoach broadly in line with MMC recommended remedies.

Chairman and Panel Members

Mr P H Dean CBE, Mrs C M Blight, Mr J Evans CBE, Mr N F Matthews, Professor J F Pickering

LYONNAISE DES EAUX SA ("LYONNAISE") AND NORTHUMBRIAN WATER GROUP PLC ("NORTHUMBRIAN") 26.07.95

Activities

A11.088   Supply of water and sewerage services.

Jurisdiction

In order to determine whether "arrangements" were "in progress", the MMC considered the difference between the meaning of "arrangements in progress" under the 1991 Water Industry Act and "in progress or in contemplation" under the Fair Trading Act 1973. The MMC attributed the distinction to the fact that the Secretary of State is under a duty to make a reference under the 1991 Act whereas his power is discretionary under the 1973 Act.

When Lyonnaise announced its intention to acquire Northumbrian, it would specify the terms of its offer only once the outcome of the MMC inquiry was clear. Under the Takeover Panel rules, if it had made its offer public, the offer would have lapsed once the reference had been made. Lyonnaise provided the MMC with a considerable amount of evidence relating to the intended bid, including a Board resolution authorising named directors to take certain relevant steps. The MMC concluded from the evidence that arrangements were not simply "in contemplation", but actually "in progress".

Assessment

The merger qualified for investigation under the EC Merger Regulation, although the UK had applied under Article 21(3) for permission to examine the regulatory impact of the transaction. The terms of the European Commission's decision did not allow the MMC to examine the impact on competition of the merger.

The Director General of Water Services ("DGWS") gave evidence that the availability of a wide range of comparative information had been of great importance to his determination of price caps for each water enterprise. The use of comparators was a continuing and evolving process which played a fundamental role in the regulation of the water industry. The loss of Northumbrian as a separate comparator would seriously prejudice the DGWS's ability to make comparisons and weaken the effectiveness of the regulatory system. Northumbrian, in particular, had value for comparative purposes as a medium sized enterprise with its water supply operation directly comparable to North East Water plc.

Recommendation

Against the public interest, with the particular adverse effect of prejudice to the DGWS's ability to make comparisons between companies.

If the merger was to proceed, the MMC recommended that action should be taken so that a single new appointment was made for the merged enterprise which would require it to maintain or exceed current levels of customer service. They further recommended that the new appointment should have the effect of securing substantial price reductions sufficient to compel the merged company to move to the forefront of efficiency in the industry. The DGWS was in the best position to calculate what was needed to achieve this outcome and advise the Secretary of State. The MMC also recommended that price reductions took effect from 1 April 1996, which would ensure that the advantage of creating the new comparator would inform the DGWS's analysis of average efficiency for the purposes of the next Periodic Price Review.

Secretary of State's Decision

The Secretary of State agreed with these findings and accordingly asked the DGWS to discuss with Lyonnaise the terms of a new appointment for the merged organisation.

Chairman and Panel Members

Mr D G Goyder, Mr A G Armstrong, Mr P Brenan, Mr D J Jenkins MBE, Mr J D Montgomery, Dr A Robinson

SERVICE CORPORATION INTERNATIONAL ("SCI") AND PLANTSBROOK GROUP PLC ("PLANTSBROOK") 25.05.95

Activities

Supply of funeral directing services, prepaid funerals and crematoria.

A11.089

Market Shares

SCI acquired Plantsbrook in September 1994. SCI had 4 per cent and Plantsbrook had 8.7 per cent of the UK market for funeral directing services. Both were also active in prepaid funerals but SCI's share did not substantially alter. SCI, but not Plantsbrook, had a 6 per cent share in crematoria in the UK. The merged company had a 29 to 51 per cent share in the supply of funeral services in ten localities in the south of England, with its share over the entire area ("the designated area") increasing from around 20 per cent to 28 per cent.

Assessment

Following the merger, barriers to entry in the supply of funeral directing services in the ten localities would be high and choice of funeral director for the consumer would be materially reduced. Additionally, price competition was muted such that SCI could potentially raise its prices excessively, and there was a lack of transparency of funeral directors' charges and the ownership of funeral directing outlets. Consumers in the market were vulnerable and less likely to "shop around" for the most competitive prices. Instead, funeral directors were able unduly to influence customers' choices of funeral arrangements.

Even though Plantsbrook owned no crematoria, SCI's increased market share in the supply of funeral directing services in the ten localities posed vertical integration concerns. In particular, there were concerns that SCI would channel funerals through its own crematoria.

Recommendation

Against the public interest. The MMC recommended undertakings so that SCI divested part of its funeral director business in order to reduce its market share in the ten localities to 25 per cent or less, that it should seek the DGFT's approval prior to acquiring any further such business in the ten localities, and that it should clearly disclose its ownership of funeral directing businesses. In addition, the MMC recommended that SCI should 'post' details of competing crematoria at every SCI funeral directing branch in the area of an SCI crematorium, together with the prices of competing crematoria.

Secretary of State's Decision

The Secretary of State accepted the MMC's findings and asked the DGFT to seek to obtain undertakings from SCI.

Chairman and Panel Members

Mr H H Liesner CB, Mr I S Barter, Mr J Evans, Mr A L Kingshott, Mr J K Roe

GENERAL ELECTRIC COMPANY PLC ("GEC") AND VSEL PLC ("VSEL") 23.05.95

Activities

A11.090   Military activities with the main focus on the supply of submarines, warships and warship equipment in the UK.

Market Shares

At the time there were only three operational warship-building yards in the UK. VSEL owned the only yard that could build both submarines and surface warships and also manufactured guns. GEC was a major supplier of defence electronics, including weapons systems and other equipment for warships, and also owned one of the other three UK warship-building yards.

Assessment

The warship market was unusual in that the Ministry of Defence ("MoD") was the only buyer and it was characterised by large infrequent orders whose win or loss could have a major impact on suppliers' viability. The MOD's policy at that time was to use only UK yards. The modern warship was a platform on which a range of weapons and support systems, usually provided by subcontractors, would be integrated. The MoD usually appointed the owner of the yard as the prime contractor for these orders.

The MMC examined the effects of the proposed merger on the supply of prime contracting and of shipbuilding facilities in relation to the Royal Navy's prospective orders and two tenders invited. VSEL was expected to bid for both tenders and in one would only face competition from a team led by GEC.

VSEL and GEC could act both as shipbuilders and prime contractors. The merged entity would own two (out of a total three in the UK) warship-building yards. This would result in a reduction of competition from other prime contractors, higher prices and reduced innovation. Since the defence budget was constrained it could result in a reduction in UK defence resources. The supply of warship systems and equipment would also be adversely affected. GEC acting as the prime contractor would be likely to favour its subsidiaries as subcontractors, which would result in reduced competition, higher prices and a narrower range of choice.

The MMC rejected that any increase in exports or rationalisation would offset the detriments identified.

Recommendation

Against the public interest. No appropriate remedies were identified.

Secretary of State's Decision

The Secretary of State declined to follow the MMC's recommendation that the GEC bid be blocked. He followed the reasoning of the minority members of the MMC Group which argued that, in the face of sharply declining orders for warships, the industry would almost certainly be further rationalised and that the MoD was well placed as an effective purchaser to extract value for money from the industry. Further, key contracts in the short term were all in the process of being settled, independently of the merger. The minority group had concluded that the merger was unlikely to affect competition, and might facilitate rationalisation. Therefore the Secretary of State decided not to block the proposed acquisition and cleared it unconditionally.

Chairman and Panel Members

Mr D G Goyder, Sir Archibald Forster, Sir Ronald Halstead CBE, Professor A P L Minford, Professor J F Pickering, Mrs E C Tritton QC

BRITISH AEROSPACE PUBLIC LIMITED COMPANY ("BAE") AND VSEL PLC ("VSEL") 23.05.95

Activities

Military activities and in particular the supply of warships, armaments and prime contracting services.

A11.091

Market Shares

At the time of the investigation there were only three operational warship-building yards in the UK. VSEL owned the only yard that could build both submarines and surface warships and also manufactured guns. BAe was a major aerospace and defence company, mainly engaged in the design, development and production of civil and military aircraft, guided weapons systems, ammunitions and guns and other defence support services. Its JV provided ship design services and combat management systems. BAe's subsidiary, Royal Ordnance manufactured ammunition and guns.

Assessment

The Ministry of Defence ("MoD") was the only buyer and the warship market was characterised by large infrequent orders. The modern warship was a platform on which a range of weapons and support systems, usually provided by subcontractors, would be integrated. The MoD usually appointed the owner of the yard as the prime contractor for these orders. One of the main reasons for BAe's proposed acquisition of VSEL was to enable it to secure warship orders, particularly export orders, drawing on its prime contracting experience with aircraft.

The MMC set out the main prospective warship orders of the MoD and the two tenders invited. VSEL was expected to bid for both tenders. The MMC saw no reason why the proposed merger would materially affect competition or the tender prices for the warships currently out to tender or for the other warships in the forward programme, since BAe did not own a warship-building yard and there were many uncertainties as to how the market would develop, including the possibility of new domestic or overseas competition. The proposed merger would not worsen the position of subcontractors in the supply of systems and equipment, since BAe primarily supplied combat management and missile systems in the selection of which the MoD was likely to be closely involved. The proposed merger would give VSEL access to BAe's marketing and sales skills in the defence area, which might be of benefit in competing for export orders.

Recommendation

Not against public interest.

Chairman and Panel Members

Mr D G Goyder, Sir Archibald Forster, Sir Ronald Halstead CBE, Professor A P L Minford, Professor J F Pickering, Mrs E C Tritton QC

S B HOLDINGS LIMITED ("SBH") AND KELVIN CENTRAL BUSES LIMITED ("KELVIN") 27.04.95

Activities

A11.092   The operation of bus services.

Market Shares

SBH had a 43 per cent market share and Kelvin had a 23 market share in the part of the Strathclyde region identified as the relevant area.

Assessment

Even though operations of the two companies overlapped, actual competition between them was muted. The loss of potential competition between them (Kelvin might otherwise have been bought by another bus operator) was considered to be more important. Nevertheless, any attempt by SBH to abuse its strong market position would however be constrained by the presence of a large number of small operators, heavily subsidised local rail and underground services and the possibility of potential competition from three large adjacent national operators.

Recommendation

Not against the public interest.

Chairman and Panel Members

Mr P H Dean CBE, Mr A G Armstrong, Professor S Eilon, Mr N F Matthews, Mr M R Prosser

STAGECOACH HOLDINGS PLC ("STAGECOACH") AND SB HOLDINGS LTD ("SBH") 27.04.95

Activities

The operation of bus services.   A11.093

Jurisdiction

Stagecoach acquired a 20 per cent holding in SBH. The MMC focused on the commercial reality as opposed to the formal agreement. Despite the fact that Stagecoach would not be able to influence SBH's decision through its shareholdings or board powers, the MMC found that Stagecoach had the ability to materially influence SBH for the following reasons: SBH needed support and Stagecoach was its *"white knight"* and *"clearly SBH's preferred recourse at the time"*; it wasn't necessary to show that Stagecoach would *"seek to exercise influence against the views of SBH's management and other board members"*. SBH was the smaller party and SBH would be willing to be advised by Stagecoach on how to improve its performance because Stagecoach was a significantly more powerful operator with broader experience and an impressive record. Moreover, the fact that Stagecoach mentioned two areas where it considered it would help SBH showed that Stagecoach expected to have material influence over SBH; and the threat of Stagecoach withdrawing and attacking the Strathclyde market in competition with SBH would ensure that SBH would pay close attention to Stagecoach's opinions.

Market Shares

SBH had a 51 per cent market share and Stagecoach had a 10 per cent market share in the part of the Strathclyde region identified as the relevant area.

Assessment

SBH was by far the largest bus operator in several districts in and around Glasgow. The area was surrounded by subsidiaries of three substantial bus operators, whose presence had been the main constraint on SBH abusing its market position. Stagecoach was the largest of these three, and the merger situation eliminated this constraint.

Recommendation

Against the public interest. Stagecoach should be required to divest its interest in SBH.

Secretary of State's Decision

Accepted MMC's recommendation, and prohibited the merger.

Chairman and Panel Members

Mr P H Dean, Mr A G Armstrong, Professor. S Eilon, Mr N F Matthews, Mr M R Prosser

THOMAS COOK GROUP LIMITED ("COOK") AND INTERPAYMENT SERVICES LIMITED ("ISL") 23.03.95

Activities

A11.094   Issuing of travellers cheques on a world-wide scale.

Market Shares

Cook held a 32 per cent share of the UK market in 1994 (issuing Mastercard-branded cheques) and ISL (issuing Visa cheques) held 17 per cent. The merger brought together two of the largest issuers to give Cook about 49 per cent of the UK market. The only other issuers of a range of travellers cheques through third party sales agents such as banks, building societies, travel agents and bureaux de change were American Express Company ("Amex") with 40 per cent of UK sales and Citicorp with 1 per cent.

Assessment

The merger effectively reduced from three to two the number of significant issuers of travellers cheques from which sales agents in the UK could choose to receive their supplies. The MMC concluded that for the present, travellers cheques constituted a separate market from the wider market of all methods of payment or obtaining currency overseas, but that this situation might change as newly developed electronic products with characteristics similar to those of the traveller cheques were introduced.

For the majority of sales agents, post merger, there would be a choice between Cook and Amex as a supplier and that there would be vigorous competition between them for the business of banks and building societies.

There was however concern over Cook's ownership of a major chain of travel agents and bureaux de change. In particular, Cook might not continue to offer ISL travellers cheques, and Cook's ownership of ISL might allow it to acquire commercially valuable information about sales agents' businesses. Prior to the merger, ISL had not been connected in any way to a travel business (it was a subsidiary of Barclays). Post merger there would not be any choice except to offer Amex travellers cheques if sales agents were unwilling to use Cook as a supplier. Amex would thereby have the opportunity to impose less favourable terms. Increased costs might then be passed on to customers.

Recommendation

Against the public interest. The MMC recommended that:

— Cook should maintain Mastercard and Visa as separately branded products and retain ISL as the sole issuer's name on the Visa cheques;

— Cook should not renew its agreement with Mastercard that 60 per cent (or any other proportion) of the cheques issued will be of the Mastercard brand; and

— Cook should take a number of steps to ensure that sales agents who saw Cook as a competitor were protected from the possibility of information about their customers or their business getting into the hands of Cook's retail operation.

If these recommendations could not be implemented, divestment would be the only alternative remedy.

Secretary of State's Decision

The Secretary of State accepted the MMC's recommendations and asked the DGFT to negotiate suitable undertakings.

Chairman and Panel Members

Mr H H Liesner CB, Mrs C M Blight, Mr P Brenan, Sir Ronald Halstead CBE, Professor J S Metcalfe CBE

STAGECOACH HOLDINGS PLC ("STAGECOACH") AND MAINLINE PARTNERSHIP LIMITED ("MAINLINE") 09.03.95

Activities

The operation of bus services.   A11.095

Jurisdiction

The MMC considered whether Stagecoach's purchase of a 20 per cent shareholding in Mainline constituted material influence. The parties argued that it did not because: Mainline's constitution and nature were such that Stagecoach could not materially influence Mainline's policy; Mainline's purpose in entering the transaction was to preserve its independence; Mainline's Articles of Association split the balance of power between management and employees who actively use their vote on important issues; Mainline's managing directors had special voting rights (for 5 years) allowing them to pass or block ordinary resolutions; Mainline's employee trust had a 26 per cent shareholding so they could effectively block a special resolution; and Stagecoach could only appoint one out of a possible 12 directors.

Despite the above factors, the MMC, quoting *Pleasurama plc/Trident Television plc/Grant Metropolitan plc* [December 1983] to the effect that "*commercial realities are more telling than formal agreements and structures*", found that Stagecoach did have material influence over Mainline because: of the relative size of the enterprises (Stagecoach was the biggest operator of bus services in the UK, highly profitable, fast growing and efficient whereas Mainline was small, short of capital and unprofitable. The link with Stagecoach was important in strengthening Mainline's business); Mainline was willing to take advice from Stagecoach (Mainline recognised that it needed to improve its performance and was willing to be advised by Stagecoach); and Mainline's alternatives to dealing with Stagecoach were unattractive (in this context the MMC took into consideration factors including Mainline's position if Stagecoach withdrew and Stagecoach's reputation in the industry for aggressive behaviour).

Market Shares

In South Yorkshire and certain districts of North Derbyshire and North Nottinghamshire (the reference area), Mainline had a 46 per cent share and Stagecoach 10 per cent. The MMC focused primarily on Sheffield (South Yorkshire) where Mainline had a 64 per cent share and no other operator had over 10 per cent.

Assessment

The merger situation reduced actual and potential competition between the two operators, weakened existing small operators, and substantially reduced the prospect of new entry in South Yorkshire. The perceived benefits were an improvement in the quality of Mainline's service, increased reliability and stability in local bus services and a reduction in congestion and pollution. However, it was essential that there would be a real potential for competition from substantial outside operators in Sheffield and these would be likely to be deterred by Stagecoach's reputation for aggression against competitors.

Recommendation

The benefits identified did not offset the weakening of competition but divestment would be disproportionate to the adverse effects. The MMC recommended that Stagecoach be prohibited from increasing its holding in Mainline above the 20 per cent level in order to change the perception of other operators that Mainline was now identified with the Stagecoach group.

Secretary of State's Decision

The Secretary of State accepted the MMC's findings but was not persuaded that the remedy recommended by the MMC would be sufficient to address the adverse effects identified which arose from StageCoach's existing 20 per cent shareholding in Mainline. He therefore asked the DGFT to seek undertakings from StageCoach to divest its 20 per cent shareholding in Mainline and its seat on the Mainline Board, and not to re-acquire shares in Mainline subsequently.

Chairman and Panel Members

Mr P H Dean CBE, Mr A G Armstrong, Mr J D Montgomery, Mr L Priestley, Dr A Robinson

DAILY MAIL AND GENERAL TRUST PLC/
T BAILEY FORMAN LIMITED 31.10.94

Activity

Publication of local newspapers.   A11.096

Market Share and Increment

The market share of Northcliffe (a subsidiary of DMGT) in sales of local newspapers in the three counties of the East Midlands triangle (Nottinghamshire,
Derbyshire and Leicestershire) would increase from 36 per cent to 58 per cent.

Assessment

The MMC considered that two concerns arose from the increase in regional
concentration. The first related to the consequences for free expression of opinion,
in particular for diversity of opinion in the press, and the second related to the possibility of Northcliffe using the very considerable market power it would acquire in a
way which could result in competing weekly publications being forced to close or
to reduce their editorial expenditure, leading to a further reduction in the diversity
of opinion or a decline in editorial standards. In addition, the MMC were concerned
that any closure of a newspaper would result in reduced choice for advertisers.

Recommendation

Against the public interest. The only condition which could be attached to a
consent to the merger that would adequately protect diversity of opinion was divestment of certain titles. However, DMGT had rejected this out of hand and the MMC
therefore recommended that the Secretary of State should not give his consent to the
proposed transfers.

Secretary of State's Decision

Consent to the transfer would not be given unless conditions could be agreed with
DMGT to remedy the adverse effects, notably the risk to diversity of opinion in the
region. The Secretary of State's final decision was delayed to allow DMGT time to
agree to conditions and third parties were invited to make their views known.
Satisfactory undertakings were ultimately agreed which covered the following:

- establishment of a new editorial board to ensure editorial independence at
  one of the titles;

- divestment of certain other titles and a commitment not to re-enter the
  market for weekly paid for newspapers in the East and Midlands area;

- a commitment not to act in a way which prevents, distorts or restricts
  competition in the relevant markets;

- a commitment not to introduce a regional edition of the Daily Mail in the
  area.

Chairman and Panel Members

Mr G D W Odgers, Mr D G Goyder, Professor S Eilon, Dr A Robinson

JOHNSTON PRESS PLC/HALIFAX COURIER HOLDINGS LIMITED 17.06.94

Activity

A11.097 Publication of regional and local newspapers.

Market Share and Increment

Following the merger, Johnston would account for 2.5 per cent of local newspapers published each week in the UK. There was no overlap in the circulation areas of the parties' newspapers.

The parties' newspaper circulation areas which were of closest proximity were in West Yorkshire, and even in West Yorkshire, Johnston would still account for less than 20 per cent of local newspapers circulated each week and other leading newspaper groups were represented in the area.

Assessment

In view of the lack of overlap in the parties' newspaper businesses, the MMC concluded that the merger would not significantly increase concentration in the ownership nor have any adverse effects on competition or choice. The MMC also concluded that the acquisition would not have an adverse effect on the accurate presentation of news or on the free expression of opinion.

Recommendation

Not against the public interest.

Chairman and Panel Members

Mr D G Goyder, Sir Peter Gibbings, Mr R Kernohan, Professor S Eilon, Mr J D Montgomery

ALCATEL CABLE SA/STC LIMITED 24.2.94

Activity

A11.098 Supply of long and short haul submarine cable telecommunications systems.

Market Share and Increment

Alcatel's worldwide share of the long haul sector would increase by 19 per cent to 38 per cent, and its share of the short haul sector would increase by 22 per cent to 44 per cent.

Assessment

The MMC concluded that submarine cable and satellite systems are separate markets. Within the long haul sector, the MMC noted that there were already few competitors and that barriers to entry were high. However, the MMC concluded that some reduction in the number of competitors might be inevitable, given the increasing need for R&D and capital investment. The MMC added that any tendency which the merged group might have to abuse its market position would be kept in check by competition between suppliers and the strong countervailing power of purchasers.

In the short haul sector, the MMC noted that there is a greater number of suppliers, and that market entry is relatively easy as the technological demands are not as great.

The MMC accepted that STC would need the long-term wholehearted support of a strong parent company if it was to continue to thrive, and also recognised Alcatel's intention to support STC's UK operations. The MMC concluded that the proposed merger was likely to be a means of preserving STC's presence in the UK as a significant exporter and employer at the leading edge of telecommunications technology.

Recommendation

Not against the public interest.

Chairman and Panel Members

Mr G C S Mather, Mr I S Barter, Mr N H Finney OBE, Mr D J Jenkins MBE, Mr G C S Mather, Professor G Whittington.

NATIONAL EXPRESS GROUP PLC/SALTIRE HOLDINGS LTD 17.02.94

Activity

Scheduled coach services.   A11.099

Market Share and Increment

NEG's acquisition of Saltire's subsidiary, Scottish Citylink Coaches Ltd ("SCC"), increased NEG's share of the supply of scheduled coach services in Great Britain from some 70 per cent to about 80 per cent.

In considering the effects of the merger, the MMC focused on those routes on which both parties competed directly prior to the merger. On the Glasgow/Edinburgh to London routes, NEG's subsidiary (NEL) and SCC were the only operators before the merger, although a new operator had commenced a service. The only other route on which the parties both operated a service was the Glasgow/Edinburgh route to Aberdeen, and a subsidiary of Stagecoach also operated on part of that route.

Assessment

On the Glasgow/Edinburgh to London route, the MMC concluded that the ability of NEG to raise fares is constrained by competition from British Rail's InterCity

East and West Coast operations, and in particular their discounted fares. On the Scottish routes the MMC concluded that there was only limited competition between NEL and SCC, because NEL's services were primarily "feeder services" operated as part of its cross-border services.

The MMC expressed some concern about the future level of fares on NEG's Scottish network as it considered that ScotRail is a less effective competitor than InterCity. The MMC also expressed concern about the future level of fares on NEG's network in general. However, they concluded that the concerns primarily arose because of the dominant positions already enjoyed by SCC and NEL, and not as a result of the merger itself. The MMC recommended that the DGFT keep the market under review.

Recommendation

Not against the public interest.

Chairman and Panel Members

Mr J D Montgomery, Mr A G Armstrong, Mrs C M Blight, Professor S Eilon, M J D Montgomery, Dr L M Rouse

THE GUARDIAN & MANCHESTER EVENING NEWS PLC/THAMES VALLEY NEWSPAPERS 22.12.93

Activity

A11.100 Publication of regional and regional and local newspapers.

Market Share and Increment

At the national level GMEN's share of regional and local newspapers would increase from 3.9 per cent to 4.3 per cent but would leave its position as the eighth largest supplier of such newspapers unchanged. The transfer would reduce the market share of TVN, the largest UK publisher of regional and local newspapers, from 11.3 per cent to 10.9 per cent.

GMEN's share of 38 per cent of circulation/distribution in the Crowthorne/Sandhurst/Yateley area would increase to 77 per cent. GMEN's share of 4 per cent of circulation/distribution in the rural area around Basingstoke would increase to 10 per cent.

Assessment

Whilst the transfers would result in a limited increase in concentration of ownership and some diminution in competition for readers and advertisers in the Crowthorne/Sandhurst/Yateley and Basingstoke areas, the MMC were satisfied that the presence of competing newspapers published by Trinity International and Southern Newspapers would ensure adequate competition. In particular, Trinity International had recently acquired titles from Argus which competed in the two areas, and these titles were expected to compete more vigorously. The MMC concluded that rationalisation of employment was likely to be necessary if TVN's titles were to become economically viable, and, so far as employment and related matters were concerned, there was no justification for opposing the proposed transfers.

Recommendation

Not against the public interest.

Chairman and Panel Members

Miss P K R Mann, Mr CC Baillieu, Mr A L Kingshott

TRINITY INTERNATIONAL HOLDINGS PLC/JOSEPH WOODHEAD & SONS LIMITED 26.10.93

Activity

Publication of regional and local newspapers.   A11.101

Market Share and Increment

At national level the proposed transfers would increase Trinity's share of regional and local newspapers from 3.5 per cent to 3.9 per cent. It would remain the eighth largest UK publisher of regional and local newspapers. The proposed acquisition of the newspapers published by Argus Press Ltd, on which the MMC was reporting separately, would improve its ranking to sixth.

Assessment

At regional and local level there was no overlap between the areas in which the Trinity and Woodhead newspapers were circulated/distributed, nor were their respective circulation areas contiguous. There would be no adverse effect on competition for readers or advertisers and only a minimal effect on employment.

Recommendation

Not against the public interest.

Chairman and Panel Members

Mr P H Dean CBE, Mr D C Churchill, Mr T R C Willis, Mr A Armstrong, Mr N H Finney OBE

ARGUS PRESS LTD/TRINITY INTERNATIONAL HOLDINGS PLC 26.10.93

Activity

Publication of local and regional newspapers.   A11.102

Market Share and Increment

At national level the proposed transfers would increase Trinity's share of regional and local newspapers from 3.5 per cent to 4.9 per cent; improving its ranking from eighth to sixth. The proposed acquisition by Trinity of the local newspapers of

Joseph Woodhead & Sons Limited, on which the MMC was reporting separately, would increase Trinity's share to 5.3 per cent, leaving its ranking unchanged.

Assessment

At regional level and local levels there was no overlap between the geographical areas in which the Trinity and Argus Newspapers were circulated/distributed, nor were their respective circulation areas contiguous. The MMC noted that Trinity agreed its broad editorial and advertising policies with the management of its newspapers, based on the perceived requirements of readers and advertisers in the communities where the newspapers were published. The MMC did not believe that Trinity's policy of editorial independence would change. Argus had yet to take advantage of efficiency gains available from introducing direct input technology, and therefore job losses were inevitable regardless of the transfers.

Recommendation

Not against the public interest.

Chairman and Panel Members

Mr P H Dean CBE, Mr D C Churchill, Mr T R C Willis, Mr A Armstrong, Mr N H Finney OBE

STAGECOACH HOLDINGS PLC/LANCASTER CITY TRANSPORT LIMITED 01.12.93

Activity

A11.103   Local bus services in Lancashire and Cumbria.

Market Share and Increment

Stagecoach's share of registered bus miles in the reference area would increase from 46 per cent to 49 per cent. Stagecoach's share of commercial services in the reference area would increase from 48 per cent to 51 per cent.

Assessment

Whilst competition between Stagecoach and LCT before the merger was weak (the two companies having entered into a timetable agreement) the MMC nevertheless believed there was still the potential for competition. This potential would have increased had LCT been acquired by a company other than Stagecoach. Potential competition from other new entrants and competition from other forms of transport did not provide as effective a constraint as having the two operators remain independent.

Recommendation

Against the public interest. The MMC recommended that Stagecoach should undertake that: (i) if it reduced fares below those of a competitor it would not raise them in real terms for a period of at least 3 years if the competitor withdrew from the market; (ii) if it increased frequencies of services on any route, it would not reduce commercial frequencies for at least 3 years if a competitor withdrew; (iii) if a competitor entered a route operated by Stagecoach, Stagecoach would not, *inter alia*, operate an additional rescheduled journey before the competitor's service within a shorter interval than the competitor had timetabled its service before an existing Stagecoach service.

Secretary of State's Decision

Accepted the MMC's findings.

Chairman and Panel Members

Mr H H Liesner CB, Mr A Ferry MBE, Mr A Robinson, Dr L M Rouse, Professor G Whittington

THE GILLETTE COMPANY/PARKER PEN HOLDINGS LIMITED 10.02.93

Activity

Supply of refillable writing instruments.

A11.104

Market Share and Increment

Gillette's market share would increase from 7.4 per cent to 62 per cent of all refillables by value; from 3.6 per cent to 77.5 per cent of refillables in the £2.50-£9.99 sector by value; from 9.2 per cent to 54.9 per cent of refillables in the £10-£49.99 sector by value; from 9.1 per cent to 39.8 per cent of refillables in the £50-£99.99 sector by value; and from 17.8 per cent to 42.9 per cent of refillables in the £100 plus sector by value.

Assessment

The MMC were primarily concerned with the potential effect on the market for refillable writing instruments. They observed that at least 40 brands of refillables are supplied to the UK market through three trade channels: the business use, business gifts and retail markets. Refillables play a small part in the business gifts and retail markets. Refillables play a small part in the business use market which is dominated by sales of cheaper disposables and where price is the main factor. The business gift market is large and competitive and competition will continue from a wide range of pen suppliers and suppliers of other gifts. The merger would therefore not adversely affect competition, price or choice in the business use or business gifts markets.

In the retail market, the MMC found that writing instruments are sold through a wide range of outlets and by two main methods, self-service and from under glass by assistants at pen counters. In the self-service (mainly "blister" pack) sector, Parker is particularly strong with an estimated two-thirds of retail sales of refillables price between £2.50 and £10 (this segment accounts, however, for less than one-quarter of the total retail market for refillables). Moreover, market shares are not static and there are 30 existing suppliers, and a range of potential new entrants.

In the under glass sector, the MMC similarly found that there are many suppliers, both long-established and new entrants, and that the larger retailers in both the under glass and self-service sectors enjoy significant purchasing power. The merged company would therefore be kept in check by retailers' bargaining strength as well as by actual and potential competitors and the merger would not adversely affect competition, price or choice in the retail market.

Recommendation

Not against the public interest. The MMC observed that the practice where consultants are not clearly identified as representing their sponsoring suppliers may mislead the consumer and may deserve further investigation on consumer protection grounds.

Secretary of State's Decision

Accepted the MMC's findings and noted that the DGFT would be pursuing the MMC's suggestion concerning the use of in-store consultants.

Chairman and Panel Members

Sir Sydney Lipworth, Mr CC Baillieu, Miss P K R Mann, Mr G C S Mather, Mr L Priestley

SCOTTISH MILK MARKETING BOARD/CO-OPERATIVE WHOLESALE SOCIETY LIMITED 08.12.92

Activity

A11.105   The processing and wholesale supply of fresh milk and production of dairy products ("commercial operations") in Scotland.

Market Share and Increment

The market share of SMMB's commercial operations would increase from 32 per cent to 41 per cent in relation to the supply of processed fresh milk in Scotland.

The market share of SMMB's commercial operations would increase from 27 per cent to 31 per cent in relation to the purchase of raw milk in Scotland.

Assessment

Although the MMC found that sufficient safeguards existed under the current legislation, which protected independent buyers of raw milk and competing processors, the expected deregulation would remove these safeguards and would result in the potential for abuse by SMMB's successor of its dominant position and vertically integrated structure. The MMC found that Scotland is a separate market for the purchase of raw milk and supply of processed fresh milk.

Recommendation

Following deregulation, the merger would operate against the public interest unless new safeguards or a change in structure was introduced.

Secretary of State's Decision

Undertakings were accepted to the effect that SMMB would not proceed with the proposed acquisition.

Chairman and Panel Members

Sir Sydney Lipworth, Mr A Armstrong, Mr F E Bonner CBE, Mr P Brenan, Mr J Evans

EMAP PLC/UNITED NEWSPAPERS PLC 13.10.92

Activity

Publication of regional and local newspapers. A11.106

Market Share and Increment

EMAP's share of regional and local newspapers at a national level would increase from 2.8 per cent to 3.4 per cent and place it in equal ninth position. United would remain fourth with a slightly decreased share.

EMAP's share of circulation of paid-for and the distribution of free newspapers in Cambridgeshire would increase from 32 per cent to 50 per cent.

EMAP's share of circulation of paid-for and the distribution of free newspapers in Northamptonshire would increase from 36 per cent to 71 per cent.

The transfers would increase United's share of newspaper circulation/distribution in South Wales from approximately 20 per cent to about 22 per cent.

Assessment

The transfers were effectively an exchange of United's newspapers in Northamptonshire and Cambridgeshire for EMAP's newspapers in south-west Wales, with additional cash being paid to United. EMAP's wide spread of ownership of newspapers in areas contiguous with those immediately affected by the proposed transfer was noted. It would be the strongest publisher in several counties but would face competition in each of them and thus would not be able to exploit its position. United's interest in South Wales as a whole were considered. There would be no adverse affect on competition in this area as there was no overlap of EMAP's and United's titles, there was no contiguity in the circulation/distribution areas, United's share of circulation would only increase from 20 to 22 per cent, and there were strong competitors. There would be accretion of EMAP's market share in two counties but at local level there was little overlap of the two sets of titles and there was substantial competition. The accurate presentation of news and free expression of opinion would be unaffected. Employment reductions were small and likely to occur regardless of the transfers and there was some indication that medium term employment prospects in each company would be improved.

Recommendation

Not against the public interest.

Chairman and Panel Members

Mr P H Dean, Mr D C Churchill, Mr R D Kernohan, Mr F E Bonner CBE, Miss P K R Mann

BOND HELICOPTERS LTD/BRITISH INTERNATIONAL HELICOPTERS LTD 16.09.92

Activity

A11.107   Helicopter services to the UK sector of the North Sea.

Market Share and Increment

Bond's share of turnover from the supply of North Sea helicopter support services would increase from 29 per cent to 49 per cent.
One other supplier would remain following the merger, Bristow Helicopters Ltd.

Assessment

The MMC found that high barriers to entry resulting from extensive start up requirements (finance, proven safety record, and aircraft and staff meeting stringent safety requirements) existed, which were compounded by the difficulty in finding suitable bases. Successful entry on a scale likely to provide effective competition was therefore unlikely in the absence of a promise of firm contracts. Business is mainly acquired through contracts and it appeared that competition was primarily in terms of price. If the number of suppliers were reduced to two, competition would be weakened and prices would be likely to rise.

Recommendation

Against the public interest.

Secretary of State's Decision

Undertakings accepted from Bond and BIH not to proceed with the merger.

Chairman and Panel Members

Mr B C Owens, Mr C C Baillieu, Mr J Evans, Mr D J Morris, Mr B C Owens, Mr C A Unwin MBE

SARA LEE CORPORATION/ RECKITT & COLMAN PLC 13.08.92

Activity

A11.108   Supply of shoe polish and related products in the UK.

Market Share and Increment

Sara Lee's share by value of the overall market for shoe polish products in the UK would increase from 24 per cent to 53 per cent. The next largest supplier, Punch Sales Ltd, enjoyed 26 per cent. Sara Lee's share of the self-selection sector of the shoe polish products market would increase from 44 per cent to 74 per cent by value.

Sara Lee's share of sales of shoe polish products in the special trades sector by value would increase from 9 per cent to 37 per cent.

Assessment

The MMC found that the market is divided into two sectors: the "special trades" sector comprising shoe retailers, repairers and the wholesalers which serve them, and the "self-selection" sector, which comprises predominantly well-known supermarket chains. Competition is effective in special trades and entry is relatively easy.

There were no formal barriers to entry to the self-selection sector, but a strong practical barrier in the strength of the familiar brand names, especially Kiwi and Cherry Blossom. The MMC found that the products are low-value, low-volume, and price insensitive. There is limited countervailing purchasing power or incentive for supermarkets to constrain prices through the introduction of own-label products or otherwise, given the strength of the Kiwi and Cherry Blossom brands together with the other relevant factors. The MMC considered that in the self-selection sector, the merger would lead to a loss of competition between the two dominant brands and would allow scope for a substantial increase in prices before Sara Lee's high market share would be put at risk.

Recommendation

Against the public interest in the self-selection sector. Sara Lee should be required to divest itself of the Cherry Blossom brand. Sara Lee should be permitted to retain the Meltonian and other acquired brands.

Secretary of State's Decision

Undertakings to divest accepted.

Chairman and Panel Members

Mr P H Dean, Mr R O Davies, Mr J Evans, Professor A P L Minford, Mr R Young

ALLIED-LYONS PLC/CARLSBERG A/S 28.07.92

Activity

Brewing and related wholesaling activities.

A11.109

Market Share and Increment

The merged group (Carlsberg-Tetley) would enjoy 16 per cent of overall beer production and 21 per cent of lager production. Following the merger, 67 per cent of lager and 59 per cent of beer would be produced by the three largest national brewers.

Assessment

The MMC considered that lager is a distinct sector from ale and therefore assessed the merger primarily by reference to its effect on the supply of lager. Carlsberg was one of only two large brewers without a tied estate, and its main brand was in the three top-selling lager brands. The removal of Carlsberg as an independent brewer in a market dominated by national brewers outweighed the expected benefits of the merger arising from the creation of a more effective brewer (with a better balanced portfolio of brands than Allied or Carlsberg would have in the absence of the merger) which would be able to compete more vigorously with the two largest brewers, Bass and Courage.

Recommendation

The merger should not be permitted to proceed unless: (i) Carlsberg-Tetley undertook not to worsen the terms of supply to Carlsberg's existing customers which were regional and local brewers or independent wholesalers for a period of three years; (ii) the term of the supply agreement between Carlsberg-Tetley and Allied was reduced from 7 to 5 years; and (iii) Allied amended its tenancy or lease agreements so that its tied tenants/lessees would be free after two years to purchase up to half their lager requirements from suppliers of their own choice.

Secretary of State's Decision

The first two undertakings were accepted. The Secretary of State accepted the DGFT's advice in relation to the third undertaking that it would be preferable that Allied should be required to free from tie a further 400 licensed premises over and above those it had already been required to free in complying with the Supply of Beer (Tied Estate) Order 1989.

Chairman and Panel Members

Sir Sydney Lipworth, Professor M E Beesley CBE, Mr A Ferry MBE, Mr A L Kingshott, Mr L Priestley

TRINITY INTERNATIONAL HOLDINGS PLC/SCOTTISH & UNIVERSAL NEWSPAPERS LTD 10.07.92

Activity

A11.110   Publication of daily and weekly regional newspapers.

Market Share and Increment

SUN published one daily and 22 weekly local newspapers from four centres in central and southern Scotland. Trinity International enjoyed 2.7 per cent of total sales of regional newspapers in the UK and was thus the twelfth largest regional newspaper publisher. If SUN's share were added to Trinity's the combined group would be the eighth largest in the UK.

Assessment

There would be no risk to the continued free expression of opinion or accurate presentation of news in the SUN newspapers. There would be increased concentration of weekly newspaper ownership following the merger, but there was no overlap in the type and range of SUN's titles with those of Trinity. There would be no reduction in competition for readers, in terms of choice, or for advertisers, in terms of rates, and new entry would be unaffected. There would be no adverse effects on employment.

Recommendation

Not against the public interest.

Chairman and Panel Members

Mr D G Goyder, Mr M Kersen, Mr T R C Willis, Mr C C Baillieu, Mrs C M Blight

HILLSDOWN HOLDINGS PLC AND ENTERPRISES BELONGING TO ASSOCIATED BRITISH FOODS PLC 07.07.92

Activity

The canning of fruit and vegetables, and the production of ambient stored meals. **A11.111**

Market Share and Increment

Hillsdown's share of UK sales of all fruits canned in the UK by value would increase from 49 per cent to 74 per cent.
Hillsdown's share of sales of canned UK seasonal vegetables (and processed peas) by value would increase from 39 per cent to 51 per cent.
Hillsdown's share of UK sales of canned raspberries by value would increase from 32 per cent to 90 per cent.
Hillsdown's share of sales of "wet" ambient stored meals and snacks by value would increase from 19 per cent to 28 per cent.

Assessment

There were only five canners of seasonal fruit and vegetables in the UK and new entry was unlikely but the multiplier retailer customers enjoyed strong buying and bargaining power (and such purchasing power could be effectively exercised given the five alternative suppliers, and the possibility of foreign sourcing). Hillsdown was thus unlikely to be able to raise prices on most types of seasonal fruit and vegetables after the merger. The ambient stored meals market was growing rapidly and given its structure there was no likelihood of any adverse effects on the public interest from this aspect of the merger.

Recommendation

Not against the public interest.

Chairman and Panel Members

Mr D G Goyder, Mr A Armstrong, Mr I S Barter, Mr F E Bonner CBE, Mr J D Montgomery

AAH HOLDINGS PLC/MEDICOPHARMA NV 07.05.92

Activity

A11.112 The (primarily wholesale) supply of pharmaceuticals.

Market Share and Increment

The MMC estimated that AAH's national share of sales by value of ethical pharmaceuticals to retail pharmacies and dispensing doctors increased by about 4 per cent to over 30 per cent. In the Grampian and Highland regions of Scotland, AAH's share of the supply by full-line wholesalers by value of ethical pharmaceuticals to retail pharmacies increased by approximately 40 per cent to approximately 80 per cent.

Assessment

Medicopharma N.V. had ceased trading and AAH had acquired certain assets of two of its subsidiaries. The MMC considered that had the acquisitions not been made these subsidiaries would have been placed in receivership, in which case AAH would have increased its sales of ethicals to retail pharmacies and dispensing doctors by only about 2 per cent. However, the increase due to the merger (a further 2 per cent) was unlikely in itself to have any material effect on competition at the national level or to affect materially AAH's purchasing power. The merger had led to a reduction in competition in the Grampian and Highland region significantly greater than would have occurred had the subsidiaries been placed in receivership. The MMC considered that this would result in an increase in prices to retail pharmacies and dispensing doctors in the region and would also result in the service to such purchasers being of a lower standard than would otherwise have been the case.

Recommendation

No significant public interest benefits were likely to arise from the merger, and in the light of its adverse effects in the Grampian and Highland region the merger might be expected to operate against the public interest.

AAH should divest itself of a business approximating as closely as practicable to the business of Medicopharma as carried on from its Aberdeen depot just before the acquisition.

Secretary of State's Decision

Undertakings, protecting new entry into the market until April 1, 1993 were accepted in accordance with the DGFT's advice. Divestment was no longer necessary following the appearance of a new entrant in the market.

Chairman and Panel Members

Mr H H Liesner CB, Mr R O Davies, Mr J Evans, Mr A Ferry MBE, Professor A P L Pickering

UNICHEM PLC/MACARTHY PLC AND LLOYDS CHEMISTS PLC/MACARTHY PLC 26.02.92

Activity

The wholesaling and retailing of pharmaceuticals (both ethicals and over-the-counter (OTC)) and the wholesaling and retailing of health food.

A11.113

Market Share and Increment

UniChem's share of the retail ethical market would increase from 1.1 per cent to 2.6 per cent. Lloyds' share of the retail ethical market would increase from 5.7 per cent to 7.2 per cent. (The largest supplier, Boots, enjoyed 11 per cent.)

UniChem and another each had a share of the wholesale market for pharmaceuticals of about 30 per cent.

Lloyds/Macarthy would enjoy approximately 20 per cent of sales of health food products by specialist health food stores.

Assessment

UniChem and Lloyds both made offers for Macarthy. The MMC observed that prices, profits, discounts and entry are controlled by voluntary and Department of Health (DH) measures and that therefore the normal competitive pressures in many respects do not apply. The MMC observed that the wholesale pharmaceutical market had become more concentrated, and that the position of some of the regional wholesalers is not strong and may weaken further. They also noted the increasing degree of vertical integration between wholesalers and retailers.

UniChem/Macarthy: the merger was not likely materially to weaken the competitiveness of the wholesale market and there would be no conflict of interest between UniChem as a wholesaler and as a retailer. As the UniChem and Macarthy chains operated in different areas there was no reason for concern regarding the effect of the merger on retail competition.

Lloyds/Macarthy: the competitiveness of the wholesale market would not be materially weakened and on the retail side there would be no adverse effect on the public interest. Adverse effects in individual areas would not arise due to the particular features of the localities concerned, competition for the supply of OTC products from non-pharmacy outlets and the fact that controls on dispensing and the existence of complaint procedures afford some protection to consumers. The MMC found that there are no significant barriers to entry into health food retailing and that some health foods are also sold in a range of other outlets; adverse effects would therefore not arise.

Recommendation

Neither merger would be against the public interest.

The DH should consider the role of regulations in affecting competition, especially in relation to increasing vertical integration and concentration of the wholesale market.

The DGFT should monitor competitiveness in the pharmaceutical sector.

Chairman and Panel Members

Mr H H Liesner CB, Mr R O Davies, Mr J Evans, Mr A Ferry MBE, Professor J F Pickering

SOUTHERN NEWSPAPERS PLC AND EMAP PLC, PEARSON PLC, REED INTERNATIONAL PLC AND TRINITY INTERNATIONAL HOLDINGS PLC 27.11.91

Activity

A11.114   The publishing of local newspapers in Hampshire, Dorset, Wiltshire and Somerset, including evening newspapers in Southampton, Bournemouth and Weymouth.

Market Share and Increment

With 2.5 per cent of the UK market, Southern was the thirteenth largest publisher of paid-for and free regional newspapers. Reed had a 8.7 per cent share of the UK market for paid-for and free regional newspapers, and was the second largest publisher. Westminster Press (Pearson) had a 6.3 per cent share, and was the fifth largest publisher. EMAP had a 3.8 per cent share, and was the seventh largest publisher. Trinity had a 2.7 per cent share, and was the twelfth largest publisher.

Assessment

EMAP, Reed and Trinity did not have a controlling interest in any national newspaper and therefore no issue arose as to concentration of ownership as between national and regional newspapers.

The MMC were not concerned by the increase in concentration of ownership of regional newspapers at the national level which would result from the proposed transfers. In addition no issues arose in those three cases over increased regional or local concentration. There was no threat to the accurate presentation of news and free expression of opinion; any employment consequences would be minor.

In the case of Pearson the concentration and competition issues raised additional considerations. However, neither its ownership of the Financial Times, its other media interests or the additional concentration of ownership of regional newspapers gave cause for concern. Westminster Press Ltd. (Pearson's subsidiary) was in competition with Southern in several localities where the distribution areas overlapped, but in three of those places there would continue to be significant competition and in the other two Westminster would not be able to increase its advertising charges after the merger.

Recommendation

The transfer to EMAP, Pearson, Reed or Trinity would not be expected to operate against the public interest.

Chairman and Panel Members

Mr D P Thomson, Sir Alastair Burnet, Mr R D Kernohan, Mr J D Keir QC, Mr R Young

AVENIR HAVAS MEDIA SA/BRUNTON CURTIS OUTDOOR ADVERTISING LTD 20.11.91

Activity

The supply of roadside poster advertising services.   A11.115

Market Share and Increment

Mills & Allen's (a subsidiary of AHM, which in turn was a subsidiary of Havas SA) share of 48-sheet and larger roadside panels would increase from 26.6 per cent to 33.8 per cent. (The second largest supplier of such panels, Maiden, enjoyed 19 per cent.)

Assessment

The MMC concluded that 48-sheet roadside panels, together with larger sizes, constitute a distinct sector of the roadside advertising market. Entry on a small scale is easy but significant barriers to growth exist (particularly as a result of planning regulations which limit the number of new panels which can be erected), and the threat of potential entry will not act as a constraint upon the behaviour of existing contractors. M&A's dominance would, therefore, lead to reduced competition, reduced choice and higher prices in the supply of 48-sheet and larger roadside panels.

Recommendation

Against the public interest; AHM and M&A should be required to divest all the 48-sheet and larger panels owned or otherwise under the control of Brunton Curtis at the date of its acquisition by M&A.

Secretary of State's Decision

The Secretary of State considered that Havas SA should also be required to divest. Undertakings were accepted from Havas SA, AHM and M&A.

The companies subsequently disposed of 2768 panels and AHM requested that they be released from their obligation to dispose of any further panels. In accordance with advice from the DGFT the undertakings were modified. The companies remained subject to an undertaking not to re-acquire any of the poster panels which they had already sold.

Chairman and Panel Members

Mr P H Dean, Mr A Ferry MBE, Mr J D Montgomery, Professor J F Pickering

THE ENTERPRISES OF ALAN J. LEWIS/ JARMAIN & SON LTD 13.08.91

Activity

The supply of wool scouring services to third parties ("commission scouring   A11.116 services").

803

Market Share and Increment

Alston's (one of Mr Lewis's companies) market share of commission scouring services in the UK would increase from 20 per cent to 52 per cent (the other leading suppliers were Hamworth (29 per cent) and Bailly—Ancion (13 per cent)).

Assessment

The MMC concluded that the merger had given rise to a significant loss of competition for several reasons. These included: the top two commission scourers enjoyed 81 per cent of the market, and the top three 94 per cent; customers have little bargaining power; in-house scourers do not compete with commission scourers; new entry was unlikely in the face of the present high level of concentration, relatively high start-up costs, and the physical problem of effluent treatment; and there was limited scope for increased competition from imports of scoured wool.

Recommendation

Against the public interest. Alston's (another company controlled by Mr. Lewis) three scouring lines should be sold by public auction to the highest bidder.

Secretary of State's Decision

The Secretary of State did not consider sale by auction to be necessary, and decided that the assets be sold to a purchaser approved by the DGFT. Undertakings were later given that Mr Lewis would decommission for 12 months, but not sell, the Alston line transferred to Jarmain. Undertakings were also given that the two remaining Alston lines be sold or rendered inoperable within 18 months and that no merchants controlled by the British Wool Marketing Board should be obliged to place their scouring business with any company under Mr Lewis's control.

Chairman and Panel Members

Mr P H Dean, Mr P Brenan, Mr A Ferry MBE, Professor J F Pickering

PROSPER DE MULDER LTD/CRODA INTERNATIONAL PLC 01.08.91

Activity

A11.117   Animal waste rendering.

Market Share and Increment

PDM's share of the animal waste rendering market in England and Wales would increase from 60 per cent to 65 per cent.

Assessment

There would be adverse effects on competition in the collection of high-grade waste in the south-west and south-east of England and the merger would modestly enhance PDM's position in the overall waste collection market in England and Wales. However, the adverse effects were marginal in relation to the structural defects in competition which existed within the industry before the merger. Moreover, Croda was no longer an effective force and was leaving the industry. PDM was likely to improve efficiency after the merger and it would bring wider public health and environmental benefits.

Recommendation

Not against the public interest.

Chairman and Panel Members

Mr D G *Goyder*, Mr F E Bonner CBE, Mr L A Mills, Mr D P Thomson

THE MORGAN CRUCIBLE COMPANY PLC/ MANVILLE CORPORATION 29.05.91

Activity

Supply of refractory ceramic fibre (RCF) in Europe and the US.   A11.118

Market Share and Increment

Morgan's share of the UK bulk and blanket RCF market would increase from 22 per cent to 41 per cent by value. (The Carborundum Company Ltd had a 43 per cent share, and there was only one other significant supplier).

Assessment

Competition in the market for bulk and blanket RCF was unlikely to be impaired despite the increase in concentration. The MMC found that competition was healthy; supply capacity was twice the level of demand; buyers could change source easily; and the third largest supplier had steadily increased its UK market share. These factors were likely to have an important constraining effect on prices in the UK.

Recommendation

Not against the public interest.

Chairman and Panel Members

Mr P H *Dean*, Mr A G Armstrong, Professor S Eilon, Mr A Ferry MBE, Mr J D Keir QC

AMOCO CORPORATION/SOCIETE NATIONALE ELF AQUITAINE 03.05.91

Activity

A11.119   The refining, wholesaling and retailing of oil and petroleum products (downstream activities).

Market Share and Increment

Elf's share of UK refining output would increase from 0 per cent to 2.4 per cent. Elf's share of deliveries of petrol to retail petrol outlets would increase from 3.1 per cent to 4.9 per cent and Elf's share of all UK retail petrol outlets would rise from 2.3 per cent to 3.7 per cent.

Assessment

The merger was concerned with "downstream" activities. Elf had become an integrated oil company in the UK (both upstream and downstream) but its market share of all petroleum products was relatively small (in the 3 per cent to 5 per cent range following the merger). The market was competitive due to the presence of a number of strong companies, notably the five majors (Esso, Shell, BP, Texaco and Mobil), and the growing importance of hypermarkets.

Although SNEA was 56 per cent owned by the French Government, it was run in a normal commercial way, and no distortion of competition or other public interest issues would be likely to arise.

Recommendation

Not against the public interest.

Chairman and Panel Members

Sir Sydney Lipworth, Mr L Britz, Mr B C Owens, Professor J F Pickering, Mr L Priestley

STORA KOPPARBERGS BERGSLAGS AB/SWEDISH MATCH NV, AND STORA KOPPARBERGS BERGSLAGS AB/THE GILLETTE COMPANY 20.03.91

Activity

A11.120   The supply of razors and razor blades in the UK.

Market Share and Increment

Gillette enjoyed 60 per cent by value of the supply of razors and razor blades in the UK. Wilkinson Sword (its only full range competitor) enjoyed 20 per cent. The only other supplier of significance, Biro Bic Ltd, enjoyed 15 per cent (disposables only).

Assessment

The reference arose from a leveraged buy-out of the Consumer Products Division of Stora (which included the Wilkinson Sword businesses), initiated by Gillette, using a shelf company (later called Swedish Match NV). Swedish Match controlled the non-EC businesses of Wilkinson Sword and Gillette held 22 per cent of Swedish Match equity in the form of non-voting convertible loan stock. This holding could convert to voting shares in certain circumstances and Gillette had pre-emption rights to acquire Swedish Match's equity on a sale or listing and to acquire the wet-shaving business and assets of Wilkinson Sword in the event of their sale.

The MMC found that the arrangements would be likely to result in a reduction in competition between Wilkinson Sword and Gillette due to:

(i) Wilkinson Sword's management being likely to take into account the fact that Gillette was a major shareholder in and the largest creditor of its parent company and had important rights concerning significant decisions by Swedish Match, notwithstanding certain limitations;

(ii) the structure of the transactions effectively determined by Gillette, which resulted in a heavy debt burden being placed on Swedish Match which was likely to reduce the competitiveness of Wilkinson Sword; and

(iii) the involvement of Gillette in the transactions and the corresponding improvement of its competitive position in relation to Wilkinson Sword.

This reduction in competition was unlikely to be mitigated by any new entry into the market or the development of existing suppliers and there were no significant benefits from the transactions.

The MMC also considered that it would be against the public interest for Gillette to have a significant influence over the potential flotation of its principal competitor in the UK or sale of its shares or assets

Recommendation

Against the public interest. It was recommended that Gillette should be required to divest its equity and creditor interests in Swedish Match, and, pending divestment, should waive its pre-emption and conversion rights and options.

Secretary of State's Decision

The Secretary of State accepted the MMC's recommendations, but subsequently revoked the interim orders that were adopted by him following removal of competition concerns through the unconditional sale by Eemland (formerly Swedish Match) of the Wilkinson Sword business to Warner Lambert.

Chairman and Panel Members

Mr M S Lipworth, Mr J S Bridgeman, Mr R O Davies, Mr J D Keir QC, Mr G C S Mather

SLIGOS SA/SIGNET LTD 26.02.91

Activity

A11.121   The processing of payment card transactions.

Market Share and Increment

Signet, the processing business jointly owned by four of the major clearing banks, processed 23 per cent of all payment card transactions to cardholders' accounts and enjoyed a 47 per cent market share of processing of credit cards to cardholder's accounts. It also processed 63 per cent of credit card transactions on behalf of retailers and enjoyed a 39 per cent market share of the processing of all payment card transactions of these "merchant accounts".

Sligos did not have any business in the UK, and the merged company, like Signet, would be the largest processor after merger.

Assessment

Barriers to entry were found not to be sufficiently high to deter the entry of major firms to the market, and several new firms, both domestic and foreign, had recently entered the market.

The Secretary of State's concern over Sligos being a subsidiary of the French state-controlled bank, Credit Lyonnais SA ("CL"), was held to be unfounded by the MMC. The French authorities were found to accord a high degree of independence to CL and to expect it to operate commercially. Signet's position in the market was not as strong as might be supposed from its market share as it owed the latter to the business of its present shareholders; Lloyds Bank, Midland Bank, National Westminster Bank and The Royal Bank of Scotland, who would be committed to Signet for a period of only around five years after its sale. After that period Signet would have to compete to keep the four banks custom.

Recommendation

Not against the public interest.

Chairman and Panel Members

Mr H H Hunt CBE, Mr C C Baillieu, Mrs C M Blight, Mr F E Bonner CBE

BRITISH AEROSPACE PLC/THOMSON-CSF SA 30.01.91

Activity

A11.122   The manufacture and sale of guided weapons systems.

Market Share and Increment

The parties agreed to merge their guided weapons business into a joint company owned equally between the parties. At the prime contract level (where responsibility is taken for the complete weapons system) there was one potential competitor, Shorts, which competed only in respect of a narrow range of weapons, and there had been no French prime contract competitor in the past. Prior to the merger, BAe and Thomson had not been competitors for defence sub-contracts. Competition at sub-contract level was actively encouraged by MOD measures.

Assessment

The MMC observed that competition was possible at two levels: prime contracting and sub-contracting, and assessed the merger against trends in the defence industry such as falling demand and over-capacity, the increasing sophistication of technology, the inter-nationalisation of procurement through consortia and the introduction of competitive tendering procedures by the MOD for the award of contracts. The MMC considered it was inevitable that there would be increasing collaboration between the major participants in the industry, and the joint venture was therefore a response to these trends. There was no evidence that the joint venture would give rise to adverse effects in the prime contracting market. Competition in the sub-contracting market would be stimulated by the merger.

The Secretary of State had been concerned over the ownership of Thomson-CSF's parent, Thomson SA, by the French Government. However, the MMC found that Thomson-CSF was managed in a commercial manner and they could not foresee circumstances in which the French Government would intervene in its affairs.

Recommendation

Not against the public interest.

Chairman and Panel Members

Mr P H Dean, Professor M E Beesley CBE, Mr J Evans, Mr L A Mills

TATE & LYLE PLC/BRITISH SUGAR PLC 6.2.91

Activity

The refining of British sugar beet and imported raw cane sugar and production of related products.

A11.123

Market Share and Increment

Tate & Lyle's share of UK sugar sales would increase from 40 per cent to 92 per cent by volume (42 per cent to 94 per cent by value).

Assessment

The existence of quotas and price support mechanisms under the EC sugar regime severely limited competition in the UK sugar market. However, the MMC found that the two companies did compete on price and service to secure particular accounts. The merger would result in higher prices for sugar in the UK and would rule out the prospect of greater competition between the two companies if the present EC sugar regime were relaxed.

The MMC considered Tate & Lyle's argument that the merger would give them the confidence to undertake the investment needed to secure the future of cane refining and the port refineries in the UK, which would otherwise be at serious risk. They accepted that it might increase the security of both in the next few years but did not think that it would by itself have any significant effect on their long-term future.

Recommendation

Against the public interest. There were no effective remedies, and the merger should not be permitted to proceed.

Secretary of State's Decision

Accepted the MMC's findings.

Chairman and Panel Members

Mr H H Liesner CB, Professor S Eilon, Mr A Ferry MBE, Mr D P Thomson

CALDAIRE HOLDINGS LTD/ BLUEBIRD SECURITIES LTD 30.01.91

Activity

A11.124   The supply of local bus services in the counties of Durham and Cleveland.

Market Share and Increment

After the merger, Caldaire's share of local bus services in the reference area would increase from 38 per cent to 49 per cent, in terms of mileage.

Assessment

The merger may be expected to lead to removal of competition for commercial services on a number of routes in the south-east Durham area, which was likely to lead to higher fares and lower standards and quality, reduced frequency of service, and less choice. The existence of potential competition from other operators and the sensitivity of passenger behaviour to fares or service levels did not constitute as effective a constraint on performance as would the maintenance of competition. It was not sufficient to rely on the county council to provide contract services should there be any deterioration in Caldaire's commercial services in the area. The merger had also resulted in a loss of potential competition in other parts of the reference area.

Recommendation

Against the public interest. A number of measures were recommended in relation to south-east Durham: to limit any increase in fares or reduction in services for two years, to improve accountability, to encourage competition, and to require advance notification to the DGFT of any further acquisitions in the area by Caldaire.

Secretary of State's Decision

Action to implement the recommendations was suspended pending the outcome of an appeal by another bus company against an MMC report on its own acquisitions. Subsequent to this DGFT re-assessed the competitive situation and undertakings were accepted in accordance with this advice.

Chairman and Panel Members

Mr J S Bridgeman, Mr L Britz, Mr M R Hoffman, Miss P K R Mann

CREDIT LYONNAIS SA/ WOODCHESTER INVESTMENTS PLC 23.01.91

Activity

The provision of financial services, including equipment leasing, instalment credit, mortgage and trade finance markets.

A11.125

Market Share and Increment

Crédit Lyonnais' and Woodchester's shares in the various financial services markets in which they operated were generally less than 5 per cent. The parties' activities only overlapped in two sectors, in each case giving a joint share of less than 1 per cent.

Assessment

The parties enjoyed low market shares and there was a substantial presence of competing institutions. Therefore the merger would not enable Crédit Lyonnais to distort the market. The low-level of state intervention in Crédit Lyonnais by the French Government meant that commercial decision-making would prevail.

Recommendation

Not against the public interest.

Chairman and Panel Members

Mr H H Hunt CBE, Mr C C Baillieu, Mrs C M Blight, Mr F E Bonner CBE

KEMIRA OY/IMPERIAL CHEMICAL INDUSTRIES PLC 23.01.91

Activity

The manufacture and sale of solid and liquid chemical agricultural fertilisers.

A11.126

Market Share and Increment

Kemira's share of the UK fertiliser market by volume would increase from approximately 18 per cent to upwards of 40 per cent. The third largest supplier, after Kemira and ICI, enjoyed 19 per cent.

Assessment

The merger would reduce the number of leading manufacturers from three to two, which would enjoy between them some two-thirds of the market, with other suppliers having low market shares and with little prospect of new entry occurring.

The MMC recognised that if the merger were not to proceed, there was a real prospect that ICI would sooner or later withdraw from the fertiliser market with a loss of employment and of domestic productive capacity. However, the MMC did not consider that such a consequence would outweigh the detriments to competition arising from the merger.

Recommendation

Against the public interest. The merger should not be allowed to proceed.

Secretary of State's Decision

Accepted the MMC's findings.

Chairman and Panel Members

Mr M S Lipworth, Mr A Armstrong, Mr K S Carmichael CBE, Mr A Ferry MBE

VALHI INC/AKZO NV 09.01.91

Activity

A11.127   The sale of organoclys, organics and organic pastes for the manufacture of, *inter alia*, solvent-based paints and the production of oil-based drilling fluids.

Market Share and Increment

The UK market share of Rheox International Inc. (a subsidiary of Valhi) by volume or organoclys for solvent-based systems would increase from 66 per cent to 92 per cent.

Rheox's share of organics for solvent-based systems would increase from 27 per cent to 36 per cent.

Rheox's share of organic pastes for solvent-based systems would increase from 21 per cent to 67 per cent.

Assessment

Organoclays, organics and organic pastes are used in two separate markets: the manufacture of solvent-based paints, coatings, inks, adhesives, etc. (solvent-based systems); and the production of oil-based drilling fluids (known as "muds"). The MMC found that there were no close substitutes for the products used in the solvent based systems market. In relation to organoclays for oil-based muds, the merger would result in drilling mud suppliers not linked to an organoclay manufacturer losing their main independent source of organoclay supplies. Although, in relation to both markets, existing suppliers might increase their activities in the UK to some extent and imports might increase, these factors would not counteract the detriments to competition. The merger would be likely to result in higher prices and a distortion of competition between drilling mud service companies.

Recommendation

Against the public interest. The merger should not be permitted to proceed.

Secretary of State's Decision

The Secretary of State accepted the MMC's conclusions and asked the DGFT to seek undertakings from Valhi not to proceed with the acquisition, and from Akzo not to dispose of its organoclays, organics and organic pastes business to Valhi or any of its subsidiaries. These undertakings were subsequently given and accepted.

Chairman and Panel Members

Mr B C Owens, Mr A Armstrong, Mr B C Owens, Mr C A Unwin MBE, Mr R Young

STAGECOACH (HOLDINGS) LTD/FORMIA LTD 20.12.90

Activity

The supply of local bus service.   A11.128

Market Share and Increment

Stagecoach's share of total registered bus miles in the reference area (East Sussex and parts of West Sussex and Kent) would increase from 26.5 per cent to 36.3 per cent. The other leading service providers enjoyed 20.4 per cent (Brighton & Hove) and 9.5 per cent (Brighton Buses).

Assessment

The merger virtually eliminated competition on many commercial services in Hastings and Rother and reduced sharply competition for contract services in Hastings and Bexhill. There was little prospect of new entry or expansion by existing operators. The strength of Stagecoach's position could weaken its competitors.

Recommendation

Against the public interest. The divestment of Hastings and District Transport Ltd (a subsidiary of Formia and the main operator, prior to the merger, in Hastings and Rother) from Stagecoach was not recommended. The MMC considered that divestment was likely to result in the replacement in this limited area of one dominant supplier by another and would also risk disruption of services and inconvenience to passengers while the change was being effected. Therefore, a number of other measures were recommended to improve local accountability, to prevent short-term retaliation against new entrants, to monitor further acquisitions and to limit the cost of tenders.

Secretary of State's Decision

Action to implement the MMC's recommendations immediately following publication of the report was suspended pending the result of an application for judicial review by another bus company, South Yorkshire Transport, which could have affected the outcome of the case. The House of Lords ruled against SYT in December 1992 and the DGFT reassessed the competitive situation in relation to Stagecoach. Undertakings closely following the original recommendations were subsequently given and accepted.

Chairman and Panel Members

Mr B C Owens, Mrs C M Blight, Mr A Ferry MBE, Professor G Whittington

TRELLEBORG AB/MCKECHNIE EXTRUDED PRODUCTS LTD 19.12.90

Activity

A11.129   The production of semi-finished extruded brass (referred to as "brass semis").

Market Share and Increment

Trelleborg's share of UK brass semis sales to users in the "free market" would increase from 7 per cent to 52 per cent.

Assessment

The market had become increasingly competitive due to an increase in competition from imports (18 per cent of the total market in 1989). The merger would remove one main supplier, but Delta Extruded Metals Company Ltd, the leading UK producer, competed effectively, and there were active independent stockholders.

Recommendation

Not against the public interest.

Chairman and Panel Members

Mr H H Liesner CB, Mr I S Barter, Mr K S Carmichael CBE, Mr D P Thomson

ELDERS IXL LTD/GRAND METROPOLITAN PLC 16.10.90

Activity

A11.130   The brewing and supply (through on-licensed premises) of beer.

Market Share and Increment

Elders' share by volume of the supply of beer as a whole to the UK market would increase from 9 per cent to 20 per cent.

Elder's share by volume of the supply of lager to the UK market would increase from 10 per cent to 23 per cent.

The Government's Beer Orders, adopted following the MMC's March 1989 Beer report, would bring about some changes, but for some years Courage (an Elder's subsidiary) would have easily the largest number of tied on-licences amongst the national brewers.

Assessment

The merger would result in the loss of one of the national brewers, reducing their number to five, and would, therefore, significantly increase concentration. The MMC expressed concern over the strong vertical links that would exist following the merger. Some sharpening of competition in the beer market at the retail level was observed but it was unclear how significant this development was in relation to the effects at wholesale level.

The MMC also expressed concern over the increase in concentration at the retail level resulting from the merger of the parties' retail interests.

Recommendation

Against the public interest. The MMC recommended that Elders and Grand Met should: (i) amend the transaction by disposing of beer brands and/or brewing capacity so that the merged brewing interests, to be owned by Elders, immediately after the proposed merger, would have a market share of around 15 per cent of the supply of beer; (ii) release from tie more of Inntrepreneur Estates Ltd's ("IEL") (a company owned jointly by Elders and Grand Met which would own all of Courage's and Grand Met's public house estates apart from some 1,160 managed houses retained by Grand Met) tied houses than was required under the Tied Estate Order; (iii) reduce the period of exclusive supply of beer under the beer procurement and supply agreements between, respectively, Grand Met and Courage (under which Courage would supply beer to Grand Met's retained houses) and IEL and Courage (under which Courage would supply beer to IEL's houses); (iv) reduce the local concentration of houses in their ownership and tied to Courage for the supply of beer; and (v) make more remote Courage's shareholding in IEL.

Secretary of State's Decision

The Secretary of State asked the DGFT to negotiate appropriate Undertakings with the parties confirming proposals made by them during the preparation of the report, but with certain amendments. Undertakings were subsequently given and accepted which would result in, *inter alia*: the shortening of the period of secured supply by Courage to IEL under the beer supply agreement from 10 years to seven years; termination of the beer procurement agreement after four years; a reduction in the local concentration of Courage tied houses; and a reduction in the number of tied houses in the IEL estate to 4,350 by November 1, 1992. Undertakings to divest beer brands and/or brewing capacity and to make Courage's shareholding in IEL more remote were not given.

The undertakings were subsequently varied at IEL's request. The variation permitted IEL to re-tie pubs which were previously free of tie, but which had fallen vacant, as long as the total number of tied pubs did not exceed the original limit of 4,350. The other requirements of the undertakings remained unchanged.

Chairman and Panel Members

Mr H H Liesner CB, Professor M E Beesley CBE, Mr F E Bonner CBE, Mr L Britz, Mr J Evans

WESTERN TRAVEL LTD/
G & G COACHES (LEAMINGTON) LTD 04.10.90

Activity

A11.131   The supply of local bus services in Warwickshire, Coventry and Solihull.

Market Share and Increment

Western Travel's share of registered bus miles in commercial services in the reference area increased from 29 per cent to 33.7 per cent.
Western Travel's share of registered bus miles in commercial services in the Warwick and Leamington area increased from 65.9 per cent to 86.5 per cent.

Assessment

The MMC analysed competition in the provision of both commercial and contract bus services and found that the merger had eliminated competition in commercial services in Warwick and Leamington, and between those towns and Coventry. They also found that the merged companies accounted for the majority of contract services in Warwick and Leamington. However, they concluded that an adjacent dominant operator, West Midlands Travel Ltd, would be well placed after privatisation to enter the market if Western Travel abused its position. The strengthening of Western's position could also itself enhance potential competition by providing a more effective challenge to West Midlands.

Recommendation

Not against the public interest.

Chairman and Panel Members

Mr B C Owens, Mrs C M Blight, Mr A Ferry MBE, Professor G Whittington

WILLIAM COOK PLC ACQUISITIONS 30.08.90

Activity

A11.132   The supply of steel castings in the UK.

Market Share and Increment

William Cook's share of the UK steel casting market by tonnage increased from approximately 35 per cent to approximately 45 per cent. No other UK foundry out of the remaining 52 supplied more than 4 per cent of the market. Between 20 per cent and 33 per cent of the market by tonnage was accounted for by imports.

Assessment

Whilst the market share created by the acquisitions was high, the potential threat of price rises was likely to be mitigated by the potential for increased imports of steel castings and the presence of effective competition from other UK suppliers. Customers could obtain castings from foundries other than those owned by Cook, and foundries could expand their product ranges if opportunities arose.

Recommendation

Not against the public interest.

Chairman and Panel Members

Mr L A Mills, Mr A G Armstrong, Mr C C Baillieu, Mr K S Carmichael CBE, Mr L A Mills

SOUTH YORKSHIRE TRANSPORT LTD
ACQUISITIONS 01.08.90

Activity

The supply of local bus services. A11.133

Market Share and Increment

SYT's market share of local bus services in the reference area, including the acquired operators, was 50 per cent of bus miles. Its share excluding the acquired operators was 44 per cent. In one part of the reference area, Sheffield, SYT's market share increased from 73 per cent to 87 per cent of bus miles.

Assessment

The MMC considered that the mergers had reduced competition in bus services in Sheffield, but were less concerned about the effects elsewhere in the reference area. The reduction in competition in Sheffield resulting from the mergers had removed a major constraint on the fares that SYT could charge, as well as an important stimulus to efficiency and improvements in services. The acquisitions were therefore expected to lead to higher fares, lower standards, quality and frequency of service and less choice than in the pre-existing more competitive situation.

Recommendation

Against the public interest. A number of remedies were considered but the MMC recommended that SYT be required to divest the assets and business it had acquired, as the most effective means to restore competition in Sheffield.

Secretary of State's Decision

Action to require remedies was suspended pending the outcome of an appeal by SYT against the report on the basis that the acquisitions did not qualify for investigation. The House of Lords found against SYT and the OFT reassessed the case. A number of behavioural undertakings were then accepted from Mainline Group Limited (formerly SYT).

Chairman and Panel Members

Mr B C *Owens*, Mrs C M Blight, M J Evans, Mr A Ferry MBE, Professor Whittington

BRITISH AIRWAYS PLC/SABENA SA 25.07.90

Activity

A11.134   The provision of air transport services.

Market Share and Increment

BA carried 36 per cent of all traffic between the UK and Belgium. Sabena World Airlines (SWA), a subsidiary company formed by Sabena to take over all its air transport operations, carried 32 per cent. The share of the next largest carrier, Air Europe, was 19 per cent.

The busiest UK/Belgium route, in terms of numbers of passengers, was London Heathrow-Brussels. BA's share on this route was 55 per cent, SWA's was 44 per cent. The remaining 1 per cent of traffic was taken by fifth-freedom carriers.

Assessment

BA purchased a 20 per cent stake in SWA (KLM took a further 20 per cent stake). The main purpose of the arrangement was to develop a "hub and spoke" operation at Brussels airport thereby linking through Brussels some 75 provincial cities in Europe. The main effects of the merger fell outside the MMC's jurisdiction and the MMC only considered those effects bearing upon the UK public interest, in particular the extent to which the merger was likely to lead to reduced competition between the parties to the detriment of the UK customer. The MMC concluded that the changes brought about were unlikely to lead to any significant change in competition between BA and SWA on the Heathrow-Brussels route and any attempt to increase fares would be an incentive for another carrier, British Midland, to come on to the route. There were substantial potential benefits to UK consumers from the hub and spoke operation and the MMC considered that the proposed long-haul arrangements between BA and SWA would increase the choice of services, particularly for passengers from certain regional airports.

Recommendation

Not against the public interest. The EC was also investigating the transaction and its recommendations might lead to changes in the arrangements.

Chairman and Panel Members

Mr M S Lipworth, Professor A P L Minford, Mr J D Montgomery, Mr D P Thomson, Mr S Wainwright CBE, Mr R Young

BICC PLC/STERLING GREENGATE CABLE COMPANY LTD 13.07.90

Activity

The manufacture and supply of cables.   A11.135

Market Share and Increment

Following the merger, BICC's share of the market for mains cable of 1kV to 22kV would increase from 21.1 per cent to 34.8 per cent; BICC's share of the market for elastomeric wiring cable would increase from 29.0 per cent to 36.7 per cent; and BICC's share of the market for PVC armoured wiring cable would increase from 15.3 per cent to 23.4 per cent.

Assessment

The MMC considered whether the merger would affect competition in the three markets where the parties' activities overlapped: mains; elastomeric wiring; and PVC armoured wiring cables. Despite the merger removing the only remaining medium-sized supplier of power cables from the market, competition would remain effective because at least three major UK competitors would remain in each of the three markets where BICC's and Sterling's activities overlapped. In addition, purchasers were knowledgeable, the potential for increased imports existed, and Sterling Greengate was unlikely to have had sufficient underlying strength to remain a competitive force in the longer term if it had remained independent. The MMC observed that further mergers reducing the number of competitors in any of the three markets would give rise to concern.

Recommendation

Not against the public interest.

Chairman and Panel Members

Mr D G Goyder, Mr R O Davies, Mr M R Hoffman, Mr L A Mills, Professor J F Pickering

RANSOMES PLC/CUSHMAN INC, BROUWER EQUIPMENT INC AND BROUWER TURF EQUIPMENT LTD 13.07.90

Activity

A11.136   The manufacture and distribution of commercial grass-care equipment.

Market Share and Increment

Ransomes' share of the commercial grass-cutting equipment market would increase from 32 per cent to 34 per cent. Ransomes' share of the turf-maintenance equipment market would increase from 0 per cent to 11 per cent.

Assessment

The MMC found that commercial grass care equipment is divided into three distinct markets: grass-cutting equipment; turf-maintenance equipment; and turf harvesting equipment. A number of mainly international firms competed in the grass-cutting market and new firms continued to enter. In these circumstances Ransome's small increase in market share was not material. The MMC also considered the effect of Ransome's enhanced position in the related grass-cutting and turf-maintenance markets and, in particular, the impact of Ransome's decision to use its dealer network to sell Cushman and Brouwer products. Customers generally obtained their equipment from a number of suppliers and exhibited little brand loyalty. The extended product range may have strengthened Ransomes' dealer network but there were other actual and potential dealers to compete with Ransomes' dealers. In addition, the relationship between Ransomes and its dealers was one of mutual dependency and this had not been upset by the merger. Ransomes' dealers were independent businesses usually with other interests and, on average, the sale of Ransomes products accounted for less than one-fifth of their total turnover.

Recommendation

Not against the public interest.

Chairman and Panel Members

Mr P H Dean, Professor M E Beesley CBE, Mr F E Bonner CBE, Mr P Brenan, Mr C A Unwin MBE

RANSOMES PLC/WESTWOOD ENGINEERING LTD AND LASER LAWNMOWERS LTD 13.07.90

Activity

A11.137   The manufacturer and sale of domestic ride-on and walk-behind mowers.

Market Share and Increment

Ransomes' share by value of sales of petrol-powered walk-behind lawn movers in the UK was 26 per cent. Market concentration of such products was not affected as

Westwood no longer sold such machines. Ransomes' share by value of sales of ride-on mowers in the UK increased from 4 per cent to 33 per cent and it became the largest supplier.

Assessment

The MMC found that the market for domestic ride-on mowers is separate from that for domestic walk-behind mowers, although the distribution system is common to both. In the ride-on mower market, Ransomes faced competition from a wide range of mainly international firms: the largest competitor enjoyed a 25 per cent market share and the next four largest suppliers had appreciable shares amounting in aggregate to 21 per cent. In those circumstances Ransomes' position was not dominant and the established strong competition between suppliers was likely to continue. Ransomes would not be able to put undue pressure on its dealers because the greater part of their income came from selling competitors' mowers and customers expected to see a number of makes on display.

Recommendation

Not against the public interest.

Chairman and Panel Members

Mr P H Dean, Professor M E Beesley CBE, Mr F E Bonner CBE, Mr P Brenan, Mr C A Unwin MBE

STAGECOACH (HOLDINGS) LTD/ PORTSMOUTH CITYBUS LTD 12.07.90

Activity

The operation of local bus services.   A11.138

Market Share and Increment

The MMC found that, following the merger, Stagecoach subsidiaries supplied over 40 per cent of local bus services in the reference area. Before the merger Southdown (a subsidiary of Stagecoach) and PCB accounted for almost 90 per cent of commercial bus miles in the Portsmouth and Havant area, and about two-thirds of contract services, with extensive competition on many routes.

Assessment

The MMC concluded that, following the merger, competition had been significantly reduced in Portsmouth and Havant, particularly on commercial services. The resulting market structure lent itself to further market dominance, enabling Stagecoach to deter other firms from entering the market and threatening the position of the remaining few competitors. Whilst the merger had not at the time of the inquiry had adverse effects on the public interest, and indeed had produced benefits, in the longer term there was the potential for anti-competitive behaviour in the Portsmouth and Havant area which would be contrary to the public interest.

Recommendation

Against the public interest. The MMC recommended undertakings and other steps with a view to making Stagecoach's activities more transparent and deterring predatory action. If such undertakings were agreed, divestment of the assets of PCB or imposition of any more formal regulation of fares would not be necessary.

Secretary of State's Decision

The Secretary of State decided that the remedies recommended by the MMC were insufficient and requested the DGFT to enter into negotiations with Stagecoach to secure the divestment of assets corresponding to the former PCB business. Undertakings from Stagecoach to do this were later accepted.

Chairman and Panel Members

Mr M S Lipworth, Mrs C M Blight, Mr A Ferry MBE, Mr B C Owens, Professor G Whittington

GENERAL UTILITIES PLC/ THE MID KENT WATER COMPANY 04.07.90

Activity

A11.139   The supply of water and sewerage services.

Market Share and Increment

Not applicable.

Assessment

GU's shareholding in Mid Kent Water increased from 15 per cent in June 1988 to 29 per cent in March 1989. In March to May 1989 shareholders of Mid Kent Water exchanged their shares for equivalent holdings in Mid Kent Holdings plc resulting in Mid Kent Holdings acquiring 99 per cent of the shares of Mid Kent Water. GU was the largest shareholder in Mid Kent Holdings with 29 per cent of its shares. The MMC concluded that GU had acquired the ability materially to influence the policy of Mid Kent Water.

Under the Water Act, the MMC must have regard to the principle that the number of water enterprises under independent control should not be reduced so as to prejudice the ability of the Director General of Water Services (DGWS) to make comparisons between water enterprises. As a result of various mergers that had already occurred, some 15 of the 29 statutory water companies (SWCs) were already under the control of four major groups, which also had major shareholdings in five others SWCs. Only about eight SWCs appeared to be independent of control or major influence by other water enterprises. The MMC concluded that GU would become more directly involved in the management of Mid Kent Water over time thereby prejudicing the DGW's ability to make comparisons between water enterprises. The benefits of the merger would not outweigh this detriment to the public interest.

Recommendation

Against the public interest. The MMC recommended that if undertakings were given that CGE (GU's parent) and GU were not to be involved in the management of Mid Kent or in the formulation of policy, that neither CGE nor GU were to be represented on the board of either company and that GU was not to use its voting rights to block special resolutions of Mid Kent Holdings, the merger should be allowed to proceed. If no such undertakings could be negotiated, the only alternative remedy would be for CGE and GU not to be represented on the board of either Mid Kent company and for GU to divest its shareholding to a level at which it could not materially influence policy.

Secretary of State's Decision

The Secretary of State accepted undertakings requiring, *inter alia*, GU to reduce its stake in Mid Kent Water from 29 per cent to 19.5 per cent and not to nominate any director of either Mid Kent company.

Chairman and Panel Members

Mr H H *Hunt* CBE, Mr A G Armstrong, Mr R O Davies, Mr J D Keir QC, Mr D P Thomson, Mr C A Unwin MBE

SOUTHERN WATER PLC/
MID-SUSSEX WATER COMPANY 04.07.90

Activity

The supply of water and sewage services.   A11.140

Market Share and Increment

Not applicable.

Assessment

Southern had increased its holding of Mid-Sussex's voting stock from 14.9 per cent to just over 25 per cent.

The transaction had created a merger situation qualifying for investigation as Southern's shareholding had given it the ability materially to influence the policy of Mid-Sussex (as Southern had the ability to block special resolutions).

The MMC concluded that the merger had reduced the number of independent water enterprises but that this reduction may not be expected to prejudice the Director General of Water Services' (DGWS) ability to make comparisons between different water enterprises (the test required by the Water Act to determine whether a merger situation involving water enterprises operates or may be expected to operate against the public interest). An important consideration was that Mid-Sussex was already controlled by SAUR Water Services PLC and accordingly Southern's shareholding could have no effect upon Mid-Sussex's value as a comparator.

Recommendation

The transaction resulted in no overall prejudice to the DGW's functions nor was it in any other way against the public interest.

Chairman and Panel Members

Mr M S Lipworth, Mr A G Armstrong, Mr J D Montgomery, Mr D P Thomson, Mr S Wainwright CBE

MR DAVID SULLIVAN/
THE BRISTOL EVENING POST PLC 31.05.90

Activity

A11.141   The publication of a number of paid-for and free newspapers in the South-West of England.

Market Share and Increment

Not applicable.

Assessment

Mr Sullivan proposed to increase his shareholding in BEP from 7.5 per cent and had indicated his intention to proceed to a possible bid. The MMC observed that the main public interest issue for consideration was the effect of the transfer on the character and content of BEP newspapers. The MMC considered that Mr Sullivan could be expected to influence editorial policy and the character and content of the newspapers and that this would harm both the accurate presentation of news and the free expression of opinion. In addition, the acquisition could harm the standing of the newspapers in their community and there could be some adverse effects on circulation. Given the different readership of Mr. Sullivan's existing newspapers and BEP's titles the acquisition would raise no significant competition concerns. However, Mr. Sullivan did not provide sufficient evidence as to the effect of the transaction on BEP's efficiency and profitability for the MMC to assess whether there would be any benefits offsetting the detriments to the public interest which had been identified.

Recommendation

Against the public interest. The MMC were unable to recommend the imposition of any conditions on the basis of which the merger could proceed.

Secretary of State's Decision

Accepted the MMC's findings and refused to consent to the transfer.

Chairman and Panel Members

Mr H H Hunt, Mr J D Keir QC, Sir Alastair Burnet, Mr M Kersen, Mr R D Kernohan

KINGFISHER PLC/DIXONS GROUP PLC 23.05.90

Activity

The retail distribution of electrical appliances and photographic equipment.   A11.142

Market Share and Increment

Kingfisher's share of the UK retail market for "electrical appliances" would increase from 9.4 per cent to 26.2 per cent. The only other major electrical appliance retailer competing on this market had a share of around 5 per cent. A broader market definition (adding, *inter alia*, gas cookers, gas space heaters, electrical garden and power tools, and the retail sales equivalents of new TV and VCR rental agreements) reduced the combined share to about 21 per cent.

Assessment

The MMC found that there existed very strong competition between Dixons Group and Comet (Kingfisher's principal subsidiary) in terms of price and other terms of sale, including in-store and after-sales service. The rivalry between them was centred particularly around national press advertisements and the MMC believed that local competition was decisively influenced by the national competition between, above all, Comet and Dixons Group. The merger would lead to higher retail prices and less favourable terms of sale and, by giving the merged company greater bargaining power with manufacturers, would effectively worsen the terms of supply by manufacturers to competing retails, which would further enhance the ability of the merged company to bring about higher levels of margins and prices.

Recommendation

Against the public interest. No effective remedies could be identified.

Secretary of State's Decision

The Secretary of State agreed with the Commission's findings and recommended that the DGFT seek undertakings that Kingfisher would not proceed with the merger nor acquire more than 15 per cent of the shares of Dixons. Undertakings were later given and accepted that Kingfisher would not acquire directly or indirectly through its subsidiaries more than 9.9 per cent of the shares of Dixons.

Chairman and Panel Members

Mr H H Liesner CB, Sir James Ackers, Mr C C Baillieu, Mr L Britz, Mr J Evans, Mr D G Goyder

TIPHOOK PLC/TRAILERENT LTD 02.05.90

Activity

Trailer rental in the UK.   A11.143

Market Share and Increment

Tiphook's share of the UK trailer rental market by fleet size would increase from 23 per cent to 34 per cent. The next two largest competitors would be TIP Europe with 31 per cent and BRS Trailer rental with 8 per cent. The merged company and TIP together would have a 2/3 share of the transient rental market and a 70 per cent share of refrigerated trailer rental services.

Assessment

The MMC found that the trailer rental market was broadly split between transient rental (hire for less than a year) and contract rental (hire for periods of a year or more). Following the merger, both sectors of the market would remain competitive. The market was characterised by vigorous price competition and knowledgeable consumers. In relation to contract rental, prices were constrained by the alternative options available to customers of leasing or purchasing. In relation to the transient sector, competition would continue to come from smaller trailer rental operators with the additional constraint of the customer's option of sub-contracting in the wider road-transport market. There was also an attractive niche market for existing and new operators in refrigerated trailers. There were low barriers to entry and the overall market was growing.

Recommendation

Not against the public interest.

Chairman and Panel Members

Mr P H Dean, Mr J Evans, Miss P K R Mann, Mr S Wainwright, Mr R Young

GENERAL UTILITIES PLC/THE COLNE VALLEY WATER COMPANY/RICKMANSWORTH WATER COMPANY 27.04.90

Activity

A11.144 The supply of water and sewage services.

Market Share and Increment

Not applicable.

Assessment

Colne and Rickmansworth were two of the 29 statutory water companies (SWCs). Lea Valley Water Company, another SWC which had common boundaries with Colne and Rickmansworth, was one of four SWCs controlled by Compagnie Générale des Eaux (CGE), the parent of GU.

Colne, Lea and Rickmansworth had been associated for a number of years in a scheme utilising water from the River Thames. They proposed to merge with a view to expanding the scheme and in order to benefit from greater economies of scale. The arrangements involved a share exchange by Three Valleys Water Services plc, which had been set up for that purpose. If the merger proposals were accepted,

Three Valleys would be controlled by CGE through GU. The Water Act provides that, in determining in relation to a merger between water enterprises whether any matter operates or may be expected to operate against the public interest, the MMC are required to have regard to the desirability of giving effect to the principle that the number of water enterprises which are under independent control should not be reduced so as to prejudice the ability of the Director General of Water Services (DGWS) to make comparisons between them. The MMC concluded that unless the cost savings arising from the merger were passed on to the consumer the benefits of the merger would not outweigh the prejudice to the DGWS's ability to carry out his duties under the Water Act and could not be brought about except in a manner which conflicts with that principle.

Recommendation

Against the public interest. However, the MMC recommended that the merger should be allowed to proceed if the parties undertook to seek a new appointment for Three Valleys as a water enterprise and also ensured that the benefits of some £60m which they expected to result from the merger were taken into account in setting price increases for that company. The effect of this would be that after 10 years prices should be at least 6 per cent lower than if the merger had not taken place.

Secretary of State's Decision

The Secretary of State was not convinced that the benefits of the cost savings to the consumer identified in the report counterbalanced the detrimental effects of the merger arising from the reduction of water enterprises available for comparison. He asked the DGWS to explore the matter further. The subsequent report identified further cost savings which the parties were prepared to undertake that would result five years after the merger in charges 10 per cent less than they would have been if the companies had remained separate. The Secretary of State then decided to allow the merger to proceed subject to undertakings to ensure that the cost savings were passed on to consumers.

Chairman and Panel Members

Mr H H Hunt CBE, Mr A G Armstrong, Mr R O Davies, Mr J D Keir QC, Mr D P Thomson, Mr C A Unwin MBE

BRITISH STEEL PLC/C.
WALKER & SON (HOLDINGS) LTD 04.04.90

Activity

The stockholding of steel products in the UK.   A11.145

Market Share and Increment

British Steel's share of the total stockholders market would increase from around 15 per cent to 34 per cent.

The MMC found that British Steel supplied 58 per cent of the total purchases by UK stockholders and about four-fifths of the purchases made by both Walker and British Steel Distribution ("BSD").

Assessment

After noting that steel products not covered by the Treaty of Paris fell to be considered under the Treaty of Rome, the MMC observed that they only had jurisdiction to report on the merger situation as it related to Treaty of Rome products. Therefore, only one-fifth of the steel products sold by Walker and BSD fell within the MMC's jurisdiction under the Fair Trading Act. In relation to the tube sector, horizontal competition issues arose from the market share of the merged company and vertical issues from British Steel's position as a major supplier. BSD/Walker supplied about one quarter of stockholder sales of all tubes, and within this category 43 per cent of sales by stockholders of structural hollow sections (SHS), 12 per cent of other welded tubes and 17 per cent of seamless tubes. Competition in these last two sectors would not be adversely affected by the merger. The market for SHS would also not be adversely affected by the merger for a number of reasons including: strong competition from overseas producers through stockholders; local competition from smaller firms for customers who would "shop around" and were prepared to split orders; and low entry costs.

Recommendation

Not against the public interest.

Chairman and Panel Members

Mr M S Lipworth, Mr R O Davies, Mr M R Hogman, Mr G C S Mather, Mr C A Unwin MBE

THE BRITISH UNITED PROVIDENT ASSOCIATION LTD/HCA UNITED KINGDOM LTD 21.03.90

Activity

A11.146   Private hospital services.

Market Share and Increment

Following the merger, BUPA's share of private acute hospitals and private sector beds in the UK would increase from 9 per cent to 14 per cent. (The leading competitors were Nuffield with 16 per cent and AMI Healthcare with 7 per cent). BUPA's share of private sector beds in the UK would increase from 10 per cent to 14 per cent. (Both Nuffield and AMI enjoyed around 11 per cent each).

BUPA was the largest health insurer in the UK, with some 52 per cent of health insurance premiums by value.

Assessment

The MMC were unconcerned by BUPA's increasing share of private hospitals and beds, and focused on the issue of vertical integration between BUPA Insurance and BUPA Hospitals. The MMC found that BUPA's share of the health insurance market gave it strong negotiating powers which enabled it to secure lower charges from private hospitals than other insurers.

However, the MMC concluded that BUPA's limited share of private hospitals (as well as the small increment brought about by the merger) and the arm's length operation of its insurance and hospital businesses meant that competition would be likely to be maintained following the merger.

Recommendation

Not against the public interest. Further investigation by the DGFT might be required if BUPA were to change its policy of operating its Hospitals and Insurance businesses on an arms length basis, use its position to the detriment of its competitors or increase its share of private hospitals by more than it currently intended.

Chairman and Panel Members

Mr D G Richards CBE, Sir James Ackers, Mr F E Bonner CBE, Mr D G Goyder, Mr J D Montgomery, Mr B C Owens

MICHELIN TYRE PLC/
NATIONAL TYRE SERVICE LTD 07.03.90

Activity

The supply and distribution of tyres. The supply of tyres included supply both as original equipment ("OE") to be fitted to new vehicles and as replacement tyres.　　A11.147

Market Share and Increment

Car tyres accounted for over half of the value of replacement tyre sales, and Michelin as manufacturer and importer supplied about one-fifth of this market. ATS (a subsidiary of Michelin) and NTS together distributed some 26 per cent by value of replacement car tyres.

The supply of replacement truck tyres accounted for about one-third of the value of replacement tyre sales. Michelin had somewhat over one-third of the value of sales of replacement truck tyres manufactured or imported into the UK. ATS and NTS together distributed some 33 per cent of replacement truck tyres by value.

Assessment

The MMC found that although the vertical integration of Michelin in the supply of car tyres raised several concerns, these were offset by the number of effective competitors in the distribution of car tyres (including several that were independent of any manufacturer and who had recently entered the market), the existence of local firms, the lack of significant barriers to entry, and the fact that the effect of the merger on local competition was likely to be limited.

However, the MMC found that Michelin's truck tyre replacement business faced considerably less competition: the combined company would be four times larger than its nearest competitor; few competitors had more than 50 outlets and only one was independent of any manufacturer; in addition some customers required nationwide coverage and larger distributors therefore possessed an advantage. The MMC also found that in certain local areas there would be little competition to the merged group and that there had been little new entry. In addition, the vertical integration between Michelin as a manufacturer and a distributor strengthened Michelin's position, weakening the degree of competition between distributors and manufacturers.

Recommendation

The MMC reached no adverse conclusions as regards the distribution of car tyres but concluded that the reduction in competition in the distribution of replacement truck tyres would be against the public interest. The MMC recommended that Michelin should be required to divest as a going concern the NTS outlets involved in the distribution of replacement truck tyres.

Secretary of State's Decision

The Secretary of State accepted the MMC's findings but also considered Michelin's subsequent announcement of the sale of NTS wholly to Uniroyal Englebert Tyres Ltd. The Secretary of State and DGFT believed this would remedy the adverse effects of the merger identified by the MMC. The Secretary of State asked the DGFT to monitor the sale and seek undertakings from Michelin that it would divest NTS outlets involved in the distribution of the truck tyres and not to seek to re-acquire those outlets.

Undertakings were subsequently given and accepted from Michelin involving the disposal of all NTS outlets engaged in the distribution of replacement truck tyres through the sale of NTS to Uniroyal Englebert Tyres Limited, a UK subsidiary of Continental AG.

Chairman and Panel Members

Mr M S Lipworth, Mr C C Baillieu, Mr A Ferry MBE, Mr D G Goyder, Mr G C S Mather, Mr J D Montgomery

ATLAS COPCO AB/
DESOUTTER BROTHERS (HOLDINGS) PLC 25.01.90

Activity

A11.148   The supply of industrial pneumatic power tools.

Market Share and Increment

Atlas' share by sales of the supply of pneumatic power tools would increase to 36 per cent, about three times as large as that of the next largest supplier, Ingersoll-Rand. The second largest supplier was Ingersoll-Rand with 12 per cent.

Assessment

The merger brought together the two leading suppliers of pneumatic tools. The parties contended that they competed in a broadly defined market for industrial power tools including electric, pneumatic and hydraulic tools. However, the MMC considered the market segment by segment. The MMC found that competition was maintained by the existence of other suppliers; the availability and increasing importance of electric tools; the purchasing power of customers in certain product segments; and the relatively low barriers to entry for pneumatic tool suppliers.

Recommendation

Not against the public interest.

Chairman and Panel Members

Mr H H Liesner CB, Mr F E Bonner CBE, Mr R O Davies, Miss P K R Mann, Mr L A Mills, Mr S Wainwright CBE

BLUE CIRCLE INDUSTRIES PLC/ MYSON GROUP PLC 21.12.89

Activity

The manufacture of domestic gas central heating boilers.   A11.149

Market Share and Increment

Potterton's (a subsidiary of BCI) share of the UK market for gas boilers (by units sold) increased from 16 per cent to 29 per cent.
Potterton's share of the UK market for floor-standing boilers (by units sold) increased from 24 per cent to 34 per cent.
Potterton's share of the UK market for wall-hung boilers (other than combination boilers) (by units sold) increased from 22 per cent to 42 per cent.

Assessment

The MMC found that the practice of distributing gas boilers through merchants, a number of whom were nationwide businesses with substantial bargaining power, and the role in the market of the many installers would make it difficult for the merged group to exploit its market position. In addition, there was strong competition from imports and between the different types of boiler. Other UK manufacturers could increase output if required, and switching from the production of one type of boiler to another would not generally create many difficulties.

Recommendation

No against the public interest.

Chairman and Panel Members

Mr H H Liesner CB, Mr F E Bonner CBE, Mr A Ferry MBE, Mr J D Montgomery, Mr B C Owens, Mr R Young

YALE & VALOR PLC/MYSON GROUP PLC 21.12.89

Activity

The manufacture and sale of domestic gas fires.   A11.150

Market Share and Increment

The merged company's share of sales of gas fires by volume would increase from 25 per cent to 35 per cent. No competitor had a market share of more than 15 per cent.

Assessment

The MMC found that gas fires were a distinct market. Other forms of heating, especially electric fires, were substitutes for gas fires, but gas fires had sufficient distinguishing characteristics in the eyes of the consumer to place them in a separate market. The merger would not enable the merged group to dominate the market for a number of reasons including the fact that about three-quarters of traditional gas fires in the UK were sold through British Gas, which had a strong interest in purchasing on the most favourable terms. In addition there were no significant barriers to entry into gas fire manufacture; three of the leading competitors were subsidiaries of major British companies; and the decorative flame effect fire market, in which neither Yale & Valor nor Myson had yet been active, had recently been expanding. Yale & Myson would as a result of the merger obtain a 13 per cent stake in the central heating market. The MMC found that this might have a beneficial effect on competition in that market.

Recommendation

Not against the public interest.

Chairman and Panel Members

Mr H H Liesner CB, Mr F E Bonner CBE, Mr A Ferry MBE, Mr J D Montgomery, Mr B C Owens, Mr R Young

COATS VIYELLA PLC/TOOTAL GROUP PLC 26.10.89

Activity

A11.151 Production distribution and retail sales of textiles and clothing.

Market Share and Increment

Coats' share of sales of industrial thread in the UK would increase from 19 per cent to 43 per cent within the EC from 16 per cent to 25 per cent; and worldwide from 9 per cent to 16 per cent.

Coats' share of sales of domestic thread in the UK increase from 18 per cent to 55 per cent. The only other major supplier, Gütermann, had a market share of 20 per cent but Coats owned 20 per cent, had a seat on the supervisory board, and held certain pre-emption rights over the remaining shares of the share capital of Gütermann.

Assessment

The MMC found that in many of the individual textile markets in which it would be operating the merged group, despite its overall size, would have had relatively low market shares and there would therefore be no adverse effects on competition on those markets. The MMC concluded that competition from both domestic and foreign firms and the structure of the industrial thread market would keep the UK market competitive. However, the domestic thread market was dominated by three major suppliers and detrimental effects could be expected following the merger in relation to choice and the supply of product at reasonable prices.

Recommendation

The MMC concluded that the merger could be expected to have adverse effects in the domestic thread market and recommended that Coats should be required to divest its domestic thread business and its shareholding in Gütermann.

Secretary of State's Decision

Undertakings were accepted.

Chairman and Panel Members

H H Liesner CB, Mr A Ferry MBE, Mr J D Keir QC, Miss P K R Mann, Mr S Wainwright CBE

MONSANTO COMPANY/RHONE-POULENC SA 18.10.89

Activity

The supply of analgesic chemicals. In the UK, particularly, the supply of salicylic   A11.152
acid methyl salicylate and bulk aspirin.

Market Share and Increment

Monsanto's market share by value would increase from 44 per cent to 84 per cent in the UK salicylic acid market; from 58 per cent to 81 per cent in the UK methyl salicylate market; from 70 per cent to 87 per cent in the UK bulk aspirin market; and from 3 per cent to 15 per cent in the UK paracetamol market.

Assessment

The MMC expressed concern over the removal of competition between the two main suppliers whose market shares were already high but concluded that Rhône-Poulenc would be unable to exploit its predominant position as there is worldwide oversupply, freedom of entry and general available technology and imports at competitive prices are available from Eastern European and Third World countries. There was also more likelihood of security of employment for the salicylates workforce at Monsanto's Ruabon, North Wales plant if the merger went ahead.

Recommendations

Not against the public interest.

Chairman and Panel Members

Mr H H Hunt CBE, Mr F E Bonner CBE, Mr P S G Flint, Mr D G Goyder, Mr L A Mills, Mr B C Owens

GLYNWED INTERNATIONAL PLC/JB&S LEES LTD 30.08.89

Activity

A11.153 Supply in the UK of hardened and tempered steel strip (H&T strip).

Market Share and Increment

Glynwed's share would increase from 52.9 per cent to 63.5 per cent by value of direct sales of H&T strip in the UK. (There were three other suppliers in the UK with 22.7 per cent of the market by value between them and imports accounted for 13.8 per cent by value).

Assessment

The MMC analysed the supply of H&T strip by reference to its end use. In some product areas Glynwed's and Lees' activities did not overlap. In two areas, band woodsaws and hand tools, there was a substantial increase in market share but also competition or potential competition from imports. In the remaining area, there was a possibility of monopolistic abuse but the MMC believed that the potential threat of price rises in this area could be mitigated by the existence and potential for increased imports of H&T strip and finished products.

Recommendation

Not against public interest.

Chairman and Panel Members

Mr D G Richards, Mr L Britz, Sir Robert Clayton CBE, Mr P S G Flint, Mr G C S Mather, Mr D P Thomson

GRAND METROPOLITAN PLC/ WILLIAM HILL ORGANISATION LTD 23.08.89

Activity

A11.154 Off-course bookmaking services.

Market Share and Increment

As a result of the merger, Grand Metropolitan's share of the UK market by turnover for off-course bookmaking would increase from 10.8 per cent to 23.2 per cent. Together with Ladbrokes Racing Ltd and Coral Racing Ltd, the merged company would account for almost 60 per cent of the industry's turnover.

Assessment

The market was characterised by limited price competition and the fact that the main attraction of betting offices to their customers is one of location. The MMC concluded that, in view of the nature of the industry, the merger would not put Grand Met in a position to exert undue market power. They also concluded that although thee may have been grounds for unease about various characteristics of the industry the risks of abuse were not increased by the merger.

The MMC found that betting offices were little affected by price competition as their markets were highly local. Following the merger, certain localities would be served only by offices belonging to the merged company and this would have detrimental effects on competition. These localities were limited in number.

Recommendation

Against the public interest. Where the two betting offices within a given locality were under the common ownership of Grand Met following the merger, Grand Met should be required to divest one of those offices within six months.

Secretary of State's Decision

After the report was published Grand Met announced that they were selling the majority of their betting offices to Brent Walker, and the remainder to Ladbrokes. Brent Walker in turn proposed that the William Hill Group, a separate company under its control, should make the acquisition. Brent Walker, William Hill Group and Grand Met each gave undertakings in terms similar to those recommended by the MMC in relation to Grand Met and these were accepted by the Secretary of State. The acquisitions by William Hill Group and Ladbrokes were therefore not referred to the MMC.

Chairman and Panel Members

M S *Lipworth,* F E Bonner, K S Carmichael, J D Keir QC, H H Liesner, L A Mills

CENTURY NEWSPAPERS LTD/
THOMSON REGIONAL NEWSPAPERS LTD 27.04.89

Activity

Publication of regional newspapers.   A11.155

Market Share and Increment

TRN's share of the regional daily newspaper market in Northern Ireland would increase from 63 per cent to 81 per cent.

Assessment

The loss of approximately 80 jobs was insufficient grounds for an adverse finding on the public interest but the MMC considered that the merger would reduce competition for readers and advertising. The balance of expression of political opinion would also have been reduced through a reduction in diversity in the Northern Ireland press.

Recommendation

Against the public interest.

Secretary of State's Decision

Refused his consent to the transfer.

Chairman and Panel Members

Mr D G Richards, Mr J D Keir QC, Mr L A Mills, Mr S D Jenkins, Mr M Kersen

THE GENERAL ELECTRIC COMPANY PLC/ SIEMENS AG/THE PLESSEY COMPANY PLC 21.04.89

Activity

A11.156 Defence electronics, telecommunications, electronics components and traffic control equipment.

Market Share and Increment

GEC and Plessey accounted for 75 per cent of payments made by the MOD to major UK electronics companies.

Assessment

GEC and Siemens intended, through a jointly held company, to launch a bid for Plessey. They revised their proposals to place Plessey's radar and military communications, businesses and traffic control equipment business under the ownership and management of Siemens (although GEC would have participation rights, subject to regulatory approvals, in Siemens defence electronics business as expanded). Plessey's naval systems, avionics and cryptographic equipment businesses would be placed under the ownership and management of GEC.

GEC and Plessey were strong and sometimes sole competitors in many aspects of the defence electronics business in the UK where the Ministry of Defence was the only purchaser. The MMC had previously reported on a bid by GEC for Plessey in 1986 and concluded that the merger would be against the public interest primarily because of its adverse effect on competition in defence electronics as well as in the supply of telecommunications and traffic control equipment.

The MMC thought that the merger raised concerns similar to those expressed in their 1986 Report in relation to competition in defence radar, military communications and traffic control equipment. Additional competition concerns were expressed in relation to a large avionics defence project called JTIDS and, having regard to Siemens being a non-UK company, potential conflicts with national security requirements.

Recommendation

Against the public interest. GEC and Siemens were required to give undertakings that GEC would not acquire any interest in or influence or control over the management of Plessey's radar and military communications businesses and traffic control activities; that access to technology and licences for production (JTIDS equipment) be available on terms satisfactory to the MOD to competing companies designated by the MOD; that, regarding ownership of Plessey's defence, R&D and semiconductor businesses, arrangements were made in order to satisfy the Secretary of State's national security concerns.

Secretary of State's Decision

Undertakings accepted in accordance with MMC's recommendations.

Chairman and Panel Members

Mr M S Lipworth, Mr F E Bonner CBE, Mr P H Dean, Miss P K R Mann, Mr G C S Mather, Mr C A Unwin MBE

HILLSDOWN HOLDINGS PLC/ PITTARD GARNAR PLC 11.04.89

Activity

The purchase of raw lamb and sheep skins; and the removal in fellmongeries of wool from skins and the preservation of pelts by pickling.　　　A11.157

Market Share and Increment

Hillsdown's share of UK purchases of raw skins increased from 4 per cent to 13 per cent.
Hillsdown's share of supplies of salted skin in the UK increased from 6 per cent to 13 per cent.
Hillsdown's share of total salted skin purchases by fellmongers increased from 29 per cent to 51 per cent.
Hillsdown's share of supply by UK fellmongers of pickled pelts increased from 22 per cent to 42 per cent.

Assessment

Competition would be maintained after the merger by other UK operators and by imports and through the lack of barriers to entry. There was also a ready market overseas for UK exports of salted skins and pickled pelts. There was no evidence that PG's export performance would be affected adversely and Hillsdown had said that it would maintain PG's level of commitment to research.

Recommendation

Not against public interest.

Chairman and Panel Members

Mr D G Richards, Mr C C Baillieu, Mr A Ferry MBE, Mr J D Keir QC, Miss P K R Mann, Mr S McDowall CBE

STRONG & FISHER (HOLDINGS) PLC/ PITTARD GARNAR PLC 11.04.89

Activity

A11.158   The purchase of raw sheep and lamb skins; the salting of raw skins; the removal in the fellmongeries of wool from skins and the preservation of pelts by pickling; and the production of wool-off clothing leather by the tanning of pickled pelts.

Market Share and Increment

Strong & Fisher's share of total purchases of raw skins would increase from 25 per cent to 34 per cent.

Strong & Fisher's share of total purchases of salted skins by fellmongers would increase from 27 per cent to 49 per cent.

Strong & Fisher's share of purchases of pickled pelts by tanners would increase from 41 per cent to 64 per cent.

Assessment

Competitiveness in the UK market was maintained through domestic and foreign firms and a lack of barriers to entry.

In addition there was a ready market overseas for UK exports of salted skins and pickled pelts. The MMC were divided over: the effect of the merger on the competitiveness of UK clothing leather in overseas markets; the impact of research and development; S&F's proposed divestment of PG's bovine businesses; and Strong & Fisher's plans to reduce its gearing.

Recommendation

The MMC concluded by a majority of four to three (including the Chairman's casting vote) that the merger was not against the public interest.

Chairman and Panel Members

Mr D G Richards, Mr C C Baillieu, Mr A Ferry MBE, Mr J D Keir QC, Miss P K R Mann, Mr S McDowall CBE

ELDERS IXL LTD/SCOTTISH & NEWCASTLE BREWERIES PLC 21.03.89

Activity

A11.159   Supply of beer in the UK.

Market Share and Increment

Courage (a subsidiary of Elders) market share of beer consumed in the UK would increase from 9.4 per cent to 20.1 per cent.

The six largest UK brewers (of which Courage and S&N were two) supplied some 75 per cent of beer in the UK.

Assessment

The MMC found that S&N and Courage were major competitors in the supply of beer to the "free" trade. Loss of the independence of S&N would reduce competition and consumer choice. The public interest required that competition, particularly for the business of free public houses, should be maintained and enhanced.

S&N and Bass (another of the six largest brewers) supplied 80 per cent of the beer in Scotland and the merger might have reinforced the duopoly and increased the difficulty of entry into the Scottish market. It would also remove the possibility of Courage entering this market on its own. The creation of a large group, which together with Bass would supply over 40 per cent of the market, would result in reduced competition and increased difficulty of supply for other brewers and distributors. The MMC did not accept Elder's view that, given the wide range of ales and lagers that were required by the consumer in the UK, the existing UK brewers would be severely disadvantaged after 1992 when competing with continental lager brewers in supplying the UK market. Elder's policies might have resulted in the sale of certain of S&N's subsidiary companies which would have little effect on competition within the brewing industry, but would affect the spread of interest which attached to S&N's position as a large independent company directly managed in Scotland.

Recommendation

Against the public interest. Elders should be required to reduce its shareholding in S&N to 9.9 per cent within 12 months.

Secretary of State's Decision

The undertakings were given and accepted in accordance with the DGFT's advice.

Chairman and Panel Members

Mr R G Smethurst, Mr K S Carmichael CBE, Miss A M Head, Mr C A Unwin MBE, Mr S Wainwright CBE, Mr R Young

BADGERLINE HOLDINGS LTD/
MIDLAND RED WEST HOLDINGS LTD 08.03.89

Activity

Supply of bus services in and around Bristol.

A11.160

Market Share and Increment

Badgerline's share of registered bus miles in the specified area would increase from 40 per cent to 82 per cent.

Following deregulation, 35 per cent of Avon County Council payments for local bus services were made to Badgerline with 43 per cent made to City Line (the trading name of MRWH's Services in Bristol).

Assessment

The market was assessed in two parts; commercial services and local authority supported services (contract services). There would be no loss of competition in commercial services after the merger. The County of Avon was concerned that the reduction in competition for its contracts would drive up prices leading eventually to some curtailment of contract services. This concern was shared by the MMC which identified serious detriments to competition for Avon's contract services as a result of the merger.

Recommendation

Against the public interest. Divestment was seen as unnecessarily drastic, and instead the MMC recommended that the DGFT should seek undertakings from Badgerline regarding its future behaviour in regard to Avon's contract services. If these were not obtained, the merger should not be allowed to proceed and Badgerline should be required to divest itself of MRWH in part by selling City Line to a third party or to dispose of MRWH as a whole to a third party.

Secretary of State's Decision

Undertakings were given and accepted in accordance with the MMC's recommendation.

Chairman and Panel Members

Professor S C Littlechild, Mr L Britz, Mr D G Goyder, Mr J D Keir QC, Mr N L Salmon, Mr D P Thomson

TR BECKETT LTD/EMAP PLC 22.02.89

Activity

A11.161   The printing and publishing of local newspapers in Sussex.

Market Share and Increment

Beckett enjoyed 12 per cent and EMAP enjoyed 23 per cent of the circulation of all weekly newspapers and daily newspapers in Sussex (30 per cent and 32 per cent of paid-for weeklies).

Beckett enjoyed 43 per cent and EMAP enjoyed 27 per cent of the circulation of all weekly and daily newspapers in Eastbourne and its surrounding district (83 per cent and 17 per cent of paid-for weeklies).

Beckett enjoyed 7 per cent and EMAP enjoyed 39 per cent of the circulation of all weekly and daily newspapers in Seaford and its surrounding district (43 per cent and 57 per cent of paid-for weeklies).

Assessment

The MMC were not in agreement about the increased concentration of local newspaper groups at the national level. They were not concerned about the increased concentration of paid-for weeklies in Sussex as a whole, but were concerned about the high concentrations of paid-for weeklies in Eastbourne and Seaford, and concluded that competition would be reduced in those areas.

Recommendation

Against the public interest. The acquisition of shares should be allowed to proceed on condition that any further acquisition of shares that gave EMAP control should be subject to consent by the Secretary of State. In such circumstances the Secretary of State should consider whether consent should be conditional on EMAP divesting its titles in Eastbourne and Seaford so that its share of circulation of paid-for weeklies in each area did not exceed 60 per cent.

Secretary of State's Decision

Consent to the acquisition given subject to the conditions recommended by the MMC.

Chairman and Panel Members

Mr D G Richards, Miss P K R Mann, D Churchill, J Clement Jones, R Halstead

MINORCO/CONSOLIDATED GOLD FIELDS PLC 02.02.89

Activity

High value minerals and metals.   A11.162

Market Share and Increment

Anglo American's (including Minorco) share of total western world gold production would increase from 20.2 per cent to 32.2 per cent. An Anglo-American group company accounted for almost 50 per cent of western world mine production of platinum. Gold Fields at the time of the merger did not produce platinum but had an involvement with the new Northam mine. Renison (a Gold Fields company) had 24.4 per cent of world production of chlorinatable titanium feedstocks. Renison also had 41.3 per cent of the western world production of zircon and in excess of 40 per cent of western world production of monazite. Gold Field's wholly-owned subsidary ARC had 18 per cent of the supply of aggregates in the UK, 42 per cent of the supply of concrete pipes and 26 per cent of the supply of concrete bricks.

Assessment

There was no reason why Minorco should, as had been suggested to the MMC, perform less efficiently that any other company in its position (it was part of the Anglo-American group and had South African associations). The MMC considered the effects of the proposed merger on competition in the world markets for a number of high value minerals and metals and aggregates concluded that the merger would not operate against the UK public interest by reason of any effects on the markets for gold or platinum. The acquisition by Minorco of Gold Field's interests in Renison would not significantly increase collusion in the markets for titanium, zircon or rare earths given the availability of other reserves of these minerals. Minorco would not be any more likely than Gold Fields to encourage or condone anti-competitive practices in the UK market for aggregates and related products.

Recommendation

Not against the public interest.

Chairman and Panel Members

Mr D G Richards, Professor M E Beesley CBE, Mr F E Bonner CBE, Sir Robert Clayton CBE, Mr B C Owens, Mr N C Salmon

THOMSON TRAVEL GROUP/ HORIZON TRAVEL LTD 11.01.89

Activity

A11.163 The supply of foreign air inclusive tours (AITs), the operation of charter airlines based in the UK and the operation of chains of retail travel agents.

Market Share and Increment

Thomson's share of the AIT holiday market would increase from 30 per cent to approximately 38 per cent.

Assessment

The MMC considered the effect of the merger on foreign AITs, on leisure travel by air including charter flights, and on retail travel agents. The MMC also considered the implications of vertical integration between these sectors. The markets were found to be highly competitive, characterised by strong if variable growth and continued entry by new firms. The merger would therefore not reduce competition.

Recommendation

Not against the public interest.

Chairman and Panel Members

Mr D G Richards, Professor M E Beesley CBE, Sir Robert Clayton CBE, Mr M R Hoffman, Mr C A Unwin MBE, Mr R Young

THE GOVERNMENT OF KUWAIT/
THE BRITISH PETROLEUM COMPANY PLC 04.10.88

Activity

The oil industry (upstream activities of exploration and production of crude oil and downstream activities of refining, delivering and marketing of petroleum products to final consumers).　　A11.164

Market Share and Increment

Not applicable.

Assessment

The Government of Kuwait acquired some 21.6 per cent of BP's ordinary share capital. BP's share capital was widely held and Kuwait's holding dwarfed all others. The holdings gave Kuwait the ability materially to influence the policy of BP. BP's ability to operate independently and free from external government influence was a matter of public interest. Unlike other shareholders, Kuwait was a sovereign state which could be expected to use its influence to support its own national interests. This would be detrimental to both BP's and to the UK's public interest.

Recommendation

Against the public interest. Kuwait should be required to reduce its shareholding to the level of 9.9 per cent of BP's issued share capital over a period of 12 months. At this level the capacity to exercise material influence would be removed.

Secretary of State's Decision

The Secretary of State accepted the MMC's conclusions, and undertakings from the Kuwait Investment Office, on behalf of the Government of Kuwait, that Kuwait would reduce its shareholding to 9.9 per cent were later given and accepted.

Chairman and Panel Members

Mr M S *Lipworth*, Mr F E Bonner CBE, Mr A Ferry MBE, Mr J D Keir QC, Mr S McDowall CBE, Mr S Wainwright CBE

PARRETT & NEVES LTD/EMAP PLC 17.08.88

Activity

The production and distribution of local newspapers in East Kent.　　A11.165

Market Share and Increment

EMAP's share of the average circulation of all newspapers in the reference area would increase from 14.2 per cent to 20.8 per cent. EMAP's share of circulation in Kent and Sussex combined would increase from 20.7 per cent to 23.5 per cent.

Assessment

The transfer would add to concentration in East-Kent but there was no overlap between EMAP'S existing titles and those it was to acquire. There was also competition between newspapers and other media, and opportunities for small companies to grow. There was no reason to believe that EMAP would compete unfairly in East Kent or elsewhere. Editorial freedom and employment were also secure and this outweighed any possible disadvantages that might arise from the small increase in concentration which was involved.

Recommendation

Not against the public interest.

Chairman and Panel Members

D G *Richards*, P K R Mann, D Churchill, J Clement Jones, R Halstead

MITEK INDUSTRIES INC/ GANG-NAIL SYSTEMS INC 20.07.88

Activity

A11.166   The supply of punched metal connector plates and related machinery in the UK.

Market Share and Increment

Hydro-Air (a subsidiary of Mitek) and Gang-Nail Systems Ltd (a subsidiary of Gang-Nail Systems Inc.) together accounted for some 76 per cent of sales of punched metal connector plates and related machinery in the UK.

Assessment

The MMC concluded that prior to the merger, competition between Hydro-Air and Gang-Nail, the market leaders, was strong. Competition from the remaining two competitors could not be as effective and new entry was unlikely to be on a sufficient scale to compensate for the loss of competition. The market was small and specialised and therefore the choice of available fabrication systems, the incentive to maintain the development of products and services, the price and standards of service all depended critically on healthy and active competition.

Recommendation

Against the public interest. Mitek should divest itself of Gang-Nail Systems Ltd.

Secretary of State's Decision

Gang-Nail Systems Ltd was sold to Eleco Holdings plc (which had no previous involvement in the reference market) and the merger was allowed to proceed.

Chairman and Panel Members

Mr H H Hunt, Mr K S Carmichael CBE, Mr B C Owens, Mr N L Salmon, Mr C A Unwin MBE, Professor G Whittington

WARNER COMMUNICATIONS INC/ENTERPRISES BELONGING TO CHAPPELL & CO. INC 28.01.88

Activity

The publication and recording of music in the UK.   A11.167

Market Share and Increment

Warner's share of music publishing turnover in Great Britain (including the Irish Republic) would increase from 9.8 per cent to 20.2 per cent.

Assessment

The MMC concluded that while the possibility remained of Warner/Chappell misusing such market power as they would possess after the merger, the evidence given fell short of the expectation that they would behave in such a way. There was also considered to be legal remedies available, both through the courts and through action taken by competition authorities, if the situation was to change in the future.

Recommendation

Not against the public interest.

Chairman and Panel Members

Mr D G Richards, Mr F E Bonner CBE, Mr M B Bunting, Mr D G Goyder, Mr J D Keir QC, Mr C A Unwin MBE

BOOK CLUB ASSOCIATES/LEISURE CIRCLE 22.08.88

Activity

The sale of books in the UK to the public through book clubs.   A11.168

Market Share and Increment

Between them, BCA and Leisure Circle accounted for about 70 per cent of total book club sales and over 70 per cent of book club membership.

Assessment

The MMC concluded that book clubs were essentially a separate market operating in parallel with the rest of the book market. Benefits for the public interest in terms of increased efficiency were not enough to outweigh the detriments caused by: the elimination of Leisure Circle as an effective competitor of BCA; the removal of

Leisure Circle as a separate and effective purchasing centre; and the reinforcement of a high level of exclusive access to titles for long periods to the detriment of existing competitors and the discouragement of new entry into the market.

Recommendation

Against the public interest. The MMC concluded that it was not open to them to recommend that Bertelsmann AG (which had a major interest in BCA) should be required to dispose of Leisure Circle nor that it would be appropriate to suggest to Bertelsmann AG that it should voluntarily dispose of Leisure Circle. The MMC did recommend, however, a number of measures to reduce exclusivity of access to book clubs to certain titles under the Concordat, the agreement which sets out the conditions under which they compare with each other for books. These measures were: an increase in the minimum number of copies required to be ordered before exclusivity might be enjoyed; a reduction in the period of time during which exclusivity may be maintained; and the removal of a book club's ability to renew exclusivity for every new edition however modest the revisions. The MMC also recommended that the Concordat should have an improved disputes procedure. If the DGFT could not obtain a satisfactory modification of the Concordat the merger should not be permitted to proceed.

Secretary of State's Decision

The proposed acquisition should not be allowed to proceed as allowing it to proceed only after the satisfactory conclusion of negotiations on the Concordat could led to an unjustifiably long period of uncertainty for the companies involved. Undertakings were subsequently given and accepted from W H Smith Group plc that it would not, and would procure that its subsidiaries would not, carry out any agreement which would result in Bertelsmann, or any subsidiary or associate of it, acquiring any interest of W H Smith in BCA.

Chairman and Panel Members

Mr R G Smethurst, Mr C C Baillieu, Miss A M Head, Miss P K R Mann, Mr N C Salmon, Mr R Young

MAI PLC/LONDON AND CONTINENTAL ADVERTISING HOLDINGS PLC 25.11.87

Activity

A11.169   Supply in the UK of roadside posters.

Market Share and Increment

MAI's share of 48 sheet poster sites in London had increased from 8 per cent to 32 per cent (6 per cent to 43 per cent share in the Southern region).

Assessment

The 4 and 48-sheet sectors should be regarded as substantially different and distinct sectors of the roadside poster market. The MMC concentrated on the 48 sheet sector as the preponderant part of MAI's business would be in that sector. MAI held twice as many 48-sheet panels as its only other competitor of any consequence and therefore advertisers would have to turn to MAI to meet wholly or partly their needs for 48 sheets. MAI'S dominance in the 48-sheet sector of the market would enable it to: increase prices to a greater extent that it would be able to do in a more competitive situation; reduce freedom of choice for agencies and advertisers on 48-sheet panels; and restrict new entry into the 48-sheet sector.

Recommendation

The MMC recommended that MAI reduce to 25 per cent its share of the total number of 48-sheet panels in each of the London, Southern, North-West and South-West television regions; MAI should also be required to reduce its shares of 48-sheet panels in each of the other regions to the percentages which applied before the merger.

Secretary of State's Decision

The undertakings were given and accepted in accordance with the MMC's recommendations.

Chairman and Panel Members

Mr H H Hunt, Mr C C Baillieu, Mr L Britz, Sir Robert Clayton MBE, Mr P S G Flint, Mr S Wainwright CBE

BRITISH AIRWAYS PLC/
BRITISH CALEDONIAN GROUP PLC 01.11.87

Activity

The supply of airline passenger services.   A11.170

Market Share and Increment

BA's share of passenger capacity of UK airlines (all services) would increase from 43.4 per cent to 50.7 per cent. The three closest competitors were Britannia with 12.1 per cent, Dan-Air with 11.1 per cent and Monarch with 4.4 per cent.

BA's share of annual slots held by airlines at Gatwick would increase from 10.9 per cent to 30.6 per cent.

Assessment

The MMC concluded that removal of competition between BA and BCAL would: leave little or no competition on a number of routes; leave the merged airline with a powerful market position with opportunities of predatory or anti-competitive behaviour; threaten the position of charter operators, at Gatwick partly, through its large number of Gatwick slots, and partly because it could by diverting scheduled services from Heathrow to Gatwick; reduce the already limited scope for expansion at Gatwick of charter operations; and give the merged airline the potential to withhold maintenance, repairs and training facilities at present provided to competing airlines by BCAL. However, there were potentially beneficial results: BA could compete better in the international arena; and rationalisation and synergy effects were expected to save millions of pounds annually.

Recommendation

BA presented to the OFT both before and during the MMC's investigation a number of conditional undertakings relating to slots at Gatwick, licensing and other competition issues. The MMC subsequently concluded that the merger did not operate against the public interest.

Chairman and Panel Members

Sir Godfray Le Quense QC, Mr M B Bunting, Mr D G Goyder, Mr S McDowall CBE, Mr L A Mills, Mr D P Thomson

CO-OPERATIVE WHOLESALE SOCIETY LIMITED/ HOUSE OF FRASER PLC 21.10.87

Activity

A11.171   The supply of funeral undertaking services in Scotland.

Market Share and Increment

The Co-op's share of funerals carried out in Scotland increased from 33 per cent to 44 per cent.

The Co-op's share of supply of coffins in Scotland increased from 43 per cent to 73 per cent.

Assessment

The MMC found that non-price competition dominated the market for the reference services. The merger reduced choice in varying degrees as the market was subdivided locally. The MMC concluded, however, that it was important that there should be adequate choice as regards the provision of funeral services wherever possible. Such choice should be available at the local level. The merger would restrict this choice. There was also concern from third parties over the continued supply of quality coffins. The MMC concluded that the effects on the supply of coffins would not operate against the public interest and *inter alia*, coffin manufacturers in England had indicated that they were able to supply coffins to Scotland at competitive prices.

Recommendation

Against the public interest. CWS should be required to divest itself of particular businesses in those sub-markets most affected by the merger. The sale of the businesses should be to persons other than the retail societies.

Secretary of State's Decision

Accepted the MMC's recommendations. Undertakings on terms similar to those recommended by the MMC were subsequently given and accepted by the Secretary of State.

Chairman and Panel Members

Sir Godfray Le Quense QC, Mr M B Bunting, Mr P H Dean, Mr A Ferry MBE, Miss A M Head, Mr N L Salmon

SWEDISH MATCH AB/ENTERPRISES BELONGING TO ALLEGHENY INTERNATIONAL INC 01.10.87

Activity

The manufacture of matches and distribution of lighters in the UK.   A11.172

Market Share and Increment

The parties enjoyed combined market shares of 82 per cent of the production of matches, 65 per cent of the production of matches and disposable lighters, and 31 per cent of the production of all lights.

The parties enjoyed combined market shares in the production and distribution of matches of 82 per cent, in the production and distribution of matches and disposable lighters of 73 per cent and in the production and distribution of all lights of 41 per cent.

Assessment

The MMC accepted that the broad market definition included all lights obtained from matches, disposable and non-disposable cigarette lighters and automatic ignition devices on, for example, domestic gas appliances. However, the MMC focused on the two narrower markets of matches and disposable lighters and the interaction between them. The MMC concluded that substantially greater concentration in an already concentrated market did not operate against the public interest. The reason for this included: the fact that market decline restricted price increases; the purchasing power of the largest buyers of matches; Swedish Match's assurances that it would continue to make "small drop" deliveries; the fact that Swedish Match's plans offered a better prospect for continuing employment. In addition, the potential for exports of matches from the UK might be improved were the merger to go ahead.

Recommendation

Not against the public interest.

Chairman and Panel Members

Mr D G Richards, Miss A M Head, Mr M S Lipworth, Miss P K R Mann, Mr C A Unwin MBE

COURIER PRESS (HOLDINGS) LTD/EMAP PLC 16.05.87

Activity

A11.173   The publication of newspapers.

Market Share and Increment

EMAP's share of the circulation of weekly paid-for newspapers in two principal regions of the UK, the Midlands and East Anglia, would increase from 24.5 per cent to 31 per cent, making it the leading supplier.

EMAP's share of the circulation of free newspapers in the two regions would increase from approximately 10 per cent to 13 per cent, again making it the leading supplier.

The merged group would be the second or third largest owner of weekly or bi-weekly paid-for newspapers in the UK by circulation. However, it would publish around 5 per cent of the weekly paid-for newspapers in the UK and the increase in market share from EMAP's present 3.4 per cent would be only 1.6 per cent. The combined group would be the 12th largest by circulation and the 10th largest by titles owned in relation to free newspapers in the UK.

Assessment

Courier's shareholders had decided to realise a proportion of their shareholdings and the MMC accepted that the Board of Courier had little alternative but to seek a buyer for the company. The MMC concluded that the merger would not be likely to result in adverse effects on employment and would be likely to provide opportunities for improving the efficiency of the combined group. The MMC were satisfied that no direct reduction in competition between paid-for or free newspapers would result and that the editors would continue to have a high degree of independence. In addition, the merger would have little effect on the concentration of ownership of regional daily newspapers. As EMAP had shown that it could run local newspapers successfully and profitably and the company had an enthusiastic and effective management, the MMC considered that in the long term the benefits of allowing EMAP to apply its management would also help to maintain Courier's newspapers. Accordingly, no detriment to the public interest would be likely to arise from the increased concentration of ownership of local papers.

Recommendation

Not against the public interest.

Chairman and Panel Members

Mr D G Richards, Mr C C Baillieu, Mr M B Bunting, Miss P Mann, Mr D G Richards, Mr D Churchill, Mr M Kersen

TRUSTHOUSE FORTE PLC/ENTERPRISES
BELONGING TO HANSON TRUST PLC 04.03.87

Activity

The operation of hotels, motorway service areas and roadside catering.   A11.174

Market Share and Increment

THF's share of catering establishments on the A45 increased from 3.9 per cent to 6.8 per cent.
THF's share of catering establishments on the A1 increased from 13.0 per cent to 19.5 per cent.

Assessment

The 30 Anchor Hotels and 85 Imperial Inns (consisting of various types of restaurant) which were acquired were not in general located close to existing THF enterprises.
The MMC found that whilst THF was the largest hotelier in the country, it did not dominate the market. After the merger it controlled some 230 hotels out of 30,000 throughout the UK. The Imperial Inns tended to occupy a sector of the market in which THF was not prominent and the acquisition of Anchor Hotels would not result in THF gaining a monopoly.
With the acquisition of Welcome Break, THF operated 15 of the then 47 motorway service areas, the next largest operator having 14 sites. The MMC noted the improved standards on motorways in respect of catering quality and petrol prices and considered that it was doubtful that any operator could raise prices or relax standards without suffering reduced custom.
THF's acquisition of the Happy Eater restaurants strengthened its position in this type of roadside catering which was enhanced by strongly branded images. Happy Eater and THF's Little Chef would be in a pre-eminent position, but there were still sites for new enterprises to develop. There were a number of other operators apparently intending to enter the market for roadside catering. Entry into the market was possible. Competition from other types of roadside catering was strong.

Recommendation

Not against the public interest.

Chairman and Panel Members

Sir Godfray Le Quesne QC, Mr L Britz, Mr K S Carmichael CBE, Miss P K R Mann, Mr B C Owens, Professor R Rees

TATE & LYLE PLC/FERRUZZI FINANZIARIA SPA/
S&W BERISFORD PLC 25.02.87

Activity

The refining and distribution of sugar in the UK.   A11.175

Market Share and Increment

Ferruzzi's share of European Community sugar production would increase from 8.4 per cent to 17.2 per cent.

Tate and Lyle's share of the supply of sugar in the UK by value would increase from 41.8 per cent to 94 per cent.

Assessment

The Report covered three references: Tate & Lyle's bid for the whole of Berisford or its subsidiary British Sugar PLC; a first Ferruzzi reference to decide whether Ferruzzi's 23.7 per cent holding of shares in Berisford had created a merger situation, and a second Ferruzzi reference relating to further possible merger arrangements with Berisford which would result in the control of British Sugar by Ferruzzi.

Tate & Lyle's bid, whilst strengthening the UK industry in the face of EC restrictions and foreign competition, created too great a concentration in the refining and distribution of sugar in the UK. It would result in a single company controlling the refining, packing, marketing and distribution of about 95 per cent of the supply of sugar and sugar products in Great Britain. Accordingly, the MMC did not accept T&L's view that the merger would not involve a material reduction in competition. The second Ferruzzi reference relating to the sale to Ferruzzi of 70 per cent of the issued share capital of British Sugar was likely to lead to three adverse effects: restriction of the ability of merchants and major users to import sugar from the rest of the Community resulting in higher sugar prices; Ferruzzi's increased influence in Community institutions (which might be used to the detriment of the UK); and detriment to the maintenance of independent cane refining in the UK. In relation to the other Ferruzzi reference of Ferruzzi's existing shareholding in Berisford, the MMC concluded that the existing shareholding operated against the public interest as although Ferruzzi did not have the ability to control Berisford's policy its shareholding would deter other Community suppliers from exporting to the UK and would give Ferruzzi additional influence in the Community.

Recommendation

Tate & Lyle reference: against the public interest. No remedies applicable, but recommendations made for Government action.

The first Ferruzi reference: against the public interest. Ferruzzi should be required during a period not exceeding two years to reduce its holdings of Berisford's ordinary shares to no more than 15 per cent of Berisford's issued ordinary share capital and Ferruzzi's voting rights should be restricted to this level until the divestment.

The second Ferruzzi reference: against the public interest.

Secretary of State's Decision

The Tate & Lyle reference: undertakings were given and accepted not to acquire more than 39 per cent of the share capital of Berisford or any part of the share capital of British Sugar, or to exercise voting rights attached to more than 15 per cent of the shares in Berisford.

The Ferruzzi references: undertakings were given and accepted that Ferruzzi should not acquire more than 15 per cent of the share capital of Berisford or British Sugar or to acquire more than 25 per cent of the assets of British Sugar. The undertakings also prevent the appointment by Ferruzzi of any directors of Berisford and the appointment of directors of British Sugar to circumstances in which Berisford holds more than 50 per cent of British Sugar and controls its Board.

Chairman and Panel Members

Mr H H Hunt, Mr J G Ackers, Mr K S Carmichael CBE, Mr P H Dean, Professor S C Littlechild, Mr C A Unwin MBE

THE PENINSULAR AND ORIENTAL STEAM NAVIGATION COMPANY/EUROPEAN FERRIES GROUP PLC 03.12.86

Activity

Ferry services.   A11.176

Market Share and Increment

P&O's share of (the total market) of Northern Ireland to Great Britain freight ferry services increased from 26 per cent to 50 per cent. Sealink enjoyed a 32 per cent market share.

P&O's share of freight ferry services to the Netherlands increased from 23 per cent to 44 per cent. Its share of freight ferry services to Belgium increased from 7 per cent to 66 per cent; and its share of freight services to France (short sea) increased from 0 per cent to 43 per cent. P&O's overall share of freight services on these routes increased from 10 per cent to 52 per cent.

Assessment

P&O acquired a majority interest in European Finance Holdings Ltd which held 20.8 per cent of the shares and 16.1 per cent of the voting rights of European Ferries. In addition, the Chairman of P&O obtained a non-executive seat on European Ferries' main Board and one of P&O's executives a seat on the Board of EF International, a US subsidiary. The MMC concluded that a merger situation had been created by the ability of P&O to exercise material influence over the policy of European Ferries. The inquiry focused on the provision of ferry services across the North Sea and to and from Northern Ireland and in the provision of port facilities (being the main areas affecting the public interest where P&O's activities overlapped with those of European Ferries). The MMC concluded that the scope for the two companies to restrict or distort competition in respect of the provision of these services was limited, given, *inter alia*, the number of other competitors and low barriers to entry.

Recommendation

Not against the public interest.

Chairman and Panel Members

Sir Godfray Le Quesne QC, Mr M B Bunting, Mr A Ferry MBE, Miss A M Head, Mr M S Lipworth, Professor S C Littlechild

NORTON OPAX PLC/MCCORQUODALE PLC 24.09.86

Activity

A11.177   The supply of cheques and lottery tickets and related products.

Market Share and Increment

Norton's share of the supply of personalised cheques in the UK, by volume, (including in-house supply) would increase from 13 per cent to 43 per cent.

Norton's share of instant lottery ticket sales, by value, in the UK would increase from 31 per cent to 45 per cent.

Assessment

The MMC considered the possible effects of the merger on the markets for the printing of personalised cheques, instant lottery tickets and promotional games. The market for personalised cheques was characterised by the strong countervailing power of the banks. This would maintain a satisfactory level of competition following the merger. In the smaller market of lotteries, the merger would result in some limitation of choice, but the MMC found that entry was relatively easy. In the market for promotional games the power of the customers to dictate the design, and influence the price of tickets and the future of the market were important factors which would maintain competition.

Recommendation

Not against the public interest.

Chairman and Panel Members

Mr R G Smethurst, Mr L Britz, Mr G D Gwilt, Mr L Kelly, Miss P K R Mann, Sir Ronald Swayne MC.

ELDERS IXL LTD/ALLIED-LYONS PLC 03.09.86

Activity

A11.178   The supply of food and drink.

Market Share and Increment

Allied enjoyed approximately 14 per cent market share by volume of the supply of beer (ale and lager) in the UK.

Allied enjoyed the following market shares in the supply of wines and spirits in the UK, (although retail off-and-on licence outlets): light British wine—65 per cent (by volume); light wine—11 per cent (by volume); port—40 per cent (by volume); brandy—24 per cent (by value); Spanish Sherry—30 per cent (by volume) and dark rum—33 per cent (by value).

Allied had the following market shares in the supply of food (by volume): 19 per cent of tea, 18 per cent of instant coffee, and 24 per cent of ground coffee.

Assessment

The MMC considered the effects of the merger on the future of the Beer and Wines and Spirits divisions of Allied, together with the effects on the tied estate, employment and pensions, but decided that the merger would not in any of those respects operate against the public interest. Elders did not compete with Allied in the UK in either the food and drink industry or in the ownership of tied houses and off-licence outlets. Therefore the MMC concentrated on the financial arrangements proposed by Elders for the merger and noted that immediately after the merger the capital gearing of the merged group would be considerably higher, and its interest cover considerably lower, than is normal in the UK. However, because of the particular circumstances of the merger the MMC concluded that the proposals did not affect the future viability of the merged group in a way which would be against the public interest. There was a concern over reciprocity and the danger of a precedent being created for highly leveraged bids. The MMC considered it unlikely that any imbalance between Australian and British law would operate against the public interest. The Commission suggested that the question of highly leveraged bids be examined. No general pronouncement was made on the basis of this particular bid.

Recommendation

Not against the public interest.

Chairman and Panel Members

Sir Godfray Le Quesne QC, Sir Robert Clayton CBE, Mr D G Goyder, Mr M S Lipworth, Mr S McDowall CBE, Mr D P Thomson

THE GENERAL ELECTRIC COMPANY PLC/ THE PLESSEY COMPANY PLC 06.08.86

Activity

The supply of telecommunications equipment and defence electronic systems.   A11.179

Market Share and Increment

After the merger, the group would supply between 25 per cent and 30 per cent by value of the annual UK output of electronic capital equipment in 11 types of electronic components.

GEC's share of the supply of all public switching equipment in the UK would increase by 40 per cent to 80 per cent, by value, and its share of the supply of System × (the digital public switching system) would increase to 100 per cent.

GEC's share of the supply of multiplex transmission equipment in the UK would increase by 14 per cent to 75 per cent, by value.

GEC's share of the supply of private exchange (PABX) equipment in the UK would increase by 27 per cent to 59 per cent, by number of extension lines delivered.

In 1984/85 payments to GEC and Plessey amounted to £1.2 billion or 73 per cent of MOD direct expenditure with major electronic companies for defence electronic equipment. The next largest electronics supplier, Ferranti, received only one-sixth of that amount.

Assessment

Whilst recognising that the rationalisation of GEC's and Plessey's System × business might be beneficial and that the merged group might produce long term benefits to the UK, the MMC concluded, *inter alia*, that the merger would result in a reduction of competition to end users in the supply of PABXs and in the supply of transmission equipment. There would also be more serious adverse effects due to the loss of competition in the supply of defence electronic equipment. This could be expected to increase costs to MOD and reduce technical innovative choice.

Recommendation

Against the public interest.

Secretary of State's Decision

Accepted undertakings from GEC that it would not without the Secretary of State's consent acquire more than 15 per cent of the equity share capital of Plessey or any of its subsidiaries and would not enter without the Secretary of State's consent into any arrangement which would constitute a merger situation with Plessey or any of its subsidiaries or which would result in a substantial transfer of activities from Plessey.

Chairman and Panel Members

Sir Godfray Le Quesne QC, Mr C C Baillieu, Mr P S G Flint, Mr L A Mills, Mr B C Owens, Professor R Rees

BET PUBLIC LIMITED COMPANY/SGB GROUP PLC 16.05.86

Activity

A11.180   The supply of various types of equipment to provide access in a variety of ways to working areas for construction or maintenance—the "access" industry.

Market Share and Increment

BET's share of the UK access industry would increase from 10.2 per cent to 22.5 per cent by value.

Assessment

The MMC found no significant adverse effects to the various sectors of the access market, nor upon R&D and product development, employment, safety and training, or imports. The merger could produce some gains in efficiency which, it achieved, could sharpen competition in the industry.

Recommendation

Not against the public interest.

Chairman and Panel Members

Mr D G Richards, Mr M B Bunting, Mr P S G Flint, Professor S C Littlechild, Sir Ronald Swayne MC, Mr C A Unwin MBE

BRITISH TELECOMMUNICATIONS PLC/ MITEL CORPORATION 27.01.86

Activity

The supply of private exchange equipment (PABXs) in the UK.   A11.181

Market Share and Increment

The MMC found that the BT/Mitel group would enjoy a market share (by number of extensions delivered) of: 18 per cent of the manufacturers' market for PABXs in the UK; approximately 50 per cent of the total supply of PABXs to independent distributors; and 75 per cent of the supply to independent distributors of medium-sized PABXs.

Assessment

The MMC found that there would be likely to be adverse effects on competition between manufacturers of telecommunications equipment due, *inter alia*, to preference being given by BT to Mitel products. This would increase prices and reduce the choice of equipment for customers. The merger would also result in adverse effects on competition between distributors due to the vertical integration of BT and Mitel. They would be likely to reduce the growth of competition in the market which would have an adverse effect on telecommunications users.

Recommendation

Against the public interest. BT should undertake: not to acquire from Mitel any telecommunications apparatus for use in the UK; nor to supply telecommunications apparatus acquired from Mitel to end-users in the UK. Other undertakings relating to cross-subsidies, provision of spares, exclusive supply agreements and independence of the reference companies' marketing, sales, supply and maintenance operations were required.

Secretary of State's Decision

The merger could proceed, subject to conditions similar to those proposed by the MMC. However, competition in the UK market for telecommunications equipment would be sufficiently protected by imposing a ceiling on Mitel's marketing to and through BT rather than imposing a complete prohibition on such marketing. Undertakings to this effect were subsequently given to BT and accepted by the Secretary of State. BT was later released from certain of the undertakings and from the remainder following its sale of its shareholding in Mitel.

Chairman and Panel Members

Sir Godfray Le Quesne QC, Mr H L G Gibson OBE, Mr S McDowall CBE, Mr N L Salmon, Mr D P Thomson

PRICE CORRELATIONS

A12.001   The correlation coefficient, ρ, between two variables X and Y is defined as:

$$\rho = \frac{\sum(X_t - \bar{X})(Y_t - \bar{Y})}{\sqrt{\sum(X_t - \bar{X})^2}\sqrt{\sum(Y_t - \bar{Y})^2}} = \frac{\sigma_{XY}}{\sigma_X \sigma_Y}$$

Where σ_X and σ_Y are the standard deviations of series X and Y respectively, and σ_{XY} is the covariance of the two series. X_t and Y_t respectively denote the values of X and Y at time t. $\bar{X}$ and $\bar{Y}$ denote the mean values of X and Y respectively.

This would not typically be calculated manually, and correlation coefficients are normally calculated by inputting the pricing data into standard spreadsheet programmes.

The correlation coefficient is a measure of the linear relationship between X and Y. will be equal to +1 or −1 if and only if:

Y = aX + b, for some constants a and b with a ≠0.[1]

If, for example, pricing correlations were to be calculated with regard to the level of prices for two different goods then a pricing correlation of +1 could be observed if the price of one good were at all times to be equal to, say, 80% of the price of another good plus, say, £5. (In the above equation, this would mean that a = 0.8 and b = £5.) The point that should be noted is that if this pricing data were to be shown graphically, the two pricing trends would not be parallel to each other in the sense that a £1 increase in the price of one good would not lead to a £1 increase in the other (but only 80p) and that the percentage price difference between the two goods would also change.

Pricing correlations can be calculated in many different forms. For example, instead of being calculated with regard to the level of prices, logarithms of prices may be used, and price correlations can be calculated on the basis of changes in prices or the logarithm of price changes.

Another issue is whether price correlations are calculated using daily, weekly, monthly or even annual data. This is an issue because in many markets prices do not adjust instantaneously but after a lag (for example, due to the timing of contract negotiations or simply because it takes some time for customers to be aware of price changes), and accordingly Bishop and Walker recommend choosing the frequency of the price data used to reflect most closely the competitive process.[2]

---

[1] Correlation coefficients are described in many statistics textbooks. See, for example, Devore, *Probability and Statistics for Engineering and the Sciences* (3rd ed., Brooks/Cole Publishing Company, 1991), at pp.204–205.
[2] See Bishop and Walker, *The Economics of EC Competition Law: Concepts, Application and Measurement* (2nd ed., Sweet & Maxwell, London, 2002) at para.11.10 and p.383 of Ch.11.

It is noteworthy that the OFT research paper on quantitative techniques in competition analysis indicates that time series of price data must have at least 20 observations in order to calculate a meaningful correlation coefficient. It states that: "Computing correlation coefficients with less than 15 observations is meaningless from a statistical point."[3]

---

[3] See para.5.4 and n.92 of Ch.5 of *Quantitative techniques in competition analysis*, October 1999, prepared for the OFT by LECG, OFT Research Paper 17, OFT 266.

THE ASSESSMENT OF LOCAL COMPETITION IN THE
BATTLE FOR SAFEWAY (2003)

Introduction

A13.001   This Appendix describes the approach taken by the OFT[1] and the Competition Commission[2] in assessing local competition between large supermarkets in the context of the various competing bids for Safeway, and in particular their use of so-called "isochrones".

On January 9, 2003, Morrisons announced that it had agreed an offer to acquire the whole of Safeway. During the next two weeks, Tesco, Sainsbury and Wal-Mart-Asda announced that they were considering bids. Finally, Trackdean Investments (an investment vehicle owned by Philip Green) announced an interest in acquiring Safeway. Since Philip Green did not operate any grocery retailing outlets in the UK, Trackdean Investments' proposed bid for Safeway did not raise competition concerns, and clearance was granted by the Secretary of State on the advice of the OFT.[3] The remaining bids were all referred to the Competition Commission.

The Table below sets out the market shares of Safeway and each of the potential bidders of grocery sales within Great Britain from larger stores (above 1400m2)[4]:

---

[1] Proposed acquisition by J Sainsbury plc, Tesco plc, Wm Morrison Supermarkets PLC and Asda Stores Ltd: Director General's advice of March 13, 2003.

[2] *Safeway plc and Asda Group Ltd (owned by Wal-Mart Stores Inc); Wm Morrison Supermarkets PLC; J Sainsbury plc and Tesco plc*, Cm. 5950, (September 2003). This is referred to below as the "Commission's Safeway Report".

[3] Proposed acquisition by Trackdean Investments of Safeway plc: Director General's advice of March 13, 2003. In this regard, the Commission noted that several parties had expressed concern to the OFT about the possible break-up of the Safeway business as a result of the Trackdean bid. However, the OFT noted that Trackdean had made a commitment (although no formal undertakings were given) to continue to operate Safeway as a grocery retailer. The OFT added that Safeway was profitable and the value of its assets lay in their continued use in grocery retailing. Accordingly, the OFT was not convinced that the exit outcome was likely, and it would look at the break-up of the business by a non-trade buyer separately.

[4] See the Commission's Safeway report at Table 2.2, p.37.

	Share of GB grocery sales from large stores
Tesco	32%
Sainsbury	23%
Asda	20%
Morrisons	7%
Philip Green	0
Safeway	12%

Each of the potential bids from supermarket chains raised a number of different competition issues. In particular:

(i) local competition and choice were important because consumers tended to shop at a local level;

(ii) national competition between the major grocery retailers was important given that many dimensions of competition were set nationally, including general pricing strategies, product ranges, store facilities, product and service quality, opening hours, etc.; and

(iii) relationships with suppliers raised further potential issues, given that in 2000 the Commission had conducted an inquiry into the supermarkets industry and had recommended a code of practice to govern relationships with suppliers.[5]

This Appendix focuses on the assessment of local competition.[6]

As regards product and geographic market definition, the Commission concluded in its 2000 report that the relevant market for assessing local competition related to grocery sales from stores of 1400m^2 or above. This was because it was generally accepted within the industry that stores materially below this size would not be able to offer a sufficient range of goods in order to provide a "one-stop shop". The Commission acknowledged that certain consumers would still undertake secondary or "top-up" shopping at larger retail outlets, but the main purpose of such stores, and the majority of their business, related to the provision of one-stop shopping. In terms of geographic market definition, the Commission had found that the majority of consumers tended to travel a maximum of 10 minutes in urban areas in order to undertake their weekly one-stop shopping, and a maximum of 15 minutes in more rural areas. It was therefore concluded that catchment areas of approximately 10 or 15 minutes as appropriate would provide a useful basis for assessing local competition between supermarkets.[7]

Following the methodology employed by the Commission in its 2000 inquiry, each of the potential bidders for Safeway prepared submissions to the OFT using isochrones. An isochrone is drawn by taking a starting point (initially a large supermarket), and assessing how far a consumer could drive within a maximum of 10 or 15 minutes in order to reach stores. The isochrone will tend to be an irregular shape, reflecting the nature of the road network surrounding the store and other geographical features (e.g. the location of bridges over natural obstacles such as rivers), with assumed faster speeds on motorways than on smaller, local roads. These isochrone maps were intended to provide an illustration of the main catchment areas of stores,

---

[5] *Supermarkets*, Cm. 4842 (October 2000), at paras 2.558 to 2.596.
[6] The following text draws heavily on paras 5.193–5.333 of the Commission's Safeway report, cited above.
[7] The Commission's Safeway report, cited above.

and the basic principle is that where two stores are located within the same isochrone/catchment area they are in direct competition with one another. Beyond this, a significant number of issues then need to be considered, which are addressed in turn below.

Technical software issues

A13.002   Since Safeway and the prospective supermarket bidders operated many stores (and therefore many isochrones could be drawn), some computer software was required in order to draw isochrones. In the case of the battle for Safeway, some of the major supermarket groups already had their own computer software. In addition, commercially available software is available. However, even using the basic parameters for competition as identified by the Commission in 2000, it became apparent when each of the potential bidders made their submissions to the OFT that the different types of software tended to give different results and different isochrone maps. There were a number of reasons for this:

(i)   they used digitised road networks of varying levels of detail—some included very minor roads, others did not—and this affected drive times;

(ii)   they employed different assumptions about road speeds, again affecting drive times. For example, some packages used maximum speed limits (perhaps incorporating time penalties for junctions), whilst others used average actual drive times at certain times of the day;

(iii)   they employed different methodologies for plotting the locations of stores; and

(iv)   there were certain other unexplainable differences between the results produced by each of the different types of software.

The various practical difficulties raised by isochrone analysis made the OFT's task of assessing the relative merits of the different potential bids for Safeway very complex. The four potential supermarket bidders had each approached the OFT with their own analysis of local competition based on isochrones, and whilst each potential bidder sought to produce an isochrone analysis on the basis of the methodology set out in the Commission's 2000 report, there still remained material differences between the maps produced by each of the bidders. A key issue for the OFT was therefore to seek to determine which isochrone analysis should be deemed most accurate for the purpose of assessing the effects of the potential mergers. The OFT had received more than 600 maps during its investigation, and whilst the various bidders had offered to make divestments of local stores in lieu of a reference to the Commission, the OFT felt unable to accept divestments given that it could not identify precisely the problem local areas for each of the potential bidders. These difficulties appeared to be the key reason why Morrisons' bid for Safeway was eventually referred to the Commission, even though this bid was not deemed to raise national competition issues (unlike with the other potential bids from Safeway, Asda and Tesco).[8]

In addition to these technical issues, there were a number of other economic issues associated with assessing geographic market definition using isochrones. These are considered further below.

---

[8] The OFT's decision refers to the fact that the proposed acquisition by Morrisons appeared likely to reduce competition substantially in certain local areas (para.31). In fact, the Commission ultimately identified many more "problem" local areas than the OFT.

Defining catchment areas, and distinguishing between urban and rural areas

As noted above, the Commission concluded in 2000 that isochrones should be drawn on the basis of 10 or 15 minute drive times, depending on whether the area was urban or rural. This was based on the view that with fewer supermarkets per square mile in rural areas, rural supermarkets had wider catchment areas than urban supermarkets.   **A13.003**

This raises the important question of, applying a SSNIP[9] and assessing the impact of local mergers, if a hypothetical monopoly supermarket retailer were to attempt to raise its prices by, say, 5 per cent, what proportion of its business would it need to lose in order to render such a price increase unprofitable? This would require specific information not only in relation to the costs and margins of the supermarket store in question (such that a "critical loss" analysis could be undertaken in order to assess the sensitivity of the supermarket's profitability to small price increases and losses of sales (see further para.6.035 of Ch.6), but also data on consumers' specific purchasing patterns (*e.g.* merely observing that the catchment areas of stores overlap does not mean that all the customers within that overlapping area would switch store in response to a small price increase, as some might well have strong preferences for one supermarket chain over another). Obtaining such data is likely to be difficult in practice. This is not least because different results are likely to be achieved for different supermarkets and different locations,[10] such that it cannot be readily assumed that the same size catchment area would be appropriate for all supermarkets. In the absence of a detailed analysis of this nature, the Commission used data concerning the proportions of the parties' customers which lived at specific distances from stores. The Commission found that the main parties derived 70–90 per cent of their sales from customers who lived within 10 minutes of their stores, and confirmed that consumers tended to travel further in more rural areas.

A further consideration is that in the 2000 inquiry, the Commission used population data in order to determine whether an area should be regarded as urban or rural. In particular, in areas where there was a population of at least 200,000 people, the area was considered to be urban, with a 10 minute drive time being appropriate. In areas with a population of less than 200,000 people, the area was regarded as rural, with a 15 minute drive time being appropriate. However, this type of analysis requires specific data on population levels within specific areas. In particular, where should the geographical boundary of the relevant population area lie? Population data is very unlikely to be available which corresponds to a 10 or 15 minute catchment area.

For these various reasons, it can be seen that it can be very difficult to distinguish between urban and rural areas and, more generally, to ascertain exactly what drive time would be appropriate in each case.

As the diagram below shows, miscalculating the drive time appropriate for an area (and therefore the size of the relevant isochrone) can have a material impact of the number of stores that are deemed to be in direct competition with one another within a 15 minute drive time there is a Tesco store such that the merger between Safeway and Morrisons would result in a reduction in the number of independently owned fascias from four to three (rather than three to two within the 10 minute drive time boundary).

---

[9] Small but Significant Non-transitory Increase in Prices. See further Ch.6, at paras.6.006 in particular.

[10] For example, in certain geographical areas there will be higher levels of car ownership than in other areas and/or better public transport links. All such factors will impact on actual journey times and catchment areas.

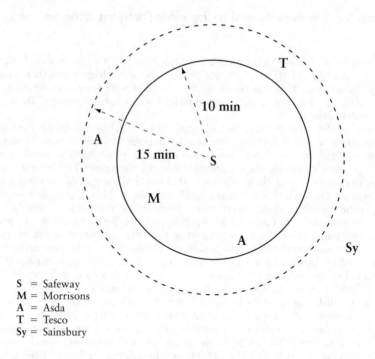

S = Safeway
M = Morrisons
A = Asda
T = Tesco
Sy = Sainsbury

Which store should be at the centre of an isochrone?

A13.004   A further practical consideration when drawing isochrones is where the isochrone should be centred. As can be seen from the diagram below and considering a merger between Safeway and Morrisons, the centring of an isochrone can have a very significant impact on the number of stores included within that isochrone:

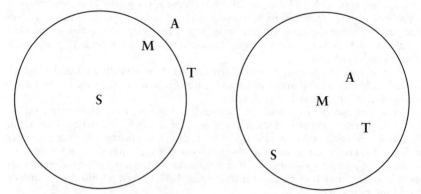

If centred on Safeway, then a merged Safeway faces no independent competition in isochrone

If centred on Morrisons, then a merged Safeway faces independent competition from Asda and Tesco

Accordingly, it is important to be clear about the specific economic question at hand. In the left-hand figure, the question being asked is "which competing stores impose a constraint upon Safeway?" It can be seen from the figure that the Morrisons store imposes a competitive constraint upon Safeway, whereas the Asda and Tesco stores lie outside Safeway's isochrone and would therefore be deemed not to be direct competitors with Safeway. The right-hand figure, however, illustrates the answer to a different question, namely "which stores impose a competitive constraint upon Morrisons?" It can be seen from this figure that each of the Safeway, Asda and Tesco stores lie within Morrisons' isochrone, and would therefore be considered to each impose a direct competitive constraint upon Morrisons.

The question then arises as to what the implications of a merger between Safeway and Morrisons would be in this case. Given that in this example the only apparent constraint upon Safeway is competition from Morrisons, then a merger between Morrisons and Safeway may well enable Safeway to raise its prices above the competitive level. This is because all of the customers which would have switched away from an *independent* Safeway in response to a price increase would have represented lost profits, whereas following the merger many of these would be retained by the merged group (*i.e.* those customers switching to Morrisons). However, Morrisons would arguably not be in a similar position to raise its prices above competitive levels given that it also faces competition from Asda and Tesco. If it were to seek to raise its prices post-merger customers would be lost to these competitors.

These arguments suggest that overlapping stores and potential "problem" stores should be assessed on the basis of centring isochrones on the stores of both the target and the acquirer.

Suppose now that Asda were to acquire Safeway and further assume that there is no overlap whatsoever in the catchment areas of the Asda and Safeway stores (the importance of this assumption is considered further in the next sub-section). If the SSNIP test applied assumes that Morrisons and Tesco do not change their prices, then Asda's acquisition will have no impact on competition as Asda and Safeway do not compete to serve any common customers. However, as set out at para.6.052 of Ch.6, this assumption might be invalid if Morrison's and Tesco's pricing decisions depend on the number of independent competitor supermarkets they each face, with this being the assumption made by the Commission.

Relevance of stores outside the isochrone

A further practical issue raised by isochrone analysis is how stores lying just   **A13.005** outside an isochrone ought to be treated in the competition analysis. Isochrone analysis assumes that stores within a particular isochrone are in direct competition with one another. Does this imply that stores lying just outside the isochrone do not represent a direct source of competition to stores within the isochrone? The diagram below provides an illustrative example of this type of problem:

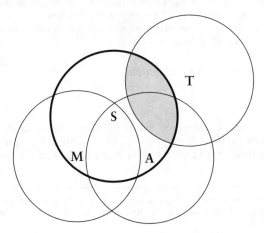

In this example, it can be seen that the isochrone centred on the Safeway store (in bold) also contains a Morrisons store and an Asda store. Accordingly, Morrisons and Asda are deemed to represent direct competitors to Safeway. The Tesco store, however, lies outside of Safeway's isochrone. Can it therefore be disregarded as an effective competitor to Safeway?

In fact, Tesco could not be automatically disregarded as an effective competitor on the basis that, as can be seen from the diagram, the isochrone centred on Tesco overlaps significantly with the isochrones centred on both Safeway and Asda. In other words, for a significant proportion of customers which regard Safeway as a viable store in order to carry out their weekly one-stop shop, Tesco is also regarded as a viable store. (These customers are located in the shaded areas.) Since supermarkets are unlikely to be able to discriminate effectively between their customers on the basis of where they live, the question then becomes "how significant are those customers which can also use the Tesco store, as a proportion of Safeway's entire customer base in the isochrone?" If there is a very significant overlap between the catchment areas of Safeway and Tesco, such that a significant proportion of Safeway's potential customers would switch to using the Tesco store[11] then Safeway should arguably take competition from Tesco into account, as well as competition from Asda and Morrisons. If, by contrast, only a very small proportion of Safeway's potential customer base would also regard Tesco as a viable competitor store, then it may be more profitable for Safeway to raise its prices and to risk losing some of these customers to Tesco. The answer to this issue lies in a "critical loss" analysis in order to determine what proportion of customers the Safeway store would have to lose in order to render a small increase in prices unprofitable (see further para.6.035 of Ch.6).

The Commission's analysis of local competition

A13.006   At the beginning of its investigation, the Commission spent some time considering how best to deal with the various practical issues raised by isochrone analysis in order to ensure maximum consistency between the assessments of each of the potential bids. The Commission concluded that the best way to undertake its analysis of local competition would be to ask Safeway to produce maps for all of the potential bidders using its own software. Safeway's software was "tried and tested", and this would resolve any inconsistency problems raised by the use of different types of software. A series of assumptions, for example concerning road speeds, rules for determining urban versus rural areas etc, were also agreed at the beginning of the inquiry, and the entire analysis was audited by an independent third party.[12]

The Commission then went on to undertake a two stage assessment of local competition. The first stage would involve a mechanical exercise of producing isochrone maps, whilst a second stage would involve discussions with the main parties on possible "problem local areas".

Stage 1 of the Commission's assessment

Map production

A13.007   At the first stage, the Commission asked Safeway to produce 10 or 15 minute isochrone maps, centred on Safeway, for each of the potential merger scenarios. The purpose of this analysis was to identify how many stores and fascias:

---

[11] This depends on the number of customers, not the geographical size of the shaded area.
[12] See Apps 5.1 and 5.2 of the Commission's Safeway report (cited above) for further details of specific assumptions.

(i)   could offer one-stop shopping in each local area pre-merger; and

(ii)   there would be in each local area following each potential merger.

In contrast to the 2000 inquiry, where urban and rural areas were identified based on whether there was a population of at least 200,000 people, during the later merger inquiry urban and rural areas were based on classifications used by the Office of the Deputy Prime Minister, responsible for planning. This led to more areas being designated as urban. The reason for this change of approach was not made clear by the Commission.

Recognising some of the practical problems raised by isochrone analysis, the Commission then made a number of refinements to the map production exercise. In particular, whilst the original set of maps had been centred on Safeway stores, the Commission then asked Safeway to produce a third set of maps, for each merger scenario, with isochrones re-centred on each potential acquirer's stores. In addition, the Commission asked Safeway to produce yet another set of maps with isochrones re-centred on other competing stores in each locality. The reason for the production of these extra sets of maps was to consider more broadly the competitive constraints faced in each relevant local area. In particular, re-centring an isochrone on other stores provided information on the direct competitive constraints faced by each individual store, and might reveal which stores, post-merger, might have the ability and incentive to raise prices above the competitive level and/or to reduce product quality/service.

In addition, the Commission asked Safeway to produce a fourth set of maps whereby isochrones were re-centred on centres of population within local areas (some as small as 1,000 people). This was rationalised in two different ways. First, to capture the issue discussed above about stores outside the isochone nevertheless competing for common customers. The second rationale was to ensure that particular centres of population faced an "effective" choice of different supermarket stores. As can be seen in the diagram below, drawing isochrones around the Morrisons and Safeway stores suggests that they are not direct competitors, whereas for consumers in the main town they are the main two stores available:

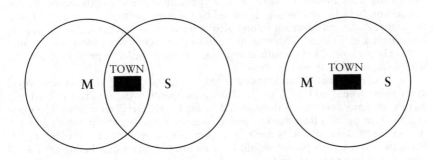

A further refinement undertaken by the Commission, known as the "regional concentration rule", involved areas where there would be no overlap between the catchment areas of a target store and a bidder store, or where there would be only one other competitor. In these circumstances, the isochrone was to be extended by 5 minute increments until the "next best alternative" store was identified. The rationale behind this was that if consumers were faced with less choice as to stores, they may be prepared to travel further in order to reach the next best alternative store. This can be illustrated by the diagram below:

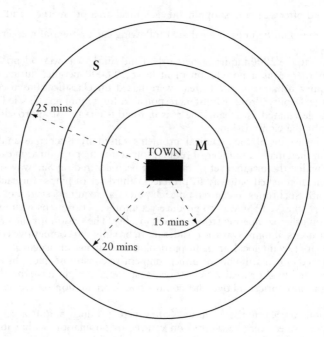

Identifying potentially problematic areas

A13.008   Having completed their first stage assessment, the Commission's preliminary conclusions were that in particular local areas, each of the proposed mergers would reduce the number of fascias available to consumers by one. The Commission concluded that "effective competitors" in local areas would include large stores (with a size of (i) 1400m² or more, or (ii) 75 per cent of the size of the Safeway store in question (whichever is smaller)) owned by the main parties (*i.e.* Safeway, Tesco, Sainsbury, Asda and Morrisons), and also large stores of Budgens, Booths, Co-op, Somerfield and Waitrose. This was on the basis that each of these companies would, in their larger stores, have a sufficient product range in order to provide consumers with a viable one-stop weekly shop.[13]

The isochrone analysis undertaken at Stage 1 revealed that whilst in some local areas there would still be 6 or 7 effective competitors (*i.e.* fascias) following a merger, in many other areas there would be far fewer fascias remaining. The question the Commission then had to consider was the circumstances in which a reduction in the number of fascias could be a competition problem. In considering this issue, the Commission placed weight on a number of factors, including the loss of consumer choice of fascias and grocery offers within a particular area, how to quantify the loss of Safeway as an independent competitor in the context of a market where each of the different supermarket groups had different price/quality strategies, and the possibility of unilateral or coordinated effects in different localities. The Commission's provisional conclusion was that a reduction in the number of independently owned fascias to four or less in any local area was *potentially* prob-

---

[13] Other retailer groups, such as Iceland, Marks & Spencer, Aldi and Lidl were excluded on the basis of their more limited product ranges.

lematic and required further consideration. On this basis, a large number of potentially problematic areas were identified for each of the possible bidders: 79 for Morrisons; 198 for Asda; 256 for Sainsbury and 284 for Tesco. In this way, the Commission could rule out unproblematic areas, although it had yet to take a final decision as to how many fascias were required in a locality following a reduction in fascias, for competition not to have been substantially lessened in that locality (or, considering relevant local areas together, nationally).

Stage 2 of Commission's assessment—consultations with the main parties

During the Commission's consultations with the main parties, a number of issues arose concerning the interpretation of isochrone maps. Some of these issues are considered further below.

A13.009

The 'five to four' fascia rule

At the consultation stage, before examining specific local problem areas, each of the parties argued to the Commission that a rule whereby a reduction in the number of fascias from five to four was too demanding and inconsistent with the Commission's approach in its 2000 report. The Commission observed that whilst in the 2000 report it had concluded that the existence of three fascias in a local area provided "adequate" competition, this was a different question from whether a reduction in the number of fascias from five to four would lead to a substantial lessening of competition, or a material reduction in choice, in each local area. In particular, the Commission emphasised that since the 2000 report, Somerfield and the Co-op had retreated from one-stop shopping to some extent. Moreover, for each of the proposed mergers, the Commission was considering competition at the local level in the context of a reduction in the number of national (or regional) players in the industry. For three of the mergers in contemplation, this would result in the loss of a national player, whilst for the Morrisons merger, four national players would be retained but a strong regional player would be lost. The Commission emphasised that this was a different question to that asked in the context of the 2000 complex monopoly inquiry.

A13.010

Morrisons argued that, in the context of its proposed acquisition, in those areas where there might be a loss of a fascia, the loss of that fascia would be compensated for by a strengthened national competitor in the form of a combined Morrisons/Safeway. A number of other arguments against the use of a five to four fascia rule were considered. These included that:

(i) a five to four fascia rule was too demanding a rule because only the companies identified by the Commission as effective competitors were considered in the reduction in the number of fascias (some of the parties argued that other companies such as Marks & Spencer, Aldi, Lidl and Netto all provided a competitive constraint on one-stop shops in certain areas);

(ii) in some areas, stores below 1400m² might also be expected to supply some degree of competitive constraint on one-stop shops;

(iii) in some areas, stores outside the isochrone might also be expected to supply some degree of competitive constraint on stores inside the isochrone;

(iv) the various decision rules applied at Stage 1 of the Commission's analysis were rather more demanding than those used in their 2000 report;

(v) the benefits from the mergers outweighed the detriment of a reduction from five to four fascias in a limited number of areas; and

(vi) a five to four fascia rule was impractical, given the high number of stores required for divestment and the number of parties ruled out from acquiring such stores (because of the various decision rules) which would result in the divestment of stores out of the industry or to weak parties—neither of which would be conducive to increased competition.

The Commission, having considered these various arguments, concluded that a reduction in the number of fascias from five to four might be too demanding a rule, and that a reduction in the number of fascias from four to three might be more relevant.

Multiple Safeway stores

A13.011   The main parties each argued that in potentially problematic local areas where there was more than one Safeway store within an isochrone, if one Safeway store was divested, that would restore the status quo and therefore should be sufficient in order to restore competition. The Commission accepted this argument in principle, but indicated that the divestment of just one store in these circumstances would be acceptable only if the divested store were sold to a supermarket retailer whereby the isochrone rules described above would be met (*i.e.* there would be at least three fascias in the local area post-merger), and where the acquiring party raised no national competition concerns.

Regional concentration rule

A13.012   Another issue which was discussed during consultations with the main parties concerned the regional concentration rule. As described above, this rule was applied in local areas where a 10 or 15 minute isochrone would not identify a target and bidder store as being within the same catchment area (and therefore in direct competition with one another), or where a target and bidder store would face competition from only one other fascia. In this case, the Commission proceeded to extend isochrones by 5 minute increments until the next best alternative store was identified. However, the parties argued that the analysis should not stop once the next best store was identified. Indeed, if the Commission had continued to extend isochrones, then other stores would also be brought into the analysis. In other words, in the context of a merger between Safeway and Morrisons, their stores may lie within 20 minutes of one another, but extending the isochrone by another 5 minutes (to 25 minutes) would ignore other competing stores just one or two minutes further away (*e.g.* Asda and Tesco in the diagram opposite):

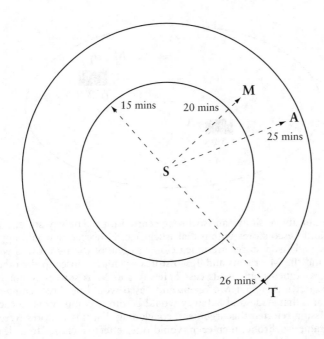

The Commission accepted this argument in principle. However, it said that whilst isochrones of 20 and 25 minutes would be considered in these circumstances, the Commission would not go beyond 25 minutes in determining whether there existed more regional competition between stores.

Stores on the edge of an isochrone

The parties contested a number of potential problem areas on the basis that there was an additional fascia just outside the boundary of an isochrone. As described above, in these circumstances, a store located outside an isochrone can still represent a competitive constraint provided the respective catchment areas of different stores overlap to a sufficient degree. The Commission did not accept that in every case a store that was just outside an isochrone actually offered an alternative to stores within the isochrone. However, the Commission did consider further the extent to which the boundary of isochrones should be considered as fixed, and concluded that a store would not be classified as a problem if it would *neither* be classified as a problem on the basis of a slightly smaller isochrone (one minute smaller), *nor* of a slightly larger isochrone (one minute larger).

A13.013

"Distant" competitors within isochrones

A further issue which was discussed with the main parties was how apparently distant competitors located within the same isochrone should be treated. Some of the main parties had argued that even if two stores were located within the same isochrone, they could serve distinct local markets. The logic here was that 10 or 15 minute isochrones could be very large, and may include a number of distinct population concentrations. It was quite possible that in certain local areas, there would be a large isochrone containing two or more smaller towns, with each town having its own supermarket outlets, and consumers rarely going to another town to do their shopping:

A13.014

871

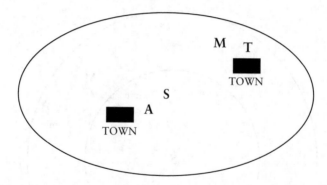

The diagram above shows an isochrone centred on a Safeway store, and Asda, Morrisons and Tesco stores within that isochrone. However, it would appear that the Safeway and Asda stores are much closer to one of the two towns within the isochrone, and the Morrisons and Tesco stores are much closer to the other. Some of the parties argued that in this case Safeway and Morrisons may not be direct competitors, but rather that Morrisons and Tesco would be direct competitors to each other and that Asda and Safeway would be direct competitors to each other. The Commission rejected this argument, concluding that if two stores were located within the same isochrone, then each would offer effective choice to at least some consumers within that isochrone.

Chains of substitution

A13.015   Morrisons and Tesco also raised the issue of chains of substitution with the Commission. It was argued that in certain instances, there were clear chains of substitution, where the stores in question were constrained by the overlapping catchments of the stores located around the perimeter of the relevant isochrones. For example, in the diagram below, it was argued that whilst stores A and B were located within the same isochrone, and were therefore considered to be direct competitors, store B was also located within the same isochrone as store C. Accordingly, store C would represent a competitive constraint upon store B, and this in turn would serve indirectly to constrain store A. Extending the analysis, store D would represent some competitive constraint on store C, and thereby on store B and, so on.

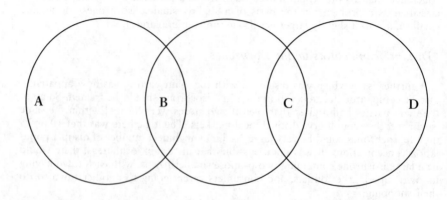

The Commission, however, considered the extent to which isochrones overlapped in practice, and found that there were few instances of significantly overlapping isochrones. The Commission pointed out that at stage 1 of its analysis, out of a total of 337 Safeway one-stop shops in Great Britain, 120 of them were in an isochrone with only one or two fascias. The Commission also observed that the main parties had indicated that between 70 and 90 per cent of their sales derived from customers located within 10 minutes of their stores. Given this, isochrones drawn around stores would have to overlap very substantially in order to constrain one another. The Commission considered that the degree of overlap required in order to create a strong chain of substitution was likely to be significantly greater than that depicted in the diagram above—where each store is at the edge of each isochrone. If it was assumed that the figure above depicted 10 minute isochrones, then stores A and B, for instance, would be over 10 minutes apart because they are at the edges of the isochrone. The Commission also noted that in other instances, the parties had argued that two stores did not necessarily compete with one another despite being located within the same isochrone on the basis that they were located at opposite edges of the isochrone. Taking all of these points into account, the Commission concluded that there were unlikely to be strong chains of substitution covering much of the country.

The Commission's conclusions

As a result of its consultations with the main parties, the Commission concluded **A13.016** that certain of the potential problem areas that had been identified for each of the potential bidders could be eliminated. However, for each bidder there remained a number of potentially problematic areas: 55 for Morrisons; 145 for Asda; 201 for Sainsbury; and 222 for Tesco.

As regards Morrisons, the Commission concluded that the local competition issues raised by Morrisons' bid could be resolved by the divestment of local stores in these identified areas. However, for each of the other bidders, concerns were raised not only in relation to local competition, but also in relation to national competition and their buyer power vis-à-vis suppliers. Local divestments would in this case be insufficient to remedy the other competition concerns identified, and the other potential bids were blocked by the Secretary of State following the advice of the Commission.

It will be interesting to see whether isochrone analysis is used more commonly going forward in cases which involve local competition, and how the regulators will refine their approaches to this type of analysis in the light of the experience of the OFT and Competition Commission in this case.

THE CALCULATION OF CRITICAL LOSSES AND ELASTICITIES

A14.001   Suppose that prior to a merger, two competing firms supplying a specific product or service in a certain geographic area were charging a price of £10 per unit and they faced identical and constant marginal production costs of £8 (so that selling less units would reduce total costs by £8 for each fewer unit sold, regardless of whether sales fall by 10 units or 100 units). These firms would thus be earning a gross margin, or contribution to their fixed costs (which, by definition, do not vary with output) and profits, of £2 per unit (£10-£8), with their total contribution being £2 multiplied by the total number of units they sell (Q1). (Implicit in this is that the regulator in applying the SSNIP test would extrapolate from these results to those that would apply for a hypothetical monopolist.)

Initial contribution prior to the price increase = (£10-£8) × Q1 = £2 × Q1

Suppose the regulator then wishes to assess what is the critical minimum sales loss that would be necessary to render a, say, 5 per cent price increase unprofitable, with 5 per cent of £10 being 50p. In these circumstances, the contribution to fixed costs following the price increase would be £2.50 multiplied by the new sales volume Q2.

New total contribution margin after price increase = (£10.50−£8.00) × Q2 = £2.50 × Q2

For such a price increase not to be profitable, the resulting percentage fall in sales volumes must at least offset the impact of the percentage increase in the gross margin. This can be expressed as:

£2 × Q1 (*i.e.* total contribution prior to the price increase) £2.50 × Q2 (total contribution after the price increase).

Thus, at a minimum: Q2/Q1 = £2/£2.50 = 0.8 (or 80 per cent of the original sales volume)

In other words, the break-even critical loss in sales volumes must be at least 20 per cent for profits not to increase following a 5 per cent price increase.

The break-even "critical" own price elasticity (with "own" price elasticity being the percentage fall in sales volumes that would be caused by a small price increase divided by the percentage increase in price) can be approximated by the critical percentage sales loss divided by the percentage price increase envisaged. In the example given above, this would be calculated by dividing the 20 per cent break even critical percentage sales loss by the 5 per cent price increase envisaged, which yields a break even critical elasticity of approximately 4 (20 per cent/5 per cent).[1] This critical break even elasticity figure would then be compared with any estimates of the actual own-price elasticity of market demand for the relevant product in the area in question.

Generally, the higher the gross margin prior to the price increase, the lower the critical loss and price elasticity and vice versa. For example, if in the above example the gross margin had been 50 per cent of the price (*i.e.* £5 instead of £2), then the break-even critical loss would have been only approximately 9.1 per cent (*i.e.* 1— (£5/£5.50) = 9.1 per cent) for a 5 per cent price increase and the critical elasticity would have been substantially lower at approximately 1.8 (*i.e.* 9.1 per cent/5 per cent). The intuition behind this relationship is that the higher the gross margin:

(i)   the smaller the proportionate increase in the gross margin from a given percentage price increase, so that the proportionate increase in contribution per unit from retained sale volumes following the price increase will be smaller[2]; and

(ii)   the greater the contribution earned from existing sales prior to the price increase, so that losing existing sales volumes has a greater negative impact on contribution and thus profitability.

It should be noted that the critical loss calculated depends on the size of the price increase. For example, in the original example outlined above, the firm made a gross margin of £2 per unit on a selling price of £10 per unit and, for a 5 per cent price increase, the break-even critical loss was calculated as being 20 per cent for profits not to increase. If instead prices were to increase by 10 per cent, then the price increase would be £1 and the gross margin would increase to £3. In order for profits to remain constant:

£2 × Q1 (contribution prior to the price increase) = £3 × Q2 (contribution after the price increase).

Thus, at a minimum: Q2/Q1 = £2/£3 = 0.67 (or 67 per cent of the original sales volume).

---

[1] The gross margin (m) can be expressed relative to price (p) so that $m = (p - c)/p$ (where c is marginal cost). If marginal cost is half of price then $m = 0.5$. The percentage increase in price can be denoted as t, so that if the price increase is 5 per cent then t will be 0.05. As above, Q1 and Q2 denote sales volumes before and after the price increase respectively. Accordingly, the break even critical loss can be expressed as $m \times Q1 = (m+t) \times Q2$, which can be rearranged to $Q2/Q1 = m/(m+t)$, or $1-Q2/Q1 = t/(m+t)$. The critical break-even market own price elasticity (implicitly assuming a linear demand curve) (where sales volumes are linearly related to price) is simply the percentage change in sales volume $(1- Q2/Q1)$ divided by the percentage change in price (t), which is $1/(m+t)$. Werden also shows that the profit maximising critical elasticity can be calculated as $1/(m + 2t)$ with a linear demand curve and $(1+t)/(m+t)$ (where own price elasticity of demand is constant at all prices, whereas with a linear demand curve price elasticity of demand increases as prices rise). Werden shows that the profit maximising critical loss and elasticities are lower than break-even critical loss and elasticities. For example, with a pre-merger gross margin of 50 per cent, a 5 per cent price increase would be profit maximising with a sales volume loss of under 8.3 per cent (for a linear demand curve) and 8.9 per cent (with constant elasticity of demand), but would break-even with a volume loss of 9.1 per cent.

[2] For example a 5 per cent price increase leads to a 25 per cent increase in the gross margin per unit in the first example above, where the gross margin was initially £2 per unit, but only a 10 per cent increase in the gross margin per unit in the second example where the gross margin was initially £5 per unit.

In other words, the critical loss in sales volumes must be at least 33 per cent for profits not to increase following a 10 per cent price increase.

Any assessment of gross margins requires an assessment of marginal costs. This information may not be readily available from accountancy information, not least because costs tend not to be neatly characterised in accountancy information as fixed or variable in nature. In addition, firms which are active in a number of markets might not produce segmented financial analysis which identifies the variable costs associated with supplying specific markets. Also marginal costs may not always be closely approximated by average variable costs, with average variable costs simply being total variable costs divided by sales volume, unless marginal cost is roughly constant and does not materially increase or decrease with volume. In addition, the extent to which costs are fixed or variable will also be influenced by the decline in sales volumes contemplated. For example, a substantial fall in sales might permit the closure of a factory etc. leading to savings in fixed factory costs, whereas a smaller sales fall might permit no such cost savings. A further issue is the time frame considered, since in the long run when fixed cost investments come up for renewal, a firm might be able to achieve savings in both fixed and variable costs by reducing output.

INDEX

INDEX